The
Class of 1953
Endowed Library
Fund

U. Grant Miller Library
Washington and Jefferson
College

WITHDRAWN

THE CAMBRIDGE HISTORY OF AMERICAN LITERATURE

The Cambridge History of American Literature addresses the broad spectrum of new and established directions in all branches of American writing and includes the work of scholars and critics who have shaped, and who continue to shape, what has become a major area of literary scholarship. The authors span three decades of achievement in American literary criticism, thereby speaking for both continuity and change between generations of scholarship. Generously proportioned narratives allow at once for a broader vision and sweep of American literary history than has been possible previously. And while the voice of traditional criticism forms a background for these narratives, it joins forces with the diversity of interests that characterize contemporary literary studies.

The *History* offers wide-ranging, interdisciplinary accounts of American genres and periods. Generated partly by the recent unearthing of previously neglected texts, the expansion of material in American literature coincides with a dramatic increase in the diversity of approaches to that material. The multifaceted scholarly and critical enterprise embodied in *The Cambridge History of American Literature* addresses these multiplicities – social, cultural, intellectual, and aesthetic – and demonstrates a richer concept of authority in literary studies than is found in earlier accounts.

This volume covers a pivotal era in the formation of American identity. Four leading scholars connect the literature with the massive historical changes then underway. Richard H. Brodhead describes the foundation of a permanent literary culture in America. Nancy Bentley locates the origins of nineteenth-century Realism in an elite culture's responses to an emergent mass culture, embracing high literature as well as a wide spectrum of cultural outsiders: African Americans, women, and Native Americans. Walter Benn Michaels emphasizes the critical role that turn-of-the-century fiction played in the re-evaluation of the individual at the advent of modern bureaucracy. Susan L. Mizruchi analyzes the economic and cultural representations of a new national heterogeneity that helped forecast the multicultural future of modern America. Together, these narratives constitute the richest, most detailed account to date of American literature and culture between 1860 and 1920.

THE CAMBRIDGE HISTORY OF AMERICAN LITERATURE

Volume 3
Prose Writing
1860–1920

General Editor
SACVAN BERCOVITCH
Harvard University

CAMBRIDGE
UNIVERSITY PRESS

CAMBRIDGE UNIVERSITY PRESS
Cambridge, New York, Melbourne, Madrid, Cape Town, Singapore, São Paulo

CAMBRIDGE UNIVERSITY PRESS
The Edinburgh Building, Cambridge CB2 2RU, UK

Published in the United States of America by Cambridge University Press, New York

www.cambridge.org
Information on this title: www.cambridge.org/9780521301077

© Cambridge University Press 2005

First published 2005

Printed in the United Kingdom at the University Press, Cambridge

A catalogue record for this book is available from the British Library

ISBN-13   978-0-521-30107-7 hardback
ISBN-10   0-521-30107-6 hardback

CONTENTS

ILLUSTRATIONS

ACKNOWLEDGMENTS

FROM THE GENERAL EDITOR

My thanks to Audrey Cotterell of Cambridge University Press for her extraordinary copy-editing skills, to Sean McCreery, my superb research assistant, and to Harvard University, which provided the funds over the past twenty years for this project. This volume is the last in a series of eight volumes, published out of sequence, that began publication in 1986. Some of the contributors finished their sections much earlier than others, and had to wait longer than normal patience would allow until their particular volume was ready for publication. I am grateful for their generosity, forbearance, and understanding, to Richard H. Brodhead, then at Yale University, now President of Duke University, and to Walter Benn Michaels, then at Johns Hopkins University, now at the University of Illinois, Chicago Circle, both of whom completed their work by 1992 (though of course both have reviewed and revised their typescripts for this publication).

I want to take this opportunity to express my gratitude to a great Americanist of an earlier generation, Daniel Aaron, with whom I first discussed this project, and whose wisdom, insight, and encouragement have been a mainstay for me, personally and professionally, over the past two decades.

Finally, my thanks to John Tessitore, representative of the best of the new generation of Americanists, who wrote most of the second part of the Introduction, summarizing the connections between the different sections of this volume.

Sacvan Bercovitch

THE AMERICAN LITERARY FIELD, 1860–1890

Because the Select Bibliography to these volumes excludes single-author works, I want to acknowledge here three books that I found particularly helpful: Hamlin Garland, *A Son of the Middle Border* (New York: Macmillan, 1917), Martha Saxton, *Louisa May: A Modern Biography of Louisa May Alcott* (Boston:

Houghton Mifflin, 1977), and Gary Scharnhorst, *Horatio Alger, Jr.* (Boston: Twayne, 1980). I also extend my thanks to the members of the graduate seminars at Yale with whom I first worked through the materials treated in this section.

Richard H. Brodhead

LITERARY FORMS AND MASS CULTURE, 1870–1920

I am grateful for the support I received from the University of Pennsylvania while working on this history. Past and present graduate students at Penn played a crucial role in deepening my account of the generative relations between literary writing and mass culture in the United States. A special debt is owed Justine Murison and Mark Sample, whose research in the archives of American mass culture introduced me to two of the texts I examine in this study. Martha Schoolman, Kendall Johnson, and Hannah Wells supplied research assistance and instructive conversation. Of the vast scholarship on modern mass culture, the work of Tony Bennett, Andreas Huysmann, and Richard Salmon has been particularly important to my account. Critical studies by Philip Barrish, Philip Fisher, Nancy Glazener, Amy Kaplan, and Susan Mizruchi are central to my analysis of some of the literary and intellectual institutions of this period in American history. I am grateful to Carol J. Singley and Oxford University Press for the opportunity to develop some of my ideas about the role of imperial travel and mass transit in the work of Edith Wharton. The essay "Wharton, Travel, and Modernity" appeared in *A Historical Guide to Edith Wharton*, ed. Carol J. Singley (Oxford: Oxford University Press, 2003), pp. 147–79. I owe special thanks to Elaine Freedgood, friend and interlocutor, for her pivotal questions and shared enthusiasms, and to Sacvan Bercovitch for his editorial guidance and encouragement.

Nancy Bentley

PROMISES OF AMERICAN LIFE, 1880–1920

I want to thank Sharon Cameron, Frances Ferguson, and Michael Fried, all of whom read and suggested revisions to the penultimate draft of this study. I also want to thank Mark Schoening, then a graduate student at Johns Hopkins, and Caleb Spencer, currently a graduate student at University of Illinois, Chicago Circle, who helped me prepare it for publication. And I am grateful to the editors of *Representations* and *New Literary History* for permission to reprint the slightly different versions of chapters 1 and 3 that they first published in 1989 and 1990.

Walter Benn Michaels

BECOMING MULTICULTURAL: CULTURE, ECONOMY, AND THE NOVEL, 1860–1929

I want to express my gratitude to the John Simon Guggenheim Foundation for a fellowship that enabled me to complete this work.

Susan L. Mizruchi

CHRONOLOGY

Many thanks to Sacvan Bercovitch, for his thoughtful collaboration on the Chronology and Introduction, for advice both literary and professional, and for including me in this wonderful project; to Susan Mizruchi, for her unflagging enthusiasm, her steadfast support, and her generosity as a mentor and friend; and to my wife Kelly, whose love enriches my life and work.

John E. Tessitore

INTRODUCTION

THIS MULTIVOLUME *History* marks a new beginning in the study of American literature. The first *Cambridge History of American Literature* (1917) helped introduce a new branch of English writing. The *Literary History of the United States*, assembled thirty years later under the aegis of Robert E. Spiller, helped establish a new field of academic study. This *History* embodies the work of a generation of Americanists who have redrawn the boundaries of the field. Trained in the decades between the late 1960s and the early 1980s, representing the broad spectrum of both new and established directions in all branches of American writing, these scholars and critics have shaped, and continue to shape, what has become a major area of modern literary scholarship.

Over the past three decades, Americanist literary criticism has expanded from a border province into a center of humanist studies. The vitality of the field is reflected in the rising interest in American literature nationally and globally, in the scope of scholarly activity, and in the polemical intensity of debate. Significantly, American texts have come to provide a major focus for inter- and cross-disciplinary investigation. Gender studies, ethnic studies, and popular-culture studies, among others, have penetrated to all corners of the profession, but perhaps their single largest base is American literature. The same is true with regard to controversies over multiculturalism and canon formation: the issues are transhistorical and transcultural, but the debates themselves have often turned on American books.

However we situate ourselves in these debates, it seems clear that the activity they have generated has provided a source of intellectual revitalization and new research, involving a massive recovery of neglected and undervalued bodies of writing. We know far more than ever about what some have termed (in the plural) "American literatures," a term grounded in the persistence in the United States of different traditions, different kinds of aesthetics, even different notions of the literary.

These developments have enlarged the meanings as well as the materials of American literature. For this generation of critics and scholars, American literary history is no longer the history of a certain, agreed-upon group of

American masterworks. Nor is it any longer based upon a certain, agreed-
upon historical perspective on American writing. The quests for certainty and
agreement continue, as they should, but they proceed now within a climate of
critical decentralization – of controversy, sectarianism, and, at best, dialogue
among different schools of explanation.

This scene of conflict signals a shift in structures of academic authority.
The practice of all literary history hitherto, from its inception in the eighteenth century, has depended upon an established consensus about the essence
or nature of its subject. Today the invocation of consensus sounds rather like
an appeal for compromise, or like nostalgia. The study of American literary
history now defines itself in the plural, as a multivocal, multifaceted scholarly, critical, and pedagogic enterprise. Authority in this context is a function of disparate but connected bodies of knowledge. We might call it the
authority of difference. It resides in part in the energies of heterogeneity: a
variety of contending constituencies, bodies of materials, and sets of authorities. In part the authority of difference lies in the critic's capacity to connect: to turn the particularity of his or her approach into a form of challenge
and engagement, so that it actually gains substance and depth in relation to other, sometimes complementary, sometimes conflicting modes of
explanation.

This new *Cambridge History of American Literature* claims authority on both
counts, contentious and collaborative. In a sense, this makes it representative
of the specialized, processual, marketplace culture it describes. Our *History* is
fundamentally pluralist: a federated histories of American literatures. But it is
worth noting that in large measure this representative quality is adversarial.
Our *History* is an expression of ongoing debates within the profession about cultural patterns and values. Some of these narratives may be termed celebratory,
insofar as they uncover correlations between social and aesthetic achievement.
Others are explicitly oppositional, sometimes to the point of turning literary
analysis into a critique of liberal pluralism. Oppositionalism, however, stands
in a complex relation here to advocacy. Indeed it may be said to mark the
History's most traditional aspect. The high moral stance that oppositional criticism assumes – literary analysis as the occasion for resistance and alternative
vision – is grounded in the very definition of art we have inherited from the
Romantic era. The earlier, genteel view of literature upheld the universality of
ideals embodied in great books. By implication, therefore, as in the declared
autonomy of art, and often by direct assault upon social norms and practices,
especially those of Western capitalism, it fostered a broad ethical–aesthetic
antinomianism – a celebration of literature (in Matthew Arnold's words) as
the criticism of life. By midcentury that criticism had issued, on the one hand,

in the New Critics' assault on industrial society, and, on the other hand, in the neo-Marxist theories of praxis.

The relation here between oppositional and nonoppositional approaches makes for a problematic perspective on nationality. It is a problem that invites many sorts of resolution, including a post-national (or post-American) perspective. Some of these prospective revisions are implicit in these volumes, perhaps as shadows or images of literary histories to come. But by and large "America" here designates the United States, or the territories that were to become part of the United States. Although several of our authors adopt a comparatist transatlantic or pan-American framework, and although several of them discuss works in other languages, mainly their concerns center upon writing in English in this country – "American literature" as it has been (and still is) commonly understood in its national implications. This restriction marks a deliberate choice on our part. To some extent, no doubt, it reflects limitations of time, space, training, and available materials; but it must be added that our contributors have made the most of their limitations. They have taken advantage of time, space, training, and newly available materials to turn nationality itself into a *question* of literary history. Precisely because of their focus on English-language literatures in the United States, the term "America" for them is neither a narrative *donnée* – an assumed or inevitable or natural premise – nor an objective background (*the* national history). Quite the contrary: it is the contested site of many sorts of literary-historical inquiry. What had presented itself as a neutral territory, hospitable to all authorized parties, turns out upon examination to be, and to have always been, a volatile combat-zone.

"America" in these volumes is a historical entity, the United States of America. It is also a declaration of community, a people constituted and sustained by verbal fiat, a set of universal principles, a strategy of social cohesion, a summons to social protest, a prophecy, a dream, an aesthetic ideal, a trope of the modern ("progress," "opportunity," "the new"), a semiotics of inclusion ("melting pot," "patchwork quilt," "nation of nations"), and a semiotics of exclusion, closing out not only the Old World but all other countries of the Americas, north and south, as well as large groups within the United States. A nationality so conceived is a rhetorical battleground. "America" in these volumes is a shifting, many-sided focal point for exploring the historicity of the text and the textuality of history.

Not coincidentally, these are the two most vexed issues today in literary studies. At no time in literary studies has theorizing about history been more acute and pervasive. It is hardly too much to say that what joins all the special interests in the field, all factions in our current dissensus, is an overriding interest in history: as the ground and texture of ideas, metaphors, and myths; as the substance of the texts we read and the spirit in which we interpret them. Even if we acknowledge that great books, a few configurations of language raised to an extraordinary pitch of intensity, have transcended their time and place (and even if we believe that their enduring power offers a recurrent source of opposition), it is evident upon reflection that concepts of aesthetic transcendence are themselves timebound. Like other claims to the absolute, from the hermeneutics of faith to scientific objectivity, aesthetic claims about high art are shaped by history. We grasp their particular forms of beyondness (the aesthetics of divine inspiration, the aesthetics of ambiguity, subversion, and indeterminacy) through an identifiably historical consciousness.

The same recognition of contingency extends to the writing of history. Some histories are truer than others; a few histories are invested for a time with the grandeur of being "definitive" and "comprehensive"; but all are narrative conditioned by their historical moments. So are these. Our intention here is to make limitations a source of open-endedness. All previous histories of American literature have been either totalizing or encyclopedic. They have offered either the magisterial sweep of a single vision or a multitude of terse accounts that come to seem just as totalizing, if only because the genre of the brief, expert synthesis precludes the development of authorial voice. Here, in contrast, American literary history unfolds through a polyphony of largescale narratives. Because the number of contributors is limited, each of them has the scope to elaborate distinctive views (premises, arguments, analyses); each of their narratives, therefore, is persuasive by demonstration, rather than by assertion; and each is related to the others (in spite of difference) through themes and concerns, anxieties and aspirations, that are common to *this* generation of Americanists.

The contributors were selected first for the excellence of their scholarship and then for the significance of the critical communities informing their work. Together, they demonstrate the achievements of Americanist literary criticism over the past three decades. Their contributions to these volumes show links as well as gaps between generations. They give voice to the extraordinary range of materials now subsumed under the heading of American literature. They express the distinctive sorts of excitement and commitment that have led to the remarkable expansion of the field. And they reflect the diversity of interests that constitutes literary studies in our time as well as the ethnographic diversity that has come to characterize our universities, faculty and students alike, since World War II, and especially since the 1960s.

The same qualities inform this *History*'s organizational principles. Its flexibility of structure is meant to accommodate the varieties of American literary history. Some major writers appear in more than one volume, because they belong to more than one age. Some texts are discussed in several narratives within a volume, because they are important to different realms of cultural experience. Sometimes the story of a certain movement is retold from different perspectives, because the story requires a plural focus: as pertaining, for example, to the margins as well as to the mainstream, or as being equally the culmination of one era and the beginning of another. Such overlap was not planned, but it was encouraged from the start, and the resulting diversity of perspectives corresponds to the sheer plenitude of literary and historical materials. It also makes for a richer, more intricate account of particulars (writers, texts, movements) than that available in any previous history of American literature.

Sacvan Bercovitch

Every volume in the *History* displays these strengths in its own way. This volume does so by providing a multilayered analysis of a pivotal era in the formation of American cultural identity. Like the writers of that time, all four contributors – Richard Brodhead, Nancy Bentley, Walter Benn Michaels, and Susan Mizruchi – foreground race and gender as the best available lenses for investigating the industrial and demographic changes then underway, along with anxieties arising from new Darwinist and social scientific conceptions of human nature. This volume may therefore be read as an exploration of difference itself, here manifested in the typologies of Naturalist novels, in the embattled domesticities of sentimental fiction, and in the nearly universal dependence on racialized language. It may also be read as a study of the totalizing forces bearing down on American individuality. Throughout, these contributors treat the relationship between culture and economy as decisive, for writers in particular, and in general for both producers and consumers in an age of marketing and advertising. Indeed, all four contributors recognize the market as a central locus of cultural interaction at a time when the dynamics of identity and the dynamics of commerce became inextricably entwined.

The result is a remarkably coherent portrait of the era, one that is enriched by a variety of critical approaches. Brodhead focuses on the emergent literary genres of the era. He depicts an anxious writer class as it was being shaped by, and was in turn shaping, the commercial interests of publishers. These writers, he shows, succeeded in manipulating both the supply and the demand of the literary market to their own ends, and they gained recognition by writing to and for specific literary niches. Bentley's narrative yields a different kind of cultural dialectic. In her account, Realism becomes the point of conflict between an entrenched cultural establishment and an upstart mass market, with important consequences for the both high literature and popular culture. Realism is also a main focus of Michaels's narrative. However, he emphasizes the social functions of literature, stressing the incorporation of literature into broad institutional hierarchies. That process of incorporation, he argues, became the site of conflicts that could no longer be contained by the nation's political structures. Mizruchi's perspective might best be termed anthropological: she demonstrates how literature defined the ways in which the nation addressed the costs and benefits of its growing cultural diversity – and how, in doing so, it helped redefine America itself as a modern nation, the land of multicultural modernity.

For Richard Brodhead, the story of postbellum American literature becomes a study in cultural stratification. His overview of the professional literary field follows a loose chronological structure, introducing new modes of writing in the order in which they were accessed by successive emergent social groups: women in sentimental fiction, the working class in its "books for the million," immigrants in the urban theater, the middle class in "high literature," provincials and African Americans in "local color." In effect, Brodhead describes the foundation of a permanent literary culture in America – featuring hierarchical, profit-driven systems of production and distribution – as well as the subsequent fragmentation of American literature into plural literatures of diverse styles, thematics, intentions, and social significances. Stressing the importance of publication as a public act, subject to the needs and desires of a reading (and paying) audience, Brodhead defines the professional spaces, or the "cultures of letters," within which writers as diverse as Horatio Alger, Charles Chesnutt, and Sarah Orne Jewett operated, both acceding to and resisting professional demands. These cultures of letters often served to limit the creative possibilities of the writers who worked within them. Yet just as often, we learn, they provided opportunities for writers who had been excluded previously from the literary field.

Nancy Bentley locates the origins of nineteenth-century Realism in an elite culture's responses – both affirmative and antagonistic – to an emergent mass culture. Her narrative embraces high literary practitioners like William Dean Howells, whose dispassionate, analytical work created a new aesthetic of social-scientific types, and Henry James, who turned his analytical gaze inward to explore the impact of a potentially chaotic modernity on matters of mind and taste. More broadly, her narrative traces a shift in American methods of "seeing," from the early postwar years, dominated by the claims of objectivity inherent in museum culture, through the crucible of modernization, to an intensely subjective relation between writer and culture. In all cases, she argues, Realism was a strategic rejoinder to the sentimentality, sensationalism, and publicity of popular culture. Yet as Bentley also shows, it turned out to be a surprisingly permeable category, creating a space in elite culture for socially marginal figures, and a surprisingly brittle category as well, susceptible to the excesses of mass culture. Realism provided an opportunity for outsiders like Charles Chesnutt to address social concerns in a context of artistic respectability, and it invited the passionate provocations of intellectuals like W. E. B. Du Bois. This deployment of Realist methods by the very types they were designed to contain – African Americans, women, Native Americans – gradually forced literary elites to abandon Realism for more self-conscious modes of writing. By the end of the century, Realism had led them into the radical ironies of American Modernism.

In Walter Benn Michaels's narrative, turn-of-the-century fiction assumes the functions of well-established cultural institutions; it becomes the contained space within which American society fights its social and political battles. Moving beyond the standard contrast between Naturalism and Realism – Naturalism as an obsessive engagement with biological and social determinism; Realism as the translation into fiction of a new journalistic ethos – Michaels uncovers their institutional value by arguing for their functional similarities. His Naturalist and Realist texts are allied insofar as they defined the terms according to which "new forms of social existence were imagined and articulated." In particular, he emphasizes the critical role that fiction played in the re-evaluation of the American individual at the advent of modern bureaucracy. Organizing his study around three basic tropes – visibility and race, desire and capitalism, work and careers – Michaels chronicles the gradual blurring of the distinction between social dependence and social independence in literary representations (as well as in the society at large). In his readings, Mark Twain's Connecticut Yankee, Kate Chopin's Edna Pontellier, and Owen Wister's Virginian all self-consciously facilitate the transition from the idealism of Emerson's heroic Individual to the hard realism of the mid-twentieth-century Organization Man.

Susan Mizruchi dramatizes the social fragmentation of the era. She presents the decades following the Civil War as the time when "the specific stakes of this diversity [were] widely conceptualized and debated," and proceeds to display the literary responses to a new national heterogeneity – social, ethnic, racial, aesthetic, religious, economic. Beginning with an analysis of the fragmentary, insistently personal evocations of the Civil War, she examines each successive crisis of dissociation – emancipation and Reconstruction, the influx of immigrants, the extermination of Native Americans, the ubiquitous influence of advertising in the creation of a consumer nation, the reappraisal of work in the age of great factories, and the altered significance of the individual in a society governed by trusts and robber barons. In short, she details the full range of literary responses to a dramatically altered social reality. Her readings range from the assimilationist impulses of Booker T. Washington and Mary Antin, to the cultural resistances of Winnemucca, to the Anglo-Saxon fantasies of Thomas Dixon, and (in a section describing the proliferation of utopian novels between 1880 and World War I) to the corporate idealism of Edward Bellamy. And she links her readings throughout to an ongoing evaluation of the nascent social sciences and the growth of corporate capitalism. Mizruchi concludes, persuasively, that the insistence on discourses of difference, even among writers who wished to inspire a greater cultural homogeneity in the nation, ultimately issued in the "multicultural becoming" of modern America.

Mizruchi's insight reinforces a central theme of the volume as a whole. All four contributors trace the movement from the homogenized mainstream culture of the antebellum years towards a fragmented, genuinely pluralistic, and finally multicultural concept of what it means to be American. To that end, they all highlight the sustained relationship, even reciprocity, between text and context, revealing the many ways in which the literature performed crucial cultural work. Together, they offer the richest, most detailed account we have of American literature and culture from 1860 to 1920.

Sacvan Bercovitch
John S. Tessitore

THE AMERICAN LITERARY FIELD,
1860–1890

Richard H. Brodhead

I

❦

THE AMERICAN LITERARY FIELD, 1860–1890

CULTURES OF LETTERS

Toward the end of his 1879 biography of Hawthorne, Henry James has this to say about Hawthorne's support of the presidential bid of the pro-slavery Franklin Pierce:

> Like most of his fellow-countrymen, Hawthorne had no idea that the respectable institution [slavery] which he contemplated in impressive contrast to humanitarian "mistiness," was presently to cost the nation four long years of bloodshed and misery, and a social revolution as complete as any the world has seen. When this event occurred, he was therefore proportionately horrified and depressed by it; it cut from beneath his feet the familiar ground which had long felt so firm, substituting a heaving and quaking medium in which his spirit found no rest. Such was the bewildered sensation of that earlier and simpler generation of which I have spoken; their illusions were rudely dispelled, and they saw the best of all possible republics given over to fratricidal carnage. . . . The subsidence of that great convulsion has left a different tone from the tone it found, and one may say that the Civil War marks an era in the history of the American mind. It introduced into the national consciousness a certain sense of proportion and relation, of the world being a more complicated place than it had hitherto seemed, the future more treacherous, success more difficult. At the rate at which things are going, it is obvious that good Americans will be more numerous than ever; but the good American, in days to come, will be a more critical person than his complacent and confident grandfather. He has eaten of the tree of knowledge. He will not, I think, be a sceptic, and still less, of course, a cynic; but he will be, without discredit to his well-known capacity for action, an observer.

This passage is useful at the start of a history of mid nineteenth-century American literature because it states so plainly the usually unspoken assumptions through which that history has been known and told. Two tenets have continued to shape the understanding of this field. The first and stronger of these, what might be called the periodization hypothesis, is that American literature breaks at the Civil War – that the war's convulsion caused a rupture in American experience and marks a boundary between different phases of "the American mind." The second assumption, what might be called the realism hypothesis, reinforces the first by specifying a difference of character between the periods so split. By its account, the postbellum differs from the antebellum by being more tempered, more ironic, more unillusioned, in short more realistic: so that in crossing the boundary from prewar to postwar we also cross over from Romanticism to the more chastened domain of Realism.

This scheme of understanding, like any intellectual convenience that has held continuing authority, speaks to a certain amount of historical truth, and a rival account will have to find its own way of talking about the realities it addressed: the succession of styles in the nineteenth century, the rise of "Realism," and so on. Nevertheless, the assumptions just named have been so unreflectively taken for truth that it might be well to underline their historiographical limits. To think of history at large: did the Civil War "mark an era?" In some realms of American experience the answer is clearly yes. In moving four million men, women, and children from the category of slave to the category of freedman the war produced a substantially new historical situation for Southern blacks, conferring on them a new status in theory and enmeshing them in the new struggle to make that status a reality. Through its devastations the war also marked an era for Southern whites, inserting them in the new history of hardship, humiliation, the attempted reconstitution of an old economy on new grounds, and the attempted resuscitation of violated social hierarchies that is this group's version of the Gilded Age.

But in other phases of nineteenth-century American history the war had a less decisive impact, and so has less meaning as a marker of bounds. The pacification and spatial containment of the Great Plains Native Americans is another American history exactly contemporaneous with Reconstruction and its successor Redemption, and these two histories cross at certain points – in the redeployment of Union soldiers like Generals William Tecumseh Sherman and Phil Sheridan as Native-American fighters in the 1870s, for instance, or in the modeling of Native-American training schools on the industrial training schools designed for freed blacks. But the subjugation of the Native American did not begin with the Civil War, and it did not change course in a decisive way through the intervention of that war. If we thought of other characteristic postwar cultural developments – the growth of great cities, the spread of industrial production, the transportation revolution, immigration – the war would be even less relevant as a chronological divide. The foreign immigration and the country-to-city mobility that are such striking facts of postbellum American history really continue an antebellum development. Boston, it might be remembered, saw its population grow tenfold – from 18,000 to 180,000 – between 1790 and 1860.

The point that even so cursory a review would make is that there is no such thing as "American history" in the sense of a uniformly shaped experience of a whole people. At any moment American history has been composed of different American histories playing themselves out at the same time: histories not fully autonomous, since they share common determinants and impinge on one another; but histories not identical either, since they represent workings through of different issues in different social locations. The lesson for literary history is that the attempt to produce homogenized historical unities – the effort to specify "the American" or the character or bent of a period – inevitably simplifies an always mixed, always multiple phenomenon. American literature's full history can only ever be the story of the different things that literature was and was becoming and of the interactions among its different strains.

But what would be the principle of division in a history of this sort? If chronological oppositions like prewar/ postwar or literary-philosophical ones like Realism/Romanticism force locally relevant distinctions onto a whole they fit less well, what way of marking difference would be more faithful to that whole's historical shape? This chapter assumes that the most significant lines of division within the literary field are produced not by differences between authors or styles or periods or movements but by literature's responsiveness to the different *places* built for literature in American cultural life. At any historical moment American society has subtended several partly distinct worlds of reading and writing, each sponsoring its own set of operative genres, each gathering its own differently composed audience around such writing, each inserting writing in a different field of extraliterary cultural forces, and each conferring on writing a different form of value and support. Such cultures of letters are not literary creations, but they are also not wholly external to literary creation, since any act of writing shapes itself within some shared understanding of what writing is and does.

This chapter attempts to survey the whole American literary terrain of the later nineteenth century. It tries to find a place in its picture not just for celebrated texts but for the whole activity of imaginative writing at this time. But it is particularly concerned to specify the array of overlapping yet differently constituted literary cultures that were operative in America at this time – the cultural configurations American works formed themselves in and against.

AFTER THE AMERICAN RENAISSANCE

A survey of American writing in the years after 1865 might begin by looking at one point of strong divergence from what came before. Modern consideration of antebellum writing has until recently focused on what F. O. Matthiessen dubbed the American Renaissance: the emergence in the 1830s of American Romantic writers of great individuality and power, particularly Emerson and Hawthorne, then in the 1850s of their more exuberantly eccentric followers – Thoreau, Whitman, Melville, Dickinson. But the American Renaissance was an affair not just of strong individual authors but of writers working out the implications of a certain literary-cultural situation. The most salient facts about Romanticism in its American incarnation are that this highly mobile intellectual strain reached the United States belatedly, flowering in the 1830s, not (as in England or Germany) in the 1790s, and that in America it found a soil that gave it quite distinctive growth-habits. Arriving when it did, in the United States Romanticism was conjoined with other urgencies that powerfully amplified its cult of the originary imagination. It intersected with the frantic nationalism of the American 1830s and 1840s. It interacted with this time's acute post-colonial anxiety over cultural dependencies that had survived political independence, and with the 1840s hunger for non-derivative forms of American expression. Most fatefully, Romantic artistic thought intersected with the highly charged ethos of reformation and perfectionism – the veritable culture of reformist experimentation – rife in America at this time.

This distinctive ethos has at its center the belief that the fundamental forms by which human life is organized need not be received from traditional practice but can be re-envisioned and re-formed in spiritually superior ways, here and now, by people like oneself. It finds its religious expression for instance in Joseph Smith, the founder of Mormonism, with his belief – outrageous at another time and place but much less peculiar in this one – that he could experience true scriptural revelation and so found the new, true church. This ethos finds its civic expression in the school and prison reform movements of the 1830s and 1840s, with their earnest conviction that such elementary social operations as education or deviance management could be reinstituted in redeemed forms. It finds its social expression in experimental communities of the American 1840s like John Humphrey Noyes's Oneida Community or Bronson Alcott's vegetarian and sexually abstentive Fruitlands, with their belief that the most elemental arrangements of daily life – divisions of labor, eating habits, erotic relations, childrearing methods – could be reimagined and re-formed.

Literary study has tended to hold American literature apart from such developments. But the authors of the so-called American Renaissance lived in close proximity to the reformatory-experimental phases of antebellum culture. And their work can be thought of as a working out, in the medium of literary expression, of a more general imperative to radical re-envisioning. The marks of this surrounding ethos can be seen in features wholly characteristic of their work:

in the extravagant vision of men and women as originators, not the receivers but the creators of the history and law they live by, found in Emerson's "Self-Reliance" or the forest scene of Hawthorne's *The Scarlet Letter*; in what might be called the testamentary attitude, the sense of writing as the medium through which the ground of being can be seen and proclaimed anew, so strong in *Walden* or *Leaves of Grass* or *Moby-Dick*; and finally in the persistent formal radicalism of this work, its brash sense that the ordering forms of literary expression exist for it fundamentally to reinvent – as Melville writes novels that reinvent what a novel is; or as Whitman writes verse that remakes the properties of verse; or as Dickinson, in conjunction with many other heterodoxies, rewrites the rules of English syntax and punctuation.

The features just enumerated are not characteristic of postbellum American writing. One of the reasons they are not is that the ethos of spiritually earnest reformatory experimentalism still forceful in the American North in the 1840s had become, by 1865 if not earlier, something more of the past than the present. (One of the great by-products of this ethos and by 1860 the principal channel for its surviving energies, the American antislavery movement, considered declaring its work over in 1865.) Many facts would suggest that the literary emanation of this culture came to its end around 1860. Thoreau, founder of a utopian community for one at Walden Pond in 1845–47, died in 1862. Melville, lover (in his words) of all men who *dive*, virtually ceased to publish in 1857. Emerson, whose last major volume *The Conduct of Life* appeared in 1860, lived on to become a well-behaved citizen of a much more orthodox literary establishment and a wan repeater of his earlier gospels of originality. Hawthorne died in 1864 but had published only one novel since 1852.

In reality this antebellum literary formation did not wholly die out with the War. It persisted in part, but as something now marginal, if not anachronistic. Walt Whitman lived all through the period I will be discussing (he died in 1892), and since he wrote up until his death, Whitman too can be counted as an author of the later nineteenth century. But Whitman's postbellum poetry, with the memorable early exceptions of the elegy for Lincoln and the war volume *Drum Taps*, takes the form either of self-imitation or the touching, repetitious farewells of an author who knows that his strong poetic life is already behind him. (These poems – including the superb "So Long!" and "After the Supper and Talk," with its splendidly Whitmanian conclusion: "Soon to be lost for aye in the darkness – loth, O so loth to depart!/ Garrulous to the very last" – appear in the valedictory annexes late Whitman built for *Leaves of Grass*: "Songs of Parting," "Sands at Seventy," "Good-Bye My Fancy," "Old Age Echoes.") Whitman's prose work from this period, while always vigorous, adopts a point of view that aligns it with a cultural moment now increasingly past. *Democratic*

Vistas (completed 1871), his review of the present failures and future prospects of American social life, addresses the America of the Grant Administration, but the form of its expression – especially its supercharged vatic prose and its millennial-nationalist inflections – makes it read like a belated instance of ways of thinking and talking dateable to the 1840s. *Specimen Days* (1882), Whitman's last sustained writing project, is overtly reminiscent.

By common reputation Melville ceased to be an author in the late 1850s. But Melville too lived all through the Gilded Age (he died in 1891), and in a full period history he too would be recognized as embodying one of the forms that American authorship took in the later nineteenth century. In a sense he embodies the author as non-author, the author in the state of renunciation or refusal of his career. After his failures to find public support for his most ambitious literary experiments – the great non-sellers *Mardi* (1849), *Moby-Dick* (1851), *Pierre: or, the Ambiguities* (1852), and *The Confidence Man* (1857) – Melville stopped writing novels and took another job: from 1866 to 1885 he was Deputy Inspector of Customs for the Port of New York. During this time he underlined this passage from Maurice de Guérin in an essay by Matthew Arnold: "The literary career seems to me unreal, both in its essence and in the rewards which one seeks from it, and therefore marred by a secret absurdity."

In fact this apparently "silent" writer kept finding new writing projects through these years. (Melville's career as a poet, like Whitman's as a prose-writer, dates from the end of the War.) But in Melville's case as in Whitman's these late-century projects seem less of that time than revisitings of problems framed in an earlier world. *Clarel* (1876), a long verse-narrative of a pilgrimage to the Holy Land and a *tour d'horizon* of available contemporary positions towards the problem of faith, is one of the most ambitious works attempted in the American 1870s. But in form and theme it takes its departure more nearly from the 1840s novel *Mardi* than from writings more nearly its contemporaries. Similarly *Billy Budd*, the prose fable Melville left in manuscript when he died, reworks in the late 1880s an imaginative issue set in the 1840s. *Billy Budd* replays in a more detached mode a problem of discipline Melville had addressed with partisan humanitarian outrage in the 1850 novel *White-Jacket*.

The culture of reformatory idealism that provided a dominant scene of American literary production in the 1840s and 1850s had become a weakly surviving force in the 1870s and 1880s, this is to say. Its ethos did not wholly die out. The continuing spawning ground of distinctive American radicalisms in religion, politics, literature, and family and community organization, this many-times-reactivated culture persisted even in the very differently oriented Gilded Age, but as something increasingly marginal and eccentric: witness the journal *Woodhull and Claflin's Weekly* (1870–76), a surviving organ of expression of 1840s spiritualism and free love communitarianism ("Progress! Free Thought! Untrammelled Lives!," its motto read in part), and the first place of American publication of Karl Marx's *Communist Manifesto*. But this culture did not inspire major new literary projects in the postwar decades, nor could it deliver a significant public base for literary programs conceived at an earlier time. Whitman, an obscene and incompetent poet in the eyes of the dominant culture of this period, remained an object largely of cult appreciation through the nineteenth century, and Melville the object of no appreciation at all.

Nevertheless, the very different writers who emerged after the war in many cases had this culture's reformatory idealism built into their experience from their 1840s childhoods. Louisa May Alcott lived through all her father Bronson Alcott's educational and communitarian experiments; Henry James had a well-to-do Swedenborgian visionary for a father; the urbanely professional William Dean Howells had lived in a utopian community in his Ohio youth. Thanks to this survival, a literary culture residual through most of this period retained the power to be reactivated at later moments of social strain. It came back to life in the resurgent utopianism of the late 1880s and early 1890s, promoting books like Edward Bellamy's *Looking Backward, 2000–1887* to bestseller status.

DOMESTIC LITERARY CULTURE

If one literary culture assembled in the antebellum period was largely deactivated by the end of the war, another one persisted at full strength into the postbellum decades, creating one of the chief socially structured worlds of reading and writing in nineteenth-century America.

We now know to remember that what the twentieth century termed the American Renaissance was only one of several contemporaneous literary developments, one product of a larger reformulation of the literary field that produced equally new writing situations for other zones of practice. In particular, the *anni mirabili* of the American Renaissance witnessed the coming together of another world of reading and writing composed around different values and relations, a domestic literary culture that created fewer authorial overreachers but a more firmly established system of authorial support. This development has in its background the emergence of a new social audience: the new middle-class family of the antebellum decades in which the father goes out to work and the mother stays in a home newly exempted from heavy domestic production, her new work being to project a strong moral presence into this now-leisured home and to instill a strong religious and moral character in the children in her charge. The spread of this social model from the 1830s on had many consequences, but in literary terms its chief effect was to create a potential new literary public – a socially particularized leisure space that reading could help fill.

By the early 1850s the scale of this potential public began to come clear. In the year in which *Moby-Dick* sold perhaps 2,000 copies and the critically well-received *The Scarlet Letter* around 5,000 copies, Susan Warner's classic domestic novel *The Wide, Wide World* had an early sale of around 50,000, a figure soon exceeded by the 300,000 run of Harriet Beecher Stowe's *Uncle Tom's Cabin* (1852). In face of such receptions publishers began fitting together new publication mechanisms designed at once to regularize the production of such family entertainment and to mobilize the family as a regular entertainment market. After the first successes of Warner and Stowe, for instance, a publisher contracted in advance for a domestic bestseller from Fanny Fern and planned a massive advertisement campaign for this novel also in advance of its com-position. (The resultant book, *Ruth Hall*, sold 55,000 copies in 1854.) These commercially aggressive new schemes of literary production helped consoli-date the set of mutually reinforcing relationships that defined America's first mass literary market. The logic of this market was that an author who knew the middle-class home's concerns (most often a woman) could reach the large public of middle-class readers and so achieve financial success on the condi-tion that (s)he write within a certain literary program: on the condition that her writing address domestic subjects and assist the mother's work of making middle-class values seem compellingly real.

The domestic literary economy organized around 1850 provided the first predictably stabilized audience for literary goods in America, and so supplied the first reliable support for writing as a full-time activity. (Before the 1840s, it will be remembered, only one American author – James Fenimore Cooper – had succeeded in supporting himself exclusively from his writing.) And this system of exchange among readers, publishers, and authors continued in effect through the succeeding decades. It is notable that one of the most popular of all nineteenth-century domestic novels – Augusta Evans (later Wilson)'s *St. Elmo*, with its characteristically contradictory projection of a strong heroine who embraces domestic restriction as her final proper career – was published after the Civil War, in 1866. (*St. Elmo* is alleged to have been read by one million people in 1866 alone, or by one American in every thirty-six. Two generations later it was still so widely read that Eudora Welty remembers her mother's rule for making sure she watered her roses long enough as: "Take a chair and *St. Elmo*.") Elizabeth Stuart Phelps (later Ward)'s peep-into-heaven novel *The Gates Ajar* incorporates the trauma of recent war deaths into the domestic novel's long-perfected address to the loss of family members, bereavement, and faith in a God who takes loved ones away. It was a bestseller in the year 1868.

The continuing vitality of the middle-class-family-oriented literary market is witnessed by the fact that the first cohort of domestic authors stayed in production long after the war. Susan Warner lived and wrote until 1885, and her sister Anna until a much later date. Mrs. E. D. E. N. Southworth wrote until near her death in 1899. Marion Harland (the pseudonym of Mary Virginia Hawes Terhune), author of the popular 1854 novel *Alone*, went blind in her late eighties but continued to dictate novels as late as 1919. (She died in 1922.)

But the strongest evidence of domestic literature's historical persistence is that this form continued to recruit new authors in the postbellum generation. Louisa May Alcott is a principal example. If the category of American literature were composed of books Americans actually read, the author of *Little Women* (1868–69) would always have been regarded as one of its major authors. The interest of Alcott in this context is that this enduringly popular writer so perfectly exemplifies the *figure* of the writer projected in mid nineteenth-century domestic literary culture. Alcott knew intimately the world of antebellum experimentalism: daughter of the incessant educational innovator Bronson Alcott, hostess of the daughter of the martyr John Brown, and admirer of her neighbor Thoreau (she eventually purchased Thoreau's house for her widowed sister to live in), Alcott can remind us that the differently inflected cultures of nineteenth-century America were not separate entities but shared social space. Nevertheless, in her work Alcott reproduces the world imaged by middle-class domestic ideology, not the radicalism adjacent to it. In keeping with this ideology's specifications of "women's sphere," *Little Women* and its sequels make their literary space be domestic space, a women's and children's world bounded off from a male public and historical world outside. (In *Little Women* Mr. March is absent at the unseen Civil War.) This family space is intensely affectionate, an island of mother-centered warmth, but as in nineteenth-century domestic ideology and all the novels it supported, this island of warmth is also a strongly tutelary space, a world where character is always being reshaped in the direction of parental ideals. In the home, *through* the home, the March sisters learn the standard lessons of women's domestic education: mandatory other-directedness, the cure of "temper," the curtailment of selfish will, and so on. Amy, Beth, Jo, and Meg grumble over their missing Christmas presents until they remember their unselfish mother Marmee, then realize they would rather give her a gift than get anything themselves. When initially tomboyish Jo feels rage, her mother helps win her to the cause of self-control by confessing to her own frequent anger, now successfully contained. When the newly married Meg chafes against the constraints a small budget puts on consumeristic acquisitiveness – "I can't resist when I see Sallie buying all she wants, and pitying me because I don't. I try to be contented, but . . . I'm tired of being poor," she says, thirty years before Sister Carrie – a loving but firm family world teaches her to curb exorbitant desires.

Alcott writes without the heavy moralism practiced by many writers in her genre, but moralization – the incorporation of the mother's cultural values as controlling presences within the daughters' personalities – is the dominant drama of Little Women and its successors. (In the last March family volume, Jo's Boys [1886], Jo – now Mother Bhaer – preaches a maternal moral revival scarcely outdone by Stowe's Little Eva). Of course the real target of edification in these books is not the March daughters but the reader who enters into their situation – the book itself, like the home it idealizes, functioning as a space for warm sharing, high-spirited entertainment, and the instilling of normative ideals.

Within Little Women and its sequels – An Old-Fashioned Girl (1870), Little Men (1871), Eight Cousins (1875), Rose in Bloom (1876), and Jo's Boys (1886) – Alcott gives the topoi of 1850s domestic fiction a classic literary expression. In a continuity quite as striking, in the writing life behind her books she also exemplifies classic features of the author as mid-century domestic culture helped define that term. One of the historical peculiarities of nineteenth-century domestic authorship is that its purveying of an ethic of unselfishness traveled together with keen-eyed appreciation of and heightened attention to its own market position: the writer-heroine of Fanny Fern's Ruth Hall is portrayed less as an artist than as a literary businesswoman, rewarded, at the end, with a reunited family and shares of stock in the bank. Perpetuating this tradition, Alcott too thought of her work less as an aesthetic object than an economic instrument. In the veiled histories of her career in the Jo March stories Alcott always implies that economic need gave the first spur to her writing and that economic success was the reason for continuing: by the time of Jo's Boys, writing, that "golden goose whose literary eggs found such an unexpected market," has brought Jo a "snug little fortune," and she has learned that "she merely had to [re]load her ships and send them off" to win a renewed "cargo of gold and glory." (She has learned, in other words, how to regularize production of a profitable commodity and make writing a successful mercantile venture.)

The featuring of the economic dimensions of authorship in the literary consciousness of domestic writers typically travels together with the insistence that writing is subservient to women's traditional family obligations – that one writes and earns money not for pleasure but to support the family. This notion, too, strongly dominates Alcott's literary self-conception. Jo's pleasure in her income is that she can send her ailing sister to healthful places and fill her mother's hard life with "every comfort and luxury." Alcott, similarly, made herself into the daughter as good provider, persuading herself that she wrote to support first her parents, then her sisters, then her sisters' children. When Bronson Alcott, the aged father who needed her support, died in 1888, Louisa May Alcott died two days later.

But if Alcott strongly continues themes and role-conceptions forged early in the domestic tradition, she can also be taken to indicate historical shifts in this literary culture. Alcott's novels are much less militantly religious than such 1850s domestic texts as *The Wide, Wide World* and *Uncle Tom's Cabin*, suggesting a cooling of the Protestant evangelicalism so ardent in middle-class culture at the time of that group's self-organization. Her books are more tolerant of theater games, outdoor exercise, and other forms of play (their tone is itself newly playful), and so signal the easing from an earlier strict self-discipline towards the greater self-indulgence licensed in later middle-class life.

But the most crucial historical change embodied in Alcott's work lies in its intended audience. As part of its general hyper-attentiveness to the moral formation of the young, the new middle class of the antebellum decades devised a literature written specifically for children that could help the parent with the work of edification, thereby creating the first specialized institutions of children's literary production. (Fanny Fern's father founded and edited one of the earliest children's papers, *The Youth's Companion*.) The domestic bestsellers of the 1850s were not conceived as children's novels, however, even if children were welcome to read them. By contrast, Alcott's works, though profoundly similar in content, were clearly directed toward the juvenile market ("moral pap for the young," she disparagingly called them). This suggests that by Alcott's day, the middle class had relegated to a children's subculture imaginative activities that it once put on center stage.

In larger terms, this change implies that as the domestic subsystem of mid nineteenth-century American literature continued its operation in the postbellum years, it also underwent internal reorganization, spinning several increasingly separate developments out of a once unified whole. Alcott's juvenile market – also colonized by Martha Finley, author of the *Elsie Dinsmore* volumes that sold five million copies in the Dodd, Mead edition alone – would be one such development. A second would be the emergence of a more specialized literature of household management in the later nineteenth century, as witnessed in Marion Harland's progression from a novelist who also wrote domestic advice to a domestic advice writer who sometimes wrote novels. Harland, who had a syndicated column in the *Chicago Daily Tribune*, wrote the million-copy-selling cookbook *Common Sense in the Household* [1871] and such later works as *Everyday Etiquette* [1905], making her the Irma Rombauer and Emily Post of the later nineteenth century all in one.

Neither young adult fiction nor household advice, however, filled the central space of middle-class reading culture that popular domestic fiction had occupied. If we ask what did supply this gap we enter an almost wholly uncharted territory, but *St. Elmo* might help us to a speculative answer. The theme of the proper shape of woman's career links this book to the first hugely successful domestic novels. Nevertheless, put next to *The Wide, Wide World*, or *Uncle Tom's Cabin* or *Ruth Hall*, *St. Elmo* seems quite a different sort of work. The home-management obsession and evangelical piety so prominent in the earlier books are largely in remission in Evans's novel; on the other hand, this book sponsors a degree of imaginative indulgence unknown to its predecessors. Like Ruth Hall, Evans's heroine Edna Earle becomes a bestselling author, but while Ruth Hall struggled against hardship, Edna Earle is endowed with almost magical gifts of mind: this youthful prodigy writes a highly acclaimed essay on Greek iconoclasm at the time of Alcibiades, among other feats of erudition. As it more freely indulges fantasies of female powers, *St. Elmo*'s prose also caters to a less chastened appetite for readerly luxury. "She could not understand why, in the vineyard of letters, the laborer was not equally worthy of hire, whether the work was accomplished in the *toga virilis* or the gay kirtle of *contadina*" is Evans's characteristically unsimple way of saying that women can write as well as men.

If *St. Elmo* reflects an emerging literary taste, and its immense popularity suggests that it does, it implies the advent of a middle-class reading world where books are no longer so obligated to recite and reinforce class-defining values (though they must of course not violate such values) – a world where such social definition is largely achieved, freeing entertainment to be more purely entertaining. This in turn would suggest that one historical yield of the domestic literary culture of the 1850s is the American middlebrow reading culture of later periods: the culture that likes to read, has the leisure to read (and the funds to buy books), wants its entertainments to be uplifting and improving, but lacks the training to find entertainment in work that defines itself as "art." This historically new organization of consumption is one of the most enduring literary consequences of the Gilded Age. Already in that age it made a new kind of book a bestseller: not *Uncle Tom's Cabin* but (for instance) General Lew Wallace's *Ben-Hur* (1880).

BOOKS FOR THE MILLION

The huge sales figures of the books just discussed tell us that in the mid nineteenth century a popular culture of letters was founded in the United States within the ethos of the family-centered middle class. This fact carries the further lesson that "popular culture" is not historically invariant. Neither an entity with fixed characteristics nor a stable opposite of "high" culture, popular culture has taken different forms at different times and places, in response to the changing social configurations that have supplied its potential homes. But the other lesson the literary history of this time can teach is that popular culture is also not historically unitary. For in the mid nineteenth century another literary system operated alongside the one just discussed that achieved circulations and readerships at least as large but that established "the popular" in very different forms and relations.

This rival to domestic fiction is found in the world of cheap reading materials. These materials in their nineteenth-century forms stayed in vigorous life up through the 1890s, but like the domestic bestseller they were brought into existence before the war, as part of the general reorganization of the industry of literary production in the 1840s. The story-paper, a newspaper-sized journal with multiple stories serialized in columns of dense print, was devised in America around 1840. Within a few years the most long-lasting and widely circulating avatars of the story-paper were founded: Frederick Gleason's (later Maturin Ballou's) *The Flag of Our Union* (1845), Robert Bonner's *New York Ledger* (1855), *Frank Leslie's Illustrated Newspaper* (1855), Street and Smith's *New York Weekly* (1859). Shortly after, another new publishing instrument was devised that would supplement the story-paper in later years. In 1860 Erastus Beadle pioneered the paper-covered pamphlet novel issued at weekly intervals, and by 1865 the first twenty Beadle's Dime Novels had sold over 4,300,000 copies. The great empires of mass-circulation fiction would rely on both vehicles. The House of Beadle and Adams eventually ran seven story-papers and twenty-five dime-novel series. Street and Smith, the industry giant of the later nineteenth century, ran fifty separate dime-novel series in addition to the *New York Weekly*.

At their inception, these new forms of production were not sharply differentiated from the domestic literary world. Robert Bonner published Fanny Fern in the *New York Ledger*; Beadle printed the magazine *The Home Monthly*; *The Flag of Our Union* announced itself as "A Paper for the Million, and a Welcome Visitor to the Home Circle" as if detecting no difference between these markets. But these once-overlapping literary economies soon became differentiated, and the story-paper and pamphlet novel became the vehicles for the profoundly different literary culture they helped hold together until the century's close.

The difference of this body of writing can be located first in its subjects. As the chivalric epic had its Matter of Britain and Matter of Troy, story-paper and dime-novel fiction makes a few topics its set generic subjects. One is frontier adventure and Indian war, as in Edward S. Ellis's *Seth Jones: or, the Captives of the Frontier*, or Joseph E. Badger, Jr.'s *Old Bull's-Eye: The Lightning Shot of the Plains*, or "Ned Buntline's" (E. Z. C. Judson's) *Buffalo Bill, the King of the Border Men* (to name three titles from ten thousand). Another is historical romance and costume drama, as in A. J. H. Duganne's *Massasoit's Daughter: or, The French Captives. A Romance of Aboriginal New England* or Lieutenant Murray's *Rosalette; or, The Flower Girl of Paris. A Romance of France*. Still another set genre is detective fiction, as in Albert W. Aiken's *The Phantom Hand; or, The Heiress of Fifth Avenue. A Story of New York Hearths and Homes*, or Judson R. Taylor's *Gypsy Blair: or, The Western Detective* (two genres in one), or Street and Smith's later *True Detective Stories*, which were marketed as "absolute chapters of experience taken from the notebooks of the greatest and most noted Chiefs of Police in the largest cities in America." The genres of the western and detective fiction strongly link this material to the film and television industries of the twentieth century, suggesting that this literary system had its historical sequel in a modern mass culture no longer based in print. But its set subjects also sharply differentiate this writing from the domestic fiction contemporaneous with it, whose parallel generic "matters" – the management of the home, missionary work and conversion, the formation of female character – it shows no signs of knowing.

Differentiated by subject, story-paper and dime novels are also marked by a certain way of making a story in words. The uncountable works in these formats are literally action-packed, filled with highly charged plot sequences and largely emptied of other ingredients: characterization in excess of plot function, narrative rumination, and so on. (Louisa May Alcott testifies that when she began writing fiction for this market her editors edited out of her manuscripts "all the moral reflections" – an ingredient essential to the work of domestic fiction proving irrelevant in this other venue.) While fiction of every cultural level has identifiable conventions, this fiction also stands apart from its contemporaries in its extreme lack of effort to hide its conventional apparatus. Its individual works fail to stand out from one another not so much because they are poorly written as because their writing makes little effort to individuate them. Their point as stories is that they replay a formula already fully known – what else did the ninety-fourth Deadwood Dick, Junior adventure do? – and so offer an experience of iteration, not of novelty or originality.

If this popular literature is identified by the different properties of its writing, however, it is just as crucially defined by the different terms on which it was brought to public life. It is an essential, not an incidental, fact about this work that it was printed in formats and materials associated with newspapers. By these means it was produced into a likeness with the most everyday form of reading, and produced as well into the category of the ephemeral: unlike the hardbound book of middlebrow or elite reading culture, embodiment of the premise that writing might be a good to preserve (and an object to own), these works in their very materials invited themselves to be consumed, traded around, then disposed of, to be replaced by another day's new issue. (The fact that this fiction was produced not individually but in series, a new work in the same format every week, reinforced this message about its consumption.) The cheapness of this fiction, similarly, is no accidental property or extraneous trait. It was designed to cost and it was advertised as costing a price with a precise market meaning: a nickel or dime, not the dollar or more of contemporaneous hardbound volumes. It was also brought to the market of readers through its own distinctive means. Story-papers and dime novels were distributed through the network of newsdealers, mass-circulated with the most everyday of printed commodities.

The different terms of this work's cultural production did more than market it more widely. They established a different public as this work's social audience. Its cheapness made this the form of literature available to those with little surplus income for entertainment or "culture." Its length – an hour or two's reading, not the 600 pages of *St. Elmo* or *The Wide, Wide World* – suited it to those with a correspondingly small command of leisure. The minimally varied formulaics of its writing made it the possible reading of those less advantaged in yet another way, readers with poorer command of literacy skills.

For these reasons, this form composed the reading experience of a different social sector than popular domestic fiction. Real historical audiences are notoriously difficult to establish, but such evidence as survives suggests a sharp divergence in the social character of these two publics. Domestic fiction had its chief audience among people (usually women) already possessing, or newly aspiring to, or at least mentally identifying with, the leisured home of middle-class life. Cheap fiction incorporated into its audience many groups situated outside such feminized ease. Beadle's Dime Novels are known to have been preferred reading in the Union Army. Irish and German-minded variants suggest that such works had immigrant readers. Nineteenth-century reports on the laboring classes find story-papers prominent in working-class culture. Memoirs show such works to have been read by boys on farms.

One wants to be careful not to unduly harden this opposition of audiences. In historical reality both the domestic and "cheap" literary markets must have contained a mix of social elements, and there was no doubt some overlapping of their readerships. Nevertheless, to catch the logic of the two popular literary systems of mid nineteenth-century America it is essential to grasp the difference of the social bases they produced writing towards. The single most fundamental fact about literature's life in America after 1840 lies in the way new segmentations and stratifications in the literary realm became correlated with emerging social differences. The reorganization of American publishing around 1850 had its most decisive yield not in the new spectrum of literary modes it generated so much as in the subsequent linkage of those modes with socially distinct audiences.

In the wake of this development, different forms of reading took on the power to help differentiate their readers in social terms. When the late nineteenth century genteel investigator Dorothy Richardson learns that a woman worker in a New York box factory has never heard of *Little Women* and finds its story pointless (her favorite fiction is Laura Jean Libbey's *Little Rosebud's Lovers; or, The Cruel Revenge* [1886]), the gap between domestic and dime-novel literacies focuses the estrangement for both women between a working-class and a middle-class "self." When Harriet Beecher Stowe writes Alcott in 1872 that "In my many fears for my country and in these days when so much seductive and dangerous literature is pushed forward, the success of your domestic works has been to me most comforting," Stowe all but explicitly uses the literary difference dangerous/domestic to mark the class boundary of the middle and lower classes. ("Dangerous" was a mid nineteenth-century genteel word for the lower strata, "the dangerous classes.") In *Little Women*, Jo's ability to recognize story-paper fiction as morally beneath her marks her growth into an approved social identity. Writing such work is in Alcott's words a form of "living in bad society" that "desecrate[s] some of the womanliest attributes of a woman's character." Jo finds her "true" womanly career when Professor Bhaer shames her out of the work he brands "bad trash."

Subliterary to those "above" it, dime novel and story-paper fiction nevertheless supplied a literature to those who consumed it, feeding, with its millions of densely printed pages, the immense appetite for reading a low-literate mass audience displayed throughout the nineteenth century. On the writer's side, the meaning of this mass market was that it created another place for authors in America. The publication schedules of cheap fiction's many competing organs created a heavy demand for writing in these formats, and after 1850 such publications yielded the support for a certain kind of American literary career. Dime-novel writing gave work literally to hundreds. Its practitioners range from Emerson's cousin Mrs. Ann Emerson Porter to the celebrated Mrs. E. D. E. N. Southworth (a hugely popular writer more properly categorized as a story-paper than as a domestic author), and from Buffalo Bill Cody and his literary inventor "Ned Buntline" to the later-to-be-muckraker Upton Sinclair. (Sinclair, author of a series of military cadet novels for Street and Smith, wrote his first such work at age fourteen.)

But beyond supporting nameable individuals, this mode of production structured a certain role for the author and enforced a particular version of authorship on practitioners in its forms. If nineteenth-century domestic fiction supports the author as moral edifier or surrogate mother, this rival system renders the author something more like a wage laborer or industrial hand. Writing in this form paid a standard amount for a standard job of work. Its insistence on pre-established formats narrowly delimited the space for authorial self-expression, in effect making a trademarked generic formula the work's creator and the writer the more or less interchangeable performer of a pre-set task. (This separation of the work from any real individual author could be pressed to great lengths. The popular Street and Smith author Bertha M. Clay never existed except as a house-controlled name various unnamed others could publish under. The author of Beadle's Deadwood Dick series, Edward L. Wheeler, apparently died around 1885, but the firm continued to publish new work in his name long after his death.) In such records of them as survive, writers in these forms are typically silent about their artistic aspirations but explicit about the productivity they sustained. We know, for instance, that Joseph E. Badger, Jr. commonly completed an 80,000-word novel in a week, writing in six-hour shifts with two-hour breaks for sleep; that Ned Buntline wrote 60,000-word novels in six days; that Prentiss Ingraham wrote a half-dime novel in a day and a dime one in five days; and that Upton Sinclair wrote something near a million words – the equivalent of the output of Sir Walter Scott – in a year and a half's work for Street and Smith. These records show the extreme subordination in such writers' thinking of the work's intrinsic interest to an overriding imperative of maximized productive efficiency. Put another way, they display the industrialized mode of authorship that presided in this nineteenth-century literary economy.

But no culturally enforced model of authorship can wholly dictate the experience an author can attach to it; and if the main tendency of this popular literary system was to disindividuate the author, it should not be assumed that all such writers were depersonalized successfully. The two most fully known of such authors' lives, while admittedly atypical, can suggest something of the range of personalizations men and women could achieve for these forms.

Horatio Alger, Jr. continues to hold a mistaken reputation as a dominant author in this nineteenth-century mode. In fact his works were unspectacularly successful in their time, and had their great vogue in an early twentieth-century revival. But Alger was indeed an author *in* this mode. Alger wrote around 400 novelettes between the late 1860s and the 1890s, an average-sized corpus for a dime novelist, including the books he wrote in series – the Ragged Dick series, the Tattered Tom Series, the Luck and Pluck Series, and so on. Alger worked through the main-line vehicles of this literary form: the *New York Weekly* began serializing Alger in 1871. And Alger followed the historical evolution of his chosen form's market: when western formulas became more popular in the 1870s, Alger too went West in search of local color.

But if his career follows standard patterns, Alger brings idiosyncratic personal content to those patterns. Alger had a lifelong infatuation with boys. He was released from his first career – as a minister – for immoral conduct with boys in his parish. He persisted in tutoring boys (among them the eventual Supreme Court Justice Benjamin Cardozo) during his writing years. Late in life he adopted a group of boys, and when he died he left them the proceeds of his work. Since the dime novel was strongly marked as a boy's genre in his time, Alger could express an attraction highly problematic in social terms by channeling it through this form. "I leased my pen to the boys," he said of his career, in a phrase that links writing with self-commercialization and a semierotic homophile transaction.

Within his work, as well, Alger is able to produce highly individualized imaginative content within highly standardized forms. The virtuous boy promoted towards respectable status is Alger's tirelessly repeated formula. But caricaturizing accounts of the Horatio Alger Rags to Riches story scarcely do justice to the mix of ingredients that gives his works their power. His first and most successful book, *Ragged Dick* (1868), combines proto-realist reportage of the lives of the urban poor with an exemplary fiction of capitalist biography (Dick begins to be a new person when he begins to save his money) and a strain of fairy-tale magic: Alger is the great author of the mysterious benefactor, downtown avatar of the fairy godparent. His mode of magical capitalist realism, as it might be called, is his own invention, and one of the distinctive literary inventions of the American Gilded Age.

A. M. Barnard exhibits a different but comparably personal usage of this apparently depersonalizing format. A. M. Barnard – another name of no real person – was the pseudonym behind which Louisa May Alcott briefly wrote (and hid her writing of) story-paper fiction in the later 1860s. The twentieth-century penetration of her disguise has revealed Alcott to have been not the writer of juvenile domestic fiction alone but of both that genre and its popular antithesis: of *Little Women* and *Little Men* and of the Cuban thriller *Pauline's Passion and Punishment* and the Russian melodrama *Taming a Tartar* (both for *Frank Leslie's Illustrated Newspaper*), as well as *A Marble Woman: or, The Mysterious Model* and *V. V.: or, Plots and Counterplots*, printed in *The Flag of Our Union*.

Alcott provides a fascinating reminder of these genres' adjacency in the literary culture of her time. Her career also illustrates the fact that authors did not inevitably fall into one or another of these forms but could choose between them, and so between their different audiences, commercial circuits, and forms of literary labor. Alcott's familial duteousness eventually led her to choose domestic writing as her proper work, and when she succeeded with *Little Women* she renounced her hidden writing. But before that time, another form had made another writing life available to her, carrying quite other experiential content. Alcott's anonymous thrillers gave outlet to a luxurious and aggressive imagination curbed by the more realistic, quotidian, moralized, and restraint-oriented domestic genre. Small wonder that she associated story-paper writing with uninhibited pleasure instead of self-sacrificial service. When Alcott rewrote the morally exotic *A Modern Mephistopheles* as a kind of story-paper art novel in 1877 she told her publisher: "Enjoyed doing it being tired of providing moral pap for the young."

In a sense, to read story-paper and dime fiction in terms of individual authors is to read it against the grain of its literary organization; and Alcott and Alger are certainly not representative figures. They can remind us, however, that any socially structured role of authorship can be made the vehicle for personal meanings – and that all writing however individualistic has some historically structured role at its base. The cheap fiction of the period 1840 to 1890 created a new form of literary production in America; it inserted imaginative writing into the lives of previously little-served social segments; and it created one possible avenue for authorial self-realization and support. If it is still a kind of dark continent to later literary history, it represented a major subsystem in the American literary system of its time.

ONSTAGE

These brief histories of domestic and "cheap" literature underline the sheer prevalence of reading in nineteenth-century America. However differentiated they were among themselves, the popular literary cultures of the mid nineteenth century both served huge audiences, reminding us that reading formed a principal recreation for many millions of people. But if it was heavily print-centered, literary entertainment was not confined to print at this time, and a thorough survey of the literary field would need to consider the nineteenth-century life of the American theater.

Like print culture, the American theater became more internally stratified in the middle of the nineteenth century. Once characterized by programs mixing high and low artistic content played to an equally mixed social audience, after 1850 American theater became progressively more separated into a so-called legitimate theater and its now-differentiated popular opposite. The legitimate theater of the Gilded Age, marked by its somewhat greater artistic seriousness and the more decorous behavior of its audiences, has left little mark in American literary history. Though a prosperous institution in its time, it produced no continuingly remembered authors – no Chekhov, no Ibsen, no Oscar Wilde, not even a Sardou – and gave no works to a continuing dramatic repertoire. It is revealing that the playwright portions of high-literary writers' oeuvres from this time, the stage efforts of Henry James and William Dean Howells, have passed into complete forgetfulness.

John Augustin Daly might be mentioned as a near-exception. Manager of a New York theater company, Daly wrote or adapted at least 100 plays, one of which, the 1867 *Under the Gaslight*, was frequently revived. (Sister Carrie, it will be remembered, debuted in an amateur performance of this play by a Chicago Elks Lodge.) The Dublin-born and London-trained Dion Boucicault – writer of 200 plays during his two American stints, 1853 to 1860 and 1870 to 1890 – was this theater's other principal celebrity. Like Daly's, Boucicault's work is interesting in part for revealing how much the culturally designated "serious" theater of this time retained of its popular background. In *Under the Gaslight* Daly gave American stage life to the man tied to the railroad track as a train approaches. Boucicault was famous for similar *coups de théâtre*: the burning building in *The Poor of New York*, the blazing ship in *The Octoroon*, and the underwater rescue in *The Colleen Bawn*. Boucicault has the further interest of suggesting that mid nineteenth-century American literature, a nativist enterprise in all its published branches, high, middle, or low, made room for immigrants in the theater. The only immigrant author to have won success beyond his ethnic group in America before the twentieth century, Boucicault regularly dramatized Irish immigrant situations to a general American audience.

After the 1850s the more unchastened production modes and the rowdier audience etiquette that had earlier characterized most American theater continued in a now-segregated popular theater; and this theater, though more ephemeral in its creations and so harder to reconstruct, seems to have been the more vital nineteenth-century tradition. Its large and faithful audience appears to have overlapped significantly with the readership of dime novels and to have included even lower social strata. All surveys of the urban underclass in the late nineteenth century insist on the centrality of theatrical melodrama to its entertainment culture. In addition to melodrama, its principal fare, such theater had its dramatic staple in vaudeville, a newly consolidated entertainment form rationalized into a true entertainment industry by the mid-1880s. It also regularly presented dime fictions reworked as stage shows. Edward L. Wheeler wrote a stage version of *Deadwood Dick*. "Ned Buntline" (E. Z. C. Judson) produced Buffalo Bill Cody onstage in the 1872 *Scouts of the Prairie*. Laura Jean Libbey wrote both print and stage versions of *Little Rosebud's Lovers*, as Albert W. Aiken did with *The Molly Maguires* and other works. His brother the dime novelist George L. Aiken devised and acted in the hugely successful stage version of *Uncle Tom's Cabin* in 1853, origin of the Tom troupes that supplied a major subform of American theater into the twentieth century.

Such crossovers imply that at the popular level, printed fiction and theater were not truly separate spheres of cultural production but formed parts of an integrated entertainment complex. This complex was the spawning ground of the early twentieth century's mass entertainment forms. Stage melodrama and the staged western gave the movies their early expressive forms, as vaudeville's nationally integrated theater chains supplied them with their places of performance.

Late nineteenth-century popular theater appears to have had a largely lower class, urban, ethnically mixed audience. But the ethnic components of this audience were also served by another literary-cultural institution distinctive to this time: the foreign-language theaters fostered by nineteenth-century immigrant groups. Within immigrant cultures, theater was often a much more primary communal institution than it was for nativized Americans. Like the church schools and social clubs it was often associated with, the immigrant theater provided a gathering point for "our people" and a place where "our" language could be spoken and heard. In this setting, plays performed the work of keeping a distant cultural heritage in fresh life, while also articulating the plights and opportunities of life in a New World. They served as mediators of cultural identities under severe stress, agents of perpetuation, self-differentiation, and adaptation all at once.

Beyond such generalizations, no single history can be offered of nineteenth-century American immigrant theater, for the reason that this theater took different shapes from different groups' different cultural histories. To survey a few instances only: The Chinese imported as laborers on the American West Coast occasionally gathered the funds to bring Chinese actors to the United States. An account of a Chinese theater in San Francisco survives in the memoir of Mary Anderson, an American actress who visited it. She writes:

We visited the Chinese theatre, which is built far underground. In what we know as the green-room we found many Chinamen crowded together . . . the whole atmosphere stifling with the odor of opium smoke and frying food. I was introduced to the great attraction of the Chinese stage, a favorite impersonator of women, who had been paid an immense sum by his countrymen in San Francisco to leave China . . . It was impossible, on seeing him with his delicate features and shining black wig, to believe him to be a man . . . We witnessed the play from the stage (they have no wings or curtain), in full sight of the audience. We saw but little of it, though we remained a long time, for the Chinese often take a year to act a single play. But we had the good-fortune to see several artists come from behind a door at the back of the stage, go through a scene in which one of them was killed, and the corpse, after lying rigid for a moment, spring up suddenly, bow, smile, and make his exit through the same door, all to the melancholy scraping of a one-stringed instrument and the dismal howl of a human voice.

The theater described here is heavily foreign to its recorder, and she clearly sees it through an ethnically stereotyping lens. But even with distortions, a picture emerges of the performance styles and audience participation forms distinctive to theater in its Chinese-American form. The non-realistic style of Oriental theatrical representation is vividly if rather quizzically evoked in this account. Female impersonation, another alien tradition in nineteenth-century America, may have entered American theater through its Chinese subsidiary.

Chinese theater appears to have remained heavily dependent on the theater of the homeland. The Polish case shows a theater imported and further elaborated in its new American setting. By 1900 there were two million Polish immigrants in America (the number reached four million in 1914) and a Polish-American theater was well established before that time. In its Polish variant, the theater was strongly associated with church-community locations like the parish hall or parochial school auditorium, and it was heavily infused with the Polish national-liberation ethic. Early Polish theater groups took patriotic military names: the Towarzystwo Gwiazda Wolnosci (Society of the Star of Freedom), for instance, or the Towarzystwo Kosciuszki (General Kosciuszko Society).

This theater remained an amateur one throughout the nineteenth century, but it was able to draw on the highly developed professional theater of nineteenth-century Poland in various ways. Its fusion of levels is revealed in the 1892 performance, before a crowd of 6,000 in the auditorium of St. Stanislas Church in Chicago, of the internationally acclaimed actress Helena Modjeska in the patriotic *Jadwiga. Krolowa Lechitow* (*Jadwiza, the Queen of Poland*), by Szczesny Zahajkiewicz – a parochial school teacher who before his 1889 emigration had been a noted intellectual, playwright, and literary figure in Lvov. After this performance, a Polish newspaper records,

no one left. Endless applause greeted the star, and eventually, the author. He came upon the stage with the script in his hand. With great effort he quieted the audience, and finally said: "After such a magnificent performance no one else should ever portray the heroine of this play. In tribute to Madame Modjeska, I tear up the manuscript. And he actually tore it up into shreds and tossed the pieces from left to right over the audience" – a great moment, by any measure, in the life of American letters.

Polish-American theater elaborated a strongly developed European tradition. By contrast, the Jews of Eastern Europe had no indigenous theater tradition, and Yiddish theater was virtually born in the United States. The first play in Yiddish, by Abraham Goldfaden, was performed in Romania in 1876;

but already by 1882 New York had seen its first stage production in Yiddish, Goldfaden's *The Sorceress*. By the 1890s New York had well-established Yiddish theater houses, acting companies, and repertories, and the theater had become a central element of New York Jewish life. In terms of literary history, a curious feature of this development lies in the way theatrical behaviors that were already old-fashioned in America found new life in a group just now mastering the theater. Yiddish theater perpetuated, at the end of the century, the mixed forms and improvisatory acting styles that characterized most American theater in the antebellum decades. This theater's staples included a mixture of tragedy and vaudeville, melodrama and farce: the pathetic climax of the 1891 tragical-musical melodrama *Exile from Russia*, thus, was followed by a humorous comic duet. Yiddish theater also perpetuated the participatory audience etiquette that had become passé in the legitimate theater by the century's end. A highly expressive display of responses was encouraged, even mandated, from this theater's audience.

American Yiddish theater had its fullest life in the twentieth century and only partly falls within the period surveyed here. But already in the 1890s, as it grouped together its own formal vehicles, social audience, and means of cultural production, this literary system created its own space for authors. Jacob Gordin exemplifies the author as this culture of letters gave shape to that figure. Gordin, who had never seen a Yiddish play in Russia, had his literary aspirations kindled by the Yiddish theater when he emigrated to America in 1891. In plays like *Siberia* and *The Jewish King Lear* he infused the formulas of popular melodrama with Russian soulfulness and made them enact contemporary Jewish ordeals. For his work, he became what no native-born author fully became in late nineteenth-century America: a full-fledged hero of the culture he expressed.

Chinese, Polish, Yiddish, and other theaters are not usually mentioned in histories of American literature. But if "literature" is understood to include all word-based imaginative expression and "American" the whole people of the United States, such theaters must form an integral part of that history. One of the peculiarities of nineteenth-century America is that many linguistic cultures besides the dominant one led a fully elaborated cultural life there. When the foreign-born wrote in the situation of the immigrant they wrote another American literature, whatever language they used.

LITERARY HIGH CULTURE

Literature as it is customarily understood may seem to be strangely missing from this survey of mid nineteenth-century American literature. Its absence from the fields surveyed thus far is explained by the fact that such writing

became the object, at this time, of its own separate literary-cultural arrangements. The same midcentury cultural reorganization that established a middlebrow sphere of reading and writing and a low-literacy sphere alongside it
formalized another literary world historically just as novel: a well-marked and
well-supported zone of serious artistic authorship. As a result of this development, in the post-Civil War generation American literary writing for the
first time acquired its own stabilized audience and secure social support – the
place made for such writing involving it, as always, in a certain set of social
relations.

    Like its contemporaneously created rivals, the high culture of letters orga-
nized near 1860 and strongly perpetuated into the 1890s coalesced around new
instruments of literary production. Soon after America's first well-capitalized
publishing houses were put together in the 1840s, some publishers began to
identify themselves specifically as literary publishers. A new kind of periodical supported by the more literary publishing houses also came into existence
at this time. The Boston-based *Atlantic Monthly*, founded in 1857 and taken
over by Ticknor and Fields in 1859, published intelligent writing across a
broad range of subjects but associated itself principally with "the fine air
of high literature." (The phrase is William Dean Howells's.) Through the
rest of the nineteenth century the *Atlantic* shared the market identity of
"quality journal" with two other periodicals that had somewhat different
menus of offerings but similar editorial standards: *Harper's New Monthly
Magazine*, founded as an adjunct to Harper and Brothers in 1850, and *Scribner's Monthly*, the Charles Scribner and Company journal founded in 1870 and
transformed into *The Century Magazine* in 1881.

    Like the family journals and story-papers they were born shortly after, these
periodicals gained their cultural identity by electing to publish certain bands
from the whole spectrum of available writing. And like their contemporaries,
their different principles of selection reflected not just different editorial policy
but the different social audiences they served. The writing of these journals
makes virtually no address to the dominant readers of cheap fiction. They
contain no adventure-fiction for boys or young men; they have no interest in
the farmer's life; except in rare features on how that "other" half lives, they
ignore the working classes; they speak to an audience decidedly native-born,
not to immigrants. In their publication choices, these magazines do almost as
little to court the audience of domestic writing. The work they publish is much
more secular, much less attuned to the evangelical pieties of the midcentury
middle class. Unlike domestic writing's fixation on a highly charged home
space, their writing is vigorously cosmopolitan, traveling freely to Europe and
beyond. In its absorption in tourism and vacationing, this work speaks to a

leisure conspicuously more affluent than the middle-class housewife's. Not unrelatedly, it also presumes a higher degree of aesthetic cultivation. It posits an interest in high art and a cultural literacy in art appreciation not assumed elsewhere.

It is easy to see how these criteria should have led the journals that adopted them to favor a more aesthetically oriented kind of writing in their selections. But the same values that identify their more literary criteria for *writing* also link them to a particular *public*: the newly modeled upper class that came together in the Northeast after 1850, distinguished from the working and middle classes just by such traits as its greater secularism, greater affluence, greater cultivation and attachment to culture, and correspondingly reduced investment in the home. Not every reader of the later nineteenth century's "quality" periodicals belonged to this newly formed elite, as not every member of this group read the *Atlantic, Harper's*, or *The Century*. But in their nineteenth-century lives these journals powerfully identified with this class's distinctive ethos, and every evidence suggests that their readership was heavily centered in this group.

The forging of a circuit linking high-cultural periodicals, a more literary grade of writing, and a gentrified audience forms one more chapter in the larger story this survey has been telling. It provides yet another exhibit of how, at the time that literature became securely founded in American life, it was founded in stratified form, with differences in the literary realm coming to mirror and reinforce differences of social identity. But if this development consolidated yet another class-correlated literary system – a socially upscale parallel to middle-class and lower-class reading worlds – the result was not simply one system among others. In terms of its social force, the high literary culture of the postbellum decades was distinguished from its contemporary rivals in two ways: first, by the extremely high premium it put on litera-ture and the other arts; and second, by the vigor with which it set about enforcing this sense of value on others. High culture was America's mes-sianic or imperialist culture in the later nineteenth century. This culture's proponents were the builders of the monumentalized cultural institutions of their time, the great new museums like The Metropolitan Museum of Art and the great new symphony orchestras like the Boston, Cleveland, and Pittsburgh Symphonies, structures that presented their aesthetic values not as their tastes only but as general public goods. By means of their institutional self-assertions – through the museums, orchestras, libraries, and schools they founded and directed – this group built massive prestige for the arts as it envisioned them, and won deference to them *as* Art from those outside its bounds.

Within the literary realm, this institutional effort had the effect of creating a set of new social positions for writers, each carrying a particular degree of public status. All nineteenth-century periodicals were managed by someone; but since the quality journals represented their content as Culture itself, their managers took on a prestige not matched by editors of other organs. One yield of the establishment of a separate high-literary culture in the mid nineteenth century is the historical emergence of the editor as conspicuous man of letters: a figure embodied by such men (famous in their time) as Richard Watson Gilder, editor of *The Century*; William Dean Howells, editor of *The Atlantic* from 1871 to 1881 and then editorial columnist for *Harper's*; Mark Twain's neighbor and sometime-collaborator Charles Dudley Warner, another *Harper's* columnist; and Thomas Bailey Aldrich, Howells's successor at *The Atlantic*. The ability of such figures to be taken as the guardians of literature in its highest grade is well attested at this time. When the farm boy Hamlin Garland came East to the literary centers, he looked to these institutional administrators as the appointed validators of an aspiring literary career: in his memoir *A Son of the Middle Border* he recalls finding Howells's encouragement like "golden medals" and Gilder's editorial praise "equivalent to a diploma."

All the literary systems of this time had their favorite authors, similarly, but only the socially aggressive high culture undertook to institutionalize its preferences in an official canon. In consequence, another yield of this culture's consolidation of social authority was the creation of the figure of the American literary immortal. This culture, it will be remembered, had its own historiography of an American Renaissance. To its eyes, American literature first came to greatness not in the works of Melville, or Dickinson, or Whitman, or Poe but in the Boston-based authors of the antebellum generation: Oliver Wendell Holmes, James Russell Lowell, Henry Wadsworth Longfellow, Nathaniel Hawthorne, James Greenleaf Whittier, and Ralph Waldo Emerson. The high culture of letters of the postbellum period vigorously identified itself with these writers and made a special project of asserting their special worth. The group just named were regularly featured in *The Atlantic*, and, largely through the efforts of another *Atlantic* editor (Horace E. Scudder), they were successfully installed in the required reading of American public schools.

By such means, these authors took on a new kind of authorial life in the postbellum period. They became, many of them while they were still alive (all but Hawthorne survived into the 1880s), national classics, their names and faces embodiments of American literary achievement – a status reflected in anthology selections, deluxe editions, public statuary, author's cards, and popular lithographs for the home. The national prestige these authors held in the later nineteenth century is a chief proof of the power that had been attained by the culture that valorized their work. When that culture lost its value-producing power in the early twentieth century, the writers it canonized lost standing in direct proportion.

In addition to the editor as cultural arbiter and the older author as at least temporary immortal, the institutionalization of an official high culture of letters in the later nineteenth century created new stations for aspiring authors. The quality journals of the Gilded Age provided a place of publication for poetry with artistic pretensions, and publication *in* these journals helped consolidate the reputations of the poets officially recognized as poets at this time: authors like Edmund Clarence Stedman, the official laureate of the postbellum generation (and a stockbroker who used the Romantic poets' names as codenames for his accounts); or the then-highly-regarded Thomas Bailey Aldrich, Bayard Taylor, and George Henry Boker.

The stiffly orthodox Victorian taste that governed such journals' verse selection has guaranteed that the minor Victorians they made America's chief contemporary poets have since disappeared from sight; but the same literary arrangements made a place for more enduringly remembered writers of prose fiction. Virtually all of the fiction writers still read from the American 1870s, 1880s, and 1890s had the high-cultural journals of this time as their literary base. Henry James was an *Atlantic* staple for over thirty years, as was Sarah Orne Jewett. (His *Spoils of Poynton* and her *Country of the Pointed Firs* were serialized alongside each other in 1896.) Howells reached an audience first through *The Atlantic*, then through *The Century*, then through *Harper's*, which also published the bulk of the fiction of Constance Fenimore Woolson and Mary Wilkins Freeman. The New Orleanean George Washington Cable was a *Scribner's* discovery and a Gilder protégé. Gilder's *The Century*, which later printed *Pudd'nhead Wilson*, serialized Howells's *The Rise of Silas Lapham*, James's *The Bostonians*, and Mark Twain's *Adventures of Huckleberry Finn* in one memorable year (1884).

The postbellum writers then as later distinguished as the more *literary* writers all found audiences through the quality periodicals, this is to say, and those journals and their publics gave support for the more literary aspirations these writers entertained – this formation being the home of the author self-defined as bearer of an artistic vocation, not as mass-producer or tutelary family aid. This support was in part financial but in part a matter of a more intangible valuing, since the prestige of these journals let them mark their authors as "the" writers of note for the American public at large. Henry James, accordingly, had a much smaller readership than many of his contemporaries, but he held the status of major author in America far beyond the circle of his actual readers. High culture's monopolization of artistic prestige meant that this culture had the power to define positions outside its sphere as well. Paradoxically, another role it created was that of the disparaged writer or writer below the salt.

Whitman's case can remind us that as this cultural formation put some authors in exalted positions, it simultaneously denied those positions to other contenders. With his frantic sexual democracy and seeming anarchy of form, Whitman embodied almost everything this ethos did not value. In a typical dictum, Harvard's Professor Barrett Wendell proclaimed Whitman's verse "faulty hexameters bubbling up through a sewer." Among high-cultural critics even the more liberal-minded Howells only ever got as far as to admire Whitman's prose. When nineteenth-century high culture's adherents canonized Lowell and Longfellow, therefore, they simultaneously erased Whitman as a great American poet. When a Centennial Ode was commissioned for the Philadelphia Centennial celebrations of 1876, the commission was offered to Lowell, William Cullen Bryant, Longfellow, Holmes, and Whittier, and finally to Bayard Taylor after the others declined – a high-culturally inflected nomination process that left Whitman off the list of national bards. When President Rutherford B. Hayes chose to honor great men of letters with diplomatic posts, he sent Lowell to Spain, Taylor to Germany, and Boker to Russia – and left Whitman in his Camden, New Jersey obscurity. In the school readers of the later nineteenth century Whitman was presented to young Americans only as the author of his most unrepresentative poem, the metrically regular "Oh, Captain, My Captain!" He was admitted to canonical status, in other words, just to the extent that he fit the-then canon's alien principles of taste.

During the time of its ascendancy this system not only controlled other authors' public standings. It infiltrated other systems with its frames of value, and so took on the power to shape their authors' self-estimations. When Rebecca Harding Davis, author of the pioneering industrial novel *Life in the Iron Mills* (1860), was dropped by *The Atlantic*, which had at first published her and wooed her, she found an alternate place of publication in the popular domestic magazine *Peterson's*. But she experienced this change as a fall into a degrading form of labor: she continued to accept the hierarchizing by which high literary culture marked popular domestic writing as beneath the dignity of art. Horatio Alger, similarly, shared the perception that dime-fiction writing was lower-class work even as he embraced that work. In an 1875 letter to Stedman he places himself in a commercialized zone set below Stedman's high artistic province: "I am afraid you do me too much honor in calling me a fellow craftsman. . . . The *res angusta donis* of which Horace speaks compelled me years since to forsake the higher walks of literature, and devote myself to an humbler department which would pay me better." Louisa May Alcott appears to have been almost systematically snubbed by *The Atlantic's* high-literary publisher, James T. Fields. Fields rejected an early writing attempt of Alcott's and urged her to stick to teaching; Ticknor and Fields later agreed to publish a volume of her fairy tales, then lost the manuscript. (Henry James, Sr., perhaps reflecting a more general disparagement of her among the culturally well placed, called Alcott's novel *Moods* by another name: *Dumps*.) But Alcott too largely shared the perception of the literary system she was excluded from on the value of her work. In *Jo's Boys* Jo's self-disparaging naming of herself "only a literary nursery-maid" follows a tribute to Emerson and Whittier as authors of a different, non-servile grade.

Such cases show that in the later nineteenth century high literary culture was an element *in* the American literary field that took on the power to set the meaning *of* the field: the power to designate various zones as high, middling, and low not just in its own eyes, but in others' eyes as well. In later history, this once-dominant culture became an object of a corresponding derision. Tarred with the label "genteel," in the twentieth century it was represented as a system more or less exclusively of inhibition, a kind of conspiracy of the respectable to force their tidy decorums on the literary expression it devitalized as it praised. Sinclair Lewis meant as much when he said in his 1930 Nobel Prize Address that Howells, the most visible embodiment of this culture in his generation, "had the code of a pious old maid whose greatest delight is to have tea at the vicarage."

It is of course easy to produce evidence of this culture's work of inhibition. James R. Osgood and Co., the successor-firm to Ticknor and Fields, agreed to publish the sixth edition of *Leaves of Grass* in 1881 but also agreed with the Boston District Attorney's office to omit Whitman's "obscenity." (Whitman removed the volume from Osgood in a huff – but thus also deprived *Leaves of Grass* of its first established literary publisher.) Richard Watson Gilder rejected Charles Chesnutt's miscegenation novel *Rena Walden* (published in 1900 as *The House Behind the Cedars*) on the grounds that it lacked "mellowness": was too dissonant, we might translate, with a white elite's self-approbation. When *The Rise of Silas Lapham* was running serially in *The Century*, Gilder made Howells cut a remark that the city houses left empty by the summering rich were enough to provoke the disgruntled poor to throw dynamite into their grand pianos: too forthright an expression of a latent social challenge. Howells himself monitored Mark Twain's vernacular to guard against obtrusions of proscribed vulgarity and slang.

But to think of this literary world exclusively in terms of its repressions gets its historical meaning fundamentally wrong. For one thing, the censure of overt expression of rebellious sexual and social energies does not characterize the genteel tradition as opposed to other literary systems of its time.

Nineteenth-century domestic fiction and dime novels are hardly paradises of a more licit expressiveness: the decorums twentieth-century deriders have fastened on genteel culture represent Victorian values all literary systems of this time largely deferred to. Further, the chief distinction of high-literary publication in the Gilded Age is really not that it is fastidious. Fairly considered, this culture's production might be found remarkable instead for the level of intelligence it sustained across a not uncatholic range of views. The twentieth century certainly did not generate a journal that produced such various writings as James's *The Portrait of a Lady*, Davis's *Life in the Iron Mills*, Twain's fable of the superego "The Recent Carnival of Crime in Connecticut," and Charles Chesnutt's conjure tales. These works ran in the nineteenth-century *Atlantic* together with Charles W. Eliot's essays on university reform, source of the since-standard elective curriculum; Thomas Wentworth Higginson's "Ought Women to Learn the Alphabet?," a major spur to the development of women's higher education; Melusina Fay Pierce's witty critiques of American family practices; and the germinal essays of W. E. B. DuBois's *The Souls of Black Folks*.

Part of the historical meaning of the high-literary culture of the Gilded Age, such titles remind us, is that it created a medium for work of large resonance: a channel through which the most deeply thoughtful writing of this time could be brought forward to an attentive audience. For literary authors especially, this achievement was a great enabler. High culture's instruments provided them – to an extent quite new in American literary history – with an organized paying public for serious art and with social validation of their artistic ambition. These are not trivial achievements; but they did entail certain corollaries. For the literary arrangements that made such provisions for writing directed it preferentially to a certain portion of the American public – to the well educated and well-to-do, not Americans at large. These arrangements also made provision for only some writing, not all: they conferred their benefits on the work that best fit with this group's cultural agendas. That it enabled in some ways as it inhibited in others, that it at once yielded real support for writing and tied writing to the class programs of an elite social fragment: this is the double meaning that high-literary culture's advent had for nineteenth-century American writing.

OUT OF THE CENTER

This chapter has undertaken to survey the conditions for literary creation in mid nineteenth-century America. Its point has been that the literary practices of reading and writing are always the object of historically particular social organizations. Such organizations do not absolutely determine what is written at a given time and place. But they do determine what kinds of support the writings then attempted can obtain and what encouragement they can find for further, similar production.

The literary-cultural arrangements of the mid-nineteenth-century United States shaped American literary creation in this sense, and they help explain what it did and did not include. Notably missing from American writing after 1850, for instance, is Victorian England's version of the novelist both artistically deliberate and popularly received. One would have to combine two antithetical writers, a Louisa May Alcott and a Henry James, say, to make an American George Eliot. This literary separation in part reflects the stratification of literary levels so much more insisted on (paradoxically) in the mid-nineteenth-century United States than in England, where literary readerships were organized across, not along, class lines. In comparison with contemporary France, which had a stratified reading culture, nineteenth-century America is conspicuously lacking a Bohemia, a prestige-bearing *milieu artiste* defined in opposition to social respectability. In America high art was founded within, not in opposition to, the milieu of an *haute bourgeoisie* – explaining why the aesthete and the gentleman tend to be the same person in the American case, and why Gilded Age literary culture has so little the character of a counterculture.

But this survey of American writing worlds has not been exhaustive, and at least a few more variants might be named to round it out. Over against its other mass markets, mid-nineteenth-century America had another scheme of mass literary marketing: the system of subscription publishing, in which hired agents hunted up individual orders for new books. Subscription publishing exploited a market not yet rationalized in the literary system proper. Its main targets were people either without access to or without the habit of frequenting bookstores. Motivated by their often-sizeable commissions, the highly persuasive subscription agents created in this paraliterary public a hunger for book ownership clearly linked to the status concerns of the not poor yet not cultured: books sold through this route were often quite expensive and always large and showily bound, making them conspicuous objects of home display. (The encyclopedia sold door to door as proof that its buyer was not unconcerned with the life of the mind was the twentieth-century survivor of this publishing form.) Horace Greeley's Civil War tome *American Conflict* sold over 200,000 copies through subscription canvassing. *The People's Book of Biography* by James Parton (Fanny Fern's husband) and Henry M. Stanley's *Livingstone* were other popular titles.

In literary terms, this mode of publication's significant figure is Mark Twain. Lured by the subscription publisher Elisha P. Bliss's promise that "we have never failed to give a book an immense circulation," Twain created his first book – *The Innocents Abroad* (1869) – in the subscription-publishing format, which is to say that he padded it out to an appropriate prescribed bulk. The huge success of *Innocents Abroad* committed him to this mode of self-production. From the mid-1870s on, Twain was an author welcomed in high culture who consciously chose this more *déclassé* means to public life. His reasons were partly financial: Twain's revenues were greatly larger than those yielded by "literary" publication, and in the 1880s Twain went so far as to found his own subscription house, Charles L. Webster & Co., to capitalize on such publishing's lucrative returns. (*Personal Memoirs of Ulysses S. Grant* was Twain's great business success.) But his choice was partly also a matter of cultural politics. Twain liked to think that through this form of publication he made himself an author of the people, not of the privileged classes. In an 1889 letter he writes: "I have always catered for the Belly and the Members. . . . I never cared what became of the cultured classes; they could go to the theatre and the opera. They had no use for me and the melodeon."

Twain's career could also remind us of another literary culture of the Gilded Age, this one sited in the West. One consequence of the history this chapter has sketched is that in the second half of the nineteenth century, literature was a highly centered practice in the United States, its means of production and validation heavily gathered in one place: the Northeastern metropolises of Boston and New York. Because of this concentration, the postbellum decades were not a time of strong regional literary cultures of the sort that later grew up around Chicago, New Orleans, and Carmel, California. For a time, however, nineteenth-century American literature had a minor center in San Francisco. In the post-Gold Rush period, San Francisco journals like *The Overland Monthly* and *The Golden Era* purveyed a kind of regional literary cuisine, the free-and-easy, funny work famously embodied in early Bret Harte and Mark Twain. By the late 1860s Harte and Twain had both jumped ship for the richer rewards of the East, and the journals these transients had illuminated faltered. But a kind of literary culture survived in San Francisco, if with less *éclat*. In the lull between its 1860s heyday and its end-of-the-century revival, the Bay Area was the home of the frontiersman-poet-*poseur* Joaquin Miller, "The Poet of the Sierras" or "Byron of the Rockies," who lived in the hills above Oakland. (Miller, who got himself lionized and his *Pacific Poems* published in London in 1871, was known into the twentieth century as author of the school-recitation piece "Columbus," with its once-famous refrain: "Sail on! sail on! sail on! and on!") Charles Warren Stoddard, the poet-idler who introduced Robert Louis Stevenson to the South Seas, was another figure of this world. So was Daniel O'Connell, author of the literary-culinary *The Inner Man, Good Things to Eat and Drink and Where to Get Them* (1891). So was Ambrose Bierce, author of the blackly ironic *Devil's Dictionary* (1906).

James Whitcomb Riley could exemplify another literary world set away from metropolitan centers. Riley, author of dialect poems of an idyllic Midwest and of a comparably idyllic childhood, was, after Longfellow, America's most beloved poet in the postbellum decades, writer of poems like "Little Orphant Annie" and "The Old Swimmin' Hole" that thousands of Americans knew by heart. The Indiana-born Riley won his eventual national success with the help of Eastern channels: the Redpath Lyceum Bureau organized his public readings after 1881, and his 1882 Boston reading marked his acceptance as a folk favorite of "serious" culture. But before this turn Riley had spent at least ten years as a poet in the Midwest, and he shows the conditions for literary life that prevailed in nineteenth-century small towns. Riley got his first practice as an entertainer as a jingle writer and singer traveling with a patent-medicine show, a literary origin America alone provided. Thereafter, besides giving recitations in Indiana schools and churches, he found a public base for his work in papers like the *Indianapolis Journal* and the *Kokomo Tribune*, from whose columns his more broadly published poems were later reprinted. These papers, like most nineteenth-century newspapers, made a daily place for short poems and humor pieces of folksy appeal. Riley makes visible the now almost wholly invisible writing of men and women who wrote for the day-to-day local press.

Joaquin Miller and James Whitcomb Riley point towards geographical variants on the nineteenth century's dominant literary cultures. Frances E. W. Harper can remind us of a writing world differentiated by race instead of region. Born in 1825, Harper had a considerable career as an antislavery lecturer before the Civil War, and after the war she was a prominent speaker for many causes: for the Women's Christian Temperance Union, the American Woman's Suffrage Association, and many more. As part of this larger program of social activism Harper also wrote literary works – poems, stories, and the novel *Iola Leroy, or Shadows Uplifted* (1892), the best-selling novel written by an African American in the nineteenth century. In its thematics of family separation and reunion and in its refusal to separate the novel as an aesthetic form from a family-based social agenda, *Iola Leroy* harks back to the literary practice of domestic novelists of the 1850s like the Stowe of *Uncle Tom's Cabin* – indeed Harper perpetuates that model more fully than any other writer of the postwar years. In this fact, Harper suggests that the family-politics plan of authorship survived as an empowering base for black women's writing after white women had largely reconceived their work as a more depoliticized "art." Harper wrote before specialized black cultural journals were founded around 1900, and she wrote before a black culture consolidated itself into a fully productive literary matrix, as it did in the Harlem Renaissance. But she shows that an African-American women's writing world was already operative in the late nineteenth century, organized on other terms than the white cultures of that time.

It would be tempting to argue that the variants just named represented alternative literary cultures in the Gilded Age, and in a sense they did. But if the term "alternative" suggests a socially powerful form of difference and resistance, they only very partially deserve this label. For each of these writing worlds had a severely limited ability to encourage literary production or command it social attention. Subscription publishing put commodity marketing values over literary ones at least as controllingly as the dime novel did: when Mark Twain added the padding necessary to give his books the proper heft for this market, as he did again in *Roughing It* (1872) and *Life on the Mississippi* (1883), he was accepting that the work of art be dictated by market require-ments, not the internal necessities of its design. This system did the writer in Twain no good – it helped make Twain an author only of great parts of books – and in its light it is not surprising that no other literary author came out of the subscription-publishing channel. The San Francisco culture of letters, which might seem to embody an appealing antithesis to Eastern high-mindedness, in fact offered little alternative. After the East absorbed its livelier writers it could command only an extremely local attention for new work, and its cult of relaxation largely discouraged such work's production in any case. (This culture's principal historian, Kevin Starr, has commented that San Francisco blunted ambition in its nineteenth-century artists.) In terms of the sheer bulk of the text it printed, small-town newspaper publishing may have been one of the largest literary producers of the nineteenth century. But except when its products were reprinted elsewhere, as Riley's were, such publishing had no power to establish literary values beyond a circumscribed local sphere, and it condemned would-be writers to the ephemeralism of one-day notice. The very terms of its constitution made it too a weakly supportive literary base. The politicized women's culture Harper wrote in had little power to set a larger culture's literary or social agenda in the 1890s (though Booker T. Washing-ton, W. E. B. Du Bois, and Ida B. Wells found more effective channels for black social expression soon after *Iola Leroy*'s year.) *Iola Leroy* likely had some audience beyond the black intelligentsia it principally addressed, but in 1892 such work lacked the means to make itself present to a general readership.

The United States did not have a homogenous literary culture in the later nineteenth century, this is to say, but it did not have a totally pluralistic culture either: for even though it included several separate literary worlds organized on quite different principles, these worlds were not each other's equals in cultural force. Admire or deplore it as we may, the principal historical fact about American literature from the mid nineteenth century to the century's end was that its social life was given in a highly selective form: a form that said that writing could receive strong support within and only within the dominant systems outlined here. This social history did not dictate what authors could imagine, but it did set the conditions on which their work could reach a public. To understand American literature in the later nineteenth century is to understand its relation to the terms of its public life.

A CASE STUDY: LITERARY REGIONALISM

Europe, European travel, and art conceived on European terms were of almost obsessional interest to American literature in the post-Civil War years. This development was a product less of Europe itself than of the new value that was attached to "Europe" in America at this time. In the period after the war, acquaintance with Europe and its fine arts became a principal mark of social superiority in America, such that those aspiring to elite status felt the need first for wealth, then for the cosmopolitan initiations that turn wealth into class. The interest in Europe regarded as the home of superiority and refinement drove many Americans with disposable income to foreign travel, a pastime that had reached such proportions by the end of the century that Henry James could growl of Venice: "the bark of Chicago disturbs the siesta." But Europe in this sense could also be accessed vicariously at home through the new institutions of high culture: the art museums filling up with newly imported Old Masters, for instance, or the symphony halls and opera houses that served up European music as an upper-class American entertainment.

The new American literary organs also ministered to this interest in things European, and writers were quick to see the opportunity this created. Beginning novelists of the postwar years spotted the fact that the surest way to rise in the American literary world was to put oneself forward as someone who knew something about Europe. William Dean Howells, a son of Ohio whose eyes were eagerly fixed on the Boston literary establishment, found his way to literary success and the editorship of the *Atlantic* by writing a book about Venice, where he had served as Consul during the war. Mark Twain started out as a writer in the silver fields of Nevada, then in California, then Hawaii, but he made his first great strike by writing up a tour of Europe and the Holy Land that he took with an upscale Brooklyn congregation, the hugely popular *Innocents Abroad*. Henry James lit on the "international theme" of American innocents encountering the complexities and corruptions of Europe in the early 1870s and continued to work it throughout his long career.

What this absorption with Europe and cosmopolitanism would not lead us to suspect is that the literary field of this time is organized equally powerfully around another notion, so opposite as to be the virtual negative of these loaded terms. If the desire to overcome American provincialism drives one phase of American writing in the post-Civil War decades, another phase is driven by the urge to make writing a provincial affair. The literary work devoted to leading the way out of local enclosure into the refinements and complications of international civilization finds its historical companion in a body of work that aims to perfect itself in the customs of the country: to locate those interior American communities that have maintained a distinctive ethos and to make literature the record of their local accents and ways.

The effort to memorialize the particularities of cultures remote from cultural centers is by no means an invention of this time. This effort has American precedents in the sort of chronicles of regional life that Cooper made for central New York State in its frontier stage in *The Pioneers* (1826), or that Caroline Kirkland wrote for a frontier Michigan being built on speculation in *A New Home – Who'll Follow?* (1839), or that Susan Warner made for the household-economy phase of Northern rural development in *The Wide, Wide World* (1850), or that Hawthorne gave for a New England slipping into the status of cultural backwater in *The House of the Seven Gables* (1851). From abroad this effort could find analogues (among other places) in Turgenev's politically charged notations of Russian rural life in *A Sportsman's Sketches*; in the border country novels of Sir Walter Scott, the Midlands novels of George Eliot, and the Wessex novels of Thomas Hardy; or in a great painterly gesture like Gustave Courbet's *Burial at Ornans* (1849), which confers on a homely provincial event the dignity of treatment heretofore reserved for the grand and the great.

In the second half of the nineteenth century artistic localism represents, paradoxically, an international movement; and it is important to remember that the American painting of provincial life is in no sense an American innovation. What is distinctive about this effort in its postbellum American context is not the project itself but the extent to which it dominates the field of literary creation. Immediately after the Civil War the local-color story emerged both as a fully stabilized genre and as what might be called the genre of high visibility in American literature. In the late 1860s Bret Harte landed an enormously lucrative contract with the success of his California mining tales "The Luck of Roaring Camp" and "The Outcast of Poker Flat." The first writer to earn full-fledged star status in the postbellum era, Harte's success said that the ability to deliver news from the provinces would now become grounds for American literary celebrity. (Harriet Beecher Stowe, an author who achieved celebrity under the different conditions prevailing in the antebellum decade, shifted her base of literary operations to regional reminiscence in *The Pearl of Orr's Island* [1862], and so might be said to found the vein that Harte exploited.) In the postwar decade the new American writers who did not make Europe their literary base virtually to a man (and woman) took regional fiction as their project, using their knowledge of some yet-unrecorded indigenous culture as the capital with which to launch a career. Edward Eggleston projected himself into authorship as the laureate of backwoods Indiana in *The Hoosier Schoolmaster* (1871). In the early 1870s Sarah Orne Jewett began chronicling the coastal Maine region first known in her fiction as *Deephaven* (1877). In 1874 George Washington Cable entered the public domain as fictive historian of what his first collection (1879) calls *Old Creole Days*. A year later Constance Fenimore Woolson worked up her knowledge of the old settlement around the Mackinac Straits and the Zoar community of rural Ohio into her first volume, *Castle Nowhere: Lake-Country Sketches*. 1875 is also the year of "Old Times on the Mississippi," Mark Twain's first exploitation of the region he would make his chief literary property.

The form in which author after author saw his or her way into literature, and for most of them the form they continued to work throughout their careers, regional fiction also represents, from the Civil War well into the 1890s, a form for which the demand always exceeds the supply. The pages of literary publications after 1865 are filled with writing in this mode, and they seem only to want to be able to fill themselves with more. In an 1878 review Howells spoke of the dialect tale as a worn-out form, but in that same year Howells's *Atlantic* gave a kind of hero's welcome to Charles Egbert Craddock (the pseudonym of Mary Noailles Murfree) for having discovered a new regional vein, the Appalachian hill cultures of Eastern Tennessee, and so shown that the resources of regionalism were not exhausted after all. Impressed by Murfree's success, a Mississippi-born writer pen-named Sherwood Bonner visited Tennessee for two weeks so that she too could produce this shade of local color. So strong was the market for such writing that even this quite shameless manufacturing of regional "knowledge" as a product for the market found ready placement, as did Bonner's equally quickly worked-up later tales of rural Illinois. When Hamlin Garland sold a Midwestern regionalist story to the *New American Magazine* in the mid-1880s the editors told him they would like a series of such sketches – proof not of Garland's irresistible talents but of the insatiable demand for the commodity Garland too found a way of supplying.

As these facts suggest, the fiction of regional life represents not a genre among others but a dominant form of literary production and consumption in the post-Civil War decades. Accordingly, it is important to ask what charge it carries *as* a form: what weight it bears or what function it performs to make it so central to the life of its time.

Whatever else it does, regionalist writing makes an issue of the local, and an inquiry into the form's cultural life might begin with the reflection that it rose to literary prominence just when the local was becoming an issue in America in a new way. It seems no coincidence that the Civil War should mark the starting point of such writing's emergence as a dominant mode. The great public event in the lives of the postbellum generation, the Civil War, was a contest over the form the local would be allowed to take in an emerging United States. As a struggle over the South's peculiar institution, the regionally particular organization of labor and human status in black slavery, the war was a violent physical debate over the tolerable limits of regional difference. As a struggle to affirm either the inviolability of Union or the right of secession, the war also fought out the root issues of local separateness: the power of included cultures to make themselves self-governing entities, their right to control the terms on which they would submit to a larger collectivity. The American South – occupied by Federal troops until 1877 as a sign of the crushing of its claims to the privilege of difference – was not regional writing's first subject. But writers found the South as literary material soon after the war. And the parade of authors who came to writing by embracing the South as an object of regional meditation – the twice-wounded Confederate soldier Cable; Murfree and Bonner, both daughters of the Confederacy; the child of North Carolinian free negroes Charles Waddell Chesnutt; Woolson, who moved South in the 1870s and whose identification with the despoiled South is the source of her strongest work: this partial list can suggest how much the regionalist project is animated by the South's postwar status, and by the meaning of the local for which the war made the South the sign.

Literary regionalism resonates in nineteenth-century America, as it does not, say, in nineteenth-century England or France, with an actual regional war fought in the very recent past. But the war was only the most visible phase of a more general assault on local cultures that proceeded from many other social causes. No history of the Gilded Age fails to take as its central story the extraordinarily accelerated processes of capitalist-industrialist development that transformed America from the 1830s on. As its emergence to leadership in world industrial production in the 1890s proclaimed, America became the leading case of a developed economy by the end of the nineteenth century, and its history all through this time is the history of the reformation of relations that marks a developing nation. The supersession of artisanal or home production by new forms of industrial manufacture is one part of this nineteenth-century history. Another is the amassing of new concentrations of wealth in America, and the articulation of a national financial system to supplement or supplant community-based supplies of credit. Another phase of this history involves the great American construction project of the later nineteenth century, the building of a more and more tightly webbed national railroad network – an event that every year brought more previously isolated localities into a national and international scheme of market relations. (Four transcontinental railroad routes were constructed in the 1880s. The South so to speak joined the national market system in 1886, when it converted to nationally standardized track widths.) The birth of chain stores and national-brand advertising campaigns displays another phase of this process: the beginning of the amalgamation of a dispersed and heterogeneous populace into a coherent market for mass-produced goods.

We usually look to see the workings of these developments in the places where they are most intensely concentrated: in the department store or the factory, the industrial city or the great financial center. But the economic processes that produced the nineteenth-century urban-industrial world as their most visible symbol also encompassed that world's apparent opposite, and they produced just as decisive a new history for preindustrial rural America. In some instances, development's effect was simply to eradicate what preceded it and erect its forms in their place. Cleveland, Ohio, Chesnutt's home during the Civil War and Woolson's early home as well, was a settlement of 6,000 in 1840. During their early lifetime, it was made over into an industrial city: a city where iron for railroads and other heavy industries was smelted from Lake Superior iron ore and Pennsylvania and West Virginia coal brought to this junction by a new transportation system. Standard Oil, the paradigm of the Trust and so of the new concentrations of corporate power that emerged in America in the 1880s, had its headquarters in this former village.

In other instances, development's effect was to leave a region to agrarian production and the culture centered on such production but to redraw the horizon this traditionalism operated in. After the Civil War the Georgia hill country just south of Murfree's Tennessee mountains remained a place where farms were worked by family units. But the growing concentration of these farmers on cotton reveals their steady shift towards producing, through household labor, for a translocal market – a conversion furthered by the conversion of their principal creditors to Cash-or-Cotton as a scheme of payment.

In a third nineteenth-century scenario, development's effect was not so much to infiltrate and reorient a local economy as simply to draw off its human resources. Rural New England towns not unlike Stowe's Orr's Island or Poganuc experienced population declines of up to 40 percent in the late nineteenth century. Here local culture persisted, but the growth it stood out-side of afflicted it with an unstanchable drainage of strength.

Even where a local community stayed substantially the same through this time, by *keeping* its form it could become different through the process of development. Randolph, Massachusetts, home town of regional writer Mary Wilkins Freeman, lost fewer than 100 of its 4,000 residents between 1880 and 1900. But during this time the nearby town of Brockton, adopting more modern versions of the shoe-manufacture that Randolph had led in its proto-industrial phase, increased in size from 13,000 to 40,000: so that Randolph became something else – became secondary, became (comparatively) underde-veloped – by staying much the same.

These transformations of preindustrial American cultures did not begin in 1865. But the acceleration of capitalist-industrial development after the war intensified these pressures on traditional organizations of local life. And the stressing of the local through this large historical action is nineteenth-century regional writing's most important social occasion. Many authors in this vein make clear that they want to write down local particularities because they know them to be historically endangered. Murfree is recorded to have said that she wanted to make East Tennessee known before the railroads penetrated it entirely. Stowe's *Oldtown Folks* (1869) offers to fix the image of the New England of "ante-railroad times, the impress of which is now rapidly fading away." Regional fiction is the product of the moment when local culture is still known but known to be being abolished. And in many cases this transformation is not only regionalism's spur to recollection, but the story it tries to piece out.

Cable's fiction finds its subject in that mixed or creolized culture – part French, part Spanish, part African and Native American, but not Anglo-Saxon – that dominated New Orleans before the Louisiana Purchase. But the *work* of fiction in Cable's hands is to tell this culture into a plot of Ameri-canizing modernization. In the early story "Jean-ah Poquelin" Cable restages post-Purchase development's incursions on an old Creole enclave. Out of loy-alty to the leprosy-infected brother he shields from public knowledge, the title character of this story seals his plantation off from the outside world. But changes in the outside world change the meaning of his property. The city grows out to incorporate it; the Building and Improvement Company needs his land to complete the transportation system it is building to further the city as a commercial center. In the guise of traditionalism (it feigns to be a Creole charivari), this group of developers finally breaches Poquelin's anti-development defenses. When it does so a traditional culture reveals itself in its full cultural difference – the secret brother is brought to light: an ethos that puts family bonds over the imperatives of profit or progress manifests itself with dramatic force. But in this same moment it is literally dislodged, giving way to the otherwise-constructed uses and values that now take its place. In the powerful "Bras-Coupé" chapter of Cable's ambitious novel *The Grandissimes* (1880), the buried determinations of an older cultural order – here involving Creole slaveholders' mutilation of their slaves and slaves' resorting to the African-Caribbean heritage of voodoo for their revenge – are brought back up for contemporary knowledge, again with an exorcising effect. Cable's Creole hero renounces family vendettas; embraces his brother-in-miscegenation in a new kind of house, the business corporation; and joins the American free enterprise system forming around the representative of rationalism and economic rationalization, the Anglo-Saxon pharmacist Frowenfeld.

Helen Hunt Jackson's *Ramona* (1884), a novel written to popularize the case against Native-American abuse that Jackson had made in such non-fiction works as *A Century of Dishonor*, tells a different version of Cable's story. Jackson locates in California what Cable finds in New Orleans: a place where the prior racial and ethnic cultures that American entrepreneurial culture has superseded are visible still. But in Jackson's account such entrepreneurialism subsumes its historical rivals not through its moral progressiveness or "natural" inevitability but through the rawer action of conquest and expropriation. Jackson (unlike Cable) wholeheartedly sympathizes with the California Mexican and Indian orders that are her victims of Anglo development: her book illustrates how a regionalist's identification with an alien culture can provide the base for a powerful dissent from capitalism's "progressive" ideology. But Jackson's fiction does to her region exactly what Cable's does to his. She too images an American society organized on other grounds than that of modern economic development; and she too makes its story be the story of its supersession.

Mary Noailles Murfree describes a much less obviously conflicted region in *In the Tennessee Mountains* (1884), and in some of her tales she treats this region as a kind of self-enclosed precinct of bumpkinism. But in her most ambitious story, "Drifting Down Lost Creek," she uses this region to focus that other development that economic development produces for rural enclaves. Falsely accused and wrongly convicted, the inventive ironsmith Evander Price is sent down from his native mountains to the state penitentiary. But in penal restriction his world is thrown open. Introduced to industrial technology in the prison work program, he finds that he has a natural calling towards an industrial mode of production. While the countrywoman who loves him gets him freed, Price returns not to her but to the world he more deeply desires: "he lowed ez he hed ruther see that thar big shed an' the red hot puddler's balls a-trundlin' about, an' all the wheels a-whurlin', an' the big shears a-bitin' the metal . . ." As Murfree now plots it, Cynthia Ware's country world closes back in on itself, but it has been robbed, through contact with this other world, of the means for its cultural perpetuation. (Having lost Price to industrialism Cynthia Ware becomes a spinster.) She continues her culture's distinctive ways, but that continuation itself has been changed into something neurotic and elegiac. Cynthia weaves, in other words she perpetuates the handwork and household mode of production Price's industry has rendered obsolete, but her weaving is now less a functional than a compulsive and consolatory labor, the gesture of an energy deprived of other outlets.

Murfree writes the history of economic development as the story of the drainage of regional primacy and life. Sarah Orne Jewett might be said to write it as the story of the creation of local cultural separateness. No trace of modernity – no train, factory, bank, or store-bought good – appears in Dunnet Landing, the coastal town of Jewett's *The Country of the Pointed Firs* (1896). Except for the unrepresented movement of the summer visitor who tells these stories, nothing crosses either in or out of Dunnet Landing's wholly local human economy. Region here is a protected, not invaded, enclave; but part of the genius of this book is to suggest that Dunnet Landing's self-enclosedness is not its inherent nature but a condition that has been created through an economic-historical process. Captain Littlepage, the Ancient Mariner of this now drowsy seaport, recalls the time when this town was a shipping center and its residents great ships' captains, full participants in the commercial enterprise of their day; and as Littlepage expresses it what this gave the town was not prosperity or power so much as experiential range: "in the old days, a good part o' the best men here knew a hundred ports, and something of the way folks lived in them." With the loss of its shipping business, the town has become mentally "narrowed down" and "shut up i' its own affairs": its once-wider horizon of action and knowledge has become local through its slippage from economic centrality. The predicament of a culture become localized in this sense is what Littlepage's compulsively told story "The Waiting Place" reveals. The story of an encounter with a ghostly other world, menacing yet wholly unresponsive, this tale realizes in a gothic or fantastic mode the experience of coming to find the living world of one's time wholly alien or other. In another sense it realizes not just what the developed world must look like to those who stand outside of development but also what their own known world has become: "a place where there was neither living nor dead," an inanimate, undeveloping limbo alongside but mysteriously untouched by the bustling activity outside.

Such instances establish that there is no single history of the cultural effects of development in postbellum regional fiction. But they show how much such development stands as this fiction's historical referent. And this in turn helps explain the genre's tenacity in this period. This quite specialized literary form has a peculiar hold over authors and readers in the postbellum decades because it speaks to the great extraliterary experience of this time. In the years when capitalist-industrial development not only formed its own new commercial economy but transformed every previously established American cultural economy, regional fiction took on the role of registrant and articulator of this great change. Not the local and traditional by themselves but the local and traditional as processes other to them worked to change their nature is the subject regional writing really addresses. In this sense the fiction of regions is precisely a literature of development: one of the principal nineteenth-century means by which the forces of social change were imaged, grasped, and known.

The way it speaks to the Civil War's legacy accounts for part of regional fiction's peculiar power in this time. The way it formulates contemporary economic history and its range of social by-products accounts for another part. But we would get a rather different understanding of the literature-of-the-local's postwar life and function if we localized it in a more differentiated way. In the post-Civil War period, when its brief seems to have been to leave no indigenous culture unreported, such fiction was produced for virtually every state. But however various its subjects, it was itself produced in certain places, not others. If we ask where regionalism was produced at this time, the answer is, overwhelmingly, in the organs of literary centers. Cable was the historian of Creole life, but it was the New York-based *Scribner's Monthly* and its successor *Century Magazine* that found Cable and brought him to a public. The *Atlantic Monthly*, bastion of Eastern refinement, was the high bidder for Bret Harte's "Western" literary output. It also published Twain's "Old Times on the Mississippi," Woolson's superb "Rodman the Keeper" (what Rodman keeps is a Union cemetery in the subdued but still-hostile northern Florida), Murfree's "Dancin' Party at Harrison's Cove" and "Drifting Down Lost Creek," and a virtually monthly work by Jewett, including all of *Deephaven* and *The Country of the Pointed Firs*. *Harper's*, the journal that published Sherwood Bonner, had a comparable monopoly on the works of Mary Wilkins Freeman.

In the later nineteenth century, this is to say, a literature of cultural enclaves was produced *as* culture not *in* those enclaves but in their antithesis. It too was produced through the journals of literary high culture, the instruments that strove to establish the ethos of a dominant social group as "culture" itself. Given this placement, we must assume that its original action was as part of this historically particular cultural program.

Thinking nineteenth-century regionalism back into the site of its operation helps clarify its involvement with the ideology of the vacation. The urbanized upper class that emerged in America after the Civil War was in a crucial sense defined by its vacation habits. The postwar decades in which this class perfected the arts of international tourism are also when it laid out its characteristic summer places, the mountains and the seashores that it colonized as its resorts. These vacation practices took on further weight as the feature of this group's way of life that most fully expressed the difference of its social identity. Its secularized outlook, mandating a pursuit of worldly pleasure not yet tolerable in rival American cultures; the easy mobility that differentiated it from more rooted social formations; its peculiar ability to exempt its members, particularly its women and children, from economic productivity; above all its wealth, its command – not universally shared – of surplus financial resources: these features were summarized and given visible expression in the vacation, which became an emblem of this class's social prerogatives.

Not all readers of the Gilded Age's prestigious literary publications belonged to the social group marked in these ways. But the "world" as this class understood it is the one these periodicals formulated and projected. And one of the clearest ways in which they indicate the group ethos they are in the service of is in the centrality they confer on the idea of vacation. One virtually mandatory feature of such journals' tables of contents is the kind of piece represented in such titles as "The Lakes of Upper Italy," or "A Little Tour in France," or "The Adirondacks Verified," or "Summer Resorts on the St. Lawrence." Through such features these journals present themselves virtually as a travel supplement, seeking out ever-new vacation venues and making them mentally visitable in print. The fact that international theme novels of the Gilded Age were serialized alongside such travel pieces suggests that they elaborated on the same socially based touristic interests. And the fact that the regional fiction of the Gilded Age was produced together with these two genres, as a virtually mandatory ingredient in the same textual recipe, implies that it cooperated with them in producing the same sense of the world.

Such writing often explicitly grasps its subject from the vantage of the summer person. Murfree "knows" Tennessee mountain culture because she summered in the Cumberlands. (An urban vacationer frames the telling of "Dancin' Party at Harrison's Cove.") Jewett, though actually from Maine, recreates Maine in her fiction as something known by a visitor from the city – in *Deephaven*, a girl who summers at the shore as a change from the monotony of European travel. But whether this origin is explicit or not, it is easy to see Gilded Age regional fiction as articulating the world in vacationers' terms. Read with its original companions in print, this writing appears as one part of a larger textual action devoted to creating a steady supply of new places – "unspoiled" and hitherto "undiscovered" – for the reader to resort to in mind. Mount Desert Island provided a real place to visit; Dunnet Landing was vicariously visible in print.

As one phase in a larger body of contemporaneous vacation writing, region-alist fiction might be said to help remake the world in the image of a particular group's prerogatives of leisure. But we could also see this vacation writing as reenacting not just this group's pleasures but its placement in cultural power. No American culture of the nineteenth century was so insular as to be unaware that cultures constructed on other principles existed all around it. One distinc-tion of the emerging postwar upper class is that it positively cultivated this awareness. This formation differentiated itself by its insistence on going out of its sphere to find worlds with other horizons. But this organized cultivation of the foreign worked, paradoxically, to establish its own cultural centrality. Tourism in print fills the pages of the high-cultural journals of the Gilded Age for the reason that it performs this feat so efficiently. In its monthly-renewed "discovery" of Italian hill towns or Appalachian enclaves or French-Canadian provinces or lost New England villages, such writing supplies not just poten-tial resorts but a steady supply of cultural otherness. Its operation is to produce a world marked as foreign; but also to make that foreignness fully graspable; and so to confirm the superior inclusiveness of the culture in which the reader is positioned.

The way regional fiction performs this underwriting of the regional's cul-tural opposite is revealed in an early example of the form. In the preface to *The Hoosier Schoolmaster*, Edward Eggleston recollects how, as a Hoosier school-boy, he resented the cultural dominations that excluded Midwestern life from books. His announced goal is to resist a narrow New England cultural hege-mony by extending American literature's social and linguistic franchise, giving literary representation to "the back-country districts of the Western states" and recording a "*lingua rustica*" other than the "New England folk-speech" of James Russell Lowell. Using the provincial to dispute the reign of the center is the professed motive for this regional writing; but in practice Eggleston works in virtually the opposite way. Within *The Hoosier Schoolmaster*, backwoods Hoosier culture is grasped through another outlook that makes it appear barbaric and grotesque. Specifically, it is grasped through the conceptual grid of the New England-born hegemonic culture of this time. The emotionally hot and rhetor-ically hyperactive religion of backwoods revivalism appears in this novel – Eggleston is one of the first writers to realize that in America, writing about regional culture will often mean writing about evangelical Protestantism – but it appears as a monstrosity next to the form of piety the book prefers: a cooled-down, non-sectarian religion of good deeds descended from Bostonian Unitarianism. The backwoods school of the book's title is measured, similarly, against the chief institution by which a New England model of civilization was normalized and disseminated in nineteenth-century America: the graded public school, presided over by a certified instructor and repudiating the discipline of the rod, devised by Horace Mann and his fellows around 1840.

A provincial or vernacular culture is made known in *The Hoosier Schoolmaster*, then, but this is inseparable from the process by which the superiority of another culture is ratified and confirmed. It is not surprising then that Eggleston's happy ending takes the form of the reestablishment in the backwoods of dominant culture's instruments of control: the new graded school in which the schoolmaster will now acculturate the young and the new asylum in which his partners in virtue will manage social aberrants.

Not many works renew the domination of dominant culture so overtly as *The Hoosier Schoolmaster*. But in a sense this process does not need to be overt, since it is embodied in regionalism's nature as a form. The very idea of making other cultures' particularities available in print implies a fundamental imperialism, an attitude of annexation and consumption towards the different or remote. (The flow of knowledge that regional fiction effects runs only one way, towards the culture of the center.) Further, this genre's formal properties insure that the regional will be represented on terms that mark it as secondary or subordinate. Dialect speech is the major requirement of this form. One of the chief qualifications nineteenth-century regionalists need to possess is the ability to produce authoritative transcriptions of vernacular speech. (Authoritative-sounding ones, at least: since the whole point is that this speech is not known to its readers otherwise than through the regionalist's transcription.) Their pages, accordingly, teem with unfamiliar American tongues – Creole: "Dat marais' billong to me; Strit can't pass dare"; Deep South black English: "you jes take keer o' dis chile while I'm gone ter de hangin'"; New England country talk: "I thought mebbe Alfred would relish 'em fur his breakfast; an' he'd got to have 'em while they was hot"; Appalachian drawl: "Fur ye see, Mis' Darley, them Harrison folks over yander ter the Cove hev determined on a dancin' party"; Midwestern farm speech: "*Good* land o' goshen, if you ain't the worst I *ever* see!"; California miners' tongue: "Wa-al, I knew a Jim Smiley, and he were the durndest fellow." But in virtually every instance, this tongue is set over against the correct literate speech of the cultural center, a language its vagaries help reestablish *as* correct (the very conception of these tongues as dialect implies the standardness of some other speech); so that its "authentic local" usage persistently validates the notion that some other usage is not local but the norm.

Regional fiction might be said to stage a detour into foreignness in order to reinforce the authority of the center. If we now ask what actual foreignness this fiction refers to, we can grasp the work it performs more concretely. It is a little hard to believe that the literary audience of the Gilded Age cared quite as much about Maine fishermen and Tennessee mountaineers as such figures' recurrence in their reading matter would imply. But it is possible to imagine other American strangers who impinged on them much more nearly: namely the immigrants who brought their increasingly foreign cultures to America in the later nineteenth century. Sarah Orne Jewett perfected the image of her Old High Yankee Dunnet Landing in the decade of massive immigration of Italians, Jews, Slavs, and Poles from Southern and Eastern Europe. Helen Hunt Jackson wrote her romantic nostalgia piece about old Mexican California in the decade when California passed virulent Restriction Laws against Chinese immigration. Mary Wilkins Freeman produced her Massachusetts village tales in the decade when the Irish first seized control of Boston city government. The dialect tale in general thrived in the decade when Northern and Midwestern state legislatures debated laws to require English-language instruction in parochial schools.

Dominance, linguistic and otherwise, was an issue for the social sector addressed in Gilded Age literary journals because that dominance was being challenged at this moment, challenged by the threat of a massive decentralization of American cultural power. That threat – more properly, that development felt by the native culture-making classes *as* a threat – is another determinant of regional fiction's nineteenth-century American life; and it is partly as a way of coping with that threat that it performed its office. Peculiarly among the genres of this time, this form addresses the strangers in the land. It deals with those who talk strangely, those Americans whose lives betray an ethnic (one meaning of "regional") difference. But as it deals with "the" foreign this genre's operation is to make it not so foreign: first by substituting old, native ethnicities for disturbingly unfamiliar ones – Downeasterners for Eastern Europeans, backwoods Protestants for Confucians or Jews; then by making "their" difference something "we" can appreciate and grasp. Regionalism acknowledges the existence of rivals to American urban-gentry culture but acknowledges it symbolically, by representing one sort of rival in the image of another; and through this representation it also makes this other something its audience can mentally master, absorb into the empire of its growing cultural knowledge. In this sense regional literature was not only written for the cultivated classes but worked imaginatively on their behalf; and the way it negotiated this group's contemporary position explains why it became their preferred literary mode.

REGIONAL WRITING AND THE ROLE OF THE AUTHOR

The social placement of a literary genre by no means delimits what an author can make of that genre. When they engaged this form, writers brought their own concerns to it and made it yield their own kind of sense. Jewett used the fiction of un-self-renewing places to produce some of the most powerful elegiac writing in the postbellum decades. Taking this form to the 1880s northern Great Plains, the scene of killing droughts, falling wheat prices, declining land values, and a massive farm debt crisis, Hamlin Garland used it to document a contemporary agricultural depression, making regionalism a literary extension of the Populist Movement. Twain made his Mississippi River country a far softer version of pastoral but then compulsively reengaged it to grapple with the presence of slavery in this regional idyll: a vision worked out with deepening clarity and force from *Tom Sawyer* through *Adventures of Huckleberry Finn* to *Pudd'nhead Wilson*.

But writers alone do not set the terms of a literary form's public life. That is established through the ordering of a culture, and through the play of social interests in the cultural sphere. In America in the second half of the nineteenth century, cultural circumstances created a position of great complexity and power for regionalist fiction. Circumscribing the individual acts through which it was imagined, this genre had a role created for it in which it assumed such contradictory functions as to image industrial development and to project imaginatively entered getaway places; to open up isolated native regions to public knowledge and to figure a new population of foreigners; to dramatize the pluralism of contemporary American culture and to put such pluralism under the sway of a culture concerned to maintain its rule.

These are the main terms of regionalism's life in the Gilded Age; but one further fact needs to be added. This is that in addition to its many other roles, regional fiction supplied late nineteenth-century America's primary point of literary access. Short in length, simple in its conventions, this was a genre it was comparatively easy to learn to write. And it was the peculiar nature of this genre not only not to bar the disadvantaged from writing, as the novel of European travel did, but to make disadvantage itself a sort of resource. The fiction of underprivileged areas and marginal lives, this genre made the first-hand knowledge of culturally subsidiary situations into a valuable literary asset, with important literary-historical results. For all its orientation towards the upper social strata, this is a time when the American literary world opened the door to writers from a variety of non-elite literary backgrounds. They gained this access through the regionalist genre, and through the value it conferred on the experience of outsiders.

The roster of late-century local color writing is crowded with women's names. Sarah Orne Jewett, Mary Wilkins Freeman, Constance Fenimore Woolson, Mary Noailles Murfree, Helen Hunt Jackson, Sherwood Bonner (Katharine Sherwood Bonner MacDowell), Rose Terry Cooke, Grace King are only the most obvious members of the list. Their number indicates that regionalism supplied the "door" for women into letters in late nineteenth-century America that domestic fiction had supplied a generation earlier. The reason is not far to seek. In its separation from the larger contemporary world, the regional backwater yielded an imaginative equivalent to another enclosed precinct, women's traditional domestic space. This likeness supported a new version of women's work: chronicling everyday life in unmodernized places.

Such writing set the norm for women's literary labor in the Gilded Age, but women were not the only ones to be enabled by this form. Hamlin Garland came from a social origin far more distant from literary high culture than most women writers of his time. He grew up on a succession of farms in the upper Midwest, and it was not until he was sixteen, when his father took a job as a grain elevator operator and moved into town, that he was exempted from manual labor and freed to devote himself to reading and writing in school. Garland was cringingly self-conscious of his uncultured origins ("you're the first actual farmer in American fiction," Joseph Kirkland told him early in his career), but regionalism gave him an entrée to the world he craved. The fact that he could supply literary fare from an untapped region made him able to place his work with Eastern publishers, and Garland eventually established himself in the literary world by purveying images of life far outside that world.

Garland achieved his literary role at the price of uprooting himself from the origins he imaged, and the emotional complexity of this situation fuels his richest work. The story that dominates Garland's first volume *Main-Travelled Roads*, "Up the Coulee," gives painful expression to the guilt induced by his flight from the farm and its (in his eyes) hard, degrading labor. Garland's best book, the 1917 autobiography *Son of the Middle Border*, is the story of how he became an author of regions: a story of flight and cultural reaffiliation that paints the conditions of authorship in the Gilded Age with unusual clarity and detail.

Garland's near contemporary Charles W. Chesnutt is usually called the first African-American author to have won a place in mainstream literary culture. Chesnutt too secured this access through the mediation of the regionalist tale. The son of free blacks from Fayetteville, North Carolina, the prodigiously self-educated Chesnutt won early advancement in the world of education, becoming head of the institution of highest learning open to blacks in North Carolina, the State Colored Normal School, by the age of twenty-two. But he hungered for another form of career: "It is the dream of my life – to be a writer!," he confided to his journal in 1879.

The emergence of a new Southern variant of the dialect tale just as Chesnutt's ambitions were taking shape gave him a way to realize this dream. Joel Chandler Harris's *Uncle Remus: His Songs and Sayings*, published in New York in 1880 and hugely popular in the North, and Thomas Nelson Page's Virginia stories like "Marse Chan'," published in *Century Magazine* in 1884, deliver the power of storytelling over to a locally rooted Southern black. The vivid vernacular of these tales made a place for black voices in literature, but it met other and even opposite needs as well. Published just after the North abandoned the program of Reconstruction, leaving Southern whites to repeal the social gains blacks had won since the war, these stories have an obvious function of easing the trauma of this desertion. The black speaks in these stories, but only to state his contentment with the old Southern order to which the North had just handed back his social fate.

But the establishment of a market for black dialect among white readers and publishers had a further and quite different effect as well. It created a need a Southern black could fill, and so made an opening for an African-American author. Though Chesnutt had virtually no prior experience as a published fiction-writer, his ability to fill out the Harris-Page formula with fresh vernacular materials enabled him to place his work in the most prestigious literary journals. "The Goophered Grapevine" was printed alongside Horace Scudder's polemics for mass instruction in the New England literary canon in the 1887 *Atlantic*, and "Po' Sandy" was published together with Henry James's *The Aspern Papers* in the same journal the next year.

Few writers have experienced such a rapid arrival. As Chesnutt was to learn, however, there was more to this enablement than met the eye. After this heady debut, it was Chesnutt's hope to work free of the dialect folk-tale form, or in his words to "drop the old Negro who serves as mouthpiece" and "get out of the realm of superstition." The reasons for this wish are not hard to grasp. Though he had subtly ironized the formula of a white speaker from the dominant classes and his "colorful" black subordinate, Chesnutt was reluctant to circulate the fiction of race relations that these conventions put forward, which occluded the actual history taking place in the South: the creation of institutionalized racial segregation. An exquisitely educated person, self-taught in Latin, French and German, Chesnutt was also reluctant to accept that "the" black could only ever be imaged as the illiterate, the lower class, or the folk black: realities as far from him as from any of his white readers.

But when he attempted to exit from his work's first form, Chesnutt found that the literary world that was happy to receive him in black-dialect folk garb was less willing to receive him without colorful ethnic dress. When he sent a novella about life in the Southern mulatto professional class to the *Century* in 1890, Richard Watson Gilder rejected it as "unmellow" and "uninteresting." Stymied throughout the 1890s, at the end of the decade Chesnutt found a publisher willing to do a volume of his stories "if you have enough 'conjure' stories to make a book" – in other words, if he would return to the genre he had found constricting ten years before.

Chesnutt did what he was told, and the resultant volume, *The Conjure Woman*, ranks with the most important works of American regionalism. But Chesnutt was not the only writer to find that the literary-cultural field that surrounded regionalism delimited his authorship at the same time that it enabled it. Demand for this genre let people from hitherto excluded origins become authors in the late nineteenth century, but virtually no one who entered literature through this form was able to escape the constraints of this form. A writer like Jewett shows far less restiveness with the genre than Chesnutt, but it remains a fact that she had virtually no literary life outside this form. In a publishing career stretching over almost forty years, Jewett was first and last the writer of unmodernized coastal Maine, making only the most minor literary forays out from this base.

The work of Mary Wilkins Freeman suggests the self-consciousness such constraints produce. Freeman borrows from Jewett the sense that one of the most characteristic human types produced in regional backwaters is the obsessive-compulsive. Jewett's Captain Littlepage has one story he is driven to tell; her Elijah Tilley has one interest in life, the memory of "poor dear"; Abby Martin has concentrated her life in one relationship, her imagined twinship with Queen Victoria. Freeman takes a strain of obsessiveness already strong in Jewett and makes it virtually the only operative dramatic element. A Freeman story begins when a character falls into an inflexible, inescapable insistence. The mother of Freeman's "The Revolt of 'Mother'" *will have* the nicer house she was promised. The hero of "A Conflict Ended" *will sit* on the church steps in silent protest against a long-forgotten turn of church politics, even if it costs him his marriage and his happiness. The aged crones of "A Mistaken Charity" *will have* their own hovel to live in and their own vegetables to eat, even if they have to break out of a charitable welfare institution to get them.

Such obsession carries a meaning about the world these tales address. Freeman suggests that in cultural backwaters, the human energy that would normally be put into action flows into self-rigidifying eccentricity for lack of other outlets. But it is impossible not to feel that these tales are charting the terms of their own existence quite as much as the places they portray. Freeman's authorship has in common with its obsessive heroes that it is immitigably committed to repetition. Enclosed in the genre that enables her career, writing for Freeman means telling *again* about the aging engaged couple who have not yet managed to marry, telling *again* about the aging woman who refuses to be supplanted from her minor cultural function, and so on. The fiction that results from this iteration is often powerful, but Freeman's writing is, and knows that it is, circumscribed. In Freeman's hands regional fiction measures the narrow space its author commands and explores the identity that can be achieved in narrowness, not by breaking but by fiercely adhering to its narrow bounds.

Together with the cultural work the genre performed, then, Gilded Age regionalism also had complex consequences on the author's side, and both the genre and the authorship it sponsored made continuing marks on American literary history. Already recognized as a cliché by the late 1870s, this genre managed not to die the death its familiarity seemed to condemn it to, and it was still going strong well into the next century. (Has it ever wholly died?) Sherwood Anderson's Winesburg, Ohio, Zora Neale Hurston's Eatonville, Florida, Faulkner's Yoknapatawpha County, Mississippi, and Laura Ingalls Wilder's Little House on the (Dakota) Prairie are obvious successors to the workspaces of nineteenth-century regional writers, and it would be easy to name a hundred more.

But later writers inherited the patterns of authorship the regionalists consolidated quite as much as their topics or themes. Edith Wharton was determined not to be the sort of self-repeating, self-delimiting author that she saw in Jewett or Freeman, and she avoided the regionalist genre as a way of resisting their form of career. (She returned to write a classic work of regionalist revival, the novella Ethan Frome, after the danger of being taken for a woman regionalist was past.) But later authors took a different tack. Flannery O'Connor and Eudora Welty are writers in the Freeman–Jewett mold: writers who returned to their home town to work, lived in their family homes rather than starting families of their own, wrote fiction of their local place whatever the literary vogue, and regarded such choices as acts of intentional self-definition. ("All vocation implies limitation," O'Connor wrote in a letter her predecessors would understand.) The fact that their choice of subject should be so intimately bound up with these choices of career form is the result of a complex history: one more yield of the life regionalism led in late nineteenth-century American letters.

LITERARY FORMS AND MASS CULTURE, 1870–1920

Nancy Bentley

I

❦

MUSEUM REALISM

William Dean Howells, in an 1887 editorial column for *Harper's Monthly*, noted that four prestigious American periodicals – *The Century, Scribner's*, the *Atlantic Monthly*, and his own *Harper's* – had all simultaneously published new stories by Henry James. "The effect," Howells writes, "was like an artist's exhibition." This "accidental massing" of James's fiction, in other words, reminded Howells of a unique kind of public place, the museum or exhibit gallery: "one turned from one masterpiece to another," viewing "a high perfection" on display in each one. Howells's trope, comparing published fiction to a museum exhibit, was not in itself unusual. A century earlier, for instance, a New York City serial that included fiction and poetry appeared under the title *Weekly Museum* (1788–1817). But the assumptions that motivate Howells's trope in the 1880s differ sharply from those that had informed the title of the earlier serial. The New York weekly was a "museum" because it collected for the reader heterogeneous materials of general interest, advertising itself as a "repository" or "assemblage of whatever can interest the mind." By 1887, however, the figure of the museum no longer connotes eclecticism but rather a consistency of "high perfection," aesthetic purity rather than diversity. Howells's use of the museum trope, moreover, bespeaks a new kind of cultural authority also absent from the earlier era. By invoking the museum, he claims for fiction the imprimatur of a defining modern institution whose authority is based first and last on the importance of disciplined representation, the specialized exhibition of images and objects. Howells's analogy draws on the currency of what his contemporary George Brown Goode, director of the Smithsonian, called "the modern Museum idea."

As Goode's phrase suggests, in the later nineteenth century the museum is not just an institution or site but a resonant, organizing idea with a profound influence on cultural perception itself. The "museum idea" is also a literary idea: an ability to distill the values of high cultural authority and distinction makes the museum an important *topos* in the pages of fiction. Henry James opens the first scene of his novel *The American* (1877) in a room in the Louvre, one of innumerable gallery scenes in his novels. Henry Adams's novel *Esther* (1884) aggressively recasts New York's Cathedral of Saint John into a secular "gallery" for viewing religious art as treasures of humanist culture. Edith Wharton in *The Age of Innocence* (1920) locates a crucial meeting between lovers in front of a glassed-in collection of antiquities in the New York Metropolitan Museum of Art. The museum's importance as a symbolic site also makes it a setting for some of the most penetrating critiques of dominant cultural values. Jane Addams makes the art galleries of Europe her site for challenging the social sensibilities of affluent Americans. W. E. B. Du Bois includes in his masterwork *The Souls of Black Folk* (1903) a race fable played out in a New York concert hall, and uses the Chicago Institute of Art as a setting in his novel *Dark Princess* (1928).

Even more significant than their museum settings, these works address a reader who shares, or should aspire to share, the savvy of the novels' cosmopolitan characters. Unlike most of the fiction that preceded them, such works expect of their readers the same subtle discriminations of observation, the specialized tastes, and the acts of trained attention required of visitors to metropolitan museums. The museum-goer's habits of perception, moreover, are presumed by these writers to be indispensable for understanding the wider world. When the narrator of one of James's novels says that the characters form a "little gallery" (one woman is a "pastel under glass"), when he calls the country villa where they gather a "museum," James supplies an index to a much broader field of cognition. The museum idea is a transportable belief that the world is most legible whenever the right kind of observer confronts and understands selected objects – within the walls of the museum or without. Thus Venice can be for James a "vast museum," complete with crowds passing through imaginary turnstiles and gondoliers and beggars who serve as custodians and ushers while "they are even themselves to a certain extent the objects of exhibition."

Bridging institutions and cognition, the museum idea is fundamental to understanding literary production in the later nineteenth-century United States. Literature in this period succeeds as never before in claiming autonomy – fiction-writing becomes a recognizable profession, literary pursuit earns the dignity of a national academy, and the history of American letters secures its place as a worthy object of study in the university. Yet that very autonomy is symptomatic of a new integration of cultural, political, and social domains. The museum is the secular temple at the center of an American society in which the arts are at once more independent and more closely integrated into mechanisms of civic governance. For this reason the era's most consequential literary development – the emergence of a sphere of high literary culture – can be described as occurring under the sign of the modern museum, as witnessed by the fealty paid to the museum in the plots and tropes of the literature itself.

It is more than a casual analogy, then, to describe an editor like Howells as undertaking the new work of a literary curator. The most influential critic in high literary circles, Howells helps establish a new understanding of fiction in which selected works emerge not only as extraordinary art objects but also as artifacts of a special *order* of representation, an order which, like museum exhibits, claims access to knowledge unavailable in other forms of display. By the 1880s, efforts by Howells and others to distinguish and elevate that order of representation had acquired the status of a literary movement or school labeled Realism, after the *Réalisme* writing of European novelists. In retrospect, Howells's attempt to identify a definitive set of formal features and methods for American Realist fiction was not altogether successful, but he succeeded beyond question in acquiring for fiction precisely the same civic prestige associated with the museum. Offered in the name of advancing a democratic public, his essays and reviews install a literature intended not for amusement but for the higher rewards of discernment and cultural enrichment. Howells's most important critical work, *Fiction and Criticism* (1891), details the principles of this high Realist venture. In it Howells distinguishes a literary sphere in which a form of leisure, novel-reading, is converted to an accumulation and preservation of high cultural value. It has become the task "for realism to assert that fidelity to experience and probability of motive are essential conditions of a great imaginative literature. It is not a new theory," Howells writes, "but it has never before universally characterized literary endeavor." Only with this distinctive literary sphere in place could Howells greet brand-new magazine stories like James's as the equivalent of the works of old masters – instant "masterpieces."

Crucially, Howells's curatorial authority over the masterworks of prose gave him a related authority – far more tenuous but still propitious – over a sphere he reviled: the unruly theatrics of an emerging mass culture. His responsibility as a leading man of letters, as he saw it, was not only to publish and disseminate masterpieces of fiction but to save fiction from the degenerative effects of a vast machinery of "shows and semblances" appearing everywhere in the American landscape. *Fiction and Criticism* reveals Howells's keen attention to the effects of mass forms on readers' sensibilities. "Love of the marvellous," Howells laments, had produced a species of fiction on a par with the circus and burlesque theater. Conceding that even a cultivated person may like "the trapeze" in occasional "moments of barbarism," Howells is nevertheless adamant that circus-like attractions of unreal spectacle and melodrama, when absorbed into fiction, produce a literature of distortion. "In a world which loves the spectacular drama and the practically bloodless sports of the modern amphitheatre," novelists too often fall into the "service of sensation." Like "burlesque and negro minstrelsy," such literature will inevitably "misrepresent life."

The mark of worthy fiction, in contrast, is precisely its aspiration to "represent life" – the same goal pursued, through their respective professional methods, by museums of ethnology, natural history, and fine art. Modern literature, the advocates of Realism hold, is on the side of science. Howells enlists for fiction his era's supreme confidence in the power of expert representations. Realism has cultivated an audience of serious novel-readers, readers who "require of a novelist . . . a sort of scientific decorum. He can no longer expect to be received on the ground of entertainment only." Howells claimed his friend Mark Twain for the campaign to cultivate American fiction, but it was Henry James who represented the "finished workmanship" and "dispassionate analysis" that were central to the highest Realism. The only aesthetic pleasure to be trusted is the "beauty in literature which comes from truth alone." For critics and editors seeking to advance a new Realist aesthetics, the important distinctions are not between genres – the novel as opposed to the poem, or fiction against non-fiction. The real gulf is between true and false cultural sites or systems of representation. The struggle is between the fidelity of authoritative signs and depictions in opposition to the distortion and excess of mass spectacle – the museum against the circus. Only fiction like James's, possessing the kind of mastery on view in museum exhibitions, will be able to adequately "represent life."

In truth, however, this fundamental opposition between real and unreal representation was itself a false conception, though a powerful one. Howells's lament that the "cheap effects" of mass entertainment too easily infected literature belies his anxious awareness of the frequent traffic between high and low arts, between Realist artistry and commercial artifice. To be sure, the rise of an autonomous high culture in this period is a momentous fact; high art's authoritative claims on beauty are of a piece with science's claims on empirical truth, a second passage to the real. But high culture's achieved autonomy should not be mistaken for any imperial indifference to the ragged, proliferating materials of popular arts. On the contrary, the very autonomy of high culture – art's self-defining, self-justifying value – forms itself against those promiscuous materials. From the first, high culture carries an acute and formative interest in what it opposes: the dime novels and nickelodeons, the sprouting commercial posters and veiled peep shows, the acres of newsprint and the unreal worlds of amusement parks. With varying degrees of awareness, Realist authors recognize that the phantasms of this early mass culture are fast becoming one of the most unyielding facts of the modern world. The untethered, protean commercial signs and images of that sector had come to constitute a reality-shaping force of enormous magnitude. With this awareness, the disciplined institutions of high culture retain a complex tie – a mix of antagonism and envy, even imitation – to the unruly world of commercial entertainment they oppose.

The museum itself may be the institution that expresses most vividly the vexed kinship between high culture and its mass-culture antagonists. Lurking just outside the preeminence of the great metropolitan museum was the popular dime museum, devoted to precisely the pleasures of eclectic spectacle that so distressed Howells. P. T. Barnum's establishment, the American Museum, had revealed an enormous public appetite for factitious visual images and for sheer performance brio in a society that was then still officially suspicious of the theatrical. Launching the venture in New York during the 1840s, Barnum made the most of this ambivalence by introducing his curiosities under the auspices of the museum and calling his performance hall a museum "lectureroom." The institution of the museum was capable of serving as something of a facade in those decades, allowing audiences to dodge any of the potentially troubling associations of commercial theater. All museums have a more or less suppressed theatricality, a latent sensationalism; Barnum's genius was to make the museum's surface disavowal into the very means for staging sensational commercial entertainment. The tactic is reflected in Barnum's *Struggles and Triumphs* (1869), an autobiography that became the most widely read book in the later nineteenth century after the Bible. Despite proudly acknowledging the kinds of "constantly diversified" exhibits in his "great Lecture Room" (from "industrious fleas, automatons, jugglers, ventriloquists, living statuary, tableaux, gypsies, Albinoes, fat boys, giants, dwarves" to "mechanical figures, fancy glass-blowing, knitting machines and other triumphs in the mechanical arts [and] American Indians"), Barnum still claimed the august national museums of Europe as his counterparts and rivals: "I frequently compared the annual number of visitors with the number officially reported as visiting (free of charge), the British Museum in London," Barnum boasts, "and my list was invariably the larger."

By the 1880s, with the establishment of metropolitan museums in most leading American cities, the institution of the museum had finally rid itself of what Henry James called the open "Barnum associations and revelations." But even in this later era the museum was not a pristine, autonomous space, a "classifying house" that merely ordered and preserved authentic specimens of art and nature. It remained linked, in invisible but structurally important ways, to the more unruly world of commercial exhibition it opposed. The same animal-collecting agencies that supplied Barnum with animal attractions for his circus, for instance, also provided natural history museums with specimens for their scientific displays. There were even direct transfers between circus and museum: when one of Barnum's most famous elephants died in the middle of a tour, for instance, naturalists and museum taxidermists rushed to transform the gigantic corpse into one of the prized attractions of New York's American Museum of Natural History. The plate glass for that museum's exhibitions was supplied by one of the trustees, Theodore Roosevelt Sr., whose company manufactured the large glass sheets behind which the ornate displays of department store goods were staged for urban crowds. In many of their techniques of architectural design, crowd control, and exhibition display, museums shared the habits and tactics and even the selfsame materials of the world of amusement parks, fairs, and commercial spectacles. These sub rosa exchanges with mass-cultural forms, together with a critical opposition to it, gave museum displays of this period their particular texture, authority, and appeal.

That the prestige of the museum was indebted to the mass culture it opposed points to enduring puzzles. How are we to understand the effects of this historical entanglement between opposed spheres? Does the profit motive driving mass culture nullify all but commercial values in popular works and venues? Do high cultural forms encourage an active transformation of thought and feeling, an enlarged freedom of consciousness, or do they serve an agenda of social exclusion and control? Still unresolved, these questions make their first appearance in the later nineteenth century and take a particularly stark form in the United States, the birthplace of major innovations in mass culture. At stake in this history is the formation of the modern category of the literary, its function and fate in our own media-reliant society.

When Henry James traced the "earliest aesthetic seeds" of his creative consciousness, he revealed that among the origins of his art was an extensive "Barnum background" of circus acts and Broadway spectacles. In a remarkable chapter from his memoir *A Small Boy and Others* (1913), James recalls his still vivid responses to the acrobat shows and staged chariot races, to the sights of Barnum's "halls of humbug," with their "bottled mermaids, 'bearded ladies,' and chill dioramas," and to the popular stage dramas with the "creak of carpentry" audible in their more ambitious scenic effects – all thrilling stops in the excursions of his New York childhood. James seems by turns amused and dismayed by the fact that "sordidities and poverties" of vulgar entertainments could have produced in him such deep stirrings, "from the total impression of which things we somehow plucked the flower of the ideal." Although he conveys with considerable wit his adult knowledge of the "meanness" of what he once took for glamour, James is still at pains to stress that the "crude scenic appeal" of such spectacles could engender the highest kind of critical and aesthetic sensibility. It was in such places, he writes, that the young James "got his first glimpse of that possibility of a 'free play of mind' over a subject which was to throw him with force at a later stage of culture, into the critical arms of Matthew Arnold" – a high distinction born of low theatrics.

Even the supreme "majesty" of Europe and European art turns out to be something James first experiences as an American spectacle. James's memory of Niblo's and Franconi's gardens, and "circuses under tents on vacant lots," leads directly to his recollection of visits to the nearby Crystal Palace, a New York recreation of the London exhibition hall, where "showy sculpture" in "profuse exhibition" produce for him the effect of Europe and "big European Art" before he ever travels in a European country. It is here, then, that European art is first experienced through American artifice: "I remember being very tired and cold and hungry there . . . though concomitantly conscious that I was somehow in Europe, since everything about me had been 'brought over' . . . If this was Europe then Europe was beautiful indeed." A gaudy American showplace literally stages for the young James the idea of Europe and conjures a future self who will be shaped by the continent he has not visited since his infancy. "The Crystal Palace was vast and various and dense, which was what Europe was going to be; it was a deep-down jungle of impressions that were somehow challenges."

Against the contention that high and low spheres were inherently at odds, here James insists that they possess a kinship, an essential relation binding their distinct identities. His close analysis of his own artistic "initiation" through mass spectacle recognizes a complexity in aesthetic experience that is missing from Howells's tenets. These popular entertainments, James claims, were "a brave beginning for a consciousness that was to be nothing if not mixed, and a curiosity that was to be nothing if not restless." Confessing an "adverse loyalty" to these origins in popular spectacle, James locates an important context for the questions of representation that preoccupied literary and cultural critics of his generation. It suggests that the distinctive aesthetics of various high arts of this period, the polished realism of museum displays and accomplished novels and paintings, may in fact owe something fundamental to their rival forms in mass culture.

The dual tendencies towards exchange and disavowal were a controlling influence on literary production. In the new institution of the Realist novel, as in the metropolitan museum, the imperative to "represent life" was never simply a matter of mimesis, of rendering a close transcription of social reality. At a deep and formative level, Realist writing also enacted a mimetic rivalry with other compelling cultural systems. Realism is a conventional name for a body of literature, but in the formation of that writing "realism" is less a descriptor than a watchword, a talisman that guides a historical process of differentiation alert at every point to the ungoverned mass-cultural productions to which it opposes itself. The high Realist novel is a museum-like institution, haunted by its own kinship with an emergent mass culture, and shaped in fundamental ways by the disorderly mass pleasures it both imitates and disavows. It is an institution committed to public pedagogy and a new disciplined kind of reading, the inverse of which is its own unacknowledged tutelage from popular entertainment and media. It is a form concerned with the refinement of taste and distinction, which is nevertheless drawn to the vulgar glamour of publicity. The Realist novel claims the detached mastery of the scientist while it vividly dramatizes fragmented zones of experience and vertiginous states of feeling. It aspires to transparency and authenticity while being obsessed with artifice and simulation. High Realism presumes for its reader a strict bodily decorum of controlled manners despite its keen absorption in the sight of the "alien" ungoverned bodies it imagines for certain women and immigrants and people of color. The impressive reach of this prose, its often astonishingly perceptive explorations of consciousness and social life, comes in no small part from an emergent mass culture that was a basis for its close elaboration of distinctions.

In assessing this writing, James's account of the birth of his cultural consciousness in the halls of Barnum supplies an index to a critical history of high Realism and its cognate arts. Three related topics stand out as key concerns. First, the memoir invokes in detail a landscape of early mass-cultural forms, a site for James in which diffuse pleasures and feelings stir closer calibrations of aesthetic judgment. A second topic, then, is the aesthetic consciousness born in a dialectical relation to that mass landscape: out of low theatrics emerges a power of discernment that will become identified with spaces of refuge such as the writer's study, the metropolitan museum, and the high art object itself. James's memoir identifies a third concern, finally, in his recollection a phantom "Europe," where Europe is an idea or effect that precedes the place itself. This notional Europe is the geography that orients American high culture and US transnational ties and territorial expansions. A powerful spur for a mixed transatlantic traffic in culture and capital, a record of racial valances that go largely unspoken and unchallenged, America's projected fantasy of Europe exerts a controlling force during the country's debut as, in W. E. B. Du Bois's words, a "vast economic empire." In mass spectacle, in cultural distinction, and in the magnetic force and racial charge of Europe, James's tale contains a grammar for articulating the history and possible meanings of high literary culture and its others.

LITERATURE FOR THE BILLION

In Edith Wharton's novel *The House of Mirth* (1905), Lawrence Selden disparages the New York elite for staging their social life in the "glare of publicity," the high visibility of the mass-circulation press and showy public appearances. Selden is not particularly bothered by wasted wealth or class snobbery in these circles. Rather, he is critical of the "ideals of a world where conspicuousness passed for distinction," where sheer public visibility counts for more than sensibility and fame eclipses character. In opposing "conspicuousness" to "distinction," Selden names a pair of key terms that define one of the abiding obsessions of the Northeastern literary establishment in its uneasy alliance with the economically driven host culture of the later nineteenth century.

Both "conspicuousness" and "distinction" describe prominence or social recognition, but placed in opposition to one another they mark two divergent sources of that recognition. For the new class of literate professionals like the urbane lawyer Selden, "distinction" had become a complex, almost circular idea. To be a man or woman of distinction no longer meant one possessed a secure claim to membership in the leading propertied class, as it would have meant to the antebellum gentry. In the increasingly dynamic, competitive culture of postbellum America, the superiority of true distinction became a more elusive quality. Neither birth nor wealth alone could secure it; as Selden's note of disdain for the wealthy elite suggests, one could be rich and well born but still found wanting. Instead, distinction is now rooted in inward qualities of mind and perception. To possess real distinction is to be able to *make* distinctions, to discern aesthetic richness from commercial blandness, to value achievements of mind over merely material advances. Selden has a striking name for men and women of distinction: they are citizens of a "republic of the spirit." Membership in this invisible nation depends on immaterial traits of refined seeing and understanding. "There are sign-posts" to this "country," Selden explains, but "one has to know how to read them."

The attributes of true distinction, then, cannot be universally recognized or read; conspicuousness, in contrast, is what we cannot help reading. Like advertising and celebrity and other creations of modern publicity, conspicuousness supplies its own self-interpreting signs. Whereas distinction resides in exceptional discernment, conspicuousness is the insistent, iconic visibility that precludes any need for discernment. Hence the urgency felt by cultivated people like Selden for a semantic opposition between the two terms, for conspicuousness threatens to make distinction irrelevant, even obsolete. Cultural leaders believed that the "glare of publicity" present everywhere in the new commercial society was a direct threat to the softer, private illumination of the best aesthetic and moral judgment.

Language, though inherited, is alive to historical change. The splitting of related words into disparate concepts, or the blending of unique terms into a new and unified meaning, can signal reordered social possibilities and conditions. A deep shift of this kind may be behind the need to articulate a starker difference between notions of conspicuousness and distinction in the later nineteenth-century English lexicon. It is in this period that cities become centers of not only an enormously enlarged sphere of commerce but also of an unprecedented production of communication, the commerce of signs and meanings – a mass circulation of words and photographs, faces and trademarks, visual styles and commercial rituals, all following paths of profit rather than the reasoning of deliberative politics or educated opinion. Under these conditions – conditions most obvious in the mass-circulation press, in rapidly rising book sales, in the visual landscape of cities dominated by commercial display and advertising – an earlier cohesive idea of Enlightenment rationality is strained to the breaking point. Previously, the ideal of Enlightenment presumed a perfect compatibility between human reason and human progress; an advance in one would secure an advance in the other. Now, the material changes wrought by rational modernization appear able to dwarf the power of personal reason and judgment. What was previously imagined as a sphere of shared, public reason, if only as a realizable ideal, is now viewed as a world divided between the indiscriminate fame conferred by public display and individual powers of reasoned discrimination. Enlightenment as an ideal illumination gives way to a self-generated rivalry: conspicuousness at war with distinction, the glare of signs against the lights of discernment.

Were these forces really so antithetical? While the writers who describe the stark opposition were rendering a profound cultural experience, there are good reasons to see the matter in rather different, less polarized terms. The belief that enlightened perception – the subtle cognitive capacities of aesthetic judgment, taste, and distinction – had become uniquely imperiled is a belief that animates the most resonant works of high culture in this period. But we need to recognize this conviction as a complex and deeply ironic truth. Its inverted truth lies in the fact that the conviction of peril actually helped *create* what was thought to be under threat: specialized judgments of taste and closely calibrated forms of cultural perception. The critic and educator Charles Eliot Norton lamented that "no one knows how to think anymore" and laid the blame on the public appetite for popular magazines. His 1888 essay in *The New Princeton Review*, "The Intellectual Life of America," is representative indictment of the popular publications that were "largely addressed to a horde of readers who seek in them not only the news of the day, but the gratification of a vicious taste for strong sensations; who enjoy the coarse stimulants of personalities and scandal, and have no appetite for any sort of proper intellectual nourishment." Yet Norton's judgment issued from a new critical establishment that owed its increased authority in no small part to its opposition of that expanding popular sphere. For that reason, the sorts of thinking and reflection cultivated in Norton's world – the world of highbrow cultural journals, university programs in the humanities, professional and artistic networks connecting New York City and Boston to European cultural capitals – these modes of thought were just as surely the products of the new commercial conditions as the seeming lapses that Norton so lamented.

To read the literary elite of the period is to realize that the scope and scale of popular writing – "literature for the billion" as James puts it – irrevocably changes the measurement of literary achievement. At one extreme, the sheer volume of printed matter in this period appears to foretell an extinction of the literary. In an essay from his *Literature and Life* (1902), Howells invents an interlocutor who wryly praises magazines and Sunday supplements by way of warning the editor against his foolish predilection for "intellectual" books: "If you don't amuse your readers, you don't keep them; practically, you cease to exist." Beginning with a sharp rise at mid-century, magazine sales swelled exponentially. In 1885 the four American magazines with a readership of over 100,000 together sold 600,000 copies a month; by 1905 five times as many magazines enjoyed sales of that order and their aggregate circulation reached 5,500,500 per month. In roughly the same period, Joseph Pulitzer's *New York World* rose from 15,000 readers (in 1883) to a circulation of over a million by 1900.

Norton's complaint that the floodtide of magazines had somehow washed away the ability to think is perhaps more accurately an admission of his own feelings of submersion, for certainly such numbers meant that far more readers than before were spending more time with the printed word – just not with the words of Norton and his peers. They were reading instead such works as the working-girl novels of Laura Jean Libbey who pushed her sales past sixteen million books with titles like *Only a Mechanic's Daughter, Madcap Laddie*, and *Plot and Passion*. They were buying the books of Sylvanus T. Cobb, who parlayed his newspaper writing for the New York *Ledger* (2,305 pieces in all) into a career as the producer of over 122 novels. Reform fiction of all kinds – temperance novels, potboilers about urban degeneration, divorce novels, and labor stories – continued to prompt Americans to buy and consume books as reading became a more widespread form of mass social engagement. It was a form of religious engagement as well: religious novels like the bestsellers from the minister Harold Bell Wright were often adapted for tent-show plays, where the millions inspired at the revivals could buy the book after the show. Mass-produced fiction, in other words, had not lowered readers' tastes so much as turned popular tastes to the work of creating new readers in unprecedented numbers.

Although men of letters like Norton were far from becoming extinct, then, the explosion in print and in book buying did produce a new readership for whom elite authors were largely outsiders. Hence the writers' recorded sense of exile from what James called a "commonschooled and newspapered democracy." The new consumption had reordered the map of literate America and elite authors existed on its margins, unread luminaries if not unknown names. The genre of the urban exposé, begun in the antebellum period by George Lippard and E. Z. C. Judson, flourished expansively in the post-Civil War era, and books like Edward Crapsey's *The Nether Side of New York* (1872), J. G. Grant's *The Evils of San Francisco* (1884), and George Stevens's *Chicago: Wicked City* (1896) disclosed to the new readers a fictional underworld that now reached as far as the West coast. The revelation of these unfamiliar urban underworlds in fiction mirrored the unforeseen massing of the new population of readers who consumed them, and if the readers were less menacing than the urban underworld, they were hardly less mysterious, at least to the literary establishment. Where had they come from? Unbidden by literary gatekeepers, this new nation of readers seemed to materialize from nowhere.

They had not, of course. Technology, impersonal and largely invisible, played a foundational role. The introduction of linotype machines in 1885, and new printing presses of lightning speed enlarged capacity beyond what anyone had foreseen. Print was not only voluminous but cheap. Newspapers and paperbacks were suddenly everyday purchases for a public with steeply rising rates of literacy. The completion of national transportation routes ensured that readers were amassed not through localized bookselling alone but increasingly through the long reach of advertising campaigns, transcontinental distribution, and improved transatlantic trade. These developments meant that the local place where readers bought and read their books mattered little; members of a sewing circle in Oregon Territory, stockyard supervisors in Chicago, and domestics in South Florida hotels might all spy the same ad or book cover and be enlisted into the readership for a given dime novel. The importance of location was displaced, as it were, from the site of the reader to the setting of the book. The shift may be one of the reasons historical romances fared especially well in the new mass market, as their exotic fictional settings – the Jerusalem of Jesus' day in Lew Wallace's *Ben Hur*, the Renaissance Italy of Francis Marion

Crawford's novels – became a common ground for millions living in disparate places.

In this unbinding of people from the determinants of local place, mass fiction and journalism made vivid one of the signal developments of modernity. By making physical place less consequential, mass publishing illuminates a transformation that one current theorist describes as "a 'lifting out' of social relations from local contexts of interaction and their restructuring across time and space." As a mass form, the historical romance in vogue in the later nineteenth century is an incarnation of this new mediation of social relations: the genre produces a fictional locale whose specificity is the inverse of the dispersed location of its massive audience. The reader's freedom to traverse time is likewise a sign of these modern conditions. Despite the return in *Ben Hur* to the zero degree of Christian history, the life of Jesus, Wallace's bestseller reflects a decidedly secular appropriation of time, a paperback tourism that made the Jerusalem of Jesus merely one site alongside Rider Haggard's fantastic African jungles in *King Solomon's Mines* (1887) and the medieval England of Charles Major's *When Knighthood Was in Flower* (1898). Self-declared Realists like Howells saw the huge popularity of historical romance as a troubling flight from modern life. In fact, the genre is a harbinger of an intensified modernity, an early rehearsal of habits of mind increasingly cut loose from more immediate proximities of place and time. The backward gaze of historical fiction, in other words, exemplifies the way technology and modern markets were rapidly encroaching on the authority of the local, the here and now of the congregation, the municipal bank, and the rural county calendar.

POPULAR SPECTACLE AND THE SPACE OF THE STUDY: HENRY JAMES AND MASS CULTURE

For cultural leaders, these results of modernization seemed starkly opposed to modern progress. Whereas Realist writers saw themselves painting in the lines of social history, inscribing causal continuities and logical probabilities, mass fiction seemed riveted by mere sensation, an infantile regression. In Howells's words, a "spectacle muse" was the deity of the age. The phrase appears in one of his most interesting meditations on the fate of literature, an essay entitled "At a Dime Museum" (1902). A distillation of the worst impulses of an emerging mass culture, the dime museum for Howells exposes the imperative to amuse that was pulling down all cultural expression to "the level of show business." As Howells knows, tact and humor are required in any critique of popular culture; to fulminate is to risk being cornered as a prig and thus to forfeit the grounds of sophistication that is the critic's only cultural advantage. To sidestep that trap, Howells invents an urbane "friend" who, in a campy tribute to "cheaper amusements of the metropolis," relates to the editor the knowing pleasures he found at an afternoon's visit to a dime museum, a jaunt during an idle hour "between two appointments."

A report from the cultural wilds, the friend's account details the crowded collection of "clever" things on display at the popular establishment, from "two gloomy apes" to contortionists "of Spanish-American extraction." Howells's readers, however, are implicitly asked to find a sharper cleverness in the friend's account itself. Delivered from the comfort of an easy chair in the editor's study, an intimate space into which the reader has gained privileged entry ("finding room for his elbow on the corner of my table he knocked off some books for review"), the friend's story conveys the second-order enjoyment of recognizing the naïveté of "popular taste." All of the friend's avowals of delight are thus subtly – and instructively – disingenuous. His reported pleasure is real but always double: the discerning reader must hear two notes, the stated report and its damning overtones. To know, for instance, that his description of the "unflagging energy" of the toiling actors in a museum theatrical is not a piece of praise but a superior smile is the reader's reward for finding herself at home with a Howells essay rather than at a dime museum.

The subtle pleasures from Howells's structure of layered discriminations become especially complex when the friend is able to mock – and thereby simultaneously affirm – his sense of his own superior sensibilities at viewing an exhibit of Australian aborigines:

On a platform at the end of the hall was an Australian family a good deal gloomier than the apes . . . staring down the room with varying expressions all verging upon melancholy madness, and who gave me such a pang of compassion as I have seldom got from the tragedy of the two-dollar theatres. They allowed me to come quite close up to them, and to feed my pity upon their wild dejection in exile without stint. I couldn't enter into conversation with them, and express my regret at finding them so far from their native boomerangs and kangaroos and pinetree grubs, but I know they felt my sympathy, it was so evident. I didn't see their performance, and I don't know that they had any. They may simply have been there ethnologically, but this was a good object, and the sight of their spiritual misery was alone worth the price of admission.

Exposing the coarseness of the racist exhibit, the passage is nonetheless primarily a striking extension of Howells's analysis of taste. The speaker's mockery of his own feelings of compassion, in other words, is Howells's sign that taste is a surer moral index than raw sentiment. At stake here is finally not the exhibit's racism (which is matched by the narrator's own slicker version, evident in the glib evocation of tree grubs and boomerangs) but rather Howells's indictment of the bad taste of a moralism got on the cheap.

Virtuosity can be tactical, an inoculation. Howells's demonstrated mastery of taste in this essay clears the way for his cultural criticism. The fictional "friend" and alter ego (who, as Howells's creation, displays the editor's own urbanity as author) becomes the figure to pose the strongest – because most knowing – challenge to the critic's concerns about mass culture: "Isn't all art one?" he asks. "How can you say that any art is higher than the others?" If spectacles like Australian savages, lady inventors, and South American contortionists give ephemeral pleasure at appropriately low prices, the friend argues, what is the harm? "Why is it nobler to contort the mind than to contort the body?"

This challenge, of course, is really Howells's well-dressed strawman. "I am always saying that it is not at all noble to contort the mind," is Howells's reply, "and I feel that to aim at nothing higher than the amusement of your readers is to bring yourself most distinctly down to the level of the show business." To equate all arts as merely different branches of entertainment is to risk delivering up literature to the "spectacle muse" of a commercial age. In its witty tour of a dime museum, the essay is Howells's brief against the distortions of a commercial culture attuned only to the principles of "show business" – to the allure of novelty and the freakish (the contortionist), the power of ignorant wishes (a fortune-teller) and fraud (a perpetual motion machine), the appeal of indiscriminate display and visual shock (a curio hall). Relatively harmless in itself, the dime museum for Howells bespeaks a world where success in literature is measured by the commercial criteria that govern mass spectacle, a world where the dime-store drama is simply a more affordable *Hamlet*, and the literary author is no more than a glorified Barnum. As the figure of the friend puts it to the editor, "You do your little act, and because the stage is large and the house is fine, you fancy you are not of the sad brotherhood which aims to please in humbler places." Howells's protest essay is at once a recognition of cultural commodification and a display of a new species of literate wit, namely, Howells's own cultural fluency and polyglot taste that can take up the myriad pleasures of mass culture and go them one better. He thus anticipates the strategies of those postmodern artists who, dropping protest, build intricate layers of literate discrimination out of the acknowledged power and disparate forms of mass culture.

In "At a Dime Museum," then, mass forms represent not an obstacle but an occasion for an exhilarating performance of literary sensibility. For discriminating readers, Howells's multivalent tones and nimble reversals trump the sensational productions of show business. Alongside this literate display of fluency, however, is the essay's indirect acknowledgment of certain generative capacities in mass culture, capacities that can be said to outstrip the "intellectual character" of the literary. Unwittingly, Howells in this way identifies a certain limitation to literary writing. It comes in a mock defense of the circus, when Howells's imaginary friend admits only one complaint about that form of mass entertainment, namely the "superfluity" of the circus's three rings: "Fancy reading three novels simultaneously, and listening at the same time to a lecture and a sermon, which could represent the two platforms between the rings." The absurdity of the conceit pits mass-culture excess against literary profundity. Literature wins, of course. But the image also recognizes a circumscribed quality of the literary. The high fiction Howells has in mind works by focusing the reader's full attention through a single object, the text in hand. Reading of this sort requires the elimination of competing stimuli. Relative silence, bodily stillness, and physical comfort are its necessary if not sufficient conditions. Literary reading favors an individual mental concentration that acquires imaginative leverage by excluding other somatic and social realities. In contrast to this monopoly on the reader's attention, however, mass forms like the circus and the dime museum seek to multiply objects and stimuli. In their very excess such sites open out to multiple zones of experience and feeling, zones to which the high cultural novel has no imaginary access. By itself, the blunt sensation of spectacle may be literature's opposite number. Yet the simultaneous visual, aural, and kinetic stimulation of a circus suggests an aesthetic heterogeneity in mass culture that is closer to a counterpart to the literary, if not a rival. Fancy reading three novels, indeed!

If Howells harbors any sense of a rival complexity from this quarter of popular culture, his essay downplays it. But his decision to focus most of the essay on the dime museum may betray a more defensive posture than Howells means to show. By making the dime museum his representative site, Howells chose a venue of popular culture that by 1902 would have been seen as rather outdated, even quaint. Already on the scene and flourishing were other forms in thrall to the "spectacle muse" that promised a wider, more aggressive cultural reach. The subculture of the urban dance hall, the enveloping world of the amusement park, the planned mayhem of deliberately staged train wrecks – these and other forms of entertainment convey the complex power of popular spectacle in the late nineteenth century. Far from fostering infantile retreat, the affective experiences available at these commercial sites are innovations in feeling that respond to the social and material technologies from which they spring. Howells's mock fantasy of reading three novels simultaneously is a piece of satire, to be sure, but the image may harbor a wish that high literature had the ability to match the multiplicity of physical and mental experiences newly available at the sites of mass culture.

The dime museum offered its pleasures under a single roof, producing an "intimacy" among the visitors that Howells's interlocutor wryly likens to "a domestic circle." In contrast to the dime museum's homeliness, amusement parks like Coney Island, Dreamland, and Luna Park captured the scope and complexity of the modern city. During the 1870s and 1880s, the smaller (and seedier) carnivals and Atlantic seaside resorts of the immediate postwar years grew into the amusement parks that became the unofficial capitals of America's emergent mass culture. By the century's end, millions passed annually through the turnstiles of these enclosed but extensive worlds, make-believe cities with their own fantastic architecture and playful transport and trade. Turrets, illuminated towers, and monumental statues in these parks anticipated the skyscrapers that would later dominate cityscapes. Water chutes and small-scale railways alluded to mechanized urban transportation while supplying controlled bursts of exhilaration. These fabricated cities were, as one visitor put it, "crazier than the craziest part of Paris," replications of the modern metropolis in which the scale, variety, and sensory assaults of urban spectacle could be manipulated for pleasure. Unlike a dime museum or even a circus, an amusement park was less a staged spectacle than a spectacular total environment, replete with landmarks, maps, and guides.

Though intended to evoke the size and heterogeneity of a real city, the amusement park importantly recast the most daunting elements of modern urban life. The density and speed of industrial cities, their outsized scale and purposeful chaos, were refashioned as the ingredients of mass entertainment. A Coney Island hotel in the shape of an enormous elephant could, through sheer whimsy, tame the increasingly massive size of urban buildings. The human crowds at amusement parks were themselves an exciting attraction. By the time the new parks were in full swing in the 1890s, over 200,000 people were descending daily on each of the leading parks. Whereas the audiences for such mass phenomena as the newspaper, the bestseller, and later the radio remained invisible and disembodied, amusement parks allowed mass consumers to see themselves gathered as a visible social body, one that resembled a leisure class, at least for a day. Rides and attractions turned the hazards of industrialism into kinetic pleasures that millions were eager to purchase with their industry wages. Patrons who rode the Leap Frog Railway at Luna Park, for instance, rushed along in small, open-air railcars that appeared certain to crash into other oncoming cars until the tracks prevented the collision at the last second. Disasters and large-scale accidents, all too frequently emblazoned in newspaper headlines, became their own live theatrical spectacles at the parks. One production at Dreamland, "Fighting the Flames," involved a cast of 4,000 characters (including 300 "midgets"). Any and all park spaces were a potential stage. Why limit the services of the ocean to providing waves for bathers when it could also serve to present the reenactment of a famous shipwreck? Why not build a raised platform over the man-made lagoon at the foot of the Shoot-the-Chute as the site for a three-ring circus, complete with equestrian acrobatics and cakewalk competitions on a stage suspended in mid-air? Although visitors felt they had entered "another world," amusement parks offered not an escape from modernity but rather a temporary mastery of modern experience made possible by a canny multiplication of the visual and kinetic stimulations of urban settings.

The park's larger-than-life dimensions, its massing of populations, its offer of unbounded and frenetic activity – these features closely match the traits that literary critics most condemned in popular literature. Henry James remarked often on the "colossal" and "deafening" daily production of fiction and journalism, and was both repelled and intrigued by the "mere bulk and mass" of the print industry of his day. In James's mind the print world, no less than the amusement park, flaunted extremes of scale and mass volume as ends in themselves, tributes to the "immense public" courted by both industries. Edith Wharton professed a lifelong aversion to "crowds," a distaste central to the distinct ambivalence she felt at the popular success of her own novels. The massiveness of objects and crowds at sites like the amusement park allowed everyone to see the otherwise invisible transformation of American life into a mass society. A parallel transformation of scale was simultaneously remaking the world of publishing, but rather than producing pleasure the altered landscape startled and distressed elite authors.

For James, the new print industry was not only outsized but suggested something dangerously kinetic, a "cataract" or "flood of fiction" that "swells and swells" until readers are sure to be "smothered in quantity and number." In a typical essay, "The Future of the Novel" (1899), James announces with alarm that "the book is everywhere." Print has become an unbounded medium and the novel seems to "penetrate the easiest and furthest," leaving hapless readers immersed and disoriented. The landscape of popular culture, with its rides, novelties, and crowds, suggests that millions of Americans sought out precisely the sorts of kinetic sensations and enveloping environments that provided the terms of James's condemnation of publishing. So much the worse, then, for modern letters: the "future of the novel" looked too much like the future of the amusement park.

But if the print industry evoked a paper Coney Island, literature in this era also had its modern-day sanctuary: the author's study. The private office or study of the writer became an iconic space, the site most removed from modern "quantity and number." James wrote of the relief of entering his study as a "blessed and uninvaded workroom," a "sacred and solitary refuge." The writing rooms of scholars and artists have always received elevated importance, from the philosopher's "studie" in Chaucer's tale ("there-as his bookes be"), to the indoor retreat where Wordsworth recollected in verse the beauty of nature. But in the late nineteenth century the study becomes emblematic not just of creative thought but also a pointed opposition to a mass-mediated public. As such, its connection to private life takes on new aesthetic and social meaning. If the amusement park was mass culture's capital, the private study was the nerve center for a high civilization under threat. Dedicated to creative work rather than raucous play, to silence or quiet conversation rather than the noise of crowds, the study was antithetical to the world of popular spectacle. The private office or study thus became a literary space of a complex kind – not just a space for literary production but a flexible symbol of the literary as such. When Howells began his editorial column for *Harper's Monthly*, he called it "The Editor's Study." There was an impressive efficiency (if not circularity) to this trope: the image of a personal study supplied a concrete location and visual "look" for Howells's literary authority, just as its use as a title of the editorial column of *Harper's* confirmed the space of the study as a symbolic repository of literary value. The California writer Gertrude Atherton even kept a photograph of Howells's real study on the writing desk in her own, as if to channel through a visual image the otherwise abstract and intangible property of the literary. When the scholar James Russell Lowell published *Among My Books* (1870) and *My Study Window* (1871), the titles not only announce Lowell's subject, his venerable literary understanding, they also offer readers an entrance to that knowledge through the image of the intimate space of his personal study. Such titles allowed critics and authors to circulate literary judgment – including implied judgment about what is literary – as a kind of personal, almost unmediated sensibility, despite its distribution through the medium of print.

As both a symbolic site and a real room, the author's study is a significant *topos* for Realist novelists as well. And when imported into narrative fiction, the figure reveals what the private study really housed as a symbolic space: not merely books and writing desks but conceptual differences, the marked distinctions necessary to isolate and distinguish the literary. In fiction, the personal study is a setting that functioned as a literal *setting apart*. In Wharton's novel *The Age of Innocence* (1920), for instance, which harkens back to the New York of the 1870s, Wharton establishes the difference between the protagonist Newland Archer and his more conventional wife by enumerating the features of his study. With its "sincere Eastlake furniture, and the plain new book cases without glass doors" holding volumes of Herbert Spencer and Dante Gabriel

Rossetti, Archer's study is distinguished as an intellectual's preserve in the midst of a quietly stultifying bourgeois household. To the discerning reader, these interior details certify the value of dedicated reading by way of an implicit contrast: the knowing taste that created Archer's study is distinguished from the merely good taste of his genteel family and social circle. The study is thus a place for the active interplay of thought and feeling – for literary openness – as opposed to a repetition of inherited forms.

That the space of the study functions to showcase literary meaning through a kind of formal narrative relief is even clearer in a Howells novel, *The Minister's Charge* (1886). The Reverend Sewell, a literary man, accidentally encourages the poetic ambitions of a farm hand, the untutored (and largely untalented) Lemuel Barker. Sewell is at a loss when Barker unexpectedly turns up on his Boston doorstep one day, but he invites the young man into his study in an attempt to show kindness.

"Come upstairs with me into my study, and I will show you a picture of Agassiz. It's a very good photograph."

He led the way out of the reception-room, and tripped lightly in his slippered feet up the steps against which Barker knocked the toes of his clumsy boots. He was not large, nor naturally loutish, but the heaviness of the country was in every touch and movement. He dropped the photograph twice in his endeavor to hold it between his stiff thumb and finger.

Whereas Howells's "Editor's Study" and Lowells's *My Study Window* invite readers into a shared textual space for a meeting of the minds, here the invitation to enter a study serves inversely to expose Barker's incomprehension. The very "heaviness" of his footfalls on the stairs bespeaks an inherent friction, a cultural resistance or drag that all but stops him in his tracks and foretells his inability to grasp (even to hold on to!) the cultural touchstones collected in Sewell's study. His entry into the space of the study reveals, as if by natural law, just who he is – or rather, who he is not. Nothing of Barker, body or soul, belongs in the study.

[Sewell] went on pointing out the different objects in the quiet room, and he took down several books from the shelves that covered the whole wall, and showed them to Barker, who, however, made no effort to look at them for himself, and did not say anything about them. He did what Sewell bade him to do in admiring this thing or that; but if he had been an Indian he could not have regarded them with a greater reticence.

The analogy with a silent "Indian" is hardly casual; Barker's stoic unresponsiveness is paradoxically expressive of deep cultural difference. Like a photographer's dark room, Sewell's study brings into focus the absence of literary sensibility that will define Barker's life and defeat his poetic aspirations. Here and elsewhere, Howells's Realism makes personal qualities of taste and perception serve as the surest index to social realities.

Conceived in this way, the literary is defined less through books or authors than through distinctions in taste and cognition, differentials that identify literary meaning with a species of interiority. So conceived, the literary is also the opposite of the poetics of spectacle – invisible rather than visual, private rather than publicized, subtle and cumulative rather than blaring. In contrast to the self-display of a Barnum performer, the author's study signifies a self-effacement characteristic of refined creation (critic Thomas Sargeant Perry identified the Russian novelist Ivan Turgenev as a "realist in the sense of hiding himself" while he practiced "painstaking accuracy"). But while the *topos* of the author's study suggests the chaste work of the mind, it also locates a quiet glamour that is never directly claimed but everywhere implied: the disavowed glamour we call authority. And in modernity, where there is glamour, there is likely to be iconic display – in other words, spectacle. A predictable paradox follows: the author's private study in this period became a site of concentrated interest for tourists and celebrity-seekers as well as literary devotees. Newspaper and magazine pieces like the British journalist Edmund Yates's *Celebrities at Home* series in the 1870s and 1880s often presented the homes of famous American authors by illustrating the "literary workshop" with lavish photographs and reverent captions. Yates's books and similar photo essays in popular magazines were an extension of the tourist pilgrimages to the "home of the author" that had been popular in England and America since the 1850s. As James notes of his protagonist in "The Private Life" (1892), an author's fame might come from the unobserved act of writing in a "darkened room," but for any writer who achieved public acclaim, that room was also a spectacle in its own right, at least for the author willing to give the public an "inside" glimpse. For dead authors, of course, the home study often became an iconic shrine – a frozen scene with carefully placed desk, inkwell and pens, a pair of folded spectacles – whether or not they had wished for that particular tribute.

Precisely the seclusion of the study, then, could be put on display. The privacy of the private study could have an almost irresistible mass appeal. But what, then, of the authorial privacy that made the study a symbolic site of the literary to begin with? In one respect, public tours and magazine photos of writing rooms altogether missed the point that the setting of the study identifies literary meaning with interior sensibility and a refuge from mass exposure. Only reading and writing offer entry to the literary; buying magazine photo spreads, seeking out interviews with famous writers, or visiting an author's home – seeking, in other words, what James called "the person of the author" – is at best a mistake, at worst a violation. In another respect, however, the mass marketing of the author's study revealed an important truth: that the association of literariness with privacy (interiority, refuge, singular perception) was itself mediated. The intimacy of the literary was established and circulated in print, not kept untainted in a preserve of individual sensibility. The figure of the study was a site of Realist publicity, an aggressive advertisement for a new oppositional understanding of literature.

James frequently satirized as a kind of excited voyeurism the popular interest in seeing the inside of the author's study. In his story "The Death of the Lion," a journalist eager to market an "intimate" view of a literary celebrity is gleeful at gaining an entrance to the writer's study:

> I was shown into the drawing-room, but there must be more to see – his study, his literary sanctum, the little things he has about, or other domestic objects or features. He wouldn't be lying down on his study table? There's a great interest always felt in the scene of an author's labors. Sometimes we're favoured with very delightful peeps. Dora Forbes showed me all his table-drawers, and almost jammed my hand into one into which I made a dash!

As this passage suggests, few authors could match James in skewering what he deemed the wrong kind of readerly enthusiasm, an eagerness to know (profitable) details about the personal life of an author. (The desire to reach a hand into "private drawers" of the writer's desk is one of his favorite – and most suggestive – images, appearing several times in his authors' tales and notebooks.) It is not too much to say that James was obsessed with what he called "the pestilent modern fashion of publicity." Moreover, for James the corrosive power of publicity was most evident when it invaded high literary values and institutions, the domain he believed should be antithetical to the "prodigious machinery" of mass forms. Interviews, advertisements, book tours, and publisher's photographs, in James's view, all fed a desire to consume the privacy of the author as a mass-produced object while pretending to offer readers a view of the secluded life where the literary is born.

The culprit for James was a mass print industry that distorted literary meaning into celebrity spectacle. As he noted in a notebook entry, the "devouring publicity" generated by modern media threatened the "extinction of all sense between public and private." For James nothing illustrated this threat as vividly as the press's transformation of an author's study into a popular spectacle, a stage for the entertainment ("delightful peeps") of strangers. And yet no author publicized the study – returned to portray it repeated times, in myriad ways – as frequently as did James. Virtually all of James's many tales of "literary life" feature an author's study as a charged narrative site. But James's obsession with "devouring publicity" is no doubt also the source of his exceptional insight into this most critical aspect of modernity. For all his satire, James in his fiction undertakes a profound exploration of the way authorial privacy – the source of high literary expression – might not be able to exist apart from the mass pressures arrayed against it. For James, complex relations tied modern literary creativity to modern mass publicity.

The defining connections here are subtle but consequential. Certainly James believed with figures like Howells and Wharton that serious engagement with literature was impossible without some shelter from the onslaught of modern conditions (the "false voice of commerce and cant"). Like those other writers, James associated that shelter with the intimate space of the author's study. In "The Right Real Thing" (1899), for instance, a biographer undertakes his nightly research on his subject in that famous author's study. Ashton Doyne's private study, the biographer believes, still holds the "personal presence" of the now dead author. So forceful is this "presence" for him (and so "personal" the space of the study) that the biographer awaits these hours of work in the study "very much as one of a pair of lovers might wait for the hour of their appointment." With a characteristic irony, James confirms the value of authorial privacy by dramatizing the way an outsider – here a biographer – tries to acquire intimate knowledge about an artist by physically entering his study. When the biographer sees (or believes he sees) Doyne's own ghost blocking his entry to the study, the phantasm is both a rebuke to the intrusive biographer as well as James's confirmation of the symbolic importance of the private study.

Clearly, James is the source of the prohibition, the author-ghost who means to warn away the too-personal reader. For the Realists, to insist on the privacy of the author's study is to defend the autonomy of narrative art. Located at a reflective distance from the complex social world it depicts, the novel requires impartial vision and aesthetic independence – "the beauty that comes from truth alone," as Howells wrote – in order to qualify as high art. Like a room dedicated to the work of writing, the worthy novel can serve no other purpose than the illumination created from the art of fiction – not social advocacy, not market success, not the attention of people of fashion, certainly not the courting of mass publicity. And yet while the author's study represents authorial privacy and autonomy, in his fiction the Jamesian study is above all a place of the *violation* of privacy. That is, his stories always feature an intrusion or interruption in the space of the study that serves to entice readers with the possibility of deep literary knowledge rather more than warn them away with stern threats. The intrusions are sometimes comic ("The Death of a Lion," "The Altar of the Dead," "The Figure in the Carpet"), sometimes insidious ("The

Aspern Papers," "The Lesson of the Master," "John Delavoy"), and often both. Like the biographer in "The Right Real Thing," the central characters in these stories are possessed of an overweening desire to enter into a study or a locked desk drawer where they are convinced they will find hidden knowledge. And yet the prohibition itself seems to signal the presence of some sort of defining knowledge, usually hinted to be sexual or marital. In James's tales, then, the pursuit of literary meaning is the pursuit of a secret, of prohibited meaning. The sense of hidden or prohibited knowledge – a secret and the desire to know it – becomes the very sensibility James explores in his sustained treatment of "literary life."

Taken together, these stories show that the pursuit of a secret is for James a literary matter, the very substance of this fiction. In the most famous of these stories, "The Aspern Papers," the narrator attempts to acquire a poet's private papers, convinced that they hold a suppressed secret about the artist's life. He is convinced, too, that it is a romantic or sexual secret. But James makes sure that his readers are far from being certain on either count – is the narrator's theory of Jeffrey Aspern's sexual secret really a reflection of the narrator's own intense desire to possess and publish the papers? That puzzle opens into another: is his desire to possess the private papers our sign of the narrator's own sexual secret, his impossible desire for the dead poet himself? This is the ambiguously sexual secret James embeds in his own tale. To read James's story is necessarily to want to know this secret; readers are allowed no superior position from which to avoid a "personal" wish to know that is exactly like the voyeuristic narrator's. In "The Aspern Papers," the desire to know is a state of mind far more complex than the "mania for publicity" linked with mass culture, even as it is marked as inseparable from that culture. The prospect of what James calls the "extinction of all sense between private and public," however worrying, is also generative. The threat itself is the origin of a new aesthetic "sense," a consciousness generated out of the very erosion of clear demarcations between desire and knowledge, between privacy and print. The instability (yet continued importance) of this boundary becomes the very ground of the literary; readers of James must possess this new "sense" to be able to follow the intricacies and ambiguities of the fiction. Indeed, to read James is to cultivate this sense, a sublime "perception of incongruities" that sharpens as it plays across the uncertain boundaries of private and public.

Examining this narrative structure, many recent studies have turned to questions of James's own sexuality and the cultural prohibitions on homo-sexual intimacy that kept it largely veiled. This biographical explanation is compelling – no less so for the way it fulfills James's fictional warning (or is it a teasing invitation?) that scholars are wont to find literary meaning in sexual biography. But the conditions of mass print with their energies of exposure are the more fundamental historical grounds for James's aesthetics of secrecy and publicity. To be sure, Realists like James remained opposed to the "irreflective and uncritical" drive to expose and display that they saw in mass culture. But James in particular came to see the modern "desire to know" as a profoundly reflective state of mind that springs from the conditions it opposes. Rooted in the same conditions, literary meaning is not opposed to mass culture but is rather meaning that relies on that commercialism for its work of "eternal distinction-making." James's own study was a "refuge," but in composing and publishing his writers' tales he helped to make the author's study a distinct "place of exhibition" (as he dubs it in "The Lesson of the Master"), a Realist site at which private sensibility becomes a spectacle for others' eyes. James's fiction is nothing short of an exhibition of the impulse to expose – to "snap at the bait of publicity" – presented as entangled with the literary forms those impulses engender, and "collected in such store as to stock, as to launch, a museum." For James, the display of these intricacies of cultural perception was as much a "thrill" and an "adventure" as any mass spectacle.

EUROPE, RACE, AND TRAVEL: JANE ADDAMS, ALEXANDER CRUMMELL, AND THE AMERICAN NEGRO ACADEMY

The literary autonomy championed by Realists is founded on a contradiction. Identified as it is with individual thought and expression, the domain of literature is open to any qualified author. Racial caste, sex, and social standing are all extraneous to the creative literary consciousness. But the same literary autonomy depends on constrained patterns of mobility. Access to education is one obvious restriction; for whole categories of Americans, the distance to a requisite education is almost always too far to traverse. Less obviously, high literary expression – to qualify as such – must also be informed by an implicit geographical map, by specific routes of travel and their terminal cities. One need not have traveled those routes in person, but literary understanding must embrace what an observer called "travel-improved taste." The contours of the literary in this period follow specific links between travel and writing, connections that trace possible avenues for change even as they mark entrenched lines of racial and imperial power.

Even before appearing in print, novelist Charles Chesnutt recognized the affiliation he could claim through the autonomy of the literary. "Shut up in my study," he records in his journal, "without the companionship of one congenial mind, I can enjoy the society of the greatest wits and scholars of England, can revel in the genius of her poets and statesmen, and by a slight effort of the imagination, find myself in the company of the greatest men of earth." Here the space of the study identifies a peculiarly social solitude, a belonging or kinship that is cognitive and therefore unconstrained by time or place. Unconstrained, too, by color: for Chesnutt, an African American living in the post-Reconstruction South, the space of the study also means a temporary release from the stigma attached to blackness. But this literary privacy is emphatically not a retreat or withdrawal. Chesnutt's recently published journal illustrates instead the way his study is a point of departure. "I will go to the Metropolis," he writes, and the generality of the phrase is apt: high literary aspiration in this moment is a simultaneous ambition for the literal and cultural mobility of a metropolitan life. Part of Chesnutt's literary sensibility is his recognition of the continuity between authorship and the self-projection realized in travel. "I worked hard, worried Susie [Chesnutt's wife] into a positive dislike for me, reading so much, [then] packed my valises, and the following week took the train for Washington [,] N.Y. etc." The national recognition Chesnutt would receive through his published short stories and novels proved his ambitions were warranted. Yet even the fulfillment of Chesnutt's desire for travel and authorship confirmed patterns of national and global restriction. The pursuit of high authorship would eventually leave Chesnutt stranded outside of national literary institutions, just as it would leave Pauline Hopkins excluded from a magazine editorship and push W. E. B. Du Bois into exile in Africa.

Patterns of travel encourage national feeling while separating cultural strata. Just as immigrants share rites of arrival and inspection, the oceanic travel of the new professional classes in this era consolidates a distinct cultural identity for those Americans who depart from the same US ports where immigrants come ashore. Transatlantic crossings, more than any other travel routes, come to define a zone of shared experience for the American elite. "A voyage across the Atlantic is today such a common undertaking that most travellers make as brief preparation for it as if they were going by train from New York to Chicago," the poet Edmund Clarence Stedman wrote. A leisure voyage to Europe was not common, of course; it was still a luxury open to a relatively small number of Americans of means. But as an idea and cultural symbol, the transatlantic travel of these affluent Americans also articulated a wider national significance. It represented an accreditation for American artists and thinkers (James Russell Lowell wrote that Howells's stay in Venice was "the University in which he has fairly earned the degree of Master"); it signified an American claim on a notion of transnational "civilization" in an age of empire; and it was a sign of the arrival of the United States as a global economic power.

Circuits of transatlantic travel also formed the literal field of production for high literary art. The work of writing travel sketches, literary translations, and reviews of foreign books was the standard apprenticeship for the high literary career, and writers dispatched manuscripts from European cities to publishers in Boston, New York, and Chicago. The travel impressions Howells wrote in Italy and sent to the *Atlantic* and the *Boston Advertiser*, for instance, became the material for his first books, *Venetian Life* (1866) and *Italian Journeys* (1869). James's travel writing for E. L. Godkin's *The Nation* in 1870–71 were collected in his *Transatlantic Sketches* (1875), the first of several travel volumes James would produce in his career. Constance Fenimore Woolson, Henry Adams, John DeForest, Edith Wharton, and John Hay all made transatlantic travel integral to the shape and substance of their works. Howells's first novel, *Their Wedding Journey* (1871), was fashioned explicitly as an extension of his travel writing, a "form of fiction" he describes as "half-story, half-travel sketch." His protagonists, Basil and Isabel March, return from Europe to embark upon a tour of the diverse scenes of American life. They undertake this venture, the reader is told, as "very conscious people," and it is clear that their consciousness, their manner of seeing and feeling, is informed by their recollected "passages of European travel."

"Very conscious people" – the word "conscious" acquires a particular semantic density in the high literary writing of this period. As Howells's plot suggests, the valence attached to the word is inseparable from Europe as symbol and cultural site. When James defined the novelist as "the historian of fine consciousness," he was sure that the deepest source for such a history was the "thicker civility" of Europe. The American, he asserts, "*must* deal, more or less, even if by implication, with Europe." But exactly what was the substance of this travel-enriched "consciousness"? There are clues in the grammar of James's formulations. "Consciousness" has a history (recorded in novels) and an ancestral home (Europe) but, as James's use of the abstract noun suggests, consciousness can be conceived as something transpersonal or transcendent with the capacity to rise above the determination of any particular origins. In this sense, the idea of "fine consciousness" is the heir of the Enlightenment belief that human understanding, if developed and intensified, can free itself from partisan interest and local blindness. Following the "trained judgment of the wisest and the best," one *Atlantic* writer insisted, "leads us towards, though never quite to, a rounded perfection of mind and soul."

British author Matthew Arnold was the most famous proponent of this secular perfectionism. His *Culture and Anarchy* (1869) was a text of enormous influence in American literary circles, and Arnold's own 1883 transatlantic journey, for a lecture tour through a series of major American cities, made his ideas available to an even broader US audience. The wide acceptance of Arnold's ideas among educated Americans suggests something of the eagerness in this

moment for thought and expression more expansive than the era's nationalist pieties and commercial values. From another perspective, the appeal of a
perfected "mind and soul" is the appeal of a fantasy, a desire for an impossible
wholeness or omniscience. But the force of the notion is also recognizable in
the wariness – sometimes it was hostility – with which many in the United
States greeted the cultural dictates of the new transatlantic consciousness.
Walt Whitman spoke for the wary when he dissented from the new authority
of an Arnoldian "elegance, prettiness, propriety, criticism, analysis: all of them
things which threaten to overwhelm us." The consciousness advocated in high
culture was not simply the "general humane spirit" of the human race, to
use Arnold's phrase, but a particular framework of thought – particular, and
therefore partial, for all its expansiveness. Forgetting its own particularity is
the risk for transatlantic consciousness.

Jane Addams analyzes this risk in her remarkable book, *Twenty Years at
Hull-House* (1910). In the chapter "The Snare of Preparation," the activist and
urban reformer looks back to her own transatlantic travel in the 1880s (Henry
James was a fellow passenger on one crossing). It was a time, Addams remembers, when American daughters (unlike their mothers' generation) "crossed
the seas in search of culture." But not long after her arrival, the "pursuit of
cultivation" begins to seem a blinkered insularity. Addams visits a London
slum and sees a large massing of the poor gathered to receive cheap vegetables, "clutching forward for food which was already unfit to eat." The shock
of the experience creates a stark shift in perception. The ideal of a cultivated
consciousness suddenly appears not as a universal subjectivity but rather a particular "attitude" that springs from distinct class conditions. The transatlantic
attitude, as Addams now views it, mistakes a narrow set of tastes for broad
understanding. The cultivated young American woman travels across Europe
unable to make a "real connection to the life around her" and is "only at ease
when in the familiar receptive attitude afforded by the art gallery and the
opera house." Artistic and intellectual acuity now reappear as a hardened and
diminished object. The young American's "trained and developed powers" of
perception, Addams sardonically writes, find use only "as she sat 'being cultivated'" in concert halls or museums, spaces which are merely "sublimated and
romanticized" classrooms.

As if viewed through the wrong end of a telescope, the supposed
enlargement of vision in "travel-improved" consciousness suddenly looks
like a timid provincialism. The new perspective is damning. Transatlantic consciousness might not be simply narrow; it might actually disguise willful self-interest as high aesthetic understanding. Yet importantly,
Addams shifts her perspective once again. Her own realization about "the

feverish search after culture," she writes, was a revelation that came through art.

It was doubtless in such moods [of "moral revulsion"] that I founded my admiration for Albrecht Dürer, taking his wonderful pictures, however, in the most unorthodox manner, merely as human documents. I was chiefly appealed to by his unwillingness to lend himself to a smooth and cultivated view of life, by his determination to record its frustrations and even the hideous forms which darken the day for our human imagination and to ignore no human complications.

If objects in art galleries (Dürer's works) help her to discover that art galleries cultivate insularity (as blinkered classrooms), is Addams's critique self-defeating? Recognized as an unfolding process of understanding, the contradiction is only apparent. What Addams associates with Dürer's paintings is a distrust of any mode of consciousness that would detach itself from darker and more complicated worldly conditions. A meaningful work of art is not a "smooth" or prettified form but rather a "human document" created out of complex life conditions. With this insight, Addams's critique actually confirms the "eternal distinction-making" function of high art, even as the distinction she finds through Dürer permanently alters her way of seeing high art.

The best fiction in the transatlantic mode achieves a similar reflexivity of critical insight. To read at all widely in the postbellum decades is to recognize a marked shift in the compass points of American letters. The literary nationalism of the antebellum years has not dimmed; but the work of "making us a real American novel" (as Howells articulates the goal) is staked less on achieving the innate expression of a native homeland and more on cultivating the comparative sensibility of a transatlantic traveler. (The emergence of distinct regional literatures in this period – America represented through separate and contrasting localities – reflects the same comparative reorientation of the national.) With its querying of the role of museums, Jane Addams's narrative identifies one of Realism's most formative sites. The visit to a European art gallery forms a pivotal site for the formation of consciousness in a transnational context. One of James's favorite shorthand phrases, "'doing' a gallery," conveys through its telegraphic brevity something of the way European museum-going is assumed to be in the background of any serious cultural analysis, part of the infrastructure of high consciousness.

The opening scene in James's early novel *The American* (1877) offers a glimpse into this transatlantic frame, for the novel's protagonist is presented to the reader through his own attempt to "do a gallery" in the Louvre museum in Paris. Sitting before a painting on a large circular divan, Christopher Newman experiences "profound enjoyment" – not, however, an enjoyment of the famous

painting but a relief in his relaxed bodily "posture": "The gentleman in question had taken serene possession of its softest spot, and, with his head thrown
back and his legs outstretched, was staring at Murillo's beautiful moon-borne
Madonna in profound enjoyment of his posture. He had removed his hat, and
flung down beside him a little red guidebook and an opera-glass." Newman's
tour of Louvre paintings ("he had looked at all the pictures to which an aster-
isk was affixed in those formidable pages of fine print in his Badeker") has
left him with an "aesthetic headache." His first real pleasure is this languid
extension of his physical frame on the divan. Newman's lack of responsiveness
to the art is thus made to correspond to the prominence given his body, and
the reader quickly recognizes that Newman is not a museum patron but the
novel's equivalent of a museum specimen, an object exhibited for the close
scrutiny of an interested observer.

The largest significance of the gallery, then, is not as a setting for Realist characters but as the ground for the consciousness of Realist readers. James's text
brings to the surface what is usually subtextual: that understanding national
meaning depends on extranational sites such as the Louvre. The museum
gallery is a second transnational home for a reader who possesses the requisite
trained sight. "An observer with anything of an eye for national types would
have had no difficulty in determining the local origin of this [gentleman] . . .
a powerful specimen of an American":

He had a very well-formed head, with a shapely, symmetrical balance of the frontal
and the occipital development, and a good deal of straight, rather dry brown hair. His
complexion was brown, and his nose had a bold, well-marked arch. His eye was of a
clear, cold gray, and save for a rather abundant mustache he was clean-shaved. He had
the flat jaw and sinewy neck which are frequent in the American type; but the traces
of national origin are a matter of expression even more than of feature, and it was in
this respect that our friend's countenance was supremely eloquent.

The superabundance of visual detail here, characteristic of Realist writing,
establishes what the narrator calls "the conditions of his identity" as an
American "specimen." Sympathetic but superior, the "eye" of the presumed
reader who has the acuity to appreciate great European paintings also has the
experience to discern national "types." These two kinds of visual objects are
aesthetically distinct (the narrator emphasizes that the sprawled Newman "is
by no means sitting for his portrait"). Nevertheless, museum-trained sight is
a key faculty for the Realist "observer" and reading the national type presumes
an international museum tutelage.

Whitman's warning against the tyranny of elegance makes itself felt here.
Could it be that the transatlantic consciousness of this sort passes off a rarified

aestheticism under the banner of Realist insight? Certainly in *The American*, Newman is marked out as less knowing than the cosmopolitan "observer" who is invited to take Newman's measure against the backdrop of the Louvre. The observing consciousness is expansive, reflective; the national "specimen" a more inert representative object. Importantly, though, the positions of observer and social specimen need not be mutually exclusive. In a private letter, the thoroughly urbane James identified his own Americanness through a self-reflective moment in a Venice gallery, "a certain glorious room at the Ducal Palace, where Paolo Veronese revels on the ceilings and Tintoret rages on the walls": "I feel as if I might sit there forever (as I sat there a long time this morning) and only feel more and more my inexorable Yankeehood." Still, there are Yankees and Yankees. The transatlantic context often functions for American authors as a species of disavowal, a means of distinguishing one's self from the felt strictures of national identity – even from the identity of the transatlantic American traveler. Such is James's aim when, in a travel essay for *Century* magazine entitled "Venice" (1882), he conjures the image of a "huge Anglo-Saxon wave" of travelers, a mass of "five thousand – fifty thousand – 'accommodated spectators'" that throws into relief the singular Henry James, a figure satisfied to sit, unhurried, "in the immense new Hotel National and read the *New York Times* on a blue satin divan."

The other side of disavowal is critical vision. Picturing American travelers as "trooping barbarians" may be snobbery or self-exemption. It may also be a flippant instance of what is elsewhere a more careful analysis of the American as a "commercial person" (the label James gives Christopher Newman's sub-species of American). The distinct consciousness associated with European travel at times represents an effort to find a position of critical distance, a way of seeing and thinking outside of the habitual perceptions encouraged by a commercial culture. Europe is the site for an alternative vision, its "thicker civility" a contrasting means through which to analyze the energies and dis-tortions of a Gilded Age America. High art, localized in the idea of Europe, could challenge the values of modernization, the beliefs and habits of thought endemic to the commercial culture that Matthew Arnold saw epitomized in the United States. In early novels such as *Roderick Hudson* (1875) and *The American* (1877), James's European settings serve to point up subtle insuffi-ciencies and distortions engendered by American modernity while picturing alternative possibilities of meaningful experience available "up to the brim" in Europe. The same perspective acquired a greater critical intensity in late works such as *The Ambassadors* (1903) and *The Golden Bowl* (1904).

Edith Wharton's most sustained transatlantic novel, *The Custom of the Country* (1913), makes the critique unmistakable – and darkly comic.

Wharton uses the cross-cultural perspective to embody brilliantly the destructive capacity of the energies of American capitalism. Her thoroughly commercial protagonist, Undine Spragg, is a rich American divorcee who blazes a path of ruin through Europe. With a "business-like intentness on gaining her end," Undine sees absolutely everything as a form of commodity in one vast open market, whether it is pearls, paintings, or husbands. In Undine, Wharton shows the instrumentalist nature of a market society as wondrously corrosive. Undine possesses a cultural Midas touch under which every custom, human relation, or aesthetic creation is converted to brittle gold and thus destroyed.

The very extravagance of Undine's portrait as a "commercial person," however, hints at a degree of unease. Here and elsewhere, Wharton is at pains to sort the transatlantic sheep from the goats – that is, to separate those who travel for culture from those who travel for profit (the "buccaneers," as Wharton labeled them). But the distinction is hard to maintain. Captains of industry and connoisseurs of art literally traveled in the same transatlantic circles. Indeed, the most famous art collectors, such as Henry Clay Frick and Andrew Carnegie, were also the most famous "commercial persons" of the age. American travelers were, in a sense, merely the human objects in a larger field of transatlantic commerce and communication. Cyrus Field laid the first transatlantic cable in 1866, making possible the almost instantaneous exchange of stock prices and securities, diplomatic communications, and syndicated news, and this rapid electronic exchange made possible a new transnational economy that underwrites the leisure travel on land and sea. Although travelers to Europe frequently conceived their journey as a "return" to a premodern way of life (illustrated in stories such as James's 1875 story "A Passionate Pilgrim"), even the search for a cultural inheritance was never outside this new circuit of economic development. Americans may have gone to European countries in search of thatched cottages and old paintings but their appetite for Old World travel was part of a thoroughly modern development of intercontinental economic ties.

How, then, to distinguish travel from transatlantic trafficking? In moments of the sharpest self-awareness, novels of the period reflect the knowledge that high consciousness itself can be subject to the instrumentalities of the "blaring" commercial world it seeks to transcend. In many stories and novels, the transatlantic context seems suddenly to stand exposed as little more than a debased trade route, an economic circuit in which art and aesthetic feeling become no different than brokered goods. In Wharton's novella *The Touchstone* (1900), for instance, artistic consciousness is made to undergo the starkest commodification. The private letters of a famous expatriate novelist, Margaret Aubyn, undergo an "alchemistic process" that transforms these literary inscriptions into an economic object of transatlantic theft and sale – they become, variously, a "check," a "bribe," a "weapon," and a collection of "stolen goods." Wharton holds out the hope for a counter-magic: the "inexhaustible alchemy" of human love may be able to redeem the sale. Yet even these "luxuries" of human feeling (they are drawn from a "funded passion") bear the imprint of the commodity form they try to overcome. The alchemy of money is the stronger transformative power. In James's fiction, this self-reflexive question about aesthetic consciousness intensifies in tone and reach over the course of his career. His Gilbert Osmond in *Portrait of a Lady* (1881) is only one of James's many connoisseurs whose appreciation of art and beauty – including, in Osmond's case, his wife – is inseparable from a desire for ownership. Any real distinction between beauty and property has collapsed. In *Portrait of a Lady* this erosion is a clear sign of Osmond's amorality, but by the time of his late novel *The Golden Bowl* (1904), James removes any such moral delimitation. The American millionaire Adam Verver makes London his headquarters for a campaign to collect the greatest European art treasures – not for personal property but for the national prestige of an American Museum. But, like the snake that swallows its own tail, Verver's ambitions for "a museum of museums" makes aesthetic history a self-consuming institution and the great museums of Europe little more than warehouses poised for a monopoly takeover by a commercial empire.

Transatlantic fiction also finds commercial traffic in what is supposed to be the intimate sphere of marriage and home. Almost by generic definition, novels depicting European travel or settings are compelled to contemplate prospects of international marriage, and narratives of cross-cultural marriages – most often involving American women wedding European men – become a notable subgenre. Journalists take up the theme, too; stories of American heiresses abroad are a favorite of the mass press. But in high Realist novels, the specter of a flourishing industry in transatlantic fortune-hunting is less entertaining than internally corrosive to the genre. In fiction by writers such as Woolson, Wharton, and James, the cross-cultural marriage provides a lens through which the novel's traditional subject matter, the social and affective material of middle-class life, is seen at least momentarily to be penetrated to the core by the instrumentalizing values of a market culture – its habits of display, its idolizing of quantity and novelty, its supreme principle of property. Testing these forces, James's novels and stories of transatlantic marriage such as "The Siege of London" (1882) and "Lady Barberina" (1883) put pressure on every kind of domestic sentiment, however genuine or duplicitous, to discover its degree of infiltration by the modern marketplace. As sentiment is tested, the fate of the marriage novel as a genre is at stake, too, and the fiction betrays a self-consciousness that the genre may not survive the test. And the genre does not survive, at least according to the consensus of literary historians. After Wharton's *The Custom of the Country* and James's *The Wings of the Dove* (1902) and *The Golden Bowl* (1904), the Anglo-American novel's traditional reliance on a separation of private family feeling and public systems like the market will no longer pretend to hold.

The cross-cultural marriage in James's "Lady Barberina" uncovers another crucial aspect of the matter of travel. "Intermarrying" between Americans and Britons is "quite fair play," one observer declares, because "they were all one race after all." The felt need to articulate rules of "fair play" for British-American marriages, spoken as if to establish fair trade policy, is one more instance of a transatlantic ironizing of the marriage novel. But the story's open acknowledgment of the rules for marriage as racial – "they were all one race after all" – taps a second, deeper subtext. As a conceptual category, "race" in this moment was pliable to a fault. The term was used variously to signify nation-states, genetic populations, historical cultures, family lines, and designated color groups. James is following a standard usage when he describes his travel writing about European countries as the work of "comparing one race to another." The same sense of a national people as a race is the governing meaning when James describes the American-British couple as "*inter*marrying." But significantly, meanings shift gear in mid-sentence: Britons and Americans *can* intermarry without fear of breaking any taboo because these national races are, from another semantic perspective, finally "one race." With this slip into a biological or genetic understanding of race, the story momentarily alludes to a world of relations structured by color, a global world that always subtends affluent transatlantic travel but usually remains out of view in the fiction.

What is a subtext in transatlantic fiction was highly visible in transatlantic politics. Stories about British-American marriages echo proposals in the same period for a literal "Race Union" between Great Britain and the United States. The rapid expansion of US industries in the later nineteenth century astonished and frequently alarmed other nations. By 1902, British author W. T. Stead describes an imminent "Americanisation of the world" and predicts that US economic expansion will outstrip the reach of the British Empire. For Stead, the prospect called for the creation of a new polity. With Britain as "the cradle of the race," and America the industrial empire of the future, Stead and others (including Matthew Arnold) urge that the two nations should forge a new political union on the basis of race. Radical as the proposal may sound today, it was a logical extension of the widely held belief that the United States was already a race union, a nation consisting of "allied varieties of the Aryan race." Hence, for many, a more formal uniting of the US with Britain was all but preordained. The proposed union is "as natural as marriage between man and woman," wrote New York lawyer John R. Dos Passos. "It consummates the purpose of the creation of the race."

No such united Anglo state was ever created, of course, but the proposal reflected an emerging global order that was altogether real. Any map that charted the world according to the economic centers ringing the Atlantic and the imperial territories that lie beyond would have been a map of "race union" – that is, a federation of white-controlled economic capitals united by their competition for the labor and land of non-white peoples. W. E. B. Du Bois called this kind of uncharted global demarcation "the color line." A third global axis, the color line not only traced a geography of power, it also marked a power of mobility. American travelers favored routes among North Atlantic countries but US-European travel also offered gateways into imperial regions beyond. At the 1876 Philadelphia Centennial exhibition, the Cook's American World Ticket and Inquiry Office advertised the patterns of mobility available to the leisure-class traveler: "Tourist tickets to all parts of the United States, the continent of Europe, Egypt and Palestine, and around the world traveling East or West . . . no matter how extended and complicated the route." Transatlantic travel was embedded in a larger global mobility structured by race, and the politics of the color line meant that the tourists in possession of a "World Ticket" were almost always white travelers.

Was the "consciousness" in transatlantic fiction therefore a racial consciousness? Was high literary culture white? Empirically, the answer is no; historically, the racial logic that answers yes is both a tacit truth and a generative problem. The vexed racial logic is most clearly seen in the effort of a number of African–American writers to advance the cause of black people through intellectual leadership and cultural achievement. Their productive attempts to wrestle with the color-line dilemmas in the pursuit of "the highest arts" illuminates much of what is ignored or disavowed by white authors. The works they produce, moreover, create a strikingly different American portrait of the "travel-improved" consciousness.

When in 1897 a number of leading African–American intellectuals gathered to establish the American Negro Academy, their organized effort to "promote the publication of literary and scholarly works" by black American authors was a dual political challenge. In their charter, the group's stated goal is directed at white racism: the Academy will refute "vicious assaults" on the race. Their unstated aim is intra-racial. The dedicated purpose of fostering "higher culture, at home and abroad" is a gauntlet thrown down to the accommodationist policies of Booker T. Washington. An accomplished black educator and activist, Washington had leveraged political retreat and an emphasis on industrial training to acquire white support for his black vocational institutions. The academy members, opposing both Washington and the "caste-ridden" white establishment, now set their sights on making high literary expression and culture a vehicle for promoting full political equality for African Americans.

The triangular struggle reflects a racial politics of high culture that is contingent and relational. With shifting responses directed towards two different racial fronts, the academy members marshal notions of Arnoldian cultivation for use in black nationalism, and hold up elite learning in the name of enfranchising the black masses. Internal tensions result from this constellation, but so do vital and uncompromising prospects. Both are registered with particular clarity in the writings of academy founder Alexander Crummell, whose books *The Future of Africa* (1862) and *America and Africa* (1891) are among the first works to make West Africa visible in US transatlantic writing. A revered leader and clergyman, the seventy-four-year-old Crummell was in his last year of life when he headed the effort to establish a scholarly society for African–American intellectuals. His credentials as a man of letters included his classical education at Cambridge University and authorship of books of essays and sermons, among other publications. Crummell's stature and long career helped him to enlist in the academy such young talents as poet Paul Laurence Dunbar, the essayist and Howard University professor Kelly Miller, and Du Bois, then a lecturer in sociology at the University of Pennsylvania. Anna Julia Cooper, a scholar of Latin and Greek who was the principal of the successful M Street School in Washington, D.C., was the only female member. Her collection of essays, *A Voice From the South* (1892), argues for the importance of defending the "untrammeled intellect of the Negro" as a political as well as human right.

As a younger man, Crummell's attachment to Victorian ideals of "civilization" formed a keystone of his vision of racial uplift for black Americans and racial "regeneration" for the peoples of Africa. Civilization ("the scientific processes of literature, art, and philosophy") was for Crummell the heaven-born twin of Christian evangelization, an instrument of the universal redemption God held out to all peoples. And like Christianity, civilization had been given first to European peoples, who had the obligation to disseminate its gifts to darker races still living in "heathenism." Although Crummell could be famously caustic about European domination ("For three hundred years the European has been traversing the coast of Africa" and "the whole coast . . . has been ravaged wherever his footstep has fallen"), he shared the Victorian view that the historical fates of races were subject to what he called "God's economy." For Crummell, holding to this view had a particular urgency: how else to explain the devastation experienced by so many native peoples "whenever European civilization has been taken in any country," except through the hand of God? For the Christian clergyman, to give the power to any other agency than God would be to concede intolerable tenets of white superiority.

With a typical ambivalence of tone, Crummell articulates his view in an 1851 address to the British Anti-Slavery Society: "There is something exceedingly sorrowful in this funereal procession of the weak portions of mankind, before the advancing progress of civilization and enlightenment." Although Crummell's acceptance of this "progress" at times leaves him just short of a blasphemous bitterness, it also supplies a providential vision of a future for "the African people" across the globe. "The aborigines of the South-Sea Islands, of New Zealand, and Australia, are departing like the shadow before the rising sun of the Anglo-Saxon emigrant," Crummell writes, but "amid all these melancholy facts, there seems to be one exception," the "negro," whose survival and spreading emancipation from slavery bespeaks a divinely chosen role in the future history of the world. The same religious underpinnings that compel Crummell to accept white domination as a providential design also give him the language to predict black cultural ascendancy. The "noblest" future civilization will be produced by African peoples: "It may be tardy in its arrival" but it "bids fair to be peculiarly bright and distinct in its features and characteristics from any form of civilisation the world now witnesses."

High cultural achievement in this context is far more than a matter of taste or refinement. Black accomplishments in "letters and cultivation" will be an index to the social progress of the race and a marker of a providential history. A white teleology of progress, fated but still incomplete, cannot be reserved for white supremacy. By 1882, Crummell has gone as far as sounding an eventual black triumphalism, in an essay he calls "The Destined Superiority of the Negro." But Crummell in this period more characteristically uses the Victorian discourse of civilization to articulate a vision that draws West Africa and the Caribbean into the transatlantic circuit of travel and cultural exchange already joining the United States and Britain. It was a circuit Crummell himself had hoped to cultivate when, immediately after receiving his degree from Cambridge, he left England for Liberia, where he spent the next two decades teaching at Liberia College in Monrovia. The steamship journey from Liverpool to the West Coast, as Crummell portrays it, enlarges the reach of civilized travel rather than departing from it. The voyage "is a grand panorama of sights and incidents," Crummell writes, "bringing to the traveller's sight the Channel with its several isles, the Bay of Biscay, the peak of Teneriffe, Madeira,

with its varied and cosmopolitan life, and its beautiful scenery[,] and its aristocratic society." In bringing before the "eye" of the transatlantic traveler the
scenery and cities of Liberia and Sierra Leone ("the grand civilization which has
sprung up on that benighted coast"), Crummell recasts the Victorian grammar
of race and progress to allow black participation in a no-longer-white civilization. African peoples are the latecomers by this reckoning, to be sure, and by
its measures the traditional arts and institutions of African peoples count for
little. Still, Crummell's rhetoric makes the language of race hierarchy undercut
its own absolutism. "Black Yankees" like Crummell, he writes in *The Future
of Africa* (1862), for all their "trials" at the hands of whites, have "not been
divorced from [American] civilization," and in their fitness for free governance are superior "to the Russian, to the Polander, to the Hungarian, to the
Italian."

More important than this recalibration of color, Crummell's version of a
Victorian global historiography insists on an independent role for diasporic
black people: "America is deeply indebted to Africa." Like William Ferris, a
Yale graduate who was another academy member, Crummell's investment in
high culture led him to articulate a variant of black nationalism that made
the history of civilization impossible to conceive without Africa. Crummell's
influence is clear in Ferris's two-volume study *The African Abroad: or, His
Evolution in Western Civilization* (1913), an encyclopedic work that recasts world
history by making African military and cultural achievement an indispensable
part of the ancient world and that narrates a modern history in which the
Americas are the second home of the African "abroad." Ferris's image of "the
African abroad" refashions the black historical subject in a striking way. In
Ferris's history, the exported black slave is supplanted by the black traveler, a
figure with agency, mobility, and a savvy consciousness.

"How hopeful are the scenes of travel!" Crummell's exclamation in an 1894
letter to a friend signifies the way an Anglo-African transatlanticism remained
to the end the frame for Crummell's hopes. "Since my return to London I have
been visiting the galleries, the great churches, the Law courts," he writes. Meeting "two black gentleman" from the Gold Coast in the famous Lincoln's Inn
law library and later encountering an impressive "West India gentleman" during his visit in London are travel "scenes" that bolster his faith in transatlantic
uplift. Crummell's hope for white recognition of the black "race-capacity,"
however, had become increasingly hard to sustain, especially when Crummell
returned from Liberia to reside in the United States. Living in the US, Crummell's commitment to high cultural advancement changed markedly in its
focus. By the time Crummell began his short tenure as the first president

of the American Negro Academy, he had become doubtful that the gifts of learning and letters could join black and white in a shared civilization. Given the contemporary public calls for a "Race Union" of two white empires, Crummell employs a trope that is all too fitting when he decries "the divorce of the black race from all the great activities" in American life: "It is a state of divorcement from the mercantile life of the country; from the scientific life of the land; from its literary life; and from its social life."

Yet Jim Crow conditions and global imperialism only heighten the importance of high cultural pursuits for Crummell. He rejects Washington's strategy of accepting the civil "divorce" in exchange for white people's help with training black labor. "This miserable fad of industrialism," he wrote in the late 1890s, is but a white "pretext" for blocking any substantial advancement of African Americans. At one time Crummell had viewed "letters and cultivation" as the way African peoples would join Europeans on a single "grand plane of civilization." No longer. In an essay published in the *American Negro Academy, Occasional Papers*, "The Attitude of the American Mind Toward Negro Intellect" (1898), Crummell declares that black advancement is a process of active "warfare" and "its main weapon is the cultivated and scientific mind." High culture is not an elevated plane but an arena of "struggle." The emphasis on conflict in this essay is relevant to the argument of some historians that the high cultural concerns of black intellectuals like Crummell were rooted in a worship of gentility. Was it possible that the American Negro Academy was in essence a gentleman's club to prove the class bona fides of the black bourgeoisie, with little relevance for the largely unlettered black population? Resentments and aspirations inflected by class are no doubt part of the mix of academy motives. But Crummell's "Negro Intellect" essay shows his advocacy of the "highest arts" for what it was: a counteroffensive against a systemic white campaign directed at the race as a whole. The "Negro curriculum" prescribed by whites, Crummell insists, is no curriculum at all but a "caste education" to make the population an "unthinking labor-machine." Its intent is to make African peoples the only race without intellectuals and thus the world's permanent "serfs." Jim Crow education is not a matter of white "indifference or neglect," then, but the latest instance of a deliberate, sustained effort to "stamp out the brains of the Negro": "There is no repugnance to the Negro buffoon, and the Negro scullion; but so soon as the Negro stands forth as an intellectual being, this toad of American prejudice, as at the touch of Ithuriel's spear, starts up a devil!"

Crummell's call for black intellectual cultivation goes hand in hand with his urging of "intelligent impatience" at the exploitation of black labor. A striking phrase, "intelligent impatience" suggests that black scholars and artists share with working-class laborers the need "to demand a larger share of the wealth which [the Negro's] toil creates for others." Crummell makes the idea explicit in another American Negro Academy publication, "Civilization, the Primal Need of the Race" (1898), where he expands upon the broad "work of intelligence" that is the special responsibility of "scholars and thinkers." The labor of intellectuals finally produces not creations of the mind or ornaments of beauty, Crummell argues, but forms of action (the work of those "who have got insight into the life of things, and learned the art by which men touch the springs of action"). Crummell's concern with high culture is not a bid for acceptance by the white "cultured classes" ("they have left us alone," as he bluntly puts it); it is rather an enterprise in the service of "the entire social and domestic life of our people."

The overt political context of Crummell's late essays exposes the tacit "white" consciousness behind most transatlantic high culture. "Seeing that the American mind in general, revolts from Negro genius," Crummell writes, "the Negro himself is duty bound to see to the cultivation and the fostering of his own race-capacity." By the end of his career, Crummell's Anglo-African transatlanticism is no longer the domain of an abstract civilization but the geography of a black public sphere – "*our* world of intellect," as he stresses it. He closes his "Negro Intellect" essay by recounting scenes of black artistic achievements in Europe – Henry Tanner's prize for his painting "Raising of Lazarus," awarded in Paris and destined for the "famous Luxembourg Gallery," and the several occasions of "triumph" that Paul Laurence Dunbar received in the "grand metropolis of Letters and Literature, the city of London." The effect of the litany transforms the contours of transatlantic culture. Invoking these scenes, Crummell recasts the European gallery as an exiled outpost of a black "world of intellect" and calls up an African-American "republic of letters" that is flourishing most visibly outside of the borders of Jim Crow America. High culture will be the home in exile for the "intellectual being" of the race in a hostile age.

W. E. B. Du Bois, whose own consciousness had been deeply shaped by his years of study in Europe, extended Crummell's analysis of the connections, now visible, now erased, between race and high culture. In his "Criteria of Negro Art" (1926), Du Bois looks back to his own late-century transatlantic travel. Like some white American writers, Du Bois makes the beauty of a European setting – in his case, the "enchantment" of the Scottish landscape – serve as a site from which to critically challenge Gilded Age values. Unlike others, however, Du Bois makes the travel *topos* a site at which to link a commercial critique with the question of racial consciousness.

In the high school where I studied we learned most of Scott's "Lady of the Lake" by heart. In after life once it was my privilege to see the lake. It was Sunday. It was quiet . . . Around me fell the cadence of that poetry of my youth. [But there came] a sudden rush of excursionists. They were mostly Americans, and they were loud and strident. They poured upon the little pleasure boat, – men with their hats on a little on one side and drooping cigars in the wet corners of their mouths; women who shared their conversation with the world. They pushed other people out of the way. They made all sorts of incoherent noises and gestures so that the quiet home folk and the visitors from other lands silently and half-wonderingly gave way before them. They struck a note not evil but wrong. They carried, perhaps, a sense of strength and accomplishment, but their hearts had no conception of the beauty which pervaded this holy place.

The perception of beauty has become a test of a type of national character represented by white American travelers. "We want to be Americans," he writes to a black audience, "with all the rights of other American citizens. But is that all? Do we want simply to be Americans?" Not if it means resting in the "present goals and ideals" illuminated in "the tawdry and flamboyant" manners and blunted perceptions of those rich travelers. For Du Bois, the cross-cultural scene of beauty is not a site for the cultivation of an abstract "consciousness" but for a specific work of critical seeing. Examining America's commercial values is part of a black culture-building alert to its own desires and conditions. "Suppose, too, you became . . . rich and powerful," he writes, "what is it that you would want?" Du Bois makes transatlantic travel a test for "that sort of a world we want to create for ourselves and for all America." Aesthetic apprehension is for Du Bois always a contextual consciousness that moves between the universal appeal of beauty and the rooted social particulars he calls "the facts of the world." Transatlantic consciousness is historically, but not essentially, a white consciousness, and in a sweeping gesture of revision, Du Bois follows his description of Scotland with a lyrical meditation on beauty that breaks open the closed circuit of white transatlantic consciousness:

After all, who shall describe Beauty? What is it? I remember tonight four beautiful things: The Cathedral at Cologne, a forest in stone, set in light and changing shadow, echoing with sunlight and solemn song; a village in the Veys of West Africa, a little thing of mauve and purple, quiet, lying content and shining in the sun; a black and velvet room where on a throne rests, in old and yellowing marble, the broken curves of the Venus of Milo; a single phrase of music in the Southern South – utter melody, haunting and appealing, suddenly arising out of the night and eternity, beneath the moon.

For Du Bois, the consciousness brought to life by beauty and travel was to become a critical tool for an enduring question: "What has this Beauty to do with the world?" It is the primary problem of aesthetics and Du Bois never presumes to answer it. Rather, in posing the question, Du Bois is able to articulate these very disparate global sites, from the Louvre to the African Veys and back to the Black Belt of the South, as a single constellation. The aesthetic problem of beauty is a means of distinguishing and, at the same time, uniting what he elsewhere calls plural "centers of culture." Du Bois urges the creation of "Negro art" not in order to ascend a ladder of civilization but to sharpen the sense of connection among recognizable worlds.

2

HOWELLS, JAMES, AND THE REPUBLIC OF LETTERS

THE CIVIC USES OF HIGH CULTURE

Matthew Arnold's *Culture and Anarchy* (1869) gave new meaning and prominence to the word "culture." "I shall not go so far as to say of Mr. Arnold that he invented it," Henry James wrote of the word, "but he made it more definite than it had been before – he vivified it and lighted it up." Surely part of what "vivified" culture in the educated vernacular was Arnold's pairing of the word with "anarchy" as its defining antonym. The red-flag urgency of "anarchy" made "culture" its cool and tranquil opposite, an antidote against social and political turmoil. Culture was conceived as a neutral or "disinterested" sphere of human experience, a sphere in which the warring interests of factions could recede in favor of a shared light for intelligent reflection on modern life. W. E. B. Du Bois had such a sphere in mind when he wrote in *The Souls of Black Folk* (1903) that African Americans wished to be "co-workers in the kingdom of culture" rather than being relegated to the role of "problem" in the sphere of politics. But Du Bois also alerts us to a certain faultline in the Arnoldian notion of culture. So long as the "kingdom of culture" is segregated – even so long as it is a solution to segregation, as Du Bois wishes – it partakes of the fractious problem of race. Even as the transcendence or resolution of politics, the sphere of culture is necessarily political.

Hence the doubleness in Wharton's image of a "republic of the spirit," which makes elegantly ironic use of a political figure, a republic, to signify a cultural space beyond the "material accidents" of politics. Arnold employs a similar turn when he identifies from among the British middle classes a "certain number of aliens, if we may so call them," individuals whose developed discernment gives them a special office transcending any narrow interests. Cultural aliens, spiritual citizens, a kingdom of co-workers – these paradoxical figures begin to capture something of the tension present in any attempt to imagine aesthetic culture in relation to matters of social power or justice. They are also reminders that the aesthetic and the social each exert a gravitational pull on the other in the critical imagination. Rarely are they conceptually isolated.

Whether out of protest, class disdain, or political hope, the proliferating talk of culture among the educated classes of Britain and America in this period made aesthetic matters into a new kind of national concern. When, only a few years after the Civil War, Thomas Wentworth Higginson published "A Plea for Culture" (1867) in the *Atlantic*, this man of letters was redirecting the energies he had previously used as a Union colonel into a campaign for strengthening art and taste in the nation – for an "America of Art." "Our brains as yet lie chiefly in our machineshops," Higginson writes. "What we need is the opportunity of high culture somewhere." His manifesto, a call for the United States to produce "better galleries" and "nobler living," is an early example of the postwar discourse that represented what Arnold called the "inward operations" of culture as a special kind of national resource.

Higginson's "America of Art" is the unrealized aesthetic republic that stands for the perfected potential of the actual society. The desire to cultivate a "literature truly American" had carried over from the nationalism of the antebellum era, but in an Arnoldian milieu that literary nationalism was now joined with an emphasis on cultural stratification. Only "higher" expression could manifest the national character. Even more incongruously, high art in this moment was charged with bringing harmony to conflicted cities and cultivating fellow feeling in an extraordinarily diverse population. John Sullivan Dwight declared in an *Atlantic* essay that the best music can be a "civilizing agency" for the "mixed people of all races" in American democracy, restraining radicalism by implanting an "impassioned love of order." The finest art, according to Metropolitan Museum of Art founder Joseph Choate, serves directly "to humanize, to educate, and refine a practical and laborious people." Properly designed parks and civic museums offer the public "a class of opposite conditions" to counter chaotic streets and workaday shops.

Confidence in the social powers of art is nowhere so clear – or so curiously literal – than when it was advocated as direct form of mob control. Aesthetic culture, it was proposed, could not only promote national unity, a oneness of heart and purpose, but also ensure "fewer strikes" and industrial labor "more faithfully performed." The secretary of the Academy of Arts and Sciences in New York urged the creation of "Theatres, Operas, Academies of Arts, Museums &c." as the solution to the "gross dissipation" that results "where refinement is not cultivated." Such pronouncements, issued with aplomb, are puzzling to the present-day ear. They sound a strange amalgam of faith and fear. Were such calls made in good faith or were they disingenuous? Did they reflect a species of hope or merely self-delusion?

To understand the matter requires not a sorting of disparate motives but an understanding of their conjunctions. A sincere belief in national uplift through art coexisted with a vision of social breakdown as two variants of the same mindset. In either scenario, American progress or American doom, the projection sharpened a sense of cultural leadership and conferred legitimacy on elite tastes and interests by presenting them as national standards. Social obligation and class retrenchment were frequently dual aspects of the same impulse. When Henry Lee Higginson, the founder of the Boston Symphony Orchestra, requested a $100,000 donation to Harvard College from a "public-spirited" relative ("you . . . owe it to yourself, to your country, and to the Republic"), his express motive for the philanthropy was the specter of an "intense and bitter" class struggle: "Educate and save ourselves and our families and our money from mobs!"

Such sentiments reveal the way cultural advocacy and philanthropy could be enlisted for social control. But to see high culture in this period as a program of imposed class domination is to miss the most important aspects of its social power. Advocates of high art recognized that cultural forms invite a transformation of some of the deepest, most vital of human responses. "Culture is infectious," one *Atlantic* author wrote. The appeal to culture was ultimately an appeal to pleasure and affect, to visceral senses we appropriately call by the name of taste. Though a misnomer, taste is an apt signifier for the range of subtle cognitive judgments and perceptions that make up cultural understanding. Like the sensation of sweetness or bitterness on the tongue, aesthetic taste seems more spontaneous than reflective, belonging more to the body than the mind. Poet William Cullen Bryant, addressing a New York audience on the place of art in countering urban ills, stressed the responsive "sense of beauty," the "perception of order, symmetry, proportion of parts" that inwardly renews the spirit. The deliberate, nationally oriented campaign to elevate American culture in this period represents an attempt at governance through intimate emulation: the purpose is not to rule but to entice, to refashion feeling and pleasure into a personality possessing "an impassioned love of order." It goes without saying that the "order" assumed here was not just any order; whatever fell outside of the pleasures and restraints of middle-class norms was likely to count as disorder, if not anarchy. But the rhetoric of a "love of order" endows those norms with the appeal of universal feeling. The persistent plea for an "America of Art" was not a calculated gambit for imposing the power of one class over others but a program of inner transformation urged upon a broad citizenry.

The emphasis on interiority meant that the pleasures of high culture were impossible to coerce but effective as an offered gift – and effective whether or not the gift was accepted. Essayists such as Higginson, Thomas Sargeant Perry, and Agnes Repplier saw their charge as a genuine broadening of shared feeling.

William Dean Howells was the most tireless on this theme. The highest art, Howells insisted, will "widen the bounds of sympathy." The belief he expressed in a review of Paul Laurence Dunbar's work, that "prejudices [are] destined to vanish in the arts," has become something of an article of faith today. At one level, high cultural institutions, much like religions, sought to create a oneness of experience in the multitude. A *Scribner's* essay stated "there is such a thing as 'the witness of the spirit,' in art as in religion." The same analogy governs Edith Wharton's retrospective story *False Dawn* (1924), in which a man returning to 1840s New York after a stay in Europe has experienced "something of the apostle's ecstasy" from his awakening to the beauty of Italian Primitive paintings. After experiencing his conversion he is prompted to "go forth and preach the new gospel" of a rediscovered aesthetic.

The other side of the desire to convert, to encourage oneness, is the desire to identify and mark out difference. The same publications that urged the wide dissemination of the arts also featured attacks on the multifarious expressions of America's "crowd civilization":

First of all, abolish the music halls in which vulgar tunes set to still more vulgar words provide the musical milk upon which the young of the masses are reared. Abolish the diabolical street pianos and hand organs which disseminate these vile tunes in all directions and which reduce the musical taste of the children in the residence streets to the level of that of the Australian bushman, who thinks noise and rhythm are music. Abolish the genuine American brand of burlesque . . . Abolish the theatre orchestra which plays the music hall stuff . . . Abolish those newspapers which degrade art by filling their columns with free advertising of so-called musical performers who are of the freak genus.

Though rhetorical, the call to "abolish" mass forms is still revealing. The imperative grammar, the extravagance and sweep, and the repetitive rhythm all attest to an impulse towards total control of cultural expression. Its practical effect is to focus aversion and reify difference, a process hidden under a taxonomic language pretending to describe what it invents, the "genus" of the grotesque and the freakish in art. Moreover, whole populations were deemed outside the realm of high art. As W. E. B. Du Bois made a point of reminding readers in *The Souls of Black Folk* (1903), "to most libraries, lectures, concerts, and museums, Negroes are either not admitted at all, or on terms peculiarly galling to the pride of the very classes who might otherwise be attracted."

To widen bounds; to mark the vulgar: these matched imperatives define the controlling energies behind the effort to build an "America of Art." Because it is often compelling only to the few, high art is commonly described as exclusive. But, with the exception of direct bans of the kind Du Bois underscores, the operative principle behind the emphasis on high culture was not exclusion but choice. That art and literature are embraced only voluntarily made them an effective gauge of the inner life. High art's wide diffusion, not its restriction, was the cornerstone for bringing high culture into use in social discipline, and its rejection by popular tastes was as significant as its (far less frequent) acceptance. An editorial Howells published in an 1878 *Atlantic*, "Certain Dangerous Tendencies in American Life," begins to illustrate the consequences of these principles. "We are in the earlier stages of a war upon property, and upon everything that satisfies what are called the higher wants of civilized life." Workers tend to regard "works of art and instruments of high culture, with all the possessions and surroundings of people of wealth and refinement, as causes and symbols of the laborer's poverty and degradation, and as things to be hated." This perception, the editorial argues, is a confusion of categories that mistakes ennobling works of art for the spoils of luxury. Art and high culture are properly a commonwealth, and as such they represent a civic responsibility rather than an exclusive possession. Those "who believe in culture, in property, and in order, that is in civilization," the essay declares, "must establish the necessary agencies for the diffusion of a new culture, a culture of a higher order" to bring about the "moral education of the people."

The call for new "agencies" to diffuse high culture is symptomatic of a profound historical innovation that wed liberal governance to the field of culture. The notion that art and culture could promote the social good was hardly a new one, of course. Scholars such as Jürgen Habermas have traced the way new genres of aesthetic criticism, emerging in the eighteenth century, encouraged the gradual detachment of art from the authoritative traditions of church and monarchy, a process that created an independent public sphere (though still a restricted one) in which the aesthetic judgments of propertied citizens were harnessed to social debate and civic improvement. By the time Matthew Arnold called art a "criticism of life" the idea was a commonplace. What was new at this time, however, was a widespread belief that aesthetic culture, with its power to produce a deep self-transformation of individuals, had a distinctive place in the practical agenda of civil governance. When Howells published the 1878 editorial column, only a small number of major metropolitan museums, civic symphony orchestras, and municipal opera companies had recently been founded. Within just a few years, however, an astonishing number of these organizations were established, creating a web of professional institutions that dominated the production and distribution of fine art and artistic performance in the United States. Whereas aesthetic institutions had detached themselves from bishops and kings, they were now increasingly organized in relation to city and state governance.

It was largely local groups of private patrons who organized this system of quasi-public cultural enterprises, but its kinship with institutions like public schools formed quickly. New York's Metropolitan Museum of Art was founded by financiers and artist consultants in 1870. The Boston Museum of Fine Art, established soon after in 1873, was similarly the venture of leading city figures, as was the founding of the Boston Symphony Orchestra in 1881. Philadelphia's Museum of Art, because it was established (in 1877) in the wake of the Centennial Exhibition, represents an early case in which a state legislature was centrally involved in creating the museum. Although the Smithsonian Institution was incorporated in the 1840s, according to director George Brown Goode it was not until 1876 that "the existence of a National Museum, as such" was established in Washington. Like other cultural leaders, Goode stressed that a museum must be able to transform human subjects from within. "The museum of the past," he declares in an 1888 report, "must be set aside, reconstructed, transformed from a cemetery of bric-a-brac into a nursery of living thoughts." If this potential is fulfilled, "the museum of the future may be made one of the chief agencies of the higher civilization." Circulating collections of specimens were created for schools as the authority of museums flowed "beyond galleries to the lecture hall and beyond the lecture hall to the suburban school."

Seen in this context, it is clear that literary production was another of the "chief agencies" to disseminate a national pedagogy of higher civilization. High literary culture was organized around a group of leading magazines, most of them the house organ for one of the major publishing companies. These literary publications – the *Atlantic*, *Harper's*, *The Century*, and *Scribner's* were the recognized leaders – reinforced each other's authority by reviewing the same books, publishing many of the same authors, taking up a similar range of topics (and mutually ignoring others), and hiring each other's writers and editors. Like other cultural institutions, these journals saw their work cultivating a higher national literature as a public mandate. High culture, in the view of these agencies, was neither a princely possession nor a form of entertainment but a moral resource for the nation, to be administered by professionals who hold a public trust. Howells in particular put forward the novelist as someone uniquely suited for the cultural elevation of the public: "He assumes a higher function, something like that of a physician or priest," and "bound by laws as sacred as those of such professions."

The success of this association of high art with civic order and professional agencies was unequivocal, but what of its effects? No single criterion can evaluate the efforts to make fiction into an agent of national uplift. The "quality" magazines and the authors they promoted won recognition as the leading literary authorities, though not without challengers. Their prestige drew in readers and introduced Americans to writers rarely given exposure in US periodicals, including French, German, and Spanish authors as well as a wider range of American authors than is usually recognized. Just as notable, even the failures of these critics and authors – their failure to acquire a wider readership, for instance – could produce a species of success. Even when ignored, their promotion of high culture served to articulate social distinctions in the public it was aiming to convert. That process is illustrated in Wharton's *False Dawn* when the would-be art "apostle" Lewis Raycie fervently hopes to win adherents and astonishes New York by turning a Manhattan home into an open gallery for exhibiting his collection of Italian paintings. But Raycie is a cultural prophet without a country. As the story describes his desire to share his discovered treasures, it formally traces new lines of cultural difference. For Wharton's readers, Raycie's gallery serves finally to assemble and name the "dumb and respectable throng, who roamed vacantly through the rooms and out again, grumbling that it wasn't worth the money." Raycie's failure frames a self-damning population – the "throng" that is the middle-class version of the "mob" – whose rejection of Raycie's paintings ironically confirms his status as Wharton's culture hero. The story illustrates one of high culture's unique advantages: an ability to win for losing. Prestige can accrue to failure in a mass society.

But the advantages of prestige should not obscure the realities of cultural competition. The new array of "agencies" created to administer the high arts saw themselves in an acute contest with commercial culture. Their efforts to attract were genuine. "The great mass of readers now sunk in foolish joys of mere fable," Howells declares in *Fiction and Criticism*, "shall be lifted to interest in the meaning of things through a faithful portrayal of life in fiction." The rivalry with commercial culture for the "great mass" of Americans, though, points up a structural vulnerability. In such competition, the inwardness of high culture, its defining difference, becomes its distinctive problem. How is it possible to make the spiritual property of cultural discernment available as a model? How do the invisible competencies of taste and judgment become visible objects for emulation, or, failing that, for intimidation? The solution is ironic, and not without risk: in order to harness the power of culture, put discernment on display. Organized through new agencies and spaces, high culture in this period set out to exhibit itself – to make distinction conspicuous.

Once again the museum offers an apt historical analogy. The metropolitan museum had become a space for instructing the public in selective discernment not simply by exhibiting objects but, even more importantly, by making visitors and non-visitors alike aware of the invisible knowledge – expertise in operation behind the scenes – that had chosen and assembled the objects exhibited. Museums, in other words, also house what they do *not* overtly display: expert cultural authority. Goode formalized this function when he asserted that museums should have "two great classes" of holdings. The "exhibition series" is visible to the public, "attractively arranged" behind "the clearest of glass." The "study series" ("tens of thousands of specimens"), on the other hand, is "hidden away perpetually from public view" but provides the "foundations of the intellectual superstructure" for the museum. The hidden holdings are the guarantors of museum authority, while the public displays are a visible witness of the curatorial expertise that has assembled the exhibition from out of the storehouse. ("The public," Goode writes, "will take pride in the possession by the museum" of the cache of objects available only to the specialist but "necessary for proper scientific research.") At the same time, public exhibits also make canons of cultural expertise available for study and emulation. "The people's museum should be much more than a house full of specimens in glass cases. It should be a house full of ideas, arranged with the strictest attention to system." Museums offer not only material objects but also the possibility of acquiring a restricted, intangible mastery for the dedicated visitor.

Developments in literature offered similar instances of the direct and indirect display of higher discernment. In an era of competing forms of authorship, books themselves could be a form of artistic exhibition. Private collections and public libraries sought out rare books as well as books of rare learning. Volumes such as Charles Eliot Norton's *Historical Studies of Church Building in the Middle Ages* (1880), Bernard Berenson's *Central Italian Painters of the Renaissance* (1897), Percival Lowell's *Occult Japan or the Way of the Gods* (1894), and Edith Wharton's *In Morocco* (1920) are material embodiments of the unique knowledge and experience described in their pages. Unlike rare editions, such works were not in short supply, but as an object in the hands of a reader or on the shelves of a library they could still advertise a restricted cultural knowledge even as they offer to share it.

The fiction promoted by the leading periodicals redesigned the novel around the same paradoxical imperatives of display and discrimination. Though Realist novels carry over much of the same thematic materials of the fiction that precedes them – explorations of courtship, family life, and social conduct, representations of moral and social conflicts – the champions of high Realism reposition the genre as a form for *challenging* conventional or popular fiction. A less obvious form of exhibition than the museum, the novel is nevertheless made over into a space of instruction through display, a new kind of quasi-public space where fictional representation can counter the "distorted and misleading likeness in our books," plays, and commercial spectacles. The

Realist novel not only holds out "a faithful portrayal of life," but also establishes that there is a specialized knowledge – Howells explicitly calls it "a sort of scientific decorum" – necessary to distinguish accurate representations from distortions, fact from fable. That knowledge lies not in the stories themselves but in the habits of perception required to read them. The Realist novel makes representation itself not only a medium for fiction but also a distinct cultural practice and a contested terrain. Reading novels with the proper discernment offers the possibility of mastering a special kind of knowledge – according to Howells, nothing less than the "the meaning of things."

Once the novel is deliberately recast as the antidote to "shows and semblances," however, it competes on the same territory of public visibility as the "effectists" of mass culture. This paradox – that to rescue high culture from conspicuousness, culture must make itself conspicuous – locates the generative rivalry that accounts for much of the controlling energy and creativity of the literature in this period. With varying degrees of perception, Realist works recognize that mass culture was remaking the order of the real. Under the pressure of the rivalry, Realist fiction begins to resemble the world of spectacle it opposes. But the resemblance is not simply a risk to high-culture fiction, it is also that fiction's precondition: the proximity is precisely what makes Realist discernment the increasingly specialized, valuable property – in short, the property of *distinction* – that it is.

WILLIAM DEAN HOWELLS, REALISM, AND THE MODERN INSTANCE

Like other novels of its time, Howells's *A Modern Instance* (1882) is about a bad marriage; unlike others, the source of the marital trouble is not adultery but publicity. The three-year marriage between newspaperman Bartley Hubbard and his wife Marcia reaches a crisis when Marcia accuses him of infidelity. Her suspicions are wrong, and within moments she knows it. Still, the false accusation has the same effect as if it were true: it sets off an enraged confrontation, an impulsive separation, and a dramatic divorce. Howells here could be said to draw on a standard plot device, the threat of adultery, to point beyond it to an even deeper disruption of traditional domesticity. The Hubbards' marriage is not destroyed by intimate betrayal – Bartley is incapable of possessing any fidelity of private feeling to betray. Instead, his only consistent interests and gratifications are the internalized energies of mass publicity, or what the narrator calls Bartley's "newspaper instinct." Similarly, Marcia's "domestic instinct" is female sentiment that has been distorted by commercial culture. Her unrealistic expectations and emotionalism are "distempered imitations" of the melodrama Howells saw as endemic to the era's popular fiction. After publishing more conventional marriage novels such as *A Chance Acquaintance* (1873) and *A Fearful Responsibility* (1881), Howells reinvented the marriage novel in *A Modern Instance* by presenting an American marriage whose partners are in thrall to the desires and forces of an emergent mass society. He would later call it his first truly "Realist" novel.

Bartley's "newspaper instinct" has the blind but canny force of erotic feeling, with which it is explicitly compared. A reporter for an aggressive Boston newspaper, Bartley dreams of starting an even racier paper that will operate on a method of public seduction. His plan for "spicy" journalism consists of minutely calibrating the desires of different groups of readers – "local accident and crime" for the lowest sorts, political affairs for those in the city machines, religious gossip for the next higher stratum ("it interests the women like murder"), fashion and financial reports for the social elite – in order to entice a mass audience to buy the same publication. Bartley defines his journalistic "principle" as simply a matter of meeting demand – "you must give the people what they want" – though it relies on carefully inciting the desires it hopes to gratify. Bartley's credo is echoed by a theater manager he meets in a bar, a man who stages a new kind of variety show, a "burlesque," performed by all-female troupes. "I give the public what it wants," the burlesque manager announces, which turns out to be "legs, principally." Bartley answers that "it's just so with newspapers, too."

Howells plays the scene for humor, but the comparison of mass-market journalism with burlesque is a pointed critique. By the mid-1870s, the novel's time frame, burlesque troupes had won a large American audience by offering eclectic theatrical novelties that stopped short of any open indecencies. During the 1868–69 theatrical season in Boston, for instance, five of the city's seven theaters featured burlesques imported from England, prompting Howells to write an analysis in the *Atlantic* of the "spectacle muse" of burlesque that had reigned over the season. The troupes consisted of female performers playing male roles in an incongruous collection of skits, songs, dances, minstrel "walk arounds," and topical parodies. Howells's review indicted the burlesque manager's "ideas of public taste," though not without an ironic awareness that the productions actually seemed to have gauged the taste of the public ("honest-looking, handsomely dressed men and women") with distressing accuracy. Howells's objection to burlesque was less its potential for sexual titillation than its deliberate incoherence – the distortions of gender as well as the disconnected jumble of sensational sights. "A melancholy sense of the absurdity, of the incongruity, of the whole," he wrote, "absorbed at last even a sense of the indecency." Burlesque swept in and left nothing untouched: "no novelty remains which is not now forbidden by statute."

With its heedless collection of novelties, burlesque was the antitype to Howells's notion of literary Realism. A classical performance of *Medea* Howells attended in 1875 sparked the idea for *A Modern Instance* ("I said to myself, 'This is an Indiana divorce case'") and his "New Medea" was meant to explore sexual and emotional disruptions of the modern age. Like Howells's novel, a famous burlesque called *Ixion; or the Man at the Wheel* (1863) also took up the theme of modern divorce by way of classical allusion, but did so with the intention to mock and dazzle. In *Ixion*, parodic fragments from classical myth are thrown together in a farcical narrative taking aim at the penchant for divorce among the social elite. Written by F. C. Burnand, the comic production featured popular actress Lydia Thompson in the role of Ixion, king of Thessaly, and her visit to Mount Olympus was the pretext for topical jokes, songs, and dance numbers. The burlesque's deliberate cultivation of incongruities led another critic to label the genre a "monstrous" form of entertainment, and "by monstrous I do not mean wicked, disgusting, or hateful, but monstrously incongruous and unnatural . . . Its system is a defiance of system."

For Howells, the same "spectacle muse" in burlesque governed mass journalism. The problem with this brand of journalism was not its popularity but rather the source of that popularity in the frisson that comes from gratuitous public exposure. Like a burlesque revue, Bartley's newspaper relies on the excitement generated by the display of what is normally unseen. Howells identifies as the "vice" of mass journalism its compulsion to gather, reproduce, and circulate an indiscriminate constellation of sensational sights: "Why should an accurate correspondent inform me of the elopement of a married man with his maid-servant in East Machias?" asks one of Howells's disapproving characters. "Why should I sup on all the horrors of a railroad accident, and have the bleeding fragments hashed up for me at breakfast?" And, in a revealing inclusion, "Why should I be told by telegraph how three negroes died on the gallows of North Carolina?" The newspaper is a burlesque show in disguise, serving up for entertainment the same flavors of racial shock, domestic scandal, and novel sights that spiced the popular stage productions. Driven by visibility for its own sake, mass journalism is for Howells a burlesque of the real.

Howells's novel indicts a long list of the sensational topics exploited by newspapers, naming elopements and railroad accidents as well as suicides, detectives in pursuit of criminals, divorce trials, and murders. But remarkably, this same list of topics is a virtual index to Howells's own plot. The story of the Hubbards' marriage begins in an elopement and, before the novel ends, features Marcia's thoughts of suicide, Bartley's pursuit by detectives, a minor train accident, a major divorce trial, and even a report of Bartley's own murder by gunshot. The novel thus unfolds by way of an uncanny doubling with the very spectacles it names and condemns. It may seem curious that Howells's plot is structured by these scandals – are these not the gratuitous novelties that Realist novels are expressly to shun? But properly understood, the narrative doubling does not compromise Howells's Realism; rather, it can be said to *constitute* Realism, to show the complexity of its historical formation. For Howells, subjects like divorce do have a genuine claim on the highest public interest, but only in the right kind of narrative frame. *A Modern Instance* is designed to properly expose distorting newspaper exposure, in order to permit the discerning reader to tell the difference. The doubling represents a compressed version of the cultural contest that is the very ground for high literary Realism, a competition for control over the recently enlarged power of public representation. Howells's aversion to mass forms was not simply a puritanical reflex against low pleasures. Rather, Howells saw that behind the ever more numerous commercial displays and pulp-fiction titles was the power of an expanded market sector to dissolve and rearrange the materials of more traditional institutions of acculturation. Realism was to be a bulwark against the power of the market to remake the real.

Bartley's acuity as a newspaperman gives him a "masterly knowledge" of Boston places and people. But the novel also insists readers realize that Bartley acutely lacks another order of understanding: he had "scarcely any knowledge of the distinctions and differences so important to the various worlds of any city." These additional "worlds," and the "distinctions" necessary to understand them, are not explicitly named. But the comment directs attention to a more expansive point of view than Bartley's, a synoptic vision the novel itself will eventually realize. Through its plot, the novel develops a picture of distinct but interdependent social regions: Bartley's reporter's haunts; the small-scale households of the Hubbards' neighborhood; the indoor-world of polite Boston society; a male precinct of professional offices and clubs; and the public space of saloons, restaurants, and theaters, among others. The result is a totality that Howells in his criticism calls "life in its civic relations," and the ability to grasp these "various worlds" as a whole is at the heart of Howells's understanding of fiction. Rivals like burlesque and mass journalism also present social life but only by offering incoherent aggregations of events and scenes. What is needed, in Howells's view, is the ability to conceive the increasingly diverse urban worlds as a total social body.

A paradigmatic test of Bartley's "knowledge of distinctions" occurs in the peculiar public space of Boston's new institutions of high culture. The narrator details the way Bartley and Marcia went sometimes to the Museum of Fine Arts, where [Marcia] became as hungry and tired as if it were the Vatican. They had a pride in taking books out of the Public Library, where they walked about on tiptoe with bated breath; and they thought it a divine treat to hear the great organ play at noon. As they sat there in the Music Hall, and let the mighty instrument bellow over their strong young nerves, Bartley whispered to Marcia the jokes he had heard about the organ; and then, upon the wave of aristocratic sensation from this experience, they went out and dined at Copeland's, or Weber's, or Fera's, or even at Parker's . . .

The distinctions in this passage are all implicit. The passage is meaningful only when one sees the meanings *not* grasped by Bartley and Marcia. Readers know that the "aristocratic sensation" the couple experiences at the organ recital actually measures their lack of aesthetic feeling, since those who understand art and culture, who live and breathe in its atmosphere, would never experience the kind of discrete sensation of "aristocratic" elevation felt by the Hubbards. Travel-savvy readers know that Marcia's weariness at the Boston museum means she would experience a fatigue many times greater at the Vatican. By requiring readers to understand by way of the gaps or distinctions in the scene, Howells posits the existence of a larger, unspecified field of knowledge that turns those differences into legible social relations. The effect is to set off the Hubbards' perceptions as examples of a certain kind of (insufficient) understanding, intelligible only to a higher order of sight. Bartley and Marcia are not fictional subjects, alternative selves we might emulate or envy or upbraid. Rather, these characters become fictional objects, figures carefully "isolated and analyzed," in Howells's critical formula, against a more encompassing horizon of social relations. These are not just objects to be seen but to be *seen through* to a whole that is graspable only by implication. This kind of structure pulls the reader away from the impulse of identification – the immediacy of "reading for the plot" – and instills a habit of what might be called reading for distinction.

Extending and deepening the analysis of "distinctions and differences" is the task of the novel as a whole. The novel will turn the distressing exigencies of the Hubbards' lives into a "modern instance," a representative object that can illuminate a broader social order. It is a mistake to see Howells as a scold or a snob; the Hubbards' deficits in higher taste are important only insofar as they help define "modern" persons who have been formed by their responsiveness to mass culture. The younger American writers who succeeded Howells's generation sometimes painted him as the guardian of a too narrow Victorian gentility, but the primary importance of aesthetic taste for Howells was not propriety or personal refinement. He insisted he was "outside of the rank of the mere *culturists*, followers of an elegant literature," and it was a fair enough claim. For Howells, aesthetic feeling is an index to social differences – a crucial index, it turns out – that points up a defining order of "civic relations" through patterns of difference. Those contemporaries of Howells who complained that his Realism was given to excessive analysis ("Boston under the scalpel" was the way one critic described Howells's fiction) were closer to the mark than those who portrayed him as a fussy defender of genteel reticence.

That analytic bent is the reason Howells underscores the Hubbards' failed marriage as a meaningful "instance" of modernity. Howells's notion of the fictional "instance" – Henry James speaks of the "expressive particular" – is a key unit of analysis in Realism. The representative or resonant instance (also the "type" or "trait") allows the reader to "seek the universal in the individual." Howells's confidence in a logic of metonymic representation presumes the existence of accessible orders of historical and social relations, orders against which carefully drawn figures could be critically analyzed. In this way Howells realizes in fiction the same "modern museum idea" that George Brown Goode defined for curators and art exhibitors. Goode's definition of a well-organized museum as "a collection of instructive labels illustrated by well-selected specimens" attests to the prime importance of the representative type as the basic unit of meaning. The properly selected specimen is a witness of an underlying system or series. Without such series, Goode emphasized, the museum is little more than a "cemetery of bric-a-brac."

The museum object, as Goode described it, is also a specimen of history, an artifact of time. Its ability to represent relies on its place in a temporal sequence, a known cultural history. Howells shares the belief that historical measurement should be one of the structuring principles of fiction. An "instance" is only meaningful as an instance of an epoch, here the order of the "modern." In truly meaningful art, Howells insists, techniques of skillful narration will reveal "the laws of evolution in art and society." In all, Howells's Realism shares the museum "idea" of the power of disciplined representation. The categories of type and historical sequence operated as a powerful nineteenth-century syntax for converting the amorphous (and wildly overdetermined) concept of "civilization" into vividly realized displays of its constitutive orders – the cultural histories of great nations, the evolution of fine art, the growth of science and technology, the succession of "primitive" cultures that make up the prehistory of civilization. Modeled after the powerful evolutionary principles that had made biology and natural history the supreme sciences, these museum disciplines embodied the desire to give the things of culture the determinate order of an organic law. When Howells asserts that fiction requires "a sort of scientific decorum," he expresses a widespread belief that specialized metonymic display could impart knowledge of the real, invisible order of things. Writers who fail to "body forth human experience" according to Realist decorum fall into the error of "falsifying nature," modeling life "after their own fancy." (Tellingly, Howells relegates these popular forms to the "stone age of fiction.") The same principles must govern the literary critic as well as the writer. The critic is "to identify the species and then explain how and why the specimen is imperfect and irregular," Howells writes in *Fiction and Criticism*. Literary criticism must restrict itself "to the business of observing, recording, comparing; to analyzing the material before it, and then synthesizing its impressions."

Yet as powerful as these principles of authoritative display were for agencies of culture like Howells's fiction, Realist exhibition never reliably served only one master. Even museum representation could break from the "law of evolution in art and society" into other, more wayward paths. Cultural leaders were acutely aware of this possibility. Boston's first museum, established in 1791, featured wax figures of Franklin and Washington together with oil paintings and live animals. The early museum was likely to offer oddities of natural history, ornaments from exotic places in Africa or China, and sensational technological displays such as a guillotine. Live performances at these museums made unabashed attempts at drawing in large popular audiences; in 1819 the Boston Gallery of Fine Arts featured the "Lilliputian Songsters," two dwarfs whose singing presented "genteel deportment." And, as we have seen, Barnum made the most of the early museum's penchant for eclectic spectacle when he launched himself in show business.

The modern museum defined itself through a strenuous differentiation from this kind of array of curiosities. As one museum administrator put it in 1888, "The orderly soul of the Museum student will quake at the sight of a Chinese lady's boot encircled by shark's teeth" or "an Egyptian mummy placed in a medieval chest." Such sheer spectacle is an affront to the discriminating observer. And yet the sting of the affront hints at the museum's lingering affiliation with popular spectacle that prompts the need for disavowal. In 1888, the visual novelties of a Chinese boot or a boxed-in mummy could signify not merely the museum's buried past but its current cultural rival, mass-culture spectacle. Howells's *A Modern Instance* gives an incisive view of this rivalry between institutions and its place in the formation of high literary culture. On the first night of their arrival in Boston, Bartley and Marcia visit Moses Kimball's Museum theater, a nine-hundred-seat auditorium for popular plays and variety shows. The theater maintained a vestige of its earlier incarnation as a museum in the exhibition gallery lining its first-floor lobby.

They passed through the long colonnaded vestibule, with its paintings and plaster casts and rows of birds and animals in glass cases on either side and she gave scarcely a glance at any of those objects endeared by association if not intrinsic beauty to the Boston play-goer: Gulliver, with the Lilliputians swarming upon him; the painty-necked ostriches and pelicans; the mummied mermaid under a glass-bell; the governors' portraits; the stuffed elephant; Washington crossing the Delaware; Cleopatra applying the asp; Sir William Pepperell, at full length on canvas and the pagan months and seasons in plaster, – if all these are indeed the subjects – were dim phantasmagoria, amid which she and Bartley moved scarcely more real.

The lobby's unsorted "phantasmagoria" is antithetical to Howells's Realist "instance." The exhibition disregards any distinction between the mythical and the natural, whimsy and solemnity, art and grotesque artifact. Belonging to no one order of nature or history, the objects represent nothing but their own singularity. In *Moby-Dick* Melville often uses something very like this cataloging of curious objects and incongruous exotic allusions to fashion a new lyrical symbolism for his distinctive literary art. For Howells, in contrast, the combined display of disparate artifacts remains an inert if instructive fossil, an example of the "stone age" of popular taste. The fact that a public "appetite for the marvelous" seemed to be growing rather than dying out made such taste only more unnatural. In their distortions and factitiousness, these objects are figures for the many kinds of "fantastic and monstrous and artificial things" in contemporary life that Howells identified in his novels and essays, from women's fashions to artificial new American "tastes and moods."

And yet the fact that Howells reproduces this jumbled sight in detail suggests that the curiosity of spectacle may not be simply the outdated phenomenon that Howells suggests. A "phantasmagoria" of various urban spectacles is also a central preoccupation of the novel, and, indeed, of all of Howells's subsequent novels. *The Minister's Charge*, for instance, includes a closely rendered picture of the pandemonium of a hotel fire, the bathos of a criminal courtroom, and the shocking street theater of a bloody trolley accident – all topics Howells's characters frequently criticize as too sensational when they appear in a tabloid paper. High Realism remains intimately bound to what it nominally excludes from the order of the real. The literary Realism Howells championed was established in a moment when newly defined orders of culture, high and low, were facing off in open competition. Realism is, in that sense, a literary language that emerges from the proximity of high and low culture in rivalry, a proximity that calls for vigilant codes of distinction. This is the self-conscious office of Howellsian Realism. For all its urgency to purge "distempered imitations," then, Realist discourse can never rid itself of what it deems unreal without sacrificing the very basis for Realist distinction.

For Howells, Realist distinction is also needed for understanding the genre's bedrock institution: marriage. Characters see the Hubbards' marriage variously as vaguely unsatisfactory (Bartley's view) or inscrutably lacking in intimacy (Marcia's view) or fatally short on domestic propriety (Marcia's father's view). But readers are asked to see it as something closer to what another character calls the "hideous deformity" of marriage – marriage in the form of the modern spectacle of divorce. This "deformity" of marriage is not simply the scandal of a divorce. Rather, divorce is the deformation of marriage, or marriage *scandalized*. This is the distinction readers are to grasp in this Realist novel: for Howells the trouble with the Hubbards' marriage is not its singularity but its instructive and representative vulnerability to the energies of a rootless commercial society. Howells's novel contends that marriage, like other traditional institutions such as churches and republican politics, is no longer an effective shield against the fantasies of mass culture that, left unchecked, invade intimate relationships and even consciousness itself.

This insight, then, requires one of the finest distinctions in the novel. The Hubbards' marriage is finally not to be seen as a singular "hideous deformity" but as an instructive "modern instance." It is not, that is, a freakish anomaly (however rare divorce was at the time) but a representative case, the result of what Howells said was his "practical and modern" treatment of marriage in the age of mass culture. Only this difference – the analytic value of the "instance" – protects the novel from being what it adamantly opposes, a narrative that exploits for "cheap effects" the "fetid explosions of the divorce trials" (a condemnation Howells penned in a critical essay). This is a rather fine line to maintain, to be sure: the same writer who complains in his editor's column of the divorce trials in the tabloids is the writer who concludes *A Modern Instance* with a long and dramatically engaging divorce trial. Yet drawing this line, the line that makes visible second-order distinctions about representation, is precisely the point. Howells represents a divorce trial not for cheap effects but for Realist effects, which is to say, the effects on the discerning reader, who acquires a mastery over the distortions of mass culture and with that mastery gains a purchase on a social whole – modernity – that is otherwise ungraspable.

This Realist aesthetic springs from mixed impulses. Howells's pronouncements on Realism carry the exhilarated conviction of a truth revealed, even as they convey a profound anxiety in the lower registers. Each was a genuine sentiment, each a tonal counterpoint that increased the resonance of the other. Howells's claims for the social power of high art were astonishingly large. His convictions about Realism amount to a romancing of the power of disciplined representation. "The highest fiction treats itself as fact." To hear the imaginative promise in this phrase requires recognition of the new excitement and authority ascribed to fact in this era. The prestige of the natural sciences and the recently established social sciences, the remarkable rational leverage derived from statistics, the new professional recognition accorded art and humanities in the university – these and other enterprises held out a disciplinary glamour for the work of fiction. For Howells and many of his contemporaries, Realism ("the movement in literature like the world is now witnessing") promised a gradual, solid-seeming materialization of an otherwise invisible totality.

Not everyone found an intellectual glamour in the Realist "movement." Some observers found Howellsian Realism given to cold, bloodless analysis. Critics such as Agnes Repplier and William Roscoe Thayer greeted the renewal of more romantic fiction in the 1890s as a welcome alternative to the fiction of Realism's dissecting "anatomists." Debates about Realism were waged in competing magazines and other venues, as when a congress on literature organized for the 1893 Chicago Columbian Exposition brought together figures such as Hamlin Garland, Mary Hartwell Catherwood, and Charles Dudley Warner to take sides on what one observer termed the "passion for realism." Despite the detractors, however, those who felt the "passion" saw Realism as a singular and truly exciting advance in American letters. With something like the exhilaration of watching a developing photograph, proponents believed Realism was bringing into view a social world usually too changeable and fast-paced to be seen steadily.

For Howells, the Realism "movement" also made fiction a collective enterprise, the work of a whole class or profession. "American life especially is getting represented with unexampled fullness," Howells claims, because fiction is the labor of a group of specially qualified authors. "It is true that no one writer, no one book, represents it, for that is not possible; our social and political decentralization forbids this, and may forever forbid it. But a great number of very good writers are instinctively striving to make each part of the country and each phase of our civilization known to all the other parts." Like Goode's notion of the museum as an "illustrated encyclopedia of civilization," Howells looked to fiction as a broad cultural enterprise able to make the enormous diversity of American society legible through a comprehensive record in letters. A generous mentor, Howells encouraged the careers of writers from outside the cultural capitals of the Northeast – Tennessee's Mary Noailles Murfree, for instance, and Hamlin Garland and Edward Eggleston who portrayed the rural Midwest – and supported cultural outsiders like immigrant Abraham Cahan, who took up the cause of Realism as editor of New York's *Jewish Daily Forward*, and African-American writer Charles Chesnutt. This collective enterprise would meet the era's "social and political decentralization" with a fully realized map of the nation in letters.

The other side of this hopeful expectation was a motivating anxiety. With-out a language or agency to realize the underlying orders of culture, social life may appear to be only a collection of heterogeneous fantasies and desires. Howells's efforts to make literature an institution of the real was born out of a deep sense that other social forms were failing to portray, or worse, wholly distorting, contemporary social life. Through the strange eloquence of his per-sonal anxieties, Howells was among the first intellectuals to articulate what are still unresolved questions about the social power of mass culture. His cultural moment, and the institution of Realism it spawned, form the prehistory of our own continuing struggle to understand the efficacy of cultural representation and to grasp the relation – whether corrosive or unifying – between mass cul-ture forms and diverse modern societies. Howells's solution was to define and embrace the literary as a social agent by strenuously distinguishing it from mass rivals deemed unreal. In the disciplinary accents of Realism's "order and system," Howells's Realism is a dream of reconciliation, an imaginary museum to house desire in the guise of the real.

The utopian impulse in Howells's particular brand of literary nationalism (a "republic of letters where all men are free and equal") tended to cover over its own contradictory premise. Moral force was inherent in the Realist vision, as Howells conceived it: the Realist writer "feels in every nerve the equality of things and the unity of men; his soul is exalted, not by vain shows and shadows and ideals, but by realities, in which alone truth lives." And literary expression of that vision, Howells believed, would make readers' cultivated perceptions into a route to social transformation. Only Realism signified "democracy in literature" because, rather than pandering to a mélange of popular tastes, it promised "the unity of taste in the future." The prospect of a "unity of taste," however, also contains an irreducible discrepancy between theory and practice. Howells's genuine democratic ideals were attached to a specialized literary practice whose effective end was necessarily to produce a delimited, self-selecting readership. Howells increasingly felt the strain of the resulting tension. His ideal "republic of letters" was the simulacrum of a unified culture, an artifact whose principle aim – to join citizens through "taste" – also belies its debt to the market culture he opposed.

The same tensions can be glimpsed in the development of Howells's career. Raised in Ohio with a fairly rudimentary education, he worked at a local newspaper office while writing literary reviews for Ohio publications. He eventually published some of his own poems in the Boston-based *Atlantic* and the New York *Saturday Press* and set his course for a life in the literary centers of the Northeast. Near the end of his life he would turn to his Ohio childhood in self-revealing volumes such as *A Boy's Town* (1890) and *Years of*

My Youth (1916), but most of his work focused on Europe and the Northeastern United States where he established his remarkably successful career in letters. Howells wrote the campaign biography of Lincoln and received as his reward the consulship of Venice, where he resided for much of the Civil War. His travel essays from Italy helped to cultivate his ties to the literary circles of Boston and New York, and upon his return to the United States he won a position as a columnist for the New York *Nation* and served next as an editor for the *Atlantic* (1866–81) in Boston.

Howells's success was held up as an example of the national integration that literary culture could foster. Here was a son of the "rough-and-ready West," as James Russell Lowell put it, whose inborn gifts had been recognized and welcomed by the highest literary lights in the East. It is probably more accurate to say that Howells's talent had inspired in the ambitious young writer a keen-eyed study of the Eastern literary establishment he deliberately prepared himself to join. Howells was an outsider whose intense observations from a distance helped him cross the threshold to the inside, and this particular path of career advancement left its mark. For the young Howells, Boston was an object of desire and intense analysis, a combination that energized him and would sharpen his fiction and criticism. His outsider's critical mastery of its "civic relations" was a continuing source of the insider's cultural success. Understanding Howells's work – his social vision and critique, and his later sense of his own critical impasse – requires careful attention to the way the mastery of social distinctions could signify for Howells both open mobility as well as implacable difference. It was a contradiction he would never completely resolve.

THE MILLIONAIRE IN PRINT: BARNUM AND HOWELLS

In *The Rise of Silas Lapham* (1885), Howells's rivalry with commercial culture takes the form of an open competition. The novel's central topic coincided with an established genre of the mass press: the portrait of the new American millionaire. Biographies and newspaper profiles of millionaires were tremendously popular in this era, as were capitalist wisdom books such as Andrew Carnegie's *Gospel of Wealth* (1889) and Orison Swett Marden's *Pushing to the Front* (1894). By portraying a millionaire, *The Rise of Silas Lapham* challenges commercial culture on its own turf, and Howells's *tour de force* Realist portrait of Silas Lapham demolishes the competition. It is a fixed fight, certainly, but no less illuminating for that fact. Recognizing the competitive motive underscores both the novel's literary control as well as its spirited, almost combative literary energies. Howells lets the press have the first go at his central character

Lapham, a paint manufacturer with a "colossal fortune." Bartley Hubbard is resurrected for the task: he reappears as a young reporter, still in his early years of marriage, on assignment to interview Lapham for the "Solid Men of Boston" series. Bartley's fatuous sketch describes Lapham as a "fine type of the successful American" in rote formulas. Howells, taking his turn at portraying Lapham, will then expose Bartley's journalistic language as a false kind of representativeness – neither a true understanding of "type" nor a real apprehension of the phenomenon of Gilded Age success. The newspaper sells a polished distortion of a millionaire's life story, one that Howells will first expose and then rewrite, as if to give a whole popular genre its comeuppance.

Howells's novel unfolds as a besting of this shallow newspaper portrait. Where Bartley's Solid Man is blandly genteel, Howells's is brought to life through the quirks of his vernacular speech and manners. Where Bartley's portrait consists of formulaic praise, Howells's presents a closely shaded picture of Lapham's moral hesitations and humiliations as well as his personal recoveries. Nothing in Howells's fiction illustrates quite so well as *The Rise of Silas Lapham* the way his understanding of Realism is oppositional, an art defined by the task of uncovering and displaying precisely what rival commercial forms distort or omit. Yet to see the matter through these oppositions – surface and depth, distortion and real representation – is to define things in Howells's terms. All responsive readers *will* see them in these terms, to be sure; being able to perceive these distinctions is the chief measure of having successfully read the novel. But Howells's defeat of Bartley's vapid journalism is also a backhanded tribute to the power of popular culture. The contest itself tacitly recognizes that other criteria exist for evaluating writing, criteria which, though dead letters to Howells, are alive for vast numbers of readers.

That Howells's distinctions carry with them their own blindness is clear when *Silas Lapham* is compared alongside the single bestselling narrative about the "rise" of an American millionaire. Howells's Lapham is the alter ego of the century's most famous businessman, Phineas T. Barnum, and Howells's novel can be read as the high culture counterpart of Barnum's own narrative. Barnum's autobiography, *Struggles and Triumphs* (1869), is the equal of *Silas Lapham* in the skill with which it manipulates the conventions of the popular success narrative. Both Howells and Barnum rely on the generic figure of the "solid man" for their own very different ends. Howells's novel shows how the attempts by the popular press to grasp the new figure of the rich American are largely bland and undiscerning (Bartley's flat praise of Lapham's "trials and struggles" barely conceals the reporter's derision). The fatuous journalistic language is proof of the need for Realist distinctions. On Barnum's side, his self-penned *Struggles and Triumphs* also leverages the popular interest in millionaires' stories, and in doing so manages the feat of representing his career in humbug as the very definition of solid success. With deft skill, Barnum enlists readers in a game of overlooking the showman's difference from the bankers and industrialists who usually signify American wealth and "solid" success. Inside details of Barnum's advertising tricks and occasional outright lies are to be accepted as proof of the showman's exemplary "integrity, energy, industry, and courage." This apparent erasure of distinctions, however, actually calls for discernment of another kind. Barnum's readers must distinguish between the chicanery of his shows and the shows' innovative success, and between Barnum's bombast and the business acumen that recognized in publicity itself a new and expanding national market.

The art of boasting illustrates the difference in these competing narratives. Howells's novel is able to recognize Lapham's tendency to brag as a vernacular trait with its own species of charm. The reader's guide in this respect is Lapham's daughter Penelope, whose affectionate mimicking of Lapham's boasts manages to convey both her better social judgment and her filial loyalty. No reader of Howells, however, can doubt the fact that Lapham's bragging is a liability – not because it is a sign of bad character, but because Lapham is unconscious of the fact that he boasts and therefore blind to its effects on others' view of him. Every lapse into boasting proves that he lacks the asset that counts the most in Howells's Boston, the capacity of cultural discernment. Bragging is an art in *The Rise of Silas Lapham*, but it is not Lapham's art; it is the reflection of Howells's art as author. But for Barnum, in contrast, bragging is a self-conscious art of considerable complexity. Readers credit Barnum with knowing and exploiting the varying kinds and effects of boasting and recognize the difference between his self-publicized hubris and his profitable mastery of the arts of publicity, the latter as sophisticated as the former is bombastic.

Barnum's account of the building of his new house, for instance, is a study in the manipulation of different forms of self-glorification. As Barnum's readers knew (and Barnum knew they knew), a boastful show of modesty was a prerequisite for any extended self-vaunting. "In deciding upon the kind of house to be erected," Barnum writes, "I determined to consult convenience and comfort. I cared little for style, and my wife cared less." Readers would have recognized Barnum's wink when, in the very next paragraph, he informs readers that the very "style" for this homey domicile was "the Pavilion erected by George IV," the "only specimen of Oriental architecture in England." Barnum calls his estate "Iranistan," a choice that, like the structure itself, stands as a permanent boast. But bragging can neutralize its own offenses if it feeds curiosity. Barnum's account of building the house satisfies his readers' desire to know the details of his extravagance (the real offense would be to withhold them). He describes the furniture, the "expensive water works," and the grounds, with their stables, conservatories, and outer buildings ("all perfect in their kind"), including the "many hundreds" of transplanted trees. If he withholds the most desirable fact, the mansion's actual cost, he offers the next best thing: the preposterous fantasy of possessing an indifference to cost. "The whole was built and established literally 'regardless of expense,' for I had no desire even to ascertain the entire cost. All I cared to know was that it suited me." He ends the passage with a self-deprecating boast, which resolves in a pleasing key any potentially dissonant notes in the self-aggrandizing performance: "When the name 'Iranistan' was announced, a waggish New York editor syllabled it, I-ran-i-stan, and gave as the interpretation that 'I ran a long time before I could stan!'"

In all, the swagger works because Barnum wholly controls it. Like all lovable rogues, he charms because he doesn't hide his sins but dresses them to best effect as an added seduction. The rhetorical performance is also an index to Barnum's cutting-edge business savvy. The description of the house – like the house itself – turns expenditure into profit, as the structure becomes an advertisement for Barnum's enterprises (a drawing of the house headed his stationery) and a sign of success itself. Responsive readers consumed the boastful writing as entertainment at the same time as they studied the book as a manual for career success.

The construction of a millionaire's house is also a central episode in *The Rise of Silas Lapham*. Howells's genius in this plot development is to uncover precisely what a figure like Barnum must suppress if he is to remain in control of his own self-display, namely, the fear of class humiliation. Barnum's narrative conjures for his readers a picture of the showman giving decisive instructions to his master architect. Lapham's architect, in contrast, hearing the rich man's plans for materials and floor designs, is barely able "to conceal the shudder which they must have sent through him." The "shudder" is not concealed from readers, of course; for readers, that glimpse of the architect's aversion is offered them as a sign of recognition of their own superior discernment. To read the novel is to find oneself privy to the discriminations of feeling, crosscurrents of taste, and finely calibrated responses that are wholly invisible to Lapham. Readers also recognize the limits to some highly cultivated tastes. When the Brahmin observer Bromfield Corey remarks upon the "bestial darkness of the great mass of people," his overrefined views, like Lapham's coarser ones, become an object of critical scrutiny, an example of perception without feeling. Most significantly, the reader's position of higher discernment makes Lapham himself transparent, opening to view the panic and embarrassment that Lapham wants desperately to keep hidden from more cultivated observers (his ignorance about whether to wear gloves to a dinner-party at the Coreys' home is a prolonged misery, but "he would rather die than ask this question" of his young employee, Tom Corey). Lapham's own series of "shudders" – and these are far more deeply felt – are a record of the distress of a self-made man made helpless by his own upward mobility. Readers are exposed to the "agonies" of his social uncertainty, the risks of self-exposure that "made Lapham sick." His own desires are also self-imposed taboos. When Lapham's wife warns him against acting on his deep wish that their daughter marry Tom Corey, he recoils, "shuddering at the utterance of hopes and ambitions which a man hides with shame."

The house is an emblem of Lapham's insufficient taste and not, as with Barnum's, of the prowess of his money. But the house's fate also shows the way Howells recognizes manners as a crucial ingredient of capitalism. Taste is a species of wealth. When the house burns down, in a fire accidentally set by Lapham himself, it is not a symbol of the futility of worldly vanity, as a moral interpretation might have it. To the contrary, the sudden ruin is a witness that Lapham lacks sufficient cultural capital. Building the new house has drained him of his money but, more to the point, it has overextended his very limited powers of taste. The property disaster is counterpart to his personal meltdown at the Coreys' dinner-party, where, much like his inadvertent sparking of the fire, his social anxiety leads to accidental drunkenness and his drunkenness to an exposure of his inadequate manners. In Boston, Lapham was not a man of means and he never was; he possessed only money. Late in the novel Howells revives a subplot that permits Lapham a moral recovery to counter his economic and social ruin. As in many Howells novels, the moral resolution has a certain prominence but also carries a strong sense of extraneousness. It is hard to deny that the novel's real dramatic energies lie in Lapham's crucible of taste as the inside story of Gilded Age capitalism.

Lapham's deepest struggles actually stem from the rewards of wealth. If Barnum's *Struggles and Triumphs* is a hymn to the era's new ways of wealth, *Silas Lapham* is its cautionary tale. But it is not clear exactly what the novel is warning against – is it a condemnation of the excessive desires and errant speculations of post-Civil War capitalism? Or is it a red flag for a discerning reader, a tacit pedagogy in which the Lapham "type" is the reader's antitype to warn against the pathos of cultural ignorance? This is one distinction the novel will not draw. The novel seems to protest the harsh terms of failure visited upon the Laphams in a capitalist culture, but the specter of Lapham's failure also generates competitive energies from within the same narrative, energies that compel the reader to seek success where Lapham fails. Sympathy with

Lapham is possible only if the reader disavows any likeness to him; to move past sympathy towards a feeling of identity (as a sentimental fiction would ask) is either to invite self-contempt or to refuse the novel's own terms of Realist distinction. Lapham's fear of humiliation serves as a kind of vaccination: his anxieties are the reader's protection, his failure the reader's advance. Howells's novels are among the most brilliant anatomies of class anxieties, feelings that had intensified in the economic boom of the later nineteenth century. But these energies are emotions his novels incite as well as analyze. As a reading experience, *The Rise of Silas Lapham* can be said to consist of moments of marked or unmarked "shudders" as a system of internally felt distinctions. The cumulative effect is to create Lapham's rounded character as an object of the reader's complex discriminations. The secondary effect, less overt but of a more fundamental significance, is the process that fashions its ideal reader as the discriminating subject, a process enacted through internal cues, deflected embarrassment, and sharpened literary apprehension.

The desire that governs Barnum's reader – the open, unembarrassed desire for upward mobility – is what the reader of Howells must most strongly disavow. But from another angle, this difference is also a resemblance. In its way, *Silas Lapham* is, like Barnum's book, a handbook that offers rules for emulation. As one would expect, Howells's rules are nothing like those of Barnum, who codifies his advice as positive axioms ("The Art of Making Money") and submits his own triumphs as proof positive of their correctness. Howells's rules are never stated – they exist only in negative form as the unspoken directives for the reader's acts of distanced empathy and disavowal. But it is no coincidence that the characters who are the novel's keenest social readers, Penelope Lapham and Tom Corey, are also the characters most clearly positioned for success. By the end of the novel, Penelope and Tom appear poised to make distinction pay. Tom has recognized the ironic provincialism of his own superior Brahmin tastes; absolving Lapham's shame and marrying Penelope opens up for Tom expansive prospects in the more glamorous form of international trade. And Penelope earns her "rise" into a higher social stratum by making a marriage match equal to her own gifts of sharp perception.

Howells's novel exhibits a culture of money. But it is also a document from within that culture that partakes of the same economics of cultural taste it critically portrays, even as the cultural dimensions of American capitalism were increasingly troubling to Howells. His views of both life and literature became darker in the years after he published *The Rise of Silas Lapham*. Labor unrest and economic strife were personally distressing to him, almost as much for the feeling of helplessness they seemed to produce in him as for the suffering they caused for others. Howells was almost alone among American intellectuals in his public opposition to the hanging of the anarchists charged in the Haymarket riot of 1887. His profound grief at his daughter Winifred's death in 1889 was another darkening influence. Howells's biographer calls him an "ambidextrous" writer; he continued to write farces and other light fare in this period, but his novels show a new sense of social dislocation and drift even as he attempts to represent through his Realist art an even larger social landscape. In *A Hazard of New Fortune* (1890) and *The World of Chance* (1893), the costs and violent conflicts of an economics of culture would come in for direct examination. The realities of American life, as much as "unreal" mass forms, were beginning to seem distorted and incongruous. In an oft-quoted 1888 letter to Henry James, Howells wrote that "'America' seems to be the most grotesquely illogical thing under the sun":

After fifty years of optimistic content with "civilization" and its ability to come out all right in the end, I now abhor it, and feel that it is coming out all wrong in the end, unless it bases itself anew on a real equality. Meantime, I wear a fur-lined overcoat, and live in all the luxury my money can buy.

As his dark self-satire suggests, Howells's own aesthetic discernment threatened to symbolize not a future social cohesion but a continuing history of inequality. His belief in the benevolent cultivation of consciousness had begun to seem ever more distant from the dream of a "republic of letters," leaving taste and distinction as capacities that amount to little more than an eye for a fine overcoat.

HENRY JAMES AND THE CIVIC IMAGINATION

The rift Howells faced between his principles of Realism and an unrealized dream of civil unity is instructive. In formal terms, the rift was foundational. Realism's reliance on the mass forms it opposes ensures that it never achieves the closed mastery it seeks. But that dilemma also motivates the Realist vigilance for maintaining perceptions of cultural difference, and the process of erecting and displaying the difference between literary values and mass forms is what the Realist novel itself performs. Lack of mastery was thus the energizing tension through which Realist writers created increasingly complex literary codes of distinction. Writers achieved their distinctive styles by risking – at times even courting – a confusion in readers' minds between their use of literary irony and the cultural objects they ironize. Charles Chesnutt and Edith Wharton offer critical portraits of social worlds (the South and the coteries of the rich) that were already objects of mass fascination and, by doing so, flirted with the voyeuristic market desires they mean to critique. The exotic reversals and elaborations of ironic distinctions in James's moral dramas often spin away to form a melodrama of their own, an aesthetic effect that made many contemporary readers suspect James himself of moral perversity. Henry Adams, whose novels and early essays endorse Howells's faith in analytic distinctions, later finds apocalyptic collapse in that very analytic cast of mind.

While the "analytic instinct" that, in James's words, "rises supreme" in the later nineteenth century failed to dominate cultural tastes, then, it allowed Howells and others to reinvent fiction writing as a special vocation and a vital cultural authority, an authority structured from within by the modernity it profoundly, warily examined. This position in the social landscape, more than any set of features or unified worldview, gives high literary Realism its shape and force. Yet the question that haunts Howells's vision of a "grotesquely illogical" America remains: high literary culture acquired authority, but to what end? The critical force of Realist analysis is more difficult to pin down than its historical origin and position. For the novelist, to recognize a "unity of taste" as a wholly quixotic goal would likely lead to Howells's late sense of futility. On the other hand, to concede that talk of a civic dimension to high art is disingenuous would be to accept and embrace high art as an instrument of social control. And yet to give up any claim of art's social relevance would reduce high literary values to nothing more than the self-satisfied preferences of the elite.

A threat of an impasse of this sort lurks within high literary Realism almost from its inception. The actual "America of Art," as it turned out, preferred the commercial arts of mass culture; could the "analytic impulse" cultivated in Realism then achieve anything other than a sense of disappointment or disdain? Henry James, the artist who developed the most analytic narrative style, was also the observer who offered the most far-sighted suggestions about the "possible fine employments" for literature in an age of mass culture. His ideas on the "civic use of the imagination" never persuaded him to look on mass forms as benign; James continued to indict the mass press and other institutions for breeding debased motives and mischief of all kinds. In one of his harshest condemnations of newspapers, for instance, he wrote to his brother William that behind the US press coverage of the Spanish–American war of 1898 he could perceive "nothing but the madness, the passion, the hideous clumsiness of rage, the mechanical reverberation; and I echo with all my heart your denouncement of the foul criminality of the screeching newspapers. They have long since become, for me, the danger that overtops all others." Yet it is also in this moment that James begins to write essays that meditate on a rather different, less hostile role for the "high aesthetic temper" in the changed landscape of mass expression.

In "The Question of the Opportunities" (1898), James never drops what he calls his "slightly affrighted" view of the "flood of books" claiming their place in American literature, for he recognizes that their vast numbers and the expanded reading public they address have altered forever what "literature" actually is. The "comparatively small library of books" that defined literary value in the past can no longer serve as an adequate measure. The quantity of print and the "huge American public" that consumes it have made fluid and unfixed the very qualities that constitute the literary: "Whether, in the conditions we consider, the supply [of texts in print] shall achieve sufficient vitality and distinction really to be sure of itself as literature" is all but impossible to say, especially when "all this depends on what we take it into our head to *call* literature." But at the same time as he records his apprehension, James emphasizes his sense of excitement – "the drama and the bliss, when not the misery" – at viewing the dizzying changes. The very contingency of literary value, James stresses, means the possibility of unexpected creativity, of "new light struck out by the material itself."

The prospect that altogether new literary values might spring from mass conditions brings a sense of critical exhilaration, an escape from "foregone conclusions and narrow rules." To be sure, a reading audience counted in the millions ("or rather the fast-arriving billion") brings no guarantee of literary achievement – and for James, we have seen, it brings positive dangers, such as the "mechanical reverberation" of the war lust he heard in the American press. Yet whatever the risks, for James such massive numbers are also certain to bring artistic "opportunities": "But if the billion give the pitch of production and circulation, they do something else besides; they hang before us a wide picture of opportunities . . . It is impossible not to entertain with patience and curiosity the presumption that life so colossal must break into expression at points of proportionate frequency. These places, these moments will be the chances."

The forms of expression likely to emerge from such conditions, moreover, represent not just possibilities for fresh literary illumination but also a new kind of literary field. Although the gargantuan scale of print production is likely to foster "extravagantly general" writing, James argues that the same threat of homogenization may well encourage counteracting strains of innovation, strains that "may get individual publics positively more sifted and evolved than anywhere else." The introduction of plural "publics" here is crucial. James imagines multiple kinds of literary value able to coexist, related yet distinct, on a plane "subdivided as a chess-board, with each little square confessing only to its own *kind* of accessibility." The metaphor of a chessboard conveys James's attempt to think his way past a purely hierarchical scheme of literary value without severing the link between literature and cultural criticism. James's chessboard figure insists that literary value must remain social; an image of congruent literary "varieties" permits him to conceive of a reading public with at least potential communication among its parts, even as it recognizes that the force of "individual genius" may work in different ways to draw in disparate kinds of readers. Accepting multiple "varieties" of the literary means the notion of a uniform system of privileged literary representation – a Realist museum – must be sacrificed. But the sacrifice brings returns: the more dynamic model of a multiform field of literature developed through a creative "reaction" to mass leveling is able to preserve a critical function for literature now recognized as contingent.

James would explore a similar notion of the creative or "productive" reaction in his Preface to the New York Edition of "The Lesson of the Master" and other tales (1908). The "operative irony" of James's brand of Realism, he asserts, takes as one of its offices the conjuring of the "possible other case," the exceptional act or sentiment that can be imagined within conditions that otherwise favor venality and hypocrisy. Making a "record" in fiction of the "honorable and productive case," he proposes, represents "the civic use of the imagination": "How can one consent to make a picture of the preponderant futilities and vulgarities and miseries of life without the impulse to exhibit as well from time to time, some fine example of the reaction, the opposition, or the escape?" Irony here favors the better or nobler instance rather than the lesser. Fiction in such a case has not abjured the actual, nor is it blind to what James calls the bloody "arrears" of history. But in recording the "possible other case," fiction becomes the imaginary history of the could-be-real. It conjures on the page a saner, nobler version of civil society that is conceivable within already existing conditions.

Literary possibility is also the keynote in "The Lesson of Balzac" (1905). James claims in this essay that a "critical spirit" can survive in the novel despite the genre's transformation into a mass "article of commerce." The commercial machinery of innumerable publishers, editors, interviewers, and producers, he asserts, has made the novel a thing of "easy manufacture" and a "bankrupt and discredited art." In these conditions, James turns to the example of Balzac to recover the figure of an "emulous fellow-worker," of the novelist as a "craftsman" and the novel as a "handmade" object of deliberate care. In the course of the essay, however, James's most insistent lament – that at present an enormous "array of producers and readers" together generate "production uncontrolled" and uncritical – gradually becomes his most striking and hopeful suggestion. All the talk of producers and production prompts James to realize that a novel can be conceptualized not as an object at all but as a practice or activity, one that is necessarily shared by readers as much as by the novel's author. The "faculty of attention" that makes for the vitality of the worthy novel, James argues, is replicated in those readers prepared to go as far as the author in the critical pursuit of a given literary subject.

Balzac is thus the "fellow-worker" of any individual who rises to the bait of his "intellectual adventure." No other novelist, for James, equals Balzac in offering an "intensity of educative practice." The practice is never without the reward of pleasure; James insists that Balzac offers "entertainment" as much as instruction. But so comprehensive and penetrating is the picture of life produced by Balzac that an extraordinary density of "significance, relation and value" is opened for the reader's analysis:

It is a prodigious multiplication of values, and thereby a prodigious entertainment of the vision – on the condition the vision can bear it. Bearing it – that is *our* bearing it – is a serious matter, for the appeal is truly to that faculty of attention out of which we are educating ourselves as hard as we possibly can.

By reconceiving the novel as a literary practice rather than an object, James presents literature as the creative labor that produces a public as it multiplies relations of shared "significance." Hence the essay's concluding image that recasts the space of the novel from a museum or exhibit to a collective workshop: "It will strike you perhaps," James notes to his audience, "that I speak as if we all, as if *you* all, without exception were novelists, haunting the back of the shop, the laboratory, or, more nobly expressed, the inner shrine of the temple; but such assumptions, in this age of print – are perhaps never too wide of the mark." Although James retains his allegiance to the distinctions of literary discernment, the "uncontrolled" production in the age of mass print supplies the very conditions for a collective, indeed a "civic" creativity able to foster multiple publics. There is no single "America of Art" in this vision, no authoritative museum for national tutelage. If he were king of art in America, he might well command otherwise. But James recognizes opportunities as well as costs in the conditions of a mass society. The "great extension of experience and consciousness" that James deems the office of art would only occur through the reality of mass forms and not in spite of them.

3

❦

WOMEN AND REALIST AUTHORSHIP

"IMPUDENT NOVELTIES": WOMEN AND PUBLICITY

In his *Atlantic* essay on the 1869 Boston theater season, "The New Taste in Theatricals," Howells described the actresses impersonating men in the popular comic plays called burlesques. Although "they were not like men, [they] were in most things as unlike women, and seemed creatures of a kind of alien sex, parodying both. It was certainly a shocking thing to look at them with their horrible prettiness, their archness in which was no charm, their grace which put to shame." For Howells, these cross-dressing performers were vivid proof of popular entertainment's ability to deform even the most fundamental of human categories, the identity of sex. By creating the illusion of an "alien sex," neither woman nor man, the burlesque impersonations stood out as one of the "monstrous and artificial" inventions that Howells found everywhere conspicuous in commercial culture. Yet, as Howells surely knew, the burlesque shows told a truth, even if it was the skewed truth of a visual pun. The "unreal" creatures on stage, that is, bespoke a new social reality: the striking presence of women in public life. As the male-costumed actresses moved and spoke on stage, they evoked the recent entry of women into what had been male roles and traditionally male social spaces outside of the home.

The increasing participation of middle-class women in public life was one of the most striking features of post-Civil War American culture. Observers of this phenomenon stressed the changed look of American society, its transformed countenance. In the workplace, one journalist writes, there is "scarcely an occupation once confined almost exclusively to men in which women are not now conspicuous." Commercial consumption, too, had a female face. The advent of the highly theatrical world of department stores, for instance, was perceived as a feminine transformation: "The lady-element of Broadway is one of its most dazzling features." Sociologist Thorstein Veblen even contended that the essential purpose of the middle-class wife was no longer to nurture and instruct in private but to advertise affluence in public through her clothes, accessories, and manners, so even as wives, women had become public creatures.

In 1904 when Henry James returned to the United States after a long absence living abroad, he described an American "scene" in which the presence of the "new" woman had become "the sentence written largest in the American sky."

As James's image of sky-writing suggests, women were one of the "impudent novelties" of modern life whose new visibility provoked as well as dazzled. Indifferent to traditional forms and cultural authorities, such novelties pushed their way into public view, taking shape in theatrical shows and urban street scenes that seemed to rival or mock – or to simply ignore – the more composed portraits of modern life penned by literary authors. In the United States during this period it was not the elite authors who composed the culture's most recognizable features for a national audience, it was rather a burgeoning commercial world – stage shows, advertising, mass-market fiction, journalism, and, sometime later, the medium of film – that made most legible the features in which a national audience would see itself writ large. For all their outsized exaggerations, the commercial expressions of post-Civil War society often provided the earliest record of new social realities. This precociousness in popular culture is especially evident when it comes to portrayals of those who were appearing for the first time in the established spaces of public life – not only women, perceived as an "alien sex" when they entered previously male-dominated social spaces, but also additional classes of what might be called alienated American subjects. Such alien public persons include the African-American citizens created after the formal end to slavery, the foreigners who immigrated to American cities in masses, and the Native Americans, those supposedly "vanished" Americans, who returned to national visibility in Wild West shows and sentimental narratives. Despite its giddy disregard for mimetic fidelity and a near-reflexive racism, mass culture nevertheless represented the presence of these Americans with an immediacy that high literary writing, with its careful distinctions and measured perspectives, never grasped.

Popular spectacles, moreover, were never merely representations or detached images. A commodity itself, public visibility was one of the strongest forces transforming social life. The dynamic energies of the new mass culture – energies from the magnified spaces of commercial display, from the audiences created through mass circulation as well as specialized publishing niches, from the transformation of cityscapes by sudden accumulations of wealth and enormous new foreign populations – these forces were themselves actively remaking what Howells called the "civic relations" of postbellum society. For this reason, the commitment in high art to representing civic relations as a social whole meant that authors had to confront the mass culture they distrusted.

As Howells's distress at the "monstrous" actresses suggests, the confrontation with popular spectacles could be dissonant, even hostile. Yet social novelties such as the public woman are also part of the very structure of high literary narrative, crucial to its internal circuit of reciprocal shock and mastery. High Realist writing achieves its impressive literary power through an armature of historicizing techniques: sharply etched social types, disciplined categories of place and time, the interlocking narrative links able to join disparate worlds and populations in a fullness of social vision. These governing techniques extend protocols of disciplinary reason into the territories of literature. They evoke a secular understanding that pushes aside the religiously derived symbology of earlier fiction and poetry. They master a social vision that successfully asserts authority over the often flat or crass representations in popular forms. But precisely because high Realism is so successful at bringing a certain rationalizing discipline to the work of literary imagining, it repeatedly finds itself confronting what James calls "impudent novelties," the unsorted materials that fall outside of established protocols of representation. Like Howells's stare at the "horrible prettiness" of the female performers, high Realism is vulnerable to a recurrent shock from phenomena it encounters as disordered and unreal. Crucially, though, such objects are not obstacles that hinder creativity. To the contrary, the body of literature aspiring to high culture can be said to form itself through a process of careful cultivation of the shock of the new. The public woman, the new Negro citizen, the curious unspoken speech of advertising and headlines, the strange living personhood of the corporation, the clothing and furniture and objects that suggest a new density of meaning in things, the extremities of human psychology that seem to spring from modern conditions – these and other hitherto unclassified phenomena, at odds with established civil relations, are the perceived riddles of culture that spur a high literary creativity. Inventing intricate styles of analysis, authors develop an aesthetic reach – sometimes in highly ironic or politically pressured forms such as Henry Adams's dispossessed "manikin" or W. E. B. Du Bois's "double consciousness" – able to turn cultural shock into the polished exhibits of high art and new canons of critical distinction.

Perhaps no single issue was as important to the formation of high Realism as the social identity of women. A figure of charged and contested value, the American woman became one of the focal points through which a high literary culture defined its characteristic styles and its critical authority. In contemporary social debates, it is important to remember, talk about "woman" referred to the lives of only a relatively limited group: middle-class white women, who were lucky enough to receive (or, less happily, merely to desire) the kind of education their brothers received, women who might contemplate paid work as a route to autonomy or status rather than a means to survival. These women and their concerns acquired a capital-letter conspicuousness – a startling legibility as the Woman Question, a revolutionary profile as the New Woman, an international publicity as the American Girl, a threatening incarnation as an atavistic Amazon. The fact that working-class women, present all along in the world of labor and in city streets, did not figure in these debates about womanhood is a telling omission. Their elision tells us that it was not simply the physical presence of women in offices and department stores that was at issue. The newness of the New Woman, rather, concerned a kind of status or agency previously attributed to men and now conspicuously claimed by some middle-class women who were restive in the role that writer Charlotte Perkins Gilman called the "amiable but abortive agent" of middle-class wife. The question of women's agency, their relation to social forces and paths of power, is one of the profound subjects through which high literary Realism develops its characteristic repertoire of narrative styles and patterns. The puzzle of women's agency is a vexation and a motive for close literary analysis, a spur to develop methods of narrative dissection able to reach new depths of human interiority. As a topic in letters, women are a touchstone for gauging the sensibilities and the national health of a nation now resolutely commercial. Gender and sexuality are more than themes in this corpus; they are also points of leverage for the cultural authority of high American art through which social urgency could join forces with stylistic innovation.

The highly public profiles women gained in the 1870s and 1880s had an unlikely origin. In antebellum culture, women had developed a distinct sense of womanhood that was private and domestic. A spiritualized identity, the femininity they invoked had its essence in a piety defined against sexuality, in domestic instincts that were opposed to marketplace calculations. But in the name of this transcendent femininity, middle-class women laid claim to a sphere of action that extended their nominally domestic work into new territory outside of the home. The Civil War was an important catalyst for accelerating this change. Answering civic needs during wartime, women gained administrative expertise by supplying hospitals, serving on sanitary commissions, and raising money for charities. Feminine nurturing was cast as a national resource. With ordinary politics suspended, public life behind the battle lines was reconfigured as a home life – albeit a divided one – in need of healing services.

In Clara Barton's memories of her ordeals as a battlefield nurse, published in the posthumous *Life of Clara Barton* (1915), the feminine arts of caring for the sick make up a field of work that is finally indistinguishable from male soldiering: "I was strong and thought I might go to the rescue of the men who fell." The confusions and bloody horrors of wartime make for a liminal period in which gender roles are less vigilantly maintained. "If you chanced to feel, that the positions I occupied were rough and unseemly for a *woman*," Barton writes, "I can only reply that they were rough and unseemly for *men*." War also permits women an acceptable posture of defiance. In *A Southern Woman's Story* (1879), Phoebe Yates Pember proudly remembers that "the women of the South had been openly and violently rebellious from the moment they thought their state's rights touched." Still, when Pember was appointed superintending matron at a Richmond, Virginia, hospital, she began her work with a fear that "such a life would be injurious to the delicacy and refinement of a lady – that her nature would become deteriorated and her sensibilities blunted." Hands-on experience running the hospital in fact does change Pember. But the work likewise alters her traditional understanding of feminine capacities, and she soon comes to resent the "ill-concealed disgust" of the men who chafe under her supervision in the workplace. New public duties, assumed temporarily during wartime, could not but effect permanent changes at the level of feeling and perception, transformations that in turn had the potential to reorder institutions.

An understanding of womanhood that was still keyed to hearth and home, then, helped middle-class white women extend putatively feminine roles and skills into the world beyond the household. The emergencies of wartime became established features of postbellum society. Women's clubs, educational unions, and Christian associations organized in the 1860s and 1870s helped to define the emergent urban world as a field that needed the perpetual services of women. That perceived need in turn prompted a call for institutions that could educate and train women to so serve. Demands for more overtly political powers for women followed as well, an unsurprising next step for women who were, after all, already hard at work in the sphere of social services.

Just as a domestic identity helped women become increasingly public actors, a parallel irony operated in the world of letters. In antebellum United States, the short stories, sketches, and novels written by women made up an increasingly large proportion of the published works until, by the 1850s, women authors supplied much of the market for fiction. But women writers also changed that market. Domestic fiction by women helped establish a new kind of book, one that was capable of selling ten or twenty times the number of copies that other successful works managed to sell. Authors such as Susan Warner, Harriet Beecher Stowe, Catherine Sedgwick, Fanny Fern, E. D. E. N. Southworth, and Maria Cummins became public celebrities by writing best-sellers about the spiritual power of the private home ("all that is pure and saving in the midst of the selfishness of man: one love, one hearth, one home") and in the process realizing a public audience unmatched in size or in the potential for profit. These women authors repeatedly effaced their professional status, taking pseudonyms, disclaiming any aspirations to high art, and expressing anxiety about their public exposure ("I have a perfect horror of appearing in print," as Sedgwick wrote) – all disavowals that actually aided their rise as public figures. While their ambivalence about publicity was no doubt real, their disclaimers about fame also made that fame possible: only by circulating a private, spiritualized model of women's identity did women authors achieve public attention both for themselves and for their vision of womanhood.

Popular domestic fiction also gave women a worldly visibility in even more material ways. Domestic authors compared their literary production to needle-work and other intimate fireside occupations, yet their commercial success ensured that their names and faces became icons in a mass marketplace. For authors like Stowe and Fern, the machinery of advertising, sales figures, bio-graphical sketches, lithographs, tours and personal appearances, press sight-ings, and celebrity photographs made the women's home lives, and even their bodies and styles of dress, into objects for public display and consumption. Unauthorized reprinting of their essays and stories produced self-perpetuating circuits of publicity; like their visual image, their words spread through an almost automatic, decentralized production that further heightened their pub-lic recognition. The champions of women's spiritual, home-centered identity acquired a status that was decidedly public, commercial, and often political.

For many traditionalists, this change amounted to an alarming female inva-sion through print and image. As one writer, the Rev. James Weir, described it, "we see forms and phases of [women's] degeneration thickly scattered through-out all circles of society, in the plays which we see performed in our theatres, and in the books and papers published daily throughout the land." As Weir's warning suggests, public visibility for women was not limited to hearthside writers. The dancer Fanny Elssler and singer Jenny Lind were among the first female performers in America to acquire national celebrity through new net-works of mass publicity. The personal lives of stage performers such as Lydia Thompson and Ada Isaacs Menken began to supply material for secondary dra-mas that ran in syndicated gossip columns. In the footsteps of reformers like Stowe, women lecturers became celebrities whose activities on behalf of vari-ous causes also brought attention to their lives. The anti-lynching activist Ida B. Wells and the feminist Charlotte Perkins Gilman were as often condemned as lauded, but both responses heightened the women's public profiles.

In a multitude of forms, femininity thrived in modern publicity. To observers like the Rev. Weir, however, the public nature of print or the stage necessar-ily compromised a woman's true identity. Francis Leiber, an influential writer on political topics, declared that "woman loses in the same degree her natural character . . . as she enters into publicity." Henry James gives the same sentiment to his character Basil Ransom, a Southern traditionalist, in *The Bostonians* (1885). When Basil observes Verena Tarrant give a public speech, the sight of a "virginal" young woman addressing a crowded assembly produces for Basil a paradox of "sweet grotesqueness." For Basil the incongruity of female subjectivity showcased in a public exhibition was not just an irony but a freakish provocation. Howells's reaction to the "horrible prettiness" of the female burlesque troupe was rooted in the same feeling of witnessing a public transgression of a fundamentally private or domestic female identity.

There is a note of gender panic if not of misogyny in the chorus of voices raised against women's increased public visibility. But something important distinguishes their condemnation from earlier currents of animus against women. After all, the conservative critics, whose ranks included women as well as men, claimed to be the defenders of a spiritually superior sex, not a low or inferior one. Their contempt was not for women but for their degradation in the new media of modern publicity, the largely ungoverned machinery of image and print that was producing what Weir calls the "thickly scattered" representations of and by women. Still, it is difficult, and at times impossible, to tease apart contemporary anti-woman sentiments from concurrent anxieties about the raft of new cultural technologies that churned profit out of the words and images "published daily throughout the land." For the things that most worried critics about the popular culture industry matched closely with what was most worrisome about women: both, it was feared, had a susceptibility to unchecked fantasy, a tendency to wander from the real. Precisely in their spiritual nature, women were apt to discount or simply fail to apprehend the necessities that determined worldly systems and orders. Similarly, the productions of mass culture, beholden only to profit, were blithely indifferent to either traditional social orders or to the rationalized orders advanced by science and professional experts. Hence the widespread tendency to see the mass-culture industry itself as feminine in nature and feminizing in cultural effect, where "feminine" signifies the unconstrained power of feelings and wishes to overwhelm the order of the real. Popular culture was, in the words of one male writer, the "iron Madonna who strangles in her fond embrace" the true American culture that concerned realists and intellectuals.

Was this association of women with mass culture anything more than a transferring of disdain for women to a new sphere of production? Certainly, the unease of male writers at a seeming feminization of culture shaped the development of an American movement of high Realism. The desire to assert a contrasting professional virility for fiction-writing can be detected in virtually every element of the Realist novel – the defining plots, styles, and characters – while it also leaves writers like Howells, James, and later male successors struggling to court an audience that includes many women readers. In *My Literary Passions* (1895), Howells observes uneasily that "literature gives one no more certain station in the world of men's activities." While Howells's novels were located solidly in the familiar fictional territories of middle-class family life, his plots are designed with an eye to sternly correcting the courtship and marriage conventions of popular fiction. Major novels such as *A Modern Instance* (1882) and *Indian Summer* (1886), for instance, are dedicated to anatomizing the unhappy results of an ill-conceived marriage. In Realist novels, the activity of novel-reading itself is usually a feminine preoccupation and a suspect one; like Flaubert's Madame Bovary, young women who love novels are usually headed for bad marriages and probably worse.

Quite clearly, then, anxiety about the cultural exposure of women – their exposure *in* popular culture as well as *to* it – is an animating energy in high Realist literature, as is unease about the power and reach of new mass-culture industries. But we miss the true import of these animating energies if we fail to notice that they were as much a conscious resource for writers as a phobic reaction. In high Realism a historical sense of sexual vertigo is subject to a profound, self-conscious analysis. Male panic is as much on display in this writing as the female exposure that produces it. Moreover, the disorienting new publicity for women was a provocative subject for women writers just as it was for men, and though the anti-popular values of Realism closed out avenues for some women writers, they helped create professional opportunities for others. Above all, the association of women with popular culture made women *representative* in an Emersonian sense. If women were exemplary cultural objects, they were also a crucial topic for exploring the vicissitudes of the thinking, feeling human subject who faced the far more theatrical, more mediated social world of the later nineteenth century. Within Realism, it is largely women and women's stories that pose the most profound meditations on human agency and the authenticity of the self that were the Realists' chief aesthetic concern.

Howells's first-person account of his confrontation with the "shocking" womanhood staged in burlesque plays offers an instructive point of entry: what can read like a phobic confession is in fact a canny delineation of the sexual dynamics and obsessions with subjectivity that would structure high cultural art. Howells makes no attempt to disguise his distress at the production. The "prettiness" of conventional feminine faces and figures performing aggressive male postures and gestures is for him a "horror to look upon." One actress dressed as a prince "had a raucous voice, an insolent twist of the mouth, and a terrible trick of defying her enemies by standing erect, chin up, hand on hip, and right foot advanced, patting the floor. It was impossible, even in the orchestra seats, to look at her in this attitude and not shrink before her." As Howells's emphasis on his own act of looking suggests, the performance requires a literal seeing – a forced revision or recognition – of women as active agents. After decades of rhetoric underscoring an ethereal, transcendent femininity, the sight of women possessing erect, defiant bodies and insubordinate voices makes them seem an altogether different sex. One woman who had appeared to shrink in the opening sketch "seemed quite another being when she came on later as a radiant young gentleman in pink silk hose and nothing of feminine modesty in her dress except the very low corsage." The transformation did not come from any illusion that the actresses were men – if anything, the body-revealing costumes emphasized their identity as women. Rather, it was the comic but pointed sight of women inhabiting the role of the worldly, self-possessing and self-asserting agent that converted the performers into an "alien sex."

Howells is confounded by the change, as much for what it reveals as what it distorts. The theatrical staging seems to unveil a species of interior truth, not in spite of the artifice of the performance but through it. "A strange and compassionable satisfaction beamed from her face," Howells writes of one of the actresses. "It was evident that this sad business was the poor thing's *forte*." The theatrical setting, Howells confesses, allows for glimpses of intimate insight. At one point the actresses add to their male imposture a racial mimicry of minstrel dances, a double impersonation that reveals an "infuriate grace and a fierce delight very curious to look upon." At the same time that the exhibition affords insight, however, it unsettles basic cognitive categories. When the self is unmoored from conventional sex and racial identities, the foundation of subjectivity is for Howells thrown into question. The stage role seemed to bring one woman such pleasure that she must be "at something of a loss to identify herself when personating a woman off the stage." The power of play-acting – of "personating" – cannot be limited to the stage, leading Howells to ponder the actress's offstage identity, only to recognize her stage role as the more fitting – because for her happier – context for the woman she is.

Similarly, Howells's own identity as a man, as he openly portrays it, begins to seem a corresponding act of impersonation. In the face of the "fierce delight" of the female performers, Howells describes his own reaction as a parody of traditional male agency. The sight of an actress who, "coldly yielding herself to the manager's ideas of the public taste, stretched herself on a green baize bank with her feet toward us or did a similar grossness," evokes a chivalrous alarm: "It was hard to keep from crying aloud in protest, that she need not do it; that nobody really expected or wanted it of her. Nobody? Alas! there were people there . . . who plainly did expect it, and who were loud in their applauses of the chief actress." As if joining the performance in a hapless role of his own, Howells casts himself as a male rescuer only to underscore the absurdity of his response in a mock-heroic self-portrait.

Howells's self-scripted melodrama of gender anxiety, then, points to a larger concern about the authenticity of the modern self, a concern widely expressed by middle-class Americans during this era. As portrayed in Howells's essay, the paradoxical artifice of a stage performance makes selfhood and human agency at once more transparent, more legible, and yet more subject to mutability. The shock of seeing an "alien" femininity, even in a comic stage play, actually provides for a new and striking inside view of male and female selves. At the same time, that interior view opens strange and disquieting questions that challenge conventional notions about the self. Howells is clearly unnerved by the funhouse distortions of the burlesque, but he also experiences the strong draw of a femininity electrified by the medium of publicity and its ability to reveal as well as refract. His fascination *and* his moral worry both reflect a broader cultural absorption in what one historian has called the "new theatricality of middle-class culture after 1850."

Howells's essay on theatrical taste speaks to new social conditions for which theater and role-playing had become primary tropes. The rapid urbanization of the later nineteenth century did more than multiply the specific media through which the culture communicated with itself. It also changed the nature of everyday social life, eroding the force of familiar social rituals and introducing more unpredictable forms of spectacle in both public and private spaces. The spontaneous dramas of urban street life – unexpected sights, novel accidents, public rows and crimes – share something fundamental with their social opposite, the carefully controlled displays of wealth and status at private dinners or elite sporting events: both kinds of encounters turned face-to-face social transactions into a species of cultural theater. Both public and private spheres were increasingly designed for displaying the self before a society conceived as an audience. These changes, adopted on a mass scale, obviously afforded certain pleasures or satisfactions for large numbers of people; had they not, urban centers and the mass media they produced would never have thrived. But a more spectatorial culture also intensified feelings that the virtues – or, for that matter, the definable vices – of the solid Victorian character were becoming hollow, improvised, inauthentic.

Nowhere were the stakes of such questions clearer for Howells's contemporaries than in matters of gender and sexuality, where it was believed that erotic energies thought to belong to the private sphere would, if exposed in public culture, bring about profound social transformations – either for better or for worse. In Howells's *The Minister's Charge* (1886), for instance, the racy humor of a popular stage play ("a farrago of indecently amusing innuendoes and laughably vile situations") is the central figure for a principle of social "complicity." For Howells the complicity of "actors and audience" in their mutual responsibility for the erotic spectacle comes to stand for the relation between cultural tastes and their ethical results, for the entanglement between individual consumption and the larger polity, the "whole social constitution." "Complicity," then, describes a kind of power in cultural representations that Howells finds troubling: the danger of a theatrical culture is its power to make the citizen by turns an "indifferent spectator" and a confused actor playing out "novel-fed fancies." For Howells, a new kind of cultural representation, the Realist novel, is needed to oppose these theatrical distortions. In this way Howells's musings on theater and the effects of burlesque begin to point up ways that gender organizes the key terms of analysis in high Realism – its terrain of psychological insight as well as exhibition, its reflection on agency as well as social determinacy, its obsession with forms of intimacy as well as with the social estrangement and disguise attributed to popular culture.

These are the oppositional terms of analysis governing James's *The Bostonians* (1885), a novel in which the figure of the public woman is the muse for the postbellum culture of spectacle. *The Bostonians* demonstrates the way Realist insight is won through opposition to a commercial theatricality that nevertheless remains Realism's most potent site for producing social knowledge. As embodied in the novel's protagonist, Verena Tarrant, the female spirituality once defined as domestic and religious in nature has become a public sensation. Under a quasi-occult inspiration, Verena gives rapturous speeches on social topics. For Verena's liberal-minded audiences, the young woman's public spirituality holds no contradiction: her talent for oratory is a feminine "genius" for feeling and speaking that quite naturally should be shared with a world in need of enlightenment about women's rights, the power of love, and other higher truths. For Basil Ransom (the "stiffest of conservatives"), on the other hand, a public femininity is an inherent absurdity. Verena's success before the era's "great popular system" of urban audiences is little more than a commercial and political scam, an "exhibition of enterprise and puffery." Her "genius" is merely the vulgar spiritualism of the mesmerist disguised as "glamor," the vibrancy of a feminine sexual attractiveness that has been improperly placed on display. "It was simply an intensely personal exhibition," Basil insists, "and the person making it happened to be fascinating." Olive Chancellor, a Bostonian, also recognizes the "danger of vulgar exploitation" in Verena's public career. But for Olive, who joins league with radical women reformers, the danger that Verena will fall victim to *private* exploitation – heterosexual marriage – is

even greater. Clearly in love with Verena, Olive gives financial backing to
Verena's career and initiates a domestic intimacy by bringing her to live in her
home, an arrangement akin to the "Boston marriage" that was a recognized
couplehood at the time for two women living under the same roof. For both
Basil and Olive, Verena's "intensely personal" exhibitions have an erotic draw
that is inseparable from a troubling publicity.

Basil insists there is "no place in public" for Verena. Yet Verena's story reveals
the postbellum public world precisely as a place of feminized spectacle. Like
the domestic novelists who became celebrities of the hearth, Verena gets her
start by embodying her spiritual "gift" before intimate gatherings in private
homes. And just as women's clubs and volunteer societies offered a bridge from
the home into spaces of greater autonomy, the next major advance in Verena's
career comes through her successful performance at a meeting of Mrs. Burrage's
Wednesday Club, a gathering of moneyed New York society. Finally, in the
climactic scene in the novel, Verena's scheduled performance before a sold-out
audience in the Boston Music Hall registers the world of full-fledged celebrity
that had been erected around women performers. Verena's public "gift" has
been converted to publicity in its most expansive, commercial sense. Even
before Verena appears onstage in front of the "roaring crowd," she is already
presented to the "gaze of hundreds" who see her in repeating form in mass-
produced theatrical posters and distributed handbills.

Though mass-produced, these images are anything but impersonal. With
an artful economy of effect, James captures the erotic attraction generated
through these multiplied reproductions by showing us Basil's fiercely jealous
reaction to the posters and handbills themselves: their sight made him "wish
he had money to buy up the stock." Verena's posters, a public site of sexual
cathexis, recall the lithographic posters that took the place of block printing
in theatrical advertisements beginning in the 1870s. The surviving posters
from this period give a bravado stylization to the charismatic sexual power of
female stage performers, featuring such sights as color drawings of gigantic
Amazon maidens or dancers towering over puny male admirers. In *The Reign
of the Poster* (1895), published in Boston, Charles Knowles Bolton compiled
a catalog of some of the pictorial posters that had become a ubiquitous form
of advertising. Bolton describes the personalized erotic attraction that had
become part of the public experience of street life through the poster displays:
"Ladies (on paper), like prospectuses, are ever attractive, and how many glad
moments these poster beauties have given us as we passed from window to
window!"

Verena's posters, of course, would have displayed a notably different
iconography; her look and public appeal is closer to the celebrity of singer

Jenny Lind ("the most popular woman in the world") who won fame through a carefully staged female artlessness, wearing her white dress as a signature costume and singing "Home, Sweet Home" before packed houses. But in picturing the multitude of posters with Verena's image, James clearly aligns her power with the magnified mass appeal of the female performer, and the narrator similarly describes her as a "rope-dancer," an "actress," a "prima donna," and a "vocalist." For Basil, these charismatic displays, their effect of "sweet grotesqueness," compel him both to pursue the soon-to-be star and to seek to terminate her public stardom.

Whereas theatrical posters celebrate the charismatic, the categories of James's novel are analytic. James at this point in his career aimed to write novels that were "very national, very typical . . . very characteristic of our social conditions." One of his most self-consciously Realist novels, *The Bostonians* brings the categories of gender, region, and nation to a story of modern exhibition. In this way, the occult energies of "the great popular system" of public performance become the object of Realist categories with their more rationalized basis for the accurate representation of social life. Such categories provide a taxonomy for "our social conditions" through which a crisis of modernity – what Basil calls the "damnable feminization" of American culture, and what James, in more neutral terms, calls "the situation of women" – can be clearly seen and measured. Significance lies in the typical rather than the extraordinary, the analytic and not the scenic or the theatrical. Or, as James summarized the Realist project, the novel provides "a more analytic consideration of appearances."

This analytic turn also prompts Realism's increasing interest in uncovering psychological depth. Against the dazzling but opaque surfaces of the stage performance or the lithograph poster, the Realist novel counters with a penetrating view of the human interior, a dissection made possible by what James calls the "discoveries" of Realist analysis that fathom "the unseen from the seen." Thus, even as *The Bostonians* is at times wickedly satirical (so much so that a good many Boston denizens felt personally insulted), its grounding in what James calls "material conditions" still yields rich portraits of motivation and feeling. Basil Ransom's character, for instance, his defining lines and tones, are always focused through the lens of his social situation as a Southern white man. The "intimate connection" Basil feels to the South opens to us a range of affect and lived relations – passions, resentments, reflexes springing from a code of honor and shame, an unconscious drive for vindication – that Basil himself keeps closed from others' view (and, at times, closed even from himself). Olive Chancellor is likewise what James calls a "representative woman" whose complexity of character unfolds along lines of a concretized "human background." Her shades of feeling and her mixed motives are the animated substance of a distinct type of modern womanhood, a social type – the reformer-spinster – that the narrator describes as "visibly morbid." The narrator takes delight in slyly ridiculing many of Olive's beliefs and contradictory motives. But, at the same time, the novel's analytic penetration also offers psychological insight into Olive that is rendered with considerable sympathy and, at times, with a breathtaking lyricism, as in the moving, anguished self-revelations that come to Olive during her isolated vigil on Cape Cod. With its "solidity of specification," the Realist novel connects identifiable social forces with resulting textures of character to create a density that is missing from – because irrelevant to – the high wattage of conspicuous fame within mass culture.

Yet even as *The Bostonians* demonstrates the potency of Realist methods, it points up a contradiction in those methods. Analysis through "social conditions" supplies a scaffold for psychological depth, but such analysis also introduces a troubling uncertainty to the question of individual agency. Self-determination begins to seem a fragile and constrained human capacity at best, and at worst a human delusion. At one level Basil and Olive represent two strong wills locked in a struggle to control Verena. But as the portrait of each character is deepened through a web of social reference, the question of just what a human will *is* becomes more equivocal. As exemplars of contrasting "social conditions," Basil and Olive eventually seem merely to be repeating in a different arena the war that had issued from the intractable differences between North and South, or from an ancient battle between men and women. Their antagonism seems scripted by larger forces, and as individuals they begin to resemble unwitting actors, mere puppets of those forces. In that sense, a theatrical culture thus begins to seem a site not for distorting but for actually apprehending a deeper historical and social truth about the tenuousness of human agency. This truth is something James's otherwise anti-theatrical novel seems forced into acknowledging in the resolution of its plot, as the representation of characters' will blurs with an overtly theatrical "personating." Basil, for instance, at the height of his determination to possess Verena, is shown repeating a role already written and performed in a fated moment of history. His sense of possessing a unique, self-directed mission is marked by the narrator through an obvious allusion to the mission of another aggrieved Southerner (and professional actor), John Wilkes Booth: "There were two or three moments during which he felt as if he could imagine a young man to feel who, waiting in a public place, has made up his mind, for reasons of his own, to discharge a pistol at the king or the president." Basil's "unique" will now looks to us like a reprised role.

Thus theatrical surface may, in its illusion, yield as much insight as does analytic depth, and depth may be as difficult to interpret as surface. Olive, too, is in the end pulled into an ambiguous stage role that seems at once a defiant act and a scripted submission to external "conditions." Rushing onto the music-hall stage when Verena fails to go on, Olive is described as repeating a historical role of martyr: "offering herself to be trampled to death and torn to pieces," she might have resembled "some feminine firebrand of Paris revolutions, erect on a barricade, or even the sacrificial figure Hypatia, whirled through the furious mob of Alexandria." Here is the Jamesian answer to the female burlesque. Deliberately overdrawn, colored by a melodrama verging on ridicule, this picture of Olive absorbs the charisma of the female performer into Realist analysis of the "visibly morbid" womanhood. Yet this culminating scene is also a moment the novel does not directly portray (nor are any of Verena's performances given more than the briefest description), as if the novel is unwilling – or perhaps unable – to dissect the actual spectacle in its moment of performative power. These Realist characters are in the end equivocal social actors. In *The Bostonians*, the analysis of women and publicity describes a broader dilemma: the more rationalized the analysis of human lives, the more uncertain the question of human agency.

INCOMMENSURATE ART: CONSTANCE FENIMORE WOOLSON

In *The Bostonians* women are caught between the distortions of publicity and the restrictions of domesticity, between crass public exposure and private efface-ment. The dilemma as James paints it is exaggerated. But its polarized terms trace for us a structure of feeling that organizes a large number of novels and sto-ries in this era, fiction in which middle-class women confront a divide between private and public worlds that makes each seem insufficient and yet unable to be bridged. In *The Tragic Muse* (1890), James replays the same dilemma in a higher theatrical culture of serious drama. But James's novels also implicitly contain a third position from which women might circumvent the dilemma – namely, *his* position, the role of Realist author with a critical standpoint from which to analyze the predicament and thus transcend it intellectually. Yet the possibility of Realist authorship as a role *for* women goes unrecognized in James's stories themselves. The omission is significant. In forming a tradi-tion of high Realism, a confluence of factors associated the elevation of fiction with the male author. The European novelists acknowledged most often in the official genealogy of American realism were men. Balzac, Flaubert, Zola, and Turgenev were among the most oft-cited models, even if Austen, Eliot, and Sand were some of the strongest influences on Realist practice. Worldly rather than religious in orientation, professional rather than commercial in status, the role of Realist writer was in large part defined in contradistinction to the women novelists who so successfully established the mass market for domestic fiction in antebellum America.

High Realism was not the sealed province of men, of course. But genres, as social creations, carry the sediments of gendered experience, silent articulations of norms for the sexes that inform their linguistic patterns. Such traces are important to a history of high Realism in American writing, in the first instance for the way they operate to encourage or to constrain would-be authors. Who gets to be a real (Realist) artist? The issue really begins from a different corner: who *wishes* to be a Realist artist? Many successful women writers – even some who sought to publish their fiction in the more prestigious magazines and publishing houses – never enlisted under the Realist banner. By the mid-1870s, fiction writers such as Elizabeth Stuart Phelps, Louisa May Alcott, and Elizabeth Stoddard were painting a wider field of experience for women than was portrayed in the domestic novels of an earlier generation. Still, in both formal and thematic ways, their stories and novels mark their own exclusion from a domain of high culture – indeed, they often count that exclusion from high art as one of the defining features of women's experience.

Harriet Prescott Spofford recalled the reordering of literary criteria as a termination of her brand of expansive psychological fiction. "You wonder why I did not continue in the vein of 'The Amber Gods,'" she wrote to a friend. "I suppose the public taste changed. With the coming of Mr. Howells as editor of the *Atlantic*, and his influence, the realistic arrived. I doubt if anything I wrote in those days would be accepted by any magazine now." At the same time, however, the constraints of the high Realist ethos could also supply conditions for an oppositional creativity. In Elizabeth Stuart Phelps's novel *The Story of Avis* (1877), for instance, Phelps measures her heroine's distance from institutions of high culture in order to create a space for a narrative mode rich in visual symbol and characterization. The protagonist, Avis Dobell, aspires to become a painter – to acquire "that most elusive of human gifts, – a disciplined imagination" – and travels to Florence and Paris, where she studies under master teachers. But unlike the expatriate artists of James or Wharton, Avis is never directly represented in a European museum or gallery. The narrative quickly forecloses any description of her artistic training and returns her to rural Massachusetts where, in the isolation of her "little bare studio," she is visited by a series of ecstatic, unformed aesthetic visions.

The tension between the fullness of Avis's artistic vision and her distance from established aesthetic institutions expresses perfectly Phelps's own creative position, as she wrote vivid, innovative fiction while remaining largely outside of the high literary establishment. Her earlier bestselling novel, *The Gates Ajar* (1868), depicts the distinctly non-Realist setting of heaven as a utopian resolution, and in works such as "The Tenth of January" (1868) and *The Silent Partner* (1871), Phelps followed the lead of Rebecca Harding Davis in combining conventions from romance fiction and religious reform literature with portraits of industrial life.

The title character in Constance Fenimore Woolson's story "Miss Grief" (1880) is a woman who has written passionate creative works – "unrestrained, large, vast, like the skies or the wind" – not unlike the visionary paintings of Phelps's Avis Dobell. In contrast with Phelps's emotionally expansive treatment of Avis, however, Woolson brings to Miss Grief's story the sharp, analytic dissection more typical of Realists. Woolson's critically penetrating style – James lauded the "high value" of her "careful, strenuous studies" and her "remarkable minuteness of observation" – brought her recognition from the high literary establishment, recognition never accorded Phelps. Even so, it is difficult to read "Miss Grief" without the distinct sense that, in disposition if not technique, Woolson was closer to the Phelps-like artist Miss Grief than she was to the successful writer who narrates the story, a man proud of his stylistic "good taste" and transatlantic urbanity. Woolson can be seen as a Realist who turns her critical eye on the high cultural establishment promoting Realism. With skillful indirection, Woolson probes precisely the kind of "high value" critics accorded fiction like hers and discovers urbane aesthetic values entangled in currents of erotic abjection and subtle cruelties that were largely invisible to cultural insiders.

"Miss Grief" is actually Aaronna Moncrief, an American woman living in Rome who makes repeated calls at the home of the narrator, an American writer, until she finally manages to meet and implore him to read her manuscripts. When his servant, having misheard the name, first reports a visit from a "Miss Grief," the narrator is bemused: "Grief has not so far visited me here." He continues to refer to her with that name even after he discovers and then conveys with an unstable sympathy that hers is indeed a life of grief: aging, living in poverty and ill health, Moncrief holds to a dim hope that her unpublished plays and poems might yet find responsive readers. This misnaming of Miss Grief distills Woolson's central ironic device, the formal distancing of a woman's misery so that its pathos cannot be viewed except through eyes of a sophisticated man of letters. Moncrief's suffering is thus realized (made Realist, it is tempting to say) but only through the storytelling of a mediating literary authority; one cannot tell her grief apart from his "Miss Grief."

How, then, to read female grief? The question is implicit in a narrative that returns to the shopworn theme of a dying woman while disabling the sentimental narrative codes for portraying female suffering. The question is also posed at the level of plot: how will an accomplished, complacent transatlantic novelist ("I model myself a little on Balzac") read the writing of an isolated, untrained woman? In essence, he cannot, Woolson answers. Initially irritated at being cornered into the task by a "shabby, unattractive" woman, as he reads the narrator is quickly "inspired and thrilled" by the strength of her passionate expression. He recognizes her superior artistic gift and tells her so: of the two, she is the "greater power." But he also finds her "unrestrained" creations literally unaccountable. He has no workable critical terms for either her "passion and power" or for what he deems her flaws. Neither sublime nor grotesque, the aesthetic logic of her art – "like the work of dreams" – is simply outside his ken. Certainly it exceeds the Realist aesthetic of his own fictional "studies," a point confirmed when he agrees to send one of her manuscripts to an editor in his literary circle. Though "impressed by the power displayed in certain passages," the editor declares that the "impossibilities of the plot" make the piece unpublishable.

Woolson in this way presents her reader with an aesthetic fissure. The story identifies extraordinary literary works but supplies no critical access to their force and beauty, no explanation of their aesthetic power. The disjunction remains to the end: Moncrief dies and her manuscripts remain unpublished and unknown. The effect is to make the reader imagine a species of literary meaning that Woolson's own story, for all its ironic perceptiveness, cannot directly tap. The narrator's Realist vision begins to seem limited, neither definitive as art nor authoritative about the real, and the values of Howellsian Realism are thrown into relief. Whereas proponents of high Realism criticized the work of many women writers as simplistic and naïve, Woolson's story in effect turns the tables: the sophisticated narrator is finally too limited in imagination to fully understand the works of this untrained woman, while her works become figures of a "greater," inaccessible literary power that is anything but simple.

And yet, another strand of Woolson's plot hints at an ironic connection between these incommensurable literary values. The narrator's failure to redeem Moncrief's powerful writing is matched by his romantic success in winning over a socially prominent younger woman, Isabel. A marginal character, Isabel is characterized only as someone unable even to intuit the force of Moncrief's artistry. The poems shown her by the narrator she deems "mixed and vague" and prompt only her condescending pity: "Her mind must have been disordered, poor thing!" Upon hearing this, the narrator experiences a subtle but crucial pattern of affective response, a pattern in which aesthetic taste and sexual feeling generate a complicated current of attraction:

Now, [the poems] were not vague so much as vast. But I knew that I could not make Isabel comprehend it, and (so complex a creature is man) I do not know that I wanted her to comprehend it. They were the only ones in the whole collection that I would have shown her, and I was rather glad that she did not like even these.

Isabel's failure to be moved by the poems that move him actually heightens his romantic attraction to her. For the narrator, it is precisely Isabel's difference from the "unrestrained, large" beauty of the poetry that makes her desirable: "Isabel was bounded on all sides, like a violet in a garden bed. And I liked her so." Behind the apparently simple matter of what one "likes," Woolson quietly insists, are rules of decorum for gender roles, rules that are tied to both artistic and erotic feeling.

Hence the skepticism Woolson invites when the narrator, in the name of fulfilling what the now dead Moncrief would "like," decides to withhold her work from ever appearing in print: "I keep it here in this locked case. I could have published it at my own expense; but I think that now she knows its faults herself, perhaps, and would not like it." What Moncrief would "like" as the fate of her poems, as with Isabel's dislike of their contents, turns out to be entangled in what the narrator likes in a wife (a "bounded" nature) and prefers in dead women writers of genius (enduring obscurity): "When I die," the narrator confides, the Moncrief manuscript "is to be destroyed unread." "Not even Isabel is to see it. For women will misunderstand each other; and, dear and precious to me as my sweet wife is, I could not bear that she or anyone should cast so much as a thought of scorn upon the memory of the writer, upon my poor dead, 'unavailable,' unaccepted 'Miss Grief.'" The narrator's elegy for Miss Grief is simultaneously a willful entombment of her writing. Though his perfect "good taste" remains in force to the end, the lines hint at his eerie satisfaction at the eternal silence of her unread works. His twin tributes to the "poor dead" writer and the living "sweet wife" sound a Poe-like note that echoes an earlier melodramatic outburst from Moncrief's grieving aunt that "all literary men" are "vampires."

There is little in Woolson's life to suggest that she herself harbored that kind of animus against "literary men." She counted Henry James, John Hay, and poet Edmund Clarence Stedman among her closest friends. After the death of her mother, Woolson – who never married – moved to Europe, where she spent time with literary men and women and their families and devoted herself to writing. She frequently shared extended visits with James when the two writers arranged to be in the same European cities. Woolson, quite unlike her "Miss Grief," also enjoyed considerable literary success. Her five published novels sold well – *Anne* (1880) was the most popular – and her short stories won consistent critical praise. Her collection *Castle Nowhere* (1875), with stories set in the Great Lakes region of her youth, and *Rodman the Keeper* (1880), which depicted Southern locales (she had also lived in Florida), were held up as first-rate achievements of local color realism. Italy became the setting for many of her later stories, which critics have tended to see as her finest work. Woolson also published her own criticism as a frequent contributor to *Harper's* and the *Atlantic*.

Yet, in spite of her popular and critical acceptance, Woolson found it difficult to escape unhappiness. Bouts of depression seem to have begun in her thirties and continued throughout her life. Like her "Miss Grief," the writer suffered from poor health and financial strain. Even though her own career was proof that women could write with a forceful literary style ("I have such a horror of 'pretty,' 'sweet' writing that I should almost prefer a style that was ugly and bitter, provided it was also strong") and garner high recognition, Woolson seemed to believe women authors were all but fated for lives of grief. "Why do literary women break down so?" she wrote to Stedman. "It almost seems as though only the unhappy women took to writing." In 1894, Woolson at age fifty-three either fell or, more likely, jumped to her death from the second-story balcony of her room in a Venice villa. She was buried in Rome.

Henry James, who had praised Woolson's talent for depicting "secret histories" ("the 'inner life' of the weak, the superfluous, the disappointed, the bereaved, the unmarried"), was horrified at the news and convinced her death was a suicide. His assessment of her work had appeared some years earlier in an extended critical essay, "Miss Woolson" (1887), which he reprinted in his book *Partial Portraits* (1888). Although he identifies her fiction with the ethos of Realism – "she has had a fruitful instinct in seeing the novel as a picture of the actual, of the characteristic – study of human types and passions" – James also singles out what is for him a distinctly feminine trait, her "dominant" focus on love and marriage: "the complications are almost exclusively the complications of love." Woolson tracks those complications to the same endpoint of human loss. Sacrifice, renunciation, sadness: these keynotes, according to James, are Woolson's chief obsessions and primary truths. The "sacrificial attitude" is a pronounced part of Woolson's fiction, to be sure. But James's view that Woolson "believes" in sacrifice ("in its frequency as well as its beauty") belies precisely the complications that Woolson insists on representing.

Just as persistent as her focus on female self-sacrifice is Woolson's close attention to the conditions and costs of achieved love. Most notably, in several of her strongest stories romantic love follows in the wake of a woman's artistic abjection. Woolson's "The Street of the Hyacinth," for instance, plays out in the tension between a naïve young woman's confident ambitions as a painter and the unspoken knowledge of the men she meets in Rome that her work is "extremely and essentially bad." Her eventual realization of her own lack of talent ("I was a fool"), bringing on her chagrin, is also the shift that brings three marriage proposals. In "At The Chateau of Corinne" (1886), even more directly than in "Miss Grief," a marriage has its source in a woman's failure as a writer. The story's resolution of the charged verbal sparring between future lovers is not the mutual surrender typical of Jane Austen's protagonists but a much sharper note of sexual antagonism. John Ford admits his attraction to Katherine Winthrop immediately after he has denounced "literary women" in general, Madame de Stael in particular, and Katherine's own poetry most directly. The story's sequence of scenes makes clear that John's erotic attraction intensifies through Katherine's visible humiliation.

When a woman's desirability is heightened in almost direct proportion to her failure or shame as an artist, what James called the "beauty" of renunciation in Woolson is an equivocal beauty at best. It is hard to credit James's claim that Woolson "believed" in sacrifice when her fiction so often figures marriage as either the public seal of a woman's artistic failure or the private burial of a woman's works of genius. For Woolson, because art was intimately joined with grief, it offered the privileged insight to recognize intimacy itself as an aesthetic medium for both love and mortification.

SCIENCE AND SELF-SCRUTINY: CHARLOTTE PERKINS-GILMAN AND ALICE JAMES

Some women writers gained a kind of halfway admission to the ranks of Realists, a result not of any failure to fully execute their aesthetic aims but because of the particular ways they fulfilled the criteria of Realist art. Writers such as Sarah Orne Jewett, Mary Murfree, Celia Thaxter, and Mary E. Wilkins Freeman published their work in the premier journals such as the *Atlantic* where it was deemed to be "truly artistic" by male editors. Yet the same virtues that earned them the status of artists – their skilled observation of distinct local cultures, their deftness of narrative touch in crafting shorter forms – also permitted the literary establishment to conceive of their work as belonging to a feminine aesthetic distinguished from a broader literary mastery. Although these writers, often classed as regionalists, hold to the Realist categories of secular time and specified place, the islands of rural life and the shorter narrative forms that characterize their work set them apart from the Realists, largely male, with their ambitions for large sociological reach.

Just as important, perhaps, the women characters in regionalist fiction were by generic definition women who *belonged*, who were indigenous to the Maine islands, the Tennessee mountains, and the New England villages that defined the horizons of social life in regionalist fiction. In contrast, the representative value of women within high Realism was precisely their ability to dramatize a loss of belonging that artists and intellectuals identified with a fraught modernity. Within high literary culture, the status of women as a literary topic was defined less by the sex of Realist writers than by those writers' disposition to look upon women as an exemplary figure of the modern. To be sure, the topic of "the situation of women" afforded male writers a degree of critical detachment that women writers could acquire only by deploying sometimes acrobatic techniques of self-scrutiny. When the status of women becomes a literary *topos* for modernity, "the most salient and peculiar point in our social life," as Henry James puts it, woman supplants nature as the phenomenon most in need of interpretation. Signifying a new mobility of selfhood, she embodies the most visible aspects of social change, from energies of organized reform (James's *The Bostonians* and *The Princess Cassimassima*, Howells's *Annie Kilburn*, John Hay's *The Bread-Winners*), to possibilities for a cosmopolitan American culture (James's *Daisy Miller*, Henry Adams's *Esther*, Wharton's *Custom of the Country*, Woolson's European stories), to the clamorous disorders of the emerging commercial culture, the "Iron Madonna" of feminized spectacle. Precisely in her mutability, the enigma of woman could contain the key to understanding the future. Finding the male domains of politics and history too narrow to grasp the emerging world, Henry Adams saw the fate of modernity in the fate of women. "I should drop the man, except as accessory, and study the woman of the future." When the commercial civilization was judged to be a flat or empty production and commercial men its flat producers, women were often made to signify depth. Within high literary culture women yield an inside view of consciousness that is at once objectified and closely realized, a literary object brought to life in deft and often astonishingly vivid detail. Women became a gendered representative of human subjectivity and its travails, a modernized counterpart to Emerson's "representative man" in a restless, unheroic age.

For women writers, of course, the "situation of women" was at once a literary topic and a condition of their lives. In the late 1880s and 1890s, women began to fashion this double status into an object of their own brand of literary mastery and to make an open claim on high culture. Their works therefore illuminate in particularly vivid ways the place of women in American society as both a modern consciousness and an enigmatic cultural object. The demand for critical detachment was, we might say, both a woman's burden and her gift. Certainly that fact explains something about why the most accomplished of these women writers all claimed to find literary wisdom in the study of science. Kate Chopin declared that "it's impossible to ever come to a true knowledge of life as it is – which should be everybody's aim – without studying certain fundamental truths" of natural science. Immersion in science, Chopin contended, is the only saving antidote for those women writers who continue to produce "hysterical" and "false pictures of life." Edith Wharton was a passionate student of Darwinism, hereditary biology, and anthropology, among other disciplines, and scientific practice was her model for successful fiction: the worthiest fiction "probes deep enough to get at the relation with the eternal laws." The literary critic, too, requires a "disciplined acquaintance with his subject" that is the equal of the professional scholar of "history or paleontology."

The appeal of science for writers like Chopin, Wharton, Pauline Hopkins, and Charlotte Perkins Gilman lies in a mix of intellectual excitement and cultural authority. Scientific knowledge for these authors bespeaks creativity, thought freed from convention. Tropes and allusions borrowed from science frequently mark the places where their fiction diverges most sharply from inherited patterns. Just at the moments when her *House of Mirth* (1905) is most vulnerable to melodrama, Wharton turns to images derived from science. She supplies a botanical description of her heroine's rootless "tentacles of self," for instance, or riffs on the "men and women . . . like atoms whirling away from each other in some wild centrifugal dance," tropes that concentrate emotion through a controlling analysis. But the more significant appeal of science for these women may have been the disposition of the scientific observer, a posture distinguished by analytic power and a keen intellectual command over external objects of study. In science's mode of critical detachment, writers found the means to dissect a social situation they also lived day-to-day from within.

Wharton called it the posture of the "drawingroom naturalist." To view lives and social relations from this position was to possess at once deep human insight and "high impartiality," with each capacity strengthened by the other. In her volume of collected criticism, *The Writing of Fiction* (1925), Wharton offers what may be the most concise distillation of Realist practice. The "creative imagination," Wharton writes, merges "the power of penetrating into other minds with that of standing far enough aloof from them to see beyond, and relate them to the whole stuff of life out of which they but partially emerge. Such an all-round view can be obtained only by mounting to a height." Giving primacy to analysis over sympathy, to discipline over identification, Wharton and others reinvented the domestic novel as an acknowledged high art open to the woman writer. To the same degree that these women acquired Realist credentials, however, their fiction frequently prompted a proportional unease – even outright distaste – in many of their contemporaries. "Mrs. Wharton sits at her desk like a disembodied intelligence," one reviewer remarked in 1905, "acute and critical and entirely unsympathetic." *Like* a disembodied intelligence, but also very much an embodied presence: note that the complaint itself pictures Wharton at her desk, a woman in the flesh. The contradiction here is an instructive one. The very success of a woman like Wharton at mastering "the impartial gaze" of the high Realist artist creates an almost reflexive return of attention to her status as a woman, placing her under the scrutiny of others' eyes. In this critical entanglement – call it the situation of woman as Realist – there are difficulties to be sure, but also unique strengths. Through it she gains an awareness of the artist's inescapable existence as a social being, an observer and a creature observed. This knowledge in turn brings a new consciousness of the internal fissures of high Realist art. For these women writers, the allegiance to science and its critical powers coexists with a keen sense of what it can mean to be a scientific object.

Both aspects of this creativity – the inspiration of science and women's status as scientific object – were dominant notes of the time. Science in the later nineteenth century was a success story, enjoying the same spectacular expansion as the national economy without its volatile cycles of boom and bust. The heightened prestige acquired enduring form in this era through the creation of professional institutions. Graduate programs in universities, museums and exhibitions, professional associations, and well-funded institutes gave scientific enterprise a new and decisive social authority. And across the disciplines there was a consensus about the scientific importance of studying sexual difference in general and women in particular. Rapid social change "necessarily induces a perturbation in the evolution of the races," scientist Paul Broca wrote in 1868, "and hence it follows that the condition of women must be most carefully studied by the anthropologist." Scholars like Broca were cautious, if not overtly fearful. Other scientists such as Elsie Clews Parsons saw in the same "perturbation" of sex roles a promise of sure progress for society and for the status of women. Parsons, the first female professor of anthropology at Columbia University, mused that the US would someday have to build a Museum of Women to show "a doubting posterity that once women were a distinct social class." In works such as *The Family: An Ethnographical and Historical Outline* (1906) and *Old-Fashioned Woman: Primitive Fancies about Sex* (1913), Parsons popularized an anthropological approach to debunking contemporary social and sexual conventions. But Parsons's confidence in an untroubled advancement for women was as almost singular as her career. Among scientists of this period, the more prevalent view held that fixed sex traits and slow evolutionary forces defined a female nature that could change only at great peril.

That more alarmist perspective imparted a sense of urgency to the collective project of defining, measuring, categorizing, comparing, and representing womankind. The result was a heterogeneous display marked by a style of representation that could be called scientific realism. Parsons fancifully imagined a museum of women for the future, but clearly the museum already existed, dispersed in the textbooks, exhibits, case studies, and lectures devoted to empirically realizing "the condition of women." Taxonomy lends an air of fixed identity to a status in flux. The "sensitive white woman" ("subsisting on fiction, journals, receptions"); the "bachelor woman" (an "interesting illustration of Spencer's law of individuation and genesis"); the "educated woman" (whose "nubility" and "fecundity" were in question); the "female hysteric" – labels such as these delineate sharp lines for the otherwise amorphous phenomenon of the modern woman. Visual representations supply a realism of physiognomy and link white women of the middle class to "primitive" women of other races. Exhibits of female skulls, life-size wax "Venuses" or medical effigies with dozens of removable parts, "absolutely lifelike" mannequins in ethnographic displays, such as the twelve life-size figures of Native American, African, and Polynesian women at the 1876 Philadelphia exhibition, were all contributions to a vast realism of gender artifact. One scientist, Edward A. Spitzka, a practitioner of the dubious anthropometric discipline of brain-weight measurement, defined a cranial hierarchy that began with the lowest brain-weight specimen, that of an anonymous Bushwoman (794 grams), and ascended to his highest specimen, which happened to be the brain of a male Realist novelist, Ivan Turgenev (2,012 grams).

The disciplined modes of observation trained on women are one measure of the seriousness with which questions about the status of women figure in scientific discourse. Suggesting by turns alarm and an exhilarated curiosity, the proliferating scientific images signify a felt need to bring women within new techniques of empirical representation ("to see is to know"). Science is thus another domain that featured a new visibility for women in this period. In contrast to the tendency of earlier scientists to subsume women under the study of mankind, in the later nineteenth century women hold a central place in efforts to empirically realize the true order of civilization, its laws, its powers, and its natural evolution. But, as is true for all scientific objects, this imperative for empirical knowledge brings with it a tendency to depict woman as static and without agency. Her passivity is axiomatic, the result of method. Efforts to explain her nature by way of social law and natural forces make woman into a product of those laws – frequently, into their manifest victim. Visually, woman as seen through the empirical lens is inert, arrested, and, at the furthest extreme, perfectly lifeless – a type, a symptom, a corpse. Perhaps the most openly aestheticized portrait in the scientific canon was offered in Johann Bachofen's influential study of ancient cults, *Das Mütterecht*, where the origin of Western law and civilization, in triumph over "the seductions of Egypt," is "imaged in the death of Candace of the Orient (Cleopatra), and in Augustus' contemplation of her lifeless body."

The iconography of the beautiful corpse is one pole of female representation. Its opposite is the galvanized actress from popular culture, all motion and outsized vibrancy, a figure that inflated women's incremental gain in social mobility into the hyperbole of a dazzling mass fame. Against Bachofen's lifeless Cleopatra, juxtapose the sensational Broadway performer Ada Isaacs Menken, who became a national celebrity in the 1860s playing the leading male role in *Mazeppa; or, The Wild Horse of Tartary.* At the famous climax of this melodrama, Menken, as Prince Ivan Mazeppa, bursts across the stage nearly nude (in flesh-colored tights) and bound to a live horse galloping full stride. In contrast with this electric spectacle, Bachofen's tableau is a frozen allegory of scientific sight. Law and the reign of reason commence in Augustus's observation of a woman, a figure for dynamic, sensuous Nature that has been arrested in death. In Menken's wild ride, the syntax of the allegory is precisely reversed. On the stage, it is the dynamism of a female spectacle that arrests the observer, who is reduced to looking on in passive wonder. To be gazed upon is a source of power, while looking is a form of subjection, an enthrallment. ("The intensely emotional situation that Miss Menken displays," wrote one editor, is expressed in grand actions whose "significance scorns interpretation.") Stillness and motion, observation and display, analysis and sensuous feeling, science and spectacle: these contraries order the field of representation that is the matrix for the portrait of woman in Realist fiction. Efforts to define her essential and unchanging traits bear indirect witness to the change and uncertainty of her status. The field defines power and passivity as exclusive properties, opposite poles that are given to sudden reversals of position.

At the heart of much Realist writing, then, by men and women alike, is an urgency to observe women that responds to the charged poles of this field of representation. In Henry James's *The Portrait of a Lady* (1881), the observation of a woman supplies both method and story. An activity the narrator calls the "conscious observation of a lovely woman" is the primary occupation of the novel's main characters, all of whom follow closely the courtship "career" in Europe of a young American woman, Isabel Archer. It is the word "conscious" in this formulation that bears the strongest accent. More than his earlier fictions about young women, *Daisy Miller* (1878) or *Washington Square* (1880), for example, this novel brings the act of watching itself under close scrutiny. The supreme importance of discernment in the literature of high culture fosters a self-reflexiveness about observation, and in James's work this secondary subject moves increasingly into the foreground.

As a result, readers found in James's fiction a sometimes startling intensity of vision. "No word or look or action in [the characters'] lives had escaped the author's attention," wrote one reviewer. "His observation and knowledge seem to grow keener with each new novel. But where will it end?" For some, James's vision was too coolly scientific, a rigor "without pity." But in *The Portrait of a Lady* the novel makes clear at all levels that the practice of watching – "the sweet-tasting property of observation," as the narrator calls it – is never dispassionate. Observing Isabel (there are "plenty of spectators") will involve efforts to know or possess or exploit or love her. Vision is transitive. It is also most often erotic, charged with pleasure, in ways both generous and sinister.

But importantly, the conscious observation of Isabel never includes the sight of her dead. The fact is significant even if it is not, in the end, definitive; as a genre the nineteenth-century Realist novel features a remarkable number of dead women. A genre that develops an increasingly dense background of social conditioning for human action, high Realism often resolves vexing questions about women's subjectivity (what does she want? is she free?) by locating a social explanation – or at least social closure – in her death. Even a woman's suicide is oftentimes less an act of agency than a nearly unwilled surrender to social or natural forces. In Realism there is an aesthetic logic, hence a beauty, in the death of a woman. Anna Karenina, Emma Bovary, Chopin's Edna Pontellier, Tess D'Urberville, Wharton's Lily Bart, James's own Millie Theal – these compelling protagonists all illuminate most clearly the cunning conditions of their worlds at the moment they cease to live.

James considers the possibility of Isabel's death and gives it a striking aesthetic resonance. By the time she recognizes her mistake in marrying Gilbert Osmond and the duplicity that engineered it, the idea of death has become something deeply affecting: "To cease utterly, to give it all up and not know anything more – this idea was as sweet as the vision of a cool bath in a marble tank, in a darkened chamber, in a hot land." Isabel's sudden wealth had given her a field for independent action rare for a woman, but in the end even her sense of having chosen and acted freely – "If ever a girl was a free agent, she had been" – has the feel of an illusion imposed from without. Even so, against the novel's own gravitational pull Isabel retains a measure of agency, a power to reflect upon the conditions that have entrapped her. "Conscious" observation, then, belongs to Isabel, too. In this she differs from Daisy Miller, the heroine of James's most popular study of the "young feminine nature." Daisy Miller's rash indifference to European decorum is less a trait of moral innocence than a lack of a discriminating consciousness, which at first appears to be a freedom to act, but ends as a vulnerability that issues in her death.

Isabel, in contrast, becomes not only the object observed but a rich source of interior perception that mirrors what James in his preface calls "the posted presence of the watcher," the penetrating "consciousness of the artist."

Consciousness for James is authorial, a form of agency if a limited one. In that respect Isabel is like Madeleine Lee, the protagonist of Henry Adams's novel *Democracy* (1880), a woman watched by others who develops an ability to see that equals the keenest of her observers. Examining closely the workings of national politics and politicians, Madeleine "got to the heart of politics, so that she could, like a physician with his stethoscope, measure the organic disease." Yet where Madeleine expects to gaze on the living, breathing body of American governance, she sees instead a Washington revealed as a series of "elaborate show-structures" peopled by mechanical mannequins and "wax images." Once again, the (Realist) truth about the social world turns out to lie in the distressing power of illusion and spectacle. The highest rule of the Republic is no better than the machinations of low entertainment.

In possessing a penetrating consciousness, these women characters share the savvy of the most discerning observers who study the "situation of women." As rich as their developing vision comes to be, however, because they are women the power of Isabel and Madeleine to observe remains a force incommensurate with what James calls the Realist heroine's "fate." The gap between her sight and her fate is revealed in women's self-examination. Observing themselves, women are at once discerning subjects and paralyzed objects: "Madeleine dissected her own feelings and was always wondering whether they were real or not; she had a habit of taking off her mental clothing, as she might take off a dress, and looking at it as though it belonged to some one else, and as though sensations were manufactured like clothes."

The paradox has its most famous expression in the "vigil" chapter of *The Portrait of a Lady*, a *tour de force* of psychological revelation. The reader in this chapter follows the furthest reach of Isabel's unfolding self-comprehension while, in the external narrative frame, Isabel neither speaks nor moves. Her consciousness painfully alive, Isabel in her person is perfectly still, locked in "motionless seeing." Her power to see is matched with a paralysis that bespeaks her final restriction in marriage. This concentrated image of Isabel's fate expresses a "far-reaching sadness." Yet it is an "exquisite" sadness, too: the beauty lies in a previously unknown fate now brilliantly realized in a completely transparent, motionless image. Isabel's vigil thus distills a whole aesthetic mode. In this Realist mode, the more a woman is consciously known, and the greater her consciousness of the social world that made her, the more likely she is to become a tragic still-life, a portrait of woman as beautiful, silent, and unmoving.

There were strains of misogyny in this literature, but the Realist desire to discover and represent the social future of women was largely sympathetic. Its strongest insights were able to bring into focus an otherwise diffuse social view that was beginning to recognize man-made constraints in what had previously been deemed women's natural sphere of being. Becoming conscious of imposed constraints is a compensation for women but not a solution; it only lends their condition the beauty of poignancy and a certain tragic dignity. The genre's most striking revelations regarding women were also the most fatalistic, its fatalism the genre's most luminous reflection.

A short story by a relatively unknown author explodes the aesthetics of paralyzed female beauty. In 1890 Charlotte Perkins Gilman wrote "The Yellow Wall-paper" in southern California and sent it to Howells a continent away. This stunning story (Howells called it "strong" and "blood-curdling") pairs a self-dissecting vision with theatrical self-display; the resulting combination seizes on the Realist property of consciousness and transforms it into a hallucinatory performance. The unnamed woman who narrates the story suffers a "slight hysterical tendency," or at least that is the diagnosis of her physician, who is also, significantly, her husband. Gilman writes the portrait of a lady as a morbid "case." Observation has become aggressively clinical. The protagonist-narrator, required to remain in a single upper bedroom, is carefully observed by her husband and by his sister, who is deputized to answer his "professional questions" in his absence. The story makes clinical observation into an unacknowledged domination, just as it makes her seeming illness and bed rest into an unnatural entrapment (he "hardly lets me stir without special direction").

Gilman's protagonist has been warned away from self-reflection – "John says the very worst thing I can do is think about my condition" – but she develops a critical consciousness nonetheless. To call it a consciousness may mislead, however. Gilman's narrator possesses none of the lucidity of Isabel Archer, none of the dark comprehension of Madeleine Lee. It is by *not* directly comprehending her "condition" that the woman creates from her mind a grotesque expression of that condition: she imagines a monstrous, living "woman" trapped in the yellow wallpaper of her bedroom. In Gilman's story, the Realist *topos* of "motionless seeing" is intensified and literalized, until the protagonist's own alienated vision becomes a collection of ugly, frenzied phantoms, which she begins bodily to mimic. In contrast with the tragically beautiful stillness at the center of so many Realist portraits, the narrator's arrested state begins in an enforced submission and ends in convulsive movement. Exaggerating the symbolic terms of the female condition allows Gilman an equally forceful denunciation of that condition. Refusing beauty generates a critical dissent animated by the sheer strength of the reader's aversion for what the story reveals. In Gilman's protagonist there is no beauty in morbidity, no self-abnegation in confronting her fate. Nor is there any power in her concluding hysterical performance – "I've got out at last!" – except as a dark parody of a self-determination she does not possess.

Gilman's protagonist lacks even the minimal agency of a character like Isabel Archer. But as a literary object, her abject condition also implies its own opposite. A woman *can* have the ability to see and act under her own powers, but this species of agency is represented in the person of the author, Charlotte Perkins Gilman. Gilman as author usurps entirely the expertise of the physician husband. The story is Gilman's superior diagnosis of his wife, a trumping of specious medical knowledge (a reviewer called it "a striking and impressive study of morbid psychology, in the shape of a story"). She examines the late-century woman and, like many social scientists of the time, describes a passive, ineffectual creature, viewing her almost as a separate "psychological species" (to quote a contemporary male scholar on women). But this morbid condition, Gilman insists, is something imposed, not organic. Physicians help to produce the morbidity they diagnose. What she elsewhere calls the aborted agency of women is the result of the sex's isolation from virtually all forms of enterprise except reproduction. What other capacities could women have, Gilman asks, when they are confined to the "little ganglion of aborted economic processes" that was the middle-class home? Identifying this condition, making it a striking literary object, was Gilman's way of mastering it.

If Gilman's story was a diagnosis, it was also a self-diagnosis and, perhaps, a self-vindication. Gilman based the story on her own experience in 1887 undergoing the "rest cure" treatment of Dr. S. Weir Mitchell. A prominent Philadelphia physician (and a novelist himself), Mitchell treated Gilman and many other New Englanders – including Edith Wharton and Jane Addams – by prescribing a regimen of extended bed rest and the near total elimination of "intellectual life" ("never touch pen, brush or pencil as long as you live"). In the aftermath of her treatment, Gilman would reverse the doctor's diagnostic: Mitchell's supposed medical cure was in fact the pathological cause. After three months of following Mitchell's instructions, Gilman reported, she "came so near the border line of utter mental ruin that I could see over."

Gilman indicts Mitchell's medical practice and thinking, but she by no means rejects scientific analysis. Indeed, she achieved her largest fame through her own brand of scientific polemic. After publishing "The Yellow Wall-paper" in *The New England Magazine* (Howells may have helped place it there, but Gilman's later account claimed otherwise), and a well-received volume of satiric verse in 1893, Gilman produced in 1898 her major study of the social evolution of women. On every page, *Women and Economics* shows Gilman's deep immersion in Darwin, in the anthropologists such as E. B. Tylor and John Lubbock her father had recommended to her, and in American sociologists like Lester Frank Ward, whose theories in works such as *Pure Sociology* (1903) Gilman considered "the greatest single contribution to the world's thought since evolution." Almost instantly successful, *Women and Economics* went through nine American printings by 1920.

The book is a serious excursion in scientific and social thought, but it is undeniably a work of Gilman's narrative imagination, with sweeping analyses of ancient history and modern institutions animated by the same kinds of creative reversals that propel "The Yellow Wall-paper." One historian of science describes the essentially literary quality of *Women and Economics* as Gilman's "talent for accepting the premises of men like Darwin and Spencer and exploding their perspectives to arrive at wickedly revolutionary conclusions." Though filled with witty ridicule (also with now disproven premises), the book affirms the "friendly forces" of evolution as proof of women's destined liberation – an adroit and courageous argument at a time when advances for women prompted dire warnings of degeneration from most evolutionists. Even death and extinction are welcomed as the cathartic elimination of "morbid conditions." If "The Yellow Wall-paper" is Gilman's diagnosis in gothic, *Women and Economics* is her scientific romance. Gilman extracted from science a tone of fearless and authoritative speech, a resource earlier women writers had borrowed from religion, and used it to critically undo what she perceived to be harmful fictions, including fictions of science itself.

Gilman also wrote out of energies of hatred and cultural contempt. She was an outspoken nativist and her scientific bent thrilled to the class purity promised in the eugenics movement. Though she voiced disapproval during the epidemic of Southern lynching, an article she published in the *American Journal of Sociology* ventured the idea that African-American men could be conscripted into state-run labor camps. Here as elsewhere, agency for middle-class white women was claimed through the exclusion of other disempowered groups, as if in a zero-sum calculus. Gilman's racial animus must be counted with the total complement of motives and ideals that give her writing its coherence and her career its public prominence.

Those diverse motives animated her work from within. The formal coherence of her great subject, women's place in modern life, came from an analytic distance she used to extricate herself from the "profound distress" she had felt when she was immersed in domesticity. Distance saved her sanity, defined her life's work, and became the structural condition of her sense of identity, "myself as a self," as she described it. Her life in California, where she moved soon after persuading her husband to divorce, is the geographical expression of this intellectual perspective of distance. Gilman was a descendant of the New England Beechers, America's first family of Protestant reform (Gilman boarded for a time with her aunts, Isabella Beecher and Harriet Beecher Stowe), and she also had connections to members of the cultural elite, such as her uncle, writer Edward Everett Hale. Like her abiding interest in science, Gilman's move to Pasadena was a form of removal that gave her Northeastern experience a discrete shape for analysis. From the edge of the continent, communication was a controlled and mediated choice; her writing, like her lecture tours, entered national circulation from a point of difference.

That point of difference was also a particular aesthetic location. Gilman self-consciously placed her work outside of the province of high art, a position where she denied herself the status of truly literary authorship but simultaneously freed herself for a prodigious literary production – well over 2,000 books, stories, essays, and poems published in her lifetime. In addition to inventing new forms for polemical works such as *Women and Economics*, Gilman, like Mark Twain, wrote books that flaunted rather than diminished or denied the central importance of commercial culture by deliberately adapting bestselling genres for her own feminist purposes. The result included surprising turns on the gothic tale, on domestic melodrama and utopian fantasy, even the murder mystery (her mystery *Unpunished* was published posthumously in 1998). Stories such as "Turned," "If I Were a Witch," and her utopian narrative *Herland* (1915) use irony to convert generic expectations into forceful critical insight. Gilman's particular writerly gifts thrive in these creative crossings, which achieve the startling force of the female stage performer, one whose moves are the flash of intellect and the shock of convention dissected and dismissed with breathtaking agility. This was a performance in the strongest sense of the word, an ideal projection of a masterful agency that possesses the power to renew belief, for the author as well as audience, in the reality of the human capacity it represents.

Gilman's public literary performance has an uncanny counterpart in the "restricted career" of Alice James, in whose life and writing Gilman's faith in agency is reflected as if through the wrong end of a telescope: diminished in all ways, but still present as an elusive yet beautiful emblem. For Alice James, the younger sister of Henry and William James, the category of career is impossibly overcharged. The phrase "restricted career" was the label James repeatedly applied to herself, and we might be impelled to hear in it only a self-deprecating sarcasm (her frequent tone) were it not for the fact that, in the end, James took herself and her ironies seriously. That James described her "career" at all is ironic because she never published anything; calling it "restricted" makes that point through a mock delicacy of euphemism. But the irony turns on itself once again when we consider that her very lack of professional authorship, together with the 1964 publication of her diary, eventually has made Alice James a singular but acclaimed literary figure. She did indeed have a career, and it was a life in letters that illuminates the general conditions of high literary authorship by way of its anomalous expression.

Alice James's surviving letters and diary show an analytic sensibility of a particularly pure sort. They also show the consequences when analysis turns purely inward. James lacked or simply abjured the kinds of techniques Gilman and others used to effect a strong critical distance from modern social experience and feeling. Instead, she makes the brand of thought we have been calling Realist distinction into something almost completely self-referential. Alice James herself, not a body of published work, would be the object giving meaningful form to the late-century puzzle of the situation of women. Her experience, her perception, and her physical condition are the stuff of an intense and finally a *literary* intellection; the life, more than the written words, bears witness to the process of Realist form-giving.

Taking what she lightly called a "scientific spirit" to the examination of her own difficult life supplied a sense of purpose and form. In a letter to her brother William and his wife Mary, Alice declared herself "perfectly grotesque . . . a wretched shriveled alien . . . But just you see if I don't have a career somewhere!" The description of her "grotesque" condition is a reference to Alice James's almost lifelong struggle with debilitating nervous attacks, and is an instance of her relieving tendency to objectify the condition that seemed to have no objective medical cause. Behind her self-dissection are habits of mind that – if and when they aren't attributable simply to James family custom – clearly partake of the shaping preoccupations of the Northeastern cultural establishment. Her experiences of transatlantic travel, her personal acquaintance with innumerable leading figures in American letters and higher education, her interest in scientific study as a model of tough-minded analysis, the depth of her knowledge of French and English authors, her enjoyment of the conditions of wealth and privilege that permitted such pursuits – these are virtually identical with the cultural ground that gives high Realist art its characteristic traits. Yet James seems always to have lived at a kind of oblique angle to her own milieu. European travel, for example, was for her less an educational initiation than a journey in the "mazes of trans-Atlantic neurasthenia." Her sense of chronic discomfiture inside the local culture that formed her, of fitting neither women's nor men's approved occupations, may account for both the intensity of her reflections and her seeming inability to direct them outward into public activity or expression. She wrote of feeling left to "stagger alone under a monstrous mass of subjective sensations." Her brother William and father, Henry

James Sr., suffered similar mental devastations, but the steadying structures of professional career, of marriage and parenthood, and of publication supplied a mechanism of recovery for those men.

James's turn inward was not narcissism. More than anyone in her family, Alice James was passionately engaged by the great political questions of the moment, which she characteristically described as affecting her somatically (her internal organs, as she wrote from Europe, "cramp themselves convulsively over every little event here"). Her inwardness is, rather, a felt imperative to provide meaningful form to the "collection . . . of fantastic and *un*productive emotions" she experienced so keenly. In her diary she described herself as a "coral insect building up various reefs of theory by microscopic additions." Her creations would be small, unpublished, hidden. But, just as much as Gilman's prolific bibliography, James's writings attest to the pervasiveness, indeed the urgency, of giving conscious, intelligible form to the uncertain situation of women.

For James, no less than for her class, morbidity and health formed the primary idiom through which to articulate the meaning of women's lives. "What an interest death lends to the most commonplace," James wrote, "making them so complete and clear-cut, all the vague and wobbly lines lost in the revelation of what they were meant to stand for." The idea and picture of death were so compelling for James, compelling precisely *as form*, that the self-understanding in her diary and letters begins to seem an eerie, second-order Realist artifact. When at age forty she learned that she was dying of breast cancer, the knowledge, she wrote, would "double the value of the event, for one becomes suddenly picturesque to oneself and one's wavering little individuality stands out with a cameo effect." In places her self-portrait can seem borrowed directly from the terms of Realist aesthetics. James described the aftermath of her anxiety attacks, for instance, as moments of transfixed stillness in which she "lay prostrate" with her "mind luminous and active."

Such language can appear to affirm the tendency towards fatalism that colored so many Realist portraits of women. Alice James's sense of vocation in defining the "wavering little individuality" through her own death catches the pressure of external forces as they appear to fix the real identity of things. This determinism was becoming a stronger and stronger note in the culture. Poet Louise Imogen Guiney expressed it in her book *Patrins* (1897), when she wrote, "we are the poor relations of every conceivable circumstance." And Alice James was certainly capable of giving the theme a dark eloquence: "What is living in this deadness we call life is the struggle of the creature in the grip of its inheritance and against the consequences of its acts." Yet James's acts of formally constructing a meaningful account of her life, of reaching towards a "revelation" of what it was "meant to stand for," also bring back the sense of an agency – limited, certainly, but also meaningful – in the conscious act of representation. Looking back on the year-long period of 1890–91, when Henry had "published *The Tragic Muse* [and] brought out *The American*" and "William's *Psychology*" had also appeared, Alice called it "not a bad show for one family! especially if I get myself dead, the hardest job of all." The conceit describing the work of "get[ting] myself dead" as a kind of authorship is certainly among the most wayward paths that Realist analysis can be said to have taken. But it is an instance that is especially alive to the Realist paradox that asserts literary mastery through an analysis of contingency and finds form in unmastered relations. Where Gilman resolves the problem of women's agency through willful projection, James magnifies the problem to make its uncertainties the terms of her creativity.

KATE CHOPIN AND THE REALISM OF DESIRE

In much Realist fiction, self-reflection tends to lift or even isolate a woman's consciousness from her immediate surroundings. As with the "motionless seeing" that transforms Isabel Archer, a woman's reflective consciousness can for a time eclipse her awareness of the quotidian world, including her own body. A distinctive reversal of this pattern, however, is one of the important innovations of Kate Chopin's fiction. Rather than bringing mental detachment, in Chopin self-reflection brings a new awareness of the body, of its immediate sensations and varying states of consciousness. A typical moment of this kind occurs in Chopin's acclaimed novel *The Awakening* (1899), when the protagonist, Edna Pontellier, lies alone on a bed during a pause in an afternoon outing. She will later realize she is in love with her afternoon companion, Robert Lebrun, one of several consequential changes for the married mother of two children. But in this moment, lying at rest yet still awake and observant, Edna's own body becomes the object of her consciousness.

How luxurious it felt to rest thus in a strange, quaint bed, with its sweet country odor of laurel lingering about the sheets and mattress! She stretched her strong limbs that ached a little. She ran her fingers through her loosened hair for a while. She looked at her round arms as she held them straight up and rubbed them one after the other, observing closely, as if it were something she saw for the first time, the fine, firm quality and texture of her flesh.

In this scene of self-reflection, "observing closely" is as tactile as it is visual, and even Edna's thoughts are reflections on the pleasurable strangeness of her sensations – the feeling of an unfamiliar bed beneath her, a sense of novelty at the sight of her own arms. Here the iconic figure of the prone woman is no longer the beautiful, lifeless object; but neither is her body merely the point of origin for her reflective thought. Observation is, once again, a woman's path towards agency, but the new consciousness Edna acquires is not the intellectual mastery characteristic of the Realist observer; her "awakening" is far more physical than analytical. Consciousness in Chopin is always sensory consciousness, awareness of and through the body's senses.

Hence the odd accuracy of the formulation, penned by a (hostile) contemporary critic, that *The Awakening* was a novel of "soul dissection." Influenced by Flaubert and Maupassant, Chopin brought the sharp delineations of French Realism to her portraits of American women. Her scalpel-like style, dispassionate and exact, was recognized as the kind of "consummate art" that elevates fiction to the status of high art. But the object of Chopin's art, the self or "soul" she depicts, is less the social identity favored by Realists than the sensuous interiority of the Romantic poets. A marriage of Flaubert and Whitman, *The Awakening* is a close analysis of the diffuse, even chaotic sensations of the embodied consciousness. By bringing sensory impressions and erotic feeling into the purview of high fiction, Chopin unsettles the principles of museum Realism. In *The Awakening* Realism is not an institution for grasping civic relations, nor a tutorial in the distinctions apprehended through high taste. Rather, by exhibiting interiority as a Realist spectacle, Chopin's fiction insists that consciousness is subject to the mutabilities of the body and its desires, a view that follows Realist truth-seeking to a point that undercuts Realist aspirations for intellectual mastery.

Chopin's literary tastes and aims were shaped less by the edicts of Northeastern editors like Howells than by her own French Catholic background. Chopin's maternal family had emigrated from France to colonial St. Louis and held considerable social prominence in the city. Her mother married an enterprising Irishman and Katharine O'Flaherty was born in St. Louis in 1850. After her father was killed in a rail accident, she was initially educated at home by her great-grandmother, who taught her French and music, and she later graduated from a Catholic academy. When she married Oscar Chopin and moved with him to New Orleans, Chopin entered a culture in which French language and literature were an even more pervasive local influence. She would read and translate French authors throughout her life.

Literary Realism thus had different compass points for Chopin than for most Northeastern writers. As it developed, Chopin's writing increasingly showed a more direct affinity with continental fiction, and a less conflicted relation to mass culture, than did the fiction of Realists like Howells and Wharton. By the time Chopin began to publish her fiction she had moved back to St. Louis following Oscar's death, but her two collections of stories, *Bayou Folk* (1894) and *Night in Acadie* (1897), were deft portraits of the rural Louisiana towns and affluent Creole culture she had known during her married years. The stories were critically praised and Chopin was received as a particularly skillful contributor to the genre of local-color fiction flourishing in the leading journals. Like most "quality" local-color writing, these stories betray little overt concern for the emergent mass culture that so often troubled (and creatively spurred) intellectuals in the Northeast. And yet, viewed as a genre, local-color writing reveals its own rivalry with mass culture precisely in its studied elimination of any trace of mass forms. By depicting rural regions and small-town life as islands of authentic culture, local-color fiction tacitly identifies mass technologies and forms with a corrosive modernity – as impersonal, soulless, indifferent to human needs, and hospitable to destructive human desires.

Chopin's Louisiana stories largely share these implicit generic values. In "At the 'Cadian Ball," a story of potential sexual exploitation brings into view class tensions between Acadian farmers and Creole planters. The culminating scene at a traditional Acadian ball, however, allows these tensions to be contained as finally harmonious parts of a distinctive regional world.

The big, low-ceiled room – they called it a hall – was packed with men and women dancing to the music of three fiddles. There were broad galleries all around it. There was a room at one side where sober-faced men were playing cards. Another, in which babies were sleeping, was called *le parc aux petits*. Any one who is white may go to a 'Cadian ball, but he must pay for his lemonade, his coffee and chicken gumbo. And he must behave himself like a 'Cadian. Grosboeuf . . . could recall but one disturbance, and that was caused by American railroaders, who were not in touch with their surroundings and had no business there. "Ces maudits gens du Raiderode," Grosboeuf called them.

As a ritual celebration, the ball shores up Acadian values and practices, not least by embracing those outsiders who can (by being white) and will (by knowing Acadian behavior) imitate and therefore honor the ways of "'Cadian" culture, while still acknowledging their outsider status (by paying for food and drink). The ethnographic rules presented in this passage are axioms. Statements of norms, they do not contemplate the possibility that someone from a higher station – a wealthy white planter, for instance – might successfully follow these rules with the intention to seduce and abuse the most desirable young Cajun woman; that dangerous possibility, though, is precisely the problem anticipated and then resolved in the narrative plot. Chopin's story works as an extension of the genre of ethnography: her fictional plot poses and then works through a potential disaster but does so in a literary form that presumes the ethnographic integrity of the local. The interests of Cajuns, Creoles, and black folk may collide, but the Cane River area – like the ball itself – has the resources to contain the conflicts within the bounds of a self-sustaining world.

What cannot be admitted into this world is modernity. "American rail-roaders," envoys of technological speed and transit, prove far too disruptive for admission to the ball. Neither are they admitted into the story: because the railroad workers are fundamentally anti-local ("not in touch with their surroundings"), the episode is never directly narrated in this local-color narrative. The modern rail system unified and transformed the postwar nation, but its speed, impersonal power, and force of dislocation have "no business" in Cane River culture and no place in local-color fiction except as a token of what is dangerous and inassimilable to local "surroundings."

Although "At the 'Cadian Ball" is inhospitable to the stories of railroaders, still it is not quite accurate to see it as hostile to the railroad. After all, it is the national rail system that transports Chopin's manuscript to the editorial offices in New York, and the same rail lines that deliver copies of *Bayou Folk* to readers from Boston to San Francisco. The discrepancy reflects a more divided position regarding modernity than is visible on the page. But the division is not necessarily a contradiction. For all its potential to disrupt locality, a national system of commercial distribution offered readers of local-color fiction the chance to witness scenes and states of feeling they would not otherwise imagine – and might not otherwise wish to. The modern mass-distribution system could be used to export ideas and sights that were neither traditional nor modern in any simple sense. In Chopin's "Neg Creole," for instance, readers are lured with conventional scenes of picturesque poverty in the New Orleans' French market, only to be taken to a room that houses the far more repellent poverty of a dying woman. There, though her life and death are not softened or made quaint, Chopin's portrait insists on the scene's accuracy and thus its dignity. In "Lilacs," Chopin in effect suppresses the urban glamor available to a Parisian singer while depicting the pleasure and "excitement" the young woman finds in her annual stay inside a provincial convent and the intense love she shares with one of the women there ("What ardent kisses! What pink flushes of happiness mounting the cheeks of the two women!"). Such scenes are not nostalgic glimpses of traditional mores but pictures that confer value on still unrecognized lives and affective bonds. Social recognition will have to come – if it comes – in a world yet to be. These scenes belong to the future, not to the past.

Other Chopin stories show a more troubling affinity between local-color conventions and the mass market. The 1890s, the decade when both of Chopin's collections appeared, also saw a broad national enchantment with the antebellum Southern plantation. Stories of a lost world of green landscapes and happy slaves afforded white Americans a soothing collective amnesia. Old South mythology was as profitable as it was pleasurable: plantation nostalgia was sustained in popular fiction and theater, in minstrel shows and sheet music, and in the mass merchandising of Mammy dolls and clocks, Old South decorative wares, and historical novelty toys. The phenomenon rested on a pronounced irony: the "memory" of a pre-industrial world of gracious rural living and racial harmony was the creation of new technologies and markets. Engines of modern industry – prodigious production advances, new systems of transport, mass advertising – produced and fed pleasing fantasies of a Southern past. Writers like Mark Twain and Charles Chesnutt would exploit the contradiction for their own ends, but for Chopin it was an irony she either failed to perceive or declined to confront. Expressing admiration for plantation novelists such as Thomas Nelson Page and Joel Chandler Harris, Chopin singled out the "child-like exuberance" of the black characters who have "furnished so much that is deliciously humorous and pathetic to our recent literature." When she held up the "whole-souled darkies" in the fiction of Ruth McHenry Stuart as part of the "wholesome, human note" of Stuart's Louisiana, Chopin echoed the implicit racial orthodoxies of the plantation school: that the ties between black and white Southerners under slavery were consensual bonds of love; that the dependent nature of African Americans made them helpless if soulful orphans in the modern South; that black lives and folkways were in essence a rich backdrop to the center-stage lives of white Southerners. These backward-looking sentiments fed a highly marketable modern fiction, and belletristic local-color writing fostered Old South iconography no less than did Aunt Jemima trademarks and Jim Crow illustrations.

In this market, Chopin, like Chesnutt, discovered a ready audience for colorful sketches of Southern life. The short fiction that launched her writing career includes tales of devoted slaves ("Beyond the Bayou") and old-timers who perform the emblematic labor of carrying fond memories of slavery days ("Aunt Polly," "The Benitou's Slave"). Also like Chesnutt, however, a number of Chopin's Southern stories can be read as slyly undercutting conventions of plantation fiction. "Désirée's Baby" replays the tale of the tragic mulatto slave who suffers from her black ancestry, but Chopin's plot then uses the myth of racial purity against itself to reveal the psychology of self-deceit upholding specious notions of white bloodlines. In the main, however, Chopin's African-American and Mexican characters are decorative figures, supplying local color in the form of human bodies of many hues.

An interior life in Chopin's fiction is almost always the portrait of a white life. The richest interior landscapes belong to white women, often women uprooted in some fashion from local moorings. Realists tend to see modern cities and consumer culture as able to transform – most likely, to flatten or weaken – the human subjects who inhabit them. Women are the most susceptible and hence the most interesting test cases of urban transformations. As Chopin began to move away from regionalist studies, her fiction increasingly featured scenes and objects from city life and viewed urban experience through women's lives. But, observed closely, these narratives exhibit a remarkable departure from the standard Realist suspicion of urban consumer culture. Mass objects and experiences are not fetishes that infect or distort human life, as depicted in most Realism. Rather, in Chopin such objects are potential portals into different states of consciousness. Consumer culture reveals rather than obscures. For viewing the lives of women in particular it offers privileged glimpses of the truths of the body, the suppressed wishes and dissatisfactions that cannot be articulated at the level of thought or language.

In "A Pair of Silk Stockings," for instance, analytic thinking is almost solely an activity to prevent self-knowledge. An unexpected windfall of fifteen dollars affords a struggling homemaker hours of "speculation and calculation" that preempt any other thoughts: "It was during the still hours of the night when she lay awake revolving plans in her mind that she seemed to see her way clearly toward a proper and judicious use of the money." But in a large department store, Mrs. Sommers's calculations give way to a revelation as affecting as that of any Realist heroine. Her revelation occurs at a lingerie counter, and comes solely through her sense of touch.

An all-gone limp feeling had come over her and she rested her hand aimlessly upon the counter. She wore no gloves. By degrees she grew aware that her hand had encountered something very soothing, very pleasant to touch. She looked down to see that her hand lay upon a pile of silk stockings. A placard near by announced that they had been reduced in price from two dollars and fifty cents to one dollar and ninety-eight cents; and a young girl who stood behind the counter smiled and asked if she wanted to examine their line of silk hosiery . . . She went on feeling the soft, sheeny luxurious things – with both hands now, holding them up to see them glisten, and to feel them glide serpent-like through her fingers.

Stroking and gazing at the colored silk transports her to a new cognitive state, one that displaces altogether her economic calculations ("she was not thinking at all") and propels her towards other pleasurable sensations – the softness of kid leather, the shine of polished boots, wine and black coffee consumed in a quiet restaurant dining room. Although Chopin parses this state of mind as closely as James does Isabel Archer's, Mrs. Sommers's consciousness is not an awareness of her social predicament but a sensory awareness that reconstructs her relation to her body: "Her foot and ankle looked very pretty. She could not realize they belonged to her and were a part of herself."

Attuned as it is to desire and bodily pleasure, commercial culture in Chopin is not dismissed as a theater of illusion. Objects in a department store can awaken unknown or forgotten internal dispositions. In their clarity and immediacy, the physical pleasures experienced by Mrs. Sommers become facts that overwhelm the reasoned motives and plans that govern her life. In turn, her life as wife and mother becomes something far more ghostly or unreal, defined by a "wish" for its endless deferral. In the story's final lines, a male observer gazes at Mrs. Sommers's "small, pale face" but cannot read her. The real cannot be grasped by even the keenest outside observer who expects to find knowledge in legible social facts or relations. "It puzzled him to decipher what he saw there," Chopin writes. "In truth he saw nothing – unless he were wizard enough to detect a poignant wish, a powerful longing that the cable car would never stop anywhere, but go on and on with her forever." Her longing exceeds the categories of high Realism, with its suspicion of the effects of consumer culture on female desire. For Chopin, it is the life of the body, its appetites, sensations, and revelations, which must be read in order to reach the real. "An Egyptian Cigarette" (1897) makes the point even more emphatically, when the hallucinatory landscape induced by smoking a narcotic cigarette, though wildly fantastic, conveys a woman's keenest feelings and social understanding.

That elliptical story was written just before Chopin began work on *The Awakening*. Though little more than a sketch, the brief story's unwillingness to heed the Howellsian opposition between fantastic image and narrative truth anticipates one of the defining features of Chopin's novel. Although *The Awakening* returns to Louisiana settings and customs, its local-color texture is in key moments overwhelmed by charged symbols expressive of Edna Pontellier's sensations and interior life. Realism loses its singular claim to represent the real. Like the Modernists to come, Chopin was prepared to see desire as expressive and bodily sensation as revelatory. In his *Remembrance of Things Past*, Proust would elevate a madeleine cake to a secular Eucharist, the taste of which turns memory into monumental narrative art. In *The Awakening*, Chopin similarly cedes to the human senses a primacy over reason that would come to characterize literary truth-telling under Modernism.

Place remains crucial in *The Awakening*. Edna Pontellier's transformation from New Orleans wife to a "Creole Bovary" (as critics quickly dubbed her), who sleeps with a man she does not love and loves still another man she will not wed, begins during a summer she spends by the sea. Grand Isle resort, a gathering place for Creole families on the Gulf of Mexico, is depicted in close detail. And yet the site is not the kind of environmental influence that setting is assumed to be in most Realism and local-color fiction. Or at least it is not so for Edna: Creole codes govern life at Grand Isle but they exert no controlling influence over the behavior and sexual identity Edna begins to fashion there. That identity, the narrator stresses, is the product of "new conditions in herself." Interior "conditions" enable Edna to live increasingly out of sync with the web of social life that surrounds her. *The Awakening* can be read as the text in which Modernist desire fractures the ethnographic authority of local-color fiction. Edna is neither an illustration of enduring Creole culture nor a "modern instance," in Howells's sense, of an anomie that can be traced back in high Realist fashion to mass culture and its discontents.

Yet while Edna's transformation issues from internal conditions, Grand Isle is still critical to that change. The music, smells, light, and sea at the resort all serve to foster her awakening. Hearing a skillful piano performance, for instance, is a key catalyst: it was "perhaps the first time her being was tempered to take an impress of the abiding truth." Her first ever swim, in a moonlit ocean, is an even more dramatic event, bringing "exultation" at her new ability to propel her body through the waves, and then an "appalled" sense of fatal isolation as she becomes aware of her distance from the shore. Edna receives "abiding truth" in these moments, but just what truth signifies in this novel is left undefined. The reason is that abstract truth has little purchase in this world. Knowledge is no longer a product of the thinker's intellectual mastery over external objects but is rather a temporal process Chopin calls "awakening," a change in a state of consciousness akin to the passage from sleep to wakefulness that cannot be abstracted from the body of the sleeper.

As if to mark her departure from the Realist coordinates of truth, Chopin twice interrupts her own narration of Edna's history to sound a lyrical refrain. "The voice of the sea is seductive; never ceasing, whispering, clamoring, murmuring, inviting the soul to wander for a spell in abysses of solitude; to lose itself in mazes of inward contemplation. The voice of the sea speaks to the soul. The touch of the sea is sensuous, enfolding the body in its soft, close embrace." Like Whitman's leaves of grass, the sea here is both nature's pastoral bower and a medium of metaphor. The poem-like passage distills the novel's aim to identify the self with the body, and meaning with affect and desire. Thought ("inward contemplation") has become erotic solitude. Voice is a medium of touch. This is Whitman's nature, not Emerson's: the natural world bespeaks the spirituality of the flesh rather than a transcendence of matter to reach ideal meaning. (Is it merely coincidence that Edna begins to drift into sleep when she tries to read a volume of Emerson?) When nature speaks, it reaches the human soul through pleasure and desire, a benevolent language of sensory "embrace." Unlike the Whitmanian soul, however, the spiritual source of Edna's awakened self is not nature alone. The same stimulus for her sanctified desire comes by way of "gorgeous" objects of the bourgeois household, including luxury chairs, a satin gown worn with diamonds, "good, rich wine" and garnet-colored cocktails. By giving lyrical affirmation to any sensuous object or medium that moves her protagonist, Chopin realizes Howells's fear that the modern marketplace would allow desire – not intellectual discernment – to ratify the real.

Whitman saw in nature and bodily desire the spiritual license to disregard law and custom and Chopin's song of the self partakes of the same radical potential. Beginning in the 1970s, feminist critics championed *The Awakening* as a literary declaration of independence from the patriarchal constraints of nineteenth-century marriage and motherhood. Edna's struggle is often seen as a dismantling of what Chopin calls the "mother-woman," a bourgeois deity whose sacralization goes hand-in-hand with women's subordination. But the novel's primary energies have less to do with a vision of gender equality or autonomy than an ethos of erotic liberation. Edna's pursuit of love and vitalist sensation leaves her indifferent to the dictates of duty. The faces of her children bring her real joy, but in their absence the bonds of kinship become negligible. Because social and familial structures matter less and less the more Edna's awakening intensifies, the novel's political valence is largely implicit. What are the consequences if female desire and feeling are authorized as literary truth, as a portrait of the real? In *The Awakening*, social roles and constraints are not so much critiqued as sloughed off and left to the side. The radicalism of Edna's story lies in the ease – and the sensuous pleasure – with which she escapes a life that had come to seem numbing and pointless.

Did white women simply have agency all along? That possibility is one of the startling implications of Edna's unhindered choices and actions. Because Chopin's novel shifts the authority of Realism from social types and civic relations to the truths of the body, Edna's will-to-desire is matched with a freedom to act. The only "inward agony" she experiences comes when she observes the bodily violence of a birth; the sight seems either to affront her with the fact of physical pain as a power superior to pleasure, or perhaps to reassert the claims of her own children as the flesh of her flesh. In either case, even this "scene of torture" leaves Edna with a power of agency. Almost immediately afterward, she enters the sea unclothed for the swim that is the novel's concluding scene and final ode to the sensuous embrace of nature. That this last act of freedom is almost certainly an act of suicide, however, clearly tempers the notion of Edna's agency. If the ability to take action is only the freedom to end her life, Edna's character is little different from the heroines in the museum of Realism, the beautiful corpses of the Anglo-European novel. Yet if Edna's choice is the last and surest expression of an ethos of desire, then the scene is not her death but a final glimpse of a consciousness that lives in the body and its senses: "There was the hum of bees, and the musky odor of pinks filled the air."

Virtually no contemporary critic saw Edna's story as heroic. A small few saw it as tragic. The fact that readers all conceded Chopin had created "flawless art" seemed only to heighten their sense of unpleasantness; the novel was deemed "sordid," "morbid," even "repellent." For these readers Edna seems to have possessed an uncanny likeness to the "horrible prettiness" Howells saw in the comic burlesque performers who exploited the incongruity of feminine bodies in male costumes and roles. For all her femininity, Edna's sexual agency struck readers as kind of Realist cross-dressing that produced an incongruous, hybrid figure of modern womanhood. Chopin was surprised and bitterly disappointed at the novel's stinging reception (though recent scholarship suggests that it was her illness and other difficulties – not social ostracism – that probably caused her to publish next to nothing after *The Awakening*). Although later critics recreated Edna as a feminist martyr, Chopin's contemporaries may have grasped something closer to the truth Chopin intended for Edna's story: the portrait of unheroic, limited agency of a protagonist who, like figures from Leopold Bloom to Faulkner's Lena Grove, lives by the vicissitudes of desire.

4

CHESNUTT AND IMPERIAL SPECTACLE

NATIVE AMERICAN LETTERS AND GERONIMO'S BOOK

The birth of an American mass-culture industry in the decades 1850–90 coincided with the "Long Death" of free Native-American peoples in the trans-Mississippi West. There was no strict causal connection; mass culture was predicated on explosive population growth and new technologies, yet even with these advantages there was nothing fated about the US dispossession of "Indian Country," which commenced soon after the Great Plains were promised to indigenous peoples at mid-century. But the conjunction in time created a certain reciprocity between the two events: the rise of mass culture is also a fitful record of the subjugation of free Native-American cultures. Mass portrayals of Native Americans form an erratic archive that is less self-serious but no less revealing than the ideological arguments or "metaphysics of Indian hating" Herman Melville sardonically identified as a national creed. Alongside demonstrations of contempt and enmity for Native Americans, mass culture enacts strains of awe, guilt, compassion, and envy never reflected in US military campaigns and policies. As regards Native Americans – and conflicted race questions broadly in the period – mass culture is the troubled unconscious mind of the white body politic, harboring desires and fears that take public shape through routes of contradiction and denial. In its new spaces of virtual existence, from photographs, dime novels, and Wild West shows to its apotheosis in the cinema, mass culture creates an expanding iconic life for Native Americans as they are steadily dispossessed of their lands and free lives.

Native Americans use mass genres for their own ends. Popular magazines and books circulate the Native-American pleas and denunciations that so often remain dead letters in governmental channels. For some tribes, Wild West performances permit the freest and fullest practice of traditional skills that had been banned on reservations. That such venues hosted genuine Native expression belies Howells's wish to equate mass spectacle with illusion. Race matters make this point with special clarity. Close attention to the history of racial conflict and coexistence refutes the elite tendency to see mass culture as a factory for producing flat images, pictures deemed simply more or less degraded and always unreal. For black people, Native Americans, and other populations, mass expressions were sometimes embraced, sometimes disowned, but never dismissed as mirage. The infrastructure and products of American mass culture possessed a reality-making power of sometimes life-or-death significance. Yet the orthodoxies of high cultural criticism left establishment intellectuals with little ability or inclination to speak to this racial power, and most literary writers chose silence. Other authors, however, turned a new analytic lens on spectacles of race and on the racial valences of literary meaning itself, in astute recognition of the generative opposition between mass entertainment and the sphere of the literary.

P. T. Barnum had quickly discovered that exhibiting Native Americans at his American Museum created a profitable sensation. His bestselling autobiography *Struggles and Triumphs* (1869) recounts several anecdotes about the Native-American companies he brought to New York and sent on to Europe, and his stories supply readers with a second-order spectacle of the novel transactions between showman and "savages." In one chapter he recounts the coup he achieved in 1864 when he managed to get a delegation of chiefs who had met with President Lincoln to come to New York from Washington. The chiefs, Barnum learns from a translator, would never permit themselves to be displayed as curiosities before a paying audience, so Barnum uses tactics that sustain the illusion that he and his patrons wished merely to pay tribute to the tribal leaders as honored guests. What Barnum offers his audience, then, is the chance to participate in staging a show for which the chiefs are the unwitting audience. The ruse amounted to a grandly enacted wink, a display of Yankee wit overcoming Native-American ferocity.

In exhibiting these Indian warriors on the stage, I explained to the large audiences the names and characteristics of each . . .

"This little Indian, ladies and gentlemen, is Yellow Bear, chief of the Kiowas. He has killed, no doubt, scores of white persons, and he is probably the meanest, black-hearted rascal that lives in the far West." Here I patted him on the head, and he, supposing I was sounding his praises, would smile, fawn upon me, and stroke my arm, while I continued: "If the blood-thirsty little villain understood what I was saying, he would kill me in a moment; but as he thinks I am complimenting him, I can safely state the truth to you, that he is a lying, thieving, treacherous, murderous monster. He has tortured to death poor, unprotected women, murdered their husbands, brained their helpless little ones; and he would gladly do the same to you or to me, if he thought he could escape punishment. This is but a faint description of the character of Yellow Bear." Here I gave him another patronizing pat on the head, and he, with a pleasant smile, bowed to the audience, as much as to say that my words were quite true, and that he thanked me very much for the high encomiums I had so generously heaped upon him.

Barnum's trick is a feat of doubling: each chief is simultaneously a fearsome killer and a fool. The double bind holds even after the men discover the ruse. Their anger at the sustained deceit and disrespect can only prove the risible pride of a savage: "Their dignity had been offended and their wild, flashing eyes were anything but agreeable."

It is hardly surprising that racist derision is easily marketed as entertainment in this moment. As the tacit US policy of dispossession breaks into episodes of open warfare and white soldiers and settlers are killed, Native-American baiting is widely practiced in the name of patriotism and outraged Christian sensibilities. Popular culture profitably follows suit. More critically revealing than Barnum's descriptions of soulless "monsters," then, is his spectacle of false homage. The Cheyenne, Kiowa, Apache, and other chiefs had been made to believe that their visit to New York was an extension of their diplomatic mission to Washington. Barnum pretends to receive them as dignitaries who had come to the East to represent the interests of rights-bearing peoples. These are not simply Barnum's false pretenses; they are his comic premise. Barnum seizes on and sells the pleasure afforded white people at the picture of Native Americans believing and behaving as if they possessed a standing that is in fact illusory.

His success at the game forces a question: just how false was the trick of Barnum's false pretenses? Barnum's ruse succeeds by finding an ingenious way to present the figure of the Native-American diplomat as a living oxymoron, without the Native Americans becoming any wiser. Inasmuch as the chiefs were in fact a Native delegation, Barnum's success cannot but have a broader significance. Did Barnum's sham praises and trumped-up excursions (carriage promenades through Central Park, ceremonial visits to schools) tell a slant version of the truth about the state visit just completed in Washington? Whether the Lincoln administration during that 1864 summit had merely pretended to recognize the delegation as leaders owed respect for their status as representatives is something that cannot be ascertained. But the historical record shows that Washington's reception of tribal heads amounted in the end to a species of official play-acting. Barnum's ruse captures the fact that the state's outward show of negotiation with Native-American leaders was structurally at variance with a white intra-racial understanding, a consensus confirmed over time that the leaders of Native-Americans peoples did not possess the status that US officials pretended to recognize and pledged to respect.

Within the year, the notorious Sand Creek massacre would make this consensus starkly apparent. After armed clashes throughout the summer between US troops and Cheyenne and Arapaho fighters, the Colorado territorial governor declared amnesty for all Native Americans willing to locate on reservations. A Cheyenne leader, Black Kettle, took his people to the banks of the Sand

Creek near Fort Lyons as directed. Despite Black Kettle's surrender, a regiment under Colonel John Chivington attacked the camp in late November and cut down ninety-eight women and children and twenty-five men. Every corpse was mutilated in some way, with body parts later displayed in a Denver theater. That scalps, breasts, and sex organs became the literal representations of the Cheyenne is a grotesque inversion of the hollow recognition given only months before in Washington to a Cheyenne chief as a living representative of his people.

Easterners were largely appalled at the massacre. Barnum could not have drawn his crowds – certainly not the same crowds, anyway – had he presented the limbs and organs from the massacre rather than the living Native Americans of his show. Yet the trophies on the Denver stage and the showman's entertainment in New York draw upon the same controlling idea of the Native American. Barnum's spectacle relied on the absence of any understanding by the chiefs of what everyone else in the Museum audience saw and heard, an absence made all the more striking by the physical presence of the men on stage. To his audience Barnum's Native Americans are bodies but they are not selves, not human subjects with full capacities to understand and communicate. In virtually the same moment, the question of Native-American comprehension is the critical factor in the events that culminate at Sand Creek. In the weeks before the massacre, Colonel Chivington had gone on record with his view that negotiation with Native Americans was a strict impossibility. The proof was their racial inability to grasp white words in any meaningful way: "It is simply not possible for Indians to obey or even understand any treaty. I am fully satisfied, gentlemen, that to kill them is the only way we will ever have peace and quiet in Colorado." Chivington's Native American is a creature whose inability to comprehend white meanings is matched by his innate propensity to kill white people. In crucial respects this representation of the Native American is also Barnum's, a double figure as fearsome as he is uncomprehending. With brutal frontier exaggeration, the notion of the Native American as all body and no soul finds its ultimate expression in the collection of body parts of dead Cheyenne and Arapaho on a stage in Denver.

At the end of the century, William James would describe the same phenomenon: the will among white Americans to imagine brown people as bodies with no "inwardness." He was referring not to the history of the US relations with Native Americans but to the imperial adventures the United States had launched in the Philippines. In his anti-imperialist essays such as "The Philippine Tangle" (1899) and "Address on the Philippine Question" (1903), James describes the primary imperial act as a cognitive one, the willful conjuring of the dark-skinned person as a being without any interior consciousness. "It is obvious that for our rulers at Washington the Filipinos have not existed as psychological quantities at all, except so far as they might be moved by President McKinley's proclamation . . . There is no clear sign of its ever having occurred to anyone at Washington that the Filipinos could have any feelings or insides of their own whatever." The Native-American wars had already proven this a fatal tautology: in confronting indigenous peoples, the absence of recognizable inwardness means perforce the absence of diplomacy – and the positive grounds for war. James identifies the same reflexive policy as the foundation of the American intervention in the Pacific. It is a reflex that turns Filipinos into "pictures," objects of mass and color only: "In short we have treated the Filipinos as if they were a painted picture, an amount of mere matter in our way. They are too remote from us ever to be realized as they exist in their inwardness."

William James's analysis here – that "pictures" pre-empt diplomacy – makes more illuminating, if more troubling, the enormous popularity in the period of pageants and live shows featuring exotic peoples. Over the course of the post-bellum decades, entrepreneurs adapted the long-standing European interest in unfamiliar peoples and customs to the technologies of the new culture industry. Native Americans remained a favorite attraction. But the small companies that toured theaters earlier in the century grew into vast outdoor extravaganzas drawing thousands of spectators. The most famous was Bill Cody's Wild West show, organized in 1883. The former cavalry officer teamed with Native horsemen and warriors in full regalia to perform feats of shooting, riding, and racing. In addition to contests and feats of skill, the casts enacted living pictures of famous Great Plains battles, engagements that had been the truest form of US recognition of Native people as estimable human agents. By invoking a history of actual warfare, the Wild West shows tacitly confirmed the fact that only Native bodies, as either fighters or as mutilated trophies, received any meaningful recognition in the eyes of official America, while state diplomacy with Native-American representatives over Native rights and claims had been a shadow play. A theater of pictures – of "mere mass," in William James's phrase – was the truest representation of US–Native-American relations, an ironic realism of racial spectacle. Here as elsewhere, the syntax of mass culture came closest to articulating the reality of race relations in American society.

Like Cody, Barnum and other showmen such as Adam Forepaugh recognized that the public appetite for racial spectacle was outstripping what could be offered on the stage of a theater. After his Museum burned down in 1865, Barnum's next large enterprise was the P. T. Barnum's Great Traveling

Museum, Menagerie, and World's Fair, which advertised "Fiji Cannibals, Modoc and Digger Indians, and representative types of Chinese, Japanese, Aztecs, and Eskimos" presented in large-scale pageants. A later racial exhibit, the Ethnological Congress of the Barnum and London Circus, launched in 1884, convened even more representatives of unfamiliar races, listed under the Barnumized taxonomy of "Cannibals, Nubians, Zulus, Mohammedans, Pagans, Indians, Wild Men." The "Congress" brought foreign men and women to US cities, but Barnum's show was not meant to cultivate a sense that people from distant points had been brought near. Instead, this larger exhibition, staged in more cavernous arenas, presented its cast as the proxies for populations that remained, in James's words, "remote from us." Barnum offered "for leisurely inspection" the "representatives of notable and peculiar tribes . . . as they can only be sought in their native countries." His participants had been found in places "where a white man never trod before." The show, in other words, was not intended to evoke an assembly of diverse peoples but to recall moments of white–native contact, in an allegory not of diplomacy but imperial discovery. In the 1890s Barnum dramatized the allegory directly in gigantic productions of *Columbus and the Discovery of America* with a cast numbering in the thousands.

When the United States organized its own allegory of Columbian origins, techniques of mass racial spectacle were annexed to national purpose. The 1893 Chicago World's Columbian Exhibition devoted its exhibit halls in the fair's neo-classical "White City" to technological displays and artistic achievement; engines, maps, and artworks were the outward expressions of inward capacities of the great state powers of Europe and the New World. In the fair's ethnological villages, non-European populations were represented not with wrought objects but with the self-evidence of their own bodies. Recreated villages of countries such as Algeria, Dahomey, and Egypt, located in the Midway entertainment zone alongside amusement rides and shops, presented brown and tan personages as the outward expressions of essential identities of blood, the only recognized "inwardness" of the darker races. But the Chicago World's Fair also affords examples of the way the practice of relegating indigenous peoples to the status of living pictures could bring unexpected results. The fair's opening-day ceremony commemorating Columbus's first voyage to America featured speeches by an array of white dignitaries, but before the addresses from politicians and fair organizers, a Native American, Simon Pokagon, came forward to ring a replica of the Liberty Bell. The resulting tableau was an elegant solution to the problem of how to express the aspirations of a democratic republic in an age of empire. The sight of a Native American sounding the state symbol of US sovereignty created a continuity of national meaning by way of balanced contrast, the red body linked with the state symbol of liberty. The visual symbol could achieve in a single moment what the speeches could only attempt in a temporal sequence: the formal equipoise necessary to contain the internal tensions of an empire of liberty.

When Pokagon delivered "The Red Man's Greeting," however, his words dissolved the visual composition – the literal composure – of an approved racial tableau. Pokagon, a Potawatoni from Southwestern Michigan, was counted a "civilized Indian" because of his education from white institutions and his conversion to Christianity. Whereas most of Pokagon's tribe had been forced out of the Midwest, a group of largely Catholic Potawatoni had managed to avoid expulsion from their lands through cooperation with federal authorities. Already considered a hybrid, a civilized Native American was deemed a fitting figure for the amalgam of Native-American origins and a US global destiny brought together in the opening ceremony. And Pokagon's "Greeting" fulfills to the letter the civilized genre requested of him, an oratory in English to mark a solemn civil occasion. But Pokagon also redefines the occasion to be commemorated: it is not an anniversary but a "funeral," the passing of a free red continent.

On behalf of my people, the American Indians, I hereby declare to you, the pale-faced race that has usurped our lands and homes, that we have no spirit to celebrate with you the great Columbian Fair being held in this Chicago city, the wonder of the world. No, sooner would we hold the high joy day over the graves of our departed than to celebrate our own funeral, the discovery of America.

The civilized Pokagon, with his command of English letters, remarks for his audience the absence of any elegy for this death: "Shall not one line lament our forest race, / For you struck out from wild creation's face?"

Pokagon's "Greeting" becomes that missing English elegy. Later printed and distributed at fairs and other sites by Pokagon and his Chicago lawyer, C. H. Engle, the address (sometimes appearing under the title "The Red Man's Lament") may have been the most widely read document of its kind before 1900. For all its ability to reduce people to pictures, the arena of racial spectacle was still a public space in which an English speaker like Pokagon could convert his value as a picture into a form of popular authority, in order to redirect his own iconic status as a representative Native American. In his speech Pokagon recasts the story of the "young republic" as the post-Columbian history of a confederated Native-American people, a sovereign "forest race." So narrated, there is no providential design to this history, only tragic contingency: "But alas! The pale faces came by chance to our shores." When "base ingratitude" is the payment for early Native assistance, Pokagon passes racial judgment on white settlers as "barbarians" and rules accordingly: "As the United States has decreed, 'No Chinaman shall land upon our shores,' so we then felt that no barbarians as they, should land on *ours*."

As that imitative "decree" suggests, Pokagon does not reject the discourse of civilization but instead effects a transvaluation of its awesome feats of material power. The city of Chicago, Pokagon acknowledges, is the "wonder of the world"; the "great Columbian show-buildings stretch skyward"; the railroad is a creation "greater in strength, and larger far than any beast of earth." Within Anglo-European thought, such improvements of land and materials are proof positive of value, creativity, and increase, the fruits by which to know and judge civilization. Pokagon does not dispute what should count as civilization nor challenge its proof in material transformation; he merely redraws the picture of its unparalleled power. "The cyclone of civilization rolled westward and the forests of untold centuries were swept away; streams dried up; lakes fell back from their ancient bounds; and all our fathers once loved to gaze upon was destroyed, defaced, or marred, except the sun, moon, and starry skies above, which the Great Spirit in his wisdom hung beyond their reach." Improvement and defacement are both synonyms for civilization, two accurate names for the same phenomenon. Pokagon speaks of both together, and in doing so traces a hitherto submerged fissure in the language of civilization. English words, conventions, and meanings contain a divided and warring world where white "success" is grammatically identical to red "sacrifice." Pokagon, as a civilized Native American, was to have reconciled this divide in his person and speech. Instead, his "Red Man's Greeting" draws in stark terms a destructiveness internal to civilization itself.

If the division cannot be resolved, it can be rationalized. Pokagon knows well this species of reason, which dictates that Native-American loss is a hard truth but truth just the same, "the unalterable decree of nature." But Pokagon rejects this appeal to nature, just as he insists on the double valence of civilization. His recounting of a past period of American peace thus becomes the most damning chapter of Pokagon's history of post-Columbian civilization.

The few of our children who were permitted to attend your schools, in great pride tell us that they read in your own histories, how William Penn, a Quaker, and a good man, made treaties with nineteen tribes of Indians, and that neither he nor they ever broke them; and further, that during the seventy years while Pennsylvania was controlled by the Quakers, not a drop of blood was shed nor a war-whoop sounded by our people.

Pokagon emphasizes a convergence of language: the seventy years of peace in Pennsylvania is the only episode for which red people and white histories recite the same version of events. As a common narrative, the Pennsylvania peace reveals that Europeans and Native Americans belong to the same history, to the same temporal order and geography, and not to different orders of nature. This brief history of peace is the exception that proves the rule of war, but it is also the anomaly that disproves the rule of war as nature's law.

Pokagon would die in 1899, just before turning seventy years old. A younger generation of Native-American intellectuals was just emerging who would enter English print culture as proponents of what one called the Native-American "thought world." Although a number of these writers published fiction, none took up the genre of the high Realist novel. The reason is not any disinclination to bring critical thought to what Howells called the "civil relations" of American life; it is rather that the authors confronted an absence of any clear Native-American relation to American civil society, a rift that compelled other modes of writing. Intellectuals such as Charles Eastman, Zitkala-Sa, Carlos Montezuma, and Laura Kellogg were among the founders of the American Indian Society in 1911 and helped launch AIS publications the *Quarterly Journal* and the *American Indian Magazine* in Washington, D.C. These scholarly institutions allowed writers to bring their education to Pokagon's stated desire to make civilization recognize and serve the Native-American world on its own terms. Yet, in one of the signal ironies of Native-American letters, the more Native-American writers cultivated high cultural institutions, the less their work reached non-Native-American audiences, while celebrities like Pokagon and Geronimo found a vastly larger audience for their dissenting words. In contrast to most prose published within high literary culture, Native-American letters developed not in opposition to mass spectacle but in the shadow of a racial theater to which Native literary expression remained openly bound.

When the Seneca anthropologist Arthur C. Parker, as editor of the *Quarterly Journal*, published a list of seven charges against "American civilization," he made the curious decision to name before all else the dispossession of Native-American thought. Parker's first charge is that the United States "had robbed a race of men – the American Indian – of their intellectual life." The choice was not the idiosyncratic concern of a bookish scholar, though Parker did prize scholarship and his collaborations with Frank Putnam of Harvard and Columbia's Franz Boas reflected his position as a leader in his field. His choice may have been a deliberate provocation, intended to defy the racist typing that assumed Native Americans had no capacity for analytic thought. But his chief reason for stressing intellectual before material or social deprivation was no doubt Parker's conviction that Native "inwardness," so discounted by Anglo-Americans, was in fact the foundation of all else in Native-American life:

In his native state the Indian had things to think about. These things in their several subjects were a part of his organized mental and external activities . . . *Human beings have a primary right to an intellectual life, but civilization swept down upon groups of Indians and blighted or banished their intellectual life and left scattered groups of people mentally confused.*

For Parker there exists a clear need for a restitution of intellectual rights: "The Indian must have his thought world given back."

The way forward to defining and recovering a Native "thought world," however, was not as clear. Charles Alexander Eastman (Ohiyesa), a Dakota Sioux author and activist, wrote of the dissonance he experienced when his field work for the YMCA in the 1890s brought him back into contact with the Native "philosophy" familiar from his youth, a style of thought which had been "overlaid and superseded by a college education" and his conversion to Christianity. As described in his autobiography *From the Deep Woods to Civilization* (1916), Eastman's discussions of Christianity with tribal elders produced unexpected results: he was at a loss to refute their "logic," while he found that his "close contact with the racial mind" was strangely consoling. By publishing collections of sketches and stories, including *Red Hunters and the Animal People* (1904) and *Old Indian Days* (1907), Eastman and his wife Elaine Goodale Eastman helped innovate a Native American species of local-color fiction, stories in English that combine a realism of ethnological detail with literary equivalents of Dakota storytelling conventions. The fiction may have been Eastman's way of attempting to combine the intellectual practices he acquired through higher education (he was a graduate of Dartmouth and Boston University medical school) with what he called the "Native philosophy in which I had been trained." But even this literary production – over nine published books – leaves opaque the question of the recovery of an original Native-American intellectual life. When Eastman eventually turned away from his life as an activist-author and lived much of his last years alone in a cabin near Ontario, was his decision to stop publishing books a sign that a Native "thought world" could not in fact be recovered? Or was his public silence proof that it could be, and that Eastman had finally recovered it?

What is certain is that Eastman's move into the Canadian woods removed any possibility of his being a visual race object or "picture." Evading the status of the iconic red body may well have required a literal disappearance from white vision, for even Native-American intellectuals were liable to be reduced to that figure in the eyes of non-Native-American audiences. Zitkala-Sa, a Dakota who had studied at Earlham College in Indiana and the New England Conservatory of Music, learned that her accomplishments as a violinist and in English oratory and letters still placed her at risk of being a racial picture, albeit "a picture to be remembered," as the *Brooklyn Times* called her. Like Eastman, Zitkala-Sa worked to craft a genre that could bring Native ideas and legends into English literary form. When she returned for a time after college to the Yankton reservation where she had grown up, Zitkala-Sa (who also went by the name Gertrude Simmons Bonnin) recognized that there was "material for stories" in the everyday Native-American life that had been ignored by showmen and other writers. In 1900 and 1901 she published fiction and autobiographical stories in *Harper's* and the *Atlantic* (pieces later collected in 1921 as *American Indian Stories*) and brought out a book of traditional Sioux tales, *Old Indian Legends* (1901).

The books of Zitkala-Sa, Eastman, and others of the era such as Arthur Parker's collections of Seneca and Iroquois folklore are credited with having begun a tradition of Native-American letters that would come to fruition in the 1960s and 1970s. A backward-looking pursuit of origins thus became the origin of a literary future; if these early authors never recovered a Native-American "thought world," it is certain they helped to found a new one. But Zitkala-Sa's writings in particular create their most striking effects when, rather than resurrecting buried knowledge, they offer an analytic account of what Parker called "deculturation," the deliberate dismantling of Native systems of meaning. Her autobiographical stories offer compressed, artful accounts of the techniques used at Native-American boarding schools for breaking apart the compound understanding, a fusion of the mental and the physical, that was the animating life of traditional Dakota society but legible in print only at moment of its dissolution.

Zitkala-Sa's "Impressions of an Indian Childhood" and "The School Days of an Indian Girl" are an intimate record of the bewilderment and fear she experiences upon entering at age eight a Quaker-run institute for Native-American children. The force of the account lies in its creation of a textual disjunction, a marked incongruity between the girl's overwhelming feelings and the school's "iron routines" that treat Native-American children as passive bodies. During Zitkala-Sa's first days at the school, for instance, the school's rooms and routines designed to cultivate order are for her a chaotic sensory assault.

We were led toward an open door, where the brightness of the lights within flooded out over the heads of the excited palefaces who blocked our way . . . The strong glaring light in the large whitewashed room dazzled my eyes . . . A large bell rang for breakfast, its loud metallic voice crashing through the belfry overhead and into our sensitive ears. The annoying clatter of shoes on bare floors gave us no peace.

Because Zitkala-Sa only rarely depicts school instructors or administrators, the narrative creates the sense of a strange, almost automated land of "large buildings" that exist to separate Native-American bodies from their beliefs and memories. An invisible, impersonal agency – a "civilizing machine," in Zitkala-Sa's words – exists just outside the range of the narrative point of view but drives everything that occurs in the story.

> I remember being dragged out [from a hiding place under a bed], though I resisted by kicking and scratching wildly. In spite of myself, I was carried downstairs and tied fast in a chair. I cried aloud, shaking my head all the while until I felt the cold blades of the scissors against my neck, and heard them gnaw off one of my thick braids. Then I lost my spirit.

Whereas the aim of Native-American education was to draw out and develop the interiority of a person who lacked a recognizable psychology, Zitkala-Sa depicts a precise inversion of that pattern: the ministrations of white schooling close down an interior "spirit" as they civilize the red body.

Yet something goes unremarked in this reversal of the meaning of education. For the school is also the site of and ironic motive for Zitkala-Sa's mastery of English literary codes, a mastery that becomes a means both of interior expression and of a critical analysis of the uses of language and symbol in a white civilization. Zitkala-Sa uses the leverage of literary irony to detach the practices of a white social order from its controlling symbols. The code of propriety governing bourgeois dress, for instance, reappears as immodest display. "As I walked noiselessly in my soft moccasins, I felt like sinking to the floor, for my blanket had been stripped from my shoulders. I looked hard at the Indian girls, who seemed not to care that they were even more immodestly dressed than I, in their tight-fitting clothes." The estranging effect becomes a critical mirror for reflecting to a largely white audience the vantage of the Native American who is otherwise made to occupy the position of visual object. That aim is realized most pointedly in a scene Zitkala-Sa describes from her college days, a state competition in which she represented her school in an oratory contest. Before she delivers her speech, Zitkala-Sa looks out at an auditorium of white faces and prepares herself to confront an audience of observers who reflexively see a Native American as a mere picture – in this case, a literal picture at its most derogatory, the sign of the squaw: "There, before that vast ocean of eyes, some college rowdies threw out a large white flag, with a drawing of a most forlorn Indian girl on it. Under this they had printed in bold black letters words that ridiculed the college which was represented by a 'squaw.'" So crudely reduced to a sign of Native-American stigma, the picture of the red body – here unmistakable *as* a picture – becomes the figure through which Zitkala-Sa gives an oppositional expression of the interiority she is not believed to possess. She does so most obviously in her speech, a superior performance of English oratory that wins the intercollegiate competition. More subtly, and with more complex implications, Zitkala-Sa also proves the point by writing and publishing her account of the event, expressing in print the interior life of feeling she will not display in the public hall. Anger, elation, and increased loneliness are the successive emotions given artful expression in her written recollection. All are signs the readers of the *Atlantic* would interpret as the marks of the literary self, the writer who disciplines thought and feeling through the uniquely public privacy of the crafted literary text.

Yet defeating the picture of the "squaw" with English eloquence does not count as success in Zitkala-Sa's work and she retreats from her own lettered persona almost as soon as she creates it. Here and throughout the narrative she reveals that every advance in her mastery of English letters widens the rift between Zitkala-Sa and her mother, who had wanted the girl to remain with her on the Yankton reservation: "The little taste of victory did not satisfy a hunger in my heart," she writes of her prize in the competition. "In my mind I saw my mother far away on the Western plains, and she was holding a charge against me." Zitkala's story suggests that the development of Native-American letters will come not from a restoration of a Native-American thought world but rather from a rift in that world, a rift that gives rise to the ineradicable, self-perpetuating desire to overcome absence through literary expression. Within the terms of the literary culture of her time, literary success leaves Zitkala-Sa in a no-man's land between mass visibility and ever-receding Native origins.

The contradictions of racial spectacle in an age of mass culture are probably sharpest in the career of Geronimo, Zitkala-Sa's antithetical counterpart. After close to thirty years of the "Apache wars," the warrior surrendered in 1886 and became a prisoner confined at Fort Sill, Oklahoma. An inmate and pauper, for two decades Geronimo was also a mass celebrity of the order of Mark Twain and Theodore Roosevelt, with a face recognized by millions from photographs and cartoons and a life of popular legend. His dictated memoir, *Geronimo: His Own Story* (1906), reached more readers than any other Native-American publication to date. Geronimo was famous, indeed glamorized, for his ferocious fighting in the wars against US and Mexican regiments. Yet he was not celebrated as a heroic outlaw in the manner of Jesse James. Rather, after his surrender Geronimo acquired an unusual legitimacy and became something of a fixture at state-sponsored events, including the 1905 inauguration parade for Roosevelt, in which he rode on horseback past crowds who hailed him by name with shouts and applause. Some along the parade route had no doubt already seen him at the 1898 Trans-Mississippi and International Exposition in Omaha, or at the Pan-American Exposition held in 1901 in Buffalo, or as recently as the St. Louis World's Fair in 1904. The public Geronimo is a coincidence of opposites: his fame as a Native-American icon gives him a public status and platform for dissent, yet he remains through it all a prisoner of the state. Geronimo's anomalous status is also the ground of his critical relevance. As one of the few people of color to acquire international fame, he illuminates the conditions of mass culture by way of his strange career as an inmate-celebrity.

Geronimo never sought his fame. He had no wish to publish his life story and turned down the white editor who proposed it until that writer, S. M. Barrett, offered money. Nor did Geronimo go willingly to the Omaha and Buffalo Expositions, though this is something Barrett reveals only in a passing footnote, where he explains that Geronimo was "sullen and took no interest in things" during that period of his life. Geronimo's "sullen" disinterest, however, presents certain puzzles for understanding *Geronimo* the bestseller. Why, for instance, does the warrior include in his book a chapter on his visit to the St. Louis World's Fair and give a detailed account of the sights and rides? Why, after several chapters of often bitter denunciation of US deceptions and poor treatment, does he conclude that World's Fair chapter with a tribute to the white American public? "I am glad I went to the Fair," he declares. "I saw many interesting things and learned much from the white people. They are a very kind people and peaceful people. During all the time I was at the fair no one tried to harm me in any way."

Barrett's explanation is simple, and simply stated. Geronimo shed his angry detachment because of a religious conversion: "The St. Louis Exposition was held after he adopted the Christian religion and had begun to try to understand our civilization." But there is nothing in Geronimo's account to suggest that either piety or an interest in civilized mores prompts the change. Indeed, what counts as the "civilization" Geronimo attempts to understand is solely the Midway world of popular entertainment: Geronimo mentions only his visit to fairground shows and amusements such as the "little house" that moves (a Ferris wheel), and the odd "canoe" (Shoot-the-Chute) he finds too unstable to set foot in. And he describes these encounters not with avid interest but rather with puzzlement and a degree of subdued distress. But even this species of interest cannot be taken at face value. By the time of the St. Louis Fair, Geronimo's third such exposition, the mechanical rides and stage shows could no longer have been the mysteries he depicts. Rather, Geronimo is "playing Indian," offering white readers the pleasure of observing the uncomprehending Native. His self-presentation in this part of the book is an extension of his role as a Native-American celebrity at the fairs: he is fulfilling the picture of the formidable Native-American warrior for whom features of urban life hold the strange wonder of the technological sublime.

Whereas Barnum exploits the unknowingness of the exhibited Native American, Geronimo leverages its value through a knowing self-exhibition in the same popular role. The reason Geronimo would reprise this role in print can be inferred from what follows it. The book's final chapter is a direct appeal to Roosevelt (to whom the book is also dedicated). "I am thankful that the President of the United States has given me permission to tell my story. I hope that he . . . will read my story and judge whether my people have been rightly treated." Like Roosevelt himself, Geronimo keenly understands that celebrity is a currency, not an identity, and that it can be traded for other things he values. Even the "sullen" Geronimo who was unwillingly exhibited at the first fair at Omaha recognized this fact well enough to sell the buttons cut off his coat, from a self-replenishing supply, for money his family badly needed. He learned to print his name in time to sell that token of himself in Buffalo, and added hand-made bows and arrows to his inventory during his six months in St. Louis. *Geronimo: His Own Story* is the print artifact he trades in hopes of gaining the returns he wants the most: permission from Roosevelt to allow the Apaches to travel back to their homeland. "Our people are decreasing in numbers here and will continue to decrease unless they are allowed to return to their native land. Such a result is inevitable." Geronimo's solemn final words are thus the terms of his largest gambit:

Could I but see this [return] accomplished, I think I could forget all the wrongs that I have ever received, and die a happy contented old man . . . If this cannot be done during my lifetime – if I must die in bondage – I hope that the remnant of the Apache tribe may, when I am gone, be granted the one privilege which they request – the return to Arizona.

Geronimo, a bitter captive, offers to trade a fiction of public contentment and balanced scales for a right of return. The terms of the barter are accepted, to the letter: Geronimo died at Fort Sill in 1909 and afterward the remaining Chihuahuas were moved to a reservation in Arizona. Pieced together from the dictation of an illiterate captive, Geronimo's book lies squarely outside of the sphere of the literary. And it must occupy that place in order to accomplish Geronimo's aims, for only the print equivalent of a racial picture – the portrait of an unlettered Native American, once fearsome and still proud but rendered poignantly powerless by white technologies of power – can acquire the mass publicity that can be leveraged for a public acquiescence to his last request.

The structure of Geronimo's book also reflects this canny understanding of an economics of mass culture and what it might yield him. After his account of the Southwestern warfare, Geronimo's book depicts a society consisting of only two kinds of spaces, prison grounds and Midway amusement parks. Geronimo's America is half penitentiary, half commercial fairgrounds and, while these are not identical sites, neither are they discrete spheres. For Geronimo they are conjoined halves of a white world that together define the possibilities and limits for a charismatic Native-American leader who, once defeated in war, acquires the currency of racial glamor in mass culture. Geronimo illuminates the operative discrepancy through which the powers of his mass publicity – a certain freedom to speak and criticize and even effect change – remain tied to a direct state control over his person. If Zitkala-Sa is the free literary author whose every written sentence perpetuates an eloquent self-division, Geronimo is the inmate-celebrity who makes prison dictation and icons of his fame into a self-selling that succeeds in securing effective change for Native Americans, though it does so over his captive body.

CHARLES CHESNUTT, STIGMA, AND THE LIMITS OF REALISM

Geronimo's account of the Midway at the St. Louis Fair captures a further aspect of the historical kinship between popular stages and colored races in the era's entertainment industry. The interests of audiences create a large market for spectacles of race; but what of the desires and interests of the racial performers, the entertainers of color who meet the demand in that marketplace? Even as Geronimo is "playing Indian" – presenting himself with an eye to the expectations of his largely white audience – he brings into focus the skills of other race performers and the peculiarities of the power they display. Geronimo in his St. Louis chapter takes up the role of fairgoer, though not before reminding readers that his celebrity status brings with it the unhappy fact of personal guards: "the Government sent guards with me when I went, and I was not allowed to go anywhere without them." Whether by design or happenstance, all of the fair performers Geronimo mentions are brown or black people; one possible exception, a man who saws women in half, is not ascribed any race. Geronimo describes Turks ("strange men with red hats") who perform sword fights; unfamiliar Native-American tribes he joins for a roping contest at the weekly Wild West show; the "little brown people" – indigenous Iggorrotes from the Philippines – "that United States troops captured on some islands far away from here," and others. From his place inside the color line, Geronimo finds the race of these performers significant enough to note, but he attends to these "strange people" not for their visual exoticism but rather for what could be called their comparative racial agency. Who possesses greater skill or strength? Who the keener eye?

The Turks with their scimitars earn respectful consideration: "They would be hard people to kill in a hand-to-hand fight." The Iggorrotes are deemed substandard performers who should not have been allowed to appear at the fair. Geronimo dwells in detail on the abilities of a black escape artist who slips free from his bonds. Geronimo's interest in these performers seems in part to be vocational, the curiosity of a fellow member of the guild. But a sense of affinity that might be vocational is hard to separate from the racial; color and ability are reciprocal concerns. Given his own history, Geronimo could not have viewed as insignificant the fact that the Iggorrotes, whom he scorns for their feeble drumming and dancing, were from a tribe that had been captured by US troops in a faraway homeland. By the same token, Geronimo's description of the black escape artist resonates as the tale of a racial captive.

In another show, there was a strange-looking negro. The manager tied his hands fast, then tied him to a chair. He was securely tied, for I looked myself, and I did not think it was possible for him to get loose. He twisted in his chair for a moment, and then stood up; the ropes were still tied but he was free. I do not understand how this was done. It was certainly a miraculous power, because no man could have released himself by his own efforts.

More than any other performance, the black man's power to free himself receives Geronimo's close notice. Though he may be partly disingenuous, he portrays the feat not as a trick but as an extraordinary capacity. His tribute to the "miraculous power" of the black performer, together with his dismissal of the Iggorrote company, comprise a muted allegory of agency. Can the brown or black man possess the ability to escape captivity? Attended by his guards, Geronimo watches a black man release himself with neither the help nor the hindrance of the manager who bound him. The moment defines a unique species of power, inexplicable but visually arresting, that acquires an ironic resonance as an instructive anomaly. An escape artist does not wield force over anyone, but neither does he suffer the passivity of the captive. His agency is exceptional – an exception from the rules of ordinary physics, and an exception to dualistic positions of the strong and the weak, of rulers and subjects. Though it is based on illusion, the performance still allows onlookers to see a special ability that frees the artist to transcend the conditions of domination and constraint that it simultaneously insists on acknowledging.

That it is a black man who displays this agency cannot be a neutral fact of the performance. In an age of imperial pageants and the Barnum-style exhibits, the performance of a black escape artist carries unfixed but inevitable racial meaning. Geronimo is unlikely to have known it, but in describing the black performer he was echoing an interest within African-American popular and literary cultures for the black magician or trickster, the figure who by vocation or avocation enjoys some form of extraordinary power. In 1900, the debut issue of the *Colored American Magazine* featured an essay on Leo Gowongo, "A Magician of Note." "He is a native of Antigua, B. W. I., with a mixture of Hindoo and Negro blood," an editor explains, "a young man of pleasing appearance, with piercing eyes, and whose every action shows energy and intelligence." Readers were invited to assess his appearance for themselves: the article includes four photographs of Gowongo performing tricks in his tuxedo. The story and pictures of a handsome man with a successful public career are pleasing in themselves, but the magazine is most emphatic about Gowongo's appeal as an entertainer and magician. The essay details several magic tricks, and the photographs capture the colorful end results, all witnesses to the special "energy and intelligence" that lie behind these extraordinary acts.

As magician, Gowongo joined two cultural types, the folkloric trickster and the modern black entertainer, both of whom risk racial stigma in order to turn their exposure before white observers into a display of exceptional skills. As magician, Gowango is also the antitype of the blackface minstrel, the white performer who ridicules a race through a trick of debased imitation. With his tuxedo and glossy photographs, Gowongo stands at the nexus of a high-stakes contest that masks itself as leisure entertainment. African-American entertainers in this moment venture into commercial theater, music, and dance for gain and recognition, but they do so when public visibility for black people is more charged than at any time in US history. Black and white people use mass culture and performance as another space in which to play out a struggle over the meaning and limits of black agency after slavery. Career, money, and cultural power are the prizes, injury and abjection the risks. And this nexus is the perhaps inevitable place towards which Charles Chesnutt and other novelists gravitate in bringing black American life into high literary culture. Literary culture offers Chesnutt the means and occasion to criticize the distortions of African-American identity occurring everywhere in public and popular spheres, though Chesnutt's literary critique simultaneously exposes the invisible racial limits in the world of American letters.

For Chesnutt, born to free mulatto parents in 1858, the career of novelist represented high cultural achievement, something European and American Realists had only recently made a plausible aspiration for the fiction-writer. From an early age, Chesnutt had viewed liberal education and literature as his route to social mobility. He attended a school for Negro children in Fayetteville, North Carolina, where the school's founder became his mentor and later assisted him in finding positions at black teaching institutions. In 1880, Chesnutt was only twenty-two when he became the principal of the Normal School for Colored Teachers in Fayetteville. The curriculum he set for his personal study in those years was even more demanding than his rapid advancement in school. Chesnutt taught himself history, music, and languages (Latin and Greek as well as French and German), mastered major English authors, practiced literary composition, and translated French novelists. When Chesnutt confides to his journal his hope to someday "secure a place in literature," the sphere of the literary is his means for conceiving both a professional vocation and a future self. In this sense, Chesnutt is the first African-American author to see himself in the terms Howells and James imagined for the fiction-writer, terms in which writing novels can bespeak one's high artistic distinction and a matching professional standing.

Chesnutt is also savvy enough to assess the field with an eye to professional success. His eye inevitably turns northward. All of his Southern opportunities teach him that Northern cultural capitals are the sites where the calibrations of literary distinction acquire institutional purchase. But Chesnutt also knows that what he calls "the Northern mind" has become newly interested in "the southern Negro." As a young black man in the South, Chesnutt had acquired his astute literary understanding against high odds; now the largely unlettered life of Southern African Americans had become an object of literary interest. Whether this turn of things represented a professional advantage for Chesnutt (as he hoped) or an added liability (as he sometimes feared) was difficult to predict when he began to pursue publication in earnest in the 1880s.

His prospects were mixed because the Northern interest in African Americans was mixed. Black folk life, like other rural cultures, had acquired an intellectual interest for some Northerners and black Southerners as a unique part of American vernacular history. Scholars and amateurs began collecting folk artifacts, stories, and beliefs for their ethnological value. Thomas Wentworth Higginson, for instance, became fascinated with Negro folk songs, which he compared to "those strange plants seen in museums alone." Chesnutt sometimes remarked dryly on the ethnological glamor that black folk life held for Northerners. Both their fascination with black culture and their concern for the black plight, he observed, has something to do with their distant vantage: "Men are always more ready to extend their sympathy to those at a distance, than to the suffering ones in their midst." But Chesnutt was hopeful that the unique social position of African Americans in the South, recently liberated from slavery but struggling against a new Pharaoh, would interest Northern readers in his fiction: "they lend a willing ear to all that is spoken or written concerning their character, habits, etc." The growing interest of the leading Northeastern magazines in regionalism also enlarged the audience for fiction about the South.

Yet, along with these strains of social and ethnological interest, Northern readers possessed a literal economic interest in the South and its black population. The propertied classes in the North had been steadily investing in Southern land and industries since the end of the war, and as the Northern economy grew, so too did their Southern portfolios. Investors did indeed wish to know the "character, habits, etc." of Southern black people, but for very different reasons than Higginson's in his hunt for rare Negro folk melodies. Finally, as economic ties grew stronger, white Northerners also began to evince a new species of *disinterest* in the South – that is, a growing tendency to look away from "the Negro Problem" in favor of more pleasing evocations of Southern pastoralism and a courtliness lost to the urban North. Chesnutt recognized that Northern attention to Southern black people, even when sympathetic, was partly a "romantic" interest in a faraway folk; he knew as well, therefore, that their sympathy and aid could easily give way to romance pure and simple.

Chesnutt's first significant publications reflect his close and canny study of these aspects of Northern interest in Southern life. The local-color tales Chesnutt began publishing in 1887 bespeak a literary tact so fine as to cross unnoticed into the tactical. Chesnutt's stories, collected in *The Conjure Woman* (1899), closely follow the narrative conventions established by authors of plantation fiction such as Thomas Nelson Page and Joel Chandler Harris, whose *Uncle Remus: His Songs and His Sayings* (1881) successfully collected African-American folk tales in a form of regionalist fiction. Like Uncle Remus, Chesnutt's Uncle Julius is a freedman with a rich collection of stories from his younger days on a plantation. For a Northern audience, the figure of the old black uncle was indispensable; certainly no white character could have called up pastoral scenes and black folkways from the Old South without suggesting a compromising sympathy with the vanquished slave system. That difficulty was resolved – or merely evaded – through the vehicle of black speech, the instrument of dialect. The typography of black dialect strikes present-day readers as tortured and denigrating, but it was precisely the opacity of the printed "black" speech that served for Chesnutt's contemporaries as a linguistic sieve to separate ethnological meanings from the abjection of slavery. Chesnutt mastered these forms and likewise their regionalist appeal; his first conjure tales appeared in the *Atlantic* and the collected volume was published by the premier Boston firm of Houghton, Mifflin.

What distinguishes Chesnutt's tales from others in the genre, however, is the way the canny assessment of a Northern audience is actually the subject or content of the stories themselves. In each successive tale, Uncle Julius recounts a different incident of plantation conjuring – a magical spell or charm that turns human beings into objects like trees and animals – to two white listeners, John and Annie. This married couple from the North had purchased a grape vineyard and moved to North Carolina. Like Chesnutt's readers, the two white Northerners are drawn to Julius's lore and absorbed by the magical transformations they do not accept as truth. Uncle Julius himself is no conjurer and never claims to be. But so skillful is Julius in understanding the psychology of his listener – John's sense of property and rationality, Anne's readiness to suspend disbelief in return for the pleasures of sentiment – that his tales always manage to win from them some prized object or opportunity. Though Julius betrays no sign of guile, Chesnutt makes clear that the black storyteller's understanding of his white audience is far savvier than their understanding of his black folk stories.

Julius's verbal dexterity, then, is its own form of charm or occult ability, and Chesnutt redoubles its ironic power by making the conventions of plantation fiction, so often apologist in tone and effect, obliquely expose the violence and humiliation at the heart of Southern slavery. In "Po' Sandy," for instance, Julius tells of a slave he once knew who could not bear to be separated from his wife and, on the eve of being sold away from the plantation, asks her to use her conjuring power to turn him into a pine tree. She does so, turning him back into a man each night under the cover of darkness. When his wife is away for a time, however, Sandy is cut down for lumber. His wife returns, and "when she seed de stump standin' dere, wid de sap runnin' out'n it," Julius recounts, "en de limbs layin' scattered roun', she nigh 'bout went out'n her min." The trope of conjure allows Chesnutt to realize in fantastic terms the dehumanization of chattel slavery without erasing the man's human subjectivity. In the bleeding sap and the horrific accuracy of the severed tree "limbs" the dialect imagery pinpoints the irrational realism of slavery's living property.

The darker tones in *The Conjure Woman*, however, are played more subtly than are the genre's romantic notes and reviewers praised the stories for their ability to "charm." It is a fitting term, if inadvertently so: Chesnutt's own dexterity allowed him to gain a foothold in high literary circles by skillfully reading the psychology of a Northern audience and using his knowledge to win interest and sales. *The Conjure Woman* shows that Chesnutt was drawn early to figures of occult or exceptional power: the conjurer, the trickster, the wily storyteller – all figures who hide canny, unsuspected abilities in the guise of a more benign-seeming capacity to entertain white people. But crucially, Chesnutt's own power was to be the exceptional agency of the literary, the secular magic that distinguished fiction as high art from mere writing. Without disavowing any kinship with the vernacular storyteller, Chesnutt still relies on the distinction in kind between the ex-slave Uncle Julius and his own standing as a man of letters. He relies, in other words, on the foundational difference of the literary, on the concentrated capacity for analytic discovery and vision cultivated in its history of narrative convention and style, in order to express what an impoverished freedman had neither the intellectual training nor the social protection to say. The sphere of the literary, Chesnutt believed, would allow him to directly address the civil relations of the contemporary South as no black or white author before him had done.

To that end, Chesnutt quickly set his sites on other genres. "I think I have about used up the old Negro who serves as mouthpiece," he wrote in a letter of 1889, "and I shall drop him in future stories, as well as much of the dialect." His aim was not merely to make a name for himself as an author of the highest kind of narrative art. Like the advocates of Realism, Chesnutt also believed that high aesthetic achievement could subtly change and develop what James called the "civic imagination." For Chesnutt, the imperative task was the "elevation of the Whites." Whatever their station or even their good will, white people in America were held back from "moral progress" by a "subtle almost indefinable feeling of repulsion toward the negro." Believing that literary forms work at the deepest levels of inwardness, Chesnutt had faith that literature could help effect a crucial social shift. "The negro's part is to prepare himself for social recognition and equality; and it is the province of literature to open the way for him to get it – to accustom the public mind to the idea; and while amusing them to lead people out, imperceptibly, unconsciously, step by step to the desired state of feeling." At this juncture, artistic achievement and civil advancement (in the unusual form of white uplift) were compatible goals in Chesnutt's mind.

Once *The Conjure Woman* volume appeared, Chesnutt began publishing other works in a more markedly Realist vein. In 1899 Houghton brought out a collection of his short stories, *The Wife of His Youth and Other Tales of the Color Line* (1899), studies of the class distinctions within an emerging black middle class, and soon after issued a novel, *The House Behind the Cedars* (1900), about a brother and sister light enough to pass for white. In November 1898, as these works were being readied for print, an incident of mass violence against African Americans occurred in Wilmington, North Carolina, an event that left Chesnutt "deeply concerned and very much depressed." He wrote to Walter Hines Page, the white editor of the *Atlantic*, that the attack was "an outbreak of pure, malignant, and altogether indefensible race prejudice, which makes me feel personally humiliated, and ashamed for the country and the state," and it galvanized Chesnutt to write a new novel. The result, a fictional examination of the November election fraud and subsequent riot, weaves the stories of fictional characters around a quite accurate retelling of the real political firestorm.

It is hard to discern whether, in taking up such a volatile topic, Chesnutt was inspired by a new professional self-confidence or by a new compulsion to probe a black man's "professional self-deception," as one critic describes the plot of the novel. Both strains of feeling, confidence and dejection, were probably contributing motives that pushed Chesnutt to write *The Marrow of Tradition* (1901), his best novel. For what distinguishes the novel most markedly from Chesnutt's other works is the fact that he produces his most uncompromising literary performance out of a far darker view of the politics of black entertainment. Chesnutt returns in *The Marrow of Tradition* to the question of the mixed and wavering interest of a Northern audience in the material of the South, but in *Marrow* the implications of feeding the Northern appetite for Southern pictures suggest a more ominous meaning for the power to charm.

Before the outbreak of open violence in the novel, the narrator describes a visit to Wellington (his fictional name for Wilmington) by a group of Northerners.

A party of Northern visitors had been staying for several days at the St. James hotel. The gentlemen of the party were concerned in a projected cotton mill, while the ladies were much interested in the study of social conditions, and especially in the negro problem. As soon as their desire for information became known, they were taken courteously under the wing of prominent citizens and their wives.

What follows is a series of "elaborate luncheons" and field trips that allow the Northern delegation to see and discuss the local conditions with their "courteous hosts." "Whether accidentally or not," the narrator notes, "the Northern visitors had no opportunity to meet or talk alone with any colored person in the city except the servants at the hotel" – these, however, "seemed happy enough." Barnum's trick with the Native-American chiefs has been played in reverse. A Northern delegation has become the unwitting audience for a rigged show, which they take to be the Southern reality. What they see in their guided visits to a selected black church, a mission school, and other sites, is the "spectacle of a dying race, unable to withstand the competition of a superior type." This "degeneracy" of the current descendants of the loyal negroes who had flourished under slavery is a sad tale and the white hosts are sorry to tell it. It is a story of largely futile attempts at black education, and of the unnamed crimes by certain black men that have brought on the "rough but still substantial justice" of lynching. The sorrowful story, however, has a happier aspect: whatever the burdens on white people, the black people are more than content. "Surely a people who made no complaints could not be very much oppressed."

The North is an audience, the South a stage, and the party of Northern visitors has been treated to a drama of "local conditions," a white fiction dressed up in blackface. Chesnutt underscores the point brilliantly when he makes the last stop on the visitors' itinerary an actual show.

In order to give the visitors, ere they left Wellington, a pleasing impression of Southern customs, and particularly of the joyous, happy-go-lucky disposition of the Southern darky and his entire contentment with existing conditions, it was decided by the hotel management to treat them, on the last night of their visit, to a little diversion, in the shape of a genuine negro cakewalk.

Offered as a "little diversion," the cakewalk is actually the last act of a pervasive, calculated diversion that places the white stage-managing of racial conditions behind the scenes of a real black performance. Through it the African Americans are unwittingly made to perform their own political contentment, in the form of a literal performance of black folk practice. As Chesnutt presents it, all dimensions of Northern interest in the South, from economic investigation (masculine fact-finding) to questions of race relations (feminine social concern), have been diverted by white fictions of race and the manipulation of pleasing black customs. The costs of this diversion, Chesnutt insists, are potentially catastrophic, and as the plot unfolds he makes his indictment even sharper: the cakewalk performance supplies the means for a white man in blackface to pin his capital crimes on a black man, an act that starts a contagion of violence.

It is not Chesnutt's career as an author that makes him portray the North as an audience, or not that factor alone. Alongside its timber, cheap labor, and other resources, the South had become a leading exporter of "pleasing customs" to a national and international audience. The cakewalk, a tradition of competitive dancing rooted in black plantation culture, was a favorite entertainment in the Northern states as well as in Europe. Madison Square Garden would draw hundreds of people to watch black dancers compete for top prizes. Elaborate recreations of plantation life, including massive "panoramas" of Old South scenes, toured widely in the North and West and were featured at World Fairs. One gigantic show billed as "Darkest America," which toured throughout the country in the same year as the Wilmington massacre, was produced by an all-black cast and management and featured a sugar plantation, a cotton gin, a prize fight, and a black ballroom scene, to mention only a few of the extensive sets. Sheet music, minstrel shows, and stage dramas were likewise cultural products that circulated in a national market for antebellum scenes and myths. In the wake of the Wilmington riot, Chesnutt views this "pleasing" entertainment industry with a sense of urgency and alarm. As portrayed in *The Marrow of Tradition* these white pleasures cannot be separated from a complex web of other passions – sexual panic, supremacist rage, a sense of righteous indignation that fuels a political coup and a racial massacre. Theatrical diversions, Chesnutt insists, are inseparable from political coercions, however much they may seem to be pleasant and even hopeful signs of good feeling.

The novel left Chesnutt's own Northern audience – readers and reviewers in literary circles – taken aback and in a state that was the print equivalent of tongue-tied. The reviews in the leading literary magazines had little praise for it and sales were tepid. Howells, an early literary mentor of Chesnutt's, wrote a review that was decidedly mixed, calling the novel a "bitter, bitter" book even as he conceded that Chesnutt's portrait of Southern race relations was wholly just and "presented with great power." Strikingly, Howells assessed Chesnutt's ability as a novelist in terms that cast the author as a black stage entertainer.

Mr. Chesnutt, it seems to me, has lost literary quality in acquiring literary quantity, and though his book, "The Marrow of Tradition," is of the same strong material of his earlier books, it is less simple throughout, and therefore less excellent in manner. At his worst, he is no worse than the higher average of the ordinary novelist, but he ought always to be very much better for he began better, and he is of that race that must first get rid of the cakewalk, if it will not suffer from a smile that is more blighting than any frown. He is fighting a battle, and it is not for him to pick up the cheap graces and poses of the jouster.

According to Howells's trope, Chesnutt should be waging the battle for recognition within the domain of Realism but has succumbed instead to playing the cakewalk performer who traffics in mannered "poses."

How is it that Chesnutt's most skeptical evaluation of racial theater earns for him this comparison with the black minstrel? *The Marrow of Tradition* clearly subscribes to the Howellsian tenets that define worthy fiction as the literary corrective for the distortions of mass spectacle. Perhaps no other work of fiction in the era offers a more pointed examination of the emergent institutions, from the national press syndicate to mass entertainment, that were drawing together all regions of the country in a single national market. Howells had criticized blackface minstrelsy for its willful projection of a theatrical "lie" that appealed to sensation; Chesnutt can be said to have expanded Howells's criticism into a full-length novel, with a plot intended to reveal the harm to lives, families, and American civil relations from the racial spectacles reuniting North and South at the expense of African Americans. Yet Howells places *Marrow* at a remove from the highest "literary quality" and closer to the theatrical gestures of a black stage performer.

The answer to the puzzle lies in Chesnutt's reinterpretation of the nature of mass spectacle. Chesnutt goes much further than Howells in his critique of the lie of minstrelsy and argues American civil relations are themselves shot through with minstrelsy's exploitative use of the black body as spectacle. The fault, then, cannot be pinned on a distortion of the real in the sphere of commercial culture, as Howells's Realism would have it. Rather, Chesnutt points to minstrelsy and other white manipulations of black life for the truth they expose about civil society, the reality that under the rule of Jim Crow all black people who enter the public sphere must present themselves, visually and otherwise, as a racial spectacle or sign – as a human stigma.

Two related moments in *Marrow* make this point most powerfully. The first comes when the innocent black man, Sandy, has been framed for a murder and presumptive rape that had been committed by Tom, a white man disguised in blackface. Chesnutt's plot thus links minstrelsy with the literal theft of a black man's identity, and to the white distortion of that identity into the phantasm of the black rapist. As the white people call for Sandy to be lynched, Chesnutt depicts the town reconstituting itself as an audience for a second racial show, another spectacle created from the appropriation of a black body. "Already the preparations were under way for the impending execution," the narrator explains.

A T-rail from the railroad yard had been procured, and men were burying it in the square before the jail. Others were bringing chains, and a load of pine wood was piled in convenient proximity. Some enterprising individual had begun the erection of seats from which, for a pecuniary consideration, the spectacle might be more easily and comfortably viewed . . . Railroads would run excursions from the neighboring towns in order to bring spectators to the scene . . . Several young men discuss[ed] the question of which portions of the negro's body they would prefer for souvenirs.

Chesnutt never gives this audience their wished-for spectacle; his plot averts the lynching at the last minute. What he makes visible instead is the avidity of a white community to become spectators at the death of a black man as a sensational visual event.

Northerners are part of this audience as well. Chesnutt emphasizes that the mass press creates its own version of the anticipated lynching as a spectacle in print:

All over the United States the Associated Press had flashed the report of another dastardly outrage by a burly black brute, – all black brutes it seems are burly, – and of the impending lynching with its prospective horrors. This news, being highly sensational in its character, had been displayed in large black type on the front pages of the daily papers.

Newsprint itself is here a visual spectacle: like the story it tells, the large type reproduces "the negro's body" in inked letters as a display of sensational blackness. These visual objects, whether a blacked-up white man, a newsprint

headline, or a Jim Crow sign hanging in a railroad car, belong to the same family
of signs: all circulate as material instances of black stigma. The doctrine finds
its fullest logical expression in the theater of lynching, in which "the negro's
body" becomes the literally self-evident sign of his own racial abjection, with
black body and stigmatic meaning made finally, wholly identical. As with
the skulls and breasts of the Cheyenne, the ability to turn body parts of a
black person into souvenirs bespeaks the social identity of African Americans
excluded from living participation in civil society.

The other black townspeople in Wellington know how to interpret such
signs perfectly, and as the preparations are made for the lynching there is a
sudden "disappearance from public view" of the black population. For African
Americans under Jim Crow, any appearance in public requires a de facto acceptance of the stigma of blackness, or what the dissenting opinion in the 1896
Plessy v. Ferguson case called "a badge of servitude." (Chesnutt, a trained lawyer,
published essays critical of *Plessy* and included an allusive fictional analysis of
the decision in one of the chapters of *The Marrow of Tradition*.) Minstrelsy and
other forms of racial entertainment, with their visual terms of performance,
merely capitalize in various ways on the conditions that already obtain in civil
society. Chesnutt's other dilation on this theme comes in his representation
of the riot. For all its fury and confusion, the hours-long rampage (planned
in advance by white supremacists) is still a form of deliberate racial spectacle.
Chesnutt's protagonist, the black physician Miller, is hurrying through the
streets during the violence when he is shocked at the sight of a black man's
corpse. What he "shuddered at was not so much the thought of death, to
which his profession had accustomed him, as the suggestion of what it signified." Miller recognizes in that moment that the "dead body of a negro" is
the truest representation of the social and legal status of black people – that
their real role in the public sphere is to perform their own non-existence as
black citizens. "The negroes seemed to have been killed, as the band plays in
circus parades, at the street intersections, where the example would be most
effective."

The corpse's "example" instructs Miller in the realism of racial spectacle. In
that moment Miller realizes that his public life as a middle-class professional
is a hollow fact with no social purchase. He had believed that his education
and accomplishments would elevate his status and help advance the cause
of African Americans, but the "circus"-like display of black abjection is the
only role that can receive any public recognition. From one perspective, *The
Marrow of Tradition* is the most far-reaching instance of the Realist ambition
to use literary distinction to critically penetrate mass spectacles. Chesnutt uses
that critical insight to profoundly reinterpret civil relations. The enormous

postwar industry of commercial entertainment and communication, Chesnutt insists, is not an unreal world of capricious fantasy. It is not a sphere apart at all but rather an instrument of modernity existing wholly within the civil relations of postbellum society and increasingly a chief engine of civil power and change.

But from another perspective, Chesnutt's literary critique succeeds too well. Chesnutt had turned to Northern literary culture both to make his critique and to escape the professional straits he described for Miller. Literature, its values and institutions, could supply a space of reflective difference for cultural criticism. "In that republic of letters," Howells writes of Chesnutt, "where all men are free and equal he stands up for his own people with a courage which has more justice than mercy in it." Chesnutt speaks freely in the world of letters, it is true, but he does not entirely escape there the conditions that bind his protagonist Miller. In writing a "bitter" novel, according to Howells, Chesnutt falls short of Realism's requirement for the "passionless handling" of social material. And yet in the same breath Howells acknowledges that no novelist, black or white, could write about an "atrocity" against his race without some degree of passion:

I am not saying that [Chesnutt] is so inartistic as to play the advocate; whatever his minor foibles may be, he is an artist whom his stepbrother Americans may well be proud of; but while he recognizes pretty well all the facts in the case, he is too clearly of a judgment that is made up. One cannot blame him for that; what would one be one's self? If the tables could once be turned, and it could be that it was the black race which violently and lastingly triumphed in the bloody revolution at Wilmington, North Carolina, a few years ago, what would not we excuse to the white man who made the atrocity the argument of his fiction?

Unable to be sufficiently detached, Chesnutt is judged too histrionic ("bitter, bitter") to qualify as a Realist. He is, in other words, too much of "the race that must rid itself of the cakewalk" – he is too black – to signify as an author of the highest "literary quality" on a subject as politically charged as Jim Crow oppression. And yet this passion is also to his credit: who would not write a bitter book, Howells asks, if he were black? But even this recognition of equal feeling posits an inequality of professional standing when literary quality rests on "passionless handling." To reveal oneself as bitter is to reveal oneself as black, and to be a black author is to be racially excluded from the detached objectivity that is Howells's prerequisite for Realist analysis. Even within high literary culture, then, Chesutt remains racially marked, a "stepbrother" with the artistic liability of his race's civil subjugation.

Chesnutt's career thus traces with some precision the racial limits of American Realism. Howells had defined Realism as the analytic representation of civil relations, but at the point at which civil relations turn into civil abjection – the point when the stigma of Jim Crow abjection is imposed through a national consensus in law and mass media – writing high literary Realism becomes impossible for a black author. Chesnutt was admitted to the "republic of letters" yet judged a professional stepchild unless he could somehow write of American civil relations with neither partisan anger nor the cakewalker's smile. Neither seems to have been a possible path for Chesnutt (or for any other African-American aspirant to the high literary novel in this moment) and he largely retreated from public view. After the publication of *The Marrow of Tradition*, Chesnutt dropped his literary career to devote himself to the stenography business he owned. And in that sphere of writing, where the formal reproduction of others' words precludes any expression of interiority, Chesnutt found wealth and professional success.

BLACK BOHEMIA AND RACIAL SCIENCE FICTION: PAUL LAURENCE DUNBAR, JAMES WELDON JOHNSON, AND PAULINE HOPKINS

The minister Charles H. Parkhurst of New York was certain that African Americans would remain a rejected race for all time: "they never, never, never will contribute, in any part, toward forming the national type of the Americans of the future." Chesnutt was equally adamant (at least in 1900) that African Americans would someday join with white Americans in "a complete racial fusion." His essay "The Future American" (1900), published in three parts in the *Boston Evening Transcript*, predicts that "slowly and obscurely" the Caucasian, Negro, and Native American populations in the US will together create a single "American race." Despite their diametric positions, Parkhurst and Chesnutt understood race in the same general terms: both saw blackness as a biological identity at odds with a "national" race. Chesnutt, of course, believed this state of things unjust, and in his essay makes a point of noting that "color" in the United States reflected "a social structure" only. Skin tone has "proved no test of race." Moreover, "the concept of a pure Aryan, Indo-European race has been abandoned in scientific circles." But he is convinced that race in its "popular sense" would remain a tacit foundation of the national identity. The make-up of the American race, however, will be transformed. In a far-distant time, he argues, the "Negro element" will have been so thoroughly absorbed into the general population that color will signify no social opprobrium, for all Americans will be a people of color, regardless of whether they are called "white" or something else.

Chesnutt's understanding of race, like Parkhurst's, is genetic and generational. By their reckoning, the facts of descent will determine over time the natural history of a single "American race." But in contrast with this racial realism, other representations of blackness, less tethered to categories of color and descent, were emerging in the same moment from the spaces of mass culture, even as mass venues trafficked in some of the most racist depictions of African Americans. In theaters, dance halls, and commercial music it is possible to see the marks or signs of a denigrated blackness loosed from the logic of natural history and revalued as the material for creative expression.

Urban culture was central to the new improvisations of race. A density of sites for commercial entertainment in major cities permitted black musicians, nightclub performers, and songwriters to make a living in show business, or at least to attempt it. In an 1887 *New York Sun* article, the Sixth Avenue district of mid-town Manhattan was described as "black Bohemia," an area with clubs, dance halls, and cabarets that formed the African-American cultural center for some decades before the rise of black Harlem. The writer and composer James Weldon Johnson recalled that "black Bohemia had its physical being in a number of clubs" in an "alluring world" where "the great prize fighters were wont to come, the famous jockeys, the noted minstrels, whose names and faces were familiar on every bill-board in the country." The billboard conspicuousness of black fighters and vaudevillians made the area a destination for pleasure-seekers, while the concentration of black audiences drew aspiring performers and artists. Johnson arrived in 1899 with hopes of producing a comic opera he had written with his brother. Both Johnson and poet Paul Laurence Dunbar wrote novels about black Manhattan, works that highlight a creative tension between literary values and commercial culture that carried special relevance for African Americans. Beholden only to profit, mass culture rewarded novelty, visual flair, and self-display, and thereby produced a paradox: African-American performers in New York, Chicago, and other urban centers discovered that racist styles and caricatures of mass culture yielded more easily to creative transformation than did the more staid racial typing of literary culture.

Dunbar's novel, *The Sport of the Gods* (1902), portrays the ragtime clubs and theaters of New York as a seductive world of black self-destruction. In most respects, the novel was an unlikely work to come from "the Poet Laureate of the Negro race," as Booker T. Washington had dubbed him. Several books of poems, including *Oak and Ivy* (1892) and *Lyrics of Lowly Life* (1897), had established Dunbar's reputation as a deft poet of Southern scenes and vernacular language. Championed by Howells and feted on an 1897 reading tour in Great Britain, Dunbar earned the acclaim of international audiences and the pride of the black intelligentsia; Alexander Crummell recruited the poet for the American Negro Academy. By any measure Dunbar was a success, especially for the son of former slaves who was raised in poverty (in Dayton, Ohio) by his mother, a domestic laborer. Yet he was increasingly frustrated that editors seemed interested only in his dialect poems and in local-color stories that depicted the rural simplicity of Southern folkways. When *The Sport of the Gods* appeared, the novel was a marked departure from the gentler tones of his other published works. If *The Marrow of Tradition* was "bitter," Dunbar's novel verged on nihilistic.

An important shift in genre accompanies the change in tone. *The Sport of the Gods* is the first African-American "great migration" novel, with a plot that follows a black family from its "own beloved section" in the South to a bewildering world in the urban North, the same journey masses of African-American migrants were beginning to undertake. Like Theodore Dreiser and other novelists of modern city life, Dunbar finds an impersonal destructiveness concentrated in American cities. But, crucially, the ruin of the Hamilton family begins in the South; urban life only extends and intensifies it. When Berry Hamilton, a butler, is accused of theft, his employer (and former master) has the "good-living negro" sent to the penitentiary and his family forced from their home. The Hamiltons' thrift, having steadily built up the family savings account, has only made them more vulnerable to the false accusation. Even crueler ironies follow. Berry's wife Fannie and teenaged son and daughter attempt a new life in New York ("a city that, like Heaven, to them had existed by faith alone") but come to grief when real crime – son Joe's murder of his lover – and family estrangement are the ultimate issue of the father's false imprisonment.

"Whom the gods wish to destroy," the narrator proclaims, "they first make mad," and the tragic note is apt. The relentless misery visited upon the Hamiltons, however, is rooted in the work of white perfidy and betrayal, not the design of capricious gods. Dunbar uses allusions to Greek and Shakespearean tragedy to pointedly misname the white racism that causes the family's destruction. Still, the narrator's dark turn on ancient drama signifies something more than this ironic critique. *The Sport of the Gods* is not only a caustic debunking of Southern local-color myths but is also, more subtly, a memorial to the unwritten high epic of black American life. Enslaved and excluded, the mass of African Americans had been relegated to the "lowly life" of vernacular culture and shut out from what one white character calls "higher civilisation" in America. Thus the Hamiltons' arrival in New York is for Dunbar the grim start to what can be only an ironic tragedy, the fall of the already low.

Awaiting them are the destructive worlds of "coon-show" theater and whiskey joints. "If he be wise," the narrator warns the "provincial" from the South, "he will go away" and shun New York:

But if he be a fool, he will stay and stay on until the town becomes all in all to him . . . Then he is hopeless, and to be elsewhere would be death. The Bowery will be his romance, Broadway his lyric, and the Park his pastoral, the river and the glory of it all his epic, and he will look down pityingly on all the rest of humanity.

The pride of Joe Hamilton, a shallow dandy, and the dreams of Kitty Hamilton, an aspiring stage singer, are the self-damning ambitions of people who can know nothing else. James Weldon Johnson, who became an intimate of Dunbar, reported that the poet spoke with "self-reproach" of the limits of dialect writing, and that his ambition had been "to write one or two long, perhaps epical, poems in straight English that would relate to the Negro." Dunbar's blues tragedy (it has its own Tiresias in a drunk named Sadness) is simultaneously a lament for the higher work of art that Dunbar could never write.

But strangely, though the novel's indictment of the "social cesspool" of black club life is clear, Dunbar himself was a leading figure in the rise of popular black theater. He created the "Senegambian Carnival" for the famous dance troupe of Bert Williams and George Walker who, with Walker's celebrated wife Aida Overton Walker, became a phenomenal success in the US and Britain. Dunbar's all-black musical *Clorindy, or The Origins of the Cakewalk*, written with Will Marion Cook, toured the country in 1898 and propelled the cakewalk into a national dance craze. When one knows this fact of Dunbar's biography, his novel's harsh judgment on black Bohemia (whereas Kitty had formerly sung "simple old songs," in New York she turns to "detestable coon ditties which the stage demanded") poses an apparent contradiction. Does the Hamiltons' degradation in black New York signify Dunbar's displaced anger at restrictions imposed by white literary culture? Like the cruelty of white "gods" who destroy black lives for sport, Dunbar permits his characters no real escape from "dishonor" and isolation, as if to act out the ability of those above him to insist that a black author keep to vernacular forms.

More suggestive, however, are the hints in *The Sport of the Gods* that Dunbar knew well the creative excitement in black urban culture, the "sense of triumph" and exhilaration released in stylized expressions of black street life. When the Hamiltons are taken to a show on one of their first evenings in Manhattan, Dunbar's description of the music and dancing betrays an almost ineffable appeal the narrator is loath to admit. The performers are oddly costumed and poorly made-up, but "they could sing, and they did sing, with their voices, their bodies, their souls. They threw themselves into it because they enjoyed and felt what they were doing, and they gave almost a semblance of dignity to the tawdry music and inane words." Kitty is "enchanted." Joe is "lost, transfixed." Even their fretful mother is "divided between shame at the clothes of some of the women and delighted with the music." The moment seals their unhappy fates, but the same instant supplies a "grand" feeling that gives them new hope and self-regard.

The division was central to Dunbar's own life. He clearly knew the stirring feelings that could be conjured through popular song. Moreover, he was skilled enough to help turn minstrel music and stagecraft towards more artistic productions. Like *Abyssinia, Sons of Ham, Octoroons*, and other black-authored shows, Dunbar's *Clorindy* was recognized as moving away from the coarser racism of white minstrelsy. This is "a coon show in name only," one white critic wrote of *Abyssinia* for "in reality, it was a most serious near-grand opera for which we were totally unprepared." Yet the urban culture that was the origin for black popular theater was a destructive milieu for Dunbar, an alcoholic, and it enticed and gripped him as much as it appalled him. His sketch in the *New York Sun*, "The Negroes of the Tenderloin," depicts "careless, guffawing crowds" that threaten moral and social ruin, even as letters from Dunbar's fiancée (later his wife), the author Alice Dunbar-Nelson, urge him to give up his penchant for the "sporting" people and pastimes of that section of New York.

Dunbar's life and writing thus captures conflicted divisions in black America – the divide between blocked ambitions for higher cultural expression and the profits from popular art; between a middle-class "dignity" always out of reach and a vital urban aesthetic that risked shame and stigma from its proximity to the low; and between the inhospitable conventions of high forms and the euphoric beauty of a street life that could also bring grief. Ill and deeply depressed, Dunbar died at age thirty-three some five years after *Sport of the Gods* appeared. His blues novel speaks the poet's sense of exile from a cultural authority he could never possess. Yet the cultural and racial oppositions so personally painful for Dunbar were also a matrix that gave shape to his groundbreaking narrative form alongside wildly popular musicals.

When Dunbar's Kitty Hamilton becomes a "celebrity" of the black stage, it portends ill; the novel's only other female performer, Kitty's mentor Hattie, has just been murdered. But the real-life star of Dunbar's cakewalk musical *Clorindy*, Aida Overton Walker, enjoyed a markedly different fate. Walker was able to deftly exploit divisions that Dunbar was compelled to battle. Although her early career was restricted to cabaret musicals like *The Cannibal King* and *A Lucky Coon*, she came to be heralded as an innovative choreographer and a performer who starred in mainstream Broadway productions. *Variety* called her "the foremost Afro-American stage artist." A career on the stage, though, violated the rules of propriety that many middle-class African Americans believed would help advance the race. "I am aware of the fact that many well-meaning people dislike stage life, especially our women," Walker wrote in a 1905 article in the *Colored American Magazine*. Urging bourgeois deportment and behavior, educated "race leaders" tended to shun the signatures of black identity – styles of speech, dress, and gesture – that white people had long distorted and ridiculed. But Walker in effect reversed this tactic, using theatrical self-display to reclaim signs of blackness as markers of modern grace and professional skill. Arguing that the contemporary stage was a true profession, Walker's essays in the *Colored American Magazine* present her career as precisely the sort of "uplift" work that dominated the black middle-class agenda. There are many "honest and well deserving men and women of color in professional life," she wrote of black entertainers, "who will compare favorably with men and women of other races in this profession or other professions." "Those before the lights must do their part," and we must "work together for the uplift of all."

Still, asking black stage performance to signify bourgeois mobility was a tall order when pleasure, profit, and sexuality were the undisguised energies of the urban stage. The break in Walker's early career came when, as a young unknown, she agreed to be photographed dancing the cakewalk for the American Tobacco Company's trading card. The other models for the photo shoot were a team from California recently arrived in New York, Walker and Williams. The trio that became the first black star entertainers thus had its origins in a commercial venture of the most straightforward kind, an advertisement, in which the mass reproduction of their stylized dance moves – the angled limbs, the costumes and brown faces – were circulated purely for the sake of trade. But paradoxically, the commercial nature of urban black performance may have made it easier to detach and transform images of the black body in mass culture than was possible in other spheres. Aida Walker's beauty, for instance, and her savvy in presenting it, allowed her to refashion the sensual appeal of her stage roles in such a way that African-American dance moves signified a trans-racial feminine charm. Her cakewalk steps, her Salome dance and other movements were widely imitated, especially among affluent white women. In private lessons, public demonstrations, and magazine interviews, Walker transmitted her gestures and techniques ("don't forget your eyes, [for] a little flirtation – just a little – is a prime requisite") along these commercial routes to a large audience that not only consumed but also themselves performed her "black" styles.

The success enjoyed by Aida and George Walker and Bert Williams was an anomaly. More often it was white performers and producers – Johnson called them "pirates" – who profited from popular interest in the innovative styles of African-American performers. In addition to their easier access to mainstream venues and financial backers, white people could more freely negotiate elements of sexuality in the music and dances than could the black performers they imitated. In a 1906 interview Aida Walker noted that, while white companies featured love scenes in virtually every production, during her ten years in professional musicals "there has never been even the remotest suspicion of a love story in any of them" because of "popular prejudice against love scenes enacted by negroes."

The color line fostered vigilance, on the stage as well as off. "You haven't the faintest conception of the difficulties which must be overcome," Walker said to her interviewer, "of the prejudices which must be left slumbering, of the things we must avoid whenever we write or sing a piece of music, put on a play or a sketch, walk out in the street or land in a new town. No white can understand these things, much less appreciate them." While black and white entertainers could perform the same "black" numbers, African-American performers had to have a sharpened self-consciousness about the social meaning of possessing a brown body. The need for constant self-reflection was a burden. But it is also likely that "the ten thousand things we must think of every time we make a step," as Walker phrased it, gave black performers a unique analytic understanding of the nature of racial signs. Black styles were marketable as well as punishable, exciting and upsetting, richly creative as well as vulnerable to racist ridicule. As a result, black performance was appropriated quite as often as it was disdained, and this highly dynamic field of meaning demonstrated that blackness was not the rooted biological identity proclaimed by scientists.

Johnson's novel about black New York emphasizes the changeable nature of racial signs. *The Autobiography of an Ex-Coloured Man* (1912) represents the division between high and low spheres not as the cruel snare that Dunbar depicted but rather as a permeable boundary, a cultural divide permitting forms of transmission even while it further segregates black and white America. His protagonist, a sheltered young man light-skinned enough to pass for white, arrives in Manhattan after an aborted college career in the South. Johnson is even more direct than Dunbar about the "fatally fascinating" power of the city: "To some natures this stimulant of life in a great city becomes a thing as binding and necessary as opium is to one addicted to the habit." But "the Club" at the center of Johnson's novel, based on the real Ike Hine's, is more than the haunt of drinkers and hustlers. Among its patrons are people like "the Doctor," an African-American medical school student from Harvard unable to give up gambling, and the black "minstrel" who will "never essay anything below a reading from Shakespere" when he agrees to perform at the Club. White producers and performers who "made fortunes" from publishing ragtime and who "came to get their imitations first-hand from the Negro entertainers they saw there" are regulars as well. Like the photographs on the Club wall, which group portraits of boxers with giants like Frederick Douglass, the Club houses a promiscuous mix of high and low figures. Vital differences thrive.

The unnamed protagonist, a trained pianist, is dazzled by the music and creativity of a black world he has never before known. At the same time, the "millionaire friend" he meets at the Club becomes his entry to the world of the white elite (in whose penthouses he performs the ragtime he has only recently learned) and his ticket to Paris, London, and Berlin, where he lives as a white man himself. Crossing color and class lines in this way teaches him the possibilities for fertile cultural transmissions (the wealthy Germans he meets in Berlin are expert ragtime players; the black people of Martinique and Haiti are often "more Frenchy" than Parisians). But Johnson's narrator does not lose sight of the way cultural hierarchies still operate to limit and define the meaning of a "Negro" life. Having been typecast as "laughing, shuffling" clowns, black people's efforts to elevate themselves socially are viewed as risible play-acting:

In this respect the Negro is much in the position of a great comedian who gives up the lighter roles to play tragedy. No matter how well he may portray the deeper passions, the public is loath to give him up in his old character; they even conspire to make him a failure in serious work, in order to force him back into comedy.

Like Dunbar, Johnson objects to the reflex that placed black expression in opposition to the higher forms of a putatively white civilization. Exclusion from forms such as epic and tragedy is symbolic of the tragic deformation of black lives.

But the false exclusion, the narrator stresses, is also an "opportunity." The "future Negro novelist and poet" who pushes past artificial restrictions can "give the country something new and unknown, in depicting the life, the ambitions, the struggles and the passions of those of their race who are striving to break the narrow limits of traditions." The passage can be said to gloss the fictional *Autobiography* itself; Johnson's novel, with its plot conjoining Cuban cigar factories and black nightclubs with Berlin opera houses and Paris cafés, was the first work of fiction to portray the real cosmopolitanism that was part of African-American life. But Johnson was also the rare intellectual who saw opportunities for critique in mass culture as well as more literary genres. After his early life in Jacksonville, Florida, where he studied classical music, became a black educator, and began a law practice, Johnson moved to New York to become a songwriter. He had traveled to Manhattan with his brother Rosamond with hopes for staging their musical *Toloso*, a humorous but critical take on American military expansionism. "The United States had, the year before, annexed Hawaii, and was at the time engaged in the Spanish-American War," he wrote in his memoir *Along This Way* (1933), and "we decided to write a comic opera satirizing the new American imperialism."

The musical was never produced, perhaps due to producers' fears of seeming "unpatriotic." If so, the aborted production may be evidence of an even lower tolerance for political dissent in mass culture than in the world of letters. But Johnson, who met Dunbar and other luminaries such as Oscar Hammerstein in this period, became a successful figure in entertainment circles, and it was in the "alluring world" of black commercial culture – a world of "greatly lessened restraints" but "tremendous artistic potentialities" – that Johnson "began to grope toward a realization of the importance of the American Negro's cultural background and his creative folk-art, and to speculate on the superstructure of conscious art that might be reared upon them."

The same desire to bring formal artistic resonance to vernacular forms such as ragtime, the rural black sermon, and Jubilee songs becomes the central obsession of Johnson's narrator in *Ex-Coloured Man*. Richly beautiful in themselves, these "lower forms of art," the narrator predicts, also "give evidence of a power that will some day be applied to higher forms." Johnson's aim was not to erase the distinction between higher "conscious art" and vernacular forms; instead, the commercial milieu of New York convinced him that black forms reflect aesthetic power and critical insight conducive to the highest aesthetic expression, and he sought to translate the signature styles of African-American identity into the recognized artistry of "higher forms." His goal was to have black cultural forms retain racial meaning – to bespeak collective African-American experience and feeling – but to cease to signify all that falls short of civilization.

Johnson's work and life went far towards realizing that goal. He somehow navigated the disparities between literary culture and black urban life more nimbly than Dunbar was able to do. After his life in Manhattan, he went on to a career as a diplomat in Nicaragua and Venezuela and later became the first African American to head the National Association for the Advancement of Colored People, but he continued throughout his life to write songs, poems, and histories that mined the aesthetic possibilities of black vernacular art. Among his best-known works were *God's Trombones: Seven Negro Sermons in Verse* (1927), and *Black Manhattan* (1930), a history of the city's African-American cultural life from its colonial origins through the Harlem Renaissance. At his death in 1938 he was dividing his time between teaching at the predominantly black Fisk University and serving as the first professor of African-American literature at New York University, bringing to academia the creative interplay of black and white worlds that he had pursued in his career in the arts.

For Johnson, any question of race opened questions of imagination. In *The Autobiography of an Ex-Coloured Man*, race is as much a matter of imaginative force as one of fact. Despite his own ability to live as a white man, the narrator never loses sight of the sometimes fatal realities of life for black people; his witnessing of a lynching makes the point with horrific vividness. (Johnson's own seizure by a lynch mob in Jacksonville had a similar life-altering effect.) But the novel also allows the reader to see the nimbus of invisible, almost magical belief and assumption that always surrounds the real-world facts of race. There is a "dwarfing, warping, distorting influence which operates upon each and every coloured man in the United States," the narrator writes. Its power stems from the fact that virtually all "thought and activity must run through the narrow neck of this one funnel" of race status. This influence is irrational and destructive, yet it is also a force that makes African Americans a "mystery" to white people. Echoing Aida Walker's comments about the "ten thousand things" in the mind of the black performer, Johnson's narrator states that black person's thoughts "are often influenced by considerations so delicate and subtle that it would be impossible for him to confess or explain them" to a white person. African-American subjectivity is thus a kind of "freemasonry," an interior knowledge that is not a racial trait or a fact of birth but a manner of seeing and understanding akin to a sixth sense and shared by black people alone.

This element of mystery or opacity at play in racial difference, Johnson suggests, has a creative dimension. The "warping" effect of racial stigma has as its other side the power to imaginatively bend or refashion the collective fantasies that define racial identities. Interestingly, what Johnson calls the "freemasonry" alive in the world of black entertainment had its counterpart in a notable subgenre of racial science fiction produced in the same era. These works tended to be produced by literary intellectuals who were far less comfortable than Johnson with the sphere of popular culture. The *Colored American Magazine*, a Boston publication that aimed to join political critique with cultural elevation, featured a number of short stories in this vein. Like white intellectuals, many black authors perceived a voracious leveling power in the market motives driving mass culture and feared its effects. But black intellectuals faced a double bind: science and high culture were as apt to stigmatize black people as the sphere of popular culture. The realism of science and letters offered them no real haven from the distortions of black identity. And one effort to surmount this dilemma can be seen in the fantastic narratives produced by African-American authors who yoked scientific discourse with fiction for the task of reimagining the facts of race.

An unpublished story by W. E. B. Du Bois is a notable example of this species of fiction. "A Vacation Unique" was likely written around 1889 while Du Bois was studying in the philosophy department at Harvard. The story, which exists only in incomplete fragments, tells of two Harvard undergraduates, one white and one black, who decide to earn money during their summer vacation by touring as "two readers giving 40 or 50 entertainments" around the country. The black student has convinced his classmate that the most profitable course would be to undergo a "painless operation" that temporarily renders him a Negro. The novelty of two black Harvard students will provide a unique spectacle ("Niggers at Harvard!"), and they will profit from the world's "gaping" surprise.

The cynical plan, no doubt reflecting Du Bois's experience of racist condescension in Cambridge, diverts the theme of black entertainment to a framework of scientific speculation. In a reverse minstrelsy, the Harvardians will turn the "astounding incongruous role" of black intellectuals into public entertainment. Moreover, by becoming a black man, the white student enters the "fourth dimension of color," a position from which to view white America from a radically new perspective. Direct allusions make it clear that Du Bois had borrowed from C. H. Hinton's "What Is the Fourth Dimension?" a story from his *Scientific Romances* (1884), and from Edwin A. Abbott's *Flatland*, a widely read science-fiction novel that had appeared in a second edition in 1884.

Like Hinton and Abbott, Du Bois uses fiction to frame a counterfactual world of theoretical ideas. "Outside of the mind you may study mind, and outside of matter by reason of the fourth dimension of color," the black student tells the other, "you may have a striking view of the intestines of the fourth great civilization." But in the story itself, Du Bois offers little theoretical speculation of the kind written by Hinton and Abbott. Instead, the fantastic operation that has turned a white man black opens to the real-world experience of black life in America. Scorn and abjection are basic conditions of that life, something immediately made clear from the caustic way the black student addresses his newly transformed "fool." "By becoming a Nigger," he tells him, "you step into a new and, to most people, entirely unknown region of the universe – you break the bounds of humanity." To exist in this dimension is to live in a limbo in which the world, for all its gaping, does not recognize you as a subject: "your feelings no longer count, they are not a part of history." To live in this dimension is also to glimpse the amorality that is the hidden secret and future "death warrant" of "Teutonic civilization."

Because the black student, as narrator, addresses his "fool" in second person ("you"), the reader experiences by proxy what it is to be addressed as a creature belonging to the "fourth dimension" of blackness. When you are not receiving taunts or stares, you are subject to demands to recognize white magnanimity: "Hostess is cordial: letting you know how nice she can be to colored people; she mentions casually the vast debt owed to Anglo-Saxon race because of the interest her people had in your people and pile of clothes sent to Tuskegee last winter." The story, with its second-person narrative structure, thus requires any white reader to undertake his or her own experiment in racial transformation – or would have, if the story had ever reached print. That it was not completed and published is a reminder that the "fourth dimension" was a reality: what Du Bois called the "inner life" of African Americans was obscured or ignored in most public life and was thus an invisible dimension of human existence for most white Americans. Through his scientific parable, Du Bois turns inside out the stage performances of blackness, exposing the warping force that constantly conditions what appear to white eyes to be the objective facts of black identity. The mocking invective the narrator directs at his now-black "fool" is a mimicry of the white hostility and contempt that trains the black subject in the arts of self-staging.

Other examples of racial science fiction, almost as provocative, did succeed in coming into print. Sutton Griggs's novel *Imperium in Imperio* (1899), originally self-published, imagines a secret organization of black people devoted to building a powerful "empire" within the United States. This black nation, a kind of inverted image of the invisible order of white supremacists who make up the Ku Klux Klan, imagines the scattered strength of the black US population as an organized political power to be reckoned with. Through the creative license of fiction, *Imperium* and other Griggs novels turn the imposed "freemasonry" of internal racial vigilance into a stealthy armed force and a potential black republic.

A similar transformation occurs in James Corrothers's story "A Man They Didn't Know" (1913). Corrothers, a Chicago author and pastor, had earlier teamed with Bert Williams and others in the world of black vaudeville. His insider's knowledge of black popular culture shows through in his comic tale of black urban life, *The Black Cat Club* (1902), a parody in dialect about a literary society whose members are razor-toting toughs from the Chicago streets. Corrothers later regretted publishing a story with such low subject matter and language, and when he committed himself to "literary English," he wrote more serious-minded stories that included historical fantasy. In "A Man They Didn't Know," Japan and Mexico have formed an alliance with Hawaii, now in secession, to declare war on the United States. African Americans, deserting the US army in large numbers, become a kind of independent armed force that is initially inclined to side with the invaders. Eventually, though, the title character leads ten thousand black men against Japanese troops in a decisive battle in southern California. Ninety thousand more black troops help secure the victory. For Corrothers and Griggs, fiction is an aggressive weapon against history. Faced with the defeat and humiliation of black people in the post-Reconstruction era, Corrothers and Griggs imagine African Americans as a dominant national power. Blackness no longer signifies the low and the dependent; instead, those values are precisely reversed as black men step forward and become the new embodiment of American will and military potency.

Literary realism had proved too restrictive, commercial culture too unliterary; for Du Bois, Griggs, and Corrothers, then, science fiction was a creative alternative, a genre in which the topic of race could draw on an aura of higher scientific authority while allowing the free transformation of racial signs and hierarchies. One of the most fascinating texts in this regard is Pauline Hopkins's novel *Of One Blood* (1903). Appearing in serial form in the *Colored American Magazine*, where Hopkins was the literary editor, the novel is a deliberate amalgam of scientific speculation and exotic romance. Like Du Bois's story, the novel begins at Harvard, where a young "genius," Reuel Briggs, suffers a keen awareness of his abjection as a black man. He passes for white among his fellow students but still carries the shame of his subordinate status. Asked what he thinks of "the Negro problem," he refuses comment: "I have a horror of discussing the woes of unfortunates, tramps, stray dogs, cats and Negroes – probably because I am an unfortunate myself." In the logic of Realist and Naturalist narrative, early death is the likely fate for most urban "unfortunates" and, ominously, Reuel possesses "morbid thoughts."

Hopkins thus initiates her story with the codes of Howells's literary Boston, invoking the "self-possessed, highly cultured New England" elite and the achievements of Harvard scholarship. In the first scene Reuel is even studying a psychology text written by William James ("The Hidden Self," later reprinted in *The Will to Believe*), from which Hopkins quotes several passages. But, as if reversing the inside of a glove to make the lining become a new exterior, Hopkins takes from the James essay a notion of spiritual identity ("the hidden self lying quiescent within") that brings about a wholesale inversion of the anticipated narrative structure. "The wonders of the material world," Reuel tells a friend, "cannot approach those of the undiscovered country within ourselves" that normal science has yet to explore. From this metaphor of a *terra incognita*, Hopkins spins out an Africanist fantasy of mesmeric visions, secret birthmarks, the recovery of an occult science, and the restoration of a rightful king – Reuel's "hidden self" and true identity – to an ancient black civilization surviving within a secret city in Africa. Hopkins trades museum realism for archeological fantasy of the most romantic kind.

The setting in an ancient African city, however, reflects a serious scholarly interest. Like many black intellectuals, Hopkins was drawn to theories of "Ethiopianism" that argued ancient Egypt was a civilization derived from black Africa. Her study *A Primer of Facts Pertaining to the Early Greatness of the African Race* (1905) surveys the scholars and classical authors who supported the claims for a black Egypt. But Hopkins is distinctly aware of the fact that imagery of Africa and ancient Egypt had become a mainstay of mass culture. A joking (and racist) white character who has joined Reuel on the North African journey looks around him and pronounces it a fit set for "Barnum's circus." The "Arabs, camels, stray lions, panthers, scorpions, serpents, explorers, etc.," he cracks, are his chance to break into show business: "There's money in it." Regardless of her own interest in Egyptian classicism, Hopkins was prepared to enlist the proven entertainment value of imperial spectacle, and her story features familiar plot turns such as pouncing leopards and the discovery of heaps of jewels. But the Barnum joke turns out to be on the white jokester when the discovery of Telassar, the secret city, reveals African art that rivals "the galleries of Europe" and an occult science only "in its infancy" in the West. Deliberately transposed from Realism to science fiction, her retelling of the "story of the Negro" is a praisesong to the dignity and cultural wealth of a civilization "hidden" in the fourth dimension of world history, an African past that is the superior source for a fallen West.

Hopkins's novel puts excess in the service of critique. Where Dunbar felt caught in the divide between literature and spectacle, Hopkins fuses both high and low materials in an ungainly doubling, confident that both spheres will bear witness to the same truth: that behind the stigma of blackness is an unrecognized dignity and agency, a noble "blood" that her novel reclaims and redeems. The novel multiplies its signifiers of race almost past the point of legibility. By the end of the novel, the "blood" that explains and defines Reuel Briggs has acquired almost every conceivable association: biological descent, an inherited mesmeric power, Ethiopian civilization, Christian universalism, a pan-African nationalism, and an aristocracy of royal lineage. Despite any number of internal contradictions, all remain suspended together as affirmed meanings of black racial identity – all except for African-American blood defined as the caste stigma of a subordinated people, the one identity codified in US law and custom. That meaning, of course, could not be dissolved by fiction, however inventive. But fiction could expose by way of contrast the poverty of the racial imagination fixed and enforced by the law.

5

WHARTON, TRAVEL, AND MODERNITY

Edith Wharton loved the sensation of speed. In *The Custom of the Country* (1913), when Wharton writes of the "rush of physical joy" that comes from flying in an open car at twilight through the wintry boulevards of Central Park, the passage bespeaks her own infatuation with motor cars and their mechanical power. For Wharton, local motor-flights and transatlantic travel were fundamental conditions of living. Henry James always pictured her "wound up and going"; in alarm and bemusement his letters define her through "her dazzling, her incessant braveries of far excursionism." Edith Wharton loved speed almost as much as she loved stillness – the contemplative space of gardens, the quiet stimulation of indoor conversation, the nearly motionless concentration necessary for the work of writing. These contraries – mobility and reflective stillness – inform Wharton's complex stance as an observer of modern life. Her taste for speed and travel on one hand, and the rooted critical focus she achieved in her writing on the other, reflect Wharton's divided attitude towards the kind of world she saw emerging in the first two decades of the twentieth century.

Critics generally agree that Wharton possessed an "anti-modernist" outlook, a skeptical and largely disapproving perspective on the changing mores of her time. In Wharton's eyes, the erosion of traditional social orders and the rise of mass culture threatened to damage beyond repair the kind of rich interior life she prized most. But whereas some scholars see these sentiments as the fears of an entrenched conservative, others see Wharton's anti-modernism as part of her forward-looking analysis of misogynist and totalitarian impulses that came to fruition in the 1930s. Was Wharton reactionary or was she politically prescient? As a cultural observer, Wharton exhibited neither blind nostalgia nor a consistent progressivism. Instead she wrote with a profound ambivalence about what one critic calls "the increasing speed of cultural production" in the twentieth century. Wharton was fascinated as well as alarmed by the rapid changes in customs, family life, and material culture – the buildings, landscapes, and polyglot populations – she confronted in modernity. Wharton's own day-to-day living could be as divided as her views. Writing in the morning quiet of her bedroom, she would satirically dissect the modern "goddess[es] of velocity" who traveled on yachts and in high-speed automobiles and the men of wealth they pursued, married, and divorced. She then emerged in the afternoons to instruct her driver to prepare the Panhard motor car for the swooping journeys that prompted friends to dub her the "Angel of Devastation."

Modernity, then, was not only an object or topic for Wharton but a set of formative energies that shaped her work from within. The energies of modernity animate her novels with a sense of risk just below the surface of social routine. Featuring rapid shifts in location and increasingly curious, deracinated (anti)-marriage plots, Wharton's fiction transforms the Realist novel of manners, the genre she inherited from nineteenth-century fiction. Combining sympathy with mordant satire, her novels depict a startling reinvention of family and erotic relationships. As reimagined by Wharton, the novel of manners is less about local social patterns than about the disruption and global dispersion of those patterns. While Wharton was an acute observer of the "spectacle muse" of modern culture, she develops Realist insights about social theatricality through her own recognition of the importance of modern mobility. Some of her deepest cultural and artistic concerns, therefore, can be grasped in Wharton's preoccupation with high-speed travel – the journeys that structure her plots, the travel-related tropes that are keynotes for her characters, and the specific forces of travel (mechanical speed, imperial reach, intercontinental communication) that were the very conditions for Wharton's writing.

As defined by social theorists, modernity is less an epoch than a tempo. The modern life confronting Wharton and her contemporaries was the result of specific accelerations, velocities of change fueled by wealth and new technologies. Faster steamships, telegraph cables, the expansion of European empires and of US territorial reach, the rapidly growing volume of print and consumer goods that spanned these global territories: these and other innovations created a global geography of rapid transit, a new alignment of space that resulted from technologies of speed. Between 1875 and 1925 (a period roughly matching the span of Wharton's lifetime), the global travel and contact that had been underway for several centuries entered what one historian terms a "take-off phase." The exponential change meant that the category of place was increasingly transformed by new modalities of time. Living in Rome or Bombay, traveling to North Africa or New York, all became very different enterprises when cables, phones, and motor cars made these places of local dwelling into sites of instant relay. Social theorist Anthony Giddens describes this transformation as "a 'lifting out' of social relations from local contexts of interaction and their restructuring across time and space."

It is impossible to conceive of either Wharton or her writings outside of this modern world of transit. Her own addiction to travel – she may have crossed the Atlantic as many as seventy times – meant that Wharton lived a good portion of her life in the mobile space of travel routes. But, more fundamentally, her career and the novels themselves are the product of this modern mobility. Because she spent her adult life largely in Europe but published her work in the United States, Wharton's literary production was quite materially transatlantic. The same between-ness of travel frequently serves as the connecting ties in the plots of her novels. Trains, steamships, and yachts are the settings for dramatic discoveries or crucial evasions, as movement through space intensifies or resolves the particular human problems under view. Even the works that present a single locale – the precincts of wealthy Manhattan or rural New England enclaves – are described with an ethnographic cast that presumes the gaze of a traveled observer.

To take up the question of Wharton's relation to modern travel, however, is to confront a certain paradox. Wharton's affinity for intercontinental travel is an index to her class privilege, her membership in the moneyed elite. Only the wealthy few could make globalization a means for pursuing personal aspirations; for the vast majority the increasing connectedness of the world's cities and regions was experienced largely as impositions of imperialist domination and global trade. Wharton was one for whom these developments in travel offered a number of rare freedoms – the liberty to leave a stifling marriage, for instance, and the opportunity to cultivate close friendships with European and expatriate American writers, not to mention the chance to write successful travel books on France, Italy, and Morocco. Yet while Wharton embraced her own freedom of movement, in her writing travel also became one of her most charged objects of satire. In her later novels in particular, Wharton savages the class of rich travelers who "inter-married, inter-loved and inter-divorced each other over the whole face of Europe" and beyond.

There is an apparent irony in the fact that Wharton, a wealthy, divorced expatriate and inveterate traveler, cast such a critical eye on the jet set of her age. Yet the irony gives way when we recognize that both Wharton's life and her satirical portraits show us two sides of the same phenomenon. Wharton can be said to critically explore in her writings the very conditions she negotiated more warily, if at times more blindly, in her own life. The fictional velocities in Wharton's work, the many continental and marital crossings that structure her plots, can serve as a kind of index to the global powers that are otherwise absent from her novels of manners. These mechanical, commercial, and imperial forces supply to Wharton's stories a particular narrative texture, a record of modernity as embodied sensation and lived experience. The novels' evocations of rapid change and dislocation are sensations her characters find variously thrilling, reckless, and disastrous while only vaguely recognizing any connection between these sensations and their underlying conditions.

Ships, cars, and trains are machines that transform manners in Wharton's fiction. In *The House of Mirth* (1905), for instance, Lily Bart is saved by a yacht. An invitation from her friend Bertha Dorset to travel the Mediterranean on the Dorsets' steam-yacht allows Lily to escape the threat of ruinous gossip in her Manhattan circle. Though she knows Bertha's social world is ignoble it is the only world in which Lily can imagine finding security and pleasure. Carrying her away from the danger of social ruin, the transatlantic cruise seems to embody both safety and luxury – indeed, safety is for Lily the ultimate luxury. Yet at the moment she believes herself most secure, Lily is headed for a fall. An episode in Monte Carlo is marked, in no less than four passages, by the metaphor of a disastrous crash. When Lawrence Selden gets his first glimpse of Lily, for instance, he sees a young woman "on the verge of disaster" and thinks of her as someone about to be "fatally involved" in a "possible crash." The yachting trip, promising safety, instead delivers Lily into a danger that Wharton expresses through the trope of a violent accident.

The theme of the disastrous wreck or car crash would become a major focus for modernist and postmodernist fiction, from F. Scott Fitzgerald's *The Great Gatsby* with its fatal auto accident, to the work of present-day writers like J. G. Ballard, whose novel *Crash* features characters who violently desire the ironic star status of car-accident victims. As a theme and trope, the travel accident signifies the tremendous powers and desires, seductive as well as menacing, generated by the velocities of twentieth-century and twenty-first-century life. In most respects, these impersonal forces are not directly visible in *The House of Mirth*. The novel's dramatic action is supplied not by modern forms of mechanical power but by the more compressed and coded field of manners – the drama of subtle gestures, allusive speech, the covert glance. Lily's is still a world governed by the reign of social appearances, overseen through the mutual surveillance of a community of recognized insiders. But the modernist poetics of disaster figure at the margins of Wharton's fiction and mark her use of the dynamic energies of an industrialized mass culture. In *The House of Mirth*, for instance, Lily's "crash" in Monte Carlo, a public humiliation in a fashionable restaurant, precipitates her descent to the less illustrious society of the "Gormer set" whose social life is organized around "motors and steam-launches." The members of the Gormer circle imitate the cosmopolitan mobility of the established elite, but in doing so they reproduce cultivated travel as merely frantic, heedless movement, a social life in a constant state of near violent transit. In this world a crash seems just a matter of time:

Lily experiences the "sense of having been caught up into the crowd as carelessly as a passenger is gathered in by an express train."

It is instructive that Wharton here stylizes the heedlessness of the Gormer set not merely through the figure of the speeding train, but more specifically through Lily's internal "sense" of train travel, the remembered sensation of being hustled impersonally into a powerful mechanical vehicle. Evoking kinetic excitement as well as foreboding, the figure identifies with surprising precision a species of human consciousness that is born of modern travel. Wharton places a good deal of weight on this figure. Lily's "sense" of being caught up in an express train echoes an earlier description of her anxious foreboding in Monte Carlo. When Bertha Dorset and a male guest one night fail to return to the Dorsets' yacht, Lily feels an immediate sense of alarm – as well she should, since she will become the scapegoat for the lovers' exposed affair and will be expelled from both the yacht and the Dorsets' social circle. Lily first expresses her alarm as the fear of a train wreck: "What happened – an accident to the train?" What the narrator calls "the peril of the moment" is a marital and social peril, but the sense of danger reverberates through the chapter and indeed the whole novel as the physical danger of an accident. The trope returns, for instance, in Lily's subsequent "sense of being involved in the crash, instead of merely witnessing it from the road." And the same figure governs Lawrence Selden's internal thoughts. His musing likewise derives a distinct "sense" from the anticipation of a violent accident: Selden wonders "to what degree was [Lily's] dread of a catastrophe intensified by the sense of being fatally involved in it?" and concludes that "whatever her . . . personal connection" with the "disaster" to come, she "would be better out of the way of a possible crash."

Through tropes of disaster and speed, Wharton revises the ancient meaning of dread. Instead of the fear of an absent or invisible power like a god, dread in *The House of Mirth* is expressed through the anticipation of a distinctive kind of modern event, the high-speed accident. The travel accident, though befalling relatively few, carried a far broader mass meaning. The fear of a "possible crash" shared by the characters in *The House of Mirth*, that is, had become a "sense" shared by millions In 1905, when *The House of Mirth* appeared in print, passenger travel had been recently revolutionized. Though train travel in particular had introduced a new order of speed early in the nineteenth century, it was only in the 1880s and 1890s that inland and intercontinental travel had become a phenomenon involving massive numbers of passengers and far higher rates of speed than ever before. Through her tropes of travel and its risk, Wharton inscribed both a history of modern travel and a record of modernity as embodied sensation which that history brought into existence.

The increasing coordination of railway and ocean steamer lines in the later half of the nineteenth century produced significant new levels of international trade, but it was ultimately passenger travel, the transport of humans, that had the most profound effects. British railway travel increased twenty-fold the number of passengers during 1840–70, with a comparable rate of increase taking place in America during a somewhat later period. Oceanic travel surged with the mass emigration from Europe to America and the British Dominions, with spectacular increases in 1880–83 and 1900–13. Ocean liners grew rapidly in size and, more importantly, grew more diversified in accommodations: the most successful companies learned to combine a large capacity for steerage bookings with luxuriously appointed cabins for wealthy tourists and businessmen. Eventually the famous Cunard Company innovated the tourist-class accommodations to reach middle-income shipboard travelers. As other steamship companies followed suit, transatlantic travel became so widespread as to verge on the commonplace.

A "rediscovery of America" by elite Europeans meant that tourist traffic flowed both ways across the Atlantic. In 1895, for instance, a total of 96,558 cabin-class and 258,560 steerage passengers arrived in New York alone. Though emigration and tourism made North Atlantic routes the most heavily traveled, in the wake of imperial expansion steamship lines were increasingly adding passenger routes in the Pacific, to South and Central America, and to the Caribbean. Just how closely passenger travel was related to commerce and military ventures is illustrated in 1899 in the wildly successful effort by the American Line to book its luxury liner *Paris* for a West Indies cruise to the sites of the Spanish–American War. After stopping in Haiti, Puerto Rico, Trinidad, and Jamaica, the *Paris*, which only a year before had served the US Navy as the auxiliary cruiser USS *Yale*, took its 400 passengers to excursions of famous war sites along the Cuban coast. The highlight of the March cruise was the formal ball aboard the *Paris*, anchored in Santiago Harbor, with music supplied by a Cuban band and the Fifth United States Infantry band. *Mirth's* Lawrence Selden, in response to his ambivalent feelings for Lily Bart, flees to this newly reopened Caribbean travel route, something Lily learns when she reads a newspaper announcement that Selden was one of the passengers to set sail "for Havana and the West Indies on the Windward Liner Antilles."

Lily's own escape – hers across the Atlantic to the Mediterranean – is never described in the narrative, but its very omission can be read as an indicator of the revolutionary speed that distinguished modern travel. No sooner does Lily receive the yachting invitation than we turn the page to find her in Monte Carlo. The wax seal Lily uses for personal letters, "a grey seal with *Beyond!* beneath a flying ship" could have served equally well as a travel industry logo as it does a signature for Lily's personal yearnings. Steamship lines vied for the "Blue Ribbon" for the fastest transatlantic trip, an industry competition that eventually reduced the Atlantic crossing to four and a half days. At times steamers found themselves in head-to-head races, with passengers on deck doubling as spectators for their own competitive journey, though on more than one occasion such races ended with a ship run aground during the final race to port.

It was the motor car, however, that gave the new speed of travel its greatest immediacy. The ability of personal motors to supply a close-up sensation of speed and daring gave the car both a glamor and class hauteur. Nevertheless, the "breath-snatching" beauty of the machines was widely praised. The speed and power visible in these modern forms of transport gave travel a new charisma. An appeal formerly reserved for celebrities was transferred to specific ships and makes of automobile. The Panhard motor car and the Lusitania ocean liner were names as famous as Houdini and Edison. This mechanical glamor had as its inverse a public apprehension about the potential for mechanical havoc. Both elements, the fascination and the fear, made the 1912 sinking of the *Titanic* into what may still be the most famous travel accident in history. The symbolic capacity of high-speed travel transformed the *Titanic* into an international icon of modernity and its risks.

By evoking Lily's social risk through the dangers of high-speed transport, Wharton makes us aware of what otherwise remains largely invisible in this novel. As in most Wharton novels, the actual sources of wealth for the rich – the economic markets and the era's rapid imperial expansion – are nowhere depicted. But in the "motors and steam-launches" that propel the plot, the novel locates the mechanical power, speed, and economic expansion that were transforming the globe. As a result, Wharton's fiction is structured around a tension between closely observed communities, with their local rituals and inherited gender roles, and the sweeping forces of a new economic world seen only obliquely but felt on every side. The latent power in these forces, their significance for her characters as for Wharton herself, was a persistent anxiety and an enduring interest. The figure of the anticipated crash pinpoints a convergence of impersonal powers and anxiety about those powers.

Lily's "sense" of an impending wreck, then, can be seen as an internalized register of powers that remain out of sight. The crash that eventually ruins her is precipitated by gossip and social intrigue, old-fashioned harms to be sure. But whereas Wharton *could* have glossed Lily's expulsion as a ritualistic sacrifice (as she does Ellen Olenska in the backward-looking *Age of Innocence*), she paints Lily instead as a modern accident victim caught in forces far more impersonal, contingent, and ruthless – and, in the end, makes her an actual fatality. Unlike Ellen Olenska, Lily's vulnerability to Bertha's social power is finally an economic vulnerability. If she is to travel at all, Lily must travel on someone else's yacht, according to someone else's itinerary. As a result, she is in the wrong place at the wrong time and, as the scandal of Bertha's affair begins to surface, Lily grasps that she will not be able to remain a mere bystander. It is precisely because she is *standing by*, a body on the margins of the plans and power of the rich, that she will take the force of the crash. When the scandal hits, Bertha virtually throws her overboard: she announces to the dining party in Monte Carlo that "Lily will not be going back to the yacht." As deliberate as are Bertha's actions, Lily's fate is not a structured, ritual punishment (like Ellen's nineteenth-century expulsion) but an incidental harm, the indifferent destruction that comes to the accident victim. Lily and Selden's diffuse fears about train wrecks and metaphorical crashes are realized in the wake of the Dorsets' yachting trip and in the callously wielded power that their yacht makes visible on the social scene.

Little wonder that Wharton's evocations of rapid transport become signs of the social recklessness and potential for destruction in a mass society. The narrator calls the Gormers' journey to Alaska a "tumultuous progress across their native continent," a phrase that allows the forward motion of mechanized travel to signify the agitated, ungoverned energies of modernity that make the overtones of "progress" ironic if not wholly false. Figuring nouveau-riche society as "the rush of travellers," Wharton condemns a world that "scarcely slackened speed – life whizzed on with a deafening rattle and roar."

Yet, while the novel indicts this "life" as crass and thoughtless, it is hard to deny that the energies signified in the "possible crash" – motion, power, suspense, the anticipation of novel sensations and arresting sights – are the very energies that give the novel its dramatic tension and excitement. It is hard to deny, in other words, that Wharton herself recognizes and indeed *uses* as a source for her art the modern currents of feeling that Selden and Lily both register as the sense of impending accident. This tone of absorbing yet anxious anticipation is the novel's keynote. Generated as it is through evocation of mechanical speed, the "possible crash" as a structure of feeling can be said to transform – to modernize – the genre in which Wharton wrote. The nineteenth-century novel of manners was built on the close examination of local social life, the contained worlds of Jane Austen's parishes and George Eliot's country towns. In *The House of Mirth*, intercontinental travel and the evocation of travel disaster make us see social worlds not as self-contained locales but as communities cut through by larger, far more impersonal governing forces. In Wharton's fiction the questions of most concern are no longer social regulation and marital resolution but reckless pleasure and potentially fatal risk.

Thinking about matters of risk in Wharton's fiction, however, may well give pause. Compared to the vast majority of people who inhabit the lands that travelers merely visited, the wealthy had the means to protect themselves from the most serious kinds of harm. Like Selden's escape from New York through the reopened Caribbean route, the journeys of wealthy travelers taking flight from personal disaffections or romantic failures followed a set of military and economic routes that were the grid, as it were, for the global powers in Wharton's era. Her characters often flee their sense of personal risk or loss, the merely metaphorical "crash," by making literal journeys along these intercontinental routes, tracing paths in which losses and upheaval were far more likely to fall on the poor or on native populations than on the leisure-class travelers. How then should we read the irony that in Wharton's works the dread associated with modern risk is felt so strongly by those in least danger of physical harm, the class who profited from those risks and the damage they inflicted?

Wharton's fiction can be said to enact a distribution of risk, a careful managing of the modern sense of danger through a narrative process that is both revealing and evasive. In contrast to earlier narratives in the genre, the stakes in Wharton's novels of manners are dizzingly high. When Lily Bart flirts with Lawrence Selden, she also flirts with real poverty, and eventually with the question of her own survival. When the much-married Undine Spragg uses up a husband, the result is usually cataclysmic, a suicide or the abandonment of a child. The gentler ironies attending courtship and marriage in Austen's novels have given way to harsh, sometimes strange incongruities and startlingly destructive forms of kinship: compulsive serial divorces (*The Custom of the Country, Glimpses of the Moon*), bizarre intergenerational love triangles (*The Mother's Recompense*), and forms of incest (*Summer, The Children, Twilight Sleep*). Though these novels tend to focus on the affluent, Wharton can be said to reintroduce internal class lines by depicting extreme consequences that fall overwhelmingly on the most economically vulnerable: children and single women. Even the most socially polished woman can find herself, like Lily Bart, facing privation and physical threat. A very young and poor woman like Charity Royall in *Summer* is doubly at risk. The downward mobility and the sexual vulnerability that shadow the lives of so many of Wharton's women make the inequities of modern conditions visible within the white middle and leisure classes.

At the same time, however, these internal fault lines can be said to obscure as much as they reveal. Absent from Wharton's novels is any appreciable recognition of the people most at risk in modernity: the poor and the colonized populations for whom travel routes represent labor rather than leisure, and imperial intrusion rather than escape. Is it possible that the spectacular nature of the dread and exhilaration of the "crash" is a cover-up of modern risks rather than a revelation? Wharton's novels also acknowledge – not always fully consciously – the possibility that part of the modern experience is a temptation to exaggerate or, alternatively, to displace or transform a sense of personal danger as a way to avoid confronting the real risks and damage in modernity.

Once again, the "possible crash" is a pivotal trope in this regard. Like the narrator, Selden in *The House of Mirth* views Lily as someone headed for a smash-up. But it is significant that the novel's most complex rendering of Selden's position is also rooted in the trope of the travel accident. Selden practices a technique of "personal detachment," as the narrator calls it, designed to protect him from romantic feelings he wishes to keep at a distance. When he sees Lily as a woman "on the brink of a chasm," his concern for her is also a feeling of self-protective removal from her plight. He is, as it were, on the other side of the chasm. But even his sense of detachment carries a trace of the emotional risk he wishes to acknowledge only in Lily's life: "The feeling he had nourished and given prominence to was one of thankfulness for his escape: he was like a traveller so grateful for rescue from a dangerous accident that at first he is hardly conscious of his bruises. Now he suddenly felt the latent ache, and realized that after all he had not come off unhurt." As the passage suggests, the practice of viewing others as potential victims of an unseen physical harm ("on the brink") may betray one's own sense of threat. The habit of detachment may be entangled in a wish to disavow feelings of vulnerability.

As Wharton's readers, we can never quite escape this habit of mind, either. Like a car accident, the extreme, sometimes astonishing spectacles in Wharton's novels are able to shock at the same time that they prompt a complex form of interest, a readerly fascination or even pleasure. The sight of the social wreckage and bizarre forms of harm evoke our sympathy at the same time that they trigger relief and a reassuring interest in destructiveness that can be enjoyed from a protective distance. Like Selden, we are made to see characters on the brink. Yet also like Selden, our very interest as readers/spectators is also an ironic sign of our shared sense of the "general insecurity" that is Lily Bart's vulnerability to economic and social power, an insecurity felt by so many of Wharton's women and children. Tellingly, the trope of the traveler at risk returns in Wharton's later works as almost an authorial tic. In *The Mother's Recompense* (1925), for instance, when evoking the crisis of the protagonist Kate Clephane, the narrator returns again and again to the trope of the travel accident as if by compulsion. Kate is compared to a "traveller" who has "skirted an abyss" and glimpsed "the depths into which she had not fallen"; to a "traveller" on a "ledge above a precipice"; and finally to a "traveller" who has "fallen asleep in the snow" and wakes to great pain. The structure of feeling Wharton identified with the anticipation of an accident captures a convergence of dread and fascination pervasive in modern life. For Wharton, the freedoms symbolized by travel are simultaneously the threats, personal as well as social, that she saw at the heart of modernity.

NATIONAL, INTERNATIONAL, GLOBAL

In at least one respect, it was possible for the spectacularity of the "possible crash" to obscure the profound changes signified in the modern culture of travel. Though she saw destructive effects in modern commercialization, Wharton was largely blind to the damage that global travel inflicted on colonized peoples. This blindness is thus an unstable ground on which Wharton's sense of internationalism was founded. Her sophisticated sense of the international is, we might say, a cover or alibi for her inattention to the global. If a position of detachment can mask feelings of vulnerability (as with Selden), by the same token Wharton's attention to fault lines of leisure-class vulnerability could blind her to the far more pervasive risks facing the poor populations, risks that go largely unnoticed in her picture of modernity.

In an essay of 1927, Wharton cited the motor car as one of the machines to "internationalize the earth." Mechanical power and modern commodities had created a "new order of things," an order Wharton found both absorbing and repelling. "The whole world has become a vast escalator, and Ford motors, and Gilette razors have bound together the uttermost parts of the earth." But as the American brand names suggest, for Wharton this international "order" was also national, the result of a distinctly American process of commercial globalization. "The universal infiltration of our American plumbing, dentistry, and vocabulary has reduced the globe to a playing-field for our people; and Americans have been the first to profit by the new facilities of communication which are so largely of their invention and promotion." Wharton's picture of this commercial global order as an Americanized order is crucial, since it is the source of both blindness and insight in Wharton's understanding of modernity. By casting the "new class of world-compellers" as Americans, driven by distinctively American excesses, Wharton judged as destructive the "infiltration" of the globe by US interests. "We have, in fact, internationalized the earth, to the deep detriment of its picturesqueness, and of many far more important things."

At a moment when most Americans greeted US expansions as an unequivocal force of progress, Wharton's view was far more wary and critically discriminating. But while this way of reading globalization prompted a disapproving view of American commercial powers, Wharton's critique rested on a distinction that allowed her to embrace European empires as America's opposite, as global orders that cultivated rather than destroyed the things Wharton found most important. Yet this crucial distinction – between America and Europe, between empires that raze and empires that preserve – was not only a political distinction but also an aesthetic one. The criterion for telling the difference was for Wharton the criterion of beauty: while Americanization destroys beauty, European imperialism reveres and protects it. Art and beauty are the key to her understanding of global politics, a fact that put art and artists more deeply within the sphere of the political than Wharton was otherwise prepared to admit.

To understand these interrelated criteria, we need to begin with Wharton's sense of the beginning: her own transatlantic childhood. Wharton describes herself in her memoir, *A Backward Glance*, as "the offspring of born travellers." Her deepest sensibilities, as she saw it, were formed by the "happy misfortune" that forced her parents to leave for Europe when she was a very young child in order to live more economically abroad than was possible in New York in the years after the Civil War. Living and traveling in Europe, Wharton believed, imprinted on her for life a "background of beauty and old-established order." And from the first Wharton conceived this order of beauty through an opposition to New World "ugliness." In an autobiographical piece, "Life and I," Wharton writes of her return from her early years abroad that "I shall never forget the bitter disappointment produced by the first impressions of my native country. I was only ten years old, but I had been fed on beauty since my babyhood, & my first thought was: '*How ugly it is!*' I have never since thought otherwise, or felt otherwise than as an exile in America."

Significantly, though, Wharton eventually came to see a "pathetic picturesqueness" in the New York world of her youth. As she described it in her memoir, this was a beauty she perceived only after world war and modernization brought about its "total extinction." But the moment when Wharton sees the "compact [American] world of my youth" as one of beauty is also the moment she identifies that vanished America with Europe. This lost American world is defined not only in opposition to modern technology ("telephones, motors, electric light, central heating . . . X-rays, cinemas, radium, aeroplanes and wireless telegraphy were not only unknown but still mostly unforeseen") but is remembered as a transatlantic outpost of "an old tradition of European culture."

America and Europe, then, are less geographic places for Wharton than they are movable sites of contrasting aesthetic value. Seeing a belated beauty in nineteenth-century New York makes that spot a lost island of European culture. By the same token, Wharton saw the "standardizing" practices of modern American trade opening the world to vast commercial "infiltration." What Wharton called "the growth of modern travelling facilities" meant the dissemination throughout the world of a set of commercial habits that she associated with the national culture of the United States. Indeed, Wharton saw "the modern American as a sort of missionary-drummer selling his wares and inculcating his beliefs from China to Peru." The results were for Wharton largely lamentable, even though the drama of American commercial imperialism was the subject she urged as worthy of serious fiction. But the most striking thing about the way Wharton cast global trade as American is that it supplied a national explanation for what were far more complicated global processes. Conceiving global trade as American allowed Wharton to separate cultivated travel – the source of her own aesthetic perceptions – from a destructive commercial travel, when in reality both art and commerce (like the Europeans and Americans who largely controlled them) were quite literally traveling in the same global circles.

In her memoir, for instance, it is Americans who pursue "feverish money-making" and get rich in "railway, shipping or industrial enterprises." For these Americans, travel means cash and movement means profit. Even leisure travel for the rich American is merely a displaced form of acquisitiveness, an insatiable appetite for novelty. Wharton's *Custom of the Country* offered a fully drawn portrait of moneyed Americans as a "new class of world-compellers" who were also world travelers. In this novel, which follows the transatlantic adventures of the divorcée Undine Spragg, Wharton explored the "taste for modernity" that theorist Walter Benjamin identified both with fashion and with travel. An analysis of fashion, Benjamin argued, "throws light on the significance of the trips that were fashionable among the bourgeoisie during the second half of the [nineteenth] century." The most "trifling symptoms" of fashion, even the "switch from a cigar to a cigarette," reflect an enthrallment with the "tempo of modern life," the "yearning for quick changes in the qualitative content of life." Like travel, fashion is finally an attraction to speed, a "switching – at high frequency – of the tastes of a given public." Benjamin thus concurred with the sociologist Georg Simmel that the essential drive behind fashion "is fully manifest in the passion for traveling, which, with its strong accentuations of departure and arrival, sets the life of the year vibrating as fully as possible in several short periods."

Travel, in short, gives speed – gives a vibrating "life" – to time itself. Though Benjamin and Simmel saw the twin passions for fashion and travel as characteristic of bourgeois culture generally, Wharton's *Custom of the Country* presents the merger of feminine fashion and intercontinental travel as a distinctively American phenomenon. What attracts Undine to Europe is not only the literal fashions of Paris couture but the fashionable hotels where Americans gather and enclose themselves in a luxe life of their own making. Undine's restlessness represents an appetite for sheer novelty, for change in everything from dresses to husbands, which the novel identifies as characteristically American.

As more than one critic has observed, while Undine's cultural ignorance makes her nothing like Edith Wharton there is still something about the character's voraciousness and love for the "rush of physical joy" that echoes portraits of Wharton offered by some of her contemporaries. And in her memoir, Wharton herself owns up to the "state of euphoria" she enjoyed for over two months when she indulged in a chartered yachting trip in the Aegean. Although she stresses that the trip was an uncharacteristic extravagance ("my prudence vanished like a puff of smoke"), she also describes her travel as a wondrous excess of joy akin to the excessive wealth of the rich industrialist. On "that magical cruise nothing ever seemed to occur during the day to diminish my beatitude, so that it went on rolling up like the interest on a millionaire's capital." Mobility and money, Wharton saw, were interchangeable. (Tellingly, Wharton used some of the proceeds of her first novel to buy her beloved Panhard motor car.)

But in contrast with these portraits drawn by friends – and perhaps in part because they contain truth – Wharton tended to present herself not as a restless traveler but as someone far more rooted and home-centered. In her letters, her memoirs, and even her photographs, Wharton emphasizes her devotion to personal dwelling places – to gardens and rooms and local surroundings. Put another way, Wharton recasts herself from an American traveler to a settled expatriate, a transformation that converts transatlantic travel into a form of dwelling, a rooted way of life. In her descriptions of "the compact and amiable little world" of her social circle in prewar Paris, Wharton's life seems to stand as an antidote to the rootlessness of modernity. Whereas London society reminded Wharton of the rush of travel – "the stream of new faces rushing past me often made me feel as if I were in a railway station rather than a drawing-room" – Paris represented an increasingly rare "continuity of social relations," a place for the cultivation of intimate and enduring human ties. France was a place where Wharton cultivated not only lasting friendships but also the domestic arts of gardening and home decoration, first in her Paris town house and later in the country home of Pavillon Colombe she built in 1922.

These ties distinguished Wharton from most American tourists and even from the younger, flashier Paris expatriates such as Fitzgerald and Hemingway. Yet to accept at face value Wharton's description of her Paris circle as a small society of homey Old World seclusion would be to overlook the astonishing degree to which members of this "amiable little world" directed power in the world at large. From the political writings of the members of Wharton's coterie in the Faubourg Saint Germain it is clear that the French journalists, diplomats, and writers in her circle were some of the chief architects of the empire erected by the Third Republic. Similarly, Wharton's American intimates in Paris were strong proponents of US expansionism and wrote some of the most influential works in favor of solidifying an American empire. The American scholar Archibald Coolidge, for instance, whom Wharton credits with having introduced her to Parisian literary circles, gave a lecture series at the Sorbonne that later became his pro-imperial volume *The United States as a World Power*. Wharton's one-time lover, the political journalist Morton Fullerton, wrote a series of articles urging the US to become a "predominant" power in the Caribbean. Naval superiority in the Atlantic and Pacific, Fullerton announced, was necessary in order to fulfill the nation's "destiny." In *Problems of Power* (1913), the book Fullerton published from his articles, he declared that Americans "are marching to the step of an imperial movement."

The closed circle of Wharton's friends and acquaintances turns out to have possessed a remarkable global reach. It was through this "little world" that Wharton met General Hubert Lyautey, a leading figure in the French expansion into Indochina, Madagascar, and Algeria. When Lyautey was serving as the Resident-General of the French Protectorate in North Africa he invited Wharton to travel through Morocco under the auspices of his colonial office. Wharton's account of that trip, her travel book *In Morocco* (1920), might be described as an aesthetic revisioning of the facts of empire. While Wharton prized the "continuity of social relations" she found in her Parisian society, the imperial relations these men and women promoted globally brought discontinuities of the most profound kind. Wharton recognized the contradiction, if obliquely. Her own attempt at a resolution in her Morocco book, however, elided as much as it admitted. Wharton acknowledged the destructive effects of colonialism only to set that destruction in opposition to an imperial "appreciation" for beauty, a force of aesthetic preservation and discernment that Wharton located in French colonial rule.

Unlike imperial enthusiasts such as Fullerton or her friend Paul Bourget, Wharton never justified European expansion in the name of progress. In fact, Wharton puts the notion of the colonizer's modern improvements under the scorn of quotation marks: "Before General Lyautey came to Morocco," Wharton writes, "Rabat had been subjected to the indignity of European 'improvements,' and one must traverse boulevards scored with tram-lines, and pass between hotel-terraces and cafes and cinema-palaces, to reach the surviving nucleus of the once beautiful native town." The greatest sin of the "modern European colonist," Wharton insists, is the "harm" he does to "the beauty and privacy of the old Arab towns."

However, just as the destruction of beauty is for Wharton the most damning fact about colonialism, so too does aesthetic value become Wharton's chief criterion for defending the most recent "French intervention" in North Africa. For Wharton, General Lyautey is exceptional because of his exceptional sensibility: he possesses "a sense of beauty not often vouchsafed to Colonial governors." In Wharton's Morocco book, French military occupation figures almost wholly as aesthetic preservation. Elaborating Lyautey's cultural qualifications for colonial rule, Wharton writes that

a keen feeling for beauty had prepared him to appreciate all that was most exquisite and venerable in the Arab art of Morocco, and even in the first struggle with political and military problems he found time to gather about him a group of archeologists and artists who were charged with the inspection and preservation of the national monuments and the revival of the languishing native art-industries.

Wharton does not deny France's colonial occupation so much as fold it into a curatorial role that is preoccupied with preserving national treasures that Moroccans themselves are unfit to protect. Rhetorically, the "French administration" in Wharton's book is elided with "the Ministry of Fine Arts" and Lyautey is less a colonialist than a connoisseur. "Were the [colonial] experiment made on artistic grounds alone," Wharton writes, "it would yet be well worth making."

"Artistic grounds" become for Wharton the Moroccan cultural territory that only select Westerners value and thus can rightfully possess. Wharton's travel book is a map of the same artistic geography, surveying the aesthetic grounds of enlightened French rule. Yet Wharton also seems to know just how precarious these "grounds" are for a defense of colonialism. Her preface acknowledges that her own travel had been contingent upon military occupation ("the next best thing to a Djinn's carpet, a military motor, was at my disposal every morning"). At the same time, she attempts to distinguish her travel from a debased future tourism sure to ruin Morocco through "the corruption of European bad taste." The preface, then, recognizes uneasily that the uniqueness of Wharton's brand of travel lies in the fact that she visited in "the brief moment of transition between [Morocco's] virtually complete subjection to European authority, and the fast approaching hour when it is thrown open to all the banalities and promiscuities of modern travel." The preface sounds a note of melancholy that the rich "mystery" of Moroccan culture will "inevitably vanish" with the coming onslaught of Western travelers. But the same wistfullness belies Wharton's own suppressed knowledge that the artistic grounds on which she justifies colonial subjection will culminate in little more than routinized sites for an army of tourists that would follow the occupying troops and Wharton herself.

KINSHIP IN TRANSIT

In a peculiarly telling sentence from her memoir, Wharton writes that "at the end of the second winter in New York, I was married; and thenceforth my thirst for travel was to be gratified." The sentence virtually erases her marriage from the account of her life. Any expected mention of a courtship, wedding, or honeymoon – not to mention a husband – has been swallowed up in the space marked by the terse semi-colon. The first clause is passive ("I was married"), while the second joins the fact of her marriage not to the gratifications of love, sex, or companionship but to the excitement and satisfactions of travel. This rather curiously constructed sentence was no doubt Wharton's attempt to sidestep with proper discretion the misery that was her failed marriage to Theodore Wharton. But the sentence also tells a truth about Wharton, the truth that travel was for her a passion and a mobile institution, a kind of substitute for marriage that ordered her relations to people and places.

The grammar that articulates a marriage, an elided divorce, and a passion for travel in this sentence illustrates a central feature of Wharton's later fiction. In these novels the weave of departures and returns that make up her characters' perpetual traveling provides a striking picture of modern marriage and kinship. The institution of the family was changing as rapidly as any other social institution in this time. Anthony Giddens notes that modernity introduces a dynamism into human relationships, an instability that brings both ruptures and potentially freeing innovations. Divorce, new kinds of sexual latitude, women's increasing autonomy from men, non-traditional forms of family and association – all are instances of a human mobility as characteristic of the modern as is the speed of motor cars. Wharton's ambivalence about such dynamism is plain enough, both in her life and her fiction. With caution and a marked anxiety, Wharton traded on the freedoms from traditional family and gender strictures that modernity was making available to women of wealth, and she finally divorced Theodore in 1913. Yet these dynamic features of modern sexuality and family in turn become the objects of a deft, funny, and often penetrating scrutiny in Wharton's novels. Behind her most pointed moments of satire we can read a disavowal, an attempt to indict a recklessness she wanted to distinguish from her own chosen life as a divorcée. Yet the disavowal itself is also an indirect acknowledgment that Wharton knew from the inside, as it were, the exhilaration as well as the damage that could come from ruptures in conventional family structures and more locally rooted ways of life.

Wharton found an ingenious way to capture this dynamism in fiction by severing the conventional marriage plot from local place and supplanting it with stories of divorces, remarriages, abandonments, and adoptions that transpire across time and space. Wharton's narratives of the affluent Americans that "inter-married, inter-loved and inter-divorced each other over the whole face of Europe" together distill one of her chief insights about modernity, her understanding that modern travel is a kind of index to the radical change within marriage and family. The ability in travel to rapidly exchange closeness for distance and to combine estrangement with intimacy reflects the mobile nature of modern kinship ties. Marriage and even blood relations are detachable, transplanted, improvised.

To this end, the travel plots of her later novels often deliberately induce a kind of disorientation in her readers as an initiation into the unsettled and often unsettling relations among the characters. Wharton's 1928 novel *The Children* opens on board an ocean liner bound for Italy. From his deck chair Martin Boyne observes a collection of children who defy his attempts to puzzle out their relation to one another and to the "little-girl-mother" who cares for them. Martin's confusion is our own, as children with differing accents, coloring, and last names behave as siblings. Their baffling presence on the steamship eventually becomes the most telling fact about their family identity. Crossing the Atlantic without any parent, the group of heterogeneous children is the product of a myriad of marriages, divorces, affairs, and remarriages among adults from at least three continents. The ocean liner is thus an appropriate host to children who owe their relation to siblings and "steps" – indeed, owe their own lives – to the couplings and break-ups that are inseparable from their parents' incessant travel. Similarly, the striking absence of any mother or father on board reflects Wharton's emphasis on the losses and disruptions that can come with modern mobility. Where do these children belong, and to whom? These puzzles only deepen into more existential questions as the novel explains the complex "marital chessboard" that is the children's varied parentage.

The novel also poses a further question: Are "the children" in fact children? Like Henry James in his *What Maisie Knew*, Wharton reconsiders what we understand as the nature of childhood. In the placeless context of travel, age and identity are no longer aligned. The oldest of the group, Judith Wheater, is variously "a playmate, mother, and governess all in one" and Martin has difficulty conjecturing her age. The more Martin saw of her, the narrator notes, "the more difficult he found it to situate her in time and space." Identity has become changeable and indistinct: "Whatever she was, she was only intermittingly." This mutability of the otherwise certain identities of kinship and age becomes increasingly charged as the middle-aged Martin unwittingly falls in love with Judith. He acts upon his unacknowledged desire by agreeing to guide and protect the children as a "father." As others force him to confront his sexual love for the teenage girl, Martin becomes enraged and then resigned, withdrawing from a world out of joint. In *The Children*, the vicissitudes of travel not only figure for us a new distance between parent and child but also forge new intimacies that shade into the taboo of incest.

Wharton's families and lovers supply fables of the "restructuring" of social relationships across the large-scale dimensions of time and space that Giddens identifies with modernity. In Wharton's world, kinship is geography, a spatial reordering of the responsibilities and rights of the generations and the routes of intimacy and sexual access. Rather than offering a haven from a commercialized culture (as in domestic novels) or a resolution to class tensions (as in novels of manners), the family is a central site for the explosive forces unleashed during the "take-off period" of global modernization. Absorbing these forces, the family in Wharton's fiction is transformed by strains of vertigo, satirical farce, and an increasingly literalized vision of incest.

Modern dislocation has a specific site in *The Mother's Recompense*. Wharton both begins and ends the narrative in a French Mediterranean town that is a colony for "uprooted, drifting women." The unnamed Riviera resort is an archipelago for the social exile of women who had, as it were, traveled too much: in this "female world," an international collection of adulterers and divorcées do their time for having fled marriages or traveled as mistresses. Kate Clephane, Wharton's American protagonist, had escaped from the "thick atmosphere of [her husband's] self-approval and unperceivingness" by agreeing to set sail from New York for the West Indies on another man's yacht – as the gossips put it, Kate had "travelled" with "another man." It is clear that for Wharton, as for Kate herself, the real transgression was Kate's temporary abandonment of her young daughter, Anne. Soon after she fled her marriage, Kate had returned to reclaim her child from her husband's family, but found that mobility was no longer on her side: upon arrival she was told that the Clephane family had left with little Anne "in a private car for the Rocky Mountains."

With exile and abandonment as backdrop, however, *The Mother's Recompense* begins by holding out the possibility of their redemption. The novel opens with travel as a trope of homecoming: the ruling Clephane matriarch has died and Kate receives a telegram from her daughter asking her to sail back for New York. When an elated Kate descends on "the gang-plank of the liner" in the New York port, she feels herself "born again." She has been delivered, as it were, from a homelessness of geographical and family exile. What she discovers, however, is a terrible distortion of kinship rather than the redemption of a mother and her daughter. Kate learns that Chris, her former and much younger lover from her days in France, has been courting Anne in New York, unaware that Anne is Kate's own daughter. The prospect of a marriage between Anne and Chris is the horrific "recompense" awaiting Kate upon her return to New York society.

Kate's decision to flee her husband for Europe has given rise to a quasi-incestuous tangle with her daughter and former lover. Distance in space collapses into a damaging hyper-closeness in human relations. The secret that Kate's daughter might unwittingly marry Kate's one-time lover brings "instantaneous revulsion" to anyone who suspects it. Wharton conveys these distortions of kinship through a sense of the physical nausea of rapid transit: in one scene in which Kate rushes out of New York by train, her state of alienation in time and space is so profound that it is literally sickening to her. From this vantage the world is nothing but "meaningless traffic."

At the same time, Wharton's kinship stories are more than merely cautionary. That is, they measure risks and warn of dangers but they also imagine a modern kinship that holds the possibility for altogether new forms of intimacy. When family relationships are chosen rather than merely inherited, Wharton suggests, they carry the promise of a reciprocity or pure affinity free from the petty tyrannies that mar traditional family relationships. Kate regains her status as a mother, for instance, only because Anne invites her to resume it, and as a result Kate conceives of their tie as a relation of "perfect companionship." She "could not picture having any rights over the girl." The depth of her love finally compels Kate to relinquish even her cherished role as a mother and to return to her European exile. The freedom of modern kinship, its foundation in consent rather than in birthright, offers a tantalizing vision of unalloyed love. Only when relations are freely chosen can they have the affective depth that seems to stimulate Wharton's imagination. In contrast to her mockery of the adults who produce the motley "tribe" in *The Children*, for instance, Wharton reserves a profound if tenuous heroism for the children in their determination to assert their status as a family against all other claims. It is precisely the absence of any clear legal or even blood relation that makes their choice to love and protect each other a poignant exception to the debased forms of kinship pervading the novel.

Wharton's portrait of family is fundamentally ironic: the radical instability of the modern family, its institutional fragility, is precisely what creates the possibility for believable bonds of love. In her *Glimpses of the Moon* (1922), for instance, it is only the pervasiveness of divorce that reintroduces the option of marrying for love. Nick and Susy Lansing, both without wealth of their own, undertake an "experiment" to marry for only as long as they can live on the wedding gifts and hospitality of their rich friends. By agreeing to relinquish the other when either of them has the opportunity of marrying for money, they rely on divorce to license their temporary marriage. In some respects Wharton holds out their bond as an attenuated form of love, a mere "bargain" to "stick to" when secure luxury beckons. Yet the novel finally suggests that such an extraordinary if not perverse agreement is in fact the proof of an exceptional intimacy: the couple's "free-masonry of precocious tolerance and irony" is in the end the reader's only guarantor of authentic love in a world of dislocation.

A proleptic agreement to divorce is the only way of contracting real love. Such ironies are permanent features of Wharton's modernity, where human relations and identities are rootless and mercurial; the Lansings circulate "among people so denationalized that those one took for Russians generally turned out to be American, and those one was inclined to ascribe to New York proved to have originated in Rome or Bucharest." Among these creatures shaped by modern "detachment and adaptability," their essence is realized most vividly in their twin appetites for changing partners and travel locations. Yet though Nick and Susy's eventual renunciation of their divorce agreement is a critique of the impermanence of modern marriage, they really only escape this critique because they recognize in each other a superior adaptability to the ungrounded nature of modernity. Their finally confirmed marriage is not a return to marital tradition but a glimpse of its uncertain future.

In *The Children* and *Glimpses of the Moon*, the improvised familial bonds in modernity can offer a "troubled glory," at least for the lucky few. Yet the Wharton novel most self-consciously about modernity, *Twilight Sleep* (1927), also contains her darkest portrait of modern intimacy. In *Twilight Sleep*, the usual finesse of Wharton's social satire has been deliberately converted into blunt-edged narrative sarcasm. The modern adaptability of Mrs. Pauline Manford, for instance, is manifest in her reliance on a succession of debased fads, from the sham spiritualism of her guru the "Mahatma," to the "eurythmic exercises" she practices to reduce hip size. The norms assumed by early domestic Realism – the naturalness of the nuclear family, the pull of the marriage plot – are so far removed from the Manfords' world as to be wholly strange if not forgotten. Indeed, the normative category of the family can be said to reappear in the metaphor of the freak show: Mrs. Manford "was used to such rapid adjustments [in her beliefs], and proud of the fact that whole categories of contradictory opinions lay down together in her mind as peacefully as the Happy Families exhibited by strolling circuses."

Even more starkly than her other late novels, Wharton's *Twilight Sleep* presents modernity as distortion. The Manford drawing room looks "more like the waiting-room of a glorified railway station than the setting of an established way of life," and modern mobility has begun to appear limiting rather than freeing or seductively risky. The "breathless New York life" of ocean liners and motor travel has created a static world of mass-produced discontent:

Today [Mrs. Manford] really felt it to be too much for her: she leaned back [in her car seat] and closed her lids with a sigh. But she was jerked back to consciousness by the traffic-control signal, which had immobilized the motor just when every moment was so precious. The result of every one's being in such a hurry to get everywhere was that nobody could get anywhere. She looked across the triple row of motors in line with hers, and saw in each (as if in a vista of mirrors) an expensively dressed woman like herself, leaning forward in the same attitude of repressed impatience, the same nervous frown of hurry on her brow.

Significantly, though, the affinities of kinship in this world still look like the best – perhaps the only – refuge for human feeling and fellowship. In the "oddly-assorted" Manford family, divorce and remarriage have actually produced a wider extension of mutual family sentiment. Pauline Manford and her two husbands "had been drawn into a kind of inarticulate understanding by their mutual tenderness for the progeny of the two marriages." Divorce actually produces a family rather than producing a "broken home"; indeed, in *Twilight* one young woman's *refusal* to grant her husband a divorce is the novel's yardstick for measuring acts of cruelty. But, as if to exploit the reader's relief at finding "mutual tenderness" in the Manfords' checkered kinship, Wharton gradually undermines the shared affection of this "dual family" through a relationship of quasi-incest.

When Dexter Manford falls in love with his stepson Jim's wife, even the regenerative relations of family succumb to what one character calls the "slippery sliding modern world." Dexter deceives himself that his feelings for Lita are brotherly. They share "the same free and friendly relation which existed, say, between Jim and Nona [Dexter's daughter]," he tells himself, in a reflection that does more to bring doubt upon the mutual fondness of the Manfords than to exonerate Dexter. The narrator glosses the thought as Dexter's "sense of having just grazed something dark and lurid," a metaphor of danger whose overtones reverberate with the fact that he is at this moment driving Lita at high speed in his private motor. With his hands on the steering wheel, he refrains from touching her. But pages later, the near miss becomes a "crash" when he throws off constraint and acknowledges his desire: "'Lita – ' He put his hand over hers. Let the whole world crash, after this . . ."

In the novel's climactic scene, the violent trope of the "crash" is realized in the literal violence of a gunshot that shatters the family. During a stay at the Manfords' country house, Pauline's first husband, Arthur Wyant, attempts to kill Dexter for his betrayal of Jim, Wyant's son. But in the nighttime attack Wyant manages only to shoot and injure Nona Manford, Jim's half-sister. Prostrate and bleeding, Nona makes her radically ambiguous plea: "It was an accident. Father – an accident!"

Accidents, we know, are never merely the products of chance in Wharton's fiction. In a Wharton narrative, rather, the accident is a violent symptom of modern conditions. With its power to distract, the spectacle of an accident can cover up those conditions at the same time as it registers their force and potential for damage. Real or imagined, the accident is a sign of the velocities of change, the extraordinary power, and the resulting potential for destruction that accelerated in Wharton's era. In *Twilight Sleep*, Wharton makes the complexities of modern kinship into the scene of a wreck. Nona's hysterical claim that the shooting was an "accident" burdens her with the work of collective disavowal that frees the rest of the family for the "remedy of travel" prescribed "when rich people's nerves are out of gear." While Nona lies immobile, the Wyants and Manfords scatter from Vancouver and the Rockies to Ceylon and Egypt.

The "possible crash" that animates Wharton's fiction combines the visual excitement of the popular spectacle with the sensations of risk inherent in modern mobility. Much more than Max Weber's image of modernity as a static, restrictive "iron cage," Wharton's figure captures for us the cultural energies it also critiques, recreating in art the speed and dread, the exhilaration and violence that make up the phenomenology of modern culture.

6

❦

ADAMS, JAMES, DU BOIS, AND
SOCIAL THOUGHT

B Y THE START OF the new century, fiction was as secure a cultural institution as any museum of brick and mortar. The proof was not only that the genre had earned public recognition as a high art, as when novelists were among the artists elected in 1898 to the newly founded American Academy of Arts and Letters. Beyond its new civil recognition, fiction itself was also now widely deemed a unique resource for civil society. "It is fair to assume," Meredith Nicholson wrote in a 1902 *Atlantic* article, "that in the nature of things we shall rely more and more on realistic fiction for a federation of the scattered states of this decentralized and diverse land of ours in a literature which shall be our most vivid social history." Nicholson limited this office of literary federation to "realistic" fiction, but critics in growing numbers were ready to dispute the primacy of Realism. Even so, it was largely under the watchword of Realism that this rather extraordinary notion – that the United States had a unifying meaning and history best grasped in fiction – had become by century's end an almost commonplace idea.

William Dean Howells received much of the credit for the new esteem accorded fiction. The younger novelist Frank Norris claimed that Howells had produced "the foundation for a fine, hardy literature we could call our very, very own." But in a 1915 letter Howells described himself as "a dead cult with my statues cut down, grass growing over them in the pale moonlight." The high literary status he had promoted for fiction endured. But in the new century the museum-like function he had helped establish for Realism – the work of supplying "exact" representations to instruct and cultivate the American public – would lose much of its authority.

The erosion of Realist tenets is part of a deeper realignment of aesthetic and social meaning in American letters. Social concerns were no less pressing for American novelists in the new century, but for many writers who perceived what Henry James called "the great modern collapse of all the forms," faith in Realist observation and notation no longer seemed either adequate or wise. Howells's wish to see literary sensibility enlisted as a searching means of social understanding, however, would find ironic fulfillment in new genres – not in

Realist novels but in hybrid works of social analysis. While novelists began experimenting with incongruous narrative styles, trained social thinkers such as Henry Adams and W. E. B. Du Bois turned to literary perception and expression precisely at the point at which disciplinary systems of social thought seemed to them to fail. The dream of a scientific novel was the broken idol of Howells's dead cult, but literary analysis became a rigorous mode of thought for defectors from the ranks of science's true believers.

IN EXCESS OF REALISM: LATER WRITINGS OF HOWELLS AND HENRY JAMES

Howells referred to Realism as "democracy in literature." The claim, though not altogether false, has been misleading. Howells's novels, it is true, feature common people and shared institutions – landladies and bookkeepers, courtrooms and flophouses. As a man, Howells had democratic sympathies, and as an editor, he translated the international "movement we call realism" into a call for US fiction writers to contribute the broadest possible record of American life. But in his pursuit of a common America, Howells's notion of the common is far closer to that of social scientists than of populists: it is a unit of analysis rather than a measure of democratic value. Howells's pursuit of the real follows something like a fictional law of averages; as Henry James put it, he "holds that in proportion as we move into the rare and the strange we become vague and arbitrary; that truth of representation, in a word, can be achieved only insofar as we can test and measure it." Ordinary objects and human types carry for Howells the virtues of frequency and probability, statistical regularities that managers and analysts value distinctly more than the populace. It is the anomalous, not the elite, that is Howells's defining antonym for the common; in James's words, he "looks askance at exceptions and perversities and superiorities, at surprising and incongruous phenomena in general."

Though Howells sought a literary understanding of the totality of American society, then, his Realist fiction is not democracy in literature any more than sociology is democracy in science. Howells's attachment to critical reflection is the likely reason his fiction, unlike Twain's, never reached a popular audience, and why Howells's novels, like James's, were judged by some readers to be overly analytic. It was James, however, who noted that Howells's critical bent could also produce a characteristic flaw, a tendency in his fiction towards including "factitious glosses." Howells's penchant for reflective meaning is manifest in the role given intellectuals in his novels. Almost always writers or literary devotees, and almost never women, his intellectuals tend to comment to one another on the narrative action, a gentlemen's chorus for the modern age. Like curators or museum guides, Howells's intellectuals have the pedagogical role of helping readers to frame the narrative phenomena to best interpretive effect. The worthy novel, according to Howells, must "make us look where we are standing, and see whether our feet are solidly planted or not. What is our religion, what is our society, what is our country, what is our civilization?" The Realist vision should compel these questions, and Howells's Realist intellectuals are so compelled to ask and ponder them.

James's charge of a "factitious" element in Howells's fiction hits the mark in two ways. If intellectuals supply a gloss on what is already convincingly represented in the arc of the narrative, they will be little more than extraneous talkers. If their commentaries are not extraneous, however, but rather are necessary for the coherence of the narrative, then such characters may be abetting the author in presenting a legible reality – a vision of "our society," country, or civilization – that is actually imposed rather than observed and represented. Can a modern society be accurately inscribed in a novel? For that matter, can it even be observed so as to inductively conceive a social whole from representative parts? James's hedged praise for Howells's "love of the common" also hints at his emerging doubts about this central tenet of Realism, for in shunning "incongruous phenomena" Howells may have been eliminating the quotidian messiness of reality and leaving Realist novels vulnerable to becoming mere solipsism, more deluded than any popular romance. Was Realism possibly the most "factitious" style of all?

Howells wrestled with the question himself in his most ambitious novel, *A Hazard of New Fortunes* (1890). In a striking departure, Howells made literary intellectuals his central narrative actors, thereby testing through the pressures of plot the Realist capacity to discern governing civil relations amidst the welter of modern phenomena. The "hazard" of the novel's title refers to a venture undertaken by a group of writers, artists, and their backers to launch a new literary magazine in New York City. The storyline is a significant innovation for Howells, for the plot is at once more forthright about the true subject of his Realism – namely, the powers of social discernment of literary intellectuals – and more willing to be skeptical of those powers in order to explore them. Howells was hazarding his own literary precepts in this novel: was the sensibility encouraged and rewarded in high Realism – nuanced critical reflection, a consciousness of close distinctions among cultural objects and textures – adequate to gauge an underlying civil order in modern America?

The task of answering would require a higher tolerance for disorderly material than Howells had previously demonstrated. His depiction of the

Manhattan setting in the novel amounts to a concession that incongruous sights and objects could not be attributed solely to the deliberate distortions of the mass-culture industry. When his central protagonist Basil March and wife Isabel move from Boston to New York (as Howells himself had done some two years before the novel was published), they are engulfed in a crowded and confusing milieu that has few rules of protocol and even fewer people who notice. The new setting corresponds with a shift from Howells's earlier preoccupation with mass culture and entertainment to a new focus on mass society as a whole, its shifting, hard-to-grasp features, its absent causalities and uncertain implications. Basil and Isabel are the central figures through which two individual minds encounter two million other residents living and working in the same locale. As they attempt to make their personal experience and reflections into a meaningful point of purchase on "the future of our heterogeneous commonwealth," Howells can be said to test at the outermost limit the capacity of the novel form to supply persuasive correlations between human consciousness and social conditions.

Henry James saw in mass society a "collapse of all the forms," a loss of the consistency of conventions and shared assumptions that risks disabling altogether the metonymic architecture of the novel. Howells depicts a similar loss of grounding in Basil's confrontation with "the frantic panorama of New York." Strange sights and novelties are not limited to places such as a dime museum, for fantastic objects and scenes are visible at every turn; the simplest train ride or city stroll holds "an uproar to the eye." Cheap print is as pervasive as air or bricks. When Basil happens upon a vendor selling ballads stacked high on the pavement, he buys up a "pocketful." Most striking of all, human lives come into view as massed lives, visible in "swarming" populations in which even the members of a "vast prosperous commercial class" look like replications of a single pattern.

Isabel voices distress at these conditions – New York "distracts and disheartens me" – though Howells tends to qualify the nature of her response as one of feminine feeling: "I couldn't make my sympathies go round two million people." Basil, the editor of the new publication, takes an analytic point of view that seeks for some intelligible order or design but finds none.

Accident and then exigency seemed the forces at work to this extraordinary effect; the play of energies as free and planless as those that force the forest from the soil to the sky; and then the fierce struggle for survival, with the stronger life persisting over the deformity, the mutilation, the destruction, the decay of the weaker. The whole at moments seemed to him lawless, Godless; the absence of intelligent, comprehensive purpose in the huge disorder, and the violent struggle to subordinate the result to the greater good, penetrated with its dumb appeal [Basil's] consciousness . . .

The passage conveys a fundamental shift in Howells's art. Rather than evoking a civil order that needs protection from unreal mass spectacle, the New York setting depicts everyday urban spectacle as a new reality that makes doubtful the possibility of grasping any governing order. Rather than a fabric of civil relations, society is now conceived as a field of outsized forces – energies, struggles, domination and defeat. Consciousness, that key Realist capacity, is no longer an acuity of thought and feeling able to calibrate cultural values but an intelligence that can recognize all too keenly the disruptive forces of contingency and chance. Howells is still at pains to represent defining social relations, but in A Hazard of New Fortunes the social issues multiply into tangled lines of conflict rather than supplying narrative structure. Tensions between labor and capital are an important strand, but the issue is suspended together with questions about the uncertain relations between men and women; about the divide alienating the South from the North; the vexed relations between art and commerce; immigration's effects on existing US cultures; and the ethics of poverty and wealth. Appearing in fragmentary ways, the issues do less to define the fabric of civil society than to suggest a society that far outstrips Realist categories.

In this decentralized world, literary culture is the closest thing to a center. Basil March absorbs the "huge disorder" of New York by viewing the city's scenes and inhabitants with an eye to their possible use as literary material. The tactic allows him to find "picturesque raggedness" in otherwise distressing conditions and to appreciate the exuberant life amidst ugliness and disorder. But Howells recognizes the irony that Basil, in the name of literary value, cultivates the disposition of spectator and converts his unease into visual pleasure, the very habits of the mass-culture consumer. The same uncertainty about literary values lurks in the magazine venture itself. The enterprise provides the only point of contact among the novel's disparate characters, and literary circulation appears as one of the few remaining vehicles for shared reflection among Americans. The magazine's organizer, Fulkerson, characterizes the publication as "something in literature as radical as the American revolution in politics; it was the idea of self-government in the arts." The pronouncement is close enough to Howells's own sentiments to recall his claims for Realism as "democracy in literature." But Fulkerson, a slangy ad man and entrepreneur, hits upon his description in a pitch intended to advertise the magazine among literary celebrities and journalists, a context that gives "self-government in the arts" the air of a commercial slogan. Presented as a piece of publicity, the formulation gives pause. Exactly what could it mean to speak of self-government – or any sort of government – "in the arts"? The resolution of Howells's plot does little to clarify things. Relations among the magazine staff members break down just as street violence erupts during a labor strike, a parallel that suggests that the association of Realism with democracy may be either a faulty analogy (literature cannot be democratic nor democracy literary) or a logical error (literature does not foster self-government in politics).

Basil March, a savvy literary intellectual, can offer no gloss on the state of civil relations because his efforts to grasp those relations simply fail. That failure, however, also means the successful elimination of the possibility of Realist solipsism: even if he wanted to, Basil cannot pass off an artifact of order as the truth of the real. In that respect, A Hazard of New Fortunes points towards a new office for the cultivated literary sensibility. The perceptive reader is still one who will attempt to read society, but the truth of literary insight will tend to lie in perceiving the mutability or absence of any controlling design among social phenomena, even in the face of increasingly powerful authorities that might wish to dictate otherwise. James would describe it as the "perception of incongruities," a recognition of slippage or shortfall, of ironic misalignment rather than the transparency of representative forms. Basil and Isabel, after leaving the home of a bright, keen-eyed young woman, witness policemen grappling in the street with a female drunk. Can the two women "really belong to the same system of things?" Basil asks. The tacit answer is that there is no system of things, at least none that will reveal itself through what Howells in 1871 had called "the secret of art," namely, "to observe with the naked eye." The liberal individual's powers of direct observation and reflection are no longer the sure origin and arbiter of positive knowledge, and A Hazard of New Fortunes is something of an elegy for Howells's Realist project of defining truth in fiction.

Realist observation emerges as a far more tenuous means of gauging civil society, but it also produces a resulting paradox: with this loss of sure social vision, the literary observer becomes newly open to history – history grasped not as observable law or system but as the irruption of historical forces. When the labor strike begins, Basil takes to the streets to observe the "great social convulsion" but finds only accidental injury and misdirected violence. There is nothing in the way of regular objects or events for him to analyze; the literary observer is no longer an unacknowledged legislator of civil relations. Still, he is the unexpected witness when clashing social forces erupt into a historical event. His is the consciousness that sees and remembers the explosive effects of a history he could have neither controlled nor foreseen through a discourse of "system." The concluding scenes in Hazard hold to Howells's practice of having his characters comment on the implications of the nearly completed story. But in contrast to his earlier novels, what Basil and his fellow intellec-tuals recognize most keenly is the gulf between what they apprehend in the surrounding "world of chance" and that world itself. They turn to Christian themes instead, invoking love and redemptive sacrifice as an alternative language of reflective meaning. Ethical disposition rather than cognitive mastery becomes the defining test for the literary intellectual. "What I object to," Basil proclaims, "is to this economic chance world in which we live and which we men seem to have created."

The turn to moral evaluation allows Howells to forge an alternative connection between character and social setting now that Realist interpretation has failed. For Howells, an otherworldly realm of meaning came to seem the necessary supplement to modernity if coherent contemplation of social life was to remain at all possible. Other writers in this era – William Butler Yeats and William James, for instance – also saw a need to reserve a place for unverifiable belief if one were to construct any adequate frame of interpretation for modern life. But few novelists followed Howells's attempt to annex religious meditation to the social categories of the Realist novel. And eventually Howells himself seems to have judged it an unworkable amalgam, for his later works leave off from close social observation in favor of more overtly symbolic forms such as his utopian fable *A Traveler from Altruria* (1894). Howells's most ambitious effort to translate Realist discernment into a synoptic museum of American modernity ends up eroding what had been his fundamental critical premise, that the novel was uniquely fitted to delineate and display the features of a modern society in its civil relations. In dramatizing the failure of Realist metonymy, *A Hazard of New Fortunes* becomes an inadvertent record of the modernity it could not represent.

Henry James would attempt his own portrait of the "huge jagged city" of New York in his book *The American Scene* (1907), a book based on his 1904–05 visit to the United States after some two decades of living abroad. For James, as for Howells, New York is a crucible in which the literary consciousness confronts "the flood of the real." Also like Howells, James discovers that an attempt to master "the great American spectacle" through close description or classification is certain to fail. Streets, buildings, and crowds are objects of intense interest and analysis, but the city's "too defiant scale" casts James back upon his own "excess of impressions" and extravagant "waste of speculation." Reviewers complained at the results, a book that offered no coherent picture of American landscapes nor any consistent judgment on American society; as one critic wrote, the book does not give a "synthetic view of life seen from a certain centralizing point of view." Unlike Howells, however, giving a centered and synthetic representation of American modernity had not been James's aim.

Despite its similarities to Howells's novel, *The American Scene* displays a markedly different set of assumptions about what is possible and desirable when a literary mind confronts the "monstrosities" of modern New York. In his fiction James had already abdicated many of Realism's techniques of fictional documentation, and by the century's end his novels no longer resembled the Realist chronicle that readers had come to expect from the author of *The Bostonians*. The appearance of *The American Scene* in 1907, however, was proof that James remained absorbed by social questions and still attached to the analytic reflection prized within high Realism. But whereas the failure of intellectual mastery of social phenomena in *A Hazard of New Fortunes* is a failure of Realism and a turn from the social to the religious, in *The American Scene* that lapse is the basis for a strikingly different species of social analysis. Its premise is not cognitive mastery but a mode of reflective thought that results from a "surrendered consciousness" open to the imprint of New York's excesses. This process of surrender yields a different species of critical knowledge at the same time that it also risks a deliberate self-display that makes James himself a literary object open to the reader's interpretation.

Innovations in James's fiction were vital to this shift in method. In the 1880s James was still pursuing the Realist imperative of social notation; an entry in his notebook records his sense of the novelist's duty to "sketch one's age." Major novels in this period, including *The Portrait of a Lady* (1881), *The Bostonians* (1886), and *The Reverberator* (1888), give close scrutiny to the pressures that "the situation of women" and new institutions of mass publicity exert upon a broad expanse of social relations. James had never been as deliberate an exponent of Realism as Howells, but many of the traits he observed in European writers – Balzac's confidence that "there is a law in these things," Zola's ability to create a "totally represented world" – were clearly among his own operative principles at that stage. But over the course of the following ten years, James would grow either impatient or skeptical of the Realist project and its techniques of social description.

One of his most telling novels in this regard is also one of his strangest. In *The Sacred Fount* (1901), James exaggerates the terms of Realist method until its notes of scientific detachment and confidence give way to panic and uncertainty. James depicts an observer who is convinced that he can detect "a law governing delicate phenomena" as the key to "our civilized state." This observer, who is the story's unnamed narrator, attends a weekend gathering at an English country estate where, in his close scrutiny of his fellow guests, he pursues "the joy of the intellectual mastery of things unamenable." The glimpse of a personal motive is striking. Recognition that supplying an explanatory law can be a source of pleasure – the "joy" of cognitive mastery – is one hint that James will question the notion of a science-like pursuit of truth in Realism. Even more arresting is the nature of the narrator's theory of a governing "law."

When he observes a woman who appears years younger than at his last sighting of her, he becomes convinced that her astonishing new youthfulness has come from a corresponding aging in her husband. "Mrs. Briss[enden] had to get her blood," and "Mr. Briss . . . can only die." Similarly, the new wit and intelligence of a man who previously had been dull, he deduces, must be explained by a recent loss of intelligence in an as-yet-unidentified woman at the gathering. A sexual secret – probably an affair between Mrs. Brissenden and the newly intelligent Gilbert Long – is the presumed mechanism: "intimacy of course had to be postulated." With his confidence in a predictive symmetry of social relations, this "expert observer" devotes himself to learning the identity of the missing woman in the quartet. A sense of discovery and metonymic order feeds his intellectual excitement as he relies on "that special beauty in my scheme through which the whole depended so on each part and each part so guaranteed the whole."

The narrator's outlandish theory is presented in the most scrupulous analytic language, which makes for a puzzling discrepancy between content and style. Is the novel an allegory of a vampire culture of affluence, encoding the "beauty and the terror of conditions so organized"? Or are readers to reject the narrator's theory and read his hyper-intellectualism as a symptom of insanity? Many of James's contemporary readers found the novel's ambiguities exasperating or worse; one reviewer announced that James's previous leanings towards "morbid" fiction had now reached a "chronic state of periphrastic perversity." But the evidence suggests that, for all its oddities, James had something serious in mind in the design of this novel. For, in the story's most important development, the reader's uncertainty is matched by the narrator's own eventual uncertainty about his theory. In a moment of crisis he experiences what he calls a "full revolution in consciousness," a sudden, devastating shift that occurs when he expands his theory of desire and its consequences. Turning his analysis on himself, he recognizes that he may well have fallen in love with one of his subjects. His own intellectual pleasure could be entangled in the very kinds of erotic forces he was attempting to track, and the insight propels him towards another dizzying possibility: he may actually be the unidentified "woman" he has been looking for – that is, the guest whose intelligence is being sapped to supply Gilbert Long with a new fund of wit. Panicked, he thinks he detects a rapid draining of his analytic powers, though of course this fact (if true) may either confirm his theory or else disprove it as nothing but the fantasy of a weakening mind.

The narrator discovers a law of desire only to realize that the nature of desire undermines his search for an observable law. The self-knowledge he gains from his intense analysis leaves him unable to stand outside of the relations he wished to master, and by the end his "palace of thought" has become a "heap of disfigured fragments." James's detractors conceded the "scientific exactitude" of the novel's treatment but complained that the book itself must be a species of hoax. But James defended the novel as "very close and sustained." Although the narrator's wish to prove a system of hidden relations comes to naught, the novel is not a satire on either the search for system or the passion for analysis. Within the world of the novel, the narrator's theory may in fact be correct; the plot never rules out the possibility that some kind of social economy or system links the characters. (Although James gave little or no notice to his contemporary Sigmund Freud, his novel's scheme of attraction and displacement among erotic subjects was not all that far from Freud's young science of unconscious drives and erotic transference.) But while the novel does not dismiss the possibility of a system of relations, it does undercut the narrator's certainty that he will be able to observe and master such a system. The loss of that governing assumption is the plot of the novel.

That plot is also the death of the Realist narrator. *The Sacred Fount* is the only James novel to use a first-person narrative point of view. The unnamed narrator has his time on the stage and afterward vanishes; James's succeeding novels contain virtually no reflective observations or descriptions from an anonymous narrative voice but present the story through the eyes of the fully participating characters. The failure of the narrator's theory in *The Sacred Fount* is James's departure from Realist narrative. In so changing his methods, James did not disown the Realist emphasis on social analysis but rather shifted the object of analysis from external phenomena to the observing consciousness, its risks, entanglements, and responsiveness to the social world it observes.

Some critics have seen this change of direction as James's retreat into a sealed sphere of formalism where aesthetic experimentation and lush language push out any concern with the social. Very little of the quotidian world – park benches, carpets, passersby – appear in James's later fiction. In syntax and structure his narrative style grows increasingly complex, at times to the point of opacity. But it is a mistake to assume that the focus in the later fiction on depicting states of consciousness cuts off any narrative interchange with the external world. Rather, James turns around the telescope, as it were: he makes a world of largely unrepresented social relations and external powers into an aperture through which to view a particular human consciousness. The reader is left with the task of reading the portrait of consciousness as a register of invisible social conditions. In a number of works, James makes the mind of a girl or young woman the "reflector," in which her efforts to absorb new experiences serve to indirectly record lines of coercion and domination in the social arrangements that surround her. In *What Maisie Knew* (1897) and

The Awkward Age (1899), for instance, James makes a young woman's limited but sometimes canny apprehension of adult society reveal the vulnerability of women and the young to the designs of others more powerful. In *The Wings of the Dove* (1902), *The Ambassadors* (1903), and *The Golden Bowl* (1904), close depictions of interior states gradually unveil a landscape of hidden erotic alliance and material motive, an estranged world that forces readers to abandon bourgeois codes of moral condemnation but still requires ethical evaluation of the actions of the refined Anglo-Americans and the social class they illuminate.

A map of that landscape, alongside others, reappears in *The American Scene* (1907). Even with its overt social topics and scrutiny, then, that book is not a departure from the concerns of James's late fiction. James in this book inhabits the role he had honed for his characters as a social "reflector": he substitutes for mimetic description of external objects a portrait of his own intense, sometimes besieged consciousness as a narrative object, and offers that object for the reader's social interpretation. *The American Scene* is a self-portrait of the artist as a "restless analyst." It depicts James's habits of unceasing, even obsessive intellectual reflection. His is not the kind of analysis that will find and extract order from disorderly material; he cannot, he warns the reader, supply the regularities of "reports and statistics." Neither can the resources of the nineteenth-century Realist novel serve his purpose. The "multitudinous life" compressed into a single skyscraper leads him to think of "the great wonder-working Emile Zola, and his love of the human aggregation" and of "artificial microcosm," but the recollection of Zola serves finally to convince James that not even that novelist could master the "monstrous phenomena" that now exceed "any possibility of poetic, of dramatic capture." That past order of literary meaning has "perished and lost all rights."

James's brand of analysis, then, is meant neither to abstractly regularize nor concretely represent "this most extravagant of cities." Instead, he offers riffs of thought (a "wild logic," a "fluid appreciation") that risk incoherence but that attempt to read and assess modernity on its own terms, without reference to any compensatory religious ideas or invidious comparisons to other eras. In practice, that means he must attempt to understand a new "epic order" of social history that as yet lacks any epic – any sufficiently expansive genre or set of expressive conventions. Novelties and elisions are the city's most definitive features. The visual obliteration of churches is akin to an "Abyssinian" mystery, an exotic disappearance that makes urban landscapes markedly unlike those of Europe. The Waldorf-Astoria is a new thing under the sun, an instance of a modern "hotel-world" of total organizational enclosure. The high quality of the sweets enjoyed by immigrants at Bowery theatricals is an expression of modern citizenship through literal consumption.

Topics of this sort are hardly social features in the ordinary sense. Candy, shoe sellers, and the superabundance of windows become analyzable forms only insofar as James sees and articulates them through the contours of his own reflective thought. There is no law that governs proper analysis; "mishaps and accidents" contribute as much as hoped-for "felicities." But the book's constellation of topics signifies more than a collection of James's idiosyncrasies. On the contrary, he claims that the book has issued from his "intimate surrender" to the external environment. Objects and cultural moods exert a pull on his mind as if of their own accord. James conveys this sense of the power of external phenomena to command attention through his use of *prosopopeia*, the representation of the speech of inanimate objects, and records what he "hears" spoken by a skyscraper, a New Jersey mansion, and by the air itself.

The point is not that his receptive disposition precludes any critique of the "great commercial democracy." James does not withhold his dismay at the "new remorseless monopolies" and the "icy breath of the Trusts" of America's high-octane capitalism. Nor does he censor his alarm at such democratic transformations as the changes to English wrought by the masses of Americans indifferent to the forms and fate of the language. But by absorbing the "vociferous" strangeness of American modernity, James attempts to make a place for history's alterity, its inassimilable otherness, within the record of his own thought. He offers a "surrendered consciousness" that is unmistakably his own at the same time that it mediates what is alien to him as an "agent of perception."

In his preface, James asserts accountability for his observations: "I would in fact go to the stake for them." The image, though whimsical, still suggests a particular seriousness about James's project in *The American Scene*. His attempt to open himself to history will also make a historical object out of Henry James. He may be judged either a heretic or a prophet for his book, and James himself cannot know which he is. His effort to make his consciousness a reflector of history also turns James the man into a literary object properly subject to critical analysis. The implications can be seen in the two topics that proved to be among the most telling tests of high literary writing in the period: mass culture and the matter of race.

Mass publicity is for James an elemental substance of modernity, as fluid and pervasive as air. The ability of commerce and accumulated wealth to multiply ways of making itself visible has spawned "unmitigated publicity, publicity as a condition, as a doom, from which there was no appeal." Even the more workaday face of New York is "a prolonged showcase" and, like Howells, James suggests that the spectacles of mass entertainment have become the generalized condition of an altogether "outward" society. Such an atmosphere leaves

Americans with a drastic attenuation of what James calls "literary desire"; he is aware of "how little honour they tend to heap on the art of discrimination." At the same time, in writing as a serious interlocutor of "the great American spectacle," James makes his prose into what can best be called literary spectacle: the strange, prodigious, misshapen, incongruous, and deliberately sensational images and language of his late style. James is not directly imitating with his style the "sword-swallowing" conspicuousness he attributes to everyday life in New York; indeed, his sentences are most likely to be illegible to "eyes accustomed to the telegraphic brevity of the newspaper." But in a number of implicit ways, James's prose reflects his tutelage in mass forms. (At times the debt is explicit: touring in New Hampshire, like a Wild West show trick, calls for "great loops thrown out by the lasso of observation from the wonder-working motor-car"). James's literary language is his backhanded homage to the freedom of mass culture to invent incautious, ad hoc forms to meet the exigencies of the age. He learns the lessons of its lack of deference, its alacrity in reading subcultures, the strategic virtues of its disproportionate and outsized dimension, its intensity of effect and rapidity of change. James "take[s] his stand" for literary discrimination with its commitment to analytic thought, but in his work the literary lives through a critical collaboration with the extravagant, impudent novelties of mass culture.

James is also a deliberate interlocutor of the "inconceivable alien." The accounts of his visits to Ellis Island and the Jewish ghetto, and his reflections on the "hotch-potch of racial ingredients" on American streetcars and sidewalks, have provoked critical controversy. They are key passages in the book, and James will stand or fall on the deliberateness of his effort to think "ethnically" about American modernity. He does not pretend the new immigrant populations are other than "alien," strangers to his own habits of thought and feeling. The "intensity of aspect" of the immigrant Jew, or the rebuff he feels from an Italian laborer, trigger in James a sense of personal distance that he records in close detail. The emphasis on otherness in these passages can read like patrician recoil and may be just that. Yet, like James's treatment of other features of modernity, preserving the immigrant's "inconceivable" aspect is a strategic moment in his brand of literary analysis, as his thought opens itself to realities of difference that it cannot master but will not elide. There is, he confesses, something that attracts him in the "close and sweet and *whole* national consciousness as that of the Switzer and the Scot," but for an American no such consciousness is possible unless it seals itself against history. That immigrants are to "share the sanctity of an American consciousness" is certain, the one "fixed element" that grounds James's thought. The same certainty, then, requires a radical change in what is assumed about the nature of a national consciousness, and "the idea of the country itself underwent something of [a] profane overhauling" to admit the realities of history.

The puzzle devolves upon James, not the "alien." Refusing a facile assimilation of the foreigner into an assumed American destiny means James is thrown back upon the limits of his own comprehension, and he records a "conscious need of mental adjustment": "He doesn't *know*, he can't *say*, before the facts . . . It is as if the syllables were too numerous to make a legible word. The illegible word, accordingly, the great inscrutable answer to the questions, hangs in the vast American sky, to his imagination, as something fantastic and *abracadabrant*." The nonsensical adjective, creative yet opaque, is the modifier James would attach mentally to everything "American." Something unknown and unknowable hangs in the American sky, an anti-symbol to the certainty of a transparent American destiny that had been the guiding sign from the time of the Puritans. To take in the "great ethnic question" is to admit the resistances and opacities of history, something inevitably corrosive to the transparency of national myth. For James, the matters of ethnicity and race are inscrutable signs that interrupt the otherwise unbroken prospect or "sky" that would figure a "sweet and whole" but falsified national future.

New York makes "inscrutable" the temporality of the future; in the South James is interrupted by residuum from a suppressed past. Outside the Capitol building in Washington he encounters "a trio of Indian braves, braves dispossessed of forest and prairie, but as free of [the Capitol grounds] as they had ever been of these." In their bowler hats, and (as he imagines) with tobacco and photographs in their pockets, the modern appearance of these supposedly "vanished" Americans shatters the smoothed over, monumental aura so deliberately cultivated at the Capitol. The strangeness of the sight – the men's ironic "freedom" to possess the grounds, their resemblance to "Japanese celebrities" – create a rift that opens out to an unacknowledged history of violence:

They seemed just then and there . . . to project as in a flash an image in itself immense, but foreshortened and simplified – reducing to a single smooth stride the bloody footsteps of time. One rubbed one's eyes, but there, at its highest polish, shining in the beautiful day, was the brazen face of history, and there, all about one, immaculate, the printless pavements of the State.

Traveling further south on a train, James exercises his "perception of incongruities" in another racial encounter, this time directed towards the incongruities of his own position as observer. From his seat in a Pullman car crossing rural fields, he considers his view of the "subject populations" – poor whites and the far more numerous poor blacks – he can see from the window. To observe this scene is to view a racial history that "ruled out" freedom for the poor and that ruled in, as it were, the economic "ease" of the observer: "The grimness with which, as by a hard inexorable fate, so many things were ruled out, fixed itself most perhaps as the impression of the spectator, enjoying from his supreme seat of ease, his extraordinary, his awful modern privilege of this detached yet concentrated stare at the misery of subject populations." James does not evade the fullest implications of the insight: that his "supreme seat of ease," in such a moment and at such a location, will be historically closest to the position of the Southern slave master. "It was a monstrous thing, doubtless, to sit there in a cushioned and kitchened Pullman and deny to so many of one's fellow-creatures any claim to 'personality'; but that was in truth what one was perpetually doing." Whether in the spirit of callousness or confession, the statement accurately identifies James's omission of any real consideration of African Americans in the book. But James is also underscoring the conditions that impede the black laborers from lavishing "care" on the world, the activity that signifies "personality" in this literary context. At the same time, he points to the fact that his own manifest personality as "restless analyst," possessing the "awful modern privilege" of social and literary observation, rests on the same material conditions.

James omits the lives of black laborers from his book, then, but makes his own privilege as their observer serve to articulate the historical plight of "subject populations." He uses and intensifies the same technique when he writes of meeting a white Southerner with pleasing manners. The gentle personality of the man becomes an interior view into an ungentle history: "though he wouldn't have hurt a Northern fly," James writes, "there were things . . . that, all fair, engaging, smiling, as he stood there, he *would* have done to a Southern negro." History resides in the conditional tense as well as the past tense: what the genial white man "would have done" to a black man or woman is a grammatical passageway into the acts of terror that were accumulating into a suppressed history of lynching, the history activist Ida B. Wells called a "red record." Like other forms of passage in *The American Scene*, James will require his consciousness to open to the wounds and irregularities of history. Originally conceived as an "agent of perception" for civil relations, high literary discernment will need to read inscrutable facts and "bloody" incivilities or it will read no more than what is already written on the "printless pavements of the state."

That James is compelled to read those uncivil signs is made clearest in the last pages of the book. Seated once again in a Pullman car he depicts himself as forced to the task by a "lucidity" he cannot evade. The train itself speaks to him of the "general conquest of nature and space," and this voice of the confident triumphalism of a commercial age "appeared to invite me to admire the achievements it proclaimed": "See what I'm making of all this – see what I'm making, what I'm making!" What James offers in return is an "eloquence of exasperation" that constitutes one of the most remarkable interrogations of American modernity. Importantly, James does *not* speak on behalf of those who have been most harmed by these forces of "conquest." "If I had been a beautiful red man with a tomahawk I should of course have rejoiced in the occasional sandy track, or in the occasional mud-channel, just in proportion" as the landscape escaped the transformations wrought by commerce and technology. "Only in that case I shouldn't have been seated by the great square of the plate-glass through which the missionary Pullman" invited his approbation.

Careful as he is to make the Native's position legible in his record, James does not criticize from any social position but his own. It is as an heir of modernity who accepts the fact of "ravage" that James makes his reply to the train's boast. He does so by calling to account what America has chosen to undertake as its project of civilization.

If I were one of the painted savages you have dispossessed, or even some tough reactionary trying to emulate him, what you are making would doubtless impress me more than what you are leaving unmade; for in that case it wouldn't be to you I should be looking in any degree for beauty or for charm. Beauty and charm would be for me in the solitude you have ravaged, and I should owe you my grudge for every disfigurement and every violence, for every wound with which you have caused the face of the land to bleed. No, since I accept your ravage, what strikes me is the long list of the arrears of your undone, and so constantly, right and left, that your pretended message of civilization is but a colossal recipe for the *creation* of arrears, and of such as can but remain forever out of hand.

This long closing section was not included in the US edition of *The American Scene*. Only the edition published in Britain contained the meditation and the open question with which it ends: "Is the germ of anything finely human, of anything agreeably or successfully social, supposably planted in conditions of such endless stretching and such boundless spreading as shall appear finally to minister but to the triumph of the superficial and the apotheosis of the raw?"

PRAGMATISM AND THE LITERATURE OF CONSCIOUSNESS

In a 1913 essay entitled "The Social Self," philosopher George Herbert Mead wrote that "it is fair to say that the modern western world has lately done much of its thinking in the form of the novel." Few other professional philosophers would have characterized the novel as a mode of thinking available "for social science." But Mead counted himself among those who practiced pragmatism, a school of thought that had a distinct kinship with literary culture.

Pragmatism's most obvious tie to the literary world was the literal kinship between Henry James and his older brother William, a professor of philosophy at Harvard who, along with Charles S. Pierce, John Dewey, and Mead, developed a new framework for asking questions about the nature of human thought. As pragmatists they sought to evaluate the soundness of a particular idea not by way of abstract systems of reason, as traditional philosophers do, but by anticipating the consequences that the idea would have in the world of lived experience. As Pierce wrote, the truth of an idea lies in "the conduct it dictates or inspires." Our ideas and beliefs are not abstract postulates we hold in our heads but implicit rules that direct our behavior. What counts most for pragmatists are the concrete effects of an idea, the extent to which it "works" in the world.

Pragmatism's turn to real events and conduct as the truest testing ground for ideas suggests something of its affinity with the novel. Yet, curiously, it was not the brother of Henry James but rather George Mead who pointed to the novel as contributing to "a general theory of self-consciousness." In their ideas about fiction, Mead and Henry James were the closer intellectual siblings; Henry and William seem to have viewed novels in something like rival terms. Despite internal differences, though, pragmatism belongs to high literary culture as it has been set forth in this study: it belongs, that is, to a new culture of American letters that had elevated the novel from a form of entertainment to a serious vehicle of thought and recognized social analysis. To place it in that company is also to recognize how pragmatism, as a literature of consciousness, was speaking to the fate of discernment in a mass society.

Like Howells and other intellectuals, William James worried about novel-reading. The wrong sorts of novels, consumed for the wrong kinds of reasons, pose a danger to one's faculties. "The habit of excessive novel-reading and theatre-going" risks creating a personality that luxuriates in feelings at the cost of decisive action. James spoke against "the nerveless sentimentalist and dreamer, who spends life in his weltering sea of sensibility and emotion, but who never does a manly concrete deed." The warning appears in James's famous chapter "Habit" in *Principles of Psychology* (1890), a groundbreaking study of the nature of consciousness that contains many of the theoretical foundations for what he called the "pragmatist method." Behind James's focus on habit is the pragmatist determination to rid philosophy of the enduring problem of the separation between thought and deed, between the mind and the world. How accurately does the mind really read what is "outside" in the world, and how real is the belief that our minds give us a free will to choose and act in that world? For James, human habit points to the ultimate continuity between thoughts and actions. At bottom the two are as unified as a brain nerve and its direction or "line of discharge," and James contends that traditional philosophers had argued for centuries over a distinction that could be effectively erased. But his comments on the risks of reading novels also reveal an underlying anxiety, an uneasiness that the mind can indeed be all too easily cut adrift from the world of action. Like the advocates of literary Realism, pragmatists hoped to show that reflective thought could make sense of what John Dewey called "a complicated and perverse world," but the fate of discernment in that world was none too certain.

What good, after all, does thinking do? If the thinking is of the sort that most professional philosophers do, the pragmatists believed that in the end it offered no real value. In his essay "The Need for a Recovery of Philosophy" (1917), John Dewey summarizes the pragmatist claim that philosophical systems, in their search for the absolute truth of things, bring people no closer to reality. What he calls "the spectator notion of knowledge" leaves philosophers standing apart from the world and merely looking on, spinning out abstract rules and systems in the hope of producing a "transcript" of what is real. Such thinking cannot cope – does not try to cope – with a world of "specific events in all their diversity and thatness." Dewey had begun his career influenced by Hegel and other German philosophers, but reading James's *Principles of Psychology* triggered a new direction for his work. When he began teaching at the University of Chicago in 1894, joined there soon after by his friend Mead, Dewey turned his attention to whether reflective thought could address "contemporary difficulties" that philosophers had "left to literature and politics." "Philosophy recovers itself when it ceases to be a device for dealing with the problems of philosophers and becomes a method, cultivated by philosophers, for dealing with the problems of men."

Of course, literature, too, was struggling with the unsorted welter of things – Dewey's "diversity and thatness" – in modern life. In *A Hazard of New Fortunes*, the progress of Howells's literary pilgrim through contemporary New York largely comes to grief, and Basil March's turn to Christian ethics marks the finite limits to what human observation can disentangle in an "economic chance world." Pragmatists also recognized limits to what even the most perceptive of observers could know, be they novelists or philosophers. But it is at this point that pragmatists introduce their most radical proposition: it is precisely those limits that allow perceptions and ideas to be true. Discernment *is* the real. It is an audacious notion, as many contemporary philosophers were quick to declare. But the validity of this core principle, pragmatists argued, lies in the fact that human speculation does indeed have limits, a fact that has for centuries locked thinkers into interminable "metaphysical disputes." And because no human thinker can ever possess omniscience, one can safely predict that a whole class of philosophical problems will never be solved. The sensible conclusion is that that class of problems then ceases to matter. As James put it, "There can *be* no difference anywhere that doesn't *make* a difference elsewhere."

The "principle of Pierce" defined a new landscape of possibilities for the work of thought. In *Pragmatism* (1907), James sums up the pragmatist as "one who turns away from fixed principles, closed systems, and pretended absolutes and origins. He turns towards concreteness and adequacy, towards facts, towards action and towards power. It means the open air and possibilities of nature, as against dogma, artificiality, and the pretence of finality in truth." The new criteria for validity redefine the aims of thought. Ideas worth pursuing are "those things we can assimilate, validate, verify" within the existing body of currently accepted truths while seeking to project new possibilities. As James makes a point of stressing, this requirement places a good deal of restriction on what can pass for a valid idea. But because the goal of thinking is not to erect a permanent description of the "truly Real," thought is freed to address what Dewey calls "the actual crises of life." Knowledge is not a copy of the world to be judged for accuracy (impossible to do, since no one possesses the master "transcript"). Knowledge is rather that thought which "affords guidance to action and thereby makes a difference in the event" it contemplates. "Intelligence develops within the sphere of action for the sake of possibilities not yet given," as Dewey puts it. "A pragmatic intelligence is a creative intelligence."

The creativity the pragmatists described sounded exhilarating to some, wrongheaded or crassly utilitarian to others. It had its foundation in a view of consciousness that James had put in place in his *Principles of Psychology*. Because there are no metaphysical first principles with which to define consciousness, James begins with the sensory data experienced in the individual mind. But unlike the British empiricists who held that sensation consists of discrete, atomistic building blocks, James insists that our senses confront a "teeming multiplicity of objects and relations," an "indistinguishable, swarming *continuum*, devoid of distinction." James's famous chapter on "the stream of consciousness" is recognized even by detractors as one of the most impressive pieces of writing to attempt to describe the mind. In it he distinguishes remarkably subtle tendencies and activities within consciousness that, once described with all of the shaded detail of his language, become startlingly familiar. His vivid analytic distinctions and lyrical descriptions have prompted critics to remark on the "literary richness" of the prose. The work possesses a literary structure as well, the structure of the German *Bildung* narrative that assumes a final fulfillment in the formed individual possessing will and agency. In James's story, individual consciousness is the protagonist and hero. The "swarming" nature of the given world would overwhelm any conceivable meaning were it not for the saving work of the individual mind. James's almost gothic invocation of the original "black and jointless continuity of space and moving clouds of swarming atoms" finally serves to make all the more impressive the "agency of attention" and human will that create a world out of that "inexpressive chaos." Through the "phenomena of selective attention" and "deliberative will," the mind carves out "a world full of contrasts, of sharp accents, of abrupt changes, of picturesque light and shade."

The metaphor of carving is James's. "The mind, in short, works on the data it receives very much as a sculptor works on his block of stone." The human mind is creative, the universe malleable. There are moments when James acknowledges a degree of collective agency in this world-building: "the world we feel and live in will be that which our ancestors and we, by slowly cumulative strokes of choice, have extricated" from the same "given stuff." But in the main, James depicts the work of the mind as the labor of the singular individual, achieved through the agency of "choice." It has seemed odd to some readers that James's insightful analysis of the largely involuntary operations of sense and habit become the ground for his hymn to the creative power of personal choice. In the conclusion of the chapter he shifts his focus from habit to choice in a direct way. Choice is the real principle behind reason ("reasoning is but a selective act of mind"), behind aesthetics ("the artist notoriously selects"), and at the root of "hortatory ethics." The resolution of reason, art, and ethics into the act of choice returns the liberal individual to the center of a "teeming" and indifferent universe, but it largely negates the powerful vision of multiplicity with which James begins.

Something of the same tension is present in James's important discussions of pluralism. One of the largest consequences of pragmatist thinking is that one must surrender the assumption that the world is a unified "monism," a single reality that harmonizes all truth as one. The pragmatist must accept instead an irreducibly plural universe of incommensurable worlds. "Other sculptors, other statues from the same stone! Other minds, other worlds from the same monotonous and inexpressive chaos!" The principle of pluralism became part of James's impassioned defense for tolerance of human differences in the name of the "sacredness of individuality." The inherent dignity of the existing human life condemns any forced subordination to another's world. In *Pluralism* and other writings James argues for the ethical and political truths that can be grasped by recognizing the plural nature of the world.

And yet a fractured, multiform universe also holds unsettling implications not easily dismissed with a celebration of plenitude and choice. The recognition of other worlds from other minds can also mean the loss of any synthesizing perspective and a resulting psychological vertigo. The decentered nature of a plural universe also presupposes, as its constitutive unit, an insulated existence in a world of one's own making. At once too open and too hermetic, a plural universe can threaten to nullify the premise of a unified mind and world. James himself describes something close to this nullification when he warns against the "ontological wonder-sickness" that can befall those who become lost in "mazes" of their own speculative thought. "Discharging" thought in action is James's prescription, but it can have the ring of an anxious afterthought.

Against any seeming inconsistency between pluralism and individualism, though, James would warn with Emerson of the larger error in following a "foolish consistency." The only meaningful consistency adheres in pragmatist results. Does holding to a belief in the sovereign individual produce untenable actions or consequences? On the contrary, for James's belief in the primacy of the individual allows thought to meet the "crises of life" and hence to validate itself as a truth. James had experienced a debilitating depression as a young man, and the mental devastation is often cited as the motive behind his philosophical commitment to an untrammeled individualism. But James's fealty to the integrity of selfhood is as much a social concern as a personal value. "Excessive novel-reading and theatre-going" is only one symptom of the dissolution of active selfhood that seems to be the most worrisome specter on the social scene. In *The Will to Believe* (1897), he invokes the "thousands of innocent magazine readers [who] lie paralyzed and terrified in the network of shallow negations," the martyrs of mass print. These "thousands" who thereby lose the firm outlines of character become something lesser or indistinct than individuals and congeal into a single mass body.

His counter image, presented in *The Will to Believe*, is "the intellectual republic." This federation of inviolate selves becomes a social body through reasoned tolerance for the differences in belief and outlook among individuals. Yet in this republic of minds, individuals are so autonomous as to be difficult to imagine in any serious human association. James's attempts to write about human life in its social dimensions are among his weaker creations. His "principle of partaking" offers reassurance that individuals, however disparate their conceptual worlds, are living congruent lives insofar as they are "partaking" of the same dimension of time. But when James wishes to depict a world of face-to-face interaction, the results can be hollow or strained: "If the poor and the rich could look at each other" with sympathetic understanding, "how gentle would grow their disputes! What tolerance and good humor, what willingness to live and let live, would come into the world!" The passage presents a scene of possibility: here is what a rich person and a poor one might conceivably do

when standing face to face. Like Henry's imagining of what a white Southerner "would have done" to a black Southerner, William is writing a social
encounter in the conditional voice. But William's scenario is sealed against
the past, with its accumulated record of animosity between labor and capital.
It offers hope and futurity, but does so by allowing pragmatist optimism to
trump a pragmatist principle of consequences that must reckon with the past.
As a scene of social relations, the imagined moment leaves actors looking and
knowing without ever speaking and, indeed, without ever needing to speak.

A far more intimate model of social existence is at the center of George
Mead's pragmatism. It is not a coincidence that Mead regarded novels as
important "data" for understanding human consciousness. Like Howells, Mead
holds that a serious sort of thinking occurs in the novel, and that the images it
depicts help create a form of knowledge. But for Mead it is not the narrative
display of a settled order of social types and relations that offers knowledge.
Not the novel as a finished artifact but rather the process of novel-*reading*, the
literal unsettling and reordering of the reader's consciousness that occurs in
the brain – that is the real source of the value to be gathered from fiction. The
activity of reading novels deepens and extends the very "processes of reflective
thought" that characterize modern selfhood. Behind Mead's ideas about the
novel was a theory of "social consciousness" that he developed in published
papers and in his lecture courses at the University of Chicago, where he taught
from 1894 until his death in 1931. The self is social, as Mead puts it, because
the "inner consciousness" imports the "outer world."

Mead's starting-point is the paradox of selfhood. We experience ourselves
as individuals, as a singular "me." But even our most intimate sense of self,
Mead insists, is social to the core. That is because our recognition of who
we are comes from other people. There is no real content to our sense of
self without interaction with the people who surround us, for we only grasp
concrete impressions by imagining ourselves as others see us, much as we only
know the features of our own face by looking in mirrors. In Mead's words, the
individual "has to get the consciousness of the 'me' through the eyes of others
to make up his social consciousness." To do so, the individual imaginatively
inhabits the perspective of some other person. "We take the role of another and
respond to ourselves." In the moment of looking at oneself through another's
eyes, the "me" becomes a kind of external thing, a projection or object that we
"see" rather than an interiority we inhabit. This reflected image of the self is
something Mead calls an "alteri." Even though the repertoire of such images or
"alteri" exists in our own consciousness, our interior sense of self is constantly
formed and reformed by way of the world without: "the 'me' is the common
individual for all of the 'alteri' that exist in consciousness." I dwell within the

singular "me," but even while living in my own skin I am incorporating a world of other people.

A "social procedure" is the very stuff of consciousness. For Mead this fact carries importance for social life as much as for psychology. The responsive nature of our consciousness means that the self can enlarge its own cognitive reach to recognize ever more diverse groups and relations. Our thinking and conduct can be a creative part of the external social world. Mead's central example is reform. Labor movements and other organized reforms force the rest of a community to recognize others in their fullest social identity, to see them as parents and neighbors and not simply as workers. In the process, individuals in the larger community will incorporate a new sense of self as reflected through the eyes of those seeking reform. The result is an expansion of the social self and "the introduction of values which were not recognized before."

Literature is vital to this social change. The novel and other "realistic" art forms allow for a further extension of the self into the social field. "The social function of the artist is to provide imagery for thinking from all points of view." As the complexity of society has grown, so have the demands on the artist, and "modern realistic literature is the result of the enormous number of social problems forcing themselves upon us":

The great need is for imagery to present [others] to us. The drama and the novel do this, make people talk to us, and we to them. It carries on the mental process of thinking. Greek tragedy presented scenes . . . of distant social situations. Our realism reflects the new series of problems, which are not typical but novel. They require setting up types which had not been set up before, carrying out lines of thought which we had not carried out before.

With its density of social images, the novel is first among literary equals, but other genres also stimulate the social thinking at the heart of Mead's theory. "Hence the short story, the photograph, the one-act play answer to the data in the science which cannot yet be fully organized or put into full relation with the rest of the field. Realism is helping us to develop imagery for social science."

Mead's aim was to describe and help cultivate a "democratic consciousness." True to the pragmatist orientation towards real-world consequences, Mead and John Dewey sought to test their ideas of psychology and social life in the "outer world" of institutions like schools and cultural organizations. Their hope was that pragmatism would prove its own truth by increasing the possibilities for a shared social consciousness among as large a group as possible. As Dewey put it, knowledge is an "instrument or organ of successful action." Mead's posthumous collection of essays, *Mind, Self, and Society* (1961), and Dewey's many works directing pragmatist thought towards education and practical politics, including *Democracy and Education* (1916) and *Liberalism and Social Action* (1935), are a record of some four decades of intellectual work devoted to examining social possibilities for the future.

But what, if any, force does history carry in understanding the possibilities of "democratic consciousness" and future social action? Was it from necessity that the pragmatists gave little space to considerations of history in order to realize a philosophy of the future? The relative neglect of historical questions by William James and other pragmatists suggests an economy of thought whereby insight into the world of the future rests on an occlusion of the facts of the past. It may be that same economy shaped the imagination of a writer almost wholly at odds with the pragmatists. History was the personal and professional obsession of Henry Adams, a writer whose ability to imagine a continuing future was as foreshortened as his historical imagination was rich.

HENRY ADAMS AND INCOMMENSURABLE KNOWLEDGE

In *The Education of Henry Adams* (1907), a book of personal and historical reflection, Adams calls the death of his sister "the sum and term of education." The knowledge learned from this first real acquaintance with death is nearly identical with William James's gothic description of the "given" world that confronts consciousness with an "inexpressive chaos." Adams writes:

The first serious consciousness of Nature's gesture – her attitude toward life – took form then as a phantasm, a nightmare, an insanity of force. For the first time, the stage-scenery of the senses collapsed; the human mind felt itself stripped naked, vibrating in a void of shapeless energies, with resistless mass, colliding, crushing, wasting, and destroying what these same energies had created and labored from eternity to perfect. Society had become fantastic, a vision of pantomime with a mechanical motion; and its so-called thought merged in the mere sense of life . . .

That Adams's self-described education arrives at the dark place where William James's education of the senses only begins is a notable irony. The two men, who shared a friendship as well as an allied Boston background and a common employer (Adams was for a time a history professor at Harvard), came to precisely inverse conclusions about the same question. How can I understand the relation of my mind to the world it inhabits? For William James, to think and act in the world is perforce to create that world's meaningful shape as the only knowable universe. Adams's education, in contrast, leads him to uncover the sheer materiality of shapeless mass and force in a world indifferent to human meaning. "Education went backward." The passage on his sister's death represents only one of many moods in the book; Adams recovers from the blow to continue his "accidental education" into the twentieth century. But the devastating "lesson" prefigures the final fruits of his education as embodied in the book's concluding laws of social entropy.

The extensive annotations Adams wrote in his copy of James's *Principles of Psychology* show something of how sharply he diverged from James's way of thinking. And without too much distortion one can read *The Education of Henry Adams* as a book-length annotation on the principles of James's philosophy. James's faith in the oneness of mind and world becomes Adams's realization of the cheap "stage-scenery of the senses" that collapses the closer one approaches reality. The social world figured in James's "republic of intellect" is overturned by Adams's "pantomime" society in which social activity is reduced to vacuous "mechanical motion." In one respect, the difference between the two thinkers is easily accounted for. Adams is a historian who insists that the heterogeneity of human events and institutions be explained by way of intelligible laws, a demand that is almost certain to founder against what Henry James called "modernity, with its terrible power of working its will." For William James, in contrast, history is subsumed into "experience," the common matrix that generates both new events and their congruent laws. His pragmatism is thus better fitted to modernity than Adams's historicism, and is intended to be. From another perspective, however, these diametric thinkers evince a striking similarity. Both are drawn by a kind of gravitational pull towards the vanishing point at which history disappears into mind, but for Adams that point is the end rather than the beginning of any meaningful human consciousness.

The *Education* is a new genre: autobiography by default. Adams writes from the position of one who intended to offer the first truly scientific history of his age but is able to deliver only a record of his own failure at the task. It is not a coy pose; his certainty about having failed is real enough. But because the book presents what Adams believes is the highest considered wisdom on the matter, his rhetoric of personal failure cannot be taken at face value. Adams's education teaches him aright by revealing that the promise of intelligibility was wrong. The periods of Adams's life are thus the only means of ordering the broken remainders of a unified field theory of history that could not be written, and the progression of his ironized education presents fragments of Darwinist theory, medieval history, American diplomacy, far West travel and European tourism, Washington satire, pedagogy, thermodynamics, economic history, and poetic musings on women, Whitman, and sex.

William James, for one, found the form too eccentric: "There is a hodgepodge of world-fact, private fact, irony (with the word 'education' stirred in too much for my appreciation!)" The art historian Bernard Berenson, though captivated by the book, called the style "over-Jamesian for my intelligence." This was certainly a reference to James the novelist rather than the philosopher: as Henry James had done in *The American Scene*, Adams seizes his own failure to master the modern world and uses it to confront the incongruities of history from within the space of consciousness.

Few people could have felt as much in possession of history as Henry Adams, which may explain why almost no one renders with as much vividness the sensibility of historical displacement. Life as the great-grandson of one president, John Adams, and grandson of another – "Quincy" to the Adams kin – meant that the town of Quincy, Massachusetts, the city of Washington, the US State Department (where he served under his father in the British legation in London), and the White House were all at various times extensions of "home" in the most literal and intimate sense. Because of his family, Adams calls himself a "child of the seventeenth- and eighteenth-centuries" fated to "wake up to find himself required to play the game of the twentieth." He enters the world, that is to say, expecting it to adhere to an "eighteenth-century fabric of *a priori*, or moral, principles," the regularities of fixed law that bind politics and virtue and promise to harmonize nature and knowledge. Recognizing those principles makes one an heir to the nineteenth century as well, or at least it appears that way to a boy who as yet "had no idea that Karl Marx was standing there waiting for him":

> The boy naturally learned only one lesson from his saturation in such air. He took for granted that his sort of world, more or less the same that had always existed in Boston and Massachusetts Bay, was the world which he was to fit. Had he known Europe he would have learned no better. The Paris of Louis Philippe, Guizot, and de Tocqueville, as well as the London of Robert Peel, Macaulay, and John Stuart Mill, were but varieties of the same upper-class bourgeoisie that felt instinctive cousinship with the Boston of Ticknor, Prescott, and Motley . . . The system [was] the ideal of human progress.

The young Adams makes the understandable assumption that the universal subject of human progress is "the boy," Henry Adams. He is right, which makes the assumption of universality wrong. That is, there was no one closer than Henry Adams – closer in sex, race, family position, education, and opportunity – to the "individual" assumed by classic liberalism, unless it were Mill himself. The passage displays Adams's technique of exploiting his unique place in the history of transatlantic liberalism to reveal that the human consciousness envisioned by classical liberal thought is in reality the mindset of a particular social class and its "instinctive cousinship" with a transatlantic class kin. The most notable family trait, Adams confides, is the willful mistake of assuming that the thought of their clan is destined to be the mind of the whole world. "Boston had solved the universe; or had offered and realized the best solution yet tried. The problem was worked out."

Adams learns otherwise, and the figure of "the boy" disappears as soon as the mistake does. In its place Adams offers a series of stand-ins ranging from the whimsical to the bizarre. He is a "French poodle on a string" pulled from "one form of unity or centralization and another." He is a "worm." He "should have been a Marxist" but, no longer believing himself a universal subject, he recognizes that "some narrow trait of the New England nature" made him unable to convert. He is a "Conservative Christian anarchist," a "pilgrim of power," a circus "acrobat" on a high wire, a "posthumous person" in the world of the living. All are different incarnations of what he calls in his preface a "manikin" self, the tailor's dummy in a human shape and a passive model useful only to take the measure of someone else's suit of clothes. The figure comes from *Sartor Resartus*, Thomas Carlyle's inventive exploration of a post-Romantic self that is no longer an organic and indivisible soul. But Adams's fondness for presenting and then rapidly changing such vivid models of self also suggests the department-store manikin that was already a familiar object behind plate-glass windows. Though he infrequently addresses directly the materials of commercial culture, they make themselves felt in such moments as his discovery of the false "stage-scenery of the senses" and his commentary on the "monthly-magazine-made American female." For Adams, who admitted "haunting the lowest fakes of the Midway" and a fondness for "snake charmers" and "gladiatorial contests," the discontinuities of twentieth-century mass culture become the aesthetic style he adapts to review his adulthood in the nineteenth century.

The effect is striking. Like Henry James and Du Bois, Adams converts the disorder he apprehends in mass culture into an analytic image for his own literary purposes. But Adams's motive for it is less clear. What prompted such an ironic self-portrait, detached and dispersed among a set of absurdist effigies? Some of the evidence is supplied by omission. His darkly ironic portrayals of himself and the world have much to do with the suicide of his wife, Marian Adams, an episode he acknowledges in the *Education* only by excising a twenty-year period from his account. The more overt evidence lies in his struggle with history. From an early age the puzzles of history are a provocation or spur, a disruption that is also a motive for thought. One such disruption comes at age twelve on a family journey to "the slave states" where Adams confronts the "moral problem that deduced George Washington from the sum of all wickedness" inherent in slavery. Another occurs at the Black District of Birmingham, England, with the "revelation of an unknown society" among the industrial poor. The problems inherent in history afford him a remarkable productivity if not any final resolution. He capped a distinguished career as a historian with his nine-volume *History of the United States during the Administrations of Washington and Jefferson* (1889–91). Adams also anonymously published two successful novels, *Democracy* (1880) and *Esther* (1884), which adapt contemporary political and social debates to the intimacies of the novel. And his immersion in twelfth- and thirteenth-century Europe became the basis of his *Mont Saint Michel and Chartres* (1904).

As presented in the *Education*, however, Adams's success as a historian seems only to deepen the problem of historical fact. One "must either teach history as a catalogue," he writes, "or as an evolution" with inherent moral meaning. But "he had no theory of evolution to teach, and could not make the facts fit one." The dilemma is keenest for the teacher of history: "In essence incoherent and immoral, history had to be taught as such – or falsified." Making sense of the "debacles" of the nineteenth century, and of the American past and future ("the nightmare of Cuban, Hawaiian, and Nicaraguan chaos"), comes to seem more urgent and yet more quixotic.

It is in this light that we should consider Adams's scientific theorizing. Adams's lifelong study of science represents his effort to find a domain to supply the "ultimate Unity" he had never expected from religion and found fruitless to try to extract from history. Darwin promises to offer the truer unities of a planetary history obedient to natural law. But Darwinism, too, turns out to look suspiciously like a god: it is worshiped as omniscient by supplicants looking to share its power. In the retrospective view of the *Education*, Adams relies on literary analysis when science, too, has appeared to fail him. Yet his turn to the literary is not a retreat from the rational but rather a means of placing the revelations of science together with the problems of human consciousness and history, a conjunction that scientists must refuse as the precondition of doing science. This is the larger reason for his sustained grappling with Darwinism and other branches of science. Displacing his "troglodytic" origins in the Adams family, he restarts a family history from his "earliest ancestor and nearest relative the ganoid fish, whose name, according to Professor Huxley, was *Pterapsis*." This "oldest friend and cousin" will supply an "impersonal point for measure" with which to reconstruct a world of meaningful regularities.

Darwinism's effects on the imagination are the real interest for Adams. "For the young men whose lives were cast between 1867 and 1900, Law should be evolution from lower to higher, aggregation of the atom in the mass, concentration of multiplicity in unity, compulsion of anarchy in order." Adams here is both confessing and mocking. He was certainly among the young men who learned to look to science for a new principle of unity. But as a radical ironist, Adams underscores the wholly human motives that made those men eager to believe in evolution's promise of order. History, in all its corrosiveness, extends to even the furthest reaches of speculative thought. The "seduction" of Darwinism lies not in its science but in its historical moment in the aftermath of the Civil War, a war that Adams had helped conduct as an aide to the Union delegation to England.

Unbroken Evolution under uniform conditions pleased everyone – except curates and bishops; it was the very best substitute for religion; a safe, conservative, practical, thoroughly Common-Law deity. Such a working system for the universe suited a young man who had just helped to waste five or ten thousand million dollars and a million lives, more or less, to enforce unity and uniformity on people who objected to it.

The power of Adams's method, an avowedly anarchic power, lies in his insistence on linking even the most monumental natural phenomena with the finitudes of history, not to reconcile them but to pursue the implications of their disjunction. In nature, the implications of evolution are what they are; in history, the implications of belief in evolution are of an altogether different order of meaning. And in that space of difference operate all the motives, aggressions, and ideals endemic to the conflicted sphere of human history. Adams's reference to the war dead, as casual as it is brutal, recalls us to the violence that cannot be sealed off from the meditations on far distant operations of natural law. Adams's "manikin," the disinherited human subject, has been pushed out of the center of the universe, just one more kinfolk of the Pterapsis fish. But so demoted, the human figure remains on the scene as the ineradicable subject of history in order to register the collusion, resistance, and denial that human subjects try to transact with an indifferent universe. The technique represents Adams's attempt to hold human actors accountable even when the sphere of human action can no longer be judged by moral law.

To look at the world this way is neither commonsensical nor comfortable. The historical consciousness in *The Education of Henry Adams* is committed to thinking analogically about incommensurable orders and thus to remaining suspended between terms that cannot otherwise meet. No one is more aware than Adams that it is a difficult posture to endure, not to mention an awkward one. "His artificial balance was acquired habit. He was an acrobat, with a dwarf on his back, crossing a chasm on a slack-rope, and commonly breaking his neck." Like so many of Henry James's tropes, the image is self-deprecating, transforming a patrician's disdain for circus-style entertainment into a picture of his own analytic consciousness. It is also altogether serious. The image of a broken neck appears again when Adams describes his visit to the Paris World Exposition of 1900, the site he uses for the final lesson in education. With its collection of objects and images, the Exposition presented "a new universe which had no common scale of measurement with the old." The facts of radium, radio waves, Daimler motors, kinetic gas, and giant electric dynamos declare a universe of "occult" energies that are literally unfathomable and distinctly threatening: "He found himself lying in the Gallery of Machines at the Great Exposition of 1900, with his historical neck broken by the sudden irruption of forces totally new." The moment is a kind of death for the "Henry Adams" who has journeyed through the book. The magnitude of force he has encountered signifies the end to any consciousness that might articulate a principle of unity. Henceforth it will be "force," rather than consciousness, that is the true subject of history. "Continuity was broken."

Adams's "force" is both scientific and literary. His method of grasping historical disjunctions through a literary "scale for the whole" allows him to compare different "lines of force that attract the mind," from medieval Christian faith and erotic inspiration to the mechanical energies of the modern age. But after the rupture in Paris, "force" becomes the principle that defeats literary intelligence, and hence historical consciousness, as it ascends to become the true subject of history. Force, clearly, is a non-human subject and obeys only what Adams calls a "law of acceleration," an internal logic that places it outside of any scale for the whole. When Adams, in his final chapters, restarts his narrative to present a compressed history of force, human beings appear as the incidental figures that comprise what might be called a race of manikins: small objects of mass who await, all unconscious, for whatever will befall them in a world ruled by "bombs."

Whether or not Adams was right that the acceleration of force would capture and overtake human history, the idea had clearly captured his historical imagination. He can project, against the grain of his own thought, the notion that the reign of force in the twentieth century might produce a new kind of consciousness and thus a continuation of the human story: "he was curious beyond all measure to see whether the conflict of forces would produce the new man, since no other energies seemed left on earth to breed." His invocation of "a new social mind" is a placeholder for a human future, but it has little ability to move Adams to any hopeful speculation: "the style of education promised to be violently coercive." Still, the difficulty Adams has in assuming the continuation of history also suggests a final irony, perhaps the only one that escapes Henry Adams: that his historical imagination tends to see history itself end with the death of his own kind of social mind. Despite his unparalleled ability for historical reflection, there is still a limit to what he can conceive about history, namely, its future, though that may be the cost of seeing history too well.

W. E. B. DU BOIS, CONSCIOUSNESS, AND LITERARY FORM

When Adams tries to convey the "debacle" of nineteenth-century history, he describes it as a trauma to his body: history breaks his neck. As with the image of his mind as an acrobat carrying a dwarf on his back, Adams uses the trope to place himself in the history he is narrating and to acknowledge his own vulnerability and complicity with its forces. He uses such language deliberately to avoid the temptation of playing a mere onlooker at the "circus" of modernity, the disposition he took in a 1906 letter to John Hay: "My lunacy scares me. I am seriously speculating whether I shall have a better view of the *fin-de-siècle* circus in England, Germany, France or India, and whether I should engage seats to view the debacle in London or Paris, Berlin or Calcutta." The attitude is one he would renounce, but the picture of his person as a seated spectator is distinctly more accurate than an acrobat-Adams risking his neck. The menu of global options bespeaks the exceptional latitude Adams enjoyed both for his mind and his body, the freedom that conditioned his ability (and, indeed, his felt need) to choose intellectual engagement rather than inured detachment. That he could choose was a luxury.

For W. E. B. Du Bois, the vulnerability of the body is never safely a trope, and for that reason his thought can be said to begin in a special subset of the mind/body problem. In his account of a black education in the post-Civil War nineteenth century, *The Souls of Black Folk* (1903), his first chapter describes the dawning self-consciousness of the "dark pupil": "For the first time, he sought to analyze the burden he bore upon his back, that dead-weight of social degradation partially masked behind a half-named Negro problem." Du Bois might wish he could offer this figure as mere metaphor, but the "dead weight" of possessing a black body is too apt to become literal truth, as *The Souls of Black Folk* proceeds to show. To be an African American in 1900 is to defy Descartes and discover that one's being has been relegated to the body rather than the mind – I think, therefore I know I am a body despised. From this enforced epistemological starting-point, Du Bois takes as his task the writing of a new philosophy of history and of American social thought. In the end this would not be the history of African Americans alone but of "the future world," the global history that would have to reckon with the facts of "industrial slavery and civic death" that the nineteenth century had bequeathed to the twentieth. Du Bois's aim in *The Souls of Black Folk* is to show that the "problem of the Negro" encodes the broader "harvest of disaster" faced by the world as a whole.

By his own account, Du Bois would have evaded the Negro problem if he could have. In his autobiography, *Dusk of Dawn* (1940), Du Bois writes that, "had it not been for the race problem early thrust upon me and enveloping me, I should have probably been an unquestioning worshipper at the shrine of the social order and economic development into which I was born." Raised in Great Barrington, Massachusetts, he attended the black institution Fisk University, then made his way to Harvard for graduate study in the philosophy department, where his mentor was William James. Like James and Adams, he was able to study in Berlin, and like them secured a post at a research institution, the University of Pennsylvania. This path permitted Du Bois to acquire possibly the best training available in the world for his field. Although his status as a black man at times impinged on the direction of that path – James counseled him to change his study from philosophy to historical research, for instance, and the University of Pennsylvania omitted his name from their catalog – Du Bois succeeded in the same world of education and scholarship as James and Adams. It was a world that suited a bookish young man who loved opera and Europe and who was writing a novel about Harvard in his spare time. But the problem of the Negro body, as he describes it, "broke in upon" his academic life most forcefully at the turn of the century "and eventually disrupted it."

Lynching was at its peak in 1899 when a black Georgia farmer, Sam Hose, was hanged and set on fire. Du Bois, at the time a professor at Atlanta University, wrote a measured letter against the lynching and left his university office with the intention of mailing it to the editor of the *Atlanta Constitution*. On his way through the streets of Atlanta, Du Bois learned that Hose's charred and severed knuckles were on public display in the shop window of a white proprietor. He turned back and never delivered the letter. "One could not be a calm, cool and detached scientist while Negroes were lynched." The spectacle of Hose's body parts on display in a shop window bespoke a set of historical conditions and relations that the academic disciplines had no capacity to analyze. Du Bois had already published landmark works in history and sociology, and there was no scholar better qualified to undertake an academic study of the current crisis. His *Suppression of the African Slave-Trade in the United States* (1896) is a history of the origins of the Negro problem; the work he published from his research at the University of Pennsylvania, *The Philadelphia Negro* (1899), is a sociology of the problem. But it was precisely the Negro problem as it was conceived by social science and white America that Du Bois needed most urgently to redefine if he were to identify the conditions of Hose's exhibited body. Du Bois would have to begin from a different point of departure. Those who had "faced mobs and seen lynchings" – those who internally recognized the "dead weight" attendant to being black – would be the subject of the history Du Bois needed to write.

"How does it feel to be a problem?" The question, posed in the first paragraph of *Souls*, becomes a lever or gear enabling Du Bois to shift the position of black people from sociological object to literary and historical subject.

Between me and the other world there is ever an unasked question: unasked by some through feelings of delicacy; by others through the difficulty of rightly framing it. All, nevertheless, flutter around it. They approach me in a half-hesitant sort of way, eye me curiously or compassionately, and then, instead of saying directly, How does it feel to be a problem? They say, I know an excellent colored man in my town; or, I fought at Mechanicsville; or, Do not these Southern outrages make your blood boil?

To displace this false form of "the Negro problem," Du Bois situates himself on the social divide between black and white and locates the origins of that false form in the "other world" of white inquiry. In response to those who see a problem in the instant they "eye" a black man, Du Bois declines to answer. "I smile, or am interested" but "I seldom answer a word."

And yet his status as problem is a fact of black historical life and a key to understanding the authentic problem as Du Bois will redefine it: "the problem of the color line." Having refused a binary system that would define white observers who learn and know against the black objects of their knowledge, Du Bois returns to analyze on his own terms the "strange experience" of "being a problem." That it *is* a status and not an essence is Du Bois's central point. But he will also insist, as no disciplinary discourse yet could or would, that an abject social status is a distinct shaping force within the interior consciousness of the person who bears that status – that it is a determinate species of "experience." To recover that sphere of experience, Du Bois draws upon memory wed to analysis and, like Adams, uses his own experience to open out unexamined social relations that structure historical inquiry.

His earliest New England memories tell of his painful discovery that he was "shut out" from the world of his white playmates by a "vast veil." Like Adams's "force," the "veil" will become a governing literary figure that allows Du Bois to synthesize human consciousness and historical fact in an analytic space that lies outside both philosophy and historical record. One result is his well-known conception of "double-consciousness":

After the Egyptian and Indian, the Greek and Roman, the Teuton and Mongolian, the Negro is a sort of seventh son, born with a veil, and gifted with second-sight in this American world, – a world which yields him no true self-consciousness, but only lets him see himself through the revelation of the other world. It is a peculiar sensation, this double-consciousness, the sense of always looking at one's self through the eyes of others, of measuring one's soul by the tape of a world that looks on in amused contempt and pity. One ever feels his twoness, – an American, a Negro; two souls, two thoughts, two unreconciled strivings; two warring ideals in one dark body, whose dogged strength alone keeps it from being torn asunder.

The passage recalls Hegel's framework for merging history with collective consciousness, and anticipates George Mead's analysis of "social consciousness" as a sense of oneself created "through the eyes of others." But the systems of both Hegel and Mead assume a normative subject, the self or "son" unconstrained by any veil. The reality of the veil for the "Negro" in America, in contrast, places him or her apart from the world of subjects as an isolated race object, a being deemed "less than human."

In Du Bois's analysis, in other words, subjects are already historical and social beings who live on one or the other side of the veil. The history of slavery is part of the veil that created enslaved African Americans as "a thing apart." The history of Reconstruction and its aftermath is part of the veil that re-enslaves the freedman and seeks to "inculcate disdain for everything black." Absent as a philosophical subject, and present as a social scientific problem, the black subject goes unrecognized by the "other world" and is left an unprotected and stigmatized body. Only by explaining the veil, or color line, can one explain the phenomenon of Sam Hose and the "death and isolation" that is one of the historical fates of the African in America. Meanwhile, as "the sociologists gleefully count his bastards and his prostitutes, the very soul of the toiling, sweating black man" endures "a vast despair."

It falls to a literary analysis to recover the excluded black subject, which Du Bois will reintroduce in a vernacular idiom as the black "soul." But merely recognizing and writing the African American as a subject will not remove the veil. On the contrary, it is the realization of the souls of black folk that makes the veil appear for what it is: an immaterial but impermeable wall of historical signs and perceptions, the "imaginings of that other world that does not know and does not want to know our power." Behind the veil, the black person knows himself or herself as both a conscious subject and as a despised object, and the disharmony creates doubt and "vain questionings." The resulting double consciousness is the critical category that can properly illuminate the "havoc" and despair in the lives of African Americans.

But Du Bois also describes the same double consciousness as a gift of "second-sight." The synthesis of self and "other world" that characterizes Du Bois's black subject becomes a powerful instrument of historical analysis at a "critical point in the Republic." Du Bois returns to the domains of history and sociology to address anew the social questions that had been too narrowly conceived as "the Negro problem." Historical chapters on the Freedmen's Bureau, on black political leadership and the loss of suffrage, and on liberal education become sites of critical reflection that open towards broader questions of American modernity. Second sight means that a history of the American republic must include the veiled history of American slavery. *Souls* thus begins history when "the slave ship first saw the square tower of Jamestown," and its doubled historiography records lines of continuity connecting antebellum slavery with the "triumphant commercialism" of the present, a moment in which human beings of all colors are increasingly viewed "with an eye single to future dividends." Du Bois's subsequent chapters on "the Black Belt" – the rural territories of the South inhabited by an isolated black peasantry – are similarly a literary reinvention of the disciplinary methods of sociology. As a field observer, Du Bois uses fable and metaphor to capture in the everyday fabric of black life what "our crude social measurements are not yet able to follow." And he charts the costs and distortions of an administrative structure that has made the South an "armed camp for intimidating Negroes." The second sight of the black subject can thus apprehend many of the "unanswered sphinxes" closed to science.

In a statement about *Souls*, Du Bois acknowledged that he had dropped the "impersonal and judicial attitude of the traditional author." The "subjective" tone and style, he wrote, meant a loss "in authority but a gain in vividness." Aesthetic textures of memoir, poetic image, and story do the primary work of analysis and synthesis in the book. Yet for all the obvious importance of literary expression in *Souls* and in his novels *The Quest of the Silver Fleece* (1911) and *Dark Princess* (1928), Du Bois has not been an easy figure to place in relation to institutions of literary and aesthetic culture. He was an unabashed devotee of European high art, urging African Americans to undertake "soul-training" by making their way to art galleries to contemplate paintings. Yet his insistence that art must serve political ends as higher "propaganda" led some younger black artists to see him as too narrow in his views on aesthetic culture. He championed the "song and story" of black folk expression and made black spirituals the unifying motif of *Souls*. He even claimed his own style in the book is "tropical – African." Yet the language in *Souls* tends towards the ornate, mannered prose of a Victorian stylist. Almost as many critics have seen Du Bois as an elitist distant from the black masses as have claimed him for an authentic racial tradition of black expression.

His unfixed position in the terrain of cultural hierarchies makes Du Bois a particularly illuminating figure for investigating the dynamics of literary value in the period. Indeed, he can be said to formulate the question of those dynamics himself when he places dual epigraphs at the head of every chapter, one an excerpt from canonical Western literature and the other bars of music from an unidentified "sorrow song," a black spiritual transcribed in musical notation only. The pairings pose an unasked question at the heart of the book: what is the place and value of high literary culture in a society recalled to its "red past" and to the civil death of a contemporary "second slavery"?

Du Bois seems unable or unwilling to say, at least directly. Sharing an intimate proximity on the page, the paired epigraphs nevertheless appear as autonomous fragments from opposing worlds with no obvious relation of meaning. But in the chapter "Of the Coming of John," Du Bois conducts an experiment in bringing the disparate cultural locations into a dialogue. The notion of double-consciousness is turned into a fable of "the two Johns," two young men and former childhood playmates – one black and one white – who have both returned to their small Southern town after receiving education in the North. John Jones, the black man, struggles to endure the subordination of life behind the color line after his awakening in the cosmopolitan milieu of New York City to new worlds of art and experience. The white John is merely bored, the confinement of the privileged.

Then the fable's crisis: when he intercepts the white John attempting to rape his sister, Jones kills him. In this reversal of the lynching scenario, the white man becomes the lifeless and nameless body and "a thing apart." The racial order will right itself, of course, and the fable ends as Jones succumbs to a white lynch mob. But the poetic evocation of the lynching, presented from within Jones's mind, merges the destruction of the black man's body with his ecstatic memory of Wagner's opera *Lohengrin*, which he heard in a "great hall" in Manhattan. "Was it music, or the hurry and shouting of men?" The "last ethereal wail of the swan" from the aria is replayed in the "strange melody" – perhaps the wail of his own cries – that accompanies the mob killing.

The Wagnerian lynching is a startling way to render the "peculiar sensation" of double consciousness. Du Bois's fable deploys "story and song," the forms he identifies as the gifts of black America, but operatic song comes from a world alien to the Southern black person, as the tale makes a point of noting. A braiding together of Wagnerian opera and an inside view of Southern black life required knowledge that few Americans possessed, white or black. But the alignment is deliberate; Du Bois is in fact relying on the perceived disparity between high aesthetic consciousness and the historical fact of violence against black bodies. For it is the shock of the unexpected conjunction that creates a meaningful effect and that allows the reader to experience a literary version of double consciousness. The value of high aesthetic culture is not in its status as high art (nor for that matter is the value of the "song and story" of black folk merely its lower place in the cultural hierarchy). Rather, the value of high art for Du Bois in this instance is precisely its aesthetic distance from the history of black lynching, a distance that makes possible the transformative effect of their doubling.

High literary writing becomes a means of perceiving through cultural rupture a history that has been obscured. This was Du Bois's gift of literary second sight to a larger American culture of segregated vision. In the book's final chapter, he speaks from a seat near "these high windows of mine," the scholar's study that is the scene of his writing and the site from which he hears the song of "free" black voices "welling up to me from the caverns of brick and mortar below." The figurative tableau, allowing the singing below to reach and inspire the writer above, gives a spatial expression to Du Bois's aim in writing *The Souls of Black Folk*: the aim to make the distance between high art and despised lives into a veil that could be imaginatively rent. Having opened that literary veil to reveal the sorrows of history, he now relies on the figure to open to a future that can offer hope. Partaking as it does of religious symbolism, the figure of the veil allows Du Bois to imagine "boundless justice" and the redeeming of souls: "in His good time America shall rend the Veil and the prisoned shall go free."

In 1940, Du Bois's autobiography *Dusk of Dawn* offered another fable of the veil, this time with the barrier figured as a wall of plate glass. After four decades, segregation is still a reality though the veil is now transparent and less easily described or identified. But the transparency does nothing to facilitate recognition or sympathy with those behind the glass.

It is difficult to let others see the full psychological meaning of caste segregation. It is as though one, looking out from a dark cave in a side of an impending mountain, sees the world passing and speaks to it; speaks courteously and persuasively, showing them how these entombed souls are hindered in their natural movements, expression, and development; and how their loosening from this prison would be a matter not simply of courtesy and sympathy, and help to them, but aid to all the world. One talks on evenly and logically in this way, but notices that the passing throng does not even turn its head, or if it does, glances curiously and walks on. It gradually penetrates the mind of the prisoners that the people passing do not hear, that some thick sheet of invisible but horribly tangible plate glass is between them and the world. They get excited, they talk louder; they gesticulate. Some of the passing world stop in curiosity; these gesticulations seem so pointless; they laugh and pass on.

White America and the larger world have not acquired the second sight Du Bois had articulated in *The Souls of Black Folk*. Instead, observers who notice the people behind the glass reflexively become spectators who see objects of curiosity or entertainment only. They remain spectators until the moment the glass is shattered, whereupon they perceive only threat:

Then the [imprisoned] people may become hysterical. They may scream and hurl themselves against the barriers, hardly realizing in their bewilderment that they are screaming in a vacuum unheard and that their antics may actually seem funny to those outside looking in. They may even, here and there, break through in blood and disfigurement, and find themselves faced by a horrified, implacable, and quite overwhelming mob of people frightened for their own very existence.

The religious metaphor of a veil has been replaced with a sleeker, more modern barrier of glass. Without the veil figure, the moment of breaking the barrier can only be an image of violent injury, not of revelation, and the intimation of a future that portends more violence still. The substitution of plate glass for the veil raises the question of why Du Bois now turns to this particular figure to represent the "psychological meaning" of segregation. Does it come from a repertoire of images with their source in a higher cultural sphere (as with the image of Plato's cave) – from the experience, say, of gazing through the plate glass of a museum display, or through the "high windows" of a scholar's study? Or is the image derived from less lofty worlds – the glass of a zoo cage, or a street-level department store window? The story contains no clues of association. But in contrast with the final tableau in *The Souls of Black Folk*, the difference between higher and lower in this fable is no longer legible, and thus of no help in articulating the possibility of transforming perception.

Regardless of the cultural setting from which the image is drawn, the plate glass of the modern age instills a uniform structure of habitual perception. It stands for the reflex of cultural spectators who have no ability or will to see abject people as souls. Like glass itself, there is no tension or texture in the trope, no internal differences that Du Bois can exploit to allow the world to perceive those behind the glass in different terms. In the scenario there is only looking, no writing or singing, and no apprehension of differentiated worlds of high and low production that had been Du Bois's informing energy in *Souls*. Neither the analytic resources of high literary culture nor the charismatic courage of mass culture or the vernacular seem to be available. Significantly, one of the terrors for the prisoners is the experience of a "vacuum" that leaves them voiceless and panicked. A fable of continuing racial stigma, the story is also a negative fable of the creative purchase that could be achieved through the interplay of high and low expression, evoked in a picture of the deadening, airless world where they have been lost.

PROMISES OF AMERICAN LIFE, 1880–1920

Walter Benn Michaels

I

🎋

AN AMERICAN TRAGEDY, OR THE
PROMISE OF AMERICAN LIFE

CLASSES AND INDIVIDUALS

Young women in Dreiser's *An American Tragedy* (1925) talk baby talk to the objects of their desire; that is what alerts us to the connection between Sondra Finchley's desire for Clyde Griffiths – "Sondra so glad Clydie here," she tells him, and Hortense Briggs's desire for the coat in the window of Rubenstein's fur store – "Oh, if I could only have 'oo," Hortense says to the coat. Whether the girls understand themselves or the objects as infantilized by their desires is unclear; Clyde calls Sondra his "darling baby girl" but what Sondra likes about Clyde is how "dependent" he is "upon her" – which one is the baby? Things are a little more straightforward between Hortense and the coat but only, perhaps, because what the coat has to offer Hortense is so much more obvious than what Clyde has to offer Sondra. The coat is the "darlingest" because it is the "classiest"; where Clyde represents for Sondra a social problem, as we will see, analogous in its double-edgedness to the psychological one of dependency, the coat represents to Hortense an unambiguously upward transformation of her "social state." The coat has "class" and wearing it, Hortense imagines, she will begin to belong to the class it has.

As the analogy between the coat and Clyde suggests, class transformation and erotic attraction are deeply linked in *An American Tragedy*, which, in concerning itself with love affairs that cross class boundaries, sees those boundaries not as obstacles to love but as the conditions of its possibility. And this point is insisted upon even more fiercely in Jack London's great narrative of class mobility, *Martin Eden* (1909); introduced by her brother to a "daughter of the bourgeoisie" – "Ruth, this is Mr. Eden" – Martin's first "thrilling . . . new impression" is "not of the girl, but of her brother's words," especially the word "*Mister!*" The way that "people in her class" talk produces love before first sight, and it continues – even after he has looked into her "spiritual blue eyes" – to underwrite their romance. In a scene that reenacts the great moment in the *Inferno* when Paolo and Francesca da Rimini are seduced for each other by reading the story of Lancelot and Guinevere ("Galeotto fu il libro e chi lo scrisse: / quel giorno più non vi leggemo avante"), Ruth and Martin are brought together over a grammar handbook: "she drew a chair near his – he wondered if should have helped her with the chair – and sat down beside him. She turned the pages of the grammar, and their heads were inclined toward each other. He could hardly follow her outlining of the work he must do, so amazed was he by her delightful propinquity." And the point of this passage is not just the sufficiently witty replacement of *La Morte d'Arthur* with the grammar. For the sentence after the one noting Martin's sense of Ruth's distracting "propinquity" begins, "But when she began to lay down the importance of conjugation, he forgot all about her," and continues, "He had never heard of conjugation, and was fascinated by the glimpse he was getting into the tie-ribs of language." It is, of course, impossible not to read Martin's discovery of "conjugation" as, at least in part, a grammatical (or rather, etymological) displacement of his sexual interest in Ruth. But surely the passage's real wit is in insisting that learning to conjugate verbs – like being called "Mister" – has its own charm; or even in suggesting that the love of Ruth might just as well be understood as a displacement of the erotic attractions of middle-class grammar. At the very least, one should see in this passage a commitment to the collaboration between eros and class mobility: "He leaned closer to the page and her hair touched his cheek . . . Never had she seemed so accessible as now. For the moment the great gulf that separated them was bridged." If a grammar is your Galeotto there may be no need to choose between definitions of conjugation.

Martin Eden is not the only ungrammatical man to conjoin the love of letters and the love of a middle-class woman; Owen Wister's Virginian spends a snowbound winter practicing "spelling" and "penmanship" to make himself acceptable to his schoolmistress from Bennington. When she finally agrees to marry him, it's in the course of a series of what Wister – with an irony unavailable to London – calls "Browning meetings". But the irony is accompanied by a defusing of cross-class desire and indeed by a kind of repudiation of it. For if Molly Wood's "descent" from the Revolutionary War hero General Stark entitles her to membership in the "Green Mountain Daughters, the Saratoga Sacred Circle, and the Confederated Colonial Chatelaines," the Virginian too will turn out to be from "old stock," whose eagerness to fight "when they got the chance" (under Old Hickory, in Mexico, and in the revolutionary war) makes them a match for the Starks. From this standpoint, the only real avatar of class mobility in *The Virginian* is "the most rising young man in Hoosic Falls" whose offer of marriage Molly declines before she heads out West. Supporters of the rising young man maintain that her behavior is "snobbish," that he probably had "a great-grandmother quite as good as hers"; Molly's defenders acknowledge the possibility but point out that "we don't happen to know who she was." From this perspective, the Virginian, despite his grammatical and literary shortcomings, is Molly's way out of a marriage "below her station"; when he becomes delirious after being wounded by "Indians" and Molly has to persuade him to come back to the settlement with her, she does so by reminding him that "A gentleman does not invite a lady to go out riding and leave her." *The Virginian* is finally not about a lower-class man who wants to marry a middle-class woman; it is about the revelation that the lower-class man is really a "gentleman" and the middle-class woman is really a "lady."

So when the Virginian finally arrives in Bennington, Bennington, anticipating a cowpoke in spurs and chaps, is "disappointed"; "To see get out of the train merely a tall man with a usual straw hat, and Scotch homespun suit of a rather better cut than most in Bennington – this was dull." Neither the hero of a "wild-west show" nor a "ready-made guy," the Virginian dresses better than the rising young men of the East because he does not need to rise. The point of his clothes is that they are "exactly the thing" for him. But the rising young men, and Hortense Briggs, want clothes that are "exactly the thing" for others, the others they plan to become. So the fur coat in Rubenstein's window represents to Hortense the possibility of purchasing a transformation in class by purchasing a transformation of the self. And for Martin Eden (like Clyde, more "ambitious" than Hortense), grammar and etiquette, new "neck-gear" and "tooth-washing" are only the first steps in a regime designed to produce "personal reform in all things."

But the end result of "personal reform" is not merely translation into the middle class, it is also what London calls "self-realization." Which is to say that class mobility is understood as a way of becoming one of "the people from up above" and also as a way of becoming an "individualist." "Actually, this is a special coat," Mr. Rubenstein tells Hortense. "It's copied from one of the smartest coats that was in New York last summer . . . You won't find no coat like this coat." The coat is "special" both because it's unique (there's none like it in Kansas City) and because it's not unique (there's at least one just like it in New York), and it's the simultaneity of these facts that gives it "class." Hortense wants the coat both because it has been "fashioned in such an individual way" and because, individually fashioned, it looks just like the equally individual coats of a lot of classy ladies in New York. Wearing it, she will belong at the same time to the class of the other women wearing it and to no class at all.

From at least one perspective this position is best understood as a contradictory one. Recent studies of class formation in the United States have, for example, achieved a certain degree of success in delineating a working-class consciousness but have encountered difficulties in extending their analysis to the middle class. The problem, as Stuart M. Blumin analyzed it in a 1985 essay in the *American Historical Review*, stems from "the individualism that lies at the heart of the middle-class system." Students of working-class consciousness experience no difficulty in discovering evidence of that class's sense of itself as a class but insofar as "middle-class formation" has involved "the building of a class that binds itself together as a social group in part through the common embrace of an ideology of social atomism," evidence of its sense of itself as a class and hence of its existence as a class has been hard to come by.

The difficulty of identifying the middle class is thus built into the process of defining it, or at least into the assumption that underlies that definition, the assumption of an essential incompatibility between individuals and classes. And this assumption plays an even more crucial role for those who, untroubled by the apparent logical problems of middle-class individualism, are troubled instead by the fate of middle-class individuals. For here, the incompatibility between individual and class is turned into a *contest* between individual and class, or, more generally, between the individual and what had come to be known as "social organization." Martin Eden, in his disillusioned Nietzschean phase, predicts the triumph of "individualists" over "social organization" but the Progressive Era (that period extending roughly from Roosevelt's accession to the Presidency in 1901 until the United States entered the First World War in 1917) has been more frequently characterized as a crucial moment in the subordination of the individual to the developing bureaucratic institutions of modernism. From this standpoint, what I characterized above as the tension between Hortense's desire to be "individual" and her desire to be "classy" must be redescribed as the compromising of her aspirations towards individuality by a society increasingly hostile to the individual and increasingly committed to structures of classification and control.

But the necessity for compromise is something Hortense cannot see, and, in fact, in *An American Tragedy*, no tension is present and no compromises are needed. Rather, the terms of contradiction are redeployed as forms of the complementary. The possibility of purchasing coats like the one in Rubenstein's window links class mobility to the fate of individualism, and if from one perspective (say, that of *The Virginian*) the rise of the "ready-made guy" looks like the destruction of individuality, from another (Hortense's and Clyde's) it looks – precisely through the technology of the ready-made – like the possibility of individualism. *An American Tragedy* rewrites the threats to a genteel individuality represented by rising young men and ready-made guys as the reconstitution of what might be called a mass individuality through grammars and mass-produced coats. It marks a moment when the transformations undergone by the opposition between the individual and the social culminates in the disappearance of that opposition. By 1925, I will argue, individuality appears as an effect of standardization. The incoherence of Hortense's desires – she does not realize that you can't be individual and classy at the same time – is dispelled by an understanding of classes and individuals which insists that in order to be either classy or individual you have to be both at the same time.

ARMIES AND FACTORIES

"Training is everything," says Mark Twain's Connecticut Yankee in an extraordinary speech that begins by asserting the absolute determination of the individual by society – "Training is everything . . . Training is all there is to a person" – and ends by asserting the absolute autonomy of the "one microscopic atom" of a person that is "original," that is, in other words, *not* a function of training. Hence the enormousness of the Yankee's opportunity – he can train an entire people – and hence the enormity of his failure – they can resist his training.

For despite its frequent proclamations of the "power of training! of influence! of education!" it is with the power to *resist* training that *Connecticut Yankee* is most concerned. The Yankee's notorious reliance on violence and physical force in his efforts to "civilize" the "white Indians" of Arthurian England and his failure in these efforts are both effects of a conception of individuality that systematically denies any power at all to training, influence, and education. "A man *is* a man at bottom," the Yankee reflects happily. "Whole ages of abuse and oppression cannot crush the manhood clear out of him." The man in question here has resisted the tyranny of the sixth century but the Yankee's admiration is as great for those who resist the democratizing of the nineteenth: "English knights," he tells the faithful young products of his "man factory," "can be killed, but they cannot be conquered." They cannot be conquered because no amount of physical abuse or coercion can ever produce in them the educational advance that even an acknowledgment of defeat would serve to mark. They are monuments to an individuality defined by nothing but the powers of resistance.

It is for this reason, rather than for their lack of civilization, that they are plausibly seen as "white Indians." "The Indian is hewn out of the rock," Francis Parkman had written in 1851. "You can rarely change the form without destruction of the substance." In principle ineducable, such men could only be subdued by violence. Hence, as Michael Rogin argued in *Fathers and Children*, "Indian hunters" like Andrew Jackson identified with the "Indian" in the very act of – actually *by means of* the very act of – hunting them; the violence of the "Indian" required the violence of the "Indian-hunter"; who, in killing the "Indian," became a version of him. It is not hard to see a similar identification in the "withering deluge" of machine-gun fire that kills the last ten thousand "white Indians" at the end of *Connecticut Yankee*. But this massacre, so often identified by critics and historians as a critique of late nineteenth-century industrialism, what Twain called "machine culture," is in fact a tribute to that culture and to its machines. Native Americans in Progressive America were increasingly identified as paradigms of the American individualism that was understood to have created Twain's machine culture just because of the absolute inflexibility that Parkman in 1851 had predicted would cause their "ruin." Thus in Thomas Dixon's anti-socialist dystopia *Comrades* (1909), it is the "Indian" Saka, in addition to the capitalist Colonel Worth, who emerges as a hero of "individuality": having tried and failed to order him about, the socialist "Brotherhood of Man saw Saka no more for many moons, but the crack of his rifle was heard on the mountain side and the smoke of his teepee curled defiantly from the neighboring plains." Morgan's recognition that *his* "Indians" can be neither trained nor conquered is thus a recognition of their rock-like character and his commitment to exterminating them is not an attack on their savagery but a tribute to their individuality. Only by means of the massacre can Twain acknowledge the "microscopic atom" that is "truly me," the selfhood that cannot be altered and so must be destroyed.

Twain's "Indians," however, are made out of metal, not rock. Twain's financially disastrous involvement with technology and, in particular, with that "mechanical miracle," the Paige Compositor, is well known, and just as the end of *Connecticut Yankee* is often read as a repudiation of late nineteenth-century industrialism, it is often read also as a proleptic repudiation of the typesetter: "In bringing Morgan to death Twain was symbolically killing off the machine madness which possessed him," as James Cox has put it. But what was most striking about Twain's involvement with the Paige was not that it took the form of an excessive (financially or ethically) and hence punishable enthusiasm for technology as such. Had Twain been backing the Paige's competition, the Mergenthaler linotype machine, he would have made the fortune he expected to make. The problem was that he chose the wrong machine, and his reasons for choosing that machine are crucial to an understanding of the individual that emerges triumphant in *Connecticut Yankee*.

The Paige Compositor, as Twain's financial savior H. H. Rogers described it many years after its final failure, "was the nearest approach to a human being in the wonderful things it could do of any machine I have ever known." Unlike the Mergenthaler, which cast its own type, melted it down at the end of each run, and then re-cast it, the Paige performed all the acts of a human typesetter – setting, justifying, and distributing individual types – automatically and, when it was working, very quickly. Where the seventeen-year-old Mark Twain had been able to set only 10,000 ems a day (more proficient typesetters could do 15,000), the Paige could set 12,000 ems an *hour* (the Mergenthaler could only do about 8,000). But it was not working very often for, as H. H. Rogers went on to say, its wonderful similarity to a human being was "just the trouble; it was too much of a human being and not enough of a machine. It had all the complications of the human mechanism, all the ability of getting out of repair, and it could not be replaced with the ease and immediateness of the human being." With its 18,000 parts (still a record), the Paige would never be able to function economically; eventually, it helped drive Twain to bankruptcy. But its real significance was not so much financial as intellectual; the Paige marked a nineteenth-century high point in the attempt to represent human actions in metal. As a strategy for building effective machines, this proved to be a failure; the success of the Mergenthaler was a function of its by-passing what Justin Kaplan has called "the human analogy." But as a thesis about what sort of thing a person is – the sort of thing that can be represented in machinery, if not a typesetter then a computer – the thinking that produced the Paige was not and has not been in any definitive way discredited: at least one segment of the artificial intelligence industry of the late twentieth century is committed to insisting upon not by-passing the human analogy. And as a thesis about the nature of individuality – the "truly me" is the mechanical me, as immune to training as Dixon's Native Americans are to socialism – the Paige provided a valuable bulwark against those who really did think that training was everything and who argued, as John Dewey did in *The School and Society* (1900), that the trick to effective training was to "get hold of the child's natural impulses and instincts," "saturating him with the spirit of service," and so fitting him for life in the "larger society."

Dewey here articulates the idea of a total education – an utterly "saturated" self – that Twain's imagination of the mechanical self is designed to make impossible. Indeed, progressive education, conceiving "individual mind as a function of social life," is devoted precisely to exploiting the possibilities for training neglected by an "earlier psychology" which "regarded mind as a purely individual affair." The disciplinary techniques of that earlier psychology treated the individual as a self-contained entity in need of "external" control; they are replaced in the "new education" by techniques of "guidance" which, instead of "forcing the child from without," attempt to shape her from within. Once you "get hold" of the child's "interests," you have no need for the tactics of "external imposition."

Dewey himself, however, manifests some reluctance to accept this account of the shift from traditional to progressive education as a shift from "forcing" the child to appealing to her "interests," not, however, because of the difficulty involved in producing an educational system that was continuously interesting but rather because of the difficulty involved in producing an educational system that was not. For even the disciplinary practices that are usually understood as forms of "external imposition" – keeping the child after school, giving her low marks, refusing to promote her – are in fact indirect appeals to interest or appeals to interest "in its obverse aspect": "to fear, to dislike of various kinds of physical, social, and personal pain." For Dewey, then, even the most apparently coercive educational methods turn out to rely, like progressive education, on some version of the appeal to interest (turn out to be, from the standpoint of *Connecticut Yankee*, insufficiently coercive).

In education, he would write some fifteen years later, "purely external direction is impossible." External direction may elicit a "physical result" (as when a man is locked up to prevent him "breaking into other persons' houses") but we must not "confuse a physical with an educative result" – locking the man up "may not alter his disposition to commit burglary." The point here is not to deny that locking a man up may be an effective way of keeping him from committing burglary; it is rather to remind us that as educators we are interested in the disposition that produces the action rather than in the action itself. But, of course, locking the burglar up (or threatening to lock him up) may, after all, alter his disposition (just as threatening to keep the child after school may alter hers), so the purest negative example is action without disposition of any kind.

Suppose that conditions were so arranged that one person automatically caught a ball and then threw it to another person who caught and automatically returned it; and that each so acted without knowing where the ball came from or went to. Clearly such action would be without point or meaning. It might be physically controlled, but it would not be socially directed.

Where the physical control over the burglar's actions (his incarceration) might after all appeal to his interest (in avoiding incarceration), the physical control over the ballthrowers can appeal to no interests since the ballthrowers are imagined from the start as having no interests – that is what it means for their actions to be described as proceeding automatically. The ballthrowers are better examples than the burglar because, while the burglar may resist education, the ballthrowers are immune to it; with them, the only possible results are "physical," the only possible changes in their behavior a function of "force."

Seeking a philosophically satisfactory (although pedagogically irrelevant) alternative to progressive education, Dewey is thus driven to Twain's solution; the world of his ballthrowers is the world of Twain's knights who can be killed but not conquered because (like the ballthrowers but unlike the burglar) they are immune to even the attenuated appeal to their interest implicit in the threat of violence. Since no education can be "purely external," in *Connecticut Yankee* there can be no education; schooling is redescribed by Twain as manufacture, training as production – it takes place in the "man factory" or the "civilization-factories." And the conflict between cultures is really a conflict between machines: the ones made in the Yankee's factories and that "political machine," the Church; Merlin's "magic" and the Yankee's "science." As such, this conflict is intrinsically and essentially violent; because they are immune to the threat of violence, the knights are susceptible only to the fact of violence. The "microscopic atom" that is "truly me" can be altered only by being transformed (by dynamite) into "microscopic fragments of knights and hardware and horse-flesh," uncountable "because they did not exist as individuals, but merely as homogeneous protoplasm, with alloys of iron and buttons." The "error" of the old psychology, Dewey thought, was to see "no alternative between forcing the child from without, or leaving him entirely alone." Refusing any alternative to the microscopic atom that is the individual or the microscopic fragments that do not exist as individuals, Twain commits himself to this "error." The triumph of social atomism in *Connecticut Yankee* is his ability to represent any transformation of the atom as its destruction. The world in which the only actions are violent ones is the world made safe for individuals.

It may be, however, that the characterization of these transformations as "violent" is as inappropriate as the language of "force" and "external imposition" turned out to be in connection with the old education's disciplinary appeals to punishment. It was inappropriate with respect to punishment because the appeal to, say, the burglar's fear of jail in no way by-passes the question of his interest, it just alters the interest that is being appealed to. And it is inappropriate with respect to the knights and ballthrowers because it makes no sense to think of them as having been coerced or even externally imposed upon. Having no interests in the first place, automatic ballplayers can no more have their interests violated or ignored than they can have them appealed to. They cannot be directed "from without" because they do not really have a within – in Dewey's terms, a machine is *all* without. Twain's mechanical "Indians" thus represent not only an extension but a perfection of Parkman's "Indians" hewn out of rock. In Parkman, the "Indians'" "substance" is destroyed when their "form" is altered; substance is simultaneously different from and dependent on form, and it is this difference combined with dependence that produces the possibility of violence. But in Twain, form is either absolutely identical to or absolutely independent of substance; the response of the victim is in both cases irrelevant.

Thus St. Stylite, the hermit, "bowing his body ceaselessly and rapidly almost to his feet" can be hooked up to "a system of elastic cords" and used "to run a sewing-machine." The hermit is praying but he is at the same time engaged in "one of the most useful motions in mechanics, the pedal-movement." The example is parodic but the principle – the irrelevance of what St. Stylite knows and wants to what he can be used to do – is not. Think of the difference made to what the inventor of "Scientific Management," Frederick Winslow Taylor, called "The Art of Cutting Metals" by the slide-rule: "By means of these slide-rules," Taylor wrote in 1911, intricate mathematical problems "can be solved in less than half a minute by any good mechanic, whether he understands anything about mathematics or not." Fitted out with a slide-rule, as St. Stylite is fitted out with elastic, the mechanic can become a part in a calculating machine as St. Stylite became a part in a sewing machine.

Indeed, the mechanic is from this perspective a more extreme example of mechanization than St. Stylite since with St. Stylite the difference between form and substance more or less corresponds to the difference between body and mind (as if the mind were immune to mechanization) whereas the slide-rule makes the distinction between body and mind irrelevant. Taylor is often accused of producing a "schism" "between the mind and the body of the industrial workman" and the workmen in plants undergoing Taylorisation routinely complained about being reduced to automata, unable to think or move for themselves. Taylor's response to such complaints was not to deny them but to generalize them: "The same criticism and objection," he argued, could be "raised against all other modern subdivisions of labor." The actions of a surgeon, properly understood, were as mechanical as those of a brick-layer or metal cutter. Replacing "rules of thumb" with "rigid rules for each motion of every man" – in effect, by-passing individual judgment and sub-stituting for it something like a slide-rule – was scientific management's goal for human action at all levels. The "instruction cards" for every factory worker that became one of the hallmarks of scientific management specified not only the rules according to which work would be performed but the rules by which that work would be evaluated. The cards call, Taylor's disciple, Frank Gilbreth wrote, for "a definite quality. They do not call for having the 'work done to the satisfaction' of anybody." The manager's satisfaction is as irrelevant as the worker's initiative. In scientific management, management was to be as mechanical as the work it managed; the mind was as much a machine as the body. The discrepancy between what St. Stylite is think-ing and what his *body* is doing thus appears most powerfully in Taylor as a discrepancy between what the mechanic is thinking and what his *mind* is doing.

Perhaps the most extreme example of mechanization, however, is the Yankee himself, whose character is so much a product of Twain's own identification with the Paige Compositor. Readers have often noted the extraordinary incon-sistencies in Twain's presentation of the Yankee, for example the juxtaposition of his lachrymose sympathy for Morgan le Fay's victims and his cheerful will-ingness to be "reasonable" by letting her hang the band that plays "Sweet By-and-By" so badly. Attempts to explain such inconsistencies by appealing to the complexities of the Yankee's character are unconvincing. The execution of the band, like the hanging of Sir Dinadan the Humorist, is a joke, and it is a joke made possible by indifference to consistency, by a conception of character as mechanical and as thus susceptible only (but absolutely) to external change: the transformation produced by Hercules's crowbar (the transformation that takes the Yankee from Bridgeport to Camelot) is a prototype of the trans-formations produced by Mark Twain's typewriter. To put it another way, the Yankee does not exactly *have* a character, he *is* the character he can be described as having, incapable of behaving "out of character" because his character is defined by nothing but his behavior. If St. Stylite and the mechanic embody the priority of form to substance, the Yankee embodies the identity of form and substance. And when the only identity is formal identity, there can be no question of consistency – only repetition or difference, staying the same thing or becoming something else. To alter him is thus to destroy him but at the same time to replace him. The Yankee is like the Native American in that he cannot be trained, but he is unlike the Native American in that he can be retooled; he perfects the "immutability" of the Native American by making it mutable.

Connecticut Yankee does not, then, express an attitude towards technology, either the optimistic one of a Mark Twain who loved machines or the pes-simistic one of a Mark Twain who was getting nervous about the Paige Com-positor and beginning to worry about the ultimate value of machine cul-ture. Rather it embodies a commitment to the essential likeness of persons to machines, a commitment embodied also in Twain's own identification with the Paige and in his vision of himself as a kind of writing machine: "I started the mill again 6 days ago and have ground out a good average," he wrote Rogers, while waiting for news of the Paige's last try-out, "11,800 words" in a week. "It is the aim of Scientific Management," Gilbreth wrote in 1912, "to induce men to act as nearly like machines as possible." In the Yankee's failure,

Twain predicts Taylor's success; defending individuals, he prepares them for the factory.

In Edward Bellamy's *Equality* (1897), the sequel to his phenomenally successful utopian novel, *Looking Backward* (1888), the narrator asks again a version of a question he had asked in 1888: what is done with people who do not acknowledge their "social duty" and refuse to join the "industrial army" that (according to Bellamy) in the late twentieth century provides equal work, equal pay, and equal rights to all citizens. His answer in 1888 to the question whether "universal military service" was "compulsory" had been first that it was more "a matter of course than of compulsion," and then, less evasively, that "A man able to duty, and persistently refusing, is sentenced to solitary imprisonment on bread and water till he consents." By 1897, however, bread and water – "compelling someone to work against his will by force" – has come to seem "abhorrent"; in *Equality*, such a man would be provided with seeds and tools and "turned loose on a reservation expressly prepared for such persons," corresponding, perhaps, the voice of the twentieth century says to the nineteenth, "with the reservations set apart for such Indians in your day as were unwilling to accept civilization."

The "Indian" here is once again a figure for the resisting individual, but the Bartleby-like refusals so admired by Twain and Dixon are condemned by Bellamy as "excessive individualism" or, forgetting even the "excessive," as symptoms of that "incapacity for cooperation which followed from the individualism on which your social system was founded." "Who has not often felt . . . as if the sense of personal identity, i.e. sense of his connection with his particular individuality, were slipping from him?" Bellamy wrote in an early essay. This appeal to a "religion of solidarity" in which the individual would be reduced to "an atom, a grain of sand on a boundless shore, a bubble in a foam flecked ocean," may be understood to express what Arthur Lipow describes as Bellamy's "deepgoing revulsion against individualism in all its forms," a revulsion that motivates his attempt in *Looking Backward* "to solve the problem of the individual in modern society by the suppression of individuality and personality in the warm embrace of a bureaucratic society" and which can serve as counterpoint to *Connecticut Yankee*, an attack on the individualism Twain defends.

At the same time, however, that *Looking Backward*'s doctrine (and most of the book is doctrine, a series of lectures by the twentieth century's Dr. Leete in response to the questions of the nineteenth century's Julian West), seems to preach against individualism, what there is of its narrative works in a somewhat different direction. For when Julian West awakens after his first night in the twentieth century, he finds himself "staring about" in "anguish," "unable to regain the clew" to his "personal identity": "I was no more able to distinguish myself from pure being during those moments than we may suppose a soul in the rough to be before it has received the earmarks, the individualizing touches which make it a person." The desire to lose one's identity is here matched by the fear of losing it and by the hope that one will "never know" that fear again; the utopian society in which individualism has been eradicated is at the same time imagined as a society in which individualism has been secured.

It is this reversal, rather than the search for an alibi, that makes sense of Bellamy's claim that service in the industrial army "is more a matter of course than of compulsion." Dixon's anti-socialist Native American is a hero because he lives according to "natural law" under which "no man, even the poorest, could be commanded to work by a superior power. He could always quit if he liked. He might choose to go hungry . . . but he was still master of his own person. His will was supreme. He, and he alone, could say, I will, or I will not." In this characteristic defense of freedom of contract (socialism, Dixon complains, replaces "contract" with "command"), Dixon identifies individuality with the possibility of independence, and that possibility – the refusal to serve – is just what Bellamy denies. He denies it, however, not because he cannot countenance it but because, in the end, he cannot imagine it. Service in the industrial army counts in *Looking Backward* less as a choice one can make than as the ground of the choices one can make. Thus the refusal to serve seems like "suicide," not a refusal on behalf of individuality but a refusal of individuality. "Nowadays everybody is a part of a system with a distinct place and function. I am outside the system," Julian complains, "and don't see how I can get in." By no means a declaration of independence, this complaint is not a renunciation of individuality either. Rather, the yearning for a "distinct place" within the system (like the "anguish" induced by being unable to "distinguish" yourself from "pure being") marks the assertion of an individuality that only some "system" can make available.

In *Looking Backward*, that system is the army. Where Dixon's war-hero Colonel Worth hates the army's "organization," hates "its iron laws of discipline, its cruel machinery devised for suppressing the individuality of its members," the peace-loving citizens of *Looking Backward* think of it as essential and regard its "perfect organization" as a way of producing what they call "self-devotion." Divided into three "grades" which are in turn divided into two "classes," within which are "many minor distinctions of standing," the industrial army is more committed to producing individuality than to suppressing it. But the individuality it produces is defined by difference rather than independence. What the industrial army offers is a system of finely graded distinctions, an "organization" that makes "self-devotion" possible because it defines the terms in which "self-devotion" can be pursued. Outside the system you cannot know who you are because you are not yet you – you are "pure" (i.e. undifferentiated) "being." But the system allows for differences – indeed, it consists of nothing but differences – and by making difference possible, it makes identity possible.

From this standpoint, what used to look like individuality comes instead to look like the inability to achieve individuality. After Taylor's initial presentation of "A Piece Rate System" before the American Society of Engineers in 1895, one of the discussants, admitting the virtues of Taylor's system, nonetheless waxed nostalgic for a time when scientific management was "unnecessary," when the

machine shops of this country were individual shops . . . There was a certain community of feeling, in those days, between the boys in the shop and the master, which I think passed away when machine-shop owners became corporations, when they were managed by a board of directors who never saw the workmen, who knew nothing of them, individually, and, as I fear, cared less.

Taylor, however, redescribes workmen in individual shops as "workmen" in "isolation," unable to profit from the scientific study of time and motion and, in this respect (strikingly enough) in exactly the same situation as workmen in "gangs"; the subject of scientific management, Taylor maintains, is neither workmen in "isolation" nor workmen in "masses" but, rescued from the undifferentiation of isolation and the equal undifferentiation of the mass, the "workman as an individual."

What is even more striking here, however, is scientific management's simultaneous compatibility with the defense of individualism and with the attack on it: the "white Indian," defined by his resistance to "organization," mechanized, becomes the ideal factory worker; the industrial soldier, defined by nothing but his participation in the system, also becomes the ideal factory worker: the machine provides the transfer through which the resistance of the individual to the system can emerge as the creation of the individual by the system and the threat to independence can emerge as the achievement of independence. Hence the appropriateness both of Herbert Croly's contradictory complaint about American individualism and of his vision of that complaint answered. The complaint was that America was both excessively and insufficiently individualistic and the response is one that represents individuals defined by difference as individuals who have achieved independence. "Individuality is necessarily based on genuine discrimination," he writes, and "In every kind of practical work specialization . . . is coming to prevail; and in this way individuals . . . are obtaining definite and stimulating possibilities for personal efficiency and independence." Discrimination and specialization clearly invoke the Bellamyite conception of individuality as difference but Croly, rather than exchanging (as Bellamy does) independence for difference, imagines difference as providing a new basis for independence. Thus the non-union laborer, characterized by employers as the "independent working man," is regarded by Croly as "a species of industrial derelict" who, if he were a truly "independent industrial individual" would demonstrate both his independence and his individuality by "joining the union."

In Croly, then, as in Taylor, the opposition between attacking individuality and defending it, or more importantly, between defining it by difference and defining it by independence, is overcome. Which is not to say that it disappears entirely or that it never mattered in the first place. The sense that individuality was threatened helped to make possible the enthusiasm for turning men into machines; the sense that individuality was threatening helped to make possible the enthusiasm for turning men into soldiers. But the compatibility of the products is in the end more striking than the incompatibility of the motives. What emerges from the defense and the attack combined is a transformation of individuality, one in which the mechanical defense of independence becomes itself a part of the machinery that reimagines the loss of independence as the access to individuality. It is this individuality that Hortense Briggs can want by wanting to belong to a class; in fact, she can want it *only* by wanting to belong to a class. The "classy" fur coat in Rubinstein's shop window thus embodies not the problem of a class that can be a class only by consisting of individuals who belong to no class but the solution of an individual who can be an individual only by belonging to some class.

STANDARDS AND INDIVIDUALS

In the industrial army, everybody wears a uniform. That is one of the things that recent writers like Arthur Lipow cite as evidence of Bellamy's anti-individualism, and Herbert G. Gutman has noted the case of a Pittsburgh railway worker complaining about the tendency to make "our men wear uniforms": "A uniform . . . constantly reminds them of their serfdom, and I for one would rather remain out of work than wear one." For the Pittsburgh brakeman, the uniform reduces you to an anonymous member of a class ("serfdom") and the refusal to wear it counts as an assertion of one's "rights as a free-born American"; for Dreiser's Clyde Griffiths, however, the bellhop's uniform he is required to wear when he gets his first job at a hotel marks his escape from his family and his achievement of a "position," enabling him to sense for the first time "the delight of personal freedom." Indeed, the bellhop's uniform is just the introduction to the uniform Clyde learns to wear when he is off-duty – the "new brown suit, cap, overcoat, socks, stickpin and shoes" purchased "in imitation of" the most "attractive" bellhop and conferring upon Clyde some of that "individual('s)" attractiveness. Outfitted in clothes "as near like those of his mentor as possible," Clyde is able, for the first time in his life, to "look different."

For Dreiser, the uniform makes difference possible – just as for Taylor, "uniformity" of "method" made individuality possible – and in making difference possible it makes possible new areas of what he will call "personal" experience. There is a sense, of course, in which uniforms had already done this. Mass mobilization for the Civil War had produced, among other effects, the first reliable standards for clothing sizes. Before the war and before Brigadier General G. H. Crosman's attempt in 1865 to "fix the sizes" of "the various articles of equipment" supplied by the Quartermaster, most Americans wore clothes crudely made at home or bought second-hand, except, of course, for the wealthy whose clothes were made to order by professional tailors. (The Virginian's best suit, made of homespun but to a tailor's "measure," ingeniously combines both the alternatives to ready-made; it embodies the upper-class enthusiasm for folk [as opposed to mass] art that one can find also in the "democratic" but custom-made furniture of the Arts and Crafts Movement.) The effort to uniform the Union army, however, made available for the first time "sufficient data" "to set up standardized tables of proportions," and, by 1889, as the publication of the Quartermaster General's *U.S. Army Uniforms and Equipment* shows, soldiers could get coats in four sizes, shirts in five and trousers in six. With ready-to-wear replacing both homemade and the primitively sized clothes available in antebellum stores, it became possible for the first time for the average American to wear clothes that fit. From the standpoint of made-to-order, standard sizing may have seemed like a loss of individuality; from the standpoint of homemade, however, it made a certain degree of individuality possible for the first time.

But the real individualizing power of standard sizing may have had less to do with making available clothes that really fit than with creating a whole new set of individualizing and intimate facts about the wearers of those clothes, a set of facts made newly available to the rich as well as to the poor. For it now became possible to have a size and it would soon become almost essential to have not only the size but a set of beliefs and desires about it, that it was too large, say, or too small, or just right. And the individual's ability to have a size was, of course, made possible only because he or she could also be treated not as an "independent" individual at all but as a member of a large class, large enough, anyway, to make it profitable for someone to produce thousands of shirts with your measurements. Thus, on the one hand, coming to have a size meant becoming a member of a substantial community while, on the other hand, the effect of standardization was hardly communal: the phenomenology of sizes involved not belonging to a group but being singled out.

This conception of individuality as an effect of standardization helps make clear the inadequacy of the Tocquevillean tension between the individual and society as a way of understanding the transformation of individuality in the Progressive Era. The workman being trained under scientific management, for example, was to be judged not by the results of his labor – a standard that appealed to the intrinsic worth of his efforts – or by comparison to what other workmen achieved – an explicitly social standard – but by his "accuracy in conforming to the standard method," by the standard, in effect, of the standard itself. Scientific management, seen in this light, was as hostile to the individual in society as to the independent individual since it was the managerial measurement of workers' performance in competition with each other that produced the group pressure to keep performance down; the workers feared (correctly) that the performance of a particularly skilled and energetic man could lower pay for all of them. The goal of scientific management was thus to make social comparison as irrelevant as isolated achievement.

In other words, having redescribed independence as "isolation," Taylor replaces it with "ambition," which cannot be "stimulated" when workmen are "herded into gangs instead of being treated as separate individuals." Taylor's point is that once scientific management has established the motions with which and the time in which a "task" should be accomplished, it has also established a standard according to which each individual's performance can be judged, not only by his employers but, more tellingly, by himself. The development of the standard enables each workman to "measure his own progress" and thereby achieve not just the "highest standard of efficiency" but the "greatest satisfaction." The pig-iron handler, to use one of Taylor's most notorious examples, spends his day carrying pig-iron from a pile to a railroad car, walking back to the pile and carrying more pig-iron to the car. Under the rules developed at Midvale Steel, when he has been taught exactly how to carry pig-iron, how much to carry at a time, how fast to carry it, and how long to rest before carrying some more, he can go from carrying twelve and a half tons a day to carrying forty-seven. And he can now be paid $1.85 a day instead of $1.15. But the most striking change is neither physical nor economic, it is psychological: scientific management makes it possible for the worker to experience satisfaction or dissatisfaction with his performance. It makes it possible (albeit in what would come to seem, by the end of the twentieth century, a somewhat primitive way) for him to know what it means to do his best and so be able to tell whether or not he has done it.

Uniformity makes available a whole new area for what Bellamy called "self-devotion." When Clyde tries on his bellhop's cap, he sees (even before his boss can tell him) that his hair is "too long"; "His hair certainly did not look right in the new cap. He hated it now." The introduction of the standard (the uniform) produces a new intensity of response to one's own appearance. Just as standard sizing made it possible for clothes to be the wrong size, the bellhop's uniform makes it possible for Clyde's hair to be the wrong length and so makes it possible for him to hate it. This experience of the self is made possible only by the mediation of the standard. Gilbreth, describing a point the worker reaches where his fingers can "do the work with no other assistance than the command from his brain to proceed," had spoken of an "automaticity of motion"; automaticity of motion in Dreiser begins to become something like an automaticity of emotion.

Indeed, this progress from motion to emotion could itself be understood as a form of automatism, as it was in the writings of the eminent neurologist (he invented the rest cure) and bestselling author (of the historical novel *Hugh Wynne* [1896]), S. Weir Mitchell. In a pair of books centering on a "character-doctor" (*Characteristics* [1891], *Dr. North and His Friends* [1900]), Mitchell argued that such automatism marked the limits of human sanity. Concerned to celebrate "originality" and "individuality" ("the amazing way in which every man remains a thing apart from every man"), Mitchell's Dr. North is at the same time interested in the "automatic imitativeness" that he acknowledges to play a role in "the developmental growth of character." The danger of this "very human" automatism emerges in mental disease, "in hysteria, and in rare cases of insanity, where a man repeats automatically the words he hears, or the gestures of the man at whom he chances to be looking." The danger is not just that automatic imitation can produce bizarre behavior but that it can also produce, by way of the behavior, the emotions that are usually thought themselves to produce the behavior. "If . . . you pinch together the frontal muscles," of someone who has been hypnotized, Dr. North points out, "so as to imitate the facial expressions of a frown, he will at once become angry . . . If you make his cheek-lines assume the curves of mirth, this suggests amusement, and he roars with laughter." The emotions here are automated not in the sense of having been turned into automatic responses but in the sense of being enabled by automation: we automatically imitate the facial behavior of others and this imitation produces as a kind of side effect the emotion appropriate to the behavior that has been imitated.

For those, like Dr. North, concerned to preserve "originality" and "individuality," the moral is clear: "to allow our features to assume the first slight expression of passion is a step toward failure in self-control." Emotion here is no longer regarded as an expression of individuality; rather, insofar as automation and imitation make individuals' emotions possible, emotion becomes the chief threat to individuality. And by the same token, standardization – the attempt, as Mitchell puts it, "to produce complete identity of product" – becomes the great technology of "passion."

The standard may thus be said to alter automaticity in producing it. Automaticity of motion was supposed – like the slide-rule – to bypass the worker's mind, and scientific management's managerial project was, as we have seen, to replace psychological notions like "satisfaction" with the mechanical specificity of the standard. But even in Taylor, the mechanical specificity of the standard ended up replacing the manager's satisfaction as a criterion of whether the job was done with the worker's satisfaction at how well he was doing it. And in Mitchell and Dreiser, it is automaticity that makes the conditions of satisfaction possible while the introduction of standards creates new realms of psychological experience, at the same time suggesting a new technology for standard (and hence individual)ization. The Dreiserian novel – with its interest neither in individuals as such nor in the social order as such but in what Dreiser called "order[s] of individuals" – would itself be an instance of this technology, as would, more generally, the late nineteenth-century novel, with what Mitchell describes as its commitment to "characterization."

For although the account of automatic imitation in *Characteristics* emerges from a discussion of poetic influence designed to show that only "great genius" can transcend "imitativeness," a subsequent discussion of George Eliot's novelistic "genius in characterization" somewhat alters the terms of the argument. In response to the remark that novelistic representation requires above all an effort of "associative memory," Dr. North asserts that "There must also be some power to do far more than memorize. There must be power to reject and modify assembled memories, so at last to create that natural oneness of the being described which ends by making a living thing, not a mere photograph." Genius is still the ability to transcend imitation, and imitation is still identified with a certain automatism (the photograph) but here the transcendence of imitation turns out to be automatic too – "Abidingly true power to characterize in fiction is automatic," Dr. North goes on to claim. The automatism that threatened genius now appears as its true mark. Furthermore, the genius it marks is "genius in characterization," the ability to create the real individuals whose individuality has been said to consist in their ability to avoid automatism. And literary genius is now said to consist not in resisting imitation but in manipulating it. "There are plenty of bright books nowadays in which a man represents the people he knows"; the genius in characterization takes these representations, these "memories," and "assembles" them into a character, "building" out of them "a living thing." Although, according to Dr. North, machines represent man's attempt to make things alike, "to make watches or engines so as to deprive the thing made of individuality," novelistic representation – in George Eliot as in Dr. North's own book on "building" character – is a machine for producing individuals.

It might thus be argued – against what have been the two dominant hypotheses: the novel as agent of social liberation, the novel as agent of social control – that the realistic novel should best be understood as participating in the broader project of standardization, and that the commitment to characterization in particular can best be understood as a commitment to constructing the standard. I want to end this section, however, not by pressing this argument but by epitomizing it, albeit in a highly simplified form.

The greeting card industry, which began with the Victorian practice of exchanging Christmas cards, has in recent years moved beyond its traditional link to that holiday and to others and has begun to produce a wide array of cards, designed to express appropriate sentiments not only for a wider but for a more personal array of sentiments. In some degree, this recapitulates a development that itself originated in the Progressive Era, beginning with the appearance first of Mother's Day cards (initially celebrated in 1908, Mother's Day was proclaimed an "official" holiday by Woodrow Wilson in 1914) and then (in 1911) of more personal "Friendship" cards, containing what a greeting-card historian calls "specially written sentiments." These more recent cards are, in effect, refinements of the old Friendship cards; instead of wishing people happy birthday or hoping that they get well soon, they say things like: "In this world it's very scary to be open and vulnerable," or "I want to please you, but first I have to please myself," or "You hurt me. I feel better just telling you." On one account, these new, or at least new-age, cards originated in a visionary experience undergone by "radio therapist and author (*The Making of a Psychiatrist*)" David Viscott. Viscott told *Time* Magazine, "Once I heard a voice saying, 'Someday you will tell people what they really feel inside,' and that's what I do." Now the reproduction of this voice in millions of greeting cards makes *Time* nervous: "It may be," their reporter comments, "that the card companies are busy establishing the emotional range for many Americans with one-size-fits-all feelings."

The comparison with clothing sizes is appropriate but the fear of one-size-fits-all misses its point. That fear is based on the assumption that people already have many varied and differentiated emotions which will be compromised by being reduced to catchphrases on cards. But the argument for the cards is that people no more come equipped with emotions than they come equipped with clothing sizes. Just as Viscott needed a voice to tell him what he would do, the consumers of these cards need his voice to tell them what they "really" feel; just as people can be instructed on how to experience the physical process of lifting and carrying large weights of pig-iron, they can be instructed on how to experience hormonal changes in their bodies. Viscott's greeting cards update the original Friendship cards and they update their industrial equivalent, Taylor's instruction cards, too. As one member of the card industry puts it, "We never create a card line; we create real feelings." If this claim seems inflated, it is not because real feelings cannot be created but because so much work – from the comparatively minor contribution of the old Friendship and Mother's Day cards (indeed, of Mother's Day itself) to the major contribution of the realistic novel – has already gone into creating them.

CLASSES AND MASSES

Hortense wants the fur coat as a way of improving her "social state"; at once individual and a copy, the coat is classy, and Hortense imagines that, owning it, she will be too. But why does Sondra want Clyde? Clyde does not have more class than Sondra, but he does not, unambiguously, have less either. For he is, after all, a Griffiths, even if a poor relation, and so the town of Lycurgus and the Griffiths themselves are uncertain how to feel about him. Within the Griffiths family, the two extremes of possibility are represented by Mr. Griffiths and his son Gilbert, the father liking and encouraging Clyde, the son disliking and discouraging him. Sergei Eisenstein, preparing a script for a never-produced movie of *An American Tragedy*, explained the difference between father and son by noting that in Mr. Griffiths

> there still prevails the patriarchal democratic spirit of the fathers, who have not for-gotten how they themselves came to the town in rags to make their fortunes. The succeeding generation is already approximating to a money aristocracy; and in this connection it is interesting to note the difference in attitude towards Clyde adopted by his uncle and his cousin respectively.

The extraordinary physical resemblance between Gilbert and Clyde makes this new snobbery all the more marked but it also suggests that there is more at work here than the hardening of class lines. Clyde's near identity to Gilbert helps constitute (especially for Sondra) a kind of slippery class erotics: Clyde's resemblance to Gilbert identifies him as one of Sondra's own class, indeed as someone who – coming from money a little older than the Finchleys' – is in certain respects socially superior to her; at the same time, however, Sondra is attracted to Clyde because he is a *lower-class* Gilbert – unlike Gilbert's "hard" eyes, Clyde's "seeking" eyes mark him as wanting from Sondra something of what Hortense wants from the fur coat and thus make him a further object of interest to Sondra, who sees her own class reflected in those eyes. Clyde is thus simultaneously above and below Sondra, attractive as the embodiment of an almost utopian class fluidity – utopian not in imagining that class lines can be crossed (the history of the Griffiths and the Finchleys testifies that they can) but in imagining the possibility of belonging to more than one class, or rather, of a single person (Clyde and, through him, Sondra herself) embodying the moment of crossing. F. O. Matthiessen convincingly describes Sondra as responding to "an intensity in [Clyde] beyond that of the college boys she is used to," but this intensity is not exactly personal, or is personal only in a way that is simultaneously structural. What Sondra responds to in Clyde is his desire for her (a reflection of her own class from below) coupled with her desire for Gilbert (reflecting her own class from above). She complicates the relatively straightforward dynamics of Hortense's desire to change her "social state" by wanting not so much to move from one class to another as to experience the phenomenon of class in the context of class mobility, to experience through class difference her own "class."

Eisenstein was right, however, to emphasize the hardening of class lines in Lycurgus. For although the Griffiths are determined to start Clyde out at "the bottom of the business" and the business is run on a piece-rate system, Clyde himself does not do piece work; "I don't want him put on piece work," Samuel Griffiths tells Gilbert. "It wouldn't look right. After all, he is related to us. Just let him drift along for a little while and see what he does for himself." The Griffiths associate good "character" with "material manufacture" but piece work is the mark of the blue-collar laborer and a certain distance from piece work marks the white-collar worker, a distance the Griffiths extend beyond the factory walls by forbidding their white-collar boys to date their blue-collar girls. In Lycurgus, the "line of demarcation" between "the rich and the poor" is like a "high wall." So when Roberta's father hears that she has been killed, he can only imagine that it was "in the factory, by a machine"; and what eventually emerges as the apparent truth – that she has been murdered by one of the "idle rich" – seems a particularly horrible but not altogether unpredictable consequence of the breaching of that wall between rich and poor, management and labor, white collar and blue.

In fact, however, the wall is breached almost from the start, within the factory and without, by the "system" designed to protect it. The employees are "drilled" "sharply and systematically in all the details and processes which comprise" the "constructive work" of the factory. The point of this drill is to produce "characters" as well as products, workers "inured to a narrow and abstemious life." The effect, however, is quite different. Far from becoming inured to the narrow and abstemious, the better drilled he is, the more white-collar Clyde finds it impossible "to keep his mind on the mere mechanical routine of the work or off of this company of girls." And the blue-collar girls are themselves "employed so mechanically as to leave their minds free to roam from one thought of pleasure to another," fixing mainly on the "nearest object," Clyde. Taylor had imagined that the mechanization of the worker would encourage the qualities exhibited by men like Samuel Griffiths, "individual character, energy, skill, and reliability"; critics of scientific management had charged that mechanization would drive the workers crazy or had predicted hopefully that it would encourage them to repudiate the whole factory system: in a famous passage in his *Prison Notebooks*, Antonio Gramsci suggested that when factory work becomes "mere mechanical routine," the worker can achieve "a state of complete freedom" leading to "a train of thought that is far from conformist." According to Dreiser, however, factory work produces neither abstemious Samuel Griffithses nor non-conforming revolutionaries – it produces Clydes. And it produces them on both sides of the "high wall" between blue collar and white.

Thus while Roberta's parents have been envisioning her "quietly and earnestly and happily pursuing her hard, honest way" (living, in other words, the lives envisioned for the workers by management), Roberta herself – "taken with the charm" of Clyde's "personality" and "seized with the very virus of ambition and unrest that afflicted him" (not to mention all the other factory girls) – has been "drifting" into an affair with Clyde. As he describes their sexual relations, "I never had any real plan to do anything . . . And neither did she, of course. We just drifted, kinda, from the first . . . And then there was that rule that kept me from taking her about anywhere, and once we were together, of course we just went on without thinking very much about it, I suppose . . ." Juxtaposing the classes, the factory creates the sexually charged atmosphere of cross-class desire; it participates in producing Clyde's and Roberta's shared eagerness "for something better than ever had been." Insisting that the classes be kept apart, it requires and so produces the secrecy of Clyde's and Roberta's relations, the enforced privacy that leads to the intimacy of their sexual relations. Finally, more powerful even than this collaboration between proximity and separation, the factory produces the difference between the classes within each class: it produces drift as the condition of white-collar labor – "I don't want him put on piece work . . . Just let him drift along . . ." – and drift as the product of blue-collar labor – Roberta has been killed not by a machine but by the desiring dreams: "we just drifted, kinda" – that machines and the mechanical quality of her own labor have turned out to make possible.

"Drift" in the Progressive Era is a charged term. The "policy of drift" had marked for Croly the great threat to his national ideal, a threat he identified with the Jeffersonian anti-federalism that, he thought, had reached its apex in the years before the Civil War when Jefferson's Jacksonian heirs had "failed to grasp the idea that the Federal Union would not take care of itself": "They expected their country to drift to a safe harbor in the Promised Land, whereas the inexorable end of a drifting ship is either the rocks or the shoals." It took Croly's great hero, Abraham Lincoln, lifting himself above "a system of individual aggrandizement, national drift, and mental torpor," to save the Union and to proclaim Croly's own thesis, that "American nationality was a living principle" and that "Americans were responsible for their own national integrity."

Croly's interest in drift, then, was essentially as an antonym to his ideal of the American nation, but the "mental torpor" and the desire for "individual aggrandizement" that formed the background for "national drift" could easily move to the front as the discussion took a less nationalist turn. Thus, by 1914, Walter Lippmann (about to go to work for Croly's new "New Republic") could ignore the question of national identity while continuing – in *Drift and Mastery* – to identify drift as the great enemy: "The scientific spirit is the discipline of democracy, the escape from drift, the outlook of a free man." Where Croly opposed the ideal of the nation to drift, Lippman opposes the ideals of administration and management: the "scientific method, the careful application of administrative technique, the organization and education of the consumer for control, the discipline of labor for an increasing share of the management." Where Croly advocated new choices, Lippman advocates choice itself: "We can no longer treat life as something that has trickled down to us. We have to deal with it deliberately, devise its social organization, alter its tools, formulate its method, educate and control it." For Lippman, then, "mastery" goes beyond the formulation of a political program to the formulation of a "theory" of "man's life" and a "method" for living it.

Croly's drifters are laissez-faire businessmen who think that if they are left to themselves democracy will flourish; *The Promise of American Life* proposes a political alternative to laissez-faire. Drift in Lippman is more pervasive – "We drift into work, we fall in love . . . Of almost no decisive event can we say: this was our own choosing" – and so the opposition to it will involve managing not only others but ourselves: we must not allow "accident" to master us, we must "penetrate the dreaming brute in ourselves," we must become "self-governing." At the same time, however, opposing drift not only to state intervention but to action itself, Lippman's logic makes available a new sphere for drift, a sphere in which drift can be rehabilitated, in which, as a 1922 advertisement headed "The Waterway to Happiness" could put it, the whole point could be to "Just drift."

The ad is for canoes and the sphere is leisure. Just as for Croly and Lippman the sphere of productive action comes increasingly to be defined by the absence of drift, so for the makers of "Old Town Canoes" the sphere of leisure is defined by the absence of anything like action: "No effort. No work. Just pleasure!" Which is not to say that work and leisure are entirely edited out of the scene of leisurely drift; rather they are transferred from the canoers to the "Old Town Canoe" itself: "For an 'Old Town' is the easiest of canoes to paddle. It answers instantly the slightest pressure of the blade. Speed, too, is built into every 'Old Town Canoe.' And strength, and steadiness." The work is thus built into the technology, and the young couple paddling in the canoe "up winding streams" may be understood as avatars of Clyde and his factory girls, looking out on the Mohawk "swirling and rippling," freed by the "mechanical routine" of their work to "roam from one thought of pleasure to another." If then the increasingly rigorous attempt to exclude drift from the realm of action turns out to rehabilitate drift as the defining criterion of leisure, the conditions of leisure turn out to be indistinguishable from the conditions of factory labor. The aggrandizing ambitions, the mental torpor, the unconscious desires of what Lippman calls "the dreaming brute" – these are expressions of the drift that in Croly and Lippman "modern civilization" must either segregate or eliminate and that in *An American Tragedy* reappears not only as a product of modern civilization but as a product of that civilization's technologies for segregating or eliminating it.

Clyde himself is "fascinated" by "canoeing," which is to say that he is "pleased by the picturesque and summery appearance he made in an out-ing shirt and canvas shoes paddling about Crum Lake." He and Dreiser regard leisure activities like canoeing, swimming, and diving as "social accomplishments"; the "appearance" they produce marks Clyde's eligibility for class transformation since, of course, the pleasure of drifting is a class pleasure. The couples at Crum Lake only "lease by the hour" the canoes that the readers of "The Waterway to Happiness" are urged to buy, but both the advertisement and the possibility of rental are institutions of class transfor-mation. They are, in this respect, like the Griffiths' factory itself, which, in Gilbert's description, has a mission of some "social importance," "making and distributing collars, giving polish and manner to people who wouldn't other-wise have them, if it weren't for cheap collars." The rhythm of factory life, I suggested earlier, produces Clydes as well as collars since it makes its workers

into "passionate" consumers, and Gilbert's description of the "social importance" of "cheap collars" reminds us of the intimacy between the factory's two
products: the consumers it produces consume the products it produces; Clydes
buy cheap collars.

We can imagine Clyde and Roberta at Crum Lake as the couple in the "Old
Town Canoe" ad; "This is the magic hour," say the makers of Old Town canoes;
it is like a "dream" "realized," think Clyde and Roberta. And we can imagine
the climactic scene of Clyde and Roberta, "drifting, drifting" in the rowboat
at Big Bittern, as the moralized culmination of the affair they "just drifted"
into; "Just drift . . . Just pleasure," says the canoe ad, but "the inexorable
end of a drifting ship is either the rocks or the shoals," says Croly. From this
standpoint, dramatizing the consequences of drift, *An American Tragedy* seems
to reaffirm the managerial morals of Croly and Lippman. But, as we have already
seen, for Dreiser the choice between drift and mastery, work and pleasure is
compromised by the irreducible interdependence of the terms between which
one is supposed to be choosing. And nowhere is this entanglement more
dramatic than in the scene of Roberta's death. For, of course, the "drifting,
drifting – in endless space where was no end of anything – no plots – no plans –
no practical problems to be solved – nothing" has itself been planned as the
prelude to "The moment of action – of crisis!" And the "moment of action" is
not only preceded and precipitated by drift, it is inhabited by it – the "action"
is an "accident," an "unintentional blow" that knocks Roberta into the water.
And then, in the wake of the action that has become an accident, there is a
moment of thought – "Do nothing" – while Roberta drowns, a commitment
to inaction that will prove to the Rev. McMillan and to Clyde himself that he
really is guilty of murder, a doing nothing that is a doing something until,
putting to work one of the "social accomplishments" acquired at Crum Lake,
Clyde swims to shore.

It is, of course, usual to understand Dreiser and American Naturalism more
generally as concerned with the limits of human agency; indeed, it is almost a
definition of Naturalism to characterize it as a literature devoted to determinism and to the critique of conventional morality and idealist metaphysics such
a determinism seemed to entail. But the genealogy of drift that we have been
tracing suggests that the preeoccupation with the limits of agency should be
understood less as a metaphysical obsession than as a point of access to new
patterns of constraint and possibility. When Lippman worries that "accident"
will become "master," he is worrying that professionals will be unable to control the nation's economy; when Clyde wants to be "free," he wants to be free
of Roberta. The genealogy of drift thus marks not so much a persistent return
to the questions of free will and determinism as a transformation of the social

formations in which these questions could once again become urgent. The technocratic fantasies of (self)control embodied in the Progressive cult of the scientific manager emerge in opposition to what looks (to Croly and Lippman) like the drift of free-market individualism, and the technologies of control brought into being by these fantasies give birth in turn to the white-collar drifting of Clyde and Roberta.

"For true to the standard of the American youth," Clyde "felt himself above the type of labor which was purely manual"; "if only he had a better collar, a nicer shirt, finer shoes, a good suit, a swell overcoat like some boys had!" The distribution of standards makes collars themselves a standard; the dissemination of Taylor's "personal ambition" makes every American too ambitious to carry pig-iron. Clyde is "one of those interesting individuals who look[ed] upon himself as a thing apart"; he experiences his individuality as proleptic membership in a class higher than the one he also experiences himself as belonging to. Like the Green-Davidson Hotel which, "someone" says "sarcastically," supplies "exclusiveness to the masses," Clyde embodies a consciousness of class difference turned into an instrument of mass identification. Imagining himself, like everyone else, "a thing apart," he imagines himself not as independent but as exclusive. In Clyde's career, then, we see the insistence on class difference as a rehearsal for the relentless and alluring individualism of the mass society.

"The white-collar people slipped quietly into modern society," wrote C. Wright Mills in 1951, as if he were describing in true Cold-War style the arrival of insidious but, in this instance, pitiful pod-people: "morally defenseless," "politically impotent," without any "culture" except "the contents of a mass society that has shaped him and seeks to manipulate him to its alien ends." Mills saw the Progressive Era as the moment when the "old middle classes" ("old independent entrepreneurs") "made their last political stand" against bureaucratic mass society. They lost, and nowadays "the individual . . . feels dangerously lost." The loss of individuality is, perhaps, the dominant theme of American cultural studies, rivaled only by the triumph of individualism, which is only to say that social change in American life characteristically presents itself as an event in the history of the individual. We have seen how the defense of individuality against the "group" took the form in Twain of imagining persons as machines (independent because inflexible, mechanical instead of social) and how this conception of individuality as independence from society both repudiated and complemented Bellamy's conception of individuality as difference within the "system." For Twain and Bellamy both, the group – they tend to call it the "mob" – poses a threat to the individual, but where the alternative to the mob in Twain is the man alone (think of the Sherburn episode in *Adventures of Huckleberry Finn*), the alternative to the mob in Bellamy is the army, consisting not of independent individuals but of individuals individualized only by their place within the system. It was mechanization, I argued, that in enabling the imagination of an individuality that resisted society made possible at the same time the vision of an individuality that was "systematic" and so enabled hostility to the group to find expression as enthusiasm for the organization. And this transformation of the independent individual's disruptive energies into the organized individual's ambitious energies produced its own disruptions: Hortenses and Sondras became Clydes and Robertas; the stabilizing differences of "mastery" made possible the destabilizing desires of "drift."

So the arrival in American culture of the white-collar people cannot be understood either as a victory or a defeat for individualism; it must be understood instead as an episode in the transformation of individuality. And insofar as the literature of the period participates in those transformations, it must be understood as a literature of white-collar promises and tragedies, like the promises and tragedies – the white-collar people and the white collars – produced in the Griffiths Collar and Shirt Company.

THE PRODUCTION OF VISIBILITY

COLORED LINES

Realism's concern with vision is by now a kind of truism, and for no writer is it more true than for Stephen Crane, whose contemporaries frequently described his writing as a kind of "photography" and whose major works reveal an ambition to make visible not only certain things that did not seem suitable to be seen (for example, the slums) but also certain things that did not seem available to be seen (for example, mental states). Thus in *Maggie: A Girl of the Streets* (1893), dreams have colors (Jimmie's are "blood-red") and "sounds" can be "seen": one of the most striking of *Maggie*'s realistic effects is its Bowery dialect – "Dat Johnson goil is a puty good looker." Indeed, the prestige of dialect as a mark of Realism was so great in the 1890s that Abraham Cahan, making his novelistic breakthrough from Yiddish to English, at the same time sought to overcome the fact that the English he was now writing was being required to represent Yiddish by italicizing bits of dialogue that were to be understood as really sounding like what they looked like. Thus *Yekl: A Tale of the New York Ghetto* (1896), contains sentences like "But what will you say to *baseball*? All *college boys* and *tony peoplesh* play it," in which, as a helpful footnote informs us, the standard English represents Yiddish and the "Italics" represent "English words incorporated in the Yiddish of the characters." These italics mark Cahan's ambition to transcend the novelistic conventions that substitute standard English for Yiddish and instead to present the reader with the real thing.

In contrast to Cahan, Crane seems both less desperate and more determined. No italics are needed in *Maggie* because no Yiddish is spoken, but at the same time the desire to make the reader see goes beyond making him see the sound of speech. The stylistic device most noted (in praise, criticism, and parody) by Crane's early readers was his use of color – not only "blood-red" dreams but "crimson oaths," "red years," and "blue demonstrations." It was as if he thought (in the words of Mark Twain's old collaborator, C. D. Warner) that you could "somehow dye the language and make it more expressive to the reading eye." And an 1898 parodist imagined a Crane text in which "the descriptive color words" were replaced by "a thick line printed in ink of the adjectival hue." The culmination of Crane's Realism was here imagined as a technique that would transform the printed page itself into the object of the reader's vision by turning words into "colors . . . impressed upon the paper."

Warner jokingly called this "local color"; "given a theme or a motive for a story or sketch," he wrote, "the problem was how to work it out so that it would appear native and Real." The solution to the problem was "pigment," a combination of "views" and "dialect" which together would guarantee that the story was "a real story of real life." Cahan's italics provide a certain justi-fication for Warner's mockery but the effect in more skillful hands could be a powerful one. Kate Chopin's "La Belle Zoraïde" proclaims itself a "true" story by describing itself as told by an "old negress" to an audience (her mistress) that will, like the audience for local color, "listen to no stories but those which [are] true." At the same time, however, it is a story written for an audience that, if it wants the truth about Creole life (in the way that *Maggie* might have been understood to provide the truth about the Bowery) is bound to be disap-pointed since the story Chopin writes is in English whereas the story the "old negress" tells is in "the soft Creole patois, whose music and charm no English words can convey." The formal problem of the story is thus to match its claim to be "true" with an ability to produce the effect of the "Real," a problem Chopin solves by ending with an act of reverse translation. Having recounted the closing conversation between mistress and servant in English, she writes, "But this is the way Madame Delisle and Manna-Loulou really talked to each other: – 'Vou pré droumi, Ma'zelle Titite?' 'Non, pa pré droumi; mo yapré zongler. Ah, la pauv' piti, Man Loulou. La pauv' piti. Mieux li mouri!'" It is as if Cahan had written his first English novel in Yiddish, or as if Crane really had replaced English words with colored lines. Dialect, from this per-spective, appeals to "the reader's eye" (as much as, or even rather than, his ear) by staging temporarily the disappearance of English in the form of the reader's momentary inability to understand the words on the page: before "Tooby sho de pa'm er my han's w'ite" becomes Uncle Remus's way of saying, "To be sure, the palm of my hand is white," it remains for a moment an empty (because incomprehensible) sequence of letters. If, then, the point of dialect was a kind of transparency – enabling the reader to see through the marks on the page to the sound of a particular speaker's voice – that transparency was characteristi-cally accompanied by a certain opacity. All phonetic writing requires you to see the letters in order to hear the sound. Dialect, however, insisting on the primacy of what you hear, paradoxically emphasizes the primacy of what you see. The "hideous puty goil" on Crane's page thus testifies not only to his desire to make language a medium through which one can see what would otherwise be invisible (the sound of Maggie's voice) but also to his desire to make language itself visible. And it is in fact this radicalization of Conrad's "before all, to make you see" that Michael Fried (in *Realism, Writing, Disfiguration*) has identified at the heart of Crane's Realist ambitions.

But if Crane's formal project is to make the reader see (formal in that the reader will be made to see not only the scene represented by his writing but the scene of writing itself), his major texts, as almost all critics have agreed, are marked also by a relentless thematization of seeing, recurring narratives of the desire to see and not to see, to be seen and not to be seen. And although these narratives may indeed represent the formal conditions of writing they do so only by transforming them into what writing represents. That is, the desire to make the reader see the writing on the page in front of him cannot finally be satisfied by making him see the colors themselves or the provisionally incomprehensible letters of dialect since the point is to make him see not colors and letters but writing. And writing, as a system of representation, can never be properly seen if it is seen only as what is "impressed upon the paper."

Thus in *Maggie* the project of representing writing is made possible only by being transformed into the project of representing something else – the Bowery; and – by way of this transformation – we find the desire to see invested with concerns not strictly limitable to the desire to see writing. We find ourselves confronted, in other words, not only with our desire to see the Bowery (which might be understood as a displaced version of our desire to see writing, a thematic disguise for a formal ambition) but also with questions like, What difference will it make to the Bowery if it is seen by us? What difference might it make to us if we were seen by the Bowery? – questions which, although they may arise out of the impulse to represent writing, cannot be answered by an appeal to that impulse. Crane's commitment to making writing visible is, in other words, necessarily transformed by the requirement that to represent writing one must represent it as a representation. And a writing that doubles its formal ambition to make us see *it* by an ambition to make us see *something else* necessarily alters that formal ambition, providing what are at the same time additional and essential motives for seeing, and making possible scenarios which will link the desire to see (through the Bowery, writing) with the desire to be seen (through writing, by the Bowery).

Crane's middle-class audience had a number of answers to at least some of the above questions. A few simply did not want to see *Maggie* at all; the reviewer for the *Tribune* thought it ought to have been "suppressed." The reviewer for *The Nation* found "little that is interesting" in anything of Crane's and found Maggie in particular "impossible to weep over. We can feel only that it is a pity that the gutter is so dirty, and turn in another direction." Such responses, not only to *Maggie* but to texts like *The Awakening, Sister Carrie*, and even the relatively genteel *The Damnation of Theron Ware*, were not typical but they were frequent, frequent enough to make it clear that part of the excitement surrounding Realism in the 1890s was the sense that Realists were making people see things they did not want to see. And, of course, in the wake of such texts as Jacob Riis's *How the Other Half Lives* (1890), with its accompanying illustrations and explicit agenda for social reform, the political point of making people see both the Bowery and the failure thus far of missionary attempts to improve it seemed quite clear. "What are you going to do about it?" Riis asked his readers. Realists wanted the middle classes to see the slums so they would finally be moved to "do something" about them. The Realist text appears here as a cousin of the newspaper and magazine exposé, and it is, of course, the case that the two genres were intimately related – produced often by the same authors, composed sometimes of the same words (a chapter of *Sister Carrie*, for example, was partially transcribed from an article Dreiser wrote for *Demorest's Magazine*).

But there is a sense in which *Maggie* resists almost from the start this account of Realism as an appeal to the middle-class conscience. Or, better, it complicates one's sense of that conscience and of the "somethings" it might be moved to "do." For *Maggie* begins by staging a series of scenes of seeing in which vision is above all *aggressive*, as Pete, observing "with interest" the fight between Jimmie and the boys from Devil's Row, comes up behind "one of the most deeply engaged" and hits him "on the back of the head," and as Jimmie's father, watching the fight between Jimmie and Billie, is moved to begin kicking at "the chaotic mass on the ground" and gets Billie on the back of *his* head. The power of both these scenes derives from the fact that the ones being watched are so absorbed in what they are doing that they are unaware of being observed, while the "interest" of those watching – Pete, Jimmie's father, the children waiting "in ecstatic awe" for Jimmie's father to "belt" his "life out" – is not only focused on a scene of violence but expresses itself in an act of violence, performed by the observer on the observed.

Moreover, the role of observer is by no means limited to Pete, Jimmie's father, and the other boys:

From a window of an apartment house that upreared its form from amid squat, ignorant stables, there leaned a curious woman. Some laborers, unloading a scow at a dock at the river, paused for a moment and regarded the fight. The engineer of a passive tugboat hung lazily to a railing and watched. Over on the Island, a worm of yellow convicts came from the shadow of a grey ominous building and crawled slowly along the river's bank.

This catalogue of observers suggests that Pete *et al.*'s "interest" in the fight is hardly anomalous and, indeed, it reminds us that Crane's reader (who is the only one who can see the convicts and whose position at the end of the chain of observation – outside the Bowery – is thus explicitly marked) is being understood to share that interest. At the same time, however, the paragraph does suggest at least one anomaly, for the list of observers includes the convicts who are not observers and who thus occupy the structural position of the boys fighting – they are being watched. Part of the point here is no doubt to suggest a certain narrative continuity between the boys and the prisoners, but the more immediate effect is both to remind the reader of his or her own position as an observer and to emphasize the power implicit in being an observer who is not himself observed, a power made explicit in the blows to the head that follow. And insofar as the reader's interest in Realism can be (as I am suggesting it is) emblemized in a figure like Pete, that interest may be understood to bring out the violence in reform. The object in making us see the Bowery is to prick our consciences, to make us do something about it, but what we want to do about it is to assert our power over it. And one way of enabling us to do that is by making the Bowery interest us in the way that the "deeply-engaged one" interests Pete.

On this account, the project of Realism is an essentially political one, insisting on and working from the social difference between the readers of the Realist text and the figures made visible in that text. In *Maggie*, however, Realism also has a slum variant in the "theatre" which, staging the triumph of the "poor and virtuous" over the "wealthy and wicked," makes Maggie "think"; she wonders "if the culture and refinement she had seen imitated . . . by the heroine on the stage, could be acquired by a girl who lived in a tenement house and worked in a factory." The answer given by what Crane calls the "melodrama" and what *Maggie* and its audience call "transcendental realism" is yes: the "representative of the audience" does indeed triumph over "the villain and the rich man"; that is why its Realism is "transcendental." But *Maggie*'s answer is no. The slums like to see their own exclusion ("Joy always within, and they like the actor, inevitably without") staged, but only if that exclusion is temporary; their "melodrama" represents not only what Riis diagnosed as the "gap between the classes" but also (what Riis recommended) a "bridge" over the gap. For Maggie, whose dead body must be fished out of the East River, there is no bridge.

But what appears in *Maggie* only as the slum fantasy of crossing class boundaries found less qualified expression elsewhere. In Edward W. Townsend's *A Daughter of the Tenements* (1895), for example, the heroine does indeed escape the slums, as does virtually every other character in the book. In fact, the tenements, as Townsend depicts them, are little more than way-stations for "aristocrats" on their way to that "other world of homes" above Washington Square or out on Long Island. Furthermore, the "aristocrats" of the slums turn out to be the natural allies of New York's real uptown aristocrats in what the novel amazingly depicts as their common battle against dishonest social climbers. Thus the true villain of the book is "the false sportsman" Mark Waters, who tries (successfully) to defraud the sons of Washington Square and (unsuccessfully) to corrupt the daughter of the tenements. By presenting every problem (moral and economic) as a consequence of Waters's machinations, *A Daughter of the Tenements* manages to make his exposure and death the solution to all social ills, as if the gap between "the masses and the classes" was caused by social climbing "swells" trying to pass themselves off as real "gentlemen."

Maggie was often compared to Townsend's slum writings, particularly with respect to its use of what contemporary criticism called "tough dialect." ("Tough," as in "tough girls" and "tough dancing," would be a term increasingly applied to the culture of the working class.) But where Maggie says things like "Dis is outa sight," the daughter of the tenements is "frequently . . . charged with having an affected accent" because she talks like the settlement worker Eleanor Hazlehurst from whom her accent has, Townsend explains, been acquired. The explanation is somewhat implausible; more important, it is supererogatory: none of the other tenement women in *Daughter* speaks with the "accent of her surroundings" either – when the opium-addicted bartender Bill Williams tells his opium-addicted paramour, Molly, that "Dis mug, Waters, has been collarin all de boodle," Molly responds, in accents graphematically identical to the settlement worker's (but without benefit of her tutelage), "How do you know he collared the boodle? How do you know Teresa didn't get it?" And the difference between accents is more than a matter of gender since, despite Townsend's reputation as a master of dialect, Bill Williams is the *only* character in *Daughter* who does speak in the Bowery dialect (one or two of the others occasionally and inconsistently produce an Irish brogue or a little Italian). And Bill Williams is also the only character who does not escape the Bowery; he talks like Maggie and, like Maggie, he dies at the end. The other "aristocrats of Mulberry Bend" talk like aristocrats right from the start and end up living on Long Island.

A Daughter of the Tenements thus replays *Maggie*'s slum "melodrama" of escape from the Bowery as a middle-class fantasy of never actually being trapped in it; it solves the problem of the slums by imagining (not altogether unprophetically) slum-dwellers as embryonic suburbanites – the reason they can be reformed is that they do not really need to be. Indeed, the most powerful image of such desired transcendence is embodied in the Realist himself, who is enabled, as Townsend put it, to "get such a hold" on Bowery "types" because "he's lived there," but whose ability to represent the slums – in all their presumed "toughness" – is at the same time his ticket out of them: Carminella, the *Daughter*, makes herself a star by enacting on Broadway a version of the "actual performances of children dancing before a street organ," and her brother Tom makes a career in art sketching his friends and relations. Realism's implied narrative thus involves at least two chapters, one in which the Realist lives there and one in which he or she does not live there any more. There is a sense, then, in which the condition of Realism's possibility is the "melodrama" of transcendence denied by Maggie's death. Maggie may die, but insofar as the Realist himself must – really to be a Realist – have been a slum-dweller, the production of his text testifies to his own survival and thus to the possibility of escape.

Maggie, as we have seen, also alludes to this project of effacing the distinction between Riis's two halves but it requires us at the same time to understand our desire to see the life of the other half as a desire not to efface but to enforce the distinction. It would be a mistake, however, to think that *Maggie* requires us to choose between these two social readings of Realism. For the most powerful scene of seeing in *Maggie* (the childrens' encounter with the "prostrate, heaving body" of their mother) appeals neither to the benevolently controlling interest of the observer in what he sees nor to the aggressively controlling one. Jimmie and Maggie "stare" at their sleeping mother. Like the boys fighting, the mother is definitively an object of vision, which is only to say that since she is asleep she is, without effort of attention, as "deeply involved" as the boys, who are too deeply involved to notice the approach of Pete and then of Jimmie's father. But where with the boys this self-absorption seems both to constitute and exhaust their interest as objects of observation, with the mother it does not. What makes Jimmie stand, "as if fascinated," over his mother's face is the expectation (experienced as "dread") that she will "open her eyes." The fascination of looking includes, indeed is (at least in part) produced by, the possibility of being looked at: "Suddenly her eyes opened. The urchin found himself looking straight into that expression, which, it would seem, had the power to change his blood to salt." And when her eyes close again, Maggie and Jimmie remain crouching beside her through the night, "drawn, by some force, to stare at the woman's face."

This "force" is not the reader's own, and the power experienced here is not simply the power of middle-class vision; perhaps one could think of it as the power of the slums. Where the boys are so "deeply involved" – so much the objects of vision – that they become, ipso facto, the objects of violence, the mother's self-involvement seems always on the verge of dissolving into aggression; the fascination of her closed eyes is that they might at any moment open. Even in Townsend's *Daughter*, the Bowery was understood to pose a threat – "the pillage and burning of your peaceful, diamond-back district homes" – and Riis's "Man with a Knife" offered "the solution of violence" to the problem of reform: "Our only fear," Riis wrote (quoting the 1887 *Report of the Association for Improving the Condition of the Poor*), "is that reform may come in a burst of public indignation destructive to property and to good morals." Maggie's mother certainly represents a threat to good morals and property; furthermore, the visual fascination she exercises over the children who watch her sleeping is a function of this threat – it is the "force" by which the "eyes of both were drawn . . . to stare at the woman's face." If, as figured in Pete, the Realist reader's "interest" in looking at the slums involves the exercise of a certain violence against them, the fascination of the slums, as figured in Maggie's mother, involves a threat of violence that goes the other way.

Maggie thus offers two answers to the question about why we want to look at the slums: we want to experience our power over them (when they do not look back); we want to experience their power over us (when they do). Both these answers are essentially political in the sense that both involve inserting the interest of Realism in an essentially political narrative, albeit not quite the same narrative. But as the potential discrepancy between narratives (does Realism stage the beginnings of proletarian revolution or the extension of bourgeois hegemony?) indicates, the interest of the Realist text itself is not quite identical to the political meaning it will turn out to bear. Which is only to say that the appeal to the reader's eye could appear in the context of and be mobilized on behalf of more than one political project.

The formal breakthrough to Realism in Chopin's "La Belle Zoraïde," for example (the emergence of Creole out of English), is accompanied by a quite differently marked thematic desire for the "Real." For if Chopin's story requires that Manna-Loulou's Creole (like Maggie's tough talk) be made visible, Manna-Loulou's story produces a visibility located neither in language nor in class. The story Manna-Loulou tells is about Zoraïde, a beautiful slave "the color of café-au-lait," raised by her mistress to be "as charming and as dainty as the finest lady of la rue Royale" and intended by her to marry "a little mulatto," with "shining whiskers like a white man's" and with "eyes that were cruel and false as a snake's." But Zoraïde detests the mulatto, and wants instead to marry "le beau Mézor," whose body is "like a column of ebony." "I am not white," Zoraïde reminds her mistress, and she does not want to marry an imitation white man; her desire for the ebony Mézor is in this respect a commitment to what Chopin in another story calls "maintaining the color line" (a commitment entrusted in that story as in this one to a black woman). When Zoraïde bears a child by the black Mézor, her mistress punishes her by sending the child away and telling her that it has died. The result is not to make Zoraïde more tractable but to make her crazy; she becomes attached to "a senseless bundle of rags shaped like an infant in swaddling clothes" that she calls her "piti." And the thematic climax of the story is when Madame in remorse has "the real baby" brought back and Zoraïde rejects it: "Nor could she ever be induced to let her own child approach her; and finally the little one was sent back to the plantation, where she was never to know the love of mother or father."

It is this climax that gives rise to the formal one — "the poor little one! better had she died!" translated back into "La pauv' piti! Mieux li mouri" — and although the two are not identical, they are clearly related by something more than narrative cause and effect. For the emergence here of Creole patois, "the way Madame Delisle and Manna-Loulou really talked to each other" both parallels and inverts Zoraïde's rejection of "the real baby"; where Chopin chooses the real (Creole instead of English), Zoraïde chooses a "dummy" (the "doll" instead of "her own child"). And this "demented" choice is itself the consequence of her mistress's preference for another kind of imitation, for the mulatto with "whiskers like a white man's" instead of the "ebony" Mézor. The pathos of "La Belle Zoraïde" thus consists not only in the traduction of its heroine's taste (from the real father to the false child) but also in the contrast between the narrated selection of imitations (the mulatto, the "piti") and the narrator's selection of the real (Creole). Chopin as Realist defines herself in opposition both to the "demented" Zoraïde and to the "wicked" mistress whose own preference for imitations overcomes Zoraïde's initial preference for the real. Indeed, the very category of the mulatto is rendered suspect by this story which, insofar as they resist being subsumed under the master categories "white" and "not white," identifies and rejects mulattoes as imitation whites; American segregation (unlike South African apartheid) would have no room for the racially mixed. If Realism had triumphed, if Chopin and Zoraïde had had their way, then a women who was "not white" would have married a man her mistress can only name as "That negro." The "color line" would have been "maintained."

In "La Belle Zoraïde," then, the demand for "true" stories is rendered indistinguishable from the demand for racial distinction. Crane's colored lines become Chopin's color line and the production of visibility is focused on racial identity; if the color line is to be maintained, racial identity must be made visible. Thus in Sutton Griggs's black separatist novel *Imperium in Imperio* (1899), the child of its "dark" hero and "brown" heroine is born "white" but his skin grows "darker by degrees" until finally he is the "very image" of his father. The miscegenous threat to racial identity is turned into a miraculous display of racial visibility. And in Chopin's own "Désirée's Baby," Désirée, a foundling married into "one of the oldest and proudest" families in Louisiana, gives birth to a baby that, apparently white, has by the end of three months, "changed" enough to be perceived by his father as "not white." The triumph of visibility here, however, has less to do with the baby's color than with its parents'. For although Désirée's skin is "whiter than" her aristocratic husband's, her "obscure origin" leads him and everyone else to believe that she too must be "not white." The trick of the story is that they are wrong. As the aristocratic Armand discovers in Chopin's Maupassant-like surprise ending, it is his own mother who was "cursed with the brand of slavery." Thus, whatever its pathos from Désirée's standpoint, with respect to the project of maintaining the color line, "Désirée's Baby" is profoundly reassuring; its central irony – the whiteness of black Désirée, the darkness of white Armand – turns out not to be ironic at all. Insofar as the point of Realism is the truth of color, when Désirée says, "I am white," she is right.

COLORED SOULS

Returning for a visit to his home town, Kingsborough, the Democratic nominee for governor of Virginia, Nick Burr, travels in an "ordinary car of a Southern railroad" among the "usual examples of Southern passengers": across the aisle, "a slender mother" holding "a crying baby"; further off, "several men returning from business trips"; across from them, "a pretty girl, asleep"; and, slouched in the seat in front of him, "a mulatto of the new era – the degenerate descendant of two races that mix only to decay." Nick Burr is the hero of Ellen Glasgow's novel *The Voice of the People* (1900), and if, in 1899 (when Glasgow wrote most of the book), such scenes were still "ordinary" and such passengers "usual," by the time of the novel's publication, they were not. In the wake of the Supreme Court's decision in *Plessy v. Ferguson* – denying the mulatto Homer Plessy's right to ride in a car reserved for whites only and so upholding the Louisiana statute providing "separate but equal accommodations" for each race – the Southern states rushed to enact Jim Crow laws for trains; Virginia's, passed in 1900, was one of the last. Part of what would be genuinely new about the "new era" would be the disappearance of such "usual" scenes; not until 1946, with the Court's decision in *Morgan v. Virginia*, could Governor Burr have seen another black man in the seat in front of him, and even then only if their train was going on past Kingsborough (Williamsburg) into North Carolina. Intra-state travel would not be desegregated for another ten years.

    Thus Belton Piedmont in Griggs's *Imperium in Imperio* is thrown off a train for riding in a white-only railway car in Louisiana and nearly lynched by the local "Nigger Rulers" for other violations of segregationist practice. The "Anglo-Saxons," proclaims Belton's friend Bernard, "have chosen our race as an empire," and both he and Belton, speaking, Griggs says, on the same day "on which the Congress of the United States had under consideration the resolutions . . . which meant war with Spain," echo the imperialist call to extend the American Empire with the anti-imperialist call to free blacks from it. The racism invoked on behalf of Jim Crow could not, in this view, be separated from the racism invoked, say, to justify the suppression of Aguinaldo in the Philippines and the replacement of his government with American rule. Like blacks and Indians, as Senator Albert J. Beveridge put it, "The Philippinos are not a self-governing race."

But if the racism of internal oppression and the racism of external conquest were not separable, they were not exactly identical either. Thus a Northern anti-imperialist could urge the American people to pause before undertaking "the task of giving the advantages of our civilization to the Negritos, Moslem pirates, and other mongrel Asiatics of the Philippines. They are all inferior races . . . [and] Wherever we have touched an inferior people we have, without exception, come into violent and bitter antagonism with them." And thus the widow of Jefferson Davis could announce that her "most serious objection" to the annexation of the Philippines was that "three-fourths of the population is made up of negroes," who, "without benefit of slavery," were a "semi-savage" and "predatory" people. From this standpoint, Jim Crow might be seen not only as anti-expansionist but also as hostile even to a more local imperialism. One of the heroes of Thomas Dixon's popular racist novel, *The Clansman* (1905), is, surprisingly enough, Abraham Lincoln, whose freeing the slaves is understood by Dixon as the essential prerequisite not to making them citizens but to getting rid of them altogether. Just as the nation could not exist "half slave and half free," it cannot exist "half white and half black," says Dixon's Lincoln. "We must assimilate or expel." And since assimilation is unthinkable, expulsion – a kind of visceral or emetic anti-imperialism – becomes essential.

There is, furthermore, an even more active sense – ideological as well as biological and geographic – in which American racism cannot be identified with expansionist imperialism. The Civil War, as Lincoln describes it in *The Clansman*, was a war of "self-preservation" rather than "conquest." Indeed "The Constitution," he asserts (as if speaking in the voice of those who insisted on the illegality of annexing the Philippines) "makes no provision for the control of conquered provinces." Hence the federal government has no right to enfranchise the blacks, and hence, in *The Clansman*, Reconstruction is presented as the attempt, after the anti-imperialist Lincoln's death, to colonize the South.

The Invisible Empire of the Knights of the Ku Klux Klan arises in rebellion against the "visible" empire of the North and its black soldiers like the rapist "Gus" who, as his full name – Augustus Caesar – makes clear, is to be regarded as an imperial stormtrooper. In *The Clansman*, then, white Americans are understood not as imperialists but as the victims of imperialism.

This way of putting the point, however, does not quite get at the complexity of the situation. After all, Americans have customarily imagined themselves as the victims of imperialism, whether the empire is British – as it was throughout the nineteenth century – or Russian, as it was for much of the twentieth. But Reconstruction goes beyond the mere victimization of white men; it not only enables white men to imagine themselves as the victims of an imperial power, it enables them to imagine the imperial power as their own government. Thus the evil empire is in its essence neither British nor Russian but American, and the task of resisting it is revolutionary as well as nationalist. (This too has persisted: against what government was the Reagan Revolution of the 1980s directed?) Reconstruction makes it possible to replay the Revolutionary scenario of casting off the chains of empire and building a new nation even when there is no empire and when the nation is not new. Thus, unlike Joel Chandler Harris's Uncle Remus stories or Thomas Nelson Page's plantation tales a generation earlier (and unlike *Gone With the Wind* a generation later), *The Clansman* makes no appeal to nostalgia for the prewar South and for the more amicable race relations of slavery. As committed as any abolitionist to the impossibility of a nation half slave and half free, Dixon represents the Civil War not as the ultimate expression of sectional, political, and economic differences but as the site on which those differences are erased and replaced with racial difference. What he calls the "prejudices" of the Northern Phil Stoneman and the Southern Ben Cameron are "melted in the white heat of battle," enabling each to see that a single man like either one of them "is worth more to this Nation than every Negro that ever set his flat feet on this continent." Jim Crow thus marks not a return to but a final repudiation of paternalist prewar race relations, casting blacks out of the family so that Northern and Southern whites – Phil Stoneman and Ben Cameron look "as much alike as twins" – can finally become brothers. Insofar as the political, economic, and sectional differences caused by slavery had forestalled true nationhood, the racial difference rendered visible by abolition made the birth of a nation possible. For Dixon as well as for D. W. Griffith and Woodrow Wilson, the Klan embodied the complete coincidence of racial identity with national identity. In the past the country had been divided on political, economic, and sectional issues; from now on, as Dixon wrote in his first novel *The Leopard's Spots* (1902), "there could be but one issue – are you a White man or a negro?"

The identification of American with white (and the colonization or, failing that, segregation of blacks) marked by its appeal to what the court in *Plessy* called "physical differences," a new development in racial thinking. For the doctrine of "separate but equal" affirmed racial distinction *as such*; it affirmed, that is, racial distinction independent of any other legal consideration so that the relation between black and white was radically distinguished from the relation between master and slave. Forty years earlier, ruling unconstitutional a statute called "An Act relative to slaves and free colored persons," the Louisiana Supreme Court had asserted that there was "all the difference between a free man of color and a slave, that there is between a white man and a slave." But where in 1856 the line was drawn between slave and free, the point in 1896 was to draw it between black and white. Slaves, in principle, could become free (Louisiana had, in fact, always had a large population of free blacks); blacks could never become white.

Thus the absence of any difference *grounded* in law (master and slave) became powerful testimony to the irreducibility of a difference only *reflected* in the law (black and white); legal equality became the sign of racial separation: "A statute which implies merely a legal distinction between the black and white races – a distinction which is founded on the color of the two races, and which must always exist so long as white men are distinguished from the other race by color – has no tendency to destroy the legal equality of the races or reestablish a condition of involuntary servitude," the court wrote in *Plessy*. The transformation here of the difference between master and slave into the difference between white and black marks a crucial step in the separation of racism from slavery, in racism's emancipation from the forms of a feudal economy. Freed from its embarrassing entanglements with the "peculiar institution," racism could now take its place as a distinctively modern phenomenon. Which is presumably what W. E. B. Du Bois meant by his famous remark, "The problem of the twentieth century is the problem of the color line."

But as *Plessy* also made clear, the question posed by the color line – Dixon's question, Are you white or black? – and the questions on which this one depended – What makes a white man white? What makes a black black? – were not always easy to answer. In some states, the court wrote, "any visible admixture of black blood stamps the person as belonging to the colored race." But that test would not do for Homer Plessy, whose "mixture of colored blood was not discernible." Hence one principle established by *Plessy* was that distinctions based upon color were not necessarily visible and therefore that it was up to the individual states to determine what "proportion of colored blood" was necessary to constitute a colored man. "Legislation is powerless to eradicate racial instincts or to abolish distinctions based upon physical differences," the court asserted. But the question of what race Homer Plessy actually belonged to and so of what ineradicable racial instincts might be his could be determined only under the laws of the State of Louisiana.

To put the case in this way is only to highlight what is already evident, the stunning incoherence of *Plessy v. Ferguson*. But it would be a mistake to understand this incoherence as fundamentally embarrassing to the emerging racist ideology. For to read the slippage between Homer Plessy's color (white) and his race (black) as a reproach to racism would be to miss the point of the Invisible Empire's invisibility. The Clan is invisible partly because its organization is secret but more importantly, according to Dixon, because its identity is based from the start on a racial principle that transcends visibility – it consists of "the reincarnated souls of the Clansmen of Old Scotland." Or, as the freedman Aleck describes the "Ku Kluxes" who persuade him to resign his office as sheriff, "Dey wuz Sperits, ridin' white hosses wid flowin' white robes, en big blood-red eyes!" Identity in *The Clansman* is always fundamentally spiritual. Thus, for example, marriage and "the close sweet home-life" can make people more "alike in soul and body" than can any physical relation: "People have told me that your father and I are more alike than brother and sister of the same blood," Mrs. Cameron writes to her daughter, "in spirit I'm sure it's true." This is why the Civil War, customarily represented in, for example, John Fox Jr.'s bestselling *The Little Shepherd of Kingdom Come* [1903], as turning brothers into enemies, is represented in *The Clansman* as turning enemies like Phil Stoneman and Ben Cameron at least into brothers-in-law and at most into "twins."

The tragedy of the war, according to Fox in *The Little Shepherd*, was that it was "fratricidal"; the consolation was that at the war's end, "Son came back to father, brother to brother . . ." And, indeed, the point of *The Little Shepherd* as a whole is that what it calls "blood" will tell. Beginning some ten years before the war with the "wood-colt" Chad abandoning the graves of his substitute hillbilly parents, it moves through the recognition that Chad, despite his unknown ancestry, must be "a gentleman born" and ends, at the war's end, with Chad restored to the graves of the Bluegrass "aristocrats" who turn out to have been his real parents. The war has turned the "ragged mountain boy" into a "highbred, clean, frank, nobly handsome" officer, or, rather the war has provided the setting in which Chad's true nobility could emerge: "The change was incredible, but blood had told."

The Clansman, by contrast, is indifferent to blood. The identity of soul that makes husband and wife "more alike than brother and sister of the same blood" and that brings the Stonemans and Camerons together transcends biology, replacing the natural unity of the family with a spiritual unity that, unlike the family, is genuinely indivisible. This is why the Klan is more than a clan. Aleck's account of them as "Sperits" corroborates Dixon's; his superstitious fear of the spirits must be understood as a response to the terrifying representation of an essentially invisible racial identity, an identity that ("Désirée's Baby" to the contrary notwithstanding) cannot be seen in people's skins (it could not be seen in Homer Plessy's) but can be seen in the Klan's sheets. The purpose of the sheets is not really to conceal the identities of individual clansmen; there is even a sense in which – with racial "twins" like Phil Stoneman and Ben Cameron – whiteness has already accomplished this: the elaborate melo-drama that leads up to *The Clansman*'s climax depends upon Phil and Ben, undisguised, substituting for each other as freely as if they were wearing their hoods. Instead, then, of hiding individual identity, the sheets in *The Clansman* subsume it under racial identity; rather than making the visible identities of individual clansmen invisible, the sheets make their invisible identities visi-ble. The Klan wear sheets because their bodies are not as white as their souls, because *no* body can be as white as the soul embodied in the white sheet.

And this redefinition of the racial body is by no means limited to anti-Negro texts like Dixon's. In Frances E. W. Harper's *Iola Leroy* (1892), for example, the central characters are blacks whose outstanding physical characteristic is whiteness: "what is the use of you're saying you're a colored man," the white Dr. Gresham asks the black Robert Johnson, "when you're as white as I am," and "I see no use in your persisting that you are colored," the same doctor says to Iola Leroy, "when your eyes are as blue and complexion as white as mine"; Iola's brother Harry is so white that he is jokingly urged to "put a label on himself, saying 'I am a colored man,' to prevent annoyance" on street cars. This insistence on fair-skinned heroes and heroines has been criticized as an expression by Harper of those "complexional prejudices" which, as Harper herself pointed out, "are not confined to white people." But in the context of Dixon's (literal) idealization of whiteness and of what Harper calls the effort "to detect the presence of negro blood when all physical traces had disappeared," the predominance of the fair-skinned mulatto can better be understood as an element in the general investigation into and redeployment of racial identity. "The slogan of the hour is 'Keep the Negro down!'" wrote Pauline Hopkins in *Of One Blood* (1902), "but who is clear enough in vision to decide who hath black blood and who hath it not?" The point of the mulatto – making it unclear who has "black blood" – is to raise the question of what – in the absence of the appropriate "physical traces" – black blood is.

One answer, the answer suggested by Hopkins's title and by its biblical source ("Of one blood have I made all nations of men to dwell upon the whole face of the earth" [Acts 17:26]), is that there is no such thing as black blood, or at least that, given the history of black and white "amalgamation" in North America, there is no such thing as black blood any more: "No man can draw the dividing line between the two races, for they are both of one blood." On this account, the mulatto marks the disappearance of racial identity, and the "white" skin of Hopkins's central characters (in *Contending Forces* [1900] as well as in *Of One Blood*, they are as "fair" as Harper's) is an emblem of the disappearance of "the color line" in the face of the universal "brotherhood" that writers like Dixon imagined blacks to desire. But *Of One Blood*'s amazing gothic plot – the (apparently white) hero's (apparently white) bride turns out to be his (black) sister; the (apparently white) best friend who seduces her turns out to be his (and so, her) (black) brother – puts a new twist both on brotherhood and on the claim that Hopkins's protagonists are "all of one blood." Hero, heroine, and villain all bear a birthmark that, despite their whiteness, "proves" their "race" and "descent" from ancient kings of Ethiopia and that guarantees a racial identity no amount of miscegenation can obscure. Their indistinguishability from whites in color only accents their absolute distinction in race.

For Hopkins, then, the family romance involves the discovery of an identity that survives "amalgamation with other races," an African identity that remains pure despite the fact that "on the American continent," as a character in *Contending Forces* remarks, "there is no such thing as an unmixed black," no one who can "trace an unmixed flow of African blood." *Of One Blood* makes such a survival possible by its commitment to "spiritualistic phenomena," to a world in which the dead communicate with the living and those with "the power" cross from one world to the other. Hopkins's doctor-hero has discovered "by research" that "life is not dependent upon organic function as a principle" and he has "inherited" from his mother the "mysticism" and "occult powers" that, transcending the organic, connect him to the "race of African kings": "the mystic within him . . . was a dreamlike devotion to the spirit that had swayed his ancestors." The organic language of identity by "descent" is here invoked on behalf of a non-organic, "spiritual" identity; what you inherit from your mother is not biological but the "principle" that supersedes biology. Racial purity, for Hopkins as for Dixon, thus requires the transubstantiation of "blood" into "spirit"; biologically corrupted by 250 years of compulsory miscegenation, the black race can "conserve" itself only by repudiating biological principles of identity and insisting on "a new principle," "an idea." Amalgamation destroys races; "Ideas only save races." The predominance of the mulatto in Harper and Hopkins thus marks the transformation of race into an idea, the disappearance of the mulatto as imitation white and her emergence as paradigmatic black. Rather than expressing "complexional prejudice," the white skin of the mulatto "race woman" embodies a blackness that black skin cannot record; it is the sheet she wears to face down the Klansman in his.

Roxy, the "very fair" "Negro" heroine of Mark Twain's *Pudd'nhead Wilson* (1894), articulates what looks like an alternative to Dixon's conception of racial identity when, volunteering to sell herself back into slavery to save her free son Tom, she says to him, "Ain't you my chile? En does you know anything a mother won't do for her chile? Dey ain't nothin' a white mother won't do for her chile. Who made 'em so? De Lord done it. En who made de niggers? De Lord made 'em. In de inside, mothers is all de same." Roxy speaks here for a racial identity that disappears when you move from the outside to the "inside." Or, more powerfully – since Roxy is only one sixteenth black and "that sixteenth," Twain says, "did not show" – she embodies a racial identity that, since it does not manifest itself on the outside (Roxy looks white) or on the inside (where Roxy is the "same" as white), can be nothing more than what Twain famously called "a fiction of law and custom." But it would be a mistake to identify *Pudd'nhead Wilson* or even Roxy herself as opposed to *The Clansman*'s discourse of racial invisibility. For it is Roxy who, when Tom refuses to fight the Italian twin who has insulted him, identifies Tom as a "nigger" since, although "Thirty-one parts o' you is white an on'y one part nigger," that "po' little part is yo *soul*." *The Clansman*'s white soul turns out to be matched not opposed by *Pudd'nhead Wilson*'s black soul.

Really to find souls without color, one has to look, despite the apparent paradox, to W. E. B. Du Bois's *The Souls of Black Folk* (1903). In the extraordinary chapter on his young son's death, Du Bois registers his own dismayed response to the child's racially ambiguous appearance (he looks like Twain's Tom Driscoll) as the father's *infliction* of race on the son:

Why was his hair tinted with gold? An evil omen was golden hair in my life. Why had not the brown of his eyes crushed out and killed the blue? – for brown were his father's eyes, and his father's father's. And thus in the Land of the Color-line I saw, as it fell across my baby, the shadow of the Veil.

But the pathos of the victimized father helplessly victimizing the son is first subsumed by the greater pathos of the boy's early death and then erased by Du Bois's interpretation of that early death as an escape from racial identity. For in this text, racial identity is exhausted and so rendered meaningless by skin color, and the young boy, imagined by Du Bois as not yet aware of skin color, is also imagined as not yet belonging to a race: "He knew no color line . . . He loved the white matron, he loved his black nurse; and in his little world walked souls alone, uncolored and unclothed." Black folks have souls but their souls are not black – or white. Like the writers of racial difference, Du Bois sees the inadequacy of skin color as a mark of that difference, but unlike them he finds no invisible colors, no racial souls. In *The Souls of Black Folk*, or, at least, in the chapter "Of the Passing of the First-Born," racial difference really is a "fiction of law and custom."

Pudd'nhead Wilson devotes a great deal of Twain's considerable energy to asserting the ineradicable difference between two baby boys who look exactly alike, employing the famous fingerprints ("Nature's autography," Twain calls them) not only to identify the criminal behind the mask of innocence but the black man behind the mask of whiteness: as Pudd'nhead accuses him, Tom's face turns "ashen" and his lips turn "white" but to no avail – the whiter he gets, the blacker he is. When he faints dead away, the novel reads it as a confession (the fingerprints put by nature to serve the "fiction" of "law" in constituting race). Tom is sentenced to life imprisonment but that will not satisfy the requirements of racial identity; since white men can go to prison, he has to be "sold down the river," a fate reserved for blacks. It was Roxy's attempt to spare him that fate that started the story off. Du Bois proposes a more radical rescue for his son, whose death he interprets as a transcending of the "Veil": "All that day and all that night there sat an awful gladness in my heart . . . and my soul whispers ever to me, saying, 'Not dead, not dead, but escaped; not bond, but free.'" Insisting that what is invisible is uncolored, Du Bois imagines his son's death as freedom not only from racism but from race. He imagines, that is, the reduction of race to visibility.

As Du Bois himself realized, however, and as the examples of Dixon and Twain made clear, that reduction had become impossible; the twentieth-century question of the color line could not be answered by an appeal to color. Indeed, the notorious Mississippi Plan succeeded in disfranchising blacks precisely by separating race from color. The state Supreme Court that approved the plan explicitly acknowledged the illegality of discrimination by color: "Restrained by the Federal Constitution from discriminating against the negro race," the court wrote, "the convention discriminates against its characteristics." And the United States Supreme Court could find no fault with this color-blind racism, ruling that the supposed "peculiarities of habit, of temperament and of character" that distinguished blacks from whites were acceptable targets of legislation in a way that skin color was not.

In the hands of the Mississippi legislature, then, the invisibility of race became an opportunity not an embarrassment, an opportunity that could be put to even broader use by writers less concerned with the reorganization of Southern politics. For if the identification of American with white made Reconstruction the necessary condition of anti-imperialist nationalism, the transformation of skin color into "character" made the technology of racism available for a more general and more radical rewriting of biology as ideology. The "constructive ideas of our civilization are Anglo-Saxon ideas," as the reformer Washington Gladden put it. Where the new racism of skin color never tired of invoking the unchangeability of the leopard's spots, the new racism of ideas transcended such appeal: "You may change the leopard's spots," wrote the anti-imperialist Senator John Daniel of Virginia in 1899, "but you will never change the different *qualities* of the race." One culmination of this process of rendering race invisible was the creation of a new racial identity: Teddy Roosevelt called it "the American race." "Our object," he told the New York Knights of Columbus in 1907, "is not to imitate one of the older racial types but to maintain a new American type and then to secure loyalty to this type." Only the transformation of a body into a soul could authorize the political project of securing racial loyalty. It was the invisibility of racial identity that – making the question, are you white or black, possible – made the translation of that question – are you American or un-American – possible.

Dixon called *The Clansman* "An Historical Romance" and its predecessor, *The Leopard's Spots* (1902), a "Romance of the White Man's Burden – 1865–1900." Ellen Glasgow, in contrast, thought of herself and was thought of by others as a Realist. She characterized her early Virginia novels as turning away from the "historical pageant" with which "American fiction entertained itself" in "the first decade of the Twentieth century" and "to the people who had really lived and loved and hated and died under all the literary brocade of the period." Under the "costume," she found the "character of a civilization." And it was for this discovery, this move from historical romance to Realism that she was praised. She conveys the impression of "real life," a reviewer said of *The Battle-Ground* (1902); "among the many novels dealing with the period of the Civil War," this one is "something new."

Indeed, the question of the "new" was Glasgow's real subject in all the early Virginia novels. Although *The Battle-Ground* takes place before and during the war, it is fundamentally about the war's role in the making of the "New South." And, although we have already seen that part of what she herself thought of as new in *The Voice of the People* (mulattoes sitting next to governors in railroad cars) was about to become old, it was not the mulatto but the governor on whom Glasgow's attention was focused. It is Nick Burr, the son of a poor white peanut farmer who represents what she calls "the intrusion of the hopelessly modern into the helplessly past," and it is the sons and daughters of Virginia's first families (especially Eugenia Battle, with whom Nick falls in love) who represent the past into which Nick is striving, not altogether successfully, to intrude. For even though he is elected Governor, he cannot win Eugenia, who, at the novel's emotional climax, realizes that "the gigantic gulf between classes" cannot, after all, be bridged. Glasgow's comparative indifference to race is thus accompanied by an increased concern with class; she is interested less in the relations between whites and blacks than in the relations between whites and whites.

Which is not to say, however, that in Glasgow's Realism the question of class displaces the question of race. For Glasgow's key word for class *is* "race." When she looks in *The Battle-Ground* beneath the "literary brocade of the period" to the "character" of the "civilization" that lies underneath, what she finds is "race": women, "shaped" from generation to generation "after the same pure and formal pattern"; men, who, even when they appear first as "half-starved" boys with "white, pinched" faces and Huck Finn-like bundles swinging from sticks over their shoulders, are immediately recognizable as "gentlemen". Thus (in *Voice*) recognizing the irreducibility of the difference between her and Nick, Eugenia's response is to seek "the shelter of the race – to cling more closely to that unswerving instinct which had united individual to individual and generation to generation." The difference between classes is here understood as a difference between races, or rather – since Nick, as the free Negro Uncle Ish puts it, is one of "dese yer new come folks es hev des' sprouted outer de dut" – as the difference between those who have a racial identity and those who, unconnected to previous generations, do not.

From this perspective, having reimagined people who belong to the wrong class as people who belong to no race, Glasgow's project in *Voice* is to find (that is, create) a racial identity for them. And this creation is, in a deep sense, political. For where Eugenia Battle finds eventual happiness in becoming "what each woman of her race had been before her – a mother from her birth" (finds happiness, in other words, not only in racial identity but in becoming herself the vessel of racial transmission and so, since race is transmission, the principle of racial identity), Nick finds his in party affiliation: "'He was born a Democrat, he lives a Democrat, he will die a Democrat,'" proclaims one of the speakers at the convention that nominates him for Governor. The difference between being born a Battle and born a Democrat is real but not necessarily essential. Nick had realized early on that becoming a lawyer instead of (like his father) a peanut farmer would not in itself enable him to transcend his class; it is instead his passionate identification with the revolutionary fathers of Virginia – Henry, Madison, and above all Jefferson – that makes it possible for him to "rise above his work." Hence despite his sympathy for poor white farmers and despite even his unwillingness to eliminate Negro suffrage, he disdains both Populists and Republicans, remaining true to the "Virginia Democracy." For even though it contains men like Nick – men, in effect, of no race – a "composite photograph" of that Democracy would nevertheless present "a countenance that was unerringly Anglo-Saxon." At the Democratic convention, then, "the steadfast qualities of the race" may be invoked not to distinguish between Eugenia's family and Nick's lack of one but to suggest a level of racial identity at which that distinction will disappear, to suggest, in effect, the technology by which a man (through his family) of no race might come to belong (through his politics) to the white race.

This was something new in American literature. Before the war, Nick Burr's father had been an overseer, and both the overseer and the overseer's son are highly charged figures of social ambition in the fiction of Reconstruction. In Thomas Nelson Page's *Red Rock* (1898), for example, the overseer cheats his employer out of a plantation, and his son, derisively referring to the displaced "aristocrats" as "lords" and "ladies," nevertheless attempts to marry one. "De overseer is in de gret house, and de gent'man's in de blacksmiff shop," complains a faithful old "servant." *Red Rock* imagines Reconstruction as the revolt of lower-class whites and it ends with the defeat of their ambitions and the restoration of the lords and ladies to the great houses, aided and abetted by those blacks who are assigned by Page the task of policing the line between the "quality" and the "trash." *Voice* is enough like *Red Rock* that *its* overseer's son also tries and fails to marry quality but so much unlike *Red Rock* that he succeeds in becoming Governor. The point of *Red Rock* is to insist on "pride of family"; it is uninterested in race and interested in blacks only insofar as "quality-niggers" testify to the quality of the families they belong to. The point of *Voice*, however, is to problematize pride of family, and, although blacks play even less of a role here than in *Red Rock*, they are nonetheless essential to the novel's racial project, which is, detaching the slaves from their masters, to replace family with color.

Racial identity is thus a way of managing class difference, since race, however counter-intuitively, turns out in *Voice* to be a more flexible category than class. There are two reasons this seems counterintuitive: first because racial categories – rooted in biology – seem a lot less flexible than essentially social categories like class; second because poor whites like Nick Burr already are "Anglo-Saxon" – what does it mean for Nick to *become* Anglo-Saxon? But we have already seen (in *The Clansman*) how the transfer of racial identity from skin to soul loosened up the requirements of biology, and in *Voice* the transformation of different families into one race involves a similar replacement of "blood" by spirit: Nick's descent from Jefferson and Madison (instead of from his father) is understood as a kind of "Apostolic Succession." And Glasgow's usual scene in the ordinary southern railroad car of the "new era" suggests the conditions under which one might be imagined to achieve Anglo-Saxonness. "New come folks" in the "new era" require "new negroes." The "new negro" is a black man not a slave and in the presence of the black man the raceless son of a peanut farmer can emerge out of the dirt as a white man. So "new come folks" need "new negroes" to make the "new come folks" "Anglo-Saxons." Class mobility depends on racial identity.

The way the African-American writer Charles Chesnutt puts this point is by imagining a world in which the term "white man" is declared "synonymous" with the term "gentleman." So, although *The Marrow of Tradition*'s (1901) Captain MacBane is, like Nick Burr, the son of an overseer, "the abolition of slavery" (which, Chesnutt says, had "opened the door of opportunity" "even more" to "the poor-white class . . . than to the slaves") has made him equal (in whiteness and hence in gentility) to the son of his former employer. But where *Red Rock* laments the *déclassement* of upper-class whites and where *The Voice of the People* (nervously) celebrates the rise of lower-class whites, *The Marrow of Tradition* is disturbed by the fate of middle-class blacks. Chesnutt's hero is a black doctor raised to be a gentleman despite the fact that his grandfather had been a slave and, of course, no profession, at least since James's *Washington Square*, has been as central to the American legitimation of class ambition as the medical one (its distinctive combination of selflessness and profitability appears to be irresistible). But when the train on which Dr. Miller and his white colleague have been traveling gets below Richmond, the new rules of rail travel interrupt their conversation, reminding "the two doctors" of the differences between them and reminding the black one in particular that "his people" are not the other members of the American Medical Association. They are instead the "noisy, loquacious, happy, dirty, and malodorous" "negroes" with whom he gets to share the "Colored" car. The "White" car rescues the overseer's son from his people; the "Colored" car returns the black doctor to his.

And poor whites are not the only "new come folks" who benefit from the replacement of slavery with Jim Crow. "In 1865," Faulkner's Jason Compson would joke, "Abe Lincoln freed the niggers from the Compsons. In 1933, Jason Compson freed the Compsons from the niggers." Glasgow's *The Battle-Ground* anticipates Jason's joke and goes it one better, eliminating the seventy-year gap between emancipations, imagining that the war freed slaveholders as well as slaves. For slaveholders in *The Battle-Ground* are like slaves; the pampered men, cut off from the reality of "work," develop a "childlike trust" in their property that mimics the "childish" psychology of that property; their wives, on the other hand, are exhausted by slavery, "grown older than [their] years" caring for "the souls and bodies of the black people that had been given into [their] hands." Glasgow's heroine demands of her hero that he become a "man," a demand that the outbreak of the war makes it partly possible for him to meet and that the South's defeat makes totally possible, since it is only in defeat that what a reviewer in *The Bookman* called the "lords of the soil" can be required to engage in what Glasgow called "honest work."

Heading home to Virginia accompanied by the still faithful black man who had been his slave, Dan Montjoy sets out to earn himself a dinner by splitting logs. "Go 'way, Marse Dan," his old slave protests "in disgust":

"Gimme dat ar axe en set right down and wait twel supper. You're jest' es white es a sheet dis minute."

"I've got to begin some day," Dan returned, as the axe swung back across his shoulder. "I'll pay for my supper, and you'll pay for yours, that's fair isn't it? – for you're a free man now."

If Dan Montjoy is as white as a sheet at the moment of his (and his slave's) entrance into the "free" world, his color (and even the conventional simile by which it is described) have a new significance in that world. The emancipation of blacks gives rich as well as poor the chance to become white; indeed, remembering a young Dan who vowed to free the slaves even if he had "to fight to do it," *The Battle-Ground* seems to suggest that *both* sides fought the war in order to end slavery. *The Bookman*'s reviewer praised Glasgow for her depiction of the "relationship" between "the lords of the soil and the representatives of the childlike race" but, in his phrasing, missed her point. Glasgow's racial achievement consists not in her representation of the relations between masters and slaves in the old South but in her representation of the transformation of those relations in the new South, the transformation of masters and slaves into whites and blacks.

The "typical progressive reformer rode to power in the South on a disfranchising or white supremacy movement," C. Vann Woodward wrote in *The Strange Career of Jim Crow*. Woodward himself regarded racism as the "blind spot" of Progressivism but he cited others who conceived it as Progressivism's "very foundation"; Edgar Gardner Murphy, one of the most articulate and cultured of Southern progressives, thought of "'the conscious unity of race' as 'the broader ground of the new democracy,' and believed that . . . it was 'better as a basis of democratic reorganization than the distinctions of wealth, of trade, of property, of family, or class.'" (In contrast to Murphy, one could cite Du Bois, who, insisting on equality between the races, insisted also on "the rule of inequality" between individuals: some are "fitted to know and some to dig," he reminded black educators.) Indeed, racism in Glasgow, and even more strikingly in Dixon, is as hostile to economic inequality as it is to racial equality. *Uncle Tom's Cabin*'s Simon Legree reappears in *The Leopard's Spots* first as a born-again scalawag, the leader, amazingly, of "the Black Man's Party," and, when that party is defeated, he flees to New York, where "he opened an office on Wall Street, bought a seat on the Stock Exchange, and became one of the most daring and successful of a group of robbers who preyed on the industries of the new nation." Not content merely with turning slaveholders into scalawags, Dixon turns them both into speculators, thus transforming the old demon of abolitionist New England into the new demon of Progressive New England. What the two demons have in common is indifference to race and love of slavery; the old Legree bought "handsome negro girl(s)" in the New Orleans slave market; the new Legree "selects his victims" from "the innocent girls" in his mills.

And just as Legree's indifference to the difference between blacks and whites emerges as an eagerness to exploit class differences, racism's alertness to the difference between blacks and whites emerges as an egalitarian hostility to class difference. Indeed, Dixon imagines racism in itself as the destruction of class difference. Defining itself by its difference from blacks, the "white race" is "fused into a homogeneous mass of love, sympathy, hate, and revenge. The rich and the poor, the learned and the ignorant, the banker and the blacksmith, the great and the small, they were all one now." The lynch mob embodies the egalitarianism of the New South and thus answers both of the "two great questions" that Dixon saw as "shadow[s] over the future of the American people": the conflict between "Labor and Capital" and the even more "dangerous" conflict between "the African and the Anglo-Saxon race." Enforcing difference between the races, the lynch mob eliminates difference within the races.

We have seen the crucial role played by racism in the establishment of a plausibly American identity (Roosevelt's "American race"); the difference between whites and blacks could be understood as replacing the difference between Northerners and Southerners, indeed as replacing the differences between native-born Americans and newly-arrived "aliens"; Dixon was almost as eager to assimilate immigrants as he was to segregate blacks. We have also seen racism's contribution to the reimagining of class difference: Glasgow's Governor Burr dies "for a damned brute" whom he is defending *against* a lynch mob but the translation of a peanut farmer's son into a governor is made possible only by the subsumption of them both into the Anglo-Saxon "Democracy." The fusion of the white race that makes Dixon's lynch mob is the same fusion that makes Nick Governor; it is no accident that when he looks into the mob he sees the faces of boys "he had played with in childhood," "features that were as familiar as his own." And, finally, his very commitment to defending "the Law" whose "guardian" he is marks the transubstantiation of racism into the political apparatus of Progressive Americanism. Racism is here a modernizing force, replacing the old organic ties of family and region with the bureaucratic obligations of party and state. Thus Dixon's conservatives think of politics as a "dirty" business and urge their children to stay out of it. But the children, insisting that "the people of the South had to go into politics . . . on account of the enfranchisement of the Negro," argue that "the State is now the only organ through which the whole people can search for righteousness."

Requiring white men to enter the service of the state, the enfranchisement of blacks completes in Dixon the transformation of a slave-holding sectionalism into a racist nationalism; the aristocratic clan becomes the egalitarian Klan. And this nationalizing racism would quickly find a more national expression – in Griffith's *The Birth of a Nation* (1915), in the segregation of the Federal bureaucracy following Woodrow Wilson's election in 1912 (Wilson sat next to Dixon in Herbert Baxter Adams's political science seminar at Johns Hopkins) and, soonest of all, in Herbert Croly's "New Nationalist" manifesto *The Promise of American Life* (1909). Discussing the relation between the "people" and the "nation," Croly insists on the tension between "popular Sovereignty" and "national Sovereignty"; we can say that "the people are Sovereign; but who and what are the people?" If we define the people as the "living people of today," we commit ourselves to the principle of "majority rule" and so, Croly thinks, to "a piece of machinery which is extremely liable to get out of order." For majority rule is really only "one means" (and an often "arbitrary and dangerous" one") to the "extremely difficult, remote and complicated end" of American "national" life. In order, then, to turn "popular Sovereignty" into "national Sovereignty," we should recognize (following Bismarck, whom he quotes) that "the true people" are not the "living people of today" and we should replace the "living people of today" with the "invisible multitude of spirits" who constitute "the nation of yesterday and tomorrow, organized for its national historical mission." Croly's "invisible multitude" mainstreams Dixon's "invisible empire." The technology of race could turn immigrants into Americans and the son of a white-trash peanut farmer into "the voice of the people." In *The Promise of American Life*, it turns the people into a nation; the clan that became the Klan now becomes the State.

THE BEARER OF COLORS

The Red Badge of Courage (1895) opens, even more directly than *Maggie*, with a rendering visible – "The cold passed reluctantly from the earth, and the retiring fogs revealed an army stretched out on the hills, resting" – and it may be understood as committed to making the hitherto unrepresentable realities of war available as *Maggie* had made visible the slums. "It seems as if the actual sight of a battle has some dynamic quality in it which overwhelms and crushes the literary faculty in the observer," wrote Harold Frederic in a brilliant review of *The Red Badge*. Just as the "real motion" of horses had gone unseen until Eadweard Muybridge, so real battles had been obscured by "conventional account(s) of what happened" (determined not by what the "observer" "really saw" but by what "all his reading ha[d] taught him he must have seen"), until the "photographic revelation" of *The Red Badge*. "War is the test-case for realistic fiction," Harry Levin would write some seventy years later, "No other subject can be so obscured by the ivy of tradition, the crystallization of legend, the conventions of epic and romance." Frederic's review inaugurated a tradition of reading *The Red Badge* as an exemplar of demystifying Realism, stripping away convention to make visible what is really there.

But Frederic also noted what seemed anomalous about *The Red Badge* as well: most "commentators" had taken it "for granted that the writer of the *Red Badge* must have seen real warfare," a supposition that Frederic regarded as "wholly fallacious" not because he had better biographical information (Frederic and Crane did not meet and become friends until 1897) but because he really did think of the "actual sight" of a battle as overwhelming and crushing "the literary faculty in the observer." In fact, according to Frederic, it was only because Crane had *not* (as he correctly inferred) ever seen a battle that he was able to "put the reality into type." And although this analysis may make the analogy to Muybridge and "his instantaneous camera" look a little odd (after all, what is the appeal of photography if not an appeal to what we actually see), it actually makes it more powerful since it was the "instantaneous camera," not Muybridge himself, that "saw" (or that recorded for Muybridge to see) the motion of the horse galloping. It is the "imaginative work" of a writer who has "never seen a gun fired in anger" that produces the "photographic revelation" of *The Red Badge*. Rather than piercing or discarding the literary conventions that make war a "test-case for realism," *The Red Badge*, on this account, is itself a product of those conventions, made possible not by the personal experience of war but by the photographic technology of the literary imagination.

Thus *The Red Badge* itself tends to transform the Realistic demystifying of war into an equally Realistic re-mystifying. Henry Fleming is "disappointed" when, having responded to newspaper reports of "a Greeklike struggle" and enlisted, he cannot get his mother to make the appropriate Greeklike remarks about "returning with his shield or on it." But while it is true that she keeps on "doggedly peeling potatoes" and promising to mend his socks, she does eventually produce a country equivalent of the Spartan mother's exhortation:

"If so be a time comes when yeh have to be kilt or do a mean thing, why, Henry, don't think of anything 'cept what's right, because there's many a woman has to bear up 'ginst such things these times, and the Lord'll take keer of us all." Realism here consists in a translation not a repudiation of mythology, and the Realistic interest in producing visibility takes the form of an injunction against inappropriate behavior: "Jest think as if I was a-watchin yeh," Henry's mother urges him. "If yeh keep that in yer mind allus, I guess yeh'll about come out right." If Crane's photographic revelation is made possible by the photographer's failure to see an actual battle, it begins to look as if the battle itself is only made possible by the participants' sense that they are indeed being watched by what will turn out to be a series of instantaneous cameras.

For it is not only the mother's gaze that is evoked in connection with the project of Realist representation, it is also the "observant regiment's" (which is why Henry is "drilled and drilled and reviewed, and drilled and drilled and reviewed"), and, more generally, society's (as embodied, for example, in the "simple questions of the tattered man," asserting a "society that probes pitilessly at secrets until all is apparent"). And, finally, it is Henry's own, as he stands "persistently before his vision," examining himself in an act of introspection that, following Frederic's analogy, turns the camera into an instrument of psychological research.

If, then, *The Red Badge* is like *Maggie* in its commitment to making things visible, it differs from *Maggie* in its sense of the uses to which the production of visibility may be put. The Realism of the slums involves the management of a social problem and the production of a social difference between observers and observed; its concerns are seeing and being seen by "the other half." In *The Red Badge*, however, one is oneself the "unknown quantity," which is to say that one is oneself the social problem. Riis's desire to add to the "information" that "has been accumulating" rapidly on the subject of the tenements is replaced by Henry's desire to "accumulate information of himself." From this standpoint, to characterize Realism's camera as an instrument of psychological research may make no sense, as it would make no sense to think of Riis's slum photographs as psychological portraits; instead of characterizing Henry as the object of psychological interest, we should think of him as the object of something like an internalized sociology. Except that "internalized" is not quite right either; for while the object of the Realist's gaze in *The Red Badge* is internal in the sense that Henry wants to accumulate information of himself (not "the other half"), it is at the same time external: Henry is first "forced to admit that as far as war was concerned he knew nothing of himself," and then forced to acknowledge that the only way he will learn about himself will be "to go into the blaze, and then figuratively to watch his legs to discover their merits and faults."

"Figuratively" here is a psychological concession, a step back from the photographer's claim that "merits" and "faults" can be discovered by watching legs. Just as war can be understood to provide a test-case for Realism, so it can be understood as a test for the psychological subject who may be identified as Realism's central character. Henry's question about himself – will I or will I not run – may be understood to anticipate what has certainly been a question for many readers of *The Red Badge* – is Henry really a coward or a hero? For these readers, the question about whether Henry will run is a question about his character that is not answered by watching his legs (hence the "figuratively"); they have been concerned instead with the motives presumed to underlie the movements of those legs. The text of *The Red Badge*, however, makes those motives as literally superficial (as easily visible) as the actions themselves. Thus the head wound that is "the red badge" is not a sign of courage but the cause of it. It is less a visible mark of invisible character than a visible motive of actions which are rendered as if they themselves are above all moving "bits of color": "waving blue lines" encountering a "grey obstruction," the "youth" carrying the "red and white" flag into battle, helping to seize the "red brilliancy" of the enemy flag, making himself literally into "the bearer of the colors." Just as (translating the Spartan mother into Henry's mother) Crane commits Realism not to exposing the "conventions" of heroism but to updating them, so (turning the body into something like a flag) he transforms the truth about one's character into the appearance of one's body: "He saw that he was good." Making character visible, *The Red Badge* makes it superficial, and makes the debate over Henry's deeper motives irrelevant.

William James's *Principles of Psychology* (1890) had explicated at least one theory according to which internal psychological states (like fear) might be more plausibly understood as external "bodily" ones. "Our natural way of thinking" about the emotions, James wrote, is "that the mental perception of some fact excites the mental affection called the emotion, and that this latter state of mind gives rise to the bodily expression"; "Common-sense says . . . we meet a bear, are frightened and run." According to James, however, common sense was mistaken; we do not run because we feel afraid, we feel afraid because we run: "we feel sorry because we cry, angry because we strike, afraid because we tremble." When Henry's legs run, then, they should be understood as producing rather than expressing his emotions. Identifying fear as the expression rather than the cause of a "bodily state," James imagined for motives an ontology that met the Realist requirement of visibility: photographs are pictures of bodies, Realism can make motives visible because psychology has made them physiological. In James and in Crane, character is on the outside; the red badge is a wound because wounds, removing the outside of the body to reveal the inside, turn everything into the outside.

But the point for Crane is not simply that Realism finds truth in surfaces instead of depths (what the body does rather than what it expresses), for the "photographic revelation" requires not only that character be visible but that it be seen, and the fact of observation makes a material contribution to the character of what will be observed. "Jest think as if I was a-watchin yeh": to imagine yourself observed by your mother is to imagine your behavior determined as well as observed, determined by being observed. And "drilled and drilled and reviewed" mobilizes the structure of maternal authority on behalf of military discipline; it is the imagination of being observed by his critical officers that will provoke Henry's almost suicidal acts of courage – "it was his idea, vaguely formulated, that his corpse would be for those eyes a great and salt reproach." Henry's "idea" takes the form not only of his dead body but of his dead body observed; not only is his character visible, it gets to be the character it is only by being seen.

Hence the question of what Henry did when his legs ran can be answered only by an appeal to what Henry was seen to do when his legs ran. For if the truth about Henry does not consist in what he feels irrespective of what his legs do (what he is on the inside), it does not consist either in what his legs do irrespective of what they are seen to do – they must be "watched." So the question about Henry does not get answered until, hearing the sounds of his victorious regiment, he "cringe(s) as if discovered in a crime." It is the watching that determines what one's legs have done; the discovery (not the feeling or the physiology) is constitutive because the character of the action cannot be determined without reference to the assessment of it implicit in the actions of others – if everybody else runs, it is "strategy"; since nobody else ran, it is cowardice. Cowardice (or bravery) consists neither in what one feels nor in what one does but in what one can be seen to do and so instructed to feel.

That is why Henry's response to the discovery is a retreat from the sounds and sight of the regiment into a "Nature" so quiet and dark that nothing will "bring men to look at him." But when, having moved "from obscurity into promises of greater obscurity," he arrives at the threshold of a "chapel" to "the religion of peace," he is stopped, "horror-stricken," by what Crane calls "the sight of a thing." The thing is a dead Union soldier and the horror might be understood exclusively as a response to the body's advanced state of decay ("Over the grey skin of the face ran little ants") if Crane did not insist in the next sentence that it is the thing's sight that makes the sight of the thing horrible – "He was being looked at by a dead man . . ." The attempt to escape the regiment's vision turns into a particularly horrifying encounter with vision, horrifying precisely because, in the "long look" "exchanged" by "the dead man and the living man," it becomes obvious that no escape is possible. And the reason that no escape is possible, the reason that Fleming's own "power of vigilance" cannot "defend" him against the power of "a society that probes pitilessly at secrets until all is apparent," is, of course, that the novel makes Henry himself into the source as well as the object of vigilance. The dead soldier can reproach Henry because the dead soldier is himself one of several dead Henrys who will populate Henry's imagination, who, receiving "laurels from tradition," will be for the eyes of others "a great and salt reproach." By way, then, of the dead soldier's "liquid-looking eyes" reproaching Henry, Henry's eyes and the eyes of those for whom *his* "dead body" will be a "salt reproach" become identical. The look exchanged by the dead man and the living one is thus a look of introspection, but, inasmuch as it picks up and extends the maternal and regimental looks, it is also a social and even socializing look.

What is the interest of Realism? We saw in the project of making the slums visible an interest in social control and an interest in seeing that control threatened. We saw also, in the image of Maggie and Jimmie not quite exchanging looks with their sleeping mother, an interest that, although saturated with social power, derives its own power from its difference from any particular social project, or at least from the two social projects it has itself evoked. Realism here cannot be identified with the desire to control the slums (by containing or reforming them) or with the desire to see them erupt in anarchic or revolutionary violence; it fascinates by identifying itself both with the assertion of power and with its violation. It makes the fear of being looked at part of the pleasure of looking, and it enforces with a certain political luridness the requirement that we occupy only one and not both of these positions, that we be middle-class controlling subjects about, perhaps, to become the objects of lower-class violence. (Perhaps we should read *Maggie* as a training manual for middle-class residents of the twenty-first-century city, a set of instructions on how – when walking the streets of New York, Chicago, or Baltimore – to experience the appropriate oscillations between confidence and nervousness, sympathy and disgust, pity and fear.)

The long look exchanged by Henry Fleming and the dead soldier suggests that in *The Red Badge* the situation is somewhat different, and their common identity as Union soldiers suggests what at least one component of that difference is. What is at issue in texts like *How the Other Half Lives, A Daughter of the Tenements,* and *Maggie* is always, at some level, the question of the difference between the two halves, between seeing and being seen. In *The Red Badge*, however, the two halves are turned from identities into functions and the experience of performing them both – simultaneously seeing and being seen – is made normal and normalizing in the experience of a visual self-consciousness, seeing oneself. By "normalizing" here (as by "socializing" above), I mean to suggest that insofar as introspection is here a kind of introjection – of the maternal and regimental gazes – it produces an inevitable, because structural, identification with the mother and the regiment; to see yourself you must become the person who can see you. The interest of Realism on this account is in the production of subject/objects like Henry Fleming, that is, Realism itself is understood as a part in the technology (alongside the family and the army) for producing the readers it represents, for producing them by representing them. Henry's desire "to go close" to the battle "and see it produce corpses" (a desire expressed immediately after his encounter with the dead soldier) should thus be understood as the desire of the Realist reader to participate in the production of Realist readers.

From this perspective, against the readings of *The Red Badge* that see it in opposition to "ideological" accounts of the war – as one critic once put it, "Reading *The Red Badge* relieves us of our ideology and, to the extent that this is ever possible, replaces it with raw experience" – we should read it as playing a crucial role in the production of our ideology precisely by organizing experiences that are above all real insofar as they are not raw. If Crane disdains the rhetoric of the old soldier, the politician's waving of the bloody flag, and the historian's appeal to the "role the war played in the formation of national character," it is only because, in Crane, it is literature, rather than the war or even the modern army prefigured in the war, that provides the exemplary instance of ideological production.

We have seen in chapter 1 how the army provided a model of organization for the utopian society of Edward Bellamy's *Looking Backward*. But the attraction of the military model was not entirely formal; "The army of industry," Dr. Leete tells Julian, "is an army not alone by virtue of its perfect organization, but by reason also of the ardor of self-devotion which animates its members." In the industrial army, honor replaces money as the object of ambition, and, indeed, the primary point of the army's organization is to encourage the pursuit of honor. The army is divided into three grades which are in turn subdivided into classes within which there are in turn "many minor distinctions of standing." Promotion is accompanied by rewards which range from the relatively material ("special privileges and immunities in the way of discipline") to the purely honorific: every member of the army wears a "metallic badge" and promotion from one grade to the next is accompanied by transformation of the

badge – from "iron" to "silver" to "gilt." The industrial army's goal is to guarantee that "no form of merit shall wholly fail of recognition" and its technology
for achieving this is a visible "ranking system" that has "the effect of keeping
constantly before every man's mind the great desirability of attaining the grade
next above his own." Thus the "organization" is, above all, an organization of
"incitements"; it is a kind of advertisement for itself and at the same time a
mechanism by which each member of the organization can become himself or
herself. The "metallic badge" of rank is "so small that you might not see it
unless you knew where to look," but, in the intensity of their "self-devotion,"
the inhabitants of the twentieth century can be counted on to know where to
look.

  We have also seen, earlier in this chapter, how the war could be understood
as having made possible the invention of white men and the creation of an
American "state," indeed how the replacement of slavery by Jim Crow racism
could be understood as having made Americans American by making them
white. The Thirteenth Amendment (1865) had outlawed "slavery and involuntary servitude" and, in their brief on behalf of Plessy before the Louisiana
Supreme Court, Albion Tourgee and James Walker had argued that Jim Crow
laws violated the Amendment because they "imposed and perpetuated" "a
badge of servitude." But the court in *Plessy* denied that "the enforced separation of the two races stamps the colored race with a badge of inferiority." The
point of Jim Crow was to make a badge out of color; the refinements in *Plessy*
and in texts like *The Clansman* (transferring race from skin to soul) or *The Voice
of the People* (creating race out of class) made racial identity itself a badge – of
American democracy.

  "He wished that he, too, had a wound, a red badge of courage." The point of
wishing for a wound is wishing for a visible mark of courage, a mark that should
be understood to constitute rather than reflect courage. Both the army and the
war play important roles in *The Red Badge*: the imagined looks in his officers'
eyes are the "incitements" to Henry's increasingly courageous acts of "self-
devotion"; the differences between the North and the South are as irrelevant
to *The Red Badge* as they would be to *The Clansman* and the emergence of a
generalized "man" as hero at *The Red Badge*'s end was in no sense inimical
to the racist desire to see the war as a victory for both the North and the
South. But it is Realism rather than the army or the war that finally makes
a man out of the "youth" who becomes a man by "seeing" himself "truly,"
becoming a color and then becoming the colors. Indeed, racism itself must
be understood as deeply compatible with the Realist production of visibility,
not only in Chopin's insistence on the color of people's skins but especially in
the subsequent project of colorizing their souls: the black or white soul makes

your race as visible to a sociologized introspection as the red badge does your character. Realism turns body, mind, and soul into the exposed surface of the wound. Thus the managerial work of encouraging production by distributing the metallic badges of the industrial army and the political work of creating American citizenship by affixing to people's skins the racial badge of servitude are subsumed in Realism by the literary work of making men men by making them badges, making them visible by making them see themselves.

3

❦

THE CONTRACTED HEART

"They all knew each other and felt like one large family," Kate Chopin writes of the "society of Creoles" Edna Pontellier marries into in *The Awakening* (1899). Edna is not quite a member of this family and is in some degree scandalized by its behavior, which is to say, by the general "absence of prudery" that characterizes Creole conversation and by the particular profusion of "intimate detail" in the "harrowing story" of the "mother woman," Madame Ratignolle's *"accouchements."* When a sexually explicit book makes the rounds of the *pension*, she is "moved to read [it] in secret and in solitude, though none of the others had done so" and when Madame Ratignolle tells about the *accouchements*, she blushes. But Edna's blush does not exactly express a prudery about sex, any more than her desire to read the novel in private expresses disapproval of it. It is to the public – the familial – discussion of such topics that she objects, and this on grounds that *The Awakening* only gradually makes clear.

For "solitude" is not only the condition in which Edna reads, it is the name she gives to a piece of piano music she particularly likes, a piece that evokes in her imagination the figure of a naked man "standing beside a desolate rock on the seashore . . . His attitude was one of hopeless resignation as he looked toward a distant bird winging its flight away from him." And where solitude is identified with the inability to get what you want, family (the opposite of solitude) is identified with the inability to want in the first place. Despite the sexual candor of their wives, Creole husbands, Chopin writes, are "never jealous"; "The right hand jealous of the left! The heart jealous of the soul!" The family is understood here as a single body, an understanding that makes jealousy impossible because it makes difference (hence solitude) and hence desire impossible. In Chopin's extraordinary short story, "A Pair of Silk Stockings," a woman embarking on an utterly unanticipated and unwise shopping spree finds herself gazing intently at her own legs: "Her foot and ankle looked very pretty. She could not realize that they belonged to her and were a part of herself." In this story, desire (at least the desire to buy) is connected with the ability to think of one's own body as separate from oneself; in *The Awakening*, the failure of desire is connected with the inability to think even of one's family (one's husband, one's children) as separate from oneself.

Indeed, it is the existence of children and especially the facts of child-birth that constitute the great threat to the powerful desires mobilized in *The Awakening*. Assisting, towards the end of the novel, at another of Madame Ratignolle's *accouchements*, Edna remembers the birth of her own children, "the heavy odor of chloroform, a stupor which had deadened sensation, an awak-ening to find a little new life to which she had given being." What makes this awakening a "scene of torture" is not so much the pain; rather, "revolting against the ways of Nature," Edna revolts against the complicity between two phenomena that she has imagined to be opposed – sexual desire and families. "The trouble," as Dr. Mandelet diagnoses it, "is . . . that youth is given up to illusions. It seems to be a provision of Nature; a decoy to secure mothers for the race." The illusion is that sexual desire represents an escape from the family; the truth is that it is the means by which the family is itself produced. Sex makes families; desire gives birth to its own death.

There is an important sense, then, in which the narrative of *The Awakening* is marked by Edna's inability to escape that death, to escape her own ability to get what she wants. She wants to be an artist and within weeks a New Orleans dealer is begging for her paintings; she wants to escape the tedium of child care and the children's grandmother immediately hustles them off to her house in the country; she wants, above all, to be free of her husband and no sooner is the desire to live on her own expressed than she is established in the little "pigeon-house" which "at once assumed the intimate character of a home." If, as many readers have felt, there is a certain fairy-tale quality to *The Awakening*, it consists primarily in Edna's magical ability to make her wishes come true. But, at the same time, it is just that ability that makes the promise of wishes fulfilled into the threat of desires destroyed. For the relation between desires and their satisfaction mirrors in *The Awakening* the relation between sexual passion and the family; the latter is understood as both the enemy of and the result of the former.

It is for this reason that unrequited passion is the privileged emotional state of *The Awakening*. "Never more [will] the cries of unsatisfied love be absent from me," Walt Whitman had written in "Out of the Cradle Endlessly Rocking," a text remembered almost as explicitly by the end of *The Awakening* (the "voice of the sea is seductive, never ceasing, whispering, clamoring, murmuring") as its own end remembers "The Raven." Chopin describes Edna's romantic life until her marriage as a series of infatuations – with a "sad-eyed cavalry officer," an "engaged young man," and a "great tragedian." The "hopelessness" of all these relations is their essential element, coloring the last especially "with the lofty tones of a great passion" and thus contributing to Edna's arrival in "the world of reality" as the wife of Léonce Pontellier. For it is "in the midst of her secret great passion" that she meets and marries Léonce, and the world of marital "reality" can thus be understood to consist in a double portion of unsatisfied love, Edna's unrequited passion for the tragedian mirrored by Léonce's unrequited passion for her.

But infatuations fade: "it was not long before the tragedian had gone to join the cavalry officer and the engaged young man and a few others," and, experiencing "anew" (when she falls in love with Robert) the "symptoms" "which she had felt incipiently as a child, as a girl in her earliest teens, and later as a young woman," Edna experiences also the transience of those symptoms: walking down to the beach, she has already begun to anticipate the day on which the thought of Robert will "melt out of her existence" just as the cavalry officer had once "melted . . . out of her existence." "Out of the Cradle" celebrates the mocking-bird "singing uselessly, uselessly" in his attempt to bring back the "she-bird"; "uselessly" guarantees "never more" – because the song will not bring back what has been lost, the desire for what has been lost will live forever. But in *The Awakening* even unsatisfied desires die; of Edna on the verge of suicide, Chopin says, "There was no one thing in the world that she desired," imagining that suicide not as a consequence of Edna's inability to get what she wants but of her inability to keep on wanting.

The modern woman, complained Charlotte Perkins Gilman in *Women and Economics* (1898), had been made into a "priestess of the temple of consumption"; "forbidden to make, but encouraged to take," she had been rendered a parasite, deprived of "free productive expression." But in the wake of a series of economic depressions and recessions attributed almost universally to "over-production" (to the failure, that is, of the public's desire), the "consuming female" could seem as essential as Gilman thought her marginal. (Indeed, even in *Women and Economics*, the transformation of women into producers is imagined simultaneously as an extension of consumption. The housewife and "amateur" mother who leaves the home to produce becomes at the same time a consumer – not only of restaurant food and professional cleaners but of what Gilman herself begins by deploring, "motherhood as a business, a form of commercial exchange.") From this standpoint, Edna's suicide looks like a confession of her inability to live up to the ideal of consumption.

There is also a way, however, in which the failure of one's desire for things and people need not be understood as exhausting all desire's possibilities. When Edna says to Dr. Mandelet, "I don't want anything but my own way," she describes a more abstract and potentially more powerful version of her desires – a desire that can survive both the presence and the absence of any desirable things. Listening to Madamoiselle Reisz play Chopin, Edna is described as waiting "in vain" for the "pictures of solitude, of hope, of longing" that the music usually evoked in her imagination. Instead of pictures of the passions, the music evokes this time "the very passions themselves," passions which lash her "soul" "as the waves daily beat upon her splendid body." The experience of desire is here unaccompanied either by an image of the desiring subject (say, the naked man on the seashore) or of a desired object (say, Robert). And the assertion that the passions are to Edna's soul what the sea is to her body suggests that her suicide may best be understood neither as the repudiation of a society in which one cannot have all the things one wants nor as an escape from a society in which one cannot want all the things one can have but as an encounter with wanting itself.

When the boy in "Out of the Cradle" asks the sea for the "word" ("final, superior to all") that will not only name what has been lost (and is thus desired) but will also, in naming it, produce it (that is, by naming it bring it back), the sea says "Death." Death is the metaphysically onomatopoetic word that is what it means, but what death means is loss; the one word that is not useless (that will satisfy love) is the word that – in being what it means – is nothing but the loss that "awaked" the love and the process of naming in the first place. In *The Awakening*, this double function of the word "death" is assumed by Edna's body which, dying to "elude" its children, at the same time becomes a child, a "new-born creature"; the mother's desire, killed by the child, is reborn in the child. Death by water thus marks not exactly a failure of desire but a submersion in it and an idealization of it, an idealization that immortalizes desire by divorcing it both from the subject (which dies) and the object (which is death) that it seems to require.

Beginning with a woman who one day finds herself "the unexpected possessor of fifteen dollars" that she sets out to spend on much needed clothes for her children, the short story "A Pair of Silk Stockings" ends with the same woman, having spent every penny on luxuries for herself, riding home on a street car that she wishes "would never stop anywhere, but go on and on with her forever." Mrs. Sommers's desire to shop forever anticipates by several years Edna's swim into the infinite but the spirit of consumption and the attempt to take seriously the responsibilities of consumption predominate in both texts. On one account, these responsibilities involve knowing, as Mrs. Sommers begins by knowing, "the value of bargains"; "she could stand for hours making her way inch by inch toward the desired item that was selling below cost." The "exceptional" housewife, some contemporary home economists argued, "could reduce spending by hunting for bargains," and it was the responsibility of every housewife to "check unrestricted expenditure on unessentials." But other home economists disdained such "niggardliness," urged "more spending and less saving," and advised against "doing without things." On this account, the account that Mrs. Sommers ends up embodying and that Edna pushes to the limits of embodiment, the responsibility of consumption is to mobilize desire at any cost, to rescue it from indifference and satiation. From this standpoint, the end of *The Awakening* must be regarded as both a success and a failure, a success in that the ideal of consumption is preserved, a failure in that it can only be preserved in death. No one can shop forever; no body in Chopin can embody the infinite.

But Carrie Meeber's body in Dreiser's *Sister Carrie* (1900) can. The comparison of endings is illuminating here. Recent scholarship has shown that at least one version of *Sister Carrie* ended with the scene of Hurstwood's suicide in a New York flophouse, an event that Dreiser regards as the consequence of his "lack of power," which is itself a consequence of the failure of his "passion," the disappearance of "the burning desires of youth." But the published version ends with Carrie "singing and dreaming"; for her, Dreiser says, there is "neither surfeit nor content." Edna's Gulf has become Hurstwood's flophouse, Mrs. Sommers' cable car has become Carrie's rocking-chair: "In your rocking-chair, by your window, shall you dream such happiness as you may never feel."

Chopin made a brilliant short story out of the desire to shop; Dreiser, seeing in the "feminine love of finery" an absolutely generalizable principle of self-transformation, made an epic out of it. Hence the continuity between Carrie's desire for a "peculiar little tan jacket with large mother-of-pearl buttons" and her desire to get out of musical comedy and into a "serious play," one more like the Balzac (*Pere Goriot*) that her intellectual "ideal" Ames has urged her to read. "If I were you . . . I'd change," Ames says to Carrie, repeating the message of the tan jacket and reminding the reader that the desire to buy a jacket that's "all the rage" is the desire to transform oneself into the person who wears such a jacket. It is the insatiability of Carrie's appetite for such transformations that distinguishes her from Hurstwood and from Edna too.

She is distinguished from them also by her success; in contrast to them and to Gilman's "consuming female," condemned to "economic dependence," Carrie sells as well as buys. Of course, even Gilman's women sell; "women's economic profit comes through the power of sex-attraction." They sell themselves, that is what she means by calling them economically dependent. But although Carrie too sells something like herself, the consequence for her is economic independence, the entry into a market that transforms rather than repeats the sale of oneself to one's husband. Selling "sex-attraction" to thousands instead of just one, Carrie leaves the restricted economy of the marriage market for the general economy of show business.

The mark of her theatrical success, as Dreiser describes it, is the appearance of her picture in one of the "newer magazines" just beginning to pay "illustrative attention to the beauties of the stage." Such attention had only recently become technologically possible and had not yet become universally welcome. "Instantaneous photographs and newspaper enterprise have invaded the sacred precincts of private and domestic life," Samuel Warren and Louis Brandeis complained in "The Right to Privacy" (1890), calling for "some remedy for the unauthorized circulation of portraits of private persons." (Chief among the "circulating portraits" they cite is that of Marion Manola, taken "surreptitiously" "while she was playing in the Broadway Theatre, in a role which required her appearance in tights.") Previous remedies, insofar as there were any, had involved extensions of "the principle of property"; thus a British court prohibited both the reproduction and description of etchings made by Prince Albert and Queen Victoria on the grounds that they were intellectual property. Approving the decision but disapproving the grounds, Brandeis and Warren argued that the prohibition in particular of the description of the etchings made clear the irrelevance of the argument based on property. "Suppose," they wrote, "a man has a collection of gems or curiosities which he keeps private: it would hardly be contended that any person could publish a catalogue of them, and yet the articles enumerated are certainly not intellectual property in the legal sense . . ." The articles are property but they are not intellectual property and the enumeration of them is intellectual but it is not property. So what would be violated by such publication would not be the right to property but "the right to privacy." And it was this "more general" right that guaranteed the sanctity of one's "thoughts, emotions, and sensations," Carrie's "facial expression," or Marion Manola's "appearance in tights."

But the effect of "The Right to Privacy" was in this regard quite different from what its authors intended. For its authority was invoked (in dissent) in a 1902 case in support of a young woman named Abigail Roberson's "property right" in "her face" (a flour company had used her photograph in its ads) and that dissent became the basis of a 1905 decision (the first in which a right to privacy was upheld) in which the 1902 plaintiff's "property in the right to be protected against the use of her face" reappeared as the claim that the "form and features of the plaintiff are his own." The "right to privacy," Brandeis and Warren had claimed, derived not from "the principle of private property but [from] that of an inviolate personality"; by 1912, however, they could be understood by legal writers like Wilbur Larremore as having established instead that property rights were "the derivative basis of the right of privacy" and thus having successfully extended property rights to areas (like facial expressions) that Brandeis and Warren themselves thought could only be safeguarded by some prior (non-property) right. Where the unsuccessful plaintiff in Roberson had been left with nothing but what a New York judge called the "compliment" to her "beauty," it was now possible for a Missouri judge (in *Munden v Harris* [1910]) to ask why the possessor of a "peculiarity of appearance" that could be made "a matter of merchandise" should not "exercise it for his own profit?" By this new logic, one's "appearance" could be understood to have what the Missouri Court of Appeals called "value," a value invented and produced by the conjunction of new legal and reproductive technology. For the technology that made it possible to affix Abigail Roberson's photograph to an advertisement for Franklin Mills Flour created value out of what had just been beauty, and the right to privacy made personal property out of personality.

Carrie's success, then, is in selling something that it was only just becoming possible for her to own, not her labor but her "look," and it is a further refinement that this "look" is "natural," i.e. utterly unrelated to any feeling she might have or might, as an actress, seek to represent: "The mouth had the expression at times, in talking and in repose, of one who might be on the verge of tears. It was not that grief was thus ever-present. The pronunciation of certain syllables gave to her lips this peculiarity – a formation as suggestive and moving as pathos itself." The absolute arbitrariness of this sign – produced by phonemes not morphemes, physiology not psychology – suggests why Brandeis and Warren were uneasy about claiming facial expressions as property. Asserting the right of women like Abigail Roberson to their own image, the Missouri court asked, "If there is value in it, sufficient to excite the cupidity of another, why is it not the property of him who gives it value and from whom the value springs?" But Carrie has not given her face its value, that is, she has not *produced* the value her face has. What is it then that makes her face valuable? And what is it that makes its value hers?

Gilman, with her commitment to "economic production" as "the natural expression of human energy," answers these questions by denying the premise on which they are based. What naturalizing production means in Gilman's short story, "The Yellow Wallpaper" (1892), is that women *do* produce their own value and they do it by producing their own bodies. Written out of an attack of what she called "nervous prostration" and as an attack on Dr. S. Weir Mitchell's attempt to treat her hysteria with his famous "rest cure," "The Yellow Wallpaper" depicts a woman suffering simultaneously from the disease and its cure – both of which, as Gilman understands them, are effects of women's being denied "free productive expression." The "breakdown" is brought on by the birth of her child, the sign that for women "production" can be nothing more than "reproduction." And the cure, absolute rest at Mitchell's Philadelphia Clinic followed by a return home with instructions to "Live as domestic a life as possible. Have your child with you all the time . . . And never touch pen, brush or pencil as long as you live" is a distillation of the conditions that caused the disease.

But the woman in "The Yellow Wallpaper," refusing to see her child and confined herself to a nursery, transforms her inability to produce into the condition of production. Gilman remembers herself in her *Autobiography* "shaking and crying" if she so much as tried to dress her baby; instead, she "made a rag baby, hung it on a doorknob and played with it." Women's "desire to produce," she would write in *Women and Economics*, can no longer be "satisfied with a status that allows only reproduction." The making of the rag baby is both a pathetic substitute for reproduction and a first step toward production. In "The Yellow Wallpaper," creeping around the childless nursery, rubbing herself against the wallpaper and peeling it off, freeing the woman she imagines imprisoned on the other side of the wallpaper and, finally, understanding herself as the woman she has freed ("'I've got out at last,' said I"), she makes neither a baby nor a rag baby but herself. As parturition becomes parthenogenesis, reproduction becomes production. And if you can imagine yourself as having made your body, you can imagine also that your body is yours.

What, in Gilman, the confining rest cure turns out to do for the hysteric – paradoxically transform the domestic reproductive space of the nursery into the public productive market place – "The Right to Privacy" does for women like Marion Manola and Carrie Meeber – defending the "sacred precincts of private and domestic life," it transforms those precincts into commodities for sale on a public market. Edna Pontellier's love for her "great tragedian" had found its focus in a "picture" of him which "stood enframed upon her desk." "Any one may possess the portrait of a tragedian without exciting suspicion or comment," Chopin remarks, and goes on to characterize this "reflection" as a "sinister" one which Edna "cherished." Edna's possession of the portrait marks a public not a private relation with the tragedian (which explains "sinister" and, given *The Awakening*'s hostility to reciprocity, "cherished" also); you do not have to be loved by him to be able to buy his picture. Sales of Carrie's picture mark her emergence out of domesticity – selling herself to Drouet and Hurstwood – and into the market – selling herself to "the public." She is like the tragedian and like Edna too, like the tragedian in selling, like Edna in desiring. But where the tragedian sells his "exalted gifts," Carrie sells the expression on her face, and where Edna's desires require privacy or "solitude," Carrie's emerge in public, in department stores, in restaurants, or on the stage. Indeed, the difference between the public space of selling and the private space of wanting is bridged by Carrie's ability to make a career not only out of selling her "look" but out of the particular "look" that she sells. The look she sells, the accidental "expression" of her 'mouth,' is "representative of all desire," Dreiser says. "It's a thing the world likes to see because it's a natural expression of its longing." For this representation of the desire for commodities itself to become a commodity, someone has to want it and be able to buy it and someone has to own it and be able to sell it. "The Right to Privacy" and "The Yellow Wallpaper," *The Awakening* and *Sister Carrie*, begin to imagine a world in which those conditions can be met.

SOMEBODY'S GIRL

Jerusha Abbott (in Jean Webster's *Daddy-Long-Legs* ([1912], Bess Oldring (in Zane Grey's *Riders of the Purple Sage* [1912]), Susan Lenox (in David Graham Phillips's *Susan Lenox* [1917]), and Charity Royall (in Edith Wharton's *Summer* [1917]) are all born "nameless"; they do not know who their fathers are. But Charity, at least, knows something – two things – about her name; "She knew that she had been christened Charity . . . to commemorate Mr. Royall's disinterestedness in 'bringing her down,' and to keep alive in her a becoming sense of her dependence . . ." There is, however, a certain discrepancy between these two things that Charity knows: on the one hand, her name is to serve as a commemoration of Mr. Royall's "disinterestedness," his indifference to obtaining any benefit for himself by bringing Charity down and then bringing her up; on the other hand, her name is supposed to impress upon Charity a sense of "dependence" amounting to obligation so that when, for example, she complains to Miss Hatchard about Royall's sexual advances, she can be urged to bear with him since, after all, he brought her "down from the Mountain." The name "Charity" thus asserts that Charity owes Mr. Royall nothing while at the same time it reminds her of how much she owes him. Or, to put the point more generally, it raises the question of the difference, if any, between gifts (which incur no obligation) and payments (which do), a difference that is subtly articulated in the series of exchanges that begins with Charity's lover, Lucius Harney, offering Royall ten dollars as "payment" for board and the use of his buggy, and continues when Royall passes the money on to Charity as a "gift," but is problematized by the novel's plot, which makes it possible to think of Harney as buying Charity from the closest thing she has to a father (Royall) and which makes it possible to think of Lawyer Royall himself – by bringing her down from the Mountain, by providing a father for her child – as having bought her. Does Charity receive presents or payments? Does she give herself away or does she sell herself?

There is, furthermore, a sense in which Charity's full name – Charity Royall – makes these questions even more vivid. Her last name as well as her first comes to her from the guardian who is himself never given a first name by the story – he is usually called "Lawyer Royall." He needs no other name, as Sandra Gilbert says in her essay, "Life's Empty Pack," because "he is, ultimately, no more than the role his professional title and allegorical surname together denote: a regal law-fixer." Juxtaposed with "Lawyer," however, "Royall" does more than mean "regal"; it anagrammatically echoes the professional designation, repeating as well as modifying "Lawyer" and thus giving Lawyer Royall two names that are the same. But with Charity, the identity of Lawyer Royall's first and last names turns into a difference, the difference between a gift and a payment that was one of the central issues of contemporary contract law and, that, insofar as the enforcement of contract was itself central to Anglo-American law, determined what came under the purview of the law. If the first element of contract was a promise, the second was "consideration," the requirement, as Oliver Wendell Holmes Jr. analyzed it in *The Common Law* (1881), that for any promised service there be a "reward." For if there was no promise of reward, no "understanding that the service was to be paid for," then "the service was a gift" and there was no contract and no legal obligation to be enforced. From this standpoint, then, the question of Lawyer Royall's "disinterestedness" and of Charity's "sense of dependence" can be seen as a question about contract – did he bring her down from the Mountain as a gift or in return for some "consideration?" And Charity Royall's name, with its simultaneous insistence on the gift (for what else is an act of Charity?) and (by way of its anagrammatic allusion to "Lawyer") on the legal world of services performed for considerations, remarks the distinction – it might better be called the tension – between gifts and bargains.

My point here is not to suggest that we read *Summer* as an allegory of contract; if we read it as an explanation of how Charity and Lawyer Royall come to be "lawfully joined together," we require no allegory to see its preoccupation with what had come to seem, since Lewis Morgan's *Ancient Society* (1877), the origin of all contracts, the marriage contract. Tracing the history of the family from "a condition of promiscuous intercourse" through the intermediary stages of "polygyny" and "polyandry" (including the marriage of brothers to sisters), to plural marriages (excluding siblings) and finally to what he called the "monogamian family," Morgan linked this history to "the growth of the idea of property." The desire to pass on what property they had accumulated to children they could be certain were theirs led men to eliminate polygyny;

the extension of incest taboos and the consequent restriction on the supply of marriageable women made "wives" "scarce" and transformed them into objects "to be acquired" "by capture," "by negotiation," and "by purchase." Monogamian marriage was thus both an effect and a cause of the increased importance of property: monogamian wives enabled their husbands to transmit the property they had acquired while at the same time they themselves became an essential portion of that property. And if the purchase of wives had come to seem "primitive," it was not because of doubts about whether they were bought but because of a change in who they were bought from. In the opening scene of Robert Herrick's *Together* (1908), the question "And who gives this woman in marriage" is regarded as an "outworn form" because "She gave herself of course!" Marriage for the middle-class woman of *Together* is offering some man "her very handsome person, and her intelligence, in exchange for certain definite powers of brain and will"; in *Together*, the "happy couple" is reduced to "the contracting pair."

What got lost in this reduction, according to some writers, was love. "True marriage," wrote the Rev. John Haynes Holmes in 1913, "means love between mate and mate – nothing more and nothing else. Where love is, there is marriage – where love is not, there is prostitution." Or, as the heroine of David Graham Phillips's *The Price She Paid* (1912) puts it to a man who wishes both to marry her and to finance her career as a singer: "I'm not going to marry you. Now let's talk business." This novel begins by asserting the proximity, not to say identity, of business and marriage, at least for society girls like its heroine, Mildred Gower, who, because they have learned no other form of "money-making" are only "a step apart" from "women of the pariah class." In lieu of going "on the streets," Mildred sells herself to the wealthy General Siddall and becomes one of his "employees," but leaves him when she finds that, despite his wealth, "there's nothing in it." The moral of this failure is that marriage cannot be a business proposition after all: "I could not belong to a man unless I cared for him," Mildred tells a subsequent candidate for her hand, "I tried it once. I shall never do it again," and she embarks instead on a "career" that must be kept as separate from love as marriage is from money: no man, her mentor tells her, must be allowed to "spoil your career"; no man must be allowed to "touch your career."

Although it begins by asserting that for (middle-class) women, marriage is the only career, the point of the novel is thus to separate them: Mildred begins by learning that you should marry for love and ends by learning that you should work for a living. These entirely conventional lessons perform the service of rescuing marriage from contract and career from sex, of "keeping," as Mary Austin put it in *A Woman of Genius* (also published in 1912 and also about a woman who makes a career on the stage, albeit as an actress instead of as a singer) "love and my career in two watertight compartments." Austin's version of "I won't marry you. Let's talk business," is an inquiring telegram "Will you marry me? Signed: Garrett" and an answering one "If you marry my work. Olivia." The answer is a no because the presumption is that work should not be married, or, to put it another way, that marriage should not be work. Olivia gave up marriage for work; her feminism consists in treating Garrett as if he has done the same. For Austin as for Phillips, marriage and career must be defined by their opposition to one another, an opposition that in freeing women to pursue careers saves marriage from degenerating into prostitution.

But the project of saving marriage from prostitution found an even broader social articulation in what might be described as the project of saving prostitution from prostitution. The urgency of this project stemmed from the general perception that the ages-old problem of "the social evil" had become a new and "infinitely complex phenomenon." In "ancient" and "medieval" times, as New York's Committee of Fifteen (in a report edited by Columbia University professor Edwin Seligman) put it, prostitutes were customarily slaves or "aliens," "secured from foreign countries"; today, however – and this is the novelty of modern prostitution – they are what the Committee calls "citizens." Thus the traditional attempt to regulate them is, as the Committee sees it, bound to fail. Regulation tries to deal with prostitution by mitigating its "effects" (primarily medical) on "decent society," identifying the prostitutes and subjecting them to periodic examinations in order to reduce the transmission of venereal disease to the decent population. With slaves and aliens, this project of identification and control was a feasible one; and indeed, if all prostitutes were the "hideous, blear-eyed, degenerate creatures, recognizable at a glance" that the advocates of regulation painted them as being, the project would still be feasible. In fact, however, the modern prostitute is more likely to look like "an attractive shop girl" and it would be "a grievous error" to suppose that she and her sisters could be "easily distinguished from the decent classes of society."

Regulation is ineffective, then, because the modern prostitute looks too much like the decent working girl to be distinguished from her, and when we remember that, according to the Committee, the distinctive feature of the modern prostitute is that she is neither a "slave" nor an "alien" but a "citizen," we can see that the superficial resemblance between her and the working girl is the sign of a deeper identity; it is confusing but not deceptive. For not only is the prostitute likely to look like an attractive shop girl, she is likely to have been an attractive shop girl and to become one again: "With perhaps the majority of prostitutes, the life of shame is only a temporary state." Unlike the slave and alien, the modern prostitute does not belong to a separate population – she is "recruited . . . from the ranks of the virtuous" and motivated by the same needs that motivate them. Against "criminal anthropologists" like the Lombrosos and the Tarnowskys who maintained that prostitutes were impelled to the street by their "innate perversity," the Committee claims that their motives are essentially economic: "it is not passion or corrupt inclination, but the force of actual physical want, that impels young women along the road to ruin." And even this explanation exaggerates the difference between the prostitute and the "decent" girl: the "more or less typical" American prostitute is not driven to prostitution by "absolute want"; rather, she is "employed at living wages, but the prospect of continuing from year to year with no change from tedious and irksome labor creates discontent." She is not depraved, she is not even all that deprived – she just wants a better job.

The significance of this rejection of Lombroso-style appeals to perversity as the cause of female criminality and of the turn instead to economic motives emerges most clearly in a text that somewhat confuses the two, Frank Norris's *McTeague* (1899). Trina McTeague is not, of course, a prostitute but, in her miserliness and her masochism, "her passion for her money and her perverted love for her husband when he was brutal," she embodies the simultaneity of sex and money that groups like the Committee of Fifteen found so disturbing. And if, from one standpoint, both Trina's desires are perverse, from another they enact the transformation of what Lombroso called "biological" "anomalies" into what seemed to the Committee economic normalcy; indeed, they enact the prostitute's development from slave to citizen.

The miser was an old figure, given new meaning by what everyone thought of as the contraction of currency in the depression of the early 1890s, a contraction that threatened, according to free-silver partisans like Ignatius Donnelly, to return the world to "barbarism," turning free "American citizens" into "slaves." Donnelly and the others blamed this threat on the disappearance of gold into the vaults of Wall Street bankers and even on its use for decorative and medical purposes: hence McTeague is a dentist and the origin of Trina's hoard is "a spot of white caries on the lateral surface of an incisor" that he "fill[s] with gold." But masochism was a recent invention; described by Krafft-Ebing in the 1880s and named by him after Leopold von Sacher-Masoch, its founding text was Sacher-Masoch's *Venus im Pelz* (1870), and its original practitioners, his protagonists, the masochistic Severin and his "cruel mistress," Wanda. Severin wants to be Wanda's "slave," and he and Wanda lament the disappearance of slavery from modern Europe, contemplating a trip to Constantinople, until Wanda realizes that a "contract" can do for them in the West what slavery could do in the East. Indeed, a contract can do more, making Severin's enslavement an effect not of "law" or "power" but of "choice." The "curtailing" of "Imperative Law" and the "enlarging" of "Contract" had led, Henry Sumner Maine wrote in *Ancient Law* (1861), to the development of "modern" "liberty"; when Severin agrees to become Wanda's "property" and she, "in exchange," agrees to appear "as often as possible in furs, particularly when she is being cruel to her slave," they are performing the disappearance of "Imperative Law" and the "movement," in Maine's famous phrase, of "the progressive societies . . . *from Status to Contract.*" Decisively identified by Sacher-Masoch with contract, masochism is not only recent but modern. In *Venus im Pelz*, it is possible only to the "free," and the masochistic contract, producing enslavement by "choice," is a sign of that freedom.

The juxtaposition of Trina's masochism to her miserliness makes that point in *McTeague*. As a masochist, Trina wants, like Severin, to be owned: her passion for McTeague consists in her conviction that "*she was his.*" But as a miser, she wants above all to own; when McTeague remarks of their savings that "it's all in the family. What's yours is mine and what's mine is yours," Trina responds, "No, it's not; no, it's not; no, it's not . . . It's all mine, mine." In *McTeague*, these perversions normalize each other; the desire to own is not only compatible with but is fulfilled by the desire to sell and so be owned. So if the miser is an atavism (Norris describes Trina as reverting to the peasant condition of her ancestors), and if the disappearance of money produced by misers was leading to a return to "barbarism," the linking of the miser's desire to own with the masochist's desire to be owned turns hoarding back into circulating and barbarism into civilization. "Prostitution is a phenomenon coextensive with civilized society," wrote the Committee of Fifteen, asserting that "barbarous and semi-barbarous" peoples are usually free of it. The Committee, like Donnelly, identifies civilization with exchange; like Maine, it identifies progress with contract. And in Trina's "economical little body," the emergence of masochism from slavery is simultaneously the transformation of slavery into citizenship.

What the Committee called the "intangible" and "indefinable" character of modern prostitution thus turns out to be its essential similarity to other less obviously reprehensible forms of urban economic activity, and what used to be called "the pariah class" – "women formally put beyond the pale" and "men with the brand of thief or gambler" – now seems to include, as David Graham Phillips put it, "almost the whole population – all those who sell body or soul in an uncertain market." Faced, then, with the difficulty of eliminating an "evil" that seemed virtually indistinguishable from the everyday activities of its "citizens" – the campaign against prostitution took an interesting turn: it sought, through the medium of the "White Slave Narrative" and related texts (for example, the Mann Act of 1910) to eliminate prostitution by denying that – in the "modern" form diagnosed by the Committee of Fifteen – it existed.

Thus although crusaders like Clifford Roe – in his compendium, *The Great War on White Slavery* (1911) – followed the Committee in conceiving prostitution as a "business," a "commercialized institution" produced not by "lust" but by "greed," the focus of Roe's attack (the specificity of the obsession with white slavery as opposed to a more general worry about "the social evil") is "the traffic in girls and women" as a *male* business in which the girls and women appear only as victims. "An America commercialized has commercialized its daughters. Who would ever have prophesied a century ago that today like hardware and groceries the daughters of the people would be bought and sold?" The prostitute is no longer a "citizen" but a "slave" once again, and the target of prosecution is the slave trader; the Mann Act prohibits the transportation across state lines of "any woman or girl for the purpose of prostitution or debauchery or for any other immoral purpose"; its target is not the prostitute but the "professional seducer," the "pimp" or the "cadet."

Where the Committee of Fifteen addressed itself to the motives for becoming a prostitute, the attack on white slavery denies there can be any such motives. White slavery is commerce between men in women, and (in *The Great War on White Slavery*) the suggestion that women might themselves have commercial interests is allowed to appear only in the mouth of a shyster lawyer unsuccessfully defending a notorious procurer. The victim, a "Jewish girl" named Sarah, is, according to the shyster, no victim at all; rather, "with all the characteristics of her race," she is "coolly and calmly planning as to how she shall get the dollar." And her desire for the dollar is by no means exclusively racial, for she shares it with her Irish friend Mollie Hart with whom she goes to the dance house and to parks and to chop suey houses: "And of course while they were at the dance house they were engaged in repeating the Lord's prayer," the lawyer jeers, or else they were trying to memorize the Declaration of Independence.

And when they were at the Parks of course they were thinking of Shakespeare's plays, or they were reading or recalling one of the great poems of the past. Now, at these chop suey places and the parks and the dance halls what were they thinking about? What were they doing? Were they planning and scheming for the dollar? Yes? And she did plan and scheme for the dollar day and night, and is not easily deceived. Not being easily deceived she cannot be easily procured . . . She procured herself . . .

This argument fails in court and, indeed, the whole point of *The Great War on White Slavery* is to guarantee that it fail, to guarantee that no woman be imagined as procuring herself. Thus Roe's section on "economic causes," the section that would appear to offer the greatest opportunity to consider prostitutes as "independent" economic agents and which even contains a plea to the employers of shop girls and clerks to pay them "living wages," ends instead with a poem (written by Kate Jane Adams) that makes clear the real economic commitments of the war against white slavery: "No matter how wayward her footsteps have been," Adams reminds her readers, "No matter how deeply she has sunken in sin; / No matter what elements may canker the Pearl, / Though lost and forsaken she is somebody's girl." Whosoever "somebody's girl" is, she is not, like Trina, her own girl, and whatever "somebody's girl" may do, she will never, like Sarah, "procure herself"; as long as the "social evil" is white slavery, all prostitutes will be slaves, not citizens.

"At last the great public is coming to recognize that there is a White Slave Traffic infinitely more inhuman than the black slave traffic," wrote J. G. Shearer in an introduction to *The Great War*. More inhuman than black slavery but nowhere near as bad as prostitution. And, indeed, from this standpoint, the white-slavery craze can best be understood as a gendered expression of the nostalgia for slavery that had dominated the Southern plantation writings of the 1890s. Progressive racism, as we have seen, would welcome the disappearance of slavery as a prelude to the expulsion of blacks. But in novels like Opie Read's *My Young Master* (1896) one finds the reverse: instead of antislavery accompanied by "Negrophobia," anti-"Negrophobia" accompanied by a certain tolerance for slavery. Furthermore, the affection for the "negro" is at the same time the expression of a certain distaste for the immigrant. Thus where Dixon welcomed Eastern Europeans into the melting-pot, Read has his black narrator and hero praise the Southern army (in which he proudly serves as a slave) because, "more Anglo-Saxon," it "fought with brighter fire and bravery than the miscellaneous nationalities gathered in the North." And, more striking still, Read demonstrates his hero's own nobility by placing him repeatedly in situations where he can decline, out of "devotion" to his "master," the opportunity to escape slavery.

"You are a negro, but you are a gentleman," his master's father tells him. The way to be both a gentleman and a negro is to recognize that one is bound to one's master by "fetters of honor" not iron. Even when offered a great deal of money with which to find a new life in the North, the narrator refuses. Just as a gentleman who owns slaves will not sell them (it is "against my principles to sell a slave," the Old Master says), a gentleman who is a slave will not allow himself to be bought; he would rather wear chains than know that his master had "lost confidence" in him. Inhabited by aristocrats – black and white – who will not take your money, the South in *My Young Master* is the redeemed nation of the white-slave narrative: the slaves do not sell themselves and their owners will not sell them either.

The narrator of *My Young Master* is black but its author was white; the author of *The Sport of the Gods* (1902), however, Paul Laurence Dunbar, was himself black, and his ambivalence about the benefits of freedom is a good deal more shocking – and compelling – than Opie Read's. *The Sport of the Gods* begins by distinguishing itself from the kind of "fiction" (Page's, Harris's, to some extent, Read's) that "has said so much in regret of the old days when there were plantations and overseers and masters and slaves," contrasting Berry Hamilton's "neatly furnished, modern house, the home of a typical, good-living Negro" to the "old cabin in the quarters" of slavery. But the contrast is also a comparison; the house is located "back in the yard some hundred paces from the mansion of his employer," a fact that has led the Hamilton children themselves "to draw unpleasant comparisons between their mode of life and the old plantation quarters system." Where the father is "one of the many slaves who upon their succession to freedom had not left the South," the children want "a home off by themselves" and they end up in the North. From one perspective, this is progress; just as Berry has gone from being a "slave" to a "servant," the children, "inspired with a desire to go to work and earn money of [their] own," will become "independent." From another perspective, however, one the novel begins by placing in the mouths of unreconstructed white Southerners and ends by adapting and adopting as its own, it is disaster.

What sends the Hamilton family north (expelling them from their Uncle Tom-like but retrospectively happy home) is a false accusation of theft against Berry, a crime that the novel represents as impossible for slaves but virtually inevitable for servants. "We must remember that we are not in the old days now," observes Berry's employer. In the old days, of course, slaves did some-times take things, but in such a way that "there was no crime committed." The "old Negro" was not culpable because "he knew nothing of the value of money. When he stole, he stole hams and bacon and chickens. These were his immediate necessities and the things he valued." Now, however, he is "ambi-tious," "he has learned to value other things than those which satisfy his belly." The slave, having no property rights in himself, had no interest in the property rights of others; when he took a ham, he did not assert a property right in it, he just ate it. The servant, however, has a property right in himself and so a potential interest in the property rights of others; hence although in twenty years Berry has shown no sign of infidelity, "No servant is beyond suspicion." The slave, who can own nothing, can steal nothing; the slave who becomes the "ambitious" servant asserts his property right in himself only at the expense of the property right of his master – the fact that he is a servant is itself the sign that he is a thief.

Coming from his old master, this attack on Berry's ambition sends him to jail; coming from Dunbar, it sends his son to jail. Moving north in the wake of their father's disgrace, the Hamilton children (like Dreiser's Carrie or like the Committee of Fifteen's shop girls) are themselves seized by "ambition": the musically talented Kitty stops singing the "simple old songs" of home and starts practicing the "detestable coon ditties which the stage demanded"; Joe, his "independence" "harden[ing]" into "defiance," becomes a drunk and a murderer. The closest he comes to redemption is when a woman from back home arrives in New York and starts spreading the story of his father's crime; what had earlier been identified as the intolerant voice of the small town (a voice associated by Dunbar with "the influence of slavery") now appears as the saving voice of conscience: "Somehow old teachings and old traditions have an annoying way of coming back upon us in the critical moments of life, although one has long recognized how much truer and better some newer ways of thinking are." The irony is double here; the point is, of course, that the old ways are really better than the new, but the old ways are the ways of the unreconstructed South and the story being spread – a story that is supposed to remind Joe of the importance of honor and "a good reputation" – is *false*. Joe is here being asked to save himself morally by remembering a crime committed against his father (the false accusation) as if it were a crime committed by his father (the theft); he is being asked to save himself from freedom by condemning his father for the crime of having become free.

Imagining "some" who would "sermonize" about Joe's fate, Dunbar characterizes them as wanting to

preach to these people that . . . it was better and nobler for them to sing to God across the Southern fields than to dance for rowdies in the Northern halls. They wanted to say that the South has its faults – no one condones them – and its disadvantages, but that even what they suffered from these was better than what awaited them in the great alleys of New York.

In *The Sport of the Gods*, the attraction of New York, the desire to live your "own life," is inevitably disastrous but the only alternative to it is the "reopened and refurnished" slave cabin to which Berry Hamilton and his wife return "without complaint" at the end. In *My Young Master*, Read imagined slaves so free they were restrained only by the "chaffing" of their "fetters of honor"; Dunbar has less respect for "Southern honor," and he knows that "Down there, the bodies were restrained, and they chafed . . ." But, like Read, he would have his former slaves prefer the chafing.

As a literary genre, however, the attempt to substitute the lesser evil of slavery for the greater evil of the free market found its most popular expression in a story not of New York nor the slave South but of Utah, and of a girl kidnapped and abused "till she give in" not by cruel slaveowners, Italian pimps or Jewish cadets but by a Mormon "proselyter." "She became a slave," the gunman Lassiter says of his sister, Milly Earne, and Zane Grey's *Riders of the Purple Sage* (1912), which begins as the story of Lassiter's revenge on the Mormons plays itself out as his attempt to save two more women – Milly Earne's daughter and her best friend – from being "broken" by them. To be broken is to be compelled to marry a Mormon and in this sense, although the Western is sometimes characterized as either indifferent or hostile to the domestic novel ("The Western *answers* the domestic novel," Jane Tompkins has written in *West of Everything*. "It is the antithesis of the cult of domesticity that dominated American Victorian culture"). It is in fact (like the novel of the career woman and like the nostalgia for black and white slavery), an extension and modernization of domesticity; the point of Zane Grey's early novels is to save women *from* forced marriages to Mormons and *for* love marriages to "gentiles." "Obedience," "humility," and "fear" are the lot of Mormon women, kidnapped into polygamy as white slaves are kidnapped into prostitution; Grey's gunslingers (like the new urban social workers) rescue them, earn their love and (going the social workers one better), marry them: *Riders of the Purple Sage* ends with one gunman taking his intended "home to Illinois – to my mother" and with the other taking *his* (complete with her adopted child) to the even more domestic setting of "Surprise Valley." Indeed, it is the child who has brought Jane and Lassiter together, making the gunman "daily" "more gentle and kind" with remarks like "Why don't oo marry my new muvver an' be my favver?" And Bern Venters, Grey's other gunslinger, has also become "softer, gentler" through his relation with Milly's daughter, Bess; "I'm a man," he tells her, "a man you've made." If men go west to become men, they become men, in *Riders of the Purple Sage*, by finding women; they become men by becoming husbands.

If the point of the career-woman novel was to save marriage from contract (by defining a career as anything but marriage) and the point of the white-slave narrative was to save prostitution from contract (by transforming prostitutes into non-contracting slaves), the Zane Grey Western combines these by imagining marriage as the saving alternative to career and slavery both. One of *Riders'* heroines, Jane, is remarkable for her independence: the village in which the novel is set is "her private property"; the gunman Lassiter works for her, agreeing to "take" her "orders," and she has not a single "relative in Utah." Its other heroine, Bess, occupies a position that is the polar opposite of

Jane's – where Jane is nobody's girl, Bess is the bandit "Oldring's girl"; where Jane seems to be "an absolutely free woman," Bess is a prisoner in Oldring's cabin. But the Western that makes men men by making them husbands must also make women wives; slavery, as *Riders* understands it, is being "forced" into marriage, freedom is the right to marry the man you love: Bess is freed so that she can love and marry Bern Venters, Jane is "broken" ("No woman can love like a broken woman") so that she can love and make a family with Lassiter. Marriage is the happy escape from freedom and slavery both.

This point is made even more explicit in the sequel to *Riders*, *The Rainbow Bridge* (1915), whose hero has come west "to find a wife" and whose heroine, Fay, like Bess and Jane before her, must be rescued for marriage from Mormonism. Most of the action in this novel takes place not in what is sometimes characterized as the "womanless milieu" of the western but in a town of some fifty Mormon "sealed wives" ("almost every one of them . . . attractive and some of them . . . exceedingly pretty") and three men. The women are the plural wives of polygamists, hiding from Federal prosecution, and the men – including Shefford, Grey's hero – are there to guard them. When one of the women turns out to be Fay, it looks like rescue is impossible, but when Fay turns out not yet to have been forced into marriage (not yet to have "give in"), the mission is back on. "You're not a wife! . . . You're free," Shefford exclaims and, almost in the same breath, "You're a slave. You're not a wife." Being a slave may be the opposite of being free but both enslavement to a man and the freedom to sell yourself to him are defined by opposition to being married. Thus one village of "sealed wives" is called Fredonia, the "village of free women": by the Mormons as an alibi – in the way that the "white slaver's" defense lawyer described the Jewish girl as free; by Zane Grey and by the discourse of white slavery as an alibi but also something more, an alibi that tells the truth. Any freedom but the freedom to marry is slavery.

Or rather, any freedom but the freedom to marry the man you love, for "Where love is there is marriage – where love is not, there is prostitution." And the proof of this freedom is loving a man to whom you are not married. Grey is hardly casual about sexual relations; Bern Venters is prepared to accept the fact that Bess has been "Oldring's girl" and to marry her anyway but he is incredibly relieved to discover that instead of exposing her to the bandits' "vileness," Oldring had shielded her from it – her imprisonment in his cabin was in fact a kind of protective custody. Although the white-slave crusaders preached the importance of society re-accepting the girls rescued from slavery, Grey may not have been in fact ready for the sight of *Riders*' young hero galloping home to mother with his new prostitute bride. Grey was ready, however, to imagine love without marriage. If white slavery and the loveless

Mormon marriage were to be condemned because they represented exchanges of women between men, even love marriages might come to look too much like exchanges – too much like contracts – to be permitted. Jane Withersteen begins by hiring Lassiter not (although he proclaims his love for her) by loving him; she pays for his services with one of her prize Arabians. She ends with all her property – even, at the very last, the Arabians – gone; unable to hire Lassiter (broke and so "broken"), she finally is able to love him. In this respect, the novel might be said to radicalize domesticity; it is from this perspective that *Riders* goes beyond imagining marriage as the alternative to the choice between slavery and freedom. Jane proclaims her love for Lassiter at a moment – entering Surprise Valley and urging Lassiter to roll the great stone that will cut off all pursuit and seal them forever within – when that proclamation will result in them cutting themselves off forever not only from the world of freedom and slavery but from the world of marriage as well: in Surprise Valley, "marriage" is "impossible." If at the heart of the monogamous family one can find (the marriage) contract, *Riders* is prepared to rescue marriage from contract by, in effect, rescuing it from marriage.

OLD HOME WEEK

Surprise Valley is Zane Grey's version of the domestic precincts that the right to privacy had been devised to defend and that it was turning out instead to make available for public sale. And the West in general, a place where, as a trader says to the hero of *The Rainbow Bridge*, "not a white man . . . would ever take a dollar from you," represents a response not only to the emergence of women from domesticity but to the transformation of domesticity itself. It is like Opie Read's old South or, with a twist, like Dunbar's, where no *black* man will take a dollar from you. Read's racial utopianism imagined the black man as the slave of love; before rejecting the money that would help him to freedom, his hero proclaims that his "heart" is his "real master." The gendered utopianism of Progressivism turns the black man into a white woman: against the prospect of women selling either what could not or what should not be sold, the western and the white-slave narrative insist that, whatever women do, they do not do it for money.

Along with the story of the career woman, they represent three different strategies for separating love from contract, for distinguishing between marriage and prostitution. The career woman chooses contract instead of marriage; she does not marry, she becomes, one might say, a prostitute instead of a bride. The white slave, on the other hand, never even becomes a prostitute; she is defined by her inability to sell herself, her inability, if she can not be a bride, to be anything else. And the western – by breaking the career woman and freeing the slave – makes them both available for a marriage in which love means so much that the marriage contract – indeed, contract itself – becomes expendable. All three, in other words, keep *Summer's* distinction between giving yourself and selling yourself intact by imagining marriage as nothing but a gift, but, as the radicalization of marriage (its transformation into something like free love) in *Riders* suggests, the imagination of marriage as nothing but a sale could perform the same function.

Thus in the novel Wharton wrote just before *Summer*, *The Custom of the Country* (1913), Undine Spragg's "career" consists of nothing but a series of marriages to men she does not love, marriages which, when they break up, are "dissolved like a business partnership." Undine's "inalienable right to 'go around'" amounts here to more than a Daisy Miller-like propensity for the society of "gentlemen"; it is an inalienable right to alienate herself in marriage. Having inherited "her father's business instinct" and having been named after one of his products, Undine feels in moments of passionate negotiation just as "Mr. Spragg might have felt at the tensest hour of the Pure Water deal." In *The Custom of the Country*, there are no gifts, only exchanges, and love and contract are just as securely separated from one another as they are in *Riders of the Purple Sage*.

This transformation of marriage into contract is condemned as "unnatural" by those characters in *Custom* who cannot accustom themselves to the "modern drama of divorce." And there is, as we have already seen, a sense in which this characterization of both divorce and marriage as "unnatural" could not help but seem accurate. For virtually the founding gesture of the anthropological study of the family had been to identify marriage as a kind of business arrangement – the first exchange of property – and then to see that exchange of property as, in Morgan's words, "the power that brought the Aryan and Semitic nations out of barbarism into civilization." Before marriage there had been no property (the Polish anthropologist Bronislaw Malinowski would say that Morgan believed in "the communism of savages") and before property there had been no marriage (the American anthropologist Robert Lowie calls this Morgan's commitment to "sexual communism," a "condition of perfect promiscuity, in which sexual lust [is] unrestricted by any incest rule"). In *Summer*, North Dormer (where Lawyer Royall is the "strongest man") is "civilization," in contrast to the Mountain, the home of "outlaws," "squatters" (with no respect for property) who "herd together like heathen" (with no respect for the rule of incest). The distinction embodied in "Charity Royall" between gift and contract is thus imagined geographically as the distinction between the Mountain and North Dormer and anthropologically as the distinction between nature and culture.

But there is at the same time an important sense in which the difference between the Mountain and North Dormer – insisted upon though it is by the residents of both places – is not altogether straightforward. For if the Mountain, as the site of "passive promiscuity," is a place where one might end up sleeping with a member of one's family, North Dormer turns possibility into fact. Charity's lover, Lucius Harney, is ostentatiously given the same initials as a Mountain man, Liff Hyatt, she suspects might be her brother; more striking still, while Harney's initial interest in Charity is described as "more fraternal than lover-like," on the occasion of their actually making love, he is said to embrace her "tenderly, almost fraternally" – the conjunctive opposition between brother and lover has disappeared. And, of course, her eventual husband, "fatherly old" Lawyer Royall, stands to her throughout in an explicitly paternal relation. He came to her bedroom that night, Charity tells Harney, "So's' t' he wouldn't have to go out," and, indeed, the relations between Charity, Harney, and Mr. Royall are arranged so that, in the best endogamous fashion, none of them has to "go out." The novel thus converts North Dormer's "civilization" into primitive "promiscuity"; Charity sleeps with her brother and marries her father.

But *Summer* goes beyond transforming North Dormer into the Mountain, it converts the Mountain into an image of North Dormer and even of that center of commerce and "litigation," Nettleton. This is most obvious in the crude but effective counterpoint at the Mountain funeral of Charity's mother: "We brought nothing into this world and we shall take nothing out of it" pronounces the minister against the background of a quarrel over who actually owns the deceased's stove that culminates in the claim, "I wen' down to Creston'n bought it . . . n' I got a right to take it outer here . . . ." But it is more disturbing in the strange doubling of Charity's mother by the "motherly" abortionist in Nettleton. Not only does she speak to Charity as her "own mother might" (and offer to get rid of her child as Charity's mother got rid of her), she speaks as "a lady that's got to earn her living" in a novel where the only real way for a lady (especially a mother) to earn her living is the way Charity's mother earned hers – prostitution. If, then, civilized North Dormer turns out to provide an image of primitive "communism," the Mountain – with its disputes over private property – images a kind of sexual capitalism, that of the prostitute who sells herself, as opposed to the sister–daughter who gives herself away.

In *Summer*, these distinctions – between giving and selling, endogamy and exogamy, primitive and civilized – are always in place, but they are not always in the same place. Harney pays Royall ten dollars for board and the use of his coach; Royall gives the money as a "present" to Charity; Charity buys clothes with it, and when Harney sees her in her new white dress, "she read(s) her reward in his eyes." The ten dollars has been both payment and gift; when it comes back to Harney in the form of Charity in her new dress it is both gift and payment – a gift to him (in excess of what he bought with it) and a payment to her (the price of the "reward" in his eyes). Harney gives Charity a brooch which she then uses as a pledge at the abortionist's; Royall gives Charity forty dollars which she uses to redeem her pledge: Charity has been given the brooch and she has paid for it: is it a purchase or a gift?

The emergence of women into the market had been accompanied by two quite different understandings of the "modern" marriage contract and of what it meant for women to give themselves. The western and the white-slave narrative rescue marriage from prostitution by denying that prostitution exists; marriage is either slavery or the mere epiphenomenon of a love that exists without it. *The Custom of the Country* and a feminist critique of marriage identify marriage with prostitution: "the personal profit of women," Gilman wrote in *Women and Economics*, "bears but too close a relation to their power to win and hold the other sex. When we confront this fact . . . in the open market of vice, we are sick with horror. When we see the same economic relation . . . established by law . . . we think it innocent, lovely and right." Marriage is either all love and no contract or all contract and no love; brides are either lovers or prostitutes.

But if the lover and the prostitute may be described in theory as occupying two quite different positions with respect to sexual relations – one gives, one sells – *Summer* may be said deliberately to court a certain confusion between these positions, and even to insist – in the figure of the wife – that as theoretically different as giving and selling may be, they cannot in practice be separated from one another. In *Argonauts of the Western Pacific* (published in 1922, written in 1921, and based on research conducted between 1914 and 1920), Malinowski would propose a taxonomy of economic dealings among the Trobriand Islanders ranging from "pure gifts" (characteristically between "husband and wife" or "parents and children") to "trade pure and simple" (characteristically between people of different villages). Responding to Malinowski in his 1925 monograph *The Gift*, Marcel Mauss denied that there were any such things as pure gifts and affirmed that Malinowski was particularly misguided in thinking of gifts from husband to wife as "disinterested"; such gifts should be understood instead on the model of what the Trobrianders called *mapula*, "the sequence of payments by a husband to his wife as a kind of salary for sexual services." This debate is resolved in *Summer* by the insistence that marriage is *both* a gift and a sale.

Another way to put this is to say that the attack on marriage as nothing more than a contractual relation (distinguishable from prostitution only because the one is a "transient trade" and the other a "bargain for life") and the defense of it as the expression of a love defined above all by the absence of any element of exchange (as indistinguishable, as we shall see, from "free love" as contractual marriage is from prostitution) together contribute to a transformation in the modern sense of what a marriage is. Thus, although readers like William Dean Howells attacked Robert Herrick's *Together* for what they took to be its "sympathetic treatment of adultery" and of "free love" and although Herrick denied any such sympathies, both the attacks and the defense missed what was genuinely new in *Together*, the *irrelevance* of adultery. Adultery, as Tony Tanner characterized it in *Adultery in the Novel* (1979), is "the main . . . topic for the bourgeois novel," since, separating "desire" from "contract," adultery launches a "frontal assault" on "the social structure." "Society," Tanner remarks, "came to cope with adultery" by way of divorce, but in none of the novels he discusses (*Elective Affinities, Madame Bovary, Anna Karenina*, etc.) "does divorce occur, nor is it felt to offer any *radical* solutions to the problems that have arisen. It is as if the novelist realized that divorce was a piece of surface temporizing, a forensic palliative to cloak and muffle the profoundly disjunctive reverberations and implications of adultery." In *Together*, too, no divorce takes place; nevertheless, *Together* is entirely committed to the phenomenology that would make divorce popular – the requirement that one's legal obligations and one's sexual desires be rendered identical. And its repudiation of adultery is from this standpoint a repudiation of the "bourgeois" novel's plot, a plot contrived, if we accept Tanner's account of it, to dramatize the discrepancy between form and feeling, law and love.

Together denies this discrepancy by first insisting upon it, presenting modern marriage as if it already were adultery. When the minister in *Together*'s opening scene asks "who gives this woman in marriage?" the question is felt, as we have already seen, to be "primitive": "She gave herself of course! The words were but an outgrown form . . ." It is precisely their transcendence of the form that is understood by the "contracting pair," and by modern couples in general, to make their marriages "different" from their parents', to make these new marriages "strike deeper." Since it is not "the words" but their "desire" that brings them "together," modern couples seem already to have rejected the social forms, and in this respect modern marriage seems already adulterous, a commitment to desire at the expense of contract. But the marriage in question is loveless; instead of "passionate and complete union" there is a "strange division"; "feeling" without "form" is accompanied by "form" without "feeling". *Together* thus takes as its premise the problem of adultery and goes on to imagine marriage as the solution to the problem.

In Tanner's account the repudiation of adultery involves a conservative retreat to "forms" at the expense of "passion," but *Together* transforms the contract into desire's text. It rescues the marriage contract not by insisting on its priority over people's feelings but by constructing in its people the feelings appropriate to the contract, indeed by imagining those feelings not only as something that can be expressed in contract but as something that can *only* be expressed in contract. For the ideal of modern marriage, the contract as the expression of "desire," does not only unite form and feeling, it undoes the possibility of an opposition between them. What Herrick's contracting pairs want above all is *to contract*. This is what it means for Isabelle to want at the end of the novel really to become what she began it by only seeming to become, a "real wife." The marriage contract is both the instrument and the object of her desire. Hence neither love as such ("free love" in the terminology of those pro-divorce polemicists who looked forward to "the day when sexual acts would be regarded as entirely private and free from any form of state regulation") nor marriage as such (the "sacred bond" of anti-divorce polemicists in the Catholic and Episcopal Churches) would suffice. The point of both these positions was to separate love from law, to promote the marriage contract to a "sacrament" or to get rid of the contract altogether. For the "contracting pairs" of *Together*, however, love without contract is finally unimaginable. The renovation of marriage at its end (her "new interest in business" enables his new interest in her) is a kind of clumsy rehearsal for the dramas of divorce and remarriage that would come to be called serial monogamy. The marriage contract in *Together* is less the legal form of a desire than it is the enactment of a desire for legal form.

In the beginning, or at least, emerging from the "condition of promiscuous intercourse," "Men did not seek wives as they are sought in civilized society, from affection, for the passion of love, which required a higher development than they had obtained, was unknown among them." "Marriage," Morgan wrote, "was not founded upon sentiment but upon convenience and necessity." Convenience and necessity but not property, for what Morgan will call the "passion" for property, like the "passion" of love, required a higher state – "The growth of the idea of property in the human mind commenced in feebleness and ended in becoming its master passion." "It was the power that brought the Aryan and Semitic nations out of barbarism into civilization." The distinctive mark of monogamy, as it begins to be understood in late nineteenth-century America, is thus the imbrication of love in property. This is what it means for *Summer* to imagine that all gifts can also be understood as purchases and all purchases understood as gifts; this is what it means for Charity to marry

Lawyer Royall, for him to tell her she is "a good girl" and for her to tell him that he is "good too." In this exchange of "goods," there can no longer be any question of choosing between presents and purchases.

In fact, Wharton goes Morgan one better, imagining the passionate relations of property as inhabiting, not succeeding, the condition of primitive promiscuity. Hence the particularity of *Summer's* representation of incest, what distinguishes it not only from Morgan's primitive promiscuity but from more popular texts (like Jean Webster's *Daddy-Long-Legs* [1912]) and more esoteric ones (like Wharton's own unpublished "Fragment of 'Beatrice Palmato.'") Like Susan Lenox and Charity, Webster's heroine is born without a father's name; the name she has, Jerusha Abbott, she got from the head of the foundling asylum in which she was raised and from which she is sent into the world under the auspices of an "unknown" benefactor who (wishing to "remain unknown") has instructed her to address him as "Mr. John Smith." Her doubled distance from "real" names encourages Jerusha to invent new ones: she becomes "Judy" and Mr. Smith becomes, of course, "Daddy-Long-Legs," to whom the letters that make up *Daddy-Long-Legs* are addressed. There is not much ambiguity about contractual commitments here: the letters are "absolutely obligatory"; they are the "payment that Mr. Smith requires" in return for Judy's college tuition and her allowance. But the name Judy chooses makes a father ("Dear Daddy") out of her employer, out of the man who, under his own name (Jervis Pendleton), will subsequently be imagined also as her brother ("Master Jervie"), and who will emerge climactically, under *all* his names ("My very dearest Master-Jervie-Daddy-Long-Legs-Pendleton-Smith"), as her husband. If to be born without a name is to be born without a father, choosing a name for yourself turns out to mean choosing a husband, which means in *Daddy-Long-Legs*, choosing the name of the father you were missing in the first place. An orphan's contractual obligation to write to a "stranger" transforms him into her "whole family" and so eliminates the contractual obligation; incest does for the college girl what white slavery was doing for the prostitute – it saves her from citizenship: "Are women citizens?" Judy asks Daddy. "I don't suppose they are," she cheerfully answers her own question. Jervis Pendleton comes along just when, in the ordinary course of things, Judy would have been pushed out of the orphans' "Home" to look for a job; making him her Daddy before making him her husband, Webster makes sure that she never really has to leave "Home" and that marriage not be understood as the job she has found.

And Wharton, in the "Fragment," goes even further toward establishing the distance between love and contract. "My little girl," Beatrice Palmato's father murmurs to his daughter, as he "plunge[s] into the deepest depths of her thirsting body" and as she sinks "backward into new abysses of bliss." The father's desire for the daughter is shockingly matched by her desire for him. It is not enough, however, for Beatrice's passion (like Judy's) to be incestuous; it must be defined explicitly in opposition to the sexual disgust she feels for her husband; her "passionate eagerness" for her father is a reaction to the "dull misery of her marriage"; the incest is also adultery.

But *Summer*, like *Together* (only with much greater power), has no use for adultery and no use for a marriage unveiled, and hence legitimated, as nothing more than incest. Lawyer Royall emerges for Charity as what Wharton calls a "*man*" insofar as he is more than just a father (which is to say, more than just a lover) and also more than just a husband (which is to say, more than just a prostitute's client). "That was a *man* talking," someone says of Royall's speech on the day of the "Old Home Week" celebration, the same day, Wharton says, that the "rocky firmness" of Royall's "presence" first pierced the "burning mist" of Charity's "dreams" and "stood out with startling distinctness." The speech is about men who go away to make their careers and then, having "failed to get on elsewhere," return home "for *good*," as Royall puts it, "and not for bad . . . or just for indifference . . ." It is, in other words, about the conjunction of domesticity and ambition, about making a career at home and about dissolving the difference between what Wharton elsewhere called "personal" and "business" "relations." In this respect, *Summer* is almost as much a rehearsal for the business psychology that would require people to love their work as it is a rehearsal for the marital psychology that, encouraging people to divorce their spouses, would require them to marry their lovers.

Where Susan Lenox, refusing (like Phillips's other career girls) to marry, remains Susan Lenox, and where Bess Oldring and Jerusha Abbott, by marrying, become Bess Venters and Judy Pendleton, Charity Royall, exchanging her father's name for her husband's name, both remains and becomes Charity Royall. The construction of Charity's love depends neither on the return to those incestuous relations that characterized the prehistory of marriage nor on the repudiation of them but instead on the transformation of them into marriage. What *Summer* does repudiate is the rescue of passion from property accomplished in *Daddy-Long-Legs* by the reduction of marriage to incest and guaranteed in "Beatrice Palmato" by the doubling of incest with adultery. Passion in itself is no more interesting than property in itself. Which is why *Summer*'s commitment to convention is ultimately more powerful than "Beatrice Palmato's" unconventionality. Marriage is made new, as Wharton's inquiry into the origins of the family turns out to be a technique for reorganizing it.

4

✲

SUCCESS

"What will she do?" is a question Henry James asks twice about Isabel Archer in his Preface to the New York Edition (1908) of *The Portrait of a Lady* (1881). The answer is marry, a conventional enough response for the heroine of a nineteenth-century novel, but one also that echoes inversely a concern of James's: "I shall not marry," he wrote Grace Norton while he was writing and she was reading *Portrait*, and, several months earlier, enclosing a copy of the first chapters of *Portrait*, he wrote William Dean Howells, "The only important things that can happen to me are to die and to marry, and as yet I do neither." What he *was* doing was writing; his letters of 1880 are filled with the sense of confidence and achievement that seem to have accompanied the production of *Portrait*. "I must try and seek a larger success than I have yet obtained in doing something on a larger scale than I have yet done," he had written Howells the year before, and by the time he wrote Grace Norton announcing his intention never to marry, he was able also to characterize *Portrait* as "much the best thing I have done," just the "success" he had been looking for. Thus the question of what Isabel will do arises as an answer to the question of what Henry will do, and *The Portrait of a Lady*, by answering the first question, becomes the answer to the second.

It might, of course, be argued that these answers should be understood as contrasting with as well as paralleling each other; the fact of his not marrying is always identified by James with an absence of "personal news" and the inevitability of Isabel's marriage no doubt derives from the difficulty of a young woman in her circumstances doing anything that would not be personal. But we have already begun to examine the development in the late nineteenth century of technologies that would transpose the personal into the public and we have also seen how marriage itself could begin to be understood as a way of entering the market rather than withdrawing from it. Which is not to say that Isabel marries for money (she does, in some sense, just the opposite) but is to say that *Portrait* treats the question of whom she will marry (what she will "do") very much as a career choice. That is, the question of finding "something to do" in (and, ultimately, with) *Portrait* is essentially a question about finding a way to satisfy what Madame Merle calls one's "ambitions" and so is inextricably bound up with the question of finding what she calls a "*carrière*."

Indeed, the problem with marriage as an answer to the question of what Isabel will "do with herself" is not so much that marrying will not seem like doing much but rather, as our analysis of the white-slave panic has already suggested, that, if it seems like doing at all, it will be doing too much. "Most women," Ralph Touchett observes, "did with themselves nothing at all; they waited, in attitudes more or less gracefully passive, for a man to come that way and furnish them with a destiny. Isabel's originality was that she gave one an impression of having intentions of her own." The passage out of the passivity of white slavery leads into the marriage market, and, of course, although writing, like marriage, could be understood to have a value that transcended the market (Howells, in "The Man of Letters as a Man of Business," described business as the "opprobrium" of art, insisting that "work which cannot be truly priced in money cannot be truly paid in money" [1902]), it could be more easily understood as having nothing but market value. Even in the utopian society of Bellamy's *Looking Backward*, based on the abolition of "buying and selling" and hence on the disappearance of the market altogether, literature survives as virtually the only commodity with a market value; authors receive work "furloughs" proportionate to their "royalties" and, of course, the amount of royalties is fixed by the demand for (although not the sales of) their books. "Kissing . . . goes by favor," Howells had remarked, intending to dissuade young writers from striving for any success other than that of intrinsic merit while identifying instead the principle of value that undid the notion of intrinsic merit.

It is from this perspective, then, the perspective of the art or marriage market, that writing and marrying can each count as a "carrière," but it is also from this perspective that they are each deeply flawed as things "to do." Frank Cowperwood, the hero of Dreiser's *Trilogy of Desire* (*The Financier* [1912], *The Titan* [1914], *The Stoic* [1947]), sees "buying and selling stocks" as "an art," which is to say, as "gambling pure and simple," or, in the terminology of the new futures markets, "fictitious dealing." The fiction in fictitious deals was a consequence of the fact that the exchanges made it possible for a man to sell commodities that he did not own and that did not, perhaps, even exist, instead of what farmers and sympathetic legislators called "the real thing" and so to make a living not by "producing" commodities with a certain value but by "betting" on what their value would be if and when the commodities came into existence. From the 1880s through the 1920s, farmers and their representatives sought to limit the activities of these "parasitic" "speculators" but they were continually thwarted by the difficulty of distinguishing "legitimate" hedges against price fluctuations from "illegitimate" speculation in fluctuations. Hedgers and speculators were both gamblers, both betting on prices they could not themselves determine. Thus the main events of Cowperwood's career – his love for Aileen Butler, his loss of a fortune in the brief panic set off by the Chicago fire of 1871, and his recovery of one in the more "widespread and enduring" panic set off by the collapse of Jay Cooke in 1873 – are events over which, as he himself insists, he had no "control."

More striking still, in Edith Wharton's *The House of Mirth* (1905) (the nickname of a firm on the New York Stock Exchange), the element of "risk" counts first as the necessary condition of erotic attraction (Lily Bart and Lawrence Selden excite themselves by assuring one another of the extraordinary "risk" they would take in marrying each other), second, of moral impeccability (the "essential baseness" of the blackmail scheme that would bring Lily to financial, and return her to social, success but that she nobly refuses to go along with is said to consist in its "freedom from risk"), and, third and most surprising, as the necessary condition of "power" (the triumph Lily experiences in the famous *tableau vivant*, where she displays herself as Reynolds's "Mrs. Lloyd" before an appreciative and excited audience, is a direct consequence of her sense that "she was risking too much"). What Isabel wants is the pleasure of doing, but the experience of entering the market is the experience of (at worst, like the farmers) giving up that pleasure or (at best, like the speculators, like Cowperwood and Lily Bart) exchanging it for the "intoxicating sense" of "power" that comes not from doing but from betting.

Lily's "power" depends upon her having something to sell – herself – and someone to sell it to; the plot of *The House of Mirth* consists largely in her increasingly desperate and ingenious attempts to make a market in herself. But Isabel's desire "to do" depends upon her *not* selling and so requires her to deny that anything she can own is her. "Nothing that belongs to me is any measure of me; everything's on the contrary a limit, a barrier, and a perfectly arbitrary one." The fact of ownership is here understood as a kind of obstacle and so successful acquisition is transformed into an encounter with constraint. As Harold Frederic says of his newly wealthy hero in *The Market-Place* (1899), "He could eat and drink a little better than the poor man . . . but only within hard and fast bounds. There was an ascertained limit beyond which the millionaire could no more stuff himself with food and wine than could the beggar." Frederic here is repeating a conventional bewilderment about the ambitions of "plutocrats"; it was easy to understand why people wanted enough money to buy themselves whatever they wanted, harder to understand how they kept on wanting. But in gesturing towards the "ascertained limit" of rich men's desires, Frederic is answering as well as asking the question of what plutocrats want. They want what Isabel wants: not to experience limits.

This desire was, in a certain sense, traditional in American life and literature, expressed often in Emerson and made most spectacularly manifest in Whitman's *Song of Myself*, where the impulse to "incorporate" everything outside the self ("I find I incorporate gneiss, coal, long-threaded moss, fruits, grains, esculent roots") commits the writer to a logic of all or nothing that understands the very idea of externality as a limit and hence a threat to the self; anything unincorporated by the self is a potential incorporator of the self. In Emerson and Whitman, this phenomenology of expansionism accompanied the actual expansion of the United States to the Pacific Coast; by the 1890s, however, the Superintendent of the Census had declared the "western movement" of Americans at an end, and in 1893 Frederick Jackson Turner had identified the closing of the frontier with the end of "the first period of American history." Where the "development" of other nations had taken place within "a limited area," the development of the United States had thus far consisted in expansion beyond its established limits; that "new product," the "American," was the result of this continual transgression. Now, with the closing of the frontier, the experience of limitlessness had to be sought elsewhere, and if Cuba, Hawaii, and the Philippines seemed to some of Turner's contemporaries to offer themselves as one kind of location, the financial world seemed to offer another, somewhat closer to home.

Thus the scene of "triumph" on which *The Market-Place* opens (its first words are "The battle was over") is a scene of "unchecked, expanding conquest stretched away in every direction" produced by a stock deal that is structured to provide not only a great deal of money (as might any successful transaction) but also an experience of apparently limitless power. Thorpe has got "a corner on the bears"; he controls all the shares of a stock that other traders have been selling short and when these traders have to deliver the shares they have sold, they will have to buy them from him at whatever price he names. The price will, of course, be high, but the point here is that, whatever it is, it will be set by Thorpe; hence his "pleasure" consists not in imagining how high the price will be but in contemplating his own power to set it. Which is why Frederic characterizes Thorpe's triumph as "somewhat shapeless to the view," and why Thorpe himself experiences "a sense of fascinated pain when he trie[s] to define to himself what its limits would probably be." The sense of pleasure and power is unimaginable without the moment of payment, but payment can only be experienced as an end to pleasure and power – "he would not give it room in his mind tonight."

What Thorpe enjoys, then, is an experience that may be sometimes available in the market but is by no means characteristic of it; he cannot be understood as sharing Cowperwood's interest in speculation. For although he describes himself as "dealing in differences" and thus indifferent to the actual "value of the property" whose shares he sells ("If there wasn't any such property in existence, it would be just the same"), he himself is not a speculator; he does not bet on the rise and fall of stocks. The pleasure of speculation involves taking advantage of situations over which you have no control, but the pleasure of the corner (like that, for example, of the monopoly) involves the contemplation of nothing but your control. The monopolist's "triumph" is less a victory *in* the market than a victory *over* the market.

Hence Thorpe's ambition is to be transfigured into "a being for whom all City things [which is to say, all *market* things] were an abomination, a 'gentleman.'" But being a gentleman, even though it gets him called "master," does not get him the experience of mastery he got "grinding" the Jews in the market. Life at his country estate, "High Thorpe," produces only boredom and the sense not of having expanded but of having "deliberately shrunk," and in response to this sense of encroaching limits Thorpe finds himself for the first time interested in the "social question." Andrew Carnegie's "The Gospel of Wealth" (1889) had urged upon the rich the moral and social advantages of philanthropy but the appeal to his conscience registers more convincingly on Thorpe as an appeal to what Frederic calls his "old dormant, formless lust for power." It is formless because, as we have seen, form can appear to it only as a limit, like a house (e.g. High Thorpe) that, once bought, testifies only to the limits of one's need for housing, the limit, as one might put it, of one's power to be housed. Philanthropy, however, knows no such limits: "What other phase of power carried with it such rewards, such gratitudes, such humble subservience as far as the eye could reach – as that exercised by the intelligently munificent philanthropist?" Thorpe's pleasure in making money, the experience of power in grinding the Jews, is equalled only by the pleasure in giving money away; except that the pleasure of giving it away may be even greater than the pleasure of accumulating it since, eventually, the Jews get all ground up (the limit on their ability to pay is a limit on one's power over them), while the "humble subservience" of the recipients of one's philanthropy may go on forever.

"He had achieved power . . . He had an excess of wealth" but "What could he do with it?" Isabel Archer's answer is the same as Thorpe's – "to be rich," she thinks, "was a virtue because it was to be able to *do*," and if at first the only act commensurate with such limitless power seems to be the act of refusing (Lord Warburton, Caspar Goodwood), Madame Merle reminds her that "accepting's after all an exercise of power as well." Indeed, accepting

Osmond is an exercise of power that continues the logic of Isabel's refusals and Thorpe's philanthropy; where to marry Goodwood or Warburton would be to accept the limits produced by *their* power (their wealth, position, even masculinity), to marry Osmond is to exercise her own, the "power to marry a poor man." Osmond provides the opportunity for an acceptance as free of constraints as the refusals that precede it. But just as the "beautiful" and "interesting" "difficulty" of what a "frail vessel" like Isabel can do is resolved in the New York Preface by the author's "really 'doing' her," so Isabel's moment of action turns out to be a moment of being acted upon: "What have you to do with me?" she will ask Madame Merle, only to receive an answer as absolute as the power she had imagined herself to exercise in marrying Osmond, "Everything."

Seeking to transcend the market thus proves to be as compromising as entering it was. In *The American* (1877), James had imagined a pretty young woman hired by the "millionaire" Christopher Newman to copy pictures in the Louvre standing before one of her efforts (apparently an Italian portrait), confessing to Newman and his friend Valentin de Bellegarde her incompetence, and, to drive home her point, covering the picture with first a "horizontal" and then a "vertical" "daub" of "red paint." Newman, no "judge" of painting, protests that she has "spoiled" her picture; Valentin, who is a judge, likes it "better that way than as it was before." "Now it is more interesting," he says, "It tells a story." Identifying himself with Turgenieff in the Preface to *Portrait*, James described himself as an artist more committed to "character" than to "story" (or, calling it by its "nefarious name," "plot") and indeed it is just because the "germ" of *Portrait* consisted so notably in a vision of Isabel as an "unattached character" in "perfect isolation" that the "difficulty" of making her "interesting" arose. In the event, of course, Isabel becomes interesting in the same way that *The American*'s portrait does; the "group of entertainers" James brings on to "make" her "interesting," the "*ficelles*" who are like "wheels to the coach" that carry "the subject alone," turn into "the fishwives who helped to bring back to Paris from Versailles . . . the carriage of the royal family." What James called the "essence" of his work is destroyed by its "form," "character" is crossed out by "story"; independent Isabel can become interesting only by ceasing to be independent.

There is an important sense, then, in which *The Portrait of a Lady* allegorizes the formal problem of its production, but there is an important sense also in which the formal problem of its production is in no sense exclusively formal. After observing that the crossed-out portrait is now, because it tells a story, more interesting, Valentin asks the artist if it is "for sale," and she replies, "Everything I have is for sale." One aspect of the "larger success" that James looked forward to in 1879 was financial; he anticipated asking more for the serial rights to *Portrait* than he had for "any of its predecessors": at the same time, however, he was mystified by the sales record ("not brilliant") of his books. By the time of the Preface (although James had by no means given up his hopes for financial success) his ambivalence about his market had been translated into ambivalence about his readers and had assumed the form of something like resignation: the artist must be content "to work for but a 'living wage,'" "the least possible quantity of attention required for consciousness of a 'spell'"; anything more can only come as a "gratuity," a "mere miraculous windfall." The radically diminished sense of what Isabel can do is accompanied by a less radically diminished sense of what "really 'doing' her" can be. And Isabel's sense that, with the world all before her, she can do whatever she chooses, is replaced by the "dream of some Paradise (for art)" where, irrespective of what the artist has done, he may enjoy the occasional "tip," the unearned "fruit of a tree he may not pretend to have shaken." The fruit fallen from the unshaken tree rewrites as windfall the profits of art; the imagined Paradise is a market that no one can corner.

THE ORGANIZATION MAN

James's last novel, *The Golden Bowl*, was published in 1904; its sales numbered in the hundreds. The American bestseller of that year, selling 40,000 copies even before publication (on the strength of the great success in 1903 of *The Call of the Wild*), was Jack London's *The Sea-Wolf*, precisely the kind of adventure story – "surprising caravans and catching pirates" – that *The Portrait of a Lady* was not. But the question about Isabel – "what will she do" – nevertheless finds its place in *The Sea Wolf*, even if in a slightly more explicit fashion: "What do you do for a living?" Wolf Larsen asks Humphrey Van Weyden. The answer is nothing (Humphrey is a "gentleman") and from one standpoint the story of *The Sea-Wolf* is the story of his learning "to do," a story that raises, in its own way, something like the technical difficulty of *Portrait*; the problem of imagining a woman who can do is matched by the problem of imagining a man who cannot. London's solution is to begin by insisting on Humphrey's effeminacy: his response to the sinking of the ferry *Martinez* is "hysterical" shrieking that repeats the screaming of "an hysterical group of women," his status as "housekeeper" on board the *Ghost* is a function of the fact that his muscles are "small and soft, like a woman's," and his bachelordom at the age of thirty-five is a consequence of his "monkish" and "abnormal" inability to love any of the women he has spent his life surrounded by. All this changes on the *Ghost*, especially the inability to be "amative": "fascinated" first by Wolf Larsen's "masculine" beauty, Hump finds himself, when the poet Maud

Brewster falls into Larsen's clutches, even more "fascinated by the fascinated look" Larsen turns upon her. In the best triangular fashion, Humphrey learns to desire a woman by desiring a man who desires a woman. When Humphrey in a moment of triumph at the end of *The Sea-Wolf* thinks to himself "I did it!" and is echoed aloud by Maud's exclamation, "You did it," they are celebrating his having become a man, an achievement made possible only by his first having been "like" a woman.

What is virtually the paradigm of the adventure novel that *The Portrait of a Lady* sets itself against involves, then, not exactly the adventure of a man among men but the adventure of a man becoming a man. And it involves also the adventure of a man becoming more "like a woman," as Wolf Larsen is reduced by the brain tumor that "wastes" him like a "strong anxiety" to absolute immobility. Larsen is a "materialist," mocking Humphrey's idealistic belief in the "soul" and continually defeating him in argument, but the disease that paralyzes before it kills him is the triumph of Hump's idealism: "Walled by the living clay, that fierce intelligence . . . burned on; but it burned on in silence and darkness. And it was disembodied. To that intelligence there could be no objective knowledge of a body. It knew no body. The very world was not. It knew only itself and the vastness and profundity of the quiet and the dark." The proof of Wolf's soul lies not in its escaping his body but in its being entombed by it. Wolf's materialism has consisted in his conviction that there was nothing more to "living" than "doing" ("to be rich was a virtue," Isabel Archer thinks, "because it was to be able to *do*, and . . . to do could only be sweet"); the defeat of that materialism is the reduction of "to do" to "to be": "To be was all that remained to him." Confronting in his paralysis the transformation of "the world" into "the vastness and profundity" of "no body," Wolf becomes Humphrey, "no sensation" in his legs, his hands growing "numb," and "a chilling numbness" "wrapping about" and "creeping into" his "heart," as he floats in the "grey primordial vastness" of the San Francisco Bay. Wolf at the end is ontologically incapable of answering the question that Humphrey is socially, professionally, and sexually incapable of answering at the beginning: "What do you do?" Thus *The Sea-Wolf*'s counter-plot repeats and distills *Portrait*'s plot: "the world all before" Isabel Archer becomes "very small"; Wolf Larsen's world disappears altogether.

But the absoluteness of Wolf's end suggests at the same time a difference from Isabel's, since even though Isabel's world has become small, in that world, she has become "free." What she is free to do is to follow the "very straight path" back to her marriage and to her role as Pansy's stepmother. "There's no such thing as an isolated man or woman," Madame Merle had told Isabel, and Isabel's return to Osmond involves a repudiation of the fantasy of omnipotent isolation more decisive than any imagined by Madame Merle or even than the reduction of that fantasy to Wolf's paralysis. Indeed, the failure of Madame Merle's own "great" "ambitions," like the failure of Wolf's, might be said to mark a turning point in the modern history of ambition. Wolf's "ambition" was Napoleonic but, although he "dreamed as greatly as the Corsican," the "opportunity" never came. The highest he can rise to is "master and owner of a ship," a parody of the imperial self-aggrandizement that is itself parodied in the paralysis that reduces him to nothing but self. The Napoleonic ambition to conquer the world is here (as in *Portrait*, where Madame Merle is described as "the great, wide world itself") understood to culminate in becoming the world; the attempt to overcome external constraints culminates in the disappearance of externality itself. But this desired disappearance of the "limits" on what one can do is represented instead as the impossibility of doing anything at all. Madame Merle, who has had "Everything" "to do" with Isabel, can do nothing but give up the world for "America"; Wolf Larson, who embodies "the verb 'to do,'" had "not done something." It is left to Isabel, whose world is "very small," to marry Pansy, and it is Humphrey van Weyden, not Wolf Larsen, who, working his way up to mate and eventually master of the reduced *Ghost*, will experience "the joy of success."

From this perspective, it is significant that *The Sea-Wolf*, like *Portrait*, ends with the commitment to marriage. For if marrying Napoleon might be understood as the closest the heroine of the nineteenth-century novel could come to being Napoleon, marriage in *The Portrait of a Lady* and *The Sea-Wolf* might be said to provide the technology through which the desire to be Napoleon begins to seem obsolete. It revises the dream of independence by revising the nightmare of dependence, transforming what had hitherto looked like the latter into what would henceforth look like the former. So, although readers since Ambrose Bierce have complained about *The Sea-Wolf*'s "sexless lovers" (and although Humphrey himself, as we have already seen, makes a good deal out of his inability to be "amative"), it is essential to London's rewriting of ambition that Hump marry and almost equally essential that his marital desire both imitate and revise Wolf Larsen's. The imitation consists, of course, in a kind of inspiration; it is only Wolf's desire for Maud that produces Hump's. But Wolf's desire (like his great ambitions) induces paralysis; at the moment that he is about to rape her, he gets a headache so bad that he is "helpless and frightened . . . for the first time in his life." The revision, then, consists in the replacement of the desire to possess Maud with the desire to marry her, a desire that transforms the impotently "infinite ambition" of all-consuming independence into the narrowed and hence empowering ambition of marriage.

The requirements of the Napoleonic imagination can only be met by the transcendence of what James calls "limits" and London calls "walls," a transcendence embodied for Isabel in the "power to marry a poor man" and embodied (or rather "disembodied") for Wolf in the liberation of his soul that is at the same time the paralysis of his flesh. But the Isabel who returns, "free," to Osmond turns the constraints upon her actions into the condition of their possibility. In order for her to do anything at all, the world in which she can do whatever she chooses needs to be transformed by her marriage to Osmond into a world in which the most she can do is try to help Pansy marry Ned Rosier. And Humphrey, reduced from a "gentleman" to a wage "slave," rises out of slavery to become not a gentleman again but a "mate," first Wolf's and then Maud's, making out of the apparent reduction of independence to dependence a transformation of what used to count as dependence into what will now count as a way of "standing on your own legs." What we see in these texts is finally not a failure of ambition but the failure of a certain idea of what ambition is, the disappearance of a certain kind of ambition, the Napoleonic ambition that characterizes the nineteenth-century novel, and the beginning of its replacement by a new form of ambition, one identified not with the elimination of "limits" but with the "success" of a career defined by them.

Another way to put this might be to say that in Isabel's and Hump's marriages we begin to see something like the bureaucratization of success. That the perceived replacement of the self-employed entrepreneur with the salaried worker was a source of general concern has long been an important theme in American social history. Daniel T. Rodgers quotes Samuel Eliot's insistence, in 1871, that "To put a man upon wages, is to put him in the position of a dependent," and goes on to point out that, in 1903, when the president of the United Mine Workers remarked that "the average wage earner has made up his mind that he must remain a wage earner" and has "given up the hope" of becoming "a capitalist," "he evoked a storm of middle-class protest." Indeed, as late as 1912, Woodrow Wilson could make a campaign issue out of the fact that most Americans no longer worked "for themselves" or "as partners" but instead "as employees," as "the servants of corporations." In this context, Isabel Archer's love of her "independence" and – through loving it so much – her loss of it enacts one of the most common nightmares of the "old" middle class metamorphosing into the "new." But it is in this context also that Madame Merle's advocacy of the career (and Hump's and Isabel's eventual access to one) achieves its full force. For the career – with its promise of promotions and professional recognition, its rewriting of jobs as vocations and its eroticization of work – would do for the new middle-class wage-earner (in life, if never quite so powerfully in art) what the narrative of endless accumulation had done for the old middle-class capitalist.

This is not to say that the story of accumulation had utterly lost its charm, any more than had its paradoxically accompanying ideal, the "gentleman." The paradox consisted in the difference between the man who was born to wealth and the one who had to struggle to achieve it, but this opposition could be ironed out by time (no remark in the nineteenth-century novel is more frequent than the observation that the parents of today's gentility were yesterday's tradespeople) or, more ingeniously (if less convincingly), rearranged as complementarity. As early as Hawthorne's *The House of the Seven Gables* (1851), the poor but honest working-man, Holgrave, could be transformed into a wealthy landowner both as a way of restoring to him what, by family right, should really be his and as a way of paying tribute to his integrity, and as late as Horatio Alger Jr.'s *Struggling Upward* (1890), the poor but honest Luke Larkin is rewarded for exhibiting his "good qualities" by an employer who turns out to be his cousin and so becomes his "guardian." In Alger, "accumulating money" can be so easily interchanged with inheriting it because the accumulating capitalist and the inheriting gentleman are both understood as essentially independent; the defining difference is between them and salaried socialites like Prince Duncan (also called "Squire") who pretends to be an aristocrat but is not even, since he will not pay his son's gambling debts, a "gentleman," and who is led by his aristocratic ambitions into disastrous stock-market speculations that only make manifest his pre-existent lack of self-reliance. It has often been observed that the Alger "myth" of the self-made man is somewhat compromised by the importance of blind luck to the success of his virtuous young men, but, of course, the point in Alger is that luck is not blind. *Struggling Upward* can be subtitled *Luke Larkin's Luck* because luck is represented as a sign of "good qualities" and so Luke's "success" can be better understood as a mark of what he is than as a reward for what he has done or as a condition that he has achieved.

And by the same token, anyone in *Struggling Upward* who really has to struggle is revealed, by the mere fact of his struggling, as someone who is unworthy of being at the top and who will not be allowed to stay there. The aspiring Prince and his "aristocratic" son Randolph are exposed as dishonest (hence unlucky) frauds and are "removed to the West," where "Randolph is now an office boy at a salary of four dollars a week." Randolph will not rise; more important, the very possibility of rising – the possibility, that is, of an alternative to genteel and/or entrepreneurial independence – has been identified with dishonesty.

Rising, as we saw in chapter 1, was viewed with suspicion also by writers with more convincing claims to gentility than Horatio Alger's. In Hoosic Falls, the Virginian is rumored to be a *"rustler,"* a word with "many meanings," according to Wister, but not found "in any dictionary." None of the many meanings fits the Virginian, however; he is not "some kind of horse"; he is not "a cattle thief"; above all, he is not one of those new young men who are aggressively "alive and pushing." It is this that distinguishes the Virginian, in Wister's (and the aristocratic Molly's) eyes from the "most rising young man in Hoosic Falls." The Virginian is a "gentleman" who does not need to push because he does not need to rise.

At the same time, however, *The Virginian* imagines a certain kind of space for "rising": partly of the kind the West had long been supposed to provide – the Virginian saves his money and takes up land on the way to becoming an independent rancher in Montana – and partly of the kind that was becoming more usual in places like Hoosic Falls. For the story of the Virginian is above all the story of his promotion – from cowhand to acting foreman and from acting foreman to the position of foreman. The humiliation of Trampas with the famous frog-ranching tale is explained from the perspective of office politics – "as boss of the outfit he beat Trampas, who was settin' up for opposition boss" – and when a "savage" "pulse of triumph" makes itself visible on the Virginian's usually "gentle" face, it is brought on not by gunplay or the famous ("When you call me that, *smile*") threat of gunplay, but by the news that Trampas's "powerful friend," the "old foreman," has taken a new job. Thus although the Virginian is in an important sense defined by his genteel difference from the rising young men of the East, he is in an equally important sense not simply their opposite but their redemption: in the West, office politics can be understood as tests of manliness and disgraceful dependence on one's "employer" becomes admirable loyalty to him.

Most important, "rising" becomes remaining true to yourself. *The Virginian* begins with the Virginian and his best friend Steve as simple cowhands, working and playing together; it moves towards its end with Steve become a rustler and the Virginian required by his employer and his own sense of "justice" to lynch him. "You have a friend and his ways are your ways," the Virginian says, but then he gets "disturbed over getting rich quick and becoming a big man in the Territory. And the years go on, until you are foreman of Judge Henry's ranch and he – is dangling back in the cottonwoods." Although it is the Virginian who has in fact risen, it is Steve who tried to get rich and become a big man: "I have kept my ways the same. He is the one that took to new ones." Rustler's meanings collapse into each other as the "pushing" man becomes a "cattle thief." The alternative to being a rustler is being a foreman; "What is a foreman?" Molly's mother had wondered upon hearing of the engagement: "a sort of upper servant," is her sister's dismayed reply. But the sister, unable to see past the old opposition between self-employment and dependence, does not understand. The absorption of the pushing young man into the rustler and the opposition of the rustler to the foreman saves the foreman from having to push. The foreman's is a purified "ambition," a rising that is a staying the same, a "career" for a "gentleman."

From this standpoint, the difference between Alger's Luke Larkin and Wister's Virginian is real but not absolute. It is real because, unlike the Virginian, Luke does not get paid and he does not get promoted; he is rewarded for the work he has done by a generous "gift" and the only "promotion" in the story belongs to the dishonest drummer J. Madison Coleman, who ends up in the State penitentiary at Joliet. But it is not absolute because the Virginian's career, replete with salary and promotions, is nonetheless like Luke Larkin's in being imagined as an effect of his "good qualities." Indeed, the whole point of *The Virginian* might from this standpoint be understood as the attempt to reforge the link between success and character that the disappearance of self-employed self-reliance had seemed to break. The transformation of the independent agrarian/entrepreneur into the speculator, "trading in differences," made all actions look like accidents. From this standpoint, the tribute to "hard work" and "self-denial" supposedly embodied in Luke's luck could just as easily be seen as an acknowledgment of their irrelevance. In the market, it is better to be lucky than to be good. But the Virginian's career makes work pay again; putting the hired man on the managerial track, it saves him from wage-slavery and speculation both. The Virginian's condition as an employee is the source of rather than an obstacle to "everything": "recognition, higher station, better fortune, a separate house of his own, and . . . the woman he wanted." And "games of chance" (like the poker game that ends with Trampas being instructed to smile, or like the rebellion of Trampas, analogized to "poker," that ends with the Virginian's promotion) turn out to be occasions for the assertion of those "good qualities" that playing the market makes irrelevant. Texts like *The Sea-Wolf* and *The Virginian* are experiments in the rescue of middle-class agency.

James on his deathbed, delirious, dictated to his "esteemed Brother and Sister" a letter he signed "Napoleone"; it described his "plans" ("of a great scope, a majesty unsurpassed by any work of the kind yet undertaken in France") for the Louvre and the Tuileries and ended by assuring his correspondents that there would be "no question of modifications either economic or aesthetic" in these designs or in any "further projects of your affectionate Napoleone."

Madame Merle too had ambitions that would have seemed "ridiculous" if she had spoken of them. James's own career represented, in the intensity with which he pursued them, both the destruction and the renovation of those imperial ambitions. The failure of the New York Edition marked the final stage in the Master's inability to impose his will on the market, and the "Preface" to *Portrait* reads as a proleptic admission of that failure. The emperors of the market, acknowledging, like Isabel, no limits on what they can do, get, like Isabel "done." Indeed, so close is the fantasy of absolute helplessness to the fantasy of absolute omnipotence that, in a text like Frank Norris's *The Octopus* (1901), even the narrative difference between them – the time it takes for what Isabel does to turn out to be what is done to her – begins to disappear; Magnus Derrick's desire to make himself "the master" is identified with his gambler's excitement at seeing his "Chance." "To know it when it came, to recognize it as it passed . . . grip at it, catch at it, blind, reckless, staking all upon the hazard of the issue, that was genius." Agrarian rhetoric opposed the farmer to the speculator, but Derrick is a farmer *and* a speculator. He represents the extension of the farmer's commitment to autonomy into a market that rendered the conditions of absolute independence identical to the conditions of absolute dependence. Magnus imagines himself "controlling the situation" by imagining himself, "blind, reckless," in a situation over which he has absolutely no control. This is Norris's version of Wolf Larsen's paralysis, an omnipotence indistinguishable from impotence.

But if in writing *Portrait*, James had proclaimed the extent of his own ambition by insisting on his "single individuality" and deciding that it was better to succeed than to marry, in *Portrait* itself, marriage destroys a "single individuality" and yet begins to look like a way of succeeding. And as Wolf Larsen sits on deck growing increasingly comatose ("the wires," "as he phrased it," "were like the stock market, now up, now down"), Humphrey and Maud rebuild their reduced version of the *Ghost* and discuss what Maud calls the "dismantling" of her "old Pantheon" of heroes ("Napoleon and Caesar and their fellows") and its replacement with a "new Pantheon" containing, they agree, one "modern hero" ("and a greater because modern"), Stanford's "Dr. Jordan." David Starr Jordan was the president of Stanford University, best known beyond Stanford for his racist anti-imperialism. His hostility to the annexation of Cuba or the Philippines is nothing really to the point of *The Sea-Wolf* – it is his pragmatic test of truth, "Can we make it work? Can we trust our lives to it?" that brings him to Maud's mind – but his anti-imperialism is not altogether irrelevant either. In a speech before the Stanford graduating class of 1898, printed and then reprinted as the lead essay of his *Imperial Democracy* (1899), Jordan had placed himself in opposition not only to "keeping" Cuba and the Philippines but to imperial ambition as such, to the "delicious" and "intoxicating" "dream" that motivated the "Roman emperors," "Nelson," Wellington," and "Napoleon." Of the three reasons he gave for resisting imperialism – "First, dominion is brute force; second, dependent nations are slave nations; third, the making of men is greater than the building of empires" – it is the third that mattered most to him and that resonates through the literature of the period.

Indeed, the commitments to imperialism abroad and monopoly at home – this double expression of the "American energy" that Frederick Jackson Turner thought the frontier had created and that would, in the wake of its closing, have to find a new outlet – appear from this standpoint as the expression also of a certain nostalgia for an older form of "dominant individualism." The *new* individualism would find its frontiers within, structuring limits instead of eliminating them. Thus, nothing is more characteristic of the Progressive "figure of heroic proportions," the "man of force," than that, like Dreiser's "Genius," he turn out to be "a good administrator" who can "handle men." Eugene Witla is supposed to be a great painter but most of *The "Genius"* (1915) is devoted to an account of his successes and failures as a "manager": "I love to manage men," he tells one of his first employers on his way up the corporate ladder and "Oh Flower Face," he complains to his eighteen-year old girl-friend as he is about to lose both her and his job, "This has been managed wrong." All that is left of Napoleonic ambition in *The "Genius"* is a Jamesian hostility to marriage, and even this disappears in a text like *Philip Dru, Administrator* (1912) which takes Dru (like Eugene, a "genius" and a "leader of men"), sets him at "the head of a committee to perfect not only a state, but a national organization as well," and culminates in his marriage to the beautiful and idealistic young fund-raiser, Gloria. In *Philip Dru*, even the bankers and politicians whose old-time Gilded Age rapacity made necessary the revolution that brings the "Administrator" into office turn out to be more committed to "organization" than to money or power; their chief ends up as the Administrator's best friend and closest advisor.

"Imperialism . . . belongs to the past," Jordan thought; Philip Dru favors the annexation of Canada and Mexico as a contribution to "efficiency." But the differences in foreign policy disappear in the face of the more general enthusiasm for making and managing men, and even greater differences tend to get subsumed by the greater effort to reimagine the limits of ambition as the conditions of its possibility. Anonymous at publication, the author of *Philip Dru* was widely rumored to be Theodore Roosevelt but was in fact Col. Edward House, who would wind up as the right-hand man of Roosevelt's successful opponent in the election of 1912, Woodrow Wilson. And the crucial difference between Wilson and Roosevelt in that election, at least as Wilson presented it, was precisely over the question of ambition. Articulating his vision of America as a land of "absolutely free opportunity, where no man is supposed to be under any limitation except the limitations of his character and of his mind," Wilson attacked Roosevelt as an agent of the monopolies which were leaving Americans with the choice of being "employees or nothing." The "New Freedom" promised salvation from this "dependence" and a return to the principles of the last President to have earned Wilson's approval, the "free" and (like Isabel in James's "Preface") "unentangled" Lincoln. It was for this reason that commentators like Walter Lippmann thought of him as essentially reactionary, committed to the "old ideal" of the individual entrepreneur rather than to the new "collective organization of industry"; he makes no mention, Lippmann complained, of "the new type of administrator, the specialist, the specially trained business man." At the same time, however, Wilson insisted that the "New Freedom" involved "something more than being left alone." For, although he spent much of the campaign excoriating the political "machines" that were, he thought, depriving the people of their freedom, he found his own best articulation of that freedom in the image of "a great piece of powerful machinery" whose "great piston" could run with "absolute freedom" only because of its "absolutely perfect alignment and adjustment with the other parts of the machine."

Wilson criticized Roosevelt for his corporate paternalism, his willingness to accept the dictatorship of the trusts if only it could be made benevolent, and so Lippmann criticized Wilson for seeming to hearken back to a Jacksonian model of the self-reliant entrepreneur. But what was new about the "New Freedom" was precisely its revision of self-reliance, its reimagination of freedom as the observation of limits and its redefinition of the free man as the perfectly adjusted cog in the machine. Opposing Roosevelt, Wilson follows James, who rewrote the novel of marriage, producing the ambitious manager out of the adulterous wife, and he follows London and Wister, who rewrote the adventure novel, producing the successful executive out of the fearless pirate and gunslinger.

CHOPIN'S SIXTHS

In 1881, Madame Merle urges upon Isabel the importance of a "career"; by the time of the New York Edition (in 1908), the word had become so common that in order to mark its dangerous novelty James (like Wister putting "rustler" in italics) was compelled to translate it into French: the problem with Americans abroad, Madame Merle tells Isabel, is that they lack "something to do"; Ralph

Touchett's consumption makes him the fortunate exception "because it gives him something to do. His consumption's his *carrière*." At least part of what is at stake in this change is the fact that the increasingly ordinary use of the word has been accompanied by a sense of the increasingly extraordinary importance of the phenomenon it names. In Robert Herrick's *The Real World* (1901), a sexy young social climber recommends the law to the idealistic hero, Jack, because it is more "worldly" (less of a "calling" than teaching or the ministry) and Jack smiles "at her conception of choosing a career, as if it were a practical affair like selecting a house-lot, over which one should not waste too much time coquetting with the soul." The point is not that Jack wants to become a minister – in fact, he does become a lawyer – but that he conceives of becoming a lawyer as more like becoming a minister than like "selecting a house-lot." Although, by the end of the century, the ministry had ceased to be a plausible career option for most ambitious young men, in *The Real World*, the exemplary appeal of the ministry is not so much diminished as it is generalized; the lure of the "worldly" consists increasingly in its resemblance to rather than its difference from the call to the ministry.

The difficulties of this transformation – understood from the standpoint not of the professional who feels himself a kind of minister but from that of the minister who feels himself a professional – are nowhere more clearly on display than in Harold Frederic's *The Damnation of Theron Ware* (1896), where entry into the ministry represents both the possibility of a career and the repudiation of that possibility. The young Theron's "early strenuous battle to get away from the farm and achieve such education as would open to him the gates of professional life" culminates in a "wave of religious enthusiasm which caught him as he stood on the borderland of manhood, and swept him off into a veritable new world of views and aspirations." But what is here presented as biographical narrative is elsewhere understood as social conflict – between professionalism and religious enthusiasm or, more specifically, between middle-class culture (Frederic calls it "civilization") and "the severely straight and narrow path of primitive Methodism." By "primitive" Methodism, Frederic means "Free Methodism," one of what the historian of fundamentalism, George M. Marsden, has called the "numerous denominations" formed in response to "the radical demands of the varieties of Holiness teachings" which in the late nineteenth century "seemed to be everywhere in American revivalist Protestantism." The Holiness Movement opposed both "modernism in theology" and the "cultural changes that modernism endorsed"; thus Theron Ware's congregation resents "growth in material prosperity," refuses "the introduction of written sermons and organ-music," and deplores "the development of even a rudimentary desire among the younger people of the church to be

like others outside in dress and speech and deportment." Since Free Methodism requires its ministers to repudiate civilized professional goals as a threat
not only to what Marsden calls "a dying way of life" but to the possibility
of religious belief itself, there turns out to be a certain tension between the
young Theron Ware's search for a profession that will get him off the farm
and into "civilization" and his choice of the ministry as that profession. Hence
one version of the "damnation" of Theron Ware: drawn away from the farm by
professional ambition (the ambition, that is, to have a profession), he under-
goes the kind of religious experience that revivalists like Dwight L. Moody
were urging upon middle-class America; then, drawn away from revival by the
blandishments of "civilization," – organ-music, even – he falls and becomes,
in his wife's word, a "backslider."

The immediate cause of this backsliding is not, however, middle-class civilization as such but the beautiful Celia Madden (it is she who plays the
organ and, in a more intimate moment, the piano – Chopin) and, surprisingly, the Catholic Church. To most middle-class American Protestants, of
course, Catholicism seemed suspiciously un-American and un-middle-class.
But Frederic imagines for his Methodists a Catholicism that – for all its exotic
medievalism – is as modern in its theology as the liberal Protestantism the
revivalists despised. In what Theron Ware thinks of as the Catholic "world
of culture and grace," "creeds" are "not of importance": "Father Forbes could
talk coolly about the 'Christ-myth' without even ceasing to be . . . a very
active and effective priest." And it is the encounter with this "world of
culture" that Theron Ware understands as "the turning-point in his career,"
a turning-point in his career precisely because it seems to offer what evangelical Protestantism seems to deny – the possibility of what will in fact
be a career instead of a "calling" away from the world in which careers are
possible.

Like the "practical" young woman in *The Real World*, Theron Ware prefers
careers to callings, but Frederic goes beyond her and beyond Theron Ware as
well by suggesting – first in Catholicism and then in the professional revivalists brought in to put Ware's church on a sounder financial basis – that the
opposition between callings and careers has become obsolete. The Soulsbys
introduce Theron Ware to the "machinery," the "organization," that makes a
revival go, shocking and thrilling him with their analogy between a revival
and a theatrical performance (he has never seen a play – Moody put the theatre
ahead of the atheistic teaching of evolution in a list of the four "great temp-
tations" threatening modern Christians). But what Theron takes to be their
exemplary lack of "sincerity" – exemplary because it marks the transcendence
of (religious) belief by (show) business – is understood quite differently by the

Soulsbys themselves. For when asked if she and her husband have ever been "sincerely converted," Sister Soulsby replies, "Oh, bless you, yes! . . . Not only once – dozens of times – I may say every time." And she adds, "We couldn't do good work if we weren't." In the person of the Soulsbys, the opposition between "belief" and "business" is undone; indeed, religious enthusiasm is understood as crucial to doing "good work." If "primitive" Methodism and Theron Ware are both convinced of the need to choose between religious enthusiasm and middle-class careerism (albeit committed to different choices), the Soulsbys embody a vision of career in which that choice need never be made – a reciprocal mobilization of belief in the service of career and career in the service of belief. The plot of damnation – giving up belief for profession, enthusiasm for machinery – is thus replaced by a plot of continuous redemption: career moves become indistinguishable from conversion experiences.

In this light, the proto-fundamentalist revival looks less like an anti-modernist defense of "a dying way of life" than like a technique of modernization, and the difference between Methodism and Catholicism ceases to be the difference between primitive belief and civilized skepticism and becomes instead the difference between two different kinds of organization and two different styles of management. A church, "like everything else," Sister Soulsby says, has "got to have a boss, a head, an authority of some sort, that people will listen to and mind." The Catholic Church, as she describes it, is "chuckfull of authority," which is to say that there is a chain of command from Pope to priest to parishioner, and so, people "do as they're told." Protestants, however (especially Methodists), do not want such authority, "won't obey any boss." So, to get Methodists to do anything, those who are "responsible for running the thing" have to "put on a spurt every once in a while, and work up a general state of excitement" and "*that* is the authority, the motive power . . . by which things are done." Revival, in other words, replaces hierarchy as a management tool. Where the bureaucratic structure of the Catholic Church requires obedience to a chain of bosses – that is Catholicism's "organization," its "machinery" – the Methodist revival creates a boss within; it both establishes and appeals to an internal authority. "Truly, something is needed besides church organization and machinery and culture and pulpit oratory," complained A. M. Hills in *Holiness and Power* (1897), sounding here like the most primitive of primitive Methodists. But what was needed, Hills thought, was "multiplied holiness camp-meetings, and the increasing holiness literature of Methodism, and the appointment of such men as Keen and Durham to go from conference to conference . . ." The remedy for want of "Holy Spirit power" was better "administration"; the opposition imagined by Theron Ware between belief and organization will not stand. Because the revival makes belief itself the organization's machinery, the return to "old-time" "holiness" is also the way to success in the "next generation": "The Methodists have the theology of the future." And because entrance into the professional classes depends on mobilizing belief not abandoning it, you can only "do good work" if you are "sincerely converted."

The Methodist revival thus appears in *Theron Ware* as an exemplary technology of modern management, one that improves upon Catholicism's distribution of authority by substituting what efficiency experts like Robert G. Valentine called "organized consent" for "compulsion." Methodism (unlike Catholicism), Sister Soulsby says, is a "voluntary system," so managing Methodists is a matter of making them want to be what you want them to be, and, since good work requires sincere conversion, of making yourself be what you want them to be. Managing the managers as well as the managed, the revival undoes the opposition between business and belief and, as practiced by the Soulsbys, it does the same for the opposition between belief and "culture." Culture in *The Damnation of Theron Ware* is the seductive Celia Madden, playing the organ in the church and the piano in her bedroom. "I divide people up into two classes, you know – Greeks and Jews," Celia tells Theron Ware. Her version of the Hellenic and the Hebraic translates the distinction between Catholics and primitive Methodists into aesthetic terms; indeed, the basis of the distinction is the presence or absence of the aesthetic – to be a "Greek" is to recognize that "beauty is the only thing in life that is worth while," and "the Greekiest of the Greeks" is Chopin, a selection from whom Celia proceeds to play as a first step toward "Hellenizing" the Reverend Mr. Ware. But if Chopin marks a high point for the "Greek idea," he is also identified in this text with the most Hebraic of events, the "old-fashioned, primitive" "Methodist lovefeast." For it is at one of these that the Soulsbys make their first appearance in Octavius, winning over the crowd by singing "Rock of Ages" to a "tune" that "no one present had heard," producing "harmonies of sound" so "moving and delightful" that by the time they are done they have "captured Octavius with their first outer skirmish line." The tune, of course, is Chopin's – Sister Soulsby has taken "all sorts of melodies out of his waltzes and mazurkas and nocturnes and so on." And her reasons for choosing Chopin are as aesthetic as even Celia Madden could wish; more aesthetic, really, for while Celia talks about Chopin as a poet of "love" and compares him to Heine, Soulsby focuses on the formal, not the literary, qualities of the music: Chopin is "full of sixths" and so perfect for Brother Soulsby who "can't sing by himself any more than a crow" but who learned "those sixths so as to make the harmony" and has now got them "down to a hair." "Now that's machinery," Sister Soulsby says, that is "management, organization."

SHOP TALK

Theron Ware reimagines conflict as complementarity: professional ambition and religious enthusiasm require rather than oppose each other, the mechanics of administration produce rather than constrain passion. In this context, art emerges as a contested but also privileged site for the renegotiation of the relations between love and work, even in texts as concerned to keep them apart as the Progressive journalist William Allen White's "moral entertainment," *A Certain Rich Man* (1909). White presents the success story of the "hard, grinding, rich man," John Barclay, as a choice between two souls, one with a "passion" for music and Emerson, the other, a "born trader" of "Yankee blood" with a knack for swapping, trading, and saving: it was only when his childhood sweetheart died, White explains, that Barclay "closed his Emerson and opened his Trigonometry, and put money in his purse." But this defining choice never quite manages to be definitive; indeed, what makes John Barclay so "horrible" to his creator is the continued and contradictory existence of the "poet" alongside the captain of industry – a contradiction embodied in a portrait of Barclay whose most "wonderful feature" is "the right hand": "a long, hard, hairy, hollow, grasping, relentless hand . . . a horrible thing with artistic fingers, and a thin, greedy palm indicated by the deep hump in the back." And even the grotesquerie of the greedy and artistic hump-backed hand does not quite capture the power of John Barclay. For what is finally most striking about *A Certain Rich Man* is neither the choice of money over art nor the inability to make that choice but the power represented by the denial that any choice is necessary. John Barclay businessman gets his best ideas, it turns out, as John Barclay artist: "He thought out the whole plan of the Barclay Economy Door Strip about midnight, sitting in his night clothes at the piano after reading 'Abt Vogler,'" and the music of Wagner not only "inspires" his best ideas but embodies them: "Wagner's work is the National Provisions Company set to music." Barclay likes Chopin too but he prefers "new music" "with go to it"; in *A Certain Rich Man* the Wagnerian avatar of the avant-garde is the trust.

And not only can art be mobilized on behalf of a career in business; it can also be understood as itself a kind of exemplary career. "Love Beauty for its own sake," the poet Brissenden tells London's Martin Eden (in the novel of the same name), "and leave the magazines alone." Brissenden, like Celia Madden, defines art in opposition to "go ahead," middle-class America. But nobody wants to go ahead faster than Martin Eden, who only feels he is writing "great stuff" when he is "at last" "turning out the thing at which the magazines would jump." Martin's way of objecting to Brissenden's analysis is to criticize him for neglecting "love" ("'Love seems to have no place in your Cosmos; in mine, Beauty is the handmaiden of Love'"), a criticism that counts as a defense of the magazines because love, to Martin, means love of Ruth, the "daughter of the bourgeoisie," and the appeal of a life spent in pursuit of beauty has been that it seems to offer him simultaneously a "career and the way to win Ruth."

The point is not that writing should be understood as a "job"; indeed Martin has contempt for those "slaves" whose "highest idea of right conduct" is to "get a job," even when the job ends up paying very well. Ruth holds up to him the example of a Mr. Butler who, starting to work in a printing office at three dollars a week, worked himself up to thirty thousand a year: "How did he do it? He was honest, and faithful, and industrious, and economical. He denied himself the enjoyments that most boys indulge in." Martin, however, is "dissatisfied with Mr. Butler's career"; there is something in it that "jar[s] upon his sense of beauty and life." The problem with Mr. Butler's career is that it is too much like a job; with its denial of the "enjoyments that most boys indulge in," it renounces "love" just as surely as does Brissenden's pursuit of beauty. Martin is most like Butler and Brissenden both not when he finally begins to achieve literary success but when he is slaving in the hotel laundry north of San Francisco. The work is hard, but no harder than the regime Martin puts himself through when writing and studying. What is harder is the structure of denial; "life" can only be found outside the laundry. So where, for Martin's partner Joe, the alternative to the laundry is to become a hobo – hobos "don't work" – the alternative for Martin is to become a writer. Unlike hobos, writers do work, but unlike laundry men and unlike Mr. Butler, their work does not deny beauty in the service of money, and unlike Brissenden, it does not deny money in the service of beauty. In fact – just the opposite – Martin's work consists in nothing but loving, making, and marketing beauty. Where the Butler-like laundry leaves no time for love, and where Brissenden's aestheticism leaves no place for love, Martin, writing three thousand words of fiction a day and a poem every evening, is "a lover first and always"; he loves his work.

Thus London's extraordinary descriptions of Martin's attempts to write are matched in power only by his description of Martin's attempts to sell what he has written. To separate these two things would be to destroy the concept of work that the career exists to makes possible. And, indeed, this concept is in *Martin Eden* a very fragile one, threatened by the resemblance between trying to publish one's writing and betting: what Martin calls the "editorial machine" is too much "like the slot machines"; "One slot brought checks and the other rejection slips." Martin writes only to publish (it is only publishing that makes writing work) but the presence of the machine introduces a discrepancy between writing and publishing, a discrepancy that plays in *Martin Eden* the role of the gap between intention and consequence in the discourse of gambling. It is as if, through Martin, London imagines that publishing is part of the act of writing and that writing for publication is ontologically different from writing without regard to publication. Where for Brissenden, the act of writing is complete when his "great and perfect" poem is finished (he declines Martin's offer to "market it" for him), for Martin, no writing can be writing until it is published (he submits Brissenden's poem to the magazines anyway). And if writing can only be writing when it is published, the inability to publish must eventually count as the inability to write. For that matter, even success in publishing – insofar as that success turns out to be a function of luck at the "editorial machines," like Cowperwood's luck on the stock exchange – will also count as the inability to write.

Hence Martin's dismay at the success he eventually does achieve which seems to him a tribute to "something that is outside of me . . . something that is not I." And even one's own body can become part of the "not I": Martin's suicide is represented as a victory over his "automatic instinct to live"; the automaticity of the "editorial machine" that made writing too much like gambling reappears in the automaticity of one's own body that leads one's "arms and legs" to start swimming "quite involuntarily" in despite of one's attempts to drown oneself. But where in Wharton's *The House of Mirth* – another text that ends with a suicidal encounter with the uncontrollable – the loss of control is exciting, as is the vision of one's body as the site of that loss, in *Martin Eden* the body turns out to be the set of limits which make the triumph of what London calls the "will" possible. Lily's death is more hoped for than intended; she is killed by the "capricious and incalculable action of the drug" she takes to help her sleep: Martin's death is carefully planned; to defeat his body, he dives so deep that when his "will" fails and his hands and feet start swimming up, it is too late – "He was too deep down. They could never bring him to the surface." In what turn out to be the last months of his life, confronted by the discrepancy between his writing and his success, between what he wanted to do and what happened to him, Martin is unable to work. His suicide puts an end to that not because it puts an end to his life but because, restoring the connection between "will" and event, producing and selling, it gives him what London calls "work to do."

The writer's success imagined by *Martin Eden* is thus the success neither of the entrepreneur nor the gambler; no more is it the success of the artist who, refusing to trade or gamble, imagines himself as a kind of "gentleman." In contrast, Herrick's novels of upward mobility – *The Memoirs of an American Citizen* (1905) and *The Real World* – are dominated by the sense that these categories exhaust the options and energized by their contempt for the first two and their difficulty in imagining the third – a gentleman who is upwardly mobile. *Memoirs*, the story of a poor farm boy who becomes a rich meat-packer, understands upward mobility as making money in "the great game of the market"; its much admired realism consists above all in a simultaneous commitment to and distaste for the model of success as the accumulation of property. Unable to imagine any other form of social mobility and unwilling to approve the only one it can imagine, *Memoirs* insists on the conflict between the requirements of the market and the requirements of morality, inverting Horatio Alger by keying virtue to failure.

The Real World, however (more autobiographical and more intensely imagined), turns the son of a disappointed music teacher into a Wall Street lawyer by sending him to Harvard, where he imbibes not law but "the intangible spirit of the college"; "more than lectures or courses, more than information or scholarship . . . that spirit was a sense of catholic, high-minded living, a feeling that the world was a fine and noble place to live in, if you lived in it like a gentleman." In the effort to imagine mobility without vulgarity, Harvard replaces the market as a technology of social promotion; the spirit of gentility replaces "information," and the "coquetting with the soul" that culminates in the choice of a legal "career" replaces the sacrifice of soul that culminates in success as a meat-packer.

But even lawyers require some "information" and having to choose any career at all implies some distance from gentility, so the problem for Herrick and his hero Jack is to reconcile career and gentility, to save Jack's career from the contamination that emerges when the practical young woman who first taught him the word ("I wish you would tell me – more, what you mean by 'career,'" he begs her) turns out to be an unscrupulous and, as Jack learns to see her, "vulgar" social-climber. "My career is as much to make as yours" the social climber tells Jack, which is precisely the problem: how can anyone with a career to make count as a gentleman instead of a social-climber? The novel answers this question, solving the problem of Jack's simultaneous gentility and social mobility by insisting above all on his "hatred of privilege, of class" and by making this hatred of all class his path to the upper class: spurned as a child by the "dainty aristocrat" Isabelle Mather, Jack separates himself from his own family and joins hers by refusing in successively crucial moments to save first his own "vulgar" brother and second Isabelle's *arriviste* fiancé from going to jail on charges of embezzlement. His reason for declining to intervene on his brother's behalf is his desire to help him "become a little more of a man"; his reluctance to help Isabelle's fiancé stems from the hatred of privilege and class mentioned above – why should criminals with "rich and influential friends" be let off the hook? And his reward for these principled stands is marriage to Isabelle: idealistic contempt for class distinction is in *The Real World* the ticket out of the petit bourgeoisie and into the aristocracy.

In the other real world, however, the rescue from vulgarity was not so easy; the "intangible spirit" of gentility was the only thing (in his early years teaching at the brand-new University of Chicago) that set Herrick and the rest of the "Harvard crowd" apart from the majority of their colleagues who, seduced by "success," were behaving more like the American Citizen, "imitating the business world" and transforming the university into a kind of "trade school." In Herrick then, the Harvard "spirit" is the only alternative to "trade school"; when the "fresh, eager minds" of the "Harvard crowd" meet to discuss, they talk about anything "except shop." But when Martin Eden meets an English professor from Berkeley, he literally "make[s] him" "talk shop." His reasons have nothing to do with a preference for trade schools, however. On the contrary, he is thrilled to be sitting with "well-bred, well-dressed men and women" and talking with "an actual university professor." But, unlike Herrick (and unlike Ruth, who prefers "topics of general interest to all"), Martin thinks that no one should talk anything but shop. Although the difference here looks like (and would be understood by Herrick as) a difference of class, the distaste for "shop vulgarity" is identified in *Martin Eden* with Mr. Butler's separation of work from "life": reimagining "the thing by which they make their living" as "the best that is in them," Martin argues for a conception of work that leaves nothing of interest outside it. And the aesthete Brissenden, with his denunciation of Ruth's family and friends as nothing more than a "trader's den," provides the confirming alternative, the desire to escape shop talk on the other side. But to Martin Eden, debates about Herbert Spencer no more count as an alternative to shop than does discussion of the "latest novels, cards, billiards," etc. The latter is just "the shoptalk of the idlers," the former the shoptalk of intellectuals – culture, to anticipate a later formulation, is the shoptalk of culture workers.

The literary historian Christopher Wilson has convincingly called *Martin Eden* an "attempt to unravel a working-class writer's simultaneous introduction to career and culture," describing in these terms "the novel's essential dramatic tension . . . between alternative approaches to ideas: one, Ruth's, which views art as a cultural item of status and respectability . . . and another, the one Martin gains, which views art as an enterprise and a career." But the attraction of art is precisely that it represents the possibility of organizing an identity that transcends such tensions; the artist in *Martin Eden* is the avant-garde for the professional whose work is his life, for the inseparability not only of status and career but of identity and career. It is from this standpoint that the distinction between culture and career – Brissenden (with his aesthete's hostility to career) and Butler (with his careerist's indifference to culture) – begins to look distinctly retro. And it is from this standpoint also that the career (as opposed to the writing) of Robert Herrick begins to look advanced.

Herrick was a university professor and a novelist, which is to say that he was one of the first "creative writers," a job description made available only by the conjunction of art and the university curriculum. He was, as we have already seen, appalled by the commercial spirit of the University of Chicago but, as we have also already seen, there was nothing all that new or shocking in the vision of artists having commercial interests or ambitions: in *Looking Backward*, the novelist is virtually the last entrepreneur. In fact, by the turn of the century, the assertion of the artist's commercial interests could function not to demystify art but to idealize it: "an artist stands on his merits," says the financier/philanthropist of *The Market-Place*, unlike "doctors" and "parsons," whose "profession[s]" are nothing but "a confidence trick." The artist here is a figure for the independent businessman at a moment when the independent businessman seemed to be on the verge of disappearing. What is new in Herrick, however, and in texts like *Martin Eden* and *The "Genius,"* is the emergence of the artist not as the tradesman Frederic admires but as the professional he deplores. Indeed, for Herrick, it is only the transformation of the writer into a professional that saves him from being reduced to a wage-slave.

In *The "Genius"*, this emergence of the artist as manager instead of Napoleonic "owner" or servile "henchman" is figured in the easy translate-ability of Eugene's success as an "artist" into his success as an "art director." Although the text makes periodic attempts to separate these out – "his was the artistic temperament, not that of a commercial or financial genius" – it provides no criteria according to which such a separation might take place. For Eugene's "artistic temperament" means also that he is "an art director by temperament," which is to say, in the end, that he is a "natural-born . . . organizer." Indeed, in Dreiser, the resistance to the organization man finds no professional expression at all and appears only in the privatized form of Eugene's equally temperamental hostility to marriage. It is almost as if, mir-roring the procedure through which James imagined marriage as the formal site of anti-entrepreneurial experimentation, Dreiser reduces the fear of losing one's autonomy to the desire to sleep with a lot of women instead of just one.

For Herrick, however, the switching mechanism is the university. On the one hand, professors are wage-earners and so they run the risk, as one of the characters in Herrick's academic novel, *Chimes*, points out, of being "rated socially in the white collar class." On the other hand, as Herrick also says, "Something in his occupation set apart the college professor and his family from the ordinary wage-earner and the successful capitalist." This, of course, expresses a hope as much as it states a fact. The "something" is "a wider perspective of life's possibilities," which turns out to manifest itself concretely in European summer vacations: "For the professor there was always at the close of every academic year the vision of European wanderings, to be repeated or begun. 'When we go to Europe,' or 'Next time I am over,' they said to one another, recognizing thus the home of their spirits." That professors are not capitalists is obvious enough without the European vacation criterion. The professor is a salaried employee; the "creative writer's" new book is an occasion for promotion, not a speculation in the market-place. But that professors are not "ordinary wage-earners" is less obvious, and it may easily seem that the European vacation is at worst a feeble attempt to establish a difference that does not exist or at best an attempt to turn a style of consuming leisure into a definitive mark of class status.

As Herrick describes it, however, Europe is more than a place for professors to tour, it is the "home of their spirits"; and the fact that Europe is where their spirits live is a defining aspect of their professional identity. What is striking about the European vacation, in other words, is not what it means as an escape from work but what it means as an extension of work. Which is not to say that the professor is doing "research" and so not really vacationing; rather the pleasure the professor takes in "wandering" is inseparable from his "research." The professor's vocation – an emblem initially of finding one's true identity away from one's work – becomes an emblem instead of the breaking down of distinctions between work and pleasure, and finding one's identity as a professional in precisely the indistinguishability of the two. "When we go to Europe," is the way the professor begins talking shop.

Americans in Europe, according to Madame Merle, are "a wretched set of people" because they "do nothing"; his consumption is Ralph Touchett's saving grace: "it gives him something to do. His consumption's his *carrière*; it's a kind of position." According to the *Oxford English Dictionary*, "position" was used as early as 1865 to signify "social state or standing," but the first citation of it signifying "official situation, place or employment" is not until 1890. Ralph's consumption is not exactly a social state, but if it is not exactly a form of employment either, it is certainly headed in that direction. Martin Eden makes fun of Ruth for using the word "position" instead of "the homely word *job*" but, as we have seen, much of what *Martin Eden* is about is the repudiation of jobs in favor of positions. From the economic standpoint, this transformation of "the industrial worker's job" into "a 'position' with circumscribed rights and duties" may be understood as what Sanford Jacoby has described as the "shifting back from contract to status." But it is not, of course, as if buying and selling had disappeared; it is rather that the position totalizes the job, taking the economic exchange and turning it into a way of life.

"Who are you?" Martin asks his reflection in the mirror one night after taking Ruth to a lecture. "He gazed at himself long and curiously. Who are you? What are you? Where do you belong? . . . And are you going to make good?" Herrick's coquetting with the soul emerges here as enabled by and enabling careerism in the sense that only a career is imagined as the answer to all those questions and so only the idea of a career makes it possible to ask them as if they were all ultimately the same question. The opposition between status and contract is here transformed into the relocation of status in contract. Questions about what you will do appear now as questions about who you are and curiosity about yourself emerges as the newest form of self-interest.

THROUGH THE LOOKING-GLASS

Who are you? What are you? Where do you belong? Are you going to make good? Martin Eden asks these questions in front of a mirror, here imagined as a technology of both external and internal reflection. Indeed, it is not clear that the difference between these two forms of reflection or between their two domains – the internal and the external – entirely survives. The young Clyde Griffiths is obsessively interested in his "appearance"; he thinks about "how he looked and how other boys looked" by appealing to the occasional glimpse of himself in a mirror that his wandering in the streets has made available to him and to the mirrors provided by the looks of those "other boys" as well as the "interested looks" occasionally directed toward him "by young girls in very different walks of life." An older Clyde, loved by Roberta and making his way in Lycurgus society, now can look "at himself in a mirror . . . with an assurance and admiration which before this he had never possessed." Showing him how he looks, his mirror shows him how he has come to feel. And in the death house, reduced to the mirrorless state of his youth, the identification of looking and feeling has become so strong that Clyde, who began by needing a mirror to tell him how he felt, no longer needs a mirror to tell him how he looks: "There was no mirror here . . . but no matter – he could feel how he looked." Feelings have become mirrors; introspection goes beyond looking at oneself in a mirror (seeing one's feelings made visible in a mirror) and becomes looking at oneself as if one were a mirror (seeing oneself made visible in one's feelings, seeing one's "look" in one's feelings).

The mirror helps to produce the look; it is one of those devices, like standard sizing, for renegotiating the relations between the external and the internal, understood here as the seen and the felt, and producing here the effect of a new individuality. To many, of course, this effect seemed false. Sinclair Lewis's *Babbitt* (1922) is in large part a polemic against standardization; "standard advertised wares," ("toothpastes, socks, tires, cameras") "fix the surface" of Babbitt's life and then, substituting for "joy and passion and wisdom," "fix what he believed to be his individuality." The implication here is that true individuality lies elsewhere, away from the surfaces revealed in and as mirrors, away from the "incredibly mechanical" "way of life" that constitutes Babbittry. In *Babbitt* itself, such individuality is unattainable, glimpsed only in moments of regret, as in a tar-roof's salesman's expression of his "dark soul" through the violin or a doggerel-writing ad-man's imagination of the real poems he "could have written." Art, in other words, is understood as offering the alternative to the standard, the machine, the mirror. But, as we have just seen, the ambition to produce great art in this period was more often articulated as an element in, not a repudiation of, the general reorganization of interiority and exteriority embodied by Dreiser and London in the mirror. If one way to write the history of American literature is as a series of more or less compromised attempts to oppose, subvert, or resist the "dominant" culture, another way to write it is by tracing its participation in that culture.

Which is not to say that the processes described here – the externalization of the individual, the internalization of the contractual, the sociologizing of introspection, and the bureaucratizing of ambition – should be celebrated rather than deplored. When the fair-skinned narrator of James Weldon Johnson's *The Autobiography of an Ex-Coloured Man* (1912) is first classed among the "niggers" at school, he hurries home to his "looking-glass." What the looking-glass shows him is a "beauty" that he has heard about but that he can now see and become "conscious" of "for the first time": the "ivory whiteness" of his skin, the "softness and glossiness" of his "dark hair." And this new consciousness is made complete by his mother's admission that he is "not white"; "From that time . . ." he says, "my thoughts were coloured," "I looked out through other eyes." School, mother, and mirror make visible what otherwise could not be seen, what otherwise would not exist – not what his *old* eyes could see, a man whose skin is a certain color – but what only his *new* eyes can see, "a *coloured* man." Transferring color from the exterior of the body to its interior makes races as surely as standards make sizes. Thus racial identity is as much a product of the processes described here as is the desire for a "classy" fur coat, but the consequences of understanding people as essentially white or black have surely been graver than the consequences of understanding them as size tens or size eights, as forty regulars or thirty-eight longs.

In any event, and for better or worse, literature played a role in these and other transformations. It was in many of the texts discussed here that the new forms of social existence were imagined and articulated. By "social existence" I do not necessarily mean political existence; although, in the wake of *Looking Backward*'s great success, the utopian novel enjoyed a considerable vogue, its various visions of a new political order are now, as they were then, of only limited interest. More ambitious efforts were made at a more intimate level. Thinking through the analogy between human beings and machines, for example, made more difference than inventing fictitious new political systems or even than inventing fictitious new machines. Whatever the motives of those involved in this effort – and, as I have tried to show, their motives varied, from Twain's attempt to preserve what seemed to him a vanishing independence to Taylor's attempt to enforce industrial efficiency – the effect was to produce a new model of individuality, one which revised rather than rescued the old independence and which, if it increased efficiency, also unleashed eroticized energies that undid the dreams of Progressive experts from the inside, that is, through the dreams themselves, the dreams of class transformation that standardization had made possible.

Whether these dreams really are "inside" or what they are inside of is, of course, a problem since, as the proliferations of forms in chapter 1 and of visible surfaces in chapter 2 makes clear, interiority is a contested space. But contested is not the same as eliminated. And by the same token, the effort, described in chapter 3, to think through the relation between the sentimental and the economic, between emotions and exchanges, ends up reconfiguring without, however, eliminating the interior. Indeed, insofar as buying and selling can be shown in a text like *Summer* to be integral rather than incidental to love, this reconfiguration might be understood as a kind of expansion; even buying and selling can be claimed for emotional life. Isabel Archer begins by thinking of the things that "belong" to her as "barriers," the boundaries between where she ends and externality begins, but she ends by being unable to conceive herself without those things. The barriers have not been overcome – there is no Emersonian triumph of the internal over the external – but they have been reimagined as constitutive instead of prohibitive. The organization you work for frustrates your dreams of doing whatever you want but without it you could not want to rise in the organization.

From the 1890s until World War I, transformations like the ones I have described were central to American culture and to American literature, and for a writer like Dreiser, whose greatest work, *An American Tragedy*, was published in 1925, they remained central. But *An American Tragedy* is, I would argue, crucially different from the major books by younger authors (*The Great Gatsby*, *The Professor's House*, *The Sun Also Rises*, *Spring and All*) that were published more or less contemporaneously, and different even from works like *The Waste Land* and *Mauberley* that were written still earlier. One way to understand this difference is formal; many ambitious works of art in the 1920s were concerned to make explicit the relations between their thematic concerns and their material existence in a way that most of the works discussed in this book were not. William Carlos Williams's slogan – "not 'realism' but reality itself" – articulated a desire for works of art which, asserting their ontological autonomy, would have an existence and a value independent of the mimetic function that he associated with the realism he called "plagiarism." Demanding a "new form" for both poetry and the novel, Williams asserted the necessity for the break with "traditional" forms of "representation" that is often thought to characterize the novelty of Modernism.

But it would be a mistake to think that this critique of representation and the consequent reflection upon the more general relation between a thing's materiality and its identity were questions of indifference in the earlier period. On the contrary, Norris's *McTeague*, conceived and mainly written at the height of the debate over the gold standard, is obsessively interested in interrogating the relation between what a thing is and what it represents, which is, after all, what the money debates were about: was gold, because of its "intrinsic value," "nature's money"? Or could a less precious metal like silver, or an almost worthless material like paper, serve instead of gold, representing as well as embodying value? Norris's two misers, Trina who collects gold and Zerkow who collects junk, are answers to those questions. Reducing things to the material they are made of (turning money to gold), while at the same time insisting that the immateriality in money is irreducible (turning junk to money), *McTeague* stages the emergence of an economics of identity. And one could, in fact, understand Norris's entire career, from *Vandover and the Brute* through *The Octopus* and *The Pit*, as a series of experiments in the ontology of difference and identity: why is a person not just the material the person is made up of, i.e., a "brute"? Why is a corporate person not just its material embodiments, i.e., its officers and shareholders? The juxtaposition of these questions and the assertion through that juxtaposition of parallel differences between persons and brutes on the one hand, corporate persons and "natural" ones on the other, had the effect of suggesting that corporate persons were at least as real as ordinary persons: the triumph of the "monstrous" Pacific and South Western Railroad at the end of *The Octopus* is understood as a triumph for personhood as well.

From this standpoint, it might be argued that American Modernism's characteristic preoccupation with the materiality of the work of art, with what Williams understood as the "reality" of words themselves rather than with the reality they represent, might more plausibly be understood as a culmination of Naturalism than as a departure from it. Where Norris investigated the relation of materiality to identity in a range of artifacts from money to corporations, at least one element in Modernism brings into play the materiality of the written artifact itself. And from this standpoint also, the difference between *An American Tragedy* and its contemporaries begins to look a little less absolute. For the attempt to imagine an ontologically perfected identity finds expression in the 1920s not only in a certain conception of the relation between signs and their referents but also in a certain conception of what it means to be or become an American. Thus the novels of the mid-1920s tend to pair characters who achieve this identity (Jake Barnes through *afición*, Tom Outland through the Indian ruins on Blue Mesa, Nick Carraway through the Dutch sailors who first encountered the New World) with characters who do not (Robert Cohn, Louis Marsellus, Gatsby), and to the list of those characters who fail one could easily add Dreiser's Clyde Griffiths. Indeed, there is a certain sense in which these novels, all of which involve, at least at a crude level of description, the failed attempt of some outsider to become an insider, could be understood as the same novel. What Clyde hopes to get through Sondra is what Cohn hopes to get through Brett, or Marsellus through Rosamond, or Gatsby through Daisy.

But the crudity (although not, I believe, inaccuracy) of that description suggests also at least one crucial difference between the ambitions of the Progressive period and those of the 1920s. It is striking (and strikingly new) that what Marsellus and Cohn want is best understood as a change in blood; that is what it means for them to be Jewish, and if Gatsby, né Gatz, is not Jewish, his desire for Daisy nonetheless provokes in Tom an attack on miscegenation which suggests that the issue between them is racial or ethnic rather than class mobility. It is not insignificant that the central couples in these texts tend to be represented as brothers and sisters: Tom, whom Rosie should have married, was already "one of the family," Nick, the attractive version of Tom Buchanan, is Daisy's cousin, and the passion between Jake and Brett has been converted by the famous war injury into a fraternal one; as a couple, they find fulfillment three years later in Faulkner's Quentin and Caddie. America, as one of the racial propagandists of the 1920s put it, was "a family matter," and the classic literature of the period is a literature of exclusion from and constitution of the family.

Clyde, however, already belongs to the family; it is because he is a Griffiths and because he looks so much like his cousin Gilbert that he gets his job at the

Griffiths Collar Factory. Which is not to say that he succeeds where Gatsby and the others fail; on the contrary, he does not even want what they want. Membership in the family is not for him an object of desire, it is only a means of obtaining the objects he does desire: "a better collar, a nicer shirt, finer shoes, a good suit, a swell overcoat like some boys had." Clyde's better collar can serve as an emblem for all the transforming objects and activities that the preceding pages have produced: Henry Fleming's wound, Mrs. Sommers's silk stockings, the Virginian's promotion, and the rest. To want that collar was to live in a world where producing and consuming and buying and selling were being reinvented and where their reinvention required the invention also of new producers and consumers, buyers and sellers.

That world did not disappear in the 1920s; on the contrary, it flourished. But it is almost as if, the imaginative effort to produce the buyers and sellers, workers and players having succeeded, serious – by which I mean ambitious – literature turned in a different direction. Lewis dedicated *Babbitt* to Edith Wharton; its primary function is to deplore what Wharton, Dreiser, London, Crane, and Chopin created. But other writers were less concerned to deplore what Willa Cather dismissively called the "new commercialism" than they were to recast it as a form of racial and/or cultural inadequacy, contrasting it to the racial and cultural purity achieved by figures like Tom Outland, self-created heir of the Anasazi Indians. Thus, although the resemblances between *An American Tragedy* and its contemporaries are real and although the Modernist critique of representation clearly derives from and in part repeats the Naturalist debate over persons and brutes, money and gold, the great texts of American Modernism do nonetheless represent a decisive shift away from the formal and thematic concerns, the transforming obsessions, of Dreiser, London, Wharton, *et al*.

Or, to put it another way, they represent a revision and aesthetic vindication not of Dreiserian commercialism but of something more like Dixonian racism. Racial identity was for Dixon the key to national identity and, although the constitution of that identity involved the proliferation of surfaces that we have identified with such writers as Crane and Dreiser, neither Crane nor Dreiser put that technology to primarily national use: *The Red Badge of Courage* is compatible with but hardly committed to remembering the Civil War as the origin of the modern American state, and Dreiser meant the "American" in *An American Tragedy* to suggest the way in which American society encouraged careers like Clyde's; he did not imagine, through Clyde, the constitution of a uniquely American identity. If then, as has sometimes been argued, the South's sense of its own difference from the rest of the nation gave us our model for a regional rather than national literature, it might also be argued that the defeated but Progressive South's desire to erase that difference gave us a new model for what a national literature, a literature that sought to establish and enforce the conditions of national identity, might be.

For the literature of the period that I have been describing, however, the question of American identity was a distinctly minor one. Gazing at himself in his "looking-glass" and asking himself who he is, Martin Eden is not wondering about his racial or ethnic origin. The only origin that matters to him is class origin ("You belong with the legions of toil, with all that is low, and vulgar, and unbeautiful") and it matters only as a condition to be transcended: "Who are you? and what are you? . . . And are you going to make good?" What it would take to make good, what might happen to you if you did not make good, what exactly making good was, these are the questions that animated the literature of the turn of the century.

BECOMING MULTICULTURAL: CULTURE, ECONOMY, AND THE NOVEL, 1860–1920

Susan L. Mizruchi

I

❦

INTRODUCTION

THE TITLE OF my narrative registers the novel's grounding in a broad spectrum of cultural and economic developments. These include: the end of slavery; the intensification of foreign immigration; the labor unrest catalyzed by the expansion of industrial capitalism; the revolution in transportation and communication; the rise of mass production and distribution; the process of standardization and professionalization; the emergence of the corporation and with it of "corporate culture"; and the dramatic extension of media forms, among them, newspapers, magazines, and advertising. Of these historical developments, none is more significant than the growing awareness of American multiculturalism. This country has "always already" been multicultural. Yet not until the second half of the nineteenth century were the specific stakes of this diversity widely conceptualized and debated. Novels of the time provided a critical forum for these conceptualizations and debates. Sometimes they did so through a focus on the death industries of slavery and war; sometimes through a concern with the work of mourning for a lost culture; sometimes through descriptions of the inner workings of new business enterprises such as magazines or clothing manufacture, or through pleas for industrial reform. Cross-cultural comparison was a mainstay of social observation not only in notoriously heterogeneous urban settings, but in towns and rural areas as well. This was the era of America's self-consciousness about its extraordinary diversity – the era, that is, of its multicultural becoming – and rising rates of immigration and growing perceptions of the world's interconnectedness served as a daily assault on the forces of parochialism.

The challenge here is to convey the breadth and complexity of such developments, while at the same time capturing the variety of ways in which American novels responded. To this end, I have divided my narrative into eight chapters, each of which encompasses a large cross-section of cultural and economic activity during this time. Chapters 2 (Remembering Civil War) and 5 (Native-American sacrifice in an age of progress) focus on the national confrontation of mass death during the Civil War, and afterward, when the Native American inhabitants of the West were forced to migrate or annihilated to make way for settlement. Chapter 3 (Social death and the reconstruction of slavery) explores the social, economic, and legal customs and institutions that extended the subordination of American blacks well beyond the era of enslavement. Chapter 4 (Cosmopolitan variations) explores the varieties of dislocation and disenchantment that accompanied the late nineteenth century experience of modernization. Chapters 6 (Marketing culture) and 8 (Corporate America) explore the rise of advertising and media forms, and the revolution in business methods, including corporate expansion and the establishment of trusts, that were so integral to the transformation of culture from the 1870s onward. Chapters 7 (Varieties of work) and 9 (Realist utopias) represent different responses to the extraordinary capitalist development of the period, from laborers and those who championed their cause, and religious and political idealists whose utopian schemes promoted complete social and economic reorganization.

Each chapter highlights specific developments critical to the culture and economy of the period. Each chapter also provides a unique perspective on the following themes that run through all eight chapters. First, there is the prevailing interest in cultural difference. A fascination with difference – its capacity to generate new images, ideas, commodities, and markets – is a thread that runs through every major cultural and economic development in this period. It runs equally through some of the era's most adverse trends and events, from the Civil War fought for slave emancipation to the reconstruction that failed to extend full social rights and opportunities to those emancipated, to the treatment of Native Americans and nativist hostility toward immigrants. Second, there is secularization and the spiritual and ethical questions that arise from major intellectual challenges to faith. Religious historians are understandably divided about the depth and range of secularization in America from the late nineteenth century through the early twentieth. Just how far beyond the ranks of intellectual elites did the skepticism initiated by the Darwinian scientific revolution extend? Ordinary Americans, and extraordinary Americans as well, remained profoundly religious. One of the primary concerns of this book is the religious beliefs of the novelists and thinkers whose works are analyzed here, since for all their reservations about religion, many of these authors, and the characters (or alter egos) they created, were devoted to religion (ranging from Christianity and Judaism to the nature religion of the Dakota Sioux). Third, there is the combined fascination with and fear of technology and technological change. The inescapable fact of this era was the impact of new inventions: the introduction of electricity on a large scale; the extension of railroads and steam travel; the increased availability of telephones, telegraphs, typewriters, sewing machines, cameras, automobiles, and other means of both speeding up American life and recording its highpoints.

This is a story of exceptional and mediocre artists: it concerns novelists who have been fixtures in traditional literary study (Mark Twain, Henry James, Willa Cather); those who have benefited from revisionist approaches to canon building (Elizabeth Stuart Phelps, Charles Chesnutt, Pauline E. Hopkins); and those who have been overlooked by traditional as well as revisionist approaches (Albion Tourgee, Maria Ruiz de Burton). It treats the theories of philosophers, social scientists, business and religious leaders, who remain central to their respective fields (Helen Keller, Mary Baker Eddy) and those who were pivotal in their own day but are little discussed now (Henry George, Ida Tarbell, Walter Dill Scott). And it differs from previous histories of this period in four major respects. First, it explores many different types of texts through a historically minded criticism that is as alert to the aesthetic qualities of advertising images and social scientific theory as it is to the economic and political implications of the literary. Second, it recognizes artistic, scientific, and commercial narratives as analogous parts of a common conversation about the nature of society, and the experience of social change during this period. While my narrative brings together a varied collection of works, and treats each one as a unique and complex artifact, it also privileges literature, without apology. It demonstrates that literary form can do things to history as it absorbs it that differs from the cultural work of sociology or anthropology or muckraking journalism. Third, women authors (literary, journalistic, social scientific, etc.) are neither marginalized nor relegated to a separate section, but are recognized as critical instigators and analysts of the developments it charts. Fourth, the category of universality is interrogated here, rather than assumed (traditional literary criticism) or dismissed (recent historicist literary criticism). I believe that one cannot recognize what is universally shared unless cultural forms and ideas are grasped in their particularity. And I believe, too, that certain preoccupations and ideas may in fact be universal, trans-cultural and trans-historical.

My main methodological claims may be plainly stated. First, literary history can be told principally through literature itself, in this particular case through novels. The task of the literary historian as understood here, is to reveal the histories that are deeply embedded in literary works; it is a process of excavation and retrieval, archaeological rather than critical. While this claim is demonstrated through sustained analysis of an American novelistic genre that is extraordinarily engaged with contemporary historical developments, it is also meant to hold for other times and places, and for other literary forms. History is everywhere in the American novel of the Realist period: what makes this observation more than a cliché is the fact that historical meaning of the most complex kinds is shown to exist not only in the most obvious places, books that draw on actual historical events, such as John Hay's *The Breadwinners* and Frank Norris's *The Pit*, but equally in the least obvious places, books whose concerns seem more individual or fanciful, such as James's *The Ambassadors* and Baum's *The Wizard of Oz*. Second, literary history can be relatively comprehensive. The obligation of the literary historian, so understood, is to cover a vast territory in depth, accounting for a broad range of developments. Literary history must give voice to a wide variety of works: the more intricate and detailed the presentation of those works, the more authoritative the claims.

Such assumptions require that the works foregrounded have a certifiable prominence in their own time. Four characteristics of the texts that predominate in my narrative confirm their importance in this sense. First, at least a third of these books were designated as best or better sellers based on early sales figures equivalent to or close to one percent of the total United States population, adjusted by the decade. This includes books as diverse as Louisa May Alcott's *Little Women* (1868) and Owen Wister's *The Virginian* (1902). Albion Tourgee's *A Fool's Errand* (1879) and Helen Hunt Jackson's *Ramona* (1884) were designated better sellers, with sales nearly reaching the one per cent mark. Second, more than half of these books were serialized in installments in leading magazines (some elite, some popular) prior to their publication in book form. Third, because these serials were published in magazines that almost always included advertisements for consumer products, sometimes interspersed with fiction and articles, these books joined inevitably a larger cultural dialogue about the changes wrought by capitalist development. Fourth and finally, it is worth noting that one author ranged with an incomparable energy, intelligence, and liberality across the various divides that may have limited other writers to representing specific cultural spheres.

Mark Twain is a central figure in this history as a writer who seems to have been engaged firsthand with every important phenomenon of the era: journalism, inventions, the affairs of the Standard Oil Trust, book publishing, stockholding, and self-promotion through advertising (i.e. the commercialization of his own career). He mastered almost every available literary genre: western adventure, travel, juvenilia, utopian fiction, historical romance, short story, the novel, essay, satire, and parody. He addressed in his fiction most major social conflicts: race relations in the eras of slavery and reconstruction, political corruption, western migration and "Indian Resettlement," industrial and capitalist expansion, in both their positive and negative aspects. And he was personally acquainted, often familiar, with an astounding number of leading writers, businessmen, statesman, intellectuals, and celebrities of his time.

The specific role of novels here involves the recognition of how they functioned through their serialization in magazines prior to their book publication, as an analogous form that is engaged, like advertisements themselves, in locating and also creating a market for their goods. In selling their stories and novels to magazines, for the sake of self-advertisement, literary authors were helping to enhance the authority and appeal of the magazines themselves, and the goods that were advertised in them. The literature – high and low, popular and obscure – that was serialized in American magazines, particularly from the 1890s through 1920, entered into a continuum of promotion. By appearing there, literary works helped to establish the cultural level of the magazine, and to sanction the commodities they advertised.

What this does to the understanding of American novels of all kinds produced during this period is to confirm their place in the pervasive advertising impulse of the era, and their specific role in the acceleration of consumer capitalism. Both the advertisements and the novels are telling stories about modernization: its effects, its values, the formal shape that it takes in both visual and written materials – advertising images, slogans, fiction. Writers such as Theodore Dreiser and Abraham Cahan (who worked as magazine editors or started their own magazines), were participants with advertisers in a process of translation, translating the terms of a new market culture to a motivated yet ambivalent populace. These translations took a variety of complex forms, and sometimes featured businessmen characters as main protagonists, allowing for the direct representation of business practices and values. At the same time that they were representing the world of business to consumers, they were also representing their profound understanding of their consumer audiences, and of the American class system in general. For as William Dean Howells perceived, the attempt to sell cultural commodities like magazines and the literature they feature, confronts one inevitably with the deeply stratified condition of American society. The pursuit of markets, in other words, involves one as a matter of course in class analysis. American novelists were helping to shape class identity and consciousness at this historical moment, and were well aware of this fact.

My largest claim is that the period from, roughly, the Civil War to the First World War was the era when America's expanding multiculturalism was self-consciously recognized and debated, especially in literature, which here refers to literary writing of various kinds, from novels, short fiction, memoirs, and essays, to political tracts and social criticism; as well as in an expanding culture industry, which included magazines, newspapers, photography, illustrations, and advertising. I try to give voice to these recognitions and debates by seeking

to recapture within its own terms a wide variety of perspectives on major historical developments of the era. That is to say, that for any particular subject matter, I focus in depth on a range of works by authors from different cultural, class,
and professional backgrounds. The primary criteria used to include a work in
this history is importance in its own time, a judgment made on the basis of
critical reception, popularity, and the life experience of its author. If an author
was in a position (ethnically, racially, regionally, by class or gender), to provide
a particularly valuable and alternative perspective on a given event or development, then his or her book is included. The variety of authors and types of works
discussed in each section is determined by their engagement with major historical episodes: Civil War, Reconstruction, urbanization and immigration,
"Indian removal" and genocide, the development of advertising and magazines, the conditions of work, the rise of big business, the utopian response.
The design of chapters, and the recurrence of specific writers from chapter to
chapter, many in multiple chapters (for example, Henry James in chapters 2, 4,
6, 7, and 8 and Mark Twain in chapters 3, 4, 5, 8, and 9) – is designed to reveal
continuities of form and content. It is my hope that those reading this history
will have the feeling that they have entered upon an ongoing conversation,
and that their acquaintanceship with the historical personages, characters, and
events here introduced builds over the course of the book.

   Three main theses about America's emerging multiculturalism in this period
have arisen from my years of research and analysis of a varied range of sources
(literary, economic, social scientific, photographic, and commercial). *Thesis One:
capitalism's romance with the exceptional diversity of American society dates back to this
historical period.* The American economy and business system as it developed
from 1860 to 1920 habitually capitalized on the nation's growing multiculturalism. This opportunism took many forms, including the incorporation of vast
numbers of immigrants into the American work force. This not only ensured
labor power for expanding industries, but facilitated the control of all laborers
by owners and managers who could count on a regularly refreshed supply of
aliens, willing to work for low wages. At the same time, these immigrant
populations also provided a critical mass of new consumers, eager to spend
their new wages, however small, on the magical commodities of the American
market place. American advertisers also capitalized on widespread nervousness
about high immigration rates among previous generations of American-born
("native") citizens by filling their images with assorted "aliens." By constantly
invoking the source of anxiety and fascination, through various racial and
ethnic figures, advertisers sought to capture the attention of Americans by
familiarizing what they feared.

Thesis two: America's extraordinary cultural diversity spurred widespread resistance to the development of a full-fledged welfare system. At a time when other Western countries with highly developed capitalist economies (Britain, Germany, France) were instituting extensive welfare systems – old age pensions, workers' compensation, health coverage – American efforts lagged far behind. Even by the late twentieth century, long after the New Deal welfare programs of Franklin Delano Roosevelt, the American "welfare state," according to business historians, remained far less entrenched than its European counterparts. A powerful and persistent national ideology of individualism, which throughout American history has energized a deep resistance to taxation and "big government," was no doubt partly responsible. But the attractions of populism and other radical plans for social and economic redistribution confirm that other stakes were involved. My claim is that the key lay in America's extreme cultural diversity, which made most Americans reluctant to support an extensive welfare system designed to protect the considerable populations of non-kin they believed most likely to benefit from it. It is telling that in the social renovation schemes set out in utopian novels of the period, the first step en route to a system of comprehensive social welfare is the purification of the body politic. There are no aliens in the social worlds of these novels; Native Americans, African Americans, and the immigrants who came from Europe during this period, have disappeared.

Thesis Three: the striking rapidity of cultural and economic development from 1860 to 1920 was largely understood as requiring essential cultural sacrifices. Among these were the sacrifices of disproportionate numbers of working-class soldiers during the Civil War. The traumatic fraternal conflict that produced so much misery and bloodshed also liberated full-scale industrial development, while the victory of Lincoln's Union served to empower the agents of unrestrained capitalism. This exchange of war dead for capitalist development occurred at the most local level of warfare as higher casualties translated into a greater demand for uniforms, munitions, and transport, and thus higher profits for business. The Native American genocide carried out over the course of this period was represented consistently as the fulfillment of a universal pattern – sacrifice for the sake of progress. African Americans – whose social and political exclusion after the war overshadowed their emancipation during it – were similarly cast, in W. E. B. Du Bois's words, as a collective "sacrifice on the altar of progress," and deliberately barred throughout this period from civil rights. The gains made during this period by African-American elites were *in spite* of prevailing customs and laws, not because of them.

The pages that follow tell the story of a vast economic and cultural transformation involving the onset of both modernization and modernism. At the center of this story – its substance and texture – is the development of a literary culture that in myriad ways expressed its unique sense of obligation to bear witness, and its unique capacity to shape, to celebrate, condemn, and re-create.

2

🙚

REMEMBERING CIVIL WAR

THE CIVIL WAR INITIATED a publishing industry. The war between the
Northern Union and the Southern Confederacy inspired chronicles –
photographic, historical, journalistic, and literary – at a rate unmatched
by previous wars. As one soldier noted of his appetite for "cheap literature . . . I,
certainly, never read so many such before or since." Dime novels written for soldier audiences and run in series such as "Dawley's Camp and Fireside Library"
and Redpath's "Books for the Camp Fires," sold in the hundred thousands.
More conventional novels such as Metta Victor's *The Unionist's Daughter* (1862);
Charles Alexander's *Pauline of the Potomac* (1862); John Trowbridge's *The Drummer Boy* (1863); Edward Willett's *The Vicksburg Spy* (1864); and Sarah Edmonds's
Unsexed: or, The Female Soldier (1864) provided those at home and at war on
both sides with a steady stream of courageous soldiers, wartime courtships, and
cross-dressed spies. Newspapers and magazines featured dramatic war testimonials, such as Oliver Wendell Holmes Sr.'s account (*Atlantic Monthly*) of his frantic search for Oliver Jr. (the future Supreme Court Justice), who was wounded
at Antietam. Editors like Joseph Medill of the *Chicago Tribune*, Horace Greeley
of the New York *Tribune*, and Henry J. Raymond of the *New York Times*, assumed
the role of elder statesmen, as they reviewed military and diplomatic strategies,
while one Alabama editor warned those corresponding with soldiers to avoid
news "that will embitter their thoughts or swerve them from the path of duty."

The most significant Civil War writing was retrospective. The literary
avalanche of Civil War remembering began, it seemed, with the drying of
ink on General Robert E. Lee's April 9, 1865 surrender. This prodigious production continued to the end of the decade and through the 1870s. The most
significant reconsiderations were even more remote, appearing in the 1880s
and 1890s, and extending so far into the twentieth century that a recent historian characterized the Civil War as "unfinished." In this sense, the chief
cultural effect of the Civil War was to keep Americans permanently fixed in
the four years (1861–65) of traumatic conflict. The array of novels and memoirs
published in the decades after the war by such varied and prominent authors
as Elizabeth Stuart Phelps, Ellen Glasgow, Frances Harper, Paul Laurence

Dunbar, Henry James, and Ulysses S. Grant lend support to this view. At the same time, however, the war played a critical role in accelerating capitalist development and modernization (in part through its eradication of the anti-quated institution of slavery), and thus seemed to all who witnessed it to speed the nation rapidly into the future.

At the start of the war, the country was largely rural and agrarian, with only the railroads qualifying as a "big business." Between 1865 and 1895, most competitive industries – from textiles, oil, iron, and steel, to glass, paper, liquor, and sugar – entered into forms of cooperation that led to their formation as trusts. The need for managing and transmitting information both within and between growing business networks required ever more complex and efficient systems. The development in this period of new methods for typing and copying, filing and storage, gave way to a communications revolution that can be traced to the twentieth-century computer and beyond. The most revolutionary invention of the Civil War era was the telegraph, an advance in communications technology unrivaled even by the telephone (introduced in 1876 by Alexander Graham Bell). The telegraph, like other industries, profited greatly from the war, emerging at its end as a genuine monopoly under the auspices of Western Union. Many financiers made fortunes through bond purchase and speculation, wartime investments that helped to bring about a uniform national currency and to fortify a national banking system.

On the eve of the Civil War, the North was substantially more advanced than the South: more industrialized and urbanized, with twice the amount of cultivated land and a vast and well-consolidated railroad network. Because Southern secession eliminated a key legislative barrier to economic develop-ment, President Lincoln was able during the war to usher various modern-izing measures through Congress and sign them into law. These included the 1862 Homestead Act, which spurred Western development, tariff leg-islation to promote Northern industry, and the Pacific Railroad Act, which allowed for the building of the transcontinental railroad. The South's great military resource was slave labor, which kept their lead, salt, and iron mines as well as agriculture fully productive. Slave labor also enabled an astonishing 80 percent conscription rate among the Confederacy's white population. Yet this resource proved unreliable (as fictionalized by Frances Harper in *Iola Leroy*). Over time slaves became increasingly identified with the Union campaign as emancipation was embraced as its purpose. Frederick Douglass had predicted this in 1861: "The American people and the Government at Washington may refuse to recognize it for a time, but the 'inexorable logic of events' will force it upon them in the end; that the war now being waged in this land is a war for and against slavery." On January 1, 1863, Lincoln signed the

Emancipation Proclamation, a measure that resulted in a major escalation of what had been a limited war. Ulysses S. Grant called it "the heaviest blow yet given the Confederacy." In all, 180,000 blacks served in the Union Army, 34,000 of them freemen prior to the war. The desperate Confederate decision near the war's end, to arm slaves and grant them freedom for fighting, nullified the very principle upon which the South had staked its rebellion.

The end of the Civil War plunged America into a double-edged mourning – for catastrophic losses, personal and national, and for a way of life. While the war in itself could hardly have provided the impetus to an industrial and technological transformation at once so complex and so rapid, the Civil War and modernization remained intertwined in many minds. The literature that was produced in the postwar years registered a view of an American society that had grown increasingly diverse and splintered. It was as if the great rift between North and South had yielded a series of aftershocks, resulting in many smaller cleavages and separations. Thus, in novels, memoirs, biographies, even in photographs, the war was portrayed as a highly particularized experience rather than a nationally definitive event. Stephen Crane's *The Red Badge of Courage* was typical: it focused on the working classes who either volunteered, or were forced to fight because they could not hire substitutes like their wealthier counterparts. Crane's war fiction was not the archive of a nation but of a class, the class that in his view gave most. This perspective was characteristic of many literary works which foreground the experiences in turn of free blacks in Ohio (Dunbar's *The Fanatics*) the genteel poor in New England (Alcott's *Little Women*), subversive slaves in the South (Harper's *Iola Leroy*), and Northern war heroes (Wister's *Ulysses S. Grant*).

WAR STILLS

Perhaps no single late nineteenth-century device was more indicative of the changes the Civil War came to symbolize than the camera. Photography was a key instrument in distinguishing both what was different about the Civil War, and how the nation was transformed by it into a modern nation-state and industrial power. Moreover, the camera provided Americans with a distinctive perspective on war – the ability to witness the carnage from a position of detachment, as a spectacle orchestrated with a viewer in mind. All the narratives discussed below, which represent the most popular and/or critically acclaimed late nineteenth-century works about the war, exploit the aesthetic prospects of mass death and mourning. The story of remembering the Civil War begins with Matthew Brady and Alexander Gardner, two photographers who recognized the dramatic possibilities of this fraternal strife and helped to make it memorable while it was still ongoing. Not much is known about the early life of Matthew Brady. He was the son of Irish immigrants who was born "near 1823–1824," as Brady wrote, "in the woods about Lake George." He turned up in New York City at sixteen in the company of a portrait artist, William Page, who had been an early mentor, and with whom he had worked in Albany. In 1840 Brady met Samuel F. B. Morse, the inventor, who was deeply engaged with the beginnings of photography in the United States, and became his disciple. In 1844 Brady opened his first daguerreotype studio in New York and published his portraits the next year under the title, *The Gallery of Illustrious Americans*. He managed from early on to identify his studio with social distinction: to sit for a photographer at Brady's was a status symbol. Brady's forte was entrepreneurship, and he reigned supreme in his time as a commercial emissary of photography. He was quick to recognize the great transformative potential of his new technology and to embrace the main chance when it came to innovations.

Brady's business manager and ultimate rival, Alexander Gardner, was born in Scotland in 1821, trained as a scientist, and became involved as a young man in business and finance. Employed by a savings and loan company in 1847, Gardner developed skills in bookkeeping and general business management that proved indispensable to his subsequent work in Civil War photography. At the same time, Gardner was an idealist, and was deeply involved in social reform movements designed to improve the situation of the laboring poor. By 1851 Gardner was working as a journalist at the *Glasgow Sentinel* and supporting working-class interests in his editorials. Gardner appears to have met Matthew Brady at the Crystal Palace Exhibition in London in 1851, where Brady was awarded a prize for his *Gallery of Illustrious Americans*. By 1855, Gardner was earning praise for his own photography in Glasgow. The next year he emigrated to New York with his family, sought out Brady, and became his assistant, working in all areas of Brady's operation.

Both Brady and Gardner grasped the commercial potential of the Civil War as subject, and took steps to make Brady's the official war photography. Exploiting his acquaintance with Allan Pinkerton, head of the intelligence company that became the secret service, Brady secured a meeting in 1861 with President Lincoln, who signed a pass that allowed Brady to travel with Union troops. Meanwhile, Gardner, who was managing their Washington offices, ordered quantities of four-tube *carte de visite* cameras in anticipation of soldiers desiring to be photographed (perhaps for the last time) in their uniforms. He also signed a contract with a commercial photography establishment in New York to buy negatives of major war personalities that could be mass-distributed in card form. Given their mutual aptitude as businessmen and photographers,

Brady and Gardner's eventual rivalry was probably inevitable. Both claimed credit for the idea of photographing the war, and both petitioned Congress separately and almost simultaneously in February 1869 to sell their collections of negatives to the government.

Brady's achievement was to establish the category of "Civil War photography," and make his name synonymous with it. According to the *New York Times* (1861),

Mr. Brady was the first to make photography the Clio of war . . . His artists have accompanied the army on nearly all its marches, planting their sun batteries by the side of our Generals' more deathful ones, and taking town, cities, and forest with much less noise, and vastly more expedition. The result was a series of pictures christened, "Incidents of the War," and nearly as interesting as the war itself: for they constitute the history of it, and appeal directly to the great throbbing heart of the north.

The subjects that predominated in "Incidents of the War" were respites, conferences, pre-battle scenes, and corpses. This is explained in part by the fact that photographers were barred from live combat. Yet it also exposes the extent to which photography specialized as an art form in the cultural activity of making sense of a war whose effects were pervasive, but which was experienced by so many as a remote, indeed frozen event. An example is Gardner's "The Burial Party," dated April 15, 1865 at Cold Harbor, Virginia, the day after Lincoln's assassination, and less than a week after Lee's surrender at Appomattox (April 9, 1865).

The monumental import of *this* picture taken presumably at *this* moment suggests that its memorializing effort is both collective and particular. It captures a collective, national obligation to bury the war along with the war dead, in addition to capturing a specific group ritual. The picture's top horizon is framed by a dark row of trees, so lush that it appears as a beard or ruff for the landscape, and, in its background, just below the trees, four African American men dressed in white shirts, dark pants and hats, holding shovels, dig or stand poised to dig in the sandy grassy surface. In the foreground, another African-American man, dressed in a coat and wool seaman's cap, poses deliberately, crouching beside a stretcher upon which five skulls are neatly arranged. The nearest skull is straight up and grinning. There are no corpses in this image of burial, only the hint of one – a shoed foot, and partial leg, extending out from the middle of the stretcher.

This elaborately composed photograph is accompanied by an enigmatic caption that appears as confused about the identity of these men as about what they are actually doing. Are these former soldiers engaged in collecting the remains of their comrades? Are they local inhabitants seeking to provide a proper burial for the martyred dead, fallen so far from the families who might

FIGURE 1. "Burial Party. Cold Harbor, Virginia, April 15, 1865,"
Photographic Sketch Book of the War by Alexander Gardner (1865).

have performed this function? Or are they professional gravediggers, hired to
roam the country burying the dead who remain above ground ten months after
the battle has ended (June 1864)? These "native dwellers" recall what most
representations of the war assiduously repress – the economic transformation
of African-American slaves into free laborers. But what kind of work are these
men engaged in? While the caption implies a labor of ritual respect, these
workers might as easily be exhuming for scientific purposes as burying for
religious ones.

"The Burial Party" suggests the profound ties between death practices and
ethnicity that had prevailed in America from the nation's founding. One such
tie is ceremonial, voluntary, and honorific. Another is scientific – the use of
dead bones and skulls as keys to human diversity – methods common to natural
philosophers like John William Draper and anthropologists like Lewis Henry
Morgan in the nineteenth century. A third tie between death practices and
ethnicity calls up the theories of Social Darwinism. To the extent that the
photograph identifies a certain ethnic group as especially suited to the labor
of death, it may identify that group as moribund.

The Gardner photograph allows us to make a critical distinction between universal and historically specific understandings of death. In all cultures, death rituals serve to negotiate the ultimate experience of estrangement – the conversion of what is intimate (child, mother, spouse, friend) into the other. But in post-Civil War America such rituals also worked to distinguish relative states of kinship and strangeness among native, migrant, and immigrant. This is why death practices were central to ethnography in these decades. For followers of Samuel George Morton, the antebellum originator of scientific ethnology, skulls and bones provided an encyclopedia of knowledge about human diversity. In keeping with dominant theories on the plural origins of humankind, death was understood increasingly in this postwar period as an expression of prevailing class and racial hierarchies as well as of religious and cultural differences. Scientists measured skulls and charted the assorted immunological characteristics and mortality rates of racial and ethnic groups. Social scientists provided typological classifications of the vast array of customs and beliefs surrounding death and mourning. Philosophers speculated about contrasting notions of death as a universal versus death as a social particular. Literary authors, painters, photographers, and even advertisers provided representations that staged prevailing efforts to make what seemed ever more inseparable yet ever more incoherent – death and human difference – amenable to aesthetic and scientific form. Above all, making sense of death in this era was an interdisciplinary affair, which explains why Stephen Crane (whose early career is discussed below in chapter 7) pored over Brady's war photographs before writing his own second-hand retrospective account of the Civil War.

Indeed, Crane's *The Red Badge of Courage: An Episode of the American Civil War* (1895), a bestseller, seems situated squarely in an era of mechanical reproduction. The novel depicts a common soldier, Henry Fleming, who enlists in the Union army, eager to prove his "manhood" by displaying courage in battle. Henry flees from his first encounter with Confederate troops, however, and rejoins his regiment to discover that others have fought intensely and been killed or wounded. Rage and guilt fuse the subsequent near-hysterical pitch into battle that transforms Henry into a "true hero." Crane's persistent irony towards the novel's ideals (courage, cowardice, etc.) undermines the closing suggestion that war is the making of men. The mind of Crane's protagonist works at times like a camera, alternately distancing and intense.

It seemed to the youth that he saw everything. Each blade of the green grass was bold and clear. He thought that he was aware of every change in the thin, transparent vapor that floated idly in sheets. The brown or gray trunks of the trees showed each roughness of their surfaces. And the men of the regiment, with their starting eyes and sweating faces, running madly, or falling, as if thrown headlong, to queer, heaped-up corpses – all were comprehended. His mind took a mechanical but firm impression, so that afterward everything was pictured and explained to him, save why he himself was there.

Crane's description suggests that photography is a competing aesthetic form for recollecting war: the attention paid to focus, the ambition to capture texture and surface, all those details of piercing sight cataloged for the sake of retrospective contemplation. What this mechanical art cannot apprehend is meaning, the "why" of things. Crane sprinkles his text throughout with observations like "He was the picture of an exhausted soldier after a feast of war." In *Red Badge*, the written word often has the feel of the caption: arty, clever, pithy, definitive. It is as if Crane set his novel in dialogue with Brady's photographic enterprise – at once admiringly, competitively, and ironically – over the meaning of both the Civil War and the recording of its events.

Brady made a career of photographing death, yet he appears never to have contemplated the metaphysical or ethical implications of his enterprise. Such questions absorb Crane. His novel might be seen as a literary accounting for all the things that photographs do not account for. Crane makes the voyeuristic aspect of representing death, the vulnerability of the dead, an ongoing concern in his narrative. This element of voyeurism is inherent in the poses of live subjects in Brady's photographs: Civil War soldiers baring their wounds for the camera. There is something seductive, subtly exhibitionist in the carefully draped bodies with pants pulled down just enough to expose a "flesh wound of the hip" or pant leg drawn up to expose a "flesh wound of leg," or sleeve rolled up to expose a "shot forearm." The subjects stare directly at the camera, their glances partly aggressive, partly provocative. The living but rent soldier bodies in these photographs highlight what remains implicit in the images of the war dead: that injuries, like the death they mime, are excruciatingly private. The pain or deadness of a particular body that is inaccessible even to direct witnesses is doubly removed from spectators remote in setting and time, whose attitude towards that pain or death can seem callous or salacious. The act of looking, these images suggest, must be prurient, since aid or empathy are not options. Crane's novel invests looking from a remove with moral purpose. Henry Fleming's repeated inadvertent confrontations with corpses, moments when he happens upon their utter strangeness yet striking calm, afford richly textured efforts to claim the moral element that is occluded by war photography.

The Red Badge of Courage is haunted by the ethical predicament of representation, which is intensified where the representation concerns a bloody war that has been neither witnessed nor suffered first-hand. Representing the Civil War is an ethical dilemma because, as is clear from the novel's beginning, it is a war fought by working-class substitutes, whose idiom is noticeably inferior to that of Crane's middle-class and elite readers. The wealthy regularly hired the poor to fight in their place during the Civil War. The business titans whose careers were launched in the flush war economy, and who built immense fortunes in the years after it – Andrew Mellon, John D. Rockefeller, Pierpoint Morgan, Philip Armour, or Jay Gould – relied, in the words of Mellon's father, on "lives less valuable or others ready to serve for the love of serving."

The novel's ninth chapter, which ends with the notorious simile of the sun pasted like a wafer in the sky, invokes the Ultimate Substitute, the Christian God who died for the sins of all. The chapter opens with Henry, whole and wandering "amid wounds," a "mob of men . . . bleeding." He stands for everyone who has either missed or deliberately eluded the Civil War, including Crane himself. He is uninjured, and therefore stigmatized by shame. Indeed the chapter might be seen as a running comparison of these two kinds of injury. "The spectral soldier" who walks beside Henry "like a stalking reproach" has a "gray, appalling face." The hand of "the tall soldier" is a "curious red and black combination." Meanwhile Henry imagines his shame as visible to all: "the letters of guilt . . . burned into his brow." While each death recorded in the novel is exquisitely prolonged, like a sacrament, the death of Jim Conklin, whose body becomes the Eucharist sun wafer at the end, fills almost a whole chapter and some of another. Henry is the principal observer of Jim Conklin's death, and his somatic responses contrast with the dying bodies surrounding him. Henry's feelings are anatomized, like body parts – "heart," "face," "tongue," – as a means of registering their intensity. They are not limited to any one part but are all-encompassing. In keeping with the novel's narrative tense, which is always present, Henry's overflowing emotions capture the totalizing character of war.

Critics have noted that despite the novel's obvious historical significance, it appears deliberately drained of historical specificity. There are no place names, no recognizable battlefields or battles, no mention of leading personages or events. The one black character in the novel, the "negro teamster" at the outset, seems there for the sole sake of announcing his insignificance. He is in fact a diversion, distracting the men from the impending battle, until more seductive diversions present themselves. Blacks slave or free, the novel seems to suggest, were incidental to the war and its aftermath. The abstractness of the novel's approach to the Civil War is also due to its particular historical focus. For *The Red Badge of Courage* is far more concerned with the historical developments ushered in by the war than with the events of the war itself.

Among the most significant of these developments is the changing nature of work in the post-Civil War era. Crane's understanding of war as the most extreme form of worker objectification, whereby the worker becomes inextricably bound up with the materials of his labor – indistinguishable from his regiment, his military affiliation, his nation, merged with the qualities of his environment (for the sake of survival) – is especially relevant to the 1890s context of the novel's writing. The novel's soldiers represent the working classes who labored in the modern industries that were currently being infused with rational principles of efficiency. These methods were subsequently codified in Frederick Winslow Taylor's *Principles of Scientific Management* (1911), which described the making of industrial labor and managerial classes as war in its own right. Taylor's ideas were consistent with the contemporaneous rise of the "Boy Scouts" (incorporated in US, 1910) and of Theodore Roosevelt's "Rough Riders" (Roosevelt's *The Rough Riders*, published 1899) – all "Strenuous Age" efforts (Roosevelt's *The Strenuous Life* published 1900) to invigorate modern Americans through institutionalizing ties to nature and the wilderness. These new strategies for training working-class and immigrant populations in the factories were thought to strengthen society in general, for inefficiency was considered unnatural. *The Red Badge of Courage* is pervaded by management rhetoric as Henry Fleming internalizes his superiors' supervision of himself. This administrative control is even maintained by corpses: in one scene, a particularly gruesome yet still vigilant corpse drives the guilt-ridden Henry back into battle.

Another marked sign of the modernity of *The Red Badge of Courage* is its nostalgia, which is expressed in an antiquarian spirituality: images of soldiers as "sheep for slaughter," ritual objects of a war machine whose appetite is at once murderous and divine. War is a God whose preferred food is men. Crane displays a profound understanding of sacrifice as a ritual that stages the dependence of social ideologies on live bodies. His portrayal of the Union Army as composed principally of men from the working classes likewise confirms how the spiritual economies of sacrifice that were so prevalent in Crane's time served to reinforce divisions between the fortunate and the bereft. Ultimately, however, there is no redemption in *The Red Badge of Courage*. In this novel, religion has become as tenuous and childlike as the Eucharist-sun "pasted" in the sky at the end of chapter 9. Technology (in the form of the camera) and art (in the form of Crane's distinctive style and theatrical scenes) predominate at the expense of the religious questions raised by this spectacle of death.

For those seeking spiritual consolation from their fiction, there was plenty to be had in two other bestselling Civil War novels by authors who were, like

Crane, the offspring of ministers. Written in the war's immediate aftermath, *The Gates Ajar* (1868) and *Little Women* (1868), by New Englanders Elizabeth Stuart Phelps and Louisa May Alcott, respectively, found more optimistic answers to the problems of faith raised by the Civil War. Phelps sought to give substance to a heaven where President Lincoln presided to greet soldiers upon arrival; Alcott detailed the myriad sacrifices required of the genteel poor on the home front. The great popularity of *The Gates Ajar* and *Little Women* were due, in no small part, to what they omitted. Phelps and Alcott offered fantasies of wartime domesticity avoiding casualties and battles, as well as the problems of race, slavery, and emancipation. Civil War novels that foregrounded race, and went so far as to represent the prospects of interracial romance and marriage, were far less enthusiastically received. Lydia Maria Child's *The Romance of the Republic* (1867), Rebecca Harding Davis's *Waiting for the Verdict* (1868), and Anna Dickinson's *What Answer* (1868), resolved their risky plots in various ways. Child married her beautiful and multi-talented octoroon heroines to a German (whose nationality freed him from American-bred racism) and a Boston abolitionist. Davis emphasized the strong bonds between white and black matriarchs, while withholding marriage between the mulatto doctor, John Broderip, and his white beloved, Margaret Conrad. Dickinson married her mulatto heroine Francesca Ercildoune to the white officer, William Surrey. William's parents, who tell him that prejudice against blacks "is a feeling that will never die out, and ought never to die out, so long as any of the race remain in America," disown the couple. And their judgment is reinforced when racists in the New York Draft riots of 1863 murder Francesca and William.

The Civil War novels of Phelps and Alcott were influential because they mined the conventional, searching within familiar territory for therapeutic remedies to war. They did not challenge readers to look outside themselves or into the future. They did not ask readers to imagine, for instance, how black people, whose status had been radically altered by the war, might be accommodated socially, economically, or politically. Instead, they depicted worlds of women from highly specified cultures and regions – white Anglo-Saxon Protestant New Englanders – shaping their Christian beliefs into coping strategies. In both novels, the Civil War is safely remote: it may kill a brother (Phelps), or debilitate a father (Alcott), but the novel's social sphere on the whole remains immune to its effects. The power of these books lies in their claims for the ongoing vitality of certain traditional American legacies whose principles were tested and strengthened by the trials of wartime.

Elizabeth Stuart Phelps (1844–1911) was a pivotal cultural figure of the post-Civil War era because of her immersion in its most important religious developments. She was an ardent feminist: producing a voluminous body of fiction, poems, and essays, and avoiding marriage until the advanced age of forty-four to a much younger seminary student. A Boston native, christened at the Pine Street Church where her father was pastor, Mary Gray Phelps (who changed her name at age eight to memorialize her mother) grew up near the Andover Seminary. Her father, Austin, a minister, married Elizabeth Stuart in 1842 and joined the faculty of Andover in 1848 as a Professor of Sacred Rhetoric and Homiletics, a post he held until his retirement in 1870. The author of many books on religion, Austin Phelps appears in his daughter's 1891 autobiography, *Chapters From a Life*, as a tormented figure, with a morbid sense of guilt, and various physical illnesses. The mother, Elizabeth Stuart Phelps, was a popular writer, whose novel about a parsonage, *Sunny Side* (1851), brought her fame just before her death. Phelps was the granddaughter of Moses Stuart, who introduced the study of Hebrew at the Andover Seminary in 1810 and encouraged the study of German philosophy and the higher criticism. Moses Stuart believed that if Andover was to become "the sacred West Point," its students needed modern weapons at their disposal. While Andover was renowned from its founding in 1808 as a citadel of orthodox Calvinism, its theology had always been more hybrid than that. The school's rather incongruous blend included Darwinism; Unitarianism and Methodism; Common Sense, Kantian, and Hegelian philosophies; German Romantic theology; and Calvinist notions such as predestination, total depravity, and the limited atonement of Christ. One of the most important influences on Phelps was her tutor, Edwards A. Park, who taught theology at Andover from 1847 to 1881. His famous sermon, "The Theology of the Intellect and That of the Feelings," delivered in Boston in 1850, was an attempt to reconcile Andover's official insistence on the absolute truth of the Bible with the appeal of sentiment or heart. Despite her gender, Phelps was thoroughly integrated into the Andover community, where intellectual seriousness was a way of life. Inspired to pursue writing by the example of her mother, Phelps invested it with a theological rigor she identified with her father. Her paternal grandfather, Eliakim Phelps, who had a Congregational parish in Stratford, Connecticut, became famous when official investigators of spirit possession confirmed that his parsonage was overrun by poltergeists. The incident had a profound effect on his granddaughter, who continued to follow the research of the Psychical Society to the end of her life, seeking evidence of clairvoyance and communication with the dead.

The Gates Ajar is a work of religious protest whose ultimate aim is to reform Christianity, not to overturn it. The novel's clergy succumb rather weakly at the end to the more responsive and fulfilling doctrines of women. Emotional and supple in their interpretation of the Bible, women alone are capable of fashioning a loving Christianity with wide appeal. Phelps spent "two or three years" reading up on mourning and eschatology before beginning *The Gates Ajar*, which she saw in part as a means for making the liturgy amenable to the sufferings of women during the war. To this end, the novel draws on a number of philosophical and theological theories: Joseph Butler's inductive rationale for the probability of life after death; Schleiermacher's Romantic interpretation of faith; and Liberal Christianity's emphasis on God's immanence and human perfectibility. Formally, Phelps's book is a mix of sermons, dialogues, poems, hymns, and allegory, with the diary predominating. The plot concerns Mary, a young woman who wavers spiritually following the death of her soldier brother Roy. Her learned Aunt Winifred stands for the Heartfelt Reason that guides Mary's return to Faith (the name of Winifred's soon-to-be motherless daughter). Aunt Winifred allows Phelps to display her own learning, and to earn theological respect for her sentimental Christianity.

The supposed materiality of Phelps's heaven has long been a source of critical controversy. The book was disparaged as "a Biedermeier paradise," "a Gilded-Age heaven," a "celestial retirement village," and admired as "a carefully crafted argument for the literal interpretation of the Bible." What has often been overlooked, however, are the subtle distinctions between literal and figurative language in Phelps's account of heaven. It fulfills what her grandfather Moses Stuart termed, "a *tropical* use of words, at the foundation of which some analogy *real* or *supposed* lies." Every description of heaven in *Gates Ajar* is conveyed in qualified, provisional terms, as in the following discussion between Aunt Winifred and Mary.

About those trees and houses, and the rest of your "pretty things?" Are they to be like these? . . . I don't suppose that the houses will be made of oak and pine and nailed together, for instance. But I hope for heavenly types of nature and of art. *Something that will be to us then what these are now* . . . You remember Plato's old theory, that the ideal of everything exists eternally in the mind of God. If that is so, – and I do not see how it can be otherwise, – then whatever of God is expressed to us in this world by flower, or blade of grass, or human face, why should not that be expressed forever in heaven by something corresponding to flower, or grass, or human face?

The Gates Ajar liberates the figural imagination, by confirming its divine authorization. "The mystery of the Bible," Aunt Winifred observes, "lies not so much in what it says as in what it does not say." Fundamental to her view is the assumption that heaven and earth correspond in an ultimate display of reason, and that God's heaven would inevitably be continuous with God's earth. God is a divine functionalist; his world is a unified plane. Hence the novel's title, which Aunt Winifred explains: God "has obviously not *opened* the gates which bar heaven from our sight, but he has as obviously not *shut* them; they stand ajar, with the Bible and reason in the way, to keep them from closing." The Bible remains accessible to successive generations of interpreters, a living document, renewed by everyone who takes inspiration from it.

In this context, the directness and simplicity of the protagonist's emotional life makes for the novel's powerful appeal. The protagonist's grief is so vast that it nullifies the rhythms of the sun, and transforms a familiar domesticity into a sterile cell. Mary responds in her mournfulness to authentic comfort – the comfort of Aunt Winifred's divinely inspired imagination. Yet this secular bond proves to be as fleeting as Mary's tie to Roy, and to all the unmentioned family members (mother, father), whose deaths can be inferred in their absence from the narrative. It is only a matter of time before Aunt Winifred dies as well, of breast cancer, leaving her daughter, "Faith," in Mary's care. The sign that Mary is liberated from the prison of mourning is her ability to see Aunt Winifred's daughter, comprehensively and objectively, a "picture" so clear as to be "photographed" in her mind. The sun has resumed its rhythms, a celebration of light that is recalled at Aunt Winifred's death. Phelps offers this photographic prospect of faith to her readers as a familiar consolation for an all-too common war-induced grief.

Louisa May Alcott shared Phelps's rich theological legacy though hers was less formal and institutional as befitted the daughter of a transcendentalist. Alcott was the second child of the educator, philosopher, and social reformer Bronson Alcott. The self-educated son of a poor Connecticut farmer, who had tried his hand at factory work, peddling, and schoolteaching, Alcott became notorious for his radical theories about nutrition and for his brief utopian experiment, Fruitlands. It was Louisa's mother, Abba May Alcott, who seems to have been the principal breadwinner for her four daughters, pursuing a variety of occupations available to women of her day (social work among them), while her husband wrote and lectured. Though the Alcott family could depend to some extent on Abba May's wealthy relatives, poverty always threatened, and there were repeated crises in the Alcott marriage. During the family's sojourn at Fruitlands, for instance, when the harvest had failed and all the other adherents had deserted the snowbound utopia, Abba forced Bronson to choose between his family and his experiment: the family returned to Concord without him. Alcott appears to have preferred the harmonious family of theory, described in his book *Concord Days* (1872), to the conflicted family of fact, invariably clamoring for food and shelter. While Louisa adored her mother, immortalizing her in *Little Women*'s Marmee, her relations with her father were ambivalent. As the focus of his first psychological experiment, "Observations on the Life of My Second Child during the First Year," she was subjected to both positive and negative reinforcement – psychological seduction, manipulation, and intimidation. Bronson obviously admired his daughter, describing her at two as extraordinarily decisive and forceful, but he was also intimidated, even repelled by her.

Among Abba Alcott's gifts to her daughter was the encouragement of her writing. She wrote in a letter that Louisa's art was "a safety valve to her smothered sorrow which might otherwise consume her young and tender heart." Louisa's art was also a means of contributing to the meager family coffer. "I am trying to turn my brains into money," she announced in 1855. She produced a voluminous body of writings, drawing on a variety of genres and techniques, including fairy tales, gothic thrillers, personal sketches, and sentimental fiction. Her writings had a common subject, women's experiences in work, love, and marriage, and a common perspective on those experiences – unconventional and often feminist. Before she was thirty, Louisa had published over twenty sensational stories, many under pseudonyms, and short fiction under her own name, in respectable magazines such as the *Saturday Evening Gazette* and the *Atlantic Monthly*. Prior to *Little Women*, she published almost a hundred fictional pieces, most of them sentimental Realism, featuring young heroines who sacrifice all for their families or young heroines who pursue independent existences in place of traditional roles as wives and mothers. Alcott's writing seems from the first to have been a means of liberating her from the conventions of femininity. Her father had decreed that boys and girls alike at Fruitlands wear trousers. He also held that any person in whom the intellect dominates was a man, and anyone ruled by the heart was a woman. Deciding that her own soul was ruled by the intellect, Louisa concluded, like her heroine Jo, that she had been born "with a boy's spirit." She intended to take "her little talent in hand and force the world again." Alcott was the first woman in Concord to register as a voter, and spoke derisively of women who failed to exercise this prerogative.

A major breakthrough in her writing career, *Little Women* spawned a series of books on the March family, and brought Alcott the fame and fortune she craved. As a domestic account of women during the Civil War, the novel showed how life at home in those straitened times required its own form of valor from the genteel and working classes. The novel opens at Christmas, and the holiday is presented as an opportunity for sacrifice: the modesty of the March sisters' celebration is insufficient; their mother Marmee insists that they give it to a family poorer still. Each daughter is compensated in some self-completing way for denying her desires, and quelling her resentment about it. Meg attains domestic bliss, Jo finds a satisfying husband and a fulfilling vocation, Amy marries Laurie, a good and wealthy man, and Beth goes to heaven. The novel promises future reward for present sacrifice at the same time that it counsels gratitude. Learn to appreciate the small good things, and you will set yourself up for deeper enjoyment of the bigger things when or if they come. The novel's governing morality repudiates modern economic aspirations, in part by parodying novelty, consumption, and advertising. Modern commodities are mocked, for example, in the account of the gifts bought by the wealthy Laurie for Meg and John's new home, which regularly break or frustrate expectations. Opposed to these flawed manufactured items are the handmade gifts fashioned by her industrious sisters.

While there are many sources of social unity in the Marches' world, the novel emphasizes divisions, most prominently divisions of class. Gender is a far more elastic category: many characters fulfill conventions, but many others blur them. This is true most strikingly of Jo and Laurie, but also of Aunt March and even of Mr. and Mrs. March. Marmee fully controls the home front without Father March, who upon his return is a shadowy, intellectual figure. Much is made of his lost fortune, very little of his ministerial career. Class remains definitive; no one questions why the poor tutor John Brooke goes to war when Laurie goes to college. Meg experiences a variety of humiliations at the home of the wealthy Moffats, although Alcott underscores the dullness and crudity that "all their gilding could not quite conceal." Amy too is susceptible to the lure of wealth, and Alcott is here also adamant about the distinctions between those who are truly genteel and those who just have money.

Alcott's ideals are Christian renunciation, inner fortitude, and resistance to the appeals of materialism and celebrity. Thus Jo must learn to limit her literary aspirations, eschewing the type of writing she finds empowering and financially rewarding. Her savior is Mr. Bhaer, who adheres to his Christian faith with a military intensity. When he convinces Jo of the worthlessness of her saleable fiction, she pitches it into the fire in a gesture of self-mastery. Mr. Bhaer is his own best example, as homely as he is poor, but generous. The novel's society is readily responsive to the simple morality of the Marches. Poverty protects from the extravagant desires that are the source of all misery. The poor are represented consistently as richer than the wealthy. The married life of John and Meg Brooke is far superior to that of Ned and Sallie Moffat, who inhabit a "great house, full of splendid loneliness." Jo learns true self-control in the face of the greatest loss of all – that of her beloved Beth – renouncing on Beth's deathbed her "old ambition" of literary fame. She also manages to write a book that is moral as well as popular, addressed "straight to the hearts of those who read it." Hence the novel's message: in giving up, all is gained. Following their collective sacrifice of Beth, Marmee and Father March reap their "Harvest," a nest of happily married daughters and grandchildren.

The submission to fate celebrated in *Little Women* was reinforced in many accounts of the war, even the unlikeliest: biographies of war generals such as Owen Wister's on *Ulysses S. Grant* (1900). Wister's primary emphasis is the air of helplessness and inevitability that marks Grant's life leading up to the war, and through his startling transformation into a war hero. Wister begins with the extraordinary sense of failure that marks Grant's life to his thirty-ninth year. His family had grown used to overlooking him as a source of support; he is a nonentity in his provincial home town. A mere four years later his picture hangs in homes across the country. His subsequent Presidency is beset by scandal and he leaves office in disgrace, dying of a stroke at sixty-three; but he is redeemed yet again, this time posthumously. In all of these instances, according to Wister, Grant capitulates to destiny, a thesis that results in a surprisingly complex and compelling portrait. On the whole, his study follows closely the account of the war laid out by Grant himself in his bestselling *Personal Memoirs*, published in 1885 by Mark Twain's own publishing house. Wister's biography is most appropriately understood as an interpretative guide to Grant's bare facts.

Wister's subject is the inadvertent, predetermined aspect of Grant's life. It is a life almost devoid of deliberateness: the ultimate import of his instincts and actions always escape Grant. Grant's great accomplishments – planning and executing battles, handling his men, negotiating with the opposition, consulting with Lincoln, drafting the terms of Lee's surrender – are simple manifestations of character, humbly carried out and humbly regarded by Grant himself. This case for the man's essential passivity allows Wister to minimize his responsibility for the scandals – both military and political – that dogged Grant in life and shadow his historical profile: stories about his drinking, his responsibility for some of the war's ugliest and most costly battles, the reputation for corruption as President.

Wister's Grant finds his element in war: displaying a genius for reading the prospects for battle in a landscape, intuiting how to penetrate Southern strongholds by conquering rivers that extend from Northern borders in Ohio deep into Southern territory. Grant at war becomes an actor in his ultimate role. Wister's account is explicitly theatrical, and he shamelessly invokes and even embellishes the apocryphal story (discounted by Grant himself) of Lee on the point of surrender, stretched out under an apple tree contemplating the Virginia sky. Though Grant considers the Southern cause unjustifiable, his generous treatment of Lee and his troops anticipate the war's ultimate purpose – union. Grant is every man who would like to imagine that he might rise to the occasion if called upon in war or peace. He represents the dream of a religious meritocracy: the common individual who has given his life up to fate, catapulted into greatness by historical circumstances.

SATIRES OF WAR

The Civil War novels of Maria Ruiz de Burton, Paul Laurence Dunbar, and Henry James, are satires that highlight the foibles of presidents and generals, and the dysfunction of American ideals, particularly religious ones, during this traumatic fraternal conflict. In contrast to the reverential perspectives of Phelps and Alcott on the role played by religion during and after the war, Maria Ruiz de Burton portrays a New England clerisy determined to exploit the upheaval for what it is worth. The dignified suffering of sisters, wives, and daughters in Phelps and Alcott is replaced by James with Northerners who revel self-righteously, even perversely, in their losses. And Paul Laurence Dunbar provides a rare view of the war as experienced by imperiled free blacks in Ohio, whose lives pivot on the edge of slavery, as close as the Kentucky border they can see but not touch. The willingness of all three authors to abandon the respect typically accorded the principals in the conflict was attributable in part to their status as social outsiders – a Mexican, an African American, and an American expatriate. While Phelps qualified religious orthodoxy in highly controversial terms, she did so as a member of that orthodoxy. *Who Would Have Thought It?* (1872), which is set in Massachusetts on the eve of the war, is the first novel of Mexican-American author, Maria Amparo Ruiz de Burton (whose career is discussed in full in chapter 5), a stranger to the Eastern religious and cultural establishment. Published anonymously because of its satirical content, the novel is the product of Ruiz de Burton's sojourn on the East coast, where she traveled from her home in California with her husband, an American army officer. Her stance in this novel as in her subsequent novel is relentlessly critical of American culture. *Who Would Have Thought It?* exposes the corruption of the Union military establishment, the clamor for enrichment during the war, the racism of the genteel Northern middle class, and the hypocrisy of the Eastern clergy.

Ruiz de Burton's focus on economic development in the context of colonialism provides a unique novelistic approach to the Civil War: the acceleration of industrialization, investment, and speculation is explored through the conquest of gold and silver in the West and Southwest. The novel's plot hinges on the theft of a theft of a theft: the gold of the Mohave Indians is stolen by Lola's mother, and is stolen in turn from Lola by the New England

Norval family, and then is stolen from the Norvals by the treacherous Reverend Hackwell. Ruiz de Burton includes another facet of the war that is omitted from other war romances: extensive descriptions of Confederate prison camps, where Union soldiers died regularly from cold, starvation, and disease. She emphasizes the Union army's complicity in these prison casualties through its policy of refusing to exchange captured soldiers with the Confederacy. Reputedly Grant's idea, the policy was designed to reduce Southern manpower since returned Confederate prisoners typically reenlisted, while their Union counterparts went home. Ruiz de Burton is equally hard on the profiteering that went on during the war.

The novel begins with Dr. James Norval, a geologist, returning to his New England home after four years of research with a dark-skinned child, Maria Dolores Medina, known as Lola, and a massive bundle of what appear to be rock specimens. Overtaken by hostile Indians during his travels on the Colorado River, he is brought to their camp, where he finds Maria Medina and her daughter, victims of kidnapping who have been kept in degraded servitude, their skins dyed black. Before her death, Mrs. Medina recounts her harrowing tale, and secures a promise from Dr. Norval that he will care for her daughter and the vast fortune in gold (the massive bundle) she has accumulated in captivity. Dr. Norval's racist wife, Jemima, refuses to take Lola in, but is placated by her gold, which she proceeds to spend. The Norval family includes two evil stepsisters, and a handsome princely son, Julian, who falls in love with Lola. While her skin gradually lightens, as the dye wears off, her initial coloring allows Ruiz de Burton to indict Northern racism. The novel's principal clergy are especially striking given the historical proximity of *Who Would Have Thought It?* and the Henry Ward Beecher trial for adultery. The hypocritical and malevolent Reverend John Hackwell, who will subsequently draw Jemima Norval into an adulterous relationship, and his sidekick, Reverend Hammerhard, are the novel's villains.

The start of the war complicates these already tumultuous social relations. Dr. Norval continues his unorthodox ways: having implied some sympathy for the slavery cause, he is charged with disloyalty to the Union and departs in haste for Africa and Abyssinia. Free speech is a luxury for a nation at war. Ruiz de Burton's critique of the Union dwells on the Presbyterian ministry and the female congregants who ensured its wealth and success. But it also features searing criticism of the War Department, the Congress, and even President Lincoln, who is portrayed as a vain and ineffectual hayseed, whose dedication to 'the people' is a myth. Ruiz de Burton's most severe criticism is reserved for Puritan influences in nineteenth-century American life. Everywhere she looks — in the rigidity of middle-class matrons and the hypocrisy of their ministers, in the greed of politicians and the racism of those who mount rhetorical defenses of abolition – Ruiz de Burton sees remnants of the seventeenth-century religion that energized a colonial empire.

The Civil War in *Who Would Have Thought It?* is an assault in its own right upon whatever values – loyalty, democracy, free speech – the American nation was thought to stand for. Julian Norval gazes around the lobby of the War Department where he has come to plead the overturning of an unjust dismissal, wondering how many injustices will stand due to the poverty and insignificance of their victims. In *Who Would Have Thought It?*, the war on the battlefield is echoed by the government's war at home against its own citizens. Julian is admitted to a hearing with the President, and pardoned, only because of his wealth and connections. The greatest casualty of the Civil War, according to Ruiz de Burton, are the principles of the nation as a whole, which, she strongly implies, were never that secure to begin with. And she argues that as the nineteenth century wore on, the nation's moral condition only worsened. Is it any wonder that Julian Norval, in the company of his new wife, Lola, chooses the life of an expatriate in Mexico over a future in post-Civil War America?

Ruiz de Burton's portrait of America during the Civil War was rare among American novels in the candor and acerbity of its portrait. But it was not unique. In his 1901 novel, *The Fanatics*, Paul Laurence Dunbar represented the sufferings of blacks in Ohio, who had been free before the war's start, as well as the traumatic discord within white families whose members took opposite sides in the conflict. As Dunbar's novel demonstrates, war always causes division, but such divisions never fall into neat binaries.

Paul Laurence Dunbar was born in 1872, in Dayton, Ohio, the town that is called "Dorbury" in *The Fanatics*. His parents were former slaves from Kentucky; his father, a plasterer who taught himself to read, served in the 55th Massachusetts Infantry and the 5th Massachusetts Colored Calvary Regiment during the Civil War. His mother, who worked as a washerwoman for the family of Orville and Wilbur Wright, liked poetry though she was apparently illiterate. A precocious child, Paul wrote poetry from the age of six. In high school Dunbar was the only African American in his class, but his talents were recognized, and he served as editor of the school paper and president of the literary society. His first jobs were in journalism, working for community newspapers, and publishing an African-American newsletter with financial support from the Wright brothers. He also worked throughout this period as an elevator operator, hoping for the breakthrough that occurred when his poetry was praised in a syndicated news piece, and caught the attention of the famous dialect poet, James Whitcomb Riley. The attention enabled Dunbar to publish his first book of poems, *Oak and Ivy* (1892), and according to legend he hawked his book to elevator riders in order to repay his publisher. The book advanced Dunbar's reputation, and in 1893, he was invited to recite at the World's Fair, where Frederick Douglass pronounced him "the most promising young colored man in America."

Dunbar's next book, *Majors and Minors* (1896), brought national recognition. In his *Harper's Weekly* editorial column, William Dean Howells welcomed "the first instance of an American negro who had evinced innate distinction in literature . . . God hath made of one blood all nations of men, perhaps the proof of this saying is to appear in the arts, and our hostilities and prejudices are to vanish in them." He assisted in the publication of Dunbar's first two books as *Lyrics of a Lowly Life*. In 1897, Dunbar, who was now living in Toledo, Ohio, toured England as a poet of international repute. Unable to support himself and his wife as a poet, Dunbar took a job at the Library of Congress. Ill with tuberculosis, his marriage in decline, he turned to alcohol, which further damaged his health. He managed to continue writing, however, and despite his premature death in 1906, he produced twelve books of poetry, four books of short stories, a play, and five novels.

Among Dunbar's best-known poems is "We Wear The Mask," which begins: "We wear the mask that grins and lies / It hides our cheeks and shades our eyes / This debt we pay to human guile / With torn and bleeding hearts we smile / And mouth with myriad subtleties." The "we" of the poem is the voice of the black collectivity, which momentarily abandons its persona in order to describe the experience of "double consciousness." For just a moment, the reader is invited to look behind the "grins and lies" that typically conceals the "torn and bleeding hearts." Pausing midway through to reconsider the wisdom of its own unmasking, the voice formally reclaims that which has become a symbol for poetic convention itself: "Why should the world be over-wise / In counting all our tears and sighs / Nay, let them only see us, while / We wear the mask." The poem suggests that aesthetic form be understood as a mask that cloaks what it represents in order to intensify its expressive force. In so doing it claims a special aesthetic office for black Americans, who by necessity have become experts in concealment.

"We Wear The Mask" provides a valuable introduction to *The Fanatics*, a novel whose narrator preserves his mask so assiduously that the author's racial identity would have been undetectable had it appeared anonymously. Set on the Ohio border, the novel depicts Southerners sympathetic to the North, and Northerners sympathetic to the South, in addition to fathers who disown sons for joining the wrong side and daughters for loving the wrong soldiers. Dunbar judiciously refuses to regionalize fanaticism. Indeed, the novel's primary claim is that black Americans, disowned by white Northerners and Southerners alike, are ideal historians of the Civil War. Abandoned by both sides, they alone are capable of representing each with accuracy and honesty. Dunbar stages this ideal capacity for detachment both in his narrative and throughout his work in his depiction of black characters. The novel's only black character, "Nigger Ed" (the pejorative always appears in quotes), goes to war as the servant of a Union captain, and is later revered for his impartial care of the wounded and dead. With the subtle exception of the quotes around "nigger," there is nothing in Dunbar's portrait that is inconsistent with the racialist assumptions of a good liberal like Howells. In other words, one would never know from the characterizations that the author of *The Fanatics* is black and critical of dominant cultural views on race.

The only indication of the author's background is the fact that the novel keeps a steady focus on the wartime circumstances of Ohio's blacks. Defined as "contraband of war" by General Butler, the former black slaves haunt the rearguards of Union troops, and pour into border States like Ohio. Sometimes finding work in the army as cooks or valets, more often destitute and homeless, these vulnerable migrants carry everything they own with them. Significantly, regardless of their difficulties, none of them are shown returning to captivity. Ohio black society also features classes that were free before the war, including Dorbury's black upper class. Cleveland has its own peculiar "aristocracy of shame." Given its convenient location close to the South but free, Cleveland was a preferred place for slave mistresses of Southern masters, who sent them there to live with their mulatto offspring. Neither established black community welcomes the newly emancipated wanderers, who are twice victimized: by whites and by fellow blacks, who fear their own inability to be distinguished from the refugees.

Dunbar's novel confirms conclusively what no other Civil War novel even addresses, that neither the North nor the South could have recruited troops to fight for the freedom of blacks. Moreover, once the war began, and for long afterward, the former slaves were repudiated by whites, as well as by more established blacks, whose security they threatened. White mobs seeking to reduce Dorbury's newly enlarged black population cared little for existing class distinctions in the black community. Dunbar recognized the subsequent role played by blacks of all classes as the social cement – the scapegoats – essential to the reunification of North and South. Dunbar gave voice in *The Fanatics* to aspects of the Civil War that were overlooked in most recollections. By confronting with relentless honesty features of the conflict omitted by other historians he also illuminated much that came after it.

The same may be said of Henry James's only novel set entirely in America, *The Bostonians* (1886, serialized in *Century Magazine*, 1884–85). Steeped in the rhetoric and agendas of the Civil War and its aftermath, the novel transforms the war into a melodramatic love contest between Basil Ransom, the ex-Confederate, and his distant cousin, Olive Chancellor, a Northern loyalist. They battle for possession of the heart of America, embodied in the working-class girl, Verena Tarrant, innocent, beautiful, talented, full of promise yet profoundly naïve. Ideas take center stage in *The Bostonians* instead of being subordinated to the demands of characterization, as in James's other novels. Olive is a pure product of New England, Basil an emblematic Southerner. While it is more than this, *The Bostonians* has been read as a thinly worked-up catalog of James's complaints about America. From his pessimistic perspective, the country is composed of greedy capitalists and political ideologues – ranging from rabid conservative (Ransom) to radical feminist (Chancellor). As a result, *The Bostonians* displays clear historical engagements. It is a novel about Reconstruction, and about the social developments that defined this era. These include changing gender roles, ideas about sexuality, the political movements that crystallized some of these changes, the rise of American consumerism, the growth of a publicity culture, the ongoing tension in America between democracy and class stratification. James displays an extraordinary alertness to small distinctions – the ways in which different forms of mobility in the novel (streetcars, carriages, walking) serve to mediate class relations – and to large ones, including class and gender. The novel also dramatizes the emergence of America as a multicultural society. The extent and subtlety of James's perspective in this regard is truly remarkable.

What seems to have impressed James most deeply about America was the limiting and even destructive nature of traditional gender roles. *The Bostonians* was the first major novel in English to deal seriously with the feminist movement, and to portray lesbian desire with respect and sensitivity. In preliminary comments on the novel, James foregrounded this element: the novel, he wrote, "relates an episode connected with the so-called 'woman's movement,'" and "should be a study of one of those friendships between women which are so common in New England." James might have been drawing on any number of couples familiar to him, including his sister Alice and her friend Katherine Loring, and Sarah Orne Jewett and Annie Fields. There is condescension in these remarks, which anticipates a consistent problem of narrative tone in the novel. But there is also real sincerity and affection in James's portrait of "Boston marriages" – the term for lesbian relationships in contemporary New England. His pervading interest in sexual identity helps to explain why the characters in *The Bostonians* appear more fixed than other characters in

James. In keeping with scientific definitions of sexual inversion set forth in the theories (then popular in the United States) of the Viennese neurologist Krafft-Ebing, James was experimenting with biological, even deterministic definitions. Thus sexual desire is an inclination that is inborn and does not change. Olive desires women; Verena desires men. Verena experiences a kind of initiatory rite as a lesbian, but her identity is heterosexual. Yet there are also hints of an alternative, more provisional understanding of sexuality, which is evident in Verena's inability to decide whom she most deeply desires. This provisional understanding is evident in the narrator's ridicule of exaggerated gender polarities such as the man-hating of Olive Chancellor, and the martial masculinity of Basil Ransom, which approaches hysteria as he stalks Verena at the novel's end.

The Bostonians begins in dialogue, an opening that is appropriate to the novel's ethnographic ambitions. The novel's very title suggests both drawing-room comedy and some effort to classify the attributes of a strange New England tribe. The emphasis on estrangement and distance is carried through in the perspectives of the first two characters introduced: Mrs. Luna, a devoted New Yorker with little fondness for her native New England, and Basil Ransom, a visitor from the defeated South. The regional contest is in play from the start, with Olive, the Northerner, exercising control over Basil, the Southerner, by making him wait. This drawing-room manipulation recalls the monumental stakes of a bloody Civil War, which was waged in part over differing conceptions of time (Northern Progressivism; Southern Traditionalism). Regional oppositions are also expressed in respective skills of deception: Northerners are too honest to be good at it, while for Southerners it is a way of life.

Regional differences are only the beginning of a host of differences that James seems eager to capture in his broad-ranging portrait of late nineteenth-century America. Social multiplicity is a fact of modern life, and reading difference, for those who seek to understand as well as to triumph in society, is a necessity. Hence, characters' struggles to classify each other as types – through region and gender, culture and class. Olive and Verena in their first private encounter perceive each other as, respectively, elite Bostonian and impoverished Bohemian. In another scene, two ladies from New York's cultivated class anticipate an upcoming lecture by Professor Gougenheim on the Talmud, while Miss Birdseye has to satisfy her nostalgia for the Underground Railroad by saving political émigrés from Europe. The perception that America is fast becoming a cultural "melting pot," comprised of Jews, Germans, Dutch, Blacks, Irish, Italians, and "natives," seems to have occurred to James long before The American Scene (1907). Like the later narrative, The Bostonians emphasizes how embattled many of the "natives" feel, a sentiment that gives rise to a general preoccupation with demography and reproduction.

Sexual preference, and its impact on marriage and procreation rates, is for this reason a major focus of *The Bostonians*. Homoeroticism in *The Bostonians* is represented as a valid alternative to heterosexuality. *The Bostonians* is different from any other novel by James because marriage and progeny here are not normative. Moreover, there is a pervading awareness in the narrative of just how threatening this omission is to society at large. James's novel seems to recognize the extent to which attitudes towards homoeroticism in late nineteenth-century America are informed by specific demographic developments. Fears that white Anglo-Saxons were losing the population battle to less desirable races and ethnicities fueled anxiety about deviations from heterosexuality. America in the 1880s had a vibrant eugenics movement, which warned that "native" groups were committing "race suicide," and promoted large families among these groups. Such "family values" reformers felt particularly threatened by the women's rights movement and the homosocial and homoerotic behaviors that were often implicitly associated with it. Leading theorists of homosexuality, such as Krafft-Ebing and Havelock Ellis, fueled their fears.

The Bostonians is not in sympathy with these theories, nor with the repressive flames they fanned. Rather it steers a course around them, by highlighting all the reasons for discord between the sexes, and insisting on the essential ambiguity and peril of sexual desire. One of the novel's critical insights is the role of fictions and fairy tales in promoting polarized and distorting gender identities. There is a story behind every idea of what it is to be a Man or a Woman in this book (Basil's self-image as a knight errant "rescuing" Verena; Verena's imaging by everyone in a range of exotic aesthetic poses; Olive's sense of herself as a heroine in a tragedy). *The Bostonians* reveals the conventional literary means by which heterosexuality is constructed; Verena's romantic attachment to Basil recalls a series of literary antecedents from *The Scarlet Letter* and *The Wide, Wide World* to James's own *Portrait of a Lady*. Hester Prynne's inability to bear the scrutiny of Dimmesdale is echoed in Verena's inability to meet the erotic gaze of Basil Ransom, though she has endured the stares of hundreds on her lecture platform. Ellen Montgomery and John Humphreys, Isabel Archer and Gilbert Osmond, supply models of women alienated from male lovers, who, apparently, will never understand them. This is in part the basis of the attraction, for both examples suggest a fundamental tie between female eroticism and self-alienation. Both lovers are identified with violence: Humphreys whips horses while Osmond's sadism is directed towards women. In keeping with this, Basil Ransom is cast as an assassin in the closing pages of *The Bostonians*;

at the point of "saving" Verena for the purposes of marriage and procreation, he is compared to John Wilkes Booth stalking Abraham Lincoln. Against these distorted heterosexual passions, James poses the more nuanced reciprocities of love between women.

Though it is clear that Verena loves and desires Basil, there has also been authentic passion in her relationship with Olive. In a late scene, Olive and Verena maintain a vigil in the dark, helpless witnesses together of Verena's heterosexual desire, which is itself imagined, in another echo from *The Scarlet Letter*, as "a kind of shame." Shame in Hawthorne's novel is adultery. Here in reversal of conventional romance, shame is conceived as the appeal of heterosexuality itself. This view may be particular to Olive and only partly shared by Verena. But the fact is that James takes it very seriously.

James's deepest respect is reserved for those who abstain from compromising love relations, exemplified by the character of Dr. Prance. Neither female nor male in aspect, Dr. Prance is passionately devoted to science and health, and utterly healthy in her own right. Her achievement is her nullification of efforts to invest gender polarities with the authority of nature. Consistently dissociated from the sickly, claustrophobic atmospheres where most of the novel's scenes take place, Dr. Prance is identified with natural settings. Her exceptional independence (personally, professionally, politically) begins with her resistance to gender. According to James, gender is a battleground, both within the self and for the self in relation to others. This is why his Civil War novel is so intimately tied to gender and sexuality, because he understands all of these phenomena, the national trauma of fraternal war, and the human matter of sexual identity and desire as fraught with conflict, leading inevitably to pain and loss. The Civil War and heterosexual and homosexual relations represent violent struggles for independence against a fearsome backdrop of interdependence. Far from psychological reductionism, James's terribly intimate exploration of romance and Civil War resulted in a powerful elaboration of their meanings.

SOUTHERN REMINISCENCES OF WAR

James's novelistic events were situated in New England and New York, where none of the fighting took place. This lends a necessary abstractness to his portrait. His contemporary, Constance Fenimore Woolson, was a New Englander who traveled South after the war for a direct view of this mythic battleground. Some of her most powerful fictions capture the experience of Northerners seeking close relationships with the scarred South. Woolson's *Rodman The Keeper: Southern Sketches* (1880) appeared in major magazines of the 1870s, where they caught the attention of Henry James. He became a confidant of Woolson, whose writing he alternately praised and slighted. Woolson's Southern works, which included *Rodman The Keeper* and *For The Major* (1883), were akin to the novels she and James set in Europe. They convey the same ethnographic sense of an observer encountering a region that is foreign but familiar: at her best, she catalogs Southern scenes and characters in nuanced detail; at her worst, she betrays Northern complicity with the South's myths and prejudices.

"Rodman The Keeper," her best story, is an extended meditation on the word "keep." What does it mean to be kept from death? What does it mean to keep or preserve the body after it? How is the honor of the dead best kept, observed? What are the acceptable proprieties for the keeper of the dead? The sketch begins with a curious dialogue without speakers or listeners, as if the only kind of conversation that can be conducted over the graveyard dead is a conversation on their behalf. The dialogue satisfies a certain fantasy about the dead – that they remain within hearing, that awareness of the living is one of the faculties kept after death. The keeper is John Rodman, a New Englander and ex-colonel appointed guardian of the national cemetery in Florida. Rodman is an Aunt Ophelia come South to impose order on the dilapidated and regionally alien territory that has become a burial ground for Union soldiers. To this end, he spends hours copying the names of the dead onto rolls in painstaking script, mowing the grass, and smoothing the gravel paths near his bare cottage.

The sketch suggests that the primary obligation of the keeper of the dead is to give voice to their needs while guiltily negating his own living condition. It helps that he is from New England, for in the sober spirit typical of the region Rodman gets pleasure from what he denies himself: the companionship of a dog (barking might disturb them); a pipe (too selfish, since the dead cannot smoke); minimal cooking (so they will not envy the aroma of his meals). There are few breaks in his isolation: the addition of an ailing ex-Confederate soldier with his servant intensifies the keeper's quiet and isolation rather than lessening it. The ex-soldiers take stock of each other's respective losses, and find peace in silence. Their quiet meals reveal another thing kept by the keeper, regional cooking, for "his prejudiced little kitchen" yields only New England fare, repudiating Southern biscuits, bacon, and hominy.

One must look to Southern women, according to Woolson, for the remnants of rebel wrath; it is they who maintain an ardent opposition to all things Northern and national. In the inadvertent community that arises among these four ruins of war – Union keeper, ailing Confederate soldier, old servant now freedman, former Southern belle – it's the belle, Miss Bettina Ward, who treasures her Southern antagonism, rejecting the keeper's generosity. The keeper insists that Pomp the freedman can only wait upon his "master" if he learns to read via a cemetery placard, the lone instance of official government poetry. While the placard anticipates a regular procession of Northern visitors come to honor their dead, the only visitors are the solemn parade of freed blacks on Memorial Day. Attired in their Sunday best, these designated mourners sing "Swing Low, Sweet Chariot" while showering the graves with flowers in gratitude for the gift of freedom. Rodman achieves a measure of victory with the still slavish Pomp when he steals out at night to place flowers on the graves of these Northern soldiers. Among the things the keeper holds is the visitors' register, meant to record the names of all mourners in attendance on the waiting graves. Its emptiness, explained by the fact that the only visitors are freedmen who cannot write, is the bane of his existence, yet it is a proper emptiness, echoing as it does the lost lives that will never be registered.

"King David" is the disheartened and disheartening account of a young man, David King, from a New Hampshire village who goes South to teach blacks after the war. The sketch, which is related primarily from David's perspective, is full of irony at his expense. He romanticizes the old cotton-fields presided over by an overseer, with a nostalgia unbefitting to a Northern reformer. He dutifully feeds two freed men who appear at dinnertime, but throws away every leftover after they leave and cooks another meal. Reform, the sketch suggests, promises no more than the reformers, and David King is as racist as those he seeks to enlighten. Other characters hinder his best efforts: a demonic Northerner manipulates David's black students with alcohol, while an aristocrat undermines David's loyalty to them. His premature departure signals the abandonment by the New England cultural elite as a whole of the defeated South and its downtrodden black population.

In *For the Major* (1883), Woolson locates a Southern world that thoroughly engages her talents. The novel is as memorable as it is strange. It dramatizes the struggle between a daughter and her very young stepmother for the love and care of the father/husband, an aged and ailing ex-Confederate Major. The setting is Edgerley, a mountain town in Virginia, which has relentlessly resisted modernization in the post-Civil War period, clinging to old Southern traditions. The contest between these two strong-willed women is overseen by the town gossips. They worship the wife, who upholds all the courtly rituals still central to Southern life, and disdain the daughter, who has been banished to New England for her teenage years by the stepmother. The stepmother's scheme of estrangement has succeeded, for the daughter is considered stand-offish and insufficiently Southern in manner. The apparently oblivious Major lives in the past, reading the *Saturday Review* and European news, because neither covers contemporary America.

This claustrophobic atmosphere is relieved by a foreign element, Marion's repressed past returned in the form of a first son she believed dead. Now a musician named Dupont, he comes to the isolated Southern mountain town to find her. The recognition of her offspring would expose Marion's previous life. Her ambivalence towards him, a fusion of alienation, fear, and adoration, is echoed by the town. From the outset, Dupont is an alluring yet suspect presence: his songs (Native American, African, Gypsy) are identified with social groups presumed inferior to the local aristocracy.

The Major's attitude towards the stranger remains a mystery. Is he perhaps more aware of his wife's history than she has supposed? The deception Marion has preserved "for the Major," presenting herself as thirteen years younger than her age, is finally revealed to Sara, who agrees to help perpetuate it. This is the sign of Sara's renewed acceptance of her Southernness. The ferocity of these two women's feelings for the Major may be read as an allegory about Southern loyalties. The novel's depiction of a wife's self-serving deception of her husband, of a daughter's complicity in it, and of the husband's willingness to be deceived reveals the post-Civil War South as a scene of historical denial and renunciation.

There was no Southern writer of the post-Civil War era who would have understood that obligation more profoundly than Ellen Glasgow. Glasgow was a Virginia writer who expressed her region, she often said, in body and soul. Yet she aspired to produce novels of universal as opposed to regional significance. Glasgow was born eight years after the end of the Civil War. Her father was a wealthy businessman, of Scottish-Calvinist descent, whose iron works factory in Richmond exemplified the economic and social forms of the new South, while her mother was a descendant of the earliest English settlers in Virginia. *The Battle-Ground* (1902) is one of Glasgow's first novels. This may account for its romantic and glorified portrait of Southern aristocracy. Glasgow did the extensive research on Richmond, Virginia battles and battle sites, but research hardly qualified her brimming admiration for the "The Lost Cause." Glasgow's white aristocrats, who address one another as "sir," are as noble and self-satisfied as the total domination of another people can make them, and their portraits are devoid of irony.

The master of Uplands was standing upon his portico behind the Doric columns, looking complacently over the fat lands upon which his fathers had sown and harvested for generations. Beyond the lane of lilacs and the two silver poplars at the gate, his eyes wandered leisurely across the blue-green strip of grass-land to the tawny wheat field, where the slaves were singing as they swung their cradles. The day was fine, and the outlying meadows seemed to reflect his gaze with a smile as beneficent as his own. He had cast his bread upon the soil, and it had returned to him threefold.

This is a slave utopia. Everyone is contented in his or her respective station; nature smiles back its beneficence on the master of it all, whose reign is confirmed by the bounty of his fields. The Governor knows how to mete out rewards to the underlings (whether black or white), who know their place, a special skill of all the reigning gentry.

The sign of a patriarch in the making is the ability to judge a good prospective horse or slave. When Dan Montjoy is offered a horse by his grandfather for having performed a chivalric deed, he chooses the slave, Big Abel, instead – a wise substitution, since Big Abel follows Dan into battle, nursing him back to health when he is wounded. This is standard for the novel's black characters. Unvarying stereotypes of the devoted slave, they speak such thick dialect that they are almost incomprehensible. While the white lower classes recognize differences between their interests and those of landowning slaveholders, they are no less willing to spill their blood for the South. As one Rebel army recruit, Pinetop, puts it, referring to the Union soldiers, "They've set thar feet on ole Virginny, and they've got to take 'em off damn quick!"

Region is region; land is land (whether you own vast tracks of it or not), and blood is blood. In Glasgow's depiction, the Confederate army is composed of the wealthiest aristocrats. Such claims represent fictional selective memory. The universal conscription decreed in February of 1862 by Jefferson Davis, President of the Confederacy, exempted slaveholders who owned twenty or more slaves. Before the draft, wealthy Southerners stayed home, for the most part. After it, slaveholders as a rule hired substitutes, as did the wealthy in the North. As the war continued, however, Southern aristocrats like the Lightfoots and the Amblers were more likely to enlist than their Northern counterparts. Dan Montjoy, the novel's hero, is a Southern hybrid descended from Jane Lightfoot, the proud aristocrat, and Jack Montjoy, a working-class Scot who beat his wife. Dan responds to war as a racial inheritance from both sides. Thus Glasgow harmonizes the traditional aristocracy of her mother with the new mercantile South of her Scottish businessman father.

The Civil War is transformative, affording a series of recognitions for all of Glasgow's aristocrats. When Dan sees Pinetop struggling over a child's primer, he recognizes the gulf of class that has divided the privileged Southerner from the white proletariat consigned to serfdom within a slave society. Betty, Dan's prospective bride, achieves perspective on the experiences of another casualty of the slavery system: free black people. Searching for food to allay the hunger on her plantation during the final stage of the war, she comes upon Levi engaged in a similar foraging expedition, and suddenly grasps the isolation of the free Negro, scorned by blacks (who fear and envy his freedom) and whites (who abhor it). The most life-altering recognition of all is that of a common humanity, conveyed by Glasgow in the portrayal of Union soldiers gently feeding starved Rebel troops in the wake of Lee's surrender. As Paul Laurence Dunbar understood, however, unity was often achieved at the expense of black people, formerly slave and free alike, who were rarely included in such images. Indeed, their peril and even death was recurrently the price paid for harmony between North and South.

Frances E. W. Harper's *Iola Leroy; Or, Shadows Uplifted* (1892) provides the perspective of the blacks who stayed at home on the plantations, while the battles so critical to their future status were waged, and built lives for themselves afterwards. Harper's novel was twice reprinted, and respectfully reviewed in major periodicals. But it fell into disrepute (dismissed by Sterling Brown for its piety in the 1940s and by the Black Aesthetics movement for its politics in the 1960s), until its rediscovery in the 1990s by a feminist critical establishment. *Iola Leroy* offers a more incisive politics and a less submissive spirituality than previously recognized. The novel can be seen as part of a larger novelistic re-imagining of the Civil War, in keeping with works like *The Red Badge of Courage* and *The Fanatics*. Harper sought in *Iola Leroy* to redirect contemporary policies on race, while teaching black youth of the sacrifices made on their behalf, which they ought not to squander.

Frances Ellen Watkins was born free in Maryland in 1825. An aunt and uncle who ran the William Watkins Academy for Negro Young, where she was educated until she went to work as a domestic in her teens, raised Watkins. Watkins was always ambitious to write, and found inspiration in abolitionism, contributing regularly to William Garrison's *Liberator*. Prior to her 1860 marriage to Fenton Harper, Watkins had both a literary and a political career, publishing poetry, prose, and fiction and lecturing on the Anti-Slavery Society circuit. Her brief marriage, ended by her husband's death in 1864, yielded three children. Harper resumed her lecturing as a single mother, and became especially well known in the South. Though she was active in the Women's Movement, she denounced the 1869 decision by major feminists (Elizabeth Cady Stanton and Susan B. Anthony) to withdraw their support for black suffrage in order to attract women of the South. In all of her lectures from this period, Harper emphasized the continuities between patriarchy, capitalism, imperialism, and racism. She presented the culture and aspirations of black Americans as clear alternatives to prevailing American values. American blacks might well be martyred by the dominant culture; if so, she argued, nations are far more indebted to their martyrs than to their millionaires.

Just as Harper drew on her poetry in lectures during her early days on the abolitionist circuit, her only novel, *Iola Leroy*, was infused with her political commitments. Actual historical figures inspired her character portraits – Ida

B. Wells, who was widely known by her pen name, Iola, for Iola Leroy; Lewis Latimer, a black poet and scientist who worked with Thomas Edison and Alexander Graham Bell for Dr. Frank Latimer; Lucy Delaney, a black woman writer and activist for Lucille Delaney. The plot of *Iola Leroy* is familiar: Iola Leroy, a wealthy white woman growing up in the antebellum South, discovers when her white father dies of yellow fever at the start of the Civil War that she is part black, and is promptly sold into slavery. Rescued by the Union army, Iola works as a nurse and is pursued by a white Northerner, Dr. Gresham, who is eager to marry her despite her parentage, which he urges her to conceal. Iola resists passing, however, as does her brother Harry. Indeed, Iola and Harry are presented repeatedly with the option of passing, which serves throughout the novel as a kind of Edenic temptation that they honorably resist. Their constancy, explained in tête-à-têtes with prospective lovers and in group conversations, is motivated by their desire to realize their race's highest potential. At the war's end, Harry and Iola are reunited with their mother, uncle, and grandmother in a stirring scene. The novel concludes with the marriages of Iola and Harry to exceptional black partners, Dr. Frank Latimer and Lucille Delaney. Together they head South to perform the redemptive work of uplift in the black community, as educators (Harry, Lucille), physician (Latimer), and writer (Iola).

The novel opens during the Civil War, with an account of the secret language used by the slaves remaining on Southern plantations to keep tabs on the fortunes of Union and Confederate sides. The quality of produce – the relative freshness of butter or eggs – supplies the means of transmitting news of victory and defeat. Indeed, there is an abundance of codes by which to read war reports. One savvy but illiterate slave needs nothing more than the look on his mistress's face to grasp the state of the war. Another slave woman manages to inform nearby Union troops of enemy intentions by hanging her sheets in prearranged patterns. These examples and others like them highlight Harper's interest in discursive systems, how they are learned, taught, and most importantly, subverted. In *Iola Leroy*, language is both a method of liberation and a means of oppression, which black folk, literate and illiterate, have either invented or penetrated because their lives depended on it. As one slave observes, the first black slaves who arrived in America spoke many different languages, a variety that was repeated in their range of complexions as well – from the near white to black. The heterogeneity of the oppressed and brutalized population on plantations made resistance especially difficult. Harper confirms how American racism spawned a particularly virulent and secure form of slavery, with diverse groups of Africans brought to America and trapped on plantations where even minimal information was difficult to obtain. Harper's historical account reveals the astonishing rapidity with which highly varied populations of African slaves managed to educate themselves and devise intricate modes of communication, despite a regime of ignorance brutally imposed.

One of the novel's most striking scenes, in Iola's classroom, gives rise to what is perhaps Harper's most radical claim: that imposed ignorance may actually confer immunity from inauthentic and oppressive forms of knowledge. Denied literacy, denied books, Iola's pupils have absorbed alternative insights, many of them subversive, which has in turn made them less susceptible to postwar educational dogmas designed to rationalize their subordination. Hence the white gentleman who has come to talk to the children about the achievements of the white race makes the mistake of engaging the children in a Socratic give and take, an exchange that reveals the children's understanding of such "progress" as having been achieved at their own expense.

Harper's predictions on interracial relations are pessimistic. Insisting on the dependence of American whites on their black brethren, as confirmed above all by the war itself where black soldiers contributed decisively to Northern victory, she concludes her novel on a note of uncertainty. Whether black Americans would be accepted as members of a collective citizenry, or held to a subordinate position that drove their aspirations inward towards more individualized, material gains, was in question well past the middle of the next century. It was an issue that would be debated famously by Booker T. Washington (on the side of intra-racial uplift) and W. E. B. Du Bois (on the side of full equality) through the turn of the century.

The Civil War represented an irreparable break for all Americans – politically, economically, and socially. Despite deceptions, treacheries, and brutalities suffered by black people after the war, despite efforts of Southern whites to institute a peonage system comparable to slavery, the fact remained that they were free and the slavery system would never be reinstituted. Civil War novels by Paul Laurence Dunbar, Frances Harper, Ellen Glasgow, Lydia Maria Child, and others, confirmed the trials and injustices in the process of transforming, as Harriet Beecher Stowe put it, "a thing into a man." But all agreed, however sober their accounts, that black people were bound to attain their rightful status as human beings. Civil War novels by Stephen Crane, Henry James, Maria Ruiz de Burton, Elizabeth Stuart Phelps, and Louisa May Alcott highlighted the material and economic revolution symbolized and unquestionably accelerated, if not initiated, by the Civil War. Whether they dwelled disconsolately on the losses entailed (Alcott, Ruiz de Burton) or anticipated more ambivalently the possibilities for art and religion in a looming modern order (Phelps, James, Crane), these novels attested that there was no turning back.

3

❦

SOCIAL DEATH AND THE
RECONSTRUCTION OF SLAVERY

IN 1861, THE YEAR THE Civil War began, Harriet Jacobs published *Incidents in the Life of a Slave Girl*. Jacobs was born a slave in 1813 in Edenton, North Carolina; her father was a skilled carpenter, and her mother the slave of a tavern keeper. Jacobs lived with both parents until the age of six, and was taught to read, but in 1824, the family of Dr. James Norcom inherited her, and she was increasingly subjected to Norcom's sexual predation. Seeking protection, Jacobs took her own lover, a white lawyer, and had two children with him. In 1835, Jacobs ran away and was sheltered by white as well as black neighbors before she entered the tiny attic crawlspace in the home of her grandmother, who was free. Jacobs remained in hiding for seven years. Sewing, reading, and writing to pass the time, she was bothered most by immobility and exposure to the elements through the thin roof. Her health permanently compromised, Jacobs escaped to the North in 1842, and after a brief reunion with her children found work as a nursemaid for a New York magazine editor. As a fugitive (under the 1850 Fugitive Slave Law, which mandated the return of all escaped slaves), Jacobs was haunted by the prospect of recapture by Norcom, who pursued her. Forced to flee New York and then Boston, Jacobs followed her brother John S. Jacobs, an abolitionist, to Rochester, New York, where she had access to an abolitionist library, and worked daily in the anti-slavery reading room just above the newspaper offices of Frederick Douglass. In Rochester Jacobs lived with the Quaker reformer, Amy Post, a women's rights advocate who encouraged her to write about her experiences under slavery. After returning to her New York employer, who bought her for $300 in 1852, to secure her safety and her service, Jacobs began a correspondence with Post that became a draft of her narrative (excerpted anonymously as "Letter from a Fugitive Slave," *New York Tribune*, 1853). When the book was published in 1861, with editorial help and an endorsement from Lydia Maria Child, its abolitionist audience was distracted by the war, but it earned Jacobs sufficient recognition to be hired as a relief worker among contraband slaves. In later life, Jacobs remained active in political causes. She died in Washington on March 7, 1897, and was buried in Mount Auburn Cemetery in Cambridge.

Jacobs portrays slavery in *Incidents in the Life of a Slave Girl* as the national horror that is "hidden in plain sight," seeking to rouse readers from their moral apathy. Though her tone is controlled, every now and then Jacobs breaks out of this calm to address her readers in direct appeals to a Northern sisterhood or to challenge a passive Northern collectivity ("In view of these things, why are ye silent, ye free men and women of the north?"). Jacobs mimes her readers' professed ignorance of American slavery in the book's Edenic opening, and proceeds methodically to explode sentimental versions of the South. The gothic horrors that Jacobs unfolds has led historians to question its authenticity; but this is to miss the book's real message. Gothic excess, Jacobs indicates, is the only proper route to a realist account of slavery. Historically speaking, American slavery is the gothic become real. And her portrait is fully supported by first-hand eyewitness accounts, such as those collected in the 1930s in the Works Projects Administration interviews with surviving slaves.

Jacobs's narrative aims to expose the dependence of an idealized nineteenth-century American domesticity on the abuse of the black body. Where food in Harriet Beecher Stowe's *Uncle Tom's Cabin* is a harmonic emblem of nurture, food in Jacobs's narrative is, literally, the slave. Throughout *Incidents*, slaves are portrayed as food – serving as wet nurses; devoured by dogs and rats; threatened by sexual predators. Many of the punishments imposed on slaves seem designed to destroy their appetites: a cook is forced to eat mush a dog has vomited into; the mistress spits into the pots of leftovers; slaves are scalded with drops of pork fat. Meanwhile, slave masters are walking emblems of appetite; Jacobs's first mention of her master's stalking of her is imaged as cannibalism. Her dream of retribution follows suit: she fantasizes the earth opening and swallowing him whole. Slave mistresses, in contrast, have anorexic tendencies: bone thin, they count and measure food, and continually deprive people of it. Food in Jacobs is a critical instrument in the alienation of the slave. To be denied food is to be denied membership in the community – it is the mechanism of social inclusion and exclusion. Jacobs makes this explicit by drawing parallels between the literal dispensing of food in the slave community and the symbolic distribution of spiritual food at church. In describing her cruel mistress taking communion, Jacobs observes that such symbolic affirmation of her faith fails to arouse a spirit of mercy. Christianity, as Jacobs portrays it, does not transcend social context, but expresses it. Far from a redemptive source of social unity as it appears in Stowe, Christianity in Jacobs reinforces racial and social divisions. Jacobs implicitly poses the question about the relationship between religious faith and oppression: are they mutually sustaining? The possibility entertained in Jacobs is that Christianity not only facilitates but sanctions oppression.

The American slavery system, according to Jacobs, is the ultimate death industry: a system organized for the purpose of killing black people. She emphasizes its impact upon the activity of mothering, which becomes under slavery a medium of death. Black women in *Incidents* invariably mother at the expense of their children, whether through a reproduction that provides commodities for the slave market, or by being forced to care for white children while ignoring their own. Significantly, Jacobs mentions her own mother only once in the narrative – when she dies. The flagrant abuse of slaves foregrounds the uneconomical, not to mention barbaric and obsolete, character of slavery. Within this brutal world, the black pursuit of freedom is presented as a fulfillment of Enlightenment ideals. Jacobs describes with grim irony how her grandmother is returned to slavery during the Revolutionary War, even though her master has liberated her. Jacobs's own live burial in her "loophole of retreat" – lodged in the house like a piece of china, just above the cupboard – is a deliberate embrace of death that issues in her rebirth as free. All the details of classic rites of passage are present, including sequestration and bodily plagues (red insects boring into her flesh, frostbite, heatstroke). Forced to lie prone almost continually, she must learn to walk anew in freedom.

While Jacobs ends her narrative free, she remains, like the nation as a whole, haunted by the institution that defined her existence well beyond slavery's official end in 1863. In a retrospective essay on the Reconstruction era, W. E. B. Du Bois describes what he calls "The Economics of Negro Emancipation," in the decades after the Civil War. The subordination of black labor was systematically institutionalized to ensure "a backward step in the organization of labor such as no modern nation would dare to take in the broad daylight of present economic thought." Disenfranchisement, imprisonment for debt and for breaking a work contract, the neglect of black education, Jim Crow laws which institutionalized complete separation of blacks and whites in public places, and finally, the most lurid form of oppression, lynching, were various measures designed to perpetuate a near medieval caste system within a modern capitalist state.

In the pages that follow, a series of novels and social treatises about the experiences of black Americans and the status of "race relations" following the Civil War will be examined. Many of their authors were aware of the impressive achievements of blacks from all classes in the post-Emancipation era, but recognized that such progress occurred in spite of prevailing social and legal institutions. Others insisted that black people were bound to remain in a condition close to enslavement until the group's eventual, inevitable demise. Because the destiny of African Americans and the question of race was always intertwined with the nation's destiny as a whole, especially in this period of political and economic expansion, it is critical to recapture the debates on that destiny. W. E. B. Du Bois, Ida B. Wells, Charles Chesnutt, and Albion Tourgee, depicted the sufferings and injustices of black folk in their novels and essays, in order to inspire political and legal forms of redress. Wells even took her anti-lynching campaign to England, after she became convinced that Americans needed international exposure to arouse their dormant consciences. William Benjamin Smith, Frederick Hoffman, Philip Bruce, Nathaniel Shaler, and Thomas Nelson Page, all renowned pseudoscientists whose claims were refuted by prominent black activists such as Du Bois and Kelly Miller, wrote racist tracts designed to rationalize the subordination and eventual extinction of blacks. Finally, Mark Twain, Pauline Hopkins, and James Weldon Johnson, provided powerful dramatic predictions of how the future of (a) race might be adjudicated.

FORMS OF SACRIFICE

The most accomplished black leader of the time was W. E. B. Du Bois (1868– 1963): public intellectual, editor, writer, reviewer, historian, and sociologist, he was truly a Renaissance man for the modern era, a man who contributed significantly to the fields of social science, journalism, as well as literature. In his writing from the turn of the century, Du Bois documents the extent of institutionalized racism, a racism whose aim is not merely the exclusion but the social extinction of American blacks. Thus, racist ethnography from this period presents the ceremonial demise of black people as the route to national cohesion and renewal. Black mortality statistics were exaggerated to support a collective image as an offering on the altar of progress. Through methods of vigilance and vigilante acts, whites sought to limit the aspirations and achievements of blacks from all classes. Identified as representative aliens, blacks became victims of ritual revenge. As recent analysts have pointed out, white Americans, principally in the South, were the last Western people to practice the ritual of human sacrifice, and black Americans were the sacrificial objects.

Through direct crusades against lynching – Ida B. Wells and James Weldon Johnson were key figures – and through their art, black activists and writers confronted the prevailing politics of sacrifice. The staging of sacrifice as an ordinary and extraordinary aspect of black American experience was an attempt to come to terms with a dominant cultural legacy. But these stagings can also be understood as ways of recuperating what was culturally indigenous about the sacrificial enterprise, as exemplified by African traditions of vengeance, with their obvious relevance for a post-emancipation context, as well as by the frank spirituality reflected in the placement of offerings at crossroads. Du Bois, like many in his era, recognized sacrifice as a dominant American tradition, at once Christian and social scientific. And he in particular emphasized its unique suitability to the purposes of an expanding capitalist nation. Yet he also sought to recover the rite as a self-actualized African-American form, and *The Souls of Black Folk* (1903) can be seen as the most prominent expression of this recovery.

When *The Souls of Black Folk* first appeared William James sent a copy to his brother Henry with a note characterizing its author as "that mulatto ex-student of mine." Henry was impressed, and pronounced the book the best by a Southerner he had read in years. *Souls* was both a popular and a critical success, widely admired by intellectuals, including the German sociologist, Max Weber. The heterogeneity of the book's readership is relevant to the difficulty of its generic classification. Du Bois's multiple vocations – sociologist, historian, journalist, editor, statesman, writer – are variously reflected in *The Souls of Black Folk*. Prior to its appearance in book form, *Souls* was published as separate essays. One way in which they cohere is through a shared thematic interest in that most privileged of literary subjects – death – and a view of black culture in America as a culture intimately associated with its rituals.

Du Bois's elegiac reflections in "Of the Passing of the First-Born," the chapter on the death of his son, provide the book's symbolic center. Here, personal loss is deflected and sustained by an apprehension of its collective ramifications. Grief assumes a monumental aspect because individual death among certain groups can never be separated from the dilemma of group survival. Du Bois's account of the dread aroused by the infant's mulatto features is a way of acknowledging that all young black lives are marked from the beginning by uncertainties about the larger group's perpetuation. In this sense, Du Bois's treatise on mourning offers a significant contrast to its Emersonian analog, "Experience." For Du Bois, it is not the elusiveness of death that appalls, but the ease with which it envelops black life, destroying an already provisional domesticity. The son's airborne illness, devastator of parental dreams, recalls passages from Du Bois's sociological works describing the perilous exposure of black homes. Emerson's complaint is that we can never be sufficiently exposed to feel the effects of our exposure. Du Bois complains that there is no way for blacks to avoid feeling the damage of their experience. He struggles to reconcile private grief and collective identity, to join black elite and black masses. The chapter includes a demographic plot that implies disproportionately lower reproductive rates among the black elite, and distinguishes the relative values of different black lives.

Constructed with a magisterial formality, in keeping with the conventions of mourning, the chapter is bound from beginning to end by mortuary ritual. The effect of this framework is less to create a sense of narrative immobility, than to recuperate an understanding of death as a journey. The chapter is filled with images of travel: Du Bois's trip from Georgia to the Berkshires to retrieve his wife and newborn son, and return South; the journey of the corpse from South to North for burial; and the journey of the son's soul heavenward. The son's first journey down South fulfills the superstitious warning that the first trip of an infant should be upward to ensure his growth to maturity. These crisscrossing secular travels – South/North; North/South; South/North – are echoed in the crossed features – blue-brown eyes, blonde-brown hair – of Du Bois's son, which Du Bois reads as a bad omen. The journey North for burial represents a desire to assist the soul's transcendent progress. At the same time, the corpse, emblem of individuality and decomposition, almost universally presided over by women, is ceremonially separated from the immortal spirit, which expresses collective endurance. Such divisions in burial rites, anthropologists have noted, help to resolve the contradictions of death: the matter of reconciling the necessary continuity of the social system with the obvious impermanence of its members. Belief in an afterlife mediates the opposition between the mortal body and the enduring body politic. Yet confidence in an immortal body politic is less assured when the mortal being in question is a black in late nineteenth-century America. Du Bois's politics of death includes the problem of solidarity within: caught by the closing contrast between the vitality of the orphaned and abject among his people and his own lost, cherished son.

Souls opens with Du Bois's declaration of affinity with his people; the chapter on his son dramatizes his resistance to such identification. The most poignant sign of Du Bois's ambivalence is the refusal to bury his son in the mass grave of the South. The body of this small black hope is separated from the doomed collectivity, just as his life is memorialized. The pollution of the anonymous multitudes is contrasted with the ascension of Burghardt Du Bois, whose soul rises like a star. Yet their destiny is a contagion, borne on the Gulf wind. It cannot be escaped, only written. Through writing, Du Bois elevates death and grief, symbolically, to the level of sacrifice. The rite pervades the narrative: from the Hebrew vow of kinship in the "Forethought," an allusion to the sacrificial meal where human and God become one, to the "After-thought," where Du Bois declares the book an offering in the wilderness. The chapter on his son recalls two biblical moments of sacrificial substitution. In one, blood drops are substituted for human bodies; in the other, God's body is sacrificed for the sins of humanity. The chapter's title, "Of The Passing of the First-Born," recalls the plot of Passover, where the Hebrews are commanded to mark their doorposts with blood, a sacrificial sign that ensures the angel of death will "pass over" their homes and spare their first-born sons. At the same time, the son is characterized in terms that associate his birth and death with the story of Christ.

The echoing lines near the chapter's beginning – "I saw, as it fell *across* my baby, the shadow of the Veil . . . I saw the shadow of the Veil as it *passed over* my baby" (my italics) – seem to equalize the sacrificial symbols of crucifixion and Passover. But of course they are not equivalent. The halting first sentence, where the infant's body, enclosed in commas, appears caught by the shadowy Veil (though perhaps also draped, as in royal robes), recalls a New Testament sacrifice that was. The second sentence, a single breath suggesting immunity through unimpeded movement, highlights a Hebrew sacrifice that was not. These two biblical alternatives provide insight into Du Bois's view of black American experience at this time: as a sacrificial possibility fulfilled or averted. The collective symbolic status glimmering through the death of this young black hope is at once the work of an uncommon fate and an all-too-common agency. His uncommon fate is that of a Christian God whose suffering served as eternal justification for the torture of innocents. The common agency is the economic and social exclusion that might well eventuate in black extinction; its brutal extension is lynch law.

The link between his son's death and Christ's sacrifice evidently resonated for Du Bois with lynching, a form of sacrifice that preoccupied him in this period. The song heard by Black John before his lynching (chapter thirteen), completes the song heard by the mourners at Burghardt Du Bois's funeral (chapter eleven). Surveying the Atlanta lands of the Cherokees earlier in *Souls*, Du Bois draws our attention to the place of Sam Hose's "crucifixion." According to Du Bois's biographer, the display of Hose's charred knuckles in an Atlanta storefront a month before Burghardt's death turned Atlanta into "a poisoned well, polluted with the remains of Sam Hose and reflecting the drawn image of Burghardt." The proximity of these two deaths highlights Du Bois's burden throughout this chapter, to accommodate his analytical distance from a black America stigmatized by high mortality with a first-hand experience that tragically confirms his own implication in it.

In biblical Hebrew, the generic term for sacrifice is "*korban*," "to bring near," which implies the effort to bring a God or gods closer to human experience. It is clear from Du Bois's bitter apostrophes throughout the chapter (to Death, Fate, and God) that he has little faith in the prospects for such intimacy. Du Bois is an unwilling Abraham: he offers up his son with a resentful eye towards all that he has given "without complaint . . . save that fair young form." Du Bois's resentment raises questions about resistance, and the place of sacrificial rites within the black community. In a chapter on teaching in the Tennessee hills, for instance, Du Bois recalls the priest's weekly offering at the altar, an obligation met as well in the elite atmosphere of Atlanta University, where a morning sacrifice is routine. There is nothing metaphorical about the sacrificial practice of black folk religion, specifically the Obi worship of slavery days. It is unclear from Du Bois's description who the victims were, or how the particular aims of such blood-sacrifices were construed. But he seems intent on confirming the lingering impact of this vengeful spirituality. American blacks have been much sacrificed, he suggests, but they are not without their own forms of sacrificial agency. Du Bois's preoccupations with death and sacrifice form a central part of his legacy: to confront them is to recognize how the identification of a negative cultural typology can be a source of creative inspiration, critique, and even renewal.

W. E. B. Du Bois was not the only American sociologist to recognize sacrifice as an ongoing social practice at the start of the twentieth century. In *Lynch-Law: An Investigation into the History of Lynching in the United States* (1905), James Elbert Cutler, a disciple of William Graham Sumner's, presented lynching as a ritual sacrifice of social strangers, worthy of scientific treatment. As a stage for the problems of mob behavior, intolerance, social integration, and a litmus test for the shortcomings of liberalism, it is easy to see why lynching caught the attention of contemporary social scientists. Du Bois's comment after learning the fate of Sam Hose – that lynching made him doubt the value of rational analysis – seems belied by a study like Cutler's. Yet Du Bois's charge is ultimately justified. For Cutler's obvious approval of lynching and his effort to explain lynching scientifically amounts to an effort to explain it away. His analysis leaves little doubt that the resemblances between American lynchings and the violent, cannibalistic rites of uncivilized peoples were deeply disconcerting to the liberal practitioners of social science. Cutler views lynching as both evidence of social instability and a critical means for managing social difference. Lynch law could not have escalated, he points out, were the majority of citizens antagonistic to the mob. Nor would lynching subside until the American legal system was forced to reconcile its abstract ideals with the social and ethnic factors underlying race conflict. Political principles were one thing, social facts another.

Cutler presented lynching as a frenzied unification of white sentiment. He extends his view to the first lynchings executed by American settlers against Indians. Lynch law prevails, he suggests, at pressure points, when society requires a reordering under new conditions. Beyond this, it is a reflexive response to extremism or crime, and Cutler clearly admires those who are sufficiently simple (as opposed to modern and scientific), and sufficiently self-righteous (as opposed to ambivalent) to take the law into their own hands. Cutler's tangled explications confirm how much safer it was for sociologists to keep the sacrificial practice of lynching at arm's length. It was rather in fictional form – in novels by Charles Chesnutt and Albion Tourgee, for example – and in more direct political censure – the speeches and pamphlets of Ida B. Wells – that such racist industries could receive the deep analysis and redress that they deserved.

Charles Chesnutt's *The Marrow of Tradition* (1901) is a novel based on an actual historical incident: the Wilmington, North Carolina riots of 1898. The riots themselves were rooted in the overthrow of Reconstruction in the late 1870s and the subsequent decline of black rights and opportunities. They were the work of white Democrats who had been displaced by Republicans, including several blacks in city government. Because black voting in Wilmington had remained high throughout the 1890s, representation in government and in official agencies reflected the city's black majority. But whites objected increasingly to being arrested by black police or tried before a black judge. A key incitement to the riots was an August 1898 editorial in the *Wilmington Record* by its mulatto editor, Alexander Manly, denouncing lynching, and condemning the role of white journalists in arousing the racist sentiments that underlay it. Manly's courageous editorial went to the heart of white hypocrisy, denouncing the predation of white men responsible for mulattos, and emphasizing the masculine attractions of black men for white women. White newspaper editorials expressed the wholesale outrage generated by Manly's candor, and South Carolina Senator, Benjamin Tillman, added fuel to the fire at a Fayetteville white supremacist rally in October 1898. The result of the Wilmington riots was that thousands of blacks were driven from their homes, some were killed, and a grandfather clause (limiting voting to men whose grandfathers had voted prior to 1867), which effectively nullified black enfranchisement, was ratified by the North Carolina state legislature. Chesnutt described the riots in a letter to his editor Walter Hines Page as a display of virulent race prejudice disgraceful to both the state and the country.

The stigma of black mortality and its recuperation in common death rites; passing and its diabolic antithesis, lynching; the sacrifice of first-born sons, these are the themes and events of *The Marrow of Tradition*. As veterans of the Civil War, the novel's white characters harbor a volatile faith based on their collective sense of ruin. Major Cateret smolders in memory of the family he has sacrificed on the altar of the Lost Cause. Sacrifice here has little to do with redemption or renewal; it is part of an endless cycle of violence. The narrative is haunted by death. In the last scene of chapter one, an old black woman performs a mysterious rite on behalf of Cateret's first-born son, which culminates in the burial of a bottle under a full moon. These peculiar atavisms represent a common subculture of belief, a mental underground essential to black culture as well as white. Assimilation rituals, by contrast, are divisive and mutually diminishing. The hair straighteners and skin bleachers of the black servant, Sandy, for instance, support white supremacist doctrine. Yet the myth of black doom is portrayed by Chesnutt as a white projection designed to master Southern decline; black morbidity mirrors Southern degeneracy. This is the plot of reverse passing, where the dissolute aristocrat, Tom Delamere, who specializes in "coon" impersonations, assumes blackface in order to rob and murder his aged aunt. As suggested in so many other books of the period, black is the color of crime. The question of its retribution inevitably gives rise to the topic of lynching among the town's whites and blacks. From the white perspective, the object is to lynch a black regardless of guilt, a principle issuing from ancient Rome, where slaves were held collectively responsible for the crimes of any one of them. Chesnutt's portrayal reveals substitution as an integral modification of the sacrificial procedure. The Roman allusion confirms what is already clear: lynch law is designed to perpetuate slavery. Moreover, white civilization depends on it. Without a degraded, because constantly menaced, black community, whites could not build their temples of light.

In *The Marrow of Tradition*, blacks and whites are steeped in the logic of sacrifice, which culminates at the novel's end where the prospect of a double sacrifice – the loss of two first-born sons, one white, one black – is imminent. While Dr. Miller's son is sacrificed (killed in a riot initiated by Careret's inflamed editorial), the novel closes on the likely salvation of Careret's son through Dr. Miller's intervention. Sacrifice here is not equalized, but particularized as the black man's burden. The doctrine of white supremacy is rewritten in familiar sacrificial form: blacks provide the offering; whites reap the bounty. Yet Chesnutt endorses a Christian ideal of acceptance, in portraying Dr. Miller's repudiation of vengeance.

Ida B. Wells was perhaps the most courageous figure in the American campaign against lynching, which was organized in the early 1890s in response to the alarming rise in incidents. During the 1880s, the number of blacks lynched averaged 100 per year; in the year 1892 there were 162 recorded annual lynchings of black men and women. Wells gained notoriety in 1892 when three young black businessmen were lynched in Memphis, Tennessee, where she edited a local black newspaper, *Free Speech*. She denounced the lynchings in unqualified terms, arousing the rage of whites, who destroyed her office and forced her to remain in New York, where she had been away on business. Wells happened to be visiting Timothy Thomas Fortune, editor of the *New York Age*, who offered her a job on the paper, and published her article on lynching on the paper's front page. Thus began her role as a political crusader, among the best known of her time.

Wells was born in Mississippi in 1862, the eldest of eight children of slaves. Her mother was deeply devout and her father was a skilled carpenter who was selected as a member of the first board of trustees of Rust College. Both taught Wells to love freedom and education, and to be independent. Both her parents died in a yellow fever epidemic when Wells was sixteen, and, with help from friends, and the money left by her father, she struggled to keep her younger sisters and brothers together as a family, finding work as a schoolteacher while attending Rust College nearby. Always extraordinarily determined to stand up for her rights, Wells's first act of resistance came in 1884, when she was moved bodily by whites from a non-smoking to a smoking train car – the only car in which blacks were allowed to ride – and immediately sued the Memphis railroad. She was awarded five hundred dollars in damages by a lower court, but a higher court reversed the decision. In 1887, Wells began work on a newspaper, *Free Speech*, in which she invested her savings to become part owner and editor, while continuing to teach. In 1891 she was fired for her editorials criticizing the quality of the Memphis colored schools, and she devoted herself thereafter to journalism. Following the lynching of the black businessmen in 1892, Wells called for a black exodus from Memphis. The withdrawal of their labor and business cast such a pall on the Memphis economy that white leaders were forced to appeal to Wells, who refused to halt the exodus. In 1893 Wells was invited to England by feminists there to talk about lynching. Her tour was so successful that she was invited back the following year, and sponsored by the *Chicago Inter-Ocean* to report on the trip. Upon her return to America in 1894, Wells teamed up with Susan B. Anthony for an American lecture tour against lynching. She also became known for her protest against racial discrimination at the 1893 Columbian Exposition at the Chicago World's Fair. That same year Wells, who was now living in Chicago, married a local black lawyer, Ferdinand L. Barnet. Barnet shared Wells's interests, having started the first black newspaper in Chicago, the *Conservator*, following his graduation from Northwestern University Law School, and devoted his energies to political activism. They had four children, the first born in 1895, and from then on Wells balanced the demands of mothering with her continuing public work. In 1901, the Barnet-Wells family became the first black family to move east of State Street in Chicago, and though they experienced no life-threatening violence, white boys often attacked their sons. Wells kept a gun in the house, and taught her children the lesson that she had learned while fighting lynching in the deep South: if she must die by violence, she would be sure to take as many of her persecutors with her as possible.

Wells's *Southern Horrors: Lynch Law In All Its Phases* (1892) and *A Red Record: Lynchings in the United States, 1892–1893–1894* (1895) are companion pieces, which seek to raise national awareness of this growing outrage. *Southern Horrors* features an introductory endorsement from Frederick Douglass, praising her fidelity to facts, and Wells's opening follows suit by identifying lynching as a case for students of American sociology. Emphasizing that lynchings are most often about controlling black social mobility, she argues that emigration from areas where lynching is prevalent, along with boycotts, remain the best means of resistance. The other obvious strategy is publicity, as exemplified by the international response to her British anti-lynching campaign, which pressured white Americans into action. Here too, economic interest motivates justice, since British businessmen were clear in their condemnation of the practice as an impediment to investment.

Boycotts, publicity, the pursuit of all existing political and legal channels, were Wells's methods for assisting her people's advance. In her later years, she remained active in Chicago's Club Movement, helping to establish the Negro Fellowship League in 1910, an organization that located jobs and provided other services for poor urban blacks. Wells criticized the uncharitableness of the city's wealthy blacks, who failed to support her endeavor in the same generous terms in which whites supported Jane Addams. Wells also urged black men to vote, in a 1910 article, "How Enfranchisement Stops Lynching" for the *Original Rights Magazine*. Her children pursued professional careers in law, printing, secretarial work, and journalism. They were inspired in part by the example of their mother, who was always moved by injustice to "do something" (one of her favorite phrases). Wells's autobiography, *Crusade for Justice*, was published after her death in 1931.

Though Ida Wells never mentioned having read it, few late nineteenth-century novels were more in sympathy with her aims and activities than Albion Tourgee's *A Fool's Errand* and its accompanying appendix on *The Invisible Empire*. A near bestseller when it was published in 1879, *A Fool's Errand* remains one of the most important studies of Reconstruction and the rise of the Ku Klux Klan. It was written by a Northern lawyer and judge, who experienced these events first-hand. The novel provides the perspective of an empathetic but strong-willed Northerner come South to make his home after the war, and his reflections upon the virulent racism that took violent expression in the activities of the Klan. Tourgee settled in North Carolina, in part because the warm climate was more conducive to the healing of his war injuries, and in part to assist the Reconstruction effort. Of French and British descent, Tourgee was born in 1838 in Ohio, moved to Massachusetts in his teens, and published his first book of poems and essays, *Sense and Nonsense*, in 1857. A student at the University of Rochester, he was awarded a B. A. upon his 1862 enlistment in keeping with a common practice of awarding degrees to men who joined the Union army before completing their education. Tourgee fought with both New York and Ohio regiments, but his tour was interrupted by his arrest for insubordination after refusing to surrender a black fugitive who had saved his company. He returned to participate in a number of major battles toward the war's end including Tullohoma, Chickamauga, Lookout Mountain, and Missionary Ridge. In 1864, Tourgee was admitted to the Ohio bar, and discovered the beauties of North Carolina, one of the least devastated of Southern states, while serving as legal counsel in a court martial case. Tourgee moved his family there in 1865, and soon became a pariah among the local inhabitants given his outspokenness on behalf of black suffrage.

The fictionalized life of Comfort Servosse in *A Fool's Errand* largely mirrors Tourgee's own. Thus Tourgee helped organize the Union League of Guilford County; began a paper, the *Union Register*, espousing the ideas of radical Reconstruction; and was active in shaping the new constitution of the state. In contrast to Servosse, however, Tourgee served as a North Carolina Judge for six years, and was utterly fearless in prosecuting Klan members. When Tourgee left his judgeship in 1876, President Grant gave him an official appointment in Raleigh, which allowed him to continue his attacks on the Klan and defenses of black civil rights. Tourgee left North Carolina in 1879, after a fourteen-year residence, and turned to fiction as an almost direct expression of the limits of political activism. This period of fervent literary production in the late seventies to late eighties included *Figs and Thistles*, which served as a campaign biography for Republican presidential candidate, James Garfield. The very attributes that ensured the failure of Reconstruction, Tourgee argued in "The South as A Field for Fiction," made the region unparalled as the setting for romance. Though Tourgee sought to exploit some of that possibility, his own deeper tendencies were reflected in the realism of *A Fool's Errand*, a novel whose disheartening conclusions posited a potentially permanent rift between North and South; the transmission of the distorted psychology of master–slave relations to succeeding generations; the necessity of black political equality and Reconstruction's utter failure to safeguard it.

A Fool's Errand was published anonymously and aroused a great deal of interest from the first. Many reviewers recalled *Uncle Tom's Cabin*, declaring Tourgee's book as strong a case for Reconstruction as Stowe's had been for abolition. The novel's commercial success inspired a signed edition with a second volume, *The Invisible Empire*, documenting the activities of the Klan. *A Fool's*

Errand engages its readers not only through its vivid descriptions of a critical era in American history, but also through the compelling idiosyncrasies of its carefully drawn protagonist, Colonel Comfort Servosse. Structured by the epistolary form, some of the most profound insights of the novel are conveyed in letters written by Servosse or his wife Metta back North to interested statesmen, friends, and relatives. An astute reader of Southern society in its postwar incarnation, Servosse's wife Metta delivers some of the novel's keenest perceptions in letters to her sister, which describe the trials of Northern women schoolteachers hired by the Missionary Association to educate the former slaves; the eagerness and oppression of the slaves themselves; and the fearsome prejudice of the equally ignorant and impoverished whites, who were likewise degraded under a plantation system. Servosse introduces many schemes to aid the blacks, but the most revolutionary of all is his effort to make them landowners, by selling them parts of his land, while assisting their purchase of horses and accepting repayment in crops. From the outraged perspective of the local whites – elite and poor alike – Servosse's outspoken defense of black rights (to testify in court, serve on juries, and vote) seems comparatively harmless. But Servosse's greatest offense is his insistence that the legal rights of the freedmen are a foregone conclusion, and that Southerners would do well to meet these inevitable provisions halfway.

The ill-fated struggles of Tourgee's commonsensical fool is as masterful a portrait of an individual at odds with his setting as Twain's Connecticut Yankee. What makes Tourgee's book rare is his ability to convey the experiences of Reconstruction from both sides. Tourgee's success in this vein appears hardwon but consistent, as exemplified by the chart he reproduces at one point to outline opposing antebellum and postbellum, Southern and Northern positions. Thus, while he exposes the tyrannical order that prevailed in the South prior to the war: the rule of censorship, the denial of free speech, the training of whites as masters and blacks as slaves to the utter disregard of alternative roles, he also manages to substantiate oppositional strands of Southern society. One of these pockets of nationalism, for instance, gave rise during the war to a group called the "Red Strings," which devised signals to assist the Union cause using bits of red string, in recollection of the Book of Joshua where a red cord let down by Rahab directed warriors away from her household. Above all, Tourgee provides a vivid picture of the world of black folk and their efforts to establish viable religious and educational institutions against all odds. Prominent in his descriptions of black life is the character of Uncle Jerry, the crippled saint of the settlement who has dramatic trances during which he sees God. His special trances also allow for more local insights, including a vision that reveals the culprits in a recent Klan murder, and results in his own lynching by the Klan. The topic of the Klan arouses Tourgee's most extreme censure, in part because he believes it to have been fatally underestimated by Northern officials in its initial incarnation during the winter of 1868–69. Misconceived as a relatively controlled effort to regulate blacks by exploiting what was prejudicially believed to be their collective fear of ghosts, it quickly evolved into a reign of terror against all those white and black who dared to espouse interracial equality or even respect. Tourgee emphasizes the solemnity and operational zeal of this soldierly enterprise, which made it so difficult to oppose. Their masks – on horses as well as men – allowed them to elude prosecution for their outrages; their successful recruitment among all classes of white society ensured that the powerful would be equally incriminated and thus resist attempts to limit or punish their activities. The Klan succeeded in making itself synonymous with the best elements in any given Southern community.

The difficulty of redressing the Klan in fact no doubt inspired the most appealing sections of Tourgee's fiction: the climactic chapters on the foiling by Servosse's daughter of a Klan plot to lynch him. The episode is rich in every imaginable romantic detail – love between this daughter of Reconstruction and the flower of Southern aristocracy, a *Romeo and Juliet*-like opposition to the romance from both sets of parents, a perilous night ride to save lives – and the drama culminates in a miraculous repudiation of the Klan by Klan members. This resolution is clearly implausible in light of the Klan's gruesomely detailed aggressions. It is also difficult to square with Tourgee's largest claim – that Servosse's efforts represent a "fool's errand." In his dedication to understanding the fundamentally irrational nature of prejudice, Tourgee's Fool exemplifies the North's failure to cleave steadfastly to its ideals as against the single-minded ferocity of the South. As the novel confirms, enlightened convictions about race on the Northern side were not nearly as common or fixed as unenlightened views on the Southern side. Moreover, from a Northern perspective in particular during this postwar era, economic expansion and opportunity was bound to nullify any claim of principle. If one were a bona fide Southerner, however, nothing could defy that cultural law characterized by William Benjamin Smith as the "jewel of the southern soul," the color line.

COLOR LINES

Among the examples of racist pseudoscience against which W. E. B. Du Bois directed many of his early writings, none is as bleak as Smith's *The Color Line: A Brief on Behalf of the Unborn* (1905). A mathematician who labeled his work "an ethnological inquiry," Smith's sources show how these race debates functioned

as heated exchanges among an identifiable group of intellectuals, which primarily confirmed the irreconcilability of their different positions. In Smith's
book, science provides the script (race struggle), and religion gives it moral
color while social engineering and charity are equated and dismissed. Thus
Christianity and science are not only intertwined, they are monumentalized:
twin towers with one awesome theme. And the sacrifice of the black race is
both divine and organic necessity. Smith regionalizes the color line from the
start of his analysis, in order to take credit for what he regards as a national
remedy en route to the ultimate solution. In reviewing *The Color Line* for *The
Dial* in 1905, Du Bois remarked that the book could "easily be passed over in
silence," were it not for its reflection of "the active belief of millions of our fellow countrymen . . . This is the new barbarism of the twentieth century, against
which all the forces of civilization must contend." The new barbarism, as confirmed by the most widely cited of contemporary studies on race, Frederick
Hoffman's *Race Traits and Tendencies of the American Negro*, seemed to be
everywhere.

Race Traits originated as research on the relative "insurability" of black lives
and developed into a study of black nature, social conditions, and race prejudice. That it became an authoritative source for sociologists, was a sign of the
field's own steeping in Darwinian theory. A Prudential statistician without
social scientific training, who also wrote a *History of the Prudential Life Insurance
Company* (1900) and a book on pauper burials in large cities (1917), Hoffman
was primarily interested in survival – from the competing claims of nations, to
the social relations that grew out of belief in the natural inequality of human
kinds. *Race Traits and Tendencies* is an eccentric blend of social psychology, liberal philosophy, reformism, statistical analysis, ethnographic description, and
racist dogma. Du Bois knew the book, and refuted it repeatedly in sociological
writings that appeared between 1896 and the 1903 publication of his *Souls
of Black Folk*. The burden of *Race Traits* is the definitive association of black
culture with death, an association that supports Hoffman's developing rationale for black people's social, political, and psychological isolation in every
possible context, from rural black belt to urban ghetto. Hoffman disputes
arguments that attribute high black mortality to environmental factors, and
cites statistics from army and prison records showing that among white and
black recruits given identical food, clothing and shelter, a disproportionately
high black mortality rate persists. He finds black mortality to be highest
among the younger generation – those at greatest remove from the sustaining
framework of slavery. Yet Hoffman is convinced of the double determination
of black doom, as reflected in the book's split title. "Race traits" indicate the
inherent basis of inferiority; "tendencies" indicates the stylistic and cultural

practices that nourish these genetic predispositions. Taken as a whole, *Race Traits and Tendencies* more than fulfilled its actuarial ambitions, with pages of tables on diseases (consumption, yellow fever, malaria, smallpox) to which blacks were thought immune, but to which they succumbed as the century progressed in greater numbers. Hoffman did admit evidence of social pathologies (alcoholism, insanity, and suicide) that were rare among blacks, but he either discredited them or interpreted them in an unflattering manner.

Nathaniel Shaler was a geologist, but the prominence of his work on race among social scientists confirms the fluid boundaries of contemporary debates on the subject. Born in Kentucky, Shaler retained his Southern sympathies while fighting for the Union, just as he played the role of disaffected Southerner while studying and teaching at Harvard. Like most Social Darwinists, Shaler believed that progress was costly, and that the requisite social sacrifices could never be distributed evenly. While he regarded humanitarianism as the highest evolutionary form, he believed it could only be achieved through a dramatic reduction of social strangers. According to Shaler, a sympathetic humanitarianism would not reach its highest form until the disappearance of those who failed to inspire it. His recommendations therefore included immigration restrictions, the rapid assimilation of "valuable aliens" (Irish, German, Jew), prohibitions on interracial marriage, limitations on black suffrage, and the radical circumscription of black labor. Indeed, the tragedy of modernity, in Shaler's view, was its terrible capacity to bring strangeness ever closer, without the formal means of keeping it within bounds. The inevitable result was the rise of an outmoded intra-tribal sympathy that was nourished by modern social variety. By positing the complexity of the sympathetic impulse, Shaler was able to recognize its variability, and to understand prejudice as one of its forms, a sympathetic hatred on behalf of preservation of one's kind. A Social Darwinist, who believed that emotions were inherent not learned, Shaler suggested that sympathy evolved and adapted like any other body part. In *The Neighbor: A Natural History of Social Contacts* (1904) he attempted to shape a Darwinian approach to the emotions into a theory of social relations.

As the grandson of white men on both sides, Charles Chesnutt grew up in Fayetteville, North Carolina. His family was wealthier than most blacks in the town, since his white grandfathers had provided some property for their mixed-race children. Chesnutt was well educated as a child, studying literature and foreign languages, and early on aspired to a literary career. "The Negro's part is to prepare himself for recognition and equality," he wrote in a journal that he kept from childhood, "and it is the province of literature to open the way for him to get it – to accustom the public mind to the idea; to lead people out, imperceptibly, unconsciously, step by step, to the desired state of feeling." Chesnutt's long life spanned turbulent times for black Americans, from the Civil War and Reconstruction through World War I. As a resident of both South and North, and a professional in the worlds of law and business (part of a rising black professional class), as well as literature (among the first serious black authors), Chesnutt grew accustomed to what Du Bois termed "double-consciousness." Admitted to the Ohio State bar in 1884, Chesnutt built a successful business in legal stenography and documentation, during the same period in which he became a regular contributor to major period-icals (publishing his first story, "The Goophered Grapevine," in the *Atlantic Monthly*, 1887). Despite the necessity of dividing his time between writing and business, Chesnutt was able to publish between the 1880s and 1905 three novels, two collections of short stories, a biography of Frederick Douglass (in the Beacon Biography series that also featured Owen Wister on Ulysses Grant), and several essays on race. In a 1901 essay published in *The Boston Transcript*, "The White and the Black," Chesnutt wrote about the racial classification of passengers on trains traversing the country, emphasizing that it was only in the South that the train conductor became a tyrant ajudicating the relative humanity of white and black. The principal subject of Chesnutt's fiction was the color line: its psychological effects, particularly on those (mulattoes) who were able to escape it, its political and philosophical implications. In a 1928 acceptance speech upon being awarded the Spingarn Medal for Literature by the NAACP (National Association for the Advancement of Colored People), Chesnutt observed that the unique psychology and complex circumstances of people with mixed blood, which he knew first-hand, afforded an especially rich field of possibility for the writer of fiction.

More fully than any other novel of its time, *The House Behind the Cedars* (1900) realizes the dramatic possibilities of the color line. The narrative opens upon a common ritual invested with an uncommon twist: the North Carolina homecoming of John Walden, a young mulatto lawyer, recently widowed, who has built a successful legal and business career by passing as white in South Carolina. South Carolina shared with Louisiana the distinction of possessing a large free mixed race population of blacks, Native Americans, mulattoes, and *mestizoes*, which stood between the white slaveholders and black slaves in the antebellum era, and helped to blur the absolute divide of the color line after it. John has managed to escape army service, profited from the turmoil of Civil War, and married the daughter of a plantation owner who has preserved his fortune. He is admitted to the South Carolina bar, and wins the business of Southerners eager to avoid carpet-bagging lawyers. Independent, realistic, and rather cold, John's personality, Chesnutt emphasizes, has more to do with his marginality than with nature. An intellectual, as well as an acute observer, John is perpetually conscious of the stain of race prejudice. He fixes on his sister Rena, who can also easily pass for white, as a perfect maternal replacement for his newly orphaned son, and talks her into returning with him to South Carolina. While Rena is guilt-ridden about leaving their black mother, Molly Walden, Charleston offers the beautiful girl the prospect of an education and an entirely new life. After finishing school, Rena meets and falls in love with a wealthy young aristocrat, George Tryon, but the futility of their relationship destroys them both. Reluctant to inform George of her mixed race, Rena's secret is exposed when George visits the Waldens' North Carolina town on business while she is there visiting her ailing mother, and inadvertently discovers her true identity. Tryon struggles against his deeply prejudicial feelings, but by the time love triumphs over culture, Rena has died of brain fever. It would take decades before the color line could be publicly repudiated anywhere else but in dreams.

THE FUTURE OF (A) RACE

When the editor of the New York *Evening Post* announced in 1905 that *The Atlanta University Publications* were the "only scientific studies of the Negro question being made today," he was acknowledging the tide of pseudoscience that had preceded their publication. The Atlanta volumes were composed with a view of the social scientific frontier on race as both wide open, with vast territories of knowledge still to be charted, and closed, littered with theories and statistics, many of them inaccurate or extremist. In describing the general plan for these monographs, Du Bois concedes that the project was motivated in great part by the high black mortality rate.

It is hard to exaggerate the fascination of the series' first volume, *Mortality Among Negroes in Cities* (1896) as local ethnography: full of documentary detail and wide-ranging debate. Doctors, college presidents, mothers, and temperance reformers come together to offer their explanations for high black mortality; in a varied chorus of armchair morality and social criticism, three arguments dominate. First, black mortality is of pressing national interest. The future of a modern American nation depends on the quality of its urban life, which turns on the fate of its black inhabitants. Second, intervention is not a possibility but a demand; social science has been redefined as social renovation. Third, the case for inherence is labeled prejudicial. For the first time in a social scientific publication, a *black* doctor assesses the group's susceptibility to disease, the quality of their health facilities, and the high rate of black stillbirths. Dr. Butler paints a grim picture of his people as lone laborers in a festering urban underworld. This Dantesque hell of undesirable work features men sweeping streets, digging sewers, and collecting garbage, while pregnant women haul coal and dirty laundry. He discounts claims of parental neglect, and cites instances of desperate parents turned away by white doctors worried about their ability to pay. The wonder, Butler emphasizes, is that black mortality is as low as it is.

Despite its billing as a continuation, the second *Atlanta* volume, *Social and Physical Conditions of Negroes in Cities* (1897), replaces criticalness with defensiveness. High mortality becomes the burden of blacks; there is little mention of their deprivation. In a paper on syphilis, a Fisk University professor claims that the disease has grown to epidemic proportions among urban blacks. Professor Harris, who draws on F. L. Hoffman for support, seems driven by a hygienic self-recrimination that is typical here. On the whole, the volume touches upon many subjects that were absorbing Du Bois at the time: the idea of death as a *defining* category for blacks at the turn of the century; the new prominence of the undertaker as a community figure; the ties between mortality, declining sympathy, and segregation; and finally, the identification of an internal correlative, the distance of black bourgeoisie from black poor, to an external dilemma, the exclusion of blacks by the dominant culture. Du Bois began his editorship of *The Atlanta University Publications* with the third volume, *The Negro in Business* (1899). The next sixteen volumes continue to assess the mortality question. But they also represent a subtle shift in emphasis. In general, we find fewer death tables and more data on segregation. One significant consequence of segregation, for instance, is the development of undertaking into an exceptionally lucrative black profession. The irony of the undertaker's success does not escape Du Bois, who seems to have the two previous volumes on black mortality in mind when he comments that certain businesses owe their success to "the peculiar environment of the Negro in this land." There is no mistaking Du Bois's point. Undertaking is profitable because it is an *exclusive* concern (blacks alone can bury their dead), not because there are higher percentages of black deaths. Moreover, conventional belief in the group's affinity for death ensures a limited but steady trade in white burials. The state of affairs described by Du Bois is confirmed by a Chicago undertaker, who noted that while black burials represent a closed market, many whites will accept a black undertaker. The history of this "peculiar" tendency extends from the Revolutionary era well into the twentieth century. In the *Philadelphia Negro*, and later in *Atlanta* (*The Negro Church*, 1903), Du Bois describes two black ministers, Absalom Jones and Richard Allen, who remained behind during the 1792 Philadelphia epidemic to bury the dead. Du Bois notes with grim irony that the piety and fortitude which inspired these acclaimed acts did not prevent the pair's ejection from church worship when congregants decided on segregated services.

The significance of undertaking is not confined to its place among the most profitable of black businesses. For Du Bois, the success of the black undertaker has symbolic weight. In contrast to traditional Enlightenment values, which assign the work of death and mourning to "humanity," Du Bois recognizes them as tasks of the ethnically familiar. A major insight of *The Negro in Business* is the real compensations afforded by segregation. *Negro Business*'s portrait of black enterprises formed as morbid offshoots of the larger economy represents what Du Bois terms "the advantage of the disadvantage." Du Bois's arguments anticipate by a century those of another sociologist, Douglas Massey, who details the increasing success of businesses dependent on black enclosure.

In later volumes of *The Atlanta University Publications*, the mortality question is reconceived. Inaugurating the second cycle of *The Atlanta University Publications, The Health and Physique of the American Negro* (1906) was the most significant statement of the time on the relationship between population figures and the rise of the color line. The book opens with a stunning photographic procession of "typical Negro-Americans," ranging from the darkest black to white, a wordless narrative, articulating in the strongest possible terms the doom of racial separation. The paradoxical foundation of this display is familiar to students of race theory: the attempt to catalog racial difference, the very rise of ethnology as a field of interest, accompanied the discovery of the hopelessly mixed character of all races. Over the course of the nineteenth century, ever more sophisticated techniques for measuring and classifying human kinds were set against the realities of assimilation. The fact was that America was absorbing its different populations whose own internal variety mirrored the racial variety of "native" Americans themselves. The same historical events – immigration, colonization, capitalist-industrial expansion – which had given rise to ethnology were rapidly eroding its analytical base.

Racial ambiguity, as these developments imply, ran in all directions. The only pure blacks were those in stereotypes, as David Livingstone recognized when he declared "the hideous Negro type, which the fancy of observers once saw all over Africa" as existing only on "signs in front of tobacco-shops." Du Bois goes on to cite the data from prominent social scientists that confirm the high percentage of black blood in white. Even more alarming is Du Bois's insinuation that black population statistics are somehow dependent on this indeterminacy. In the commentary that follows his silent parade of "Negro" types, Du Bois points out that passing is so easily accomplished by large numbers of mulattoes, that black population may be impossible to estimate. *Health and Physique* thus makes short work of three dominant theories: that black and white races have become increasingly distinct; that African culture is limited to its American and African variants; that black culture is regressive. With Africa reinscribed as the first productive culture of the ancient world, black mortality statistics in modern America become an obvious outcome of social conditions. Place any other group in similar circumstances, and the results will be identical. Du Bois's comparisons range from Russia, England, and Sweden, to the Chicago stockyards, where white death rates surpass black. *Health and Physique* concludes with a series of propositions co-authored by Du Bois, Franz Boas, and R. R. Wright. First, the black death rate is on the decline; second, high mortality is a product of social conditions; third, there is pressing need for more black doctors and health facilities; fourth, the health and endurance of the nation as a whole is dependent on the fate of black Americans, and finally, there must be greater sympathy for black problems throughout America.

Du Bois's substantive challenge to the category of black mortality is qualified by fears that it had assumed a life of its own. A correspondent from the "Negro Anti-Tuberculosis League" of Georgia articulates a common concern, when he identifies high black mortality as a "stigma" on the race, a term that registered the disturbing independence of stereotypes from social facts. This may explain why allusions to the mortality issue in the *Atlanta* volumes tend to be muted, as if black analysts want to avoid feeding its flames. But it is also because these studies challenge prevailing race theory through data rather than disputation. These are works of practical sociology: confronting mortality statistics in terms of socioeconomic cause and outcome, addressing every serious qualification, from the segregation that belies black disappearance to the "passing" that defiantly stages it. The *Atlanta* volumes were designed to expose black existence to the light of empirical method. This explains their magnitude: endless tables on black businesses, hospitals, and medical schools; extended photographic series (on the evolution of the black body and home); protracted "correspondence" to close each volume. Only detail could fill the vacuum of hearsay and grim mythology, could transform black Americans from phantoms of sociological analysis to the "bone and flesh" collectivity ushered in by Du Bois at the start of *Souls*.

The stigma of mortality that attached to blacks as a group in this era helps to explain why the difference of their attitudes towards death became a special preoccupation. Contemporary studies tended to presume a black relationship to death that was uniquely intimate. Philip Bruce's *The Plantation Negro as a Free Man* (1889) was especially revealing in this respect. Like other Southerners writing on "the Negro problem," Bruce did not simply assert that blacks were different; he showed from his own standpoint what made them so. He believed that black culture was peculiarly death-tinged, that blacks lingered over the dead with a clinical fascination, and that their mourning rites recalled primitive African forms in their frenzied character. Indeed, as exemplified by mourning practices, the sensibilities of blacks and whites were so divergent, according to Bruce, as to suggest a national (not simply a cultural) divide. The enormity of Bruce's claim was equalled by his task: the transformation of overly intimate neighbors (many of them blood kin) into representative strangers. Bruce's account is especially suggestive as an explanation for why death rites were so essential to the construction of estrangement in this context. The recognition of blacks as strangers and the recognition of the living as dead are parallel processes. In both cases, one must accept a being that has been accessible and sympathetic as alien and remote. Bruce's ultimate example of a white man discovering, in the process of paying his last respects to a black friend, the difference of blacks, living and dead, is a primal scene for the recognition of estrangement. The alienating spectacle of a black collectivity's dealings with death appears here as a dramatic redoubling: the social dead looking upon their natural dead. Thomas Nelson Page sounded similar themes in *The Negro: The Southerner's Problem* (1904) but with greater ambivalence. He was prone to mournful reflection on the past rather than alienating contemplation of the present. As a novelist known for sentimental romances of the antebellum South, Page predictably praised "the Old-Time Negro," and emphasized his warm feelings for the black race. Page's patronizing generosity was afforded by his guiding assumption that blacks were brief sojourners on the American scene, a demise that was inevitable, however many generations or even centuries it might take. In Page, the white lyncher and black ravisher were part of a common "pestilence," just as both sides of the race debate shared a common ship of state. Or perhaps a common raft, which is the vehicle of choice in the next race drama under consideration, Mark Twain's *Huckleberry Finn* (1885). As a book about friendship and love; a study of freedom; an account of acculturation; a work of mourning (for its young protagonist is haunted by death and its rituals); *Huckleberry Finn* provides sustained reflection upon the intersecting subjects of ritual sacrifice, the color line, and specific cultural relationships to death, under discussion in this chapter.

Twain's bestselling novel sold 50,000 copies within three months of its publication in 1885, sales assisted by the excerpts published in *Century Magazine* (1884 to 1885) which helped to advertise it, and by the controversy generated by the book's subject matter from the outset. Banned in the nineteenth century by the Concord Public Library for coarse language and antisocial role models, *Huckleberry Finn* was condemned in the twentieth century for negative stereotyping of African Americans. The novel is invaluable for confronting so many nineteenth-century demons – from slavery and racism to the subordination and repudiation of women – which Twain portrays as a cultural legacy for the future. Language here is a means of both liberation and enslavement; a dangerous weapon and an empowering lyricism. Like so many others of Twain's works, *Huckleberry Finn* with its forgetful hero confirms the importance of cultural memory. It highlights cultural pressure points – instances of conflict and contradiction, the details that resist the coherence of mythic paradigms that keep sticking out and exposing themselves. In so doing, it fulfills Kenneth Burke's notion of literary narratives as answers to specific historical situations, answers that highlight the basic structure and contents of the situation in a way that includes an attitude toward them.

The question that has preoccupied critics of *Huckleberry Finn* most recently has to do with Twain's perspective on the racist stereotypes he portrays. Is Twain himself beholden to his culture in the way his hero Huck seems to be? Or is Twain rather investigating and subtly undermining – through a "thick description" of his culture – the stereotypes he sets forth? The novel does in some sense defy racist norms by representing them so profoundly and complexly through Huck's struggle against them. Huck progresses then falls back time and again. It is critical, for instance, that his notorious response to Aunt Sally's query, "'Anybody hurt?' 'No'm, killed a nigger,'" follows the famed "conscience" scene in which Huck tears up the letter turning Jim in, and resigns himself to Hell. In keeping with the enlightened norms of our culture, as against the racist assumptions of Twain's, Huck "progresses" then reverts. This is because the book is as much about the enslavement to prejudice as it is about the institution of slavery. Twain confined his narrative perspective to a child's for precisely the reason that children harbor the prospect of change, at the same time embodying the process of acculturation. Through their absorption of a culture's norms, they pinpoint what that culture stands for. And when they resist those norms, in response to experience, the resistance is always passionate. Twain can show how Huck comes to recognize Jim's humanity, slowly, against his will, but surely. We watch Huck gradually grasp ideas of racial equality that we now take for granted, and then pull back from those ideas. It is like watching a whole nation come to consciousness, awaken, and then recede back into darkness. Or like watching the dawn coming on near the opening to chapter nineteen, one of the most lyrical moments in all of Twain's writings.

The first thing to see, looking away over the water, was a kind of dull line – that was the woods on t'other side – you couldn't make nothing else out; then a pale place in the sky; then more paleness, spreading around; then the river softened up, away off, and warn't black any more, but gray; you could see little dark spots drifting along, ever so far away – trading scows, and such things; and long black streaks – rafts; sometimes you could hear a sweep screaking; or jumbled up voices, it was so still, and sounds come so far; and by-and-by you could see a streak on the water which you know by the look of the streak that there's a snag there in a swift current which breaks on it and makes the streak look that way; and you see the mist curl up off of the water, and the east reddens up, and the river, and you make out a log cabin in the edge of the woods, away on the bank on t'other side of the river, being wood-yard, likely, and piled by them cheats so you can throw a dog through it any-wheres; then the nice breeze springs up, and comes fanning you from over there, so cool and fresh, and sweet to smell, on account of the woods and the flowers; but sometimes not that way, because they've left dead fish laying around, gars, and such, and they do get pretty rank; and next you've got the full day, and everything smiling in the sun, and the song-birds just going it!

This passage reveals Twain at his most optimistic. Every day offers the prospect of renewal, of starting fresh, even if there always are a few rank fish lying around. The rhythm of the language here is the roll: Huck piles image upon image in a breathless heap, like the light gaining momentum as the sun rises. This is the rhythm of inspired seeing. Yet this very daylight is imperiling; for Huck and Jim must hide when the sun comes up, traveling at night to avoid Jim's recapture.

Huckleberry Finn shares the principal concern of all Twain's works in the mechanics of belief. How do people come to believe what they believe? How do they ever come to change those beliefs, if that is even possible? What mechanisms allow for change: good-heartedness, friendship, suppleness? The most prominent belief in the novel's world is the belief in slavery, and its companion doctrine, black inferiority. The book takes a heterogeneous approach to slavery, viewing enslavement as a matter of consciousness as well as a matter of institutions. Slavery in *Huckleberry Finn* is both a specific historical system directed at black people, and a universal condition, common to whites and blacks. The novel distinguishes between *freedom to* (Huck) and *freedom from* (Jim). Huck is able to free himself from his enslavement to cultural mores, at least temporarily in the conscience scene, but Jim has no avenue through which to free himself. To the extent that slavery is a stigma inscribed on black culture, it remains an enduring legacy, a view of the black condition handed down from generation to generation. This is the meaning of the excruciating ending, which Ernest Hemingway instructed readers to skip, where Tom mercilessly protracts Jim's imprisonment for the sake of a lark, and Huck participates, reluctantly, but ultimately fully. Twain's exploration of how slavery is recollected and perpetuated in the era of Reconstruction suggests that blacks can be freed by legal fiat, but remain enslaved in racist minds, both white and black. For Twain, the

Southerner become Northern entrepreneur, the son of slaveowners (his family owned one) who married into a family of abolitionists, understood slavery and freedom as an ongoing American dialectic. Only a culture that knew slavery intimately, Twain believed, could understand the deepest meanings of freedom. *Huckleberry Finn* shows how the persisting identification of black people with enslavement gets rationalized, via stereotypes and labels, such as the word "nigger," which punctuates the narrative like a whip lash.

This is consistent with the introductory "Notice" and "Explanatory Note," where language is a weapon and talk a means of trickery and aggression. Signed by "G. G. Chief of Ordnance," "ordinance" (decree) minus the "i" becomes "ordnance" (artillery). This is the drama of the West itself: the rule of law is replaced by the rule of force, power trumps knowledge, and humor undermines the authority of moral absolutes. The Explanatory Note foregrounds the importance of dialect and the diversity of tongues spoken in the book, reinforcing the Notice's identification of the book's realism. In *Huckleberry Finn* storytelling, speech, lyricism do not transcend social context but express it. Language is not liberatory, but revelatory, of who we are and of what we cannot escape – our class, ethnicity, region, and culture. Indeed, the novel's primary narrative forms – storytelling, dialect, dialogue – serve to emphasize the fact that language is a product of social interaction. Such a view of language is at odds with criticism that views Huckleberry Finn as a self-reliant hero, or the book as a celebration of the freedom from culture. Indeed, Huck, like Henry Thoreau, is culturally common in his rebellion against civilization; a conformist in his pursuit of his own unique relationship to the wild and to the cultural "other," Jim. Huck is also typically American in his tendency to talk of freedom while capitulating to forces that threaten it – e.g. acting as a pawn for Tom Sawyer, conceding to the domination of the King and Duke (parodies of the un-American constraints of aristocracy). Huck's Americanness extends to his innocence and naïveté: he has no sense of humor, he is an innocent straight man to Twain's own jokes. In this sense he is acutely vulnerable in a novel where jokes are weapons as much as sources of fun. Perhaps most important, Huck shares a national penchant for amnesia. The past is a region he would prefer to leave behind, an impulse that gets him into scrapes, such as forgetting who he is supposed to be impersonating at the moment. Some memory lapses are strategic; we know little of Huck's previous life because it is too painful to contemplate.

Huck's ambivalence towards formal religion represents a classic form of Protestant inwardness, a preference for framing an original relationship to universal forces. Institutional Christianity simply does not make sense to Huck; just as hierarchical Christianity or the Christian Science Church of Mary Baker

Eddy make no sense to the speakers of other works by Twain. But criticism of religion in Twain is more often an expression of devotion than of skepticism; for he, like Melville, was more an ambivalent or failed believer than a non-believer. And *Huckleberry Finn*, in keeping with Twain's best work, pays homage to a spiritual practice that is spontaneous and common. For the book is very much about ritual, the cultural rites that make a particular antebellum Southern community go round, and that children like Huck grow into. Huck is a great believer in a complementary order of ghosts and spirits that haunt the world, especially at night, and require propitiation when something happens that is not to their liking – for example, the burning of a spider in a candle, which demands a compensatory turning in one's tracks, breast-crossing, and tying of hair. Huck's superstition is the bond that links him to Jim, whose representativeness as a slave is confirmed by his beliefs. According to Huck, "Niggers is always talking about witches in the dark by the kitchen fire." Huck misses what the novel as a whole emphasizes: the universality of superstition as the faith of the powerless. Far from an idealized system of value, folk belief in *Huckleberry Finn* is another means of enslavement. In reading these ordinary pieties as reaction formations, opiates for the most oppressed of the masses, Twain anticipates the hard-nosed prophecy of Baby Suggs in Toni Morrison's *Beloved* minus the race politics: "There is no bad luck in the world but white folks." Still, there are critical distinctions in the applications of this ecumenical faith, which is sometimes a method of comfort, sometimes of cruelty. The band formed from Tom Sawyer's gang requires secret blood oaths, punishes disloyal members by ravaging closest kin, and marks its victims with crosses on their breasts. While the band's closing resolution, to meet again next week to rob and kill people, is only pretend, the rites themselves recall an all too real secret brotherhood in Twain's South: the Ku Klux Klan.

Indeed, lynching is a perpetual threat in *Huckleberry Finn:* a savagery that seems to express a collective state of moral disrepair. Twain's novel abounds in sacrificial scenes: scapegoat rituals; the victimization of animal substitutes; melodramas of self-sacrifice. This propensity for sacrificial theater is a main component of the novel's renowned burlesque. There may be no scene which more powerfully evokes this theater than the depiction of a sow milking her young in contented squalor until she is set upon by vicious dogs. With characteristic generosity fueled by need, Huck manages to convey the despair of the human "loafers" who initiate this small tragedy, while making us feel all the terror of the pig.

She'd stretch out, and shut her eyes, and wave her ears, whilst the pigs was milking her, and look as happy as if she was on salary. And pretty soon you'd hear a loafer sing out,

"Hi! *So* boy! Sick him, Tige!" and away the sow would go, squealing most horrible, with a dog or two swinging to each ear, and three or four dozen more a-coming; and then you would see all the loafers get up and watch the thing out of sight, and laugh at the fun and look grateful for the noise . . . There couldn't anything wake them up all over, and make them happy all over, like a dog-fight – unless it might be putting turpentine on a stray dog and setting fire to him.

The flaming dog has an obvious reference point for Twain's post-Reconstruction South: the lynching of blacks. In the hazy world of *Huckleberry Finn*, where moral discriminations are as obscure as the "dull line" of the sky at sunrise, ritual murder is possibly the only thing that makes people feel alive. The desire of readers to believe Huck superior to these people is not always satisfied by Twain. For the novel is partly eighteenth-century picaresque (and it is no surprise that Twain admired a book like Tobias Smollet's *Humphrey Clinker*), recalling that genre's quirky anticipation of the modern leisure conventions of tourism. Movement in *Huckleberry Finn* – going around the country gawking, the lark of witnessing other modes of life, checking out a lifestyle then taking off – is a means of avoiding dullness and staving off death. It is, Twain suggests, the opposite of being stuck in the mud, limited to a single place or type of existence. Yet however different in experiential terms, it is hardly distinguishable in moral terms. Utterly prepossessing, with a powerful gift-of-the-gab, good-hearted, full of empathy, Huckleberry Finn is nevertheless culturally common. And Twain never tires of reminding us that it is a commonality fraught with corruption.

Huckleberry Finn is a deeply pessimistic, antisocial novel, whose rhythm consists of continual flights from society justified by periodic sojourns into rotten-to-the core communities. Yet the power of the book is precisely its ability to invest a plot of this kind with so much humor and compassion. Jim becomes far more than the object of mockery he appears at the book's beginning, where he believes that witches hung his hat on a limb for a sign. His superstitions are eventually shown to be a rich means of managing grief and exercising control. Noting that Jim knows all sorts of signs, but that they deal with bad luck exclusively, Huck wonders if Jim knows any good luck signs. Jim's reply, that you do not need to know when good luck is coming because you do not need to ward it off, makes perfect sense. Jim knows what he thinks and believes, and most importantly, knows what he does not know or need to know. He can deal with almost any crisis that presents itself, and has good instincts about avoiding danger. Most important of all, he succeeds in substantiating the moral relativism that represents one of the morals of Twain's book. Though Huck thinks Jim is stubbornly literal-minded in resisting the wisdom of King Solomon, Twain's readers are supposed to wonder if he does not have a point. This questioning is reinforced both by Jim's judicious conclusion that both Pap and the Widow Douglas are partly right in their respective notions of stealing, and by Jim's dignity in the face of one of Huck's worst pranks. Twain's readers are set up to recognize that though Jim is black and a slave, he is a far better parent to Huck than either Pap or the Widow Douglas.

It is a mark of Twain's unpredictability and inventiveness that for all his associations with the deadly forces of slavery, Jim is the most modern character in the novel. This is partly because of his humaneness, which is all the more pronounced in contrast to the barbaric behavior of so many other characters. But it is also because Jim is specifically identified with questions about ownership, property, and speculation. Judge Thatcher invests the small fortunes earned by Tom and Huck after discovering the robber's money in the cave, and the King and Duke are among the greediest creations in fiction, but Jim alone dwells upon money, and the money that money can bring. His fortune-telling hair-ball, taken "out of the fourth stomach of an ox," will only offer predictions for a fee. Jim describes his speculations in one of his first conversations with Huck. While the scene is burlesque, the dialogue registers Jim's preoccupation with finance, and conveys his implicit awareness that the black man will make a place for himself in American society if he can master it. On the basis of his own hairy arms and chest, Jim prophesies his likely wealth. His first speculations in stock involve "live stock," which "up 'n' died" and put him off further investments of this particular kind. The small amount that he recovers from this foiled venture (from his scrappy sale of the tallow and hide), is put in a bank run by another slave (which is subsequently robbed, in allusion to the Freedman's Bank scandal) and a remaining portion goes to a slave named Balum, who donates it to charity, because the return sounds promising ("whoever give to de po' len' to de Lord, en boun' to git his money back a hund'd times"). Jim's biggest economic gamble is running away (to prevent being sold down the river), and he recognizes that in doing so he is now his own best capital investment. "I wisht I had de money, I wouldn' want no mo" he says. At the novel's end, Jim owns himself in the eyes of the law as well, but has considerably less money to show for it. He feels rich with his forty dollars, which ironically recall the forty acres and a mule promised and denied the black slaves following their emancipation. The passage confirms the rapid decline in value of black people from slavery to freedom. Twain here confirms the harsh realism that contemporary lynching made horrifically vivid: that blacks were worth far less to their white brethren free than enslaved. Moreover, in its comprehensive account of the dynamics of slavery, at once wide-ranging and prophetic, *Huckleberry Finn* anticipates the cruelest irony of slavery's abolition: that blacks had exchanged their "slavery to individuals," in the words of Frederick Douglass, "to become the slaves of the community at large."

Besides *Huckleberry Finn* and *The Adventures of Tom Sawyer*, *Pudd'nhead Wilson*, which was serialized in *The Century Magazine* from 1893 to 1894, is Twain's only major novel set in the antebellum South. While it has key affinities with *Huckleberry Finn*, *Pudd'nhead Wilson* is also informed by many of the ventures, financial and technological, that preoccupied Twain in the decade between these two novels. Thus, *Pudd'nhead Wilson* provides a curiously modern account of the slavery era, an account that brings contemporary intellectual developments to bear in its scrutiny of the most ancient, yet still most puzzling and "peculiar" of institutions. These contemporary intellectual developments include: the new science of criminal detection; social scientific theories on the relative effects of nurture and nature; and debates on race and eugenics. *Pudd'nhead Wilson* is also distinguished by the intimacy of its portrait of slavery. Blacks and whites do not have to inhabit marginal terrains aboard rafts on rivers to become interdependent. Blacks and whites in this work are thoroughly intermingled via lines of blood and kinship. In this sense, *Pudd'nhead Wilson* fulfills Twain's observation about Southern antebellum life in his *Autobiography*: "All the negroes were friends of ours and with those of our own age we were . . . comrades, and yet not comrades; color and condition interposed a subtle line which both parties were conscious of and which rendered complete fusion impossible." Yet "fusion" there was, in biological as well as in social terms, according to *Puddn'head Wilson*, a novel which is preoccupied with the effects of mixed ancestry and the prospects for its detection. Twain sets the stage for his elaborate antebellum portrait of the effects of racial ancestry with a brief satirical description of his writing quarters in the Villa Viviani in the Florentian hills, surrounded by the busts of Cerretani senators, which he imagines mutely inviting him into their family. By using this "Whisper to the Reader," as he calls it, to introduce a novel about slavery and miscegenation, Twain effectively equates various forms of prejudice. Aristocratic pretensions, fawning before the busts of long lines of Italian senators, are equivalent to European disdain for abbreviated American bloodlines, which are in turn equivalent to worry about bloodlines at all, which are, finally, equivalent to belief in white racial superiority.

Enter "Dawson's Landing, on the Missouri side of the Mississippi," a town devoted to every type of snobbery and prejudice. The novel begins with the birth of two baby boys, Thomas à Becket Driscoll, son of the wealthy Percy Northumberland Driscoll, a financial speculator and descendant of what Twain calls the FFV – first families of Virginia – and Valet de Chambre, son of Driscoll's slave, Roxana. Roxana's son is the product of her seduction by another wealthy descendant of the FFV, Colonel Cecil Burleigh Essex. Percy Driscoll's wife dies within the week of her son's birth, and Percy Driscoll himself returns to his business dealings. It falls to Roxana or "Roxy," as she is called, to tend to the two babies, "Tom" and "Chambers" for short. The plot turns on the white appearances of Roxy and her baby son. Roxy is beautiful, smart, and ambitious; the only thing that distinguishes her as a slave is socialization and experience. Fearing that her own baby son might some day be sold down river, she switches the indistinguishable babies. Henceforth, the real Tom becomes the slave Chambers, and the real Chambers becomes the heir apparent, Tom, while the novel becomes a study of the relative effects of nature and nurture. Roxy humbles herself before Tom, as do all the other characters, while Chambers is treated as a slave. Tom is a weak, spoiled, and nasty baby, who grows into a worse adult, while Chambers, his servant, is strong, healthy, and capable. Shortly after the babies are born, a stranger from upstate New York, Mr. David Wilson, an amateur scientist fresh out of law school, comes to settle in Dawson's Landing. Wilson is fond of aphorisms, which supply the epigraphs for every chapter in the novel, and identify him with Twain's own creative authority. However, because the inhabitants of Dawson's Creek, like so many other Southern townsfolk in Twain's fiction, are exceedingly dim and do not get his jokes, they respond to his first attempt at humor by branding him a fool, after which he is known around town as a "Puddn'head." Still, Wilson holds the key to the identities of the babies, having taken their "finger-marks" on various occasions (as he has for all the town's inhabitants), and his knowledge is critical to the resolution of the novel's plot.

While never fully endorsing him, Twain implies that the local reading of Puddn'head Wilson reflects more on the town's inhabitants than on Wilson himself. Since his reputation discourages legal clients, Wilson has time for scientific "experiments," including palmistry and the cataloging of people's finger-marks, which appears to be inspired by Francis Galton's *Finger Prints* (a book which Twain read in 1892). Fingerprints, according to Galton, were not only the key to racial identity but also revealed specific character traits such as intelligence. Twain's portrait of Wilson's Galtonian explorations is detailed and careful: he describes the slim box Wilson carries everywhere, with grooves for the minuscule strips of glass; how subjects are asked to rub their fingers through their hair to collect the natural oil before imprinting them on the glass strips. As both a writer and a stranger, drawn to scientific invention and patient in his pursuit of it, Wilson is identified with impulses Twain was himself invested in and valued. Moreover, he is given the role of savior at the novel's end, in providing the legal evidence and counsel that liberates the innocent and damns the culprit. Yet there is irony in the ease with which he settles down finally as a celebrated figure among the townsfolk who once condemned him, especially beside the tragic fates of the other main characters, Roxy, Tom, and Chambers. Twain's ongoing hints that though the town underestimates Wilson they are not altogether off the mark, are confirmed, paradoxically, by the town's eventual acceptance of him. There is no such thing as heroism or happiness in the world of *Puddn'head Wilson*; the best that a character can do is to avoid damnation or ruin. Puddn'head's end is clearly preferable to others: Tom is sold down south; the brokenhearted Roxy is left to find "solace" in church; and Chambers suffers the terrible contradiction of being restored to his rightful legacy, while remaining a slave in bearing and outlook. Nothing is sacred in this novel, including motherhood.

Twain's extraordinary portrait of the white slave mother Roxy provides a profound indictment of the interdependent institutions of slavery and mothering. Though Twain seems at times to be endorsing nature over nurture, much of the responsibility for Tom's character deficiencies are here laid squarely at the feet of perverse mothering. Mothering under slavery cannot be other than a perversion, in Twain's view, but Roxy's imagination is unsurpassed in this respect. "The fiction created by herself" is designed to subvert the "fiction of law and custom" that consigns her white son to slavery, since one good fiction deserves another. The problem is that like all fictions in *Pudd'nhead Wilson*, from the Franklinian aphorisms that fill Wilson's "whimsical calendar," to Twain's own "tangled" text, which he diagnoses as needing a "literary Caesarean operation," it is foiled by human interpreters. As the most uncooperative of heroes, Tom, the protagonist of Roxy's fiction, resists making good of the great opportunity she provides him in switching his identity at birth from slave to heir. Drinking, gambling, lying, thieving, and finally murdering his way into his only possible fate – slavery – Tom fulfills a conviction that runs through all of Twain's fiction: "the main structure of his character was not changed and could not be changed." To attribute Tom's deficiencies to human weakness is not to let the institutions that nourished them off the hook. For the overarching pessimism of *Pudd'nhead Wilson*, like that of *Huckleberry Finn*, is the consequence of a malignant slave system that may be capable in some instances (Jim) of keeping the slave's humanity intact, but never the master's. The effects of the institution, as Twain's Reconstruction memoirs of slavery confirm, linger long after its abolition.

The prospects for black Americans laid out in the various examples discussed, such as W. E. B. Du Bois and Charles Chesnutt, Ida B. Wells, Thomas Nelson Page, and Mark Twain, might be reduced to three distinct possibilities. One option embraced by light-skinned "blacks," exemplified by John Walden of *The House Behind the Cedars* and by countless mulattoes mentioned in Du Bois's Atlanta study, *Health and Physique of American Negroes*, was racial passing, blending imperceptibly into the white race, renouncing one's black past as if it were a bad memory. Another possibility exemplified by the life of Wells and Du Bois was tireless political advocacy on behalf of one's people, which required tremendous reserves of strength in the face of continuous setbacks, and ongoing evidence of the vitality of American racism. Indeed, both Wells and Du Bois demonstrated in their own lives how exceptional talent and determination might bring an individual in one generation from poverty and illiteracy to world fame and intellectual prominence. Yet a third possibility was a more personal and familial struggle against the indignities of life as a black American, finding consolation in religion, and exploiting the available possibilities for social and economic advance. In the next two works by James Weldon Johnson and Pauline Hopkins, two African-American authors writing at the turn of the century, all these prospects are represented. Johnson's alter ego in *The Diary of an Ex-Colored Man* (1912) chooses to abandon his black identity in favor of the racial passing that was available to him. In her novel *Contending Forces* (1900), Pauline Hopkins, a New England author educated in the Boston public schools during the 1860s and 1870s, sketches the prospects of a black middle class in a place where they might flourish. Haunted by a history of slavery and plagued by humiliations and injustices, Hopkins's characters nevertheless manage to succeed in their Boston environment. The possibility represented by Hopkins was realized by many black Americans of her time, and she can be recognized as an author who, along with contemporaries such as Frances Harper, Anna Julia Cooper, and A. E. Johnson, helped to launch a tradition of novels about black middle-class life in America.

By confronting racial passing as its main subject, James Weldon Johnson's *Autobiography of an Ex-Colored Man* reveals just how common passing is in works of the late nineteenth and early twentieth century. It is a fixture in the literature on slavery, where slaves (George Harris of *Uncle Tom's Cabin*; Harriet Jacobs of *Incidents*) regularly pass to escape. It is also integral to Reconstruction narratives, such as Du Bois's *Souls of Black Folk*, which posits a potential causal link between passing and passing, that is, the son's blue eyes and light hair are perceived as a grim omen, in a potential allusion to the myth of mulatto fragility, and Chesnutt's *The House Behind the Cedars*, which features a passing plot. Nor is passing confined to blacks in literature from the turn of the century and later, for Jews in works by Mary Antin (*The Promised Land*) and Abraham Cahan (*The Rise of David Levinsky*) sometimes seek to pass as gentiles in order to become more "American." In Johnson, however, passing is not a step towards Americanization but an escape from it. This is a definitive contrast with the bleak resolutions of the passing scenarios in Charles Chesnutt's novels. Identified with cosmopolitanism rather than Americanization, passing is the means of liberating the race problem from a provincial American context in order to frame it internationally. At the same time, there is in Johnson a pull towards ethnic and racial particularity, which, however elusive and mystifying, is nevertheless powerful. Johnson's narrating protagonist passes equally in the black world and in the white, and passing (or marginality as Chesnutt defined it in his own artistic life), is critical to his creative imagination. Yet the ex-colored man also understands talent, true artistry, as indigenous, requiring attachment to one's cultural roots. Thus, the book distinguishes between being an artist, which depends on owning up to one's ancestry, and being cultured, which depends on abandoning it. Learning languages and playing music in Europe involves a different order of cultural production than building a musical archive at home in the South. The ex-colored man describes how he teaches himself languages, devising a plan which involves memorizing three hundred essential words, along with a set of common phrases, and then forcing himself to speak exclusively in the foreign tongue. The key to a language, he concludes, is its most commonplace ideas and words. The ex-colored man's piano playing, on the other hand, has more to do with inherent talent than acquired skills. His descriptions of pianists emphasize a black legacy, which includes his mother's playing and his first memory of a miraculous ragtime pianist, a legacy symbolized by his own recollected preference for the black over the white piano keys. It is a preference overcome by his growing recognition that the piano's harmonizing of black and white, through the universal appeal of ragtime music in particular, might hold the key to compensating the racial conflicts of his life.

The art of autobiography is itself a paradoxical enterprise for Johnson's ex-colored man, for whom the representation of an extinguished self is both full of pathos and imperiling. To reveal too much is incriminating and threatens his cover. To reveal too little is to leave his necessary mourning for a lamented identity incomplete. For passing, as Chesnutt implies, and Johnson shows definitively, is a death wish, not only for the individual in question, who must nullify a cultural inheritance, but for the culture that provokes the desire, thus repudiating the cultural riches represented by the individual. Johnson's working title for his book was "The Chameleon." The ex-colored man lives up to it, as the ultimate marginal man, who resists attachments, and desires above all to remain indistinct. As a child, he seeks the origins of things, digging below the glass bottoms in his mother's garden to see where they end, obsessing about borders of all kinds, from skin colors to criminal activity. Culture is the place where he can escape boundaries, participating in artistic languages that seem to transcend the color line. Yet culture is marred in this world, just as it is in the world of Du Bois, and the moment of proof is a night at the opera, where the ex-colored man sees his father and white stepsister, and is so disturbed by his own comparative isolation and loneliness that he goes on a drunken binge.

"It's no disgrace to be black, but it's often very inconvenient": this observation might be taken as the ex-colored man's ultimate rationale for passing, until the terrible moment, the most horrific in the narrative, when he witnesses the lynching of a black man, first-hand. Down South to research black spirituals, he happens upon the burning alive of a black man for some indeterminate crime. The scene is rendered with all the vividness one might expect from an author who dedicated his political life to the ill-fated Dyer Anti-Lynching Bill, and was almost lynched himself (for sitting in a park with a very light-skinned black woman). The victim writhes, cries, and groans while the crowd cheers, until he is a pile of scorched bones and fragments of skin. The ex-colored man is convinced that the smell of charred human flesh will remain forever, as he reacts not with rage but with something more vulnerable and human – shame that he belonged to a nation (America) where something so unimaginable could occur, and that he belonged to a people (blacks) who could be so treated. Johnson understood that lynching was sanctioned in part because it distracted from more civil forms of oppression. But it also helped to rationalize these forms as the inevitable lot of a wretched group. The paradox, as Johnson articulated it in his own autobiography, *Along This Way* (1933), was that it took "such tremendous effort on the part of the white man" to keep blacks in the place where "inferior men naturally fall." At the same time, Johnson's visceral portrait of lynching confirms how this inhuman rite degraded everyone. The ex-colored man eventually marries a white woman to whom he reveals his black ancestry. They marry anyway, and have children who look white, and are never told of their father's identity. The narrative ends with the ex-colored man's attendance at a Carnegie Hall benefit, where he hears the Hampton students sing the old songs, and feels a powerful longing for his mother and her people. The featured speakers include C. R. Ogden, ex-ambassador Choate, and Mark Twain. But it is Booker T. Washington who absorbs the ex-colored man's attention, and leads him to conclude that in passing he has been exiled from his people as well as from history.

The characters of Pauline Hopkins's novel, *Contending Forces: A Romance Illustrative of Life North and South* (1900) pursue vastly different goals from James Weldon Johnson's ironically conceived alter ego, whose resolutions would have seemed to Hopkins and her characters both alienating and deplorable. Born in Portland, Maine in 1859, the grandniece of the poet James M. Whitfield, and raised in Boston, where she attended public schools, Hopkins's writing career was launched in 1874 when she won first prize for an essay on intemperance in a contest sponsored by William Wells Brown and the Congregational Publishing Society. In 1880, one of her plays about the Underground Railroad was performed by the "Hopkins' Coloured Troubadours," the family troup that nourished Hopkins's artistic ambitions. Hopkins's writing and editing work culminated in the *Colored American Magazine*, a Boston periodical, founded by the Colored Co-operative Publishing Company, which included Walter Wallace, Jesse W. Watkins, Harper S. Fortune, and Walter A. Johnson. Hopkins served as a contributing editor on the magazine, and its inaugural issue featuring her first published story, "The Mystery Within Us," appeared in 1900, along with *Contending Forces*, which was also published by the Colored Co-operative. While earning her living as a stenographer at the Bureau of Statistics, and later at the Massachusetts Institute of Technology, Hopkins served as contributing editor of the *Colored People's Magazine* (1903–04). *Contending Forces*, the only novel Hopkins published during her life, was advertised as "a race-work dedicated to the best interests of the Negro everywhere," and Hopkins understood its purpose as alleviating the degradation of her race. That the political views of Hopkins were more in keeping with the Du Bois wing of black activism than the Booker T. Washington wing of black accommodation was signaled by her resignation (possibly forced) from the staff of the *Colored People's Magazine*, when it was taken over by Washington's disciple, Fred R. Moore. Shortly thereafter, Hopkins secured work on a periodical called *The Voice of the Negro*, whose political perspective was closer to her own. Hopkins also co-founded, with Walter Wallace, a small publishing company in 1905, which issued a history book entitled *A Primer of Facts Pertaining to the Early Greatness of the African Race and the Possibility of Restoration by Its Descendants*, as well as a short-lived magazine, the *New Era*. Hopkins lived through the Harlem Renaissance, but continued her split life as a stenographer by day and a writer by night. She died tragically in a fire in 1930, her work unheralded until long after her death.

Contending Forces features a melodramatic plot and a range of settings, extending from Bermuda to North Carolina and Boston. Hopkins begins in the Americas, with the brutal slavery of the British Bermudas at the turn of the nineteenth century, which included intermarriage between landowners and their lightest and most comely female slaves. The opening "Tragedy" section recounts the story of the Monforts and their sons, Charles and Jesse, who discover their slave status after their father's death, and lose both freedom and fortune. The shift to late nineteenth-century Boston is abrupt, but enhanced by another engaging set of characters, principally Sappho Clark, a lovely mulatto who will help to reveal yet another major setting – mid nineteenth-century New Orleans with its terrible custom of slave concubinage. When Hopkins turns to her Boston plot, centered around "Ma Smith's Lodging-House," her subject becomes turn-of-the century black American society and the achievements wrested from a largely hostile environment. Excluded from every viable business and profession, black families still manage to live decently and to cultivate the talents of their children. She compares the plights of blacks with Jews and highlights the patient striving of both peoples to earn livelihoods. Despite the prevailing American preoccupation with money, she observes, citing the central questions of the day as tariff reform, the parity of gold and silver, the role of trusts and combinations, no social problem is more critical than that of race.

Hopkins seems determined to provide her own form of consciousness-raising in the novel, by invoking an unexpected hierarchy of color. Will Smith, the hero and eventual suitor of Sappho, has an almond complexion with curly black hair that unmistakably registers his black blood and depresses the wealthy white women who wonder why such manly beauty should be wasted on a racial inferior. Loosely modeled on W. E. B. Du Bois, Smith is an intellectual and outspoken in his demand for equal rights and attacks on lynching. The novel's villain, the weak and hypocritical John Langley, is contrastingly fair complexioned, easily capable of passing as white. Sappho, who lodges at the Smith house and works as a stenographer is, like Will, "gorgeous" but definitively "black." For Hopkins, the apparent ideal is to be identifiably Negro while drawing on the best and brightest. An undesirable fate is to unite the inferior blood of representatives of either race, as does John Langley, whose ancestors include low-status whites and blacks. Hopkins's variegated cast includes a Booker T. Washington figure, Dr. Arthur Lewis, a businessman with a large industrial school in the South. She also offers the story of Luke Sawyer, who endures the ruin of his father, a successful storeowner, and then the destruction of his adoptive mulatto family in New Orleans, a family that includes Mabelle Beaubean, who turns out to be Sappho herself. Hopkins manages to energize her brimming plot through the continuous promise that these characters will eventually be revealed as kin, in fulfillment of the relations that form the legacy of black people in America. This is the past; as for the future, Hopkins articulates her deepest ideals on race through Will Smith, who insists that neither subordination nor miscegenation will do. Blacks must advance as a people on their own terms, through education, political activism, and voting, using whatever means at their disposal for shaping public opinion and spreading the ideal of justice. In short, Hopkins dramatized in her novel the goals she pursued in her own active life.

Hopkins's *Contending Forces*, which insisted that any account of the black American present and future be informed by recognition of the group's enslaved past, fulfills the highest aims of W. E. B. Du Bois, who distinguished the critical scrutiny of his people's past from a preoccupation with victimization. Du Bois acknowledged Hopkins as a fellow traveler, when he noted in a piece on the *Colored American Magazine* for the *Crisis*, that Hopkins was relieved of her editorship because "her attitude was not conciliatory enough." The agenda outlined by Du Bois and Hopkins included fortifying the black community in its own right while demanding social opportunities and legal rights from the dominant culture. Both believed that only the highest ambitions and ideals, and the most radical political claims, would enable their people to embrace full citizenship in the modern era. Still, the resolution of James Weldon Johnson's "ex-colored man" remained compelling to many Americans just entering the national fold, whether from conditions of enslavement or from foreign countries. To abandon an afflicted past for an enlightened cosmopolitanism, or simply for the sake of altered consciousness itself, was the dream of many literary immigrants, whose aspirations sometimes proved deadly. But this was a sacrifice that characters – both literary and non-literary – from Abraham Cahan's Yekl to Willa Cather's Mary Baker Eddy, were prepared to make.

4

❦

COSMOPOLITAN VARIATIONS

THE WORKS DISCUSSED in this chapter include classic novellas (e.g. Jack London's *The Call of the Wild*), immigrant novels and letters (e.g. Abraham Cahan's *Yekl* and *A Bintel Brief*), social scientific studies of immigration and religious extremism (by Edward A. Ross and William James), autobiographies (Alice James's *Diary*, Helen Keller's *The Story of My Life*), biographies (of Mary Baker Eddy), and major American novels (e.g. *McTeague, The House of Mirth, The Turn of the Screw, The Wings of the Dove*). These works will be examined as narratives that draw their chief inspiration from some of the most important changes of the late nineteenth century: the human displacements issuing from urbanization, migration, and immigration. Much of the literature is set in urban locales: San Francisco, Frank Norris's *Vandover and the Brute* and *McTeague*; London and Venice, Henry James's *Wings of the Dove*; New Orleans, Chopin's *The Awakening*; New York, Cahan's *Yekl* and Wharton's *House of Mirth*; Boston, which provided a perfect environment for the flowering of Mary Baker Eddy's Christian Science. But some of it is centered in the dilapidated regions left behind (Wharton's *Ethan Frome*) or the wilderness conceived as ideal alternatives (London's *The Call of the Wild*). And some of it is located in worlds that are, for different reasons, boundless: the infinite white darkness of Helen Keller; the hyper-consciousness of Henry James's "life after death"; the heavens of Mark Twain and Elizabeth Stuart Phelps. The human characters introduced in these works are memorable, usually for their peculiarity, excessiveness, or frailty. These are people incapable of simply "getting along" in the places they are thrown into – often distinguished by their vulnerability to the elements and failure to survive. Some are suicides (Lily Bart, Edna Pontellier); some are murdered (Trina McTeague, John Thornton); some die of natural causes (Milly Theale, Alice James); some from causes beyond nature (Miles); many endure as fragments of their original selves (Yekl, Merton Densher, Ethan Frome, Vandover).

Together these texts provide intimate human variations on a central American theme of mobility and self-transformation during a time when the country was triumphing over competitors like Argentina, Brazil, and industrialized

Western Europe in the international competition for cheap immigrant labor, and averaging over five million newcomers a decade between 1880 and 1920. Due in part to extensive industrialization and technological innovation (and the jobs, housing, and modern transportation systems they produced) the total urban population during the 1880s increased by 56.4 percent. In the late nineteenth century twenty farmers moved to the city for every urbanite who moved to the land (where recurrent depressions and mechanized farming reduced job opportunities), while ten farming offspring became urbanites for every one who remained a farmer. In 1860 immigrants comprised 40 percent of the populations of major American cities including New York, Chicago, and San Francisco; by 1910, the population of immigrants and their American-born children had risen to 70 percent in major cities (New York, Chicago, Boston, Detroit etc.) The result of this rapid expansion and diversification was a certain fragmentation of urban social life, which however charged with opportunity could seem vast and unsettling to native, migrant, and immigrant alike.

These urban landscapes proved a critical testing ground for the new science of sociology, which specialized in studies of immigration and urbanization. The German sociologist, Georg Simmel, whose writings were translated and published in *The American Journal of Sociology* during the 1890s, and University of Chicago sociologists such as W. I. Thomas and Robert Park, described the new forms of social alienation issuing from urban industrial capitalism. In his pioneering study, *The Philosophy of Money* and in highly original essays on such subjects as fashion, miserliness, and marginality, Simmel described the restlessness aroused by the constant stimulation as well as the rationalization of modern society, which afforded greater freedoms at the same time that it yielded more intricate interdependencies. The problems arising from the racial and ethnic heterogeneity of cities and the escalation of social deviance were of central concern to Thomas and Park. Thomas won renown for work on the psychology of race prejudice and on delinquency among female adolescents and also for his major account of the Polish peasant in Europe and America, while Park, a close associate of Booker T. Washington's, studied the impact of popular media, journalism in particular, as well as the process of assimilation, focusing on how a common urban experience might be shaped from the diverse conditions of the modern city.

The dis-ease of cosmopolitanism is dramatized in the writings explored below, which convey the varieties of disenchantment that accompany the late nineteenth century experience of modernization. Anxieties, depression, alienation were common afflictions in a society that seemed to be changing at a relentless pace. While some writers, Jack London and Frank Norris most memorably, entertained the prospect of a wilderness life as the alternative to the suffocations of urbanity, their characters brought their dilemmas with them into the wild, and discovered that these landscapes barely resembled the pristine vacancies they imagined them to be. Migration, immigration, and urbanization become the focus here as the most concrete versions of a dislocation that many understood in more elusive and abstract terms.

NATIVE AND IMMIGRANT "CASES"

Frank Norris (1870–1902), who was born in Chicago and raised in San Francisco, specialized in maladjusted, freakish characters, whose dominant impulses – miserliness, materialism, greed, compulsiveness – seemed generated by the conditions of modernization. In his best novel, *McTeague: A Story of San Francisco* (1899), an old seamstress spends her days contemplating the thin wall that separates her from the withered bookbinder whom she loves and is therefore incapable of addressing. The ranch-owner protagonist of *The Octopus* (1901), who leads a battle against the railroad, is so distressed by women that he flees like a jackrabbit when any approach. But perhaps no character in all of Norris is more odd and entangled than the protagonist of his first novel, *Vandover and the Brute* (1894, published 1914), a study of degeneration written during Norris's sojourn as a special student at Harvard. The following year (1895–96), Norris left for South Africa to cover the events of the Boer War, his journalism reflecting his sympathies for the Uitlanders or English, whom he saw as latter-day American colonists aroused over the familiar grievance of taxation without representation. Kruger's Boers eventually defeated Jameson's Uitlanders, and Norris ended up with a severe case of South African fever that plagued him until his early death in 1902.

Like so many other Realist-Naturalist writers, Norris cut his literary teeth as a reporter for a city paper, the San Francisco *Wave*, which distinguished itself from competitors such as William Randolph Hearst's *Examiner* and Arthur McEwen's *Chronicle* by its consistent support of C. P. Huntington and the Railroad Trust. The literary department, which featured writings by Ambrose Bierce, Jack London, and Will Irwin, among others, was the pride of editor John O'Hara Cosgrove, who hired Norris to write local sketches – a carnival, a group of Italians making claret, a fresh oyster meal on the wharf at Belmont camp. The deliberateness with which Norris set out to capture the peculiar literary magic of this Western city was forecast in an 1897 *Wave* article in which he proclaimed the aesthetic potential of a city whose typical inhabitants seemed already fictional. Norris attributed this to San Francisco's unique isolation, which made its people distinctive as well as intense. Eschewing a literature of mere observation, Norris would aim, in terms derived from Zola, for the heart of reality by means of a few true touches. As his editor Cosgrave recollected, Norris "had no faculty of physical attention, but after having been to a place, exposed to its stimuli, he could describe it – *on paper* – with complete verisimiltude. I used to say that his pores served him as visual organs."

Vandover and the Brute reveals Norris's equally strong instinct for characterization. Vandover is a naturalist's Huckleberry Finn with his willed amnesia, his sensuality, his tendency to level all experience, his innocent amorality. The novel opens with the death of Vandover's invalid mother at a trainstop in western New York, during the family's "migration" from East coast to West. The eight-year-old child registers with anesthetized precision the details of the scene. Unable to distinguish the capricious from the grave, he evinces the total recall of a traumatized child who *would* remember exactly where the mother's head rested for her last breath, *would* remember where the father kept his comb and cigars, *would* know every line on the dying invalid face; *would* remember how the porter wiped his forehead and where he put the surplus sweat. The narrator's few observations are a model of restraint: a comment – "the journey was too much for her" – and an image of the patient animal-like train almost blameworthy in its brimming health, "sitting back on its motionless drivers like some huge sphinx crouching along the rails . . . steaming quietly, drawing long breaths."

The novel proceeds as a *Bildungsroman* qualified by Naturalist melodrama. Vandover's discovery of sex in an *Encyclopedia Britannica* entry on obstetrics is life-altering, while his unusual pliability and impulsive need for comfort are signs of eventual brutishness. His life is an ongoing struggle between a civil self – ambitious to paint, respectful of his father and love interest, the virtuous Turner Ravis – and animal self – preoccupied with needs, frequenting prostitutes, requiring constant vigilance. The great allegorical painting, "The Last Enemy," which the dissipated Vandover is incapable of reproducing on the point of his ultimate downward spiral, captures his predicament and that of humanity in general. Depicting a dying British cavalryman and his loyal horse, with a predatory lion closing in, tail menacingly erect, jaw hanging, the painting replicates the inner struggle between the good Vandover (cavalryman), whose refinement is set in relief by his pet dog, Cork (horse), and Vandover the Brute (lion), suffering from *Lycanthropy-Mathesis*, the technical term for a wolf-man.

The novel's main plot events serve to flesh out these Darwinian themes. The shipwreck of the *Mazatlan*, during Vandover's return from a European sojourn, highlights self-preservation rationalized via anti-Semitism: the cruel barring of a Jew from the lifeboat, a collective racialist version of Vandover's instinct. A fierce struggle ensues: the scrappy Jewish diamond-dealer tries to battle his way aboard (with some defending his inclusion) and loses, the water reddening as his body sinks. The final blow to Vandover's humanity is the death of his father, who expires, like the mother, posed familiarly in his favorite chair. The ordinariness of this imperceptible drift into death parallels the awful accessibility of Norris's characters, Vandover is an extreme within range of the typical. His inability to respond to these parental deaths erupts eventually in the most relentless kind of responsiveness.

Norris conveys Vandover's complex relationship to loss in parallel scenes following his father's funeral. The first describes the butler in the father's smoking room, opening windows, sweeping, "rearranging" furniture. The second describes Vandover, two weeks later, in the same smoking room, wondering at the ease with which he has accepted his father's death, how he has "rearranged" himself according to his new circumstances. Espying his father's effects, Vandover slips a pen and knife into his pocket, reserving cigars, gum, crumpled handkerchiefs for a special collection in his closet. The scene suggests how objects serve to mediate memories and emotions. Grief is situated in a sense, managed, but also made plain, and set in relief, by the arrangement of familiar possessions. This is an insight found in all of Norris's novels – one thinks especially here of *McTeague* – where objects are consistently invested with a great responsive capacity. It is not just that trains become animals, it is that objects are themselves packed with emotional intensity, with all the sentiment they arouse in the people who own them. In part this is because they absorb the expressiveness that has been depleted from human relations. But also, quite differently, it is because human beings cannot cope with their overwhelming feelings of loss, and find that such feelings can be valuably controlled when transferred to objects. The animation of the material world in Norris's narratives reflects the monumental intensity of his characters, who, like comic-strip superheroes, often seem outsized in the Western city streets where most of Norris's novels are set.

Rigorous laws of etiquette restrain human emotions in the novels of Edith Wharton, but similar exchanges between the human and the material prevail. Her works convey the faith in magical property that runs through literary Realism and Naturalism, resonating with Marxian economics on commodity fetishism, and with anthropological conceptions of gift exchange. Wharton's decadent New Yorkers, ever on the point of reversion to savagery, and Norris's San Franciscans, share a common destiny. Their ruin signals threats upon urban elites from without and within. Vandover, who ends up an abject janitor at the San Francisco workers' cottages he once owned, subject to recurrent bouts of lycanthropy, and Lily Bart (the protagonist of *The House of Mirth*, 1905), who ends up a penniless suicide in a shabby New York boarding house, present shocking mirrors of class decline. "To think I was a Harvard man once!" Vandover mourns, just as Lily marvels at her former socializing with women whose hats she now decorates among "the underworld of toilers." A flood of immigrants; a newly radicalized working class; a vibrant commerce and fluctuating economy that empowers innumerable parvenus – all this is matched in elite minds by their own diminishing work ethic, by moral and spiritual turpitude, and by shrinking birth rates. The somber fates of Vandover and Lily register authorial convictions of class crisis that were widespread.

Edmund Wilson's characterization of Wharton (1862–1937) as the "poet of interior decoration" confirms her dependence on beautiful objects and their owners. Wharton's first published book, *The Decoration of Houses* (1897), co-authored with Ogden Codman, a renowned home designer, argued that interiors – wallpaper, furnishings and their arrangement – should express the individuality of the woman of the house, while conforming to classical principles of proportion. This is consistent with the extent to which things in Wharton's novels, hats, jewelry, books, rugs, tea trays, speak worlds about those who wear and display them. While Wharton appreciates material splendor (she is in sympathy with her heroine Lily Bart's rapture over her dresses), she recognizes the cost of that appreciation. In *The House of Mirth*, her first major novel, which was serialized in *Scribner's Magazine* (January–November, 1905) prior to its publication as a Scribner book, Wharton treated the New York leisure class from the perspective of an intelligent observer, spawned and nourished by it but never wholly committed to its norms. When the novel first appeared, some complained that Wharton had preyed on her own circle and exposed it to the scrutiny of society at large. The bestselling novel's success was due in part to the voyeurism of ordinary Americans whose infatuation with the rich is depicted in the novel itself.

Wharton seems to have been aware that the novel betrayed class secrets. She was familiar with Thorstein Veblen's 1899 *Theory of the Leisure Class*, and the correspondence between his searing analysis of elite economic habits and Wharton's fictional critique is noteworthy. Veblen's basic claim was that wealthy urbanites acquired and maintained status by openly displaying how much they could afford to waste. Indeed, it was the specific function of wives to represent the financial power of their husbands through their conspicuous leisure and consumption. People in capitalist society, Veblen argued, were obsessively imitative, defining their well being in comparison to others, caught up in a perpetual cycle of desire fueled by the need to surpass their neighbors. In *The House of Mirth*, this culture of competitive display is sustained by publicity.

The novel's opening offers a contrast between different social spheres: New York high society, where the right people are recognized, and a vast –

international as well as national – network (of professionalism, commerce, the stock exchange), which impinges on everyone, anonymously. Increasingly pervasive engines of publicity – newspapers, magazines – which make different classes appear accessible to one another, qualify a growing sense of distance among classes, and between individuals and social institutions. By personalizing representatives of specific classes and milieus, the media makes the social world knowable. A culture where the dominant aim is exposure – of oneself and others – is a culture ruled by the market. For Wharton, it is inevitable that individuals embrace the ruthless ethos of exchange. Thus, in the novel's climactic *tableau vivant* scene, Lily and other marriageable women literalize their commodity status by personifying the subjects of famous portraits. Lily's transformation into Reynolds's "Mrs. Lloyd" liberates Selden's passion; he is able to love Lily through the temporary confirmation of her value as an artistic masterpiece. Selden's ultimate refusal to "invest" in Lily, to take risks with his emotional capital, reflects a miserliness that is epitomized by Lily's aunt, Mrs. Peniston, who disinherits Lily and seals her doom.

Wharton's ideal is an inherent nobility and traditionalism set against the indiscriminate logic of market forces. Economic poverty is only skin-deep. A deeper impoverishment lies in disconnection from one's roots, bloodlines, beliefs and loyalties transmitted between generations, regions, and homes inhabited for centuries. The Darwinian rapaciousness that characterizes her novel's social set, from this perspective, represents a modern reduction of its original greatness. This would make the mildly sympathetic yet ultimately repudiated Jewish character, Mr. Rosedale, emblematic of what must be resisted. Wharton's alternative includes an image of virtuous poverty personified by Nettie Strether, the gentle working-class mother whose interests are aligned with those of a genuine elite. The poor will always exist, she suggests, like birds building their nests on the edges of cliffs. Meanwhile, the inherently noble, that is, the Seldens and the Barts, must stick together, however meager their prospects. This is the tragic recognition afforded Selden at the novel's end. If the white Anglo-Saxon aristocratic tribe can grasp this renewed sense of obligation, then Lily Bart will not have died in vain.

Lily Bart's dilemma arises from dispossession and displacement. Her father's lost fortune, Lily's subsequent dependence on self-serving relatives and friends, her own resentment of this dependence, which leads to self-destructive behavior, all contribute to her demise. Yet the roots of Lily's doom lie in the particular plight of leisure-class women, who are raised to be objects of admiration, who are denied vocations, and who are taught to cultivate their irrelevance. To lack a sense of purpose in a society where success among all classes was increasingly defined by the possession of marketable skills or professional status was a form of deprivation unique to female members of a paradoxical American aristocracy. No figure in the late nineteenth century was more tragically representative of this situation than Alice James, who was unable to build on her talents or on the material and intellectual opportunities afforded by her distinguished family. Like other (mostly female) members of Anglo-American and European elites in the era before Freud's "talking cure" was made widely available, the search for peace and contentment itself became her life's vocation.

In 1894, shortly after Alice James's death, her friend and apparent lover, Katharine Peabody Loring, who had cared for Alice during her illness, edited the manuscript of Alice's diary and sent copies to the surviving James brothers. William never acknowledged receiving it and Henry destroyed his copy, advising Loring not to publish it because it compromised the privacy of so many. These responses typify the indifference towards her ambitions displayed by Alice's brothers throughout her life. Though she belittled them herself, these ambitions were appropriate to a family of cosmopolitan intellectuals. Born in New York City in 1848, Alice was the youngest, and only daughter of the five children of Mary and Henry James Sr. Her education, like that of her brothers, was variegated, often disrupted by their father's urge to relocate. Alice suffered from this peripatetic childhood; by her adolescence, which coincided with the Civil War, she was a semi-invalid, forecasting the physical and emotional problems of her adulthood. While brothers Bob and Wilky fought for the Union and William and Henry tested vocations, Alice suffered collective (the national spectacle of death) and individual (her vexed mind and body) woes.

It is unclear exactly what was wrong with Alice, but it appears to have been, at least in part, the neurasthenia to which all the Jameses were prone: excessive nervousness, possessions by strange phantoms, overwhelmingly direct encounters with evil personified. The fact that the least successful members of the family were the most permanently damaged by such illnesses, suggests its root in feelings of inadequacy and deprivation. Hence Henry's rather insidious characterization of Alice: "Tragic health was, in a manner, the only solution for her of the practical problem of life." Alice became familiar with prevailing antidotes for unclassifiable disease: ice and electric therapy, blistering baths, and the famed rest cure of S. Weir Mitchell – force-feeding and the cessation of all activity. When Alice met Katherine Loring in 1873 – she was twenty-six and Loring twenty-five – there was an immediate attraction. Alice discovered in Katherine the perfect blend of gender attributes, the strength to accomplish the most demanding "masculine" tasks – hewing wood and capturing runaway horses – combined with admirable feminine traits. Observing the pair in Europe in 1884, Henry James noted the benefits of the relationship, and advised his family to accept it gratefully. Alice lived as an invalid without a specifiable illness until 1891 when doctors discovered breast cancer. Alice faced what she called, "the great mortuary moment," with her usual blend of irony and reverence. She died in March 1892, with Katharine and Henry by her side, and was cremated, her ashes buried in the family plot in Mt. Auburn Cemetery, Cambridge.

Alice began her diary in December of 1886, regarding it initially as a commonplace book for copying quotations from her voluminous reading – e.g. Howells, Loti, La Bruyère, Flaubert, Edgar Quinet, Cotton Mather, George Sand, Tolstoy, Renan, Auguste Comte, works by her brothers. By 1889, however, she had begun to take it more seriously as an aesthetic means for compensating a wasted life. Having lived so long a prisoner to her body, Alice sought in her diary to convert those physical limitations into imaginative art. "The paralytic on the couch can have if he wants them wider experiences than Stanley slaughtering savages," she proclaimed. Despite Alice's apparent belief in her intellect's subjection to her body, there is much in the James family history to suggest Alice's body was a casualty of her devalued mind. Alice's biographer notes that her father underrated female intellect, and highlights a familial economy in which one member's achievement required another's failure. William and Henry's professional triumphs, as philosopher and as literary author, respectively, were measured against the inadequacies of the younger brothers and the irrelevance of Alice. This explains the abjection of the diary's speaker, who tends toward defeatist rhetoric – declaring herself a "little rubbish heap" or "mildewed toadstool." Like others who are strong-willed but overlooked, Alice is obsessed with power and politics, and at times absorbs the strength of those she admires, claiming at one point, "the potency of a Bismarck." In keeping with this, the diary is full of hostility and aggression – towards acquaintances, servants, the world at large, her family above all. Writing, in this sense, provides less a means of exorcising disappointment and despair than of staging it. Much of the diary is devoted to the time before her death and the narrative is striking in its lack of self-pity, guilt, or fear. While this may signal the emptiness of her life, it also confirms the singularity of this lone James sister. Alice confronts death without religious comfort, dismissing requests to transmit messages in heaven, and repudiating brother William's latest spiritual advisor. She is a full participant in the ritual plans for her dead body, and speaks openly of impending cremation, imagining Katharine transporting her ashes across the ocean.

Alice James, who had never felt at home anywhere, might have fancied herself an immigrant, forced to abandon her country in search of the material security that provided her little consolation. Among these immigrants, none knew better than Abraham Cahan the stresses of transplantation, and the limitations of affluence in offsetting its effects. Editor of the *Jewish Daily Forward* from its founding in 1897 until his death in 1951 and author of the first major Jewish-American novel, *The Rise of David Levinsky* (1917), Cahan was the leading proponent of Jewish-American writing and socialist culture in the major stage of Jewish immigration. Born in Padberberezer, Lithuania in 1860, offspring of orthodox rabbis and teachers, Cahan soon demonstrated that his own abilities would be best nourished by a secular education. He graduated from government schools, and worked as a teacher, until his revolutionary activity forced his 1882 emigration to America. Shortly after the twenty-two year old Cahan began work in a New York sweatshop, he joined the labor movement, and by August, 1882, he was delivering Yiddish addresses for the "Propaganda *Verein*" a group of Russian and German immigrants dedicated to promoting socialism and anarchism among their fellow Jews. He became the major Yiddish speaker for a group whose rallying cry was "in the mother tongue we must agitate among the Jews." As a writer for two Yiddish socialist weeklies, the *Neuezeit* and the *Arbeiter Zeitung*, Cahan expressed an idealism that saw in America the potential for a just social order. Such idealism aroused serious resistance, including the denunciation of its proponents as alien advocates of sedition. A veritable Renaissance man, who worked as a teacher, labor organizer, orator, editor, novelist, and journalist, Cahan was up to the challenges of life as an ethnic outsider determined to reform his new country.

Though he published primarily in Yiddish-American magazines, Cahan aspired to an English readership. In his five-volume autobiography, he described the inspiration he drew from Hawthorne, James, and Howells. His first story in English, published in 1895, earned the acclaim of Howells, who had met Cahan while gathering information for *A Traveler From Altruria*, which Cahan later translated into Yiddish and published in the *Forward*. Howells admired Cahan's fresh depictions of Jewish immigrants, and helped him to find a publisher for his first novel, *Yekl: A Tale of the Ghetto* (1896). Reviewing the book for the New York *World*, Howells called Cahan "a new star of realism," and later commended both his *Imported Bridegroom and Other Stories of Yiddish New York* (1898) and *The Rise of David Levinsky*, which echoed Howells's own *The Rise of Silas Lapham* (1885).

Because Howells was not a reader of Yiddish, he knew only second-hand what many would consider Cahan's greatest triumph, his fifty-four year editorship of *The Jewish Daily Forward*. At the beginning of Cahan's tenure, circulation was below 6,000, attributable, he felt, to the paper's intellectualized Yiddish and penchant for abstract theory, which alienated even East Side Jews whose appetite for Tolstoy, Spencer, and Darwin sustained a pushcart trade in these works. Cahan introduced colloquial Yiddish and increased the number of human interest features. As reported by the New York *Evening Post*, "within eight weeks after Cahan had taken hold of *Forward*, its circulation trebled . . . And now it has a daily circulation of over 130,000 a day" (July 27, 1912). Cahan's democratizing aims were exemplified by columns such as a "Gallery of Missing Husbands," which exposed men who had abandoned their families by printing their pictures, and a regular column called the *Bintel Brief*, or "a bundle of letters," addressed to the editor by ordinary people. Cahan had long sought to provide a forum that allowed readers to express the difficulties as well as the miracles of immigration. Begun in January, 1906, the *Bintel Brief*, Cahan noted in his autobiography, served the "hundreds of thousands of people, torn from their homes and their dear ones . . . lonely souls who thirsted for expression, who wanted to hear an opinion, who wanted advice in solving their weighty problems." The column grew so popular that writing letters (for the illiterate) to the *Bintel Brief* became an occupation in its own right. Initially, Cahan answered all the letters himself, responding to mothers searching for children, workers with tyrannical bosses, young men and women facing marriage decisions. The editor was a confidant as well as spiritual advisor, a job counselor and therapist. A wife whose husband had survived a Russian pogrom and emigrated, only to become obsessed with the Kiev ritual murder trial of the Jew, Mendel Beilis, was advised to find him a good psychiatrist; others were directed to relief agencies, unions, and back to the old country.

Whether they wrote to offer wisdom or to obtain it, *Bintel Brief* authors confirmed the trials of assimilation. Accordingly, "Americanization" is an ambivalent enterprise in Cahan's fiction, implanting values – the passion for baseball, dancing, and women in *Yekl: A Tale of the New York Ghetto* (1896), or material greed in *The Rise of David Levinsky* – that mar human fullness and authenticity. Immigration initiates the death of the old country self, which is replaced by its ghostly semblance in America. *Yekl* recurs frequently to the protagonist's religious upbringing, his mother's superstitions, his father's blacksmith shop, while highlighting the gradual process whereby "Yekl" becomes "Jake": the waning of religious convictions, the condescending attitude towards the past. Cahan's resistance to the dominant American values that dazzle his protagonist gives the novel a consistent tension and unpredictability while his account of ghetto life is rich and detailed. Cahan depicts the persistent spirituality of Jews (which may intensify as they drift from fulfillment of their religious obligations) enlivening the world around them, investing material things with awesome power. Jake's guilt feelings over his father's death lead to dread of his ghost. The helplessness of Jake's transplanted wife, Gitl, is reflected in her terror of American novelties – stoves, washtubs, painted broomsticks. Ordinary bedclothes become burial shrouds, as Jake contemplates abandoning his wife and child. These imaginings depend on Judaic and American legacies: haunted characters in *midrashic* tales, as well as the tortured souls of Hawthorne's fiction.

Cahan's multicultural realism insists on moral and psychological complexity. The abandoned wife is hardly a victim, however pathetic at the rabbinic divorce court or telling her son of his father's flight. She finds a new husband and establishes a grocery business. Meanwhile, the protagonist is made wretched at the novel's end by the recognition that his misery is just. Cahan's immigrants are harsh and ungenerous: those who suffer deserve to. Those who do not are lucky. Yet they all remain compelling. Cahan added unique elements to an American literary tradition.

The continuous prospect of revitalization represented by immigration at its best was not taken lightly by American social scientists who were professionally preoccupied with its effects. Yet these experts – for example, the Massachusetts Institute of Technology economist Francis A. Walker and the University of Wisconsin sociologist Edward A. Ross – could be the most formidable of national gatekeepers. Social scientists sought to appraise immigration from the standpoint of "native" Americans, as Ross did in his influential book, *The Old World In The New: The Significance Of Past And Present Immigration To The American People* (1914). Ross emphasized the vigor and piety of the English, Dutch, Germans, Scots, who settled a wilderness for the sake of principle, surviving hardships more recent stocks could not have tolerated. The challenges of immigration in the seventeenth and eighteenth centuries ensured that only the strong would transmit their traits to future Americans. The greater ease of immigration since the mid nineteenth century enabled the incorporation of weaker foreign strains. Citing Francis Walker's well-known statistics on the fatal relationship between high rates of immigration and falling native birth rates, Ross argued that American elites were in danger of extinction. By claiming that Americans were more imperiled by immigration than immigrants themselves, these analyses provided a curious counterpart to immigrant narratives lamenting the overpowering effects of Americanization.

Increased reproduction rates for the middle and upper classes was the solution to various social ills proposed by Anglo-American social scientists and echoed by many at the turn of the century. This is one reason why novels like Kate Chopin's *The Awakening* (1899), which portrayed a leisure-class Protestant woman devoid of maternal instinct, aroused the ire of readers. The book was removed from the public library in St. Louis, Chopin's home town, and prompted her expulsion from the city's Fine Arts Club. Most reviewers objected to a wife and mother who neglected her children, engaged in adultery, drank and gambled for amusement, and then drowned herself in an apparent fit of *ennui*. Chopin (1851–1904), forty-eight when *The Awakening* appeared, was already an author of note, having published over a hundred stories, essays, and sketches in popular and elite magazines. A widow with six children and a plantation to manage, Chopin wrote when she could spare time from her maternal and commercial obligations. There is no denying that Edna Pontellier is self-indulgent and passive in her unhappiness, inarticulate to a degree that some readers find appealing, others maddening. It is a testimony to Chopin's craft that she manages to make a heroine who behaves this way matter deeply. The novel inspired some reviewers while enraging others, but all were captivated by its intense narrative style. *The Awakening* was written with a sensuality and precision that was new in American writing at the time.

Chopin's portrait of Edna Pontellier anticipates Freud on the troubled lives of upper-class women, and complements the conclusions of modern feminists as well as more conservative social scientists. For feminists (e.g. Charlotte Perkins Gilman, Willa Cather), women are burdens to themselves and others because they are denied educational and professional opportunities that would lead to greater fulfillment. For social scientists (e.g., S. Weir Mitchell, G. Stanley Hall, Herbert Spencer), modern women are dissatisfied because they resist what comes naturally – mothering, housekeeping, modeling virtue. Chopin's narrative beckons the question of "what's wrong with Edna" by having so many characters pose it. Edna may be a classic "hysteric" or a "normal" woman driven to depression and rebellion by the meagerness of her social role. Yet Chopin also ascribes Edna's discontent to her familial and cultural background. Born in Kentucky, raised as a Presbyterian, Edna's lifelong struggle with affect and attachment makes her marriage to a Creole Catholic partly therapeutic. In contrast to the warmth and cohesiveness of her husband's culture, Edna's upbringing is a litany of losses: her mother's early death, her father's narcissism and alcoholism, the mutual hostility implied in Edna's refusal to attend her sister's wedding. Edna's isolation is cultural, issuing from the emptiness of American Protestantism and its excessive individualism, values justified by the philosophy of Emerson, which, significantly, puts Edna to sleep. Over the course of the novel Edna experiences others increasingly as encumbrances, finding human connections threatening to her self-development.

Yet what made the book so provocative was its candid account of problems that were central to modern democratic society: the position of women; the inherence of maternal self-sacrifice; the limited satisfactions of material possessions; the value of life itself. In picturing a discontented wife and mother whose comfortable existence fails to satisfy her, and whose final suicide appears preferable to her pain, Chopin raises questions about the liberal individual's relationship to death, and women's potential to *be* liberal individuals. *The Awakening* can be read as a defense of suicide, a questioning of the secular valuation of life above all else (known and unknown). Chopin's is the first American novel to confront the seductiveness of death unqualified by religious faith, in keeping with a poetic tradition that runs from Walt Whitman's "Vigil Strange I Kept on the Field One Night" to Robert Frost's "Stopping By Woods On A Snowy Evening." Death is likened to a return for Edna, to the womb of same-sex desire which is implied in Edna's attraction to the voluptuous "mother-woman" Madame Ratignolle. This is not to dismiss the significance of the ending for postmodern feminism. Standard feminist interpretations see Edna Pontellier awakened to the limits on her aspirations, whether they deem it disappointing (she might have endured to model a vividly feminist life) or valuable (yielding a feminist martyr). Yet the novel also supports a more radical feminist alternative: the story of a "consciousness raised" beyond the ideals of her society. Understood in conventional terms, nature, represented by the look and feel of the sea, prevails at the novel's end, affirming women's basic affinities with its rhythms over and above the prospects of society and civilization. By picturing the allure of nature over the dissatisfactions of modern urban life, Chopin was joining a cross-gender dialogue whose most prominent participants were novelists like Frank Norris and Jack London.

THE LURE OF THE WILD

Contemporary efforts to institutionalize the wild, in the form of urban parks and zoos, and the creation of protected wilderness territories; the popularity of groups like the Rough Riders and the Boy Scouts, which emphasized survival skills, were means of communing with nature while expressing anxieties about its projected disappearance and about the increasing artificiality of modern life. The future of American fiction, according to Norris and London, lay in the abandonment of elegant scenes and stylistics, in favor of rugged narratives of Darwinian struggle. Norris was part of a group of American writers, which included London, Stephen Crane, and Owen Wister, among others, who conceived a role for novelists in mediating the charged tensions between human nature and civilization. Norris and London modeled these fictional behaviors in their own adventurous lives, identifying with their characters' search for meaningful work in a society where production was rigorously separated from consumption. They identified likewise with their characters' preferences for intense human attachments, or no attachments at all. The urban settings of their fictions – typically miniaturized, claustrophobic – appear incommensurate with the simple power of their protagonists, who struggle against the punishing demands of society until they are released into the wilderness where they belong. The more muted and depressing regional locales of Edith Wharton provide variations on a similar theme: incongruous humans, like weeds, requiring uprooting or relocation to more congenial environments.

To pose equivalence between people and other species as these writers did, was to concede much. Ever the provocateur, Mark Twain, in an 1896 essay, "Man's Place in the Animal World," went even further, arguing for a reversal of the Darwinian theory of man's ascent from the lower animals – i.e. man's *descent* from the higher animals. Reviewing their respective consumption habits, Twain concludes that humans are inferior to all other species since they alone kill for sport. A comparison of gathering methods – humans versus squirrels, birds, and bees – yields similarly unflattering results: humans are greedy and ungenerous while these diminutive creatures are not. Human complexity, leading to melancholia, resentment, aggression, computes to loss in relation to their simpler natural brethren who are at home in the universe. A set of principles emerge: humans alone inflict pain for the pleasure of it, go to war, enslave, harbor patriotism and faith, and possess a moral sense, which exists, it seems, to be violated. The only faculty which justifies human claims to superiority is the intellect, which, Twain notes, is notably absent from accounts of heaven with which he is familiar. This is no doubt, he deduces, because higher animals alone go there. In their implicit appeal to animal lovers and detailed confirmation of scientific research on dog behavior, Jack London's renowned accounts of animals and humans in the wild echo Twain. While emphasizing the role of elites in both species, however, London's Darwinian hierarchy stops short of Twain's spirited case for "the Higher Animals."

Jack London was born in San Francisco in 1876 to Flora Wellman, a music teacher who was deserted by Jack's biological father, the astrologist William Chaney, and later married to John London, who adopted Jack. The family's poverty resulted in a nomadic life regulated by the harvests, until their move to Oakland, where access to a public library revealed ten-year-old Jack's passion for reading. From early on, London worked to help support the family while attending school. At fifteen he took a full-time job in a cannery, and borrowed money to buy a boat for oyster pirating on San Franciso Bay. London was drawn to local labor politics, joining Kelly's Army, the California Branch of Coxey's Army, a march of the unemployed to Washington, later tramping cross country, and jailed briefly for vagrancy in upstate New York, an episode recounted in *The Road* (1907). During this period, London nursed his literary ambitions, and was rewarded by a first-place finish in a San Francisco essay contest for a piece about a typhoon, evidence that his extensive reading had registered deeply. Three years later, at twenty, London attended Oakland High School to gain accreditation for admission to the University of California Berkeley, which he attended for less than a semester in 1896. London hoped to live on his writing, but ended up with a backbreaking job at a steam laundry (fictionalized in *Martin Eden*).

Still, London was extraordinarily young when his break came in 1898: the sale of his first story, "To the Man on Trail," to the *Overland Monthly*, and another the following year, "An Odyssey of the North" to the *Atlantic Monthly*. In 1900 Houghton Mifflin published his first collection of short stories, *The Son of the Wolf*, about the gold rush in the Alaskan Klondike, and in 1901 McClure Phillips published the second, *The God of His Fathers*. *The Call of the Wild* launched London into popular and critical acclaim. Over the next decade, he published a book a year with Macmillan: *The People of the Abyss* (1903); *The Sea Wolf* (1904); *War of the Classes* (1905); *White Fang* (1906); *The Road* (1907); *The Iron Heel* (1908); *Martin Eden* (1909); *Burning Daylight* (1910); *South Sea Tales* (1911); *The Valley of the Moon* (1913); *The Strength of the Strong* (1914); and in 1915, *The Scarlet Plague* and *The Star Rover*. While working at this feverish pace, London married twice, served as a war correspondent in Japan and Korea, sailed around the world, and built an 1,100-acre ranch, all the while struggling with illness. Finally succumbing to a combination of rheumatism, kidney failure, and gastro-intestinal uremia, London died in 1916, possibly of a self-induced drug overdose. London's sensational success was due in part to the close proximity between his life and fiction. When McClure's offered London a desk job and steady income, London declined, commenting, "had I taken the advice of the magazine editors, I'd have been swiftly made into a failure." London's impulsive repudiation of convention was valuably conventional in a classic American sense: e.g. his skilled pursuit of the wilderness; his work ethic as both a laborer and an exceptionally productive writer; his construction of a dream house from the fortune earned by his novels.

All of these characteristics seem to coalesce in the short novel that made London's career, *The Call of the Wild*, which was serialized in *The Saturday Evening Post* (June 20, 1903–July 18, 1903) prior to its publication as a bestselling book. *The Call of the Wild* is a *Bildungsroman* from the perspective of one of the most charismatic animals in literature. As wise as Michael Drayton's cat or Franz Kafka's dog investigator; more passionate than Twain's ironic half-breed and psychologically substantial than Kipling's jungle animals, London's Buck, 140 pounds of dog intelligence, emotion, and might, may be the only unequivocal hero in American literary Realism. The novel opens with a discrimination that is meant to imply others:

Buck did not read the newspapers, or he would have known that trouble was brewing, not alone for himself, but for every tide-water dog, strong of muscle and with warm, long hair, from Puget Sound to San Diego. Because men, groping in the Arctic darkness, had found a yellow metal, and because steamship and transportation companies were booming the find, thousands of men were rushing into the Northland. These men wanted dogs, and the dogs they wanted were heavy dogs, with strong muscles by which to toil, and furry coats to protect them from the frost.

Buck's failure to read the newspapers is just the beginning of a series of human tendencies and appetites that he lacks. Everything that mystifies Buck about human beings, and every way in which he differs from them, is a sign of superiority. The way to tell a moral story in literary Realism, it seems, is to make it a dog's life. Buck is a natural aristocrat, "king over all creeping, crawling, flying things . . . humans included." He is dragged from a life of leisure in the warm Santa Clara Valley to a life of toil in the Alaskan Klondike, carrying sled loads of mail to gold prospectors, covering up to sixty miles a day. Thrown into a bare struggle for survival, his morality is compromised but he improves in every other way.

Throughout the terrible events of the novel's fast-paced opening – Buck's kidnapping and exchange from one brutal dog-breaker to another – Buck is not pitied, but admired for his fortitude and depth of understanding. Primitive law has to be learned by this sophisticated animal, who has difficulty with the crude speech of his new owners. London emphasizes Buck's ability to profit from experience: resolving never again to be beaten by a man with a club and never to be made a scapegoat by a ruthless pack of dogs. Buck's dream life, another repository of his vast consciousness, helps to ensure that. The novel's other dogs provide a range of character more deep and varied than the novel's humans. The humans serve primarily to appreciate Buck, as when a wilderness-toughened team-driver fashions moccasins for Buck's sore frost-bitten feet, and smiles indulgently when Buck will not move after he forgets to put them on. In one of the novel's most memorable passages, describing a rabbit hunt, London celebrates Buck's transformation. The artist at the top of his creative powers, the patriotic soldier in the groove of war who has lost all sense of fear, the perfect specimen of dog strength and wisdom functioning at his highest potential, unite in a single ideal of self-integration. Yet the book's real climax comes when a gentle dog-loving prospector saves Buck's life, and Buck experiences love for the first time. Buck's responsiveness to human generosity after all of his hardening is the ultimate sign of his greatness. It is also the sign of his ultimate subordination to the dominant species.

The interdependence of Buck and Thornton is based on mutual indebtedness – Thornton saves Buck, Buck saves Thornton. What makes Thornton the best human in the novel is his preference for dogs, and his ability to arouse doglike devotion in Buck. By the time he meets John Thornton, Buck has already heard "the call of the wild," the primitive wolf howl, which confirms Buck's place in a wild fraternity that stirs the core of his being. To solve a potential dilemma – forcing Buck to choose between Thornton and his nature – Thornton is killed by Yeehat Native Americans. Avenging the murder in a single-handed massacre, Buck becomes a legend, commemorated as the Evil Spirit or "Ghost Dog" whose terrible deeds ensure that a certain select valley of the Alaskan Klondike will be forever free of Yeehats. As if to sanction Buck's final existence among his own dog kind, the appearance of Native Americans at the novel's end highlights the terrible conflicts that issue from the mingling of different peoples. London is unconcerned with motivation and there is no hint that the Yeehats may be responding in kind to some prior imperial aggression. London suggests that like must live with like, however ecstatic certain cross-species alliances (such as that between Thornton and Buck) might be. It is only with the wolves that Buck realizes his nature fully. A return to the wild is the ideal sought by the highest natural specimens.

Like Jack London, Frank Norris was drawn to the forces that seemed incommensurate with civilization, locating the future of American fiction in the "red, living heart of things." To grasp and recreate this primitivism, Norris implied, was to gain insight into the most seemingly intractable social problems and the social designs that were simply unworkable. Norris's convictions drew on a turn-of-the century social scientific perspective that feared the savagery underlying civilization (and always threatening to erupt), at the same time that it mourned modern society's distance from nature. *McTeague*, the novel which earned him respect and even celebrity as a writer, according to William Dean Howells ignored the "provincial proprieties" in favor of "the savage world which underlies as well as environs civilization . . . There is no denying the force with which he makes the demand, and there is no denying the hypocrisies which the old-fashioned ideal of the novel involved." Norris took heart in such reviews, as he did in the book's sales, 12,000 the first year. The novel's immediate inspiration was the 1893 San Francisco murder of Sarah Collins, a washerwoman at a local kindergarten, by her husband, a brute made terrible by alcohol, and enraged because she would not give him money. These facts, together with the Lombroso-inspired descriptions of the murderer from the *San Franciso Examiner*, were incorporated into *McTeague*. Cesare Lombroso's theories about criminality, which conceived the criminal as an atavistic reversion and dwelled on physical attributes of the criminal type, were popular in America during the 1890s, and Norris knew them well.

McTeague opens on a bachelor dentist's typical Sunday: dining at the saloon, and resting in his professional parlors, drinking steam beer from a pail, playing on his concertina, his only companion a canary. The novel ends with McTeague (the dentist is identified by surname alone) in Death Valley, accompanied by the same (nearly dead) canary, and a lifeless body to which he is chained. Between these bookends, Norris weaves a grim plot, with occasional moments of relief. A love story at base, *McTeague* emphasizes the gender polarities that drive love and make brutality so often its issue. *McTeague* features bestiality, miserliness, wife battery, sterility, senility, individual degeneracy, and social decline, all within the umbrella of a Darwinian social universe. The book conveys the emotional atmosphere and physical texture of life in the animal kingdom, where the animals are human and the real animals have more dignity by far. The novel's arc is primarily downward: McTeague goes from dentist to maker of surgical instruments to piano mover to miner; Trina from homemaker to toymaker to washerwoman. The characters have struggled up the social ladder only to be crushed: from the mediation and control of sensual appetites (reconceived as "tastes" and "pleasures") by bourgeois rites of passage (professionalization, courtship, marriage), to the rule of animal instinct.

The novel's desacralized sacred world resembles, in certain respects, a social scientific blueprint, though less in the Lombrosian manner usually identified than in the mode of William Robertson Smith and Emile Durkheim. Society here is afflicted with anomie. Social bonds have worn thin. Kinship ties – mother–son, cousins – count for little. Friendship counts for less. Bloodlines transmit debility rather than sustenance. In one four-block radius we find German, Scottish, Irish, Mexican, black, and Jew. Norris may be trying to ape God by including every possible human kind in his fictional Armageddon. In keeping with the air of doom that opens *McTeague*, characters betray a range of compulsions and deformities. This is a society of hoarders and misfits, all of them consumed with losses and assets, all of them devoted to the miserly prospect of self-containment. Though the book is full of misers, and no character escapes the taint of this peculiar malady, Norris feminizes miserliness, aligning this trait with a distinctive female ambitiousness. In descriptions which seem uncannily Weberian, Norris's female characters are associated with modern principles of rationalization and reduction, to which male characters are forced to submit. This is typified by the efforts of McTeague's mother, who manages to compress her son's mining trade (in Norris's words, "the caricature of dentistry"), into an expert oral "art."

Norris specifies miserliness and reduction as feminine traits, in confirmation of his belief that women harbor what is probably society's most precious commodity. Women in *McTeague* are the reproducers who do not produce, whose bodies shrivel like empty money bags, when they might expand with child. Sexuality has achieved a pure commodity status, and there is no distinguishing woman's sexuality from her identity. Thus, when her sexuality is "given out," the woman loses value and all control over her destiny. The novel affirms that female sexuality in its most obvious commodity form is reproduction, the means to the working classes' notorious advantage over Anglo-American ruling classes in this era. Yet this community's lone offspring, the frail "hybrid" of the Jewish Zerkow and Mexican Maria Macapa, dies shortly after birth. The novel's close, a fight to the death for McTeague and Marcus Schouler, provides a multiple offering in the desert. No less than three victims are laid before the desert gods – two humans and a canary. But like everything else in this book of stylized excess, the scene ends without spiritual edification, weighed down (rather than lifted) by its sacrificial machinery.

Norris's narrative opposes an idealized antisocial principle to a feminine principle of domesticity and progress, an ideal that is ultimately at odds with Trina's own monumental greed. Violence appears to be a consequence of the discrepancy between human need and social forms. To some extent this discrepancy is gendered – that is, male impulses are set against a claustrophobic and interiorized femininity. Yet what makes *McTeague* such a complex and powerful novel is that gender polarities are broken down. Trina, the promoter of social forms, is also in her miserliness the most socially resistant of characters. At the same time, the natural wilderness that overwhelms and finally extinguishes any human or social prospect is clearly feminized. The drive towards extinction in *McTeague* is shown to be independent of gender. It is both feminine and masculine: present in Trina's refusal to hand over her gold though she knows McTeague will kill her, and in McTeague's desert fight to the death with Marcus Schouler. Both are forms of suicide: flights from civilization and its trappings towards the death that is as "interminable" and "measureless" as the desert itself. In this way the plot of *McTeague* recalls Norris's characterization of San Franciso for the *Wave* as a "pinpoint" in a vast wilderness "circle of solitude." Civilization out West is provisional, almost aching to be submerged in the surrounding terrain.

Edith Wharton is known for her portraits of urban civilization, but she was also capable of the most acute accounts of its antithesis. *Ethan Frome* (1911), perhaps her most popular novel, is set in a New England wilderness as barren and threatening as any conceived by Norris. In this work, Wharton seeks the psychological and intellectual counter to East coast urbanism, in its most acute rural form. She claims a greater sophistication than her country subjects, assuming the pose of ethnographer among villagers, whose traditions are nonetheless older than hers. Yet she seeks to honor the sobering qualities of the aptly named Starkfield, and the crushed fortunes of its protagonist, Ethan Frome, the victim of a terrible accident years before the narrative begins. The narrative progresses like a detective novel – first the corpses, then the events that produced them. At fifty-two Ethan walks "checking each step like the jerk of a chain." His crippling is fully realized as a New England destiny, both metaphysical and physical, a collective rather than individual fate. The dead hover close to the living, seeming equally if not more alive: their graves "nuzzle up through the snow like animals pushing out their noses to breathe." The town is desolate partly because of the rerouting of traffic with the advent of the train, partly from the sheer magnitude of snow, which seems to drown potential vitality "in a soft universal diffusion." The novel's plot centers on the twenty-eight-year-old Ethan, unhappily married to a rigid invalid cousin, Zeena, seven years his senior, Zeena's attractive, poor relative, twenty-year-old Mattie Silver, who comes to help with the housekeeping, and the adulterous love that develops between husband and housekeeper. Mattie is the brightest thing in Ethan's life, and Wharton portrays their love as inevitable. Equally inevitable is the foiling of that love, ensured by Ethan's guilt concerning his invalid wife, and by his and Mattie's poverty. Had they a means of flight, of abandoning Zeena in relative comfort, they might have leapt. Instead, they remain in a barren land that is incapable of yielding bounty or even nourishment. Their tragic end is the consequence of whim inspired by the chance presence of a sled at the top of the sledding hill on the night Mattie is to leave for good. Whether a grim extension of this spontaneous indulgence, or a punitive reversal of it, they guide their sled into an imposing elm on the hill trail. While the crash precludes their separation, it consigns them to a living hell. The paralyzed Mattie descends into spinal disease, waited upon by the resentful martyr Zeena. To Ethan, beset with two ailing and antagonistic women, the grave looks inviting indeed.

  Ethan Frome is a drama of scarcity and sacrifice. Self-denial is an accepted way of life for the novel's crumbling humanity, and the smallest departure from convention yields extraordinary torment. Zeena's trip to a doctor, who plies her with expensive remedies, proves even costlier by enabling the adulterous union. The passionate love between Ethan and Mattie is repaid by a life of pain and disfigurement. Ethan's youthful ambition to leave town, nourished by a year away studying, requires that he be chained there permanently. Forces conspire to keep the characters bound to the dilapidated little town, whose only spark comes from an outsider: the "ambitious Irish grocer" who introduces "'smart' business methods." Starkfield natives excel in fulfilling obligations: Ethan leaves school to run the farm after his father's death; nurses his ill mother; marries the cousin who has helped him; honors a cold, barren marriage in the face of love; Zeena rises from her sickbed to nurse Mattie after the accident, despite the adultery responsible for it; Ethan stands by the miserable pair of women, to complete a circle of woe. The greater the trial, the more zealously they suffer it. They can only be overcome by complete physical assault, as in Mattie's spinal disease. As a novel about desire and its discontents, *Ethan Frome* responds to the era of consumption and modernization with a stark reminder of the region whose moral intensity and repressed passion continued to offer a powerful origin myth for Americans.

People in Wharton's Starkfield are psychologically as well as morally intense. Her characters are extremists who fear their emotions – ambition, passion, jealousy – with good reason. They live close to the edge, brushing up against the forces – snow, death, and insanity – that threaten their provisional existences. Wharton implies some grim pleasure for readers of *Ethan Frome* in the view of common people resisting the overwhelming demands of pain, trial, or desire, to remain within the border of society. The following section features some of the most distinctive voices of the period – Helen Keller, William and Henry James, Mark Twain, Elizabeth Stuart Phelps, Mary Baker Eddy – all of whom deliberately violated the borders between the familiar and the alien; the scientifically legitimate and the unexplained; the normative and the estranged. They pursued these borders invariably out of necessity: Helen Keller was deaf and blind; the James brothers were periodically subject to nervous illness; Eddy was fragile psychologically yet possessed of a uniquely charged spiritual disposition; Twain and Phelps were continually plunged into mourning for dead family and lovers. Yet all of them understood their explorations into the unknown in collective terms, and took their roles as spiritual guides seriously.

In so doing, they were also fulfilling trends that were widespread among intellectuals in this turn-of-the century era. Despite their extensive knowledge of advances in social science as well as in science, and their repudiation of conventional religious practices, they resisted thoroughly secular explanations of human experience. While each of these thinkers struggled variously in public to accommodate the challenge to religion represented by the advent of Darwinism and the establishment of the social sciences, they also provided in private, living testimonies to what such paradigms missed. In this way, they personify the limits of the secularization thesis – the idea that religion was being replaced by scientific understanding in this era. Figures like the James brothers and Elizabeth Stuart Phelps, Mark Twain and Helen Keller thus served to exemplify the persisting power of spirituality in the age of science. Their experience confirmed an observation made by Albion Small, a leading American sociologist at the time, "From first to last, religions have been men's more or less conscious attempts to give finite life its infinite rating.

Science can never be an enemy of religion . . . the more science we have the more are we awed and lured by the mystery beyond our ken."

DISTINCTIVE VOICES IN OTHER WORLDS

Mark Twain once observed that the two most interesting people of the nineteenth century were Napoleon and Helen Keller. Twain met Keller on a few occasions, and she describes in *The Story of My Life* how she "listens" to his stories by holding her hands to his lips. Keller, who became blind and deaf from scarlet fever at the age of nineteen months, is an extraordinary figure, and her equally talented teacher, Anne Sullivan, complements Keller's own account of her life and education in letters. Born into a family of poor Irish immigrants, Sullivan was orphaned at ten and sent to the Tewksbury Almshouse. Partly blind from a disease of the eyes, she brought to her vocation first-hand knowledge and an inventive intelligence. The story of Keller and Sullivan reveals the state of research on learning and education in America at the turn of the century, and also confirms the value of intellectual life, for there was no one more equipped to judge how culture could enhance experience than a blind and deaf girl shut inside, in her words, "a tangible white darkness."

Keller is a major figure in part because the account (her own and that of others) of how her darkness was relieved touches upon so many significant cultural developments in her time. An Alabama native, daughter of a Confederate officer, Keller was adopted by an Eastern educational establishment – the Perkins Institute for the Blind, the prestigious Cambridge School, and Harvard University – eager in this post-Civil War era to make amends with the South. Discovered by Alexander Graham Bell, who introduced her to Michael Anagnos, director of the Perkins Institute, Keller became the darling of Boston and New York intellectual circles, represented by such prominent figures as William Dean Howells, Oliver Wendell Holmes, and William James. Familiar with major editors, H. W. Mabee of *Outlook*, William Alden of *Harper's*, she was sponsored by the same Standard Oil trustee, Henry H. Rogers, who supported Mark Twain. Because of her Southern background, Keller was extraordinarily mindful of the racial caste system that became even more entrenched in the era after Emancipation. Charles Dudley Warner characterized her as "the purest-minded human being in existence," which may stand for her need to penetrate the logic of assumptions and beliefs in order to grasp what those with sight and hearing grasp intuitively. Anne Sullivan noted how the seven-year old Keller's fascination with racial distinctions extended to a view of how thought might be informed and limited by them. "My think is white," Helen observes, "Viney's [a black servant] think is black."

Born in 1880 in the tiny Alabama town of Tuscumbia, Keller was from an old New England family, which included the Adams and the Everetts on her mother's side, and the first child of her Southern father's second marriage. The most dramatic event in Keller's childhood was her acquisition of language, the moment when she connected the sensation of running water on one hand with her teacher's spelling of the word "w-a-t-e-r" on her other hand. Language, she later recalled, delivered her from an alien existence to "kinship with the rest of the world." Keller excelled in particular, according to Sullivan, in the "unconscious language of the emotions," divining the dispositions of others from the slightest movement, in confirmation of the fact that every thought and emotion has a physical expression, however subtle. In 1888 Keller moved to Boston to study at the Perkins Institute for the Blind, and by 1890 was learning to speak. In 1896, Keller began to prepare for Radcliffe College's entrance exams. Examined in 1897, with no special dispensations, she passed all her subjects, including French, Latin, English, Greek, and Roman History, and earned honors in German and English. Entering Radcliffe in 1900, she managed to graduate in 1904 with her entering class.

Keller's appreciation for her limited but intensified faculties are evident throughout *The Story of My Life: With Her Letters, 1887–1901 And A Supplementary Account Of Her Education*, which was partly serialized in *The Ladies Home Journal* (1901) before its publication as a book (1902). She absorbed the world through every available means, registering the collective morning arousal at a camp-out by inhaling the rich aroma of coffee, and by feeling the stamping feet of horses and the panting of dogs. She thrilled to the experience of tobogganing down steep slopes across a frozen lake. At Niagara Falls in 1893, she sensed the vibrating air and trembling earth. She toured Chicago's World Fair with a special presidential pass that allowed her to touch the exhibits so that "wonders from the uttermost parts of the earth – marvels of invention, treasuries of industry and skill and all the activities of human life actually passed under my finger tips." Keller distinguishes between deep learning, and education, which requires the ingestion of information without time to digest it. Her conventional studies serve to establish the potential of the handicapped, but they are remote indeed from the satisfactions dating back to her first "connected story," an inspiration that led her from that day to "devour . . . everything in the shape of a printed page that has come within the reach of my hungry finger tips." Keller is a great reader: she enthuses like Thoreau over the special power of the classics in the original, and considers reading an art requiring sympathy rather than erudition. In part because readers failed to grasp the depth of Keller's ironic wit, and in part because her observations *were* genuinely subversive, Keller's assessment of her college years incensed readers.

The extraordinary odyssey of Keller and Sullivan invited continual comparison with the pedagogical relationship of Laura Bridgman, a deaf and blind girl born in 1829, and Samuel Gridley Howe, an experimental scientist who devised for her the system that was later called Braille. From the outset, Keller seemed to have greater potential than Bridgman, who was also deprived of the senses of smell and taste. Strong and energetic, Keller was graceful, alert, and exceptionally intelligent. In Anne Sullivan, Keller had an innovative educator whose personality was ideally suited to hers. Sullivan was convinced that education must be based on what came naturally to children, on play and freedom rather than rote instruction and constraint. Common sense was a staple of Sullivan's method, and she devised her plan for teaching Helen on the process of conventional language acquisition. Long before they are able to speak themselves, children demonstrate their understanding of the language around them, even of highly complex patterns. Months of being spoken to and directed by others provide a critical pathway to speech, instilling an intricate grammatical edifice well before a child can speak. Sullivan decided to perform the same operations manually with Keller, "talking into her hand" with the presumption that Helen could listen and imitate. Like an educated parent, Sullivan spoke in complete sentences, modeling the speech forms she sought to instill, and relating to her pupil always on a high intellectual level. Sullivan's commitment to empathic pedagogy, her pragmatism and self-honesty, her ability to admit defeat while preserving her optimism in the face of setbacks, above all, her deep respect for her pupil, ensured her success.

Sullivan's faith in Keller's potential is moving:

Something within me tells me that I shall succeed beyond my dreams . . . I know that [Helen] has remarkable powers, and I believe that I shall be able to develop and mould them. I cannot tell how I know these things. I had no idea a short time ago how to go to work; I was feeling about in the dark; but somehow I know now, and I know that I know. I cannot explain it; but when difficulties arise, I am not perplexed or doubtful. I know how to meet them; I seem to divine Helen's peculiar needs.

Keller's greatest talents seemed to be literary and critical. Reading for Keller is a release from darkness to light, the creation of an inner sanctum where thought is wholly internal and intensified. In this way, reading also provides her a means for luxuriating in her separateness. After reading some verses from Omar Khayyam, Keller reflects, "I feel as if I had spent the last half-hour in a magnificent sepulcher. Yes, it is a tomb in which hope, joy, and the power of acting nobly lie buried." Reading entombed provides an alternative to the other kind of death towards which Keller demonstrates a primed sensitivity. Though she had never been told anything about death or burial, on entering a cemetery for the first time at the age of seven she became instantly somber and spelled "cry – cry" repeatedly into the hand of her teacher. A year later, she evinced an even greater intuition of death by perceiving, again, without being told, that the lady she and Anne Sullivan had accompanied to the cemetery had lost a daughter named Florence, and Helen walked directly to her grave. Anne Sullivan reports that "she had been told nothing about [Florence], nor did she even know that my friend had had a daughter." Sullivan knows enough to refrain from explaining what seems inexplicable. But it also seems clear that Sullivan understands this as Keller's grasp of the language of the unconscious. As Keller observed in one of the many superb essays she wrote for her Radcliffe English Professor, Charles T. Copeland, this one on the miracle of plant growth, "Now I understand that the darkness everywhere may hold possibilities better even than my hopes." Keller represented a living example for her time that the unknown and invisible might astound us with the measure of its bounty. This was a bounty that was ever apparent to the great American philosopher, William James, Keller's contemporary.

In keeping with his role as the preeminent national philosopher of his day, James was eager to challenge boundaries between professional science and the wealth of scientific interest that had become increasingly central to American popular culture. James was described by one scholar as having "a pathological repugnance to the processes of exact thought," which suggests that he may have been in his element in the series of essays on mysticism and the occult published in contemporary magazines and written in the spontaneous, collo-quial idiom that appeared natural to him. "The Hidden Self," for instance, appeared in *Scribner's Magazine* in 1890, a popular forum that welcomed some of the ties James set forth between discoveries in the emerging science of psy-chology and the popular testimony of mediums and mystics. Such testimony, James noted, posed a serious challenge to science: "Lying broadcast over the surface of history, no matter where you open its pages, you find things recorded under the name of divinations, inspirations, demoniacal possessions, appari-tions, trances, ecstasies, miraculous healings and productions of disease, and occult powers possessed by peculiar individuals over persons and things in their neighborhood." James goes on to note that while the nineteenth-century vogue of mediums seems to have originated in Rochester, New York, and animal magnetism with Mesmer in France, these practices have been known in every time and place. Despite the mass interest in the occult, and the exten-sive literature to which it has given rise, scientists have been deaf to its claims. In the few debates that have occurred between scientists and mystics, the scien-tists prevail in theory, but the mystics have a superior command of facts. James praises French scientists for their greater openness to the unexplained, which he attributes to the culture's distinct fondness for human variety. In the Havre experiments with hysterical patients conducted by Monsieur Janet, different levels of consciousness and even alternative consciousnesses within individuals were revealed, to suggest new avenues for therapy and vast potential for relieving human misery. James believed that psychic research and Christian Science held the same potential. He was especially drawn to the research of Frederic Myers, founder of the British Society for Psychical Research, which he touted in both professional and popular venues. James was impressed by Myers's holistic principle, according to which true scientific understanding required the pursuit of phenomena beyond its ken. Myers had made a system of diverse phenomena – unconscious cerebration, hypnotism, hysteria, inspirations of genius, hallucinatory voices, apparitions of the dying, medium-trances, demoniacal possession, clairvoyance, thought-transference, ghosts – and concluded that nature, as James put it, is "gothic, not classic. She forms a real jungle, where all things are provisional, half-fitted to each other, and untidy." A pioneer in the wilderness of the mind, Myers's achievement was to have staked the flag of science upon it.

In *Science and the Modern World*, Alfred North Whitehead characterized James as the leading exemplar of a new era whose dominant intellectual tendency was the repudiation of the Cartesian dualism of body and mind. One could argue that this tendency was nowhere more apparent than in *The Varieties of Religious Experience* (1902), James's major study of religious experience in all its empirical diversity. Dubbed by some contemporaries, "Wild Religions I Have Known," *Varieties* was first delivered as the "Gifford Lectures" at the University of Edinburgh, where James was the first American to be so honored. It was especially appropriate that the lectures provided a highly accessible formulation of James's deeply democratic, pragmatist ideas, specifically his aversion to metaphysics and his insistence that ideas be rooted in experience. The emphasis on experience signals James's categorical commitment to individuals; for religion, in his view, "is a monumental chapter in the history of human egotism." His examples – Tolstoy, John Bunyan, St. Francis, Rousseau, Mohammed, George Fox, Martin Luther, Jonathan Edwards, Ignatius Loyola, the Spanish Jesuit Molina, the little-known Persian philosopher and theologian, Al-Ghazzali, Walt Whitman, Joseph Smith, Nietzsche, Tennyson – traverse cultures and centuries, as do his topics – extrasensory perception, optimism, Lutheran theology, mind-cure, pessimism, self-division, conversion, saintliness, mysticism, asceticism, automatisms, anthropomorphism. A science of particulars rather than abstractions explains the abundance of concrete examples. Extremes (religion as "acute fever), not norms (religion as "dull habit"), provide the parameters of the religious temperament. The analysis must be as broad as religious belief and expression itself, and broad explorations demand broad categories: "the feelings, acts, and experiences of individual men in their solitude, so far as they apprehend themselves to stand in relation to whatever they may consider the divine."

Though James, like Emerson, was sometimes criticized for lacking a sense of evil, he is clear on the limits of evolutionary optimism: healthy-mindedness is fine as far as it goes. Significantly, James provides first-hand evidence of where it does not. In the lecture on "The Sick Soul," he offers a ghoulish image of a male asylum patient, a black-haired young man with greenish skin, whose condition horrifies a spectator drawn into deep identification with him. While the spectator, who remains a nervous wreck long after the encounter, is presented as a French writer, he is widely believed to have been James himself. Indeed, the incident resembles the terrible "vastation" experienced by Henry James Sr. when his sons were boys. Such powerful instances of melancholia, hallucinations, delusions, James observes, explain the persistence of revivalism and other orgiastic religions, since powerful anxieties require powerful religious solutions. The most successful religions – Christianity, Buddhism, Judaism – have the most highly developed pessimistic elements.

In the Postscript that he added to the lectures before their book publication, James reveals his own working belief system. He conceives a larger power beyond each individual that is friendly to him and his needs, and that might be none other than "a larger and more godlike self, of which the present self would then be but the mutilated expression." The universe might then be thought of as a collection of these various godlike selves – a kind if polytheism revisited. This makes sense because polytheism has always been the real religion of common people, regarding the world as partly lost and partly saved, which James believes a proper view of the collective spiritual state. *The Varieties of Religious Experience* exemplifies, above all, the humility of one of the great scientific minds of his time. What most scientists took as hallucinations, James treated with scientific care, because those who experienced these hallucinations were convinced they were real. The striking similarity of these descriptions across time and place lent them further credibility. Religious believers in widely varying settings experienced the same evidence for their faith in God. James's singular tolerance for religious experiences both remote and diverse is a tribute to his lifelong interest in human idiosyncrasies, and to his enduring interest in what could not be known.

John Dewey wrote of William and Henry James that "the former is concerned with human nature in its broad and common features (like Walt Whitman, he gives the average of the massed effect), while the latter is concerned with the special and peculiar coloring that the mental life takes on in different individualities." While the voluminous fiction, essays, and criticism Henry James produced over a long literary career serve as the record of his views on morality, religion, and psychology, in one distinctive essay, "Is There a Life After Death?" (1910), Henry approached the philosophical and spiritual interests of his brother. Both Henry and William framed their thoughts about death against a paternal backdrop of optimistic Christianity and Transcendentalism to which neither subscribed. Their concepts of death derived primarily from their experiences of consciousness: having inhabited their own fertile minds, and interacted with so many other such minds, neither could believe that these vital engines would simply shut off at death. As William wrote in a 1908 letter to Charles Eliot Norton,

I am as convinced as I can be of anything that this experience of ours is only a part of the experience that is, and with which it has something to do; but *what* or *where* the other parts are, I cannot guess. It only enables one to say "behind the veil, behind the veil!" more hopefully, however interrogatively and vaguely, than would otherwise be the case.

Henry shares William's conviction of consciousness beyond death, invoking an uncharacteristic religious metaphor: one prepares for the Jamesian afterlife the way one prepares for the Christian heaven of Elizabeth Stuart Phelps, by living an utterly devout life of submission to the powers of intellect. James and Phelps share a fundamental assurance of continuity: an eternal condition of ecstasy waits if one has cultivated it all along. James claims an intensification of the mental life over time, and posits death as an elite republic of consciousness, populated by the most sensitive minds. Far from a loss then, death is a triumph, the ultimate liberation of the mind from its cumbersome attachment to the body.

Henry James's preference for rarefied characters, whose intense thoughtfulness both impel and inhibit his plots, was criticized famously by his brother William, who complained that Henry had "reversed every traditional canon of story-telling especially the fundamental one of *telling* the story." William was referring specifically to *The Wings of the Dove* (1902), which Henry himself conceded in a 1902 letter was a book with "too big a head for its body," whereas he had been trying all the while "to write one with the opposite disproportion – the body too big for its head. So I shall perhaps do if I live to 150." James's dilemma was caricatured by Max Beerbohm in his famous drawing of James the Master – massive head and tiny body. Artistic authority, according to Beerbohm's James, required domination of the physical. Still, bodies in James gain dramatic intensity through the minds that conquer them. They achieve powerful expression by way of their very repression. How could it be otherwise, given a novelistic world in which the central subjects are disease and death?

At the same time, to utter in *The Wings of the Dove* is in some sense to enact, and metaphors have a special, even deadly, force. Characters control each other by attribution, naming who and what they are: Kate to Milly, "you're a dove." At the same time, words designating dangerous things become prohibitive, a conspiracy of silence prevails, seconded by a narrative habit of omission and emphasis on the unspoken. The failure to name the mortal illness of the novel's American heiress is not only a mark of discretion but of a pervasive fear of death's contagion. As Robert Hertz, a contemporary anthropologist, noted of primitive attitudes towards death, "Death is an impure cloud . . . It surrounds the deceased, pollutes everything it touches." *The Wings of The Dove*, more than anything James wrote, is preoccupied with the category of taboo: the idea that there is no distinction between the word and the thing it names, such that the utterance of a prohibited subject is equally prohibited. This awesome necessity for surreptitious speech, according to Ortega Y Gasset (*The Dehumanization of Art*) supplies the roots of metaphor itself. The resistance to articulating key words and concepts, James's penchant for obscurity, must also be recognized as part of his ambivalence towards audiences. While James was ambitious for popular acclaim, as exemplified by his failed efforts as a playwright, he also disdained it, as confirmed by his formulation of an "initiated reader." James was ever alert, in a creative rather than dismissive way, to the effects of modernization, and its impact on language in particular. Detailed studies of James's style have indicated that it abounds in contemporary speech: the clichés and turns of phrase that were on everyone's lips in the middle- and upper-class circles of his Anglo-American subjects. In keeping with this, *The Wings of the Dove* depicts a society in the throes of secularization, undergoing historical changes that undermine traditional beliefs and ethics. James's novel offers a series of dilemmas framed in starkly moral terms, while his characters search for a moral clarity that steadily eludes them. While the cast of characters might be divided neatly between innocents and plotters in any given instance, these categories shift and blur over the course of the narrative.

The Wings of the Dove provides the drama of the mind trying to wrap itself meaningfully around death. By giving us a beautiful American heroine, Milly Theale, rich, generous, good, and ill, without a single living relative, and two penniless Britons, Kate Croy and Merton Densher, handsome in their own right, intelligent, courageous, in love, and in desperate need of money to realize it, the novel raises questions: can death be fashionable or beautiful; do the dead care what is done with their money after they die; do dead people care about anything at all; can words kill; can death be overcome to the extent that people have more effect dead than alive? The story seems to have originated in an 1894 notebook sketch for the stage, and in its first incarnation was even more markedly melodramatic. Milly was a pathetic doomed innocent, while Kate Croy was more unequivocally manipulative and greedy. Both characters retain traces of this initial polarization, and key plot elements, death, deceit, and betrayal, retain the flavor of classic stage melodramas. To be sure, James's mind was at home in melodrama. As his secretary, Theodore Bosanquet, commented, "When he walked out of the refuge of his study into the world and looked about him, he saw a place of torment, where creatures of prey perpetually thrust their claws into the doomed and defenseless children of light." And James observed in an 1896 notebook entry, "I have the imagination of disaster and see life as ferocious and sinister." James's sense of horror had a historical register: he was obsessed throughout his life with war, whether the Civil War of his youth in which he failed to fight, the imperial wars of his maturity, or the impending World War of his old age. It had a theological register: his preoccupation, that of a non-believer, with religious and ethical questions, and his occasional experimentation with alternative spiritual forms (for instance, the "psychical research" of Frederic Myers). And it had a psychodynamic register: James's ongoing fascination with characters who make "conveniences" of others (Madame Merle in *The Portrait of a Lady* is the prototype). In *The Wings of the Dove*, melodramatic action meets metaphorical reflection, and is relentlessly complicated.

The Wings of the Dove is notorious for what it fails to represent: the late sexual encounter between Densher and Kate; the devastating interview in which Lord Mark reveals the plot to Milly; Milly's final meeting with Densher; Milly's letter announcing her bequest to Densher. This circuit of privacy seems to protect all the principal characters, to enfold them as it were, in "the wings of the dove." James is preoccupied with the depths that charge surfaces. Gestures, statements, looks are signs of what lies beneath them. James never treats the *content* of the depth, just the *charge* it gives the surface. This is precisely the function of his metaphorical language. This tendency, which pervades James's late fiction in general, can be understood as an approach to the ultimate abyss – death. James deprives us repeatedly of knowledge of crucial scenes in order to amplify their resemblance to the ultimate condition that cannot be known or represented – death itself. But this is not to say that his characters do not still struggle to control it. The novel's closing account of Milly's triumphant afterlife might be understood as James's ultimate fantasy of immortality. Through her own meticulously orchestrated plot, she rules all from the grave. In death, she embraces her own conception of the dove, offering her gift to Densher on Christmas Eve, enfolding all in a winged mantle that divides as much as it protects or conjoins. Milly's plot is inescapable, especially after Kate throws Milly's accompanying letter in the fire, ensuring the mythic status of Milly's bequest. James suggests at least two ways of understanding Milly's power at the novel's close. As a type of aesthetic immortality, her sequencing of events, especially without the letter, ensures a rich fund of interpretive possibility and Densher's eternal devotion. This is the Judaeo-Christian legacy of interpretation: mystifying acts that lend themselves to everlasting debate. As a form of honoring the dead, exacted in Jewish and other cultures, Milly's memory is revered through prescribed ritual acts. Whether as artist or ancestor, Milly dictates the contents of others' consciousnesses posthumously. It is significant that Densher's worship of the dead Milly replicates his masturbatory recollection of his sexual consummation with Kate. While this parallel results in the familiar alignment of sex with death, possibly suggesting an erasure of the first scene (sex) by the second (death), it seems, more profoundly, to register the novel's economy of experience. For James is ever engaged in tabulating losses and forging relations of commensurability: Kate loses purity and Densher but gains a fortune; Milly loses Densher in life but gains him forever in death; Densher exchanges a live female body he can keep for a time for a dead female body he can have forever. Yet finally the novel shows the drama of life and death to be fundamentally incommensurable, a nullification of the very idea of commensurability. It is in death, according to James, where we exist solely in consciousness, and are known only in the hearts and minds of others, that we have most power to arouse love and to control loved ones. Thus Milly Theale at the novel's end rewrites the terms of Psalm 55: "O that I had wings like a dove / then I would fly away and be at rest . . . / for it was not an enemy that reproached me / but it was thou / my companion and familiar friend." She may be gone at the novel's end, but as one of the Jamesian dead she is hardly at rest.

The Turn of the Screw, like The Wings of the Dove, is centrally concerned with the control exerted by the dead upon the living. What makes the governess's story a ghost story is the fact that she transfixes her audience with its haunting power from the grave (in a manner akin to the control exercised by the dead Milly over Densher and Kate). Throughout the story the border between the dead and the living is highly permeable. The governess, like a ghost, or a Freudian dream, is a borderline character, defining margins by crossing them. She is a mediator, conveying messages from the children, their uncle, and from officials at Miles's school. For readers, who are deprived of their contents, she is a dead-letter office preserving the unrevealed messages in her own silent vault. Like all Jamesian dead letters, these generate the urge to interpret. In a similar way, dreams, as locked messages from the unconscious to the consciousness, initiate the process of interpretation. *The Turn of the Screw* begins just after a story has ended, and anticipates the start of another. This suggests that the novel will have something to do with the appetite for story, the extent to which human beings simply endure in the breaks between stories, and that we need only catch our breath before another begins. The contiguity of the novel's beginning and ending (from "no comment uttered" to "he uttered the cry"; from "breathless" listeners to the "last breath" of Miles), which comprise a pair of bookends for what lies between, suggests a potential causal relationship between the craving for story attributed to the listeners of the opening and the death pictured at the end. It is possible to understand James as incriminating the desire for story as compulsive, voyeuristic, and potentially even murderous.

The narrative is preoccupied with boundaries, and with framing devices that enhance them (by outlining the boundary) or unsettle them (by rendering the boundary permeable). Doors, windows, corridors, stairways, all border regions that connect spaces and also provide contrasts between them, take center stage, as do natural boundaries – the use of dawn and twilight as settings for scenes – and class boundaries – between uncle and governess, servants and children, governess and housekeeper – which are regularly violated. James commonly characterized writing as a boundary crossing.

Discouragements and lapses, depressions and darkness come to one only as one stands *without* – I mean without the luminous paradise of art. As soon as I really re-enter it – cross the loved threshold – stand in the high chamber, and the gardens divine – the whole realm widens out again before me . . . and I believe, I see, I *do*.

The artist's aim is "to live *in* the world of creation – to get into it and stay in it – to frequent it and haunt it." Writing here involves the passing into an altogether different realm; it is positively ghostly, a means of communing with the dead, and of reanimating them. It seems appropriate then that the governess first apprehends the ghost of Quint – "So I saw him as I see the letters I form on this page" – while writing. Ghosts are as real as stories. James goes beyond this claim in his 1908 preface to *The Turn of the Screw*:

What, in the last analysis, had I to give the sense of? Of their being, the haunting pair, capable, as the phrase is, of everything . . . Only make the reader's general vision of evil intense enough, I said to myself – and that already is a charming job – and his own experience, his own imagination, his own sympathy (with the children) and horror (of their false friends) will supply him quite sufficiently with all the particulars. Make him *think* the evil, make him think it for himself, and you are released from weak specifications. This ingenuity I took pains – as indeed great pains were required – to apply; and with a success apparently beyond my liveliest hope.

By insisting on the imaginative complicity of writer and reader, James implies the reader's craving for the ghosts and their diabolical schemes. In keeping with Walter Benjamin's claims in his essay "The Storyteller," James confirms the necessity for recourse with the dead. We need the novel, according to Benjamin, "not because it presents someone else's fate to us, perhaps didactically, but because this stranger's fate by virtue of the flame which consumes it yields us the warmth which we never draw from our own fate. What draws the reader of the novel is the hope of warming his shivering life with a death he reads about." Novels, especially ghost stories, let us warm ourselves by looking closely at a death that is not our own. In a series of novels from this period, Mark Twain and Elizabeth Stuart Phelps present the direct experience of death, accounts which demonstrate how revealing, in a cultural and political sense, the task of representing death can be.

Mark Twain's *Extract from Captain Stormfield's Visit to Heaven* (serialized in *Harper's Monthly*, December 1907–January 1908), was one of the earliest works he wrote (a manuscript exists from the early 1870s) and the last book he published (it was issued as a Christmas gift book by Harper and Brothers, six months before Twain's death, in 1909). Twain thought of *Captain Stormfield* as a burlesque of Phelps's 1868 bestseller, *The Gates Ajar*. According to Twain, Phelps

had imagined a mean little ten-cent heaven about the size of Rhode Island – a heaven large enough to accommodate about a tenth of one per cent of the Christian billions who had died in the past nineteen centuries. I raised the limit; I built a properly and rationally stupendous heaven and augmented its Christian population to ten per cent of the contents of the modern cemeteries; also, as a volunteer kindness I let in a tenth of one per cent of the pagans who had died during the preceding eons.

Twain's critique of Phelps's afterlife centers on the exclusiveness of its clientele: Phelps's heaven is designed on behalf of her white middle-class readers who can expect to find only people like themselves there. *Beyond The Gates* (1883) and *The Gates Between* (1887), sequels to *The Gates Ajar*, go beyond their predecessor by providing protagonists who actually experience the afterlife first-hand. *Beyond The Gates* is the story of forty-year-old Mary, the unmarried daughter of a clergyman, who has contributed in a variety of significant ways to her community: as teacher, Civil War nurse, board member on the Sanitary Commission, the Freedmen's Bureau, and the State Bureau of Labor. Though she has given much to others, she has struggled to believe in God, immortality, and the history of Jesus Christ. This makes her spiritually commonplace. Mary falls ill from scarlet fever, finally achieves a deep peace and discovers her father (dead for the past twenty years) in her sickroom. All of these events are described in Phelps's usual realistic detail: the room's familiar furnishings assist Christian readers in imagining a dead parent coming to lead them heavenward.

Throughout her odyssey, Mary is careful to emphasize that her accounts are mere approximations of what she has known: there are no earthly referents to express the perfection of heaven. Yet it is in heaven where human beings are most fully realized through the patient, loving counsel of Christ. This is truly a revelation for Mary, who has in life been wracked by doubt: while Mary is not one of heaven's elect, she is better off than those who have led utterly secular lives. Because it is the fullest possible expansion of earthly time, where all eras and cultures come together, heaven is a site of endless potential. Here one might meet the great minds and leaders of all time – Loyola, Jeanne d'Arc, Luther, Newton, Columbus, Darwin – seek out the cavemen, travel the planets including the Sun and Mars, even encounter literary characters – Hester Prynne, Uncle Tom, and Jean Valjean. And heaven is also where life's disappointments are compensated. Mary is just on the point of uniting with an old beau when she is awakened, painfully, from her trip to heaven, which has been a dream. She has not died after all, and awakens to a frost-bitten New England morning, the factory bells calling the poor factory girls to work.

Yet when heaven *is* fully realized through the protagonist's actual death, as in the final work of Phelps's trilogy, *The Gates Between*, a certain dramatic power is lost. The year is 187–, the protagonist, forty-nine-year-old Esmerald Thorne, has been married four years, having met his wife after building a medical career and a fortune. While apprised of Helen's goodness and beauty, he remains a self-involved workaholic, preoccupied with power, and with status and money. He is the last candidate on earth, it seems, for heaven, which is apparently why he goes there. His first great difficulty following death is letting go: he hovers in the land of the living, witnessing the reactions to his death, poring over newspaper accounts, even keeping watch on the stock exchange. In heaven, he wanders helplessly until his son appears, though Thorne does not immediately recognize him (perhaps because he was insufficiently engaged with him while alive)? Thorne learns to care for his son, meets Christ, gains faith, and is rewarded by the ascension of his wife Helen as well. There is no waking from this heavenly dream. The book closes with a taunting epigraph. "Perceiving that inquiry will be raised touching the means by which I have been enabled to give this record to the living earth, I have this reply to make: That is my secret. Let it remain such." The force of Phelps's treatments of spiritualism and the afterlife were convincing to readers who made bestsellers of all three *Gates* books. The insistence in all three books that the spirits of the dead were accessible, that heaven was an ideal place recognizable to all Christians including the least devout, and that spiritualist ideas of the afterlife were reconcilable with orthodox Christianity, were assumptions drawn from Phelps's own experience. She also drew sustenance from the thriving spiritualist movement, which according to Harriet Beecher Stowe counted four to five million adherents after the Civil War. Most importantly, Phelps's receptivity to alternative spiritual practices was part of a lifelong intellectual commitment to making Christianity amenable to the psychic, spiritual, and scientific developments that increasingly moved people in her time.

Though he ostensibly disdained Phelps's conceptions of the afterlife, Mark Twain's, like hers, originated in struggles with deeply held beliefs. As all his writings attest, Twain was well versed in a complex religious legacy, featuring his father's free thought, his mother's Presbyterianism, and his indoctrination in a Hannibal, Missouri culture of Campbellite revivalists. *Captain Stormfield* provided a valuable account of Twain's thinking about death and the afterlife at the same time that it took satiric aim at popular accounts of heaven, while cashing in on their incredible success. Profits from the magazine publication of the novella went into a wing of a new house in Redding, Connecticut, appropriately called "Stormfield." While Twain reportedly waited to publish the book until the death of his wife Olivia (a great fan of the Phelps series), it is also likely that he was never entirely satisfied that it was done.

The novella was based on the dream of a friend, Captain Ned Wakeman, who loved the Bible, knew it through and through, and shared the details of his heavenly vision with Twain. Yet Twain's responsiveness to Phelps predominates: what seems to have irked him most about her Christian heaven was its exclusivity and parochialism. The act of imagining heaven was for her an exercise of authority and control – projecting a spiritual theory on to the universe. In Twain's hands it became the opposite: an assertion of humility, a recognition of how small a place human beings occupy in a universe whose limits are unknown. Methods of measurement conceived on earth are useless for fathoming infinities beyond it. Captain Stormfield arrives in heaven after spinning through space for countless light years, and finds himself in line behind a sky-blue man with seven heads and one leg. *His* heavenly indoctrination will involve an ongoing confirmation of human insignificance and nullification of human beliefs about it. Officials at heaven's gates have no idea where earth is, let alone the United States. When they finally manage to locate earth's solar system on a map, after days of searching, Stormfield learns that it is referred to as "the Wart."

Twain's heaven is extraordinarily heterogeneous, comprised of many and diverse customs, as befits its countless kingdoms. It argues for the "mongrel" character of all nations on earth. In keeping with its multicultural composition, heaven's luminaries come from all times and places, some of them recognizable, some of them obscure. Shakespeare, Homer, Confucius, Buddha, and Mahomet have to walk behind a common tailor from Tennessee, and a horse-doctor named Sakka from Afghanistan. The Christian precept, "the last shall be first," is taken literally: the Tennessee tailor was a scapegoat crowned with cabbage leaves and rode through his village on a rail, so humble that he never expected to go to heaven, let alone as an exalted being. This is mass-society heaven, with life forms everywhere: when Captain Stormfield perches happily on a cloud, he finds a million others perching nearby. Twain's heterogeneous heaven harbors a humbling prophecy of white global insignificance in the modern era. Stormfield wonders late in the narrative about the dearth of blond angels, and is given a quick demography lesson: white people are a blip in a human history dominated by copper-colored peoples. In order to discover this expansive heaven, Stormfield has first to free himself from all the doctrines that constrain his access to it. Suffering and pain exist in heaven just as on earth, for "happiness ain't a *thing in itself* – it's only a *contrast* with something that ain't pleasant . . . there's plenty of pain and suffering in heaven – consequently there's plenty of contrast, and just no end of happiness." Stormfield tells his guide that "it's the sensiblest heaven I've heard of yet . . . though it's about as different from the one I was brought up on as a live princess is different from her own wax figger." *Captain Stormfield* testifies to Twain's unparalleled ability to make fun of beliefs and practices while affirming their seriousness as well as his need of them. Twain's relationship to imaginary heavens followed closely the pattern of his relationship to Christian Science or Mind Cure, which dated back to his childhood. As a small boy, he watched a farmer's wife, a renowned mind healer, relieve his mother's suffering from toothache. A similar practitioner miraculously cured his wife Olivia of a paralysis that had prevented her from walking. His daughter Clara, who was a hysteric, became a Christian Scientist, and his two other daughters, Susy and Jean, sought help unsuccessfully from practitioners of the new religion.

Twain's familiarity with its successes and failures accounts in part for the confused response to his writings on Christian Science. For as much as he despised its institutional forms under the rule of Mary G. Baker Eddy, he could recognize how it had helped people. *The Philadelphia Medical Journal*, for instance, expressed dismay at what they took to be Twain's sincere respect for Christian Science, while Harper and Brothers confirmed an opposite understanding of Twain's message, when they withdrew the book from publication in 1903 for fear that it would offend the Eddy establishment. It is easy to see how Twain's *Christian Science* (excerpted in *Cosmopolitan Magazine*, October 1899 and the *North American Review*, December 1902), prior to its publication as a book (1902) could have aroused such different responses. For Twain demonstrates a powerful capacity, evident in all his writings, to make belief appear authentic, even when he is at odds with or ridiculing it. He describes how "loving mercifulness and compassion . . . heals fleshly ills and pains and griefs – *all* – with a word, with a touch of the hand" and that "any Christian who was in earnest" might "cure with it *any disease or any hurt or damage possible to human flesh and bone.*" Thus Christ's touch is revived through the ages by the simple miracle of faith. Given the wonderment Twain displays in his writings towards the tenacity of belief and his preoccupation with its dramatic possibilities, his fascination with Christian Science is understandable – his admiration as well as his disdain. Twain admired Christian Science for the way it worked against the habitual human tendency to favor the negative side of mental power, especially in matters of health. The idea of an outsider urging on the mind's positive power in cases of illness seemed marvelous.

Yet Twain was contemptuous of those who exploited human vulnerability. Eddy epitomized this type: "I do not think her money-passion has ever diminished in ferocity, I do not think that she has ever allowed a dollar that had no friends to get by her alive." A consummate businesswoman in the form of a religious leader, her astonishing success as the prophet of Christian Science raised disturbing questions about the roots of great spiritual leadership. Most damning, however, in Twain's portrait is the well-substantiated charge that she plagiarized the Christian Science bible, *Science and Health*. It is always obvious, according to Twain, which passages Eddy *has* written because she is incapable of intelligible, grammatical English. The inanity of her prose can be explained by her confusion about the spiritual issues at stake and about her own ambitions. Twain's central claim in *Christian Science*, which opens with a wonderful burlesque about a man who falls off a mountain, breaks every bone in his body, and discovers that the only doctor for miles is a Christian Scientist, is that alternative medicines provide reasonable complements to an authoritarian medical establishment that is often inadequate to the most basic afflictions. Problems arise when the alternatives themselves become doctrinaire. Twain welcomed any method, spiritual or physical, that relieved suffering; a growing concern for Twain as he aged and found himself increasingly alone.

Twain was not the only major American writer to appreciate the possibilities in Christian Science. Theodore Dreiser sent his ailing "Genius" to a Christian Science practitioner in the final chapters of his 1915 novel, and Harold Frederic, author of *The Damnation of Theron Ware* (1896) was subjected, controversially, to a Christian Science treatment after suffering two strokes in 1898 because his lover, Kate Lyon, a devotee, refused conventional medicine. But the American writer who was most profoundly conversant with the history and doctrines of Christian Science was Willa Cather, who ghostwrote a major biography

of its founder as her first assignment at the New York editorial offices of
McClure's Magazine. Cather began work at *McClure's* in 1906 at the age of
thirty-two, after having published thirty stories of her own. The materials on
Eddy's life and Christian Science had been collected by Georgine Milmine, a
newspaperwoman, who was given credit for both the Eddy articles as serialized
in *McClure's Magazine*, 1907–08, and for the book, *The Life of Mary Baker G.
Eddy and the History of Christian Science*, published by Doubleday in 1909. But
editors close to the project and Cather's companion, Edith Lewis, maintained
that Cather was the principal author. Cather scholars have recently recognized
the biography as her first long work, to which she devoted eighteen months
of sustained attention. While Cather sought to minimize her ties to the book
because of the controversy it aroused, and because she typically disdained
her journalism, *The Life of Mary Baker G. Eddy* addressed concerns that run
throughout her career. Cather was raised as a Baptist, and joined her family
in transferring this allegiance to the Episcopal Church. As her late novels
attest, Cather had extensive knowledge of Roman Catholicism. Her biography
emphasizes the significance of a woman-centered religion, while questioning
the effects of Eddy's charismatic authority. Cather appears both fascinated and
disturbed by the spiritual craving that ranged from the isolated snowbound
villages of Vermont and Massachusetts to the remote settlements of Nebraska
and Colorado, and produced converts for the patent deceptions of Mary Baker
Eddy.

Cather proves an adept biographer, combining critical toughness (her treatment of Eddy's plagiarism of Phineas Parkhurst Quimby's "Science of Health")
and understanding (capturing the pathos of the life without sentimentality).
She is at once comprehensive and precise, filling her narrative with memorable
images: Eddy's overwrought father, Mark Baker, on a tirade against neighbors
for violating the Sabbath, when he had mistaken Monday for Sunday; Mary's
childhood hysterics, which undermine her widower father's household rule; the
adult-sized cradle hauled through the streets by Mary's second husband, so she
can be rocked to sleep every night; Mary abandoned by her family and forced
to be a guest in a series of homes, where she is waited on like royalty. Eddy
inherits her father's piety, literalness, and self-righteousness, while absorbing
aspects of a rural New England religious world.

Mary Baker Eddy was born in 1821, the era before railroads and before
the modern inventions that would alleviate the punishing toil of farm life,
where everything was made by hand. Education for the boys of the family
was sporadic, fit between planting and harvest, while the girls attended a
district school. Mary, the youngest of six, extraordinarily high-strung, rebelled
against this relatively mild regime, and so received very little formal schooling

(making even less conceivable, Cather implies, her authorship of the Christian Science philosophy). Showing off seemed to come naturally to Eddy, who continually sought clothing fashions and styles which her family could not afford. Throughout her analysis, Cather draws comparisons between the facts as she found them and Eddy's own self-presentation in her autobiography, *Retrospection and Introspection*. Among Eddy's unsupported claims was that her father believed her "brain too large for her body," and kept her home to be tutored in Greek, Latin, Hebrew, Logic, and Natural Philosophy. Equally apocryphal was Mary's insistence that at twelve, after years of hearing spiritual voices, she was admitted to the Congregationalist Church, where she succeeded in repudiating the church doctrine of predestination. According to church documents, Eddy joined the church at the customary age of seventeen, without protest. Eddy, who had a talent for outlasting her husbands, married George Washington Glover, a mason, in 1843; he died of yellow fever six months later. Mary returned to her father's home, where she gave birth to her son, George Washington Glover, in the fall of 1844. From the beginning, Mary behaved in her father's words "like an old ewe that won't own its lamb." The boy was regularly dispatched to his former wet nurse, who eventually adopted him. In 1853 Eddy was married again, to a dentist, Daniel Patterson.

A hypochondriac and at the same time genuinely fragile, Eddy absorbed fads like a sponge, her various enthusiasms, for mesmerism, spiritualism, and homeopathic healing, covering the range of popular religion in mid nineteenth-century New England. Mesmerism was introduced by Charles Poyen, a French disciple of Mesmer's, who lectured throughout the area and published a book, *Animal Magnetism in New England*, in 1837. Andrew Jackson Davis, author of *The Great Harmonia* and a celebrated New England spiritualist, had also begun to attract attention to his claims for the power of mind over matter. The most important event in Eddy's life was her visit to Phineas Parkhurst Quimby in Portland, Maine, who had devised a method of healing through the simple, benevolent power of mind. A clock-maker by trade, inventor of the famous "Quimby Clock," Quimby had a natural aptitude for mechanics. "A mild-mannered New England Socrates, constantly looking into his own mind, and subjecting to proof all the commonplace beliefs of his friends," he was widely read in philosophy and science, and excited by the ideas of Charles Poyen. Drawing on Christ's mission of healing, Quimby argued that disease was false reasoning, derived not from God but from man. When Mary Glover Patterson came to Quimby in 1863, she was impoverished and emaciated. Quimby's treatment for her spinal trouble left her miraculously pain-free. Eddy became a disciple, poring over his manuscripts and writing letters to local newspapers (such as the Portland *Courier*) to champion the cure. When

Quimby died in 1866 from a stomach tumor that stubbornly resisted his own methods, Eddy was an active mourner and participant in decisions about the future of his work. Eddy's "Christian Science" would never have emerged had Quimby's other disciples been more alert. Nine years after Quimby's death, Eddy published *Science and Health*, a book largely based on Quimby's system of curing disease, which failed to identify him as its originator. Cather provides a straightforward factual history of Eddy's plagiarism, comparing passages from *Science and Health* to Quimby's original text, and quoting sworn court testimony from Quimby associates and neutral observers. The most damning evidence is letters and statements by Eddy herself confirming her indebtedness to Quimby, which she completely ignored in claiming his system as her own in the 1875 book and ever after. These details alone explain why Christian Scientists tried to suppress Cather's biography, sabotaging its library circulation, and inspiring Cather's own reluctance to claim it.

The 1875 version of *Science and Health* was riddled with errors and poor writing, and was largely overlooked, though copies were sent to famous philosophers and theologians, including Thomas Carlyle. Eddy began with the basic principle that mind is the only causation and the body is the mere instrument of spirit. Building on Quimby's association of the imperfection of matter with human beings and the perfection of mind with God, Eddy identifies Adam in the book of Genesis as "the man of error." In later editions of *Science and Health*, Eddy ignores the Hebraic origins of the name "Adam" to highlight its literal meaning – "a dam," or "obstruction." As the image of man who introduced the belief of life in matter, Adam is the source of all sickness, sin, and death. The expulsion of Adam and his product Eve from the Garden of Eden involves the separation of Matter from Mind, a breach that persisted for centuries, until the appearance of Christ, "the most scientific man of whom we have any record." A critical mediator between God and man, Christ is "the Great Teacher of Christian Science." Eddy joined numerous theologians in positing a New Testament notion of divine sentience favorably against an Old Testament notion of divine omnipotence. Two logistical conundrums presented themselves. First, if God is all, yet there is no God in matter, where does matter come from? Second, Christian Science amounted to a reliance on the healing powers of time; it proved helpless against diseases that time could not remedy, such as Quimby's own stomach tumor. The ultimate obstacle for Christian Science, Eddy conceded, was Death. While Christian Science healers must never accede to death but transcend it in their thoughts, it remained at present incontrovertible. Eddy's system, in Cather's words, amounted to "the revolt of a species against its own physical structure; against its relations to its natural physical environment; against the needs of its own physical organism, and against the perpetuation of its kind." It reflected an individual steeped in paranoia and committed to the belief that ailments liberated from her patients could be transferred to her own person. Most powerful of all was Eddy's faith in "malicious mesmerism," that malevolent people, especially vengeful former disciples, could overtake her.

Eddy's disciples, invariably male and younger, came and went. Eddy dominated them, severing their ties to others, and demanding their devotion to her needs. Their departures were often ugly, as exemplified by Eddy's break with Daniel Spofford, whom she charged with witchcraft. Spofford was brought before the Supreme Judicial Court in Salem MA, on May 14, 1878, a proceeding that was covered by the Boston *Globe*. Eddy was clearly energized by her perceived misfortunes. During the time of her purportedly worst sufferings, her Christian Science empire was expanding apace, her journal – eventually, *The Christian Science Monitor* – was launched, and revised editions of *Science and Health* (with the aid of a skilled writer the Reverend James Henry Wiggin) appeared.

Cather records with grudging admiration how Eddy improved with age, dispensing with ungrammatical habits of speech, learning to delegate in recognition of her own limitations, and sequestering herself in order to create an aura of mystery. In the final decade of her life, Eddy presided over the remarkable expansion of Christian Science across America, absorbing converts in the lonely settlements of Michigan, Minnesota, Nebraska, and beyond. "Never, since religions were propagated by the sword," Cather writes, "was a new faith advertised and spread in such a systematic and effective manner." Eddy's band of healers, primarily white, Christian, and female, tended to be from the middle classes. Male recruits were often medical school dropouts, and included a Boston sea captain who turned to Christian Science to find a cure for his wife's illness, and discovered a vocation. Captain Joseph S. Eastman, in Cather's words, "had escaped typhoons and coral reefs and cannibal kings, only to arrive at an adventure of the mind which was vastly stranger." What he found, to his surprise, upon attending a Christian Science meeting in Boston was a mixed company that included "many highly cultured people." Eddy succeeded in building "the largest and most powerful organization ever founded by any woman in America. Probably no other woman so handicapped – so limited in intellect, so uncertain in conduct, so tortured by hatred and hampered by petty animosities – has ever risen from a state of helplessness and dependence to a position of such power and authority."

Christian Science represented the reinvigoration of a truism in the art of healing: that time works wonders. Eddy's genius was to recognize the vast spiritual potential of the idea and its adaptability to the era and culture. She had an instinct for all the ways in which the body in her time had become a site of subjection, partly through images of the suffering, wounded, mutilated, and dead before and after the Civil War, partly through the trying spectacle of difference that confronted Americans in a time of mass immigration. Eddy's radical renunciation of the body and its history, her insistence that it was a mere instrument of spirit, seemed comforting to members of the middle and leisure classes in urban areas who comprised the majority of church followers. Mary Baker Eddy died of pneumonia in December of 1910, at the age of ninety. Her concern all along had been less with the theory itself than with its propagation and institutionalization as a personal monopoly. Sometime believer and habitual critic Mark Twain confirmed Eddy's success in characterizing her venture as "the Mind Trust," on a par with Standard Oil and U.S. Steel.

The significance of Christian Science for an American literary tradition goes beyond the interest displayed by numerous writers in its ideas and methods. Like other growth industries of the period, Christian Science nourished both progressive impulses and backward ones. As a woman-centered religion investing modestly trained, usually female healers with divinely infused powers that rivaled those of an emerging male medical establishment, Christian Science was consistent with a movement for women's rights that grew in a variety of cultural, legal, and political ways between the Civil War and World War I. In harking back to an era when the link between an individual's spiritual and physical state was assumed, and health care was an integral part of pastoral practice, Christian Science represented a considered reaction against a new industrial capitalist order where occupational specialization and institutional expansion were the rule. Above all, it expressed a yearning among modern urbanites for something beyond the material; it expressed needs that could not be answered by accumulation, aspirations that resisted the marketplace. This is despite the paradox that the religion's founder managed to build a substantial fortune upon these aspirations, a paradox that confirms how deeply American the movement was.

5

❦

NATIVE-AMERICAN SACRIFICE IN
AN AGE OF PROGRESS

"THE LOVE OF POSSESSIONS is a disease among them," said Sitting Bull, summarizing with powerful conciseness the essential difference he saw between whites and Native Americans. One could argue that this statement provides as apt an explanation as any for the plight of America's original inhabitants in the late nineteenth century. In 1865 at the end of the Civil War there were over 300,000 Native Americans in the United States, a figure that excluded those who had avoided enumeration. During the war, Native-American loyalties were divided regionally. Southeastern Native Americans, including Cherokees, Chocktaws, Chickasaws, Seminoles, and Creeks sided with the South, inspired by a promise of their own state after the war. The Five Civilized Tribes, as they were called, were themselves slaveholders, and this fact together with their bitterness over the government's consistent failure to honor treaties, drew them to the Confederacy. Four thousand Native Americans from other tribes fought for the North. Native Americans on both sides suffered during and after the war from the pillaging of their territory, burning of their villages, and slaughter of their cattle. At the war's end, Native Americans who had been loyal to the Confederacy were punished by the triumphant Union more harshly than the Confederacy itself. Reconstruction treaties commandeered Native-American lands for railroads and white settlement, and the Native Americans in the gold-rush territories barely survived the invasion of fortune-hunters. Lincoln's promise to improve government and tribal relations after the war, renewed in the 1867 Doolittle report, confirmed the gap between rhetoric and reality in white–Native-American affairs. The Doolittle report cataloged military brutalities against the Native Americans and acts of greed among reservation officials, and concluded with a plea for greater governmental compassion. But its fundamental message was a self-serving Darwinism that predicted the gradual displacement of the weaker race by the stronger, and belied how Native Americans had survived centuries of warfare, epidemics, and forced migration. Throughout the post-Civil War period two predominant methods, assimilation and extermination, served to further limit and extinguish Native-American ways of life. During the presidency

535

of Ulysses S. Grant, who had vowed to uphold Lincoln's promise to reform the Bureau of Indian Affairs, an assimilation policy took precedence. Reservations were expanded and specific portions of land were allotted to individual Native-American families, while a system of schooling for Native-American children emphasizing manual trades was developed. The military's role under such a policy was to ensure, in Grant's words, that "Indians should be made as comfortable on, and uncomfortable off, their reservations as it was in the power of government" to make them. Grant relied on religious organizations, particularly the Society of Friends, for Native-American education. There were moments of enlightenment and justice in Grant's administration of Indian affairs, including accounts (Piute Sara Winnemucca's, *Life Among the Piutes*, Arapaho Carl Sweezy's, *The Arapaho Way: A Memoir of an Indian Boyhood*) of generous reservation officials. Grant's personal secretary during the Civil War, who wrote Lee's surrender at Appomattox, was Ely S. Parker, a Senecan Native-American from upstate New York. Parker, who had assisted Lewis Henry Morgan in preparing his anthropological studies on the Native Americans, was a civil engineer, with legal training (he was refused admission to the New York State Bar because Native Americans were not US Citizens). Appointed the first native Commissioner of Indian Affairs, his term was cut short by a sham fraud charge, that was later revoked.

The leading doctrine for the 1880s was the allotment of Native-American lands to individual Native-American families, ostensibly the first step towards citizenship (which was not granted until 1924). Following a tribal census, the government granted each Native-American "family" 160 acres of land, the size of an average homestead. The sum of these allotments was then subtracted from the total acreage of the reservation, and leftover lands, which might come to more than half of the reservation, were sold on the open market. Every tribe lost land this way, some, the Native Americans of Iowa, as much as 90 percent of former holdings. Native Americans who thrived under these arrangements became eligible for citizenship. The Native American, according to the 1886 Commissioner of Indian Affairs, would learn "the exalting egoism of American civilization so that he will say 'I' instead of 'We,' and 'This is mine' instead of 'This is ours.'" Few seemed concerned that the plan contradicted an 1886 Supreme Court ruling in *The U.S. v. Kagema*, which declared all Native Americans wards of the nation. Moreover, as Ely S. Parker recognized, the programs codified in the Dawes Act of 1887 amounted to the dissolution of Native-American ways of life. The Dawes Act, passed unanimously by Congress and signed into law by President Rutherford B. Hayes, initiated dispossession in part because of Native-American difficulty adapting to American methods of taxation and land leasing. Neighboring cattlemen and farmers were prepared to buy up Native-American holdings at the slightest opportunity. For some

Native-American peoples – the Chippewa in the Great Lakes and the Shawnee of Indian Territory – the outcome of allotment was landlessness and destitution. As one Oklahoma Creek Native American complained, "Egypt had its locusts, Asiatic countries their cholera, France had its Jacobins, England its black plague, Memphis had the yellow fever . . . But it was left for unfortunate Indian territory to be afflicted with the worst scourge of the nineteenth century, the Dawes Commission."

In *America and the Civil War*, Karl Marx had described a course of unimpeded capitalist development, which neither traditional institutions nor revolutionary socialism served to modify. The only apparent impediments were characterized by President James Madison as "the black race within our bosom and the red on our borders." Though they were sometimes coupled in white imaginations with subjugated black peoples, Native Americans were seldom eroticized or degraded in the terms used to rationalize white violence against blacks before and after slavery. Rather, Native Americans were depicted as noble savages whose culture was obsolete. Liberal principles of contract, ideals of promise-keeping and personal responsibility, were inimical to their warlike and anarchic tendencies. Native Americans responded in various ways to the daunting transformations of their circumstances throughout the nineteenth century (by the turn of the twentieth century, a Native-American population estimated at 1.5 million in the seventeenth century had dwindled to 237,000). Some sought spiritual solutions, such as the Sioux Ghost Dances, a messianic religious movement which anticipated the return of dead relatives and a lost way of life, and the sacred Peyote rituals which blended prayer organized around the consumption of hallucinogenic cactus with a pan-Native-American politics that united adherents across the country. Others, the Cherokees and the Creeks, chose military resistance, though their efforts were largely overcome. Still another option was represented by the activities of a considerable Native-American elite that had developed by the first decade of the twentieth century. On October 12, 1911, in Columbus, Ohio, an assembly of Native Americans, some self-proclaimed full bloods, some half bloods, most graduates of industrial or boarding schools, joined common cause to form the Society of American Indians. Ely Parker's brother, Arthur C. Parker, a historian and anthropologist of Native-American culture, declared the participants in this event a "superior class of men and women and above the class of pale invaders." Parker appealed to the popular press to recognize "the call of the leaders of the race to the race to strike out into the duties of modern life and in performing them find every right that had escaped them before."

Among these leaders was Dr. Charles Alexander Eastman, a Santee Sioux of Minnesota. Eastman was a mixed-blood Sioux, whose grandmother was the daughter of Chief Cloudman of the Mdewankton Sioux and the wife of a

Western artist, Captain Seth Eastman. Eastman's mother, Mary Nancy Eastman, married a Wahpeton Sioux, Chief Many Lightnings, in 1847, and died
giving birth to Eastman in 1858. A paternal grandmother and uncle raised
Eastman after he was separated from his father, with whom he was reunited in
1873. Eastman graduated from Dartmouth College with a bachelor's degree
in science in 1887, and earned a medical degree at Boston University in 1890.
Eastman's first appointment was at the Pine Ridge Agency reservation, where
he witnessed the Wounded Knee Massacre. While working as a reservation
doctor, Eastman found time for literary pursuits, which resulted in two commercial as well as critical successes, *Indian Boyhood* (1902) and *The Soul of
the Indian* (1911). In his writings, Eastman emphasized the Native-American
capacity for great attainments and the importance of an indigenous Native-
American literature that retained the distinctive qualities of separate tribes.
He was also a strong and consistent advocate of political rights and justice
for his people. Despite the eloquence and personal magnetism that ensured
him success as a public intellectual, his two literary works provided his largest
audiences. With his personal memoir, *Indian Boyhood*, Eastman was one of the
first Native-American writers to reach a significant trade readership.

His work exemplifies both the possibilities of and the limitations upon
Native-American culture in this post-genocide era. The literature on white–
Native-American conflict and on the annihilation of the Native-American
tribes written by both white and Native-American authors in this period,
faced the difficult task of rationalizing, whether in political, philosophical, or
religious terms, the sacrifice of a people in an age of progress. Some, like Charles
Eastman, wrote from inside the culture in a tone of suppressed anger, seeking
to detail the lost rituals of a civilization, while recording a nation's crimes on
behalf of a universal posterity. Eastman's style recalled Frederick Douglass's
ambivalent autobiography: at once appreciative of dominant cultural ideals and
critical of the hypocrisy that authorized their violation in the name of principle.
Some, Louis Henry Morgan, Zane Grey, Willa Cather, wrote admiringly from
the outside, convinced that Native-American society represented a superior
social model but prepared to consign it to a heroic past. Others, such as
Helen Hunt Jackson and Sara Winnemucca, denounced governmental and
military policies, and outlined, through their fiction – *Ramona* – and non-
fiction – *A Century of Dishonor*, *Life Among the Piutes* – alternative reform
agendas. Finally, some authors depicted the remnants of Native-American
civilization in American society. Zitkala-Sa in her fiction, and Maria Ruiz de
Burton in *The Squatter and the Don*, portrayed Native Americans who managed
to assimilate, as ghosts of their former selves. In each of these examples and
more explored in the following pages, the wisdom of Sitting Bull returns as

a haunting reminder of a Native-American indifference towards possessions that persists as a larger humanitarian value in a materialist era.

RITUAL

As the first in a series of works by indigenous authors, Sarah Winnemucca Hopkins's *Life Among the Piutes: Their Wrongs and Claims* (1883) reflects in its rhetoric and politics an earlier moment in the history of Native-American affairs. There is self-consciousness about the implications of appropriating literacy, which recalls the concerns of slave narrators, as well as a certain optimism about the prospects for redressing the situation of Native Americans. While her people's imperiled condition supplies the motivation for her writing, Winnemuca inhabits a still vibrant indigenous culture. This makes her work less an exercise in elegy than in political advocacy. Where Eastman and Zitkala-Sa portray their assimilation at the delicate ages of adolescence, as the direct result of their cultures' destruction in the post-Civil War era, Winnemuca argues for the reconstitution of Native-American lands and cultures. Where both Eastman and Zitkala-Sa are products of intermarriage, Winnemuca is a full-blooded Piute who emphasizes her aristocratic lineage and the obligations imposed by her place in a tribal elite.

Sarah Winnemucca Hopkins, or Shell Flower Paiute, was born in 1844 near the Humboldt River in Nevada, the granddaughter of Truckee, the chief of all the Piutes, and the daughter of Old Winnemucca, who succeeded his father as tribal chief. Winnemucca was comfortable on stage, and when her family began to pursue commercial drama as a way of compensating the tribe's diminishing resources she figured prominently in their routines. In 1864 she appeared in a show with her father, sisters, and eight braves in Virginia City, Nevada, and later that year participated in "Tableaux Vivants Illustrative of Indian Life" in San Francisco. In press accounts of these performances, she was sometimes referred to as the "Piute Princess." Known for her fiery temper, Winnemucca, who had many husbands, was a controversial figure both among her people and in the larger society she navigated as a representative and political activist. But her passion proved highly valuable when it came to public speaking, and her first lecture in San Francisco in 1879 was such a stunning success that she embarked immediately on a tour East, where she delivered over three hundred lectures. Speaking in the homes of such luminaries as Emerson, Whittier, and Senator Henry L. Dawes, Winnemucca secured the support of Elizabeth Peabody and her sister Mary Tyler Mann, the wife of Horace Mann. The enthusiasm aroused by her lectures led to a book contract and the promise of editorial help from Mann. *Life Among the Piutes* includes an ethnographic account, "The Piutes," which Winnemucca published a year before the book's publication in *The Californian*. In 1884, she settled on her brother's farm in Lovelock, Nevada to begin a school for Piute children, which she later abandoned due to inadequate funds and illness. She died in 1891.

"The first outbreak of the American Indian in human literature . . . [with] a single aim – *to tell the truth* as it lies in the heart and mind of a true patriot, and one whose knowledge of the two races gives her an opportunity of comparing them justly," so declared Mary Mann in the preface to *Life Among the Piutes*. The book treats the Piutes' first contact with settlers, conflict, resettlement, and negotiations with the federal government. Most of Winnemucca's family is killed, and her tribe forcibly removed to a reservation; her brother is jailed in Alcatraz; and amoral reservation officials plague her people. In bearing witness to the personal and collective sufferings of the Piutes at the hands of Americans, Winnemuca's project suggests affinities between black and Native-American experiences of oppression. This is especially evident in the opening, where she highlights differences between the oral culture of Native Americans, and the literate culture of whites, who write everything down, marking and cataloging as means to conquering and possessing.

I was born somewhere near 1844, but am not sure of the precise time. I was a very small child when the first white people came into our country. They came like a lion, yes, like a roaring lion, and have continued so ever since, and I have never forgotten their first coming. My people were scattered at that time over nearly all the territory now known as Nevada.

With simple eloquence, she deflates the Darwinian argument for the "displacement" of savages by the forces of civilization. To a small Native-American girl living in the harmony and quiet of the West, the coming of whites is a violent predation. While her ever optimistic grandfather, the tribal chief, reads their appearance as a kind of ancestral deliverance –" my long-looked for white brothers have come at last" – their guns belie his open arms. Chief Truckee insists on a traditional justification for the white appearance, the promised reunion of whites and Native Americans separated by "our father" at the beginning of the world because of their shared cruelty. The white return suggests renewed faith on the part of higher powers in prospects for white–Native-American peace. This conviction aids relations at first: the chief even joins Captain Fremont in the 1848 Mexican–American War, returning with a new title, "Captain Truckee," a government issue firearm, and an admiration for the California landscape. Chief Truckee, who figures prominently in Winnemuca's account, remains committed to his belief in a universal humanity – that whites "think as we do."

Chief Truckee's death in 1859 represents the passing of an era; the new decade of Civil War and the rapid progress that accompanies it proves disastrous for the Piutes. A clear sign that their situation is hopeless is the unwritten rule among Native-American women to reproduce sparingly for fear of their inability to protect their offspring. The section of her narrative devoted to the Bannock War recounts her service as a liaison between the Piutes and the American army in June of 1878, when she drove 223 miles by horse and wagon between enemy lines, hazarding both Bannock Native-American and American hostility. Though she achieves her purpose of protecting the Piutes from both sides, she finds the Americans and the Bannocks to be equally barbaric. Winnemucca's descriptions of the Bannock War are no less riveting than the adventure writings of James Fenimore Cooper and Zane Grey. Yet her rhetorical methods on the whole are closest to the sentimental novel tradition. She appeals repeatedly to readers' sympathies: "Dear reader, I must tell a little more about my poor people, and what we suffer at the hands of our white brothers." Her pleas for justice mount in intensity, especially in her detailing of the "Yakima Affair," where the Piutes are herded like cattle to another state during the winter, dwindling to one third of their original number.

Oh, for shame! You who are educated by a Christian government in the art of war, the practice of whose profession makes you natural enemies of the savages, so called by you. Yes, you, who call yourselves the great civilization; you who have knelt upon Plymouth Rock, covenanting with God to make this land the home of the free and the brave . . . your so-called civilization sweeps inland from the ocean wave; but, oh, my God! leaving its pathway marked by crimson lines of blood, and strewed by the bones of two races, the inheritor and the invader; and I am crying out to you for justice, – yes, pleading for the far-off plains of the West, for the dusky mourner.

Recalling Frederick Douglass's apostrophe to the white ships' sails and Harriet Jacobs's petitioning of a white sisterhood in their respective slave narratives, as well as the sentimental novels of Susan Warner and Harriet Beecher Stowe, Winnemuca's narrative makes her people's sufferings legible within the terms of an American literary tradition. The book ends with the tribe's members scattered across the plains of Oregon, living emblems of broken promises. Winnemucca's political agenda is foregrounded by her closing petition for the restitution of her peoples' Nevada lands. Readers are asked to sign and forward it to Mrs. Mary Mann in Boston. There were few instances in nineteenth-century American letters where the purposes of a written record were so direct.

Charles Alexander Eastman's *Indian Boyhood* is dedicated to "the little son who came too late to behold for himself the drama of savage existence." This conveys the split perspective of a book whose assimilated narrator is ever mind-ful of the difference between a Native-American and an American childhood. At the same time, Eastman's narrative is designed to overturn conventional dis-tinctions between civilized and savage existence. Native Americans are made not born, and Native-American becoming depends upon systematic education. *Indian Boyhood* is an instruction manual for a white audience steeped in clichés. Eastman's remark, for example, that "The Indian youth is a born hunter," is countered by pages detailing how "Ohiyesa the first" is prepared for his life in the wild by a careful and knowledgeable uncle.

Eastman begins his book with a rhetorical question that sets the world of the Native-American boy within an American literary tradition of rugged scouts, whale hunters, and runaways capable of triumphing in the wilderness: "What boy would not be an Indian for a while when he thinks of the freest life in the world?" Natty Bumpo, Ishmael, Huckleberry Finn, and Ohiyesa repre-sent a single lineage of heroes schooled in nature, developing all their senses, befriending animals as well as hunting them. There are differences: Eastman's life is purposeful from the outset (the medicine man who presides at his birth prophecies his future career as a doctor); women are critical to his survival and greatly admired (the infant child is given by his mother on her deathbed into the care of her mother-in-law, an astonishingly vigorous woman of sixty); and life in the wilderness is less a story of strong individuals overcoming the odds, than a drama of collective labor and communal celebration. Spring, summer, autumn were times of bounty; winter, of deprivation. It was atypical for the nomadic Santee Sioux to prepare against want. Eastman was four years old in 1862 when his people rose up against white settlers in Minnesota, killing 800 in a month. The American military drove them into Canada, arresting most of the men, including Eastman's father and brothers. Thus, most of his memoir is focused on his upbringing in southern Manitoba, where his uncle and grandmother preside over a decade-long process of cultural transmission. An "Indian" boyhood is an ongoing tutorial: in various tree barks, bird col-oration and calls, modes of fighting bears, wild-cats, wolves. "Indian" boys learn to fast, run for days, find water in the night forest, master their emo-tions. Eastman demonstrates this final skill in the climactic chapter of the book, which affirms the centrality of religion in the life of the "Indian". At the age of eight, he is called upon to make his first significant offering to the "Great Mystery," and is urged by his grandmother to give up his beloved companion, "the jet-black dog" Ohitika, "with a silver tip on the end of his tail and on his nose." Though he is devastated by this sacrifice, he is fortified by the awe of the people, and by the overall gravity of the occasion. An "Indian" boyhood is an endurance test. Eastman ends his memoir with the shocking realization that his lifelong aim of avenging his father and brothers has been nullified by their survival. Imprisoned by the "Big Knives," they have been converted to Christianity. Eastman has long been curious about whites and their technologies, their notions of property, taxation, and exchange. On the journey to his new life however, he confesses to feeling "as if I were dead and traveling to the Spirit Land." Listening to his father singing a Christian hymn one morning in his "American home," it is clear that his will be a long and complex assimilation.

Eastman's *Soul of the Indian* (1911) begins where *Indian Boyhood* ends, with the question of how a boy schooled in Native-American ways accommodates Christianity and the alien laws of possession that complements it. *Soul of the Indian* describes the religion of "the typical American Indian" before it was blighted by contact with the white. Like Henry Lewis Morgan, Eastman emphasizes the commonality between classical Greece and contemporary Native-American ways of life. Most important is the relationship to nature, and the idea of the omnipresence of divine beings, which inhabit every plant, tree, and insect, the earth, sun, and sky. Eastman emphasizes the Native-American's repudiation of white materialism. Native Americans also differ from whites in their treatment of animals, which are respected and appreciated for sacrificing themselves on behalf of their human friends.

Contemporary Christianity is rife with hypocrisy and superstition. Despite the teachings of Christ, which are consistent with Native-American religion, whites are preoccupied with money. Eastman finds the principles of Christianity and modern values irreconcilable; were white men honest, they would admit as much. He quotes a Crow Native American:

The Wise Ones said we might have their religion, but when we tried to understand it we found that there were too many kinds of religion among white men for us to understand, and that scarcely any two white men agree which was the right one to learn. This bothered us a good deal until we saw that the white man did not take his religion any more seriously than he did his laws, and that he kept both of them just behind him, like Helpers, to use when they might do him good in his dealings with strangers. These were not our ways. We kept the laws we made and lived our religion. We have never been able to understand the white man, who fools nobody but himself.

A regime of self-denial and physical exertion, an essential moral soundness, is replaced by a culture of indulgence and cupidity. The very recording of Native-American customs and beliefs is a sign of their tragic diminishment. Eastman concludes on the subject of death, which arouses little fear. While the Native American has never doubted the immortality of the soul, he does not speculate about the future, nor does he utter the names of the dead. The proud elegiac tone of Eastman's narrative signals its primary aim: the codification of religious practices for a community of worship whose days are numbered.

Eastman's *From the Deep Woods to Civilization: Chapters in the Autobiography of an Indian* (1916) is his most pro-civilization book. This book begins with the appearance of Eastman's father, come to bring his Native-American son "home to civilization." Eastman's receptivity to the dominant culture is reflected in his openness to Christianity. He is equally approving of white literacy, and acknowledges its beneficial supplanting of his own oral culture. At the same time, Eastman laments the superior elements of Native-American culture that are left behind, and the injustices visited upon Native Americans by whites, just as he repudiates the self-serving proposition that suffering is an inevitable consequence of progress. Yet Eastman proves a man of the age by his particular receptivity to dominant-culture habits of invention and enterprise. He assumes the role of representative Native-American, but makes clear that his has been a charmed life as a member of a distinguished Native-American family, with connections through intermarriage to powerful Easterners. Few Native-American college students were introduced to Emerson, Longfellow, Parkman, and Matthew Arnold, nor were they aided, as he was, in their quests for vocations. To be sure, Eastman had extraordinary personal gifts – high intelligence, good looks – and strong discipline (a result of Native-American education preserved throughout his life in civilization). At Beloit College he identified with poor students, since he was also putting himself through school (the government had yet to adopt a policy supporting Native-American education). At Knox College, Eastman befriended such future notables as S. S. McClure, Edgar A. Bancroft (future lawyer for the International Harvester Co.), and John S. Phillips of the *American Magazine*. At Dartmouth College, which he entered in 1882, Eastman drew strength from previous Native-American alumni, including Occum, a century earlier, and Daniel Webster, reputedly part Native-American.

Eastman's extensive and varied education, together with an instinctive curiosity that disposed him towards the best features of both cultures, ensured that he would be an asset to his people. At a relatively young age, Eastman had defined lifelong goals: the Native American must relinquish exclusive loyalty to tradition, and adapt himself to opportunities made available by the dominant culture; the commitment to a liberal Christianity capable of harmonizing all languages and gathering all peoples under one faith. Like many idealists, he was a perpetual outsider, criticizing whites for failing to practice what they preached, and Native Americans for denying that white social ideals were worthwhile even if white social practices were not. Eastman's marginality made him a valuable historian of cultural conflict. His account of the 1890 events at Wounded Knee, where 250 Sioux Native-Americans, mostly women and children, were massacred by white cavalry, is a case in point. Because he was a doctor at the nearby Pine Ridge reservation, he knew the aggressive religious movement as a response to a series of injustices: the cutting of reservation rations and consequent malnutrition, the official disregard of widespread illness, the violation of treaties. Eastman makes much of the fact that the Wounded Knee Massacre occurred around Christmas, recalling how he tended wounds in a reservation church under a Christmas tree. He takes what little solace he can in his Yuletide engagement to Elaine Goodale, daughter of Puritans on one side and Tories on the other. Eastman's experience as doctor and witness at Wounded Knee, which proved to be the final battle between Native Americans and the army, resulted in a published account of the events. He considered his revisionist history an essential counter to the inaccuracies of mainstream journalistic coverage.

Throughout *From The Deep Woods To Civilization*, Eastman stresses, in the name of Christianity, how much whites have to learn from Native Americans. This is linked to his ongoing critique of modernity. Indeed, Eastman posits Native-American civilization as *the* perfect exemplum of Christian principles. Contemplating terrible poverty in New York, Chicago, and Boston, he notes that no Native-American people would tolerate the coexistence of excess wealth and utter deprivation. Eastman's liberal universalism was brought full circle through his 1911 experience as the Native-American representative at the First Universal Races Congress in London. He was pleased to discover his own faith in racial equality affirmed by his colleagues there, and distinguished himself by his demand that religious diversity be respected as well, a demand seconded by the Jewish Felix Adler and by Asian Buddhist representatives. Eastman closes his book with a characteristic appeal to whites and Native Americans. In America, "the dollar is the measure of value, and *might* still spells *right.*" Native-American civilization, however, is gone, and there is no choice but to adapt to American ways. Religion, he argues, Christianity specifically, harbors the potential salvation of modern society. A society without a strong spirituality and ethics cannot survive.

Eastman's experience of alienation as a Native-American man attempting to assimilate into American society was doubled for his contemporary Zitkala-Sa, who once referred to herself as "neither a wild Indian nor a tame one." Zitkala-Sa's sketches of growing up Native American in America at the turn of the century were published in the best American magazines, including the *Atlantic Monthly* and *Harper's*. Zitkala-Sa, or Red Bird, also known as Gertrude Simmons Bonnin, was born at the Yankton Sioux Agency in South Dakota in 1876, the daughter of a full-blooded Sioux and a white father who died before she was born. At the age of eight, Zitkala-Sa was sent to the Indiana Manual Labor Institute in Wabash, Indiana, from which her older brother had graduated, and from this point on felt herself homeless. Throughout her life, Zitkala-Sa understood this sense of not belonging as a result both of personal experience and collective circumstances. Throughout her education – at Earlham College in Indiana, where the multitalented young woman earned prizes in oratory, and developed her abilities as a violinist; during two years teaching at the Carlisle Indian School; subsequent training at the Boston Conservatory of Music as a violin soloist; and later touring in Europe with the Carlisle Indian Band – Zitkala-Sa was haunted by the recognition that her people were less than immigrants in their own land. No amount of assistance, she realized, even were it consistent, would ever reduce that injustice. Her awareness that there was no part of her life that had not been violated by educators, officials, well-meaning or not, or simply by the stereotypical expectations which people brought to their encounters, made inevitable her ultimate return to Sioux territory and her marriage to a politically active Sioux. From 1903 to the start of World War I, she lived on the Uintah and Ouray Reservation in Utah, with her husband, Raymond, Talefese Bonnin and her son Raymond, who was born in 1903. In 1916 she moved to Washington D.C., where she and her husband became lobbyists for Native-American causes. Over the next twenty years, before her death in 1938, she gained renown as a lecturer and writer. Among her most important contributions was her investigative report in the 1920s on the treatment of northern Oklahoma Native Americans whose land possessed vast oil reserves. In *Oklahoma's Poor Rich Indians: An Orgy of Graft and Exploitation*, Zitkala-Sa recounted the tale of Ledcie Stechi, a Choctaw orphan who had inherited rich oil land. Cared for at first by her Native-American relatives, when the oil was discovered she was made the ward of a white bank owner who doled out a barely livable subsistence for Ledcie and her aged grandmother. Ledcie died shortly after she came directly under the bank owner's care, apparently from poisoning.

While less shocking, the narrative events of Zitkala-Sa's own childhood, collected as *American Indian Stories* (1921), confirm the destructive impact of white guardians, and reveal a strong contrast between her early life on the reservation, where she is taught women's arts – beadwork, weaving, gathering and preparing food – and school days at the Quaker mission. Dominated by tragic images of her people driven like buffalo from their land of mass death, the stories also catalog wrongs done to Native Americans through agencies of relief administered by the inept and hostile: an alcoholic agency doctor sends his charges to early graves, while a sadistic teacher crushes the ambitions of a young Native American by reminding him that he is a mere government pauper. Despite the pleasures of life on the reservation, her closeness to her mother, and her fear of whites, Zitkala-Sa is drawn to white culture, lured by promises of red apples and a ride on the "iron horse." Life among whites is the only choice for a talented and ambitious girl, though it continually defies her expectations and sense of decency. The train ride is marred by the cold curiosity of white families, with no empathy for homesick Native-American children. The schooling features equal measures of good will and harshness, but its strongest note is disregard for the children's emotional and physical needs. She remains bitter about the neglect of their sufferings, describing how a daily teaspoon from a single large bottle is made to remedy all illness. She never quite recovers from the poor care she received at the Quaker missionary school, nor does she recover from the experience of self-alienation. This is reflected in narratives marked by images of tombs and live burial, that emphasize how she is caught between the imprisoning consciousness conferred by her white schooling and the spiritual solace of a receding Native-American culture emblemized by her mother's conversion to Christianity.

This struggle to derive succor from a world that is steadily vanishing makes "Why I Am a Pagan" the most moving of her sketches. In Native-American teachings, she points out, all things great and small are respected for their divinely conceived purpose. In contrast to Eastman, who notes the similarity between such ideas and Christian precepts, Zitkala-Sa sees only differences: the harmonious notion of universal kinship is unlike any Christian principle she has known, whether in theory or in practice. Her religious philosophy repudiates a forgiving split between Christian creed and deed, just as it foregoes the ecumenical desire to discover affinities in the religious beliefs of different cultures. With a deliberate ethnocentric flourish, she identifies her newfound peace as the legacy of "the Great Spirit," animating the world and connecting all living things. *Indian Stories* concludes with a poignant reminder of the assimilationist alternative in the tragic life of "The Soft-Hearted Sioux," who is converted to Christianity during nine years at a mission school and returns to his people as a missionary. His fellow Native Americans remain deaf to his preaching, perhaps because they are near starvation, despite the fact that the reservation is surrounded by a white settlement rich with cattle. Guilt-ridden by the spectacle of his dying father, the Gentle Sioux steals some meat, and kills the white settler who pursues him. The sketch ends with an image of bloody snow as the Gentle Sioux is led to the gallows. Clearly he mistook his role in Christianity; instead of a spokesman for sacrificial principles, he is an object of sacrificial practice.

The critical passion of indigenous writers in the post-Civil War period was shared by some white outsiders who wrote about Native-American affairs. Such was the case with Lewis Henry Morgan, a lawyer, businessman, and eventual "father of American Anthropology." A native of Aurora, New York, Morgan's ethnological interests were kindled by concern for Native Americans in his home region who were struggling in the 1840s to keep their ancestral lands. Morgan's first book, *The League of the Ho-de-nosau-nee, or Iroquois* (1851), which he wrote with the assistance of Ely S. Parker, the Seneca Native American, was, according to John Wesley Powell, head of the Bureau of American Ethnology, "the first scientific account of an Indian tribe ever given to the world." Morgan and Parker documented Native-American society in pre-colonial times and the earliest responses to whites, including the religious teachings of "Handsome Lake," a Seneca Native-American who had died in 1815. Handsome Lake's teachings grew increasingly popular among his descendants and resembled in significant respects the contemporaneous religious revivals of upstate New York's white inhabitants, stressing temperance and spiritual devotion while prohibiting divorce and abortion. At the same time, Handsome Lake discouraged interaction with whites, and emphasized the necessity of retaining Iroquois lands. Morgan's investigations of local Native Americans convinced him that a classificatory system of relationship was generally shared by their diverse peoples, and could be traced to Asia.

In 1871, Morgan pursued his theory on the Asiatic origin of the Native Americans in *Systems of Consanguinity and Affinity of the Human Family*, a six-hundred page analysis with nearly 200 tables listing the relationship terms from tribes and nations of North America, Europe, Asia, Oceania, and Africa. The book's theory of origins proved unsupportable, but Morgan had identified the category of kinship and the anthropological science that was so closely tied to it. Morgan advanced a key distinction in noting that primitive social relations were based on kinship and modern ones were based on property. His subsequent exploration of these property relations in his polemical *Ancient Society* (1877) revealed his appreciation for Native-American culture. A combination of moral fervor and scholarly substance made *Ancient Society* the most celebrated and popular of Morgan's works. He described property as a kind of Frankenstein's monster, which had become so diversified that its effects were undetectable. "The time will come," he predicted, "when human intelligence will rise to the mastery over property, and define the relations of the state to the property it protects . . . A mere property career is not the final destiny of mankind, if progress is to be the law of the future as it has been of the past." Though he tended to characterize Native-American civilization in ways that rendered it obsolete, Morgan emphasized its complexity. His receptivity to cultural pluralism anticipated assumptions about cultural differences that were not widely accepted until well after the turn of the century.

Morgan's detailed recording of Native-American customs confirmed his respect. His account of Native-American views of ownership in *Ancient Society* countered arguments that Native Americans were incapable of surviving in the modern marketplace. Morgan approached Native-American culture in terms that reinforced its continuities, while noting differences. In keeping with social-scientific understanding of the importance of homes and domestic habits in defining the values of a people, for instance, the fifth chapter of *Ancient Society*, "Houses and House-Life of the American Aborigines" (excerpted in *The North American Review*), described Native-American laws of hospitality and ideas of common ownership. Morgan called for more exploration of Native-American arts and inventions, architecture, manners, languages, religious beliefs, methods of healing, political systems. The Native-American way of life, he concluded, merited attention for its sophistication, and also for the sake of ameliorating the cultural conflict brought about by colonization.

No contemporary of Morgan's was more committed to redressing the ravages of that process than Helen Hunt Jackson, a renowned New England writer who remarked shortly before her death that her writings on the conditions of the nation's Native Americans were "the only things I have done for which I am glad now. They will live on and they will bear fruit." Jackson's conviction appears to have been shared by reading audiences who made *Ramona* (1884; serialized in the *Christian Union* May 15 to November 6, 1884) a bestseller, and responded to her treatise *A Century of Dishonor* (1881), with respectful outrage. Like Stowe's *Uncle Tom's Cabin*, a work she consciously emulated ("If I could write a story that would do for the Indian a thousandth part what *Uncle Tom's Cabin* did for the Negro, I would be thankful the rest of my life," she wrote in 1883) Jackson's novel had direct political consequences, assisting the passage of the "Act for the Relief of the Mission Indians," which preserved thousands of acres of land for California's mission "Indians." Like Stowe too, Jackson claimed a divine hand in the writing process. *Ramona* was a critical as well as commercial success. Albion Tourgee ranked it with *Uncle Tom's Cabin* as one of the century's two great ethical novels. Jackson was "converted" to her role as a promoter of "Indian rights" on October 29, 1879, at a reception at Boston's Horticultural Hall for Ponca Chief Standing Bear, who was touring the East to publicize the forced migration of his tribe from their Dakota homelands. Jackson's reform writings began as open letters to newspapers (e.g., *The New York Evening Post*, *The New York Times*, *The Springfield Republican*, and *The Boston Daily Advertiser*), and was collected in 1881 as *A Century of Dishonor: A Sketch of the United States Government's Dealings with Some of the Indian Tribes*.

Published by Harper and Brothers after Scribner's and Robert's Brothers rejected it as too controversial, *Century of Dishonor* focused on governmental dealings with seven tribes – the Poncas, Cherokees, Delawares, Cheyennes, Nez Perces, Sioux, and Winnebagoes. An introductory chapter summarized international law on the rights of prior occupancy, and claimed such rights for Native Americans. A chapter on "Massacres of Indians by Whites" revealed how often Native-American violence was provoked; a series of appendices detail "Indian Character," the extent of white aggressions; and the Native-American perspective of Sarah Winnemucca. Reviews of *A Century of Dishonor* were uniformly positive, and the book established Jackson as an authority on Native Americans. Commissioned by *Century Magazine* in the fall of 1881 to write four pieces on Southern California, Jackson began an immersion course in its history: Jesuit accounts by Miguel Venegas and Francisco Javier Alegre, J. Russell Bartlett's (a founder of the American Ethnological Society) *Personal Narrative of Explorations in Texas, New Mexico, California, Sonora, and Chihuahua*, and Edward Everett Hale's contribution on California for William Cullen Bryant's *A Popular History of the United States* (1876–80). She also researched the history of California's missions and ranchos at the Hubert Howe Bancroft Library of Western Americana.

Jackson was drawn to Southern California's multiculturalism, which she tended to romanticize, from the tragic experiences of Mission Indians to what she called "the Mexican element" – highly "picturesque . . . red tiles, brown faces, shawls over heads – dark eyes and soft voice, and the Spanish tongue." In 1882, Hunt assumed a post as official commissioner of Mission Indians in Southern California. One of the first women to hold such a position, Jackson worked without pay (her second husband, William Sharples Jackson, was a wealthy Colorado Springs banker, and later president of the Denver Rio Grande Western Railroad). Jackson's co-commissioner, Abbot Kinney, described her unique rapport with the region's inhabitants: "She could go up to utter strangers, people of the most diverse kind – diverse in nature, social position, work, education, ideals – and in a few minutes, without any leading or prompting, they seemed to pour out their inmost ideas to her." The result of these official travels was Jackson and Kinney's 1883 *Report on the Condition and Needs of the Mission Indians of California*, which endorsed their right of habitation. Jackson's report on the missions recognized the intolerable injustices of Native-American "resettlement."

The *Atlantic Monthly*, which had published Jackson's European travel writings and poetry in the 1880s, refused her Southern California writings. This was consistent with the conservative trend in the 1880s and 1890s of a

Yankee high culture that viewed literature as an exclusively aesthetic medium, irreducible to politics and ethics. Jackson had little difficulty publishing her Southern California pieces elsewhere, including the *Independent*, the *Century*, and the *Christian Union*, where *Ramona* was serialized.

Ramona was written in four months, a legendary production history that was reinforced by the production site: New York's Berkeley Hotel, where Jackson wrote surrounded by Native-American baskets and romantic busts of her hero and heroine. Colonial conflict among whites, Spaniards, and Native Americans in nineteenth-century California proved an ideal vessel for Jackson's skills as a New England regional writer. The novel features stock plots and characters: an idealized heroine (Ramona), offspring of Scottish father and Native-American mother, acquires a cold, manipulative Spanish stepmother (Señora Moreno), marries a noble Native American (Alessandro), is widowed, marries the stepmother's son (Felipe) who has always loved Ramona, and becomes head of the manor. Yet the novel is compelling in its detailing of a civilization, and its recasting in a distinctive cultural context of various foundational myths. A multicultural romance set in California during different stages in the transition to modernity, *Ramona* is a story of romantic exile. A latter-day Exodus narrative, it pictures the hapless Ramona and Alessandro wandering from one ravaged Native-American village to another, providing a long ambulatory record of the destruction of Native-American culture. The most effective characters are the powerful Señora Moreno and her weak son Felipe, while Jackson's villains are the novel's dreaded and never fully elaborated "Americans." It is Señora Moreno's anti-Americanism that reveals Jackson's sympathies with her.

It gave her unspeakable satisfaction, when the Commissioners, laying out a road down the valley, ran it at the back of her house instead of past the front . . . Whenever she saw, passing the place, wagons or carriages belonging to the hated Americans, it gave her a distinct thrill of pleasure to think that the house turned its back on them . . . a pleasure in which religious devotion and race antagonism were so closely blended that it would have puzzled the subtlest of priests to decide whether her act were a sin or a virtue.

Americans are blameworthy for their crude and violent Western culture, and as agents of a capitalist system that victimizes specific groups. The novel ends with the expatriation of Felipe, who abandons his flourishing ranch for Mexico, accompanied by his wife, Ramona, who is eager to spare her daughter the life of a "half-breed" in America. Felipe's rejection of America expresses aristocratic disdain for the greed of California's nouveaux riches; his return to Mexico is an embrace of his own class and kind. Jackson's romantic racialism sanctions interbreeding to a point, while reinforcing the special affinity of like races and classes.

America is repudiated for its cruelty towards the gentle Native Americans, as well as for its violation of a sacred (by the lights of New England and New Mexico) upper-class code. Despite their reservations about Jackson's polemics, the editors and readers of the *Atlantic Monthly* would have found much to admire in the moral vision of *Ramona*. While championing the lost cause of California's Native Americans, who survive the narrative in only limited ways (mixing their blood with those of stronger peoples), the novel affirmed many high culture ideals, including the principled racism of a New Darwinian science. In this respect, Jackson's work proved compatible with the Social Darwinism favored by members of the Eastern elite who made names for themselves in this period writing about whites and Native Americans out West.

SOCIAL DARWINISM

By far the most curious of these Western works was Mark Twain's *Roughing It* (1872), the literary by-product of Twain's experiences as aid to his brother Orion, who was appointed Secretary of the Territory of Nevada in 1861. Following his brief sojourn as a Confederate soldier, Twain embraced the prospect of Western travels with his brother, which allowed him to pursue prospecting, speculating, and journalism. Combining the methods of travel writing, autobiography, and the novel, *Roughing It* features a tenderfoot narrator who is alternately self-mocking and self-aggrandizing. Because his opinions are always rather tongue-in-cheek, his continuous slurs and displays of prejudice, towards women (the few he meets), Native Americans, Chinese, blacks, and Mexicans are difficult to assess. Do they express Twain's pre-enlightened youth, while affirming a subtle racism that runs like a noxious undercurrent throughout his career, or are they the distinct views of a literary persona, a novice from Missouri, who might be expected to believe such things? The question is significant because of the virulence of the tenderfoot's bigotry and also because he is considerably more enamored of the civilization he leaves behind in heading West than the typical Twain narrator. The Western territory, as portrayed in *Roughing It*, is a crossroads of cultural variety. Irish (sometimes called "Micks"), Chinese, Mexicans (sometimes called "Greasers"), French, Russians, and Germans come together in pursuit of the opportunities afforded by gold and land. Like all of Twain's novels, *Roughing It* has two major plots. The first is the drama of the West, still in the 1860s a region of dream and invention, the place where American fictions – the rags-to-riches story, ideals of self-transformation, independence, and freedom – come to life, at the expense of cultural aliens, Native Americans mainly. The second is the drama of authorship: Twain's launching of his career as a popular American author with claims to greatness. Twain wrote *Roughing It* in the wake of his extraordinary success as a lecturer, storyteller (of the "Celebrated Jumping Frog of Calaveras County") and travel writer (*Innocents Abroad*), and the narrative displays self-consciousness about the kind of language necessary to literary fame. To probe the book's creative explorations of this subject is to recognize the interdependence of its two major plots – the West as the ultimate in dramatic potential; the West as the place where the nation's original inhabitants are sacrificed.

Twain's drama about Western expansion, myth-making, and Native-American resettlement depends on Darwinist categories and assumptions. These include the idea that primitive peoples are closer to animals than are civilized ones and that evolutionary progress requires their displacement and even annihilation. Throughout the narrative, Twain uses animals – rabbits, coyote, cows, even species unknown to the West (e.g. camels) – as the basis of a distinctively Western language. Thus, the conductor's "picturesque" idiom yields the image of a heavily curtained coach "as dark as the inside of a cow"; the "jackass rabbit . . . is well-named"; and an exotic camel, the only animal detached enough to judge, has "choked to death" on one of the narrator's manuscripts. Animals illuminate the Darwinist rationale that deems Native Americans an indigenous species subject to population controls administered by efficient and enterprising colonists. An inventory of wildlife the tenderfoot expects to find out West – "buffaloes and Indians, and prairie dogs, and antelopes" – ominously conjoins Native Americans with the buffalo slaughtered through the 1860s. Is the coupling ironic, or rationalizing in a subliminal way, the naïve but dangerous project of the novel's tenderfoot narrator, or the implicit thought of early, unenlightened Twain?

The case for authorial bigotry is bolstered by a portrayal of Native Americans as consistently aggressive, in the classically inverted terms of "settlement" and "captivity" narratives. Consider one of the novel's most memorable descriptions:

a long, slim, sick and sorry-looking skeleton, with a gray wolf-skin stretched over it, a tolerably bushy tail that forever sags down with a despairing expression of forsakenness and misery, a furtive and evil eye, and a long, sharp face, with slightly lifted lip and exposed teeth. He has a general slinking expression all over. The coyote is a living, breathing allegory of Want. He is *always* hungry. He is always poor, out of luck, and friendless. The meanest creatures despise him, and even the fleas would desert him for a velocipede.

This metaphorically rich condemnation culminates in an analogy to Native-Americans that is among the most direct assaults on a culture in classic American literature.

[The coyote] will eat anything in the world that his first cousins, the desert-frequenting tribes of Indians, will, and they will eat anything they can bite. It is a curious fact that these latter are the only creatures known to history who will eat nitroglycerin and ask for more if they survive. The coyote of the deserts beyond the Rocky Mountain has a peculiarly hard time of it, owing to the fact that his relations, the Indians, are just as apt to be the first to detect a seductive scent on the desert breeze, and follow this fragrance to the late ox it emanated from, as he is himself and when this occurs he has to content himself with sitting off at a little distance watching those people strip off and dig out everything edible, and walk off with it. Then he and the waiting ravens explore the skeleton and polish the bones. It is considered that the coyote, and the obscene bird, and the Indian of the desert, testify their blood kinship with each other in that they live together in the waste places of the earth on terms of perfect confidence and friendship, while hating all other creatures and yearning to assist at their funerals.

Though it hardly excuses the slur, it is possible that the narrator is thinking here of one outcast group of Native American – the "desert . . . tribes"? Yet he later cites an even lower Native American, the Goshute, "the wretchedest type of mankind I have ever seen." They are "small, lean . . . a dull black like the ordinary American Negro; taking note of everything, covertly, like all the other 'Noble Red Men.'" All Native Americans, from the perspective of the tenderfoot, are essentially alike, a surmise confirmed by the following: "Whenever one finds an Indian tribe he has found Goshutes more or less modified by circumstances and surroundings – but Goshutes, after all." The possibility that the tenderfoot's prejudices are supposed to seem barbarically funny raises the prospect of humor so vitriolic that it has become something else. While laughing at bigotry was soon to become a Twain trademark, *Roughing It* does not quite reach it. But the narrative does show verbal facility to be compatible with cruelty, indeed, among its most cherished mediums, especially in the West. This is one of the most important ideas in *Roughing It*. Hence the rites of settlement: the combination of adventure, compulsive talk, fear, and loathing that help to camouflage extermination and land theft. Yet beneath the rhetoric, a stream of references to bones, skeletons, and skulls, confirm that the post-Civil War West was fast becoming a Native-American graveyard.

Roughing It looks forward to the 1870s, the decade of the most aggressive Western expansion, which provides the setting for the most important novels on the subject. Maria Ruiz de Burton's *The Squatter and the Don* (1885), Owen Wister's *The Virginian* (1902), and Zane Grey's *Riders of the Purple Sage* (1912), are all set in the 1870s and offer different perspectives on the era through their

Mexican-American (Ruiz de Burton), Virginian and New England (Wister), and Mormon (Grey) protagonists, respectively. What these three accounts of colonization and development share is a common casualty, Native Americans, who appear in all three novels as interlopers on their own land.

The Squatter and the Don, the second novel by Ruiz de Burton, and one of the first English novels by a Mexican-American author, describes the gradual displacement of the Mexican population by white settlers in the Southwest. Though Mexicans were granted full citizenship under the 1848 Treaty of Guadalupe-Hidalgo, a series of State and Congressional laws resulted in the transfer of their land to the open market, where it was snapped up by white speculators, farmers, and railroad tycoons. While de Burton portrays her Mexican aristocrats or "Californios," as they were called, as victims of California, the US Congress, and capitalist developers, she overlooks the original dispossession of Native-American lands (by Mexicans). Native Americans appear in *The Squatter and the Don* as afterthoughts, servants or day laborers, usually lazy and dishonest, while de Burton attends to the wrongs of the Mexican aristocracy in all ways superior to the unrefined Americans that seek to replace it. The parallels between *The Squatter and the Don* and *Ramona* are obvious; what is missing is Jackson's moral defense of Native Americans and fully realized Native-American characters. Jackson, like Lewis Henry Morgan, is a cultural insider bearing witness to the American sacrifice of the Native-American nations. In her concern for the grievances of her own people, Ruiz de Burton disregards those of the original inhabitants. The reformist sensibility that led to political advocacy for groups other than one's own, at least in literary circles of the time, apparently required a guilty New England conscience.

Maria Amparo Ruiz de Burton was born in Loreto, Baja California, in 1832, to a family of wealthy landowners and military leaders. The valuable California territory owned by Ruiz de Burton's grandfather, Governor of Lower California until his death in 1853, included a stretch of land in Baja, for which his granddaughter would fight until her death. Ruiz de Burton's distinguished parentage was maternal, which may explain why she took her mother's name, Ruiz, instead of her father's, Arango. Ruiz de Burton met her husband, Henry S. Burton, an American army captain, in 1847, when he came to La Paz to take over Baja California. Burton presided over the surrender of La Paz, and the articles of capitulation signed by Mexicans which conferred the right to become US citizens, while retaining their lands and forms of government. These articles were superseded by the Treaty of Guadalupe-Hidalgo, which excluded Baja California, and granted Alta California, as well as the rest of the Southwest territory, to America. During this period, Ruiz de Burton left with her mother for San Francisco, and both became US citizens. In 1849

Ruiz de Burton married Captain Burton first in a civil ceremony before a Presbyterian minister, and later before a priest. Burton was a twenty-eight-year-old widower and Ruiz de Burton was sixteen, and the marriage was celebrated as a romantic union between "natural enemies." The couple lived in Monterey, San Diego, and moved east during the Civil War when Burton became a major, then brigadier-general in the Union army. Burton caught malarial fever while fighting in the South and never recovered, dying in 1869, and leaving his thirty-seven-year-old wife with their children, Nellie and Harry. Ruiz de Burton returned to San Diego to live at the Jamul Ranch, which Burton had bought years earlier.

It is not known when Ruiz de Burton began to write, but the publication of her novels followed her husband's death. Her novels (which quote Joseph Addison, Samuel Johnson, Thomas Carlyle, Ralph Waldo Emerson, William Ellery Channing, and Herbert Spencer, among others), and voluminous correspondence, reveal extensive knowledge of literature and philosophy, as well as European and American history. Her first novel, *Who Would Have Thought It?*, (discussed in chapter 1) written from the perspective of a Mexican-American outsider on the East coast, was published by J. B. Lippincott in 1872. Though the title page lists no author (a choice probably dictated by the novel's biting satire) the book is entered in the catalog of the Library of Congress under H. S. Burton and Mrs. Henry S. Burton. Ruiz de Burton's second novel, *The Squatter and the Don*, was published by Samuel Carson and Co. in 1885 under a pseudonym, C. Loyal or "loyal citizen," a conventional signature in official Mexican correspondence, that provided ironic commentary on the unappreciated loyalty of the Mexican-American citizenry. Throughout the 1870s and 1880s, Ruiz de Burton was battling the Land Commission for possession of the Jamul Ranch. She also managed, with the aid of her son Harry, businesses – the cultivation of castor beans, the building of a water reservoir, a cement company to exploit the land's limestone deposits. Most of her time, however, was devoted to the land dispute which thoroughly informs her second novel. Ruiz de Burton wrote newspaper articles castigating her antagonists, and took them to court in New Mexico, but she died unrewarded and alone in Chicago in 1895. The sense of justice that impelled Ruiz de Burton's fight for her land infuses *The Squatter and the Don*, a narrative so intent on cataloging the facts of the Californio struggle that it is sometimes overwhelmed by them. Ruiz de Burton was limited to small readerships in her time and dropped out of the literary canon, only to be rediscovered in the 1990s when her two novels were reprinted in an academic US Hispanic Literary Heritage series. Characters in *The Squatter and the Don* are given to long speeches rehearsing their grievances, exchanges especially common between Clarence Darrell, the sympathetic eldest son of the wealthy American "Squatter," and "the Don" Mariano. Significantly, the Don's historical account touches lightly on the Native-American dispossession by the Californios. Explaining that Native Americans were divested of land to make room for Mexican enterprise, Don Mariano implicitly endorses the Social Darwinism of his American neighbors: the rightful displacement of primitive by civilized peoples. While Clarence Darrell argues that few Americans would support governmental actions in California were they widely known, the underlying facts of colonization – land-theft and extermination – prevail from region to region.

The strongest critique in *The Squatter and the Don* is directed against monopoly capitalism, personified by the four owners of the Central Pacific Railroad Company of California, Leland Stanford, Collis P. Huntington, Charles Crocker, and Mark Hopkins. In 1869, the company was granted 9,000,000 acres of free land and millions of dollars in bonds and construction costs to build a Western railroad. From the 1870s to 1910, the company appropriated a major share of the profits from virtually every business and industry in California. During this period, Stanford, Huntington, Crocker, and Hopkins amassed fortunes unparalleled even in American corporate history, and fought tenaciously to preclude all competition from other California development projects. This included the Texas Pacific Railroad, a line that would have made San Diego the Western terminus to the shortest transcontinental railway, ensuring the city and southern California a share of prosperity. Ruiz de Burton and her husband were heavily invested in the financial prospects of the Texas Pacific, which illuminates her animus. But newspaper reports from the 1880s confirm that the Central Pacific Railroad Company bribed Congressmen and members of the Southern legislature, and directed other illegal political maneuvers to ensure that the Texas Pacific Railroad would not be built. Ruiz de Burton emphasizes in her novel that the machinations of Stanford, Huntington, *et al.* went beyond greed. Two aspects of her portrait are noteworthy. Her depiction of a visit to Governor Stanford by the novel's protagonists to mount a final appeal for the Texas Pacific, reveals Stanford as arrogant and wholly devoid of social conscience. In contrast to Frank Norris, whose indictment of the railroad trust in *The Octopus* is confined to a Jewish scapegoat, S. Behrman, Ruiz de Burton places the guilt of empire-building upon California's Anglo-Saxon elite. In contrast to those of Helen Hunt Jackson, Ruiz de Burton's Mexican-American aristocrats are willing entrepreneurs, defenders of a capitalist system of healthy competition, and opposed only to the forces of monopoly that limit it. As this suggests, *The Squatter and the Don* is a valuable exposé of the illegal and unjust methods by which land was made available to settlers in the West during the late nineteenth century, illegalities and injustices that were always at the expense of Native Americans and Mexican-Americans. It is also a stirring indictment of the Central Pacific Railroad Company run by Stanford, Huntington, Crocker, and Hopkins, a detailed novelistic recuperation of a crucial and ugly part of American history that other American novelists preferred to ignore or forget.

At its best, the novel is a powerful example of the historical romance, with an intriguing cast of characters, drawn from three families, two American and one Mexican-American, and an absorbing, unpredictable plot. Women characters are prominent, and often penetrate the political mistakes and racial prejudices of their husbands. This is true of Mary Moreneau Darrell, who discerns even before her marriage to the novel's "squatter" that his violent temper will produce much misfortune. William Darrell has a history of squatting on Mexican-American lands and contesting their titles in American courts. While there is plenty of government-owned land available to settlers, the richest lands are owned by Mexican-Americans, leading Americans to "squat" on them, initiating their litigation. The struggle between William Darrell, the squatter, and Don Mariano Alamar, the owner, concerns an American settler's "right" to the richest land in the territory, and a Mexican-American's "right" to keep his lands. Darrell and Mariano both have large families of attractive children, who are drawn to one another. The narrative is full of romances and intermarriages between Darrells, Alamars, and Mechlins (wealthy New Yorkers moved to California for their father's health). The Mechlins are not squatters, and support the Alamars, in illustration of Ruiz de Burton's notion that authentic elites (a status independent of money) implicitly understand each other. The novel's hero, Clarence Darrell, surpasses his father in every way: as an entrepreneur (he is a millionaire in his twenties from speculation in mining stocks that his narrow-minded father has forbidden), as a lover, and as a moral being. Clarence's fortune allows him to pay the Alamars in secret for the land his father "squats" on, and win the love of Don Mariano's favorite daughter, Mercedes. But a confrontation between father and son over the secret payment results in Clarence's exile, and a period of wandering and illness (he contracts typhoid) that brings suffering to both families.

The novel concludes with tragic loss and hope. Don Mariano and James Mechlin become casualties of the foiled San Diego Railroad, which ruins them financially and leads to their deaths. The Mechlins return to New York. Don Mariano's family moves to San Francisco to pursue careers in banking and finance with the support of Clarence, who has amassed an even bigger fortune and married his beloved Mercedes. The ending features the mournful wife of Don Mariano comparing the Veblenian habits of America's noveau riche (details are given of "The Great Nob Hill Silver Wedding Ball" thrown by a "new" San Francisco millionaire) to the dignified pleasures of her own life at the rancho. While the novel posits a beneficial fusion of Spanish and American bloodlines, and suggests the prospect of healthy capitalist development, it laments the supplanting of a Mexican landed gentry by a commercial society with neither class nor conscience. Ruiz de Burton's version of colonizing the West is a story of Mexicans and Americans, bearing few traces of the remaining indigenous inhabitants. As confirmed by the only very recent recuperation of *The Squatter and the Don*, literary history can be as Darwinian as the colonial struggles it registers. Moreover, the most renowned novelistic treatments of Western settlement provide even less account of Native Americans. The "victors" represent the "vanquished" as ghosts haunting a landscape overtaken by progress.

Of all the novels written in the period between the end of the Civil War and the beginning of the First World War, none was a greater success than Owen Wister's *The Virginian* (1902). An immediate bestseller, the novel was reprinted thirteen times in its first year of publication. *The Virginian* recreated Wyoming between 1874 and 1890, though Wister's supposed elegy to cattle country seemed to have little to do with cattle. But most agreed that he had managed to capture in narrative form the awesome outlines of a Western landscape he compared to Genesis. The novel was the product of a rest cure Wister took on the advice of Dr. S. Weir Mitchell, a family friend who was famous for treating nervous illnesses. Born into the Eastern elite, educated at St. Paul's School, and then at Harvard, graduating in 1882 with highest honors in classical music, Wister was sent to Europe to study music, but ill health forced his return in 1884. Wister's Western trip helped to reconcile him to a law career: graduating from Harvard Law School he opened a legal practice in 1889 in Philadelphia. Wister had been raised there, the only child of Owen Jones Wister, a doctor of Pennsylvania Dutch descent, and Sarah Butler, a widely published writer and daughter of the actress Fanny Kemble and a South Carolina plantation owner. The family's standing afforded connections such as Theodore Roosevelt, who encouraged Wister's writing, William Dean Howells, who did not (at least at first), Frederic Remington, and Henry James. While working as a lawyer, Wister wrote stories about his Western experiences. The enthusiastic reception of two of these stories by *Harper's Magazine* in 1891 emboldened him to pursue an artistic career.

The Virginian, Wister's first published novel, is about the initiation of an ideal youth into a respectable occupation and marriage. As such, the novel stages the impulses and forces that require repression in the name of civilization, from homosexuality (a threatening proposition regulated through elaborate ritual controls), to over-identification with nature, to fear of death, which is portrayed as a "childlike" weakness. Because initiation is designed to confirm boundaries, from class boundaries, to gender boundaries, to sexual prohibitions, the novel's characters display dangerous urges to obliterate them. In keeping with the conventions of the Western, the West is presented in *The Virginian* as a territory of deprivation. With the exception of the scene celebrating the variety of ways to prepare and eat frogs' legs, consumption is rare. *The Virginian* promotes asceticism, picturing bodies in distress, denied sleep, food, and sex, and displays hostility towards all forms of domesticity. It is also anti-Christian, replacing God with ideals of masculine skill and fraternity. Suffering is valued, but in the name of an altogether material and human gospel. The novel's heroes aspire to silence and impenetrability approaching the condition of natural objects. Characters in *The Virginian* court death, and killing is a perpetual threat carried out invariably in a stylized way in order, it seems, to belie its violence.

Wister's embrace of these classic features of the Western reflects his alienation from a modern urban America of increasing class conflict and social heterogeneity. His correspondence is marked by nativist rhetoric, as when he describes "the encroaching alien vermin who degrade our commonwealth from a nation into something half pawn shop, half broker's office." Elsewhere he wrote, "to survive in cattle country requires a spirit of adventure, courage, and self-sufficiency; you will not find many Poles or Huns or Russian Jews in that district." The dilemma for a writer like Wister was how to reconcile his belief in Anglo-Saxon superiority (according to his essay, "The Evolution of the Cow Puncher," the cowboy represented a contemporary version of the medieval knight), with the domination of labor by capital, which required the subordination of *some* Anglo-Saxons. *The Virginian* provides a biosocial rationale for class privilege, justifying the ascent of the natural aristocrat. In this way, the novel is an American success story: a poor Virginian in the post-Civil War era wins the favor of the rich and powerful, and becomes a captain of industry, specifically, of a coal concern. *The Virginian* is based on actual historical conflict (not unlike the tension that caught Norris's imagination for *The Octopus*) between ranchers (the Wyoming Growers Association), the banks, and the railroads. In keeping with other Westerns, Native Americans are portrayed as ignorant leaders and invisible massed aggressors. Two Native-American chiefs, for instance, provide an uncomprehending audience for the Virginian's famous story about frog legs. The chiefs are tourist objects, arrayed conspicuously in traditional costumes, except when they are salesman themselves plugging their baubles. Significantly, the most degraded characters, such as Balaam, are also the most hostile towards Native Americans, while the novel's hero displays a more sympathetic, if condescending, attitude. The novel's Native Americans are not characters but types, consigned to reservations which they leave with permission and sometimes without, to commit atrocities upon undeserving whites.

While *The Virginian* is typical of Western novels, its themes of initiation, male fraternity and homoeroticism, the reconciliation of civilization and the wild, the individual and community, storytelling and rhetorical aptitude, violence as a Western and specifically American proclivity, are also staples of an American novelistic tradition that includes works by Cooper, Melville, Twain, London, and F. Scott Fitzgerald. The novel's narrator, who both idealizes and criticizes the hero and the West, resembles many reflective narrator personae in American literature from Ishmael to Nick Caraway. The novel is full of outlaws, but distinguishes good men who go bad, such as the Virginian's friend Steve who turns to horse stealing and is hung by the hero himself, from evil men like Trampas, who is killed by the Virginian in a theatrical shootout at the novel's end. As both examples reveal, the Virginian resorts to violence whenever necessary: vigilante justice or lynch law is synonymous with social order in the novel's society. This is a principle that must be accepted by the New England schoolteacher, Molly Stark Wood, if she is to subordinate herself properly to the rule of the West and to her prospective husband, the Virginian. *The Virginian* confirms the gradual transformation of lynching in the West from a "natural right" rule of law to an assertion of class and racial privilege directed against "dangerous" or marginal groups. In contrast to the racist and sacrificial lynching of blacks in the post-Civil War South, Western lynching remains a sanctioned duty when carried out by the right people. The West as depicted by Wister is unapologetically misogynistic but highly romantic: the evolution of love between hero and heroine absorbs much of the narrative. Women are the agents of culture who betray only a superficial grasp of its deepest aspects, an open book to the natural intellectuals (such as the Virginian) they seek, condescendingly, to educate. Female values are ridiculed (as in the parable of the hen Emily) or disavowed. Christian ideals of love and forgiveness, like the interior spaces and forms of confinement identified with sentimental novels, are absorbed into the Western in more (Norris's *McTeague*) and less (Wister's *The Viriginian*) obvious ways. At their best in *The Virginian*, women betray male strengths, and serve as doubles of the men they love. Molly Stark Wood's soft strength replicates that of the Virginian when she must rescue him from a Native-American attack. The prolific union of Molly Stark Wood and the Virginian ensures a Northern stake in the West that is sentimental and romantic as well as economic. The 1892 cattle wars bring ruin to the West, while the railroads build a branch to the Virginian's land to ensure his prosperity for generations to come.

Zane Grey's *Riders of the Purple Sage*, which equaled *The Virginian* in popularity, confirms the pivotal significance of the 1870s in the history of the West but focuses on a different milieu. *Riders of the Purple Sage* is set in southern Utah in 1871, where Mormonism is the way of life in most settlement towns. Native Americans are no more than a memory in the narrative, a means of celebrating the wilderness skills of different characters. In this sense, Grey's novel situates itself a century beyond the works of James Fenimore Cooper, which it consistently recalls. There are no Mohicans presented here for elegiac consideration. Instead Native-American ingenuity lingers in the atmosphere, identified with admirable characters, the hero Jim Lassiter, and the gunman Bern Venters. Mormons assume the position of deplored aliens, hypocritical, greedy, and malevolent. While the heroine, Jane Withersteen, is a daughter of the Mormon Church, her deprogramming by the gentle gentile gunman, Jim Lassiter, is applauded. Zane Grey was born in Zanesville, Ohio, in 1872. His family had settled the town two generations before, and his father was a leading citizen and dentist. Grey won a baseball scholarship to the University of Pennsylvania, where he studied dentistry. After graduation, he set up a dental practice in New York City, but grew restless and began to write fiction and non-fiction on the West, using the work of James Fenimore Cooper as a model. Grey's first four novels, *Betty Zane* (1903), *The Spirit of the Border*, *The Last Trail* (1905), and *The Last of the Plainsmen* (1908) were commercial failures, but he made money on novels for boys and magazine essays. *The Heritage of the Desert* (1910) was Grey's first commercial success. But it was his 1912 novel about religious conflict in Utah, *Riders of the Purple Sage*, that launched him into the bestseller category to stay. Grey's writing displayed his passion for the splendor of territories through which he traveled – Arizona, New Mexico, Cuba, and Mexico – before resettling in California in 1916. The plots and characters of Grey's formulaic Westerns are largely unmemorable, but extended descriptions of the land, mountains, deserts, canyons, and various climatic tempests, grant his narratives real distinction.

Riders of the Purple Sage opens with an image of nature tamed yet predominant. "A sharp clip-clop of iron-shod hoofs deadened and died away, and clouds of yellow dust drifted from under the cottonwoods out over the sage." The horse is civilized, constricted, by the "iron" that marks its possession and utility. Yet the dust and sage prevail, symbolizing the dominance of the Western landscape. However destructive the gun-toting inhabitants of this narrative, they will be subjected in turn to nature. The novel is the story of Jane Withersteen, the lone inheritor of vast wealth, a ranch with the town's main water supply, Amber Spring, thousands of cattle, the best horses in the region. The town's embattled Mormons await the invasion of gentiles, while the presence of neutral rustlers complicates this polarity. Jane Withersteen is a peacemaker, a Mormon who befriends gentile outcasts, thus antagonizing the Mormon elders. Their leader Tull, who seeks to marry Jane, arrives at her ranch, intending to expel the gentile Bern Venters, whom Jane has been protecting. But a threatening figure appears, emerging from the sage like a force of nature. This is Lassiter, whose ominous aspect sends the Mormon elders scurrying for cover. A sworn enemy of the Mormons, Lassiter recounts how they blinded his horse by holding hot irons close to his eyes. Lassiter becomes Jane's rider, caring for her horses, cattle, and ranges, under threat from rustlers, as well as from fellow Mormons who punish her disloyalty by stealing her livestock. Each of the main characters, Bern Venters and his love Elizabeth Erne, Jim Lassiter and his love Jane Withersteen, harbors a secret which must be disclosed before blissful romantic union is possible. What makes the novel something more than a formulaic Western is its self-conscious approach to its subject – conquest. Grey examines Western conflict through an extended history – thousands of years – of migration and displacement. Accordingly, his narrative is unusually attentive to the wilderness as place – snakes, frogs, beaver, rabbits as well as fauna and foliage. Venter's first sight of "Deception Pass" reveals a magical retreat that will prove the salvation of Jane Withersteen and Jim Lassiter.

Venter turned out of the gorge, and suddenly paused stock-still, astounded at the scene before him. The curve of the great stone bridge had caught the sunrise, and through the magnificent arch burst a glorious stream of gold that shone with a long slant down into the center of Surprise Valley. Only through the arch did any sunlight pass, so that all the rest of the valley lay still asleep, dark-green, mysterious, shadowy, merging its level into walls as misty and soft as morning clouds. Venters then descended, passing through the arch, looking up at its tremendous height and sweep. It spanned the opening to Surprise Valley, stretching in almost perfect curve from rim to rim. Even in his hurry and concern Venters could not but feel its majesty, and the thought came to him that the cliff dwellers must have regarded it as an object of worship . . . At length he passed beyond the slope of weathered stone that spread fan-shape from the arch; and encountered a grassy terrace running to the right and about on a level with the tips of the oaks and cottonwoods below. Scattered here and there upon this shelf were clumps of aspens, and he walked through them into a glade that surpassed, in beauty and adaptability for a wild home, any place he had ever seen. Silver spruces bordered the base of a precipitous wall that rose loftily. Caves indented its surface, and there were no detached ledges or weathered sections that might dislodge a stone. The level ground, beyond the spruces, dropped down into a little ravine. This was one dense line of slender aspens from which came the low splashing of water. And the terrace, lying open to the west, afforded an unobstructed view of the valley of green tree-tops.

Cliffs and valleys symbolize a remote yet continuous past whose different actors looked upon these cliffs with reverence as divine emblems. The "weathered stones," the majestic growths, of spruces and aspens, all reflect the natural environment's singular resistance to time. This is reinforced later when Venter discovers an entire world of stone – houses, with their fireplaces, pottery and other domestic items – probably a thousand years old or more, undisturbed and intact within the cave.

Cultural conflict, Grey suggests, is an interminable story of human vitality, survival, and extinction. In shutting up his two main protagonists, Jane Withersteen and Jim Lassiter, together with their adopted daughter, Fay, in these caves at the novel's end, in having them close off the cave's outlet (for their own lifetime at least) and rain boulders down on their Mormon pursuers, Grey highlights their place within a procession of civilizations across time and culture, whose inhabitants shared a common purpose of protecting kin against alien others. By strongly implying that the devout and submissive Jane Withersteen has simply transferred her loyalties from the Mormon elders to Jim Lassiter, Grey supplies a traditional ending for a stereotyped love affair between a strong, silent gunman and a woman who craves domination. But the novel returns the younger pair of lovers to modernity, hinting that their more supple and provisional gender identities may particularly suit the twentieth century. Venter can admit, for instance, that Elizabeth is a better horseman than he, and neither is marked by the constricting traditions of Mormonism. For this promising pair, armed with the gold they discovered at Deception Pass, modern civilization is preferable to life on the purple borderland of the West.

The Spirit Of The Border (1905), the second of Grey's Ohio trilogy novels (the first was *Betty Zane*, 1903; the third *The Last Trail*, 1905) did not advance Grey's reputation as a novelist. But it provides an exemplary historical fiction that interprets both authentic personages (Lewis Wexel, John G. E. Heckewelder, Simon Girty, and Ebenezer Zane) and early twentieth-century ideas about the future of America's Native Americans. *The Spirit of the Border* is based on the actual massacre of Christian Native Americans and white missionaries in the Ohio Valley in March, 1782. The Moravian settlement of Gnadenhutten ("Cabins of Grace") was a peaceful and flourishing oasis amidst constant strife. Among the missionaries living there were the Moravian John Heckewelder, author of *History, Manners, and Customs of the Indian Nations* (1819) and David Zeisberger, the Moravian leader. Accounts of the massacre confirm that Colonel David Williamson led the attack, assisted by the white-Native-American renegade, Simon Girty. In histories of colonial conflict at the turn of the nineteenth century, Girty is a malevolent figure, arousing Native Americans to attack white settlers, and urging American and British soldiers and Native Americans into battle against each other. In Grey's rewriting of this history, Girty's brother Jack is the villain, and the peaceful Christian Native Americans are victims of fellow Native Americans who resent their conversion. Grey's revision exculpates white militia held responsible in reliable histories, and foregrounds the subject of Native-American conversion.

According to Grey, white outcasts, equally cruel to white settlers and Native Americans, were largely to blame for the frontier's worst savageries. One of Grey's purposes in the novel is to clear the name of Lewis Wetzel, a man often identified with the outcasts, whom Grey believed to be a true hero. From youth, Wetzel reputedly roamed the forests seeking vengeance upon Native Americans for the murder of his family. So fearsome were his murderous rampages that the French-inspired Native Americans called him *Le Vente de la Mort* (the Death Wind). Grey's fiction portrays Wetzel in a sympathetic light as the savior of the Gnadenhutten missionaries, susceptible to women, and even at times to Native Americans. Setting his historical novel in a particular region, delineated with accuracy and care, drawing on authentic historical figures, and invoking a controversial historical episode, Grey pays homage to his mentor, James Fenimore Cooper. Nor do the similarities end here. *The Spirit of the Border* sends attractive white sisters into the wilderness to aid their missionary uncle and serve as pawns in the interminable warfare between white military, missionaries, "white Indians," and Native Americans. It defines heroism as the ability to navigate the wilderness with the stealth and sagacity of a Native American. It discriminates among various kinds of killing, sanctioning all but the most gratuitous forms, and in so doing distinguishes a frontier morality from the morality of civilization. *The Spirit of the Border* also promotes a male fraternity that at its most intense (the friendship of Joe Downs and Lewis Wexel) looks like marriage.

Grey's divergences from Cooper provide a key to his contemporary scene. The novel displays ambivalence towards Christianity and its missionary aims. The religion has a place but only subordinated to the deeper reality of a Social Darwinism that treats primitive peoples and ways of life through the admiring historical imagination of the novelist. Grey departs from Cooper in representing a series of harmonious frontier intermarriages between white males and Native-American women, who prove as seductive as the wilderness. There is no pairing of white women and Native-American men, in part because white women are scarce, but more deeply because these female lights of civilization are unprepared, historically speaking, to surrender to the wilderness in 1905. The biggest departure from Cooper is Grey's presentation of conflict as issuing from white theft of Native-American land, and exacerbated by other whites who simply covet warfare.

But it is Grey's depiction of the prospects for Native-American conversion to Christianity that is most consistent with the ideals of his own historical moment. In staging the Native Americans' receptivity to Christianity, as well as the admirable faith of the missionaries who journeyed to a menacing frontier hoping to save souls, Grey relies heavily on historical sources. His primary focus is the Moravian mission, which devoted its efforts in the 1870s to Western tribes, chiefly the Delawares. It was a mark of the missionaries' success in Ohio that Native-American converts were drawn from so many different tribes. The missionaries honored the dignity of Native Americans and the justice of their hostility towards the settlers. The missionary Jim Downs, brother of Joe, for instance, "desired to keep to [the Native-Americans'] ideal – for he deemed [it] more beautiful than his own – and to conduct his teaching along the simple lines of their belief, so that when he stimulated and developed their minds he could pass from what they knew to the unknown Christianity of the white man." While there is condescension here, there is also faith in the compatibility between Native-American and Christian religions. In portraying the success of Jim's preaching among all tribes, Grey seconds contemporary Charles Eastman's commitment to an assimilation that combines admiration for Native-American culture with a conviction of Native-American adaptability to Christianity. Indeed, a Christian ideal of sacrifice is portrayed as common to preachers, renegades, and military officials. Yet the Christian Native Americans prove the model devotees, embracing their sacrifice with the ecstasy of medieval martyrs.

The narrative teleology of *The Spirit of the Border* is consistent with the portrayal of Native Americans in Grey's later novels. The fact that Grey was drawing on a number of late nineteenth-century histories in writing his novel – the journal of Colonel Ebenezer Zane; Consul Willshire Butterfield's *History of the Girtys* (1890); E. G. Cattermole's *Famous Frontiersmen, Pioneers and Scouts*(1883); Theodore Roosevelt's six-volume *The Winning of the West* (1887); James McMechen's *Legends of the Ohio Valley* (1881) – reinforces what is implicit in the novel itself. It is telling that one of the most sustained dramatizations of Native Americans by a popular Western writer at the turn of the century comes in a novel set in the far distant past. Less than a century before, then President Thomas Jefferson had offered a prophesy in an 1808 address to Zane Grey's Delawares, Mohicans, and Munries:

When once you have property, you will want laws and magistrates to protect your property and persons, and to punish those among you who commit crimes. You will find that our laws are good for this purpose; you will wish to live under them, you will unite yourselves with us, join in our Great Councils and form one people with us, and we shall all be Americans; you will mix with us by marriage and your blood will run in our veins, and will spread with us over this great island.

The nineteenth century was not the first, nor would it be the last century, when literary accounts (by the likes of Grey, Ruiz de Burton, Wister, Twain, Winnemuca, Eastman, and Jackson) would belie the self-congratulating optimism of governmental spokesmen on the status of Native Americans. There is no record of the immediate Native-American response (if there was one) to Jefferson's prescriptive assimilationism. Had their own most optimistic prophecies been recorded, the leaders of the Delawares, Mohicans, and Munries would surely have provided a very different picture of Native-American existence at the turn of the century.

6

MARKETING CULTURE

URING THE TELEVISION coverage of the 1984 Winter Olympics, novelist John Updike found himself riveted, not by the Games but by the high-stakes advertising that accompanied them. "I have no doubt that the aesthetic marvels of our age, for intensity and lavishness of effort and subtlety of both overt and subliminal effect, are television commercials," he commented, adding, "except within narrow professional circles, the artists involved, like Anglo-Saxon poets and Paleocene cave-painters, are unknown by name." Updike's observation was anticipated almost a century earlier by editors at *Munsey's* magazine, who noted in a July 1895 column that

some of the cleverest writing – the most painstaking, subtle work turned out by literary men today – can be found in the advertising pages of a first rate magazine. Every word is measured, examined under a magnifying glass, to see just how big it is, just how much meaning it has, and how many kinds of meaning it has.

The rise in the aesthetic stakes of advertising coincided with the rise in its commercial stakes: in the post-Civil War era advertising expenditures grew exponentially, from $50 million just after the war to $500 million by the century's end. Magazine editors recognized how fully implicated were their cultural activities in the business end of their enterprises. The inclusion of specific advertisements in their periodicals, for instance, served as implicit endorsements of the commodities they featured, even raising concerns about liability, as confirmed when Cyrus Curtis and Edward Bok announced that their magazines would no longer advertise patent medicines. The commercial reciprocity between editors and advertisers was clear: magazines sought to sell their space to the highest bidders, just as advertisers sought the most illustrious and widely disseminated forums. "Magazines like *McClure's*," an eight-year-old-boy declared to his mother in a 1904 ad, "tell you what you want, and show you where you can get it. *McClure's Magazine* is the marketplace of the world." The ad captures the fashioning of leisure-class women as consumers, as well as the awareness among the era's advertisers of the commercial readiness of impressionable children. In examples such as these, and in many others, advertisements provided new conceptualizations of reading (as shopping), as well as new categories for classifying social experience, defining fresh areas of need (clean teeth, disposable tissues, carpet cleaners) and introducing trademarked items to satisfy them (Colgate ribbon toothpaste, Kleenex, and Scourene). In some instances – such as Amelie Rives's novel, *The Quick or the Dead*, serialized in *Lippincott's* magazine, 1888 – literary works incorporated brand-name items, forecasting "product placement" practices that have become a standard method of consumer metonymy in postmodern film, television, and theatre. Where a novelistic character might be "recognized" through his appearance in another fiction (Huckleberry Finn's dependence on *Tom Sawyer*) or her taste in reading (Catherine Morland's addiction to gothic fiction in *Northanger Abbey*), Jerry Seinfeld's credentials as *the* comedian of the commonplace are established through his cereal preferences. Boxes of Honeycomb and Cap'n Crunch on display in his conveniently doorless kitchen cabinets signal a familiar cultural resistance to growing up. The late nineteenth century was an era when advertisements and art, literary and visual images from photographic to painterly, were packaged together as mutually enhancing products. What advertisements offered the literature they appended, and increasingly bordered in widely circulating magazines, was the aura of modernity, up-to-date ness.

To appear alongside an intelligently conceived advertisement for Sapolio soap conferred upon a story by William Dean Howells a stamp of relevance. Some serials, such as Mark Twain's "Chapters from My Autobiography," functioned as advertisements for their authors while earning them money. Twain had long kept a file of autobiographical pieces framed around significant exchanges or events: his relationship with Ulysses S. Grant, his world tour, the death of his beloved daughter Susie. When George Harvey praised the pieces that Twain shared with him, and offered $30,000 to publish them in his *North American Review*, Twain began work in earnest. While Twain displays concern for many subjects personal and public, the autobiography seems above all an exercise in literary salesmanship.

This holds true in one degree or other, for most of the prominent books serialized in the period. Among other works that appeared in leading magazines (some elite, some popular) prior to their publication in book form, were Helen Keller's *The Story of My Life* (*Ladies Home Journal*), James's *The Bostonians* (*The Century*) and *The Ambassadors* (*North American Review*), Washington's *Up From Slavery* (*Outlook*), Cahan's *The Rise of David Levinsky* (*McClure's*), Norris's *The Pit* (*Saturday Evening Post*), Howells's *A Modern Instance* (*The Century*) and *A Hazard of New Fortunes* (*Harper's Weekly*), S. S. McClure, *My Autobiography* (*McClure's*), Jack London's *Martin Eden* (*Pacific Monthly*) and *The Call of the Wild* (*Saturday*

FIGURE 2. *Saturday Evening Post*, July 18, 1903, back page, text of *The Call of the Wild* by Jack London, surrounded by advertisements.

Evening Post), and Herrick's *Memoirs of an American Citizen* (*Saturday Evening Post*).

Because these serials were published in magazines that almost always included advertisements for consumer products, sometimes interspersed with fiction and articles, these books joined inevitably a larger cultural dialogue about the processes of production and distribution, the status of the commodity, the impact of innovation and technology, the nature of work in a modern industrial era, and the changes wrought by capitalist development. All of these were questions that assumed particular urgency in the three decades following the Civil War.

ADVERTISING

American business methods and values during the post-Civil War period provided a critical means of mediating the growing cultural diversity and class stratification of American society. This was vividly dramatized in the field of advertising, which extended its artistic ambitions far beyond the scope of what had previously been imagined, while joining many other fields in becoming a "science." Advertisers were especially keen to promote the "progress" of their profession. "The science and skill displayed in advertising in modern times were not thought of in colonial times" one observer commented in 1895. According to a representative from a leading Chicago ad agency, "ads in periodicals are now read with as much zest as is the reading matter." An editorial in the prominent advertising journal, *Printer's Ink*, held that an "advertisement can be made so seductive and readable that I must continue to read it whether I want the thing it advertises or don't want it. In fact, the live advertiser is now a sharp competitor of the reading-material purveyor in the race for entertainment." In the period when advertisements were still largely confined to the magazines' end pages, the perusal of advertisements was encouraged by the convention of pre-cutting the advertising pages before the magazines were shipped, leaving the remainder of the magazine pages to be cut by the recipient. Many advertising copywriters (among them Helen Landsdowne Resor, a J. Walter Thompson executive), and sometimes magazine editors as well sought to orchestrate the advertisement with the fiction and articles they accompanied. In books such as *The Psychology of Advertising* (1908) and *Effective Magazine Advertising* (1907), leading practitioners (sometimes with the help of ordinary consumers whose comments they incorporated into their analyses) addressed questions about the power of suggestion, consumption patterns, and the relation between marketing and ethnicity. Walter Dill Scott and Francis Bellamy argued that commodities not only denote but also confer lifestyle.

Racine
Canoes

are as beautiful
of line and as
thoroughly com-
fortable and dur-
able as the ideal

"Cheemaun" of Hiawatha.   We carry a complete line of every type of water craft.
RACINE BOAT MANUFACTURING COMPANY, Box 10, MUSKEGON, MICH.
122 W. 34th St., New York ; 182 Milk St., Boston, Mass. ; 38 Delaware Ave., Camden, N. J. ; 182 Jefferson Ave., Detroit, Mich. ; 1610 Michigan Ave., Chicago, Ill. ; 321 First Ave., South Seattle, Wash.

FIGURE 3. "Racine's Canoes," *Harper's Weekly*, April 18, 1908.

They proposed, too, that magazines should always aim above the actual class position of its presumed readership, since flattery is the highest inducement to consumption.

What is perhaps most striking about these advertisements is their portrayal of ethnicity. One example is the advertisement for Racine Canoes that was run in *Harper's Weekly* (1908). "Racine Canoes are as beautiful of line," the ad announces, "and as thoroughly comfortable and durable as the ideal 'Cheemaun' of Hiawatha."

The fine print lists locations on West 34th St., New York; Milk St., Boston; and Michigan Ave., Chicago, thereby pinpointing the market for this antiquated enterprise – stressed-out urbanites. The brushed edges of the image provide a reflection of an ideal family of five, and enclose it in a time warp of nostalgic potential. To own a Racine Canoe is to embrace the simplicity and peace of "primitive" existence; it is also to be liberated from the punishing pace of the modern city, and the problem of white–Native-American conflict. This advertisement is remote from the mid nineteenth-century canoe scenes painted by Charles Deas (*The Voyageurs*) and Alfred Jacob Miller (*The Trapper's Bride*) where the emphasis is on whites who have adopted Native-American ways. The whites in the Racine ad sit perfectly still, in solemn respect for the artifact, and perhaps also for the original designers who left these cultural treasures behind. Advertising fosters the illusion that the power of purchase is the only limit to what one can be: to buy a Racine canoe is to be a member of a community that possesses the wealth and the leisure to enjoy it. Another advertisement that drew on ethnic and evolutionary themes to promote a product was for Waterman Pens.

To buy a Waterman pen is to identify with progress, the ad suggested as it focused the attention of *Atlantic Monthly* readers on the 1907 Jamestown

FIGURE 4. "Waterman's Ideal Fountain Pen," *Atlantic Monthly*, June 1907.

Exposition in Norfolk, Virginia, which was sponsored by manufacturers, government agencies, railroads, even cooking schools, and featured displays, demonstrations, and samples (like the "dainty celluoid souvenir" bookmarks "free" at "Booth No. 1"). These expositions made cultural variety and product innovation appear as twin ideals of a global marketplace. In the ad itself, an avuncular John Smith gazes fondly upon his diligent student Pocahontas as the facts of genocide and displacement are transferred from ethnic bodies (Pocahontas, Smith) to writing instruments (quill, fountain pen). Pocahontas and Smith are arrayed in the seventeenth-century dress appropriate to their respective cultures and stations (hers in a Native-American hierarchy and his in a military one), but the image is dominated by a tension between feather and steel which distinguishes them irrevocably. The obsolete feather framing the left side of the ad is echoed in the headdress of the now obsolete Pocahontas, while the steel dagger protruding jauntily from Captain Smith's left hip recalls the details of empire and progress inscribed in that emblem of civilized "genius": the steel fountain pen that frames the image on the right.

The familiar ethnic characters and belongings in these advertisements (Pocahontas, canoes) serve as symbols of authenticity that reinforce the subliminal connection between buying and being. Ethnicity stands for the prospect of self-transformation through purchase that is a central message of these advertisements. Ethnicity, converted into stereotype, functions in these ads both to erase history and to validate the promise entailed by the product. To own a Waterman fountain pen is to possess the power of origins signified by the authentic person of Pocahontas, whose role is that of a benign recipient of literacy.

One of the most notorious and versatile advertising runs of this era, extending from 1884 through 1910, was for soap, "Hand Sapolio" and "Sapolio" all-purpose cleansers in cake form. Its uses ranged from bathing and skincare, to washing dishes, floors, and even tombstones, to sharpening knives and polishing false teeth. From the outset, the mass marketing of soap was synonymous with the quest for moral perfection. This is no doubt why the Reverend Henry Ward Beecher took such pride in the effects of his own 1884 advertising venture for Pears Soap. Under the direction of its chief advertising manager, Artemus Ward, Sapolio – which was omnipresent in literary journals (*Century*, *Atlantic Monthly*, *Putnam's*, *McClure's*) where important novels were serialized – was responsible for many inaugural feats in the world of marketing. Enoch Morgan's Sons selected Sapolio for widespread advertising in the 1860s, primarily in *Harper's Weekly* and Leslie's *Illustrated Weekly Newspaper*, and its expenditures grew in terms previously unimaginable. In 1871, $15,000 was spent on advertising Sapolio, in 1885, $70,000, and by 1896, Sapolio's advertising expenses reached $400,000. For variety and creativity, Sapolio advertising was exceptional in its time. In 1884, the manufacturer became the first to advertise on public transit, exploiting the boredom of captive audiences in New York's horse-drawn streetcars. In 1892, Ward engineered a reverse voyage to Columbus's Spain on a fourteen-foot dory named "the Sapolio," which was covered widely in the popular press; and in 1900, he launched the notorious "Spotless Town" campaign with its own regular production of jingles. The campaign was so successful that the image of "Spotless Town" entered the common lexicon (in newspapers, cartoons, political speeches, and on stage) as a synonym for cleanliness, order, and perfection. Sapolio was second only to the Ford automobile in the amount of free publicity it generated.

What makes the Sapolio ads especially noteworthy is their appeal to so many different social strata, and their use of such a variety of historical events. These full-page ads from *Putnam's* and *The Century* between 1904 and 1907 reveal the vast ambitions of Sapolio's promoters. They identified their product in turn with: the aggressive expansionism in Panama; the traditional superstitious wisdom of the Gypsy fortune-teller; the middle-class housekeeper who rises at dawn to clean her home; the Turkish bath where men congregate to admire and perhaps take erotic pleasure in the "sparkling eye and . . . limb" achieved by "Hand Sapolio"; and finally, the "ceremonial law[s]," "very peculiar, very strict" of the "Hebrew race." In this last image, spiritual laws of purification, and prohibition, identified "for more than 6,000 years" with Jews exclusively, are linked irrevocably with the "strictly Kosher" "vegetable oils" of Sapolio. Another image, of "The House of Sapolio," the mansion built literally, brick by brick, of soap, takes spiritual portent even further. The rhetoric of this advertisement – "in every walk of life . . . a solid foundation on which to build a reputation or to keep a home clean" – implies the accessibility of this Romanesque estate where everyone who is clean may enter, or possibly where everyone who enters becomes clean. The view here is wholly prospect: the reader is given the illusion of standing poised at the threshold. To enter is to *ascend into* this soap palace, which is itself the apparent product of wizardry performed by E. Morgan's Sons. The message here is that *everyone* who stands at this threshold, given proper washing, is welcome. Through Sapolio, the modern marketplace claims the ritual power to eradicate the dirt and pollution that divides Americans. In this era of multicultural becoming, the daily rite of soap consumption holds the promise of harmonizing disparity and difference. To contemplate the awesome power of Sapolio, "the safest soap for Toilet and Bath," is to gain a sense of the terrific anxiety aroused by mass production and commodity relations. Sapolio ads suggest that this soap has a mystical power; it can transform people.

FIGURE 5. Sapolio, "Making the Dirt Fly," *Putnam's Monthly*, June 1907.

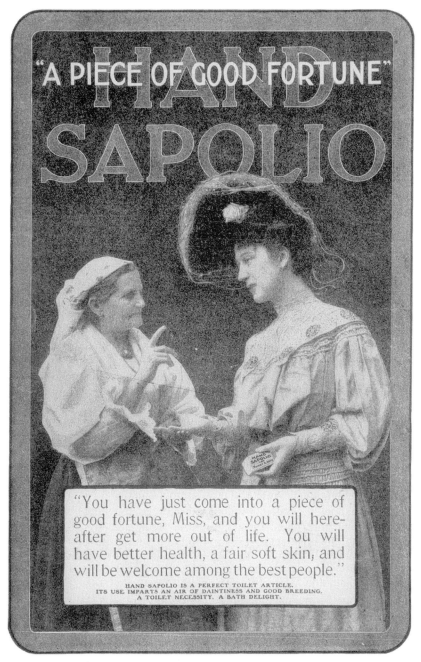

FIGURE 6. Sapolio, "A Piece of Good Fortune," *Century Magazine* 69,
September 1905.

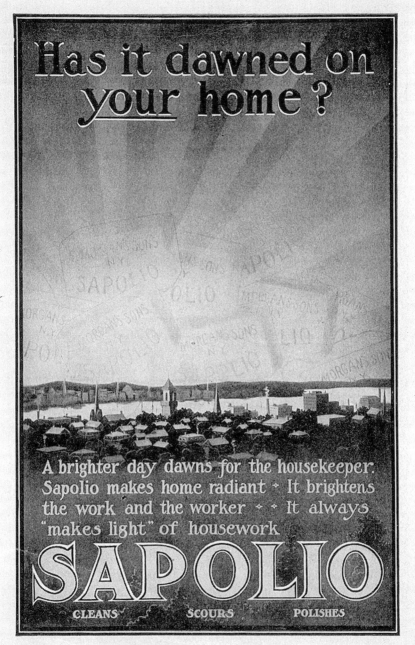

FIGURE 7. Sapolio, "Has it dawned on your home?" *Putnam's Monthly*, May 1907.

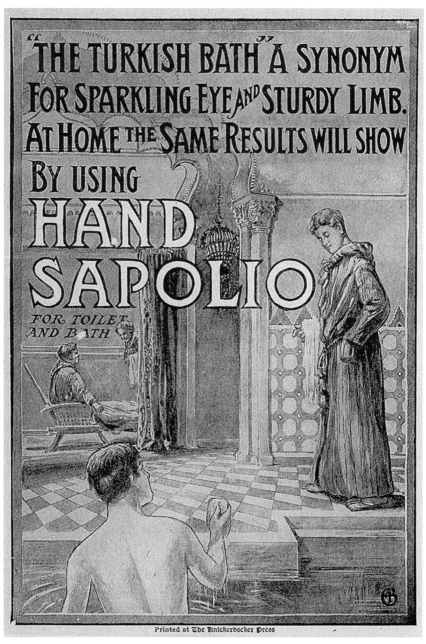

FIGURE 8. Sapolio, "The Turkish Bath," *Putnam's Monthly*, September 1907.

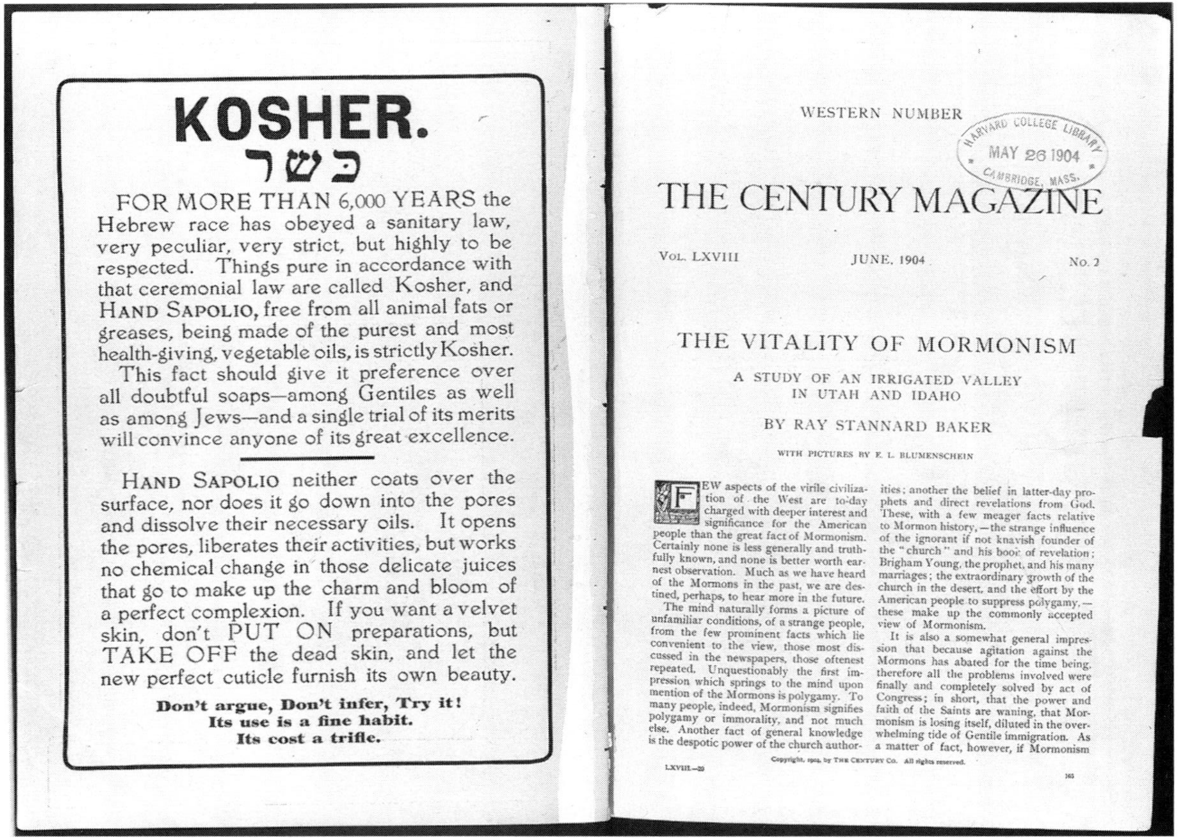

KOSHER.
כשר

FOR MORE THAN 6,000 YEARS the Hebrew race has obeyed a sanitary law, very peculiar, very strict, but highly to be respected. Things pure in accordance with that ceremonial law are called Kosher, and HAND SAPOLIO, free from all animal fats or greases, being made of the purest and most health-giving, vegetable oils, is strictly Kosher.

This fact should give it preference over all doubtful soaps—among Gentiles as well as among Jews—and a single trial of its merits will convince anyone of its great excellence.

HAND SAPOLIO neither coats over the surface, nor does it go down into the pores and dissolve their necessary oils. It opens the pores, liberates their activities, but works no chemical change in those delicate juices that go to make up the charm and bloom of a perfect complexion. If you want a velvet skin, don't PUT ON preparations, but TAKE OFF the dead skin, and let the new perfect cuticle furnish its own beauty.

Don't argue, Don't infer, Try it!
Its use is a fine habit.
Its cost a trifle.

WESTERN NUMBER

THE CENTURY MAGAZINE

VOL. LXVIII JUNE, 1904 NO. 2

THE VITALITY OF MORMONISM

A STUDY OF AN IRRIGATED VALLEY IN UTAH AND IDAHO

BY RAY STANNARD BAKER

WITH PICTURES BY E. L. BLUMENSCHEIN

FEW aspects of the virile civilization of the West are to-day charged with deeper interest and significance for the American people than the great fact of Mormonism. Certainly none is less generally and truthfully known, and none is better worth earnest observation. Much as we have heard of the Mormons in the past, we are destined, perhaps, to hear more in the future.

The mind naturally forms a picture of unfamiliar conditions, of a strange people, from the few prominent facts which lie convenient to the view, those most discussed in the newspapers, those oftenest repeated. Unquestionably the first impression which springs to the mind upon mention of the Mormons is polygamy. To many people, indeed, Mormonism signifies polygamy or immorality, and not much else. Another fact of general knowledge is the despotic power of the church authorities; another the belief in latter-day prophets and direct revelations from God. These, with a few meager facts relative to Mormon history,—the strange influence of the ignorant if not knavish founder of the "church" and his book of revelation; Brigham Young, the prophet, and his many marriages; the extraordinary growth of the church in the desert, and the effort by the American people to suppress polygamy,—these make up the commonly accepted view of Mormonism.

It is also a somewhat general impression that because agitation against the Mormons has abated for the time being, therefore all the problems involved were finally and completely solved by act of Congress; in short, that the power and faith of the Saints are waning, that Mormonism is losing itself, diluted in the overwhelming tide of Gentile immigration. As a matter of fact, however, if Mormonism

LXVIII.—20 163

FIGURE 9. Sapolio, "Kosher," *Century Magazine*, June 1904: opposite the first article, "The Vitality of Mormonism," by Ray Stannard Baker.

FIGURE 10. Sapolio, "The House of Sapolio," *Putnam's Monthly*, July 1907.

It is a truism among historians of American advertising that the profession was transformed by the Civil War. A clamor for war news greatly increased newspaper circulation, and the government war bonds that helped to ensure the success of the Union were sold via newspaper advertisements. The distribution of labor-saving machinery for harvesting and farming (to replace the men in the army), the introduction for soldiers of standardized factory-made clothing, and shoe manufacturing generated greater need and revenue for advertising. Men at war were replaced not only by machines but also by women, who had formerly devoted themselves to the domestic manufacture of family necessities. Thus both during the war and after it, people made fewer items at home, and instead worked to buy goods produced outside of it, which became increasingly known to them through advertising. Leisure-class women in particular, with time for reading as well as for consumption, provided a primed audience for advertising. The transformations in economy, commerce, and standards of living occurring over the course of the late nineteenth century are exemplified by two significant changes in methods of advertising during this time. One was the replacement of self-made copy by that of professional copywriters. When the first transcontinental railroad was built in 1869, most businesspeople were writing their own advertisements; by 1910, the vast majority was commissioning leading advertisers. The other major change was a shift in the rhetoric of advertising itself, from an emphasis on production and manufacture (which depicted manufacturers "as the heroes of progress") to an emphasis on consumption, market growth, and diversification.

Advertising catalyzed a range of economic transformations in the 1870s and 1880s: expanded distribution; renovated production processes issuing from new machinery; the replacement of wood by coal as a major energy source; increase in factory sizes to allow faster and cheaper production; new inventions such as light bulbs, telephones, streetcars, phonographs, moving pictures, development of railroad, all ensured not only a mass supply of goods, but a means of transporting them to remote areas. This period also featured the beginnings of an electrical development that was to transform industry and influence every occupation in American life, while adding to the comfort of average people. Continued economic progress required new markets and customers; advertisers zeroed in on a growing consumer population that was increasingly literate and capable of understanding print ads. By 1880, the American illiteracy rate had dropped to 17 percent, largely attributable to a public education system that was free and compulsory. Between 1880 and 1900 the volume of advertising grew from $200 to $542 million. Advertisers not only encouraged the public to buy soap, bread, clothes, and other necessities instead of making their own, but to buy the same goods repeatedly. Facilitated by the invention of the paper bag and the folding box, factory-produced, brand-name merchandise gradually supplanted bulk goods. The brand name gave rise to what advertising professionals called "the soft sell": an approach that drew on the manufacturer's reputation and sought to invest the item with memorable associations to help justify its relatively high price. But the fact that consumers no longer had direct contact with the maker of a product profoundly undermined commercial ethics. The advertiser stepped into the vacuum created by the anonymity of modern sale and purchase, an anonymity advertising sought to exploit and appease.

Advertising needed a makeover, and no one did more in the late nineteenth century to confer legitimacy on the profession than John E. Powers, who was dubbed "the father of modern advertising." Powers, who had studied advertising in England during the 1860s, introduced the practice of focus advertising: pitching ads to appropriate audiences. Equally influential was Powers's notion that advertisements should be concise, with each ad limited to one idea. This principle and the "Powerisms" it fostered, was consistent with claims that modern Americans had extraordinarily short attention spans. Hence, Ivory Soap's "It Floats"; Kodak Camera's "You Press the Button; We Do the Rest"; Prudential Insurance's "The Strength of Gibraltar." Trademarked slogans of this kind eventually came to be worth millions of dollars. Especially popular were human-interest trademarks, among them figures such as the curly-headed boy of Hires' Root Beer; the boy-in-slicker of Uneeda Biscuit; the cod liver fisherman of Omega Oil; the Cream of Wheat Chef; the Armour "Negro"; Aunt Jemima; and Sunny Jim of Force Cereal.

Another key renovator of advertising was the Bostonian Nathaniel C. Fowler, who began as a journalist and wrote a series of books in the 1880s, including *Advertising and Printing*, *Building Business*, and the encyclopedic *Fowler's Publicity*. Advertising, according to Fowler, was a science, but an inexact one. Like the physician, the advertiser aimed at best to succeed more often than he failed, for advertising was a contingent business. Fowler envisioned women as the primary household consumers, supervising the purchase of everything from oatmeal to shutters. By the 1890s, the claims of advertising had become exceedingly ambitious. One industry analyst called advertising, "the medium of communication between the world's greatest forces – demand and supply. It is a more powerful element in human progress than steam or electricity . . . Men may look forward to the day when advertising will be what it has long deserved to be, one of the world's greatest sciences." This prospect awaited the dramatic changes of the 1890s: the acceleration of production and distribution rates enabled by the development of specialized machinery, a railroad system, and more sophisticated forms of communication. These circumstances coincided with tremendous population growth. From 1880 to 1910 the US population nearly doubled (from 50,000,000 to 91,000,000, with 18,000,000 new immigrants). The country's purchasing power was increasing, as were its exports. Only one challenge remained: persuading the consumer to buy.

Among all producers, soap manufacturers took greatest advantage of advertising, helping to make it a large-scale enterprise. The sign of Sapolio's ambitions was their high aesthetic standards. Artemus Ward, who coined the most popular of Sapolio slogans ("A clean nation is a strong nation"), combed foreign languages, drawing on proverbs from across the world. Sapolio also employed Bret Harte in the 1860s. Enlisting an up and coming author to write ad copy, or a celebrity to endorse the product became integral to successful advertising plans. When the Lackawana Railroad began advertising their passenger rail service between New York and Buffalo, it exploited an endorsement from Mark Twain. As recorded in *A History of the Lackawanna Railroad*, Twain had written to them in 1899 to report "Left New York on Lackawanna Railroad this A. M. in white duck suit, and it's white yet." Twain's endorsement inspired the theme of the subsequent advertising campaign, "The Road of Anthracite," featuring a young woman, "Phoebe Snow," dressed in white, to highlight the fact that the hard-coal anthracite burned on their locomotives produced less soot than hard coal. Visual artists were equally involved in advertising: Maxfield Parrish painted for Fisk Tire; N. C. Wyeth for Cream of Wheat; Norman Rockwell for Heinz Baked Beans and Grape Nuts.

The aesthetic ambitions of advertisers went hand in hand with their commitment to professionalism and science. Like all the new "sciences" institutionalized at this time, advertising claimed command of a body of knowledge, both practical and theoretical, occupying a niche filled by no other group. Agencies such as J. Walter Thompson cultivated confidential relationships with clients while pursuing ethnographic research on their behalf, compiling a database so valuable (population and distribution statistics by category and state, "split-run" evaluations of different ad campaigns) that marketing researchers would be drawing on it decades hence. At the same time, a developing psychology of suggestion inspired advertisers to appeal directly to the mind and emotions. In so doing, they drew on the new theories of Freud and Jung, and closer to home, the work of Northwestern University psychologist Walter Dill Scott, who advanced the academic study of advertising.

Scott's first book, *The Theory And Practice Of Advertising* (1903, serialized, *Mahin's Magazine*, 1902–03) showed what the psychologist had to offer the advertising executive. Staking his claim on the big business that advertising had become at the century's turn, he emphasized the interdependence of intellectual and commercial endeavors. The enterprising manufacturer would recognize his need for theory, just as the devoted scientist would understand the value of a worldly application of his principles. Scott's theories represent the latest, *c.* 1902, understandings of how the mind works, analyzed in terms of their implications for advertising. In a discussion of "Association of Ideas," for example, he demonstrates the advantage of ubiquitous advertisements which help companies to become synonymous with the products they advertise (e.g. Pears and soap). In highlighting the importance of what he calls "fusion" advertising, he reveals the importance of class analysis to the success of advertising. The advertiser must cultivate a certain aura for the product and be mindful of the tone conferred by the medium of the advertisement, participating in the composition of the publication and securing a choice spot for their ad. Class differences require the modulation of rhetoric: expressions that prove highly successful with one class of society might fail with another class. As a social constructionist, like many of his social-scientific counterparts in this era, Scott views most psychological differences as class and environmentally based, and considers only one type of mental imaging innate and differential – the capacity to visualize. Where one individual might with ease envision the entire contents of his breakfast table, another's view might be impressionistic at best. Such differences cause one consumer to be captivated by the bold, colorful flower in an ad for perfume, while leaving another cold. Hence, *all* the advertiser's senses must be in play as he directs his appeal to a broad, heterogeneous class of consumers.

Scott's *The Psychology of Advertising* (1908) is the work of an academic who has thoroughly assimilated the perspective of big business. Commending the optimism and enterprise of the American businessman, Scott anticipates Michael Schudson's characterization of advertising as "capitalism's way of saying 'I love you' to itself." Scott's celebration of advertising as the arm of capitalism introduces a book focused on class-appropriate advertising. One of his most revealing examples confirms his theory that the preference for a commodity identified with the upper class is associated psychologically with empathy as well as with instinct. For illustration, he reproduces a Regal Shoe ad, picturing a stereotyped Irishman, pipe in mouth, shamrock hat, who quips, "Begorra – I'd Be Happy If I Could Only Get a Regal On."

Happiness seems a remote possibility given how enormous his feet (clad in yellow work boots) look next to the graceful Regal pumps. The ad dramatizes class aspirations: the advertiser does not expect the consumer to identify with the Irishman himself, but with his ambitions. He does hope that the middle-class consumer will empathize with this humble Irishman, who believes that squeezing himself into a pair of Regals will be his route to social mobility. What the ad offers the consumer in exchange for his empathy is a satisfying

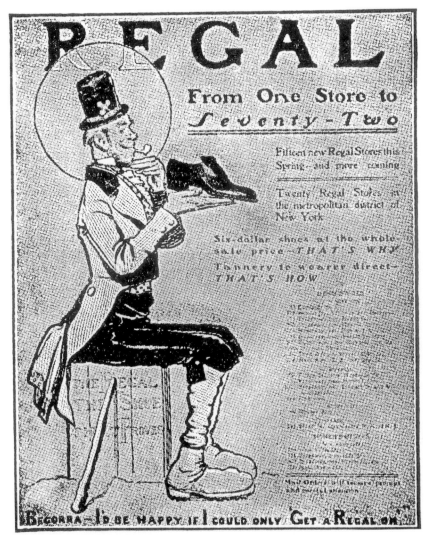

FIGURE 11. Regal Shoes ad, from Walter Dill Scott,
The Psychology of Advertising (1908).

condescension: a Regal life is wishful thinking for the Irishman, but not for him. Indeed, one could argue that the ad succeeds precisely by driving a wedge between those with like aspirations: everyone may *want* to be regal, but only some *can* be. The fact that many who want it never get it makes it all the sweeter for those who do. According to Scott, the Regal Shoe ad misses its mark, by offering for identification a stereotyped figure that can never inspire identification. But Scott misses the ad's expectation that the consumer will identify with the message (social mobility), not the medium (the degraded Irishman). Scott extends his ideas about the class stratifications of American consumer behavior in reflections on the most literal area of consumption. In a chapter on "The Psychology of Food Advertising," he is concerned implicitly with the relationship between food and distinction. Food in the modern era has more to do with anxieties about social status than with appetite; hence the preference for turkey over pork, and quail over chicken.

Scott is especially attentive to habit, which he considers the faculty most relevant to advertising. Scott's interest in habit is consistent with his conviction that advertising has greatest impact when it seeps unnoticed into the consciousness of consumers. Habit is what we do unknown to ourselves: how we dress ourselves – which arm we slide first into the sleeve of a coat; how we read the newspaper – last page first, section by section, skimming all? Such behaviors, predictable and quantifiable, have various applications to advertising. As Scott explains in a penultimate chapter, "The Unconscious Influence in Street Railway Advertising," streetcar advertising is effective because it is *the* most subliminal form of advertising.

That there was nothing accidental about the tactics used to induce that unconsciousness was evidenced by Francis Bellamy's study *Effective Magazine Advertising: 508 Essays about 111 Advertisements* (1909, excerpted in *Everybody's Magazine*, 1907). Bellamy's book was based upon a contest sponsored by a Progressive, middle-class periodical, *Everybody's Magazine* in 1907, which asked readers to judge the best advertisement in the November issue and explain why. The contest was indicative of the tremendous self-consciousness of the advertising industry by the century's turn, which sought to read the minds of potential consumers as they read advertisements. Advertisers and magazines were participants in a mutually reinforcing campaign for audiences as readers based their sense of a magazine's quality partly on the appeal of its advertisements. At the same time, advertisers recognized that their products absorbed a kind of de facto endorsement from the magazine that featured them. Indeed, every aspect of the periodical, from the paper it was printed on to its intellectual content, contributed to its value as an advertising medium. Bellamy's analysis revealed, above all, the extent of consumers' fascination with merchandise and self-conscious savvy about its acquisition. The people he quoted, while no doubt self-selected individuals drawn to advertising and marketing, nevertheless betray a mercantile literacy and sophistication that is rarely acknowledged in studies of consumption during this period.

Throughout his analysis, Bellamy stresses that the best products are adver-tised in the best magazines, and the public is well aware of this. There is an obvious circularity to advertising. The more money a company spends on it, the better its product is assumed to be; the better its product is assumed to be, the more people buy it, leading to greater profits for the company, and more money to be invested in advertising. The book that follows Bellamy's com-monsensical introduction is consistent with the main principles he outlines there. A series of advertisements, for pianos, radiators, bond paper, razors, jew-elry, coffee, asphalt paving, cameras, window shades, vacation resorts, ostrich boas, hangers, and cross-country passenger trains (and this is just the first forty pages!), are reproduced with assessments of their success as advertisements by ordinary magazine readers. The success of an advertisement is measured by the attention it generates, which depends on a combination of simplicity and ingenuity. The best ads build on commonplaces, which they present in unex-pected ways. The reviews of the ads reproduced by Bellamy are extravagant in their praise for the rhetoric of advertising; this confirms how an atmosphere of advertising can be endlessly self-replicating, in this case inspiring consumers to hawk their own remarkable powers of appreciation. The circle of advertising ultimately envelops the audience, not simply as buyers, but as participants in an adulatory climate of self- and object-love.

EDITING

Contests of this kind, which were the rule rather than the exception, helped to make advertising part of the common American culture. By the 1880s, most magazine readers understood advertising as an integral element of the magazines they read. The dramatic expansion of periodical advertising was partly due to the great increase in competition. After the Civil War, new magazines poured from the presses. From 1865 to 1870 the number of jour-nals in the United States doubled. By 1880 that number had doubled again. With the exception of *The Century*, which sought advertising actively from its outset, most literary periodicals refused to sell advertising space through the 1860s, but by 1870 magazines that had managed to limit advertisements to cultural subjects were accepting paid advertisements of all kinds. Elite mag-azines courted the advertising they had previously spurned in order to defray the costs of competing with new magazines and to pay writers and artists, whose fees rose in accordance with the availability of new publishing venues. Indeed, the survival of most journals depended on their ability to attract adver-tising. In 1879, the periodical business received a terrific boost from the US government with the introduction of bulk mailing, second-class rates that single-handedly transformed the economics of magazine publishing. At the same time, greater affordability in the 1880s of electrotype plates and halftones for illustrations gradually allowed the use of color, greatly enhancing advertising's visual effects. As a result, many magazines began to distribute advertising throughout their pages rather than isolating it at the end. By the turn of the century advertising had developed an aesthetic sophistication that reinforced its compatibility with the art and literature it increasingly bordered in magazines. Advertisers were influenced by the English Arts and Crafts Movement, which advocated medieval ideals of workmanship, and by an Art Nouveau that coupled romanticism with modern manufacturing and its products. The palpable contrast between Art Nouveau's natural forms and the mass-produced objects they were used to promote represented a contradiction that pervaded advertising throughout the twentieth century. Elaborate Art Nouveau Posters also adorned the covers of magazines such as *Harpers*, *Atlantic*, and *The Century*. Designed by French artists such as Eugene Grasset and Anglo-American artists such as Aubrey Beardsley and William H. Bradley, these covers helped to make the commercial, artistic, and literary contents into one fluent discourse. Their designs were thought to speak directly to women, the special object of advertisers at the turn of the century, who believed that they were responsible for 85 percent of all purchases. Despite the perceived necessity of attracting women consumers, female professionals in advertising generally shared the fate of their counterparts in other developing fields – marginalization.

Magazines and newspapers were invaluable to advertisers because their dramatically expanded circulation facilitated deliberate market segmentation. Some large city newspapers, like *The New York Times*, targeted affluent markets to attract both national and local advertisers. Although newspapers differed widely in their efforts to draw on various segments of their potential audiences, magazines had traditionally addressed the "better classes." The modern magazine's editorially orchestrated focus remained its greatest claim on advertising patronage. Yet in keeping with the pattern of expansion and consolidation in business generally, as magazines became increasingly prominent beneficiaries of the overall success of advertising through the 1890s, their numbers declined dramatically. Of the thousands of magazines that appeared after the Civil War, by 1900 less than a third had claimed large audiences and advertising revenue. The magazines that had established minor advantages in their ability to attract advertisers in the 1880s and 1890s continued to attract more readers and then more advertisers in a mutually sustaining cycle. Those who were successful with magazines after the century's turn, such as Cyrus K. Curtis with *The Saturday Evening Post*, had learned that success depended on attracting advertising revenue, rather than attending to subscriptions and content.

As Curtis observed in 1906, "I can hire men to conduct the editorial affairs of my magazines and to look after the circulation . . . But the *promotion* of the business is a matter I feel it is my duty to attend to myself."

This is a sentiment that Fulkerson, the syndicate businessman behind the main magazine enterprise in Howells's *A Hazard of New Fortunes* (1890), would have understood. As Howells's novel makes clear, by 1890 there was no world of letters independent of the savvy, entrepreneurial spirit of a cultural broker like Fulkerson. His protagonist Basil March, a "western man come east," who moves from Boston to New York to assume the editorship of an ambitious new magazine, struggles to reconcile his aesthetic principles with the commercial motives of its managing editor and chief benefactor. Howells's novel confirms that the magazines have transformed the American world of letters into a big business. Howells was familiar with developments such as the *New York Ledger*, a leading literary magazine of the 1870s, paying Fanny Fern $1000 for a story and Henry Ward Beecher $30,000 for his novel *Norwood* (1867). The method conceived in *A Hazard of New Fortunes* for making "the man of letters . . . a man of business" (Howells's title for a contemporaneous essay), is a magazine "run in the interest of the contributors," paying contributing authors and artists a low fee "outright," while providing them with a percentage of overall profits. The magazine is a crucial mediator, according to the novel's cynical artist, Angus Beaton, "the missing link . . . between the Arts and the Dollars." Howells, typically, makes a complex, and ultimately irresolvable, moral quandary of the confrontation. The novel is a product of Howells's experiences as an editor, in New York and Boston, first as an editorial assistant at *The Nation*, and later, at the *Atlantic Monthly*, which published his first poems. Howells served as editor-in-chief at the *Atlantic* for a decade (1871–81) and resigned the post when the owners ended their partnership in 1881. This breakup coincided with Howells's growing success as a novelist, to which he subsequently devoted himself full time. Signing a contract with James R. Osgood, Howells was ensured a regular income in exchange for exclusive rights to all his writings. When this distinguished publishing house failed in 1885, Howells signed an even more lucrative contract with Harper and Brothers. But Howells was a natural editor, and the world of magazines was one he kept his hand in to the end of his life. In 1886, he began writing "The Editor's Study," a regular column for *Harper's Monthly*; in 1892 he became co-editor, briefly, of *Cosmopolitan* (resigning after four months, complaining privately of "hopeless incompatibility" with the other editor); in 1895 he began a column, "Life and Letters," for *Harper's Weekly*, and in 1900 he launched "The Editor's Easy Chair" for *Harper's Monthly*, a column which lasted until his death in 1920.

The world of *A Hazard of New Fortunes*, like that envisioned by American advertisers of the era, is sharply divided along class lines. The man behind the novel's new magazine is Fulkerson, with entrepreneurial skills suggesting the publisher and the adman in one, who works "his interest with the press to the utmost" and ensures that "paragraphs of a variety that did credit to his ingenuity were afloat everywhere." Like other ambitious managing editors, Fulkerson understands that his magazine's future depends on its ability to identify the broadest exclusive readership. The majority of publishers and editors identified their readers as professional classes, though some, like *Frank Leslie's Popular Monthly* and *Women's Argosy*, sought to appeal to a vast working class. Editors themselves, as Howells suggests in highlighting the economy of his editor-hero, Basil March, were respected and circulated easily among wealthy urban elites, but their salaries were decidedly middle class. March is an editor of the *Atlantic* stripe, a contemplative moralist, preoccupied with art and craft, eschewing the business end of things. Recognizing that the bulk of the magazine's prospective audience is middle-class, rural America, he also understands that the contents, dictated by the expectations of readers, have a certain inevitability: a story, a travel sketch, a literary essay, a social essay, a dramatic piece, a translation, some criticism on the latest books, plays, art, fashion, some poetry, and sprinkled liberally throughout, illustrations, which were the making of any magazine. While the successful general-interest magazine, according to Howells, aims at the white Protestant middle class, it must reflect the diversity of American society, both formally (generic diversity) and socially (the cultural range of authors, artists, and subjects). The editor's object is to unite the heterogeneous elements in a satisfying coherent way, to manage a diversity of effects into an attractive whole that is rewarded by widespread purchase.

Howells's emphasis on this aspect of magazine editing – the editor's struggle to locate coherence within diversity – unifies the narrative threads of his novel. While the many passages depicting characters wandering through the streets of New York, reflecting on the contrasting lives of different classes and on the ethnic variety across neighborhoods, might seem to digress from the larger plot of this magazine novel, they are in fact integral to it. The successful magazine is distinguished by its ability to harness and exploit the tumultuous diversity of the modern city and make it available as a legible commodity to the country at large. As Fulkerson observes, "there's no subject so fascinating to the general average of people throughout the country as life in New York City." The successful periodical manages to provide "contrasts . . . for the sake of the full effect." Yet it is the very diversity – of background, politics, taste – of *Every Other Week*'s staff that ensures its collapse. When the socialist translator, Lindau, insults the capitalist owner Dryfoos, and March is ordered to fire Lindau, he is thrown into a typical Howellsian quandary. Though he disagrees with Lindau's radical ideas, March cannot work for a man who denies contributors freedom of speech. The novel ends in the ideal partnership of March, all discrimination and conscience, and Fulkerson, the ultimate businessman, who seem destined to effect the permanent reconciliation of North and South, while bringing *Every Other Week* to ever greater reaches of success.

Henry James was preoccupied with the business and culture of magazines throughout his career, thus it is not surprising that one of his most memorable novels, *The Ambassadors*, features an editor as its protagonist. James not only made his main character, Lambert Strether, an editor, but he made the practice of magazine serialization the defining structure of the novel. Serialized in the *North American Review* from 1902 to 1903, *The Ambassadors* accompanied such pieces as Mark Twain on Christian Science, Hamlin Garland on "Sanity in Fiction," Edith Wharton on reading, and Howells on Chicago fiction. That the novel was also typically Jamesian in the beauty of its narrative, in its deep renditions of character consciousness, in its penchant for psychological abstractions, and in the way it propelled its plot forward only confirmed how integral serialization had always been to James's authorship. Indeed, James's first full-length novel, *Roderick Hudson*, was initiated by a letter from an editor at *Scribner's Monthly* proposing that he write a serial novel for the magazine. James took the offer to William Dean Howells at the more prestigious *Atlantic*, who drew up a twelve-hundred-dollar contract for a novel, *Roderick Hudson*, in twelve parts, running from November 1874 to November 1875.

In *The Ambassadors*, James laments the commercialization of culture in America, while managing to profit from it. *The Ambassadors* is the aesthetic monument to James's dissatisfaction with his country – the poverty of materials, of social life, the preference for utilitarian over intrinsic value – conveying powerfully on behalf of its deprived American hero the atmospheric gravity of Paris. As James writes in his detailed preview, "Project of Novel by Henry James":

Strether's name, as the editor, is on the cover, where it has been one of the few frank pleasures of his somewhat straightened life to have liked to see it. He is known by that pale, costly cover – it has become his principal identity. A man of moods and of a very variable imagination, he has sometimes thought this identity small, poor, miserable; while at others thinking it as good as most of the others around him.

Strether's mission as the "ambassador" of his patron (and potential wife), the wealthy widow Mrs. Newsome, is to "rescue" her son, Chad Newsome, from an extended stay in Paris. Soon after arriving in Paris, Strether meets the mysterious French adulteress, Madame Vionnet, responsible for Chad's delay. For Chad, and increasingly for Strether, Madame Vionnet is everything that a prospective marriage and career awaiting him in Woollett, Massachusetts, is not. She gratifies an unrealized aesthetic and intellectual sense in Strether, who finds himself as a result perilously at odds with his mission. Madame Vionnet and the Parisian atmosphere with which she is identified arouse Strether's latent dissatisfaction with Woollett, the Newsomes, and the America they represent. The novel's chief irony, then, is that the ambassador deputized to bring the lingering sojourner home becomes in Paris consumed with the dread of dying without ever "having lived."

He comes to recognize his own editorship of the green-covered Woollett review as a meager nod to culture, in a larger "mercantile mandate" that is the Newsomes' sole concern. Despite repeated references to the Newsomes' enterprise, James characteristically repudiates a direct account of the business life, or the man of business. The novel's sympathy with Strether and Chad is expressed through its resistance to the material facts that pull them home. In an early scene, Strether invokes with mock exuberance a parade of adjectives to *avoid* describing the Newsome firm: "a big brave bouncing business . . . a roaring trade . . . a workshop . . . a great production . . . a great industry . . . a manufacture that, if it's only properly looked after, may well be on the way to become a monopoly." From birth ("big brave bouncing") to growth ("trade," "workshop" "production") to expansion, a final step that even holds the prospect of "monopoly," Strether describes the life cycle of an American business, without ever naming its purpose. Meanwhile Chad's family demands that he sacrifice Paris and the affair that has "made" him for an American scene where he must "prove himself" "an immense man of business." That Chad's rhetoric compensates for a deeper loss is suggested by the admiration he expresses in his final conversation with Strether for "the art of advertisement" which "scientifically worked" and was "a great new force."

In the form of an ambassador from modern America who foils the terms of his mission, James manages to stage a formidable contest between an American scene where commerce governs all aspects of life and culture and a European scene where life and culture have their own value. Profit may have motivated Strether's mission, with its success portending marriage to Mrs. Newsome and her vast wealth. But the novel closes with the claim that abandoning the mission was greater profit still. Loss in an economic sense is gain in a life sense. James's penchant for imagining reverse migrations from America stood out in an era when so many were immigrating to America in pursuit of the material opportunities forsaken by his characters. Yet the visions of James's novels were often at odds with his own entrepreneurial efforts on behalf of his art. Critics expecting consistency from an author's work to his life have overlooked the extent to which James's own efforts to exploit the commercial opportunities of an American literary market place belied his presentation of commerce in his novels. For James understood as well as anyone in the world of letters how an American cultural establishment was vitalized and supported by the capitalist ethos that also overshadowed it. (A fuller treatment of James appears below in the section on authorship.)

Such support was critical to the success of Samuel S. McClure, an Irish immigrant who started *McClure's Magazine* in 1893, his "only real capital" a large acquaintance with talented writers, and in a decade built it into one of the leading magazines in the world. McClure's achievement grew out of the simple belief that there was a place in America for the heterogeneous middle-class periodical that was so central to literary culture in England. A shrewd outsider, he grasped the American appetite for heroes, and encouraged Ida Tarbell's profiles of great men, which proved critical to the magazine's initial success. McClure satisfied another American niche with a series on scientific innovations, that became increasingly popular. Finally, his recognition of a cultural penchant for multiple viewpoints led to his encouragement of a type of investigative journalism that Theodore Roosevelt referred to as "muckrak-ing." Exemplified by Lincoln Steffens's essays on urban political corruption and Ida Tarbell's series on the cartel violations of Standard Oil, these pieces were designed to encourage constructive social reform as opposed to radical change. Evidently, the magazine's commercial customers were satisfied with its adversarial style, for the era of *McClure's* most notorious muckraking was also the time of its most lucrative advertising. What made series such as Tarbell's acceptable to a range of readers of varying political persuasions was their scientific rigor, comprehensiveness, and vivid prose. Combining the ben-efits of science and journalism, *McClure's* signature essays filled a gap between journalistic simplicity and expert tendencies towards insularity. McClure's scheme was to pay journalists adequately for pieces so they had time to master a subject. Thus they could write, if not with the authority of an expert, with sufficient depth and accuracy to engage an intelligent public.

McClure's own storied life was itself worthy of serialization (1913–14, pub-lished as *My Autobiography*, 1914). Co-written with Willa Cather, the serial provided a nostalgic account of his boyhood in Ireland, where he was born in 1858 to a family of poor farmers, and his immigration to the Midwest. The seeds of McClure's future work were planted by the constant challenge faced by this curious and intelligent boy finding things to read. Reading everything he could get his hands on, including "Agricultural Reports" sent to constituents by their Congressmen, McClure traced his subsequent idea of newspaper syndication to his intellectually deprived adolescence in rural America. Circulating stories across the country in urban newspapers and weekly county papers, McClure sought both to serve the needs of rural children, whose cultural impoverishment he knew first-hand, and to create new markets for writers he admired. McClure's self-education was sufficient to gain him entrance to Knox College in Illinois, which he financed with summer work as a peddler, furthering his knowledge of rural Americans. At Knox, McClure met a number of people who would figure prominently in his magazine. These included John Phillips, co-founder of *McClure's*, Albert Brady, future business manager, and Robert Mather, later chairman of the Westinghouse Electrical Companies and an important investor.

McClure's subsequent rise in Boston was a classic American success story. Soon after arriving, he managed to talk the head of Pope Manufacturing Co. (Bicycles), into launching a cycling magazine called *The Wheelman*. As cycling was the first popular outdoor sport in America, *The Wheelman* flourished accordingly. McClure moved to New York after *The Wheelman* was sold, to work at *The Century* in a menial job, which gave him time to think, leading to one of his great innovations – syndication. Syndication was not original to McClure, having already been tried by papers such as the *New York Sun*, which purchased stories by writers and published them simultaneously in cities across the country. But it had never been tried on the scale he conceived. So confident was he of his plan that he decided in 1884 to test the prospect on his own. While McClure had no difficulty securing contributions given the obvious benefits for authors both monetarily and through exposure, most editors were wary. McClure's syndicate, however, took hold after a year, and he was eventually able to sign on such reputable writers as Sarah Orne Jewett, Elizabeth Stuart Phelps, Joel Chandler Harris, and Arthur Conan Doyle.

McClure's success in the magazine business grew out of a shrewd appraisal of his adopted country and its leading institutions. His idealism, which persisted despite the many in-depth reports of social corruption uncovered by his own staff, typified the enterprising reformist spirit that drove American expansion in various fields, from invention, manufacturing, and authorship, to union organizing and journalism, during this post-Civil war era. Had McClure himself been looking for an individual to profile in any of his series, on "Great Individuals," or "Innovators in Science," for instance, had he been looking for a comparable figure in the realm of "genius," had he been interested in talking about the value, for a given community, of a vibrant magazine to express its primary interests and expand its horizons, he need have looked no further than W. E. B. Du Bois. Indeed, McClure once purchased an article by Du Bois, but failed to publish it, deeming it too politically incendiary for the liberal muckraking tastes of *McClure's* readership. Experiences like this no doubt strengthened Du Bois's conviction of the need for a magazine designed to address the circumstances and aspirations of the black community.

From early in his long career as a public intellectual, author, and social scientist, W. E. B. Du Bois dreamed "that a critical periodical for the American Negro might be founded." Du Bois's first steps towards this end were taken in 1906 in Memphis, Tennessee where he began a weekly paper called *The Moon*. In 1907 *The Moon* was moved to Washington where it became *The Horizon* (1907 to 1910). When Du Bois assumed an executive position at the newly incorporated National Association for the Advancement of Colored People in 1910, among his first initiatives was the transformation of *The Horizon* into *The Crisis* (1910-33), whose title was inspired by James Russell Lowell's poem, "The Present Crisis." In less than a decade, *The Crisis* became a fixture of the black intelligentsia. From a starting circulation in 1910 of one thousand, the magazine was generating profit within two years (boasting an annual income by 1920 of $75,000), achieving a circulation of 100,000 by 1918. The importance of *The Crisis* to the NAACP agenda and to the overall improvement of the conditions of blacks in America is clear. It enabled a consistent and prominent profiling of the facts of these conditions as well as a consistent delineation of the obvious means at the nation's disposal for improving them.

Among the examples that inspired Du Bois's *Crisis* were the first national monthlies targeted at African-American audiences: Frederick Douglass's *North Star*, William Garrison's *Liberator*, and Timothy Thomas Fortune's *Globe*. Most NAACP leaders shared the skepticism of Albert Pillsbury, who wrote Du Bois that "periodicals are as numerous and pestilential nowadays as flies were in Egypt, and most of them meet with the very same reception." But Du Bois remained dedicated to the success of a magazine whose primary aim was the exposure of the virulence of race prejudice. Oswald Villard, editor of the *Evening Post*, provided office space, and Du Bois signed Kelly Miller (Howard University dean), Max Barber (former editor of the *Voice of the Negro*), William Stanley Braithwaite (poetry editor of the *Boston Transcript*), and Mary Dunlop Maclean (staff writer for *The New York Times*), as contributing editors. Du Bois insisted on low subscription prices and varied content, mixing information and analysis with entertainment, to encourage wide circulation. Thus in the first four years of publication *The Crisis* featured a regular column, "Along the Color Line," with subsections on politics, education, social uplift, organizations and meetings, science and art; an "Opinion" section which reproduced press correspondence; an "Editorial" section; a large section devoted to NAACP activity; and "The Burden," which recorded recent atrocities against blacks. "Talks About Women" (which urged black women to join the wider movement for women's suffrage) and "Men of the Month" (portraits of black inventors, surgeons, psychiatrists, architects, and other role models) were later introduced as regular features.

The first issue of *The Crisis* placed great emphasis on lynching and murders of southern blacks for attempting to escape the peonage system. An editorial posited black participation in national politics as a means of countering such outrages. The issue included "Talks About Women," by Mrs. John Milholland, a piece which confirmed Du Bois's commitment to women's concerns; a paper by Franz Boas repudiating pseudoscientific theories on race; and a critical account of Booker T. Washington's European tour ("On landing in America, Mr. Washington announced that the Negroes in the United States were better off than the poor classes in Europe"). Advertising in this issue was purchased by Madame E. Toussaint's Conservatory of Art and Music – "The Foremost Female Artist of the Race"; Real Estate Broker Philip A. Payton – "New York's Pioneer Negro Real Estate Agents"; L. C. Smith & Bros. Typewriters of Syracuse, New York; the Henry Phipps Model Tenements for Colored Families; Marshall's Hotel on West Fifty-third Street; "The Leading Colored Restaurant in America"; and the Nyanza Pharmacy – "the only colored Drug Store in New York City." With the magazine's growing success, these advertisers were joined by major black colleges and universities – Atlanta, Fisk, Howard, Shaw, Virginia Union, Wilberforce – and by leading publishers of black writers, including the publisher of *The Souls of Black Folk*.

Over the course of his twenty-three years as editor of *The Crisis*, Du Bois was its major contributor, and his vision predominated. Indeed, some readers complained that Du Bois's race-progressive gospel was so intense that it bordered on religiosity. But few denied that *The Crisis* was first and foremost a political periodical, designed to claim for black Americans the rights due them under the Constitution and the Declaration of Independence. Du Bois described in one editorial how *The Crisis* offices were invaded just before the First World War by federal agents suspicious of blacks, whom they counted among "foreign nationals." The agents inquired, Du Bois recalls, "just what, after all, were our objects and activities? I took great satisfaction in being able to sit back in my chair and answer blandly, 'We are seeking to have the Constitution of the United States thoroughly and completely enforced.'" Nor did the periodical pull punches in its upbraiding of major reform movements – specifically, women's suffrage and organized labor – for their racist exclusion of black women and black workers. *The Crisis* was prepared to acknowledge the occasional triumph (the victorious strike of Haywood's Industrial Workers of the World, which was open to all races and trades, in Lawrence, Massachusetts), but Du Bois was relentless in his exposure of the hypocrisy of reformers who saw no contradiction between their appeals on behalf of oppressed women or workers, and their antagonism (often violent) towards even more oppressed black people. There was no subject that was more fully reviled in the pages of *The Crisis* than lynching, which Du Bois confronted aggressively. In an editorial on the lynching of a deranged black man in Coatesville, Pennsylvania, entitled, "Let the Eagle Scream," Du Bois described how on this Sunday in September, thousands of whites poured out of churches to be present at the smoking pyre. "The point is," Du Bois wrote, "he was black. Blackness must be punished. Blackness is the crime of crimes."

When Du Bois left *The Crisis* and the NAACP in 1934, following his censure for criticizing the association's policy on Pan-African solidarity (they were against it) and segregation (they were not unequivocally opposed to it), he was credited with having originated and established, "without a cent of capital . . . an unprecedented achievement in American journalism," a fully self-supporting magazine with a monthly circulation of 100,000. No less importantly, he had provided a critical new forum for sustaining a black intelligentsia, while offering more widespread enlightenment on the "race problem" in America. In recognizing the great potential of the mass-circulation magazine in helping to expand the parameters of the national conversation on African Americans both within the African-American community and beyond its borders, Du Bois proved himself once again uniquely capable of exploiting multiple media, disciplinary, and political forms, while preserving a uniquely critical perspective on all of them in the name of the true advancement of his people over the course of the twentieth century.

AUTHORSHIP

No American writer in the post-Civil War era was more alert than Henry James to the commercial prospects of literature and the role magazines played in developing those prospects. For a writer whose work through much of twentieth-century literary history has been made synonymous with abstractness, exclusivity, and aesthetic withdrawal, the story of James's preoccupation with the literary market place, his deep regard for readerships, and the significant contemporary reputation he enjoyed as a leading American writer, has sometimes been overlooked. But the details, aesthetic and political as well as economic, of James's shrewd efforts to establish himself as an American author of international repute help to illuminate the situation of authorship in general during this post-Civil War period. The tremendous expansion of reading audiences, aptly exploited by S. S. McClure, the proliferation of periodicals, the rise of publishing firms, the professionalizing of advertising, the commercialization of literature, all of these changes paralleled James's development as a transatlantic author. According to an English census in 1881, 3400 respondents identified themselves as authors, editors, or journalists; by 1901 the number had risen to 11,000. Figures in the United States were even higher. In the 1870s American publishers put out 3000 new books a year; by the turn of the century the number had doubled. An international copyright agreement between the United States and Great Britain was not signed until 1891, thus British and American authors were subjected to piracy in the transatlantic exchange of their works. Because he remained an American citizen, while residing in England, James enjoyed the copyright protections of both nations. Indeed, James effectively doubled his income by copyrighting his books in both countries, and selling them for serialization in both American and English periodicals prior to book publication. James's success in exploiting a transatlantic book industry that usually worked to the disadvantage of authors made him an especially informed advocate in this period for the professional author.

James's official entry into what he characterized as a "modern class of trained men of letters . . . the great army of constant producers" was in 1865 through William Dean Howells, who as editor of the *Atlantic Monthly* paid James $100 for the Civil War tale, "The Story of a Year." In 1875, the American publisher James R. Osgood published both *A Passionate Pilgrim* and *Transatlantic Sketches*, yielding respective royalties of $88.20 and $196.80, relatively meager sums that explain why, throughout his career, James earned far more from serialization of his books than from the comparatively modest earnings of his published volumes. Thus, for example, James was paid $1350 in 1876 by the *Atlantic Monthly* for their serialization of *The American*. When James reluctantly joined the many authors who had secured literary agents to help them navigate an increasingly diversified literary market-place with adversarial relations between authors and publishers, he informed his brother William that the agent would be used exclusively to secure serialization agreements. Though by the turn of the century, James was receiving a respectable yearly income from his family's properties in Syracuse, New York, he remained eager to exploit the market for serialization. Were you "able to arrange for the serialization of *The Golden Bowl?*" he wrote his new literary agent, James B. Pinker. "It would be a dream of bliss & I should bless your name forever!" James's ability to live for the most part on his literary earnings was due to the serialization of his works and his success in securing their British republication under secure copyright. In encouraging a fellow American author to seek British publication, James commented, "It is a patriotic fallacy that we read more than they. *We don't.*"

The English literary market place owed its comparative stability to the fact that novels were published in multiple volumes and priced at four times that of their American counterparts, then aimed at middle- and upper-middle-class readerships. Moreover, established book clubs, and libraries, both circulating and exclusive, ensured that novels would sell enough to keep them profitable for English publishers. Such was not the case in the United States, where publishers depended on significant profits up front, and continually sought bestsellers. With the exception of *Daisy Miller* (1878), which sold 20,000 copies in weeks after its release by Harpers, James was consigned to relatively modest sales of his books. In his reliance on profits from serialization and/or private supplemental income through most of his life as an author, James's experience was typical. But he hardly endured the obscurity and repudiation that have come to be associated with his career by critics in the twentieth century. As Rebecca West observed, it "was interesting to note how often in the obituary notices of Mr. James it was said that he never attained popularity . . . From 1875 to 1885 (to put it roughly) all England and America were . . . captivated by the clear beauty of Mr. James's work." There is little question, however, that James failed to achieve the celebrity to which he aspired, and the reasons for this are directly attributable to the uniqueness of everything he wrote, which often made him an easy target for both contemporary and subsequent critics.

Of the charges laid against James's novels over the course of literary history, none has been more damning than that of elitism. His characters, who are seldom represented at work, spend a great deal of time engaged in talk while drinking tea or going to museums. The opening to *The Portrait of a Lady* is representative.

Under certain circumstances there are few hours in life more agreeable than the hour dedicated to the ceremony known as afternoon tea. There are circumstances in which, whether you partake of the tea or not – some people of course never do – the situation is in itself delightful. Those that I have in mind in beginning to unfold this simple history offered an admirable setting to an innocent pastime. The implements of the little feast had been disposed upon the lawn of an old English country house in what I should call the perfect middle of a splendid summer afternoon. Part of the afternoon had waned, but much of it was left, and what was left was of the finest and rarest quality.

This is a society defined by its exclusivity. Each assertion is carefully qualified, while a consensus of style, thought, and behavior is steadily invoked. The narrator appeals to a circle of insiders, and declares the narrative open to those able to comprehend its signs and gestures. This opening makes much of the ceremonies of a particular class. In this sense the narrator's ostensible humility is a pretense: the history is far from "simple" just as the "feast" is assuredly not "little." In James, sitting down to tea is a thoroughly moral act: it is "perfect," "fine," and "rare." And for all this emphasis on purity and simplicity, and on the preservation of long-standing traditions, it is important to recognize that two of the three men in this opening scene are transplanted Americans – Daniel and Ralph Touchett – who have voluntarily adopted English rituals. They could as well be sitting down to afternoon coffee, a commodity no less imperial but certainly not English.

James's representation of transplanted Americans here forecasts one of the main concerns of his fiction in general: what does it mean to adopt a country and to assume a set of traditions? James was alert to the defining rites of different cultures. The faculty of observation was the driving purpose of Realist fiction as he conceived it, as it was of the developing social sciences that were contemporaneous with it. James made social observation into a high art. Yet Jamesian Realism was always underwritten by a Modernist relativism. All observation in James is subjective, and any perspective is relative to any other. A distinct narrative point of view is a strict principle in James's fictions; the reader's perspective is always held to that of one limited perceiver who might be able to roam among the minds of different characters, but is always indebted, for any particular insight, to a single consciousness. One could argue that it was precisely by limiting his narrative perspective to specific consciousnesses that James could dramatize the terrific power he accorded each one. As confirmed by the weight given to "Portrait," in the title "*The* Portrait of a Lady," James was deeply committed to aesthetic power, the transformative capacities of human artifice and convention. Human perceptions and forms are for him dominant and preeminent. The same goes for human emotions, which are privileged in James and provide the basis for his unique psychological realism. In his plots the principle actions consist of seeing, thinking, and feeling: violence in James is always mental.

His interest in the variability of cultural conventions was literal as well as theoretical, though his own expatriation was marked by ambivalence. He wrote optimistically, for example, in an 1867 letter to Thomas Perry:

I think to be an American is an excellent preparation for culture. We have exquisite qualities as a race, and it seems to me that we are ahead of the European races in the fact that more than any of them we can deal freely with forms of civilization not our own, can pick and choose and assimilate and in short (aesthetically etc.) claim our property wherever we find it. To have no national stamp has hitherto been a defect and a drawback, but I think it not unlikely that American writers may yet indicate that a vast intellectual fusion and synthesis of the various national tendencies of the world is the condition of more important achievements than any we have seen. We must of course, have something of our own – something distinctive and homogeneous – and I take it that we shall find it in our moral consciousness, our unprecedented spiritual lightness and vigor. In this sense at least we shall have a national cachet.

Yet it is possible to read *The Portrait of a Lady* itself, with its cast of bored and ruthless expatriates, as a more substantial articulation of the pessimistic view.

Despite James's lifelong "poet's quarrel with his native land," in Turgenev's words, he waited until the very end of it, 1915, the year before he died, to renounce his American citizenship. Henry James Jr. (1843–1916) was born on April 15 in Washington Square, New York City. His paternal grandfather, William James, emigrated from Ireland in 1789, with little money, a Latin grammar, and an ambition to visit Revolutionary battlegrounds. Due to successful land ventures in Albany, NY, where he eventually settled, and salt manufacturing in Syracuse, William James left an estate valued at three million dollars when he died in 1832. William James raised his four sons as strict Presbyterians, a harsh creed with which the youngest, the future Henry James Sr., seems to have been continually at odds. Henry Sr. studied at Union College and at the Princeton Theological Seminary, where he began his struggle to locate a benevolent divinity, and met Mary Robertson Walsh, the sister of a fellow theology student, who would become his wife. While she had been raised as a strict Calvinist, Mary was willing to forego a religious marriage ceremony at the behest of her husband to be. Henry Jr. then was born into a wealthy, and theologically skeptical family, whose restless paternal head saw to it that his children (William, Henry Jr., Garth Wilkinson, Robertson, and Alice) moved constantly, and were educated in schools with a variety of philosophical orientations, throughout the world. This seems to have had a positive intellectual effect on the two older sons, William, the Pragmatist philosopher, and his younger brother, Henry, the writer. After a year at Harvard Law School in 1862, Henry Jr. began contributing stories to American magazines, and was sufficiently successful to launch a full-time literary career.

James pursued the craft of writing with an incomparable passion and industry, producing more novels, stories, and criticism than any other major American author. Because Henry Jr. habitually opposed his own vocational endeavors to the professional activities of his father and brother, critics have consistently made more of his literary antecedents than of those closer to home. Yet James's fiction was undoubtedly influenced by the imposing intellectual presences of his father and older brother. The theology of Henry James Sr. drew heavily on the writings of Emerson and Emanuel Swedenborg, a philosopher devoted to a doctrine of moral and social responsibility. The intellectual compatibilities of the philosopher father and literary son include a shared preoccupation with the problem of individualism and the position of women, a concern for the tension between modern secularism and matters of the spirit, and an ongoing interest in the subjects of kinship and sympathy. Henry Jr. was also deeply engaged with his brother William's philosophical and social-scientific writings, as well as with the debates they generated. On occasion, Henry even provided editorial assistance, as in the case of an article "The Progress of Anthropology" published in *The Nation* in 1868.

Among available models from an American literary tradition, none had a more profound impact than the work of Nathaniel Hawthorne, the subject of a biography James published in 1879 for Macmillan's English Men of Letters Series. Though James considered his portrait "gentle and good-natured," it aroused a storm of protest in America, for its condescending treatment of the New England writer. Describing Hawthorne's diaries, James comments

I think I am not guilty of any gross injustice in saying that the picture [a reader] constructs from Hawthorne's American diaries, though by no means without charms of its own, is not, on the whole, an interesting one. It is characterized by an extraordinary blankness – a curious paleness of color and paucity of detail. Hawthorne, as I have said, had a large and healthy appetite for detail, and one is, therefore, the more struck with the lightness of the diet to which his observation was condemned. For myself, as I turn the pages of his journals, I seem to see the image of the crude and simple society in which he lived . . . It takes so many things, as Hawthorne must have felt later in life, when he made the acquaintance of the denser, richer, warmer European spectacle – it takes such an accumulation of history and custom, such a complexity of manners and types, to form a fund of suggestion for a novelist.

The *Hawthorne* biography reveals James's desire for distance – from his culture, and probably just as importantly, from his overbearing family. Psychological necessity joined aesthetic necessity: the prospect of being an American in Europe provided the detachment that was essential to his art of social observation. Yet James's biography can also be seen as enacting an aesthetic primal scene with its rhetorical case for expatriation cloaking a deep envy of Hawthorne's New England roots. In contrast to James, Hawthorne belongs – "the spell of the continuity of his life with that of his predecessors has never been broken." While James's pigeonholing of Hawthorne – as democrat, as provincial, as primitive – supplies the route to his own emergence as the nation's even greater (because sophisticated and cosmopolitan) novelist, it is also a ghostly revelation of James's feared aesthetic deficiencies. Is it possible to write as a man without a country?

At the same time, James's disparagement of Hawthorne's literary culture belied the true vibrancy of an American novel-writing and reading public, along with James's investments in it. James's writing appears not only more definitively American but also more nuanced when seen as a powerful synthesis of the cross-fertilized traditions of the sentimental novel, extending from Charles Brockden Brown through Susan Warner and Harriet Beecher Stowe, and the historical romance, stretching from James Fenimore Cooper to Herman Melville and Nathaniel Hawthorne. As one fork in an aesthetic road available to James, Warner's *The Wide, Wide World* anticipates much of what might be considered quintessentially "Jamesian": the validation of the emotional life, the foregrounding of the mind and powers of imagination; the embrace of fairy-tale motifs; the emphasis on women's bonds and friendships; the attention to female development from childhood through adolescence to young adulthood; the fascination with "the Pygmalion theme" – fashioning your ideal wife, then marrying her – the focus on the ritualized aspects of daily life, the spiritualization of the ordinary. The power of intimate relationships, the governing psychology of James's novels, where the self enacts the punitive constraints of culture, is compatible with the soul-searching and self-abnegation that underlies Warner's model of Christian charity.

The fact that James was inspired as well as haunted by the American traditions that he absorbed, partly motivated his effort to create an artistic inheritance through the eighteen prefaces he wrote, beginning in 1907, for the Collected New York Edition of his works. They became an unavoidable legacy in their own right for American writers in the twentieth century. Part autobiography (the author writing), part biography (the novel developing), the prefaces provide an aesthetic history for both author and work. Here European scenes of writing – James's memory of drafting *The Portrait of a Lady* in Venice, for example – represent the process of transforming history into a theory of fiction. Yet James's choice of photographs as frontispieces to each volume confirms his desire to locate his fictions in identifiable historical worlds. Writing to Scribner's in 1906, James emphasized his preference for a "scene, object, or locality . . . consummately photographed and consummately reproduced." James enlisted Alvin Langdon Coburn, a twenty-two-year-old photographer he had met in New York in 1905 when Coburn took his picture for *Century Magazine* to shoot twenty-four locales (St. John's Wood, St. Paul's Cathedral, Portland Place, The Luxembourg Gardens, The Arc de Triomphe) from London and Paris, to Venice and Rome. James's choice of a "young American expert" and of photography itself as the medium for introducing the various parts of his opus gave his New York Edition a specifically American stamp, serving to identify it with the expansive modernity of his native land. Its dramatic commercial failure sent James into a deep depression. Four years of revisions on major novels and stories to make them suitable representatives of his authorial principles were met by indifference. Moreover, the project he hoped might see him financially through old age left him "in bankruptcy," as he complained to Howells. Though James was hardly destitute, the failure of the New York Edition prompted Edith Wharton to arrange secretly to have $8000 diverted by Scribner's from her own bountiful royalties to James in the form of an advance for *The Ivory Tower*, a novel left unfinished at his death.

There was no American literary author of the era who enjoyed more professional prestige as an arbiter of the cultural establishment than James's exact contemporary, William Dean Howells. If James's career represents a pinnacle of American Realism for all time, Howells's career was undoubtedly a pinnacle of American Realism for his own era. Howells was a central figure in the cultural institutions that adjudicated literary production in this period, among them, magazines, publishing houses, journalism, and also advertising agencies. He was also a key broker of reputations, helping to establish the careers of such diverse writers as Mark Twain, Henry James, Bret Harte, Stephen Crane, Frank Norris, Paul Laurence Dunbar, Sara Orne Jewett, and Abraham Cahan. And he wrote one of the great American literary Realist treatments of marriage and divorce set against the backdrop of the rise of professional journalism. That novel was *A Modern Instance* (1882; serialized, *Century Magazine* 1881 to 1882), which Howells deemed to the end of his career, his highest literary accomplishment.

Howells's incomparable professionalism was partly due to his humble origins, which required that he find sources of income while pursuing literary fame. Howells (1837–1920) was born in Martins Ferry, Ohio, the son of Mary Dean and William Cooper Howells, an idealistic printer whose allegiance to Swedenborgianism and abolition alienated people in the small towns the family inhabited over the course of Howells's peripatetic childhood. Put to work as a printer at an age when his wealthier contemporaries (Cather, James, Twain) were being educated, Howells became an autodidact. Howells was drawn to literature, poetry writing in particular, and his father's profession afforded the opportunity for early publication in local newspapers. By 1860, Howells had published five poems in the respectable New England journal, the *Atlantic Monthly*, and headed East to meet New England literati. Howells visited Hawthorne, Emerson, and Thoreau, as well as Holmes and Longfellow, and was rewarded for writing a campaign biography of Abraham Lincoln with a consulate in Venice. He and his new wife, Elinor Mead, from a respected New England family, settled in Boston after the war, where he worked as an editor at *The Nation* and then at the *Atlantic Monthly*. Howells soon became head of a household whose tastes and habits made him increasingly dependent on his sizeable professional income. Yet his enjoyment of the prestige and authority accorded his editorial work failed to mitigate his struggle to reconcile the demands of an editorial career with his ambition to write seriously. Howells's preeminence as an editor afforded him a significant impact on the literary history of his era. He was equally knowledgeable about journalism. His choice to make the protagonist of his first major novel a reporter was informed by his early engagements with the literary vocation as a printer on his father's Ohio newspaper, and reporter for the *Cincinatti Gazette, Ohio State Journal*, the *Saturday Press* and the *Boston Advertiser*.

The novel was inspired by an 1875 Boston performance of *Medea*. Howells saw Medea's perverse love for the egotistical Jason, according to an interview, through the lens of "an Indiana divorce case . . . and the novel was born." Subsequent summers at a farm in Shirley, Massachusetts, where the landlord and landlady, both previously divorced, fought continuously, served to amplify Howells's feeling for his subject. Howells based his Jason figure, Bartley Hubbard, on Bret Harte, the multitalented writer, who excelled in journalism, among other things, and was known for his charm, drinking, debts, and philandering. Howells described the novel's central concern in a note to *Scribner's* prior to its serialization, "the question of divorce . . . We all know what an enormous fact it is in American life, and that it has never been treated seriously." Howells's subject was reinforced by *Century*'s simultaneous publication (January 1882) of Washington Gladden's "The Increase of Divorce." He knew little about the legalities of divorce, so he sought expert advice and traveled to Indiana (a state with distinctively liberal divorce laws) to attend a trial. The Indiana trip anticipated the Midwestern–New England regional axis that would be traversed in his novel. Howells's attraction to Northeastern village life in post-Civil War America reverberates in *A Modern Instance*.

His opening portrait of the cold, decaying New England town of Equity, Maine, is marked by admiration. Natural Maine is full, according to Howells, even when it is full of winter. Still, a former spiritual intensity has been replaced by religious liberalism: church-hopping, the conjoining of observance and pleasure, general disquietude. New England piety has become an uninspired, vaguely materialist ideal of "Equity." The town's captivating young couple, Bartley Hubbard and Marcia Gaylord, converse late into the night, a freedom, "scarcely conceivable to another civilization," covering all the concerns that later define their marriage and divorce: superstition and faith, jealousy, ambition, village versus urban life. It is no wonder these passionate lovers stand out against the gray backdrop. For passion, like belief, when authentic, has nothing to do with equity. And indeed, their passion becomes progressively unequal after marriage, with Marcia devoted to Bartley, who it seems can only care deeply about himself.

As is typical of Howells's fiction, the novel is deeply attentive to class distinctions. Representing late nineteenth-century Boston as sharply divided along class lines, Howells highlights the snobbery of a Boston elite that excludes Bartley from the best society. Bartley, the ultimate self-made man, discovers a calling in journalism, a morally ambiguous enterprise. He is ever aware of the main chance, and willing to stretch the truth. He grasps immediately the human interest appeal of their apartment-hunting, and transforms their experience into a sensational account of a significant social problem: without greater regulation, the exorbitant costs of housing in Boston would result in the loss of "those young married people of small means with whom the city's future prosperity so largely rested." Bartley also proves adept at publicizing the affairs of the wealthy. He combines flattery and exposé in a perfect balance. What makes him a natural journalist is his lack of conscience, his opportunism.

Howells's "modern instance" designates a type that transcends region as well as class. It points to the increasing turmoil of modern values and beliefs. According to Bartley, the newspaper at its best need do no more than reflect the variety of interests and classes present in any given place. It is this fundamental pragmatism that leads to his abandonment of his wife and child, and to his eventual doom. The account of Marcia's journey to Indiana, accompanied by her daughter and father, to face the divorce summons is a Realist tour de force. At the novel's conclusion, divorce is endorsed as a legal option, though repudiated for its social effects. Religion is qualified as an explanatory system, while confirmed as a source of comfort for individuals. And love, Marcia's love of Bartley, the love of her father and Ben Hallek for her, is an impulse that overrides moral considerations. The last words, in dialogue – "Ah, I don't know. I don't know" – register the chronic ambiguity that will characterize the endings of both *The Rise of Silas Lapham* (1885) and *A Hazard of New Fortunes* (1890). They confirm a preference in Howells's best works for leaving ethical situations open-ended.

Like William Dean Howells, Willa Cather served a long literary apprenticeship in the magazine business. Thirty-six years younger than Howells, Cather confronted a far more commercialized and intricate periodicals industry at the start of her career, and she became involved with a magazine whose intellectual contents were more varied than the primarily literary focus of Howells's *Atlantic Monthly* and *The Nation*. As an editor at *McClure's*, Cather became familiar with the business of literature and gained journalistic experience, but she also pursued areas of analysis she might never have expected. During this time she co-authored *The Life of Mary Baker G. Eddy and the History of Christian Science* as well as the autobiography of S. S. McClure. She also published her first novel, *O Pioneers!*, an effort to make the region she knew amenable to art. "Every one knows Nebraska is distinctly *déclassé* as a literary background," she wrote. "Its very name throws the delicately attuned critic into a clammy shiver of embarrassment. Kansas is almost as unpromising." The novel's inclusion on the *New York Times Book Review* list of one hundred best books of 1913 confirmed that Cather had managed to make Nebraska a viable, perhaps even chic, object of literary attention.

Cather (1873–1947) was born in Virginia to a family of landowners with roots in Revolutionary America. Her father was a lawyer who made a living from sheep farming and later selling livestock, farm equipment, and real estate. The family emigrated to Webster County, Nebraska near the flourishing farm of her uncle and aunt when Cather was four. Cather became familiar with the immigrant settlers from Scandinavia, Russia, Germany, France, and Bohemia, who populated the Nebraska homesteads, and was a frequent audience to the stories of pioneer farm women in particular. When she was ten, she met an English storekeeper, William Duker, who began to teach the ambitious girl Greek and Latin. Cather also attended performances regularly at the newly opened Red Cloud Opera House. She participated in local theatrical productions, but she was also interested in science, and delivered a speech in defense of free scientific inquiry at her high school graduation. Cather entered the University of Nebraska in 1891, distinguishing herself, almost immediately in literature. As a freshman, she published essays on Carlyle in the *Nebraska State Journal*, and became a regular contributor of fiction, poetry, and essays to magazines. She worked as an assistant editor for the Lincoln *Courier*, where she wrote a column on women novelists, and in 1896 she became editor of the *Home Monthly*, a magazine designed to compete with the *Ladies Home Journal*. Cather's views on other writers were fearless and unequivocal. Mark Twain was neither "a reader nor a thinker nor a man who loves art of any kind," but "a clever Yankee who has made a 'good thing' out of writing." Of William Dean Howells she remarked that "passions, literary or otherwise, were never [his] forte." But Frank Norris's *McTeague* was a "great book" and the "masterly prose" of Henry James "as correct, as classical, as calm and as subtle as the music of Mozart."

There are no Native Americans in the turn-of-the century Nebraska landscape settled by Willa Cather's multicultural "pioneers." The native inhabitants are mentioned once, when Carl Linstrum, the artist-lover of the novel's heroine, Alexandra Bergson, announces that he is going to Alaska and she wonders if he is going there to paint them. In the "windy Nebraska tableland," where Cather's Norwegian, German, French, Bohemian, and Mexican immigrants struggle with the ultimately bountiful soil, there are no longer any human claimants to complicate their ascent from toiling farmers to wealthy landowners. *O Pioneers!* synthesizes many of Cather's developing interests from the first decade of her ambitious career as a writer, reviewer, editor, opera-goer, and feminist, experimenting with same-sex romance and gender crossing. Cather, always known to her family as "Willie," was by adolescence cropping her hair, wearing boys' clothes, and signing her name William Cather, M. D. Her artistic and journalistic pursuits introduced her to an avant-garde elite that enabled her to forge sexual relationships with women. Alexandra Bergson, the heroine of *O Pioneers!*, is an exceptional character in the degree of authority she exercises over her family, her resistance to conventional romance and marriage, and her independence. Her father transfers control of the family farm to Alexandra on his deathbed because she is the eldest and most able of his four offspring (though the others are male), and because she alone shares his quasi-spiritual devotion to the land. The father's death is a boon to the family fortunes, since Alexandra is a superior manager and innovator, and the farm is transformed accordingly into an estate.

Sixteen years later, Nebraska is a picture of progress, replete with telephone wires, vast checkerboards of productive farmlands. The jewel of Alexandra's current existence is her youngest brother Emil, whom she has raised and conceived for greater things than farming. While the scene opens ominously with Emil cutting grass at the gate of the Norwegian graveyard where his parents are both buried, he is a student at the University of Nebraska, handsome, athletic, with every opportunity before him as brother of Alexandra Bergson, one of the richest farmers on the Divide. The farmers of Alexandra's neighborhood work hard, go to church, marry, have children, enjoy their various social activities, and sometimes dream about the old country. But most of all they luxuriate in the land. Their harmony with nature is as pronounced as their harmony with their own ethnic diversity, for there is no cultural strife among the region's various inhabitants, who seem to delight in their differences if they notice them at all. The implication is that the land's bounty ensures the people's harmony. Despite all this good fortune, the novel ends in tragedy. It is a tragedy based in part on the tragic flaw of its heroine, who lacks the imagination to grasp the complexities of human passion. She has an intense engagement with her land, she feels maternal devotion towards Emil, but she does not understand romance, and misses the ultimately life-threatening love that develops between Emil and the impetuous Maria Shabata. Alexandra's one passionate image is a kind of agrarian revery she lapses into from time to time, of a bronze (Native American?) warrior carrying her swiftly across ripened corn fields. But Emil entertains a less abstract passion for Maria, the Bohemian beauty he has loved from childhood, who has on a whim married a charmer she now despises. The lone, brief adulterous realization of their love on the eve of Emil's departure results in their murder by Maria's vengeful husband. The novel ends with Alexandra's marriage to Carl and the assurance that this platonic love is not destructive. Cather implies that Alexandra, in later age, may come to know the sensual pleasures she has previously denied herself. Still, the novel's ultimate union of a gentle and artistic wandering man, who has decidedly not made it in America's turn-of-the century world of enterprise and capital, with a strong-willed woman, whose energy and intelligence have ranged freely out West and earned her an agrarian estate, is hardly conventional. Alexandra seems unlikely to begin a family after forty. And the closing appeal to the "fortunate country, that is one day to receive hearts like Alexandra's into its bosom," suggests that the heroine's passion is only for the land.

In the preface that Willa Cather added to *The Song of the Lark*, seventeen years after its publication in 1915, Cather emphasizes that her central interest in the book was to tell the story of an opera singer's rise to success through "the play of blind chance" that "fell together to liberate her from commonness." The remainder of the narrative, which recounts the gradual reduction of the girl's humanity as her artistic self overtakes her, Cather confesses, should have been left to conjecture. Once an artist achieves her destiny, the self that is accessible to others becomes comparatively diminished. The preoccupation with opera singers and with the music of Richard Wagner in particular that provides the central subject of *The Song of the Lark* dates back, for Cather, to her time working for the *Pittsburgh Daily Leader*, which she served as an arts reviewer as well as a news reporter. Cather was discovering her own lesbian sexuality at this turn-of-the century moment with Isabelle McClung, the daughter of a wealthy Pittsburgh judge. The affair, that would extend throughout Cather's life, drew her to Wagner, whose powerful operatic roles for women were well known.

The Song of the Lark traces the rise to fame of a Swedish-American opera singer, Thea Kronburg, born in a small Colorado town, which Cather calls Moonstone. Thea is adored from childhood by a series of adult men. In her family, the mother is the most sympathetic to Thea's artistic needs, but is too burdened with responsibilities, and too commonplace in her own right, to appreciate her. The responses of Thea's father and siblings range from indifference to jealousy. Cather's artist is self-originating, self-taught, self-driven, and self-perpetuating. At the pinnacle of her success in New York, Thea recollects the moment when she first set out to seek her fortune, "I carried with me the essentials, the foundation of all I do now." Wagner provides a monumental confirmation of her inborn artist for whom music, simultaneously eroticized and spiritualized, is "the sole justification for life." A musical experience was meant to be transformative, ravishing, in both religious and sensual terms. The artistic agent of this ravishment was androgynous. Wagner appealed to a generation of bisexual or homosexual aesthetes through his emphasis on renunciation and sensuality, his ability to arouse both idealism and passion. Cather's novel was widely admired by famous divas, as well as by agents of culture like H. L. Mencken, who pronounced Cather among "the small class of American novelists who are seriously to be reckoned with."

Cather's contemporary Theodore Dreiser sought likewise to infuse his fiction with the expansive spirit of the Midwest and West while extending the boundaries of what was acceptable to the arbiters of American literary culture. Dreiser's efforts to represent human sexuality in terms he considered consistent with literary Realism led to conflict with censors throughout his career. Like Cather's, Dreiser's characters mimed the lives of their authors in navigating the chasm between the rural worlds of their upbringings and the urban locales that fulfilled (and sometimes thwarted) their aspirations, and inevitably compromised traditional morality. Dreiser, who endured greater poverty than any other major American writer, followed many of his generation into the magazine business to support his novelistic endeavors. The "Genius" (1915), Dreiser's most autobiographical novel, records the struggle to reconcile the values of art with the commercial purposes of successful magazines, to honor Realist aesthetic aims while avoiding charges of indecency. Dreiser was in financial distress when he began the novel in 1911, having been fired from a lucrative job as chief editor at Butterick Publications for his adulterous affair with the eighteen-year-old daughter of an assistant editor. Dreiser fictionalized this situation in The "Genius", which helps to explain why friends and prospective editors objected to the work-in-progress. He thus turned his attention to his trilogy on the life of businessman Charles T. Yerkes, publishing The Financier in 1912 and The Titan in 1914. Yet Dreiser retained faith in The "Genius", and subsequently completed a series of revisions that included changing his protagonist's profession from Realist writer to painter of the Ashcan school. Literary historian Stuart Sherman's "The Barbaric Naturalism of Theodore Dreiser" exemplified reaction to the 1915 novel. Published in The Nation, Sherman's review suggested in the xenophobic terms of these prewar years that the "animal behavior" of Dreiser's characters might be explained by the author's German heritage. While reviews like Sherman's did not harm sales of the novel and may even have helped, condemnation by the Western Society for the Prevention of Vice, which spurred a chain reaction among similar societies across the country, succeeded in shutting down publication entirely. When the book was reissued in 1923, Dreiser took the offensive, demanding in a new foreword whether "the morals of the young" were to be protected at the expense of "thousands of perfectly normal and responsible people" who enjoyed "this form of aesthetic stimulation." H. L. Mencken drafted a petition against the censors, securing signatures from such luminaries as Edward Arlington Robinson, Amy Lowell, Robert Frost, Ezra Pound, Willa Cather, and Mary Wilkins Freeman (William Dean Howells refrained, pleading ignorance of *The "Genius"*). But the publishers held the novel hostage by refusing to print more copies. Dreiser grew increasingly bitter towards a cultural establishment which he believed precluded "original thought" and rigorously excluded social outsiders. Dreiser's feelings of marginality as a poor son of immigrants disposed him towards the socialism and communism that drew the allegiance of many American writers in the 1920s and 1930s.

Dreiser (1871–1945) was born in Terre Haute, Indiana, to John Paul Dreiser, native of Mayen, Germany, and Sarah Schanab, the daughter of a prosperous Moravian Mennonite farmer. Dreiser's father was a weaver with ambition: employed at a woolen mill, he became production manager, and then bought his own mill. When the mill burned down, he struggled to rebuild it, was injured and never recuperated fully. By the time Dreiser was born, John Paul Dreiser was fifty and channeling his disappointment into religious orthodoxy. Indoctriuating his children in a punitive Catholicism, he was spurned by each in turn as they became financially independent. While more sympathetic to his father's predicament than were his siblings, the intellectually avid Dreiser resented the narrow parochialism of the Catholic schools he was forced to attend. He favored his sentimental, indulgent mother, the empathetic supporter of her eight children, who were often hungry and constantly uprooted. The public schools which Dreiser entered at age thirteen in Warsaw, Indiana, proved his salvation. There his intelligence and literary sensibility were recognized, and he was encouraged to pursue chemistry, physics, and history, and to master German so he could read Goethe and Heine.

Dreiser was only fifteen years old in 1886 when he set out alone for Chicago to make his fortune, a scene he would recreate fourteen years later in the guise of a girl (*Sister Carrie*). Like his subsequent protagonists, Dreiser drifted from one low-paying job to another (dish-washer, busboy, clerk), but was able to attend public school simultaneously. He performed well enough there to attract the attention of the high school principal, who arranged (at her own expense) to send him to the University of Indiana in Bloomington as a special student. He lacked the education to benefit fully from his courses, and was depressed by his status as a poor outsider, but the year whetted his appetite for the intellectual life. His first job was as a journalist, covering the Democratic National Convention in 1892, which led to a position at the *Chicago Globe*. A well-received piece on the Chicago slums enabled a move to the *St. Louis*

Globe-Democrat, where he interviewed such notables as Arthur Stanley, John L. Sullivan, and Annie Besant.

Two formative influences were the work of Herbert Spencer, and the encouragement of his eldest brother, Paul Dresser, a successful New York songwriter. For Dreiser, Spencer's law of progressive evolution and his mechanistic conception of human nature proved a dramatic liberation from Catholicism. At the same time, he struggled to reconcile his first-hand experience of poverty with Spencer's notion of the "survival of the fittest," which was widely adapted by contemporary Social Darwinists to the detriment of the poor. Indeed, what impressed Dreiser most about New York, when he joined his brother there, was the great gulf between wealth and poverty. During the summer of 1895, Dreiser struggled to acclimate, covering the police court for the *World*, and identifying with the down and out Bowery types who would figure prominently in *Sister Carrie*. He later became an editor on a magazine entitled *Ev'ry Month*, where he wrote about Spencer's theories, graft in municipal New York, and the horrors of sweatshops. By 1899, Dreiser was sufficiently established as a journalist and editor to make the first *Who's Who in America*.

But Dreiser's relationship with book editors was rocky from the start. Doubleday suppressed his first novel, *Sister Carrie* (1900) soon after accepting it, producing a mere one thousand copies without advertising, to satisfy an unbreakable contract. This resulted in a three-year period of emotional instability during which Dreiser shunned writing. Magazines mediated his return to the literary profession in the six years after his nervous breakdown, when he edited popular periodicals for women, an experience immortalized in *The "Genius"*. The story of Eugene Witla's rise, following *his* breakdown, through the advertising department of the *New York World* and on to a successful career in magazine advertising, provides a valuable window on this new corporate sphere. The novel is closely autobiographical, depicting Eugene's experiences as a day laborer after his neurasthenic collapse, his marriage to a devoted, placid, slightly older woman from whom he feels increasingly alienated, his promiscuity and weakness for younger women, his development as a Realist painter. Eugene is initiated at the Summerfield advertising agency with a campaign for the American Crystal Sugar Refining Company, which wants to sell sugar, powdered, grained, and cubed, in packets. "It's a question of how much novelty, simplicity, and force we can put in the smallest possible space," his boss Summerfield tells Eugene. Eugene is instructed on the intricacies of human psychology, though he remains as much artist as scientist. He moves from the Summerfield Agency to the Kalvin Publishing Company of Philadelphia, a more distinctive and expensive firm, run by Obadiah Kalvin, a devout Christian who attracts conservative customers. His big opportunity is an offer from the United Magazines Corporation to head their book business, and oversee the art, editorial content, and circulation of seven magazines.

Eugene flourishes at the United Magazines Corporation, but lacks the ruthlessness needed to survive there. He fails to recognize the necessity of a financial interest in the business, and is insufficiently manipulative with subordinates, inspiring their work but not their loyalty. Dreiser emphasizes Eugene's indifference to power and material luxuries; hence his willingness to jeopardize everything for a young woman. The "Genius"'s third book is entitled "Revolt," to suggest a repudiation of the success myth. Permanently separated from his lover, after a fierce battle with her wealthy mother, guilt-ridden about the death of his long-suffering wife, on the point of another nervous breakdown, Eugene turns reluctantly to Christian Science, lured by his sister, a follower since her "miraculous cure" from cancer. Dreiser devotes pages to the religion – the notion of God as principle, the denial of the reality of evil, the idea of pain as human error – and to the gradual conversion of his hero. His treatment is respectful and condescending. Though Mrs. Johns lives in a spacious well-equipped apartment, with an elevator operator and a maid, everything about her, from her homely face to the tasteless mediocrity of her dress and furnishings, is designed to downplay vanity and materialism. It is the very plainness, the simplicity, the banality, even, of the philosophy and its practitioners that makes it the ultimate cure for the complex material predicament of modernity.

Dreiser's choice to conclude his "Portrait of the Artist" with an exploration of Christian Science in its ideal rather than institutional form reflects the general ambivalence among major novelists towards the era's values. None of them could ignore the extent to which writing itself had become a serious business in this era, and some of them (Twain, Wharton, and London in particular) managed to maximize the personal benefits of commercialization. But all confronted these circumstances with misgivings. This dissatisfaction was expressed in some cases through alternative political agendas, in others through different kinds of aesthetic withdrawal. Howells, London, and Dreiser were actively engaged in radical politics. Tolstoy's *What To Do?* influenced Howells as did the utopian nationalism of Edward Bellamy. He gave his allegiance to Christian Socialism, repudiating a system whereby "a few men win wealth and miserably waste it in idleness and luxury, and the vast mass of men are overworked and underfed." Dreiser was too much of an individualist to be won over by the communist system (he witnessed first-hand for *Dreiser Looks at Russia* in 1928), but he was nevertheless deeply drawn to a society designed to eradicate the poverty that had plagued his childhood. London was an active socialist throughout his career, resigning from the party near the end of his life because he was convinced that there would be "no smoothly-running social-istic state" anytime soon. Cather developed an intense admiration for the rich multicultural traditions – Native American, Bohemian, German, Czech, and Norwegian – of the West. Edith Wharton and Henry James perfected the option of their class, travel and expatriation in Europe and England, through much of their lives. Their divergences from the commercial ethos they engaged so fully in their writings, professional experiences, and personal lives, confirms how exemplary these authors were. And this is what made their literary works such invaluable repositories of their time.

7

❧

VARIETIES OF WORK

THE NATURE OF WORK changed in the second half of the nineteenth century. All the advanced capitalist countries experienced the rise of the factory system, the intensification of machine production, the massing of wage laborers, and the subdivision of labor. While the beginnings of industrialization in the United States are typically marked by the 1820 founding of the first mill town in Lowell, Massachusetts, from 1850–1900 there was dramatic expansion in every industry, from locomotives, reapers, and Winchester rifles to textiles, cigars, and glassmaking. In the years between 1860 and 1920 the volume of manufactured products grew fourteenfold. The post-Civil War era ushered in what labor historian David Montgomery has called a "cult of productivity," characterized by ever increasing rates of output and scientific methods of management, imposed by a professional managerial class. While workers of the late nineteenth century were fully habituated to an industrial time sense (a transformation in the culture at large symbolized by mass-produced pocket watches from the American Watch Company of Waltham, Massachusetts) they were also aware of the power they wielded, as a deliberate collectivity, over production processes. As one efficiency consultant observed, every factory has "a fashion, a habit of work, and the new worker follows that fashion, for it isn't respectable not to." Employers could be equally tenacious: in 1885 managers at the McCormick reaper plant responded to a conflict with unionized iron molders by firing them all. Moreover, the harmony of working-class interests was subject to constraints peculiar to the American context. According to Ira Katznelson "what needs to be explained is not the absence of class in American politics but its limitation to the arena of work." He argues that American laborers, as distinct from European or British, saw themselves as workers at work but ethnics at home. Shared class solidarities were preeminent in the workplace but ethnic and territorial identifications ruled elsewhere, and tended to structure political practice and behavior. The compartmentalizing of working-class consciousness helped to diminish the prospect that welfare benefits – unemployment insurance, health coverage, old-age pensions – integral to social systems in other advanced industrial nations would be enacted in America.

While America's common laborers were less cushioned than their other Western counterparts from the hardships of industrialization, they were also less convinced than their forebears of the presumptive link between hard work and economic reward. Their doubt was fortified by successive depressions in the 1870s, 1880s, and 1890s, and extensive poverty amid productive abundance and surplus wealth (a 1901 United States Bureau of Labor survey reported between 20 and 30 percent of wage-earners at poverty level incomes). Already in 1877, an economic analyst taking note in turn of the eclipse of Western expansion, and the reserves of capital necessary to entrepreneurial success, prophesied the demise of social mobility as ideally conceived: "born a laborer, working for hire," he concluded, the typical American would probably die that way. One outgrowth of the difficulties of working-class life, and the recognition of its likely permanence, was a post-Civil War reform movement on behalf of labor cooperatives. Calling for a workers's share in policy-making and profits in an effort to restore the value and dignity of ordinary labor, the agenda produced such improbable bedfellows as Terence Powderly, head of the Knights of Labor and E. L. Godkin, editor of *The Nation*. Godkin's role in the cooperation movement signaled the reservations of many in the middle and upper classes towards a capitalist-industrial growth that threatened traditional liberal ideals. In books such as S. Weir Mitchell's *Wear and Tear; or, Hints for the Overworked* (1871) and George M. Beard's *American Nervousness* (1881), the fast-paced existence dictated by technological and economic development was equally lamented for the toll it took on American bodies.

These transformations were carefully anticipated or confirmed in contemporaneous novels, social reform treatises, and memoirs that featured work as their primary concern. Upton Sinclair's *The Jungle* (1906), Mary Wilkins Freeman's *The Portion of Labor* (1901), and Theodore Dreiser's *Jennie Gerhardt* (1911) depicted the struggles of characters to make a livelihood in, respectively, the meatpacking, shoe manufacturing, and glassmaking industries. W. E. B. Du Bois's *The Philadelphia Negro* (1899), John Spargo's *The Bitter Cry of the Children* (1906), and Charlotte Perkins Gilman's *Women and Economics* (1898) explored the specific fortunes of blacks, children, and women as workers in the new industrial order at the turn of the century. Booker T. Washington's *Up From Slavery* (1901) and Mary Antin's *The Promised Land* (1912) demonstrated the persistence of the "work ethic" in practice as well as in theory, at a point when its demise was widely proclaimed. Because these writers were profoundly aware of the changes in their own literary profession during this period, because some of them came from the working classes or struggled to support themselves and their families while building their careers, and because many were socially positioned (as women or members of minorities) to understand how their particular group's access to justly compensated labor affected their life chances, they provided rich perspectives on the experience of work across classes and cultures. Together with major proponents of labor reform and redistribution of wealth, including Henry George, Jacob Riis, and Samuel Gompers, these writers will be considered in what follows as exemplary witnesses to the transformation of work in the period between the Civil War and World War I.

FACTORY WORK/PIECEWORK

Near the end of *The Jungle* (serialized in the socialist magazine *Appeal to Reason*, February to November 1905), Upton Sinclair mounts a soapbox to denounce Social Darwinism and capitalist trusts and to declare common cause with the muckraker Henry Demarest Lloyd. An international bestseller within weeks of its publication, the popularity of *The Jungle* was due in no small part to prevailing appetites for exposés. It was also due to the ordinariness of Sinclair's subject: the health violations of the American meatpacking industry were relevant to anyone who ate sausages. Equally gripping was Sinclair's demonstration of the ties between different kinds of corruption, from municipal graft and corporate illegalities to real-estate fraud and the manipulation, both at home and at work of poor, illiterate immigrants. The novel opens in the midst of a highly ritualized Lithuanian wedding: Sinclair's effort, he explained to the *Appeal*'s editor, to evoke "an environment and an atmosphere." The scene conveys the poignancy of these immigrants who, despite their poverty, refuse to sacrifice the "*veselija*," or "grand feast," the event "in [everyone's] lifetime [when] he could break his chains, and feel his wings, and behold the sun." *The Jungle* is the story of Jurgus Rudkus, a Lithuanian peasant eager to make his way in Chicago's stockyards. Married to Ona Lukoszaite at the novel's start, Jurgus lives in two cramped rooms with an extended family of twelve. Pursuing their American Dream, they buy a house under fraudulent terms, and all from the aged Antanas Rudkus to the fragile boy Stanislovas, slave from dawn until dusk in Packingtown to meet the payments. Ona has a baby, but must return to the factory before recovering so her health is permanently damaged. Jurgus is injured at work and the remainder of the novel recounts their tragic losses – a cycle of despair featuring increasingly abject labor, unemployment, the death of Ona and their son, and Jurgis's turn to socialism. Throughout, Sinclair details the struggle to unionize Packingtown and the revolting filth of the production processes.

Sinclair's is a totalizing view of the capitalist enterprise. Every aspect of the industry is scientifically conceived and administered: from the omnipresent advertising, broadcasting the wonders of the commodities produced there, to the regulation of the beggars who pervade Packingtown, some of them wretched casualties of the meat plant, others with comfortable homes and money in the bank simply milking a corrupt system. At the center of Sinclair's portrait is the analogy between the hogs at the slaughterhouse and the immigrants who work there. A cruel functionalism predominates: the hogs themselves provide the energy that drives them up the chutes. These rivers of living creatures are transported to a death that is above all efficient, impervious to pain or uproar, devised to utilize every part of the hog with the exception of the squeal.

It was pork-making by machinery, pork-making by applied mathematics. And yet somehow the most matter-of-fact person could not help thinking of the hogs; they were so innocent, they came so very trustingly; and they were so very human in their protests – and so perfectly within their rights! They had done nothing to deserve it; and it was adding insult to injury, as the thing was done here, swinging them up in this cold-blooded, impersonal way, without a pretence at apology, without the homage of a tear . . . One could not stand and watch very long without becoming philosophical, without beginning to deal in symbols and similes, and to hear the hog-squeal of the universe. Was it permitted to believe that there was nowhere upon the earth, or above the earth, a heaven for hogs, where they were requited for all this suffering? Each one of these hogs was a separate creature. Some were white hogs, some were black; some were brown, some were spotted; and some were old, some were young; some were long and lean, some were monstrous. And each of them had an individuality of his own, a will of his own, a hope and a heart's desire; each was full of self confidence, of self importance, and a sense of dignity . . . And now was one to believe that there was nowhere a god of hogs, to whom this hog-personality was precious, to whom these hog-squeals and agonies had a meaning? Who would take this hog into his arms and comfort him, reward him for his work well done, and show him the meaning of his sacrifice?

Striking for its anthropomorphism, the passage criticizes scientific techniques designed to objectify animals so humans can consume them. Sinclair sets sentimental rhetoric against a capitalist system that crushes the dignity of living things, while exploiting every inch of them. Jurgis's recollection of dressing hogs in the Lithuanian forest contrasts vividly with this killing by assembly line. While in theory rational and utilitarian, in practice the science of meatpacking looks like barbaric torture. One "meaning" here is that capitalism unrestrained is a nightmare for "innocent" creatures. And there is no creature here more "guileless" than Jurgis, who will soon have his own leg injury to match that of the "swinging" hogs. The troubling proximity of man and beast in Sinclair's portrait explains the effort to distance the carnage with the reference to "symbols and similes." Humans are distinguished from animals precisely through their access to language; possessed of this tool, they will, hopefully, never find themselves so wretchedly abused. Irony is added to injury by the fact that animals were the source of the very first symbols used by humans, and therefore played an essential role in the original acts of communication that led to irrevocable distinctions between them.

Yet the most curious detail is the mention of "rights." Under what circumstances can hogs be understood as having them? The relevance of Harriet Beecher Stowe's *Uncle Tom's Cabin* – which Sinclair claimed his novel would "be identical with" – is unmistakable. Sinclair's hog/workers recall Stowe's slaves, whose advancement is based on their capacity to suffer. A creature that suffers, according to Stowe and Sinclair, is a creature that can be accorded "rights." The notion that like those of suffering slaves the rights of suffering animals might someday be recognized, was anticipated in 1789 by Jeremy Bentham. Responding to the decision in the French colonies to emancipate black slaves, Bentham predicted, "the day may come when the rest of the animal creation may acquire those rights." Such rights would be adjudicated, not on the basis of "can they *reason?* Nor, can they *talk*, but, can they *suffer?*" On behalf of his suffering hog brethren, in the manner of Stowe, Sinclair forges a community of empathic response. He calls, likewise, upon a notion of universal human (and animal) existence, in noting the separateness and individuality of the different hog personalities. And he ascribes a higher order of hog-dom, presided over by a hog deity, whose office is to compensate the hogs for the dignity denied them in life. Sinclair's insistence on the hogs' human qualities furthers an ongoing claim of the novel: no human being who is vulnerable is safe in a social system that tolerates such treatment of defenseless beasts.

What made *The Jungle* a literary sensation was Sinclair's extension of the novel's circle of helplessness to the American consumer – young, old, poor, rich, native and immigrant. The sign that Sinclair's consumer commonwealth includes his suffering immigrants, and that his novel is finally a work of reform rather than social radicalism, is their depiction throughout as meat-eaters. Their suffering may be *akin* to the suffering of the animals at the factory but they are not the animals' *kin*. The characters feast on sausages from the novel's start to its finish, and the animals may be said to wreak revenge when young Stanislovas, locked up asleep in the factory all night, is himself consumed by rats. Given all their meat-eating and the continuous accounts of Packingtown's gruesome production processes, it is miraculous that only one character – Elzbieta's wretched invalid child – dies from tainted meat. But there are enough deaths in the novel, and mysteries surrounding them, to convince readers that the deadliness of Packingtown is confined neither to a locale nor a species. The fear generated in consumers by *The Jungle* ensured that it would have an immediate impact. Shortly after its publication, President Theodore Roosevelt wrote to Sinclair to promise that the abuses depicted in the novel would be investigated. Roosevelt added that Sinclair's socialism was "pathetic," suggesting that its implementation would destroy, morally and physically (death by starvation and epidemic), the very classes it sought to save. A Labor Commission Report verifying all of Sinclair's charges resulted in the immediate passing of the Pure Food and Drug and the Meat Inspection Acts, which had been stalled in Congress for years.

Sinclair's narrative may have had a more limited effect than he desired. It contributed to a lasting reform rather than inspiring a socialist revolution. Sinclair was himself entirely responsible for the limitations in his conception of race and culture. Consistent with the divisions he makes between animals and humans, Sinclair describes black workers – recruited from the South by factory owners to break the union strikes – as subhuman, "human beasts." They appear closer to the factory's animals than to the white workers whose jobs they threaten. Indeed, they are responsible for introducing additional contaminants into the international food supply. Apparently, for Sinclair, it is one thing to draw analogies between black slaves and Lithuanian "wage-slaves," it is quite another to declare solidarity with working-class blacks. In keeping with his distinction between consumed hogs and hog-consuming immigrants, the workplace, according to Upton Sinclair, required careful discriminations between aliens and kin.

One of the most significant insights of *The Jungle* is also one of its least obvious: the difficulty of achieving solidarity among workers even under the most intolerable conditions. As the novel demonstrates, it was easy for factory owners and managers to foment conflicts and drive wedges between workers on the basis of racial and cultural differences. In the vast urban industrial settings of Chicago and New York with large numbers of foreign immigrant and black migrant workers, fundamental class affinities among workers, shared determinations of opportunity, livelihood, and reward, were submerged. Novels centered on factory life in smaller towns and cities, featuring more homogeneous groups of workers, afforded a view of the preeminence of class identification in America during this time. To explore the representation of class in specific novels is to understand the subtle and myriad ways it could be denied at a time in the history of American work when it was perhaps most undeniable. John Hay's *The Breadwinners* and Mary Wilkins Freeman's *The Portion of Labor* portray class as critical to individual psychology and social organization. Freeman romanticizes the working class, while Hay writes as an unsympathetic antagonist. Freeman's novel, set in a New England industrial town, is a capitalist fairy tale, culminating in the marriage of the poor factory-worker's daughter to the factory-owner's son. Hay's, set in Cleveland, is based on the labor strikes of 1877, and ends with a violent clash between labor and capital and the exiling of the strike's ringleaders. Freeman's characters transcend their class identities, assuming a particularity apart from their aristocratic or proletarian roots. Hay's characters are stereotypes, embodying the strengths and weaknesses of their antithetical class positions. In *The Portion of Labor*, the divide between rich and poor is mediated by a culture of consumption that succeeds in unifying communal desires and prospects. The stock market is also depicted as a democratizing medium, capable of enriching the deserving regardless of class.

Early in *The Portion of Labor* (1901, serialized in *Harper's New Monthly Magazine*, 1900–01) Ellen Brewster, daughter of a shoe-factory worker, runs away from home and becomes enchanted by a market window display. The lonely sister of the factory owner, Cynthia Lennox, who mistakes the mutely obedient child for an orphan, brings her home. Desperate for a child herself, Lennox keeps Ellen though the whole town is searching for her, and the disappearance becomes a local media event. When Ellen is happily reunited with her family, she refuses to implicate Lennox in any way, which spells the start of her divided class loyalty. The incident cements a bond between this daughter of the proletariat and the town aristocracy, and eventually she marries Cynthia's nephew, Robert Lloyd. Significantly, the bridge between the classes is a moment of rapt consumer attention. Through the enlarging, enhancing effects of advertising, consumption is presented as a means of freedom and social mobility. When Ellen returns to the same window later in the novel with her upper-class lover, Robert Lloyd, she has realized this capitalist myth, and the place of romance within it. Mere desire for marketplace items, the narrative suggests, enables one's ascent through the class system. Ellen's appropriate response to the window as an impoverished child is yearning, which is immediately rewarded by the appearance of her fairy godmother, Cynthia Lennox, and by subsequent marriage into the upper class. Yet her return as a young woman with her wealthy lover features her own complex resistance to the myth. Ellen vigorously repudiates Lloyd's theory of advertising as an art form, his notion that advertisers perform an essential public role, serving aesthetic as well as carnal appetites. Her argument highlights the illusoriness of a supposedly democratized consumption that merely accentuates divisions between rich and poor, by making material abundance appear accessible. While the upper-class hero, Robert Lloyd, revels in the purely aesthetic features of the scene, the working-class heroine, Ellen Brewster, recognizes in the "heaps of tomatoes, and long, emerald ears of corn" the fruits of labor her intimates at home cannot afford.

Ellen's divided loyalties are mirrored in her mixed birth, as a descendant of the aristocratic Brewsters and the shiftless Louds of Loudville. It is unclear at the novel's end how Robert Lloyd will manage the repulsion he feels toward Ellen's family. Nor is it clear how Ellen will preserve her familial bond while embracing the ideals of her new husband. It is implied that the marriage will work because cross-class marriages are the rule. Robert Lloyd's own parents are from "vastly different stock": his father from a distinguished old family, his mother, who supplies the capital for the factory, the granddaughter of a cobbler. And the long feud between Ellen's genteel grandmother and mother is resolved by the fulfillment of their shared ambition that Ellen "marry up." Yet such assurances are undercut by another ongoing claim of the narrative, that class is inherent. Cynthia Lennox's elite friend wonders about her plan of sending Ellen to Vassar College: "Why do you want to increase the poor child's horizon farther than her little feet can carry her? You might as well teach a Zulu lace-work, instead of the use of the assagai."

According to *The Portion of Labor*, class is as fixed as any inborn trait, and functions, paradoxically, to subdivide the working classes. The difference between Freeman's representation of class and Sinclair's representation of race is the ingredient of marriage, which seems designed to collapse the divisions between her characters. Marriage in Freeman's novel goes hand in hand with another magical arbiter of human fortunes – the stock market. For another plot in the novel that reinforces the marriage plot concerns Andrew Brewster's speculations in mining stocks, an investment that violates his deepest values both as an aristocrat and as a laborer committed to honest work. The vagaries of the market not only intensify the family's poverty, but also contribute to Andrew's decline.

Most importantly, this plot device supplies the necessary motivation for Ellen's own sojourn among the rank and file at the shoe factory. At the novel's end, however, it is not work that saves and ennobles but the stock market, whose dividends are redeemed, restoring Andrew Brewster's money and manhood. Robert Lloyd benefits from the same economic upswing, an improvement in business that allows him to raise the wages of his workers, and regain his proletarian beloved. One could argue that the closing picture of good fortune issuing from the growth of stock dividends suggests an alternative democratization of speculation to replace the democratized consumption the novel highlights only to repudiate. In either case, the watchwords of Freeman's fictional society are mixing and mobility, which provide a striking contrast with the rigidity of Hay's novelistic world.

The Breadwinners (1884, published anonymously) is filled with class rage, pitting aristocratic privilege against the inherent inferiority of the working classes. To recognize Hay's novel as a bestseller, serialized prior to publication in a magazine as prominent as the *Century* (1883–84), is to grasp the profundity of class resentment in America at this time. In the introduction to the 1884 Harper's edition, Hay's son Clarence reports that 1877, the year of the novel's setting, was notable for strikes among railroad employees that led to widespread riots and looting. John Hay (US Secretary of State from 1898–1905) was alarmed by the disorder, and complained in an 1877 letter about the hypocrisy of politicians, whose "sympathies were all with the laboring man, and none with the man whose enterprise and capital give him a living." *The Breadwinners* is designed to rectify the imbalance. Nobility, as Hay presents it, is a quality transmitted genetically and limited without exception to the upper classes. And anything associated with workers, including work itself, is pejorative. It is a badge of honor that the hands of Arthur Farnham, the aristocratic hero of *The Breadwinners*, "showed they had done no work." The novel opens in Farnham's living room, with a visit from Maud Matchin, the coarse but beautiful daughter of a hardworking carpenter, whose sole ambition is to marry wealth. Their dialogue provides the governing typology of dim, overreaching laborers, and polite, thoughtful elites. Maud's father, Saul Matchin, seems to supply an admirable exception, but he is undermined by his failure to transmit his values and his helpless love for the undeserving Maud. Maud is also blessed with a devoted suitor, Sam Sleeny, a dumb but decent apprentice to her father, whom she spurns mercilessly. While Maud's resistance to Sam is portrayed as class self-hatred, the bleak prophecy of their closing marriage appears to justify her behavior. Meanwhile, every politician in *The Breadwinners* is corrupt. The worst of them, a stereotyped sagacious Jew, Jacob Metzger, applies the same principle to his butchery business and to politics – getting "the most out of a carcass." The one feat of novelistic imagination is the Dickensian villain Andy Offitt, the mastermind behind the "Brotherhood of Bread-winners" that launches the labor uprising. Refusing to glorify the event with the term "strike," Hay portrays the "agitation" as the disorganized violence of the most inept laborers. Setting his narrative decisively against Mary Wilkins Freeman's ideal of social mobility and against workers themselves, Hay won an extensive and appreciative audience.

Other authors managed to undermine social mobility while expressing sympathy for the plights of their working-class characters. In a series of novels published around the turn of the century, Isaac Kahn Friedman, who was born into a wealthy Jewish family in 1870, sought to affirm his socialist views while highlighting the unknown pleasures of working-class life. *Poor People*

(1900), a novelistic account of Chicago tenement life, *By Bread Alone* (1901), a novel based on the 1892 strike at the Carnegie Steel Mills in Homestead, Pennsylvania, *The Autobiography of a Beggar* (1903), and *The Radical* (1907), the story of a man's rise from delivery boy to United States Senator, featuring his gradual disavowal of his role as "the people's champion," were all published by mainstream presses and reviewed in the best journals.

Friedman provides no evidence of his Jewish identity in his novels. He features narrators from a variety of cultures, and even invokes Jewish stereotypes. While this suggests a certain self-alienation, it also reflects an effort to capture the multicultural wealth of working-class experience. *Poor People* depicts the world of the working immigrant poor at the turn of the century. Its narrator, Thomas Wilson, a composer, who clerks in a department store by day and writes opera scores by night, manages to inhabit slum life while retaining a sense of its aesthetic possibilities. His Chicago tenement is a sea of cultures: a German alcoholic woodcarver, an Irish blacksmith, an avaricious Jewish tailor, a Polish shoemaker and healer, a Dutch fortune-teller, and a Swedish seamstress. Whether they work at nearby factories or take in piecework at home, all of these characters subscribe to the time clock of modern industry, their survival dependent on their ability to accommodate it. What makes Friedman's novel unique is its emphasis on the place of art in the lives of the laboring poor. Adolph Vogel romances Ida Wilson, cares for his alcoholic father, and battles his own taste for drink, while working on a dramatic masterpiece entitled, "Poor People."

Friedman's portrait of tenement life corroborates many assumptions of his contemporary Chicagoan, Jane Addams. They agree, for instance, that the poor are their brothers' keepers. They also share a faith that people of different cultures can live together harmoniously under the most trying conditions. Wilson speculates during a wedding feast that "the good Lord must have beamed with satisfaction to have seen the children of His various nations gathered about the tenement table in amity and friendship." The novel concludes with a series of marriages – the elder German Vogel marries the Dutch fortune-teller and the Polish shoemaker marries the Swedish seamstress. Another character ascends to the nouveau riche, and moves her parents to her nicer home, but they return to the tenement. Adolph's "Poor People," a barely disguised portrait of the tenement, is produced to critical acclaim. Friedman's novel and Adolph's play share two morals: "Once you've known the wonders of tenement life, you can't bear to leave it; to those who are sufficiently subtle, its aesthetic possibilities are rich." This is an assumption which Jane Addams would have found congenial. For one of her central aims was to liberate the artistic potential of the working-class poor, a potential located most of all in their labor. Indeed, she felt that all social classes could benefit from the development of a creativity that was stifled by modern systems of work.

Addams believed that the problems of the immigrant poor could be alleviated by a greater unity between work and home life, as well as a greater sense of purpose at work. Factory workers suffered from feelings of disconnection, from one another and from a larger industrial effort. Help the factory worker to recognize the place of his or her job in a significant enterprise; invest laborers with an understanding of their mutual interdependence, and their work would be vitalized. The labor museum that Addams opened at Hull House, which featured craft shops, exhibitions of primitive tools, and forms of artisan expertise was a testament to these ideals. And though she could never endorse vocational education with the intensity of Booker T. Washington, whom she invited to speak at Hull House, Addams did promote industrial education and training in the public school curriculum. Throughout her life, Addams exemplified an ideal union of high intellectualism with an energetic devotion to the mundane.

Built in 1856 by Charles J. Hull, a leading citizen of Chicago, Hull House, which was reputedly haunted, had been a home for the aged, a second-hand furniture shop, and a factory before it became the centerpiece of Progressive Era reform. Among the early projects initiated by Addams during the first decade of Hull House (1890–1900) was a kindergarten, clubs for boys and men and women, sewing classes, temporary housing, job counseling, a coal association, a music school, a gymnasium, a playground, a coffeehouse with adjacent theatre, an art gallery, and the Jane Club – a cooperative apartment for women. During this time Addams also served as sanitation inspector for her ward, and oversaw the fall of the death rate from third to seventh highest in Chicago.

In *Twenty Years At Hull-House* (1910, illustrations by Norah Hamilton, excerpted in *American Magazine* and *McClure's*) Addams shared the insights afforded by her long career in social reform. Most important was her claim "that private beneficence is totally inadequate to deal with the vast numbers of the city's disinherited." She also emphasized the generosity of the poor to each other, an assumption that cut across Social Darwinist assumptions that survival was the deepest human urge. In keeping with this, was the necessity of preserving and valuing the original culture of immigrants, as they were integrated into American life. To be haunted by a rich cultural legacy, as were most Hull House inhabitants, was a blessing. Addams believed that the difference of the immigrant past could help to assuage the persistent American problem of race. Describing how a group of Mediterranean immigrants attended respectfully to a Hull House lecture by W. E. B. Du Bois, Addams suggested that their race consciousness was far less acute than that of a comparable American audience.

The life and writings of Jane Addams reveal the practical prowess of the reform conscience at the turn of the century. They also exemplify the impact made by women towards improving the circumstances of the urban working class. The entrance of women, many of them charged with religious and domestic ideals, into the arena of municipal reform was critical to the assimilation of urban immigrants (from foreign countries, and from regions such as the South), and in revising general attitudes towards them. They also enabled crucial improvements for native workers, especially in the areas of housing and sanitation. These urban reformers and the institutions they ran (the YWCA and the Salvation Army were typical) mediated between the private and public realms, allowing inhabitants of neighborhoods who were familiar but not familial to come together. As "borderland[s] between charitable effort and legislation," in Addams's words, they provided temporary relief for the problems of labor, in anticipation of long-term solutions. Yet perhaps even more important than the essential services they provided was the way these reform activities channeled the energies of middle- and working-class women at a point when most American social institutions were far less prepared to exploit this valuably humane resource.

WOMEN'S WORK

Cultural ambivalence towards the professional capacities of middle- and upper-class women were particularly intense at the turn of the century. Charlotte Perkins Gilman's *Women and Economics* advanced the simple but powerful message that as long as women were dependent on men economically they would never achieve their full potential. It won its author immediate and world-wide recognition. The book was translated into seven languages and launched Gilman into the national spotlight. Fame and intellectual authority came easily to her, as the great-niece of Harriet Beecher Stowe. Even more formative was Gilman's upbringing as the daughter of a single mother, who managed to wrest a living as a part-time schoolteacher. Gilman in turn renounced Victorian ideals of marriage and motherhood to pursue professional ambitions. She entered the Rhode Island School of Design at eighteen, and later devoted herself to public service. These plans were compromised, however, when she married Charles Walter Stetson, a Rhode Island artist, and in 1885, gave birth to a daughter, Katherine Beecher Stetson. Suffering from postpartum depression, Gilman put herself under the care of the famous "rest cure" physician, S. Weir Mitchell. "The Yellow Wall-Paper" (1892), Gilman's first and most famous literary work, is the short fictional record of that ordeal. Mitchell ordered that Gilman set aside her work entirely to rest and feed, a regimen that intensified her distress. Repudiating Mitchell's prescriptions and her marriage along with it, Gilman separated from her husband and moved to Pasadena, California with her daughter in 1888. The move represented the formal beginning of her career as a lecturer and writer on behalf of women's causes.

Among the major influences on Gilman's *Women and Economics* were Charles Darwin, the sociologists Herbert Spencer and Lester Ward, and the utopian novelist Edward Bellamy. Gilman drew especially on Bellamy's *Looking Backward* (1888) for its socialist ideas and enlightened views on women. Gilman's own system of "social motherhood" consigned childrearing to trained professionals, and further radicalized domestic life through its reform of conventional clothing fashions for both genders. *Women and Economics* begins with the observation that the human female was distinctive among all living beings in depending on the male for subsistence. The consequence for women, and for the human species as a whole, warned Gilman, was crippling. The work in which middle-class women specialized – childcare, cooking, cleaning – was not only work of the most personally unsatisfying sort, but work that was unremunerated and unrecognized. As Gilman pointed out, housework did not qualify as "work" at all, since it was both unproductive and inefficient, consisting of tasks that could never be completed. But Gilman's objection to domestic labor had less to do with the work itself than with the worker's isolation. In a critique that had much in common with the ideas of Jane Addams, Gilman defined work as sociable, a cooperative activity that brought its agents into enabling ties with other human beings. Gilman dreamed of women liberated from their lonely domesticity, "working together, as they were meant to do, for the common good of all." Gilman had her share of critics. In a 1909 debate in New York City with the feminist orator Anna Howard Shaw before an audience of working-class women, Gilman's claim that women were "parasitical," was heartily refuted by Shaw. Shaw won the approval of the majority for her claim that women's work both domestic and public was the salvation of their families and their societies. Indeed, the problem, as one woman writing to *Harper's Bazar* saw it, was that American women had not learned to be "parasitical enough."

Gilman spent a lifetime perfecting and developing her ideas about women and economics together with a legion of feminist colleagues. The sign of their significance is the fact that they remain, almost a century later, powerfully relevant to American cultural debates. One sign of their viability is the portrayal of women's work in contemporaneous American novels, where the type of work available to women ranges from the high point of vaudeville theatre in *Sister Carrie* to a low point of prostitution in *Maggie*. When major writers in the decades before and after the turn of the century wrote about women and work, they wrote invariably about the lower classes. While Dreiser wrote from inside the perspective of the working class as a member of the laboring poor who had witnessed his sisters' experiences of prostitution and single motherhood, Gertrude Stein, Henry James, and Stephen Crane wrote as outsiders, their narratives marked by elitism and detachment.

Gertrude Stein is not always recognized as a keen social observer. But Stein's views on the problems of social heterogeneity – the mingling of different racial and ethnic groups, the experience of different classes in turn-of-the century America, the relationships between genders – provides a unique perspective on the meaning of work in her time. Her fiction is a literary laboratory for exploring the formal properties of immigrant working-class life; the nature of gender difference; and the costs of racial mixing. *3 Lives* (1909) is a series of case studies, which follow their immigrant and black domestics from birth to death. The subject of the first profile, Good Anna, considers herself a domestic expert and bristles at any interference into her domain. She prefers the doctor, of all her customers, because he is as ignorant of her area of specialization as she is of his. The only women she will work for are placid incompetents who allow her complete domestic authority. Anna's professionalism is expressed in her ability to classify others and judge the suitability of their lifestyles to their social stations. "Anna," the narrator observes, "knew so well the kind of ugliness appropriate to each rank of life . . . she knew the best thing in each kind and she never in the course of her strong life compromised her sense of what was the right thing for a girl to wear." The attention to social hierarchies, and their expression in personal insignia – dress, possessions, manners (like the story titles, "The Good Anna," "The Gentle Lena") – recall medieval typologies of character. But this is not nostalgia. Stein is depicting the revival of medieval forms of stratification, the insistence on the fixity of social character and rigid rules of conduct, by a nation in transition. Her delineation of the accoutrements of working- and lower-middle-class life in early twentieth-century Baltimore poses an exact correlation between social status and its material expression.

In theory, Stein's stories represent an incomparable turn of-the century confrontation with heterogeneity, highlighting the lives of two German immigrant maids and a mulatto from the black lower-middle class. Technically, however, these stories are remarkable for their relentless homogeneity. Her characters comprise a distinctly limited number of types, her categories are few and spare, her plots repetitive and monotonous. Given a writer so alert to the layered meanings of words, it is no accident that Stein is writing about maids. It is an appropriate, and characteristically literal, joke on Stein's part that each story in this work, which highlights the domestication of social difference, concerns a *domestic*. Stein's subject in *3 Lives* is the daily theatre of heterogeneity as homogeneity: the methods by which difference is made into a recognizable domestic code.

Stein is acutely perceptive about the psychological impact of this domestication. She emphasizes the process of internalization in her "servant girls" and "real Negroes" – the vicious little forms of self-hatred that permeate their relationships. "Melanctha" shows how racism has invaded the psyches of black Baltimore. Her degrading account here of storytelling among the black train porters – "their color would go grey beneath the greasy black, and their eyes would roll white in the fear and wonder of the things they would scare themselves by telling" – captures the racist type of the dominant culture. These representatives of the most respectable black service profession literally scare themselves out of their own skin (becoming "grey" and "white") in courting their superstitious terrors. When Stein describes the friendship between the Mulatto Melanctha, a genteel laundress, and the much darker Rose, that mystifies the black community, she captures the collective morality of black Baltimore. Among blacks themselves, intelligence is typed as white, and stupidity black. Similarly, Stein's immigrant maids despise themselves and each other. Stein's maids believe that servants are inhuman. According to Good Anna, every maid's life is a struggle against her own latent "servant girl nature." The maids identify with their mistresses in the typical symbiosis of master and slave. Stein's parody is complex and duplicitous, often replicating what it professes to mock. Though Richard Wright defended her portrayal of racism in "Melanctha," others found in Stein's parody a disturbing clinical distance from her subjects. Yet despite this, Stein managed to delve empathically into the "bottom beings" of her maids and laundresses.

A similar blend of detachment and sympathy marks Henry James's *In The Cage* (1895), which depicts a female telegraph operator and sticks close to the details of her working-class life. In so doing, the novella provides a unique perspective on how new technological developments impact on individuals and registers the interdependence of different classes. *In The Cage* is about the small intimacies that modern life affords through its distances, distances created by technology and also by increasingly pronounced class and racial divisions. In his notebook, James identifies the novella as a product of his prowls about London, "the thick jungle of the great grey Babylon." In his guise as adventurer or explorer, he is struck especially by the proliferation of small groceries housing telegraph machines. Observing one shop, James wondered at the access afforded these young operators to the experiences of their wealthy customers.

In the 1890s, before the use of telephones became widespread, telegrams provided a quick, though potentially expensive, means of communication in large cities such as London and New York. The telegraph office attached to a grocer's shop was one among many avenues for the intersection of classes across a chasm of anonymity, in this case, between the working-class operators and the wealthy customers who used telegrams. James's novella centers on two aristocrats, Captain Everard and Lady Bradeen, who send urgent messages concerning a potentially scandalous affair from the telegraph office where James's unnamed operator works. The telegraph operator is barely visible behind her cage, and James makes clear that these exalted personages regard her as a mere appendage to her machine. She, however, comes to feed on their comings and goings, investing their every move with fantastic intrigue. All that James allows us to know is that the telegraph operator's voyeurism enables her to rescue them (by remembering the content of a telegram) from disaster. The novella ends with her realization that she means nothing to the pair, however much they have meant to her, and that her own life is barren.

What makes the novella difficult as a reading experience, and significant as a Jamesian narrative, is its confinement to the perspective of its heroine. While she is typical of James's heroines in her intellectual vitality and self-consciousness, her options are unusually limited. Her life offers few alternatives beyond work and the predictable courtship of a plodding grocery clerk, Mr. Mudge, thus there is a complete discrepancy between her imaginative powers and opportunities. The relationship of readers to the telegraph operator reproduces her relationship to her customers; readers are given only pieces of her life, and are prevented from putting the whole story together. Telegraphy is also itself a kind of authorship, the miraculous posting of messages into the world. The telegraph operator is a Jamesian artist, both like and unlike his typical protagonists. Indeed, she is endowed with imagination, but punished for having it. The novella dwells on the dangers of excessive aspirations, out of keeping with an individual's social position.

The telegraph operator is an addict of sorts, a condition that comes naturally as the daughter of an alcoholic. She inhabits a dream world for a time, but discovers that dreams are not shared across classes. A suitor like Mr. Mudge, who sees material drives as primary and ultimate, is necessary. Need and desire, however, can be fatally opposed, and the close of In The Cage is bleak. Hovering over a parapet on the Paddington canal, enveloped in fog, the telegraph operator is regarded uneasily by a strolling policeman, whose job is to guard the borders of society from prostitution and suicide – the former regulated, the latter outlawed. It is not clear whether the telegraph operator is contemplating suicide, or merely reflecting on her own previous blindness. Nor is it clear which side of the parapet represents death. James may be suggesting that by resigning herself to a monotonous job and dull marriage, the telegraph operator might as well be.

Still, her experience looks hopeful by comparison with the life of Stephen Crane's Maggie. The bleakness of *Maggie: A Girl of the Streets* (*A Story of New York*) and its subject matter made it impossible for Crane to find a magazine for serialization or a publisher. The book's first edition in 1893 was printed privately and sent to friends, reformers, and literary critics, with an inscription that conveyed Crane's recognition of the incendiary nature of his material. This aggressive authorial pose became a staple of his writing and his career. Living up to his role as the youngest, rebellious son of a minister and an ardent temperance reformer, Crane from the beginning seemed determined to provoke readers. Raised in New Jersey, Crane (1870–1905) attended Syracuse University on a baseball scholarship, and turned to writing soon after dropping out. Reviewers of *Maggie* labeled the book "aggressive realism," and characterized Crane's as the "animalistic school" of American literature. Yet *Maggie* won Crane the admiration of such influential authors as Hamlin Garland and William Dean Howells, and provided a solid starting point for his literary career. In 1895 the success of *The Red Badge of Courage*, an immediate bestseller, enabled the reissuing of *Maggie*. The book's publishers demanded changes they considered essential to the sensibilities of genteel readers (and later excised by twentieth-century editors, who returned to Crane's original 1893 text) but ensured the book's commercial success, which added to his growing reputation.

The brutal detail of Maggie's life as Crane represents it makes the novella's spare fifty-eight pages a grim experience for the most hardened readers. Crane insists cruelly on Maggie's gentleness. She is a naturally delicate soul who strives to inject her desperate ghetto world with bits of color. She also possesses beauty, that "most rare and wonderful production of a tenement district," which attracts her brother Jimmie's friend, the self-centered and unconscionable bartender, Pete. Pete's attentions initially relieve the drabness of a life divided between her work at the collar factory and the drunken rages of her mother. The beer gardens, zoos, and Bowery theatricals she is taken to by Pete never fail to raise her spirits. She innocently worships Pete, and fails to suspect his motives. Her mother, however, suspects the worst, and disowns her daughter. Maggie is thus thrown into the arms of Pete, who abandons her after taking her virginity. With nowhere to live, Maggie turns to streetwalking.

Some critics have read Maggie's suicide into these final pages, but there is little support for such a reading. Close to the novel's end, Crane paints a ghoulish scene of Maggie searching for a customer, and settling, finally, on a frightening, leering figure, "a huge fat man in torn and greasy garments," who, Crane implies, is responsible for Maggie's death. Throughout the novella, Crane is intent on emphasizing the importance of environment to her fate. No one is blamed for Maggie's brutal end: not her sadistic mother, a hopeless alcoholic, nor the predatory Pete. Rationalizations are themselves held up to ridicule – those of vice squads, temperance leagues, and the church in particular.

Henry James once remarked that Stephen Crane entered the world of professional literature fully formed. And indeed *Maggie* exhibits all the qualities for which Crane's writing became known: cryptic irony, a tendency to mock convention, and defiance of literary expectations (e.g. predictable characters; clearly developed and resolved plots). In the worlds of Crane's fiction, no one is responsible but some, the softest, suffer tremendously. It is a situation that his writings do not seek to relieve by invoking some deeper spiritual principle. It is, for Crane, sufficient to represent it as such.

A similar preoccupation with the Darwinian indifference of the world towards its human and animal inhabitants, a similar combination of emotionalism, bordering on the sentimental but stopping short, marks the fiction of Theodore Dreiser. The harshness of these combined preoccupations is especially pronounced in his novels featuring working-women protagonists, *Jennie Gerhardt* and *Sister Carrie*. *Jennie Gerhardt*, Dreiser's second novel and the first to earn him commercial and critical success, is also, with the exception of *The "Genius"*, Dreiser's most autobiographical novel. The novel confirms more vividly than any other he wrote, the extent to which his German immigrant family was immersed in the vacillating fortunes of the laboring poor during the era of America's industrial-capitalist expansion. The story of William Gerhardt's immigration to America from Germany, his work as a glass artisan, his old-world value system, his fierce religiosity, and his injury, decline, and gradual acceptance of the looser morals of his generous daughter, Jennie, parallels the life of Dreiser's father, Johann Paul. Similarly, the loving and unsuspicious natures of both Mrs. Gerhardt and of Jennie recall Dreiser's mother and sister Mame, who had a child with an upper-class man out of wedlock, a predicament that made pariahs of the whole Dreiser family. Finally, the sense of responsibility displayed by family members towards one another, the ties that somehow became fixed despite the poverty and degradation of their upbringing, is confirmed anew in Dreiser's portrait of the Gerhardts.

Jennie Gerhardt is infused with Dreiser's nostalgia for some pre-capitalist Eden, and its main character is nearly pagan in her simplicity and passion. Dreiser's mythic treatment of Jennie's feminine passivity and genius for nurture can be cloying, but there is empathy for her situation as a working-woman struggling to survive in a harsh urban environment. What makes this novel a less powerful account of its time than *Sister Carrie* is Dreiser's insistence on a character so fully resistant to it. Jennie Gerhardt has none of Carrie's avidity or opportunism; Dreiser emphasizes her natural superiority to a materialistic society. Jennie is eighteen at the novel's start (the same age as Carrie) when she accompanies her mother to Columbus, Ohio to find work. The Gerhardts have suffered a series of blows, most importantly, the father's injury in the glassmaking works, and subsequent unemployment in the era before workers' compensation. Jennie and her mother secure jobs as scrubwomen at a hotel where the beautiful Jennie attracts a wealthy bachelor, George Brander, who is also a US Senator. When Jennie's brother Bass is arrested for stealing coal, Jennie appeals to Senator Brander, who helps the family, and also helps himself, with good intentions, to Jennie. Dreiser suggests that Brander would have readily cared for the needy mother of his child, but he dies before learning she is pregnant.

Hence the novel's plot: the struggle of an attractive working girl and her illegitimate child to survive among the condemnatory immigrants of the mid-Western laboring class. Jennie's father labels her a "street-walker" and throws her out of the house. She is rescued by a brother who initiates her move to the bigger social world of Cleveland, where she can recuperate far from the scandal. Opportunities abound in this city, and Jennie soon becomes a maid to a wealthy family. But another upper-class man, Lester Kane, this time an unscrupulous one, pursues Jennie and their affair dominates the better part of the novel. Lester Kane is the son of a wealthy carriage manufacturer, which allows Dreiser to illustrate the transformation of family-owned industries in this period of incorporation. Cincinnati, the Kanes' home base, was the setting for the largest carriage trade in the country, and the Carriage Builders' National Association was formed there in 1872. Archibald Kane, Lester's father, is the ideal self-made man. His sons, Lester, who is personable and old-fashioned in his business impulses, and Robert, stereotyped as "a Scotch Presbyterian . . . with an Asiatic perception of the main chance," are both involved in the company and headed towards inevitable conflict given their opposing conceptions of its future. Robert's plan, which includes throttling competition, streamlining production, and creating a carriage trust, is the way of history. Lester's method, based on contacts and favors, is the way of sentiment. While Dreiser's heart is with Lester, his rational judgment favors Robert. Robert prevails, Lester dies, and Jennie endures.

Despite Robert's triumph, *Jennie Gerhardt* offers an essentially nostalgic understanding of the world of business and labor, and the route to success in it. The ambitious businessman should start poor, become obsessed with one idea, and conceive an irrepressible enthusiasm for it. The highest nobility for the laboring man or woman is to be devoid of desire and disposed to self-sacrifice. Like her father, who prizes the admiration of his employer over any material compensation, Jennie abandons her dream of marriage to Lester, and refuses any remuneration for herself. The novel ends with a tribute to Jennie: her great achievement has been to love and to give. *Jennie Gerhardt* thus provides an antidote to both a ruthless market capitalism and a genteel culture that devalues passion.

Sister Carrie is a classic study of social mobility, a major novel about a working-woman's social ascent. The novel opens in August 1899 with its eighteen-year-old heroine boarding a train, the image of hope and ignorance. Her effects are modest, to suggest a person of little consequence. In modern capitalist society, possessions are material extensions of the self that are not only expressive but also constitutive. At the same time, emotions are theatrical rather than authentic. Carrie's departure from home and family inspires: "a gush of tears at her mother's farewell kiss," "a pathetic sigh as the familiar green environs of the village passed in review." This opening foreshadows Carrie's eventual rise as an actress – a melodramatic display of the fond farewell.

Dreiser was not an unqualified supporter of the theatre. He would have appreciated its attraction for urban immigrants who helped a whole new commercial industry, from vaudeville and musicals to early film, flourish. But he also would have questioned its promotion of spectatorship over responsible participation in a public and political sphere. Throughout *Sister Carrie*, he expresses disdain for the institution, by stressing Carrie's lack of genuine talent as she rises through its ranks. What distinguishes Carrie is a golden quality of passivity, the assurance she gives that she can be controlled, a quality that makes her especially appealing to men. Carrie's breakthrough involves a part without lines through which she manages to launch her career. Dreiser's biggest reservation about the prominence of acting and the cult of stardom is that it confirms and intensifies a more general thinning of human relations that is already underway.

Critics of *Sister Carrie* have debated whether Dreiser is a supporter or critic of the expanding consumer-capitalist order but most agree that his novel conveys admiration along with awareness of its limitations. This may explain why he made his capitalist seeker a female. Dreiser casts his protagonist as "a half-equipped little knight" in order to pinpoint the poignancy and tenuousness of the pursuit of wealth. Dreiser feminizes consumption itself towards the same end. Women are the consumed and the consuming prized commodities exchanged by men, ultimate connoisseurs of fashion, definitive participants in the nexus of desire and purchase that makes the novel's society go round. To lack desire is to have lost the will to live. Dreiser is alert to the fantastic power that a consumer society accords the ability to buy, just as he is alert to the fundamentally passive action that buying is. All participants in a passive consumer-capitalist fantasy of transformation are feminized. Their quest is an expression of social powerlessness, just as a typical middle- or upper-class woman's consumption in this era almost always represented a status (her husband's) she had not herself achieved.

Women, as Dreiser portrays them throughout, are born poets of a materialist aesthetic. If they fail to appreciate the natural beauty rhapsodized by poets, they never miss its artificial form. Dreiser has too much admiration for materialism, an admiration rooted deeply in his Catholic upbringing, to abstain entirely from the materialist appreciation he attributes to women. Indeed, one could argue that like F. Scott Fitzgerald Dreiser pushes us closer to an aesthetic that defies neat distinctions between the God-given and man-made. Yet Dreiser cannot disguise his disdain for women who prefer the yellow of a skirt frill to the yellow of a buttercup. The Dreiser who sanctioned such feminine choices in his role as chief editor of women's magazines (a job that, ironically, delivered the material reward that *Sister Carrie* did not) remained committed to the superiority of what money could not buy. In *Sister Carrie*, virtue and love are the most immaterial, and ambiguously represented, of these superior values.

Carrie, the female protagonist, aspires to a better life and loses her virtue in the process; Hurstwood, the male protagonist, seeks love and commits a crime in his effort to win it. According to Dreiser, Carrie's seduction is an inevitability for which she is nevertheless, somehow, responsible. Contrast this to the portrait of George Hurstwood, successful manager of a Chicago club, whose own moment of truth involves his theft of money from the club's safe, among the most renowned scenes in literary Realism. Believing himself in love with Carrie, trapped in an unhappy marriage, betraying all the signs of mid-life crisis, Hurstwood finds the safe ajar one night as he closes up, and is sorely tempted. There follows an extended scene (pages long) of Hurstwood vacillating between obligation and desire. Finally, he takes the money, manipulates Carrie onto a train, and the remainder of the novel depicts their eventual arrival in New York and Hurstwood's unraveling: financial ruin leading to abandonment by Carrie, followed by homelessness, and suicide in a boardinghouse.

What makes these two parallel falls of Carrie and Hurstwood especially complex and mystifying is that Dreiser portrays one as inevitable and the other as a mistake; one is briefly rendered from another character's point of view, the other is protracted and encourages intimate identification with the character who falls. Hurstwood is the modern individual subjected to forces beyond his control, both internal – biological, sexual, emotional – and external – his role as a cog in the machinery of a small business, controlled by his bosses and by his wife. Yet for turn-of-the century critics who condemned Dreiser's novel, the most important distinction between Carrie and Hurstwood is that she achieves wealth and stardom while Hurstwood is ruined. The plot punishes Hurstwood for his betrayal of a moral standard, while rewarding Carrie for what seemed an even worse (because less considered) violation. Dreiser's contemporaries were scandalized. To the publisher who sought to withdraw a promise of publication, it mattered little that Dreiser introduced at his novel's end a social reformer for the homeless and a rich young inventor, Bob Ames, who highlights the meagerness of Carrie's achievements, as well as her emptiness and dissatisfaction. Nonetheless, Dreiser meant by these figures to raise important questions. Why does one individual fall by the wayside and another achieve the heights of prosperity? Why does one individual continue sleepwalking to old age, enduring the same dissatisfactions that drive others to risk everything? How is it possible for people to tolerate a daily spectacle of inequity: utter deprivation for some and anesthetizing abundance for others? *Sister Carrie* is Dreiser's earliest inquiry into the contradictions of the American success myth. At this point, Dreiser remains dazzled by the myth; his more mature novels would probe its contradictions with great insight. Still, *Sister Carrie*'s portrait of a society built on a rhythm of loss and gain, a perfect equivalence between casualties of the social system (Hurstwood) and victors (Carrie), is consistent with classic works of Progressive-Era protest, such as Henry George's *Progress and Poverty* (1879) and Jacob Riis's *How The Other Half Lives* (1890).

PROTEST WORK

Two lines of argument predominated in social protest writings from the post-Civil War period. The first, exemplified by the theories of Henry George and W. E. B. Du Bois, focused on prevailing ideologies. Both targeted a prevailing "ethics of scarcity" that suggested the necessity of one group floundering while another thrived and posited a situation of destitution for some and abundance for others as integral to a healthy economic system. George located his critique in the monopoly of land, which he argued should be recognized as a collective resource of material benefit to the whole community. Du Bois identified the manipulation of labor as a central problem, specifically the deliberate efforts by managers and company owners to set different types of workers in competition with each other. The second line of argument was exemplified by the exposés of Jacob Riis, John Spargo, and Samuel Gompers. These writers argued that the exploitation of child laborers and poor immigrants, who worked long hours under dangerous conditions, without adequate air, light, or rest, was more compatible with medieval barbarism than with a modern American democracy.

The story of Henry George's meteoric rise to fame, after the tepid reception of *Progress and Poverty* by prospective publishers (it was accepted by Appleton with the proviso that George defray the costs of plates), is legendary. The book was translated into twenty-five languages and celebrated world wide; the 2,000,000 copies sold by 1905 made it one of the most popular works of economics ever. Leo Tolstoy and George Bernard Shaw, among others, claimed their lives had been changed by George's study; when George died in 1897 over 50,000 people lined the streets of New York to view his coffin. The first version of *Progress and Poverty* was published as a pamphlet entitled "Our Land and Land Policy" (1871). In forty-eight pages, George described how a single land tax could meet the costs of government, even providing surpluses, and give workers a share in the fruits of progress. By destroying land monopolies and shifting the burden of taxation from labor and capital to landowners, George's scheme promised to alleviate extremes of wealth and poverty. Such a transformation of the tax system would, he believed, increase production, ensure justice in distribution, benefit all classes, and lead to a higher and nobler civilization. George understood that his ideas contradicted prevailing laws of Social Darwinism that saw weaker civilizations and individuals naturally replaced by stronger ones, and suffering as the inevitable cost of progress. He argued that a progress kindled by association was inevitably susceptible to retrogression once widespread inequalities began to develop. Laissez-faire, in his view, ultimately led to socialism, the reconciliation of social with moral law. Recognizing the issue as deeper and vaster than he had imagined, he began work immediately on the larger study.

George's argument was revolutionary, but popular because it was consistent with democratic ideals. His was a plea for the salvation of a ship of state well worth preserving, conveyed in a common tongue. As presented here, George saw his single tax as capable of bringing about a mythical reversal. By tying all Americans once again to the land they rightly shared (minus Native American claims, of course), George's single tax had the potential to overcome the loss of the American frontier subsequently proclaimed by Wisconsin historian Frederick Jackson Turner.

For all their groundbreaking force, George's arguments were marked by political restraint. He characterized Karl Marx as "the prince of muddle heads" (his judgment was reciprocated), and expelled all socialists from his United Labor Party. His views were marked by nativist passion. In "The Chinese on the Pacific Coast" (1869), published in the New York *Herald*, George characterized Chinese immigrants as "sensual, cowardly, and cruel . . . incapable of understanding our religion" and "our political institutions." Twenty years later, in reply to William Lloyd Garrison Jr., George defended his ideals of national and racial purity.

Born into poverty in Philadelphia in 1839, George left school at fourteen to go to sea. Settling in San Francisco, he worked as a printer and then a journalist. In 1861, penniless but in love, he married, and by the time he moved to New York to launch a new branch for his small San Francisco paper, he was the father of two. George's Eastern journalistic venture failed, due to the combination of a powerful press and telegraph monopolies. But his confrontation with the raw vitality of New York and its spectacular extremes of poverty and wealth was decisive. He attributed the gap between rich and poor to the monopolizing of natural resources, land in particular. Progress had increased the value of land, enriching landowners while leaving wages untouched. The remedy seemed obvious: eliminate all taxes save those on land, allowing producers their full wages, government its natural revenue, and the community its right to land value.

In addition to its sensational triumph as a book, *Progress and Poverty* had genuine political consequences. The argument that a just state could eliminate poverty and suffering spawned a political party based on the idea of a single tax. George became a public figure, and spent the remainder of his life lecturing, writing, and trying to implement his ideas. In 1886, George ran for mayor of New York, as a candidate of the reform party, losing the election to Abram S. Hewitt, but amassing more votes than the Republican candidate, Theodore Roosevelt. While George's ideas were far more influential in his own time than beyond it, they have continued to affect tax legislation throughout the world. The measure of a work of social protest is its contemporary political effect; according to that standard, George's book was a triumph.

By the same measure Du Bois's *The Philadelphia Negro*, its impact evident only years later, was a failure. But there is no contemporary study of labor and capital that is more profoundly critical of the prevailing American economic system. The argument for the interdependence of racism and capitalist development was a staple of Du Bois's early career. *The Philadelphia Negro*, however, does not reflect nostalgically on some primordial alternative to capitalism. In every era, Du Bois suggests, prejudice displays a new shape and energy, adjusting to dominant social forces. He cites population statistics on the vitality of black Philadelphia (the largest black constituency in any American city by 1890), which help to explain the virulence of racism in the Quaker city. Du Bois's emphasis on the economic threat posed by blacks recognizes race as a secondary cause. In a developing capitalist economy, the idea is to accentuate black paupers and criminals, while denying the existence of the black middle class. The abjection of blacks and their prospects is a critical means of controlling a developing labor force. In Du Bois's reading, the degradation of black labor is circular and systematic: any occupation identified with blacks loses prestige. In contrast to many immigrant groups that were considered susceptible to assimilation, blacks were viewed as inherently incapable of advancing themselves or any line of work which they pursued. Du Bois countered such claims with a record of acts deliberately designed to undermine black labor. "Most people were willing and many eager that Negroes should be kept as menial servants rather than develop into industrial factors," he observes, "Special effort was made not to train Negroes for industry." Owners and managers encourage prejudice because it ensured surplus labor. Du Bois cites one notorious case where blacks were employed simply for the sake of unifying a crew split by ethnic tensions. High rates of black migration not only threatened whites, but also impeded black efforts to locate occupational niches.

The Philadelphia Negro represents blacks as immigrants: Philadelphia is a black Ellis Island, a racial gateway between feudal South and modern North. The book also portrays Du Bois's quest for professional legitimacy, his immigration ticket, as it were, into the newfound land of sociology. Social scientific convention required the identification of one's particular point of view in order to set it aside. But Du Bois invests a social scientific convention with racial (and political) meaning. To inhabit and then not to inhabit your "personal" point of view, to become an invisible mediator of social knowledge – this is the black definition of success. Du Bois's opening embrace and erasure of his own social position enacts in small his presentation of life as a middle-class black in turn-of-the century Philadelphia. First he will make them appear, in opposition to claims for the uniform pathology of "Negroes"; then he will make them disappear, in keeping with their own aspirations.

Du Bois recognizes invisibility as an index of achievement among blacks themselves. He ends his book with a plea, and a warning, addressed to each side of the class and color line. The black elite, he declares, must realize its responsibility to the hardworking black masses. But white America has a larger obligation – to recognize its fate as tied to that of black Americans. While enslavement did not prove the end of blacks, "economic and social exclusion might." And the potential damage to the nation as a whole would be incalculable. Du Bois in The Philadelphia Negro occupies a familiar stance among authors of protest writing – pleading on behalf of one's group. While Du Bois's professional role as a sociologist demanded that he objectify that bond, his sympathies were apparent, particularly in his profound recognition of the black middle-class plight.

John Spargo, a reform writer at the turn of the century, also wrote about what he had experienced first-hand. While Spargo was prolific, none of his books achieved the success of *The Bitter Cry of the Children* (reprinted twice in its first year of publication), one of the most popular works of social reform produced in the first decade of the twentieth century. A dedicated socialist, over a long writing career which lasted until his death in 1976, Spargo wrote books on subjects ranging from a biography of Karl Marx and an analysis of John D. Rockefeller to histories of Vermont and early American pottery. Spargo left the socialist party in 1917 due to its anti-war policy, and together with Samuel Gompers formed the American Alliance for Labor and Democracy.

The Bitter Cry of the Children grew out of Robert Hunter's more general study, *Poverty*, which offered estimates of the number of underfed children in New York City. Having suffered child poverty, Spargo felt motivated and equipped to undertake a definitive account of the subject in the United States. "When I write of hunger I write of what I have experienced," Spargo declared in his preface, "So, too, when I write of child labor." Spargo makes clear from the outset that poverty is not attributable to lack of initiative. Periods of destitution come at some time or other to all members of the working class. He recalls how during a recent address before 219 labor union members, he inquired who among them had suffered hunger, and 184 raised their hands. Spargo's primary concern in the first part of his book is to substantiate what he calls "the democracy of birth," a belief that all are born equally healthy. Spargo is familiar with prevailing medical evidence to the contrary; his strategic purpose is to challenge statistics on higher rates of inborn health defects that are used to deny aid to poor children. Hunger and malnutrition, contaminated milk supplies, inadequate supervision (because mothers are forced to work) – all of these conditions prevent poor children from gaining a foothold in an increasingly competitive industrial society.

Spargo's most impassioned rhetoric is reserved for his graphic account of child labor. American child labor at the turn of the twentieth century, he argues, is analogous to Britain's at the turn of the nineteenth, conditions so wretched that they sickened Members of Parliament who were given details of the abuses. When English philanthropy focused on the abolition of slavery, "small children were being tortured to death in the industrial pit of capital." America, always a century behind England in humanitarianism, now faces a similar crisis of industrial exploitation. The problem is nationwide, extending from the canning factories of New York State, which employ four-year olds, to the cotton mills of the South, where six-year-old girls labor overnight. Spargo refuses to concede parental responsibility, nor does he consider the role of custom. In previous centuries, he points out, children worked in nurturing domestic enterprises, which also ensured valuable education in a trade. Industrial capital destroyed the family workplace, submitting children and adults to the ruthless oversight of the factory. Parents do not want their children to work, but have no choice. Employers covet children, who can be paid less (and whose employment also depresses adult wages) and worked harder because of docility and energy. Spargo highlights instances where employers hire adults provided their children also work. Capital has no conscience; there will be no relief from this brutal regime until government decides to check it.

Reported numbers of child laborers under sixteen were almost two million in 1900 (US Census), but Spargo believes that the actual figures are closer to two and a half. In one small town in Pennsylvania alone, Spargo found 150 illegally employed "breaker boys" in the anthracite coalmines, hunched over coal chutes from dawn to dusk, picking out pieces of slate and other refuse from the coal as it rushes past them, all the while inhaling mounds of dust, cutting fingers, losing limbs. The foundation is laid for asthma and consumption as well as hunchback and other spinal deformities later in life. To experiment, Spargo took the place of a twelve-year-old boy (who worked ten hours a day for sixty cents); by the end of a brief stint, his hands were bruised and cut, and for hours afterward, he coughed up particles of anthracite.

The biggest problem is that even those who might help are blind to facts. Spargo derides the sentimental activities of women reformers, who fill the coffers of poor children with flowers. He refers to a women's guild in New York that supplied 10,000 tenement house children with "a potted plant" each, in an effort to "refine" and "spiritualize" them. The ladies offered prize ribbons to every child who could preserve a healthy plant over a year's time. "Not all the children to whom the year before they had given flowers were there" Spargo comments acidly, some having "drooped during the summer and died like flowers in parched ground." Water was abundant now, however, as many guild women wept to see the outcome of their philanthropy.

Spargo's book appeared in a field that had been gaining momentum since the 1870s. Portraits of slums and of the stresses of working-class life proved a steady diet for middle-class readers of magazines, newspapers, and bestselling books such as Charles Loring Brace's *The Dangerous Classes of New York* (1872) and Josiah Strong's *Our Country: Its Possible Future and Its Present Decay* (1885). This literature and the establishment of the highly publicized New York City Tenement-House Commission in 1884 intensified middle-class desires to know more about the laborers who congregated in urban centers. Among these works, none were more popular than photo-documentaries, and the ultimate example of the form was Jacob Riis's *How The Other Half Lives: Studies Among the Tenements of New York.* While Riis was less radical politically than Spargo, he too wrote about conditions he knew first-hand, on behalf of those excluded from affluence and consumer comforts.

How The Other Half Lives reflects the immigrant status of its author per- haps most markedly in its respect for the dominant values and institutions of American society. Born in Denmark and trained as a carpenter, Jacob Riis immigrated to America alone at the age of twenty-one to seek his fortune. From 1870 to 1873, he wandered through New York, New Jersey, and Pennsylvania, from one odd job to another, building workers' shacks for an Allegheny iron mill and ships in upstate New York, selling furniture, drumming flatirons. Despite the prejudice he endured as an immigrant, and despite the uncer- tainties of this vagabond existence, his experience confirmed his belief that anyone could find work in America. Returning to New York, Riis landed a job as a freelance journalist, and subsequently as a police reporter for the New York *Tribune.* Here he perfected his skill at the short vignette, which provided the foundation of his famous study. The human interest story that fastened on a particular character, the significance of his situation and its relevance to slum life, helped Riis to generate his book's thesis: people did not make slums, slums made people. Stephen Crane, like other "environmentalists" of the time, echoed Riis's thesis.

In the late 1880s, Riis began to gather photographs of slums, which he believed critical to appreciating the plight of their inhabitants. Riis's pho- tographs were first presented to lecture audiences in the form of lantern-slides, which produced images about ten feet square with two projectors. The accom- panying lectures featured stories about the subjects, personal anecdotes, and a pithy moral. Delivered at churches in addition to other reform venues, the lec- tures were sometimes preceded by scripture reading, prayer, and gospel music. The lectures gained widespread notoriety when the New York *Sun* published a sample in 1888. *Scribner's* followed in 1889 with nineteen pages of text and illustrations, entitled "How the Other Half Lives," which Riis expanded into his book. An immediate success, *How The Other Half Lives* (1890) launched Riis on a nationwide lecture tour. Though recent critics have questioned both Riis's sympathy for his subjects and his responsibility for all the photographs published under his name, the book was the most influential portrait of the working poor produced between the Civil War and World War I. Everyone interested in social reform read *How The Other Half Lives* – journalists, social scientists, policy makers, average citizens. Theodore Roosevelt considered the book invaluable to his tenure as the Police Commissioner of New York, and praised it as "both an enlightenment and an inspiration for which I felt I never could be too grateful."

As historians have pointed out, the Lower East Side of New York profiled in Riis's book was unique among urban slums for the density of its housing and the youth of its inhabitants. The crime rate was unusually high. A large part of the book focused on deviance, which came readily to Riis given his journalistic beginnings as a police reporter. Like most urban slums of the time, this one was, in Riis's words, a "queer conglomerate mass of heterogeneous elements, ever striving and working like whiskey and water in one glass." Riis's cataloging of this diversity featured ethnic and racial stereotypes, sometimes as acerbic as those employed by nativists. But Riis directed his moral outrage against the city's religious community, drawn to more distant and exotic suffering, the greed of landlords, and the indifference of the comfortable classes. Riis's proposed solutions included: general civic responsibility, outlawing of dilapidated tenements, and a new initiative for remodeling and building. Riis recommended private enterprise backed by municipal law, and he included testimonials from Philadelphia businessmen that tenement construction pays. This combination of ethical concerns and practicality, the vividness of his empathic documentary archive, together with the conventionality of his perspective (including his prejudices towards various immigrant poor) ensured the book's wide appeal.

But it was the quality of the photographs, the profound engagement with their subjects that gave *How the Other Half Lives* enduring significance. The first edition contained thirty-nine images: photograph after photograph capturing the intimate geography of slum life. Children rolling barrels stop to pose with wonder for the camera in a dark and narrow alley of "Gotham Court" (Figure 12).

The sunrays filtering in stand metaphorically for the camera and its reformative aim: to illuminate and thereby alleviate. The rigid angles of balconies and banisters, and the billowing clothes and sheets seem to leave no room for human inhabitants (like the three boys looking up at the camera from a ground floor balcony) in "Rear Tenement, Roosevelt Street" (Figure 13).

In "Street Arabs in Sleeping Quarters," three barelegged boys huddle asleep, two caught in an embrace, the third in profile hugging the wall.

The carefully arrayed populace of "Mullin's Alley" manages through sharp focus and casual poses to preserve independence within a deliberate arrangement (Figure 14). A blond boy with superb features and cap occupies the foreground, his slim molded hands lightly gripping his waist; a smiling boy leans against the wall, one hand in his pocket, a gesture and expression which manages to convey both bravado, and spontaneous warmth; two girls, one in white dress, another in stripes, sequester themselves secretively in a corner, one peeping directly at the camera, the other, in profile, perpendicularly

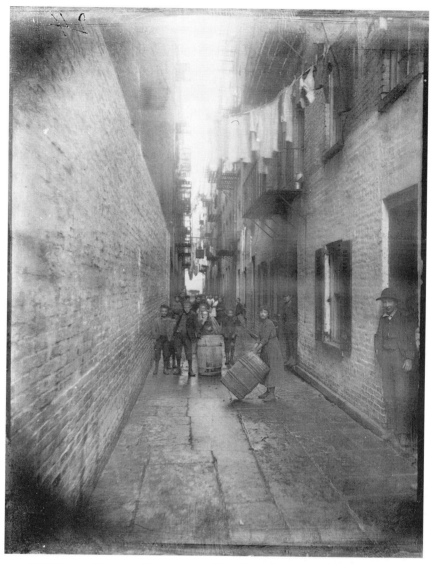

FIGURE 12. "Gotham Court," Jacob Riis, *How The Other Half Lives* (1890).

opposed to the camera angle. These images mount a reform agenda of their own, articulated nowhere else in Riis's book. This is an argument for variety. Ghetto dwellers come in all shapes and sizes: their personalities, as well as their ethnicities, by turn vibrant, curious, dull, observant, enthusiastic. They dress distinctively despite poverty, they think diverse thoughts, their parents dream different dreams on their behalf. Riis's photographic object is to detail

FIGURE 13. "Rear Tenement, Roosevelt Street," Jacob Riis,
How The Other Half Lives (1890).

and thereby to humanize the inhabitants of New York's tenements. However urgent the tones of Riis's narrative, however much they satisfy the prevailing initiatives of middle-class reform, the photographs themselves tell a deeper story. This story concerns the power to retain individuality in circumstances designed to render people uniform, to remain a self able to stare questioningly for posterity at a camera lens, to huddle close to another for comfort in sleep, to have a friend with a different colored dress. All of these aspects of being human persist in the ghetto and are captured in pictures. Not everything reflected in Riis's photographs is optimistic. The handsome boy pulling threads from silk upholstery in "In A Sweatshop" (Figure 16) has a black eye that might have been caused by any of the strong men surrounding him.

FIGURE 14. "Street Arabs in Sleeping Quarters," Jacob Riis,
How The Other Half Lives (1890).

The four laborers with the policeman burying coffins in the snow in "The Trench in the Potters Field" (Figure 17), are putting some very small bodies to rest.

The mother gazing slightly upward in "In the Home of an Italian Rag-Picker, Jersey Street" (Figure 18), her brown hands encircled around the baby wrapped inertly in its blanket (is it dead or alive?), her body utterly stilled with exhaustion, seems to lack the vigor to plead to a higher order of any kind. Each picture, whether men dressed in black huddling conspiratorially, homeless people in a five-cent a night rooming house, or sweatshop workers, is critical in conveying Riis's message. Through the formalizing scrutiny of the camera, these people become characters; thus transformed, their case for a human chance is made.

As a Danish immigrant who studied his adopted country well, Jacob Riis recognized how essential claims to individuality were to the fortune of any social group. Samuel Gompers, the founder of the American Feder-ation of Labor, born in England to Dutch Jewish immigrants, shared Riis's

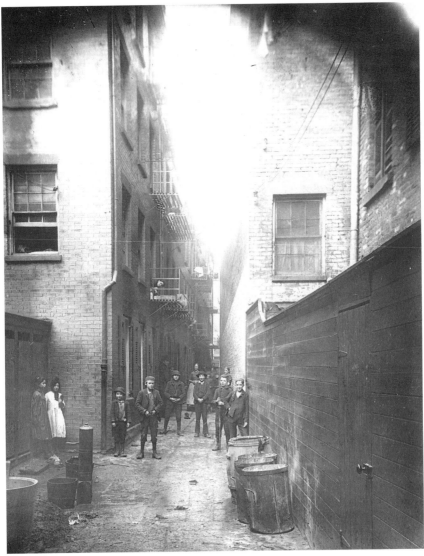

FIGURE 15. "Mullin's Alley," Jacob Riis, *How The Other Half Lives* (1890).

perspective. Gompers was credited by labor leaders throughout the twentieth century for identifying the requisite principle for an American labor organization – voluntarism. While Lenin called Gompers's method "a rope of sand," most believed it a brand of practical realism that ensured labor's success in the United States. From the beginning of his career as a labor organizer in

FIGURE 16. "In a Sweatshop," Jacob Riis, *How The Other Half Lives* (1890).

post-Civil War America, Gompers demonstrated an eagerness to work within the social and economic system, despite his awareness of its injustices. His purpose was to build a labor movement based on the opportunities of America rather than on the situation of labor abroad.

In *Seventy Years of Life and Labor* (1925) Gompers recounts his formative years in England. He recalls being greatly affected when French Huguenot neighbors, silk weavers, were ruined by machinery that replaced their skills. His education at a Jewish Free School, where he learned Talmud (in addition to basic subjects), gave him training in logic that he considered critical to his later success as a champion of labor. As the oldest son, Gompers left school at the age of ten to learn cigar-making, his father's trade. Three years later, his family was among a group assisted by the English Cigarmakers' Union in their emigration to America, a program designed to alleviate competition for English workers. Gompers's first memory of America was a scene of race conflict aroused by his father at the old Castle Garden landing area in Manhattan. For shaking hands with a black man, a boat employee who had aided the family on the difficult sea journey, Mr. Gompers was attacked by bystanders.

FIGURE 17. "The Trench in the Potter's Field," Jacob Riis,
How The Other Half Lives (1890).

His father's refusal to back down provided a lifelong lesson in defending one's beliefs, and a model for Gompers's efforts to forge alliances between black and white laborers, efforts that were violently resisted. Still, Gompers and his father found work easily in New York, and the boy was taken by the cosmopolitanism and heterogeneity of the city's Lower East Side. In 1864 Gompers joined the

FIGURE 18. "In The Home of an Italian Rag-Picker, Jersey Street," Jacob Riis,
How The Other Half Lives (1890).

Cigar Makers' Local Union, and three years later, he married another cigar-maker, Sophia Julian. Cigar-making, as described in *Seventy Years of Life and Labor*, was a sociable trade. Because one could think and talk while stripping tobacco leaves and rolling cigars, "the mind-freedom" of the work facilitated discussion and reading aloud. The strong bonds of friendship generated among workers provided an ideal ground for common interests and political organization.

The cigar shop became a forum where books by leading economic theorists – Marx, Lasalle, Henry George – were read aloud and debated. Gompers found his leanings corroborated by Marx's view of trade unions as the "practical agency, which could bring wage earners a better life." But the misery issuing from the Financial Crisis of 1873, widespread unemployment, loss of livelihood, and violence incited by extreme union factions, made Gompers wary of radicalism. Though he participated in cigar-makers' strikes in 1873 and in 1877, and in solidarity demonstrations with striking railroad workers, he continued to affirm his faith in free enterprise. Gompers became a US citizen in 1872, and it was a point of pride that in a lifelong career of union organizing he was arrested only once (in 1873). In the early years of his Federation of Labor, Gompers specialized in organizing fellow Jews, specifically, the large numbers of Jewish tailors immigrating from Russia at the time and being exploited by clothing manufacturers. But the labor reform with which Gompers became especially identified was the shorter workday. "Eight Hours for Work," went a contemporary slogan, "Eight Hours for Rest, Eight Hours for What We Will." The single most effective strike Gompers organized was an all-trades eight-hour demonstration on May Day, 1886, which was so successful it swelled the ranks of labor unions across the country. The eight-hour day, according to Gompers, was not simply a means of increasing wages and alleviating unemployment, but a human right, and he defended the American worker against the charge of declining productivity leveled by Frederick W. Taylor.

Gompers's judicious navigation of the volatile world of work and capital in the late nineteenth century was exemplified by the position he took on the controversial alliance between his Labor Federation and the Socialist Party. Insisting that party affiliations be kept out of labor organizations and charters, he nevertheless articulated his respect for socialist principles. Gompers also defended the Haymarket anarchists, as well as Eugene Debs, jailed during the Pullman strike, and later for protests against the First World War. Like other prominent immigrants, Jacob Riis and Abraham Cahan among them, Gompers sought to keep his adopted country faithful to its ideals. However challenging this task, through a long life of labor Gompers never wavered in its pursuit.

THE WORK ETHIC

Historians have explored how the advent of industrialization in late nineteenth-century America contributed to an erosion of traditional understandings of work. As codified by Max Weber, the "Protestant ethic" included the spiritu-alization of daily life, the notion that every individual had a particular vocation or calling, the obligation to be useful and make good use of time, and the tie between effort and reward. While the eclipse of Weber's "ethic" was underway by midcentury, the post-Civil War expansion of industrial capitalism intensi-fied the process. Self-denial and productivity remained important values, but America was becoming "a culture of consumption," a transformation assisted by the rapid rise of advertising. Consumer culture encouraged alternative val-ues, in particular those of abundance and leisure. In this period of changing industrial processes, and changing productive and consumptive ideals, the work ethic persisted as a significant register of Americanization. Indeed, what is particularly noteworthy about the work ethic at the turn of the century is the way in which three exemplary social outsiders commemorated its principles in classic works of literature. Through their respective bestsellers, *Up From Slavery*, *The Promised Land*, and the "Ragged Dick Series," Booker T. Washington, a former slave, Mary Antin, a Jewish immigrant, and Horatio Alger, a closet homosexual, revitalized an imperiled work ethic while using it as a guide to personal fame and fortune.

Booker T. Washington was the most powerful African-American leader at the turn of the century, his political sagacity and success unequalled by any contemporary. Washington gained renown for his program of industrial education at Tuskegee, the institute he founded in Alabama. His policy of accommodating white prejudice and relinquishing black claims for civil and legal rights in exchange for economic opportunities made him a controversial figure in his own time and long after. Indeed, materialism was a veritable religion for Washington, and his social philosophy was remarkably consistent with that described by Max Weber in *The Protestant Ethic and the Spirit of Capitalism* (1905). Washington's was no idle embrace of a prevailing capitalist ethos. He internalized that ethos and translated it into terms amenable to the conditions of Southern blacks in rural areas. Members of the Tuskegee faculty recalled how they dreaded the sound of wagon wheels signaling the principal's return from his travels, and the resumption of morning inspections. Touring the campus on horseback, Washington would note every piece of trash, every stray animal, every missing button on a student's coat. Each sign of waste or indifference would be recorded in his red notebook, and later redressed, in the name of the black Protestant kingdom on earth under construction at Tuskegee. Tuskegee was Washington's brick and mortar version of this utopia; *Up From Slavery* was the rendition made of words. He sought to invest it with a similar vision of spiritual necessity, a similar emphasis on building from the ground up, and a similar revaluation of manual labor. In arguing that the highest office of Southern blacks was doing "a common thing in an uncommon manner," Washington secured a permanent place for himself, for good or ill, as an architect of ordinariness.

Washington's policies won him extensive political authority, but also provoked attacks from fellow black leaders. Yet over the course of his highly publicized career as an accommodator, he privately financed a range of court suits, challenging injustices against blacks, Jim Crow cars, peonage, and the denial of jury service. After the publicity generated by his 1895 Atlanta Exposition Address, featuring the notorious aphorism – "In all things purely social we can be as separate as the fingers, yet one as the hand in all things essential to mutual progress" – Washington was urged to begin work on his memoirs. His first effort was *The Story of My Life and Work* (1900), which was largely ghost-written by the black journalist Edgar Webber. Dissatisfied with the result, Washington resolved to take more control and the outcome, *Up From Slavery* (1901, serialized in *Outlook*, 1900–01), became a bestselling account of his rise from slavery to national and international prominence. Washington no doubt especially appreciated the response of Kodak head George Eastman, a $5000 check to Tuskegee. One of the sharpest reviews was by W. E. B. Du Bois in *The Dial* (1901). While Du Bois acknowledged Washington's achievements, as well as key points of agreement between their positions, he emphasized what he considered the gravest danger of Washington's concessions, shifting the burden of black oppression from whites to blacks. Washington's policies, according to Du Bois, overlooked three barriers to black progress in the South: the greed of capital that reduced black workers in country districts to "semi-slavery"; the competitive fears of Southern workers which encouraged black disenfranchisement; and the passions of the ignorant and bereft, which perpetuated terrible abuses including lynching. Du Bois's criticisms did not prevent Washington from inviting him to Tuskegee for the summer, an indication of Washington's political skills, his ability to put aside differences for the sake of valuable alliances. As one contemporary observed, "Washington had no faith in white people, not the slightest, and he was most popular among them, because if he was talking with a white man he sat there and found out what the white man wanted him to say, and then as soon as possible, he said it." As a black man born a slave in the South, and intimate from childhood with the virulence of white racism, Washington developed a trademark ability to mask his feelings. It proved as useful in the writing of his life as in the living of it.

Washington was called "the wizard" by those who knew him well. The nickname suggests a complexity of character and thought that is evident in *Up From Slavery*. Written with the journalist Max Bennett Thrasher, the narrative charts the transformation of the victim, suffering from memory loss and struggling for literacy, into the agent, full of ambition and resourcefulness, and devoted to work. Generically, what begins as a slave narrative soon becomes a success narrative. The bulk of *Up From Slavery* is a story of making it in America, comparable to contemporary works like Jacob Riis's *The Making of an American* and Mary Antin's *The Promised Land*. Slavery is hardly beside the point for Washington, but the book's shape confirms his recognition, with Du Bois in *The Philadelphia Negro*, that progress for African Americans requires their redefinition as immigrants. The scars of slavery are there between the lines of his narrative, in the excessive modesty of the tone, and in the frequency with which he denies resentment towards all the people and institutions (his white father, Southern whites, the federal government) that failed him over the years. Yet Washington's tolerance is both strategic – part of his effort to recast African-American identity – and heartfelt, a consequence of his religious faith. Thus when Washington characterizes slavery as a "school," as he does frequently in the early part of his narrative, he seeks to normalize the African-American experience, so that its effects are no less indelible than a language barrier. But he also aims to suggest that, like many another evil, the institution betokens a providential design. Slavery may have been corrupt and immoral, but it had consequences underwritten by God – the education of black people. Washington's confidence is based on a faith in black election: the trials of his people signal divine favor and eventual reward. "Success," Washington observes, "is to be measured not so much by the position that one has reached in life as by the obstacles which he has overcome while trying to succeed."

Early reviews of *Up From Slavery* noted the affinities between Washington's persona and that of Franklin's *Autobiography*, which Weber considered distinctly representative of the Protestant ethic. Weber's conflation of Protestant religion and capitalist development took narrative form in Franklin, a model that was extended by Washington. Both Franklin and Washington insist on the necessity of concealment while embarking on courageous acts. God is responsible for this stance: the God who remains out of sight but encourages the observant to recognize "his finger in all the details of life." Both fear desire – Franklin, because it was potentially disruptive to a balanced and functional system (social or political), Washington, because its end could be a lynch rope. Washington's ideal of moderation and self-effacement was perfectly suited to the post-emancipation South where black ambition was considered a form of incitement.

Washington's perspective on desire and its discontents is elaborated in one of his book's most memorable vignettes, where he declares his preference for the weekly molasses doled out during slavery, over the fourteen-course dinners of the lecture circuit. The transformation, from the degraded slave craving his sweet morsel to the eminent statesman, indifferent to excessive banquets, is complete. As a child he would shut his eyes "while the molasses was being poured" in hope of being surprised by a big helping. As an adult, he knows how to conceal his yearnings, to avoid distressing Southern whites intent on preserving slave constraints on black appetites. Washington's message is, characteristically, mixed; his rhetoric comforts but twists. No matter how big this particular black man gets his appetites (and dreams) remain stuck like molasses in slavery days. He enjoys his "share" but has "never believed in 'cornering'" the market on desirable things. For the hopeful racist seeking reassurance, the anecdote promises that black folk under Washington's direction will not be claiming "shares" far beyond the allotments of slavery days. They will only consume fourteen-course dinners if required to. Yet the contrasting and more obvious point is that this former slave has become a famous man feasting on fourteen-course dinners while recollecting the lean molasses days of youth. Like a Titan (Andrew Carnegie, John D. Rockefeller) modeling the road to wealth, Washington's childhood deprivations make the fruits of success all the more sweet.

The molasses anecdote suggests that black people will develop healthy appetites for work and rewards when they are free to regulate themselves. For slavery destroyed the natural rhythms of labor and relaxation, expenditure of energy and enjoyment of one's bounty. Washington's devotion to the soil, his conviction that it is only through a profound attachment to the elemental that his people can progress, may be seen as a symbolic attempt to eradicate the stain of slavery, to cleanse and purify so as to begin anew. Blacks must start with essentials en route to higher aspirations. Washington's emphasis on the acquisition of skills and the identification of proper vocations was more a means to an end than an end in itself. He was not in fact opposed to higher education or professional training for blacks: "When a Negro girl learns to cook, to wash dishes, to sew, to write a book, or a Negro boy learns to groom horses, or to grow sweet potatoes, or to produce butter, or to build a house, or to be able to practice medicine as well or better than some one else, they will be rewarded regardless of race or color." Washington's offspring fulfilled this prescription, aspiring to professions while excelling in a variety of practical skills. His daughter was a dressmaker who dreamed of becoming a musician; his oldest son was a brickmason who wanted to pursue architecture; his youngest son was a manual worker who set his sights on medicine.

Indeed, the central purpose of *Up From Slavery* is the revaluation of work of all kinds. Work, according to Washington, was the great casualty of American slavery, a greater casualty even than black honor. One of the strongest claims of *Up From Slavery* is that black and white labor suffered equally under a system that undermined an ideal of work essential to human dignity.

The whole machinery of slavery was so constructed as to cause labor, as a rule, to be looked upon as a badge of degradation, of inferiority. Hence labor was something that both races on the slave plantation sought to escape. The slave system on our place, in a large measure, took the spirit of self-reliance and self-help out of the white people.

The implicit assertion here is that Southern whites might well benefit from a Tuskegee of their own. Washington's adaptation of the work ethic for black Americans was consistent with other aspects of a black-centered social policy.

What made Washington a singular spokesman for black Americans at the turn of the century was the intensity and narrowness of his vision. While convincing whites of his deference, his gift to fellow blacks was that he cared for them alone.

By appropriating the principles of the work ethic for African Americans, Booker T. Washington demonstrated his group's suitability to assimilation. According to Washington, the fundamental values of Protestantism provided the best means for the recovery of his people in the post-slavery era. The problem for Jewish immigrants as portrayed by Mary Antin was their tribal susceptibility to Americanization. Because of their aptitude for adaptation, as well as the compatibility between Jewish and American values, the challenge for Jews in America was the preservation of their religious and cultural identity. Beyond articulating the ideals of the work ethic – sacrifice, striving, perseverance, a sense of destiny – Mary Antin personified them. The self she presented in her bestselling autobiography was a walking embodiment of Protestant morality. But what makes the book so valuable in psychological and literary terms is the struggle waged by Antin's Russian-Jewish self against the assimilation its author so avidly pursued.

Mary Antin became an instant celebrity when *The Promised Land* was published in 1912. The book was widely and favorably reviewed, and Antin received fan letters from readers as distinguished as former president Theodore Roosevelt. Antin embarked immediately on a lecture tour in support of cherished causes: an open immigration policy, Zionism, and public education. Antin's advocacy of immigration, the subject of her second book, *They Who Knock at Our Gates: A Complete Gospel of Immigration* (1914), demonstrated her loyalty to the Jews of many nations in need of the opportunities and refuge provided by America. *The Promised Land* conveys deep ambivalence about the process of immigration and the difficulties of reconciling Jewish and American values. Among the most complex personal accounts of assimilation ever written, the book represents Americanization as a ritualized pattern and a skill to which Jews are peculiarly disposed. Some readers criticized Antin's reverence for her adopted country. The Jewish philosopher, Horace Kallen, for example, lamented her tendency to be "excessively, self-consciously flatteringly American." Brahmin cultural critic, Randolph Bourne, expressed his disdain for "the Jew who has lost the Jewish fire and become a mere elementary, grasping animal." Yet to take Antin's narrative as an unqualified portrait of self-making is to overlook its profound insistence on the suffering that issues from immigration. For all its brashness and enthusiasm, Antin's remains a sad book, even a work of mourning for the still vital forces of tradition, spirituality, and family, forsaken in her effort "to win America." Antin may emphasize her rebirth in

America, but she never lets us forget that *The Promised Land* is a primer on the immigrant experience, and as such, "a death-bed confession."

Antin was born in Polotzk, Russia in 1881, and emigrated with her family to Boston in 1894. A precocious child, she was encouraged especially by her father, formerly a businessman in Russia, who was sufficiently enlightened to seek a liberal education for his daughters. In America, Israel Antin seemed to fail at every venture he pursued, so that the family's hopes rested on Mary, whose excellent scholastic record earned her a place at the prestigious Boston Latin School for Girls. Her academic successes caught the attention of teachers and philanthropists such as Edward Everett Hale, who liked to encourage the "right" kind of newcomers. A middle-class market for immigrant narratives facilitated Antin's literary debut, after caseworkers at the Hebrew Immigrant Aid Society showed Israel Zangwill a series of Mary's letters to Russia. Translated from Yiddish to English the letters were published in 1899 with an introduction by Zangwill. Antin's double life, revolving between her slum home and the opportunities afforded by her wealthy patrons, generated predictable conflict and increased the likelihood of a rebellious marriage. At a Natural History Club outing sponsored by the immigrant agency, Hale House, Antin met Amadeus Grabau, a paleontology lecturer at Columbia University. She was nineteen and he was thirty-one when they married in 1902. Their one child, a daughter, Josephine, was born in 1906. Antin's Jewish mentors were unhappy about her intermarriage, but Antin insisted on her continuing devotion to Judaism.

Among the sacred features of the "promised land" was the American educational system. Where else but on hallowed ground could a penniless Russian-Jewish girl become a student of the classics, be mentored by publishers and philanthropists, and marry an American-born professor? The book featured not one but many conversions: from Russian outcast to American citizen; from traditional Judaism to liberal transcendentalism; from the communal ethnicity nurtured in the Pale to American individualism; from impoverished immigrant to bestselling author. Like other spiritual autobiographies with which it was compared, Antin's book is structured by a biblical typology, and treats the major events of her life as signs of election. At the same time, the life is representative; Antin is "speaking for thousands."

The origin of Antin's narrative is the funeral of her grandfather, which she identifies as her first memory. Describing the shape of her grandfather's body arrayed for burial, she worries about the authenticity of her recollection, and invokes a familiar register of guilt. Antin's narrative tendency, egomania qualified by guilt, is typical of American spiritual autobiographies. To bring one's life before God in judgment, in the tradition of Jonathan Edwards, is a humbling experience. Because Antin cannot quite conceive a divine audience, her gesture has more the quality of a fetish than of a spiritually meaningful act. Likewise, the rich symbolic portent of sacrificial ritual in the Old World is replaced by family melodrama in the New. When traditional Jews in the Russian Pale wring the necks of chickens in order to ensure a propitious marriage, or offer a "sacrifice of money, to be spent for the poor" as "insurance against damnation" they are participating in a collective form of worship. Ever the daughter of her enlightened father, Antin professes skepticism about God's willingness to transact with human beings. But she swings the chickens over her head with fellow Jews on the Eve of Atonement and believes herself redeemed in the process.

What happens to this sense of religious purpose in America? Antin's narrative shows that a legacy of religious feeling does not just evaporate. Instead it is translated into the most significant collective form still available to the Jewish immigrant: the family. Proper religious behavior in the old country becomes familial psychology in the new, as Mary Antin's sister Frieda is sacrificed for the sake of Antin's own American ascent. As a product of the Pale, Antin knows that "glory" comes to those who sacrifice. As a product of America, Antin knows that those who are called upon to sacrifice are invariably designated as inferior. Sacrifice, in a secular-materialist society built on individualism, has become a condition of deprivation experienced by some and not by others. The difference in individual apportionments must be rationalized, in this case by what Antin calls "family tradition, that Mary was the quicker, the brighter of the two, and that hers could be no common lot. Frieda was relied upon for help."

Most critics have emphasized Antin's clear preference for her adopted country, while some have detected a special lyricism in the Russian sections. This is most pronounced in Antin's portrayal of food. Chapter five, "I remember," which describes how her writing vocation is initiated by death, is full of references to food. Food in *The Promised Land* is a vehicle of loss and recovery. "It takes history to make such a cake," Antin observes of the cheesecakes baked in the Russian Pale. Composed "of daisies and clover picked on the Vall; the sweetness of Dvina water; the richness of newly turned earth," cheesecake, like any other food, expresses the particularities of time and place. Hence, the mind and body is a veritable archive of tastes, a mediator between lost and found selves. The food nostalgia that marks Antin's Russian sequences is paralleled by food revulsion in her American sequences. America is associated with "food, ready to eat, without any cooking from little tin cans," and with the "pink piece of pig's flesh" which Antin eats more of "than anybody at the table" to demonstrate her readiness for assimilation.

Consumption in *The Promised Land* is a passport that allows the narrating ego to move back and forth between the Old World and the New, between death and life, between the irretrievable and the all-too-real. For anthropologists, food has always been central to theories about boundaries. As substances that pass in and out of bodies, food helps to articulate more abstract conceptions of boundaries. Food is a universal means of distinguishing kinship and confirming acceptance. The commercialization of ethnic foods – Mexican tamales, Jewish bagels – signals, however partially, assimilation in America. In keeping with this, certain prized foods – coffee, tea, sugar, and salt – have figured prominently in the international trade that confirms national borders. While the cultivation of worldwide appetites for a country's leading commodity is certain to undermine its identity as such, the commodity usually retains its original association. But it is only an association. In its place of origin, for example, coffee is a whole product, integral to its world. As a commodity on a shelf in another land, it is something entirely different.

What makes Antin's portrayal of food revealing is that her immigrant is so fully identified with it. Metaphorically, her immigrant is the commodity, the cheesecake, rather than the consumer. Lost to Antin in America is the sense of completeness derived from the primacy of place, even a place as narrow as the Russian Pale. Like the "advantage of the disadvantage" described by W. E. B. Du Bois in *The Souls of Black Folk*, specifying the benefits issuing from the terrible oppression of American blacks positive advantages accrue to the beleaguered Jews of Russia. The compensation of the Old-World Jew was a fierce sense of belonging, a tribalism supported by religiosity so strong that it appeared to Antin "a fortress." With deprivation came the intensification of the Diaspora vision, a tremendous longing that was its own reward: "in the dream of a restoration to Palestine [the Jew] forgot the world." The paradox of Jewishness, the culture of Diaspora, is that Jews have always lived most fully and cohesively in countries that have been least hospitable to them. By evoking the intensity of life in the Russian Pale, by allowing it to upstage her presentation of life in America, Antin pinpoints the unique dilemma for the Jew in the land of material opportunity and religious toleration. Can a Jew be so much in the world and remain a Jew? Is the preservation of Jewishness to be honored at the expense of self-development and self-satisfaction? The answers to these questions are located not in the triumphant rhetoric of *The Promised Land* but in the highs and lows that define its deepest vision.

In her account of the world of reading that was opened to her in America, Antin recalls that next to books by Louisa Alcott, her favorites were "boys' books of adventure, many of them by Horatio Alger." One likely explanation for Antin's preference was the resemblance between the system of value set out in his novels and her own. The fact that a Jewish female immigrant was reading Alger suggests how omnipresent his works were by the turn of the century. In his time, Alger was one of many successful writers of books for boys, including James Otis, Oliver Optic, and G. A. Henty, whose titles are commemorated in advertisements at the back of Alger's first editions. Alger's novels alone endured because of his uniquely reproducible treatment of the American success myth: the drama of upward mobility, achieved through destiny and hard work.

Alger wrote a hundred novels between 1867 and his death in 1899, each with the same formulaic morality: poverty ennobles, inspiring thrift and ambition; virtue and diligence are always rewarded by upward mobility; merit creates its own aristocracy. In Alger's world, decency, good looks, and intelligence are inseparable. The only simpletons are spoiled rich boys, while good manners and taste are innate. Once the hero's superior qualities are established, the narratives invariably introduce a wealthy benefactor, who conceives a liking for the hero and provides means for his improvement, which always begins with the purchase of a new suit. Alger book titles – *The Train Boy*, *Dan, the Newsboy*, *Young Bank Messenger*, *Frank Fowler, the Cash Boy*, *Tom the Bootblack*, *The Errand Boy* – reflect their preoccupation with work. Though these books support a work ethic they do so without reference to actual labor. In novels whose titles foreground various occupations, the work process is rarely depicted or even discussed. Moreover, Alger ignores modern industrial developments, highlighting instead jobs that seem timeless, such as those in the spheres of mercantilism, farming, and banking. Alger's highly nostalgic conceptualizations of work during a time when its transformation aroused considerable anxiety undoubtedly contributed to their appeal. At the same time, Alger's books often featured the modern activity of speculation, whether as a distant enterprise that fascinates a character like Ragged Dick (he refers continually to his mythical shares in the Erie Railroad) or as a practice protagonists engage in themselves. In many Alger series ("Ragged Dick," "Tattered Tom," "Luck and Pluck," "Brave and Bold") heroes invest their minuscule savings in shares of some enterprise, often a mine, and by realizing a profit, manage to gain an economic foothold. Too much speculation is a bad thing, especially when engaged in by the greedy rich (*Struggling Upward*). Approached with wisdom and modesty by the humble poor, speculation is always remunerative.

Alger was born in 1832 in Marlborough, Massachusetts, the son of a poor but respectable Unitarian minister who was able to send him to a college preparatory school, and then to Harvard. Alger was an outstanding student, with ambitions to write. Though he was able to publish in good magazines – *Harper's, Putnam's, North American Review* – he could not support himself, so he turned to the ministry, graduating from the Harvard Divinity School in 1860. Securing a small congregation in Brewster on Cape Cod, he continued to write while fulfilling his ministerial duties. By the second year of Alger's tenure at Brewster, however, rumors were circulating alleging Alger's homosexuality and molestation of children. After losing his pulpit, Alger moved to New York City, devoting himself exclusively to writing.

Whether Alger was able to sublimate his passion for boys in writing about them, or discovered a more physical outlet in the anonymity of New York is unclear, but there is evidence that as an urban writer who soared to fame via tales of upward mobility, he made peace with himself. A friend of the James family, Alger was candid about his desires, though he appears to have classified them as a form of "insanity" (as reported by Henry James Sr. in a letter to Henry Jr., a probable homosexual himself). Years later, Alger could refer openly to his "natural liking for boys" and comment that he had "leased his pen" to them. In "Writing Stories for Boys" (*The Writer*, 1896), an essay often excerpted in advertisements, Alger noted that the "writer for boys should have an abundant sympathy with them . . . should learn to look upon life as they do. Boys object to be written down to. A boy's heart opens to the man or writer who understands him." Alger's first major success was the bestselling *Ragged Dick*, and one of its consequences was Alger's acquaintance with Charles Loring Brace, a philanthropist who ran a Children's Aid Society and a Newsboys' Lodging House for homeless boys. Alger became a regular at these institutions, drawing freely on their inhabitants as subjects for his books.

Ragged Dick or Street Life in New York (1868, serialized in *Student and School-mate*, 1867) is among the strongest of Alger's novels. Here Alger provided an authentic portrait of a social sphere – the highly competitive order of boot-blacks in midtown Manhattan – and a relatively realistic hero: Dick is far less angelic than subsequent Alger protagonists. He smokes, swears, and indulges in pranks at the expense of country rubes and unsuspecting old gentlemen. He is extravagant, a characteristic that becomes increasingly rare among Alger heroes. The typical Alger hero is not only limited, beneficially, by familial obligations, but thrift is his dominant instinct. Dick is also atypical in his emotional poignancy. He confesses to feelings of loneliness in his vagabond existence and sympathy towards the criminal poor, exhibiting a depth lacking in subsequent Alger heroes. Dick speaks a rough dialect that exposes his lack of education. The sign of his growing respectability at the novel's end is a new deliberateness in speech. Significantly, he is consumed with finance; his ruminations are dominated by fantasies of economic ascent, and jests about his "manshun up on Fifth Avenoo." His preoccupation with the stock market includes the opposing tactics of bulls and bears. The spur to his transformed prospects – from jests to options – is a chance eavesdropping on a conversation between a wealthy boy and his uncle, who needs someone to show the nephew, Frank, around the city. Dick offers his expert knowledge of Manhattan (apparently his ragged clothes and speech are no deterrent), and there begins a reciprocal education. Dick introduces Frank to street life and Frank introduces Dick to the upper class. Dick gradually assumes Frank's values, a transformation forecast by the uncle's first gift to Dick, Frank's old suit. As Dick improves, he is shadowed by a fellow bootblack, the bully Mickey Maguire, whose antagonistic envy highlights the complexity of social relations among working boys. The novel ends with Dick's rescue of a boy who falls from a Brooklyn ferryboat. The boy's father, a wealthy merchant, repays Dick with a job as a clerk in his counting-room. Dick's future is assured, employed by a wealthy benefactor forever in his debt. The benefactor's first gift to Dick, predictably, is the handsomest suit he has ever owned. As for the bully, Mickey Maguire, his inheritance of Dick's cast-off garments betoken that he too is on his way upward.

By the publication of Alger's next significant novel, *Struggling Upward* in 1890, the hero had changed considerably. The Alger heroes that fall between *Ragged Dick* and *Struggling Upward* reveal the slow accretion of civilized instincts and habits, including proper speech, cleanliness, and courtesy. Gone are the qualities that make Ragged Dick memorable, among them, a sense of humor, sadness, and critical intelligence. Luke Larkin, the loving son of a poor widowed mother, is flawless. He is also a thorough conformist, incapable of a fresh thought or statement. The setting of the novel is a small town, not far from New York City, and Luke's antagonist is a malevolent rich boy, Randolph Duncan, a far cry from the irritating ragamuffin, Mickey Maguire. The difference between the antagonists signals Alger's growing preference for stark moral oppositions over more subtle shades of temperament and behavior. *Ragged Dick*'s New York setting is integral to the novel's storyline, while *Struggling Upward*'s setting is irrelevant. Alger's dramatic abilities seem to have been compromised by success, the obligation to produce standard works on a tight schedule for commercial profit.

Yet there is one scene in *Struggling Upward* that suggests Alger still found ways to complicate his narratives and make important points. During his ride on the Black Hills stagecoach, Luke Larkin meets a passenger who is unmistakably homosexual, and who foils an attempted robbery. The stagecoach scene includes a Colonel Braddon, who blusters about his courage but turns out to be a coward, and a clergyman, who employs "an instrument of retribution" to aid the brave Mortimer Plantagenet Sprague, the homosexual who trounces the robbers. Sprague is introduced as "a genuine dude, as far as appearance went, a slender-waisted, soft-voiced young man, dressed in the latest style, who spoke with a slight lisp." Alger's approbation is signaled in Luke's response: "In spite of his affected manners and somewhat feminine deportment, Luke got the idea that Mr. Sprague was not wholly destitute of manly traits, if occasion should call for their display." In the extended scene of dialogue that follows, Sprague flaunts his lisp and his weakness, substituting "weally" for really; ending every sentence with "don't you know," and enjoying the "sudden sinking" of coach wheels that launches the brawny Colonel into his lap. "If it's all the same to you," he quips, "I'd rather sit in *your* lap" (my emphasis). Suddenly the robbers appear, barking orders to the terrified passengers. In classic Superman style, Sprague produces a pair of revolvers "and in a stern voice, wholly unlike the affected tones in which he had hitherto spoken said: 'Get out of here, you ruffians, or I'll fire!'" Minutes later, the "dude" is back, lavishly praising the minister and denying his own heroism. Manifesting the prized Alger traits in the guise of a homosexual, Sprague enjoys complete control over his erotic exhibitionism while demonstrating mastery in the Wild West.

Mortimer Plantagenet Sprague is not a deceiver but rather a human being in Alger's deepest sense of the term: combining the impulses of weakness and courage, the aspiration to self-display and self-effacement, passivity and assertiveness, masculinity and femininity. As an allegory for Alger's authorship, the sequence stands as both an appeal and a justification for his work. Alger himself was the dude, and he looked the part, at five feet seven, boyishly slender, with a slight stammer and an effusive manner, capable of producing, in book after book, manly little heroes who harbored supreme courage. But these manly little heroes were as needy as they were resourceful, accomplishing every task set out for them however daunting and then returning to their mothers, or turning for comfort to one another in their orphaned or abandoned state. These forms of nurture had nothing to do with uplift; they were not satisfactions an Alger hero had to earn or be worthy of. They were given as an original endowment. It was this willingness to reach beyond the parameters of success in his books that make Alger's fiction worthy of literary study in their own right.

Booker T. Washington, Mary Antin, and Horatio Alger succeeded in their respective works in extending the boundaries of the work ethic to include experiences and types of people not ordinarily identified with Protestant norms. Washington accomplished this through his revaluation of manual labor, which he believed had been so profoundly disparaged under slavery, that it required wholesale remarketing, among whites as well as blacks. Mary Antin reveled in striving and achievement for their own sake, emphasizing in her self-representation how a talented and motivated individual could exploit the opportunities of a true meritocracy. And Horatio Alger created fictional worlds comprised of pure, gentle youths justly served by fate and fortune. It was a tribute to his legacy that two of the greatest and most ambivalent novels on the American work ethic, F. Scott's Fitzgerald's *The Great Gatsby* (1925) and Theodore Dreiser's *An American Tragedy* (1925), depict their heroes as avid readers of Horatio Alger. At a time when the practical and theoretical legitimacy of the work ethic was uncertain Washington, Antin, and Alger ensured its survival by translating it into the terms of cultural mythology.

8

❧

CORPORATE AMERICA

IN HIS WIDELY INFLUENTIAL *Business Cycles: A Theoretical, Historical, and Statistical Analysis of the Capitalist Process* (1939), Joseph Schumpeter observed, "It was not enough to produce satisfactory soap, it was also necessary to induce people to wash." During the post-Civil War era Americans were induced to wash. The rise of big business and the extraordinary expansion of the American economy between 1860 and 1920 were facilitated by several factors. Between 1860 and 1900, 676, 000 patents were granted by the US Patent Office, spurred in part by the development of steel production and the application of electricity to industry. The dramatic influx of new inventions supplied techniques for converting the nation's vast natural resources into manufactured products. Long before Standard Oil, there was the American railroad; organized in the 1830s and 1840s, by the 1890s there were over 200,000 miles of track throughout the country. The national railroad educated employees, Andrew Carnegie as well as unionized workers, in the methods of big business, while transporting people and products to growing domestic and foreign markets. America's economy could not have developed as it did in the nineteenth century without the continual renewal of the American labor supply by immigrants who came for economic opportunity and helped to perpetuate economic growth. From 1800 to 1900 America was transformed into a mass society (its population increasing from 5.3 million to 76 million) distinguished by its astonishing diversity unequalled by any other nation in the world. While multiculturalism was especially identified with urban areas like New York and Chicago, where 80 percent and 87 percent, respectively, were immigrants or children of immigrants, small industrial towns like Fall River, New York, and Scranton, Pennsylvania were even more ethnically mixed. The same was true of the West, which absorbed over 8 million immigrants who came to stake land claims in places like South Dakota, Kansas, and Nebraska. These settlers brought with them foreign agricultural strains that often proved more durable than homegrown. The Kubanka and Kharkov wheat introduced by Russian Mennonites in Minnesota, for example, flourished so remarkably that by 1914 half of the winter wheat consumed in the US was of the Kubanka and Kharkov varieties.

In addition to these material and human resources, American investors and entrepreneurs benefited from a general economic commitment to diversification, towards manufacturing, banking, and services and away from agriculture. Above all, the American legal system was uniquely hospitable to business enterprise. While there were few inhibiting tariff barriers between states and regions, venture capitalists were protected against foreign competition by direct and indirect subsidies. Corporate and contractual laws, lenient bank and bankruptcy laws, and the relative freedom from the demands of organized labor and the claims of environmentalists, all made for a society unusually hospitable to business enterprise. With a government comparatively young and small, no aristocracy, no church, and no standing army, the nation had few impediments to the expansion of market forces. In 1861, the only big business in America was the railroad; by the time the Supreme Court dissolved Standard Oil, American Tobacco, and Du Pont in 1911, trusts were a fixture of the economy. Henry Adams and his brother Charles characterized the railroad as a modern form of piracy in their scathing and prophetic critique of big business, *Chapters of Erie* (1886). But critiques of this kind did little to prevent what one business historian called the great explosion of mergers between 1895 and 1905, when 300 business firms were formed into trusts, many of them firms that became household names over the course of the twentieth century, including Chiquita, Eastman Kodak, Coca-Cola, Reebok, General Electric. One hundred and eighty nine of the *Fortune* 500 firms of the 1990s were founded between 1880 and 1920. In the seven years between 1897 and 1904 alone, 4,227 American companies were reduced to 257 combinations, occasionally by force.

The theoretical purpose of the trust was to centralize management, consolidating smaller companies in order to rationalize production processes, making them cheaper and more efficient. Recurrent depressions or panics – in the 1870s, 1880s, and 1890s – also motivated a search for means of controlling prices and output, so as to regularize profits. While their methods paralleled those of industrial giants, many of the companies that participated in combinations were mainly interested in keeping their manufactures running full to compensate high capital investments and costs. But John D. Rockefeller's Standard Oil Company, which was worth almost a billion dollars by the turn of the century, epitomized the giant corporation with its conspiratorial monopolizing of production, ravaging of competition, and price-fixing. The term "robber baron" – coined in 1880 by Kansas farmers in an anti-monopoly pamphlet – expressed widespread fears that an American individualist ethos of enterprise and innovation was imperiled by trusts. Rockefeller himself was eventually prosecuted under the 1890 Sherman Antitrust law, designed to curb the worst abuses of combination and ensure healthy competition. Significantly, Standard Oil was readily revived as a conglomerate, when its services were needed by the nation upon entering World War I.

Next to the American legal system, there was perhaps no other cultural domain more interested in the affairs of business than American literature. One of the most notable features of Realist novels was their preoccupation with economic enterprise in all its facets. This was partly because writers like Howells and Phelps, Twain and Dreiser, were coming to terms with the commercialization of their own literary profession in an era when magazine serialization, advertising, larger reading audiences, and literary celebrity could yield profits previously unknown to authors. Another reason was the powerful intellectual and aesthetic claims exerted by a culture of business that was changing society in ways that were of direct concern to Realist writers, transforming American senses of time, conceptions of material possessions, as well as the conditions of opportunity and value. Every writer discussed in the following pages was profoundly ambivalent about the changes wrought by rapid capitalist development in this period. They were all as enchanted as they were repelled by it. That fascination–repulsion constitutes the very texture of their works: the economic rhetoric, particularly the language of sacrificial exchange, pervading the fiction of Henry James, the absorption with class and conscience in the novels of William Dean Howells and Elizabeth Stuart Phelps, the predominant categories of speculation, consolidation, and credit that govern the worlds of Mark Twain, Frank Norris, and Theodore Dreiser.

MANUFACTURERS

Poised between a traditional Christian disdain for rampant materialism and their profound dismay over the class conflict aroused by unrestrained capitalist development, Elizabeth Stuart Phelps and William Dean Howells offered two of the most critical portraits of manufacturers published in the post-Civil War period. In *The Silent Partner* (1871) and *The Rise of Silas Lapham* (1885), Phelps and Howells invoked familiar settings and themes to voice their apprehensions about a new and dangerous economic-industrial order. Phelps wrote about the New England mill towns close to her home in Andover, and emphasized the redemptive possibilities of bonds among women from different classes in assuaging the most destructive effects of these expanding manufactories. Howells depicted his self-made businessman, who was straight off the farm, through the lens of a strict Protestant morality. By repeatedly staging conflicts between Silas Lapham's economic interests and the demands of his conscience, Howells suggested their fundamental incompatibility. Yet the deep ambiguity of Howells's ending confirms that already the divide, that would be further obscured by subsequent American novelists, was blurring.

Elizabeth Stuart Phelps, who provided the era's starkest opposition between moral values and business practices, was inspired by an actual case where the negligence of manufacturers resulted in the deaths of employees. The novel registers her vivid memory of the Pemberton Mill disaster of 1860, when a faulty construction (overlooked by "careless inspectors") collapsed on seven hundred and fifty workers and buried eighty-eight of them alive. Phelps recalls in her autobiography, *Chapters From A Life* "how the mill girls, caught in the ruins beyond hope of escape, began to sing . . . their young souls taking courage from the familiar sound of one another's voices." Phelps's fictionalization of the tragedy was consistent with her view that "the province of the literary artist [was] to tell the truth about the world he lives in . . . that in any highly-formed or fully-formed creative power, the 'ethical' as well as the 'aesthetical sense' is developed." Phelps visited the rebuilt mills, consulted engineers, officials, physicians, journalists, and people who had survived the mill's collapse. The result of her investigations was "The Tenth of January," published in the *Atlantic Monthly* (1868). While the story was faithful to fact, Phelps felt that it failed to deal adequately with the social problems underlying the incident, raising more questions than it illuminated. What were the prospects for cross-class empathy and political alliances among women, was capital-labor conflict inevitable and what was the role of Christianity in its mediation, how far did manufacturers' responsibility toward their employees extend? *The Silent Partner* represents her effort to explore in more complex terms the relationship between factory-owning capitalists and the laboring poor who work for them in a New England mill town. The representatives of these groups are two women: a wealthy young socialite of twenty-three, Perley Kelso, whose father is an owner of the Hale and Kelso Mills; and Sip Garth, an uneducated factory worker of twenty-one, who is instinctively eloquent and preternaturally aware. Both women are orphans: motherless at the narrative's start they are soon fatherless as well. Perley's father dies in a train accident, Sip's in a factory accident – a "kindred deprivation," that stirs immediate sympathy in Perley.

The novel's opening scene involves a chance meeting of the pair on a rainy night that Perley experiences from the warmth of her coach and Sip uncovered on the street. "As Lazarus and Dives, face to face," this confrontation defines the remainder of the narrative. Perley, since her father's death a "partner" in the town's leading manufactory, comes to know Sip and other workers. Guided by Sip, Perley embarks on a Dantesque tour of the factory from the perspective of those who suffer its operations. She encounters a spirited eight-year-old boy, illegally employed, who is crunched up by a grinding machine. She sees an old laborer fired for meager productivity and forced to await death in the almshouse. And she also meets Catty, the novel's ultimate casualty and Christ figure, the younger sister of Sip, born deaf and dumb, because her mother worked punishing long hours up to the moment of her delivery. Sip's life is a round of misfortune, culminating in Catty's death by drowning. The deaf, dumb, and now blind Catty (from a hand disease contracted at her wool-picking job and rubbed into her eyes) gets lost in a flood and is killed by a log avalanche in a vivid crucifixion. Thus, "the world of the laboring poor as man has made it, and as Christ has died for it, a world deaf, dumb, blind, doomed, stepping confidently to its own destruction before our eyes."

This is the rhetoric that initiates Sip's career as a preacher, with a Christian message of peace. Perley opts for a life of genteel reform, removed from both the manufactory's elite and Sip's working class. The lone continuity between Perley and Sip is their mutual, one could argue, "feminist" repudiation of men. Perley breaks her engagement with Maverick Hale, the callous son of her father's partner, and refuses the more sympathetic Stephen Garrick, the self-made man, who has risen from poverty to part ownership of the factory. Perley's decisions have to do with her own self-realization: the pursuit of independence that makes her loath to be a "silent partner." Sip rejects marriage in recognition of her class status as inborn and inescapable. "I've heard tell of slaves before the war that wouldn't be fathers and mothers of children to be slaves like them. That's the way I feel," she tells the man with whom she has known her only happiness.

Phelps has no sympathy for the mill owners, whom she characterizes as heartless and concerned for profits alone. Nor does she have a taste for the high society their livelihood supports. But Phelps's potentially radical Christianity amounts to a strategy of appeasement just as her model of feminine self-reliance is limited to mild social reform. Finally, her ethics seem a rather nostalgic means of redress against forces whose challenge required more systematic and sophisticated tactics. Howells's *The Rise of Silas Lapham* (1885, serialized in *Century Magazine*, 1884–85) shares Phelps's moral quandary. His most renowned work, it was also the first major American novel to feature a businessman as protagonist, a tradition that extends from Howells through Fuller's *The Cliff-Dwellers* (1893), Herrick's *Memoirs of an American Citizen* (1905), Norris's *The Pit* (1903), Dreiser's *The Financier* (1912), and Cahan's *The Rise of David Levinsky* (1917). Whether these authors portray manufacturers or financiers, the question of their heroes' ethical sensibilities is invariably a central point of reference.

Howells's concern about the impact of business on social morality affirmed his sense of its cultural ascendancy, as did his designation of *The Rise of Silas Lapham* as being "typically American." What he meant by this is clarified in the words of the novel's aristocrat, Bromfield Corey, "Money . . . is the romance, the poetry of our age. It's the thing that chiefly strikes the imagination. The Englishmen who come here are more curious about the great new millionnaires than about any one else, and they respect them more." The making of large fortunes, through manufacturing, creating commodities, developing land, locating markets, had become a distinctly American activity. Building material empires in this post-Civil War period was the nation's contribution to world civilizations. Unlike Dreiser, who sought to establish the aesthetic possibilities of this materialism, Howells was concerned to delineate its moral effects. Thus his novel foregrounds costs, consequences, and compensations: the price paid by individuals and by society as a whole for the nation's material obsessions. Howells's purpose, like Phelps's, keeps his narrative at a remove from enterprise. His characters discuss their feelings about manufacturing and its products; they indulge in the pleasures afforded by their successful ventures, including house building and romance; and they torture themselves about their responsibilities to those who have been casualties of the new economy rather than beneficiaries like themselves. They question their own motives whether in charity or in moneymaking, and contemplate the larger social effects of business. The figure that focuses all this deliberation is Silas Lapham, the singular businessman whose rise – towards what? – constitutes the plot of Howells's novel.

Silas Lapham is introduced in an interview with Bartley Hubbard, the cynical journalist from *A Modern Instance*, whom Howells resurrects as a reporter doing a feature on "Solid Men of Boston." The conceit provides distance on Lapham, a morally ambiguous figure throughout, and establishes him as worthy of respect and also of sympathy, since he appears at the mercy of Hubbard. The conceit also enables Howells to relate the details of Lapham's ascent, beginning with his recognition of the commercial potential of the paint-mine discovered on the family farm. Just before the Civil War, when the need for non-flammable paint has been highly publicized by a ship explosion in the West, Lapham decides to test the properties of his inheritance. An expert review reveals the paint as fireproof, waterproof, and resistant to decay. Like all new products, Lapham's paint seems like a miraculous gift to its manufacturer. Lapham's paint business is put on hold during the Civil War, though Lapham understands that he might have gotten the product "into government hands," and seen his fortunes soar. Instead, Lapham enlists, gets wounded, becomes a colonel, and survives. Returning home he plunges into paint, "like my own blood to me," labeling the various market brands with family names. He is soon shipping "to all parts of the world," admirably compensated for his wartime sacrifice.

Yet Lapham's conscience remains unsettled. He has fired his original partner, an inept scoundrel called Milton K. Rogers, who supplied the capital for launching his paint business. Lapham atones for his guilt over Rogers by accepting his new business proposition. The proposition ultimately ruins Lapham, because it requires that he sell land to shady investors at the expense of the community, something he refuses to do. In short, he is a businessman who repudiates modern business practices, insisting on fair dealing in a system where the ruthless alone triumph. Critics have expressed skepticism towards what seems an over-idealized account of the successful man of business, and his portrait might even be called unrealistic by his own standards. In an 1891 essay "Call For Realism," Howells proclaims that fiction must "cease to lie about life; let it portray men and women as they are, actuated by the motives and the passions in the measure we all know." An ambitious man of business like Lapham who makes a fortune in paint, but finds the ultimate exploitation of his gains to be inconsistent with his Christian values, is not impossible. But it is never quite clear exactly *why* Lapham's sale of his land to Rogers's investors would be harmful to the community. What is necessary is the either/or option: either Lapham sacrifices his wealth or his morality; under no circumstances can he preserve both.

The same rigid scheme prevails in the novel's love story, which proves critical in revealing the nature of its Realism. Lapham's two daughters, Irene and Penelope, both love the same young man, Tom Corey, but Tom reciprocates Penelope's love. Like the business plot, the love story is resolved by the necessity of sacrifice for the common good. Lapham must give up his wealth in order to preserve his virtue and Irene must give up Tom Corey to Penelope, whose love is reciprocated. Both solutions honor a utilitarian morality: it is better that one person suffers than two or more. The difficulty of such a reading for the business theme is that it presumes Lapham's economic ruin is essential to his good conscience, which the novel fails to establish convincingly. The difficulty of such a reading for the love theme is that it presumes, in the manner of fairy tales (as opposed to Realist novels), that once people are married – Tom and Penelope – their troubles disappear, whereas it seems likely that both will continue to lament Irene's pain and their own role in it. All this complication of ready solutions suggests that the basis of Howells's Realism is his interest in people's beliefs about what constitutes moral behavior. Howells's novel is realistic because it focuses on the ways in which people in the late nineteenth century groped towards resolutions to their predicaments that seemed to them upright and honest, whether or not they were (or could be).

It is not Howells who believes in the concluding decisions of his characters but the characters themselves. The novel's deepest perspective opts for uncertainty and open-endedness in suggesting that the outcomes of actions remain unpredictable however morally beneficial they might appear in the present. This would make Howells's attitude towards American business ultimately more consistent with that of a Norris or Dreiser than with that of a Phelps, signaling his receptiveness to modernity in all its forms.

Howells's *The Rise of Silas Lapham* inspired Abraham Cahan's portrait of a Jewish immigrant "making it" in America, *The Rise of David Levinsky* (1917, serialized in *McClure's* 1912–13). Cahan shares Howells's ambivalence towards his businessman protagonist, emphasizing his vitality, while questioning the morality of his behavior in romance as well as in business. Moreover, both novelists highlight a prevailing ethic of sacrifice; their characters believe that their material success requires them to forfeit something significant. Thus Levinsky's wretched personal state at the novel's end is understood as the price he pays for his professional triumph. Poised on either side of a thirty-year history of literary representations of manufacturing, the novels reveal how much has changed in the business world from 1885 to 1917. Most striking among these is the increasingly central role of immigrants in the nation's key industries. Robert Herrick's *Memoirs of an American Citizen* (1905), for instance, which recounts the life of a penniless farm boy, Edward Van Harrington, who works his way up to become the head of the Meat Trust in Chicago, describes how his success is enabled in part by his recognition of the special niche market afforded by kosher meat. Going into business with German Jews, Harrington is able to gain a foothold that eventually funds his full-scale expansion. His pivotal business associate on his way up is John Carmichael, a "foul-mouthed Irishman." The fact that Herrick's "American Citizen" rides his way to fame and fortune on the backs, as it were, of these smaller immigrant businessmen, confirms the significance of David Levinsky's own "rise."

Because Cahan approached the world of American business as an outsider, profoundly aware of the opportunities it offered maligned foreigners like David Levinsky, he was more optimistic about its social impact. Such optimism, however, was qualified by anxieties about the predicament of Jews in his adopted country. These intensified during the writing of the novel. *The Rise of David Levinsky* originated in a proposal from an editor at *McClure's* that Cahan contribute to a series on immigrants in business. Neither of them could have

FIGURE 19. Illustrations by Jay Hambidge for Abraham Cahan's *The Autobiography of a Jew: The Rise of David Levinsky, McClure's Magazine*, July 1913.

anticipated that a month before the appearance of Cahan's serialized novel, an associate editor, Burton J. Hendrick would publish an essay entitled, "The Jewish Invasion of America" (covering topics such as "Intensity of Jewish Competition," "Jews the Greatest Owners of Land," "Jews as a Great Power in American Railroads"). Nor could they have known that Hendrick would announce Cahan's forthcoming serialization. The effects of Hendrick's piece were reinforced by Jay Hambidge's illustrations for *Levinsky*, which contained offensive Jewish stereotypes.

These frames, together with the aggressive realism of Cahan's portrait, led to accusations that the author had betrayed his people. While Cahan's sympathies were clear, the subject of Jews in business inevitably raised stereotypical associations that were bound to be controversial. Still, the faults of David Levinsky, the coat manufacturer who rises from rags in Russia to wealth and power in America, are a product of his author's respect. Given the opprobrium Cahan endured over *Levinsky*, it is ironic that he was haunted during its writing by the trial in Kiev, Russia, of Mendel Beilis – a Jew accused, and later acquitted,

FIGURE 20. Illustrations by Jay Hambidge for Abraham Cahan's *The Autobiography of a Jew: The Rise of David Levinsky, McClure's Magazine,* July 1913.

of murdering a Christian boy to use his blood for ritual purposes – and the case in Atlanta, Georgia of Leo Frank, a Jew convicted of murdering a Christian girl and later lynched by a mob.

Jewish persecution forms an important subtext for Cahan's novel in more ways than one. The garment industry featured in the novel was a direct beneficiary of the devastating Russian pogroms of 1881–82. The convergence of an influx of Russian tailors seeking refuge and the growing demand from American women for mass-produced overcoats, dresses, and suits galvanized clothing manufacture. And it resulted in the radical democratizing of fashion. In the words of David Levinsky,

It was the Russian Jew who had introduced the factory-made gown, constantly perfecting it, and reducing the cost of its production. The ready-made silk dress which the American woman of small means now buys for a few dollars is of the very latest style and as tasteful in its lines, color scheme, and trimming as a high-class designer can make it . . . The average American woman is the best-dressed average woman in the world, and the Russian Jew has had a good deal to do with making her one.

Cahan makes the story of clothing manufacture a multicultural story by detailing how Russian Jews became increasingly central to this critical industry. This is due in part to the incomparable hospitality of American speculators eager to supply capital to Jewish manufacturers, whom they considered good risks. Far from being exclusionary, American financiers, according to Cahan, welcomed Jews into rapidly expanding urban markets, valuing their skills in both manufacturing and sales.

The focus of American economic growth in the late nineteenth century was urban commerce, the specialty of Jewish immigrant entrepreneurs, who brought with them a history of experience with cosmopolitan consumers. Throughout the cities of Europe, Jewish workers and merchants skilled in trades and sales nearly monopolized the production of clothing and footwear. This was even true of Russian cities until the 1880s, when anti-Semitic sanctions ruined many merchants. The American marketplace offered a miraculous cessation of anti-Semitic restrictions on Jewish enterprise. Often starting out in America as peddlers, many Jews were able by the last decades of the nineteenth century to establish specialty and department stores. These included Filenes of Boston; Kaufmanns of Pittsburgh; Lazaruses of Columbus; Goldsmiths of Memphis; Sangers of Dallas; Spiegelbergs of New Mexico; Goldwaters of Arizona; and Meiers of Portland. While American observers typecast Jews as a people of business, they did little to hinder the development of what one writer for the *New York Tribune* called, a "Hebrew Hive of Industry."

Cahan's contribution to American literature was his powerful fictionalization of these economic trends. Nor is his portrait confined to clothing manufacture; his hero's ambitions take him into other business arenas, including New York real estate, where Jews again appear as a critical force. Cahan describes the Russian Jew as builder: "Under the spell of their activity cities larger than Odessa sprang up within the confines of Greater New York in the course of three or four years." Cahan's terms emphasize the magical transformation of Jews, the quintessential wanderers, into developers of land and neighborhoods. Such details reinforce Cahan's theme that America is "different" for the Jew. No other nation is more hospitable to his material genius; no other nation is more threatening to that other critical element of Jewish character – his spirituality and intellect.

"I was worth over a million, and my profits had reached enormous dimensions," David Levinsky confesses near the novel's end. "I had no creed. I knew of no ideals." Levinsky decides that he needs a wife and family. So he falls in love with the daughter of a poet, who complains to Levinsky about America's materialism and spiritual impoverishment. As it turns out, Levinsky is too assimilated for the poet's daughter, who rejects his overtures. The final book,

"Episodes of a Lonely Life," sets the hero's great fortunes against his shrunken heart and soul. The novel closes on Levinsky's paralyzing nostalgia for himself as a penniless schoolboy poring over the Talmud. Professional success and private happiness are mutually exclusive. Yet Cahan also suggests, more deeply, that there is something fundamentally isolating, religiously as well as humanly, about immigration and Americanization. Levinsky has worked himself through his material triumphs into a tragic condition he can recognize but not change. He has become by the novel's end the one commodity which he cannot sell. "In business I am said to know how to show my goods to their best advantage. Unfortunately, this instinct seems to desert me in private life. There I am apt to put my least attractive wares in the show-window." The reason for this is Levinsky's deep cultural prejudice against business and consequent devaluation of his accomplishments. Levinsky has satisfactions: the intellectual pleasure he takes in mapping the growth of American commerce and the role of fellow Jews in this expansion. He enjoys the material comforts afforded by his success. But he would readily change places with the Jewish scholar, sculptor, or musician. Cahan leaves his clothing manufacturer lonely and insecure because he believes in a higher social office for his people. In contrast to Dreiser and Norris, he cannot see the poetry in a coat or grain of wheat. The problem for Cahan lies not in the particular organization of the social economy, but in the social preoccupation with material things. What distinguishes Frank Norris's *The Octopus* (1901) from these other treatments, respectively, of the textile (Phelps), paint (Howells), and clothing (Cahan) industries, is his profound aesthetic respect for the manufacture of wheat. This is perhaps why his novel provides the era's most idealistic portrait of a manufacturing industry.

The Octopus, like *The Silent Partner*, drew inspiration from an historical incident, the Mussel Slough Massacre, and sought to expose a moral wrong identified with a specific industry, the Railroad Trust. Norris's approach to his subject recalled Phelps's: he was not interested in representing the event in historically precise terms, but in building on its dramatic potential. In May of 1880 in the Mussel Slough district of California, federal deputies representing the railroads killed five ranchers participating in a mass demonstration against impending eviction from their lands. The Southern Pacific Railroad had invited ranchers to develop the land and promised to sell it to them subsequently at a nominal cost. When the railroad priced the land years later, however, they included its *new* rather than *original* value, essentially asking the ranchers to pay for their own improvements. The incident had already inspired one novel, *The Feud of Oakfield Creek* (1887) by the philosopher Josiah Royce, a native Californian. Norris did research at the Mechanics Institute Library in the San Joaquin

Valley, and interviewed railroad magnate, Collis P. Huntington. He also spent a summer at the Santa Anita Rancho near Hollister, California, witnessing the process of modern wheat production, with one of the first combined harvesters and threshers.

It is important to recognize that the heroes of Norris's novel are capitalist ranchers with large investments in land and farming equipment, competing with the railroads for the great wealth afforded by wheat production. They have no particular love of the land; their purpose is to exploit its bounty. They respond to their loss of a critical decision of the railroad commission by resolving to "buy" their own commissioner. The complexity of this portrait befits Norris, who was a member of the Anglo-Saxon elite: his mother, a descendant of old New England and Virginia families, his father, a wealthy self-made businessman. When he covered a mining strike in Pennsylvania ("Life in the Mining Regions," *Everybody's Magazine*, 1902), for example, his perspective was not particularly pro-labor. But his father disinherited Norris when he divorced his mother in 1894, a circumstance that increased Norris's sympathies for the middle and working classes, and also made him more professionally ambitious in pursuit of the writing career his father opposed. Norris was heartened by the reception of *The Octopus*, a commercial as well as critical success. Doubleday advertised the novel well, and succeeded in selling all 33,000 copies of the first printing, while a high-profile reviewer promised that the book would "quicken the conscience and awaken the moral sensibilities." Norris's title image of the railroad as "octopus," the monstrous "colossus" swallowing up everything in its wake, became notorious as an example of "shrill, anti-corporate rhetoric." The novel's true demonic force, however, is neither technology nor the businessmen who benefit from its productive powers, but Nature itself, which is always capitalized in Norris's works.

The Octopus: a Story of California was the first novel in what Norris termed "The Trilogy of the Wheat," to be followed by *The Pit: a Story of Chicago* and *The Wolf: a Story of Europe*. *The Octopus* concerned wheat production, *The Pit*, wheat distribution, and *The Wolf*, wheat consumption. Before beginning *The Wolf*, Norris died of appendicitis, at the age of thirty-two. Norris's sprawling *Octopus* is framed by the story of a poet, Presley, who is ambitious to write the Song of the West but suffers from writer's block, which can only be overcome by a heartfelt identification with "the People." Finally stirred by the circumstances of the farmers, Presley produces a "socialistic" poem, "The Toilers," which is a huge success. The portrait of Presley paralleled the life of San Francisco poet, Edwin Markham, whose 1899 poem, "The Man with the Hoe," based on a Millet painting and published in the *Examiner*, was also life-altering. Presley becomes a celebrity: the people's champion against the Railroad Trust as well as an item on the high-society dinner circuit. This does not prevent Presley from openly and naïvely voicing his complaints about the railroad directly to Shelgrim, the head tycoon himself, who denies every principle of modern manufacture in declaring that railroads grow themselves just like wheat. Shelgrim surprises Presley with his sentimentality and devotion to art, which belie his imposing physique and personality. Indeed, the novel is full of intricately drawn eccentrics. There is the priest, Father Sarria, a latter-day St. Francis, who loves all creatures great and small, though he harbors a secret, shameful passion for cockfighting. There is the tragic shepherd Vanamee, who meets his beloved nightly under a row of trees, only to arrive one night to find her ravaged and comatose. Driven by grief to a nomad existence, a wandering Jew in the desert, it is never clear whether the mysterious ravisher was Vanamee himself, his desire unleashed and grown monstrous. And there is the rancher Annixter, a classic naturalist type: obsessed with his digestive tract, hyper-masculine, possessed of superhuman energy for all forms of intellection and physical work. He has a genius for farm management, but proves equally adept at law, once he decides to master it in order to challenge the railroad trust. Utterly disdainful of that half of humanity whom he labels "Feemales! Rot!" he becomes helplessly smitten with the lovely Hilma Tree, a milkmaid on his ranch. Yet it is Annixter who notes in a fit of disgust that the methods of the Western farmer are self-destructive in the extreme, ruining the land by never alternating crops, then bemoaning the hard times arising from the exhaustion of the soil.

The novel's central mythology is the law of Nature, the Great Force, bound to defeat the most carefully conceived human efforts: "Men were naught, death was naught, life was naught; FORCE only existed – FORCE that brought men into the world, FORCE that crowded them out of it to make way for the succeeding generation, FORCE that made the wheat grow, FORCE that garnered it from the soil to give place to the succeeding crop." This is seconded by the mythology of the California wheat growers as Nature's select beneficiaries, the suppliers of the world. Both myths are directly qualified by the novel's representation of the global status of wheat production. Norris highlights the ticker telegraph in every ranch office that connects each by wire to San Francisco, and through it to Minneapolis, Duluth, Chicago, New York, and on to Liverpool, with news on worldwide stores of wheat, the latest prices, the weather in the remotest wheat-producing areas. The telegraph confirms the ranchers' interdependence, their status as "a unit in the vast agglomeration of wheat land the whole world round, feeling the effects of causes thousands of miles distant – a drought on the prairies of Dakota, a rain on the plains of India, a frost on the Russian steppes, a hot wind on the llanos of the

Argentine." While this passage extends the myth by highlighting the hand of Nature in every region of wheat, it also undermines the monolithic wheat-producing power of the California ranchers. In keeping with this, the narrative foregrounds the various factors – local, national, international – that regularly reduce the price of wheat. These include the extension of wheat areas and competition far beyond the needs of the world population and the draining of the manufacturers' profits by intermediaries – banks, warehouses, merchants, buyers, and above all, the railroad.

The watchword of the nineteenth-century economy was production; the watchword of the twentieth is consumption. This is the main argument of the novel's leading manufacturer Cedarquist, who recognizes the necessity of creating markets. His vision spurs the ranchers to new dreams, "set free of the grip of Trust and ring and monopoly acting for themselves, selling their own wheat, organising into one gigantic trust, themselves, sending their agents to all the entry ports of China." The novel's economy is a tautology of trusts: the rancher's prospective liberation from the railroad trust enables the wheat trust. But of course there was to be no wheat trust. As business historians have pointed out, only certain kinds of industries lent themselves to trusts: those that featured economies of scale (steel, oil, automobiles) and those that featured economies of scope (pharmaceuticals, trademarked snack foods). Products in technologically advanced industries able to link mass production to mass distribution had the best chance of surviving in cartel form. National Biscuit became a successful American trust at the turn of the century; National Wheat did not. A certain degree of artificiality was required to make it as a trust.

In this light, it seems especially appropriate that the novel's dramatic ending features what might be called the Revenge of the Wheat through its live burial of the Jewish railroad agent, S. Behrman. Behrman dies from curiosity, peering into a wheat chute that sucks him down to a death by suffocation in wheat. Behrman is the ultimate Jewish middleman, the capitalist jack-of-all trades to be pitied, according to Abraham Cahan. As the front of the railroad's power, he is the ranchers' nemesis. The ultimate man of business, he is an indisputable affront to Nature. As a mediator among artificial things, he is appropriately, punitively repaid in the end by productive force. Norris gives the last word to Nature's productive abundance. But there is a profound awareness in this triumphant climax that this was indeed the last word.

CAPITALISTS

No American Realist writer was more drawn to the world of business than Samuel Clemens (1835–1910), who trademarked his own literary merchandise with the self-made pseudonym "Mark Twain" (a command for measuring the depth of a river) in 1863. Twain was the son of John Marshall Clemens, a struggling lawyer and judge who failed at every business proposition he pursued, and Jane Lampton Clemens, who was widowed young. John Clemens left his family little except for seventy thousand acres of Tennessee land upon which everyone but Twain pinned their hopes long after they had been invalidated. Twain, twelve when his father died, was raised in a Mississippi river town, Hannibal, Missouri. His life was bounded by a cosmic event, Haley's Comet (which appeared the year of his birth and death), and his maturation and success coincided with the astonishing economic and technological expansion of the country. He seemed to have had his hand in every significant economic venture of the era. Fascinated by new technologies, he often speculated: the Paige Typesetter was the most notorious of these investments, which included a domestic still for desalinating water and a new steam generator for tugboats. He also undertook the risky option of a partnership in a publishing company, which produced at its height bestsellers like Grant's *Memoirs*, but proved in the long run a financial misstep.

Twain's most significant connection to the business world was his close friendship with Henry H. Rogers, a chief director of the Standard Oil Trust, who in the 1890s guided Twain from bankruptcy back to considerable wealth, which he enjoyed until his death (Figure 21).

Rogers was a great admirer of Twain's writings, and learned of his financial troubles from mutual acquaintances. He described himself as "Capitalist" in his *Who's Who* entry, and once told a governmental commission investigating Standard Oil that "we are not in business for our health but are out for the dollars," but he made a point of patronizing the arts. Rogers took control of all Twain's business investments, and they became so close that Twain would spend the day in Rogers's Standard Oil Building office reading and smoking while Rogers conducted business. Twain also became intimate with Andrew Carnegie, who sent him cases of his special Scotch, and they referred to each other as "Saint Mark" and "Saint Andrew." Twain lived on Fifth Avenue and spent summers at Tuxedo Park (an elite estate in Westchester County), vacationing in Palm Beach and Bermuda, with the likes of Carnegie and Rogers. In 1908, Twain made a speech at the Aldine Club before fifty magazine publishers in support of the Rockefellers. This was less Twain's betrayal of an earlier democratic impulse than his embrace of plutocratic leanings he had always had. As he observed in a letter to his pastor, the Reverend Joseph Twichell, "Money-lust has always existed, but not in the history of the world was it ever a craze, a madness, until your time and mine." Twain counted himself among the mad, but his paradoxical genius enabled him to recognize it as a moral and political failing. It was this guilt towards his own capitalist

FIGURE 21. Photograph of Mark Twain and Henry Rodgers
sailing together in Bermuda (1907).

ambitions, his resistance to a world of business he was helplessly attracted to
and saw first-hand at its highest reaches, that makes him such an invaluable
witness to his era.

Mark Twain once characterized Theodore Roosevelt as "the Tom Sawyer
of the political world of the twentieth century," implying that the president
was both immature and a "show-off." But the label also highlighted a certain Yankee ingenuity. Twain was working on *The Adventures of Tom Sawyer*
(1876) around the same time as *The Gilded Age* (1873, coauthored by Charles
Dudley Warner), and the novels share an interest in inheritances, stockholding, and speculation. Twain later called *Tom Sawyer* "a hymn" to boyhood, but
he initially assumed that it would be read by those for whom it was written,
adults. Many of its paradigmatic scenes and details concern capital and its

manipulation. Exchange makes the devout world of St. Petersburg go round, seeming to drive every social interaction. But Tom is the ultimate master, managing to one-up everyone, from Aunt Polly, who invariably fails to deliver his deserved punishment, to the friends he succeeds in keeping on Jackson's Island. Tom manages to remain sweet while stealing sugar, to appear genuine while showing off, to commandeer all the tickets for the Sunday-School prize Bible though he is unfamiliar with the good book and could not care less. The one boy who challenges Tom's speculative supremacy is the "juvenile pariah of the village," Huckleberry Finn, who falls outside the town's reigning economy. Son of the town drunkard, lawless, idle, and unwashed, Huckleberry Finn arouses the envy of other boys for his ostensible "free will." Huck, who gets the better of Tom in all their trades, would never capitulate to Tom's ultimate business scheme: the redefinition of fence-painting from a chore to a privileged activity. Forced by Aunt Polly to whitewash her fence, Tom manages to make the task look so inviting that boys pay dearly for a chance. By the end of the day, Tom has succeeded in remaking himself as well, from a "poverty-stricken boy in the morning" to one "rolling in wealth," a transformation that antici-pates the novel's ending. If Tom had not run out of paint, Twain observes, "he would have bankrupted every boy in the village." Tom has educated himself in a fundamental principle of value: that value is determined by the sacrifice required to attain it. The more people are made to pay for something, the more they will covet it. It is no surprise to find Tom with a "prodigious income" at the novel's end, his fortune invested at six per cent interest. But it is a sign of Twain's idealism about money matters at this point in his career that the outsider Huck Finn is in the identical financial condition.

Though speculation and fortune-building is an activity perfected by chil-dren in *The Adventures of Tom Sawyer*, there is nothing innocent about it. This is even more dramatically true of *The Gilded Age*, which is entirely populated by adults, and set principally in the corrupt world of Washington politics. Subtitled, "A Tale of To-Day," *The Gilded Age* succeeded in coining a phrase that would come to stand for the post-Civil War era in general. Significantly, it was the first and last novel Twain would set in the historical present. Writing about the greed and profiteering that he believed typified it could only make him want to escape to other times, as he did in all his subsequent works. In his "Revised Catechism" (*New York Tribune*, 1871), Twain wrote bitterly, "What is the chief end of man? – to get rich. In what way? – dishonestly if we can; honestly if we must. Who is God, the one only true? Money is God." The bitterness extends to *The Gilded Age*, which expresses much of Twain's despair about the effects of unfettered capitalist development. The novel represents the collaboration of two Connecticut neighbors disgusted by the state of culture, reeling over the Beecher–Tilton trial (for adultery between the famed minister Henry Ward Beecher and Mrs. Theodore Tilton, the wife of an upstanding congregant), and convinced that American democracy would most likely be a failed experiment.

Warner, a newspaper editor, had never written a novel and Twain's previous experience was "Roughing It." Twain had his own family's obsession with their father's Tennessee land to build on, while Warner could draw on his time as a railroad surveyor in Missouri and a businessman in Philadelphia. Twain was responsible for the novel's satirical centerpiece, the Hawkins's speculations on their Tennessee land, and for the sequences on Washington politics. Warner wrote the love story set in Philadelphia, and also covered parts on the Missouri railroad surveyors. They wrote the sections on Laura Hawkins's career as a political lobbyist and her trial for murder together. Twain and Warner found much to exploit in the contemporary scene: the Beecher affair, the Credit Mobilier scandal (charges of stealing from the US Treasury against the Credit Mobilier company, an offshoot of the Union Pacific Railroad, with several US Congressman implicated in the corruption), and a Senate vote-buying prosecution involving a Senator Samuel C. Pomeroy (the novel's Senator Dillworthy). "I think I can say, and say with pride, that we have some legislatures that bring higher prices than any in the world," Twain observed caustically in one of his speeches. It was the point of this biting satire to present recognizable situations and personages. While the novel had a promising geographical design, sending one set of characters East in search of wealth, and the other West to pursue love and resolve questions of parentage, a surplus of personalities and plots continually threatened to overwhelm it. Indeed, it was typical of Twain that in his major indictment of his era's capitalist ethos the novel's charming speculator Colonel Beriah Sellers is the primary source of imaginative integrity. This was because of continual slippage between Twain's moral outrage against capitalism and his admiration for its harnessing of human energies and passions, including his own. Reading audiences repaid Twain's ambivalence in kind, with sales reaching 35,000 copies in the first two months, and then falling to almost nothing. Twain blamed the Panic of 1873, but he might have factored in his own deeply divided perspective.

Twain's writings are filled with animals, carrying significant moral and political weight. His novels and stories abound in pigs, frogs, dogs, coyotes, cats, horses and cows; whether dead or alive, they make heavy demands on the consciences of Twain's human characters. As this suggests, Twain was a firm believer in the law of nature. His works generally minimized free will; human beings were fallen creatures fulfilling the dictates of their nature in a degraded world. By providing the basic elements of what might be called a Darwinian aesthetic, Twain's writing offers an appropriate introduction to contemporary literary Realist accounts of the worlds of business and economy. Theodore Dreiser and Frank Norris also fulfill this generic principle by finding their inspiration and voice in the natural brutality of society. In contrast, a novel like *The Rise of David Levinsky* undermines its protagonist's commercial values by favoring religious and cultural ideals. In Phelps's *The Silent Partner* or Howells's *The Rise of Silas Lapham* ethical considerations counter the cruel rhythms of urban industries. Dreiser's novels are noteworthy for their indifference to these qualifications.

Dreiser was unparalleled as a chronicler of the business world because of his almost innocent admiration for successful capitalists. In contrast to Gustavus Myers, whose critical investigations into *The History of the Great American Fortunes* (1907–10) he read in preparing his own portrait, Dreiser was dazzled by "the great financiers." Myers stressed the ruthlessness and dishonesty of men like John D. Rockefeller, J. P. Morgan, and Collis P. Huntington, the combined result of character, harsh childhoods, and opportunity. Dreiser carefully eliminated traits Myers presented as exemplary, in particular a puritanical austerity. Despite his first-hand experiences of deprivation in a cruel American economy and the developing political radicalism that would ultimately flower into socialism, Dreiser understood these figures as true artists. The individual who was made for finance, for whom speculation was a passion, was as free of moral constraints as the poet or painter. Dreiser's Frank Algernon Cowperwood has a persistent and powerful sensuality that is reflected in his inherent good taste and attraction to women. The son of a bank teller, possessed of a native, steely aptitude for speculation and accumulation, he knows exactly what to do with a windfall from an uncle, depositing it, working it as collateral credit, enhancing its uses ten times beyond its actual worth. He even thinks of his own "self-duplication," having children that is, as "acquisitive." Cowperwood's moral immunity also derives from his condition as an embodiment of natural law, a "Superman" or *übermensch*. In an interview following the publication of *The Financier* (1912), when asked whether his protagonist had the ethical right to behave as he did, Dreiser replied that there was "in Nature no such thing as the right to do or the right not to do . . . I am convinced that so-called vice and crime and destruction and so-called evil are as fully a part of the universal creative process as the so-called virtues, and do as much good."

Dreiser's ethically neutral portrayal of a capitalist nevertheless exposed one of the most significant results of the American Civil War: an event that *unmade* so many proved the *making* of many others. The first American war to produce casualties in mass numbers was also the first to yield vast fortunes. The war affords Dreiser's protagonist a major opportunity, the handling of a state loan, resulting in a substantial profit and the growth of his reputation. But the Great Chicago Fire of 1871 induces a panic in the stock market. Cowperwood, whose speculations have been typically bold, is the fall guy, in part because he is having an adulterous affair with Aileen Butler, the daughter of a powerful boss. True to form, Cowperwood effortlessly masters the Quaker regime (emphasizing silence, solitude, self-scrutiny) of the prison where he is sent. Released just in time for the Panic of 1873, Cowperwood exploits its effects, and manages to regain his fortune just before the novel's close. *The Financier* is the first of a trilogy loosely based on the life of businessman Charles Yerkes, including *The Titan* (1914), which follows Cowperwood's re-emergence in Chicago and building of the street railway system there, and *The Stoic* (1947) which Dreiser left unfinished when he died in 1945. *The Financier* focuses on the post-Civil War expansion of the American economy, though Cowperwood's first adult economic undertakings coincide with the Civil War.

Throughout the novel, Dreiser emphasizes Cowperwood's auspicious compatibility with the principles of opportunism and risk that dominate the economy of his time. Cowperwood's first business venture at the age of thirteen corresponds exactly to John D. Rockefeller's, whose deductions from his own (quoted in Tarbell, *History of Standard Oil*, 1904) might have been Cowperwood's: "The impression was gaining ground with me that it was a good thing to let the money be my slave and not make myself a slave to money." Characteristically alert, Cowperwood happens by a wholesale auction and arranges on an intuition to buy seven cases of Castille soap, which he then sells at a thirty-dollar net gain for himself to his local grocer. Cowperwood lives up to his middle name, "*Alger*non" (in honor of Horatio Alger), in this demonstration of talent – a special knack for recognizing the main chance – determination, and ambition. Even more significant is the way the transaction anticipates a fundamental mechanism of the post-Civil War economy that Cowperwood will come to manipulate expertly, the futures contract. The futures contract allowed a product to be bought and sold before delivery, an advantage to the seller by insuring against a drop in prices and an advantage to the buyer by ensuring against a rise, while enabling both to distribute their sales and purchases over the course of a year. Its most significant effect was the creation of a new category of businessman, the speculator who stood between the producer and the buyer, never possessing or even desiring the commodity but enriching himself by way of it. In the soap exchange, Dreiser depicts young Frank enacting in small a method that was, according to business historian Alfred Chandler, devised in the 1850s and 1860s and institutionalized by 1870. His father's response to the soap episode: "are you going to become a financier already?" seems more affirmative than quizzical. By managing to get the best of a specialized niche in the new commerce, Cowperwood proves himself the young man for his age.

There is no moment in all of his writings that better captures Dreiser's sense of that age than the description of an even younger Frank Cowperwood contemplating a tank at the local fish store.

One day he saw a squid and a lobster put in the tank, and in connection with them was witness to a tragedy which stayed with him all his life and cleared things up considerably intellectually. The lobster, it appeared from the talk of the idle bystanders, was offered no food, as the squid was considered his rightful prey. He lay at the bottom of the clear glass tank on the yellow sand, apparently seeing nothing – you could not tell in which way his beady, black buttons of eyes were looking – but apparently they were never off the body of the squid. The latter, pale and waxy in texture, looking very much like pork fat or jade, moved about in torpedo fashion; but his movements were apparently never out of the eyes of his enemy, for by degrees small portions of his body began to disappear, snapped off by the relentless claws of his pursuer. The lobster would leap like a catapult to where the squid was apparently idly dreaming, and the squid, very alert, would dart away, shooting out at the same time a cloud of ink, behind which it would disappear . . . The incident made a great impression on him. It answered in a rough way that riddle which had been annoying him so much in the past: "How is life organized?" Things lived on each other – that was it.

The scene foregrounds the survival of the fittest philosophy, and the analogy between the animal and human order that is a staple of Dreiser's fiction. In formulating it, Dreiser probably drew on an early essay for *Popular Magazine* entitled "A Lesson from the Aquarium" (1906). *The Financier* is full of such lessons from the aquarium. Indeed they provide, between this account of lobster and squid, and the closing depiction of the powerfully deceptive "Black Grouper," a pair of naturalist bookends introducing and concluding the ruthless but still magnificent career of his financier. The young Cowperwood comes to the fish store daily, as if hypnotically drawn there to behold the stark drama of predation, lobster feeding on squid, squishy limb by squishy limb, gradually devouring the trapped and helpless victim. Significantly, the boy *feels* nothing, gazing coldly on a process that he perceives as the answer to a question that has puzzled him. Dreiser suggests that Cowperwood's sense of purpose, his ethical, political, psychological system, is formed by this spectacle. But there is a deeper allegory here, beyond the ken of the budding financier, in the "idly dreaming" squid releasing his protective scribe-like ink clouds. While the squid cannot prevent his inevitable demise, he manages to dream nevertheless, and to prolong his life by darting and shooting. The drama is tragic, which reinforces its undeniable artistry. Despite his admiration for his lobster-identified financier, Dreiser's sympathies are with the ink-laden squid, whose triumph is that there is any drama at all. Herein lies Dreiser's aesthetic purpose, which derives from a conviction of the brutal organization of life, and his persistence in pondering and reflecting upon it.

The Titan is an extended examination of the life of Frank Cowperwood following his relocation, with his new wife Aileen Butler, to Chicago, where he invests in the urban streetcar system. The novel is less character-driven than *The Financier*, and has a more documentary focus. This is especially evident in the detailed portrait of Cowperwood's efforts to win a franchise for his streetcars, against claims for municipal control over systems like transportation and gas so critical to the fate of the community at large. *The Titan's* powerful sense of place is also evident in its presentation of local and national politics. The novel offers a rich account, for instance, of William Jennings Bryan's campaign to establish legal parity between the value of gold and silver, in order to ensure an ample money supply, beyond the control of central banks and the Titans who ran them. Cowperwood's gift of a telescope to the University of Chicago (which recalls his star-gazing at the penitentiary) is a blatant attempt to establish his credentials as a public benefactor, to facilitate loans from reluctant Chicago banks. There are also the Irish ward bosses, Kerrigan and Tiernan, whose resistance to Cowperwood's political control of areas necessary to his expanding rails proves critical. Yet *The Titan* is a rather predictable sequel in lacking the integrity and force of its predecessor. The problem here is not as some critics have suggested, that finance is inherently abstract, lacking the reality and substance of paint or wheat, and thus incapable of keeping readers interested over two long novels. For Dreiser makes speculation into the most vital social and aesthetic activity. Nor does Dreiser give more play in this novel to historical events because his financier absorbs him less. Cowperwood is an equally compelling figure, though split by multiple love interests, which contrasts with the intense polarization of wife and mistress in *The Financier*. Indeed, he remains a credible lover despite the increasing disparity between his age and that of the youthful women who attract him.

The major drawback with the novel is that Dreiser is confined to Cowperwood amassing his great fortune (worth twenty million dollars by the time he leaves Chicago for Europe) and aging; his life in this novel enables little in the way of true dramatic action. Cowperwood's experience as Titan is about accumulation: of money, houses, women, and masterpieces. But his relationship to all of these things is fundamentally dull, because Dreiser has made the case for his suitability to finance so well. Cowperwood lives and breathes speculation, divesting, investing, and dispensing with money and the objects it buys. Speculating in romance is no substitute, since women cannot be administered in the same emotionless exacting way as currency. He has little passion for the consumptive materialism afforded by his wealth. The one time in his life when Cowperwood appears relatively content being still is his time in prison, but there, significantly, he possesses nothing, and derives pleasure from looking inward and upward at the stars. At the end of *The Titan*, Cowperwood has lost the agility of his speculating days, and assumed the stolidity of his own vast estate, a condition that is utterly at odds with the laws of his nature. His impending flight from Chicago to new foreign economic territory is for Dreiser an attempt to rekindle the animation and art of an earlier financier self. On this point, as with much else in Dreiser's free adaptation of the life of Charles Yerkes, fiction is kinder than fact. "After reducing the railway system of Chicago to chaos," Matthew Josephson reports, Yerkes "decamped forever to London."

What made Chicago a place that could transform a financier into a Titan, according to Dreiser, was the freedom of this "prairie metropolis" from the "unctuous respectability" of the urban East. It was a place where a man like Frank Cowperwood could begin anew without crossing the continent. A spacious, ever expanding gateway between East and West, every industry seemed to thrive in Chicago, from stockyards and railroads, to real estate, hotels, and hardware. After streetcars, whose "vast manipulative life" forms a principal attraction for Cowperwood, he is drawn to the Chicago stock exchange, specifically its dealings in wheat, corn, and other kinds of grain. The same wheat deals on the Chicago stock exchange also engage the energies of American literature's other great early twentieth-century financier, Curtis Jadwin of Frank Norris's *The Pit* (1903, serialized, *Saturday Evening Post*, 1902–03). Published posthumously, the novel's prepublication orders were so great that two more editions were printed before the day of publication, and first year's sales approached 95,000. The novel was not only widely and respectfully reviewed, but it gained unusual commercial notoriety, made into a play in 1904, a silent film in 1917, and a Parker Brothers card game based on the Chicago Board of Trade in 1919. *The Pit*, like *The Titan*, was part of a trilogy, but without a reappearing lead character. Norris's *Epic of the Wheat* was designed, he explained to William Dean Howells, "to keep the idea of this huge Niagara of wheat rolling from West to East."

As with *The Octopus*, Norris drew upon an actual historical event for his main plot, Joseph Leiter's cornering of the wheat market in 1897–98. Dubbed the "King of the Wheat," Leiter drove up the price of the grain, managing to dominate the Chicago Board of Trade for a full six months before capitulating to the bears, led by Philip Armour of the Meat Trust (the novel's Calvin Crookes). In addition to spending time in Chicago, observing activities at its Board of Trade, Norris was tutored in the intricacies of market speculation by a young broker who invented a game to help Norris grasp the fluctuations of a market run. Extending a wire from the radiator grate in the floor to a hook in the ceiling, he threaded a float through it, whose rise (from an influx of furnace heat) indicated a bull market, and fall indicated a bear.

Curtis Jadwin was modeled less on Joseph Leiter than on Norris's own father: his summers on Lake Geneva in Wisconsin; his Lake Michigan mansion close to those of Marshall Field, George M. Pullman, and Philip Armour; his rural childhood and self-made fortune; his sponsorship of a Sunday school for poor children; his marriage to a cultivated, histrionic woman who mystified him. In keeping with their proximity to Norris's parents, Curtis and Laura Jadwin are respected dramatis personae with few of the caricatured qualities of the characters in McTeague. Laura is passionate and beautiful; Jadwin is introduced in classic male terms by what he is capable of doing. A bachelor who has made his fortune in real estate, he occasionally takes part in wheat or corn "deals," consulted by other financiers who respect his shrewdness. The narrative is recounted from the perspective of Laura Jadwin, which seems designed to enlarge its prospective readership, since women constituted a significant portion of the novel-buying public and men might be appealed to on the grounds of subject alone. The novel's broad intent is also signaled by the foregrounding of predictable romantic situations, to accompany its detailed portrait of modern economic trends. Chicago appears grimy but impressive, containing all the rich cultural and commercial opportunities that money can buy.

But the main reason that Norris's vision of the business world is relayed through a woman's consciousness is his conviction that women enable it. Culture as well as religion, like the women who preside over it, has a pervasive influence in The Pit. The description of the Jadwins' wedding at an Episcopal church is reverential. "Not in the midst of all the pomp and ceremonial of the Easter service had the chancel and high altar disengaged a more compelling influence . . . The whole world was suddenly removed, while the great moment in the lives of the Man and the Woman began." Jadwin's unqualified pursuit of the market is enfolded in this virtuous bond. Women facilitate commercial activities precisely by their natural opposition to them. This is confirmed by an obvious detail, that Jadwin's bachelorhood requires a careful equilibration of business activity and spiritualized good works, exemplified by his sponsorship of a Sunday school for poor children. Jadwin's neglect of good works as a married man suggests that he is liberated by the cultural and spiritual activities of his "better half."

Norris's financier is never wholly ruthless; Jadwin is sharply distinguished from the character he anticipates, Dreiser's Cowperwood. Indeed, Jadwin is the farmers' champion, rehearsing their sufferings when a bear market drives down the price of wheat: loans heaped on farms already heavily papered, crops mortgaged in advance, no new farm implements, nor buggies, nor parlor organs. After Jadwin's bull market has driven up the price of wheat, he is visited by a deputation of wheat farmers bearing gifts and heralding the great wave of prosperity. As in *The Octopus*, Norris emphasizes the global inter-connectedness of economic events, and the lack of control in even the most resourceful human agents. The Pit's "centrifugal power" reverberates throughout the world. Norris invests that global system of commerce with the force of Nature. This is seconded by the conventional naturalization of the wheat pit with its rhetoric of bulls and bears, by consistent suggestions that the wheat demonstrates independent principles of growth, and by the characterization of the novel's financiers as "blooded to the game." Yet Nature also assumes a curious miniaturized form in the novel through a cat that lingers in the Pit after all the traders have gone.

The floor of the Board of Trade was deserted. Alone, on the edge of the abandoned Wheat Pit, in a spot where the sunlight fell warmest – an atom of life, lost in the immensity of the empty floor – the grey cat made her toilet, diligently licking the fur on the inside of her thigh, one leg, as if dislocated, thrust into the air above her head.

Her leg pointed straight upward, in mocking mimicry of the traders bidding gesture, this domesticated creature provides a kinder, gentler variation on a more powerful natural principle.

For Norris the categories of nature and artifice are interwoven: the most artificial things appear the most natural, and sometimes vice versa. This naturalizing appears in the novel as compensatory, designed to alleviate the anxiety generated by what Thorstein Veblen calls "a credit economy." The distinctive aspect of a credit economy is the primacy of the businessman, who no longer directs the production of real commodities but manipulates value by way of investments and markets, thus initiating an unending process of valuation and revaluation. Noting that post-Civil War America featured increasingly an economy dominated by credit and controlled by financiers, Veblen focused on the devastating cycles of prosperity and depression caused in part by specu-lators who in competing against each other sought to drive up paper values beyond real values. The credit economy that was especially dominant after the 1880s is one in which all value seems immaterial and unsettled. While *The Pit* registers admiration for the great financier, it ultimately shares Veblen's wariness about his impact. This is not in the name of the socialism Veblen endorsed. But Norris's decision to destroy his financier and his speculative impulse at the end of *The Pit*, returning him to a purer agrarian lifestyle, can be seen as a form of qualified populism.

Norris fears the state of affairs described by Henry Adams in his 1869 essay on "The New York Gold Conspiracy," where he complained about "a speculative mania . . . almost every man who had money at all employed a part of his capital in the purchase of stocks or of gold, of copper, of petroleum, or of domestic produce, in the hope of a rise in prices, or staked money on the expectation of a fall." Preoccupied with the consequences of speculative finance, Norris employs religion, culture, and femininity to counterbalance it. Norris's traditionalism did not express his belief that value was ever intrinsic necessarily, but rather his concern for the human effects of market economics. It is telling that the one novelist Curtis Jadwin admires is William Dean Howells, whose Silas Lapham elicits "all of his sympathy."

It is appropriate that Jadwin is drowned at the novel's end in a deluge of his own unmaking. Fortunately for him he is a financier, thus the wheat is only speculative and his ruin financial rather than ultimate. Moreover Jadwin is no scapegoat, like Berhman the Jew; a vast economic community shares his loss. And his domestic sanctuary is enriched, the clear beneficiary of his commercial ruin. The novel's close is suffused with tones of spiritual rebirth: the Jadwins' removal to the West, bankrupt, anticipating a new beginning built on stronger foundations. Their backward glance on "the Board of Trade building, black, monolithic, crouching on its foundations like a monstrous sphinx" is a glance on behalf of the nation as a whole. From Norris's nostalgic posthumous perspective, Americans were eager to put the speculative beast behind them. He did not live to realize that it had only just begun.

TITANS

By 1905, American big business was securely in place. It had triumphed in the post-Civil War years because it proved the most efficient method for organizing production and finance in a country which valued material progress above all things. This was Henry Adams's perception as he contemplated the great World's Fairs set successively in major Midwestern cities (Chicago, 1893; St. Louis, 1904): his nation had fully realized its ultimate faith in machines, materialism, and industrial capitalism. Henry Blake Fuller's The Cliff Dwellers (1893) and Henry James's The Golden Bowl (1904) encompass this critical period. While Fuller's novel employs the lens of his home town, Chicago, the city that captures the attention of so many literary chroniclers of business and finance, James's novel is set primarily in London, with occasional recollections of "American City," the anonymous (apparently Midwestern) home town of the novel's American business Titan, who returns there at the novel's end. These novels and the works of social analysis discussed in what follows, understand big business as an established social and economic fact. The corporate mind is less a focus of moral scrutiny, as it is in Norris and Howells, or a phenomenon to be explained in the order of nature, as it is in Dreiser. It is for Fuller and James, Thorstein Veblen, Ida Tarbell, and Andrew Carnegie, a consolidated and determining fixture of the culture. Theirs is a long view as these writers assess the place of American corporate culture in world history. They recognize that the sign of institutionalization is the presence of identifiable rituals, which they set out to catalog, each in different ways. How will these ritualized economic practices be understood years hence (Fuller, Veblen)? What are the parallels between primitive principles of gift exchange and prevailing principles of gift giving in a contemporary corporate culture, and what do they reveal about continuities between primitives and moderns (James)? Will the turn-of-the-century Titan be seen by future generations as benefactor or outlaw (Carnegie, Rockefeller, Tarbell, Lloyd)?

The Cliff Dwellers is a story of greed and social mobility featuring the Chicago elite who work at "the Clifton," the eighteen-story business building that serves as the novel's central gathering place. These latter day "cliff dwellers" (in Fuller's conceit) constitute a "tribe" distinguished by various rituals including occasional recourse to a "pipe of peace." These details confirm Fuller's perspective on the business sphere as essentially ethnographic. However large in life by their own and others' estimations, the cliff dwellers are as precariously situated as any previous human grouping, one among many social orders that has passed away over time. The result of Fuller's decision to represent the world of Chicago commerce in social-scientific terms is a largely satirical novel. George Ogden, the novel's hero, is a New Englander trying to make his way in more expansive commercial territory. This regional disparity ensures distance and explains his rather unique point of view. "In the public conveyances," he detects "a range of human types completely unknown to his past experience; yet it soon came to seem possible that all these different elements might be scheduled, classified, brought into a sort of *catalogue raisonné* which should give every feature its proper place – skulls, foreheads, gaits, odors, facial angles, ears." Forced by a rainstorm into the reading-room of the city's main public library, the reflective hero is surrounded by a "cataract of conflicting nationalities" that signals a universal brotherhood defined by a shared mortality. And indeed, as befits the novel's expansive focus, death is the ultimate referent of its narrative consciousness, always there to counter the avidity of its main actors. Ogden's plight is survival; over the course of the novel he loses every relation. In one critical scene he goes to arrange the funeral of his father with a friend who helps him to mediate between his own grief and the rapacity of the undertaker. Burying his wife and then his tiny daughter, Ogden discovers

that wealthy Chicagoans fight as aggressively for prime space in the cemetery as for real estate in the best neighborhoods. Ogden reflects accordingly
on epidemic rates of insanity and suicide, on how society's "fine-spun meshes
bind us and strangle us." It is a sign of just how enmeshed he is that Ogden's
means of retreat at the novel's end is marriage to the disaffected daughter of
the villainous bank president. The final pages offer a tragic ritualized image
of foundation sacrifice through a character whose need for lavish jewels has
required the debilitating fees charged by her architect husband. "It is for such
a woman that one man builds a Clifton and that a hundred others are martyred
in it." Aligning the habits of wealthy turn-of-the century Chicagoans with the
ritual practices of any number of extinct "tribes," Fuller predicts the imminent
demise of his "cliff dwellers."

  The Golden Bowl, considered by James and many critics to be his best work,
provides a more intricate ethnographic approach to turn-of-the century capitalism. The novel's central subject is exchange: both the exchange of men and
women across genealogical boundaries that is marriage, and the exchange of
commodities like the Golden Bowl itself. The novel is set primarily in London,
and features a young, handsome, Italian Prince, Amerigo, from a family which
has lost its wealth; an American man of enterprise, Adam Verver, who has
everything but Amerigo's celebrated ancestry; Maggie Verver, Adam's lovely
daughter, who has been given everything money can buy, including remarkable innocence; Charlotte Stant, beautiful and sophisticated, who has been
Maggie's admired older friend at boarding school. The novel's plot, which
begins with preparations for the marriage of the Prince and Maggie, is built
on a few simple details. Maggie's mother has died long ago, and she worries about leaving her father when she marries. Though their relationship is
hardly altered by her marriage, Maggie conceives a plan to marry her father
to Charlotte. Charlotte and the Prince have had a brief but intense love affair
that ended with their mutual recognition of its impossibility without wealth
on either side. The Ververs know nothing about this affair, nor do they sense
its lingering aftereffects, in part because they are preoccupied with their own
intense father–daughter bond, the novel's "open secret."

  Everything in James's novel – from princes, friends, husbands, fathers, and
daughters, to tiles, precious art, dinner invitations, sex, and love – is subject
to exchange. *The Golden Bowl* is preoccupied with the condition of the Anglo-
American empire, and with it the social and sexual form considered crucial to
its preservation – heterosexual marriage. Yet marriage, as figured in the bowl
itself, is slightly damaged, cracked. Vended by a mildly "sinister" Jew, who
keeps it ceremonially apart from the other bric-a-brac in his shop, the bowl
seems to bind the novel's social and racial plot (centered on the empire's perilous

condition and the social aliens who threaten it) with the novel's familial plot (centered on the curious arrangements – incestuous, adulterous – of the novel's principal foursome). The novel features not one but two Jewish merchants, each of whom presides over a critical moment of exchange: the unnamed antique dealer, and the tile merchant, Mr. Gutterman-Seuss, whose paternity, as father of "eleven little brown" -faced children all possessed of "impersonal old eyes astride of such impersonal old noses," contrasts menacingly with the one-child families of Adam Verver (Maggie) and Prince Amerigo (the Principino). Each exchange, the transfer of merchandise across race (Jewishness was for James a racial category), mirrors the concomitant "bride" exchanges, of Maggie and Charlotte, respectively. The economic prominence and formally pivotal roles of these stereotyped outsiders signals a potentially dangerous assimilation of alien forms and peoples. It also highlights the question of James's attitude towards Jews in general, as well as their particular symbolic relationship to the novel's pivotal action – adultery.

The novel's characters often contemplate ancient exchange rituals, as, for instance in the Prince's ruminations over his marriage and kinship ties in the opening chapters, and in descriptions of the Jewish merchants, "the touch of some mystic rite of old Jewry." Such contemplations tend to be spiritualized; many anticipate the category of "gift" in Marcel Mauss's "primitive" sense, from bride exchange to potlatch. Mauss's *The Gift* (1925) is a product of his post-World War I moment, and aims in part to draw conclusions of a moral nature "concerning certain problems posed by the crisis in our own law and economic organization." Chief among them is the troubling proximity of exchange and warfare. "Societies have progressed," Mauss writes, in so far as they

have succeeded in exchanging goods and persons . . . between tribes and nations, and, above all, between individuals. Only then did people learn how to create mutual interests, giving mutual satisfaction, and, in the end, to defend them without having to resort to arms . . . This is what tomorrow, in our so-called civilized world, classes and nations and individuals also, must learn.

Mauss shares Henry James's habit of invoking distinctions between primitive and modern systems in order to press implicit continuities. So while Mauss notes the contemporary tendency to regard the world of things as mute, inert, set in motion, made knowable only by persons and their words, he also registers a lingering modern faith in and fear of the independent vitality and power of things. When he reminds us that the first contracts were between human beings and gods or dead spirits, it is to confirm the residue of this contract in the modern world. When he recalls the derivation of charity as a moral notion of gift and fortune on the one hand and sacrifices on the other, he has modern charitable acts in mind. James in *The Golden Bowl* intuits what anthropologists have increasingly come to recognize, the commonalities between gift and commodity, between "the spirit of reciprocity" that rules the world of gift, and "the profit-oriented, calculating spirit" that rules the world of commodity.

Adam Verver in *The Golden Bowl* is the agent of that unification, a figure that stages the continuities between capitalist self-interest and primitive exchange. Adam Verver makes the ancient precept, "the rich man is rich so as to be able to give to the poor," his own. Giving is for him a way of keeping. A gift which is not matched by a counter-gift creates a lasting bond, restricting the debtor's freedom; one of the ways of "holding" someone is to keep up a lasting asymmetrical relationship of indebtedness. Verver's museum in American City has

all the sanctions of civilization . . . a house from whose open doors and windows, open to grateful, to thirsty millions, the higher, the highest knowledge would shine out to bless the land. In this house, designed as a gift, primarily, to the people of his adoptive city and native State . . . his spirit today almost altogether lived, making up, as he would have said, for lost time and haunting the portico in anticipation of the final rites.

Verver's power derives from his ability to give, a power that in turn allows for unlimited acquisition. The world appears to him as a sea of things to be appropriated, especially those most beloved. Thus his daughter recalls, some "slim draped 'antique' of Vatican or Capitoline halls, late and refined, rare as a note." And Verver regards his new grandson, the Principino, "in the way of precious small pieces he had handled." While there is no record of James having an intimacy on the order of Mark Twain's with American business Titans, his brother William, who was deeply impressed by John D. Rockefeller, treated him to detailed descriptions. William's letter to Henry of January 1904 may resonate in the portrait of Adam Verver. "A man 10 stories deep, and to me quite unfathomable . . . flexible, cunning, quakerish, superficially suggestive of naught but goodness and conscientiousness, yet accused of being the greatest villain in business whom our country has produced."

By marrying Maggie Verver to Prince Amerigo and Adam Verver to Charlotte Stant, as James does in Book I, "The Prince," he makes gift-giving, the sharing of one's fortune with "the poor," the basis of marriage, and identifies marriage as the most typical method of exchange. Marriage is also linked irrevocably to social aliens, who play critical roles in the novel's major transactions. The memorable, bilingual Jew (who eavesdrops on the Italian conversation of Charlotte and Amerigo) subsequently sells the bowl to Maggie for her father's birthday present. As an Italian speaker the dealer is aligned with the Prince (who also shares a native shrewdness in detecting the bowl's defect). They are aligned as well through their respective "conversions" in the book's second half. The Prince rededicates himself to marriage, the dealer decides to inform Maggie of the bowl's crack, acting "on a scruple rare enough in vendors of any class, and almost unprecedented in the thrifty children of Israel." This slur on the bowl dealer is consistent with the representation of the tile vender. The stereotypes of *The Golden Bowl* argue for the shifting kaleidoscope of Jewish identity in James's time: the standing of Jews in England and America as an ancient group that was also extraordinarily amenable to capital and modernity.

This striking duality in Jewish identity is captured by a contemporaneous advertisement for Sapolio soap (see figure 9 in chapter 6 above). The ad employs Hebrew script to promote the ritual purity – certified "Kosher" properties – of Sapolio soap, whose benefits as an agent of health and cleanliness are supported by its appeal to this highly traditional people. Moreover, by invoking Jews as the spur to a sale, the ad draws implicitly on a presumed Jewish facility for commerce. Henry James and E. Morgan's Sons (the manufacturers of Sapolio) together build on a presumed Jewish knack for survival and adaptation: the culture has endured since ancient times, yet is readily identified with modern economic exchange.

James's portrayal of Jews then, is hardly innocent. Indeed, what Jews seem to stand for, above all, in his novel, is a threatening modernity, which is understood as both inevitable and problematic. In this way, their position vis-à-vis society is exactly analogous to James's understanding of adultery in marriage. The plot of *The Golden Bowl* yields the following postulate: Jews are to society (Anglo-Saxons) as adultery is to marriage – transgressive, distasteful, yet necessary. By implying that the Prince's infidelity has enabled the preservation of his marriage to the Princess, by portraying complex Jewish aliens as essential participants in the exchange rites necessary to marriage, James lent his support to anthropological theories emphasizing continuities between primitives and moderns.

Such assumptions were basic to the thought of Thorstein Veblen, a contemporary of James's who shared his distaste for great American businessmen with a tendency to become profoundly absorbed by them. Veblen wrote his searing critique of the captains of industry while ensconced as a professor at the University of Chicago, the direct heir of John D. Rockefeller's philanthropy. It was a sign of Veblen's own iconoclastic refusal to be bought that he denounced the university's president, William Rainey Harper, as "a captain of erudition," the intelligentsia's variation on the robber baron. Identified by *Fortune Magazine* as "America's most brilliant and influential critic of modern business and the values of a business civilization," Veblen's originality derived from his sophisticated understanding of the range and intricacy of turn-of-the century incorporation combined with the perspective of a cultural outsider. The brilliant son of Norwegian farmers assumed a mantle previously held primarily by Brahmins like Henry Adams and Henry James. Veblen's most renowned contribution to social theory was *The Theory of the Leisure Class* (1899), in which he single-handedly invented a new class, detailing its attributes, its relationship to other classes, and its impact on society as a whole. The leisure class was defined by its exemption from industrial toil and its pos-session of a wealth sufficient to its lavish exhibition. What made "prestige behavior" so significant socially was the way it served as the glue uniting upper-class hierarchies everywhere, facilitating the seemingly effortless coor-dination of interests ranging from intra-elite marriages to executive corporate decisions.

Born in 1857 in rural Wisconsin to an artisan farmer, Veblen was one of twelve children. Both parents were devoted populists and well educated, teach-ing their precocious son Greek, Latin, and German. Because Norwegian was spoken at home and English was a late acquisition for Veblen, he mumbled well into adulthood. This did not stop him from excelling at Carleton College in Minnesota, where he was sent at seventeen, encountering there one of the great economists of the era, John Bates Clark. Following graduate work at Johns Hopkins and Yale (where he earned a PhD in philosophy), Veblen failed to get an academic job because of his atheism. Returning to the farm, he read extensively in socialism and found inspiration in Edward Bellamy's utopian nationalism. During this period, Veblen was a regular reviewer for the *Journal of Political Economy*, specializing in books on socialism. In 1891, Veblen received his first academic appointment in the University of Chicago Economics Depart-ment. Fired at Chicago, he was hired by Stanford but was soon fired there as well. Veblen's dismissals were attributed to his affairs with female students, but were also undoubtedly related to his unorthodox views. Veblen's disen-chantment with the early twentieth-century academy was expressed in *The Higher Learning: A Memorandum on the Conduct of Universities by Business* (1918), whose original subtitle, "A Study in Total Depravity," conveys much about its primary claims. At the University of Missouri, Veblen was more produc-tive, if not more successful institutionally, and managed to write a number of books while on the faculty there, including *The Instinct of Workmanship* (1914), *Imperial Germany* (1915), and *The Nature of Peace* (1917). During World War I, Veblen worked at the Food Administration, and got a job at the New School for Social Research in New York after the war. Later returning to Stanford, he lived in a shack in the woods near the campus. He died in 1929.

The Theory of the Leisure Class is properly understood as ethnography on his own society. Here he transformed various social standards – "pecuniary emulation"; "conspicuous leisure and consumption"; "the belief in luck" – into objects of ritual analysis. Veblen's method was evolutionary, tracing the development of the human species from the period of savagery, the longest and most peaceful in human history, where the dominant concern was group survival and the foremost value workmanship. The creation of tools facilitated the production of surpluses and wealth, which in turn led to class distinctions and exploitation. A predatory hunter-warrior class gave way to a feudal elite, the precursors to the owners and managers of modern industry. Modern industrial society emphasized consumption as the ultimate indicator of class status. Veblen was the first to recognize how the obligation to consume urged upon the citizens of a modern capitalist society actually intensified class distinctions and conflicts. While other economists believed that increased access to consumer goods would minimize class-consciousness, Veblen believed that it would become the major avenue for expressing it. He hoped that such invidious distinctions would lead to the overthrow of the class system and its eventual replacement by socialism. Veblen seized on evidence of counter-movements, the value of innovation in industry, the overall importance of machines and scientific culture, the challenges of the New Woman movement, to prophecy the end of leisure-class mores. Yet his thorough account of how ably consumer society generated states of false consciousness belied such hopes. Moreover, it is important to recognize that the leisure class described by Veblen was only part of an upper class, whose most elite and powerful element cultivated *inconspicuousness*. The higher and more secure the social status of a group or individual, the more subtle and reserved they could be.

Upward social mobility usually involved being noticed. This was the cardinal principle of one of the era's most notorious Titans, Andrew Carnegie, who elevated a personal craving for attention (understandable for a man who stood five feet, three inches full grown, four inches below the then national average) into a creed. Carnegie understood attention in its various meanings. He emphasized the importance of keeping the attention focused, of being devoted single-mindedly to a particular business endeavor. The maxim with which he became identified was "Put all your eggs in one basket, and then watch that basket." He also had in mind the classic Horatio Alger sense of attracting the attention of benevolent superiors eager to discover a resource in their office boy or janitor. "The rising man must do something exceptional," Carnegie wrote in *The Empire of Business* (1902), "HE MUST ATTRACT ATTENTION," teaching his employer "that he has not a mere hireling in his service . . . but one who devotes his spare hours and constant thoughts to the business."

This was the method perfected by Carnegie on his road to wealth: stamping his image in the minds of employers like his crucial mentor, Thomas A. Scott, who hired Carnegie as office manager of the western division of the Pennsylvania Railroad and took him under his wing. Referred to in the company as "Mr. Scott's Andy," Carnegie, who was only seventeen when they met, worshipped Scott, and received critical aid from him, including money for his first significant business investment. Some considered Carnegie's subsequent treatment of Scott indicative of his tenacity, even ruthlessness as a businessman. During the Panic of 1873, while he was Senior Vice-President of the Pennsylvania Railroad, Scott solicited Carnegie, who had expanded his steel business considerably due to the Panic and had previously aided Scott, for another loan. Carnegie staunchly refused, despite agonized pleas from both Scott and his supporters.

Born in 1835, in a Scottish village, Carnegie was the eldest child of a skilled weaver, a Chartist, whose craft was tragically displaced by the advent of steam-powered weaving mills. Emigrating to America in 1848, the family settled in a Pennsylvania industrial town bordering Pittsburgh. The bleak environment of Allegheny-Pittsburgh was nicknamed "slabtown" by inhabitants, but Carnegie took to it with zeal, determined to make good. His first job at the age of thirteen was bobbin boy in a cotton textile mill, for $1.20 per week; forty-three years later, he had amassed over 300 million dollars. Rising through the ranks at the mills, Carnegie's big break was a job as telegraph office manager for the Pennsylvania Railroad, which led to his promotion into the railroad's administrative ranks, where he began to invest in railroads, bridge building, and other enterprises. By 1868, with help from the Civil War, the thirty-three-year old Carnegie was worth $400,000. The recognition that launched Carnegie into the upper ranks of multimillionaires was that "steel was destined to change the material basis of civilization." Prior to the late nineteenth century, steel had been too expensive to produce in great quantities. With the 1856 discovery of an expeditious means of removing impurities from pig iron, the way was opened for wide-scale manufacture of steel. The goal remained elusive, requiring, among other things, easy access to the additional raw materials – iron ore, limestone, and coke – necessary for steel production. But by 1881, after teaming up with a leading coke manufacturer, Henry Clay Frick, and hiring an expert German chemist, Carnegie's empire was underway. Carnegie's success was built on the following principles: keep the steel mills running; hire top engineers to design the original plants (thus avoiding expensive industrial disasters); spend what is needed to maintain low operating costs; the larger the scale of operation, the cheaper the product; the larger the market, the greater the competitive advantage.

Throughout the essays he wrote for public consumption and published in popular journals of the time, Carnegie offered a pragmatically informed view of self-development, based on his own first-hand experience. Like his admirer Booker T. Washington, Carnegie repudiated college education, classical education in particular, as an unlikely avenue of success. Education, he believed, was beneficial to the extent that it prepared an individual directly for his destined vocation. When he did speculate on the potential of education for enlightenment's sake, Carnegie could sound strikingly naïve, as when he suggested that the common interests of capital and labor might be promoted by instructing working men in the laws of political economy and the shared subjection of capital and labor to these laws. Carnegie lauded the advantages of poverty in firing individuals with ambition, but again exaggerated his claim with the preposterous insistence that "you can scarcely name a great invention, or a great discovery . . . a great picture, or a great statue, a great song or a great story" that "has not been produced by an individual born poor." Abolish poverty, Carnegie concludes, and all progress would cease. Carnegie's suspicion of inherited wealth enhanced an instinctive passion for charity. As he wrote in "Wealth" (*North American Review*," 1889), "the man who dies thus rich [without having given to charity] dies disgraced." From the late 1880s to the end of his life, Carnegie threw his energies into endowments ensuring his reputation as one of the world's great benefactors. John D. Rockefeller admired Carnegie's bequests, in particular the deliberate orchestration of gifts (Carnegie's focus on cultural institutions), which he emulated in focusing himself on science and medical research.

Carnegie might well have preserved a comparatively untarnished reputation if not for crises like the Homestead Strike in July of 1892. Previously considered a friend of labor, which was unusual for an ambitious manufacturer (he opposed, for instance, the use of "scabs" to break strikes), Carnegie was confronted with a strike at his own mill, spurred by dissatisfaction with wage cuts and workers' demands that mill owners acknowledge their union. Henry Frick, Carnegie's partner and executive manager, who was anti-union and uncompromising, arranged to shift major orders to a different mill, and hired three hundred Pinkerton detectives and a force of armed guards. Following a four-month standoff, one of the bloodiest confrontations between capital and labor in history erupted, with hundreds wounded and ten killed. When the conflict was over, the union was crushed and the workers returned to work. The handling of the strike went against every tenet of Carnegie's avowed views on capital–labor relations. The sign that Carnegie perhaps recognized this was his decision to leave Frick alone to oversee the mill's long siege against labor. Frick kept Carnegie posted, reporting with pride that though their economic losses from the strike were heavy, the company showed profits of $4,000,000, immediately afterward. Carnegie's response came by telegram from vacation in Italy: "Congratulations all around – life worth living again – how pretty Italia."

By 1913 John D. Rockefeller's net worth was approximately $900 million (federal spending that year was $713 million), twice that of Andrew Carnegie's. Rockefeller's supremacy was founded in part on his ability to outmaneuver Carnegie on his own turf. Anticipating the value of iron ore (a product critical to steel production), Rockefeller managed to secure a monopoly on it, forcing Carnegie to deal with Rockefeller for a material essential to his own industry. While both Titans profited from their alliance, Rockefeller profited most. Likewise, while Carnegie blazed the path with his charitable donations ($350 million in his lifetime), Rockefeller's philanthropy far surpassed Carnegie's ($530 million before he died, $1¼ billion through his descendants). The ambition that led them to amass great fortunes and then invest much of them in philanthropic institutions bearing their names, informed their deep concern for their personal reputations. This was especially true of Rockefeller, the subject of sustained and increasingly visceral attacks from the 1880s on, which culminated in his prosecution for monopoly, conspiracy, and price-fixing, among other things. Through all of this, Rockefeller remained enormously sensitive to criticism and preoccupied with how his life and works would be read by posterity.

In 1917, when he agreed to an interview with his authorized biographer, William O. Inglis, Rockefeller suggested that the best way to revive those all-important years between 1865 and 1878 when he was establishing his company, Standard Oil, was to return to the books on that era by his two nemeses. In *Wealth Against Commonwealth* (1894) and *The History of the Standard Oil Company* (1904, serialized in *McClure's*, 1902–04), Henry Demarest Lloyd and Ida Tarbell, respectively, memorialized the greatest struggles and triumphs of Rockefeller's career. It was telling that Rockefeller, an astute reader of his own life, believed these books indispensable to an appraisal of it. The controversy generated by Standard Oil attached to everyone connected with it, including critics. One hundred years after the publication of Tarbell's 406-page book, readers disagree about its ultimate opinion of the Titan and his works. It seems clear that while Tarbell evidently followed the legendary advice given her by Henry James, "cherish your contempts," she also felt admiration for her robber-baron subject. The complexity of her response suggests that the more one knew, the more difficult it was to maintain an unequivocal attitude towards the nation-defining events of this critical time in American history and culture. The best prospects for cultural history remain therefore immersion in the most informed sources of the time, particularly those that aroused controversy and were respected by people of various political persuasions.

Prior to the mid nineteenth century in America, few recognized the manifold commercial possibilities of the petroleum oil buried deep below the surface of the earth in states such as Kentucky, West Virginia, Ohio, and, principally, Pennsylvania. The dark smelly substance discovered while drilling for salt-water was considered a nuisance. It was not until members of the new Pennsylvania Rock-Oil Company sent a specimen off for testing to a Yale chemist, Benjamin Silliman, that the commercial properties of this oil became widely known. "Your company have in their possession a raw material from which, by simple and not expensive process, they may manufacture very valuable products," was the succinct conclusion of the report, a model of scientific and literary precision prized for its commercial facts. By August 1859, oil was being pumped out of the ground in Pennsylvania at the rate of twenty-five barrels a day; within two years, it was two to four thousand a day, and the price per barrel had dropped from twenty dollars to ten cents. Related manufactories arose to accommodate this rushing substance: drills to ensure a steady stream of oil; barrels to hold it, first wooden, then iron, to be replaced gradually by oil pipelines; road, water, and rail services to transport the barrels; industries for refining the oil. In an ongoing cycle of hope, elation, and despair, fortunes were made and lost in the ruthless hit or miss expansion of the oil industry. At the end of the Civil War, thousands poured into the region: in the words of Tarbell, "this little corner of Pennsylvania absorbed a larger portion of men probably than any other spot in the United States." She might have said "larger and more varied," for it was possible to hear seemingly *any* language spoken in this region – a multicultural labor force matched by the multiculturalism of the product's markets. By 1872, oil was being shipped from rural Pennsylvania to forty European ports, the Middle East, the West and East Indies. Through the 1880s, no one grasped the value of one of oil's chief waste products, gasoline, which was usually discarded unconscionably, allowed to run into nearby rivers, making them dangerously flammable. In the 1890s a method was devised to "crack" petroleum, enabling a greater yield of gasoline, just in time for the first Ford two-cylinder automobile.

Early setbacks (Robert E. Lee's invasion of Pennsylvania; Civil War taxes; the 1870 Franco-Prussian War foiling foreign exports; fluctuations in the price of oil) never deterred the industry pioneers, who in ten years, according to Tarbell, had established an oil enterprise that was efficient as well as lucrative. The future looked bright for these self-reliant businessmen, including Tarbell's father, until "a big hand reached out from nobody knew where, to steal their conquest and throttle their future." That hand belonged to John D. Rockefeller.

What Rockefeller did was brazen and simple: step-by-step he built a monopoly of one of the world's most crucial resources. Together with Jay Gould and James Fisk of the Erie Railroad, Thomas Scott of the Pennsylvania Railroad, and Cornelius Vanderbilt of the New York Railroad, and his co-owners, William Andrews and Henry Flagler, Rockefeller created the South Improvement Company, which amounted to a unique collaboration between the freshly incorporated Standard Oil Company and the railroads. Standard Oil provided incentives to the railroads (e.g. assuming legal liability for fires or accidents; sixty free carloads of refined oil per day), while the railroads provided Standard Oil rebates on their oil shipments, while doubling the rates of their competitors. With most competitors destroyed by uneven freight rates, Rockefeller proceeded to buy out the survivors, offering them stock in Standard Oil in exchange for their refineries. In case after case, floundering companies were presented with offers they could not refuse. Rockefeller himself never saw his pursuit of a monopoly as anything but a rational and even idealistic effort to introduce order into an industry that had become self-destructively overdeveloped. His son, John D. Rockefeller Jr., summed up his thinking in a 1902 address at Brown University, a statement that Tarbell used as an epigraph to her *History*: "The American Beauty Rose can be produced in its splendor and fragrance only by sacrificing the early buds which grow up around it."

John D. Rockefeller was born in 1839 in Richford, New York, and raised in nearby Moravia, small upstate towns in the center of what was called "the Burned-Over District," a region marked by the fires of Protestant Evangelicalism. From boyhood, Rockefeller proved an astute student of finance, with an affinity for mathematics soon complemented by a love of bookkeeping. Even as a boy, he kept a book, which he called "Ledger A," where he recorded dutifully every cent earned, spent, and given to charity. His sobriety issued from the strict regime of his mother, who treated her eldest son as a small patriarch when his father was away from home (which was often). The only subject that absorbed Rockefeller, who was an indifferent pupil at the Owego Academy, was the principal's weekly report on new business inventions. Like other tycoons, ranging from Andrew Carnegie to Bill Gates, Rockefeller eschewed a college degree for a three-month course at a business college. Rockefeller's maternal legacy was a devout Baptist faith. While hers was a democratic creed that emphasized potential reformation for all, free will, and self-scrutiny, Eliza Rockefeller forbade smoking, drinking, dancing, card-playing, and theatergoing, and encouraged thrift and good works. It is hardly surprising that her famous son, in his own words, "never had a craving for anything."

Rockefeller's paternal legacy could not have been more different. A charlatan as well as charmer, sometime peddler, cure doctor, lumberman, and eventual bigamist (even indicted for rape), William Rockefeller was undoubtedly responsible for his eldest son's distrust of passion. His recurrent absences and irregular work patterns spelled perpetual financial insecurity. At the same time, the elder Rockefeller had an incurable, indeed, a deep and sensual love for money. As one contemporary recalled, "The old man had a passion for money that amounted almost to a craze," and another remembered the four-gallon pail brimming with gold pieces, that William kept at home during his solvent periods. While John D. Rockefeller minimized such testimonies, his memory of his own first look at a significant banknote, and the way he locked and unlocked the safe over the course of the day at his bookkeeping job just to gaze upon the bill, parallels the accounts of his father, not to mention pivotal moments in Dreiser's *Sister Carrie* and Norris's *McTeague*. Rockefeller's yearning makes him both a chip off the old block and highly representative of his age. Like many other ambitious young men, Rockefeller bought his way out of Civil War conscription with money for a substitute and subsequent annual contributions. His Cleveland food and farm implement business profited greatly from the conflict, with annual earnings ($17,000) four times larger than before the war. In 1863, Rockefeller (with his partner) invested $4000 in an oil-refining venture, and almost immediately recognized the prospects of the emerging industry. By 1865 he was owner of Cleveland's largest oil refinery.

John D. Rockefeller once remarked of his oil empire, "It was right before me and my God. If I had it to do tomorrow I would do it again the same way." It was left to Henry Demarest Lloyd and Ida Tarbell, individuals with strong moral and civic impulses of their own, to assess the validity of these claims. Henry Demarest Lloyd was born in 1847, to a poor Calvinist minister who became a bookseller after the family moved to New York City to live near his wife's wealthy relatives. Lloyd's childhood of genteel poverty (his mother pawned inherited silver to buy overshoes for Henry, who was later a scholarship student at Columbia), together with his developing preference for worldly Christianity, disposed him towards civic reform. Following law school at Columbia, Lloyd worked for the Free-Trade Association, editing their magazine, advocating laissez-faire liberalism and railing against governmental corruption. Soon after marrying into the wealthy family that co-owned the *Chicago Tribune*, Lloyd landed a job there. Lloyd's eventual home at the *Tribune* was a "Money and Commerce" column in which he took stands on economic issues: from abolishing grain corners at the Chicago Board of Trade, to stiffer regulatory oversight of the nation's railroads, to the Great Railroad Strike of 1878, which resulted in over a hundred deaths, thousands of injuries, and incalculable loss of property.

Like the main ideas of Henry George's *Progress and Poverty*, those of Lloyd's *Wealth Against Commonwealth* received a trial run in essay form before they were expanded into a book. In contrast to Henry George's modestly circulated pamphlet, Lloyd's essay, "The Story of a Great Monopoly," was published in the *Atlantic Monthly*, whose editor, William Dean Howells, predicted its sensational success. In a mere sixteen pages, "The Story of a Great Monopoly" (which drove the March 1881 issue of the *Atlantic* to six reprintings) managed to grant Standard Oil its "legitimate greatness," while deploring its unscrupulousness, citing a web of bribery so thick that it seemed the company had "done everything with the Pennsylvania legislature except refine it." Posing as a friend of the consumer, Lloyd adopted the position that Americans were perilously innocent of the dangers posed by corporate monopolies. Thirteen years later, Lloyd, who counted Booker T. Washington, Jane Addams, and Robert Louis Stevenson as friends, sought out Mark Twain's publishing company for his book-length version of the story. When Twain refused *Wealth Against Commonwealth* in deference to his friendship with Henry H. Rogers, Howells again stepped in, helping Lloyd secure a contract with Harper and Brothers.

Though he characterized himself during the writing of *Wealth Against Commonwealth* as "a socialist-anarchist-communist-individualist-collectivist-cooperative-aristocrat-democrat," Lloyd's allegiances placed him securely in the camp of Progressivism. Rockefeller, to whom he referred elsewhere as "the most selfish usurper that ever lived," was the central figure of the book, but Lloyd avoided direct references to preclude prosecution for libel. Lloyd's depersonalized narrative also enhanced his claim for the wider implications of his study, which he conceived as a general indictment of America's commercial civilization. Lloyd displays a fascination with the conspiratorial rituals and language of the oil business that makes the book extraordinarily revealing of its era and subject matter. He has an eye for the suspenseful theatrics of investigating committees, detailing how agents grilled a series of Standard Oil men into revealing the meaning of an oft-repeated phrase, "to turn another screw" ("to press a reluctant victim into compliance"). Lloyd appreciates the inherent drama of his story, and allows its subjects to speak on their own behalf. Thus Lloyd centered his case against the oil monopoly upon the life histories of four particular casualties of the Rockefeller empire: a poor widow; an aged inventor; a small manufacturer; and a would-be saboteur, bested by people more devious than he.

The fates of these individuals feed directly into Lloyd's conclusion, where he joined Henry George in adopting an anti-modernist stance, arguing the superiority of an earlier era, when hardworking innovators could earn good livings without threat of absorption by monopolies. America, he suggests, has bargained with the devil and sold its vocational birthright for a pittance – ever more affordable heaps of commodities. Lloyd's solution – government ownership of the trusts – was consistent with the historical trajectory of his analysis, the inexorable drive towards combination. He argued that regulatory commissions were inadequate to contend with the excesses of monopoly capitalism, which required more vigorous socialist measures. Lloyd conceived a major role for the rational managerial methods of the new social sciences. "It is not a verbal accident," he wrote, "that science is the substance of the word conscience." Led by the intelligentsia and a new professional managerial class, these social reforms would result in the replacement of "the profit-hunting Captain of Industry" by "the public-serving Captain of Industry." But Lloyd's vision was not to be. Though his book sold well and was reprinted four times in its first year of publication, Lloyd recognized dejectedly that "the trust is virtually supreme in the United States."

Less politically radical though no more enamored of monopolies, Ida Tarbell was prepared to assume Lloyd's mantle of literary trust-busting. In 1900, the editors of *McClure's Magazine* sought to make a splash in the highly competitive journalistic market by running a series on corporate trusts, destined in their view to succeed silver as *the* national topic in the first decade of the new century. Ida Tarbell, the magazine's managing editor and ace author, who had won both popular and professional acclaim for her profiles of Napoleon and Abraham Lincoln, settled on Standard Oil after considering the beef, sugar, and steel trusts. In part, her choice was personal. Raised in the oil region, she had seen her father and many others put out of business by Rockefeller's company. Even more important was the paper trail on company history (not surprising given its founder's devotion to bookkeeping), comparable, she suggested, to archives of the Civil War or the French Revolution. The availability of records covering Congressional probes of the company (1872, 1876) and state investigations (1879, 1891) further bolstered the prospects for high-profile journalistic treatment. There was one glitch: a critical piece of documentary evidence had gone missing. A pamphlet entitled "The Rise and Fall of the South Improvement Company" proved as difficult to locate as the Cather/Milmine biography of Mary Baker Eddy, for the same reason – its subject had purchased and destroyed most extant copies. When Tarbell finally tracked one down, she had proof of the crucial link between the illegal activities of the South Improvement Company and Rockefeller's Standard Oil.

Ida Minerva Tarbell was the most renowned of Samuel McClure's distinguished staff of writers, which included Ray Stannard Baker (whose articles on union abuses and on US Steel were celebrated), Lincoln Steffens (famed investigator of municipal corruption), and Finley Peter Dunne (author of the

Mr. Dooley stories). Born in 1857 into a family with ties to the *Mayflower*, Ida Tarbell moved at the age of three to the heart of the Pennsylvania oil region, where her father hoped to prosper. A devout Methodist, Franklin Tarbell's career in oil provides a history in miniature of the industry's evolution, first barrel-manufacturing in Rouseville, then oil-drilling, and finally ownership of a refinery in Titusville. Tarbell was fifteen years old when her father became one of the first victims of the South Improvement Company, his profits nullified by a 100 percent hike in railroad shipping rates. Tarbell was a brilliant girl, a voluminous reader filled with intellectual curiosity and a determination that led her to pursue evolutionary science despite its irreconcilability with her Methodist upbringing and to reject conventional expectations of women. Graduating from the Methodist-affiliated Allegheny College, she took a job as editor of *The Chatauquan*, helping the magazine's circulation grow from 15,000 in 1880 to 50,000 by the mid-eighties. This was largely owing to Tarbell's enlargement of its scope to include the major economic concerns of the day, from violent capital–labor conflict to battles over protective tariffs.

Syndicate publishing, so fruitfully exploited by her future boss, Samuel McClure, liberated Tarbell from the claustrophobia of the Pennsylvania oil region. It occurred to Tarbell that she might write articles in an exotic place like Paris and offer them for syndicate publication across the United States. In 1891, Tarbell relocated to Paris and proceeded to do just that, until McClure himself appeared at her door. He had recognized in Tarbell's syndicated piece, "The Paving of Paris," qualities of scientific precision and dramatic flair that he coveted for the magazine he had just begun in New York. By 1894 she was ready to accept his offer of a full-time position as an editor in New York. Tarbell was an immediate success at *McClure's*, where her serial biographies of famous men dramatically raised the magazine's circulation. Never one to rest on her laurels, Tarbell began research in 1900 on a serial that was destined to become one of the most important pieces of journalism in American history. Tarbell researched, reviewed, and cross-referenced sources, and employed an assistant to explore areas she could not reach herself, so that her claims would be supported by hard evidence. She submitted drafts to expert economists, John R. Commons of the University of Wisconsin, and John Bates Clark, of Carleton College, hired by McClure to ensure the social-scientific consistency of her arguments. Senior editor John S. Phillips and McClure himself also scrutinized Tarbell's manuscripts. Given a significant and gripping subject, a writer and researcher of Tarbell's talent, and experts and editors supporting her in this fashion, the serial's impact was assured. The serial's second installment (December 1902) spelled the beginning of the end for Rockefeller's reputation, by providing proof of his role in the ruthless and unlawful tactics of the South Improvement

Company. "Mr. Rockefeller has systematically played with loaded dice," Tarbell observed in her conclusion, "and it is doubtful if there has ever been a time since 1872 when he has run a race with a competitor and started fair."

Though Tarbell once commented that the editors at *McClure's* hardly "sat around with our brows screwed together trying to reform the world," she was delighted to receive praise from President Theodore Roosevelt, and to learn that her series was responsible for forcing Roosevelt's hand on the issue of trusts (Republicans in the House under his leadership voted half a million dollars to the Attorney General's office for their prosecution). In May of 1911, seven years after the publication of Tarbell's serial in a two-volume book form, the United States Supreme Court ordered the dissolution of Standard Oil. Significantly, with the exception of his recorded interview with William Inglis, which was consigned to the archives along with the prospective biography, John D. Rockefeller never responded to the charges leveled by Tarbell in her *History*. According to his most recent biographer, Ron Chernow, Rockefeller remained silent because he could not have repudiated some of the charges without acknowledging, tacitly, the justice of others.

Tarbell's exposé was celebrated in her own time and ever since as an example of a free press triumphing over a major threat to national democratic ideals. Yet it was a sign of the profundity of corporate power in America that Standard Oil was able to rise like a phoenix from its ashes in World War I, when called upon by the government to assist the war effort. With the President of Standard Oil of New Jersey serving as its chairman, a Petroleum War Service Committee was formed to pool production and coordinate resources. Though the great oil anaconda had been chopped into pieces by the Supreme Court decision, these pieces apparently retained the magical capacity to reconstitute themselves as a single corporate body. To Ida Tarbell and other observers of this model trust, it may have seemed that it had never been disturbed.

9

༅

REALIST UTOPIAS

IT IS WELL KNOWN THAT one of the most popular works of literary utopianism, Edward Bellamy's *Looking Backward* (1888), was written during the
era of American literary Realism; few are familiar with the extraordinary
outpouring of utopian novels that appeared between *Looking Backward* and
Charlotte Perkins Gilman's *Herland* (1915). From the late 1880s to the turn of
the century alone, over 150 utopian novels were published in the United States,
a figure unequalled in any other country or historical period. It may seem paradoxical, from the perspective of literary history, to find a vogue of utopian art
and thought in a culture renowned for its practicality and materialism. But
it is precisely the intensity and pace of capitalist development that helps to
explain the appeal of utopianism. The utopian novelistic form afforded writers
a distance, which facilitated their profound engagement with the economic
and social developments that both dazzled and disturbed them. In work after
work, narrators and characters experienced the detached contemplation of the
utopian perspective. They tested the institutionalization of extreme principles, sometimes radically enlightened ones, as in William Dean Howells's *The
Traveler From Altruria* (1894), sometimes dangerously pessimistic ones, as in
Ignatius Donnelly's *Caesar's Column* (1890). They imagined inventions and scientific advances beyond the ken of contemporaries, as in Alvarado Fuller's *A.D.
2000* (1890) and Arthur Bird's *Looking Forward* (1899). Or, as in *Unveiling a
Parallel* (1893) by Alice Jones and Ella Merchant, they conceived of societies
where probable but still remote political changes – women's right to vote and
occupational parity with men – had been realized.

American utopian novels written from the 1880s to the beginning of World
War I represented a cultural form that emerged in tandem with economic and
industrial expansion and helped to express the mood of Progressive Era reform.
Utopian novelists took a variety of positions on the major political issues of the
day, from the rise of big corporations and the growing chasm between rich and
poor, to immigration and women's rights. Some utopian authors were themselves businessmen: King Gillette, inventor of the Gillette Razor and author

of *The Human Drift* (1894), Bradford Peck, the owner of one of the largest department stores in New England and author of *The World a Department Store* (1900), and L. Frank Baum, a traveling salesman with expertise in advertising and author of *The Wizard of Oz* (1900). This convergence between the apparently antithetical fields of business and utopianism does more than confirm the popularity of the utopian novel (even businessmen wrote them). It also confirms one of its central purposes – to redress the harsh effects of capitalist expansion. Authors like Gillette and Peck argued that the values of innovation and enterprise needed to be reconciled with humanistic and spiritual values. Many utopian novelists were concerned with the renovation of religious ideals they believed essential to alleviating social ills. Bellamy's *Looking Backward* registers the influence of his father, a Baptist minister, Donnelly's *Caesar's Column* parodies upper-class Protestantism in the name of a more just Christianity, Howells's *Traveler From Altruria* outlines an ideal Christian Socialism, and Baum's *Wizard of Oz* reflects his faith in Theosophy, which decreed "God was Nature, Nature God." These authors sought a religion free of sectarian quarreling, readily applicable to ordinary experience, and open to Darwinian science.

The preoccupation with reproduction, ethnicity, and race in utopian novels was even more pronounced. It reveals how the genre helped to express the distress generated by rising levels of social heterogeneity (with immigration rates unrivaled by any previous or subsequent time in the nation's history). What makes the utopian novel a critical point of reference here is that it attracted authors from different cultural backgrounds – African Americans (e.g. Sutton E. Griggs, *Imperium in Imperio*, 1899), Jews (e.g. Solomon Schindler, *Young West*, 1894), and Irish (e.g. Ignatius Donnelly, *Caesar's Column*) – as well as numerous women authors. Through its obligatory account of a traveler entering an unknown and wondrous region, confronted with people and customs both alien and familiar, the utopian novel offered a literary laboratory for probing the nature of cultural difference. Utopian novels typically featured an American or group of Americans as time travelers, whether most commonly projected forward like Bellamy's Julian West, or projected backward like Twain's Connecticut Yankee, whose experiences represented direct reversals of both the colonial and the immigrant situations. Transported to new worlds, sometimes their native lands transformed, whose norms and rituals seemed counterintuitive however preferable to those left behind, these travelers became captives of the new worlds and often captivated, through sustained education and retraining, by their dominant values.

Many of the most important novelists of this generation, from William Dean Howells and Mark Twain to Jack London and Charlotte Perkins Gilman, contributed to the genre. And the genre's highpoints represent some of *the* most significant literary confrontations in any form with the tendencies of this critical historical moment. Novels such as Bellamy's *Looking Backward* and Gilman's *Herland* are regarded, deservedly, as models of the genre, but others, such as Donnelly's *Caesar's Column* were as eagerly embraced by reading audiences. Like the characters and situations they created in their literary utopias that carried their distinctive traits of personality and culture wherever they went, Twain, Howells, and Gilman retained their signature styles and concerns in, respectively *A Connecticut Yankee in King Arthur's Court*, *The Traveler From Altruria*, and *Herland*. But in helping to formulate the unique type of utopianism that flourished in their lifetimes, they also demonstrated a powerful aesthetic and political breadth.

PERFECTING MANUFACTURE

As a work that sought solutions to the gravest social and economic problems, *Looking Backward: 2000–1887* deserves to be read alongside classic social theory, from Plato's *Republic* and More's *Utopia* to nineteenth-century writings by Owen and Fourier. The novel expressed Bellamy's attraction to militarism and socialism and his sympathy for the women's rights movement. And it reflected his disdain for a society that squandered its valuable resources by exploiting labor, allowing factories to remain idle, and countenancing routine cycles of inflation and depression. Bellamy believed that the root of these ills lay not in technology and innovation but in the increasing power of plutocrats. The novel sold nearly half a million copies, and was a worldwide bestseller. Translated into many languages, it spawned a national social reform movement, and influenced seemingly every significant American intellectual of the time. Dozens of sequels appeared in the 1890s, yet another sign of the extraordinary inspirational gift of this son of a Baptist minister. Bellamy, who recalled vividly in his journals accompanying his father to Evangelical camp meetings, possessed a moral fervor that was especially suited to a late nineteenth-century society marred by scandal and corruption. Bellamy's answer to this national malaise was, in Mark Twain's words, to make "heaven paltry by inventing a better one on earth."

Twain's rhetoric located *Looking Backward* squarely in the arena of religion, which represented not only a shrewd appraisal of its deepest methods and ideas but also an understanding of its political limitations. Bellamy deliberately invoked the term "Nationalism" in all of his writings, to distinguish his agenda from the socialism that it resembled in key respects. Socialism, Bellamy wrote Howells in 1888, is a term he

never could well stomach . . . In the first place it is a foreign word in itself and equally foreign in all its suggestions. It smells to the average American of petroleum, suggests the red flag, with all manner of sexual novelties, and an abusive tone about God and religion, which in this country we at least treat with decent respect.

The hint of physical revulsion at the thought of a term at once "foreign" and incendiary is reinforced by the social purity of Bellamy's utopia. The paradox of Bellamy's novel is that utopia exists at the expense of social heterogeneity, invention, innovation, that is, all the things that made technological advance and economic expansion possible in the first place. And the novel's very success was partly due to its blandness and restraint. In a manner similar to Henry George's in *Progress and Poverty*, a work he admired, Bellamy in *Looking Backward* drew adherents to his radical agenda by appealing to audiences in commonplace and even prejudicial terms.

Like no other form of social protest in the late nineteenth century, Bellamy's *Looking Backward* supplied a rudder for a sea of discontent. By 1890 there were 162 Bellamy Clubs in 27 states, and *The Nationalist*, a Boston-based magazine, became the official voice of a movement composed of professionals and intellectuals. In 1891 Bellamy launched his own magazine, *The New Nation*, whose purpose was to outline a plan of practical reform which featured government ownership of all critical industries from coalmines and steel mills, to telegraph companies and railroads. In 1891, a new Nationalist Party founded on Bellamy's ideas sponsored a slate of candidates in New England, and joined forces with the Populist Party (sponsor of another renowned utopian author, Ignatius Donnelly) in the Midwest, a region where Bellamy was especially popular. Bellamy's political work fell off after 1893 due to poor health (he died of tuberculosis in 1898), and he again threw his political energies into novel-writing. His sequel to *Looking Backward*, *Equality* (1897), was neither a commercial nor a critical success, primarily because it was set squarely in a golden age. Bellamy's best fiction thrived on the tension between society as it was (beset with flagrant inequalities, misery amid abundance) and society as it might be (were human rationality and benevolence to prevail).

Bellamy was born in Chicopee Falls, Massachusetts in 1850, and raised in a religious household as marked by his mother's forbidding Calvinism as by his father's Baptist faith. Like many industrial towns of the era, Chicopee was full of immigrant families working long hours for low wages, and subject to constant capital–labor conflict. Because the town was relatively small, its crowded tenements, frequently hazardous factories, strikes, and epidemics, were visible to all and made a strong impression on Bellamy. Following graduation from Union College, and study in Germany (German, law, and socialist theory), Bellamy pursued a career in journalism. In 1871, he went to New York as a reporter on William Cullen Bryant's *Evening Post*, and later for Theodore Tilden's radical paper, *The Golden Age*, and for his own paper, *The Springfield Penny News*. His articles on such topics as "Riches and Rottenness," "Over-worked Children in Our Mills," and "Wastes and Burdens of Society" helped prepare for *Looking Backward*. Equally beneficial was the fiction Bellamy managed to produce while working as a journalist (four novels and twenty-three short stories) and place in the best magazines (e.g. the *Atlantic Monthly* and the *Century*).

The protagonist of *Looking Backward*, Julian West, is a bored, slightly neuras-thenic upper-class Bostonian, soon to be married once his new house is built, a prospect delayed by labor strikes as chronic, apparently, as West's insomnia. West relies on unorthodox methods to alleviate his sleep problem: mesmerism and nightly retreat to an underground vault that replicates "the silence of the tomb." Falling into an especially deep sleep one night, he awakens 113 years later in utopian America, 2000. Dr. Leete, his wife, and his daughter, Edith, whom West marries at the novel's end, guide him through the ideal particulars of this new society. Bellamy's challenge is to find convincing for-mal means of providing soapboxes so his characters can rehearse the wrongs of late nineteenth-century America and the superiority of its utopian variation. The utopia of *Looking Backward* is intriguingly prophetic, featuring numerous twentieth-century advances: shopping malls, credit cards (Edith Leete is an avid shopper), and telephonic radios that prefigure television, under a wholly equitable democratic regime. The novel even anticipates the internet-based religious worship of the twenty-first century with its image of a preacher, Mr. Barton, who sermonizes by telephone, reaching audiences of 150,000. The centralized utopian economy is designed to eliminate the excess and inef-ficiency of laissez-faire capitalism. Production and distribution are organized, everyone works until the age of forty-five, and each individual receives the same annual income. Women's work outside the home remains defined by their work within it on behalf of husbands and children, but women enjoy equal opportunity and pay. The symbol for the mass-produced abundance made uniformly available to all is the system of mechanical umbrellas covering all the sidewalks of Boston during rainstorms.

The rigid class and material distinctions of America 1887 have been eradi-cated at the expense of its multicultural variety, for America 2000 is unequiv-ocally homogeneous. Indeed, the virtual absence of characters in the novel suggests Bellamy's difficulty in conceptualizing the human types amenable to the kinds of reforms he imagines. He emphasizes systematic changes, while minimizing the human factors that complicate them. The success of utopia in *Looking Backward* depends on its being wholly theoretical. Bellamy fails to *represent* the transformed social relations – conversational forms, habits, collective rituals, and emotional behaviors – that assist and express a general accommodation of utopia. The potential success of the utopian social system Bellamy delineates in his novel is belied by his inability to depict its human dimensions. As in many utopian works, the most pressing and engaging question of the novel becomes the nature of predictability itself: can change, its consequences, the future, be predicted?

Hence the importance of religion to the novel's deepest vision. From a religious perspective, the future is fundamentally predictable. They "still have Sundays and sermons in utopia," for the sake of Bellamy's late nineteenth-century audience, which requires *some* mechanism of belief. Bellamy's own recourse to this mechanism is consistent throughout his career, which from beginning to end confirms the depth of his prophetic commitment to America. As he wrote in his 1892 "Letter to the People's Party," "Let us bear in mind that if [America] be a failure, it will be a final failure." Bellamy's biblical typology – America as the New Israel – builds on a Puritan legacy to convert the crises of the Gilded Age into prophecies of the Millennium. This is made explicit in the first of the narrative's many tutorials between the all-knowing host, Dr. Leete, and the innocent pilgrim, Julian West. As Leete observes, half-questioningly: "You must, at least, have realized . . . the general misery of mankind, were portents of great changes of some sort." Equally important is the framing of West's embrace of the utopian perspective as a "conversion." The profoundly spiritualized underpinnings of West's odyssey are especially evident in his nightmare late in the novel. Returning to late nineteenth-century America, he tries to preach to the unconverted but finds them hopelessly unresponsive. Bellamy's comparison of utopian conversion to a religious conversion, however unsuccessful, is utopian in its own right. If only human minds were as open to conversion on socioeconomic grounds as they were on spiritual ones!

The problem of how to change beliefs is fundamental to utopian novels. There was no novelist more deeply interested in this problem than Mark Twain, who made it the central concern of his greatest works, and grasped its particular relevance to utopianism. Twain had an almost scientific appreciation for how ideas are instilled and adhered to. For Twain the human–machine analogy was reciprocal; one might work back from machines to new conceptualizations of the human minds that created them. What better circumstance for testing the wondrous mental powers of humans than the traveler to utopia, a stranger in a strange land. More than any other novel by Twain, *Connecticut Yankee* fired the late nineteenth-century American popular imagination. The idea of an entrepreneurial mechanic transported to sixth-century England appealed because it combined the attributes of the historical novel with modern values of innovation and industry. In staging his clash of civilizations, Twain drew on the striking transformations he witnessed during his lifetime. Raised in the slave south, Twain saw first-hand the effects of emancipation. He experienced the revolution in transportation, from the stagecoach and steamboat to the railroad, and the advent of full-fledged industrialization, enabled by countless technological innovations and constantly changing modes of production. Twain's sense of time was equally informed by intellectual transformations initiated by major thinkers like Charles Darwin, a devotee of Twain's fiction, whom Twain visited in 1879.

Connecticut Yankee, with its vivid dramatization of historical and intellectual dislocation, is Twain's most politically radical work. The novel depicts material progress as the paradoxical route to "a new Dark Ages," and the Yankee, Hank Morgan, characterizes institutions as "civilisation-factories" and "man-factories" to express his view of industrialization as inevitably dehumanizing. These assumptions were supported by the controversial illustrations of Daniel Beard, which associated Twain's narrative with Henry George's Single Tax Plan, among other anti-capitalist measures. The most infamous of Beard's drawings was "The Slave Driver," whip in hand, foot on the breast of a prostrate woman, the unmistakable image of railroad Titan Jay Gould. Twain expressed his approval in an 1889 letter to Beard, "Hold me under everlasting obligations. There are a hundred artists who could have illustrated any other of my books, but only one who could illustrate this one." As Beard reported in his autobiography, the illustrations that so impressed Twain "grievously offended some big advertisers," and were therefore removed from future editions of the novel.

Connecticut Yankee is a powerful novel because its elaborate political and economic concerns are integral to the humanity of its characters, especially the protagonist-narrator, who for all his energy and enterprise retains a capacity for wonder. "It was a soft, reposeful, summer landscape, as lovely as a dream, and as lonesome as Sunday," Hank Morgan recounts in hushed tones at the novel's opening, "The air was full of the smell of flowers, and the buzzing of insects, and the twittering of birds, and there were no people, no wagons, there was no stir of life, nothing going on." Like Huckleberry Finn's, Hank's narrative is full of sensual detail, suggesting the goodness of a natural world devoid of human elements. The opening contrasts with a novelistic society whose barbarism and cruelty is unequivocally man-made. Hank Morgan is a Huck Finn with distinct Tom Sawyer elements: Huck's gentle reflectivity combined with Tom's entrepreneurial greed.

The dominant paradigm in *Connecticut Yankee* is that of progress. Have Americans discovered in the nineteenth century an idea so powerful that it can simply be transferred to Arthurian England and through the ingenuity of an energized Yankee, instituted there? It takes little time for Hank Morgan to establish a variety of nineteenth-century innovations. And by the narrative's end, the Connecticut Yankee has managed to modernize, single-handedly, the sixth century. There are schools, colleges, newspapers; authorship is a profession, slavery is abolished, all are equal before the law. There are telegraphs, telephones, phonographs, typewriters, sewing machines, and a stock exchange. They even have baseball. Of all the innovations that Hank Morgan introduces in Camelot, none in his view holds greater potential for collective transformation than soap and its marketing. The benign tolerance of the populace for Morgan's modern manipulations confirms the impact of King Arthur's exceptionally tyrannical regime. And the very ease of his efforts suggests a troubling compatibility between modern innovation and traditional hierarchy. The chief difference between the final massacre, initiated by Morgan (utilizing all the fruits of progress), and old-world barbarisms is the incomparable degree of slaughter afforded by new technologies. Yet he makes continual distinctions between medieval-style oppression and more recent forms, to the credit of the latter. There is no question in his mind that his native Connecticut, where power, however corruptible, resides ultimately in the people, is preferable to what he witnesses in King Arthur's court.

In its contradictoriness, the political vision of *Connecticut Yankee* is most reflective of conditions in nineteenth-century America. Morgan's orchestration of a clash between civilizations succeeds in staging, above all, the tension between tradition and modernity in American society. To what extent were Americans capable of adapting to the social, economic, political, and spiritual upheavals of their time, and what would be the result if too many were left in the wake of these transformations? And how, most importantly from Twain's perspective, did human minds accommodate change – from the most concrete (changing modes of transportation; changing commodities, from bulk to brand) to the most cerebral (Darwinian versus biblical explanations for human origins)? By attempting to introduce enlightenment on a grand scale to the most superstitious of peoples, Morgan embarks on a deep exploration of the tenacity of belief. This is why he concentrates from the outset on invention and discovery, from the patents that secure one's property in creative products to the schooling that provides the ideas and tools for innovations, to the newspaper that allows for the dissemination of new information. The Yankee ponders continually his all-powerful purpose: the transformation, bit by bit, of the Arthurian collective mentality. History intrudes on utopia in the form of the Interdict. In banning electric light, the Church threatens the very foundations of Morgan's empire. While he is able to enlist boys for an armed resistance, most of Camelot's adults capitulate. There follows a confrontation between Morgan's small band and the Church with its knights. Morgan is convinced he will triumph, a conviction fulfilled by the electrocution of the vast enemy force in a scene of utter devastation. But Morgan is finally also a casualty of this spectacle of mass death, succumbing in its aftermath.

Given the proximity of Twain's utmost obsession with the Paige Typesetter and his writing of *Connecticut Yankee* (1884–89), it is not surprising to find traces of that ill-conceived investment in the novel's apocalyptic ending. Twain's typesetter was made at the same Fire Arms Manufacturing Company in Hartford, Connecticut that turned out Gatling guns, the weapon of choice for Morgan's army at the novel's end. The technology that produced magically rapid print was intimately linked to the technology that produced magically rapid gunfire. This was not the first time that Twain had linked literary firepower to the deadlier kind, as in the epigraph to *Huckleberry Finn*. Twain's disastrous experience with the Paige Typesetter was only one of nearly a hundred new inventions that drew his apparently boundless enthusiasm for innovation. In *Connecticut Yankee*, Twain seems prepared to contemplate those enthusiasms from a distance, through the hapless persona of his protagonist-narrator. Utopias, Twain recognized, required the things that human beings believed they needed in addition to those that were good for them.

While critics have read this ending as a sign of Twain's deep disenchantment with his own era of progress, it is also a characteristically bleak commentary on the nature of humankind in general. "Human ideas are a curious thing, and interesting to observe and examine," Morgan comments. "I had mine, the King and his people had theirs. In both cases they flowed in ruts worn deep by time and habit, and the man who should have proposed to divert them by reason and argument would have had a long contract on his hands." Talk is itself one of the biggest impediments: where there is incessant, air-filling monologue, there is little room for thought, for challenge, for renovation. Moreover, the limitation on any individual experience creates an enormous barrier. Genuine empathy for unfamiliar suffering is in equally short supply in nineteenth-century America and in Arthurian England.

In keeping with the complexity and elusiveness of its main ideas, Twain's novel has eluded generic definitions, seeming as much an idiosyncratic apocalyptic romance as a bona fide utopian novel. But the novel is preoccupied with utopia, and with the prospect that the future might represent utopia to the past – the very basis of the myth of progress. *Connecticut Yankee* is more a commentary on the utopian novel than a concerted attempt to be one. Twain's novel reverses the typical utopian scenario, where a guide who translates the terms of the superior (or inferior) society befriends the protagonist, a confused alien in another world. In making his time traveler the expert among a dim populace of medieval souls, introducing a modernity that is historically inevitable, Twain twists and distorts the classic utopian message. Despite its author's proclaimed appreciation for Bellamy, Twain's utopian-dystopian novel reads as a grim disavowal of the peddlers of perfection. Utopias always fail, Twain implies, not because human beings are essentially flawed, but because any system of reformation bent on perfecting what higher powers have wrought is bound to go terribly wrong. This was not an argument for submission to Christianity, which he bitterly parodied in the novel, but rather Twain's pessimistic insistence that malicious forces beyond human beings always get the last word. Twain gives us the most practical possible agent in Hank Morgan, and still his utopia goes awry.

From this perspective, King Camp Gillette's counterintuitive argument in *The Human Drift* (1894) is directly relevant to Twain's portrait: Gillette claims that businessmen are the only appropriate crafters of utopia. Though Gillette's worldwide renown, which persists to this day, is based on his razor blades, his fame in his own time was due equally to the social reorganization schemes that seemed so much at odds with the purposes of a major manufacturer. At the start of *The Human Drift*, Gillette asserts that the tycoon is the consummate source of reform, because he understands the power of capital. He may lack motivation, but his rationality will ultimately prevail, allowing him to grasp the irreversible trend or "drift" towards financial concentration, and the inevitability that such consolidated power will in time have to be more equitably distributed along with resources themselves. Only a social system based on what Gillette called "united intelligence and material equality" was capable of realizing the potential of modern American invention and industry. Gillette's argument was similar to that set forth in any number of contemporary utopian works, many of them with greater formal claims to literary historical significance. His book is important because of the attention that it received in its time and because it remains a curiosity. How could an ambitious businessman produce a work notable for the purity of its idealism, a mere year before he invented a product that would earn him international celebrity in addition to a fortune? While many business Titans became identified with visionary enterprises of different sorts, some of them more practical than others (John D. Rockefeller's funding of cutting edge medical research versus Andrew Carnegie's quest for "world peace") these efforts *followed* their amassing of millions, and were the appropriate charitable consequences of self-enrichment. Gillette was unusual in that his idealism preceded his business triumphs, and persisted afterward.

The Human Drift offers 150 pages of impassioned political argument, historical analysis, poetry, and architectural designs to plead for a just allotment of modern industrial wealth. It was due to the openness of the utopian novel form as such that *The Human Drift* could be thus classified. For Gillette's art was in his architecture. Like Howells, who drew inspiration for *The Traveler From Altruria* from the same source, Gillette was influenced by the "White City" of the Chicago's World Fair in conceiving a city space defined by the harmonizing of diverse elements. The most revolutionary aspect of his plan, both aesthetically and socially, was the design of his apartments: spiraling high-rises with vast indoor as well as outdoor public spaces. Combinations of steel, brick, porcelain, and glass, with foliage, grass, and flowers, these aesthetically stunning buildings facilitated maximum durability and efficiency. Urbanites in Gillette's utopia enjoyed the sophistication and intensity of urban life, without forsaking nature. Rural America was restructured to facilitate large-scale production and give rural inhabitants access to thoroughly equipped and modernized facilities (libraries, theaters, restaurants, schools). Gillette's vast metropolis accommodated the whole of North America, 70 million people in 40,000 skyscrapers, each of them centered around gorgeous plant-filled atriums crowned by skylights, and bordered on their outer rings by rural areas that fed the urban populations inside. While every building and apartment was the same in terms of size and quality, parity did not equal monotony. Every building in his vast metropolis, he insisted, was a distinct work of art.

There was little in Gillette's background to explain his reconciliation of commercial ambition and utopian idealism. In contrast with many other utopian authors, religion did not play a significant role in his upbringing or in his adult life. Born in Wisconsin in 1855, to a family of modest means with seven children, Gillette was the son of a small businessman who liked to tinker with new inventions and a housewife who published a bestselling cookbook. After the family relocated to Chicago, where Gillette's father owned a hardware supply business, they lost everything in the Chicago Fire of 1871. Gillette began work at the age of seventeen, first as a hardware salesman, later selling bottle-stops and Sapolio soap. Like his father, Gillette liked to experiment, and was particularly drawn to disposable commodities, taking a hint from a successful employer to think of a throwaway item that required constant repurchasing. According to company legend, Gillette scoured the alphabet in search of some need he might fulfill with an invention. One morning in 1895, while shaving, he conceived the disposable safety blade. While the idea may have come instantaneously, it took six years for Gillette and his partner, an MIT engineer, to form the American Safety Razor Company, and another two to begin full-scale production with the financial backing of an Irish immigrant brewer.

As suggested by his trust in a disposable product – what business historians call "planned obsolescence" – Gillette proved a savvy manufacturer. In 1903, he paid $200 for the first advertisement featuring his razors, and as his company grew ad campaigns became increasingly ambitious. Because Gillette's image invariably appeared in product advertisements, and the multimillion dollar business had great success in a global market, Gillette's face was soon familiar worldwide (he described being mobbed by excited Egyptians during travels in the Middle East). With so much ingenuity dedicated to the fine points of commerce, where did Gillette find room in his mind for the altogether different intellectual demands of social renovation? For the utopian dreaming of his 1894 *The Human Drift* extended over the course of his commercial career. And what was truly distinctive about Gillette's vision was its combination of social radicalism – a system of material equalization and collective control that, despite his caveats, required a complete dismantling of the status quo – and commonsensical business methods. Gillette's capacity to balance seemingly incompatible purposes ensured the practical success of his utopian measures, which had a direct influence on urban planners in the twentieth century.

Like King Camp Gillette, Bradford Peck was a successful businessman who brought his commercial experience to bear in conceptualizing utopian alternatives. Peck took his utopia further than Gillette, both by testing it in corporate terms and by imagining it in more satisfying fictions. The year before he published his 1900 novel, *The World A Department Store*, Peck launched the "Cooperative Association of America," in Lewiston, Maine, a business partnership between producers and consumers that eliminated middlemen – bankers, speculators, advertisers – whom Peck believed drove up costs artificially. The Cooperative membership was primarily upper-class, Anglo-Saxon Protestant, focused on gradual social change. Peck was convinced that his utopian scheme, which included a cooperative restaurant, a cooperative grocery store, and a cooperative electric light company, was so compelling, that it would be reproduced nationally. *The World A Department Store*, Peck's only novel, was designed to generate support for his social model. Peck shared Gillette's combination of business practicality and utopian idealism, privileging efficiency over competition, in the name of progress. He differed from Gillette, and joined other utopian authors like Baum and Donnelly, in his embrace of religion. Peck's business utopia promoted a thoroughly Christianized commerce.

Peck was born in 1853, and raised in a home where work, of necessity, was emphasized over education. A cash boy at a department store at age twelve, Peck looked forward, in classic Horatio Alger terms, to one day having his own store. Peck worked his way up the ladder of retail, eventually opening a department store in Lewiston, Maine, which he built into the largest in New England, outside of Boston. Peck's rise from "rags to riches" and the ongoing success of his commercial ventures (in real estate, dry goods, etc.) prompts the same question raised by Gillette's career. What motivated this triumphant capitalist to pursue utopian schemes for social reorganization? In Peck's case the answer was lifelong devotion to Christianity, which he considered inimical to the competitive practices and Darwinian principles of modern capitalism.

The World A Department Store registers the influence of *Looking Backward* by depicting a hero who awakens in a utopia twenty-five years hence that has righted all the wrongs of turn-of-the century America. The hero's innocence of his new world, and competing memories of his past society, yield plentiful opportunities for detailed social comparisons. As in Bellamy and Gillette, there are no kitchens, and food acquisition, preparation, and service are professionalized. The family as a childrearing institution has disappeared; child development experts raise offspring in groups. There is no use of liquor, except for medicinal purposes. Yet most social hierarchies (specifically, those of class, gender, and race) remain. Society is strictly Christian; there are no alternative faiths. And the only non-white faces appear in a schoolroom display of past human types. The homogeneity of Peck's utopia is confirmed by the neat symmetry of the novel's romances; dark-haired male mates with blonde female, blond male with dark-haired female, in a careful balancing of attributes. The predictability of romance is matched by the predictability of the novel's chief activity – shopping. No longer challenging or enervating, no bargains, no lines at checkout, no crowds. Above all, there is no advertising, which Peck portrays as a key source of inflation in the modern marketplace.

What cooperation meant to Peck was a system organized in the interest of the efficient manufacturer and the upper classes. Middlemen who threatened the manufacturer's profits were eliminated, as were the non-Anglo Saxons, non-Christians, and working classes who threatened social harmony. Peck's utopia was not designed to improve the lot of competitive capitalism's primary victims but to eliminate the victims themselves. Though his vision failed to accommodate a Christianity open to all animal and humankind, Peck's interpretation of Christianity made it readily reconcilable with his business practices. Christianity, according to Peck, flourished in societies that were conducive to the most rational and profitable methods. In *The World A Department Store*, turn-of-the century Christianity is presented as bad business:

a system of warring creeds, competing for members and resources. In Peck's utopia, Christianity has become standardized; indeed, it looks very much like a Christian trust. This is borne out by Peck's closing celebration of none other than John D. Rockefeller and Standard Oil. Adopting a familiar corporate defense, Peck applauded the company's cooperative organizational methods. Apparently, Peck's "Cooperative" had more in common with private corporations than recognized by those who feared its socialistic ambitions. To readers of *The World A Department Store*, it all made perfect sense.

The career of L. Frank Baum, the most famous utopian author of the era next to Bellamy, has something in common with each of the previous examples. Baum had Mark Twain's boundless enthusiasm for inventions and showmanship, and even went bankrupt due to the grandiose ventures he pursued following his greatest success. Baum was highly spiritual, like Bellamy and Peck, though he was less moralistic, preferring his religion mysterious and playful. Baum also shared Gillette's knack for business, pursuing a variety of professions and always landing on his feet. In 1900, Baum published two books that were intimately related: *The Art of Decorating Dry Goods Windows and Interiors* and *The Wonderful Wizard of Oz*. The first reflected his work advising Midwestern store owners on their window displays in the rural towns he visited as a traveling salesman. As founder of the National Association of Window Trimmers of America, he had accumulated enough material on the subject to put together the small book, which he sold by subscription. The title confirmed Baum's view of advertising, particularly the highly personable and immediate form in shop windows, as an entertainment art. Window displays were narrative enactments designed to entrance potential consumers as if they were spectators at a theatre. Because people were naturally curious about mechanical contrivances, and would inevitably stop to contemplate a moving object, Baum considered them especially valuable. Capturing the interest of potential consumers was more than halfway to the sale.

Baum's passion for invention and exhibition, his advertising skill and desire to captivate, came to fruition in his world-famous novel. When asked about his inspiration for *The Wonderful Wizard of Oz*, Baum replied that he was a mere "instrument" of "the Great Author," echoing statements by many pious novelists from the century that had just ended. Baum's reply was indicative of the importance of his faith – a blend of theosophy (nature religion), mysticism, spiritualism, and renovated Christianity – to his bestselling novel. Those beliefs derived from his Methodist upbringing, the intense Evangelicalism of his native region, and the growing liberalism and religious uncertainty of his era. Baum was so confident of the book's likely success that he reportedly framed the pencil (now a stub) with which he had written it. He did not wait long for the realization of his expectations: within weeks of publication 10,000 copies were gone, and second and third printings in press. Contemporary critics were lavish: pronouncing it "the best children's story-book of the century," (*Minneapolis Journal*) and the start of a new era of writing for children (*New York Times*).

Lyman Frank Baum was born in 1856 in Chittenango, New York, a small town upstate. After the elder Baum, a barrel manufacturer, struck oil in Titusville Pennsylvania, he built a country estate just outside of Syracuse, NY, where Baum and four siblings were raised. The family's wealth and indifference to formal education liberated Baum to pursue activities such as editing and printing magazines with his own press and a fowl-breeding business. The latter led to national recognition in the field, and his first publication, *The Book of the Hamburgs* (1886). The restless multitalented Baum then turned to local theatricals, appearing in amateur productions and writing plays for a Syracuse troupe. In the fall of 1882, Baum married Maud Gage, daughter of a prominent feminist, Matilda Joslyn Gage, a participant in the Seneca Falls Women's Rights Convention, and subsequently entered his family's oil business to ensure adequate support for his wife and child. It was Baum's wife, Maud, who engineered their move to Dakota Territory, where she had relatives. In Aberdeen, South Dakota, Baum discovered his avocation for journalism, editing the *Aberdeen Saturday Pioneer*, whose opinion columns he used to explore topics such as feminism and white–Native-American conflict.

Baum sided with the Dakota pioneers, repudiating all claims of the original inhabitants. Indeed, after the 1890 massacre of Native Americans at Wounded Knee, Baum openly endorsed the extermination of the remaining Native Americans, fearing they would seek vengeance. General unrest and economic depression resulted in a mass exodus of settlers in the early 1890s, which the Baums joined, relocating to Chicago, where Baum became a traveling salesman for a wholesale china firm. The Baum family now had four sons and Baum prized the domestic intervals when he would create stories for them. His first children's book, *Mother Goose in Prose*, with illustrations by Maxfield Parrish, was published in 1897, then came *By the Candelabra's Glare* (1898), and *Father Goose, His Book* (1899), a bestseller, greatly admired by Howells and Twain.

Like these earlier books, *The Wonderful Wizard of Oz* was a departure in children's literature visually, with bold original color illustrations by William Denslow that combined Art Nouveau with the linear clarity of Japanese painting. In narrative terms, the novel eschewed didacticism and sentimentality for plainness and economy. Over his writing desk Baum kept a plaque with lines from 1 Corinthians 13:11: "When I was a child I spake as a child, I understood as a child, I thought as a child." A gentle democratic spirit rules Dorothy's world, where the bark even of witches is worse than their bite. Dorothy is a brave and resourceful product of Midwestern pioneer culture, a young orphan on a Bunyan-like journey. She succeeds in rescuing not only herself but also the friends she makes along the way, overcoming terrific odds and propelling herself towards her goal without conventional forms of male assistance. Dorothy's companions, the Scarecrow, the Tin-man, and the Lion, represent, among other things, the three states of Nature – Vegetable, Mineral, and Animal – in addition to the three personal faculties that each seeks, Intelligence, Love, and Courage. They can also be seen as emblems of contemporary social movements or developments: Agrarianism (Scarecrow), Industrialization (Tin-man), Back-to-Nature (Lion). The novel leaves little doubt that Dorothy and her companions already possess the things they seek. The emphasis on self-discovery, on overcoming a series of trials to locate the power within, is as universal as it is specifically American.

The novel's most emphatically American type is "the Wizard" himself, unmasked at the end as a "humbug," whose true occupations are ventriloquism and ballooning. The Wizard recalls any number of nineteenth-century showmen and charlatans. But he is also the capitalist par excellence, instructing visitors who come to request favors in the basic laws of exchange. Supplicants must pay dearly for the use of his miraculous powers. The Wizard's Emerald City bears comparison to the White City of Chicago's 1893 Columbian Exposition, the brainchild of American business leaders. Despite his fraudulence, the Wizard is no villain, and his portrait conveys the same respect for deceivers Baum once expressed in an editorial, "Barnum was right when he declared that the American people liked to be deceived." Baum's theories on window dressing depend on the same pleasure in deception. Yet still more powerful in Baum's famous novel is an ideal of directness and honesty. The principles he sanctioned in the various business enterprises he pursued so avidly were somewhat at odds with the pragmatic and childlike world he created in his most memorable fiction.

The sun had baked the plowed land into a gray mass, with little cracks running through it. Even the grass was not green, for the sun had burned the tops of the long blades until they were the same gray color to be seen everywhere. Once the house had been painted, but the sun blistered the paint and the rains washed it away, and now the house was as dull and gray as everything else.

When Aunt Em came there to live she was a young, pretty wife. The sun and wind had changed her, too. They had taken the sparkle from her eyes and left them a sober gray; they had taken the red from her cheeks and lips, and they were gray also. She was thin and gaunt, and never smiled, now. When Dorothy, who was an orphan, first came to her, Aunt Em had been so startled by the child's laughter that she would scream and press her hand upon her heart whenever Dorothy's merry voice reached her ears;

and she still looked at the little girl with wonder that she could find anything to laugh at . . . It was Toto that made Dorothy laugh, and saved her from growing as gray as her other surroundings. Toto was not gray; he was a little black dog, with long, silky hair and small black eyes that twinkled merrily on either side of his funny, wee nose. Toto played all day long, and Dorothy played with him, and loved him dearly.

Baum stages a classic struggle here between things that make experience bleak (from drought and want to dullness) and those that enliven it (the instinctive humor and happiness of children and their pets). The scene reveals the contradictory power of nature: draining life of color while rejuvenating it via children and animals. There is simply no way for an adult in this landscape to escape being gray. Children and animals, however, retain an inherent, untouchable vitality so alien to this world that it strains the heart. The passage endorses variety by omission: the variety of human, animal, and vegetable existence, the potential variety of worlds unknown that may exist undetected in the little cracks of the land.

Baum's emerald utopia is everything that Kansas is not. It is a sea of colorful beings, most of them alternative kinds, munchkins, walking scarecrows, talking dishes, witches, winkies, and winged monkeys. This is not to suggest that a writer who supported the annihilation of the South Dakota Native Americans was at heart a defender of multiculturalism but to affirm a critical cliché: that novels can convey messages unknown to their authors. Moreover, such sentiments *are* consistent with Baum's liberal openness to different religions. He was drawn to esoteric faiths such as Kabbalism and Rosicrucianism, as well as to Eastern ideas of reincarnation and karma. He engaged in assorted religious practices, conducting séances, participating in spiritualist groups, and remaining alert to psychic events, such as the haunting of his Chicago house. Faith, for him, was imaginative, intuitive, flexible, and synthetic as befitted an era of novelty and invention.

Most of all, Baum believed that modern science afforded a view of a more (not less) spiritualized universe. An editorial he wrote on the subject reads like a philosophical appendage to *The Wizard of Oz*. "Scientists have educated the world to the knowledge that no part of the universe, however infinitesimal, is uninhabited. Every bit of wood, every drop of liquid, every grain of sand or portion of rock has its myriads of inhabitants – creatures deriving their origin from and rendering involuntary allegiance to a common Creator." Such a faith, one could argue, amounted to an ultimate form of multiculturalism. It was perhaps owing to its author's diverse and supple belief system that *The Wizard of Oz* had a more extensive afterlife than any other novel of this period. A musical and "fairy-logue" (moving pictures accompanied by orchestra and lecture) in Baum's time, it became one of the most popular films in American cultural history. Through these different media, the novel's multi-creature utopia became familiar, indeed integral, to the imaginative life of every subsequent generation. And in this way, however inadvertently, it helped to foster greater tolerance for the growing multiculturalism of non-utopian America.

REINVENTING RACE AND CLASS

In American utopian novels of the late nineteenth century there was no single social issue that received more consistent attention than racial and ethnic differences. Written mainly by authors of Anglo-Saxon Protestant ancestry, these novels pictured ideal worlds devoid of the troubling cultural variety that increasingly marked their society. However radical the social organizations of these utopias might be in political and economic terms, they were more often than not eugenicist breeding grounds for a purified citizenry. Thus, in Alexander Craig's *Ionia* (1898), Jews are forbidden to marry each other, and any Jew who commits a crime is immediately sterilized. In Arthur Vinton's *Looking Further Backward* (1890) and John Bachelder's *A.D. 2050* (1890), evil Chinese populations launch unprovoked attacks on the United States. Frona Colburn dedicates her *Yermah the Dorado* (1897) to "WHITE KNIGHTS of all times" who are exemplified by her idealized Aryan hero. African Americans and Native Americans are rarely mentioned in these utopias, except as in Walter McDougall's *The Hidden City* (1891), where their absence is highlighted as evidence of their inability to accommodate a superior civilization. In *Anglo-Saxons, Onward! A Romance of the Future* (1898) and *Armageddon: A Tale of Love, War, and Invention* (1898), Benjamin Rush Davenport and Stanley Waterloo predict the victory of Anglo-Saxon armies in global wars of the twentieth century, whose result is the annihilation of all inferior races.

An alternative to these genocidal impulses was a strain of racial pluralism introduced by utopian authors with roots in different cultural communities. Dr. Sutton E. Griggs, an African-American author whose utopian novel *Imperium in Imperio* (1899) circulated more widely among African Americans than works by Charles W. Chesnutt and Paul Laurence Dunbar, conceived a separate state in America where blacks would fulfill their distinct destiny. Jewish author David Lubin in *Let There Be Light* (1900) staged a series of dialogues in which his hero, a Jewish laborer named Ezra, imagines a utopian harmony of classes and races. Others sought to dramatize this pluralistic agenda increasingly popular among intellectuals such as Horace Kallen and Charles Eastman, who urged the acceptance of America's multicultural character. So in Charlotte Perkins Gilman's *Herland* (1915), where care has been taken "to breed out, when possible, the lowest types," race remains a prominent differentiation, while ideal variety becomes the general aim ("Celis was a blue-and-gold-and-rose person; Alima, black-and-white-and-red . . . Ellador was brown: hair dark and soft like a seal coat; clear brown skin with a healthy red in it"). The shared purpose in these examples was the commitment to improving prevailing methods of social and racial reproduction so as to alleviate what all these authors perceived to be unhealthy heterogeneous patterns. Utopian authors trained their sights persistently on matters of race and culture, it seems obvious in retrospect, because the spectacle of cultural difference was omnipresent, and the subject was a constant source of political controversy and intellectual debate. By reinventing race, these authors paved the way for the renovation of a social system built on punishing disparities between rich and poor. Mitigating the racial distinctions that fragmented their society, many utopian authors believed, would give everyone a greater stake in a just social order. Greater homogeneity in these utopian works leads naturally to a stronger sense of collective welfare.

Ignatius Donnelly's *Caesar's Column: A Story of the Twentieth Century* (1890), a bestseller published under the pseudonym Edmund Boisgilbert, MD, has long been notorious for its anti-Semitic elements. Featuring a Jewish villain, Jacob Isaacs, known as Prince Cabano (the Italian title purchased by his wealthy father), the Prince is the most reptilian of ruling-class exploiters. Corpulent and big-nosed, with "a Hebraic cast of countenance," he is a brutal tyrant, responsible for the misery of millions. He also has an insatiable appetite for gorgeous virgins, whom he buys in a white slave market of his own making and keeps in the harem on his estate. Donnelly's Jewish villains cover both ends of the political spectrum, for the other unnamed but equally diabolical Jew is part Shylock, part Bolshevik. A hooked-nosed Russian cripple, this Jew robs the Brotherhood he has served and flees to Judea, where he seeks to "re-establish the glories of Solomon, and revive the ancient splendors of the Jewish race."

The son of Irish immigrants, Ignatius Donnelly, born in Philadelphia in 1831, knew the experience of being a foreigner in America, one generation removed. His father was an American-educated doctor, and Donnelly himself attended public schools, received legal training, and was admitted to the Pennsylvania Bar in 1853. Married to Katharine McCaffrey in 1853, they moved West, where he invested heavily in a Minnesota town called Niniger that he hoped might eventually rival Chicago as a Midwestern center of commerce. The investments failed, partly due to the Panic of 1857, and Donnelly turned to politics, where his oratorical talents led to two terms as Lieutenant-Governor and then to Congress, where he became known as a defender of the people's rights against corporate interests. Returning to Minnesota in 1874 to serve in the state senate, Donnelly started a newspaper called the *Anti-Monopolist*. Journalism whet his appetite for writing, and over the next decade, Donnelly published five utopian novels and a book arguing for Francis Bacon's authorship of Shakespeare's plays. Donnelly's vast and learned first novel *Atlantis: The Antediluvian World* (1882), sought to prove the existence of Atlantis, its role as the source of ancient mythology, and its destruction in a single natural disaster. The book was a critical and commercial success, but the string of utopian novels that followed, leading up to *Caesar's Column*, while similar in scope, were largely ignored.

Given the prominence of Donnelly's political career – he helped found the Populist Party in 1892, and was the Party's candidate for Vice-President in 1900 – one might expect Donnelly's life to have been structured by periods of great political activity offset by periods of literary production. In fact his extraordinary fund of energy ensured his parallel pursuit of both vocations. Donnelly's political activity and literary work were mutually reinforcing. As a politician, Donnelly was as ambitious and idealistic as he was in his writings, known particularly for his support of public education. The speeches of his novelistic characters often sound like Populist Party platforms. No novel of Donnelly's expressed his political views more accurately than *Caesar's Column*, the most enduring of his works. Donnelly drew on two previous literary best-sellers for inspiration: Bellamy's *Looking Backward* and John Hay's *The Breadwinners*, whose notoriety as an anonymous book may have influenced Donnelly's decision to adopt a pseudonym. The first publisher Donnelly submitted the novel to (A. C. McClurg) found it incendiary, but the second (Frances J. Schulte) read it as a cautionary jeremiad.

Indeed, despite the heated politics of its author, *Caesar's Column* is a sustained argument against extremism. The narrative consists of letters from the novel's hero, Gabriel Weltstein, to his brother Heinrich back home in Uganda, Africa. A Dantesque wayfarer in America *c.* 1988, Gabriel is a humanitarian, continuously overwhelmed by the brutal intensity of both the rapacious ruling class and the insurgent Brotherhood working on behalf of the masses as the revolution draws near. Donnelly's turbulent society displays elements of utopia. Liquor, for instance, is outlawed, though rulers imbibe freely, and a highly scientific form of consumption has dramatically increased longevity for those who can afford it, a development enhanced by the improvement of air quality in all the places frequented by the rich. The novel's plot is set in motion when its three principals collide in a street accident: Gabriel, Maximilian Petion, a former member of the elite, now leader in the Brotherhood, Estella Washington, the beautiful descendant of George Washington, who is a new (and still virginal) concubine of the evil Prince Cabano. Max takes Gabriel on a tour of the Under-World, where he sees masses of Americans living in squalor, the end result of late nineteenth-century economic policy. Meanwhile, the elites (many of them "Israelites") enjoy resplendent luxury, insulated by their control of the government, military, and media. The lone gap in this tight and intricate machinery is the (inexplicable) perpetuation of a public education system, which manages to keep the otherwise wretched working classes well educated, filling their ranks with learned and eloquent leaders.

The solution advanced by Donnelly's hero in a chapter entitled "Gabriel's Utopia," is an instrumental Christianity designed to extend the fruits of innovation and industry to all, in the name of its originator. It is left to the religion's true devotees to "take possession of the *governments* of the world and enforce *justice!*" Social improvement, according to *Caesar's Column*, depends on the fulfillment of Christianity's foundational principles. Donnelly's example of fallen Christians is a congregation of lavishly attired women who listen to a sermon on the necessity of suffering while being entertained by dancers in earth-goddess costumes wet with blood. This grossly sensual, perverse Christianity leads straight to the inevitable holocaust at the novel's end.

En route to this devastation, Caesar Lomellini, the leader of the Brotherhood, manages to triumph over the evil plutocracy and the world is turned upside down. Mob rule is even more appalling than anticipated. At the head of the mob stands Caesar, "so black with dust and blood that he looked like a negro . . . his mat of hair rose like a wild beast's mane . . . his eyes were wild and rolling." Bodies fill the streets, making them impassable, so Caesar orders that a column be built of the dead, in tribute to his power. From their electric airship, Gabriel, Estella, and Max, with his new Anglo-Saxon Protestant bride Christina, espy an horrific effigy atop Caesar's Column: the leader's head. Murdering the leader, Max explains, is the first instinct of mobs. Returning to Uganda, Gabriel and his party fortify their island against potential aggressions from abroad. Within five years their small mountainous country has become an idyll where excessive wealth and poverty are unknown. Like so many other utopian communities, theirs is safe from "the dark and terrible throngs" of urban America. How Donnelly reconciled this purified idyll with his own Irish Catholic background remains a mystery. Secure in the bounty of their rural retreat, Donnelly's homogeneous island community is free to realize Christ's message on earth. True to its author's Populism, *Caesar's Column* endorses an agrarian democratic ideal against a modern pluralism ultimately devastating to rich and poor alike.

The setting of Charlotte Perkins Gilman's exclusively female utopia in *Herland* (1915) is equally pastoral and remote. And the prevailing method of single-sex reproduction ensures an even more perfect race of inhabitants.

Gilman's novel anticipates a recurring fantasy in American utopian novels by women (most of them, excepting Mary Lane's *Mizora*, written in the late twentieth century): a world without men. In suggesting that simply by eliminating whole categories of people certain social problems might be solved, Gilman was typical of the era's utopian novelists. Still, utopia in the hands of a seasoned author was different from utopia in the hands of a Lane or Donnelly. Though Gilman raised similar questions about race, reproduction, and social organization, she explored the issues with greater complexity. Moreover, her theoretical interests were more carefully woven into the novel's form. *Herland* has characters with contradictory tendencies, a suspenseful plot with surprising twists, an imaginatively detailed setting, and a philosophy that reflects deliberate reading and reflection. When Gilman offers renovated ideas about gender, they are presented convincingly through characters likely to contemplate such matters. What made Gilman's novel especially noteworthy in the canon of American utopian fiction was the depth of its immersion in contemporary intellectual debates.

By the time she wrote *Herland* (serialized in *Forerunner*, 1915), Charlotte Perkins Gilman was an international celebrity, known for her fiction, her polemical writings, and her lectures. A coveted speaker, Gilman had published 8 novels, 171 short stories, 9 non-fiction books, and over 1000 essays. Gilman was also editor of her own magazine, the *Forerunner*, where much of her writing appeared. Her most popular fiction, "The Yellow Wallpaper" (the *New England Magazine*, 1891), was as controversial as it was widely read. In "Why I Wrote The Yellow Wall-Paper" (*Forerunner*, 1913), she explained that the story was inspired by her ordeal as a patient of the famous Dr. S. Weir Mitchell, in an effort to persuade him of "the error of his ways." Gilman drew on her own depression both before and after her daughter's birth for her story, which shows how any experience of maternity that is less than ideal is treated as pathological. The protagonist/narrator is consigned to a rest cure by her physician husband, an eminently rational character, and forbidden to engage in work of any kind, which drives her further into madness. The story makes clear that this apparent "insanity" is in fact a displaced form of rage. The protagonist's only mental rudder is the story itself, which she records in a secret diary.

The construction of motherhood in *Herland* is a direct response to the heroine's trials in "The Yellow Wallpaper." The novel features three male explorers: Van, a student of sociology, whose penchant is social observation; Terry, a wealthy man of enterprise; and Jeff, who is trained as a doctor. Young and adventurous, they join a "scientific expedition" to a mountainous, forested region unrecorded on maps featuring dialects unknown to civilized man. Persistent allusions from their guides to a country of women that has never been visited piques their curiosity, and the trio breaks off from the expedition in search of it. *Herland* is the story of what they find.

Gilman's utopia institutionalizes her own eminently rational and innovative solutions to prevailing social problems. The effort to reconcile scientific rationalism with feminist idealism is built into the structure of *Herland*, which is narrated by Van, the social scientist. The novel's deepest implications are that all the tendencies that impede rational behavior are male traits projected onto women. Hence the primary purpose of Van's retrospective narrative: the recollection by a male consciousness of how he comes to accept a counterintuitive and disconcerting reality. Throughout, Van conveys his newfound loyalty to the civilization of Herland and his sense of wonder at discovering a country from which men have been absent for two thousand years. Because the women of Herland intend to keep it that way, Van has been deprived of his meticulous records and drawings and must write from memory. But his enthusiasm – "the world needs to know about that country" – works against them. Van's narrative consistently contrasts his own barbaric impulses (shared by his fellow male travelers) with the restrained civility of his women hosts. Van's early response to Herland, "why, this is a *civilized* country! There must be men," ironic at his own expense, reveals how much he has to learn. For the novel's main point is that Herland is the most civilized country on earth, precisely because there are none. Through Van's descriptions of his homeland to eager audiences of Herlanders, the illogic of contemporary American society is exposed by the logic of Herland.

Herland is a non-hierarchical matriarchy whose social model is the welfare state. All citizens benefit from a maternalistic government and enjoy equal access to the bounty afforded by the intelligent cultivation of national resources. The only form of reproduction is parthenogenesis, regulated with a strictness that Francis Galton would have envied. The rigorous control of human reproduction informs all other kinds of production – animal, agricultural, artificial. Childrearing is the revered work of experts; there is neither competition nor poverty; crime is unheard of; and even sickness is so radically minimized that the profession of medicine is "a lost art." The key to this ideal social order is the eradication of sexuality, which has been bred and trained out of the "race." "An endlessly beautiful undiscovered country" has replaced a modern Western sexual tradition that exaggerates "femininity." The only normative form of passion in Herland is maternal, with filial and sisterly devotion regarded as its acceptable outgrowths. So fierce is this maternal feeling that Herland women grow pale in learning of modern American production procedures that rob the cow of her calf and the calf of its natural sustenance.

Free to fulfill their instincts, the women of Herland flourish, creating a world without vice. Feminine weaknesses – "submissive monotony," "pettiness," "jealousy," "hysteria" – turn out to be male artifacts. Gilman anticipated her novel's agenda in a 1913 essay, "New Mothers of a New World," where she attributed the majority of social problems to male engendering, and concluded fervently, "we will work together, the women of the race, for a higher human type." According to Gilman, it is the male partner that inhibits the creation of a perfected citizenry of the type represented in *Herland*. Parthenogenesis is the highest form of reproductive purity, the only kind that can ensure the absolute control of genetic inheritance. As recognized by groups that define kinship through matrilineal descent, the maternal body that contains and nurtures the egg, then fetus, delivering it up after maturation, is the only infallible source of parental identity (arguably even in the era of DNA). According to Gilman, whose portrait, however male-averse, would have appealed, theoretically, to contemporary sociologists, nature is the wild card in transmission, while socialized traits are fully susceptible to control. They likewise would have approved of Gilman's view of sexuality and desire as disempowering to women, recalling a Victorian ethos that views ideal women as devoid of physical passion. They would have been pleased as well with the presentation of mothering as the primary and ultimate form of pleasure and power in Gilman's utopia, which makes the novel appear as a corrective to her own experience.

Despite such contradictions, Gilman's ingenious narrative achieves a complete reversal of the terms of encounter. Where the male visitors have everything on their side that would sustain a judgment of their superiority – civilization, science, modernity, progress, Western education, first-hand knowledge of the world – all of these advantages are found to be more finely appropriated by the isolated society of women, who have been cut off from the rest of the world for over 2000 years. What makes this credible, in Gilman's scheme, is women's innate possession of all of these qualities as a birthright. Civilization, rationality, modernity, a thirst for knowledge, wisdom, *Herland* suggests, are as natural to women as mother's milk. If allowed to develop unimpeded by male prerogatives such as patriotism, competition, sexual desire, conquest, the inevitable result would be utopia.

While racial and reproductive solutions to social problems were pervasive in realist utopias, their authors (as we have seen) were no less attentive to the need for socioeconomic renovation. Indeed, racial purification was often viewed as the precondition for radical economic change; a homogeneous culture was the first step towards a more equitable society. The majority of utopian authors advocated a transformation of the current capitalist system to achieve a more cooperative and centralized economy and a more even distribution of wealth.

While most, like Edward Bellamy, stopped short of truly radical plans for social reorganization, rejecting bona fide socialism, some, like William Dean Howells and Jack London, embraced socialism. They were convinced that the nation's expanding monopoly capitalism, which allowed the concentration of wealth in the hands of ever-smaller numbers, was creating a permanent underclass. Howells and London worried that a growing gap between rich and poor would spell the end of the American middle class. In his renowned proletarian utopian novel *The Iron Heel* (1908), London conceived a dystopian nightmare with the mass of Americans confined to poverty under plutocratic rule and revolutionary violence looming.

The Iron Heel anticipated science fiction disaster films of the late twentieth century, which predicted the state of the world after an unchecked capitalist-industrial system had reached its ill-fated end. The novel was London's message to his contemporaries that there was no time to lose; America *c.* 1908 was on the verge of Armageddon. The narrative's central conceit is the discovery of a manuscript by a futuristic historian, Anthony Meredith, from the utopian era "419 B.O.M.," seven centuries hence. The Everhard Manuscript is a first-hand account of the period between 1912 and 1932, when the proletariat challenged the vicious ruling oligarchy repeatedly, each time with disastrous results. The manuscript represents the recollections of Avis Everhard, the devoted wife of Ernest Everhard, the primary leader of the revolution. Thus the narrative combines a personal defense of socialist revolution from the perspective of its chief architect's wife, with a running catalog of notes on the early decades of the twentieth century by an historian writing from utopia. Anthony Meredith's notes provide Americans with eye-opening history lessons on the first decades of the twentieth century. Focused on corporate developments such as the rise of Rockefeller's Standard Oil, they provide an ongoing rationale for socialism. Yet Meredith at the same time exercises a consistent restraint on the glowing presentation of revolution and revolutionaries in Avis Everhardt's narrative. For his main claim is that the revolutionaries were poor readers of history, failing to consider that the fascist boot of the Iron Heel might be the most likely outgrowth of an exploitative capitalism.

The Everhard manuscript portrays Ernest Everhard as a proletarian *übermensch*, that is, a typical London hero. Much of the narrative is devoted to his animated diatribes, lovingly introduced by Avis, who never fails to describe how he looks delivering his speeches. As befits the novel's utopianism, Everhard is a full-blown radical theoretician from the start, however contradictory his agenda, a blend of Nietzschian Darwinism, socialism, and democratic idealism. As "a natural aristocrat," Everhard exhibits the usual antagonism of London's protagonists, who are always superior to their working class roots however much they champion and idealize them. Nor has Everhard's mind developed at the expense of his body, for his overpowering intellect is matched by a superb physique. His physical and mental powers fortify each other in cerebral debates that are portrayed as combat. Everhard's intellectual dominance of the elite depends on the assurance that he can pound them into insensibility.

The symbolic violence of these exchanges, where Everhard is invariably masterful and castigating, is not simply for the pleasure of his wealthy wife, who falls promptly in love after noting, "I had never been so brutally treated in my life." The triumphant dynamics of the novel's love plot are exactly reversed in the novel's political plot, where the working class is smashed to bits by the fascist Iron Heel, which, in an oft-repeated phrase, is destined to "walk upon [their] faces." Despite the persuasiveness of Everhard's rhetoric, and the self-evidence of his facts, the narrative progresses to its inexorable devastating conclusion: the obliteration of the middle and working classes in a holocaust that leaves the streets carpeted with corpses.

No class in *The Iron Heel* holds a corner on brutality, though the upper classes come very close. Perhaps the most memorable image in the novel is that of the mill hand, Jackson, who is denied compensation after his arm is shredded by a machine at work. The rule of the novel's oligarchy is everywhere, silencing the pulpit and the press, suppressing dissent at the universities, swallowing up the middle classes, making deals with the labor unions at the expense of most workers, packing the Congress and Senate with their loyalists, and swelling the coffers of the major trusts. There are fleeting moments of hope: Everhard's socialists win in a landslide in the 1912 elections, though they find themselves powerless when they arrive in Congress, and they manage to avert a war with Germany through an alliance between American and German workers who refuse to fight each other "for the benefit of their capitalist masters." These proletarian victories, however, are blips on a horizon of ruin, as the novel winds down with chapter titles such as, "The Beginning of the End," "Last Days," and "The Roaring Abysmal Beast." The end result of this dystopian class war is the transformation of humans into beasts.

The voice that speaks through Avis Everhard is the voice of Jack London, the believer, who could declare in a 1906 lecture at Yale University, "We Socialists will wrest power from the present rulers. By war, if necessary. Stop us if you can." So stirred were the students present that a group of them launched soon after it a Yale Chapter of the Intercollegiate Socialist Society. Yet the debacle that closes *The Iron Heel* affirms a more sober attitude that London articulated in a 1901 letter: "I should much prefer to wake tomorrow in a smoothly-running socialistic state; but I know I shall not." Had London survived to the 1930s, he would have seen his novel enshrined as a socialist cult object, widely viewed among keepers of the red flame as a powerful articulation of socialist principles in the face of a fascist enemy. Though both were on the same political side, as proponents of socialism, William Dean Howells's gentle utopia in his Altruria trilogy could not have been further from the violent dystopia of Jack London's *Iron Heel*. Similarly, the fierce and aggressive rhetoric of London's Ernest Everhard is replaced by the sweet reasonableness of Aristides Homos, the traveler from Altruria, in confirmation of the fact that theoretical bedfellows could be utter aliens when it came to method.

Howells's utopian imaginings provide an appropriate culmination to his career as a major Realist writer, influential editor, generous supporter of literary apprentices, and spokesman for humanitarian political causes. As an author who accomplished more in practical cultural affairs than any American writer of his time, Howells's professional activities were also marked by an incomparable idealism. He was drawn to Bellamy's "Nationalism," as well as to Christian Socialism, supported the accused anarchists in the Haymarket Affair, and expressed his dismay over the treatment of the strikers at the Carnegie Iron and Steel Company in Homestead, Pennsylvania. Between 1889 and 1891, when he lived in Boston, Howells frequented Bellamy's Nationalist meetings and Edward Everett Hale's Tolstoy Group, and endorsed Hamlin Garland's efforts to combine cultural practice and social protest. Throughout this period, Howells's concerns about the social effects of an American plutocracy and the need for sweeping change were increasingly focused on the prospects of Christian Socialism. Howells wrote approvingly of Leo Tolstoy's radical Christianity in an 1888 review of *What to Do?*, arguing that a system in which a small elite amasses wealth while the majority lives in poverty is necessarily short-lived. Howells's traveler from Altruria directly echoed the review in observing that the last straw in his country was the appalling greed of the wealthy, whose accumulations simply became intolerable.

The Altrurian narratives originated in a request from John Brisben Walker, a successful businessman who had bought the *Cosmopolitan* in 1889, that Howells write some "sociological essays" in support of the Christian Socialist creed they shared. Howells preferred the term "altruism" to socialism, a concept he introduced in his final "Editor's Study" column for *Harper's Monthly* (1892), where he described an imaginary society founded on this principle. Altruria, Howells explained, was "an outlandish region inhabited by people of heart, a sort of economic *Pays du Tendre*." Howells's Altrurian narratives sought to dramatize the possibilities of altruism were it to become the driving force in a society, a "national policy." Altrurians live "*for* each other," Howells wrote, in contrast to Americans who live "*upon* each other."

The first book of the projected utopian trilogy, *A Traveler From Altruria; A Romance* (1894, serialized in *Cosmopolitan*, 1892–94), features Aristides Homos, a traveler from the utopia of Altruria to America in the early 1890s, who is astonished by a society in which "4000 American millionaires" are "richer than all the other Americans put together." The traveler's guide is an author, who also serves as the novel's narrator. A thoughtful but naïve member of the elite, the narrator struggles to translate prevailing social customs and ideals, but in doing so finds himself entangled in the contradictions between American belief and practice. The group of upstanding friends he assembles to meet the traveler, which includes a professor, a doctor, a lawyer, a minister, a banker, and a manufacturer, appear as self-satisfied and close-minded, incapable of understanding the social order from any perspective but their own. The obvious irony at their expense is the traveler's deep grasp of their civilization, his multiple sympathies for its various members, and his overriding conviction that it is nothing short of "savage." Much of the novel's dramatic energy is invested in the narrator's gradual abandonment of his own views in favor of the traveler's. For this reason, their relationship is compelling, marked by the narrator's ambivalence towards the source of his destabilization, whose humanity he sometimes questions. As he gazes upon the traveler in one scene, for instance, the narrator wonders, "Was he really a man, a human entity, a personality like ourselves, or was he merely a sort of spiritual solvent?"

The Altrurian's distinction between their worlds captures the gulf separating the two men. "If you could imagine an Altruria where the millennium had never yet come, you would have some conception of America." Altruria, as described by the traveler in ongoing comparisons with America, is a Christian Socialist society where everyone lives in small intimate communities, traveling to urban centers for entertainment and resources uniformly available to all. There is no money, no one works for anyone else; everyone does his share of labor and shares equally in the social wealth. Moreover, chance has been entirely eradicated from economic life. Nor is there hurry, for now that people have stopped competing against one another, there is no need to rush. Recalling William Morris's *News From Nowhere* in critical respects (the professor responds to one of the Altrurian's descriptions, "He has got *that* out of William Morris"), Howells's utopia honors craftsmanship and is designed to restore the dignity of labor: mass production is gone, and the work ethic once again prevails. As these examples demonstrate, Howells's utopia betrayed nostalgia for a pre-industrial, agrarian social order that he believed characterized the Midwest of his childhood. The Altrurian's message is above all a Christian message; contemporary America is the scene of Christ's suffering upon the cross so that he might be known in a future world like Altruria.

Howells's series tapped common sentiments, and he reported that it was more enthusiastically received than anything he had written in years, with letters coming from all over the country and from all kinds of people. Among admirers of the series was Edward Bellamy, who applauded Howells's stirring critique of contemporary America. The response of the book's publisher, Harper and Brothers, was more tepid, and they refused to publish the second in the series, "Letters of an Altrurian Traveler" (*Cosmopolitan*, 1893–94, partly incorporated into *The Eye of the Needle*, 1907), in book form. A review of *A Traveler From Altruria* in the New York *Daily Herald* (September 1894), entitled "Poets Become Socialists Too: Howells Champions Socialism," suggests why. Howells was too politic not to attempt to assuage the concerns of his publishers, who were famously allergic to political controversy. Indeed, during his editorship of *Harper's Monthly* (which continued until his death in 1920), Howells reported himself always prepared to hear "the tinkle of the little bell" signaling a visit from owner J. W. Harper, when his columns expressed opinions that might irk the magazine's conservative readership. The fact that the bell never rang was a sign of how successfully he had internalized its chime.

This was perhaps why Howells, for the final book of his utopian trilogy, *The Eye of the Needle* (1907), decided to embrace the term "Romance" in the first subtitle, by providing as the novel's centerpiece a love affair between the Altrurian and an upper-class American. Eveleth Strange, the young widow of a wealthy man, is beset with an exceptionally active social conscience. Anticipating the women of Gilman's Herland, Eveleth lacks the flirtatiousness typical of the women the Altruian meets, and is also fiercely independent and outspoken. While she is engaged in continuous charity work, she is frustrated by its obvious limitations. Overwhelmed by the social misery she is incapable of ignoring and convinced that nothing other than complete social reorganization will do, she is drawn to the fair-minded utopian traveler. Eveleth's instinctive altruism is the fruit of her relationship with her mother. Her mother, with whom she lives, is a devout Christian who takes the teachings to heart, and compares the American present to the American past with the same intensity expressed by the Altrurian in his social comparisons. Howells struggles to preserve the complexity of this romance between people of two worlds, insisting that however idealistic, Eveleth is a product of her environment, wedded to a world of status and luxury. Part one of *Through The Eye of the Needle*, set in America and narrated by the Altrurian, ends with him forcing Eveleth to choose between her love and her money, a choice he fears will preclude their marriage. Part two, set in Altruria and narrated by the blissfully happy bride, dissolves all doubt. The remainder of *Through The Eye of the Needle* is Eveleth's cheerful recounting of life in Altruria, which her mother (whom she has convinced to accompany her) deems just like the America of her childhood. Although some critics noted that the Altruria recalled by the traveler in the recollections of *A Traveler From Altruria* looked more inviting than its first-hand rendition in *The Eye of the Needle*, the novel was respectfully reviewed.

Despite his commitment to social justice and genuine sympathy for socialist agendas, Howells remained temperamentally a moralist, who found the task of reconciling his idealism with the unvoiced constraints imposed by *Harper's* relatively congenial. His comments in a 1907 letter reveal that his appraisal of utopia and of social reorganization in general was always more ambivalent than his zealous fellow travelers were capable of recognizing. Howells could not help discovering, he noted, "imperfections even in Utopia." This did not make his vision any less courageous or complete. Like those of writers of comparable stature, Howells's utopia reflected his own ongoing interests: in the nature of social obligations and the role of sympathy in collective life. In keeping with this, Jack London's *Iron Heel* expressed his passion for class politics, and became a cult work whose rhetorical fervor inspired subsequent generations of socialists. The charming originality of Baum's *The Wizard of Oz* managed to extend spiritual meaning into unfamiliar territory. Charlotte Perkins Gilman's powerful engagement with major social problems and theories in *Herland* grew out of her role as a public intellectual. Finally, the imaginative brilliance of Twain's *Connecticut Yankee*, which incorporated so much of philosophical, economic, political, and religious significance into its formal structure, demonstrated the unique range of its author.

Perhaps what was most distinctive about all of these writers was what their utopian designs resisted. None of them embraced the racial and ethnic stereotypes or purification schemes that yielded cultural homogeneity in the ideal communities of writers like Peck and Donnelly and so many others. Gilman came closest with her method of parthenogenetic reproduction, but the society of *Herland* was resolutely pluralistic, indeed it celebrated colored people. Howells and London, Gilman, Baum and Twain seemed to recognize that even in utopia, history had to be reckoned with. They grasped implicitly that a utopia in which cultural differences stood in the way of social welfare was utopia in name alone. Though they viewed this fact with varying degrees of trepidation, they understood that America would endure in the future as *the* multicultural nation among the nations of the world.

CHRONOLOGY 1860–1920

John E. Tessitore

	American Literary Texts	American Events, Texts, and Arts	Other Events, Texts, and Arts
1860	Davis, Rebecca Harding (1831–1910), *Life in the Iron Mills* (novel) Hawthorne, Nathaniel (1804–1864), *The Marble Faun* (novel) Holmes, Oliver Wendell (1809–1894), *The Professor at the Breakfast Table* (miscellany)	Emerson, Ralph Waldo (1803–1882), *The Conduct of Life* (philosophy) The 5 story Pemberton Mill in Lowell, Massachusetts collapses; 88 people are killed and hundreds are injured. Abraham Lincoln is elected President.	Eliot, George (1819–1880), *The Mill on the Floss* (novel) Mill, John Stuart (1806–1873), *Considerations of Representative Government* (political philosophy) Great Britain asserts its neutrality in the US Civil War.
1861	Holmes, Oliver Wendell (1809–1894), *Elsie Venner* (novel) Jacobs, Harriet (1813–1897), *Incidents in the Life of a Slave Girl* (personal narrative) Winthrop, Theodore (1828–1861), *Cecil Dreeme* (novel)	Confederate forces fire on Fort Sumter, beginning the Civil War. Jefferson Davis is elected President of the Confederacy.	The Russian Czar, Alexander II, emancipates the serfs. Victor Emmanuel II is proclaimed King of a unified Italy. Louis Pasteur develops the germ theory of disease. Dickens, Charles (1812–1870), *Great Expectations* (novel) Eliot, George (1819–1880), *Silas Marner* (novel) Maine, Henry Summer (1822–1888), *Ancient Law* (legal history)
1862	Alexander, Charles (1837–1927), *Pauline of the Potomac* (novel) Stowe, Harriet Beecher (1811–1896), *The Pearl of Orr's Island* (novel) Victor, Metta (1831–1885), *The Unionist's Daughter* (novel)	Henry David Thoreau dies. Crummell, Alexander (1819–1898), *The Future of Africa* (political essays) President Lincoln signs the Homestead Act, opening 270 million acres of the American West, in 160 acre parcels, to settlers.	Otto von Bismarck is appointed Prime Minister of Prussia and delivers his "Blood and Iron" speech. Léon Foucault measures the speed of light on earth. Hugo, Victor (1802–1885), *Les Misérables* (novel)

		Spencer, Herbert (1820–1903), *First Principles* (evolutionary biology)
	Jefferson Davis, President of the Confederacy, decrees a universal conscription of Southern men between the ages of 18 and 35.	Turgenev, Ivan (1818–1883), *Fathers and Sons* (novel)
	Matthew Brady opens an exhibition of battlefield photography, *The Dead of Antietam*, at his New York gallery.	
	Howe, Julia Ward (1819–1910), "The Battle Hymn of the Republic" (poem/popular song)	
1863	Alcott, Louisa May (1832–1882), *Hospital Sketches* (short stories)	France establishes a protectorate in Cambodia.
	Hale, Edward Everett (1822–1909), "The Man Without a Country" (short story)	Archduke Maximilian of Austria becomes Emperor of Mexico.
	Hawthorne, Nathaniel (1804–1864), *Our Old Home* (travel)	
	Trowbridge, John Townsend (1827–1916), *The Drummer Boy* (novel)	President Lincoln signs the Emancipation Proclamation, ending slavery in the Confederate states.
		West Virginia becomes a state. Arizona and Idaho are organized into territories.
		Huxley, T. H. (1825–1895), *Evidence as to Man's Place in Nature* (biological anthropology)
		Four days of draft riots in New York City end in over 1,200 deaths.
		Manet, Edouard (1832–1883), *Olympia* (painting)
		A Union victory at the Battle of Gettysburg turns the tide of the Civil War. At the subsequent dedication of the battlefield and cemetery, President Lincoln delivers his Gettysburg Address.
		Burnand, F. C. (1836–1917), *Ixion; or the Man at the Wheel* (burlesque)
		Mill, John Stuart (1806–1873), *Utilitarianism* (ethical philosophy)
1864	Edmonds, Sarah (1841–1898), *Unsexed; or, The Female Soldier* (novel)	Greeley, Horace (1811–1872), *The American Conflict* (history)
	Thoreau, Henry David (1817–1862), *The Maine Woods* (travel)	Dickens, Charles (1812–1870), *Our Mutual Friend* (novel)
		Abraham Lincoln is re-elected President.
		Tolstoy, Leo (1828–1910), *War and Peace* (novel)

(cont.)

	American Literary Texts	American Events, Texts, and Arts	Other Events, Texts, and Arts
	Willett, Edward (1830–1889), *Vicksburg Spy* (novel)	Ulysses S. Grant is appointed Commander of the Union armies.	Louis Pasteur invents the antibacterial process known as "pasteurization."
		General Sherman begins his "march to the sea," destroying Confederate lands from Chattanooga to Savannah.	The first Geneva Convention creates the Red Cross Society to treat those who are sick or wounded in battle.
		Nathaniel Hawthorne dies.	French workers are granted the right to strike.
			The First International Workers' Association is formed in London.
			The Metropolitan Railway, the world's first subway system, opens in London.
1865	Thoreau, Henry David (1817–1862), *Cape Cod* (travel)	Robert E. Lee surrenders his Confederate forces to Ulysses S. Grant at Appomattox Courthouse, on April 9, ending major combat of the Civil War.	The US demands the withdrawal of French forces from Mexico.
	Trowbridge, John Townsend (1827–1916), *The Three Scouts* (novel)	President Lincoln is assassinated on April 9. Vice President Andrew Johnson becomes President.	Karl Benz designs the first automobile not adapted from a horse-drawn carriage.
		P. T. Barnum's first American Museum is destroyed in a fire.	William Booth establishes the Salvation Army.
		The ratification of the 13th Amendment abolishes slavery.	Carroll, Lewis (1832–1898), *Alice's Adventures in Wonderland* (novel)
		The Ku Klux Klan is founded in Tennessee.	
		Alexander Gardner publishes his *Photographic Sketchbook of the War*, a volume of battlefield photos he took while working for Matthew Brady.	

1866	Evans, Augusta (1835–1909), *St. Elmo* (novel) Howells, William Dean (1837–1920), *Venetian Life* (travel)	Cyrus Field lays the first transatlantic cable. The National Labor Union, comprised of skilled and unskilled workers, is founded to lobby for the 8-hour work day. Winslow Homer completes *Prisoners from the Front* (painting).	The Seven Week War begins between Prussia and Austria. Alfred Nobel invents dynamite.
1867	Thoreau, Henry David (1817–1862), *A Yankee in Canada* (travel) Child, Lydia Maria (1802–1880), *The Romance of the Republic* (novel) Daly, Augustin (1838–1899), *Under the Gaslight* (drama)	Higginson, Thomas Wentworth (1823–1911), "A Plea for Culture" (criticism) The Doolittle Report documents the mistreatment of Native Americans by the federal government and recommends a policy of greater compassion.	Dostoevsky, Fyodor (1821–1881), *Crime and Punishment* (novel) Mexican Emperor Maximilian is executed. Benito Juárez is re-elected President and restores republican rule. Fenian violence increases in Ireland.
1868	Finley, Martha (1828–1909), *Elsie Dinsmore* (novel) Harte, Bret (1836–1902), *Condensed Novels and Other Papers* (short stories) Twain, Mark (1835–1910), *The Celebrated Jumping Frog of Calaveras County and other sketches* (short stories) Alcott, Louisa May (1832–1888), *Little Women* (novel) Alger, Horatio (1832–1899), *Ragged Dick* (novel) Davis, Rebecca Harding (1831–1910), *Waiting for the Verdict* (novel)	Nebraska becomes a state. The federal government purchases Alaska from Russia for $7,200,000. Parton, James (1822–1891), *The People's Book of Biography* (biography) President Johnson is impeached, then acquitted by the US Senate. Ulysses S. Grant is elected President.	Joseph Lister introduces sterilization and antiseptic procedures in surgery. Marx, Karl (1818–1883), *Das Kapital* vol. 1 (political philosophy) Giuseppe Verdi's opera *Don Carlos* premieres in Paris. Emperor Meiji opens Japan to Western influences. The Ten Years War begins in Cuba. Collins, Wilkie (1824–1889), *The Moonstone* (novel)

(*cont.*)

	American Literary Texts	American Events, Texts, and Arts	Other Events, Texts, and Arts
	Dickinson, Anna (1842–1932), *What Answer* (novel)	The ratification of the 14th Amendment grants citizenship to all born or naturalized in the US and ensures equal protection under federal law.	Dostoevsky, Fyodor (1821–1881), *The Idiot* (novel)
	Phelps, Elizabeth Stuart (1844–1911), *The Gates Ajar* (novel)	The 8-hour work day is established in public works.	
1869	Howells, William Dean (1837–1920), *Italian Journeys* (travel)	The National Colored Labor Union is founded, when African Americans are denied membership in the National Labor Union.	The Church of Ireland is disestablished.
	Stowe, Harriet Beecher (1811–1896), *Oldtown Folks* (novel)	Barnum, P. T. (1810–1891), *Struggles and Triumphs* (memoir)	The Suez Canal opens.
	Twain, Mark (1835–1910), *Innocents Abroad* (travel)		Arnold, Matthew (1822–1888), *Culture and Anarchy* (criticism)
			Flaubert, Gustave (1821–1880), *Sentimental Education* (novel)
			Galton, Francis (1822–1911), *Hereditary Genius* (eugenics)
			Mill, John Stuart (1806–1873), *On the Subjection of Women* (social theory)
			Richard Wagner's opera *Das Rheingold* premieres in Munich.
1870	Alcott, Louisa May (1832–1888), *An Old-Fashioned Girl* (novel)	*Scribner's Monthly* is founded.	Chancellor Otto von Bismarck initiates the Franco-German War to promote German unification.
	Phelps, Elizabeth Stuart (1844–1911), *Hedged In* (novel)	Lowell, James Russell (1819–1891), *Among My Books* (criticism)	France's Third Republic is created as the empire of Napoleon III collapses.

Harte, Bret (1836–1902), *The Luck of Roaring Camp, and other sketches* (short stories)

The First Vatican Council proclaims the doctrine of papal infallibility.

Verne, Jules (1828–1905), *Twenty Thousand Leagues Under the Sea* (novel)

Sacher-Masoch, Leopold Ritter von (1835–1895), *Venus im Pelz* (novel)

New York's Metropolitan Museum of Art is founded.

John D. Rockefeller founds the Standard Oil Company.

The ratification of the 15th Amendment guarantees voting rights to all male citizens.

1871 Alcott, Louisa May (1832–1899), *Little Men* (novel)

The Commune, a league of radical socialists, controls Paris from March to May. Over 20,000 Communards are executed as the Third Republic reclaims the city.

Harland, Marion (1830–1922), *Common Sense in the Household* (domestic advice)

Darwin, Charles (1809–1882), *The Descent of Man* (biological anthropology)

Eggleston, Edward (1837–1902), *The Hoosier Schoolmaster* (novel)

Adams, Henry (1838–1918) and Charles Adams (1835–1915), *Chapters of Erie and other Essays* (history)

Lowell, James Russell (1819–1891), *My Study Window* (criticism)

Mitchell, S. Weir (1829–1914), *Wear and Tear; or, Hints for the Overworked* (health and medicine)

Eliot, George (1819–1880), *Middlemarch* (novel)

Howells, William Dean (1837–1920), *Their Wedding Journey* (novel)

Phelps, Elizabeth Stuart (1844–1911), *The Silent Partner* (novel)

Morgan, Lewis Henry (1818–1881), *Systems of Consanguinity and Affinity of the Human Family* (anthropology)

William Dean Howells becomes editor of the *Atlantic Monthly*.

The Great Chicago Fire kills approximately 300 people, leaves over 100,000 homeless and destroys thousands of buildings.

Giuseppe Verdi's opera *Aida* premieres in Cairo.

(cont.)

	American Literary Texts	American Events, Texts, and Arts	Other Events, Texts, and Arts
		James McNeill Whistler completes *Arrangement in Gray and Black* (painting).	
		Whitman, Walt (1819–1892), *Democratic Vistas* (criticism)	
		P. T. Barnum's circus, "The Greatest Show On Earth," opens in New York.	
1872	Ruiz de Burton, María Amparo (1832–1895), *Who Would Have Thought It?* (novel)	Edward Muybridge photographs the stages of a horse's gallop, prefiguring the era of motion pictures.	Financial panic in Vienna.
	Twain, Mark (1835–1910), *Roughing It* (travel)	Alcott, Bronson (1799–1888), *Concord Days* (memoir)	The third Carlist War begins in Spain over the rightful succession to the throne.
		Brace, Charles Loring (1826–1890), *The Dangerous Classes of New York* (documentary reporting)	Claude Monet finishes *Impression: Fog* (painting).
		Congress passes the General Amnesty Act, pardoning most ex-Confederates.	Nietzsche, Friedrich (1844–1900), *The Birth of Tragedy* (criticism)
			Verne, Jules (1828–1905), *Around the World in 80 Days* (novel)
1873	Eggleston, Edward (1837–1902), *The Mystery of Metropolisville* (novel)	Boston's Museum of Fine Art is founded.	Amadeo I of Spain abdicates and is replaced by an unstable republic.
	Howells, William Dean (1837–1920), *A Chance Acquaintance* (novel)	Jay Cooke, financier of the Northern Pacific Railroad, declares bankruptcy, precipitating a national financial panic.	Arnold, Matthew (1822–1888), *Literature and Dogma* (criticism)

	Twain, Mark (1835–1910) and Charles Dudley Warner (1829–1900), *The Gilded Age* (novel)		Pater, Walter (1839–1894), *Studies in the History of the Renaissance* (art history) Spencer, Herbert (1820–1903), *The Study of Sociology* (sociology)
1874	Aldrich, Thomas Bailey (1836–1907), *Prudence Palfrey* (novel)	The Society for the Prevention of Cruelty to Children is founded in New York.	The British Factory Act institutes a 56-hour work week.
	Eggleston, Edward (1837–1902), *The Circuit Rider* (novel) Warner, Charles Dudley (1829–1920), *Baddeck, and that Sort of Thing* (travel)	The Women's Christian Temperance Union is founded in Cleveland. The Chautauqua movement begins in upstate New York.	The first Impressionist exhibition is held in Paris. Hardy, Thomas (1840–1928), *Far From the Maddening Crowd* (novel)
1875	Alcott, Louisa May (1832–1888), *Eight Cousins* (novel)	Andrew Carnegie introduces the Bessemer steel-making process in the US at his plant in Braddock, Pennsylvania, insuring his dominance of the steel market.	Great Britain and Russia intervene in the conflict between France and Germany and avert another war.
	Howells, William Dean (1837–1920), *A Foregone Conclusion* (novel); James, Henry (1843–1916), *Roderick Hudson* (novel); *Transatlantic Sketches* (travel), Woolson, Constance Fenimore (1840–1894), *Castle Nowhere: Lake County Sketches* (short stories)	Madame Blavatsky founds the Theosophical Society in New York. Eddy, Mary Baker (1821–1910), *Science and Health* (theology)	Bizet's opera *Carmen* debuts in Paris.
1876	Alcott, Louisa May (1832–1888), *Rose in Bloom* (novel)	Colorado becomes a state.	Porfirio Díaz leads a successful revolution and becomes Mexico's President.

(cont.)

	American Literary Texts	American Events, Texts, and Arts	Other Events, Texts, and Arts
	Harte, Bret (1836–1902), *Gabriel Conroy* (novel); *Two Men of Sandy Bar* (drama) Twain, Mark (1835–1910), *The Adventures of Tom Sawyer* (novel)	Philadelphia's Centennial celebrations. Alexander Graham Bell invents the telephone.	The first complete performance of Wagner's *Ring* cycle takes place at Beyreuth. Johannes Brahms composes his *Symphony No. 1*. Eliot, George (1819–1880), *Daniel Deronda* (novel)
1877	Alcott, Louisa May (1832–1888), *A Modern Mephistopheles* (novel) James, Henry (1843–1916), *The American* (novel) Jewett, Sarah Orne (1849–1909), *Deephaven* (novel) Phelps, Elizabeth Stuart (1844–1911), *The Story of Avis* (novel)	The US election between Rutherford B. Hayes and Samuel J. Tilden is decided by a Congressional electoral commission. Hayes becomes President. End of Reconstruction; Federal troops withdraw from the South. Nationwide railroad strikes in July and August end in violent confrontations between strikers and the US military. Philadelphia's Museum of Art founded. Thomas Edison invents the phonograph. Morgan, Lewis Henry (1818–1881), *Ancient Society* (anthropology)	The last Russo-Turkish war begins over disputed territory; it ends in 1878. Queen Victoria is proclaimed Empress of India. British General Charles Gordon becomes Governor-General of Sudan. Auguste Rodin completes *The Age of Bronze* (sculpture). Zola, Emile (1840–1902), *L'Assommoir* (novel)
1878	Alcott, Louisa May (1832–1888), *Under the Lilacs* (novel) Harte, Bret (1836–1902), *Drift from Two Shores* (short stories)	Pierce, Charles Saunders (1839–1914), *How to Make Our Ideas Clear* (philosophy) The Knights of Labor convene their first national assembly in Reading, Pennsylvania.	Greece declares war on Turkey; the European powers intervene before major combat begins. The International Labor Union is formed.

James, Henry (1843–1888), *The Europeans* (novel)		Electric street lights are introduced in London. Gilbert and Sullivan's opera, *HMS Pinafore*, debuts in London. Hardy, Thomas (1840–1928), *The Return of the Native* (novel) Morris, William (1834–1896), *The Decorative Arts* (aesthetics) Tolstoy, Leo (1828–1910), *Anna Karenina* (novel, serialized since 1873)
1879 Cable, George Washington (1844–1925), *Old Creole Days* (short stories)	George, Henry (1839–1897), *Progress and Poverty* (economics)	The Zulu War between the independent Zulu nation and Great Britain over the control of southern Africa begins; despite suffering heavy losses, the British defeat the Zulus before the end of the year.
James, Henry (1843–1916), *Daisy Miller* (novella) Howells, William Dean (1837–1920), *The Lady of the Aroostook* (novel) Tourgée, Albion (1838–1905), *A Fool's Errand* (novel)	Pember, Phoebe Yates (1823–1913), *A Southern Woman's Story* (memoir) James, Henry (1843–1916), *Hawthorne* (biography) The postal service introduces new reduced rates for bulk mailing. Mary Baker Eddy founds the First Church of Christ, Scientist, in Boston. Thomas Edison demonstrates his improved electric light bulb.	Ibsen, Henrik (1828–1906), *A Doll's House* (drama) Meredith, George (1828–1909), *The Egoist* (novel)
1880 Adams, Henry (1838–1918), *Democracy* (novel)	James A. Garfield is elected President.	The Transvaal War (or the First Boer War) between South Africa's British and Dutch settlers begins; it ends a year later in a British defeat.

(cont.)

	American Literary Texts	American Events, Texts, and Arts	Other Events, Texts, and Arts
	Cable, George Washington (1844–1925), *The Grandissimes* (novel)	Federal deputies kill five men during a mass demonstration of railroad workers in Mussel Slough, California.	France begins initial construction of the Panama Canal, under the guidance of engineer Ferdinand de Lesseps.
	Harris, Joel Chandler (1848–1908), *Uncle Remus: His Songs and Sayings* (folklore)	Electric street lights are introduced in New York City.	Gilbert and Sullivan's opera, *The Pirates of Penzance*, debuts in Paignton, England.
	Howells, William Dean (1837–1920), *The Undiscovered Country* (novel)		Auguste Rodin completes *The Thinker* (sculpture).
	James, Henry (1843–1916), *Washington Square* (novel)		Dostoevsky, Fyodor (1821–1881), *The Brothers Karamazov* (novel)
	Wallace, Lew (1827–1905), *Ben-Hur* (novel)		Zola, Emile (1840–1902), *Nana* (novel)
	Woolson, Constance Fenimore (1840–1894), *Anne* (novel); *Rodman the Keeper* (short stories)		
1881	Cable, George Washington (1844–1925), *Madame Delphine* (novel)	Beard, George M. (1839–1883), *American Nervousness* (health and medicine)	French troops occupy Tunisia.
	James, Henry (1843–1916), *The Portrait of a Lady* (novel)	Holmes, Oliver Wendell Jr. (1841–1935), *The Common Law* (jurisprudence)	Irish Home Rule activist Charles Stuart Parnell is imprisoned by the British government for incitement to intimidation.
	Howells, William Dean (1837–1920), *A Fearful Responsibility* (short stories); *Dr. Breen's Practice* (novel)	Jackson, Helen Hunt (1830–1885), *A Century of Dishonor* (history)	In response to the assassination of Czar Alexander II, the Russian Holy Synod initiates a series of repressive policies, including the pogroms against Jews.
		Boston Symphony Orchestra is founded. Booker T. Washington founds Tuskegee Institute.	

1882	Goldfaden, Abraham (1840–1908), *The Sorceress* (drama)	The Federation of Organized Trades and Labor Unions of the United States and Canada, a forerunner of the American Federation of Labor, is founded by Samuel Gompers.	Italy establishes the colony of Eritrea.
	Howells, William Dean (1837–1920), *A Modern Instance* (novel)	President Garfield is assassinated. Vice President Chester A. Arthur becomes President.	British forces overtake Cairo.
	Twain, Mark (1835–1910), *The Prince and the Pauper* (novel)	Whitman, Walt (1819–1892), *Specimen Days* (memoir)	Richard Wagner's final opera, *Parsifal*, debuts at Bayreuth.
		Ralph Waldo Emerson dies.	Ibsen, Henrik (1828–1906), *An Enemy of the People* (drama)
			Stevenson, Robert Louis (1850–1894), *Treasure Island* (novel)
1883	Phelps, Elizabeth Stuart (1844–1911), *Beyond the Gates* (novel)	Winnemucca Hopkins, Sarah (1844?–1891), *Life Among the Piutes: Their Wrongs and Claims* (memoir)	France establishes a protectorate in Vietnam.
	Twain, Mark (1835–1910), *Life on the Mississippi* (travel)	William Cody founds his traveling show, Buffalo Bill's Wild West.	The first Russian Marxist party, the Group for the Liberation of Labor, is founded.
	Woolson, Constance Fenimore (1840–1894), *For the Major* (novel)	The Metropolitan Opera House opens in New York City.	The first volume of the *Oxford English Dictionary* is published.
		The Northern Pacific Railroad, connecting the Great Lakes and the Pacific Ocean, is completed.	Nietzsche, Friedrich (1844–1900), *Thus Spake Zarathustra* (philosophy)
		The Brotherhood of Railroad Trainmen is formed.	

(*cont.*)

	American Literary Texts	American Events, Texts, and Arts	Other Events, Texts, and Arts
1884	Adams, Henry (1838–1918), *Esther* (novel) Twain, Mark (1835–1910), *Adventures of Huckleberry Finn* (novel) Hay, John (1838–1905), *The Bread-winners* (novel) Hinton, C. H. (1853–1907), *Scientific Romances* (short stories) Jackson, Helen Hunt (1830–1885), *Ramona* (novel) Murfree, Mary Noailles (1850–1922), *In the Tennessee Mountains* (short stories)	Congress passes the Pendleton Civil Service Reform Act, ending the "spoils system" in government bureaucracy. Grover Cleveland is elected President. New York City Tenement-House Commission established.	The Redistribution Act extends suffrage to all British men over 21. The dirigible balloon is invented by the Renard brothers. The Fabian Society is founded in London.
1885	Howells, William Dean (1837–1920), *The Rise of Silas Lapham* (novel) James, Henry (1843–1916), *The Author of Beltraffio* (short stories) Ruiz de Burton, María Amparo (1832–1895), *The Squatter and the Don* (novel)	The Knights of Labor initiate their first strikes in the United States. William LeBaron Jenney's 10 story Home Insurance Building, considered the first modern skyscraper, is completed in Chicago. Grant, Ulysses S. (1822–1885), *Personal Memoirs of Ulysses S. Grant* (memoir) Strong, Josiah (1847–1916), *Our Country: Its Possible Future and Its Present Decay* (documentary reporting)	A strike of 8,000 textile workers outside Moscow is put down by Cossack soldiers. Louis Pasteur invents a rabies inoculation. Gottlieb Daimler improves the internal combustion engine, creating the first modern gasoline engine. Gilbert and Sullivan's opera, *The Mikado*, debuts in London.

1886

Vincent Van Gogh finishes *The Potato-Eaters* (painting).

Zola, Emile (1840–1902), *Germinal* (novel)

Slavery is abolished in Cuba.

Heinrich Hertz discovers electromagnetic waves.

Haggard, H. Rider (1856–1925), *King Solomon's Mines* (novel)

Hardy, Thomas (1840–1928), *The Mayor of Casterbridge* (novel)

Huxley, T. H. (1825–1895), *Science and Morals* (ethics)

Nietzsche, Friedrich (1844–1900), *Beyond Good and Evil* (philosophy)

Stevenson, Robert Louis (1850–1894), *Dr. Jekyll and Mr. Hyde* (novella); *Kidnapped* (novel)

Auguste Rodin completes *The Kiss* (sculpture).

The First Colonial Conference is held in London.

Alcott, Louisa May (1832–1888), *Jo's Boys* (novel)

James, Henry (1843–1916), *The Bostonians* (novel)

Howells, William Dean (1837–1920), *The Minister's Charge* (novel); *Indian Summer* (novel)

Standardization of track widths in the South completes the national railroad system.

The Supreme Court decides *US v. Kagema* declaring all Native Americans to be wards of the nation.

The Statue of Liberty is dedicated in New York Harbor.

Cosmopolitan magazine is founded in Rochester.

The American Federation of Labor is founded. It soon leads an all-trades demonstration for an 8-hour workday.

Ottmar Mergenthaler invents the linotype machine.

1887

The Triangle Alliance is formed between Austria, Germany and Italy.

Sardou, Victorien (1831–1908), *La Tosca* (drama)

Phelps, Elizabeth Stuart (1844–1911), *The Gates Between* (novel)

Chicago's Haymarket Riot begins when a bomb explodes during a strike at the McCormick Reaper Works.

The lead, sugar and whiskey trusts are formed.

The US obtains the right to use Pearl Harbor as a naval base.

(cont.)

American Literary Texts	American Events, Texts, and Arts	Other Events, Texts, and Arts
Royce, Josiah (1855–1916), *The Feud of Oakfield Creek* (novel)	Roosevelt, Theodore (1858–1919), *The Winning of the West* (history)	Strindberg, August (1849–1912), *The Father* (drama)
1888 Bellamy, Edward (1850–1898), *Looking Backward, 2000–1887* (novel)	Benjamin Harrison is elected President.	The Suez Canal Convention declares the canal open to all traffic in war and peace.
Howells, William Dean (1837–1920), *Annie Kilburn* (novel)	George Eastman invents the Kodak box camera.	"Jack the Ripper" murders 6 women in London.
James, Henry (1843–1916), *The Aspern Papers* (novella); *The Reverberator* (novel)	Bronson Alcott and Louisa May Alcott die, two days apart.	Nikolai Rimsky-Korsakov's orchestral suite, *Scheherazade*, debuts in St. Petersburg.
	The Burlington Railroad Strike begins in Chicago and lasts almost a full year.	Gustav Mahler completes his *Symphony No. 1*.
	James, Henry (1843–1916), *Partial Portraits* (biography)	Strindberg, August (1849–1912), *Miss Julie* (drama); *Creditors* (drama)
	Norton, Charles Eliot (1827–1908), "The Intellectual Life of America" (criticism)	
1889 Twain, Mark (1835–1910), *A Connecticut Yankee in King Arthur's Court* (novel)	North Dakota, South Dakota, Montana and Washington become states.	Pater, Walter (1839–1894), *Appreciations* (criticism)
Harris, Joel Chandler (1848–1908), *Daddy Jake the Runaway and Other Stories* (short stories)	Jane Addams founds Hull House in Chicago.	The First International Socialist Congress in Paris creates the Second International.
Woolson, Constance Fenimore (1840–1894), *Jupiter Lights* (novel)	The Daughters of the American Revolution is founded.	The Eiffel Tower rises above the International Exhibition in Paris.
	Carnegie, Andrew (1853–1919), *Gospel of Wealth* (self help)	The first Pan American Conference is held in Washington DC
	Adams, Henry (1838–1918), *History of the United States during the Administration of Washington and Jefferson* (history)	

1890

Alger, Horatio Jr. (1832–1899), *Struggling Upward* (novel)

Bachelder, John (1817–1906), *A.D. 2050*

Donnelly, Ignatius (1831–1901), *Caesar's Column: A Story of the Twentieth Century* (novel)

Fuller, Alvarado (1851–1924), *A.D. 2000* (novel)

Howells, William Dean (1837–1920), *A Hazard of New Fortunes* (novel)

James, Henry (1843–1916), *The Tragic Muse* (novel)

Vinton, Arthur (1852–1906), *Looking Further Backward* (novel)

Bruce, Philip (1856–1933), *The Plantation Negro as a Freeman* (ethnography)

The Populist Party is formed.

The tobacco trust is created.

Congress passes the Sherman Antitrust Act outlawing corporate monopolies that operate "in restraint of trade."

Approximately 300 Native Americans and 25 federal agents die at Wounded Knee, South Dakota in the last major confrontation of the Indian Wars.

The Mississippi State legislature enacts the Mississippi Plan, activating poll taxes, literacy tests and residency requirements to disenfranchise African Americans.

Brandeis, Louis (1856–1941) and Samuel Warren (1852–1910), "The Right to Privacy" (jurisprudence)

Howells, William Dean (1837–1920), *A Boy's Town* (memoir)

James, William (1842–1910), *Principles of Psychology* (psychology)

Riis, Jacob (1849–1914), *How the Other Half Lives* (documentary reporting)

Great Britain creates the first free elementary education program.

Ibsen, Henrick (1828–1906), *Hedda Gabler* (drama)

Wilde, Oscar (1854–1900), *The Picture of Dorian Gray* (novel)

American Literary Texts	American Events, Texts, and Arts	Other Events, Texts, and Arts
1891 Bierce, Ambrose (1842–1914?), *Tales of Soldiers and Civilians* (short stories) Garland, Hamlin (1860–1940), *Main-Travelled Roads* (short stories) McDougall, Walter (1858–1938), *The Hidden City* (novel) Mitchell, S. Weir (1829–1914), *Characteristics* (novel)	The Forest Reserve Act preserves several hundred acres of undeveloped land, and makes provisions for natural research. The United States and Great Britain sign their first copyright agreement. Herman Melville dies. Howells, William Dean (1837–1920), *Fiction and Criticism* (criticism) Crummell, Alexander (1819–1898), *America and Africa* (political essays) Phelps, Elizabeth Stuart (1844–1911), *Chapters from a Life* (memoir)	Brazil adopts a republican constitution. Construction begins on the Trans-Siberian railroad. Doyle, Arthur Conan (1859–1930), *The Adventures of Sherlock Holmes* (short stories) Gissing, George (1857–1903), *New Grub Street* (novel) Hardy, Thomas (1840–1928), *Tess of the D'Urbervilles* (novel)
1892 Bierce, Ambrose (1842–1914?), *The Monk and the Hangman's Daughter* (novel) Gilman, Charlotte Perkins (1860–1935), *The Yellow Wallpaper* (novella) Harper, Frances E. W. (1825–1911), *Iola Leroy; or, Shadows Uplifted* (novel)	A strike of mill workers at the Homestead Steel plant near Pittsburgh ends after a 4-month standoff; Pinkerton detectives and armed guards clash with strikers, leaving 10 dead and hundreds wounded. Cooper, Anna Julia (1858–1964), *A Voice from the South* (essay collection) Wells, Ida B. (1862–1931), *Southern Horrors: Lynch Law in All Its Phases* (documentary reporting) Alice James dies. (Her diary, *Alice James: Her Brothers – Her Journal* is published in 1934.) Walt Whitman dies.	Hendrick Lorentz discovers the electron. Paul Cézanne completes *The Card Players* (painting). Piotr Tchaikovsky's ballet, *The Nutcracker*, debuts in St. Petersburg. Hauptmann, Gerhart (1862–1942), *The Weavers* (drama)

1893	Bierce, Ambrose (1842–1914?), *Can Such Things Be?* (short stories)	Women are enfranchised in New Zealand.
	Crane, Stephen (1871–1900), *Maggie: A Girl of the Streets* (novel)	Belgian workers call a general strike in April.
		Chicago's Columbia Exposition opens; Simon Pokagon, a Potawatoni, opens the fair with a greeting, later published as "The Red Man's Lament."
	Fuller, Henry Blake (1857–1929), *The Cliff-Dwellers* (novel)	McClure's Magazine is founded by Samuel S. McClure.
	Howells, William Dean (1837–1920), *The World of Chance* (novel)	Antonin Dvořák completes his *Symphony No. 5 ("From the New World")*.
		Turner, Frederick Jackson (1861–1932), "The Significance of the Frontier in American History" (history)
		Durkheim, Emile (1858–1917), *The Division of Labor* (anthropology)
	Jones, Alice (1846–1905) and Ella Merchant (1857–1916), *Unveiling a Parallel* (novel)	A financial panic follows the failure of several major railroads. Hundreds of banks and thousands of businesses declare bankruptcy as the nation slides into a depression that lasts until the end of the decade.
		Wilde, Oscar (1854–1900), *Salomé* (drama)
1894	Chopin, Kate (1851–1904), *Bayou Folk* (short stories)	A strike of railroad workers begins in the Pullman company town outside of Chicago and spreads nationwide. In the ensuing violence between strikers and federal troops, 13 die and 57 are wounded.
		The Turkish army begins the systematic extermination of Armenians.
	Gillette, King Camp (1855–1932), *The Human Drift* (short stories)	Lloyd, Henry Demarest (1847–1903), *Wealth Against Commonwealth* (corporate history)
	Howells, William Dean (1837–1920), *A Traveler from Altruria* (novel)	Marden, Orison Swett (1848–1924), *Pushing to the Front* (self help)
		For his support of the Irish Home Rule bill, William Gladstone is forced to resign as Prime Minister of Great Britain.
		Nicholas II succeeds Alexander III as Czar of Russia.

(cont.)

American Literary Texts	American Events, Texts, and Arts	Other Events, Texts, and Arts
Schindler, Solomon (1842–1915), *Young West* (novel) Twain, Mark (1835–1910), *Pudd'nhead Wilson* (novel)		Gold is discovered in the Transvaal. Kipling, Rudyard (1865–1936), *The Jungle Book* (short stories)
1895 Crane, Stephen (1871–1900), *The Red Badge of Courage* (novel) James, Henry (1843–1916), *In the Cage* (novel)	Howells, William Dean (1837–1920), *My Literary Passions* (criticism) Wells, Ida B. (1862–1931), *A Real Record: Lynchings in the United States, 1892–1893–1894* (documentary reporting)	The Chinese–Japanese War ends in a Japanese victory. China relinquishes Taiwan and recognizes Korea's independence. Piotr Tchaikovsky's ballet, *Swan Lake*, debuts in St. Petersburg.
Townsend, Edward W. (1855–1942), *A Daughter of the Tenements* (novel)	The New York Public Library is founded. The first hydroelectric plant is installed at Niagara Falls.	Auguste and Louis Lumière invent the first motion picture camera. Wilhelm Roentgen discovers x-rays. Oscar Wilde loses his libel case against the Marquis of Queensbury and is imprisoned for sodomy. José Martí leads a rebellion in Cuba against the Spanish imperial government. Guglielmo Marconi invents the wireless telegraph. Sienkiewicz, Henryk (1846–1916), *Quo Vadis?* (novel)
1896 Cahan, Abraham (1860–1951), *Yekl: A Tale of the New York Ghetto* (novel) Frederic, Harold (1856–1898), *The Damnation of Theron Ware* (novel) Jewett, Sarah Orne (1849–1909), *The Country of the Pointed Firs* (novel)	William McKinley is elected President. Utah becomes a state. Geronimo surrenders, ending thirty years of "Apache wars."	The first modern Olympic games are held in Athens. Henri Becquerel discovers spontaneous radioactivity in uranium. The Nobel Prizes for physics, physiology and medicine, chemistry, literature, and peace are established.

Mitchell, S. Weir (1829–1914), *Hugh Wynne* (novel)

Read, Opie Percival (1852–1939), *My Young Master* (novel)

Major, Charles (1856–1913), *When Knighthood Was in Flower* (novel)

Twain, Mark (1835–1910), *The Personal Recollections of Joan of Arc* (novel)

1897

Bellamy, Edward (1850–1898), *Equality* (novel)

Chopin, Kate (1851–1904), *Night in Acadie* (short stories)

Colburn, Frona (1859–1946), *Yermah the Dorado* (novel)

Howells, William Dean (1837–1920), *The Landlord and the Lion's Head* (novel)

James, Henry (1843–1916), *What Maisie Knew* (novel); *The Spoils of Poynton* (novel)

Twain, Mark (1835–1910), *Following the Equator* (travel)

The Supreme Court decides *Plessy v. Ferguson* legalizing racial segregation in public places.

Gold is discovered in the Klondike River, Alaska.

Du Bois, W. E. B. (1868–1963), *Suppression of the African Slave-Trade in the United States* (history)

Atlanta University Publications, volume I, *Mortality Among Negroes in Cities*, is published.

Harriet Beecher Stowe dies.

Hills, A. M. (1848–1935), *Holiness and Power* (religion)

James, William (1842–1910), *The Will to Believe* (philosophy)

Henry Ossawa Tanner completes *The Raising of Lazarus* (painting)

Wharton, Edith (1862–1937), *The Decoration of Houses* (interior design)

The American Negro Academy is founded.

Atlanta University Publications, volume II, *Social Conditions of Negroes in Cities*, is published.

Hardy, Thomas (1840–1928), *Jude the Obscure* (novel)

Wells, H. G. (1866–1946), *The Island of Dr. Moreau* (novel)

The French government begins its investigation into the treason conviction of Alfred Dreyfus.

Sir Arnold Ross discovers the malaria bacillus.

Emile Durkheim founds the *Revue de Sociologie*.

Conrad, Joseph (1857–1924), *The Nigger of the "Narcissus"* (novel)

Ellis, Havelock (1859–1939), *Studies in the Psychology of Sex*, vol. I (biological anthropology)

Rostand, Edmond (1868–1918), *Cyrano de Bergerac* (drama)

(cont.)

American Literary Texts	American Events, Texts, and Arts	Other Events, Texts, and Arts
	The Jewish Daily Forward, the nation's leading Yiddish newspaper, begins publication under the editorial guidance of Abraham Cahan.	Stoker, Bram (1847–1912), *Dracula* (novel) Wells, H. G. (1866–1946), *The Invisible Man* (novel)
1898 Cahan, Abraham (1860–1951), *Imported Bridegroom and Other Stories of Yiddish New York* (short stories)	The Spanish–American War begins in February, ends in December. The US annexes Cuba and the Philippines as territories.	Emile Zola publishes "J'accuse," an open letter to the French President protesting the unjust imprisonment of Alfred Dreyfus for treason.
Page, Thomas Nelson (1853–1922), *Red Rock* (novel)	The Trans-Mississippi and International Exposition begins in Omaha, Nebraska.	Pierre and Marie Curie discover the elements radium and polonium.
Crane, Stephen (1871–1900), *The Open Boat and Other Stories* (short stories)	White supremacists in North Carolina murder African Americans during the Wilmington Massacre. The state legislature responds with a "grandfather clause," effectively disenfranchising former slaves.	Ferdinand von Zeppelin invents the rigid dirigible airship.
James, Henry (1843–1916), *The Turn of the Screw* (novella)	Congress charters The National Institute of Arts and Letters. Dunbar, Paul Laurence (1872–1906), *Clorindy, or The Origins of the Cakewalk* (musical theater) Gilman, Charlotte Perkins (1860–1935), *Woman and Economics* (sociology)	Paul Gauguin completes *Whence do we come? What are we? Where are we going?* (painting). Wells, H. G. (1866–1946), *The War of the Worlds* (novel)
Waterloo, Stanley (1846–1913), *Armageddon: A Tale of Love, War, and Invention* (novel)		

	Literature		
1899	James, Henry (1843–1916), *The Awkward Age* (novel)	Atlanta University Publications, volume III, *The Negro in Business*, is published.	The Second Boer War begins in South Africa between British and Dutch settlers. The British take control of the country in 1902.
	Chesnutt, Charles (1858–1932), *The Conjure Woman* (short stories); *The Wife of His Youth and Other Tales* (short stories)	Sam Hose, an African American who confessed to the murder of his white employer, is tortured and burned alive before a large crowd outside of Atlanta. His death inspires Ida Wells to write her anti-lynching tract, *Lynch Law in Georgia*.	The First Peace Convention at The Hague bans chemical warfare, hollow-point bullets, and air-raid bombing.
	Chopin, Kate (1851–1904), *The Awakening* (novel)	Du Bois, W. E. B. (1868–1963), *The Philadelphia Negro* (sociology)	The International Women's Conference is held in London.
	Crane, Stephen (1871–1900), *Active Service* (novel)	James, Henry (1843–1916), "The Future of the Novel" (criticism)	
	Frederic, Harold (1856–1898), *The Market-Place* (novel)	Jordan, David Starr (1851–1931), *Imperial Democracy* (political science)	
	Griggs, Sutton (1872–1933), *Imperium in Imperio* (novel)	Veblen, Thorstein (1857–1929), *The Theory of the Leisure Class: an economic study of institutions* (economics)	
	Norris, Frank (1870–1902), *McTeague* (novel)		
1900	Baum, L. Frank (1856–1919), *The Wizard of Oz* (novel)	William McKinley is re-elected President.	The Boxer Rebellion against Western political and cultural influence begins in China.
	Chesnutt, Charles (1858–1932), *The House Behind the Cedars* (novel)	Debut issue of the *Colored American Magazine*.	Great Britain annexes the Transvaal.
	Crane, Stephen (1871–1900), *Whilomville Stories* (short stories)	The United States adopts the gold standard.	Max Planck introduces the quantum theory of energy.

(cont.)

American Literary Texts	American Events, Texts, and Arts	Other Events, Texts, and Arts
Dreiser, Theodore (1871–1945), *Sister Carrie* (novel)	The Committee of Fifteen, a citizens' group dedicated to the eradication of prostitution and gambling, is founded in New York.	Chekhov, Anton (1860–1904), *Uncle Vanya* (drama)
Friedman, Isaac Kahn (1870–1931), *Poor People* (novel)	Dewey, John (1859–1952), *The School and Society* (education)	Conrad, Joseph (1857–1924), *Lord Jim* (novel)
Glasgow, Ellen (1873–1945), *The Voice of the People* (novel)	Wister, Owen (1860–1938), *Ulysses S. Grant* (biography)	Freud, Sigmund (1856–1939), *The Interpretation of Dreams* (psychoanalysis)
Hopkins, Pauline (1859–1930), *Contending Forces* (novel)	Stephen Crane dies.	Strindberg, August (1849–1912), *The Dance of Death* (drama)
London, Jack (1876–1916), *The Son of the Wolf* (novel)		
Lubin, David (1849–1919), *Let There Be Light* (novel)		
Mitchell, S. Weir (1829–1914), *Dr. North and His Friends* (novel)		
Peck, Bradford (1835–1935), *The World A Department Store* (novel)		
Wharton, Edith (1862–1937), *The Touchstone* (novella)		

	American Literary Texts	American Events, Texts, and Arts	Other Events, Texts, and Arts
1901	Chesnutt, Charles (1858–1932), *The Marrow of Tradition* (novel)	President McKinley is assassinated. Vice President Theodore Roosevelt becomes President.	Queen Victoria dies and is succeeded by Edward VII.
	Dunbar, Paul Laurence (1872–1906), *The Fanatics* (novel)	The Pan-American Exposition opens in Buffalo, New York.	Guglielmo Marconi transmits the first transatlantic radio message.
	Freeman, Mary Eleanor Wilkins (1852–1930), *The Portion of Labor* (novel)	Cuba becomes a US protectorate.	Kipling, Rudyard (1865–1936), *Kim* (novel)

Friedman, Isaac Kahn (1870–1931), *By Bread Alone* (novel)

Herrick, Robert (1868–1938), *The Real World* (novel)

James, Henry (1843–1916), *The Sacred Fount* (novel)

Norris, Frank (1870–1902), *The Octopus* (novel)

Washington, Booker T. (1856–1915), *Up From Slavery* (personal narrative)

Zitkala-Ša (1876–1938), *Old Indian Legends* (folklore)

1902   Carruthers, James (1869–1917), *The Black Cat Club* (novel)

Dixon, Thomas (1864–1946), *The Leopard's Spots* (novel)

Dunbar, Paul Laurence (1872–1906), *The Sport of the Gods* (novel)

Glasgow, Ellen (1873–1914), *The Battle-Ground* (novel)

Hopkins, Pauline (1859–1930), *Of One Blood* (novel)

J. P. Morgan organizes the US Steel Corporation.

The US buys the rights to build the Panama Canal from France for $40 million.

The Newland Reclamation Act facilitates irrigation projects in the West, including the damming of Western rivers.

President Roosevelt appoints an arbitration commission to negotiate an end to the Anthracite Coal Strike, setting a new precedent for federal intervention.

Carnegie, Andrew (1835–1919), *The Empire of Business* (business)

Eastman, Charles Alexander (Ohiyesa) (1858–1939), *Indian Boyhood* (memoir)

Mann, Thomas (1875–1955), *Buddenbrooks* (novel)

Conrad, Joseph (1857–1924), *Heart of Darkness* (novella); *Typhoon* (novella)

The Peace of Vereeniging ends the Boer War. Great Britain promises to install a representative government in South Africa.

Doyle, Arthur Conan (1859–1930), *The Hound of the Baskervilles* (novel)

Lenin, Vladimir Ilyich (1870–1924), *What Is To Be Done?* (political philosophy)

The *Times Literary Supplement* is first published in London.

(cont.)

	American Literary Texts	American Events, Texts, and Arts	Other Events, Texts, and Arts
	James, Henry (1843–1916), *The Wings of the Dove* (novel) Wister, Owen (1860–1938), *The Virginian* (novel)	Howells, William Dean (1837–1920), *Literature and Life* (criticism) James, William (1842–1910), *The Varieties of Religious Experience* (philosophy) Keller, Helen (1880–1968), *The Story of My Life* (memoir) Bret Harte dies.	Emmeline Pankhurst founds the Women's Social and Political Union in Manchester.
1903	Du Bois, W. E. B. (1868–1963), *The Souls of Black Folk* (literary ethnography) Fox, John Jr. (1863–1919), *The Little Shepherd of Kingdom Come* (novel) Friedman, Isaac Kahn (1870–1931), *The Autobiography of a Beggar* (novel) James, Henry (1843–1916), *The Ambassadors* (novel) London, Jack (1876–1916), *The Call of the Wild* (novel) Norris, Frank (1870–1902), *The Pit* (novel)	Orville and Wilbur Wright perform the first manned flights near Kitty Hawk, North Carolina. The Ford Motor Company opens its first factories. *The Great Train Robbery* (film) dir. Edwin S. Porter. Scott, Walter Dill (1869–1955), *The Theory and Practice of Advertising* (business) Ward, Lester Frank (1841–1913), *Pure Sociology* (sociology)	At a congress in London, the Bolsheviks and the Mensheviks split over the fate of radical socialism in Russia. Colombia denies the US a concession to build the Panama Canal. Panama becomes a US protectorate anyway, after a successful revolt in Panama City. Shaw, George Bernard (1856–1950), *Man and Superman* (drama)
1904	Eastman, Charles Alexander (Ohiyesa) (1858–1939), *Red Hunters and the Animal People* (short stories)	Theodore Roosevelt is re-elected President.	The Russo-Japanese War begins over control of Korea and Manchuria. Japan is victorious in 1905.

James, Henry (1843–1916), *The Golden Bowl* (novel)	President Roosevelt attaches the "Roosevelt Corollary" to the Monroe Doctrine, reserving the right of the US to police the Western Hemisphere.	The US begins construction on the Panama Canal.
London, Jack (1876–1916), *The Sea-Wolf* (novel)	The World's Fair is held in St. Louis, Missouri.	Chekhov, Anton (1860–1904), *The Cherry Orchard* (drama)
	Adams, Henry (1838–1918), *Mont Saint Michel and Chartres* (art history)	Conrad, Joseph (1857–1924), *Nostromo* (novel)
	Page, Thomas Nelson (1853–1922), *The Negro: The Southerner's Problem* (ethnography)	Weber, Max (1864–1920), *The Protestant Ethic and the Spirit of Capitalism* (sociology)
	Shaler, Nathaniel (1841–1906), *The Neighbor: A Natural History of Social Contracts* (ethnography)	Puccini's opera, *Madame Butterfly*, debuts in Milan.
	Tarbell, Ida (1857–1944), *History of Standard Oil* (corporate history)	
	Kate Chopin dies.	
1905 Dixon, Thomas (1864–1846), *The Clansman* (novel)	Congress charters the American Academy of Arts and Letters.	The first workers' soviet is formed in Russia in response to growing labor unrest and government repression.
Grey, Zane (1872–1939), *The Spirit of the Border* (novel)	Helen Keller graduates from Radcliffe College.	The crew of the battleship *Potemkin* mutinies in Odessa harbor.
Herrick, Robert (1868–1938), *The Memoirs of an American Citizen* (novel)	The Industrial Workers of the World is founded in Chicago.	Albert Einstein proposes his special theory of relativity as well as his quantum theory of light.
Wharton, Edith (1862–1937), *The House of Mirth* (novel)	Cutler, James Elbert (1876–1959), *Lynch-Law: An Investigation into the History of Lynching in the United States* (sociology)	Henri Matisse completes *Woman with the Hat* (painting).

(cont.)

American Literary Texts	American Events, Texts, and Arts	Other Events, Texts, and Arts
	Harland, Marion (1830–1922), *Everyday Etiquette* (domestic advice)	Freud, Sigmund (1856–1939), *Three Contributions to the Theory of Sex* (psychoanalysis)
	Hopkins, Pauline (1859–1930), *A Primer of Facts Pertaining to the Early Greatness of the African Race* (history)	Orczy, Baroness Emma (1865–1947), *The Scarlet Pimpernel* (novel)
	Santayana, George (1863–1952), *The Life of Reason* (philosophy)	Shaw, George Bernard (1856–1950), *Major Barbara* (drama)
	Smith, William Benjamin (1850–1934), *The Color Line: A Brief on Behalf of the Unborn* (ethnography)	Wilde, Oscar (1854–1900), *De Profundis* (apologia)
1906 Bierce, Ambrose (1842–1914?), *The Devil's Dictionary* (originally entitled *The Cynic's Word Book*) (satire)	President Roosevelt visits the Panama Canal. It is the first trip abroad by a sitting US President.	Alfred Dreyfus is found innocent of treason in a retrial.
London, Jack (1876–1916), *White Fang* (novel)	R. A. Fessenden broadcasts the first radio program in the US	Pope Pius X issues an encyclical condemning the separation of church and state in France.
O. Henry (William Sidney Porter) (1862–1910), *The Four Million* (short stories)	An earthquake in San Francisco kills 700 people and causes $400 million in damages.	Schweitzer, Albert (1875–1965), *The Quest for the Historical Jesus* (theology)
Sinclair, Upton (1878–1968), *The Jungle* (novel)	Congress passes the Pure Food and Drug Act.	
	Congress passes the Hepburn Act granting the Interstate Commerce Commission the power to regulate railway charges.	
	Atlanta University Publications, volume XI, *The Health and Physique of the American Negro*, is published.	

1907

Adams, Henry (1838–1918), *The Education of Henry Adams* (personal narrative)

Eastman, Charles Alexander (Ohiyesa) (1858–1939), *Old Indian Days* (short stories)

Friedman, Isaac Kahn (1870–1931), *The Radical* (novel)

Howells, William Dean (1837–1920), *The Eye of the Needle* (novel)

James, Henry (1843–1916), *The American Scene* (travel)

London, Jack (1876–1916), *The Road* (novel)

Parsons, Elsie Worthington Clews (1874–1941), *The Family: An Ethnographical and Historical Outline* (anthropology)

Geronimo (1829–1909), *Geronimo: His Own Story* (memoir)

Spargo, John (1876–1966), *The Bitter Cry of the Children* (documentary reporting)

Paul Laurence Dunbar dies.

President Roosevelt reaches his "Gentlemen's Agreement" with Japan, limiting Japanese immigration while easing discriminatory laws in San Francisco.

J. P. Morgan imports $100 million in gold from Europe to halt a financial panic.

Ziegfeld Follies debuts in New York City.

James, William (1842–1910), *Pragmatism* (philosophy)

Twain, Mark (1835–1910), *Christian Science* (non-fiction)

Mahatma Gandhi initiates a campaign of passive resistance among Transvaal Indians.

The first Cubist exhibition takes place in Paris.

Robert Baden-Powell founds the Boy Scout movement.

Pablo Picasso completes *Demoiselles D'Avignon* (painting).

Bergson, Henri (1859–1941), *Creative Evolution* (philosophy)

Conrad, Joseph (1857–1924), *The Secret Agent* (novel)

Gorky, Maxim (1868–1936), *Mother* (novel)

(cont.)

	American Literary Texts	American Events, Texts, and Arts	Other Events, Texts, and Arts
1908	Herrick, Robert (1868–1938), *Together* (novel) London, Jack (1876–1916), *The Iron Heel* (novel) Twain, Mark (1835–1910), *Extracts from Captain Stormfield's Visit to Heaven* (novel)	William Howard Taft is elected President. Henry Ford introduces the Model T, the first affordable automobile for a mass market. The "Ashcan school" of American painters is formed. Jack Johnson becomes the first African American heavyweight boxing champion. Mary Baker Eddy begins publication of *The Christian Science Monitor.* Scott, Walter Dill (1869–1955), *The Psychology of Advertising* (business)	The Young Turks unseat Sultan Abdul Hamid II in a bloodless coup and govern the Ottoman Empire for the next ten years. Oil is discovered in Persia.
1909	Dixon, Thomas (1864–1936), *Comrades* (novel) London, Jack (1876–1916), *Martin Eden* (novel) Stein, Gertrude (1874–1946), *3 Lives* (short stories) White, William Allen (1868-1944), *A Certain Rich Man* (novel)	W. E. B. Du Bois and others found the National Association for the Advancement of Colored People. Delaware is the first state to forbid the employment of children under fourteen. Milmine, Georgine and Willa Cather (1837–1947), *The Life of Mary Baker G. Eddy and the History of Christian Science* (biography) James, William (1842–1910), *A Pluralistic Universe* (philosophy)	Following the assassination of Prince Ito by a Korean nationalist, Japan annexes Korea. The Anglo-Persian Oil Company is founded. Henri Matisse completes *The Dance* (painting). Wells, H. G. (1866–1946), *Ann Veronica* (novel); *Tono-Bungay* (novel)

1910

Addams, Jane (1860–1935), *Twenty Years at Hull-House* (personal narrative)

Grey, Zane (1872–1939), *The Heritage of the Desert* (novel)

James, Henry (1843–1916), *The Finer Grain* (short stories)

Rockefeller, John D. (1839–1937), *Random Reminiscences of Men and Events* (memoir)

Sarah Orne Jewett dies.

W. E. B. Du Bois founds *The Crisis*, the official journal of the NAACP.

Mark Twain dies.

Charles William Eliot edits the 55-volume *Harvard Classics* series, providing a liberal arts education for people who do not attend college.

The Negro Fellowship League is established to provide services for urban African Americans.

Congress passes the Mann Act outlawing interstate travel for the purposes of "sexual activity."

Croly, Herbert (1869–1930), *The Promise of American Life* (political science)

Myers, Gustavus (1872–1942), *History of the Great American Fortunes* (history)

Pound, Ezra (1885–1972), *The Spirit of Romance* (criticism)

The Mexican Revolution begins against the autocratic rule of Porfirio Díaz.

Great Britain's King Edward VII dies. George V succeeds him.

China reclaims control of Tibet.

The World Missionary Conference convenes in Edinburgh.

Igor Stravinsky's ballet, *The Firebird*, debuts in Paris.

Forster, E. M. (1879–1970), *Howard's End* (novel)

Leroux, Gaston (1868–1927), *The Phantom of the Opera* (novel)

Russell, Bertrand (1872–1970) and Alfred North Whitehead (1861–1947), *Principia Mathematica* (mathematics/logical philosophy)

(cont.)

	American Literary Texts	American Events, Texts, and Arts	Other Events, Texts, and Arts
1911	Dreiser, Theodore (1871–1945), *Jennie Gerhardt* (novel) Du Bois, W. E. B. (1868–1963), *The Quest of the Silver Fleece* (novel) Wharton, Edith (1862–1937), *Ethan Frome* (novel)	In separate cases, the Supreme Court declares Standard Oil, DuPont and American Tobacco in violation of anti-trust law and dismantles them. Eastman, Charles Alexander (Ohiyesa) (1858–1939), *Soul of the Indian* (memoir) Roe, Clifford (1875–1934), *The Great War on White Slavery* (documentary reporting) Taylor, Frederick Winslow (1856–1915), *The Principles of Scientific Management* (industrial management) The Society of American Indians is founded. One hundred and forty-six employees of the Triangle Shirtwaist Company perish when they are unable to escape a fire in a New York factory. The tragedy initiates a nationwide effort to improve building safety codes. *The Masses*, a socialist weekly, begins publication in New York.	Radicals convene in Nanking, after the collapse of the Manchu dynasty, and elect Sun Yat-Sen provisional President of China. The First Universal Races Congress convenes in London. Ernest Rutherford proposes a model of the atom that includes electrons orbiting a nucleus. Hayford, J. E. Casely (1866–1930), *Ethiopia Unbound* (novel) Conrad, Joseph (1857–1924), *Under Western Eyes* (novel) Wagner, Richard (1813–1883), *Mein Leben* (memoir)
1912	Antin, Mary (1881–1949), *The Promised Land* (personal narrative) Austin, Mary (1868–1934), *A Woman of Genius* (novel)	Woodrow Wilson is elected President. Arizona and New Mexico become states.	The first Balkan War begins in Eastern Europe. The *Titanic* sinks on its maiden voyage.

Cather, Willa (1858–1947), *Alexander's Bridge* (novel)	US Marines invade Nicaragua.	Durkheim, Emile (1858–1917), *Elementary Forms of Religious Life* (cultural anthropology)
Dreiser, Theodore (1871–1945), *The Financier* (novel)	F. W. Woolworth Company is founded.	Jung, C. G. (1875–1961), *The Theory of Psychoanalysis* (psychoanalysis)
Grey, Zane (1872–1939), *Riders of the Purple Sage* (novel)	James Loeb funds the publication of the first 20 volumes of the *Loeb Classical Library*, a compilation of Latin and Greek texts in English translation.	
House, Col. Edward (1858–1938), *Philip Dru, Administrator* (novel)		
Johnson, James Weldon (1871–1938), *The Autobiography of an Ex-Colored Man* (novel)		
Phillips, David Graham (1867–1911), *The Price She Paid* (novel)		
Webster, Jean (1876–1916), *Daddy-Long-Legs* (novel)		
1913 Cather, Willa (1873–1947), *O Pioneers!* (novel)	The ratification of the 16th Amendment authorizes the first federal income tax.	The second Balkan War begins in Eastern Europe.
James, Henry (1843–1916), *A Small Boy and Others* (memoir)	The ratification of the 17th Amendment provides for the popular election of senators.	Following the assassination of Francisco Madero, Mexico falls into political chaos.
Wharton, Edith (1862–1937), *The Custom of the Country* (novel)	The Armory Show in New York City introduces Americans to modern European art.	Igor Stravinsky's ballet, *The Rite of Spring*, debuts in Paris.
	The Ford Motor Company begins assembly-line production of the Model T.	The trial of Mendel Beilis, falsely accused of ritual murder during a wave of anti-Semitic activity in Kiev, focuses international attention on the plight of Russian Jews. Beilis is acquitted.

(*cont.*)

American Literary Texts	American Events, Texts, and Arts	Other Events, Texts, and Arts
	Ferris, William (1873–1941), *The African Abroad: or, His Evolution in Western Civilization* (history)	Niels Bohr refines his model of atomic structure, the foundation of quantum mechanics.
		Conrad, Joseph (1857–1924), *Chance* (novel)
	Fullerton, William Morton (1865–1952), *Problems of Power* (political science)	Lawrence, D. H. (1885–1930), *Sons and Lovers* (novel)
	Mead, George Herbert (1863–1931), "The Social Self" (sociology)	Mann, Thomas (1875–1955), *Death in Venice* (novel)
	Parsons, Elsie Worthington Clews (1874–1941), *Old-Fashioned Woman: Primitive Fancies about Sex* (anthropology)	Proust, Marcel (1871–1922), *Swann's Way* (vol. 1 of *In Search of Lost Time*) (novel)
		Shaw, George Bernard (1865–1950), *Pygmalion* (drama)
1914 Dreiser, Theodore (1871–1945), *The Titan* (novel)	The Federal Trade Commission is established.	World War I begins after the assassination of Austria's Archduke Francis Ferdinand.
Lewis, Sinclair (1885–1951), *Our Mr. Wren* (novel)	Mother's Day is proclaimed an "official" holiday by President Woodrow Wilson.	The Panama Canal opens to commercial traffic.
Norris, Frank (1870–1902), *Vandover the Brute* (novel)	*The Little Review* begins publication in Chicago.	Marcus Garvey forms the Universal Negro Improvement Association and African Committees in Jamaica.
	The New Republic begins publication in New York.	Bell, Clive (1881–1964), *Art* (criticism)
Tarkington, Booth (1869–1946), *Penrod* (novel)	Antin, Mary (1881–1949), *They Who Knock at Our Gates: a Complete Gospel of Immigration* (social theory)	Joyce, James (1882–1941), *Dubliners* (short stories)

| 1915 | Cather, Willa (1873–1947), *The Song of the Lark* (novel)
Dreiser, Theodore (1871–1954), *The "Genius"* (novel)
Gilman, Charlotte Perkins (1860–1935), *Herland* (novel)
Grey, Zane (1872–1939), *The Rainbow Bridge* (novel) | Lippmann, Walter (1889–1974), *Drift and Mastery* (social theory)
McClure, Samuel S. (1857–1949), *My Autobiography* (memoir)
Ross, Edward A. (1866–1951), *The Old World in the New: The Significance of Past and Present Immigration to the American People* (sociology) | Alexander Graham Bell in New York, and Thomas A. Watson in San Francisco, execute the first transcontinental phone call.
Leo Frank, a Jewish businessman wrongfully imprisoned for a 1913 murder, is removed from his cell by a mob and lynched in Marietta, Georgia. In the aftermath, the Anti-Defamation League is formed to monitor hate groups.
Barton, Clara (1821–1912), *Life of Clara Barton* (memoir)
The Birth of a Nation (film) dir. D. W. Griffith | A German U-boat sinks the *Lusitania* off the coast of Ireland, prompting the US to question its own neutrality in World War I.
Mahatma Gandhi returns to India after spending 20 years in South Africa, litigating on behalf of Indian immigrants. | Ford, Ford Madox (1873–1939), *The Good Soldier* (novel)
Kafka, Franz (1883–1924), *The Metamorphosis* (novella)
Lawrence, D. H. (1885–1930), *The Rainbow* (novel)
Maugham, W. Somerset (1874–1965), *Of Human Bondage* (novel)
Woolf, Virginia (1882–1941), *The Voyage Out* (novel) |

(*cont.*)

	American Literary Texts	American Events, Texts, and Arts	Other Events, Texts, and Arts
1916	Anderson, Sherwood (1876–1941), *Windy McPherson's Son* (novel)	Woodrow Wilson is re-elected President.	Pancho Villa raids the US at the New Mexico border. The US invades Mexico but does not capture him.
	Glasgow, Ellen (1874–1945), *Life and Gabriella* (novel)	Congress passes the Keating-Owen bill, the first child labor law; the Supreme Court declares it an unconstitutional regulation of interstate commerce.	British troops suppress the Easter Rising in Ireland.
	Howells, William Dean (1837–1920), *The Leatherwood God* (novel)	Henry James dies.	Joyce, James (1882–1941), *Portrait of the Artist as a Young Man* (novel)
	Lardner, Ring (1885–1933), *You Know Me, Al* (short stories)	Dewey, John (1859–1952), *Democracy and Education* (philosophy)	
	Twain, Mark (1835–1910), *The Mysterious Stranger* (novel)	Eastman, Charles Alexander (Ohiyesa) (1858–1939), *From the Deep Woods to Civilization* (memoir)	
		Howells, William Dean (1837–1920), *Years of My Youth* (memoir)	
1917	Cahan, Abraham (1860–1951), *The Rise of David Levinsky* (novel)	The United States enters World War I.	The Russian Revolution begins with nationwide worker demonstrations and the abdication of Czar Nicholas II.
	Phillips, David Graham (1867–1911), *Susan Lennox* (novel)	Puerto Rico becomes a US territory.	Germany begins unrestricted submarine warfare.
	Sinclair, Upton (1878–1968), *King Coal* (novel)	Cambridge University Press publishes the first volume of *The Cambridge History of American Literature*.	
	Wharton, Edith (1862–1937), *Summer* (novel)	Dewey, John (1859–1952), "The Need for a Recovery of Philosophy" (philosophy)	

1918	Garland, Hamlin (1860–1940), *Son of the Middle Border* (memoir)	The Bolsheviks, under the leadership of Vladimir Ilyich Lenin, form the Communist Party. Russia is renamed the Union of Soviet Socialist Republics.
	Cather, Willa (1873–1947), *My Antonia* (novel)	President Wilson delivers his "Fourteen Points" address to Congress, outlining his vision of a postwar world, including a League of Nations.
	Tarkington, Booth (1869–1946), *The Magnificent Ambersons* (novel)	A worldwide influenza epidemic claims the lives of 20 to 40 million people.
	Installments of James Joyce's *Ulysses* first appear in *The Little Review*, igniting an ongoing censorship battle in the US	Mann, Thomas (1875–1955), *Reflections of a Nonpolitical Man* (political philosophy)
	Socialist activist and politician Eugene V. Debs is sentenced to 10 years in prison for "wartime sedition."	Spengler, Oswald (1880–1936), *The Decline of the West* (history)
		Strachey, Giles Lytton (1880–1932), *Eminent Victorians* (biography)
1919	Anderson, Sherwood (1876–1941), *Winesburg, Ohio* (short stories)	The Treaty of Versailles ends World War I and provides for a League of Nations.
	Glasgow, Ellen (1874–1945), *The Builders* (novel)	The ratification of the 18th Amendment prohibits the manufacture, sale and transportation of "intoxicating liquors."
	Hergesheimer, Joseph (1880–1954), *Java Head* (novel); *Linda Condon* (novel)	A five-day general strike in Seattle and a nationwide strike of steel workers contribute to a national anti-radical, anti-Bolshevik hysteria.
	Mencken, H. L. (1880–1956), *The American Language* (criticism)	Mahatma Gandhi begins his civil disobedience campaigns in India.
		Walter Gropius founds the Bauhaus School of design in Dessau.

(cont.)

	American Literary Texts	American Events, Texts, and Arts	Other Events, Texts, and Arts
1920	Fitzgerald, F. Scott (1896–1940), *This Side of Paradise* (novel)	Warren G. Harding is elected President.	Barth, Karl (1886–1968), *The Epistle to the Romans* (theology)
	Lewis, Sinclair (1885–1951), *Main Street* (novel)	The ratification of the 19th Amendment grants women the right to vote.	Hesse, Hermann (1877–1962), *Demian* (novel)
	O'Neill, Eugene (1888–1953), *The Emperor Jones*; *Beyond the Horizon* (drama)	The Senate votes against US participation in the League of Nations.	Jaspers, Karl (1883–1969), *The Psychological Outlook on Life* (philosophy)
	Wharton, Edith (1862–1937), *The Age of Innocence* (novel); *In Morocco* (travel)	Alleged anarchists Nicola Sacco and Bartolomeo Vanzetti are arrested for murder.	Maugham, W. Somerset (1874–1965), *The Moon and Sixpence* (novel)
		William Dean Howells dies.	Woolf, Virginia (1882–1941), *Night and Day* (novel)
		Brooks, Van Wyck (1886–1963), *The Ordeal of Mark Twain* (criticism)	The Russian Civil War ends with the victory of Lenin's Red Army over the anti-communist White Army.
			The International Organization of Employers is formed.
			The League of Nations meets for the first time in Paris. It establishes an International Court of Justice.
			Freud, Sigmund (1856–1939), *Beyond the Pleasure Principle* (psychoanalysis)
			Lawrence, D. H. (1885–1930), *Women in Love* (novel)
			Mansfield, Katherine (1888–1923), *Bliss and Other Stories* (short stories)

BIBLIOGRAPHY

This selected bibliography is drawn from lists provided by the contributors to this volume. It represents works that they have found to be especially influential or significant. The bibliography does not include dissertations, articles, or studies of individual authors. We have also excluded primary sources, with the exception of certain collections that present materials that have been generally unknown or inaccessible to students and scholars.

Adams, Bluford. *E Pluribus Barnum: The Great Showman and the Making of US Popular Culture*. Minneapolis: University of Minnesota Press, 1997.

Allen, Robert C. *Horrible Prettiness: Burlesque and American Culture*. Chapel Hill: University of North Carolina Press, 1991.

Barron, Hal S. *Those Who Stayed Behind: Rural Society in Nineteenth-Century New England*. New York: Cambridge University Press, 1984.

Barrish, Philip. *American Literary Realism, Critical Theory, and Intellectual Prestige, 1880–1995*. Cambridge: Cambridge University Press, 2001.

Bell, Michael Davitt. *The Problem of American Realism: Studies in the Cultural History of a Literary Idea*. Chicago: University of Chicago Press, 1993.

Bennett, Tony. *The Birth of the Museum: History, Theory, Politics*. London: Routledge, 1995.

Bentley, Nancy. *The Ethnography of Manners: Hawthorne, James, Wharton*. Cambridge: Cambridge University Press, 1995.

Boardman, Gerald Martin. *The Oxford Companion to American Theater*. New York: Oxford University Press, 1984.

Bourdieu, Pierre. *Distinction: A Social Critique of the Judgment of Taste*. Cambridge, Mass.: Harvard University Press, 1984.

Bramen, Carrie Tirado. *The Uses of Variety: Modern Americanism and the Quest for National Distinctiveness*. Cambridge, Mass.: Harvard University Press, 2000.

Brodhead, Richard H. *Cultures of Letters: Scenes of Reading and Writing in Nineteenth-Century America*. Chicago: University of Chicago Press, 1993.

The School of Hawthorne. New York: Oxford University Press, 1986.

Bush, Clive. *Halfway to Revolution: Investigation and Crisis in the Work of Henry Adams, William James, and Gertrude Stein*. New Haven: Yale University Press, 1991.

Carby, Hazel. *Reconstructing Womanhood: The Emergence of the Afro-American Woman Novelist*. New York: Oxford University Press, 1987.

Chandler, Alfred. *The Visible Hand: The Managerial Revolution in American Business*. Cambridge, Mass.: Harvard University Press, 1980.

Charvat, William. *The Profession of Authorship in America, 1800–1870: The Papers of William Charvat*. Columbus: Ohio State University Press, 1968.

Chernow, Ron. *Titan: The Life of John D. Rockefeller, Sr.* New York: Random House, 1998.

Cohen, Margaret, and Christopher Prendergast, eds. *Spectacles of Realism: Body, Gender, Genre*. Minneapolis: University of Minnesota Press, 1995.

Denning, Michael. *Mechanic Accents: Dime Novels and Working-Class Culture in America*. London; New York: Verso, 1987.

Dimock, Wai Chee. *Residues of Justice: Literature, Law, Philosophy*. Berkeley: University of California Press, 1996.

Donovan, Josephine. *New England Local Color Literature: A Women's Tradition*. New York: F. Ungar Pub. Co., 1983.

Douglas, Ann. *The Feminization of American Culture*. New York: Knopf: Distributed by Random House, 1977.

Elam, Harry Jr., and David Krasner, eds. *African-American Performance and Theater: A Critical Reader*. Oxford: Oxford University Press, 2001.

Elfenbein, Anna Shannon. *Women on the Color Line: Evolving Stereotypes and the Writings of George Washington Cable, Grace King, Kate Chopin*. Charlottesville: University Press of Virginia, 1989.

Fetterley, Judith, and Marjorie Pryse, eds. *American Women Regionalists, 1850–1910*. New York: W. W. Norton, 1992.

Fisher, Philip. *Hard Facts: Setting and Form in the American Novel*. New York: Oxford University Press, 1985.

Fox, Richard Wrightman, and T. J. Jackson Lears, eds. *The Culture of Consumption: Critical Essays in American History, 1880–1980*. New York: Pantheon Books, 1983.

Fox, Stephen. *The Mirror Makers: A History of American Advertising and its Creators*. New York: William Morrow, 1984.

Fredrickson, George M. *The Black Image in the White Mind: The Debate on Afro-American Character and Destiny, 1817–1914*. New York: Harper and Row, 1971.

Freedman, Jonathan L. *Professions of Taste: Henry James, British Aestheticism, and Commodity Culture*. Stanford, Calif.: Stanford University Press, 1990.

Fried, Michael. *Realism, Writing, Disfiguration: On Thomas Eakins and Stephen Crane*. Chicago: University of Chicago Press, 1987.

Gaines, Kevin K. *Uplifting the Race: Black Leadership, Politics, and Culture in the Twentieth Century*. Chapel Hill: University of North Carolina Press, 1996.

Garvey, Ellen Gruber. *The Adman in the Parlor: Magazines and the Gendering of Consumer Culture, 1880s to 1910s*. New York: Oxford University Press, 1996.

Gillman, Susan. *Blood Talk: American Race Melodrama and the Culture of the Occult.* Chicago: University of Chicago Press, 2003.

Godden, Richard. *Fictions of Capital: The American Novel from James to Mailer.* Cambridge: Cambridge University Press, 1990.

Glazener, Nancy. *Reading for Realism: the History of a US Literary Institution 1850–1910.* Durham, N.C.: Duke University Press, 1997.

Hahn, Steven, and Jonathan Prude. *The Countryside in the Age of Capitalist Transformation: Essays in the Social History of Rural America.* Chapel Hill: University of North Carolina Press, 1985.

Heinze, Andrew R. *Adapting to Abundance; Jewish Immigrants, Mass Consumption, and the Search for American Identity.* New York: Columbia University Press, 1990.

Hounshell, David. *From the American System to Mass Production, 1800–1932: The Development of Manufacturing Technology in the United States.* Baltimore: Johns Hopkins University Press, 1984.

Horwitz, Howard. *By the Law of Nature: Form and Value in Nineteenth-Century America.* New York: Oxford University Press, 1991.

Howe, Irving. *The World of Our Fathers: The Journey of the East European Jews to America and the Life They Found and Made.* New York: Harcourt, Brace, Jovanovitch, 1976.

Howells, William Dean. *Literary Friends and Acquaintance: A Personal Retrospect of American Authorship.* New York: Harper and Brothers, 1900.

Huyssen, Andreas. *After the Great Divide: Modernism, Mass Culture, Postmodernism.* Bloomington: Indiana University Press, 1986.

Johannsen, Albert. *The House of Beadle and Adams and its Dime and Nickel Novels: The Story of a Vanished Literature*, 2 volumes. Norman: Oklahoma University Press, 1950.

Jones, Gavin R. *Strange Talk*: *The Politics of Dialect Literature in Gilded Age America.* Berkeley: University of California Press, 1999.

Kaplan, Amy. *The Social Construction of American Realism.* Chicago: University of Chicago Press, 1988.

Kasson, John F. *Amusing the Million: Coney Island at the Turn of the Century.* New York: Hill and Wang, 1978.

  Civilizing the Machine: Technology and Republican Values in America, 1776–1900. New York: Grossman Publishers, 1976.

Katz, Mark D. *Witness to an Era: The Life and Photographs of Alexander Gardiner: The Civil War, Lincoln, and the West.* New York: Viking Studio Books, 1991.

Katznelson, Ira. *City Trenches: Urban Politics and the Patterning of Class in the United States.* New York: Pantheon Books, 1981.

Kelley, Mary. *Private Woman, Public Stage: Literary Domesticity in Nineteenth-Century America.* New York: Oxford University Press, 1984.

Laird, Pamela Walker. *Advertising Progress: American Business and the Rise of Consumer Marketing.* Baltimore: Johns Hopkins University Press, 1998.

Lears, Jackson T. J. *Fables of Abundance: A Cultural History Of Advertising in America.* New York: Basic Books, 1994.

　No Place of Grace: Antimodernism and the Transformation of American Culture, 1880–1920. New York: Pantheon Books, 1981.

Levine, Lawrence W. *Highbrow/Lowbrow: The Emergence of Cultural Hierarchy in America.* Cambridge, Mass.: Harvard University Press, 1988.

Marvin, Carolyn. *When Old Technologies Were New: Thinking About Electric Communication in the Late Nineteenth Century.* New York: Oxford University Press, 1998.

McCraw, Thomas K, ed. *Creating Modern Capitalism: How Entrepreneurs, Companies, and Countries Triumphed in Three Industrial Revolutions.* Cambridge, Mass.: Harvard University Press, 1997.

Menand, Louis. *The Metaphysical Club.* New York: Farrar, Straus and Giroux, 2001.

Michaels, Walter Benn. *Our America: Nativism, Modernism, and Pluralism.* Durham, N.C.: Duke University Press, 1995.

Mitchell, Lee Clark. *Determined Fictions: American Literary Naturalism.* New York: Columbia University Press, 1989.

Mizruchi Susan L., ed. *Religion and Cultural Studies.* Princeton, N.J.: Princeton University Press, 2001.

　The Science of Sacrifice: American Literature and Modern Social Theory. Princeton, N.J.: Princeton University Press, 1998.

Morrison, Toni. *Playing in the Dark: Whiteness and Literary Imagination.* Cambridge, Mass.: Harvard University Press, 1992.

Moses, Wilson. *Afrotopia: The Roots of African-American Popular History.* Cambridge: Cambridge University Press, 1998.

　Alexander Crummell: A Study of Civilization and Discontent. Oxford: Oxford University Press, 1989.

Mott, Frank Luther. *Golden Multitudes: The Story of Best Sellers in the United States.* New York: Macmillan Co., 1947.

　A History of American Magazines, 5 volumes. Cambridge, Mass.: Harvard University Press, 1957–68.

Moylan, Michele, and Lane Stiles, eds. *Reading Books: Essays on the Material Text and Literature in America.* Amherst.: University of Massachusetts Press, 1996.

Norris, James. *Advertising and the Transformation of American Society, 1865–1920.* New York: Greenwood Press, 1990.

Nye, David. *Electrifying America: Social Meanings of a New Technology, 1880–1940.* Cambridge, Mass.: MIT Press, 1990.

Nye, Russel Blaine. *The Unembarrassed Muse: The Popular Arts in America.* New York: Doubleday, 1982.

Ohmann, Richard M. *Politics of Letters.* Middletown, Conn.: Wesleyan University Press, 1987.

　Selling Culture: Magazines, Markets, and Class at the Turn of the Century. London: Verso, 1996.

Orvell, Miles. *The Real Thing: Imitation and Authenticity in American Culture, 1880–1940.* Chapel Hill: University of North Carolina Press, 1989.

Patterson, Orlando. *Slavery and Social Death: A Comparative Study.* Cambridge, Mass.: Harvard University Press, 1982.

Pizer, Donald. *Realism and Naturalism in Nineteenth-Century American Literature.* Carbondale: Southern Illinois University Press, 1966. Rev. ed. Carbondale: Southern Illinois University Press, 1984.

Pope, Daniel. *The Making of Modern Advertising.* New York: Basic Books, 1983.

Presbrey, Frank. *The History and Development of Advertising.* New York: Doubleday, 1929.

Porter, Carolyn. *Seeing and Being: The Plight of the Participant-Observer in Emerson, James, Adams, and Faulkner.* Middletown, Conn.: Wesleyan University Press, 1981.

Posnock, Ross. *Color and Culture: Black Writers and the Making of the Modern Intellectual.* Cambridge, Mass.: Harvard University Press, 1998.

The Trial of Curiosity: Henry James, William James, and the Challenge of Modernity. New York: Oxford University Press, 1991.

Rampersad, Arnold. *The Art and Imagination of W. E. B. Du Bois.* Cambridge, Mass.: Harvard University Press, 1976.

Rodgers, Daniel T. *The Work Ethic in Industrial America, 1850–1920.* Chicago: University of Chicago Press, 1978.

Roemer, Kenneth M. *The Obsolete Necessity: America in Utopia Writings, 1888–1900.* Kent, Ohio: Kent State University, 1976.

Rogin, Michael. *Ronald Reagan the Movie: and Other Episodes in Political Demonology.* Berkeley: University of California Press, 1987.

Ross, Dorothy. *The Origins of American Social Science.* New York: Cambridge University Press, 1991.

Scheckel, Susan. *The Insistence of the Indian: Race and Nationalism in Nineteenth-Century American Culture.* Princeton, N.J.: Princeton University Press, 1998.

Schivelbusch, Wolfgang. *Disenchanted Night: The Industrialization of Light in the Nineteenth Century.* Berkeley: University of California Press, 1988.

Schudson, Michael. *Advertising the Uneasy Persuasion: Its Dubious Impact on American Society.* New York: Basic Books, 1984.

Seller, Maxine Schwartz, ed. *Ethnic Theatre in the United States.* Westport, Conn.: Greenwood Press, 1983.

Sivulka, Juliann. *Soap, Sex, and Cigarettes: A Cultural History of American Advertising.* Belmont, Calif.: Wadsworth, 1998.

Skocpol, Theda. *Protecting Soldiers and Mothers: The Political Origins of Social Policy in the United States.* Cambridge, Mass.: Belknap Press of Harvard University, 1992.

Slotkin, Richard. *The Fatal Environment: The Myth of the Frontier in the Age of Industrialization, 1800–1890.* New York: Atheneum, 1985.

Regeneration through Violence; the Mythology of the American Frontier, 1600–1860. Middletown, Conn.: Wesleyan University Press, 1973.

Starr, Kevin. *Americans and the California Dream, 1850–1915*. New York: Oxford University Press, 1973.

Stepto, Robert B. *From Behind the Veil: A Study of Afro-American Narrative*. Urbana: University of Illinois Press, 1991.

Sundquist, Eric, ed. *American Realism: New Essays*. Baltimore: Johns Hopkins University Press, 1982.

   To Wake the Nations: Race in the Making of American Literature. Cambridge, Mass.: Belknap Press of Harvard University, 1993.

Susman, Warren. *Culture as History: The Transformation of American Society in the Twentieth Century*. New York: Pantheon Books, 1984.

Taylor, Helen. *Gender, Race, and Religion in the Writings of Grace King, Ruth McEnery Stuart, and Kate Chopin*. Baton Rouge: Louisiana State University Press, 1989.

Tebbel, John William. *A History of Book Publishing in the United States. Volume 2: The Expansion of an Industry, 1865–1919*. New York: R. R. Bowker, 1975.

Tedlow, Richard S. *Giants of Enterprise: Seven Business Innovators and the Empires They Built*. New York: Harper Collins, 2001.

Thomas, John L. *Alternative America: Henry George, Edward Bellamy, Henry Demarest Lloyd and the Adversary Tradition*. Cambridge, Mass.: Belknap Press of Harvard University, 1983.

Tompkins, Jane P. *West of Everything: The Inner Life of Westerns*. New York: Oxford University Press, 1992.

Tomsich, John. *A Genteel Endeavor: American Culture and Politics in the Gilded Age*. Stanford, Calif.: Stanford University Press, 1971.

Tractenberg, Alan. *The Incorporation of America: Culture and Society in the Gilded Age*. New York: Hill and Wang, 1982.

   Reading American Photographs: Images as History: Mathew Brady to Walker Evans. New York: Hill and Wang, 1989.

Warren, Kenneth W. *Black and White Strangers: Race and American Literary Realism*. Chicago: University Press of Chicago, 1993.

Wiebe, Robert H. *The Search for Order, 1877–1920*. New York: Hill and Wang, 1967.

Wexler, Laura. *Tender Violence: Domestic Visions in an Age of US Imperialism*. Chapel Hill: University of North Carolina Press, 2000.

Williamson, Judith. *Decoding Advertisements: Ideology and Meaning in Advertising*. London: Boyars, 1978.

Wilson, Christopher P. *The Labor of Words: Literary Professionalism in the Progressive Era*. Athens: University of Georgia Press, 1985.

Ziff, Larzer. *The American 1890s: Life and Times of a Lost Generation*. Lincoln: University of Nebraska Press, 1979.

INDEX

Abbott, Edwin A. 219

Abyssinia (show) 213

academies: American Academy of Arts and Letters 66, 247; American Negro Academy 99–100, 102–4, 210

Adams, Charles 667

Adams, Henry 91, 133, 139, 247–48, 270–77; on exhibitions 275–76, 692; *Chapters of Erie* (with Charles Adams) 667; *Democracy* 164, 274; *The Education of Henry Adams* 270–77; *Esther* 66, 158, 274; *History of the United States during the Administrations of Washington and Jefferson* 274; *Mont Saint Michel and Chartres* 274; "The New York Gold Conspiracy" 691–92

Adams, Herbert Baxter 339

Adams, Kate Jane 363

Addams, Jane 166, 465, 625–27, 628, 706; on museums and art galleries 66, 92–93; *Twenty Years at Hull-House* 626–27

Adler, Felix 545

advertising 7, 413, 414, 415, 568–98; aesthetic development 568, 571, 584, 589; Alcott parodies 436; authors' self-promotion 417, 476, 569; Baum's expertise 711, 723; to black Americans 597; for books and magazines 76, 417, 476; for canoes 311, 312, 572, fig. 3; and children 568; and class 568, 572, 575, 585–87, 589; copywriters 571, 582, 584; development 571–88; Dreiser on 613; and ethnicity 418–19, 572–74, 575, 584, 697; expenditures 568, 574–75, 582; focus advertising 583; Gillette and 721; and immigrants 418–19, 575, 697, fig. 9; in journals 416, 417, 476, 568–98, figs. 2–10; market segmentation 568, 572, 575, 585–87, 589; and packaging industry 582–83; Peck and 722; person's rights over appearance 353–54; product placement 569; professionalization 571, 582, 584–88, 598;

renovation 583–84; soap 569, 574–75, 584, 585, 697; as science 571–72, 584–88; for theater 148–49; on trading cards 214; Twain and 416, 476, 569, 584, 680–81; women and 568, 582, 583, 589; *see also* brand names

African Americans 99–106, 210–18, 414, 454–91; academy 99–100, 102–4, 210; accommodationism 99–100, 653–54; advertising to 597; agency 197–98, 201–2; in Civil War 423, 440, 441–42, 448, 451–53; communication 452–53; consciousness, double 139, 280–81, 282, 441, 471; and death 425–27, 457, 458–61, 462, 469–70, 472–74, 475, 476, fig. 1; dialect writing 200, 212, 316; education 59, 100, 103, 198–99, 217–18, 597 (industrial training schools) 12, 99–100, 103, 653, 654, 701; Ethiopianism 222; ethnology 199; Freedmen's Bureau 280; future of race 457, 472–91; "great migration" novels 211; and high literary culture 60, 99–106, 281–83 (exclusion) 90, 110, 216; labor 456, 597–98, 617, 621, 639–40, 649–50; magician or trickster figure 197–98, 201; and mass culture 138, 196–98, 210, 216–18; middle class 486, 639–40; oral culture 540; political advocacy 486, 597–98, 653 (*see also* NAACP); popular portrayal 138, 198; population figures 474–75; racial passing 485–88, 491; racial understanding 209–10, 215, 218; and racist pseudo-science 457, 468–70; and regional literary culture 6, 59–61; and religion 455, 457–61, 462–63, 479–80, 486; and sacrifice theme 419–20, 457–58, 461–62, 470; science fiction 218–23; suffrage 280, 462, 465, 596–98; theater and performers 196–98, 203, 204–5, 210, 212–14, 215, 220 (*see also* cakewalk); transatlantic travel 98–99, 101–2, 104; urban culture 210–18;